Greece

**David Willett   Kate Daly
Carolyn Bain   Rosemary Hall
Brigitte Barta   Paul Hellander**

LONELY PLANET PUBLICATIONS
Melbourne • Oakland • London • Paris

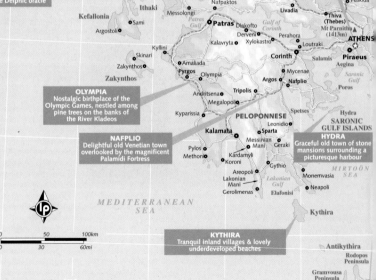

GREECE

FORMER YUGOSLAV REPUBLIC OF MACEDONIA

Durrës
◇ Tirana
Prilep
Bitola
Berat
Korça
Vlora
ALBANIA
Florina
Edessa
Kastoria
Veria
MACEDONIA
Mt Falakre (2111m)
Seres
Thessaloniki
Halkidiki
Kassandra Peninsula

Mt Grammos (2520m)
Mt Smolikas (2637m)
Konitsa
Mt Gamila (2497m)
Mt Olympus (2917m)
Lake Aliakmonas
Mt Ossa (1978m)

Erikousa
Pelekas ● Corfu
Corfu
Tigoumenitsa
Parga
Paxi
Antipaxi

Métsovo
Kalambaka
Larisa
THESSALY
Ioannina
EPIROS
Trikala
Karditsa
Farsala
Volos
Alonnisos
Skiathos
Skopelos

Preveza
Lefkada
Amfilohia
Mytikas
Lefkada
Ithaki
Agrinio
Karpenisi
Lamia
Mt Iti (2125m)
Loutra Edipsou
Mt Parnassos (2457m)

STEREA ELLADA

Nafpaktos
Messolongi
Livadia
Halkida
Thiva (Thebes)
Mt Parnitha (1413m)
ATHENS

Kefallonia
Sami
Argostoli
Skinari
Zakynthos
Zakynthos
Kyllini
Amaliada
Pyrgos
Olympia
Andritsena
Megalopoli
Kyparissia

Diakofto
Derveni
Xylokastro
Perahora
Loutraki
Corinth
Salamis
Piraeus
Aegina
Mycenae
Argos
Nafplio
Tripolis
Saronic Gulf
Poros

Patras
Patras Gulf
Gulf of Corinth
Kalavryta

PELOPONNESE
Leonidio
Sparta
Geraki
Spetses
Hydra
SARONIC GULF ISLANDS

Kalamata
Messinian Mani
Pylos
Methoni
Kardamyli
Koroni
Areopoli
Lakonian Mani
Gerolimenas
Gythio
Lakonian Gulf
Elafonisi
Monemvasia
Neapoli
MIRTOÖN SEA

Kythira
Antikythira
Rodopos Peninsula
Gramvousa Peninsula
Kastelli-Kissamos
Paleohora

Brindisi
Lecce
Otranto
40° N
38° N
36° N
20° E
22° E

0   50   100km
0   30   60mi

LP

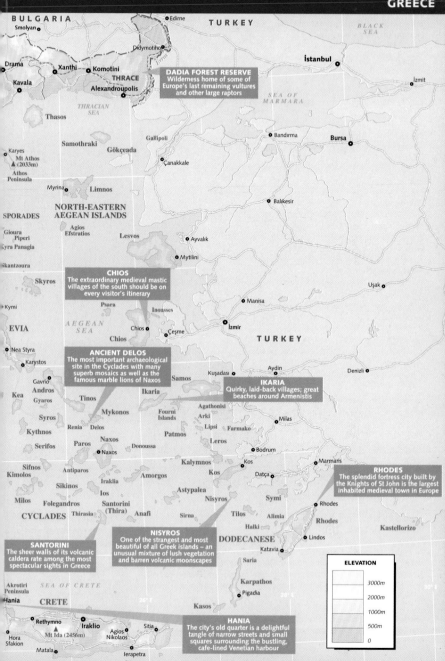

BULGARIA

Smolyan

Drama

Xanthi · Komotini

Kavala

THRACE

Alexandroupolis

Didymotiho

Edirne

TURKEY

BLACK SEA

İstanbul

İzmit

DADIA FOREST RESERVE
Wilderness home of some of
Europe's last remaining vultures
and other large raptors

Thasos

THRACIAN SEA

SEA OF MARMARA

Samothraki

Gökçeada

Gallipoli

Bandırma

Bursa

Karyes
Mt Athos
(2033m)
Athos
Peninsula

Çanakkale

Myrina · Limnos

Balıkesir

SPORADES

NORTH-EASTERN
AEGEAN ISLANDS

Agios
Efstratios

Lesvos

Ayvalık

Gioura
Piperi
Kyra Panagia

Mytilini

Skantzoura

Skyros

CHIOS
The extraordinary medieval mastic
villages of the south should be on
every visitor's itinerary

Uşak

Kymi

Psara

Inousses

Manisa

İzmir

EVIA

AEGEAN SEA

Chios

Çeşme

TURKEY

Chios

Nea Styra

Karystos

ANCIENT DELOS
The most important archaeological
site in the Cyclades with many
superb mosaics as well as the
famous marble lions of Naxos

Kuşadası

Aydin

Denizli

Gavrio

Andros

Samos

Ikaria

IKARIA
Quirky, laid-back villages; great
beaches around Armenistis

Kea

Gyaros

Tinos

Agathonisi

Milas

Syros

Mykonos

Arki

Farmako

Kythnos

Renia Delos

Fourni
Islands

Lipsi

Serifos

Paros

Naxos

Patmos

Leros

Bodrum

Sifnos

Naxos

Donoussa

Antiparos

Amorgos

Kalymnos

Kos

Kimolos

Iraklia

Kos

Datça

Marmaris

Sikinos

Astypalea

RHODES
The splendid fortress city built by
the Knights of St John is the largest
inhabited medieval town in Europe

Milos

Ios

Nisyros

Symi

Folegandros

Santorini
(Thira)

Anafi

Sirna

Tilos

Rhodes

CYCLADES

Thirasia

Alimia

Rhodes

Kastellorizo

SANTORINI
The sheer walls of its volcanic
caldera rate among the most
spectacular sights in Greece

NISYROS
One of the strangest and most
beautiful of all Greek islands – an
unusual mixture of lush vegetation
and barren volcanic moonscapes

Halki

DODECANESE

Lindos

Akrotiri
Peninsula

Hania

SEA OF CRETE

Katavia

Saria

Karpathos

CRETE

Pigadia

Rethymno · Iraklio

Mt Ida (2456m)

Agios
Nikolaos

Sitia

Kasos

HANIA
The city's old quarter is a delightful
tangle of narrow streets and small
squares surrounding the bustling,
cafe-lined Venetian harbour

Hora
Sfakion

Matala

Ierapetra

Gavdos

ELEVATION

3000m

2000m

1000m

500m

0

Greece
5th edition – February 2002
First published – February 1994

Six-monthly upgrades of this title available free on
www.lonelyplanet.com/upgrades

Published by
Lonely Planet Publications Pty Ltd ABN 36 005 607 983
90 Maribyrnong St, Footscray, Victoria 3011, Australia

Lonely Planet offices
Australia Locked Bag 1, Footscray, Victoria 3011
USA 150 Linden St, Oakland, CA 94607
UK 10a Spring Place, London NW5 3BH
France 1 rue du Dahomey, 75011 Paris

Photographs
Many of the images in this guide are available for licensing from
Lonely Planet Images.
email: lpi@lonelyplanet.com.au
Web site: www.lonelyplanetimages.com

Front cover photograph
White-washed church against skyline in Elounda, Crete (Alan Benson)

ISBN 1 86450 334 3

text & maps © Lonely Planet Publications Pty Ltd 2002
photos © photographers as indicated 2002

Printed by SNP SPrint (M) Sdn Bhd
Printed in Malaysia

Contents – Text

THE AUTHORS   9

FOREWORD   14

INTRODUCTION   17

FACTS ABOUT GREECE   19

History 19
Geography 37
Geology 37
Climate 37
Ecology & Environment 39
Flora & Fauna 39

Government & Politics 42
Economy 42
Population 43
People 43
Education 43
Science 45

Arts 46
Greek Art & Architecture 49
Society & Conduct 65
Religion 70
Language 72

FACTS FOR THE VISITOR   73

Suggested Itineraries 73
Planning 73
Responsible Tourism 74
Tourist Offices 75
Visas & Documents 76
Embassies & Consulates 77
Customs 79
Money 79
Post & Communications 82
Internet Resources 84
Books 85
Films 88
Newspapers & Magazines 88
Radio & TV 89

Video Systems 89
Photography & Video 89
Time 89
Electricity 90
Weights & Measures 90
Laundry 90
Toilets 90
Health 90
Women Travellers 96
Gay & Lesbian Travellers 96
Disabled Travellers 97
Senior Travellers 97
Travel with Children 97
Useful Organisations 97

Dangers & Annoyances 98
Legal Matters 98
Business Hours 98
Public Holidays 99
Special Events 99
Activities 101
Courses 102
Work 102
Accommodation 103
Food 105
Drinks 109
Entertainment 111
Spectator sports 112
Shopping 112

GETTING THERE & AWAY   113

Air 113
Land 120

Sea 122
Organised Tours 124

GETTING AROUND   125

Air 125
Bus 127
Train 128
Car & Motorcycle 129

Bicycle 131
Hitching 131
Walking 132
Boat 132

Local Transport 136
Organised Tours 136

ATHENS   138

Suggested Itineraries 139
History 139
Orientation 141
Information 143
Walking Tour 146
The Acropolis.....................150
Southern Slope of the
Acropolis 156

Ancient Agora 157
The Keramikos 158
Roman Athens 159
Byzantine Athens 161
Neoclassical Athens 161
National Archaeological
Museum 161
Other Museums 165

Hills of Athens 167
Parks 168
Activities 169
Language Courses 169
Children's Activities 170
Organised Tours 170
Hellenic Festival 170
Places to Stay 171

Places to Eat 175
Entertainment 181
Spectator Sports 185
Shopping 186
Getting There & Away 187
Getting Around 189
Around Athens 194

Piraeus 194
Moni Kaissarianis 201
Attica 201
Glyfada 201
Cape Sounion 203
The Mesogeia 204
Lavrio 204

Vravrona (Braouron) 205
Rafina 205
Marathon Region 206
Elefsina (Eleusis) 207
Mt Parnitha 208

PELOPONNESE   209

Suggested Itineraries 209
History & Mythology 209
Achaïa 212
Patras 213
Diakofto............................217
Zahlorou 217
Kalavryta 218
Around Kalavryta 220
Corinthia 220
Corinth 220
Ancient Corinth &
Acrocorinth 223
Corinth Canal 224
Isthmia.............................224
Loutraki 225
Nemea..............................225
Argolis 225
Argos................................225

Mycenae 227
Nafplio 229
Around Nafplio 234
Epidaurus 234
Arcadia 236
Tripolis 236
Megalopoli.......................237
Central Arcadia 238
Kynouria 240
Lakonia 241
Sparta 241
Mystras 244
Anavryti 246
Langada Pass 247
Gefyra & Monemvasia 247
Neapoli 249
Gythio 250
The Mani 252

Lakonian Mani 253
Messinian Mani 257
Messinia 259
Kalamata 259
Mavromati
(Ancient Messini) 262
Koroni 263
Finikounda 264
Methoni 264
Pylos 265
Around Pylos 267
Elia 267
Tholos To Pyrgos 268
Pyrgos 268
Olympia 268
Andritsena 272
Kyllini 273

CENTRAL GREECE   274

Suggested Itineraries 274
Sterea Ellada 274
Athens to Thiva 274
Thiva (Thebes) 276
Livadia..............................276
Delphi 277
Mt Parnassos 280
Arahova 281
Around Arahova 282
Galaxidi 283

Around Galaxidi 284
Messolongi 285
South-West Coastal
Resorts 286
Karpenisi 287
Around Karpenisi 288
Karpenisi to Agrinio 289
Lamia 289
Iti National Park 291
Agios Konstantinos 292

Thessaly 292
Larisa................................292
Volos 296
Pelion Peninsula...............299
Trikala 305
Around Trikala 307
Meteora............................308
Kalambaka........................311
Kastraki 312

NORTHERN GREECE   314

Suggested Itineraries 314
Epiros 314
Ioannina 316
Around Ioannina 320
The Zagoria Villages 322
Konitsa 325
Metsovo 326
Igoumenitsa 328
Sagiada 330
Syvota 331

Parga 331
Preveza 334
Around Preveza 336
Arta 336
Macedonia 337
Thessaloniki......................337
Around Thessaloniki 349
Pella 349
Mt Olympus 350
Veria 354

Vergina 356
Edessa 356
Florina 358
Prespa Lakes 359
Kastoria 362
Halkidiki 364
Kavala 374
Philippi 378
Thrace 379
Xanthi 381

Komotini 382
Alexandroupolis 383
Evros Delta 387

Alexandroupolis to
Didymotiho 387
Didymotiho 387

North of Didymotiho 389

SARONIC GULF ISLANDS 391

Suggested Itineraries 391
Aegina **392**
Aegina Town 393
Around Aegina 395
Moni & Angistri Islets 396

Poros **396**
Poros Town 397
Around Poros 398
Peloponnesian Mainland 398
Hydra **399**

Hydra Town 400
Around Hydra 402
Spetses **403**
Spetses Town 404
Around Spetses 407

CYCLADES 408

Suggested Itineraries 408
Andros **413**
Gavrio 413
Batsi 413
Andros (Hora) 415
Around Andros 416
Tinos **416**
Tinos (Hora) 418
Around Tinos 420
Syros **420**
Ermoupolis 422
Galissas 425
Around Syros 426
Mykonos **426**
Mykonos (Hora) 428
Around Mykonos 433
Delos **433**
Ancient Delos 434
Paros & Antiparos **436**
Paros 436
Antiparos 443
Naxos **445**

Naxos (Hora) 446
Around Naxos 450
Little Cyclades 453
Iraklia....................................454
Shinousa 455
Koufonisia 456
Donousa 457
Amorgos **458**
Katapola 458
Amorgos Hora 460
Moni Hozoviotiissis 460
Aegiali 460
Around Amorgos 461
Ios **461**
Hora, Ormos & Milopotas ..462
Around Ios 465
Santorini (Thira) **466**
Fira 468
Around Santorini 473
Thirasia & Volcanic Islets ..477
Anafi **477**
Sikinos **478**

Folegandros **479**
Karavostasis 480
Karavostasis Hora 481
Around Folegandros 482
Milos & Kimolos **483**
Milos 483
Kimolos 487
Sifnos **487**
Kamares.................................488
Apollonia 489
Around Sifnos 489
Serifos **490**
Livadi.....................................490
Around Serifos 491
Kythnos **492**
Merihas 493
Around Kythnos 493
Kea **493**
Korissia 494
Ioulida 494
Around Kea 495

CRETE 496

Suggested Itineraries 497
Central Crete **500**
Iraklio 500
Knossos 509
Gortyna 511
Phaestos 512
Agia Triada...........................512
Matala....................................512
Malia 513
Eastern Crete **514**
Lasithi Plateau 514
Agios Nikolaos.....................515
Elounda 518
Kolokytha Peninsula............518
Spinalonga Island................519

Kritsa 519
Ancient Lato 519
Gournia 520
Mohlos 520
Sitia 521
Around Sitia 522
Zakros & Kato Zakros 522
Ancient Zakros 523
Xerokambos 523
Ierapetra 524
Myrtos 525
Myrtos to Ano Viannos 526
Western Crete **527**
Rethymno 527
Around Rethymno 531

Rethymno to Spili 531
Spili 532
Around Spili 532
Plakias 532
Around Plakias 534
Agia Galini............................534
Around Agia Galini 535
Hania 537
Akrotiri Peninsula 542
Hania to Xyloskalo 543
Samaria Gorge 543
Agia Roumeli to
Hora Sfakion 544
Hora Sfakion 544
Around Hora Sfakion 545

Sougia 546
Paleohora............................547

Around Paleohora 549
Kastelli-Kissamos 550

Around Kastelli-Kissamos 551

DODECANESE 553

Suggested Itineraries 553
Rhodes **556**
Rhodes Town 561
Eastern Rhodes 568
Western Rhodes 571
Southern Rhodes 572
The Interior 573
Halki **574**
Emborios 575
Around Halki 575
Karpathos **576**
Pigadia................................577
Southern Karpathos 579
Central Karpathos 580
Northern Karpathos 581
Kasos **582**
Fry 583
Around Kasos 584
Kastellorizo (Megisti) **584**
Kastellorizo Town 585
Symi **587**
Gialos 589
Around Symi 590

Tilos **591**
Livadia.................................592
Megalo Horio......................593
Around Megalo Horio 594
Nisyros **594**
Mandraki 595
Around Nisyros 596
Kos **597**
Kos Town 600
Around Kos Town 603
Around Kos 603
Astypalea **605**
Astypalea Town 606
Livadia.................................607
Other Beaches 608
Kalymnos **608**
Pothia 610
Around Pothia 611
Myrties & Masouri 612
Telendos Islet 612
Emborios 613
Vathys & Rina 613
Leros **613**

Lakki 615
Xirokambos 615
Platanos & Agia Marina 615
Pandeli 616
Krithoni & Alinda 616
Gourna 617
Northern Leros 617
Patmos **617**
Skala 619
Monasteries & Hora 620
North of Skala 621
South of Skala 621
Lipsi **621**
Lipsi Town 622
Around the Island 623
Arki & Marathi **624**
Arki 624
Marathi 625
Agathonisi **625**
Agios Giorgios 626
Around Agathonisi 626

NORTH-EASTERN AEGEAN ISLANDS 627

Suggested Itineraries 627
Ikaria & the Fourni Islands ...**630**
Agios Kirykos 632
Agios Kirykos to The North
Coast 633
West of Evdilos 634
Fourni Islands 637
Samos **637**
Vathy (Samos) 640
Pythagorio 643
Around Pythagorio 645
South-West Samos 645
West of Vathy (Samos) 646
Chios **647**

Chios Town 649
Central Chios 652
Southern Chios 653
Northern Chios 655
Inousses **655**
Inousses Village 656
Island Walk 657
Psara **657**
Lesvos (Mytilini) **658**
Mytilini Town 661
Northern Lesvos 664
Western Lesvos 667
Southern Lesvos 669
Limnos **672**

Myrina 674
Western Limnos 675
Central Limnos 676
Eastern Limnos 676
Agios Efstratios **676**
Samothraki **678**
Kamariotissa 679
Sanctuary of the
Great Gods 680
Around Samothraki 682
Thasos **684**
Thasos (Limenas) 686
East Coast 689
West Coast 690

EVIA & THE SPORADES 692

Suggested Itineraries 692
Evia **694**
Halkida 695
Central Evia 695
Northern Evia 696
Southern Evia 696

Skiathos **697**
Skiathos Town 698
Around Skiathos 700
Skopelos **702**
Skopelos Town 702
Glossa 705

Around Skopelos 706
Alonnisos **706**
Patitiri 708
Old Alonnisos 710
Around Alonnisos 710
Islets Around Alonnisos 711

Skyros 711
Skyros Town 713

Magazia & Molos 716
Around Skyros 717

IONIAN ISLANDS 718

Suggested Itineraries 718
Corfu & the Diapondia Islands **721**
Corfu Town 724
North of Corfu Town 729
South of Corfu Town 731
The West Coast 731
Paxi & Antipaxi **734**

Paxi 734
Antipaxi 737
Lefkada & Meganisi **737**
Lefkada 737
Meganisi 742
Kefallonia & Ithaki **743**
Kefallonia 743
Ithaki 750

Zakynthos............................**753**
Zakynthos Town 754
Around Zakynthos 757
Kythira & Antikythira **759**
Kythira................................759
Antikythira.........................763

LANGUAGE 765

GLOSSARY 771

THANKS 775

INDEX 791

Abbreviations 791

Text 791

Boxed Text 799

MAP LEGEND back page

METRIC CONVERSION inside back cover

Contents – Maps

GETTING AROUND

Road Distances (km) 131   Greece – Main Ferry Routes 133

ATHENS

Athens Map Section 144-5
Acropolis (Ancient) 151
Ancient Agora 157
Athens (Ancient) 160

National Archaeological
Museum 162
Athens Metro System 192
Around Athens 193

Piraeus 196
Attica 202

PELOPONNESE

Peloponnese 210-11
Patras 214
Corinth 221

Citadel of Mycenae 228
Nafplio 230
Sparta 242

Mystras 245
Kalamata 260
Ancient Olympia 270

CENTRAL GREECE

Sterea Ellada 275
Ancient Delphi &
Sanctuary of Apollo 277
Lamia..................................290

Thessaly..............................293
Larisa..................................294
Volos 297
Pelion Peninsula..................300

Meteora, Kastraki &
Kalambaka 309

NORTHERN GREECE

Epiros 315
Ioannina 317
The Zagoria Villages 323
Igoumenitsa 328
Parga 332
Preveza 334

Macedonia 338
Thessaloniki 340
Mt Olympus 351
Prespa Lakes 360
Kastoria 363
Athos Peninsula 368

Karyes 372
Kavala 375
Thrace 380
Alexandroupolis 384

SARONIC GULF ISLANDS

Saronic Gulf Islands 392
Aegina 393

Poros 397
Hydra..................................400

Hydra Town 401
Spetses................................404

CYCLADES

Cyclades 409
Andros 414
Tinos 417
Syros 421
Ermoupolis 423
Mykonos 427
Mykonos (hora) 429
Ancient Delos 435
Paros & Antiparos 437

Parikia 438
Naxos 446
Naxos (Hora) 448
Little Cyclades 454
Amorgos 459
Ios 462
Santorini (Thira) 467
Fira 470
Anafi 477

Sikinos 479
Folegandros 480
Milos & Kimolos 484
Sifnos 488
Serifos 490
Kythnos 492
Kea 494

CRETE

Crete 498-9
Iraklio 501
Palace of Knossos 510

Agios Nikolaos 516
Rethymo 528
Hania 536

Paleohora 547

DODECANESE

Dodecanese 554
Rhodes 558
Rhodes Old Town 561
Rhodes Town 565
Halki 575
Karpathos 576
Pigadia 578
Kasos 582

Kastellorizo 584
Tilos 591
Nisyros 595
Symi 588
Kos &Pserimos 598
Kos Town 601
Astypalea 606
Kalymnos 609

Pothia 611
Leros 614
Patmos 618
Lipsi 622
Arki &Marathi 625
Agathonisi 626

NORTH–EASTERN AEGEAN ISLANDS

North-Eastern
Aegean Islands 628
Ikaria &Fourni Islands 631
Samos 638
Vathy (Samos) 641
Pythagorio 643
Chios 648

Chios Town 650
Inousses 655
Psara 657
Lesvos 659
Mytilini 661
Olive Trails 671
Limnos 672

Samothraki 678
Sanctuary of the
Great Gods 681
Thasos 684
Thasos (Limenas) 686

EVIA & THE SPORADES

Evia & the Sporades 693
Skiathos 699

Skopelos 703
Alonnisos 707

Skyros 714
Corfu Town 725

IONIAN ISLANDS

Ionian Islands 719
Corfu 722
Corfu Old Town 726
Paxi & Antipaxi 734

Lefkada & Meganisi 738
Kefallonia & Ithaki 744
Argostoli 746
Zakynthos 754

Zakynthos Town 756
Kythira & Antikythira 760

GREECE MAP INDEX

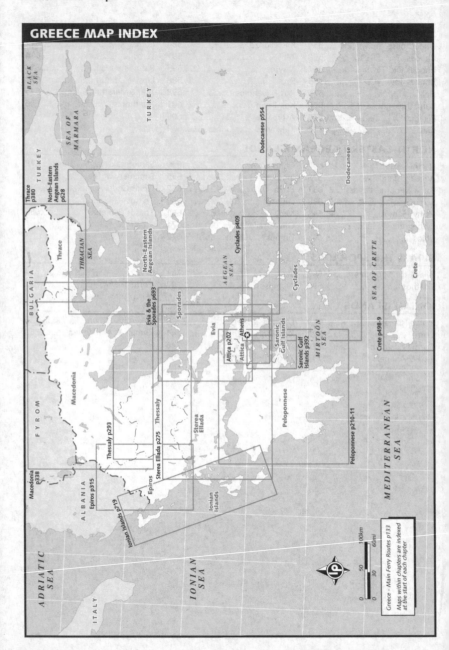

Greece – Main Ferry Routes p133

Maps within chapters are indexed at the start of each chapter

The Authors

David Willett

David is a freelance journalist based near Bellingen on the mid-north coast of New South Wales, Australia. He grew up in Hampshire, England, and wound up in Australia in 1980 after stints working on newspapers in Iran (1975–78) and Bahrain. He spent two years working as a sub-editor on the *Melbourne Sun* before trading a steady job for a warmer climate. Between jobs, David has travelled extensively in Europe, the Middle East and Asia.

He is a regular visitor to Athens as coordinator of Lonely Planet's guide to *Greece* and co-author of the Athens city guide. He is also the author of Lonely Planet's guide to *Tunisia*, and has contributed to various other guides, including *Africa*, *Australia*, *Indonesia*, *South-East Asia*, *Mediterranean Europe* and *Western Europe*.

Paul Hellander

Paul has never really stopped travelling since he first looked at a map in his native England. He graduated from Birmingham University with a degree in Greek before heading for Australia. He taught Modern Greek and trained interpreters and translators before donning the hat of a travel writer. Paul has contributed to some 24 LP titles including guides to *Greek Islands*, *Rhodes & the Dodecanese*, *Crete*, *Cyprus*, *France*, *Israel & the Palestinian Territories*, *Europe*, *Singapore*, *Central America* and *South America*. When not travelling with his Mac and Nikons, he lives in Adelaide, South Australia where he studies the history of political intelligence, listens to the BBC World Service, cooks Thai food and grows hot chillies. He was last seen plotting yet more forays to Europe's Mediterranean basin.

Rosemary Hall

Rosemary was born in Sunderland, England. She graduated in fine art, but fame and fortune as an artist eluded her, so she spent a few months bumming around Europe and India. After teaching in northern England, she decided to find something more exotic, finally landing a job in Iraq. When, after two years, the Iraqi government refused to renew her work permit, she settled in London, tried to make it again as a painter, did supply teaching, and then travelled in India, South-East Asia and Africa.

Rosemary researched Iraq for Lonely Planet's *Middle East on a Shoestring* and wrote the 1st edition of *Greece*. She is the co-author of four walking guides to London.

Brigitte Barta

Brigitte was born in Wellington, New Zealand. At the age of six months her parents took her to live in Berlin, via Naples, and she first visited Greece when she was three. She grew up mostly in Melbourne, Australia, and has also lived in England, Germany, Spain, Switzerland, the US and Greece, where she spent a year on the island of Santorini. She currently resides in San Francisco and works in the New Media department at Lonely Planet's Oakland office. One of these days, she'll stop day-dreaming about moving back to Greece and just do it.

Carolyn Bain

Carolyn was born in Melbourne, Australia (the third-largest Greek city in the world) and first visited Greece as a teenager (on a package tour from Scandinavia, no less). She was therefore eminently qualified to island-hop around the Ionians in search of the perfect beach, best kalamari and any unattached shipping magnates. Due to an unfortunate shortage of shipping magnates, she continues her job as an author for Lonely Planet and is based in Melbourne.

Kate Daly

Born in Sydney, Kate spent several formative childhood years in the remote country town of Wee Waa, in north-western NSW. She dropped out of an arts/law degree in 1985, and turned to travel instead – hitchhiking up the East Coast and through the Northern Territory. Returning to uni she studied writing and has a BA (Communications) from the University of Technology, Sydney. Kate has travelled widely in North- and South-East Asia and Europe. Her first experience of the extraordinary islands of the Aegean was via Turkey. On the work front, she's done it all, from copywriter in Tokyo, to editor in Melbourne. She has written for Lonely Planet's *Out to Eat Melbourne 2000*, and contributed to Lonely Planet's *Queensland* and *Australia* guides.

ACKNOWLEDGMENTS
David Willett

I'd like to thank all the friends who have contributed so much to my understanding of Athens over the years, especially Maria Economou from the Greek National Tourism Office; the Kanakis family; Ana Kamais; Matt Barrett; Tolis Houtzoumis; and Alex and Pavlo.

Thanks also to my friends around the Peloponnese: Petros and Dimitris in Nafplio; Yiannis in Sparti; the irrepressible Voula in Gythio; the Dimitreas family from Kardamyli; and Andreas the magician from Patras.

Special thanks to my partner, Rowan, and our son Tom for holding the fort at home during my frequent trips away.

Paul Hellander

Updating a travel guide invariably involves the input of many people. I would like to mention some who helped in ways big and small to make my work just that little bit easier: Byron & Marcus Hellander (Ioannina), Maria Haristou and Andonis Konstandinidis (Thessaloniki), Giannis Mourehidis (Konitsa), Alekos and Valentini Papadopoulos (Thessaloniki), Angeliki Kanelli (Athens), Nikos and Anna Hristodoulou (Lipsi), Raphael Delstanche (Rhodes), Alex & Christine Sakellaridis (Halki), Minas Gializis (Karpathos), Emmanouil Manousos (Kasos), Nikos Perakis, (Kato Zakros), Vasilis Skoulas (Anogia), Tony Fennymore (Hania), Vangelis Skoulakis (Kissamos), Mihalis Manousakis (Hania). Professional thanks also to Geoff Harvey, DriveAway Holidays (Sydney), Peugeot-Sodexa (Paris), Kostas Lambrianos, Dodekanisos Naftiliaki (Rhodes), Tonia Marangou, Minoan Lines (Piraeus) and finally the adept editors and designers at LP who put this book together. Stella Hellander – wife, companion and photographer – this time, this one is just for you!

Rosemary Hall

I am grateful to George (Vrachos Camping) and George Papadimitrio (Kalambaka) for getting my laptop into action again when I couldn't; the staff at the EOT and Municipal Tourist offices in Arahova, Volos and Larisa; the staff at Planet Internet Café (Larisa); the staff at Thalpos Leisure & Services (Skopelos); Pakis Athanasiou at Ikos Travel and Maria at Liadromia Hotel (Alonnisos) and Poppi at South Evia Tours, Karistos (Evia) for invaluable assistance.

Thanks to Kristina Brooks-Tsalapatani and Nikkos Sikkes for filling me in on all the changes that have taken place on Skyros in the last two years; Bridget Johnson and Dave Dix for keeping an eye on my flat while I was away and, as usual, to David Willett for support and good humour in his emails and our telephone conversations.

Finally, and most importantly, thank you to all the people who offered sympathy and practical help when, halfway through my trip, I received a telephone call telling me of my mother's death. These include my father, staff at First Choice Tours on Skiathos, David Hall and Janet Wright whose assistance at this difficult time enabled me to get back to the UK faster than I believed possible, and to everyone at Lonely Planet involved in the production of this book.

I dedicate my contribution to this book to my mother who always encouraged me in my travels.

Brigitte Barta

Many people were extremely generous with their time and insights during the course of my research. Thanks go to Margarita and Kostas Moukas, whose energy and devotion to conservation and restoration on Lesvos is an inspiration. Aristides Sifneos, also on Lesvos, provided background on history and special places. Christos Karagiannidis, clown king of Thasos, gave me a crash course on the best of his island, and Tatiana and Iordanis Iordanidis intensified my fondness for Samothraki. Anna Dakoutros (Santorini) and Theodore and Güher Spordilis (Chios) took hospitality too far, despite my protests – thank you. I would also like to thank Maria Kollerou at Myrina Tourist & Travel Agency (Limnos), Samiotis Tours (Lesvos), Smaragda at the Chios tourist office, and ITSA Travel (Samos). Dimitris Tsavdaridis, on Santorini, put me in touch with all the right people and kept my sangria cup filled – D, you are the secret ingredient in this cocktail. In Athens, Maria and Sophia Brakoulia gave me a soft landing and showed me a good time, and in London their brother, Andreas, did the same. I hope you will let me reciprocate sometime soon. Back at home my nonstop gratitude goes to Rob Guerin for patience, understanding and courage at the crossroads and beyond. And thanks to Dermot Burgess for taking my photo.

Carolyn Bain

The Greeks once again showed that while they're not too flash at adhering to advertised opening hours or providing easily decipherable ferry schedules, they more than compensate for this with their kindness and warmth. I met countless friendly, helpful Greeks who made my job a lot more pleasurable, and my heartfelt thanks go out to all of them. I must particularly thank Christina Avloniti in Corfu Town, who helped me make sense of the ferries; Noula Mouzakiti in Agios Stefanos, and her staff, who made sure I got to the Diapondia islands and also showed me a great time in their town; Dora in Nydri on Lefkada who gave me valuable help and information; and the Makis family of Poros on Kefallonia, who so kindly came to my rescue during the car debacle.

Others I must thank are Sarah Vermoolen for her excellent company and assistance on Corfu, and all the great people I met on Paxi who made it so damn hard to leave their wonderful island. Thanks to Ann Buckley, my neighbour on Ithaki, and especially to my sister, Jules Bain, for her great company and support on Kefallonia. Thanks also to Jules and John for their hospitality in London post-research. And finally, thanks to Cameron Lloyd, the Most Cultured Man in Brisbane, for sharing good lobster, bad wine and many fine ouzo-commercial moments on lovely Kythira.

Kate Daly

Thank you to all those overworked travel agents and visitor information offices (official or otherwise) who were generous with their time under hectic peak season conditions, and to all the kind souls along the way who offered information, ouzo, coffee, cake (and best of all cake & ice cream), sweets and trademark Greek wide smiles. A huge thank you to Brigitte Barta for advice along the way, and to Paul Hellander, Carolyn Bain and David Willett for advice and assistance. Melanie Dankel and Gus Balbotin, the co-ordinating editor and cartographer respectively, and their team, deserve a thousand thanks for speeding things up when I was lagging behind. Thanks also to Kieran Grogan for making it happen in the first place. Lastly, an inadequate thank you to Mikey for coping with Typhoon Katie.

This Book

This is the 5th edition of LP's *Greece* guide. The 1st edition was written by Rosemary Hall. The 2nd edition was updated by David Willett, Paul Hellander, Rosemary Hall and Kerry Kenihan, and the 3rd edition by David Willett, Paul Hellander, Rosemary Hall and Corinne Simcock, with David coordinating both editions.

For the 5th edition, David Willet was the coordinating author, and updated the introductory chapters and Athens, the Peloponnese and Saronic Gulf Islands chapters. Paul Hellander updated the Northern Greece, Crete and Rhodes and the Dodecanese chapters. Rosemary Hall updated Evia and the Sporades, Carolyn Bain was responsible for the Ionian Islands chapter, Brigitte Barta for the North-East Aegean Island chapter and Kate Daly for the Cyclades chapter.

FROM THE PUBLISHER

The 5th edition of *Greece* was produced in Lonely Planet's Melbourne office. Production was coordinated by Melanie Dankel (editorial) and Agustín Poó y Balbontin (mapping and design). A big *efcharisto* to the illustrious editing and proofing team Janine Eberle, Shelley Muir, Helen Yeates, Susannah Farfor, Bethune Carmichael, Bridget Blair, Darren O'Connell (Doc) and Yvonne Byron. Mapping prowess was lent by Sally Morgan, Csanad Csutoros, Joelene Kowalski and Yvonne Bischofberger. The chapter end was skillfully drawn by Agustín. General credits to Kieran Grogan, Tony Davidson, Adrian Persoglia, Mark Griffiths, Mark Germanchis, as well as the GIS unit for providing the data for Athens maps, LPI for the pics, Maria Vallianos for the front cover and Matt King for the illustrations.

Thanks to Emma Koch for the language chapter, to Helen Papadimitriou, Chris Tsismetzis and Anastasia Safioleas for additional Greek language pointers and to Emma Sangster for watching brief assistance.

Itan fandastika!

ACKNOWLEDGMENTS

Maps

THANKS
Many thanks to the travellers who used the last edition and wrote to us with helpful hints, advice and interesting anecdotes. Your names appear in the back of this book.

Foreword

ABOUT LONELY PLANET GUIDEBOOKS

The story begins with a classic travel adventure: Tony and Maureen Wheeler's 1972 journey across Europe and Asia to Australia. Useful information about the overland trail did not exist at that time, so Tony and Maureen published the first Lonely Planet guidebook to meet a growing need.

From a kitchen table, then from a tiny office in Melbourne (Australia), Lonely Planet has become the largest independent travel publisher in the world, an international company with offices in Melbourne, Oakland (USA), London (UK) and Paris (France).

Today Lonely Planet guidebooks cover the globe. There is an ever-growing list of books and there's information in a variety of forms and media. Some things haven't changed. The main aim is still to help make it possible for adventurous travellers to get out there – to explore and better understand the world.

At Lonely Planet we believe travellers can make a positive contribution to the countries they visit – if they respect their host communities and spend their money wisely. Since 1986 a percentage of the income from each book has been donated to aid projects and human rights campaigns.

Updates Lonely Planet thoroughly updates each guidebook as often as possible. This usually means there are around two years between editions, although for more unusual or more stable destinations the gap can be longer. Check the imprint page (following the colour map at the beginning of the book) for publication dates.

Between editions up-to-date information is available in two free newsletters – the paper *Planet Talk* and email *Comet* (to subscribe, contact any Lonely Planet office) – and on our Web site at www.lonelyplanet.com. The *Upgrades* section of the Web site covers a number of important and volatile destinations and is regularly updated by Lonely Planet authors. *Scoop* covers news and current affairs relevant to travellers. And, lastly, the *Thorn Tree* bulletin board and *Postcards* section of the site carry unverified, but fascinating, reports from travellers.

Correspondence The process of creating new editions begins with the letters, postcards and emails received from travellers. This correspondence often includes suggestions, criticisms and comments about the current editions. Interesting excerpts are immediately passed on via newsletters and the Web site, and everything goes to our authors to be verified when they're researching on the road. We're keen to get more feedback from organisations or individuals who represent communities visited by travellers.

Lonely Planet gathers information for everyone who's curious about the planet – and especially for those who explore it first-hand. Through guidebooks, phrasebooks, activity guides, maps, literature, newsletters, image library, TV series and Web site we act as an information exchange for a worldwide community of travellers.

Research Authors aim to gather sufficient practical information to enable travellers to make informed choices and to make the mechanics of a journey run smoothly. They also research historical and cultural background to help enrich the travel experience and allow travellers to understand and respond appropriately to cultural and environmental issues.

Authors don't stay in every hotel because that would mean spending a couple of months in each medium-sized city and, no, they don't eat at every restaurant because that would mean stretching belts beyond capacity. They do visit hotels and restaurants to check standards and prices, but feedback based on readers' direct experiences can be very helpful.

Many of our authors work undercover, others aren't so secretive. None of them accept freebies in exchange for positive write-ups. And none of our guidebooks contain any advertising.

Production Authors submit their manuscripts and maps to offices in Australia, USA, UK or France. Editors and cartographers – all experienced travellers themselves – then begin the process of assembling the pieces. When the book finally hits the shops, some things are already out of date, we start getting feedback from readers and the process begins again …

WARNING & REQUEST

Things change – prices go up, schedules change, good places go bad and bad places go bankrupt – nothing stays the same. So, if you find things better or worse, recently opened or long since closed, please tell us and help make the next edition even more accurate and useful. We genuinely value all the feedback we receive. A well-travelled team reads and acknowledges every letter, postcard and email and ensures that every morsel of information finds its way to the appropriate authors, editors and cartographers for verification.

Everyone who writes to us will find their name listed in the next edition of the appropriate guidebook. They will also receive the latest issue of *Planet Talk*, our quarterly printed newsletter, or *Comet*, our monthly email newsletter. Subscriptions to both newsletters are free. The very best contributions will be rewarded with a free guidebook.

We may edit, reproduce and incorporate your comments in all Lonely Planet products, such as guidebooks, Web sites and digital products, so let us know if you don't want your comments reproduced or your name acknowledged.

Send all correspondence to the Lonely Planet office closest to you:

Australia: Locked Bag 1, Footscray, Victoria 3011
USA: 150 Linden St, Oakland, CA 94607
UK: 10a Spring Place, London NW5 3BH

Or email us at: talk2us@lonelyplanet.com.au

For news, views and updates see our Web site: www.lonelyplanet.com

HOW TO USE A LONELY PLANET GUIDEBOOK

The best way to use a Lonely Planet guidebook is any way you choose. At Lonely Planet we believe the most memorable travel experiences are often those that are unexpected, and the finest discoveries are those you make yourself. Guidebooks are not intended to be used as if they provide a detailed set of infallible instructions!

Contents All Lonely Planet guidebooks follow roughly the same format. The Facts about the Destination chapters or sections give background information ranging from history to weather. Facts for the Visitor gives practical information on issues like visas and health. Getting There & Away gives a brief starting point for researching travel to and from the destination. Getting Around gives an overview of the transport options when you arrive.

The peculiar demands of each destination determine how subsequent chapters are broken up, but some things remain constant. We always start with background, then proceed to sights, places to stay, places to eat, entertainment, getting there and away, and getting around information – in that order.

Heading Hierarchy Lonely Planet headings are used in a strict hierarchical structure that can be visualised as a set of Russian dolls. Each heading (and its following text) is encompassed by any preceding heading that is higher on the hierarchical ladder.

Entry Points We do not assume guidebooks will be read from beginning to end, but that people will dip into them. The traditional entry points are the list of contents and the index. In addition, however, some books have a complete list of maps and an index map illustrating map coverage.

There may also be a colour map that shows highlights. These highlights are dealt with in greater detail in the Facts for the Visitor chapter, along with planning questions and suggested itineraries. Each chapter covering a geographical region usually begins with a locator map and another list of highlights. Once you find something of interest in a list of highlights, turn to the index.

Maps Maps play a crucial role in Lonely Planet guidebooks and include a huge amount of information. A legend is printed on the back page. We seek to have complete consistency between maps and text, and to have every important place in the text captured on a map. Map key numbers usually start in the top left corner.

Although inclusion in a guidebook usually implies a recommendation we cannot list every good place. Exclusion does not necessarily imply criticism. In fact there are a number of reasons why we might exclude a place – sometimes it is simply inappropriate to encourage an influx of travellers.

Introduction

Greece has always attracted travellers, drawn by the fascination of some of Europe's earliest civilisations. Philosophers muse that to journey to Greece is to return home, for the legacy of ancient Greece pervades the consciousness of all Western nations. Greek Doric, Ionic and Corinthian columns adorn many of our buildings, and much of our greatest early literature drew on the Greek myths for inspiration. Some of our most evocative words are Greek – chaos, drama, tragedy and democracy, to name a few. Perhaps the greatest legacy is democracy itself.

While it was this underlying awareness of Greek culture that drew the wealthy young aristocrats of the 19th century to the country, the majority of today's visitors are drawn by Greece's beaches and sunshine. Island-hopping has become something of an initiation rite for the international singles set. Their numbers are dwarfed, however, by the millions of package holiday-makers who come to Greece every year in search of two weeks of sunshine by the sea. Greece now welcomes almost 10 million visitors a year, making tourism easily the most important industry in the country.

The ancient sites are an enduring attraction. The Acropolis needs no introduction as the most remarkable legacy of the classical period. At Knossos on Crete, you can wander around the ancient capital of one of Europe's oldest civilisations: the Minoan. The many Minoan, Mycenaean and classical Greek sites, and elaborate Byzantine churches, stand alongside the legacies left by foreign occupiers: towering Venetian, Frankish and Turkish castles, and crumbling, forgotten mosques.

Reminders of the past are everywhere. The Greek landscape is littered with broken columns and crumbling fragments of ancient walls. Moreover, there is hardly a meadow, river or mountaintop which is not sacred because of its association with some deity, and the spectres of the past linger still.

Greece has clung to its traditions more tenaciously than most European countries. Through hundreds of years of foreign occupation by Franks, Venetians, Turks and others, tradition and religion were the factors that kept the notion of Greek nationhood alive. Greeks today remain only too aware of the hardships their forebears endured, and even hip young people carry on these traditions with enthusiasm.

The traditions manifest themselves in a variety of ways, including regional costumes, such as the baggy pantaloons and high boots worn by elderly Cretan men, and in the embroidered dresses and floral headscarves worn by the women of Olymbos, on Karpathos. Many traditions take the form of festivals, where Greeks express their *joie de vivre* through dancing, singing and feasting.

Festival time or not, the Greek capacity for enjoyment of life is immediately evident. If you arrive in a Greek town in the early evening in summer, you could be forgiven for thinking you've arrived mid-festival.

This is the time of the *volta*, when everyone takes to the streets, refreshed from their siesta, dressed up and raring to go. All this adds up to Greece being one of Europe's most relaxed and friendly countries. But Greece is no European backwater locked in a time warp. In towns and cities you will find discos as lively as any in Italy, France or Britain, and boutiques as trendy.

If you're a beach-lover, Greece, with its 1400 islands, has more coastline than any other country in Europe. You can choose between rocky outcrops, pebbled coves or long swathes of golden sand.

Greece's scenery is as varied as its beaches. There is the semitropical lushness of the Ionian and North-Eastern Aegean Islands and southern Crete; the bare sunbaked rocks of the Cyclades; and the forested mountains, icy lakes and tumbling rivers of northern Greece. Much of this breathtaking landscape is mantled with vibrant wild flowers.

There is yet another phenomenon which even people cynical about anything vaguely supernatural comment upon. It takes the form of inexplicable happenings, coincidences, or fortuitous occurrences. It could be meeting up with a long-lost friend, or bumping into the same person again and again on your travels; or missing the ferry and being offered a lift on a private yacht; or being hot, hungry, thirsty and miles from anywhere, then stumbling upon a house whose occupants offer hospitality.

Perhaps these serendipitous occurrences can be explained as the work of the gods of ancient Greece, who, some claim, have not entirely relinquished their power, and to prove it, occasionally come down to earth to intervene in the lives of mortals.

Facts about Greece

HISTORY
From ancient Minoan palaces and classical Greek temples to spectacular Byzantine churches and remote Frankish castles, the legacy of Greece's long and colourful history is everywhere.

Stone Age
The discovery of a Neanderthal skull in a cave on the Halkidiki peninsula of Macedonia has confirmed the presence of humans in Greece 700,000 years ago. Bones and tools from Palaeolithic times have been found in the Pindos mountains.

The move to a pastoral existence came during Neolithic times (7000–3000 BC). The fertile area that is now Thessaly was the first area to be settled. The people grew barley and wheat, and bred sheep and goats. They used clay to produce pots, vases and simple statuettes of the Great Mother (the earth goddess), whom they worshipped.

By 3000 BC, people were living in settlements complete with streets, squares and mud-brick houses. The villages were centred on a large palace-like structure which belonged to the tribal leader. The most complete Neolithic settlements in Greece are Dimini (inhabited from 4000 to 1200 BC) and Sesklo, both near the city of Volos.

Bronze Age
Around 3000 BC, Indo-European migrants introduced the processing of bronze (an alloy of copper and tin) into Greece – so began three remarkable civilisations: the Cycladic, Minoan and Mycenaean.

Cycladic Civilisation The Cycladic civilisation, centred on the islands of the Cyclades, is divided into three periods: Early (3000–2000 BC), Middle (2000–1500 BC) and Late (1500–1100 BC). The most impressive legacy of this civilisation is the statuettes carved from Parian marble – the famous Cycladic figurines. Like statuettes from Neolithic times, they depicted images of the Great Mother. Other remains include bronze and obsidian tools and weapons, gold jewellery, and stone and clay vases and pots.

The peoples of the Cycladic civilisation were accomplished sailors who developed prosperous maritime trade links. They exported their wares to Asia Minor (the west of present-day Turkey), Europe and north Africa, as well as to Crete and continental Greece. The Cyclades islands were influenced by both the Minoan and Mycenaean civilisations.

Minoan Civilisation Crete's Minoan civilisation was the first advanced civilisation to emerge in Europe, drawing its inspiration from two great Middle Eastern civilisations: the Mesopotamian and the Egyptian. Archaeologists divide the Minoan civilisation, like the Cycladic, into three phases: Early (3000–2100 BC), Middle (2100–1500 BC) and Late (1500–1100 BC).

Many aspects of Neolithic life endured during the Early period, but by 2500 BC most people on the island had been assimilated into a new and distinct culture which we now call the Minoan, after the mythical King Minos. The Minoan civilisation reached its peak during the Middle period, producing pottery and metalwork of remarkable beauty and a high degree of imagination and skill.

The Late period saw the civilisation decline both commercially and militarily against Mycenaean competition from the mainland, until its abrupt end around 1100 BC, when Dorian invaders and natural disasters ravaged the island.

Like the Cycladic civilisation, the Minoan was a great maritime power which exported goods throughout the Mediterranean. The polychrome Kamares pottery, which flourished during the Middle period, was highly prized by the Egyptians.

The first calamity to strike the Minoans was a violent earthquake in about 1700 BC, which destroyed the palaces at Knossos,

Phaestos, Malia and Zakros. The Minoans rebuilt them to a more complex, almost labyrinthine design with multiple storeys, sumptuous royal apartments, reception halls, storerooms, workshops, living quarters for staff and an advanced drainage system. The interiors were decorated with the celebrated Minoan frescoes, now on display in the archaeological museum at Iraklio.

The Minoans were also literate. Their first script resembled Egyptian hieroglyphics, the most famous example of which is the inscription on the Phaestos disc (1700 BC). They progressed to a syllable-based script which 20th-century archaeologists dubbed Linear A, because it consists of linear symbols. Like the earlier hieroglyphics, it has not yet been deciphered, but archaeologists believe that it was used to document trade transactions and the contents of royal storerooms, rather than to express abstract concepts.

Some historians have suggested that the civilisation's decline after 1500 BC was accelerated by the effects of the massive volcanic explosion on the Cycladic island of Santorini (Thira), an eruption vulcanologists believe was more cataclysmic than any on record. They theorise that the fallout of volcanic ash from the blast caused a succession of crop failures – with resulting social upheaval.

Mycenaean Civilisation The decline of the Minoan civilisation in the Late Minoan period coincided with the rise of the first great civilisation on the Greek mainland, the Mycenaean (1900–1100 BC), which reached its peak between 1500 and 1200 BC. Named after the ancient city of Mycenae, where the German archaeologist Heinrich Schliemann made his celebrated finds in 1876, it is also known as the Achaean civilisation after the Indo-European branch of migrants who had settled on mainland Greece and absorbed many aspects of Minoan culture.

Unlike Minoan society, where the lack of city walls seems to indicate relative peace under some form of central authority, Mycenaean civilisation was characterised by

independent city-states such as Corinth, Pylos, Tiryns and, the most powerful of them all, Mycenae. These were ruled by kings who inhabited palaces enclosed within massive walls on easily defensible hilltops.

The Mycenaeans' most impressive legacy is their magnificent gold jewellery and ornaments, the best of which can be seen in the National Archaeological Museum in Athens. The Mycenaeans wrote in what is called Linear B (an early form of Greek unrelated to the Linear A of Crete), which has been deciphered. They also worshipped gods who were precursors of the later Greek gods.

Examples of Linear B have also been found on Crete, suggesting that Mycenaean invaders may have conquered the island, perhaps around 1500 BC, when many Minoan palaces were destroyed. Mycenaean influence stretched further than Crete: the Mycenaean city-states banded together to defeat Troy (Ilium) and thus to protect their trade routes to the Black Sea, and archaeological research has unearthed Mycenaean artefacts as far away as Egypt, Mesopotamia and Italy.

The Mycenaean civilisation came to an end during the 12th century BC when it was overrun by the Dorians.

Geometric Age

The origins of the Dorians remain uncertain. They are generally thought to have come from Epiros or northern Macedonia, but some historians argue that they only arrived from there because they had been driven out of Doris, in central Greece, by the Mycenaeans.

The warrior-like Dorians settled first in the Peloponnese, but soon fanned out over much of the mainland, razing the city-states and enslaving the inhabitants. They later conquered Crete and the south-west coast of Asia Minor. Other Indo-European tribes known as the Thessalians settled in what is now Thessaly. Of the original Greek tribal groups, the Aeolians fled to the north-west coast of Asia Minor; the Ionians sought refuge on the central coast and the islands of Lesvos, Samos and Chios, although they also held out in mainland Greece – in Attica and the well-fortified city of Athens.

The Dorians brought a traumatic break with the past, and the next 400 years are often referred to as Greece's 'dark age'. But it would be unfair to dismiss the Dorians completely; they brought iron with them and developed a new style of pottery, decorated with striking geometrical designs – although art historians are still out to lunch as to whether the Dorians merely copied the designs perfected by Ionians in Attica. The Dorians worshipped male gods instead of fertility goddesses and adopted the Mycenaean gods of Poseidon, Zeus and Apollo, paving the way for the later Greek religious pantheon.

Perhaps most importantly, the Dorian warriors developed into a class of landholding aristocrats. This worsened the lot of the average farmer but also brought about the demise of the monarchy as a system of government, along with a resurgence of the Mycenaean pattern of independent city-states, this time led by wealthy aristocrats instead of absolute monarchs – the beginnings of 'democratic' government.

Archaic Age

By about 800 BC, local agriculture and animal husbandry had become productive enough to trigger a resumption of maritime trading. New Greek colonies were established in north Africa, Italy, Sicily, southern France and southern Spain to fill the vacuum left by the decline of those other great Mediterranean traders, the Phoenicians.

The people of the various city-states were unified by the development of a Greek alphabet (of Phoenician origin, though the Greeks introduced vowels), the verses of Homer (which created a sense of a shared Mycenaean past), the establishment of the Olympic Games (which brought all the city-states together), and the setting up of central sanctuaries such as Delphi (a neutral meeting ground for lively negotiations), giving Greeks, for the first time, a sense of national identity. This period is known as the Archaic, or Middle, Age.

Most city-states were built to a similar plan, with a fortified acropolis (highest point of a city). The acropolis contained the cities' temples and treasury and also served as a refuge during invasions. Outside the acropolis was the *agora* (market), a bustling commercial quarter, and beyond it the residential areas.

The city-states were autonomous, free to pursue their own interests as they saw fit. Most city-states abolished monarchic rule in favour of an aristocratic form of government, usually headed by an *arhon* (chief magistrate). Aristocrats were often disliked by the population because of their inherited privileges, and some city-states fell to the rule of tyrants after Kypselos started the practice in Corinth around 650 BC. Tyrants seized their position rather than inheriting it. These days they've got an image problem, but in ancient times they were often seen as being on the side of ordinary citizens.

Athens & Solon The seafaring city-state of Athens, meanwhile, was still in the hands of aristocrats, and a failed coup attempt by a would-be tyrant led the legislator Draco to draw up his infamous laws in 620 BC (hence the word 'draconian'). These were so harsh that even the theft of a cabbage was punishable by death.

Solon was appointed arhon in 594 BC with a far-reaching mandate to defuse the mounting tensions between the haves and the have-nots. He cancelled all debts and freed those who had become enslaved because of their debts. Declaring all free Athenians equal by law, he abolished inherited privileges and restructured political power along four classes based on wealth. Although only the first two classes were eligible for office, all four were allowed to elect magistrates and vote on legislation in the general assembly, known as the ecclesia. His reforms have led him to be regarded as the harbinger of democracy.

Sparta In the Peloponnese, Sparta was a very different kind of city-state. The Spartans were descended from Dorian invaders and used the Helots, the original inhabitants of Lakonia, as their slaves. They ran their society along strict military rules laid down by the 9th-century BC legislator Lycurgus.

Newborn babies were inspected and, if found wanting, were left to die on a mountain top. At the age of seven, boys were taken from their homes to start rigorous training that would turn them into crack soldiers. Girls were spared military training but were forced to keep very fit in order to produce healthy sons. Spartan indoctrination was so effective that dissent was unknown and a degree of stability was achieved that other city-states could only dream of.

While Athens became powerful through trade, Sparta became the ultimate military machine. They towered above the other city-states.

The Persian Wars The Persian drive to destroy Athens was sparked by the city's support for a rebellion in the Persian colonies located on the coast of Asia Minor. Emperor Darius spent five years suppressing the revolt, and emerged hellbent on revenge. He appealed to Sparta to launch an attack on Athens from behind, but the Spartans threw his envoy in a well and Darius was left to do the job alone.

A 25,000-strong Persian army reached Attica in 490 BC, but suffered a humiliating defeat when outmanoeuvred by an Athenian force of 10,000 at the Battle of Marathon.

Darius died in 485 BC before he could mount another assault, so it was left to his son Xerxes to fulfil his father's ambition of conquering Greece. In 480 BC Xerxes gathered men from every nation of his far-flung empire and launched a coordinated invasion by army and navy, the size of which the world had never seen. The historian Herodotus estimated that there were five million Persian soldiers. No doubt this was a gross exaggeration, but it was obvious Xerxes intended to give the Greeks more than a bloody nose.

Some 30 city-states of central and southern Greece met in Corinth to devise a common defence (others, including Delphi, sided with the Persians). They agreed on a combined army and navy under Spartan command, with the strategy provided by the Athenian leader Themistocles. The Spartan King Leonidas led the army to the pass at

Thermopylae, near present-day Lamia, the main passage into central Greece from the north. This bottleneck was easy to defend, and although the Greeks were greatly outnumbered they held the pass until a traitor showed the Persians a way over the mountains. The Greeks were forced to retreat, but Leonidas, along with 300 of his elite Spartan troops, fought to the death. The fleet, which held off the Persian navy north of Euboea (Evia), had no choice but to retreat as well.

The Spartans and their Peloponnesian allies fell back on their second line of defence (an earthen wall across the Isthmus of Corinth), while the Persians advanced upon Athens. Themistocles ordered his people to flee the city: the women and children to Salamis, and the men to sea with the Athenian fleet. The Persians razed Attica and burned Athens to the ground.

Things did not go so well for the Persian navy. By skilful manoeuvring, the Greek navy trapped the larger Persian ships in the narrow waters off Salamis, where they became easy pickings for the more mobile Greek vessels. Xerxes, who watched the defeat of his mighty fleet from the shore, returned to Persia in disgust, leaving his general Mardonius and the army to subdue Greece. The result was quite the reverse. A year later the Greeks, under the Spartan general Pausanias, obliterated the Persian army at the Battle of Plataea. The Athenian navy then sailed to Asia Minor and destroyed what was left of the Persian fleet at Mykale, freeing the Ionian city-states there from Persian rule.

Classical Age

After defeating the Persians, the disciplined Spartans once again retreated to their Peloponnesian 'fortress', while Athens basked in its role as liberator and embarked on a policy of blatant imperialism. In 477 BC it founded the Delian League, so called because the treasury was on the sacred island of Delos. The league consisted of almost every state with a navy, no matter how small, including many of the Aegean islands and some of the Ionian city-states in Asia Minor.

Ostensibly its purpose was twofold: to create a naval force to liberate the city-states that were still occupied by Persia, and to protect against another Persian attack. The swearing of allegiance to Athens and an annual contribution of ships (later just money) were mandatory. The league, in effect, became an Athenian empire.

Indeed, when Pericles became leader of Athens in 461 BC, he moved the treasury from Delos to the Acropolis and used its contents to begin a building program in which no expense was spared. His first objectives were to rebuild the temple complex of the Acropolis which had been destroyed by the Persians, and to link Athens to its lifeline, the port of Piraeus, with fortified walls designed to withstand any future siege.

Under Pericles' leadership (461–429 BC), Athens experienced a golden age of unprecedented cultural, artistic and scientific achievement. With the Aegean Sea safely under its wing, Athens began to look westward for further expansion, bringing it into conflict with the city-states of the mainland. It also encroached on the trade area of Corinth, which belonged to the Sparta-dominated Peloponnesian League. A series of skirmishes and provocations led to the Peloponnesian Wars.

First Peloponnesian War One of the major triggers of the first Peloponnesian War (431–421 BC) was the Corcyra incident, in which Athens supported Corcyra (present-day Kerkyra or Corfu) in a row with its mother city, Corinth. Corinth, now under serious threat, called on Sparta to help. Sparta's power depended to a large extent on Corinth's wealth, so it rallied to the cause.

Athens knew it couldn't defeat Sparta on land, so it abandoned Attica to the Spartans and withdrew behind its mighty walls, opting to rely on its navy to put pressure on Sparta by blockading the Peloponnese. Athens suffered badly during the siege. Plague broke out in the overcrowded city, killing a third of the population – including Pericles – but the defences held firm. The blockade of the Peloponnese eventually began to hurt, and the two cities reached an uneasy truce.

The Sicilian Adventure Throughout the war Athens had maintained an interest in Sicily and its grain, which the soil in Attica was too poor to produce. The Greek colonies there mirrored the city-states in Greece, the most powerful being Syracuse, which had remained neutral during the war.

In 416 BC, the Sicilian city of Segesta asked Athens to intervene in a squabble it was having with Selinus, an ally of Syracuse. A hot-headed second cousin of Pericles, Alcibiades, convinced the Athenian assembly to send a flotilla to Sicily; it would go on the pretext of helping Segesta, and then attack Syracuse.

The flotilla, under the joint leadership of Alcibiades, Nicias and Lamachos, was ill-fated from the outset. Nicias' health suffered and Lamachos, the most adept of the three, was killed. After laying siege to Syracuse for over three years, Alcibiades was called back to Athens on blasphemy charges arising from a drinking binge in which he knocked the heads off a few sacred statues. Enraged, he travelled not to Athens but to Sparta and persuaded the surprised Spartans to go to the aid of Syracuse. Sparta followed Alcibiades' advice and broke the siege in 413 BC, destroying the Athenian fleet and army.

Second Peloponnesian War Athens was depleted of troops, money and ships; its subject states were ripe for revolt, and Sparta was there to lend them a hand. In 413 BC the Spartans occupied Decelea in northern Attica and used it as a base to harass the region's farmers. Athens, deprived of its Sicilian grain supplies, soon began to feel the pinch. Its prospects grew even bleaker when Darius II of Persia, who had been keeping a close eye on events in Sicily and Greece, offered Sparta money to build a navy in return for a promise to return the Ionian cities of Asia Minor to Persia.

Athens attacked and even gained the upper hand for a while under the leadership of the reinstated Alcibiades, but its days were numbered once Persia entered the fray in Asia Minor, and Sparta regained its composure under the outstanding general Lysander. Athens surrendered to Sparta in 404 BC.

Corinth urged the total destruction of Athens but Lysander felt honour-bound to spare the city that had saved Greece from the Persians. Instead he crippled it by confiscating its fleet, abolishing the Delian League and tearing down the walls between the city and Piraeus.

Spartan Rule The Peloponnesian Wars had exhausted the city-states, leaving only Sparta in a position of any strength. During the wars, Sparta had promised to restore liberty to the city-states who had turned against Athens, but Lysander now changed his mind and installed oligarchies (governments run by the super-rich) supervised by Spartan garrisons. Soon there was widespread dissatisfaction.

Sparta found it had bitten off more than it could chew when it began a campaign to reclaim the cities of Asia Minor from Persian rule. This brought the Persians back into Greek affairs, where they found willing clients in Athens and increasingly powerful Thebes. Thebes, which had freed itself from Spartan control and had revived the Boeotian League, soon became the main threat to Sparta. Meanwhile, Athens regained some of its former power at the head of a new league of Aegean states known as the Second Confederacy – this time aimed against Sparta rather than Persia.

The rivalry culminated in the decisive Battle of Leuctra in 371 BC, where Thebes, under the leadership of the remarkable statesman and general Epaminondas, inflicted Sparta's first defeat in a pitched battle. Spartan influence collapsed, and Thebes filled the vacuum.

In a surprise about-turn Athens now allied itself with Sparta, and their combined forces met the Theban army at Mantinea in the Peloponnese in 362 BC. The battle was won by Thebes, but Epaminondas was killed. Without him, Theban power soon crumbled. Athens was unable to take advantage of the situation. The Second Confederacy became embroiled in infighting fomented by the Persians and when it eventually collapsed, Athens lost its final chance of regaining its former glory.

The city-states were now spent forces and a new power was rising in the north: Macedon. This had not gone unnoticed by the inspirational orator Demosthenes in Athens, who urged the city-states to prepare to defend themselves. Only Thebes took heed of his warnings and the two cities formed an alliance.

The Rise of Macedon

While the Greeks engineered their own decline through the Peloponnesian Wars, Macedon (geographically the modern *nomos*, or province, of Macedonia) was gathering strength in the north. Macedon had long been regarded as a bit of a backwater, a loose assembly of primitive hill tribes nominally ruled by a king. The Greeks considered the people to be barbarians (those whose speech sounded like 'bar-bar', which meant anyone who didn't speak Greek).

The man who turned them into a force to be reckoned with was Philip II, who came to the throne in 359 BC.

As a boy, Philip had been held hostage in Thebes where Epaminondas had taught him about military strategy. After organising his tribes into an efficient army of cavalry and long-lanced infantry, Philip made several forays south and manipulated his way into membership of the Amphyctionic Council (a group of states whose job it was to protect the oracle at Delphi).

In 339 BC, on the pretext of helping the Amphyctionic Council sort out a sacred war with Amfissa, he marched into Greece. The result was the Battle of Khaironeia in Boeotia (338 BC), in which the Macedonians defeated a combined army of Athenians and Thebans. The following year, Philip called together all the city-states (except Sparta, which remained aloof) at Corinth and persuaded them to form the League of Corinth and swear allegiance to Macedonia by promising to lead a campaign against Persia. The barbarian upstart had become leader of the Greeks.

Philip's ambition to tackle Persia never materialised, for in 336 BC he was assassinated by a Macedonian noble. His son, the 20-year-old Alexander, who had led the decisive cavalry charge at Khaironeia, became king.

Alexander the Great Alexander, highly educated (he had been tutored by Aristotle), fearless and ambitious, was an astute politician and intent upon finishing what his father had begun. Philip II's death had been the signal for rebellions throughout the budding empire, but Alexander wasted no time in crushing them, making an example of Thebes by razing it to the ground. After restoring order, he turned his attention to the Persian Empire and marched his army of 40,000 men into Asia Minor in 334 BC.

After a few bloody battles with the Persians, most notably at Issus (333 BC), Alexander succeeded in conquering Syria, Palestine and Egypt – where he was proclaimed pharaoh and founded the city of Alexandria. Intent on sitting on the Persian throne, he then began hunting down the Persian king, Darius III, defeating his army in Mesopotamia in 331 BC. Darius III fled east while Alexander mopped up his empire behind him, destroying the Persian palace at Persepolis in revenge for the sacking of the Acropolis 150 years earlier, and confiscating the royal treasury. Darius' body was found a year later: he had been stabbed to death by a Bactrian (Afghan) dissident.

Alexander The Great (356–323BC)

Alexander continued east into what is now known as Uzbekistan, Bactria (where he married a local princess, Roxane) and northern India. His ambition was now to conquer the world, which he believed ended at the sea beyond India. But his soldiers grew weary and in 324 BC forced him to return to Mesopotamia, where he settled in Babylon and drew up plans for an expedition south into Arabia. The following year, however, he fell ill suddenly and died, heirless, at the age of 33. His generals swooped like vultures on the empire.

When the dust settled, Alexander's empire had fallen apart into three large kingdoms and several smaller states. The three generals with the richest pickings were Ptolemy, founder of the Ptolemaic dynasty in Egypt (capital: Alexandria), which died out when the last of the dynasty, Cleopatra, committed suicide in 30 BC; Seleucus, founder of the Seleucid dynasty which ruled over Persia and Syria (capital: Antiochia); and Antigonus, who ruled over Asia Minor and whose Antigonid successors would win control over Macedonia proper.

Macedonia lost control of the Greek city-states to the south, which banded together into the Aetolian League, centred on Delphi, and the Achaean League, based in the Peloponnese; Athens and Sparta joined neither. One of Alexander's officers established the mini-kingdom of Pergamum in Asia Minor, which reached its height under Attalos I (ruled 241–196 BC) when it rivalled Alexandria as a centre of culture and learning. The island of Rhodes developed into a powerful mini-state by taxing passing ships.

Still, Alexander's formidable achievements during his 13 years on the world stage earned him the epithet 'the Great'. He spread Greek culture throughout a large part of the 'civilised' world, encouraged intermarriage and dismissed the anti-barbarian snobbery of the classical Greeks. In doing so, he ushered in the Hellenistic period of world history, in which Hellenic ('Greek') culture broke out of the narrow confines of the ancient Greek world and merged with the other proud cultures of antiquity to create a new, cosmopolitan tradition.

Roman Rule

While Alexander the Great was forging his vast empire in the east, the Romans had been expanding theirs to their west. Now they were keen to start making inroads into Greece. They found willing allies in Pergamum and Rhodes, who feared Syrian and Macedonian expansionism. The Romans defeated the Seleucid king, Antiochus III, in a three-year campaign and in 189 BC gave all of Asia Minor to Pergamum. Several wars were needed to subjugate Macedon, but in 168 BC Macedon lost the decisive Battle of Pydnaa.

The Achaean League was defeated in 146 BC; the Roman consul Mummius made an example of the rebellious Corinthians by completely destroying their beautiful city, massacring the men and selling the women and the children into slavery. Attalos III, king of Pergamum, died without an heir in 133 BC, he donated Asia Minor to Rome in his will.

In 86 BC, Athens joined an ill-fated rebellion against the Romans in Asia Minor staged by the king of the Black Sea region, Mithridates VI. In retribution, the Roman statesman Sulla invaded Athens, destroyed its walls and took off with its most valuable sculptures.

Greece then became a battleground as Roman generals fought for supremacy. In a decisive naval battle off Cape Actium (31 BC) Octavian was victorious over Mark Antony and Cleopatra and consequently became Rome's first emperor, assuming the title Augustus, meaning the Grand One.

For the next 300 years, Greece, as the Roman province of Achaea, experienced an unprecedented period of peace, the Pax Romana. The Romans had always venerated Greek art, literature and philosophy, and aristocratic Romans sent their offspring to the many schools in Athens. Indeed, the Romans adopted most aspects of Hellenistic culture, spreading its unifying traditions throughout their empire.

The Romans were also the first to refer to the Hellenes as Greeks, which is derived from the word *graikos* – the name of a prehistoric tribe.

Christianity & the Byzantine Empire

The Pax Romana began to crumble in AD 250 when the Goths invaded Greece, the first of a succession of invaders spurred on by the 'great migrations'. They were followed by the Visigoths in 395, the Vandals in 465, the Ostrogoths in 480, the Bulgars in 500, the Huns in 540 and the Slavs after 600.

Christianity, meantime, had emerged as the country's new religion. St Paul had made several visits to Greece in the 1st century AD and made converts in many places. The definitive boost to the spread of Christianity in this part of the world came with the conversion of the Roman emperors and the rise of the Byzantine Empire, which blended Hellenistic culture with Christianity.

In 324 Emperor Constantine I (also known as Constantine the Great), a Christian convert, transferred the capital of the empire from Rome to Byzantium, a city on the western shore of the Bosphorus, which was renamed Constantinople (present-day İstanbul). This was as much due to insecurity in Italy itself as to the growing importance of the wealthy eastern regions of the empire. By the end of the 4th century, the Roman Empire was formally divided into a western and eastern half. While Rome went into terminal decline, the eastern capital began to grow in wealth and strength, long outliving its western counterpart (the Byzantine Empire lasted until the capture of Constantinople by the Turks in 1453).

Emperor Theodosius I made Christianity the official religion in Greece in 394 and outlawed the worship of all Greek and Roman gods, now branded as being pagan. Athens remained an important cultural centre until 529, when Emperor Justinian forbade the teaching of classical philosophy in favour of Christian theology, then seen as the supreme form of all intellectual endeavour. The Hagia Sofia (Church of the Divine Wisdom) was built in Constantinople and some magnificent churches were also built in Greece, especially in Thessaloniki, which was a Christian stronghold much favoured by the Byzantine emperors.

The Crusades

It is one of the ironies of history that the demise of the Byzantine Empire was accelerated not by invasions of infidels from the east, nor barbarians from the north, but by fellow Christians from the west – the Frankish crusaders.

The stated mission of the crusades was to liberate the Holy Land from the Muslims, but in reality they were driven as much by greed as by religious fervour. By the time the First Crusade was launched in 1095, the Franks had already made substantial gains in Italy at the empire's expense and the rulers of Constantinople were understandably nervous about giving the crusaders safe passage on their way to Jerusalem. The first three crusades passed by without incident, but the fourth proved that the fear was justified. The crusaders struck a deal with Venice, which had a score to settle with the Byzantines, and was able to persuade the crusaders that Constantinople presented richer pickings than Jerusalem.

Constantinople was sacked in 1204 and the crusaders installed Baldwin of Flanders as head of the short-lived Latin Empire of Constantinople. Much of the Byzantine Empire was partitioned into feudal states ruled by self-styled 'Latin' (mostly Frankish) princes. Greece had now entered one of the most tumultuous periods of its history. The Byzantines fought to regain their lost capital and to keep the areas they had managed to hold on to (the so-called Empire of Nicaea, south of Constantinople in Asia Minor), while the Latin princes fought among themselves to expand their territories.

The Venetians, meanwhile, had secured a foothold in Greece. Over the next few centuries they acquired all the key Greek ports, including the island of Crete, and became the wealthiest and most powerful traders in the Mediterranean.

Despite this disorderly state of affairs, Byzantium was not yet dead. In 1259, the Byzantine emperor Michael VIII Palaeologos recaptured the Peloponnese from the Frankish de Villehardouin family, and made the city of Mystras his headquarters. Many eminent Byzantine artists, architects, intellectuals and philosophers converged on the city for a final burst of Byzantine creativity. Michael VIII managed to reclaim Constantinople in 1261, but by this time Byzantium was a shadow of its former self.

The Ottoman Empire

Constantinople was soon facing a much greater threat from the east. The Seljuk Turks, a tribe from central Asia, had first appeared on the eastern fringes of the empire in the middle of the 11th century. They established themselves on the Anatolian plain by defeating a Byzantine army at Manzikert in 1071. The threat looked to have been contained, especially when the Seljuks were themselves overrun by the Mongols. By the time Mongol power began to wane, the Seljuks had been supplanted as the dominant Turkish tribe by the Ottomans – the followers of Osman, who ruled from 1289 to 1326. The Muslim Ottomans began to rapidly expand the areas under their control and by the mid-15th century were harassing the Byzantine Empire on all sides. Western Europe was too embroiled in the Hundred Years' War to come to the rescue, and in 1453 Constantinople fell to the Turks under Mohammed II (the Conqueror). Once more Greece became a battleground, this time fought over by the Turks and Venetians. Eventually, with the exception of the Ionian Islands, Greece became part of the Ottoman Empire.

Much has been made of the horrors of the Turkish occupation in Greece. However, in the early years at any rate, Greeks probably marginally preferred Ottoman to Venetian or Frankish rule. The Venetians in particular treated their subjects little better than slaves. But life was not easy under the Turks, not least because of the high taxation they imposed. One of their most hated practices was the taking of one out of every five male children to become janissaries, personal bodyguards of the sultan. Many janissaries became infantrymen in the Ottoman army, but the cleverest could rise to high office – including grand vizier (chief minister).

Ottoman power reached its zenith under Sultan Süleyman the Magnificent (ruled

1520–66), who expanded the empire through the Balkans and Hungary to the gates of Vienna. His successor, Selim the Sot, added Cyprus to their dominions in 1570, but his death in 1574 marked the end of serious territorial expansion.

Although they captured Crete in 1670 after a 25-year campaign and briefly threatened Vienna once more in 1683, the ineffectual sultans that followed in the late 16th and 17th centuries saw the empire go into steady decline. They suffered a series of reversals on the battlefield, and Venice succeeded in holding onto the Peloponnese after a campaign in 1687 that saw them advance as far as Athens. The Parthenon was destroyed during the fighting when a shell struck a store of Turkish gunpowder.

Chaos and rebellion spread across Greece. Corsairs terrorised coastal dwellers, gangs of *klephts* (anti-Ottoman fugitives and brigands) roamed the mountains, and there was an upsurge of opposition to Turkish rule by freedom fighters – who fought each other when they weren't fighting the Turks.

Russian Involvement

Russia's link with Greece went back to Byzantine times, when the Russians had been converted to Christianity by Byzantine missionaries. The Church hierarchies in Constantinople and Kiev (later in Moscow) soon went their separate ways, but when Constantinople fell to the Turks, the metropolitan (head) of the Russian Church declared Moscow the 'third Rome', the true heir of Christianity, and campaigned for the liberation of its fellow Christians in the south. This fitted in nicely with Russia's efforts to expand southwards and southwestwards into Ottoman territory – perhaps even to turn the Ottoman Empire back into a Byzantine Empire dependent on Russia.

When Catherine the Great became Empress of Russia in 1762, both the Republic of Venice and the Ottoman Empire were weak. She sent Russian agents to foment rebellion, first in the Peloponnese in 1770 and then in Epiros in 1786. Both rebellions were crushed ruthlessly – the latter by Ali Pasha, the governor of Ioannina, who proceeded to set up his own power base in Greece in defiance of the sultan.

Independence Parties In the 1770s and 1780s Catherine booted the Turks from the Black Sea coast and created a number of towns in the region, which she gave Ancient Greek or Byzantine names. She offered Greeks financial incentives and free land to settle the region, and many took up her offer.

One of the new towns was called Odessa, and it was there in 1814 that businessmen Athanasios Tsakalof, Emmanuel Xanthos and Nikolaos Skoufas founded the first Greek independence party, the Filiki Eteria (Friendly Society). The message of the society spread quickly and branches opened throughout Greece. The leaders in Odessa believed that armed force was the only effective means of liberation, and made generous monetary contributions to the freedom fighters.

There were also stirrings of dissent among Greeks living in Constantinople. The Ottomans regarded it as beneath them to participate in commerce, and this had left the door open for Greeks to become a powerful economic force in the city. These wealthy Greek families were called Phanariots. Unlike the Filiki Eteria, who strove for liberation through rebellion, the Phanariots believed that they could effect a takeover from within.

The War of Independence

Ali Pasha's private rebellion against the sultan in 1820 gave the Greeks the opportunity they had been waiting for. On 25 March 1821, Bishop Germanos of Patras signalled the beginning of the War of Independence when he hoisted the Greek flag at the monastery of Agias Lavras in the Peloponnese. Fighting broke out almost simultaneously across most of Greece and the occupied islands, with the Greeks making big early gains. The fighting was savage, with atrocities committed on both sides. In the Peloponnese, 12,000 Turkish inhabitants were massacred after the capture of the city of Tripolitsa (present-day Tripolis) and Maniot freedom fighters razed the homes of thousands of Turks. The Turks retaliated with massacres in Asia Minor, most notoriously on the island of Chios, where 25,000 civilians were killed.

The fighting escalated and within a year the Greeks had captured the fortresses of Monemvasia, Navarino (modern Pylos) and Nafplio in the Peloponnese, and Messolongi, Athens and Thiva (Thebes). Greek independence was proclaimed at Epidaurus on 13 January 1822.

The Western powers were reluctant to intervene, fearing the consequences of creating a power vacuum in south-eastern Europe, where the Turks still controlled much territory. Help came from the philhellenes (literally, lovers of Greece and Greek culture) – aristocratic young men, recipients of a classical education, who saw themselves as the inheritors of a glorious civilisation and were willing to fight to liberate its oppressed descendants. The philhellenes included Shelley, Goethe, Schiller, Victor Hugo, Alfred de Musset and Lord Byron. Byron arrived in Messolongi – an important centre of resistance – in January 1824 and died three months later of pneumonia.

The prime movers in the revolution were the klephts Theodoros Kolokotronis (who led the siege on Nafplio) and Markos Botsaris; Georgos Koundouriotis (a ship owner) and Admiral Andreas Miaoulis, both from Hydra; and the Phanariots Alexandros Mavrokordatos and Dimitrios Ypsilantis. Streets all over Greece are named after these heroes.

The cause was not lacking in leaders; what was lacking was unity of objectives and strategy. Internal disagreements twice escalated into civil war, the worst in the Peloponnese in 1824. The sultan took advantage of this and called in Egyptian reinforcements. By 1827 the Turks had captured Modon (Methoni) and Corinth, and recaptured Navarino, Messolongi and Athens.

At last the Western powers intervened, and a combined Russian, French and British fleet destroyed the Turkish-Egyptian fleet in the Bay of Navarino in October 1827. Sultan Mahmud II defied the odds and proclaimed a holy war, prompting Russia to send troops into the Balkans to engage the Ottoman army. Fighting continued until 1829 when, with Russian troops at the gates of Constantinople, the sultan accepted Greek independence by the Treaty of Adrianople.

Birth of the Greek Nation

The Greeks, meanwhile, had been busy organising the independent state they had proclaimed several years earlier. In April 1827 they elected as their first president a Corfiot who had been the foreign minister of Tsar Alexander I, Ioannis Kapodistrias. Nafplio, in the Peloponnese, was chosen as the capital.

With his Russian past, Kapodistrias believed in a strong, centralised government. While he was good at enlisting foreign support, his autocratic manner at home was unacceptable to many of the leaders of the War of Independence, particularly the Maniot chieftains who had always been a law unto themselves. Kapodistrias was assassinated in 1831.

Amid the ensuing anarchy, Britain, France and Russia once again intervened and declared that Greece should become a monarchy and the throne should be given to a non-Greek so that they wouldn't be seen to favour one Greek faction. A fledgling kingdom was now up for grabs among the offspring of the crowned heads of Europe, but no-one exactly ran to fill the empty throne. Eventually the 17-year-old Prince Otto of Bavaria was chosen, arriving in Nafplio in January 1833. The new kingdom (established by the London Convention of 1832) consisted of the Peloponnese, Sterea Ellada, the Cyclades and the Sporades.

King Otho (as his name became) got up the nose of the Greek people from the moment he set foot on their land. He arrived with a bunch of upper class Bavarian cronies, to whom he gave the most prestigious official posts, and he was just as autocratic as Kapodistrias. Otho moved the capital to Athens in 1834.

Patience with his rule ran out in 1843 when demonstrations in the capital, led by the War of Independence leaders, called for a constitution. Otho mustered a National

Assembly which drafted a constitution calling for parliamentary government consisting of a lower house and a senate. Otho's cronies were whisked out of power and replaced by War of Independence freedom fighters, who bullied and bribed the populace into voting for them.

The Great Idea

By the middle of the 19th century the people of the new Greek nation were no better off materially than they had been under the Ottomans, and it was in this climate of despondency that the Megali Idea (Great Idea) of a new Greek empire was born. This empire was to include all the lands that had once been under Greek influence and have Constantinople as its capital. Otho enthusiastically embraced the idea, which increased his popularity no end. But the Greek politicians did not; they sought ways to increase their own power in the face of Otho's autocratic rule.

By the end of the 1850s, most of the stalwarts from the War of Independence had been replaced by a new breed of university graduates (Athens University had been founded in 1837). In 1862 they staged a bloodless revolution and deposed the king. But they weren't quite able to set their own agenda, because in the same year Britain returned the Ionian Islands (a British protectorate since 1815) to Greece, and in the general euphoria the British were able to push forward young Prince William of Denmark, who became King George I (the Greek monarchy retained its Danish links from that time).

His 50-year reign brought stability to the troubled country, beginning with a new constitution in 1864, which established the power of democratically elected representatives and pushed the king further towards a ceremonial role. An uprising in Crete against Turkish rule was suppressed by the sultan in 1866–68, but in 1881 Greece acquired Thessaly and part of Epiros as the result of another Russo-Turkish war.

When Harilaos Trikoupis became prime minister in 1882, he prudently concentrated his efforts on domestic issues rather than pursuing the Great Idea. The 1880s brought the first signs of economic growth: the country's first railway lines and paved roads were constructed; the Corinth Canal (begun in AD 62!) was completed – enabling Piraeus to become a major Mediterranean port; and the merchant navy grew rapidly.

However, the Great Idea had not been buried, and reared its head again after Trikoupis' death in 1896. In 1897 there was another uprising in Crete, and the hot-headed prime minister Theodoros Deligiannis responded by declaring war on Turkey and sending help to Crete. A Greek attempt to invade Turkey in the north proved disastrous – it was only through the intervention of the great powers that the Turkish army was prevented from taking Athens.

Crete was placed under international administration. The day-to-day government of the island was gradually handed over to Greeks, and in 1905 the president of the Cretan assembly, Eleftherios Venizelos, announced Crete's union (*enosis*) with Greece, although this was not recognised by international law until 1913. Venizelos went on to become prime minister of Greece in 1910 and was the country's leading politician until his republican sympathies brought about his downfall in 1935.

The Balkan Wars

Although the Ottoman Empire was in its death throes at the beginning of the 20th century, it was still clinging onto Macedonia. It was a prize sought by the newly formed Balkan countries of Serbia and Bulgaria, as well as by Greece, leading to the Balkan Wars. The first, in 1912, pitted all three against the Turks; the second, in 1913, pitted Serbia and Greece against Bulgaria. The outcome was the Treaty of Bucharest (August 1913), which greatly expanded Greek territory by adding the southern part of Macedonia, part of Thrace, another chunk of Epiros, and the North-Eastern Aegean Islands, as well as recognising the union with Crete.

In March 1913, King George was assassinated by a lunatic and his son Constantine became king.

WWI & Smyrna

King Constantine, who was married to the sister of the German emperor, insisted that Greece remain neutral when WWI broke out in August 1914. As the war dragged on, the Allies (Britain, France and Russia) put increasing pressure on Greece to join forces with them against Germany and Turkey. They made promises which they couldn't hope to fulfil, including land in Asia Minor. Venizelos favoured the Allied cause, placing him at loggerheads with the king. Tensions between the two came to a head in 1916, and Venizelos set up a rebel government, first in Crete and then in Thessaloniki, while the pressure from the Allies eventually persuaded Constantine to leave Greece in June 1917. He was replaced by his more amenable second son, Alexander.

Greek troops served with distinction on the Allied side, but when the war ended in 1918 the promised land in Asia Minor was not forthcoming. Venizelos took matters into his own hands and, with Allied acquiescence, landed troops in Smyrna (present-day İzmir) in May 1919 under the guise of protecting the half a million Greeks living in that city (just under half its population). With a firm foothold in Asia Minor, Venizelos now planned to push home his advantage against a war-depleted Ottoman Empire. He ordered his troops to attack in October 1920 (just weeks before he was voted out of office). By September 1921, the Greeks had advanced as far as Ankara.

The Turkish forces were commanded by Mustafa Kemal (later to become Atatürk), a young general who also belonged to the Young Turks, a group of army officers pressing for Western-style political reforms. Kemal first halted the Greek advance outside Ankara in September 1921 and then routed them with a massive offensive the following spring. The Greeks were driven out of Smyrna and many of the Greek inhabitants were massacred. Mustafa Kemal was now a national hero, the sultanate was abolished and Turkey became a republic.

The outcome of the failed Greek invasion and the revolution in Turkey was the Treaty of Lausanne of July 1923. This gave eastern Thrace and the islands of Imvros and Tenedos to Turkey, while the Italians kept the Dodecanese (which they had temporarily acquired in 1912 and would hold until 1947).

The treaty also called for a population exchange between Greece and Turkey to prevent any future disputes. The Great Idea, which had been such an enormous drain on the country's finances over the decades, was at last laid to rest. Almost 1.5 million Greeks left Turkey and almost 400,000 Turks left Greece. The exchange put a tremendous strain on the Greek economy and caused great hardship for the individuals concerned. Many Greeks abandoned a privileged life in Asia Minor for one of extreme poverty in shantytowns in Greece.

The Republic of 1924–35

The arrival of the refugees coincided with, and compounded, a period of political instability unprecedented even by Greek standards. In October 1920, King Alexander died from a monkey bite, resulting in the restoration of his father, King Constantine. Constantine identified himself too closely with the war against Turkey, and abdicated after the fall of Smyrna. He was replaced by his first son, George II, but George was no match for the group of army officers who seized power after the war. A republic was proclaimed in March 1924 amid a series of coups and counter-coups.

A measure of stability was attained with Venizelos' return to power in 1928. He pursued a policy of economic and educational reforms, but progress was inhibited by the Great Depression. His anti-royalist Liberal Party began to face a growing challenge from the monarchist Popular Party, culminating in defeat at the polls in March 1933. The new government was preparing for the restoration of the monarchy when Venizelos and his supporters staged an unsuccessful coup in March 1935. Venizelos was exiled to Paris, where he died a year later. In November 1935 King George II was restored to the throne by a rigged plebiscite, and he installed the right-wing General Ioannis Metaxas as prime minister. Nine months later, Metaxas assumed dictatorial powers with the king's consent under the pretext of preventing a communist-inspired republican coup.

WWII

Metaxas' grandiose vision was to create a Third Greek Civilisation based on its glorious ancient and Byzantine past, but what he actually created was more like a Greek version of the Third Reich. He exiled or imprisoned opponents, banned trade unions and the KKE (Kommunistiko Komma Ellados, the Greek Communist Party), imposed press censorship, and created a secret police force and a fascist-style youth movement. Metaxas is best known, however, for his reply of *ohi* (no) to Mussolini's request to allow Italians to traverse Greece at the beginning of WWII, thus maintaining Greece's policy of strict neutrality. The Italians invaded Greece, but were driven back into Albania.

A prerequisite of Hitler's plan to invade the Soviet Union was a secure southern flank in the Balkans. The British, realising this, asked Metaxas if they could land troops in Greece. He gave the same reply as he had given the Italians, but then died suddenly in January 1941. The king replaced him with the more timid Alexandros Koryzis, who agreed to British forces landing in Greece and then committed suicide when German troops marched through Yugoslavia and invaded Greece on 6 April 1941. The defending Greek, British, Australian and New Zealand troops were seriously outnumbered, and the whole country was under Nazi occupation within a month. King George II and his government went into exile in Egypt. The civilian population suffered appallingly during the occupation, many dying of starvation. The Nazis rounded up more than half the Jewish population and transported them to death camps.

Numerous resistance movements sprang up. The three dominant ones were ELAS (Ellinikos Laïkos Apeleftherotikos Stratos), EAM (Ethnikon Apeleftherotikon Metopon) and the EDES (Ethnikos Dimokratikos Ellinikos Syndesmos). Although ELAS was founded by communists, not all of its members were left-wing, whereas EAM consisted of Stalinist KKE members who had lived in Moscow in the 1930s and harboured ambitions of establishing a postwar communist Greece. EDES consisted of right-wing and monarchist resistance fighters. These groups fought one another with as much venom as they fought the Germans.

By 1943 Britain had begun speculating on the political complexion of postwar Greece. Winston Churchill wanted the king back and was afraid of a communist takeover, especially after ELAS and EAM formed a coalition and declared a provisional government in the summer of 1944. The Germans were pushed out of Greece in October 1944, but the communist and monarchist resistance groups continued to fight one another.

Civil War

On 3 December 1944, the police fired on a communist demonstration in Syntagma Square. The ensuing six weeks of fighting between the left and the right were known as the Dekemvriana (events of December), the first round of the civil war, and only the intervention of British troops prevented an ELAS-EAM victory. An election held in March 1946 and boycotted by the communists was won by the royalists, and a rigged plebiscite put George II back on the throne.

In October, the left-wing Democratic Army of Greece (DAG) was formed to resume the fight against the monarchy and its British supporters. Under the leadership of Markos Vafiadis, the DAG swiftly occupied a large swathe of land along Greece's northern border with Albania and Yugoslavia.

By 1947, the US had replaced Britain as Greece's 'minder' and the civil war had developed into a setting for the new Cold War as the Americans fought to contain the spread of Soviet influence in Europe. Inspired by the Truman Doctrine, the US poured in cash and military hardware to shore up the anti-communist coalition government. Communism was declared illegal and the government introduced its notorious Certificate of Political Reliability (proof that the carrier was not left-wing), which remained valid until 1962 and without which

Greeks couldn't vote and found it almost impossible to get work.

US aid did little to improve the situation on the ground. The DAG continued to be supplied through the communist states to the north, and by the end of 1947 large chunks of the mainland were under its control, as well as parts of the islands of Crete, Chios and Lesvos. It was unable, though, to capture the major town it needed as a base for a rival government declared by Vafiades, despite a major assault on the town of Konitsa in northern Epiros on Christmas Day 1947.

The tide began to turn the government's way early in 1949 when the DAG was forced out of the Peloponnese, but the fighting dragged on in the mountains of Epiros until October 1949, when Yugoslavia fell out with the Soviet Union and cut the DAG's supply lines. Vafiades was assassinated by a group of his Stalinist underlings after the fall of the DAG's last major stronghold in the Grammos Mountains, and the remnants of his army capitulated.

If this was a victory, there was nothing to celebrate. The country was in an almighty mess, both politically and economically. More Greeks had been killed in the three years of bitter civil war than in WWII; a quarter of a million people were homeless, many thousands more had been taken prisoner or exiled, and the DAG had taken some 30,000 Greek children from northern Greece to Eastern bloc countries for indoctrination.

The sense of despair left by the civil war became the trigger for a mass exodus. Almost a million Greeks headed off in search of a better life elsewhere, primarily to countries like Australia, Canada and the USA. Villages – whole islands even – were abandoned as people gambled on a new start in the suburbs of cities like Melbourne, New York and Chicago. While some have drifted back (including half the restaurant owners in the Peloponnese!), most have stayed away.

Reconstruction & the Cyprus Issue

A general election was held in 1950. The system of proportional representation resulted in a series of unworkable coalitions,

and the electoral system was changed to majority voting in 1952 – which excluded the communists from future governments. The next election was a victory for the newly formed right-wing Ellinikos Synagermos (Greek Rally) party led by General Papagos, who had been a field marshal during the civil war. General Papagos remained in power until his death in 1955, when he was replaced by Konstantinos Karamanlis, the minister of public works.

Greece joined NATO in 1951, and in 1953 the US was granted the right to operate sovereign bases. Intent on maintaining a right-wing government, the US gave generous aid and even more generous military support.

Cyprus occupied centre stage in Greece's foreign affairs, and has remained close to it to this day. Since the 1930s, Greek Cypriots (four-fifths of the island's population) had demanded union with Greece, while Turkey had maintained its claim to the island ever since the British occupied it in 1914 (it became a British crown colony in 1925). After an outbreak of communal violence between Greek and Turkish Cypriots in 1954, Britain stated its intention to make Cyprus an independent state.

The right-wing Greek Cypriot EOKA (National Organisation of Cypriot Freedom Fighters) took up arms against the British, but Greece and Turkey finally accepted independence in 1959. Cyprus duly became a republic the following August with Archbishop Makarios as president and a Turk, Fasal Kükük, as vice president. The changes did little to appease either side. EOKA resolved to keep fighting, while Turkish Cypriots continued to clamour for partition of the island.

Back in Greece, Georgos Papandreou, a former Venizelos supporter, founded the broadly based EK (Centre Union) in 1958, but an election in 1961 returned the ERE (National Radical Union), Karamanlis' new name for Papagos' Greek Rally party, to power for the third time in succession. Papandreou accused the ERE of ballot-rigging – probably true, but the culprits were almost certainly right-wing, military-backed groups (rather than Karamanlis) who feared communist infiltration if the EK came to power. Political turmoil followed, culminating in the murder, in May 1963, of Grigorios Lambrakis, the deputy of the communist EDA (Union of the Democratic Left). All this proved too much for Karamanlis, who resigned and left the country.

Despite the ERE's sometimes desperate measures to stay in power, an election in February 1964 was won by the EK. Papandreou wasted no time in implementing a series of radical changes. He freed political prisoners and allowed exiles to come back to Greece, reduced income tax and the defence budget, and increased spending on social services and education. Papandreou's victory coincided with King Constantine II's accession to the Greek throne, and with a renewed outbreak of violence in Cyprus, which erupted into a full-scale civil war before the UN intervened and installed a peace-keeping force.

The Colonels' Coup

The right in Greece was rattled by Papandreou's tolerance of the left, fearing that this would increase the EDA's influence. The climate was one of mutual suspicion between the left and the right, each claiming that the other was plotting a takeover. Finally, Papandreou decided the armed forces needed a thorough overhaul, which seemed fair enough, as army officers were more often than not the perpetrators of conspiracies. King Constantine refused to cooperate with this, and Papandreou resigned. Two years of ineffectual interim governments followed before a new election was scheduled for May 1967.

The election was never to be. A group of army colonels led by Georgos Papadopoulos and Stylianos Patakos staged a coup on 21 April 1967. King Constantine tried an unsuccessful counter-coup in December, after which he fled the country. A military junta was established with Papadopoulos as prime minister.

The colonels imposed martial law, abolished all political parties, banned trade unions, imposed censorship, and imprisoned,

Urban Guerilla Terror

Greece's deadly November 17 urban guerilla group takes its name from the date in 1973 on which the military junta used tanks to crush a student protest at Athens Polytechnic, killing at least 20 students.

It has proved the most durable of the many left-wing guerilla groups that emerged in Europe in the 1970s. To the acute embarrassment of the police, not one member of the gang has been caught in more than 24 years of activity.

The group claimed the first of its 23 victims on Christmas Eve 1975 when CIA bureau chief Richard Welsh was gunned down in the driveway of his Athens home. It has continued to strike at regular intervals ever since. Its most recent victim was the British defence attache, shot by a gunman on a motorcycle in northern Athens in May 2000. His assassination brought Britain's Scotland Yard into the case, still without result despite some promising leads.

Rocket attacks have become the group's trademark, following a raid on a military depot at Larissa in 1987 that netted a haul of antitank missiles. They have been used in a string of attacks over the years, including an assault on the US embassy in Athens in 1998.

The group remains the country's major security concern in the countdown to the 2004 Olympics.

tortured and exiled thousands of Greeks who opposed them. Suspicions of CIA assistance in the coup remain conjecture, but criticism of the coup, and the ensuing regime, was certainly not forthcoming from the CIA or the US government. In June 1972 Papadopoulos declared Greece a republic (confirmed by a rigged referendum in July) and appointed himself president.

In November 1973 students began a sit-in at Athens' Polytechnic college in protest against the junta. On 17 November, tanks stormed the building, injuring many and killing at least 20. On 25 November, Papadopoulos was deposed by the thuggish

Brigadier Ioannidis, head of the military security police.

The following July, desperate for a foreign policy success to bolster the regime's standing, Ioannidis decided it was time to play the Cyprus card. He hatched a wild scheme to assassinate President Makarios and unite Cyprus with Greece. The scheme went disastrously wrong after Makarios got wind of the plan and escaped. The junta installed Nikos Sampson, a former EOKA leader, as president, and Turkey reacted by invading the island.

The junta quickly removed Sampson and threw in the towel, but the Turks continued to advance until they occupied the northern third of the island, forcing almost 200,000 Greek Cypriots to flee their homes for the safety of the south.

After the Colonels

The army now called Karamanlis away from Paris to clear up the mess in Greece. An election was arranged for November 1974 (won handsomely by Karamanlis' New Democracy party), and the ban on communist parties was then lifted. Andreas Papandreou (son of Georgos) formed PASOK (the Panhellenic Socialist Union), and a plebiscite voted 69% against the restoration of the monarchy. (Former king Constantine, who now lives in London, didn't revisit Greece until the summer of 1993. The New Democracy government sent missile boats and a transport plane to follow his yacht. Nonetheless the ex-king said he and his family enjoyed the holiday, and he had no wish to overthrow the Greek constitution.)

Karamanlis' New Democracy (ND) party won the election in 1977, but his personal popularity began to decline. One of his biggest achievements before he accepted the largely ceremonial post of president was to engineer Greece's entry into the European Community (now called the European Union), which involved jumping the queue ahead of other countries who had been waiting patiently to be accepted. On 1 January 1981 Greece became the 10th member of the EC.

The Socialist 1980s

Andreas Papandreou's PASOK party won the election of October 1981 with 48% of the vote, giving Greece its first socialist government. PASOK came to power with an ambitious social program and a promise to close US air bases and withdraw from NATO.

After seven years in government, these promises remained unfulfilled (although the US military presence was reduced); unemployment was high and reforms in education and welfare had been limited. Women's issues fared better, though: the dowry system was abolished, abortion legalised, and civil marriage and divorce were implemented. The crunch came in 1988 when Papandreou's love affair with air hostess Dimitra Liani (whom he subsequently married) hit the headlines, and PASOK became embroiled in a financial scandal involving the Bank of Crete.

In July 1989 an unlikely coalition of conservatives and communists took over to implement a *katharsis* (campaign of purification) to investigate the scandal. In September it ruled that Papandreou and four of his ministers be tried for embezzlement, telephone tapping and illegal grain sales. Papandreou's trial ended in January 1992 with his acquittal on all counts.

The 1990s

An election in 1990 brought the ND back to power with a majority of only two seats, and with Konstantinos Mitsotakis as prime minister. Intent on redressing the country's economic problems – high inflation and high government spending – the government imposed austerity measures, including a wage freeze for civil servants and steep increases in public-utility costs and basic services. The government also cracked down on tax evasion (which is still rife!).

The austerity measures sparked off strikes in the public sector in mid-1990, and again in 1991 and 1992. The government's problems were compounded by an influx of Albanian refugees (see the People section later in this chapter), and the dispute over the use of the name Macedonia for the southern republic of former Yugoslavia.

By late 1992 corruption allegations were being made against the government and it was claimed that Cretan-born Mitsotakis had a secret collection of Minoan art. Allegations of government telephone tapping followed, and by mid-1993 Mitsotakis supporters began to cut their losses, abandoning the ND for the new Political Spring party. The ND lost its parliamentary majority and an early election was held in October, which Andreas Papandreou's PASOK party won with 47% of the vote against 39% for ND and 5% for Political Spring. Through the majority voting system, this translated into a handsome parliamentary majority for PASOK.

Papandreou's final spell at the helm was dominated by speculation about his heart condition and general poor health. Papandreou was rarely sighted outside his villa at Kifissia, where he lived surrounded by his ministerial coterie of family and friends. He was finally forced to step down in early 1996 after another bout of ill-health, and his death on 26 June marked the end of an era in Greek politics.

Papandreou's departure produced a dramatic change of direction for PASOK, with the party abandoning his left-leaning politics and electing experienced economist and lawyer Costas Simitis as the new prime minister. Cashing in on his reputation as the Mr Clean of Greek politics, Simitis romped to a comfortable majority at a snap poll called in October 1996.

Simitis belongs to much the same school of politics as Britain's Tony Blair. Since he took power, PASOK policy has shifted right to the extent that it now agrees with the opposition ND on all major policy issues. His government has focused almost exclusively on the push for further integration with Europe, which has meant more tax reform and more austerity measures – as dictated by EU bosses in Brussels. His success in the face of constant protest, and the skill with which his government handled the difficult diplomatic challenge presented by the 1999 NATO conflict with Serbia, has earned him the grudging respect of the Greek electorate, who handed him a mandate for another four years at elections held in April 2000.

The goal of admission to the euro club was achieved at the beginning of 2001, and Greece adopted the euro as its currency in March 2002.

Recent Foreign Policy

Greece's foreign policy is dominated by its very sensitive relationship with Turkey, its giant Muslim neighbour to the east.

After decades of constant antagonism, these two uneasy NATO allies were jolted to their senses (literally) by the massive earthquake which devastated the İzmit area of western Turkey in August 1999. According to geologists, the quake moved Turkey 1.5m closer to Greece. It had the same effect on the Greek people, who urged their government to join the rescue effort. Greek teams were among the first on the scene, where they were greeted as heroes. The Turks were quick to return the favour after the Athens quake which followed on September 7, 1999. The relationship has continued to blossom, despite the occasional hiccup, and at the time of research the two countries were contemplating mounting a joint bid to stage the 2008 European soccer championship.

It's really an extraordinary turn-around. It wasn't that long ago that the merest incident – trivial to the outsider – would bring the two to the brink of war. A famous incident occurred in February 1996 when a group of Turkish journalists symbolically replaced the Greek flag on the tiny rocky outcrop of Imia (Kardak to the Turks). Both sides poured warships into the area before being persuaded to calm down.

While Turkey remains the top priority, Greece has also had its hands full in recent years coping with events to the north precipitated by the break-up of former Yugoslavia and the collapse of the communist regimes in Albania and Romania.

The first crisis to arise from the break-up of Yugoslavia was sparked by the former Yugoslav republic of Macedonia's attempt to become independent Macedonia. This prompted an emotional outburst from

Greece, which argued that the name 'was, is, and always will be' Greek. Greece was able to persuade its EU partners to recognise Macedonia only if it changed its name, which is how the independent acronym of FYROM (Former Yugoslav Republic of Macedonia) came into being.

The wars in Croatia and Bosnia had little political impact on Greece, but the country found itself in an impossible position during the 1999 NATO conflict with Serbia over Kosovo. The Greek public, already strongly sympathetic towards their fellow Orthodox Christian Serbs in the battle against the Muslim Albanian Kosovars, was outraged when the NATO bombing began. The Americans bore the brunt of anti-NATO demonstrations, violent at first, that lasted throughout the war.

Although Thessaloniki was used as a shipment point for NATO equipment, Greece played no active part in the war.

GEOGRAPHY

Greece, at the southern extremity of the Balkan Peninsula, is the only member of the EU without a land frontier with another member. To the north, Greece has land borders with Albania, the Former Yugoslav Republic of Macedonia, and Bulgaria; and to the east with Turkey.

Greece consists of a peninsula and about 1400 islands, of which 169 are inhabited. The land mass is 131,900 sq km and Greek territorial waters occupy 400,000 sq km. The islands are divided into six groups: the Cyclades, the Dodecanese, the islands of the North-Eastern Aegean, the Sporades, the Ionian and the Saronic Gulf Islands. The two largest islands, Crete and Evia, do not belong to any group. In Greece, no area is much more than 100km from the sea. The much indented coastline has a total length of 15,020km.

Roughly four-fifths of Greece is mountainous, with most of the land over 1500m above sea level. The Pindos Mountains, which are an offshoot of the Dinaric Alps, run north to south through the peninsula, and are known as the backbone of Greece. The mountains of the Peloponnese and

Crete are part of the same formation. The highest mountain is Mt Olympus (2917m).

Greece does not have many rivers, and none which are navigable. The largest are the Aheloös, Aliakmonas, Aoös and Arahthos, all of which have their source in the Pindos Range in Epiros. The long plains of the river valleys, and those between the mountains and the coast, are the only lowlands. The mountainous terrain, dry climate and poor soil restricts agriculture to less than a quarter of the land. Greece is, however, rich in minerals, with reserves of oil, manganese, bauxite and lignite.

GEOLOGY

The earthquake which struck Athens on September 7, 1999, leaving 139 dead and 100,000 homeless, served as a savage reminder that Greece lies in one of most seismically active regions in the world.

The quake was just one of more than 20,000 quakes recorded in Greece in the last 40 years. Fortunately, most of them are very minor – detectable only by sensitive seismic monitoring equipment. The reason for all this activity is that the eastern Mediterranean lies at the meeting point of three continental plates: the Eurasian, African and Arabian. The three grind away at each other constantly, generating countless earthquakes as the land surface reacts to the intense activity beneath the earth's crust.

The system has two main fault lines. The most active is the North Aegean Fault, which starts as a volcano-dotted rift between Greece and Turkey, snakes under Greece and then runs north up the Ionian and Adriatic coasts. Less active but more dramatic is the North Anatolian Fault that runs across Turkey, which is renowned for major tremors like the 7.4 monster that struck western Turkey on August 17 1999, leaving more than 40,000 dead. Seismologists maintain that activity along the two fault lines is not related.

CLIMATE

Greece can be divided into a number of main climatic regions. Northern Macedonia and northern Epiros have a climate similar to the

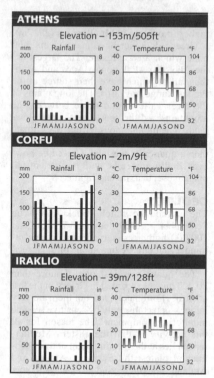

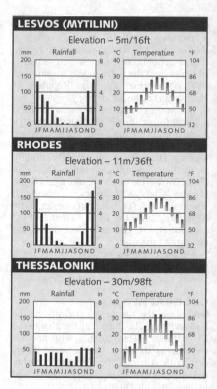

Balkans, with freezing winters and very hot, humid summers; while the Attic Peninsula, the Cyclades, the Dodecanese, Crete, and the central and eastern Peloponnese have a more typically Mediterranean climate with hot, dry summers and milder winters.

Snow is very rare in the Cyclades (it snowed on Paros for the first time in 15 years in 1992), but the high mountains of the Peloponnese and Crete are covered in snow during the winter, and it does occasionally snow in Athens. In July and August, the mercury can soar to 40°C (over 100°F) in the shade just about anywhere in the country. July and August are also the months of the *meltemi*, a strong northerly wind that sweeps the eastern coast of mainland Greece (including Athens) and the Aegean Islands, especially the Cyclades. The wind is caused by air pressure differ-

ences between North Africa and the Balkans. The wind is a mixed blessing: it reduces humidity, but plays havoc with ferry schedules and sends everything flying – from beach umbrellas to washing hanging out to dry.

The western Peloponnese, western Sterea Ellada, south-western Epiros and the Ionian Islands escape the meltemi and have less severe winters than northern Greece, but are the areas with the highest rainfall. The North-Eastern Aegean Islands, Halkidiki and the Pelion Peninsula fall somewhere between the Balkan-type climate of northern Greece and the Mediterranean climates. Crete stays warm the longest – you can swim off its southern coast from mid-April to November.

Mid-October is when the rains start in most areas, and the weather stays cold and

The Evil Olive

It is a sad irony that the tree most revered by the Greeks is responsible for the country's worst ecological disaster. The tree is the olive. It was the money tree of the early Mediterranean civilisations, providing an abundance of oil that not only tasted great but could also be used for everything from lighting to lubrication. The ancient Greeks thought it was too good to be true and concluded it must be a gift from the gods.

In their eagerness to make the most of this gift, native forest was cleared on a massive scale to make way for the olive. Landowners were urged on by decrees such as those issued in the 6th century BC by the arhon of Athens, Solon, who banned the export of all agricultural produce other than olive oil and made cutting down an olive tree punishable by death.

Much of the land planted with olives was unsuitable hill country. Without the surface roots of the native forest to bind it, the topsoil of the hills was rapidly washed away. The olive tree could do nothing to help. It has no surface root system, depending entirely on its impressive tap root.

Thus, the lush countryside so cherished by the ancient Greeks was transformed into the harsh, rocky landscape that greets the modern visitor.

wet until February – although there are also occasional winter days with clear blue skies and sunshine.

ECOLOGY & ENVIRONMENT

Greece is belatedly becoming environmentally conscious; regrettably, it can be a case of closing the gate after the horse has bolted. Deforestation and soil erosion are problems going back thousands of years. Olive cultivation (see the boxed text 'The Evil Olive') and goats have been the main culprits, but firewood gathering, shipbuilding, housing and industry have all taken their toll.

Forest fires are also a major problem, with an estimated 25,000 hectares destroyed every year. The 2000 season was one of the worst on record, particularly in the Peloponnese and on the island of Samos.

The result is that the forests of ancient Greece have virtually all but disappeared. Epiros and Macedonia in northern Greece are now the only places where extensive forests remain. This loss of forest cover has been accompanied by serious soil erosion. The problem is finally being addressed with the start of a long overdue reafforestation program.

General environmental awareness remains at a very low level, especially where litter is concerned. The problem is particularly bad in rural areas, where roadsides are strewn with soft-drink cans and plastic packaging hurled from passing cars. Environmental education has begun in schools, but it will be some time before community attitudes change.

FLORA & FAUNA
Flora

Greece is endowed with a variety of flora unrivalled in Europe. The wildflowers are spectacular. There are over 6000 species, some of which occur nowhere else, and more than 100 varieties of orchid. They continue to thrive because most of the land is too poor for intensive agriculture and has escaped the ravages of chemical fertilisers.

The regions with the most wildflowers are the mountains of Crete and the Mani area of the Peloponnese. Trees begin to blossom as early as the end of February in warmer areas, and the wildflowers start to appear in March. During spring the hillsides are carpeted with flowers, which seem to sprout even from the rocks. Spring flowers include anemones, white cyclamens, irises, lilies, poppies, gladioli, tulips, countless varieties of daisy and many more. By summer, the flowers have disappeared from all but the northern mountainous regions. Autumn brings flowers too, especially crocuses.

The forests that once covered ancient Greece have been decimated by thousands of years of clearing for agriculture, boat building and housing. Northern Greece is

Wildflowers

The Greek countryside is the showcase for a spectacular spring display of wildflowers. Autumn is often described as Greece's 'second spring'.

Of Europe's 200 wild orchid species, around half grow in Greece. They flower from late February to early June. Another spring flower is the iris. The word 'iris' is Greek for rainbow – an appropriate name for these multicoloured flowers. Greece's wild irises include the white and yellow *Iris ochreoleuca* and the blue and orange *Iris cretica*. The latter is one of 120 wildflowers unique to Crete. Others include the pink Cretan ebony, the white-flowered symphyandra and the white-flowered *Cyclamen cretic*. Other unique species include the *Rhododendron luteum*, a yellow azalea which grows only on Mytilini, and a peony which is unique to Rhodes.

Spectacular plants include the coastal giant reed. You may get lost among its high, dense groves on your way to a beach. The giant fennel, which grows to 3m, and the tall yellow-horned poppy also grow by the sea. Another showy coastal plant is the magenta-flowered Hottentot fig, which was introduced from Africa. The white-flowered sea squill grows on hills above the coast. Conspicuous thistles include the milk thistle which has green and white variegated leaves and grows in meadows and by roadsides. In rocky terrain you will see the stemless carline thistle, whose silvery-white petalled flowers are used in dried flower displays.

The beautifully perfumed sea daffodil grows along southern coasts, particularly on Crete and Corfu. The conspicuous snake's-head fritillary *(Fritillaria graeca)* has pink flowers shaped like snakes' heads, and the markings on the petals resemble a chequer board – the Latin word *fritillu* means dice box.

Interesting trees include the evergreen carob which grows to 10m. John the Baptist is said to have eaten its pods when he lived in the desert. Mineral-rich carob is sold in some countries as a healthy substitute for chocolate. The flowers of the Judas tree, unusually, appear before the leaves. According to legend they were originally white, but when Judas hanged himself from the tree they turned pink in shame.

the only region that has retained significant areas of native forest. Here you will find mountainsides covered with dense thickets of hop hornbeam *(Ostrya carpinifolia)*, noted for its lavish display of autumn cover.

Another common species is the Cyprus plane *(Platanus orientalis insularis)*, which thrives wherever there is ample water. It seems as if every village on the mainland has a plane tree shading its central square – and a Taverna Platanos.

Australian eucalypts were widely used in tree-planting programs from the 1920s onwards, particularly in the Peloponnese and Crete.

Fauna

Greece also has quite a large range of fauna, but you won't encounter much of interest unless you venture out into the prime habitat areas.

Bird-watchers have more chance of coming across something unusual than animal spotters. Greece has all the usual Mediterranean small birds – wagtails, tits, warblers, bee-eaters, larks, swallows, flycatchers, thrushes and chats – as well as some more distinctive species such as the hoopoe.

A large number of migratory birds, most of which are merely passing by on their way from winter feeding sites in north Africa to summer nesting grounds in Eastern Europe, can also be seen. Out of a total of 408 species of migratory birds in Europe, 240 have been sighted in Greece. One very visible visitor is the stork. Storks arrive in early spring from Africa, and return to the same nest year after year. The nests are built on electricity poles, chimney tops and church towers, and can weigh up to 50kg; look out for them in northern Greece, especially in Thrace.

MARTIN HARRIS

The hoopoe, part of the kingfisher family

Lake Mikri Prespa, in Macedonia, has the richest colony of fish-eating birds in Europe, including species such as egrets, herons, cormorants and ibises, as well as the rare Dalmatian pelican – Turkey and Greece are now the only countries in Europe where this bird is found. The wetlands at the mouth of the Evros River, close to the border with Turkey, are home to two easily identifiable wading birds – the avocet, which has a long upcurved beak, and the black-winged stilt, which has extremely long pink legs.

Upstream on the Evros River in Thrace, the dense forests and rocky outcrops of the 7200 hectare Dadia Forest Reserve play host to the largest range of birds of prey in Europe. Thirty-six of the 38 European species can be seen here, and it is a breeding ground for 23 of them. Permanent residents include the giant black vulture, whose wingspan reaches 3m, the griffon vulture and golden eagles. Europe's last 15 pairs of royal eagles nest on the river delta. The reserve is managed by the Worldwide Fund for Nature Ellas (☎ 21 0331 4893, fax 21 0324 7578, e webmaster@wwf.gr, w www.wwf.gr), Filellinon 26, Athens 105 58.

About 350 pairs (60% of the world's population) of the rare Eleonora falcon nest on the island of Piperi in the Sporades.

The mountains of northern Greece also support a much greater range of wildlife than anywhere else in the country, although you're extremely unlikely to spot animals such as the brown bear or the grey wolf (see Endangered Species, following). Wild boar are still found in reasonable numbers in the north and are a favourite target for hunters. Squirrels, rabbits, hares, foxes and weasels are all fairly common on the mainland; less common is the cute European suslik – a small ground squirrel.

Reptiles are well represented. The snakes include several viper species, which are poisonous. For more information on snakes in Greece, see the Health section in the Facts for the Visitor chapter. You're more likely to see lizards, all of which are harmless.

One of the pleasures of island-hopping in Greece is watching the dolphins as they follow the boats. Although there are many dolphins in the Aegean, the striped dolphin has recently been the victim of murbilivirus – a sickness that affects the immune system. Research into the virus is being carried out in the Netherlands. You can get more information about dolphins from the Greek Society for the Protection & Study of Dolphins & Cetaceans (☎/fax 21 0422 3305, e delphis@hol.gr), Pylis 75–79, Piraeus 18 533.

Endangered Species

The brown bear, Europe's largest land mammal, still survives in very small numbers in the Pindos Mountains, the Peristeri Range that rises above the Prespa Lakes and in the mountains which lie along the Bulgarian border. You can get more information from Arcturos (Friends of the Greek Bear, ☎ 231 0554 623), Ag Mina 3, Thessaloniki, 54 625.

The same organisation also has information on wolves – another endangered species, but not protected in Greece as in other countries. They survive in small numbers in the forests of the Pindos in Epiros as well as in the Dadia Forest Reserve area.

**The Mediterranean Monk Seal,
Europe's rarest mammal**

Europe's rarest mammal, the monk seal, was once very common in the Mediterranean, but is now nearly extinct in Europe – it survives in slightly larger numbers in the Hawaiian islands. There are only about 400 left in Europe, half of which live in Greece. There are about 40 in the Ionian Sea and the rest are found in the Aegean. These sensitive creatures are particularly susceptible to human disturbance, and now live only in isolated coastal caves. The majority of reported deaths are the result of accidental trapping, but the main threat to their survival is the continuing destruction of habitat. Tourist boats are major culprits.

The waters around Zakynthos are also home to the last large sea turtle colony in Europe, that of the loggerhead turtle *(Careta careta)*. The loggerhead also nests in smaller numbers on the Peloponnese and on Crete. The Sea Turtle Protection Society of Greece (☎/fax 21 0523 1342, ℮ stps@compulink. gr), Solomou 57, Athens 104 32, runs monitoring programs and is always looking for volunteers. See the Attica section of the Athens chapter for information about the society's rescue centre at Glyfada.

National Parks
Visitors who expect Greek national parks to provide facilities on a par with those in countries like Australia and the US will be very disappointed. Although all have refuges and some have marked hiking trails, Greek national parks have little else by way of facilities.

The most visited parks are Mt Parnitha, just north of Athens, and the Samaria Gorge on Crete. The other national parks are Vikos-Aoös and Prespa in Epiros; Mt Olympus on the border of Thessaly and Macedonia; and Parnassos and Iti in central Greece. Most consist of buffer zones protecting an inner wilderness area. Some activities (including hunting!) are permitted in the buffer areas, but no activities other than walking are allowed in the protected area.

If you want to see wildlife, the place to go is the well-organised Dadia Forest Reserve in eastern Thrace (see the Northern Greece chapter for details).

There are national marine parks off the coast of Alonnisos in the Sporades, and at Laganas Bay, Zakynthos, in the Ionians.

GOVERNMENT & POLITICS
Since 1975, democratic Greece has been a parliamentary republic with a president as head of state. The president and parliament, which has 300 deputies, have joint legislative power. The PASOK party of Prime Minister Simitis holds 163 seats in the current parliament. Greek governments traditionally name very large cabinets – Simitis fronts a team of 43, with 19 ministries. Papandreou had 52 in his last cabinet!

Greece is divided into regions and island groups. The mainland regions are the Peloponnese, central Greece (officially called Sterea Ellada), Epiros, Thessaly, Macedonia and Thrace. The island groups are the Cyclades, Dodecanese, North-Eastern Aegean, Sporades and Saronic Gulf, all in the Aegean Sea, and the Ionian, which is in the Ionian Sea. The large islands of Evia and Crete do not belong to any group. For administrative purposes these regions and groups are divided into prefectures or nomes *(nomoi* in Greek).

ECONOMY
Greece is an agricultural country, but the importance of agriculture to the economy has declined rapidly since WWII. Some 50% of the workforce is now employed in services (contributing 59% of GDP), 22% in agriculture (contributing 15%), and 27% in industry and construction (contributing 26%). Tourism is by far the biggest industry; shipping comes next.

Although Greece has the second-lowest income per capita of all the EU countries (after Portugal), its long-term economic future looks brighter now than it has for some time. Tough austerity measures imposed by successive governments have cut inflation to less than 3%, and the investment climate remains healthy, despite the bursting of the stock market bubble in 2000 after several years of boom. Many Greeks lost a fortune in the crash after a buying frenzy had pushed the stock index to an insupportable high of almost 11,000 points. At the time of research, it was hovering around a more realistic 6000.

POPULATION

A census is taken every 10 years in Greece. The census taken in early 2001 was the first since the 1991 census and recorded a population of 10,939,771. The 1991 census confirmed that Greece is now a largely urban society, with 68% of the population living in cities. By far the largest is the capital, Athens, with an estimated 3.5 million people living in the greater Athens area – an increase of 400,000 on the 1991 figure. The population figures of other major cities (1991 population in brackets) are: Thessaloniki (750,000), Piraeus (171,000), Patras (153,000), Iraklio (127,600), Larisa (113,400) and Volos (110,000). Less than 15% of people live on the islands, the most populous of which are Crete (537,000), Evia (209,100) and Corfu (105,000).

PEOPLE

Contemporary Greeks are a mixture of all of the invaders who have occupied the country since ancient times. Additionally, there are a number of distinct ethnic minorities living in the country.

The country's small Roman Catholic population is of Genoese or Frankish origin. They live mostly in the Cyclades, especially on the island of Syros, where they are 40% of the population. The Franks dominated the island from AD 1207 to Ottoman times.

About 300,000 ethnic Turks who were exempt from the population exchange of 1923 live in western Thrace. There are also small numbers of Turks on Kos and Rhodes which, along with the rest of the Dodecanese, did not become part of Greece until 1947.

There are small Jewish communities in several towns. In Ioannina, Larisa, Halkida and Rhodes, they date back to the Roman era, while in Thessaloniki, Kavala and Didymotiho, most are descendants of 15th-century exiles from Spain and Portugal. In 1429, 20,000 exiled Jews arrived in Thessaloniki and by the 16th century they constituted a major part of the population. In 1941, the Germans entered Thessaloniki and took 46,000 Jews to Auschwitz, most never returned. They comprised 90% of Thessaloniki's Jews and more than half the total in Greece. The small number of Jews in Athens are mostly German Jews who came over with King Otho in the 1830s. Today there are only about 5000 Jews living in Greece.

Very small numbers of Vlach and Sarakatsani shepherds live a semi-nomadic existence in Epiros. They take their flocks to the high ground in summer and return to the valleys in winter. The Vlachs originate from the region that is now Romania; the origins of the Sarakatsani are uncertain.

You will come across Roma (Gypsies) everywhere in Greece, but especially in Macedonia, Thrace and Thessaly. There are large communities of Roma in the Thracian towns of Alexandroupolis and Didymotiho.

The collapse of the communist regimes in Albania and Romania produced a wave of economic refugees across Greece's poorly guarded northern borders, with an estimated 300,000 arriving from Albania alone. These refugees have been a vital source of cheap labour for the agricultural sector; fruit and vegetable prices have actually gone down as a result of their contribution. Albanians also have a reputation as fine stonemasons, and their influence can be seen everywhere.

Athens has substantial Bangladeshi and Kurdish communities.

EDUCATION

Education in Greece is free at all levels of the state system, from kindergarten to tertiary. Primary schooling begins at the age of

Three Pillars of Western Philosophy

Socrates – 'Know thyself'

Little is certain about Socrates because he committed nothing to paper. Historians and philosophers have constructed a picture of Socrates through the writings of Plato, a one-time pupil.

Socrates was born in Athens in about 470 BC and fought in the First Peloponnesian War. Thereafter he gave his life over to teaching in the streets and, particularly, the gymnasia – a mission bestowed on him by his god, the *daimon*.

He was deeply religious but regarded mythology with disdain. The *daimon's* existence was demonstrated by the perfect order of nature, the universality of people's belief in the divine and the revelations that come in dreams.

Socrates' method was dialectic: he sought to illuminate truth by question and answer, responding to a pupil's question with another question, and then another, until the pupil came to answer their own inquiry.

He believed that bodily desires corrupted people's souls, and a person's soul was directly responsible for their happiness. The soul was neither good nor bad, but well or poorly realised. Accordingly, unethical actions were in some sense involuntary – people committed bad actions because they had poor conceptions of themselves. However, those who knew good would always act in accordance with it.

Believing that a profound understanding of goodness was a prerequisite for those who governed society, Socrates held that democracy was flawed because it left the state in the hands of the unenlightened and valued all opinion as equal.

In 399 BC, at the age of 70, Socrates was indicted for 'impiety'. He was convicted with 'corruption of the young' and 'the practice of religious novelties', and sentenced to death by the drinking of hemlock. The story of Socrates' day of execution is told in Plato's *Phaedo*.

Plato – 'Until philosophers are kings... cities will never cease from ill, nor the human race'

Plato was born in about 428 BC in Athens, or perhaps Aegina, and studied under Socrates, who had a great influence upon him.

In about 387 BC, Plato founded his famous Academy in Athens as an institute of philosophical and scientific studies.

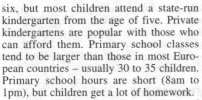

six, but most children attend a state-run kindergarten from the age of five. Private kindergartens are popular with those who can afford them. Primary school classes tend to be larger than those in most European countries – usually 30 to 35 children. Primary school hours are short (8am to 1pm), but children get a lot of homework.

At 12, children enter the *gymnasio*, and at 15 they may leave school, or enter the *lykeio*, from where they take university-entrance examinations. Although there is a high rate of literacy, many parents and pupils are dissatisfied with the education system, especially beyond primary level. The private sector therefore flourishes, and even relatively poor parents struggle to send their children to one of the country's 5000 *frontistiria* (intensive coaching colleges) to prepare them for the very competitive university-entrance exams. Parents complain that the education system is badly

Three Pillars of Western Philosophy

Plato's prolific writings take the form of dialogues and read like scripts. He never introduced himself as a character in his dialogues, but he did use real people as speakers, including Socrates.

Politically, Plato was an authoritarian. The *Republic* is, in part, given over to his view of the ideal state. He divided people into commoners, soldiers and rulers. Plato declared that all people should live simply and modestly; that women and men should be equal, and given the same education and prospects; that marriages should be arranged by the state and children be removed from their parents at birth. This would minimise personal, possessive emotions, so that public spirit would be the prime emotion that individuals felt.

Plato held that knowledge cannot be derived from the senses. He argued that we perceive *through* our senses, not *with* them. We have knowledge of concepts that are not derived from experience: perfect symmetry has no manifestation in the material world. Plato believed that knowledge was inside everybody, and claimed that all knowledge is recollection – that it comes as revelation to the intellect.

Aristotle – 'He who exercises his reason and cultivates it seems to be both in the best state of mind and most dear to the gods'

Aristotle was born in 384 BC in Stagira, Macedonia. He travelled to Athens in 367 BC to study at Plato's Academy. He remained for nearly 20 years, until Plato's death.

Aristotle then quit Athens following a disagreement with the Academy. He spent 10 years travelling before he returning to found a rival institution, the Lyceum, working there for another 12 years and writing prolifically.

After the death of Alexander the Great in 323 BC, the strong anti-Macedonian sentiment that ensued led to Aristotle being indicted for 'impiety'. He fled Athens and died a year later.

Central to Aristotle's beliefs is his distinction between 'form' and 'matter'. The sculptor of a statue confers shape (the form) onto marble (the matter). A thing's form is that which is unified about it – its *essence*. Matter without form is just potentiality, but by acquiring form its actuality increases. God has no matter, but is pure form and absolute actuality. Thus humans, by increasing form in the world, by building houses and bridges, make it more divine.

Aristotle was the first thinker to look at structures of deductive arguments, or syllogisms, and for 2000 years was unsurpassed in the study of logic, until Gottlob Frege and Bertrand Russell, the 20th century's great symbolic logicians, picked up his thread.

underfunded. The main complaint is about the lack of modern teaching aids in both gymnasio and lykeio.

Grievances reached a peak in 1991, when lykeio students staged a series of sit-ins in schools throughout the country, and organised protest marches. In 1992, gymnasio pupils followed suit, and the government responded by making proposals that called for stricter discipline and a more demanding curriculum. More sit-ins followed, and in

the end the government changed its plans and is still reassessing the situation.

SCIENCE

Ancient Greece also left its mark on the world of science, particularly in the field of mathematics.

There was a time when every student could quote Pythagoras' Theorem for right-angle triangles: that the square of the hypotenuse is equal to the sum of the squares of the other two sides. Pythagoras was an eccentric philosopher who lived on Samos at the end of the 6th century BC, but his theorem has been used by builders to create right angles ever since.

The theorem was attributed to Pythagoras by Euclid, a Greek living in Alexandria at the beginning of 3rd century BC. His *Elements* was used as a geometry text book in schools and universities until quite recent times.

Perhaps the best known of all the early mathematicians is Archimedes (287–212 BC), from the Greek city of Syracuse on Sicily. Legend has it that he ran around naked shouting '*eureka, eureka*' (I found it, I found it) after his discovery of the system of measuring volume by displacement of water when he climbed into his bath. He was also an engineer and the inventor of the Archimedes' screw, a device which used a threaded screw inside a pipe to raise water.

Hippocrates (c. 460–375 BC), from Kos, is known as the father of medicine, and as the author of the Hippocratic Oath on medical ethics (see the boxed text 'Hippocrates – the First GP' in the Dodecanese chapter). Many women today have reason to thank Dr George Papanicolaou, who developed the pap smear.

ARTS

See the following colour 'Greek Art & Literature' section for a detailed look at the history of art and architecture in Greece.

Dance

Music and dancing have played an important role in Greek social life since the dawn of Hellenism. You may even think at times that Greeks live solely for the chance to sing and dance. You wouldn't be that wrong. Whether it be at a traditional wedding, a nightclub, an Athenian *boîte* or a simple village *kafeneio*, a song and a dance are not far from people's minds.

The style of dancing often reflects the climate or disposition of the participants. In Epiros, the stately *tsamiko* is slow and highly emotive, reflecting the often cold and insular nature of mountain life. The Pontian Greeks, on the contrary, have a highly visual, vigorous and warlike form of dancing reflecting years of altercations with their Turkish neighbours. The *kotsari* is one of the best examples of this unique dance form.

The islands with their bright and cheery atmosphere give rise to lilting music and matching dances such as the *ballos* or the *sirtos*, while the graceful *kalamatianos* circle dance, where dancers stand in a row with their hands on one another's shoulders, reflects years of proud Peloponnese tradition. Originally from Kalamata in the Peloponnese, this dance can be seen everywhere, most commonly on festive occasions.

The so-called 'Zorba's dance' or *sirtaki* is a stylised dance for two or three men or women with linked arms on shoulders, while the often spectacular solo male *zeïmbekikos* with its whirling improvisations has its roots in the Greek blues of the hashish dens and prisons of prewar times. The women counterpoint this self-indulgent and showy male display with their own sensuous *tsifteteli*, a svelte, sinewy show of femininity evolved from the Middle Eastern belly dance.

The folk dances of today derive from the ritual dances performed in ancient Greek temples. The sirtos is one of these dances, and is depicted on ancient Greek vases. There are also references to dances in Homer's works. Many Greek folk dances, including the sirtos, are performed in a circular formation; in ancient times, dancers formed a circle in order to seal themselves off from evil influences.

Music

Singing and the playing of musical instruments have also been an integral part of life in Greece since ancient times, and are as widely divergent as Greek dancing. Cycladic figurines holding musical instruments resembling harps and flutes date back to 2000 BC. Musical instruments of ancient Greece included the lyre, lute, *piktis* (pipes), *kroupeza* (a percussion instrument), *kithara* (a stringed instrument), *aulos* (a wind instrument), *barbitos* (similar to a violincello) and the *magadio* (similar to a harp).

If ancient Greeks did not have a musical instrument to accompany their songs, they

MARTIN HARRIS

The Greek bouzouki is used to play
traditional rembetika music

imitated the sound of one. It is believed that unaccompanied Byzantine choral singing derived from this custom.

The ubiquitous stringed *bouzouki,* closely associated with contemporary music and which you will hear everywhere in Greece, is a relative newcomer to the game. It is a mandolin-like instrument similar to the Turkish *saz* and *baglama.*

The plucked strings of the bulbous *outi* (oud), the strident sound of the Cretan *lyra* (lyre) and the staccato rap of the *toumber-laki* (lap drum) bear witness to a rich range of musical instruments that share many common characteristics with instruments all over the Middle East.

The bouzouki is one of the main instruments of *rembetika* music – the Greek equivalent of the American Blues. The name rembetika may come from the Turkish word *rembet* which means outlaw. Opinions differ as to the origins of rembetika, but it is probably a hybrid of several different types of music. One source was the music that emerged in the 1870s in the 'low life' cafes, called *tekedes* (hashish dens), in urban areas and especially around ports. Another source was the Arabo-Persian music played in sophisticated Middle Eastern music cafes *(amanedes)* in the 19th century. Rembetika was popularised in Greece by the refugees from Asia Minor.

The songs which emerged from the tekedes had themes concerning hashish, prison life, gambling, knife fights etc, whereas cafe *aman* music had themes which centred around erotic love. These all came together in the music of the refugees, from

which a subculture of rebels, called *manges,* emerged. The manges wore showy clothes even though they lived in extreme poverty. They worked long hours in menial jobs, and spent their evenings in the tekedes, smoking hashish and singing and dancing. Although hashish was illegal, the law was rarely enforced until Metaxas did his clean-up job in 1936. It was in a tekes in Piraeus that Markos Vamvakaris, now acknowledged as the greatest *rembetis*, was discovered by a recording company in the 1930s.

Metaxas' censorship meant that themes of hashish, gambling and the like disappeared from recordings of rembetika in the late 1930s, but continued clandestinely in some tekedes. This polarised the music, and the recordings, stripped of their 'meaty' themes and language, became insipid and bourgeois; recorded rembetika even adopted another name – *laïko tragoudi* – to disassociate it from its illegal roots. Although WWII brought a halt to recording, a number of composers emerged at this time. They included Apostolos Kaldaras, Yiannis Papaïoanou, Georgos Mitsakis and Manolis Hiotis; one of the greatest female rembetika singers, Sotiria Bellou, also appeared at this time.

During the 1950s and 1960s rembetika became increasingly popular, but less and less authentic. Much of the music was glitzy and commercialised, although the period also produced two outstanding composers of popular music (including rembetika) in Mikis Theodorakis and Manos Hatzidakis. The best of Theodorakis' work is the music which he set to the poetry of Seferis, Elytis and Ritsos.

During the junta years, many rembetika clubs were closed down, but interest in genuine rembetika revived in the 1980s – particularly among students and intellectuals. There are now a number of rembetika clubs in Athens.

Other musical forms in Greece include *dimotika* – poetry sung and more often than not accompanied by the *klarino* (clarinet) and *defi* (tambourine) – and the widely popular middle-of-the-road *elafrolaïka*, best exemplified by the songs of Giannis Parios. The unaccompanied, polyphonic *pogonisia* songs of northern Epiros and southern Albania are spine-chilling examples of a musical genre that owes its origins to Byzantium. At the lesser end of the scale, the curiously popular *skyladika* or 'dog songs' – presumably because they resemble a whining dog – are hugely popular in nightclubs known as *bouzouxidika* where the bouzouki reigns supreme, but where musical taste sometimes takes a back seat.

Since independence, Greece has followed mainstream developments in classical music. The Athens Concert Hall has performances by both national and international musicians.

Comparatively few Greek performers have hit it big on the international scene. The best known is Nana Mouskouri. Others include Demis Roussos, the larger-than-life singer who spent the 1980s strutting the world stage clad in his caftan, and the US-based techno wizard Yanni.

You'll also find all the main forms of Western popular music. Rock, particularly heavy metal, seems to have struck a chord with young urban Greeks, and Athens has a lively local scene as well as playing host to big international names. The biggest local bands are *Xylina Spathia* (Wooden Swords) and *Tripes* (Holes).

Literature

The first, and greatest, ancient Greek writer was Homer, author of the *Iliad* and *Odyssey*. Nothing is known of Homer's life; where or when he lived, or whether, as it is alleged, he was blind. The historian Herodotus thought Homer lived in the 9th century BC, and no scholar since has proved nor disproved this.

Herodotus (5th century BC) was the author of the first historical work about Western civilisation. His highly subjective account of the Persian Wars has, however, led him to be regarded as the 'father of lies' as well as the 'father of history'. The historian Thucydides (5th century BC) was more objective in his approach, but took a high moral stance. He wrote an account of the Peloponnesian Wars, and also the famous *Melian Dialogue*, which chronicles talks between the Athenians and Melians prior to the Athenian siege of Melos.

Pindar (c. 518–438 BC) is regarded as the pre-eminent lyric poet of ancient Greece. He was commissioned to recite his odes at the Olympic Games. The greatest writers of love poetry were Sappho (6th century BC) and Alcaeus (5th century BC), both of whom lived on Lesvos. Sappho's poetic descriptions of her affections for other women gave rise to the term 'lesbian'.

Dionysios Solomos (1798–1857) and Andreas Kalvos (1796–1869), who were both born on Zakynthos, are regarded as the first modern Greek poets. Solomos' work was heavily nationalistic and his *Hymn to Freedom* became the Greek national anthem.

The best known 20th-century poets are George Seferis (1900–71), who won the 1963 Nobel Prize for literature, and Odysseus Elytis (1911–96), who won the same prize in 1979. Seferis drew his inspiration from mythology, whereas Elytis' work is surreal.

The most important novelist of the 20th century is Nikos Kazantzakis (1883–1957), whose unorthodox religious views created such a stir in the 1920s. See the Books section in the Facts for the Visitor chapter for a commentary on his works.

Nikos Dimou is a modern writer who has created a similar stir with his controversial observations on Greek society. His book *I Dystihia tou na Eisai Ellinas* (The Misery of Being Greek) has sold more than 100,000 copies. None of his works are available in English, but that may change. He has a Web site in English (**W** www.ndimou.gr).

Apostolos Doxiadis achieved international fame in 2000 with his unusual novel

[Continued on page 65]

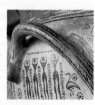

Walk around any capital city in Europe, America or Australasia and the influence of ancient Greek art and architecture is plain to see. It's there in the civic buildings, in the monumental public sculptures, in the plan of the city streets themselves. The product of a truly extraordinary civilisation, the humanism and purity of form of Greek art has inspired artists and architects throughout history. Be it in the paintings and sculptures of the Italian Renaissance or in the playful postmodernist buildings of the late 20th century, the influence of the ancient Greeks cannot be overemphasised.

Ironically, the influence of Greek art has spread throughout the world due to a reality that many travellers (and indeed the Greeks themselves) find unpalatable. This is the fact that many of the greatest works of ancient Greek art haven't had a home in Greece itself for hundreds, sometimes thousands, of years. From the Parthenon frieze taken by Lord Elgin and now displayed in the British Museum to the famous *Nike (Winged Victory of Samothrace)* in Paris' Louvre museum, the work of the Greek masters is held in the collections of the great museums of the world. Many of the great ancient Greek buildings, too, are found in countries other than Greece as they date from the time of the expansive ancient Greek world, which encompassed parts or all of countries such as Italy, Iran, Turkey, Syria and Libya.

Travellers to Greece itself shouldn't despair, however. There's plenty left to see! The buildings, paintings, pots, sculptures and decorative arts of the ancient and Byzantine worlds can be found on the country's streets, cities and islands, as well as in its wonderful museums. They may not be in their original form – it takes a stretch of the imagination to envisage arms on *Hermes of Praxiteles*, and magnificent and austere buildings such as the Parthenon overlaid with gaudily coloured paintings and sculptures – but they manage to evoke the history of the Greek nation more powerfully than a library of history books ever could.

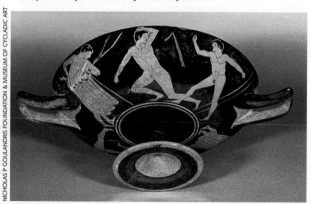

NICHOLAS P GOULANDRIS FOUNDATION & MUSEUM OF CYCLADIC ART

Preceding page:
Geometric period vase from the 6th or 7th century BC (John Elk III, National Archaeological Museum)

Left: Red-figure kylix, Attic workshop, by the 'Painter of the Paris Gigantomachy', 480 BC

ARCHITECTURE

Of all the ancient Greek arts, architecture has perhaps had the greatest influence. Greek temples, seen throughout history as symbols of democracy, have been the inspiration for architectural movements such as the Italian Renaissance and the British Greek Revival.

One of the earliest known architectural sites of ancient Greece is the huge palace and residential complex at Knossos on Crete, built in the Minoan period. Its excavation and reconstruction was begun by Sir Arthur Evans in 1900. Visitors today can see the ruins of the second residential palace built on this site (the first was destroyed by an earthquake in 1700 BC), with its spacious courtyards and grandiose stairways. They can also marvel at the many living rooms, storerooms and bathrooms that give us an idea of day-to-day Minoan life. Similar palaces on Crete, usually of two storeys and built around a large courtyard, have since been excavated at Phaestos, Agia Triada, Malia, Gournia and Zakros.

The Minoan period was followed by the Mycenaean. Instead of the open, labyrinthine palaces of the Minoans, the Mycenaeans used their advanced skills in engineering to build citadels on a compact, orderly plan, fortified by strong walls. Visitors to Greece today can appreciate Mycenaean sites such as those of the ancient city states of Mycenae and Tiryns, excavated by the German archaeologist Heinrich Schliemann in the 1870s. The famous Lion Gate at the palace at Mycenae and the stupendous galleries of the palace at Tiryns both illustrate the engineering expertise of the Mycenaeans.

The next great advance in ancient Greek architecture came with the building of the first monumental stone temples in the Archaic and classical periods. From this time, temples were characterised by the

Doric   Ionian   Corinthian

famous orders of columns, particularly the Doric, Ionic and Corinthian. These orders were applied to the exteriors of temples, which retained their traditional simple plan of porch and hall but were now regularly surrounded by a colonnade or at least a columnar facade.

Doric columns feature cushion capitals, fluted shafts and no bases. Doric temples still part extant include the Temple of Hera at Olympia, the Temple of Apollo at Corinth and the Temple of Hephaestus in Athens. The most famous Doric temple in Greece is, of course, the Parthenon.

The shaft of the Ionic column has a base in several tiers and has more flutes. Unlike the austere Doric style, its capital has an ornamented necking. In all, the Ionic order is less massive than the Doric, and is generally more graceful. The little temple of Athena Nike by the entrance to the Athenian Acropolis, and the Erechtheion, opposite the Parthenon, are two famous Ionic temples.

The distinct and ornate Corinthian column features a single or

JOHN ELK III

Left: Temple in Sanctuary of Apollo, Delphi

double row of leafy scrolls (usually acanthus). This order was introduced at the end of the classical period and was subsequently used by the Romans in many of their buildings. The Temple of Olympian Zeus in Athens, completed in Hadrian's time, is a good example of a Corinthian temple.

Theatre design was also a hallmark of the classical period. The tragedies of Aeschylus, Sophocles and Euripides and the comedies of Aristophanes were written and first performed in the Theatre of Dionysos, built into the slope of Athens' Acropolis in the 5th century BC. Other theatres dating from this period can be found at Dodoni, Megalopolis, Epidaurus and Argos (the latter seats about 20,000). They all feature excellent acoustics and most are still used for summer festivals.

In the Hellenistic period, private houses and palaces, rather than temples and public buildings, were the main focus. The houses at Delos, built around peristyled (surrounded by columns) courtyards and

Right: The massive Temple of Olympian Zeus, Athens, begun in the 6th century BC, completed in AD 131

MARK HONAN

featuring striking mosaics, are perhaps the best examples in existence.

The Roman period saw Corinth become an important Roman city, with recent excavations uncovering fountains, baths and gymnasia. Athens obtained a new commercial agora (now known as the Roman Agora) in the time of Augustus and a century and a half later the emperor Hadrian endowed the city with a library and built an elegant arch that still stands between the old and new parts of the city.

During the Byzantine period the Parthenon in Athens was converted into a church and other churches were built throughout Greece. These usually featured a central dome supported by four arches on piers and flanked by vaults, with smaller domes at the four corners and three apses to the east. The external brickwork, which alternated with stone, was sometimes set in patterns. At Mt Athos and on Patmos, where the first monasteries were built in the 10th century, the monastic buildings as well as the churches survive, though much has changed through centuries of continuous use and a number of fires. At Meteora in central Greece, the monasteries were built high on precipitous rocks and for centuries were almost inaccessible.

JOHN ELK III

Left: Moni Agias Varvaras Rousanou, Meteora, 16th century

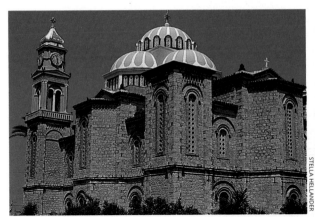

STELLA HELLANDER

Right: Karlovasi
Cathedral, Samos

After the temporary fall of Constantinople to a crusading army in 1204, much of Greece became the fiefdoms of Western aristocrats. The most notable of these was the Villehardouin family, who built castles in the Peloponnese at Hlemoutsi, Nafplio, Kalamata and Mystras. At Mystras they also built a palace which was a court of the Byzantine imperial family for two centuries prior to the Turkish conquest.

There is very little architecture of the Ottoman period surviving in Greece. The only examples are found at Kavala, Xanthi and Didymotiho near the Turkish border.

After the War of Independence, Greece continued the neoclassical style that had been dominant in western European architecture and sculpture from 1760 to 1820, thus providing a sense of continuity with its ancient past. This neoclassical style is apparent in Nafplio, initially the capital, and in Athens, notably in the Doric and Ionic ensemble of the National Library and the university. Noteworthy, too, are the old royal palace, the Polytehnio, and the mansions which are now the Byzantine, Benaki and Kanellopoulos museums.

SCULPTURE

Taking pride of place in the collections of the great museums of the world, the sculptures of ancient Greece have extraordinary visual power and beauty.

The prehistoric art of Greece has been discovered only recently, notably in the Cyclades and on Crete. The pared-down sculptures of this period, with their smooth and flattish appearance, were carved from the high-quality marble of Paros and Naxos in the middle of the 3rd millennium BC. Their primitive and powerful forms have inspired many artists since, particularly those of the 20th century.

In the Mycenaean period, small terracottas of women with a circular body or with arms upraised were widely produced. These are known to modern scholars as phi (φ) and psi (ψ) figurines from their resemblance to these letters of the Greek alphabet.

Displaying an obvious debt to Egyptian sculpture, the marble sculptures of the Archaic period are true precursors of the famed Greek sculpture of the classical period. The artists of this period moved away from the examples of their Oriental predecessors and began to represent figures that were true to nature, rather than flat and stylised. For the first time in history a sculptured shape was made to reproduce the complex mechanism of the human body. Seeking to master the depiction of both the naked body and of drapery, sculptors of the period focused on figures of naked youths *(kouroi)*, with their set symmetrical stance and enigmatic smiles. Many great kouros sculptures and draped female kore can be admired at the National Archaeological Museum in Athens.

The sculpture of the classical period shows an obsession with the human figure and with drapery. At first the classical style was rather severe, as can be seen in the bronze charioteer at Delphi and the sculpture from the temple at Olympia. Later, as sculptors sought ideal proportions for the human figure, it became more animated. New poses were explored and the figures became increasingly sinuous, with smaller heads in relation to the body.

Left: Marble statuette of a boy playing with a goose, 3rd century BC

Right: Tanagran figurine; terracotta, Boeotian workshop, 330 BC

NATIONAL ARCHAEOLOGICAL MUSEUM, ATHENS

NICHOLAS P GOULANDRIS FOUNDATION & MUSEUM OF CYCLADIC ART

Unfortunately, little original work of the classical period survives. Most freestanding classical sculpture described by ancient writers was made of bronze and survives only as marble copies made by the Romans. Looking at these copies is a bittersweet experience. On the one hand, they are marvellous works of art in their own right. On the other, copies of works such as *Diskobolos* (The Discus Thrower) by Myron, *Apoxyomenos* (Scraper) by Lysippos and the various Aphrodites by Praxiteles have made us aware of what an extraordinary body of work has been lost. Fortunately, a few classical bronzes, lost when they were being shipped abroad in antiquity, were recovered from the sea in the 20th century. These include the statue of a youth (c. 350–330 BC)

Right: Grave stele of a woman with her maid; Attica, early 4th century BC

NATIONAL ARCHAEOLOGICAL MUSEUM, ATHENS

found in the sea off Antikythira, now in the collection of the National Archaeological Museum, Athens. Also on show here is the wonderful *Poseidon of Artemision*, thought to date from 470–450 BC.

The sculpture of the Hellenistic period continued the Greeks' quest to attain total naturalism in their work. Works of this period were animated, almost theatrical, in contrast to their serene Archaic and classical predecessors. The focus was on realism. Just how successful the artists of this period were is shown in the way later artists, such as Michelangelo, revered them. Michelangelo, in fact, was at the forefront of the rediscovery and appreciation of Greek works in the Renaissance. He is said to have been at the site in Rome in 1506 when the famous Roman copy of the *Laocoön* group, one of the iconic sculptural works of the Hellenistic period, was unearthed.

The end of the Hellenistic age signalled the decline of Greek sculpture's pre-eminent position in the history of the artform. The torch was handed to the Romans, who proved worthy successors. Sculpture in Greece itself never again attained any degree of true innovation.

POTTERY

Say the words 'Greek art' and many people immediately visualise a painted terracotta pot. Represented in museums and art galleries throughout the world, the pots of ancient Greece have such a high profile for a number of reasons, chief among these being that there are lots of them around! The excavation of these pots, buried throughout Greece over millennia, has enabled us to appreciate in

Left: Red-figure pelike, Attic workshop, by the 'Painter of the Louvre Centauromachy', 450–440 BC

Right: Black-figure lekythos, Attic workshop, probably by the 'Amasis Painter', 560–550 BC

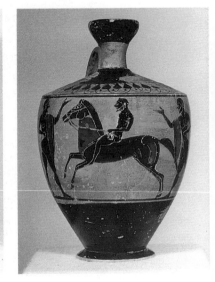

PHOTOGRAPHS: NICHOLAS P GOULANDRIS FOUNDATION & MUSEUM OF CYCLADIC ART

small measure the tradition of ancient pictorial art. Quite simply, in the absence of significant examples of Greek painting, pots are all we've got!

Practised from the Stone Age on, pottery is one of the most ancient arts. At first, vases were built with coils and wads of clay but the art of throwing on the wheel was introduced in about 2000 BC and was then practised with great skill by Minoan and Mycenaean artists.

Minoan pottery is often characterised by a high centre of gravity and beak-like spouts. Painted decoration was applied as a white clay slip (a thin paste of clay and water) or one which fired to a greyish black or dull red. Flowing designs with spiral or marine and plant motifs were used. The Archaeological Museum in Iraklio has a wealth of Minoan pots.

Mycenaean pottery shapes include a long-stemmed goblet and a globular vase with handles resembling a pair of stirrups. Decorative motifs are similar to those on Minoan pottery but are less fluid.

The 10th century BC saw the introduction of the Protogeometric style, with its substantial pots decorated with blackish-brown horizontal lines around the circumference, hatched triangles, and compass-drawn concentric circles. This was followed by the new vase shape and more crowded decoration of the pots of the Geometric period. The decorations on these pots are painted in a lustrous brown glaze on the light surface of the clay, and the same dark glaze is used as a wash to cover the undecorated areas. Occasionally a touch of white is added. By the early 8th century, figures were introduced, marking the introduction of the most fundamental element in the later tradition of classical art – the representation of gods, men and animals.

By the 7th century BC, Corinth was producing pottery with added white and purple-red clay slip. These pots often featured friezes of lions, goats and swans and a background fill of rosettes. In 6th-century Athens, artists used red clay with a high iron content. A thick colloidal slip made from this clay produced a glossy black surface that contrasted with the red and was enlivened with added white and purple-red. Attic pots, famed for their high quality, were exported throughout the Greek empire during this time. Many of these exports are the pots that grace the collections of international museums today.

PAINTING

The lack of any comprehensive archaeological record of ancient Greek painting has forced art historians to largely rely on the painted decoration of terracotta pots as evidence of the development of this Greek artform. There are a few exceptions, such as the Cycladic frescoes in houses on Santorini, excavated in the mid-to-late 20th century. Some of these frescoes are now in the collection of the National Archaeological Museum in Athens. These works were painted in fresco technique using yellow, blue, red and black pigments, with some details added after the plaster had dried. Plants and animals are depicted, as well as men and women. Figures are usually shown in profile or in a combination of profile and frontal views. Stylistically, the frescoes are similar to the paintings of Minoan Crete, which are less well preserved. Reconstructed examples of frescoes from the Minoan period can be seen at the Palace of Knossos, on Crete.

Greek painting came into its own during the Byzantine period. Byzantine churches were usually decorated with frescoes on a dark blue ground with a bust of Christ in the dome, the four Gospel writers in the pendentives supporting the dome and the Virgin and Child in the apse. They also featured scenes from the life of Christ (Annunciation, Nativity, Baptism, Entry into Jerusalem, Crucifixion and Transfiguration) and figures of the saints. In the later centuries of the period, the scenes involved more detailed narratives, including cycles of the life of the Virgin and the miracles of Christ.

Painting after the Byzantine period became more secular in nature, with 19th-century Greek painters specialising in portraits, nautical themes and pictorial representation of the War of Independence. Major 19th-century painters included Dionysios Tsokos, Andreas Kriezis, Theodoros Vryzakis, Nikiphoros Lytras, Konstantinos Volanakis and

BYZANTINE MUSEUM, ATHENS

Left: The Archangel Michael; icon, 14th century

Opposite Page:
Top Left: Presentation of Christ in the Temple and the Baptism of Christ in the River Jordan by John the Baptist; icon of the Cretan school, 16th century

Top Right: The Virgin Enthroned, with a border of scenes from the life of Christ and portraits of saints; icon of the Cretan school, 16th century

Bottom: Blind Eros and two sirens; painting on wood by Agapios Manganaris of Sifnos, 1825

BENAKI MUSEUM, ATHENS

BENAKI MUSEUM, ATHENS

BYZANTINE MUSEUM, ATHENS

BENAKI MUSEUM, ATHENS (INV. NO. 6690)

Nicholas Gyzis. Gyzis' historical paintings, which were painted at the time of the fascination with the 'Great Idea' of a new Greek empire, feature particularly interesting subject matter.

From the first decades of the 20th century, artists such as Konstantinos Parthenis, Konstantinos Kaleas and, later, George Bouzianis were able to use the heritage of the past and at the same time assimilate various developments in modern art. These paintings are best studied in the National Art Gallery in Athens.

OTHER ARTS

Though we talk predominantly of architecture, sculpture, pottery and painting when discussing Greek art, there are, of course, the many 'minor' arts as well. Examples of many of these artforms can be seen in Greek museums; they are less monumental – in both size and ambition – than the works discussed above but are no less interesting. These arts include:

Weaving and embroidery Often displaying regional characteristics, examples of weaving and embroidery survive in some quantity from the 17th century onwards. Examples can be seen in the folk museum at Thessaloniki.

Opposite page: Fisherman; fresco from Akrotiri, Santorini (Thira), c1600 BC

Decorative arts The Benaki Museum in Athens displays a fine collection of decorative arts from medieval and modern Greece, as well as some from earlier centuries.

Mosaics Mosaic wall decoration with tesserae (tiles) of coloured glass for figures and glass with gold leaf for background can be seen at the 11th-century churches at Dafni, at Moni Osiou Louka near Delphi and at Nea Moni on Chios.

Right: Embroidered cushion cover: a mermaid with two tails, floral spirals and birds, Crete, 18th century

Metalwork and jewellery Spectacular Mycenaean gold masks, diadems, cups and dress ornaments occupy the central hall of the Archaeological Museum in Athens.

Further reading:

Greek Art and Archaeology, JG Pedley, Cassell, London, 1992
The Greek Museums, M Andronicos et al, Athens, 1975
A Handbook of Greek Art, Gisela Richter, Phaidon, London 1974
Greek Art, John Boardman, Thames & Hudson, London 1996

Left: Enamelled gold pendant with pearls in the shape of a three-masted caravel, Patmos 17th century

[Continued from page 48]

Uncle Petros and Goldbach's Conjecture. Despite this success, he's better known at home as a film director. He also has a Web site: Ⓦ www.apostolosdoxiadis.com.

Drama

Drama in Greece can be dated back to the contests staged at the Ancient Theatre of Dionysos in Athens during the 6th century BC for the annual Dionysia festival. During one of these competitions, Thespis left the ensemble and took centre stage for a solo performance regarded as the first true dramatic performance. The term 'thespian' for actor derives from this event.

Aeschylus (c. 525–456 BC) is the so-called 'father of tragedy'; his best-known work is the *Oresteia* trilogy. Sophocles (c. 496–406 BC) is regarded as the greatest tragedian. He is thought to have written over 100 plays, of which only seven survive. These include *Ajax, Antigone, Electra, Trachiniae* and his most famous play, *Oedipus Rex*. His plays dealt mainly with tales from mythology and had complex plots. Sophocles won first prize 18 times at the Dionysia festival, beating Aeschylus in 468 BC, whereupon Aeschylus went to Sicily in a huff.

Euripides (c. 485–406 BC) was another famous tragedian, more popular than either Aeschylus or Sophocles because his plots were considered to be more exciting. He wrote 80 plays of which 19 are extant (although one, *Rhesus*, is disputed). His most famous works are *Medea, Andromache, Orestes* and *Bacchae*. Aristophanes (c. 427–387 BC) wrote comedies – often ribald – which dealt with topical issues. His play *The Wasp* ridicules Athenians who resorted to litigation over trivialities; *The Birds* pokes fun at Athenian gullibility; and *Plutus* deals with the unfair distribution of wealth.

You can see plays by the ancient Greek playwrights at the Athens and Epidaurus festivals (see the Athens and Peloponnese chapters), and at various other festivals around the country.

Drama continues to feature prominently in domestic arts, although activity is largely confined to Athens and Thessaloniki. The first couple of the modern Greek theatre are playwrights Thanasis Reppas and Mihailis Papathanasiou, also noted writers of screenplays and movie directors. Unfortunately, performances of their work are only in Greek.

Cinema

Greeks are avid cinema-goers, although most of the films they watch are North American or British. The Greek film industry has long been in the doldrums, largely due to inadequate funding. The problem is compounded by the type of films the Greeks produce, which are famously slow moving, loaded with symbolism and generally too avant-garde to have mass appeal.

The leader of this school is Theodoros Angelopoulos, winner of the Golden Palm award at the 1998 Cannes Film Festival for *An Eternity and One Day*. It tells the story of a terminally ill writer who spends his last day revisiting his youth in the company of a 10-year-old boy. His other films include *The Beekeeper, Alexander the Great* and *The Hesitant Step of the Stork*.

Although it produces no action films, the Greek cinema has shown in recent years that it does have a lighter side. The big hit at the time of research was *Safe Sex*, a lighthearted look at sexuality directed by Thanasis Reppas and Mihailis Papathanasiou.

SOCIETY & CONDUCT
Women in Society

Despite the positive role model provided by mythology, which filled its pantheon with equal numbers of gods and goddesses, women barely rate a mention in most histories of ancient Greece – unless they happened to have a face lovely enough to launch a thousand ships.

Women were denied the vote, and were excluded from such events as the Olympic Games – on pain of death. Their role was to rear warriors, and look after the domestics.

That role remained virtually unchanged until very recent times. Women finally got the vote in 1956, but had to wait until the 1980s for the formal abolishment of the dowry system. The 1983 Family Law Act,

Ancient Greek Mythology

Mythology was an integral part of life in ancient times. The myths of ancient Greece are the most familiar to us, for they are deeply entrenched in the consciousness of Western civilisation. They are accounts of the lives of the deities whom the Greeks worshipped and of the heroes they idolised.

The myths are all things to all people – a ripping good yarn, expressions of deep psychological insights, words of spine-tingling poetic beauty and food for the imagination. They have inspired great literature, art and music – as well as the odd TV show.

The myths we know are thought to be a blend of Dorian and Mycenaean mythology. Most accounts derive from the works of the poets Hesiod and Homer, produced in about 900 BC. The original myths have been chopped and changed countless times – dramatised, moralised and even adapted for ancient political propaganda, so numerous versions exist.

The Greek Myths by Robert Graves is regarded as being the ultimate book on the subject. It can be heavy going, though. *An Iconoclast's Guide to the Greek Gods* by Maureen O'Sullivan makes more entertaining reading.

The Twelve Deities

The main characters of the myths are the 12 deities, who lived on Mt Olympus.

The supreme deity was **Zeus**, who was also god of the heavens. His job was to make laws and keep his unruly family in order by brandishing his thunderbolt. He was also the possessor of an astonishing libido and vented his lust on just about everyone he came across, including his own mother. Mythology is littered with his offspring.

Zeus was married to his sister **Hera**, the protector of women and the family. Hera was able to renew her virginity each year by bathing in a spring. She was the mother of Ares, Hebe and Hephaestus.

Zeus produced Athena from his forehead – spear and all!

Ares, god of war, was the embodiment of everything warlike. Strong and brave, he was definitely someone to have on your side in a fight – but he was also hot-tempered and violent, liking nothing better than a good massacre. Athenians, who fought only for such noble ideals as liberty, thought that Ares must be a Thracian – whom they regarded as bloodthirsty barbarians.

Athena, the powerful goddess of wisdom and guardian of Athens, is said to have been born (complete with helmet, armour and spear) from Zeus' head, with Hephaestus acting as midwife. Unlike Ares, she derived no pleasure from fighting, preferring to use her wisdom to settle disputes peacefully. If need be, however, she went valiantly into battle.

CLINT CURÉ

Hephaestus was worshipped for his matchless skills as a craftsman. When Zeus decided to punish man, he asked Hephaestus to make a woman. So Hephaestus created Pandora from clay and water, and, as everyone knows, she had a box, from which sprang all the evils afflicting humankind.

Ancient Greek Mythology

The next time you have a bowl of cornflakes, give thanks to **Demeter**, the goddess of earth and fertility. The English word 'cereal', for products of corn or edible grain, derives from the goddess' Roman name, Ceres. The Greek word for such products is *demetriaka*.

The goddess of love (and lust) was the beautiful **Aphrodite**. Her *tour de force* was her magic girdle which made everyone fall in love with its wearer. The girdle meant she was constantly pursued by both gods and goddesses – the gods because they wanted to make love to her, the goddesses because they wanted to borrow the girdle. Zeus became so fed up with her promiscuity that he married her off to Hephaestus, the ugliest of the gods.

Poseidon, the brother of Zeus, was god of the sea and preferred his sumptuous palace in the depths of the Aegean to Mt Olympus. When he was angry (which was often) he would use his trident to create massive waves and floods. His moods could also trigger earthquakes and volcanic eruptions. He was always on the lookout for some real estate on dry land and challenged Dionysos for Naxos, Hera for Argos and Athena for Athens.

CLINT CURÉ

Apollo, god of light, was the son of Zeus by the nymph Leto. He was the sort of person everybody wanted to have around. The ancients Greeks associated sunshine with spiritual and intellectual illumination. Apollo was also worshipped as the god of music and song, which the ancients believed were heard only where there was light and security.

Apollo's twin sister, **Artemis**, seems to have been a bit confused by her portfolio. She was worshipped as the goddess of childbirth, yet she asked Zeus to grant her eternal virginity; she was also the protector of suckling animals, but loved hunting!

Bad weather was often blamed on Poseidon's temper

Hermes, messenger of the gods, was another son of Zeus – this time by Maia, daughter of Atlas. He was a colourful character who smooth-talked his way into the top ranks of the Greek pantheon. Convicted of rustling Apollo's cattle while still in his cradle, he emerged from the case as the guardian of all divine property. Zeus then made Hermes his messenger, and fitted him out with a pair of winged golden sandals to speed him on his way. His job included responsibility for commerce, treaties and the safety of travellers. He remained, however, the patron of thieves.

Hermes completes the first XI – the gods whose position in the pantheon is agreed by everyone. The final berth is normally reserved for **Hestia**, goddess of the hearth. She was as pure as driven snow, a symbol of security, happiness and hospitality. She spurned disputes and wars and swore to be a virgin forever.

She was a bit too virtuous for some, who relegated her to the ranks of the Lesser Gods and promoted the fun-loving **Dionysos**, god of wine, in her place. Dionysos was a son of Zeus by another of the supreme deity's dalliances. He had the job of touring the world with an entourage of fellow revellers spreading the word about the vine and wine.

Ancient Greek Mythology

Lesser Gods

After his brothers Zeus and Poseidon had taken the heavens and seas, **Hades** was left with the underworld (the earth was common ground). This vast and mysterious region was thought by the Greeks to be as far beneath the earth as the sky was above it. The underworld was divided into three regions: the Elysian Fields for the virtuous, Tartarus for sinners and the Asphodel Meadows for those who fitted neither category. Hades was also the god of wealth, in the form of the precious stones and metals found deep in the earth.

Pan, the son of Hermes, was the god of the shepherds. Born with horns, beard, tail and goat legs, his ugliness so amused the other gods that eventually he fled to Arcadia where he danced, played his famous pipes and watched over the pastures, shepherds and herds.

Other gods included **Asclepius**, the god of healing; **Eros**, the god of love; **Hypnos**, the god of sleep; **Helios**, god of the sun; and **Selene**, goddess of the moon.

Mythical Heroes

Heroes such as **Heracles** and **Theseus** were elevated almost to the ranks of the gods. Heracles, yet another of Zeus' offspring, was performing astonishing feats of strength before he had left the cradle. His 12 labours were performed to atone for the murder of his wife and children in a bout of madness. The deeds of Theseus included the slaying of the Minotaur at Knossos.

Other heroes include **Odysseus**, whose wanderings after the fall of Troy are recorded in Homer's *Odyssey*, and **Jason**, who led his Argonauts to recover the golden fleece from Colchis (in modern Georgia).

Xena, regrettably, does not feature anywhere. The strapping 'warrior princess' of TV fame is a scriptwriter's invention – not a myth!

which also gave women equal property rights and legalised abortion, finally put an end to a system that had remained largely unchanged since Byzantine times.

The result is young women growing up today enjoy freedoms and opportunities that were unimaginable only a generation ago. The transition has not been entirely straightforward in a society so accustomed to male domination, nor is it complete. Outside major cities like Athens, Thessaloniki and Patras, times – and attitudes – have hardly changed.

Women fill no more than a handful of seats in the nation's 300-strong parliament. Ironically, despite the built-in disadvantages of being female, many of the country's best known personalities of modern times have been women. The glamorous head of the 2004 Athens Olympic organising committee, Gianna Angelopoulos-Daskalaki, is the latest woman in a line that includes the singers Maria Callas and Nana Mouskouri, and cultural crusader Melina Mercouri.

The main women's organisations are the Greek Union of Women (☎ 21 0823 4937), Aharnon 51, Athens 104 39; the Greek Federation of Women (☎ 21 0362 9460), 120 Ippokratous 120, Athens 11 472; and the League for Women's Rights (☎ 21 0361 6236), Solonos 41, 106 72.

Traditional Culture

Greece is steeped in traditional customs. Name days (see the accompanying boxed text), weddings and funerals all have great significance. On someone's name day an open-house policy is adopted and refreshments are served to well-wishers who stop by to give gifts. Weddings are highly festive occasions, with dancing, feasting and drinking sometimes continuing for days.

Greeks tend to be more superstitious than other Europeans. Tuesday is considered an unlucky day because on that day the

Olympian Creation Myth

Olympian Creation Myth

According to mythology, the world was formed from a great shapeless mass called Chaos. From Chaos came forth Gaea, the earth goddess. She bore a son, Uranus, the Firmament, and their subsequent union produced three 100-handed giants and three one-eyed Cyclopes. Gaea dearly loved her hideous offspring, but not so Uranus, who hurled them into Tartarus (the underworld).

The couple then produced the seven Titans, but Gaea still grieved for her other children. She asked the Titans to take vengeance upon their father, and free the 100-handed giants and the Cyclopes. The Titans did as they were requested, castrating the hapless Uranus, but Cronos (the head Titan), after setting eyes on Gaea's hideous offspring, hurled them back into Tartarus, whereupon Gaea foretold that Cronos would be usurped by one of his own offspring.

Cronos married his sister Rhea, but wary of his mother's warning, he swallowed every child Rhea bore him. When Rhea bore her sixth child, Zeus, she smuggled him to Crete, and gave Cronos a stone in place of the child, which he duly swallowed. Rhea hid the baby Zeus in the Dikteon cave in the care of three nymphs.

On reaching manhood, Zeus, determined to avenge his swallowed siblings, became Cronos' cup-bearer and filled his cup with poison. Cronos drank from the cup, then disgorged first the stone and then his children Hestia, Demeter, Hera, Poseidon and Hades, all of whom were none the worse for their ordeal. Zeus, aided by his regurgitated brothers and sisters, deposed Cronos, and went to war against the Titans who wouldn't acknowledge him as chief god. Gaea, who still hadn't forgotten her imprisoned, beloved offspring, told Zeus he would only be victorious with the help of the Cyclopes and the 100-handed giants, so he released them from Tartarus.

The Cyclopes gave Zeus a thunderbolt, and the three 100-handed giants threw rocks at the Titans, who eventually retreated. Zeus banished Cronos, as well as all of the Titans except Atlas (Cronos' deputy), to a far-off land. Atlas was ordered to hold up the sky.

Mt Olympus became home-sweet-home for Zeus and his unruly and incestuous family. Zeus, taking a fancy to Hera, turned himself into a dishevelled cuckoo whom the unsuspecting Hera held to her bosom, whereupon Zeus violated her, and Hera reluctantly agreed to marry him. They had three children: Ares, Hephaestus and Hebe.

Byzantine Empire fell to the Ottomans. Many Greeks will not sign an important transaction, get married or begin a trip on a Tuesday. Greeks also believe in the 'evil eye', a superstition prevalent in many Middle Eastern countries. If someone is the victim of the evil eye, then bad luck will invariably befall them. The bad luck is the result of someone's envy, so one should avoid being too complimentary about things of beauty, especially newborn babies. To ward off the evil eye, Greeks often wear a piece of blue glass, resembling an eye, on a chain around their necks.

Dos & Don'ts

The Greeks' reputation for hospitality is not a myth, although it is a bit harder to find these days. In rural areas, Greece is probably the only country in Europe where you might find yourself invited into a stranger's home for coffee, a meal or even to spend the night. This can often lead to a feeling of uneasiness for the recipient if the host is poor, but to offer them money is considered offensive. The most acceptable way of expressing your thanks is through a gift, perhaps to a child in the family. A similar situation arises if you go out for a meal with Greeks; the bill is not shared as in northern European countries, but paid by the host.

When drinking wine it is the custom to only half fill the glass. It is bad manners to empty the glass, so it must be constantly replenished. When visiting someone you will

Name days

Name days, not birthdays, are celebrated in Greece. Great significance is attached to the name given to a child, and the process of choosing a name follows fairly rigid conventions. The idea of a child being given a name just because the parents like the sound of it is unknown in Greece. Even naming a child after someone as a mark of respect or admiration is unusual. That so many children were named Vyronis (the Greek form of Byron) was a measure of the tremendous gratitude the Greeks felt for the philhellene Lord Byron.

Children are never named after parents, but the eldest son in a family is often called after his paternal grandfather, and the eldest daughter after her paternal grandmother. Names are usually of religious origin. Each island or area in Greece has a patron saint, and people living in that area often name a child after its patron saint. The patron saint of Corfu is Agios Spyridon and it seems as if about half of the men who were born there are called Spyridon. Exceptions to this custom occur if a family is not religious – quite a rarity in Greece. A non-religious family will often give their offspring a name derived from ancient Greece or mythology. Socrates, Aristotle, Athena and Aphrodite are popular.

Each saint has a special feast day. A person's name day is the feast day of the saint after which they were named. On someone's name day, open house is held and a feast is laid on for the friends and neighbours who call. They will give a small gift to the person whose name day it is, but there is less emphasis on the giving of presents than there is in birthday celebrations.

If you meet someone in Greece on their nameday, the customary greeting is 'chronia polla!', which means 'many years'.

be offered coffee; again, it is bad manners to refuse. You will also be given a glass of water and perhaps a small serve of preserves. It is the custom to drink the water, then eat the preserves and then drink the coffee.

Personal questions are not considered rude in Greece, and if you react as if they are you will be the one causing offence. You will be inundated with queries about your age, salary, marital status etc.

If you go into a *kafeneio*, taverna or shop, it is the custom to greet the waiters or assistant with *'kalimera'* (good day) or *'kalispera'* (good evening) – likewise if you meet someone in the street.

You may have come to Greece for sun, sand and sea, but if you want to bare all, other than on a designated nude beach, remember that Greece is a traditional country, so take care not to offend the locals.

Treatment of Animals

The Greek attitude to animals depends on whether the animal is a cat or not. It's definitely cool to be a cat. Even the mangiest-looking stray can be assured of a warm welcome and a choice titbit on approaching the restaurant table of a Greek. Most other domestic animals are greeted with a certain indifference. You don't see many pet dogs or pets of any sort for that matter.

The main threat to animal welfare is hunting. Greek hunters are notorious for blasting anything that moves, and millions of animals are killed during the long 'open' season, from 20 August to 10 March, which encompasses the bird migratory period. The Hellenic Centre for the Rehabilitation of Wild Animals and Birds (☎ 2297 028 367) on the island of Aegina, reports that 80% of the animals it treats have been shot.

RELIGION

About 98% of the Greek population belong to the Greek Orthodox Church. Most of the remainder are either Roman Catholic, Jewish or Muslim.

Philippi, in Macedonia, is reputedly the first place in Europe where St Paul preached the gospel. This was in AD 49 and during the next five years he preached also in Athens, Thessaloniki and Corinth.

Transliteration & Variant Spellings: An Explanation

The issue of correctly transliterating Greek into the Latin alphabet is a vexed one, fraught with inconsistencies and pitfalls. The Greeks themselves are not very consistent in this respect, though things are gradually improving. The word 'Piraeus', for example, has been variously represented by the following transliterations: Pireas, Piraievs and Pireefs; and when appearing as a street name (eg, Piraeus Street) you will also find Pireos!

This has been compounded by the linguistic minefield of diglossy, or the two forms of the Greek language. The purist form is called Katharevousa and the popular form is Dimotiki (Demotic). The Katharevousa form was never more than an artificiality and Dimotiki has always been spoken as the mainstream language, but this linguistic schizophrenia means there are often two Greek words for each English word. Thus, the word for 'baker' in everyday language is *fournos*, but the shop sign will more often than not say *artopoieion*. The baker's product will be known in the street as *psomi*, but in church as *artos*.

A further complication is the issue of anglicised vs hellenised forms of place names: Athina vs Athens, Patra vs Patras, Thiva vs Thebes, Evia vs Euboia – the list goes on and on! Toponymic diglossy (the existence of both an official and everyday name for a place) is responsible for Kerkyra/Corfu, Zante/Zakynthos, and Santorini/Thira. In this guide we usually provide modern Greek equivalents for town names, with one or two well known exceptions, eg Athens and Patras. For ancient sites, settlements or people from antiquity, we have tried to stick to the more familiar classical names; so we have Thucydides instead of Thoukididis, Mycenae instead of Mykines.

Problems in transliteration have particular implications for vowels, especially given that Greek has six ways of rendering the vowel sound *ee*, two ways of rendering the *o* sound and two ways of rendering the *e* sound. In most instances in this book, *y* has been used for the *ee* sound when a Greek *upsilon* (υ, Υ) has been used, and *i* for Greek *ita* (η, Η) and *iota* (ι, Ι). In the case of the Greek vowel combinations that make the *ee* sound, that is οι, ει and υι, an *i* has been used. For the two Greek *e* sounds αι and ε, an *e* has been employed.

As far as consonants are concerned, the Greek letter *gamma* (γ, Γ) appears as *g* rather than *y* throughout this book. This means that *agios* (Greek for male saint) is used rather than *ayios*, and *agia* (female saint) rather than *ayia*. The letter *delta* (δ, Δ) appears as *d* rather than *dh* throughout this book, so *domatia* (rooms), rather than *dhomatia*, is used. The letter *fi* (φ, Φ) can be transliterated as either *f* or *ph*. Here, a general rule of thumb is that classical names are spelt with a *ph* and modern names with an *f*. So Phaistos is used rather than Festos, and Folegandros is used rather than Pholegandros. The Greek *chi* (ξ, Ξ) has usually been represented as *h* in order to approximate the Greek pronunciation as closely as possible. Thus, we have 'Haralambos' instead of 'Charalambos' and 'Polytehniou' instead of 'Polytechniou'. Bear in mind that the *h* is to be pronounced as an aspirated *h*, much like the *ch* in loch. The letter *kapa* (κ, Κ) has been used to represent that sound, except where well known names from antiquity have adopted by convention the letter *c*, eg, Polycrates, Acropolis.

Wherever reference to a street name is made, we have omitted the Greek word 'odos', but words for avenue *(leoforos)* and square *(plateia)* have been included.

The Greek Orthodox Church is closely related to the Russian Orthodox Church; together they form the third-largest branch of Christianity. Orthodox, meaning 'right belief', was founded in the 4th century by Constantine the Great, who was converted to Christianity by a vision of the Cross.

By the 8th century, there were a number of differences of opinion, as well as increasing rivalry, between the pope in Rome and the patriarch of Constantinople. One dispute was over the wording of the Creed. The original Creed stated that the Holy Spirit proceeds 'from the Father', which the

Orthodox Church adhered to, whereas Rome added 'and the Son'. Another bone of contention concerned the celibacy of the clergy. Rome decreed priests had to be celibate; in the Orthodox Church, a priest could marry before becoming ordained. There were also differences in fasting: in the Orthodox Church, not only was meat forbidden during Lent, but wine and oil also.

By the 11th century these differences had become irreconcilable, and in 1054 the pope and the patriarch excommunicated one another. Ever since, the two have gone their own ways as the (Greek/Russian) Orthodox Church and the Roman Catholic Church. The brief visit to Athens by Pope John Paul II in May 2001 was the first by a pontiff for more than 1300 years.

During Ottoman times membership of the Orthodox Church was one of the most important criteria in defining a Greek, regardless of where he or she lived. The church was the principal upholder of Greek culture and traditions.

Religion is still integral to life in Greece, and the Greek year is centred on the festivals of the church calendar. Most Greeks, when they have a problem, will go into a church and light a candle to the saint they feel is most likely to help them. On the islands you will see hundreds of tiny churches dotted around the countryside. Most have been built by individual families in the name of their selected patron saint as thanksgiving for God's protection.

If you wish to look around a church, you should always dress appropriately. Women should wear skirts that reach below the knees, and men should wear long trousers and have their arms covered. Regrettably, many churches are kept locked nowadays, but it's usually easy enough to locate caretakers, who will be happy to open them up for you.

LANGUAGE

See the Language chapter at the back of this book for pronunciation details and useful phrases. For a more comprehensive guide to language, see Lonely Planet's *Greek phrasebook*. The boxed text in this chapter 'Transliteration & Variant Spellings: An Explanation' takes a look at the vagaries of turning Greek into English.

The Glossary chapter at the back of the book contains some common Greek words.

Facts for the Visitor

SUGGESTED ITINERARIES

One of the most difficult aspects of travel is organising an itinerary. The following list provides a choice of two-week and four-week nationwide itineraries covering as much of the country as time and transport schedules permit. For suggested itineraries for specific areas or island groups, see the relevant chapters later in the book.

Two Weeks

Spend the first two days in Athens, visiting the Acropolis, the Ancient Agora and the National Archaeological Museum (two days); travel to Nafplio in the Peloponnese and use it as a base to visit Ancient Mycenae and Epidaurus (two days); travel across the Peloponnese to Ancient Olympia (one day); continue around the coast to Patras and catch a bus to Delphi (one day); return to Athens and catch an overnight ferry to Rhodes (one day); spend a couple of days exploring the medieval city of Rhodes and visiting Ancient Lindos then catch the evening flight to Iraklio on Crete (two days); visit Knossos (one day); catch a hydrofoil to Santorini (two days); return to Athens via Naxos or Mykonos – depending on whether you want to walk or party (two days).

Four Weeks

Spend the first day in Athens visiting the Acropolis and exploring the Plaka district (one day); visit the National Archaeological Museum and the Ancient Agora (one day); day trip to Delphi (one day); travel to Nafplio in the Peloponnese and use it as a base to visit Ancient Mycenae and Epidaurus (two days); travel across the Peloponnese to Ancient Olympia (one day); continue around the coast to Diokofto and ride the mountain railway up to Kalavyrta (one day, overnight Diakofto, Zahlorou or Kalavryta); head to Patras and catch a bus to Ioannina (one day); head north to the villages of the Zagorohoria district and the Vikos Gorge (two days); travel across the Pindos Range via the Katara Pass to Kalambaka (one day); spend the day exploring nearby Meteora and continue by train to Thessaloniki (one day); explore Thessaloniki and make a side trip to Vergina and Veria (two days); take an overnight ferry to Paros and spend a couple of days relaxing and exploring the old town (two days); continue to spectacular Santorini (two days); take the hydrofoil to Irak-

lio on Crete and visit Knossos (one day); travel west along the coast to the old Venetian town of Hania (one day); return to Iraklio and fly to Rhodes (two days); island hop north through the Dodecanese to Patmos via Nisyros or Tilos (three days); continue to the North-Eastern Aegean island of Samos, the greenest of all the islands and the closest to Turkey (two days); return to Athens (one day).

PLANNING

When to Go

Spring and autumn are the best times of the year to visit Greece. Winter is pretty much a dead loss outside the major cities. Most of Greece's tourist infrastructure goes into hibernation from the end of November until the beginning of April – hotels and restaurants are closed and bus and ferry services are either drastically reduced or plain cancelled.

The cobwebs are dusted off in time for Easter, when the first tourists start to arrive. Conditions are perfect between Easter and mid-June, when the weather is pleasantly warm in most places; beaches and ancient sites are relatively uncrowded; public transport operates at close to full schedules; and accommodation is cheaper and easy to find.

Mid-June until the end of August is the high season. It's party time on the islands and everything is in full swing. It's also very hot – in July and August the mercury can soar to 40°C (over 100°F) in the shade just about anywhere in the country; the beaches are crowded, the ancient sites are swarming with tour groups and in many places accommodation is booked solid.

The season starts to wind down after August and conditions are ideal once more until the shutdown at the end of November. Before ruling out a winter holiday entirely, it's worth considering going skiing (see Activities later in this chapter for details).

Maps

Unless you are going to trek or drive, the free maps given out by the EOT (the Greek

National Tourist Organization) will probably suffice, although they are not 100% accurate. On islands where there is no EOT office there are usually tourist maps for sale for around €1.50 but, again, these are not very accurate.

The best maps are published by the Greek company Road Editions, whose maps are produced with the assistance of the Hellenic Army Geographical Service. These maps are steadily being updated using Global Positioning Satellite technology. There is a wide range of maps to suit various needs, starting with a 1:500,000 map of Greece. Motorists should check out the company's 1:250,000 maroon-cover series covering Thrace, Macedonia, Thessaly and Epiros, Central Greece, the Peloponnese and Crete. Even the smallest roads and villages are clearly marked, and the distance indicators are spot-on – important when negotiating your way around the backblocks. Useful features include symbols to indicate the location of petrol stations and tyre shops.

Its blue-cover Greek island series includes all the main islands. The scale ranges from 1:100,000 for larger islands like Corfu and Rhodes to 1:30,000 for Syros. It also publishes a 1:50,000 green-cover Greek mountain series, produced with trekkers in mind. The series includes Mt Athos, Mt Olympia, Mt Parnitha, Mt Parnassos and the Pelion Peninsula (Pilio).

Freytag & Berndt's 15-map Greece series has good coverage of the islands and the Peloponnese.

What to Bring

Sturdy shoes are essential for clambering around ancient sites and wandering around historic towns and villages, which tend to have lots of steps and cobbled streets. Footwear with ankle support is preferable for trekking, although many visitors get by with runners (trainers).

A day-pack is useful for the beach, and for sightseeing or trekking. A compass is essential if you are going to trek in remote areas, as is a whistle, which you can use should you become lost or disoriented. A

torch (flashlight) is not only needed if you intend to explore caves, but comes in handy during occasional power cuts. If you like to fill a washbasin or bathtub (a rarity in Greece), bring a universal plug as Greek bathrooms rarely have plugs.

Many camping grounds have covered areas where tourists who don't have tents can sleep in summer, so you can get by with a lightweight sleeping bag and foam bedroll. Whether or not you are going to self-cater, a plastic food container, plate, cup, cutlery, bottle opener, water container and all-purpose knife are useful, not only for picnics, but for food you take with you on long boat trips.

You will need only light clothing – preferably cotton – during the summer months. But if you're going to climb Mt Olympus (or any other high mountain) you will need a sweater and waterproof jacket, even in July and August. During spring and autumn you'll need a light sweater or jacket in the evening. In winter take a heavy jacket or coat, warm sweaters, winter shoes or boots, and an umbrella.

In summer a sun hat and sunglasses are essential (see the Health section later in this chapter). Sunscreen creams are expensive, as are moisturising and cleansing creams. Film is not expensive, especially in larger towns and tourist areas, but the stock tends to hang around for a while in remoter areas.

If you read a lot, it's a good idea to bring along a few disposable paperbacks to read and swap.

RESPONSIBLE TOURISM

Ideally, being a responsible tourist entails an effort to minimise the detrimental effects of tourism – and maximise the benefits. This starts with such fundamental things as being polite and respectful.

The most irresponsible thing that a tourist can do is to 'souvenir' stones or small pieces of pottery from ancient sites. If every visitor picked up a stone from the Acropolis, there would soon be nothing left.

An easy way to be a responsible tourist is to economise on water use. Greece is a dry country and fresh water is a precious commodity, so turn the tap off while you're brushing your teeth and don't spend hours in the shower.

See the Society & Conduct section in the Facts about Greece chapter for tips regarding dress and how to avoid causing offence.

TOURIST OFFICES

Tourist information is handled by the Greek National Tourist Organization, known by the initials GNTO abroad and EOT (Ellinikos Organismos Tourismou) in Greece.

Local Tourist Offices

The EOT's head office (☎ 21 0331 0561, 21 0331 0562, fax 21 0325 2895, **e** gnto@ eexi.gr, **W** www.gnto.gr) is at Amerikis 2, Athens 105 64. There are about 25 EOT offices throughout Greece. Most EOT staff speak English, but they vary in their enthusiasm and helpfulness. Some offices, like that in Athens, have loads of useful local information, but most have nothing more than glossy brochures, usually about other parts of the country. Some have absolutely nothing to offer except an apology.

In addition to EOT offices, there are also municipal tourist offices. They are often more helpful.

Tourist Offices Abroad

GNTO offices abroad include:

Australia
(☎ 02-9241 1663/1664/1665) 51–57 Pitt St, Sydney NSW 2000
Austria
(☎ 1-512 5317) Opernring 8, Vienna A-10105
Belgium
(☎ 2-647 5770) 172 Ave Louise Louizalaan, B1050 Brussels
Canada
(☎ 416-968 2220) 91 Scollard St, Toronto, Ontario M5R 1G4
(☎ 514-871 1535) 1170 Place Du Frere Andre, Montreal, Quebec H3B 3C6
Denmark
(☎ 3332 5332) Vester Farimagsgade 1, 1606 Copenhagen
France
(☎ 0142 60 65 75) 3 Ave de l'Opéra, Paris 75001

Germany
Berlin: (☎ 30-217 6262) Wittenbergplatz 3A, 10789 Berlin 30
Frankfurt: (☎ 69-236 561) Neue Mainzerstrasse 22, 60311 Frankfurt
Hamburg: (☎ 40-454 498) Neurer Wall 18, 20254 Hamburg
Munich: (☎ 89-222 035/036) Pacellistrasse 5, 2W 80333 Munich
Israel
(☎ 3-517 0501) 5 Shalom Aleichem St, Tel Aviv 61262
Italy
Rome: (☎ 06-474 4249) Via L Bissolati 78–80, Rome 00187
Milan: (☎ 02-860 470) Piazza Diaz 1, 20123 Milan
Japan
(☎ 03-350 55 911) Fukuda Building West, 5F 2-11-3 Akasaka, Minato-Ku, Tokyo 107
Netherlands
(☎ 20-625 4212) Kerkstraat 61, Amsterdam GC 1017
Sweden
(☎ 8-679 6480) Birger Jarlsgatan 30, Box 5298 S, 10246 Stockholm
Switzerland
(☎ 01-221 0105) Loewenstrasse 25, 8001 Zürich
UK
(☎ 020-7734 5997) 4 Conduit St, London W1R ODJ
USA
Chicago: (☎ 312-782 1084) Suite 600, 168 North Michigan Ave, Chicago, Illinois 60601
Los Angeles: (☎ 213-626 6696) Suite 2198, 611 West 6th St, Los Angeles, California 92668
New York: (☎ 212-421 5777) Olympic Tower, 645 5th Ave, New York, NY 10022

Tourist Police

The tourist police work in cooperation with the regular Greek police and EOT. Each tourist police office has at least one member of staff who speaks English. Hotels, restaurants, travel agencies, tourist shops, tourist guides, waiters, taxi drivers and bus drivers all come under the jurisdiction of the tourist police. If you think that you have been ripped off by any of these, report it to the tourist police and they will investigate. If you need to report a theft or loss of passport, then go to the tourist police first, and they will act as interpreters between you and the regular police. The tourist police also fulfil the same functions as the EOT and municipal tourist offices, dispensing maps and brochures, and giving information on transport. They can often help to find accommodation.

VISAS & DOCUMENTS
Passport
To enter Greece you need a valid passport or, for EU nationals, travel documents (ID cards). You must produce your passport or EU travel documents when you register in a hotel or pension in Greece. You will find that many accommodation proprietors will want to keep your passport during your stay. This is not a compulsory requirement; they need it only long enough to take down the details.

Visas
The list of countries whose nationals can stay in Greece for up to three months without a visa includes Australia, Canada, all EU countries, Iceland, Israel, Japan, New Zealand, Norway, Switzerland and the USA. Other countries included are Cyprus, Malta, the European principalities of Monaco and San Marino and most South American countries. The list changes – contact Greek embassies for the full list. Those not included can expect to pay about US\$20 for a three-month visa.

North Cyprus Greece will refuse entry to people whose passport indicates that, since November 1983, they have visited Turkish-occupied North Cyprus. This can be overcome if, upon entering North Cyprus, you ask the immigration officials to stamp a piece of paper (loose-leaf visa) rather than your passport. If you enter North Cyprus from the Greek Republic of Cyprus (only possible for a day visit), an exit stamp is not put into your passport.

Visa Extensions If you wish to stay in Greece for longer than three months, apply at a consulate abroad or at least 20 days in advance to the Aliens Bureau in Athens (☎ 21 0770 5711), Leoforos Alexandras 173. Take your passport and four passport

photographs along. You may be asked for proof that you can support yourself financially, so keep all your bank exchange slips (or the equivalent from a post office). These slips are not always automatically given – you may have to ask for them. The Aliens Bureau is open 8am to 1pm weekdays. Elsewhere in Greece apply to the local police authority. You will be given a permit that will authorise you to stay in the country for a period of up to six months.

Most travellers get around this by visiting Bulgaria or Turkey briefly and then re-entering Greece.

Travel Permits
You need a special permit to visit the monasteries of the Mt Athos peninsula in Macedonia. This can be issued in either Athens or Thessaloniki. See the Mt Athos section of the Northern Greece chapter for details.

Travel Insurance
A travel insurance policy to cover theft, loss and medical problems is a good idea. The policies handled by STA Travel and other student travel organisations are usually good value. There is a wide variety of policies available; check the small print.

Some policies specifically exclude 'dangerous activities', which can include scuba diving, motorcycling, even trekking. A locally acquired motorcycle licence is not valid under some policies.

You may prefer a policy that pays doctors or hospitals direct rather than you having to pay on the spot and claim later. If you have to claim later make sure you keep all documentation. Some policies ask you to call back (reverse charges) to a centre in your home country where an immediate assessment of your problem is made.

Check that the policy covers ambulances or an emergency flight home.

Driving Licence & Permits
Greece recognises all national driving licences, provided the licence has been held for at least one year. It also recognises an International Driving Permit, which should be obtained before you leave home.

Hostel Cards

A Hostelling International (HI) card is of limited use in Greece. The only place you will be able to use it is at the Athens International Youth Hostel.

Student & Youth Cards

The most widely recognised form of student ID is the International Student Identity Card (ISIC). It qualifies you for half-price admission to museums and ancient sites and for discounts at some budget hotels and hostels. Aegean Airlines and Cronus offer student discounts on some domestic flights, but there are none to be had on buses, ferries or trains. Students will find some good deals on international air fares.

Some travel agencies in Athens are licensed to issue cards; see the Information section of the Athens chapter. You must show documents proving you are a student, provide a passport photo and cough up €7.35.

Copies

The hassles created by losing your passport, travellers cheques and other important documents can be reduced considerably if you take the precaution of taking copies. It is a good idea to have photocopies of the passport pages that cover personal details, issue/expiry dates and the current entry stamp or visa. Other items worth photocopying are airline tickets, credit cards, driving licence and insurance details. You should also keep a record of serial numbers of travellers cheques, and cross them off as you cash them.

This emergency material should be kept separate from the originals, so that hopefully they won't both get lost (or stolen) at the same time. Leave an extra copy with someone at home just in case.

There is another option for storing details of your vital travel documents before you leave – Lonely Planet's online Travel Vault. Storing details of your important documents in the vault is safer than carrying photocopies. Your password-protected travel vault is accessible at any time. It's the best option if you travel in a country with easy Internet access. You can create your own travel vault for free at W www.ekno.lonelyplanet.com.

EMBASSIES & CONSULATES
Greek Embassies & Consulates

The following is a selection of Greek diplomatic missions abroad:

Albania (☎ 42-34 290/291) Ruga Frederik Shiroka, Tirane
Australia (☎ 02-6273 3011) 9 Turrana St, Yarralumla, Canberra ACT 2600
Canada (☎ 613-238 6271) 76–80 Maclaren St, Ottawa, Ontario K2P OK6
Cyprus (☎ 02-680 670/671) Byron Boulevard 8–10, Nicosia
Denmark (☎ 33-11 4533) Borgergade 16, 1300 Copenhagen K
Egypt (☎ 02-355 1074) 18 Aisha el Taymouria, Garden City, Cairo
France (☎ 0147 23 72 28) 17 Rue Auguste Vacquerie, 75116 Paris
Germany (☎ 30-236 0990) Kurfürstenstrasse 130, D-10785 Berlin
Ireland (☎ 01-676 7254) 1 Upper Pembroke St, Dublin 2
Israel (☎ 03-605 5461) 47 Bodenheimer St, Tel Aviv 62008
Italy (☎ 06-854 9630) Via S Mercadante 36, Rome 00198
Japan (☎ 03-340 0871/0872) 3-16-30 Nishi Azabu, Minato-ku, Tokyo 106
Netherlands (☎ 070-363 87 00) Amaliastraat 1, 2514 JC, The Hague
New Zealand (☎ 04-473 7775) 5–7 Willeston St, Wellington
Norway (☎ 22-222 728) Nobels Gate 45, 0244 Oslo 2
South Africa (☎ 12-437 351/352) 1003 Church St, Hatfield, Pretoria 0028
Spain (☎ 01-564 4653) Avenida Doctor Arce 24, Madrid 28002
Sweden (☎ 08-663 7577) Riddargatan 60, 11457 Stockholm
Switzerland (☎ 31-951 0814) Postfach, 3000 Berne 6, Kirchenfeld
Turkey (☎ 312-436 8860) Ziya-ul-Rahman Caddesi 911, Gaziosmanpasa 06700, Ankara
UK (☎ 020-7229 3850) 1A Holland Park, London W11 3TP
USA (☎ 202-939 5818) 2221 Massachusetts Ave NW, Washington DC 20008

Embassies & Consulates in Greece

All foreign embassies in Greece are in Athens and its suburbs, while there are additional consulates of various countries in

Thessaloniki, Patras, Corfu, Rhodes and Iraklio. They include:

Albania (☎ 21 0723 4412) Karahristou 1, Athens 115 21
Consulate in Thessaloniki: (☎ 231 054 7435, fax 231 054 6656) Odysseos 6
Australia (☎ 21 0645 0404) Dimitrou Soutsou 37, Ambelokipi, Athens 115 21
Consulate in Thessaloniki: (☎ 231 024 0706, fax 231 026 0237) Ionos Dragoumi 20 (also represents New Zealand)
Bulgaria (☎ 21 0647 8105) Stratigou Kalari 33A, Psyhiko, Athens 154 52
Consulate in Thessaloniki: (☎ 231 082 9210, fax 231 085 4004) N Manou 12
Canada (☎ 21 0727 3400) Genadiou 4, Athens 115 21
Consulate in Thessaloniki: (☎ 231 025 6350, fax 231 025 6351) Tsimiski 17
Cyprus (☎ 21 0723 7883) Irodotou 16, Athens 106 75 (☎ 231 026 0611) Nikis 37, Thessaloniki
France (☎ 21 0361 1663) Leoforos Vasilissis Sofias 7, Athens 106 71
Consulate in Corfu: (☎ 2661 033 788) Polyla 22
Consulate in Thessaloniki: (☎ 231 024 4030, fax 231 024 4032) McKenzie King 8
Germany (☎ 21 0728 5111) Dimitriou 3 & Karaoli, Kolonaki, Athens 106 75
Consulate in Corfu: (☎ 2661 031 453) Guilford 57
Consulate in Iraklio: (☎ 281 0226 288) Zografou 7
Consulate in Rhodes: (☎ 2241 063 730) Parodos Isiodou 12
Consulate in Thessaloniki: (☎ 231 023 6315, fax 231 024 0393) Karolou Dil 4a
Hungary (☎ 21 0672 5337) Kalvou 16, Athens 154 52
Consulate in Thessaloniki: (☎ 231 0547 397) Danaïdou 4
Ireland (☎ 21 0723 2771) Leoforos Vasileos Konstantinou 7, Athens 106 74
Consulate in Corfu: (☎ 2661 032 469) Kapodistria 20a
Israel (☎ 21 0671 9530) Marathonodromou 1, Athens 154 52
Italy (☎ 21 0361 7260) Sekeri 2, Athens 106 74
Consulate in Thessaloniki: (☎ 231 093 4000) Papanastasiou 90
Japan (☎ 21 0775 8101) Athens Tower, Leoforos Messogion 2-4, Athens 115 27
Netherlands (☎ 21 0723 9701) Vasileos Konstantinou 5–7, Athens 106 74
Consulate in Iraklio: (☎ 281 034 6202) Avgoustou 23

Consulate in Rhodes: (☎ 2241 031 571) Alexandrou Diakou 27
Consulate in Thessaloniki: (☎ 231 028 4065) Komninon 26
New Zealand *Consulate in Halandri:* (☎ 21 0687 4701) Kifissias 268
Romania *Consulate in Thessaloniki:* (☎ 231 024 4793) Leoforos Nikis 13
South Africa (☎ 21 0680 6645) Kifissias 60, Maroussi, Athens 151 25
Consulate in Thessaloniki: (☎ 231 072 2519) Tsimiski 51
Sweden *Consulate in Thessaloniki:* (☎ 231 028 4065) Komninon 26
Turkey (☎ 21 0724 5915) Vasilissis Georgiou 8, Athens 106 74
Consulate in Rhodes: (☎ 2241 023 362) Iroön Politechniou 12, Rhodes
Consulate in Thessaloniki: (☎ 231 024 8452) Ag Dimitriou 151
UK (☎ 21 0723 6211) Ploutarhou 1, Athens 106 75
Consulate in Corfu: (☎ 2661 030 055) Menekratou 1
Consulate in Iraklio: (☎ 281 022 4012) Apalexandrou 16
Consulate in Rhodes: (☎ 2241 027 247) Pavlou Mela 3
Consulate in Thessaloniki: (☎ 231 027 8006) El Venizelou 8
USA (☎ 21 0721 2951) Leoforos Vasilissis Sofias 91, Athens 115 21
Consulate in Thessaloniki: (☎ 231 024 2905) Tsimiski 3
Yugoslavia (☎ 21 0777 4355) Leoforos Vasilissis Sofias 106 Athens 115 21
Consulate in Thessaloniki: (☎ 231 024 4266, fax 031 024 0412) Komnion 4

Generally speaking, your own country's embassy won't be much help to you in emergencies if the trouble you're in is even remotely your own fault. Remember that you are bound by Greek laws. Your embassy will not be sympathetic if you end up in jail after committing a crime locally, even if such actions are legal in your own country.

In genuine emergencies you might get some assistance, but only if other channels have been exhausted. For example, if you need to get home urgently, a free ticket home is exceedingly unlikely – the embassy would expect you to have organised insurance. If you have all your money and documents stolen, it might assist with getting a new passport, but a loan for onward travel is out of the question.

CUSTOMS

There are no longer duty-free restrictions within the EU. This does not mean, however, that customs checks have been dispensed with; random searches are still made for drugs.

Upon entering the country from outside the EU, customs inspection is usually cursory for foreign tourists. There may be spot checks, but you probably won't have to open your bags. A verbal declaration is usually all that is required.

You may bring the following into Greece duty-free: 200 cigarettes or 50 cigars; 1L of spirits or 2L of wine; 50g of perfume; 250mL of eau de Cologne; one camera (still or video) and film; a pair of binoculars; a portable musical instrument; a portable radio or tape recorder; a typewriter; sports equipment; and dogs and cats (with a veterinary certificate).

Importation of works of art and antiquities is free, but they must be declared on entry, so that they can be re-exported. Import regulations for medicines are strict; if you are taking medication, make sure you get a statement from your doctor before you leave home. It is illegal, for instance, to take codeine into Greece without an accompanying doctor's certificate.

An unlimited amount of foreign currency and travellers cheques may be brought into Greece. If you intend to leave the country with foreign banknotes in excess of US$1000, you must declare the sum upon entry.

Restrictions apply to the importation of sailboards into Greece. See the Activities section later in this chapter for more details.

It is strictly forbidden to export antiquities (anything over 100 years old) without an export permit. This crime is second only to drug smuggling in the penalties imposed. It is an offence to remove even the smallest article from an archaeological site.

The place to apply for an export permit is the Antique Dealers & Private Collections Section, Archaeological Service, Polygnotou 13, Athens.

Vehicles

Cars can be brought into Greece for four months without a carnet; only a green card (international third-party insurance) is required. Your vehicle will be registered in your passport when you enter Greece in order to prevent you leaving the country without it.

MONEY
Currency

Greece was gearing up for the transition to the euro at the time of research, scheduled for January 2002. Its national currency, the drachma (dr), became part of the basket of euro currencies at the beginning of 2001, fixed at a rate of 340.75 dr to €1. Already it is compulsory to display prices and issue receipts in euro as well as drachma. Prices for this book have been calculated by dividing the 2001 drachma prices by 340.75, and then rounding up to the nearest five cents.

The new euro banknotes and coins were due to be introduced on 1 January 2002, ushering in a two-month period of dual use of euros and drachma. By the end of 1 March 2002, the drachma will be withdrawn. Only euro notes and coins will remain in circulation and prices will be displayed in euros only.

There will be seven euro notes in different colours and sizes; they come in denominations of euro 500, 200, 100, 50, 20, 10 and five. These notes will be the same everywhere: the €5 note in France will be the same €5 note in Italy and Portugal.

There are eight euro coins, in denominations of two and one euros, then 50, 20, 10, five, two and one cents. Each state will be able to decorate the reverse side of the coins with its own designs, but all euro coins can be used anywhere that accepts euros.

At the time of research, people appeared surprisingly unemotional about the impending disappearance of the drachma, which has been the country's currency since independence. For the record, a collector's set of the last days of the drachma should include coins in denominations of five, 10, 20, 50, 100 and 500 dr, and banknotes of 100, 200, 500, 1000, 5000 and 10,000 dr.

Phone numbers listed incorporate changes due in Oct 2002; see p83

Exchange Rates

country	unit		euro
Albania	100 lekē	=	0.77
Australia	A$1	=	0.57
Bulgaria	1000 leva	=	0.52
Canada	C$1	=	0.71
Japan	¥100	=	0.92
New Zealand	NZ$1	=	0.48
United Kingdom	UK£1	=	1.62
United States	US1	=	1.11

Warning It's all but impossible to exchange Turkish lira in Greece. The only place you can change them is at the head office of the National Bank of Greece, Panepistimiou 36, Athens – and it'll give only about 75% of the going international rate.

Exchanging Money

Banks will exchange all major currencies in either cash, travellers cheques or Euro-cheques. The best-known travellers cheques in Greece are Thomas Cook and American Express. A passport is required to change travellers cheques, but not cash.

Commission charged on the exchange of banknotes and travellers cheques varies not only from bank to bank but from branch to branch. It's less for cash than for travellers cheques. For travellers cheques, the commission can be as much as €4.40 for amounts under €100 and €5.90 for amounts over €100.

Post offices can exchange banknotes – but not travellers cheques – and charge less commission than banks. Many travel agencies and hotels will also change money and travellers cheques at bank rates, but their commission charges are higher.

If there is a chance that you may apply for a visa extension, make sure you receive, and keep hold of, a bank exchange slip after each transaction.

Cash Nothing beats cash for convenience – or for risk. If you lose cash, it's gone for good and very few travel insurers will come to your rescue. Those that will, normally limit the amount to approximately US$300. It's best to carry no more cash than you need for the next few days, which means working out your likely needs whenever you change travellers cheques or withdraw cash from an ATM.

It's also a good idea to set aside a small amount of cash, say US$50, as an emergency stash.

Travellers Cheques The main reason to carry travellers cheques rather than cash is the protection they offer against theft. They are, however, losing popularity as more and more travellers opt to put their money in a bank at home and withdraw it at ATMs as they go along.

American Express, Visa and Thomas Cook cheques are all widely accepted and have efficient replacement policies. Maintaining a record of the cheque numbers and recording when you use them is vital when it comes to replacing lost cheques – keep this separate from the cheques themselves. US dollars are a good currency to use.

ATMs Automated teller machines (ATMs) are to be found in every town large enough to support a bank – and certainly in all the tourist areas. If you've got MasterCard or Visa/Access, there are plenty of places to withdraw money. Cirrus and Maestro users can make withdrawals in all major towns and tourist areas.

AFEMs (automated foreign exchange machines) are common in major tourist areas. They take all the major European currencies, Australian and US dollars and Japanese yen, and are useful in an emergency. Note that they charge a hefty commission, though.

Credit Cards The great advantage of credit cards is that they allow you to pay for major items without carrying around great wads of cash. Credit cards are now an accepted part of the commercial scene in Greece just about everywhere. They can be used to pay for a wide range of goods and services such as meals (in better restaurants) and accommodation, car hire and souvenirs.

If you are not familiar with the card options, ask your bank to explain the workings and relative merits of the various schemes: cash cards, charge cards and credit cards

Ask whether the card can be replaced in Greece if it is lost or stolen.

The main credit cards are MasterCard, Visa (Access in the UK) and Eurocard, all of which are widely accepted in Greece. They can also be used as cash cards to draw cash from the ATMs of affiliated Greek banks in the same way as at home. Daily withdrawal limits are set by the issuing bank. Cash advances are given in local currency only. Credit cards can be used to pay for accommodation in all the smarter hotels. Some C-class hotels will accept credit cards, but D and E class hotels rarely do.

The main charge cards are American Express and Diners Club, which are widely accepted in tourist areas but unheard of elsewhere.

International Transfers If you run out of money or need more for whatever reason, you can instruct your bank back home to send you a draft. Specify the city and the bank as well as the branch that you want the money sent to. If you have the choice, select a large bank and ask for the international division. Money sent by electronic transfer should reach you within 24 hours.

Security

The safest way of carrying cash and valuables (passport, travellers cheques, credit cards etc) is a favourite topic of travel conversation. The simple answer is that there is no foolproof method. The general principle is to keep things out of sight. The front pouch belt, for example, presents an obvious target for a would-be thief – only marginally less inviting than a fat wallet bulging from your back pocket.

The best place is under your clothes in contact with your skin where, hopefully, you will be aware of an alien hand before it's too late. Most people opt for a money belt, while others prefer a pouch hung around the neck. Another possibility is to sew a secret-stash pocket into the inside of your clothes. Whichever method you choose, put your valuables in a plastic bag first – otherwise they will get soaked in sweat as you wander around in the heat. After a few soakings,

they will end up looking like they've been through the washing machine.

Taxes & Refunds

The value-added tax (VAT) varies from 15% to 18%. A tax-rebate scheme applies at a restricted number of shops and stores; look for a Tax Free sign in the window. You must fill in a form at the shop and present it with the receipt at the airport on departure. A cheque will (hopefully) be sent to your home address.

Costs

Greece is still a cheap country by northern European standards, but it is no longer dirt-cheap. A rock-bottom daily budget would be €25. This would mean hitching, staying in youth hostels or camping, staying away from bars, and only occasionally eating in restaurants or taking ferries. Allow at least €50 per day if you want your own room and plan to eat out regularly as well as travelling about and seeing the sights. You will still need to do a fair bit of self-catering. If you really want a holiday – comfortable rooms and restaurants all the way – you will need closer to €100 per day. These budgets are for individuals travelling in high season (July/August). Couples sharing a double room can get by on less.

Your money will go a lot further if you travel in the quieter months. Accommodation, which eats up a large part of the daily budget, is generally about 25% cheaper outside high season. There are fewer tourists around and more opportunities to negotiate even better deals. All prices quoted in this book are for the high season.

Museums & Ancient Sites Most small museums and sites charge €4.40, while major sites and museums cost between €3.55 and €5.90. Museums and sites are free Sunday from 1 November to the end of March, as well as 6 March, 18 April, 18 May, 5 June and the last weekend in September.

Admission to sites and museums is free all year for anyone under 18, and for card-carrying EU students, teachers and journalists. Students from outside the EU qualify for a 50% discount with an International Student Identification Card (ISIC), while pensioners (over 65) from EU countries also pay half price.

Tipping & Bargaining

In restaurants the service charge is included in the bill but it is the custom to leave a small amount. The practice is often just to round off the bill. Likewise for taxis – a small amount is appreciated.

Bargaining is not as widespread in Greece as it is farther east. Prices in most shops are clearly marked and non-negotiable. The same applies to restaurants and public transport. It is always worth bargaining over the price of hotel rooms or *domatia* (the Greek equivalent of the British bed and breakfast, minus the breakfast), especially if you are intending to stay a few days. You may get short shrift in peak season, but prices can drop dramatically in the off season. Souvenir shops and market stalls are other places where your negotiating skills will come in handy. If you feel uncomfortable about haggling, walking away can be just as effective – you can always go back.

POST & COMMUNICATIONS

Post offices *(tahydromio)* are easily identifiable by the yellow signs outside. Regular post boxes are also yellow. The red boxes are for express mail only.

Postal Rates

The postal rate for postcards and airmail letters to destinations within the EU is €0.55 for up to 20g and €0.85 for up to 50g. To other destinations the rate is €0.60 for up to 20g and €0.90 for up to 150g. Post within Europe takes between five and eight days and to the USA, Australia and New Zealand, nine to 11 days. Some tourist shops also sell stamps, but with a 10% surcharge.

Express mail costs an extra €1.85 and should ensure delivery in three days within the EU – use the special red post boxes. Valuables should be sent registered post, which costs an extra €2.35.

Sending Mail

Do not wrap a parcel until it has been inspected at a post office. In Athens, take your parcel to the Parcel Post Office (☎ 01 2322 8940) in the arcade at Stadiou 4, and elsewhere to the parcel counter of a regular post office.

Receiving Mail

You can receive mail poste restante (general delivery) at any main post office. The service is free, but you are required to show your passport. Ask senders to write your family name in capital letters and underline it, and also to mark the envelope 'poste restante'. It is a good idea to ask the post office clerk to check under your first name as well if letters you are expecting cannot be located. After one month, uncollected mail is returned to the sender. If you are about to leave a town and expected mail hasn't arrived, ask at the post office to have it forwarded to your next destination, c/o poste restante. See the Post section in the Athens chapter for addresses of post offices that hold poste restante mail.

Parcels are not delivered in Greece; they must be collected from the parcel counter of a post office – or, in Athens, from the Parcel Post Office.

Telephone

The Greek telephone service is maintained by the public corporation known as Organismos Tilepikoinonion Ellados, which is always referred to by the acronym OTE (pronounced O-tay).

The system is modern and reasonably well maintained. There are public telephones just about everywhere, including some unbelievably isolated spots. The phones are easy to operate and can be used for local, long distance and international calls. The 'i' at the top left of the push-button dialling panel brings up the operating instructions in English.

All public phones use OTE phonecards, known as *telekarta*, not coins. The cards cost €2.95 for 1000 units, €5.60 for 2000 units, €12.35 for 5000 units, and €24.10 for 10,000 units. The 1000-unit cards are widely available at *periptera* (street kiosks),

Warning: Phone Number Changes

Greece is implementing a new national numbering plan to alleviate a shortage of numbers in the telephone system and to allow users to better understand call charges. As a result dialling numbers in Greece could be a little problematic during 2002.

The new plan means that all numbers now have 10 digits. The key features of the scheme are:

The area code now has to be dialled for every number, even when calling from within the same geographical area. So, for instance, to call an Athens number from within Athens, you need to include the area code 01.

Also, all numbers now have a 0 added at the start of the local number (which follows the area code). For example, if you want to dial the old Athens number 01-123 4567 it now becomes 01 0123 4567.

To further complicate things, from **20 October 2002**, the area code's leading 0 will be replaced with a 2 for fixed phones and with a 6 for mobile phones. So the Athens number 01 0123 4567 will change to 21 0123 4567. The numbers listed in this book incorporate this change, so if **you dial any number in this book before 20 October 2002 remember to dial 0 instead of the first digit.**

The old numbers will work until 20 January 2002; from then until 20 October 2002 callers to old numbers will get a recorded message.

corner shops and tourist shops; the others can be bought at OTE offices. A local call uses 10 units for one minute.

It's also possible to use these phones using a growing range of discount-card schemes, such as *Kronokarta* and *Teledome*, which involve dialling an access code and then punching in your card number. The cards come with instructions in Greek and English. They are easy to use and buy double the time.

It is no longer possible to use public phones to access other national card schemes, such as Telstra Australia's Telecard, for international calls. These calls can be made from private digital phones, but your time on the phone is also charged at local call rates. It's better to use Kronokarta or Teledome.

International calls can also be made from OTE offices. A counter clerk directs you to a cubicle equipped with a metered phone, and payment is made afterwards. Villages and remote islands without OTE offices almost always have at least one metered phone for international and long distance calls – usually in a shop, *kafeneio* (cafe) or taverna.

Another option is the periptero which usually has a metered telephone which can be used for local, long-distance and direct dial international calls. There is a surcharge, but it is less than that charged by hotels.

Reverse-charge (collect) calls can be made from an OTE office. The time you have to wait for a connection can vary considerably, from a few minutes to two hours. If you are using a private phone to make a reverse-charge call, dial the operator (domestic ☎ 151, international ☎ 161).

To call internationally direct from Greece, dial the Greek international access code (☎ 00), followed by the country code for the country you are calling, then the local area code (drop the leading zero if there is one) and then the number. The table below lists some country codes and per-minute charges:

country	code	cost per minute
Australia	61	€0.29
France	33	€0.29
Germany	49	€0.29
Ireland	353	€0.29
Italy	39	€0.29
Japan	81	€0.41
Netherlands	31	€0.29
New Zealand	64	€0.67
Turkey	90	€0.35
UK	44	€0.29
USA & Canada	1	€0.29

Off-peak rates are 25% cheaper. They are available to Africa, Europe, the Middle East and India between 10pm and 6am; to the

Phone numbers listed incorporate changes due in Oct 2002; see p83

Americas 11pm to 8am; and to Asia and Oceania 8pm to 5am.

To call Greece, the international access code is ☎ 30.

Ekno Communication Service

Lonely Planet's eKno global communication service provides low-cost international calls – for local calls you're usually better off with a local phonecard. eKno also offers free messaging services, email, travel information and an online travel vault, where you can securely store all your important documents. You can join online at W www.ekno.lonelyplanet.com, where you will find the local-access numbers for the 24-hour customer-service centre. Once you have joined, always check the eKno Web site for the latest access numbers for each country and updates on new features.

Mobile Phones

Few countries in the world have embraced the mobile phone with such enthusiasm as Greece. It has become the essential Greek accessory; everyone seems to have one.

If you have a compatible GSM mobile phone from a country with an overseas global roaming arrangement with Greece, you will be able to use your phone in Greece. You must inform your mobile phone service provider before you depart in order to have global roaming activated.

There are three mobile service providers in Greece – Panafon, CosmOTE and Telstet. Of the three CosmOTE tends to have the best coverage in more remote areas like some of the remoter villages, so you could try re-tuning your phone to CosmOTE if you find mobile coverage is patchy. All three companies offer pay-as-you-talk services by which you can buy a rechargeable SIM card and have your own Greek mobile number: a good idea if you plan to spend some time in Greece. The Panafon system is called 'á la Carte', the Telestet system 'B-free' and CosmOTE's 'COSMO KARTA'.

USA and Canadian mobile phone users won't be able to use their mobile phones in Greece, unless they are dual system equipped.

Useful Phone Numbers

General telephone information	☎ 134
Numbers in Athens and Attica	☎ 131
Numbers elsewhere in Greece	☎ 132
International telephone information	☎ 161 or 162
International telegrams	☎ 165
International dialling instructions in English, French and German	☎ 169
Domestic operator	☎ 151 or 152
Wake-up service	☎ 182
Weather	☎ 149
Attica Weather	☎ 148
International access code for Greece	☎ 30
International access code from within Greece	☎ 00

Toll-free 24-hour emergency numbers:

Police	☎ 100
Tourist Police	☎ 171
Ambulance (Athens)	☎ 166
Fire Brigade	☎ 199
Roadside Assistance (ELPA)	☎ 104

Fax & Telegraph

Most post offices have fax machines; telegrams can be sent from any OTE office.

Email & Internet Access

Greece was slow to embrace the wonders of the Internet, but is now striving to make up for lost time. There has also been a huge increase in the number of hotels and businesses using email, and these addresses have been listed here where available.

Internet cafes are springing up everywhere, and are listed under the Information section for cities and islands where available. Some hotels catering for travellers also offer Internet access.

INTERNET RESOURCES

Predictably enough, there has recently been a huge increase in the number of Web sites providing information about Greece. A good place to start is the *500 Links to Greece* site at Ⓦ www.viking1.com/corfu/link.htm. It has links to a huge range of sites on everything from accommodation to Zeus.

The address Ⓦ www.greektravel.com takes you to an assortment of interesting and informative sites on Greece by Matt Barrett. The Greek Ministry of Culture has put together an excellent site, Ⓦ www.culture.gr, with loads of information about museums and ancient sites. Other sites include Ⓦ www.gogreece.com/travel and Ⓦ www.aegean.ch. You'll find more specialist Web sites listed through the book.

The Lonely Planet Web site (Ⓦ www.lonelyplanet.com) gives a succinct summary on travelling to Greece, postcards from other travellers and the Thorn Tree bulletin board, where you can ask questions before you go or dispense advice when you get back. The subWWWay section links you to other useful travel resources on the Web.

BOOKS

Most books are published in different editions by different publishers in different countries. As a result, a book might be a hardcover rarity in one country while it's readily available in paperback in another. Fortunately, bookshops and libraries search by title or author, so your local bookshop or library is best placed to advise you on the availability of the following recommendations.

Lonely Planet

The Lonely Planet guides to *Mediterranean Europe* and *Western Europe* also include coverage of Greece, as does *Europe on a shoestring*. Regional titles include *Greek Islands*, *Corfu & the Ionian Islands*, *Dodecanese* and *Crete*, while *Peloponnese* will be published in 2002. *Crete Condensed* is part of the popular pocket guide series. The handy *Greek phrasebook* will help enrich your visit.

Katherine Kizilos vividly evokes Greece's landscapes, people and politics in her book *The Olive Grove: Travels in Greece*. She explores the islands and borderlands of her father's homeland, and life in her family's village in the Peloponnese mountains. The book is part of the Journeys travel literature series.

These titles are available at major English-language bookshops in Athens, Thessaloniki, Rhodes and Iraklio. See the Bookshop entries in these sections for more details.

Guidebooks

The ancient Greek traveller Pausanias is acclaimed as the world's first travel writer. *The Guide to Greece* was written in the 2nd century AD. Umpteen editions later, it is now available in English in paperback. For archaeology buffs, the Blue Guides are hard to beat. They go into tremendous detail about all the major sites, and many of the lesser-known ones. They have separate guides for Greece and Crete.

Travel

During the 19th century many books about Greece were written by philhellenes who went to the country to help in the struggle for self-determination. *Travels in Northern Greece* by William Leake is an account of Greece in the last years of Ottoman rule. Leake was the British consul in Ioannina during Ali Pasha's rule. The English painter and writer Edward Lear, of *The Owl and the Pussy-Cat* fame, spent some time in Greece in the mid-19th century and wrote *Journeys of a Landscape Painter* and *A Cretan Diary*.

Lawrence Durrell, who spent an idyllic childhood on Corfu, is the best known of the 20th-century philhellenes. His evocative books *Prospero's Cell* and *Reflections on a Marine Venus* are about Corfu and Rhodes respectively. His coffee-table book *The Greek Islands* is one of the most popular books of its kind. *My Family and Other Animals* by his brother Gerald is a hilarious account of the Durrell family's chaotic and wonderful life on Corfu.

Patrick Leigh Fermor, another ardent philhellene, is well known for his exploits in rallying the Cretan resistance in WWII. He now lives in Kardamyli in the Peloponnese. His highly acclaimed book *The Mani* is an account of his adventures in the Mani peninsula during the 1950s. By the same author, *Roumeli* relates his travels in northern Greece. *Deep into Mani* by Peter Greenhalgh & Edward Eliopoulis details a journey through the Mani some 25 years after Fermor's account.

Travels in the Morea by Nikos Kazantzakis is a highly readable account of the great writer's travels through the Peloponnese in the 1930s.

People & Society

Of the numerous festivals held in Greece, one of the most bizarre and overtly pagan is the carnival held on the island of Skyros, described in *The Goat Dancers of Skyros* by Joy Coulentianou.

The Cyclades, or Life Amongst the Insular Greeks by James Theodore Bent (first published 1885) is still the greatest English-language book about the Greek islands. It relates the experiences of the author and his wife while travelling around the Cyclades in the late 19th century. The book is now out of print, but the Hellenic Book Service may have a second-hand copy; see the Bookshops section later in this chapter.

Time, Religion & Social Experience in Rural Greece by Laurie Kain Hart is a fascinating account of village traditions – many of which are alive and well beneath the tourist veneer.

Portrait of a Greek Mountain Village by Juliet du Boulay is in a similar vein, based on her experiences in an isolated village.

A Traveller's Journey is Done and *An Affair of the Heart*, by Dilys Powell, wife of archaeologist Humfry Payne, are very readable, affectionate insights into Peloponnese village life during the 1920s and 1930s.

Road to Rembetica: Music of a Greek Subculture – Songs of Love, Sorrow and Hashish by Gail Holst explores the intriguing subculture that emerged from the poverty and suffering of the refugees from Asia Minor.

The Colossus of Maroussi by Henry Miller is now regarded as a classic. Miller relates his travels in Greece at the outbreak of WWII with feverish enthusiasm. Another

book that will whet your appetite for a holiday in Greece is *Hellas: A Portrait of Greece* by Nicholas Gage.

History & Mythology

A Traveller's History of Greece by Timothy Boatswain and Colin Nicholson gives the layperson a good general reference on the historical background of Greece, from Neolithic times to the present day. *Modern Greece: A Short History* by CM Woodhouse is in a similar vein, although it has a right-wing bent. It covers the period from Constantine the Great to 1990.

Mythology was an intrinsic part of life in ancient Greece, and some knowledge of it will enhance your visit. One of the best publications on the subject is *The Greek Myths* by Robert Graves (two volumes), which relates and interprets the adventures of the main gods and heroes worshipped by the ancient Greeks. Maureen O'Sullivan's *An Iconoclast's Guide to the Greek Gods* presents entertaining and accessible versions of the myths.

There are many translations around of Homer's *Iliad* and *Odyssey*, which tell the story of the Trojan War and the subsequent adventures of Odysseus (known as Ulysses in Latin). The translations by EV Rien are among the best.

Women in Athenian Law and Life by Roger Just is the first in-depth study of the role of women in ancient Greece.

The Argonautica Expedition by Theodor Troev encompasses Greek mythology, archaeology, travel and adventure. It relates the voyage undertaken by the author and his crew in the 1980s following in the footsteps of Jason and the Argonauts.

Mary Renault's novels provide an excellent feel for ancient Greece. *The King Must Die* and *The Bull from the Sea* are vivid tales of Minoan times.

Mistras and Byzantine Style and Civilisation by Sir Steven Runciman and *Fourteen Byzantine Rulers* by Michael Psellus are both good introductions to Greece's Byzantine Age.

Farewell Anatolia and *The Dead are Waiting* by Dido Soteriou are two powerful novels focusing on the population exchange of 1923. Soteriou was born in Asia Minor in 1909 and was herself a refugee.

The Jaguar by Alexander Kotzias is a moving story about the leftist resistance to the Nazi occupation of Greece. Although a novel, it is packed with historical facts. *Greek Women in Resistance* by Eleni Fountouri is a compilation of journals, poems and personal accounts of women in the resistance movement from the 1940s to the 1950s. The book also contains poignant photographs and drawings.

Eleni by Nicholas Gage is an account by the author of his family's struggle to survive the horrors of WWII, the civil war, and his mother's death at the hands of the communists. It was made into a film in 1985.

The third volume of Olivia Manning's Balkan trilogy, *Friends & Heroes*, has Greece as its setting. It is a riveting account of the chaos and confusion among the emigre community fleeing the Nazi expansion across Europe. In another classic, *The Flight of Ikaros*, Kevin Andrews relates his travels in Greece during the 1940s civil war. *Greece in the Dark*, by the same author, tells of his life in Greece during the junta years.

Poetry

Sappho: A New Translation by Mary Bernard is the best translation of this great ancient poet's works.

Collected Poems by George Seferis, *Selected Poems* by Odysseus Elytis and *Collected Poems* by Constantine Cavafy are all excellent translations of Greece's greatest modern poets.

Novels

The most well-known and widely read Greek author is the Cretan writer Nikos Kazantzakis, whose novels are full of drama and larger-than-life characters. His most famous works are *The Last Temptation*, *Zorba the Greek*, *Christ Recrucified* and *Freedom or Death*. The first two have been made into films.

Athenian writer Apostolos Doxiadis has charmed critics the world over with his latest novel, *Uncle Petros and Goldbach's*

Conjecture. It's an unlikely blend of family drama and mathematical theory, although you don't need to be a mathematical genius to enjoy the book. If you are and you can prove the conjecture – that every even number greater than two can be written as the sum of two prime numbers – you could be in line to collect a prize of US$1 million offered by the publishers.

English writer Louis de Bernières has become almost a cult figure following the success of *Captain Corelli's Mandolin*, which tells the emotional story of a young Italian army officer sent to the island of Kefallonia during WWII.

The Australian journalists George Johnston and Charmian Clift wrote several books with Greek themes during their 19 years as expatriates, including Johnston's novel *The Sponge Divers*, set on Kalymnos, and Clift's autobiographical *A Mermaid Singing*, which is about their experiences on Hydra.

Australian Gillian Bouras writes of living in Greece in *A Foreign Wife* and *Aphrodite and the Others*. Fellow Australian Beverley Farmer has two collections of beautifully written short stories, *Home Time* and *Milk*, many of which are about foreigners endeavouring to make their homes in Greece.

Dinner with Persephone by Patricia Storace has been well reviewed and is of particular interest to women.

The Mermaid Madonna and *The Schoolmistress with the Golden Eyes* are two passionate novels by Stratis Myrivilis, set on two villages on the island of Lesvos.

Museum Guides

Museums and Galleries of Greece and Cyprus by Maria Kontou, of the Ministry of Culture, lists 165 museums in Greek and English with about 1000 photographs to illustrate exhibits that relate to visual arts, natural history, navigation, science, technology and the theatre.

Botanical Field Guides

The Flowers of Greece & the Aegean by William Taylor & Anthony Huxley is the most comprehensive field guide to Greece. The Greek writer, naturalist and mountaineer

George Sfikas has written many books on wildlife in Greece. Among them are *Wildflowers of Greece*, *Trees & Shrubs of Greece*, *Medicinal Plants of Greece* and *Wildflowers of Mt Olympos*.

Children's Books

The Greek publisher Malliaris-Paedia puts out a good series of books on the myths, retold in English for young readers by Aristides Kesopoulos. The titles are *The Gods of Olympus and the Lesser Gods*, *The Labours of Hercules*, *Theseus and the Voyage of the Argonauts*, *The Trojan War and the Wanderings of Odysseus* and *Heroes and Mythical Creatures*. Robin Lister's retelling of *The Odyssey* is aimed at slightly older readers (ages 10 to 12), but makes compelling listening for younger ones when read aloud.

Bookshops

There are several specialist English-language bookshops in Athens, as well as shops selling books in French, German and Italian. There are also good foreign-language bookshops in Iraklio, Rhodes, Patras and Thessaloniki (see those sections for details). All other major towns and tourist resorts have bookshops that sell some foreign-language books.

Imported books are expensive – normally two to three times the recommended retail price in the UK and the USA. Many hotels have small collections of second-hand books to read or swap.

Abroad, the best bookshop for new and second-hand books on Greece, written in both English and Greek, is the Hellenic Book Service (☎ 020-7267 9499, fax 7267 9498, ⓔ hellenicbooks@btinternet.com, Ⓦ www.hellenicbookservice.com), 91 Fortress Rd, Kentish Town, London NW5 1AG. It stocks most of the books recommended here.

FILMS

Greece is nothing if not photogenic, and countless films have made the most of the country's range of superb locations. The islands do, of course, figure prominently.

Kefallonia is the latest to feature as the setting for the big budget movie version of *Captain Corelli's Mandolin*, starring Nicolas Cage in the title role.

Mykonos was the setting for the smash hit *Shirley Valentine*, featuring Pauline Collins in the title role and Tom Conti as her Greek toy boy. *Mediterraneo* (1991) is an Italian movie that achieved cult status worldwide. It was set on Kastellorizo.

James Bond came to Greece too, and *For Your Eyes Only* features some dramatic shots of Roger Moore doing his 007 impersonation around the monasteries of Meteora. Moni Agias Triados features prominently.

Those with longer memories may recall Gregory Peck and David Niven leading the assault on the *Guns of Navarone* back in 1961.

NEWSPAPERS & MAGAZINES

Greeks are great newspaper readers. There are 15 daily newspapers, of which the most widely read are *Ta Nea*, *Kathimerini* and *Eleftheros Typos*.

After almost 50 years as a daily newspaper, the *Athens News* (€1.50) has become a weekly. It appears on Friday with an assortment of news, local features and entertainment listings. The prime source of daily news is now the Athens edition of the *International Herald Tribune* (€1.35), which includes an eight page English-language edition of the Greek daily *Kathimerini*. All are widely available in Athens and at major resorts. You'll find the *Athens News* on the Web at Ⓦ athensnews .dolnet.gr, while Kathimerini is at Ⓦ www .ekathimerini.com.

Foreign newspapers are also widely available, although only between April and October in the smaller resort areas. You'll find all the British and other major European dailies, as well as international magazines such as *Time*, *Newsweek* and the *Economist*. The papers reach Athens (Syntagma) at 3pm on the day of publication on weekdays, and at 7pm on weekends. They are not available until the following day in other areas.

RADIO & TV

Greece has two state-owned radio channels, ET 1 and ET 2. ET 1 runs three programs; two devoted to popular music and news, and the third to mostly classical music. It has a news update in English at 7.30am Monday to Saturday, and 9pm Monday to Friday. It can be heard on 91.6 MHz and 105.8 MHz on the FM band, and 729 KHz on the AM band. ET 2 broadcasts mainly popular music. Local radio stations abound; the mountains around Athens look like pincushions.

The best short-wave frequencies for picking up the BBC World Service are:

GMT	frequency
3am to 7.30am	9.41 MHz (31m band)
	6.18 MHz (49m band)
	15.07 MHz (19m band)
7.30am to 6pm	12.09 MHz (25m band)
	15.07 MHz (19m band)
6.30pm to 11.15pm	12.09 MHz (25m band)
	9.41 MHz (31m band)
	6.18 MHz (49m band)

Greek TV is a prime example of quantity rather than quality. There are nine free channels and various pay-TV channels. All the channels show English and US films and soapies with Greek subtitles. A bit of channel-swapping will normally turn up something in English.

VIDEO SYSTEMS

If you want to record or buy video tapes to play back home, you won't get a picture unless the image registration systems are the same. Greece uses PAL, which is incompatible with the North American and Japanese NTSC system. Australia and most of Europe use PAL.

PHOTOGRAPHY & VIDEO
Film & Equipment

Major brands of film are widely available, although they can be expensive in smaller towns. In Athens, expect to pay about €4.40 for a 36-exposure roll of Kodak Gold ASA 100; less for other brands. You'll find all the gear you need in the photography shops of Athens and major cities.

In most countries, it is possible to obtain video cartridges easily in large towns and cities, but make sure you buy the correct format. It is usually worth buying at least a few cartridges duty-free to start off your trip.

Photography

Because of the brilliant sunlight in summer, you'll get better results using a polarising lens filter.

As elsewhere in the world, developing film is a competitive business. Most places charge around €8.80 to develop a roll of 36 colour prints.

Video

Properly used, a video camera can give a fascinating record of your holiday. As well as videoing the obvious things – sunsets, spectacular views – remember to record some of the ordinary everyday details of life in the country. Often the most interesting things occur when you're actually intent on filming something else.

Make sure you keep the batteries charged, and have the necessary charger, plugs and transformer for the country you are visiting.

Restrictions & Etiquette

Never photograph a military installation or anything else that has a sign forbidding photography. Flash photography is not allowed inside churches, and it's considered taboo to photograph the main altar.

Greeks usually love having their photos taken but always ask permission first. The same goes for video cameras, probably even more annoying and offensive for locals than a still camera.

TIME

Greece is two hours ahead of GMT/UTC and three hours ahead on daylight-saving time, which begins the last Sunday in March, when clocks are put forward one hour. Daylight saving ends on the last Sunday in September.

So, when it is noon in Greece it is noon in İstanbul, 10am in London, 11am in Rome, 2am in San Francisco, 5am in New York and Toronto, 8pm in Sydney and 10pm in Auckland.

ELECTRICITY

Electricity is 220V, 50 cycles. Plugs are the standard continental type with two round pins. All hotel rooms have power outlets and most camping grounds have supply points.

WEIGHTS & MEASURES

Greece uses the metric system. Liquids – especially barrel wine – are often sold by weight rather than volume: 959g of wine, for example, is equivalent to 1000mL.

Like other continental Europeans, Greeks indicate decimals with commas and thousands with points.

LAUNDRY

Large towns and some islands have laundrettes. They charge from €5.30 to €10 to wash and dry a load. Hotel and room owners will usually provide you with a washtub if requested.

TOILETS

Most places in Greece have Western-style toilets, especially hotels and restaurants that cater for tourists. You'll occasionally come across Asian-style squat toilets in older houses, kafeneia and public toilets.

Public toilets are a rarity, except at airports and bus and train stations. Cafes are the best option if you get caught short, but you'll be expected to buy something for the privilege.

One peculiarity of the Greek plumbing system is that it can't handle toilet paper; apparently the pipes are too narrow. Whatever the reason, anything larger than a postage stamp seems to cause a problem; flushing away tampons and sanitary napkins is guaranteed to block the system. Toilet paper etc should be placed in the small bin provided in every toilet.

HEALTH

Travel health depends on your predeparture preparations, your day-to-day health care while travelling and how you handle any medical problem or emergency that does develop. While the list of potential dangers can seem quite frightening, few travellers experience more than upset stomachs.

Medical Kit Check List

Following is a list of items you should consider including in your medical kit – consult your pharmacist for brands available in your country.

☐ **Aspirin or paracetamol (acetaminophen in the USA)** – for pain or fever

☐ **Antihistamine** – for allergies, eg, hay fever; to ease the itch from insect bites or stings; and to prevent motion sickness

☐ **Cold and flu tablets, throat lozenges and nasal decongestant**

☐ **Multivitamins** – consider for long trips, when dietary vitamin intake may be inadequate

☐ **Antibiotics** – consider including these if you're travelling well off the beaten track; see your doctor, as they must be prescribed, and carry the prescription with you

☐ **Loperamide or diphenoxylate** – 'blockers' for diarrhoea

☐ **Prochlorperazine or metaclopramide** – for nausea and vomiting

☐ **Rehydration mixture** – to prevent dehydration, which may occur, for example, during bouts of diarrhoea; particularly important when travelling with children

☐ **Insect repellent, sunscreen, lip balm and eye drops**

☐ **Calamine lotion, sting relief spray or aloe vera** – to ease irritation from sunburn and insect bites or stings

☐ **Antifungal cream or powder** – for fungal skin infections and thrush

☐ **Antiseptic (such as povidone-iodine)** – for cuts and grazes

☐ **Bandages, Band-Aids (plasters) and other wound dressings**

☐ **Water purification tablets or iodine**

☐ **Scissors, tweezers and a thermometer** – note that mercury thermometers are prohibited by airlines

Predeparture Planning

Health Insurance Refer to Travel Insurance under Visas & Documents earlier in this chapter for information.

Warning Codeine, which is commonly found in headache preparations, is banned in Greece; check labels carefully, or risk prosecution. There are strict regulations applying to the importation of medicines into Greece, so obtain a certificate from your doctor which outlines any medication you may have to carry into the country with you.

Health Preparations Make sure you're healthy before you start travelling. If you are embarking on a long trip make sure your teeth are OK.

If you wear glasses take a spare pair and your prescription.

If you require a particular medication take an adequate supply, as it may not be available locally. Take the prescription or, better still, part of the packaging showing the generic rather than the brand name (which may not be locally available), as it will make getting replacements easier.

Immunisations No jabs are required for travel to Greece, but a yellow fever vaccination certificate is required if you are coming from an infected area. There are, however, a few routine vaccinations that are recommended. These should be recorded on an international health certificate, available from your doctor or government health department. Don't leave your vaccinations until the last minute as some require more than one injection. It's recommended that everyone keep up-to-date with diphtheria, tetanus and polio vaccinations.

Basic Rules

Care in what you eat and drink is the most important health rule; stomach upsets are the most likely travel health problem (between 30% and 50% of travellers in a two-week stay experience this) but the majority of these upsets will be relatively minor. Don't become paranoid; trying the local food is part of the experience of travel, after all.

Avoid climatic extremes; keep out of the sun when it's hot, dress warmly when it's cold. You can avoid insect bites by covering bare skin when insects are around, by screening windows or beds and by using insect repellents.

Everyday Health

Normal body temperature is up to 37°C (98.6°F); more than 2°C (4°F) higher indicates a high fever. The normal adult pulse rate is 60 to 100 per minute (children 80 to 100, babies 100 to 140). As a general rule the pulse increases about 20 beats per minute for each 1°C (2°F) rise in fever.

Respiration (breathing) rate is also an indicator of illness. Count the number of breaths per minute: Between 12 and 20 is normal for adults and older children (up to 30 for younger children, 40 for babies). People with a high fever or serious respiratory illness breathe more quickly than normal. More than 40 shallow breaths a minute may indicate pneumonia.

Seek local advice: If you're told the water is unsafe due to jellyfish, crocodiles or bilharzia, don't go in. In situations where there is no information, discretion is the better part of valour.

Food & Water Tap water is safe to drink in Greece, but bottled water is widely available if you prefer it. You might experience mild intestinal problems if you're not used to copious amounts of olive oil; however, you'll get used to it and current research says it's good for you.

If you don't vary your diet, are travelling hard and fast and missing meals, or simply lose your appetite, you can soon start to lose weight and place your health at risk. Fruit and vegetables are good sources of vitamins and Greece produces a greater variety of these than almost any other European country. Eat plenty of grains (including rice) and bread. If your diet isn't well balanced or if your food intake is insufficient, it's a good idea to take vitamin and iron pills.

In hot weather make sure you drink enough – don't rely on feeling thirsty to indicate when you should drink. Not needing to urinate or very dark yellow urine is a danger sign. Always carry a water bottle with you on long trips. Excessive sweating can lead to loss of salt and therefore muscle

Phone numbers listed incorporate changes due in Oct 2002; see p83

cramping. Salt tablets are not a good idea as a preventative, but in places where salt is not used much adding salt to food can help.

Environmental Hazards

Sunburn By far the biggest health risk in Greece comes from the intensity of the sun. You can get sunburnt surprisingly quickly, even through cloud. Use a sunscreen and take extra care to cover areas that don't normally see sun. A hat helps, as does zinc cream or some other barrier cream for your nose and lips. Calamine lotion is good for mild sunburn. Greeks claim that yogurt applied to sunburn is soothing. Protect your eyes with good-quality sunglasses.

Prickly Heat This is an itchy rash caused by excessive perspiration trapped under the skin. Keeping cool, bathing often, drying the skin and using a mild talcum powder, or resorting to air-conditioning even, may help until you acclimatise.

Heat Exhaustion Dehydration or salt deficiency can cause heat exhaustion. Take time to acclimatise to high temperatures and drink sufficient liquids, such as tea and drinks rich in mineral salts, eg, clear soups and fruit and vegetable juices. Wear loose clothing and a broad-brimmed hat. Do not do anything too physically demanding.

Salt deficiency is characterised by fatigue, lethargy, headaches, giddiness and muscle cramps and in this case salt tablets may help. Vomiting or diarrhoea can deplete your liquid and salt levels.

Heatstroke This serious, occasionally fatal, condition can occur if the body's heat-regulating mechanism breaks down and the body temperature rises to dangerous levels. Long, continuous periods of exposure to high temperatures can leave you vulnerable to heat stroke. You should avoid excessive alcohol consumption or strenuous activity when you first arrive in a hot climate.

The symptoms are feeling unwell, not sweating very much or at all and a high body temperature ($39°$ to $41°C$ or $102°$ to $106°F$). Where sweating has ceased the skin becomes flushed and red. Severe, throbbing headaches and lack of coordination will also occur, and the sufferer may be confused or aggressive. If untreated, severe cases will become delirious or convulse. Hospitalisation is essential, but in the interim get victims out of the sun, remove their clothing, cover them with a wet sheet or towel and then fan continually. Give fluids, if they are conscious.

Fungal Infections These infections, which are more frequent in hot weather, are most likely to occur on the scalp, between the toes (athlete's foot) or fingers, in the groin and on the body (ringworm). You get ringworm (a fungal infection, not a worm) from infected animals or by walking on damp areas like shower floors.

To prevent fungal infections wear loose, comfortable clothes, avoid artificial fibres, wash frequently and dry carefully. If you do get an infection, wash the infected area daily with a disinfectant or medicated soap and water, and dry well. Apply an antifungal cream or powder (tolnaftate). Expose the infected area to air or sunlight as much as possible and wash all towels and underwear in hot water as well as changing them often.

Hypothermia Too much cold is just as dangerous as too much heat, particularly if it leads to hypothermia. Although everyone associates Greece with heat and sunshine, the high mountainous regions can be cool, even in summer. There is snow on the mountains from November to April. On the highest mountains in the north, snow patches can still be seen in June. Keeping warm while trekking in these regions in spring and autumn can be as much of a problem as keeping cool in the lower regions in summer.

Hypothermia occurs when the body loses heat faster than it can produce it and the core temperature of the body falls. It is surprisingly easy to progress from very cold to dangerously cold due to a combination of wind, wet clothing, fatigue and hunger, even if the air temperature is above freezing. It is best to dress in layers; silk, wool and some of the newer artificial fibres all insulate well. A hat is important, as a lot of heat is lost through the head. A strong, waterproof outer layer is essential, as keeping dry is vital. Carry basic supplies, including food containing simple sugars to generate heat quickly and lots of fluid to drink. A space blanket should always be carried in cold environments.

Symptoms of hypothermia are exhaustion, numb skin (particularly toes and fingers), shivering, slurred speech, irrational or violent behaviour, lethargy, stumbling, dizzy spells, muscle cramps and violent bursts of energy. Irrationality may take the form of sufferers claiming they are warm and trying to take off their clothes.

To treat mild hypothermia, first get the person out of the wind and/or rain, remove their clothing if it's wet and replace it with dry, warm clothing. Give them hot liquids – not alcohol – and some high-kilojoule, easily digestible food. Do not rub the victims; instead allow them to slowly warm themselves. This should be enough to treat the early stages of hypothermia. The early recognition and treatment of mild hypothermia is the only way to prevent the onset of severe hypothermia, which is a critical condition.

Motion Sickness Sea sickness can be a problem. The Aegean is very unpredictable and gets very rough when the *meltemi* wind blows. If you are prone to motion sickness, eat lightly before and during a trip, and try to find a place that minimises disturbance – near the wing on aircraft, close to midships on boats, near the centre on buses. Fresh air usually helps; reading and cigarette smoke don't. Commercial motion-sickness preparations, which can cause drowsiness, have to be taken before the trip commences; when you're feeling sick it's too late. Ginger (available in capsule form) and peppermint (including mint-flavoured sweets) are natural preventatives.

Infectious Diseases

Diarrhoea Simple things like a change of water, food or climate can all cause a mild bout of diarrhoea, but a few rushed toilet trips with no other symptoms is not indicative of a major problem.

Dehydration is the main danger with any diarrhoea, particularly in children or the elderly as dehydration can occur quite quickly. Under all circumstances *fluid replacement* (at least equal to the volume being lost) is the most important thing to remember. Weak black tea with a little sugar, soda water or soft drinks allowed to go flat and diluted 50% with clean water are all good.

Hepatitis A general term for inflammation of the liver, hepatitis is a common disease worldwide. The symptoms are fever, chills, headache, fatigue, feelings of weakness and aches and pains, followed by loss of appetite, nausea, vomiting, abdominal pain, dark urine, light-coloured faeces, jaundiced (yellow) skin and the whites of the eyes may turn yellow. **Hepatitis A** is transmitted by contaminated food and drinking water. The disease poses a real threat to the Western traveller. You should seek medical advice, but there is not much you can do apart from resting, drinking lots of fluids, eating lightly and avoiding fatty foods. People who have had hepatitis should avoid alcohol for some time after the illness, as the liver needs time to recover.

Hepatitis E is transmitted in the same way, and can be very serious in pregnant women.

There are almost 300 million chronic carriers of **Hepatitis B** in the world. It is spread through contact with infected blood, blood products or body fluids; for example, through sexual contact, unsterilised needles and blood transfusions, or contact with blood via small breaks in the skin. Other risk situations include having a shave, tattoo or having your body pierced with contaminated equipment. The symptoms of type B may be more severe and may lead to long-term problems. **Hepatitis D** is spread in the same way, but the risk is mainly in shared needles.

Hepatitis C can lead to chronic liver disease. The virus is spread by contact with blood – usually via contaminated transfusions or shared needles.

Phone numbers listed incorporate changes due in Oct 2002; see p83

Tetanus This potentially fatal disease is found worldwide. It is difficult to treat but is preventable with immunisation.

This disease is caused by a germ which lives in the soil and in the faeces of horses and other animals. It enters the body via breaks in the skin. The first symptom may be discomfort in swallowing, or stiffening of the jaw and neck; this is followed by painful convulsions of the jaw and the whole body. The disease can be fatal.

Rabies This is a fatal viral infection and is caused by a bite or scratch by an infected animal. It's rare, but it's found in Greece. Dogs are noted carriers as are monkeys and cats. Any bite, scratch or even lick from a warm-blooded, furry animal should be cleaned immediately and thoroughly. Scrub with soap and running water, and then clean with an alcohol or iodine solution. If there is any possibility that the animal is infected medical help should be sought immediately. Even if the animal is not rabid, all bites should be treated seriously as they can become infected or can result in tetanus. A rabies vaccination is now available and should be considered if you are in a high-risk category – eg, if you intend to explore caves (bat bites can be dangerous), work with animals, or travel so far off the beaten track that medical help is more than two days away.

Sexually Transmitted Diseases Sexual contact with an infected sexual partner spreads these diseases. While abstinence is the only 100%-effective prevention, using condoms is also effective. Gonorrhoea, herpes and syphilis are among these diseases; sores, blisters or rashes around the genitals, discharges or pain when urinating are common symptoms. In some STDs, such as wart virus or chlamydia, symptoms may be less marked or not observed at all in women. Syphilis symptoms eventually disappear completely but the disease continues and can cause severe problems in later years. The treatment of gonorrhoea and syphilis is with antibiotics.

There are numerous other sexually transmitted diseases, for most of which effective treatment is available. There is currently no cure for herpes.

HIV/AIDS Infection with the human immunodeficiency virus (HIV) may lead to acquired immune deficiency syndrome (AIDS), which is a fatal disease. Any exposure to blood, blood products or body fluids may put the individual at risk. The disease is often transmitted through sexual contact or dirty needles – vaccinations, acupuncture, tattooing and body piercing can be potentially as dangerous as intravenous drug use.

If you do need an injection, ask to see the syringe unwrapped in front of you, or take a needle and syringe pack with you.

Fear of HIV infection should never preclude treatment for any serious medical conditions.

Insect-Borne Diseases
Typhus Tick typhus is a problem from April to September in rural areas, particularly areas where animals congregate. Typhus begins with a fever, chills, headache and muscle pains, followed a few days later by a body rash. There is often a large painful sore at the site of the bite and nearby lymph nodes are swollen and painful. There is no vaccine available. The best protection is to check your skin carefully after walking in danger areas such as long grass and scrub. A strong insect repellent can help, and serious walkers in tick areas should consider having their boots and trousers impregnated with benzyl benzoate and dibutylphthalate. (See the Cuts, Bites & Stings section following for information about ticks.)

Lyme Disease A tick-transmitted infection, lyme disease may be acquired throughout Europe. The illness usually begins with a spreading rash at the site of the bite and is accompanied by fever, headache, extreme fatigue, aching joints and muscles and mild neck stiffness. If untreated, these symptoms usually resolve over several weeks but over subsequent weeks or months disorders of the nervous system, heart and joints may develop. The response to treatment is best early in the illness. The longer the delay, the longer the recovery period.

Cuts, Bites & Stings

Skin punctures can easily become infected in hot climates and may be difficult to heal. Treat any cut with an antiseptic such as povidone-iodine. Where possible avoid bandages and Band-Aids, which can keep wounds wet.

Although there are a lot of bees and wasps in Greece, their stings are usually painful rather than dangerous. Calamine lotion or sting relief spray will give relief and ice packs will help to reduce the pain and swelling.

Snakes Always wear boots, socks and long trousers when walking through undergrowth where snakes may be present. Don't put your hands into holes and crevices, and be careful when collecting firewood.

Snake bites do not cause instantaneous death and antivenenes are usually available. Keep the victim calm and still, wrap the bitten limb tightly, as you would for a sprained ankle, and then attach a splint to immobilise it. Then seek medical help, if possible with the dead snake for identification. Don't attempt to catch the snake if there is even a remote possibility of being bitten again. Tourniquets and sucking out the poison are now comprehensively discredited.

Jelly Fish, Sea Urchins & Weever Fish Watch out for sea urchins around rocky beaches; if you get some of their needles embedded in your skin, olive oil will help to loosen them. If they are not removed they will become infected. Be wary also of jelly fish, particularly during the months of September and October. Although they are not lethal in Greece, their stings can be painful. Dousing in vinegar will deactivate any stingers that have not 'fired'. Calamine lotion, antihistamines and analgesics may reduce the reaction and relieve the pain. Much more painful than either of these, but thankfully much rarer, is an encounter with the weever fish. It buries itself in the sand of the tidal zone with only its spines protruding,

and injects a painful and powerful toxin if trodden on. Soaking your foot in very hot water (which breaks down the poison) should solve the problem. It can cause permanent local paralysis in the worst instance.

Bedbugs & Lice Bedbugs live in various places, but particularly in dirty mattresses and bedding. Spots of blood on bedclothes or on the wall around the bed can be read as a suggestion to find another hotel. Bedbugs leave itchy bites in neat rows. Calamine lotion or sting-relief spray may help.

All lice cause itching and discomfort. They make themselves at home in your hair, your clothing or in your pubic hair. You catch lice through direct contact with infected people or by sharing combs, clothing and the like. Powder or shampoo treatment will kill the lice and infected clothing should then be washed in very hot water.

Leeches & Ticks Leeches may be present in damp conditions. They attach themselves to your skin to suck your blood. Trekkers often get them on their legs or in their boots. Salt or a lighted cigarette end will make them fall off. Do not pull them off, as the bite is then more likely to become infected. An insect repellent may keep them away.

You should always check your body if you have been walking through a potentially tick-infested area as ticks can cause skin infections and other more serious diseases. If a tick is found attached, press down around the tick's head with tweezers, grab the head and gently pull upwards. Avoid pulling the rear of the body as this may squeeze the tick's gut contents through the attached mouth parts into the skin, increasing the risk of infection and disease. Smearing chemicals on the tick will not make it let go and is not recommended.

Sheepdogs In Greece these dogs are trained to guard penned sheep from bears, wolves and potential thieves. They are often underfed and sometimes ill-treated by their owners. They are almost always all bark and no bite, but if you are going to trek into remote areas, you should consider having rabies injections (see Rabies). You are most likely to encounter these dogs in the mountainous regions of Epiros and Crete. Wandering through a flock of sheep over which one of these dogs is vigilantly (and possibly discreetly) watching is simply asking for trouble.

Women's Health
Antibiotic use, synthetic underwear, sweating and contraceptive pills can lead to fungal vaginal infections, especially when travelling in hot climates. Fungal infections are characterised by a rash, itch and discharge and can be treated with a vinegar or lemon-juice douche, or with yogurt. Nystatin, miconazole or clotrimazole pessaries or vaginal cream are the usual treatment. Maintaining good personal hygiene and wearing loose-fitting clothes and cotton underwear may help prevent these infections.

Sexually transmitted diseases are a major cause of vaginal problems. Symptoms include a smelly discharge, painful intercourse and sometimes a burning sensation when urinating. Medical attention should be sought and male sexual partners must also be treated. For more details see the earlier section on Sexually Transmitted Diseases. Besides abstinence, the best thing is to practise safer sex using condoms.

Hospital Treatment
Citizens of EU countries are covered for free treatment in public hospitals within Greece on presentation of an E111 form. Inquire at your national health service or travel agent in advance. Emergency treatment is free to all nationalities in public hospitals. In an emergency, dial ☎ 166. There is at least one doctor on every island in Greece and larger islands have hospitals. Pharmacies can dispense medicines that are available only on prescription in most European countries, so you can consult a pharmacist for minor ailments.

All this sounds fine but, although medical training is of a high standard in Greece, the health service is badly underfunded and one of the worst in Europe. Hospitals are overcrowded, hygiene is not always what it should be and relatives are expected to bring in food for the patient – which could be a problem for a tourist. Conditions and treatment are better in private hospitals, which are expensive. All this means that a good health-insurance policy is essential.

WOMEN TRAVELLERS
Many women travel alone in Greece. The crime rate remains relatively low and solo travel is probably safer than in most European countries. This does not mean that you should be lulled into complacency; bag snatching and rapes do occur, although violent offences are rare.

The biggest nuisance to foreign women travelling alone are the guys the Greeks have nicknamed *kamaki*. The word means 'fishing trident' and refers to the kamaki's favourite pastime: 'fishing' for foreign women. You'll find them everywhere there are lots of tourists; young (for the most part), smooth-talking guys who aren't in the least bashful about sidling up to foreign women in the street. They can be very persistent, but they are a hassle rather than a threat.

The majority of Greek men treat foreign women with respect, and are genuinely helpful.

GAY & LESBIAN TRAVELLERS
In a country where the church still plays a prominent role in shaping society's views on issues such as sexuality, it should come as no surprise that homosexuality is generally frowned upon – especially outside the major cities. While there is no legislation against homosexual activity, it pays to be discreet and to avoid open displays of togetherness.

This has not prevented Greece from becoming an extremely popular destination for gay travellers. Athens has a busy gay scene, as does Thessaloniki – but most gay travellers head for the islands. Mykonos has long been famous for its bars, beaches and general hedonism, while Paros (and Antiparos), Rhodes, Santorini and Skiathos all have their share of gay hang-outs.

The town of Eressos on the island of Lesvos (Mytilini), birthplace of the lesbian poet Sappho, has become something of a place of pilgrimage for lesbians.

Information

The *Spartacus International Gay Guide*, published by Bruno Gmünder (Berlin), is widely regarded as the leading authority on the gay travel scene. The Greek section contains a wealth of information on gay venues everywhere from Alexandroupolis to Xanthi.

There's also stacks of information on the Internet. For example, the Web site *Roz Mov*, at W www.geocities.com/WestHollywood/2225/index.html, is a good place to start. It has pages on travel information, gay health, the gay press, organisations, events and legal issues – and links to lots more sites.

Gayscape also has a useful Web site whic can be found at W www.gayscape.com/gayscape/menugreece.html which has lots of links.

DISABLED TRAVELLERS

If mobility is a problem and you wish to visit Greece, the hard fact is that most hotels, museums and ancient sites in Greece are not wheelchair accessible. This is partly due to the uneven terrain of much of the country, which presents a challenge even for able-bodied people, with its abundance of stones, rocks and marble.

If you are determined, then take heart in the knowledge that disabled people do come to Greece for holidays. But the trip needs careful planning, so get as much information as you can before you go. The British-based Royal Association for Disability and Rehabilitation (RADAR) publishes a useful guide called *Holidays & Travel Abroad: A Guide for Disabled People*, which gives a good overview of facilities available to disabled travellers in Europe. Contact RADAR (☎ 020-7250 3222, fax 7250 0212, e radar@radar.org.uk) at 12 City Forum, 250 City Road, London EC1V 8AF.

SENIOR TRAVELLERS

Card-carrying EU pensioners can claim a range of benefits such as reduced admission charges at museums and ancient sites and discounts on trains.

TRAVEL WITH CHILDREN

Greece is a safe and relatively easy place to travel with children. It's especially easy if you're staying by the beach or at a resort hotel. If you're travelling around, the main problem is a shortage of decent playgrounds and other recreational facilities.

Don't be afraid to take children to the ancient sites. Many parents are surprised by how much their children enjoy them. Young imaginations go into overdrive when let loose somewhere like the 'labyrinth' at Knossos.

Hotels and restaurants are very accommodating when it comes to meeting the needs of children, although highchairs are a rarity outside resorts. Service in restaurants is normally very quick, which is great when you've got hungry children on your hands.

Fresh milk is readily available in large towns and tourist areas, but hard to find on the smaller islands. Supermarkets are the best place to look. Formula is available everywhere, as is condensed and heat-treated milk.

Mobility is an issue for parents with very small children. Strollers (pushchairs) aren't much use in Greece unless you're going to spend all your time in one of the few flat spots. They are hopeless on rough stone paths and up steps, and a curse when getting on/off buses and ferries. Backpacks or front pouches are best.

Travel on ferries and buses is free for children under four. They pay half fare up to the age of 10 (ferries) and 12 (buses). Full fares apply otherwise. On domestic flights, you'll pay 10% of the fare to have a child under two sitting on your knee. Kids aged two to 12 pay half fare.

USEFUL ORGANISATIONS
Mountaineering Clubs

Ellinikos Orivatikos Syndesmos (EOS – Greek Alpine Club; ☎ 21 0321 2429, 21 0321 2355) is the largest and oldest Greek mountaineering and trekking organisation. Its headquarters are at Plateia Kapnikareas 2, Athens – on Ermou, 500m west of Syntagma. The place is staffed by volunteers with daytime jobs, but if you call or visit

Phone numbers listed incorporate changes due in Oct 2002; see p83

between 7am and 9pm on a weekday, there should be someone there.

Automobile Associations

ELPA (☎ 21 0779 1615), the Greek automobile club, has its headquarters on the ground floor of Athens Tower, Messogion 2-4, Athens 115 27. The ELPA offers reciprocal services to members of national automobile associations on production of a valid membership card. If your vehicle breaks down, dial ☎ 104.

DANGERS & ANNOYANCES
Theft

Crime, especially theft, is low in Greece, but unfortunately it is on the increase. The worst area is around Omonia in central Athens – keep track of your valuables here, on the metro and at the Sunday flea market. The vast majority of thefts from tourists are still committed by other tourists; the biggest danger of theft is probably in dormitory rooms in hostels and at camping grounds. So make sure you do not leave valuables unattended in such places. If you are staying in a hotel room, and the windows and door do not lock securely, ask for your valuables to be locked in the hotel safe – hotel proprietors are happy to do this.

Bar Scams

Bar scams continue to be an unfortunate fact of life in Athens, particularly in the Syntagma area. The basic scam is always some variation on the following theme: solo male traveller is lured into bar on some pretext (not always sex); strikes up conversation with friendly locals; charming girls appear and ask for what turn out to be ludicrously overpriced drinks; traveller is eventually handed an enormous bill.

Fortunately, this practice appears confined to Athens at this stage. See under Information in the Athens chapter for the full run-down on this scam and other problems.

LEGAL MATTERS
Consumer Advice

The Tourist Assistance Programme exists to help people who are having trouble with any tourism-related service. Free legal advice is available in English, French and German from 1 July to 30 September. The main office (☎ 21 0330 0673, fax 21 0330 0591) is at Valtetsiou 43-45 in Athens. It's open 10am to 2pm Monday to Friday. Free advice is also available from the following regional offices:

Iraklio Consumers' Association of Crete
  (☎ 281 0240 666) Milatou 1 and Agiou Titou
Kavala Consumers' Association of Kavala
  (☎ 251 0221 159) Ydras 3
Patras Consumers' Association of Patras
  (☎ 261 0272 481) Korinthou 213B
Volos Consumers' Association of Volos
  (☎ 2421 039 266) Haziagari 51

Drugs

Greek drug laws are the strictest in Europe. Greek courts make no distinction between possession and pushing. Possession of even a small amount of marijuana is likely to land you in jail.

BUSINESS HOURS

Banks are open 8am to 2pm Monday to Thursday, and 8am to 1.30pm Friday. Some banks in large towns and cities open between 3.30pm and 6.30pm in the afternoon and on Saturday morning.

Post offices are open 7.30am to 2pm Monday to Friday. In the major cities they stay open until 8pm, and open 7.30am to 2pm Saturday.

The opening hours of OTE offices (for long-distance and overseas telephone calls) vary according to the size of the town. In smaller towns they are usually open 7.30am to 3pm daily, 6am to 11pm in larger towns, and 24 hours in major cities like Athens and Thessaloniki.

In summer, the usual opening hours for shops are 8am to 1.30pm and 5.30pm to 8.30pm on Tuesday, Thursday and Friday, and 8am to 2.30pm on Monday, Wednesday and Saturday. Shops open 30 minutes later in winter. These times are not always strictly adhered to. Many shops in tourist resorts are open seven days a week.

Department stores and supermarkets are open 8am to 8pm Monday to Friday,

8am to at least 3pm on Saturday and closed Sunday.

Periptera are open from early morning until late at night. They sell everything from bus tickets and cigarettes to hard-core pornography.

Museums and Ancient Sites

The bigger the attraction, the longer it stays open. Places like the Acropolis and the National Archaeological Museum in Athens, Delphi, Knossos and Olympia are open 8am to 7pm daily during summer (1 April to 31 October). They close at 5pm during the rest of the year.

Most other sites and museums open at 8am or 8.30am, and close at around 2.30pm and 3pm. It's no coincidence that these are the standard Greek public service hours! It means that you need to get out and about early if you want to visit more than one site a day. Most places are closed on Monday.

Lots of minor sites are unenclosed – and therefore always open to the public.

PUBLIC HOLIDAYS

All banks and shops and most museums and ancient sites close on public holidays. National public holidays in Greece are:

New Year's Day 1 January
Epiphany 6 January
First Sunday in Lent February
Greek Independence Day 25 March
Good Friday March/April
(Orthodox) Easter Sunday March/April
Spring Festival/Labour Day 1 May
Feast of the Assumption 15 August
Ohi Day 28 October
Christmas Day 25 December
St Stephen's Day 26 December

SPECIAL EVENTS

The Greek year is a succession of festivals and events, some of which are religious, some cultural, others an excuse for a good knees-up, and some a combination of all three. The following is by no means an exhaustive list, but it covers the most important events, both national and regional. If you're in the right place at the right time, you'll certainly be invited to join the revelry.

January

Feast of Agios Vasilios (St Basil) The year kicks off with this festival on 1 January. A church ceremony is followed by the exchanging of gifts, singing, dancing and feasting; the New Year pie *(vasilopitta)* is cut and the person who gets the slice containing a coin will supposedly have a lucky year.

Epiphany (the Blessing of the Waters) On 6 January, Christ's baptism by St John is celebrated throughout Greece. Seas, lakes and rivers are blessed and crosses immersed in them. The largest ceremony occurs at Piraeus.

Gynaikratia On 8 January a day of role reversal occurs in villages in the prefectures of Rodopi, Kilkis and Seres in northern Greece. Women spend the day in kafeneia (cafes) and other social centres where men usually congregate, while the men stay at home to do the housework.

February-March

Carnival The Greek carnival season is the three weeks before the beginning of Lent (the 40-day period before Easter, which is traditionally a period of fasting). The carnivals are ostensibly Christian pre-Lenten celebrations, but many derive from pagan festivals. There are many regional variations, but fancy dress, feasting, traditional dancing and general merrymaking prevail. The Patras carnival is the largest and most exuberant, with elaborately decorated chariots parading through the streets. The most bizarre carnival takes place on the island of Skyros where the men transform themselves into grotesque 'half-man, half-beast' creatures by donning goat-skin masks and hairy jackets.

Shrove Monday (Clean Monday) On the Monday before Ash Wednesday (the first day of Lent), people take to the hills throughout Greece to have picnics and fly kites.

March

Independence Day The anniversary of the hoisting of the Greek flag by Bishop Germanos at Moni Agias Lavras is celebrated on 25 March with parades and dancing. Germanos' act of revolt marked the start of the War of Independence. Independence Day coincides with the **Feast of the Annunciation**, so it is also a religious festival.

March-April

Easter Easter is the most important festival in the Greek Orthodox religion. Emphasis is placed on the Resurrection rather than on the Crucifixion, so it is a joyous occasion. The festival begins on the evening of Good Friday with the *perifora epitavios*, when a shrouded bier (representing Christ's funeral bier) is carried through the streets to the local church. This moving candlelit procession can be seen in towns and villages throughout the country. From a spectator's viewpoint, the most impressive of these processions climbs Lykavittos Hill in Athens to the Chapel of Agios Georgios.

The Resurrection Mass starts at 11pm on Saturday night. At midnight, packed churches are plunged into darkness to symbolise Christ's passing through the underworld.

The ceremony of the lighting of candles which follows is the most significant moment in the Orthodox year, for it symbolises the Resurrection. Its poignancy and beauty are spellbinding. If you are in Greece at Easter you should endeavour to attend this ceremony, which ends with fireworks and candle-lit processions through the streets.

The Lenten fast ends on Easter Sunday with the cracking of red-dyed Easter eggs and an outdoor feast of roast lamb followed by Greek dancing. The day's greeting is *Hristos anesti* (Christ is risen), to which the reply is *Alithos anesti* (Truly He is risen). On both Palm Sunday (the Sunday before Easter) and Easter Sunday, St Spyridon (the mummified patron saint of Corfu) is taken out for an airing and joyously paraded through Corfu Town. He is paraded again on 11 August.

Feast of Agios Georgos (St George) The feast day of St George, Greece's patron saint, and patron saint of shepherds, takes place on 23 April or the Tuesday following Easter (whichever comes first). It is celebrated at several places, but with particular exuberance in Arahova, near Delphi.

May
May Day On the first day of May there is a mass exodus from towns to the country. During picnics, wildflowers are gathered and made into wreaths to decorate houses.

Anastenaria This fire-walking ritual takes place on 21 May in the village of Langadas, near Thessaloniki. Villagers clutching icons dance barefoot on burning charcoal.

June
Navy Week The festival celebrates the long relationship between Greeks and the sea with events in fishing villages and ports throughout the country. Volos and Hydra each have unique versions of these celebrations. Volos re-enacts

the departure of the *Argo*, for legend has it that Iolkos (from where Jason and the Argonauts set off in search of the Golden Fleece) was near the city. Hydra commemorates War of Independence hero Admiral Andreas Miaoulis, who was born on the island, with a re-enactment of one of his naval victories, accompanied by feasting and fireworks.

Feast of St John the Baptist This feast day on 24 June is widely celebrated around Greece. Wreaths made on May Day are kept until this day, when they are burned on bonfires.

July
Feast of Agia Marina (St Marina) This feast day is celebrated on 17 July in many parts of Greece, and is a particularly important event on the Dodecanese island of Kassos.

Feast of Profitis Ilias This feast day is celebrated on 20 July at the hilltop churches and monasteries dedicated to the prophet, especially in the Cyclades.

August
Assumption Greeks celebrate Assumption Day (15 August) with family reunions. The whole population seems to be on the move either side of the big day, so it's a good time to avoid public transport. The island of Tinos gets particularly busy because of its miracle-working icon of Panagia Evangelistria. It becomes a place of pilgrimage for thousands, who come to be blessed, healed or baptised.

September
Genesis tis Panagias (the Virgin's Birthday) This day is celebrated on 8 September throughout Greece with religious services and feasting.

Exaltation of the Cross This is celebrated on 14 September throughout Greece with processions and hymns.

October
Feast of Agios Dimitrios This feast day is celebrated in Thessaloniki on 26 October with wine drinking and revelry.

Ohi (No) Day Metaxas' refusal to allow Mussolini's troops free passage through Greece in WWII is commemorated on 28 October with remembrance services, military parades, folk dancing and feasting.

December
Christmas Day Although not as important as Easter, Christmas is still celebrated with religious services and feasting. Nowadays much 'Western' influence is apparent, including Christmas trees, decorations and presents.

Summer Festivals & Performances

There are cultural festivals throughout Greece in summer. The most important are the Athens Festival (June to September), with drama and music performances in the Theatre of Herodes Atticus, and the Epidaurus Festival (July to September), with drama performances in the ancient theatre at Epidaurus. Thessaloniki hosts a string of festivals and events during September and October.

The sound-and-light show in Athens and Rhodes runs from April to October.

Greek folk dances are performed in Athens from mid-May to September and in Rhodes from May to October.

ACTIVITIES
Windsurfing

Windsurfing is the most popular water sport in Greece. Hrysi Akti on Paros and Vasiliki on Lefkada vie for the position of the best windsurfing beach. According to some, Vasiliki is one of the best places in the world to learn the sport.

You'll find sailboards for hire almost everywhere. Hire charges range from €10 to €15 an hour, depending on the gear. If you are a novice, most places that rent equipment also give lessons.

Sailboards can be imported freely from other EU countries, but the import of boards from other destinations, such as Australia and the US, is subject to some quaint regulations. Theoretically, importers need a Greek national residing in Greece to guarantee that the board will be taken out again. Contact the Hellenic Windsurfing Association (☎ 01 2323 0330, fax 01 2322 3251, e ghiolman@ghiolman.com), Filellinon 7, Athens, for more information.

Water-Skiing

Islands with water-ski centres are Chios, Corfu, Crete, Kythira, Lesvos, Paros, Skiathos and Rhodes.

Snorkelling & Diving

Snorkelling can be enjoyed just about anywhere along the coast off Greece. Especially good places are Monastiri on Paros, Velanio on Skopelos, Paleokastritsa on Corfu, Telendos Islet (near Kalymnos) and anywhere off the coast of Kastellorizo.

Diving is another matter. Any kind of underwater activity using breathing apparatus is strictly forbidden other than under the supervision of a diving school. This is to protect the many antiquities in the depths of the Aegean. There are diving schools on the islands of Corfu, Crete (at Agios Nikolaos), Evia, Hydra, Leros, Milos, Mykonos, Paros, Rhodes, Santorini and Skiathos, and at Glyfada (near Athens) and Parga (Epiros) on the mainland. You can check out the Web site found at: W www.isdc.gr for a full list of diving possibilities.

Trekking

More than half of Greece is mountainous. It would be a trekkers' paradise but for one drawback – many of the paths in Greece are overgrown and inadequately marked. Like all organisations in Greece, the EOS (Ellinikos Orivatikos Syndesmos, Greek Alpine Club) is grossly underfunded (see Useful Organisations earlier for details about the club). But don't be put off by this, as the most popular routes are well walked and maintained. You'll find information on maps in the Planning section at the beginning of this chapter.

On small islands it can be fun to discover pathways for yourself. You are unlikely to get into danger as settlements or roads are never far away. You will encounter a variety of paths; *kalderimi* are the cobbled or flagstone paths that link settlements and date back to Byzantine times. Sadly, many have been bulldozed to make way for new roads.

A number of companies run organised treks. Trekking Hellas (☎ 21 0323 4548, fax 21 03251474, e trekking@compulink.gr, W www.trekking.gr), Filellinon 7, Athens 105 57, specialises in Epiros and Northern Greece, while Alpin Club (☎ 21 0729 5486, fax 21 0721 2773, e alpinclub@internet.gr, W www.alpinclub.gr), Mihalakopoulou 39, Athens 115 28, concentrates on the Peloponnese and Sterea Ellada.

Skiing

Greece provides some of the cheapest skiing found in Europe. There are 16 resorts dotted around the mountains of mainland Greece, mainly in the north. The main skiing areas are Mt Parnassos, 195km north-west of Athens, and Mt Vermio, 110km west of Thessaloniki. There are no foreign package holidays to these resorts; they are used mainly by Greeks. Most have all the basic facilities and can be a pleasant alternative to the glitzy resorts of northern Europe.

The season depends on snow conditions but runs approximately from January to the end of April. For further information pick up a copy of *Greece: Mountain Refuges & Ski Centres* from an EOT office. Information may also be obtained from the Hellenic Skiing Federation (☎ 21 0524 0057, fax 21 0524 8821), PO Box 8037, Omonia, Athens 100 10.

COURSES
Language

If you are serious about learning the language, an intensive course at the start of your stay is a good way to go about it. Most of the courses are in Athens (see the Athens chapter), but there are also special courses on the islands in summer.

The Hellenic Culture Centre (☎/fax 21 0360 3379, 2275 031 978, e hcc@hcc.gr, w www.hcc.gr) runs courses on the island of Ikaria from June to October. Two-week intensive courses for beginners cost €470 and involve 40 classroom hours. The centre can also arrange accommodation.

The Athens Centre (☎ 21 0701 2268, fax 21 0701 8603, e athenscr@compulink.gr, w www.athenscentre.gr), Arhimidous 48 in the suburb of Mets, runs courses on the island of Spetses in June and July.

Corfu's Ionian University runs courses in Modern Greek Language and Greek Civilisation in the months of July and August. Details are available from the Secretariat of the Ionian University (☎/fax 2661 087 264, e foukou@ionio.gr) located at Megaron Kapodistria 49100, Corfu Town.

Dance

The Dora Stratou Dance Company (☎ 21 0324 4395, fax 21 0323 6921, e grdance@hol.gr, w http://users.hol.gr/~grdance), Sholiou 8, Athens 105 58, runs several workshops at its headquarters in Plaka during July and August.

WORK
Permits

EU nationals don't need a work permit, but they need a residency permit if they intend to stay longer than three months. Nationals of other countries are supposed to have a work permit.

English Tutoring

If you're looking for a permanent job, the most widely available option is to teach English. A TEFL (Teaching English as a Foreign Language) certificate or a university degree is an advantage but not essential. In the UK, look through the *Times Educational Supplement* or Tuesday's edition of the *Guardian* newspaper for opportunities – in other countries, contact the Greek embassy.

Another possibility is to find a job teaching English once you are in Greece. You will see language schools everywhere. Strictly speaking, you need a licence to teach in these schools, but many will employ teachers without one. The best time to look around for such a job is late summer.

The notice board at the Compendium bookshop in Athens sometimes has advertisements looking for private English lessons.

Bar & Hostel Work

The bars of the Greek islands could not survive without foreign workers and there are thousands of summer jobs up for grabs every year. The pay is not fantastic, but you get to spend a summer in the islands. April/May is the time to go looking. Hostels and travellers hotels are other places that regularly employ foreign workers.

Volunteer Work

The Hellenic Society for the Study & Protection of the Monk Seal (☎ 21 0522 2888, fax 21 0522 2450), Solomou 53, Athens 104 32, and the Sea Turtle Protection Society of Greece (☎/fax 21 0523 1342, e stps@ compulink.gr), Solomou 57, Athens 104 32, use volunteers for the monitoring programs they run on the Ionian Islands and the Peloponnese.

Street Performers

The richest pickings are to be found on the islands, particularly Mykonos, Paros and Santorini. Plaka is the place to go in Athens; the area outside the church on Kydathineon is the most popular spot.

Other Work

There are often jobs advertised in the classifieds of English-language newspapers, or you can place an advertisement yourself. EU nationals can also make use of the OAED (Organismos Apasholiseos Ergatikou Dynamikou), the Greek National Employment Service, in their search for a job. The OAED has offices throughout Greece.

Seasonal harvest work is handled by migrant workers from Albania and other Balkan nations, and is no longer a viable option for travellers.

ACCOMMODATION

There is a range of accommodation available in Greece to suit every taste and pocket. All places to stay are subject to strict price controls set by the tourist police. By law, a notice must be displayed in every room, which states the category of the room and the price charged in each season. The price includes a 4.5% community tax and 8% VAT.

Accommodation owners may add a 10% surcharge for a stay of less than three nights, but this is not mandatory. A mandatory charge of 20% is levied if an extra bed is put into a room. During July and August, accommodation owners will charge the maximum price, but in spring and autumn, prices will drop by up to 20%, and perhaps by even more in winter. These are the times to bring your bargaining skills into action.

Rip-offs rarely occur, but if you do suspect that you have been exploited by an accommodation owner, make sure you report it to either the tourist police or regular police and they will act swiftly.

Camping

Camping is a good option, especially in summer. There are almost 350 camping grounds in Greece, and a lot of them are situated in great locations. Standard facilities include hot showers, kitchens, restaurants and minimarkets – and often a swimming pool.

Most camping grounds are open only between April and October. The Panhellenic Camping Association (☎/fax 21 0362 1560), Solonos 102, Athens 106 80, publishes an annual booklet listing all the camping grounds, their facilities and months of operation.

Camping fees are highest from 15 June to the end of August. Most camping grounds charge from €3.55 to €4.40 per adult and €2.35 to €2.95 for children aged four to 12. There's no charge for children aged under four. Tent sites cost from €2.95 per night for small tents, and from €3.55 per night for large tents. Caravan sites start at around €5.90.

Between May and mid-September the weather is warm enough to sleep out under the stars, although you will still need a lightweight sleeping bag to counter the predawn chill. It's a good idea to have a foam pad to lie on and a waterproof cover for your sleeping bag.

Freelance (wild) camping is illegal, but the law is seldom enforced – to the irritation of camping-ground owners.

Mountain Refuges

There are 55 mountain refuges dotted around the Greek mainland, Crete and Evia. They range from small huts with outdoor toilets and no cooking facilities to very comfortable modern lodges. They are run by the country's various mountaineering and skiing clubs. Prices range from around €4.70 to €5.90, depending on the facilities. The EOT publication *Greece: Mountain Refuges & Ski Centres* has details about each refuge.

Hostels

There is only one youth hostel in Greece affiliated to the International Youth Hostel Federation (IYHF), the excellent Athens International Youth Hostel (☎ 21 0523 4170). You don't need a membership card to stay there; temporary membership costs €1.80 per day.

Most other youth hostels in Greece are run by the Greek Youth Hostel Organisation (☎ 21 0751 9530, fax 21 0751 0616, ⓔ y-hostels@otenet.gr), Damareos 75, 116 33 Athens. There are affiliated hostels in Athens, Olympia, Patras and Thessaloniki on the mainland, and on the islands of Crete and Santorini.

Hostel rates vary from €4.70 to €5.90 and you don't have to be a member to stay in any of them. Few have curfews.

There is a XEN (YWCA) hostel for women in Athens.

Domatia

Domatia are the Greek equivalent of the British bed and breakfast, minus the breakfast. Once upon a time domatia comprised little more than spare rooms in the family home which could be rented out to travellers in summer; nowadays, many are purpose-built appendages to the family house. Some come complete with fully equipped kitchens. Standards of cleanliness are generally high. The decor runs the gamut from cool grey marble floors, coordinated pine furniture, pretty lace curtains and tasteful pictures on the walls, to so much kitsch, you are almost afraid to move in case you break an ornament.

Domatia remain a popular option for budget travellers. They are classified A, B or C. Expect to pay from €17.60 to €29.35 for a single, and €23.50 to €47 for a double, depending on the class, whether bathrooms are shared or private, the season and how long you plan to stay. Domatia are found throughout the mainland (except in large cities) and on almost every island that has a permanent population. Many are open only between April and October.

From June to September domatia owners are out in force, touting for customers. They meet buses and boats, shouting 'Room, room!' and often carrying photographs of their rooms. In peak season, it can prove a mistake not to take up an offer – but be wary of owners who are vague about the location of their accommodation. 'Close to town' can turn out to be way out in the sticks. If you are at all dubious, insist they show you the location on a map.

Traditional Settlements

Traditional settlements are old buildings of architectural merit that have been renovated and converted into tourist accommodation. You'll find them all over the country, including the islands. There are some terrific places among them, but they are expensive – most are equivalent in price to an A- or B-class hotel. Some of the best examples are in the Papingo villages of northern Epiros and in the old Byzantine town of Monemvasia in the Peloponnese. Hania (Crete) and Rhodes Town also have a good range of possibilities.

Pensions

Pensions in Greece are virtually indistinguishable from hotels. They are classed A, B or C. An A-class pension is equivalent in amenities and price to a B-class hotel, a B-class pension is equivalent to a C-class hotel and a C-class pension is equivalent to a D- or E-class hotel.

Hotels

Hotels in Greece are divided into six categories: deluxe, A, B, C, D and E. Hotels are categorised according to the size of room, whether or not they have a bar, and the ratio of bathrooms to beds, rather than standards of cleanliness, comfort of the beds and friendliness of staff – all elements that may be of greater relevance to guests.

As one would expect, deluxe, A- and B-class hotels have many amenities, private bathrooms and constant hot water. C-class hotels have a snack bar, rooms have private bathrooms, but hot water may only be available at certain times of the day. D-class hotels may or may not have snack bars, most rooms will share bathrooms, but there may be some with private bathrooms, and they may have solar-heated water, which means hot water is not guaranteed. E classes do not have a snack bar, bathrooms are shared and you may have to pay extra for hot water – if it exists at all.

Prices are controlled by the tourist police and the maximum rate that can be charged for a room must be displayed on a board behind the door of each room. The classification is not often much of a guide to price. Rates in D- and E-class hotels are generally comparable with domatia. You can pay from €35 to €60 for a single in high season in C class and €45 to €80 for a double. Prices in B class range from €50 to €80 for singles, and from €90 to €120 for doubles. A-class prices are not much higher.

Apartments

Self-contained family apartments are available in some hotels and domatia. There are also a number of purpose-built apartments, particularly on the islands, available for either long- or short-term rental. Prices vary considerably according to the amenities offered. The classified section of the *Athens News* advertises apartments, mostly in Athens. The tourist police may be able to help in other major towns. In rural areas and islands, ask in a kafeneio.

FOOD

Greek food does not enjoy a reputation as one of the world's great cuisines. Maybe that's because many travellers have experienced Greek cooking only in tourist resorts. The old joke about the Greek woman who, in summer, shouted to her husband 'Come and eat your lunch before it gets hot' is based on truth. Until recently, food was invariably served lukewarm – which is how Greeks prefer it. Most restaurants that cater to tourists have now cottoned on to the fact that foreigners expect cooked dishes to be served hot, and improved methods of warming meals (including the dreaded microwave) have made this easier. If your meal is not hot, ask for it *zesto*, or order grills, which have to be cooked to order. Greeks are fussy about fresh ingredients, and frozen food is rare.

Greeks eat out regularly, regardless of socio-economic status. Enjoying life is paramount to them and a large part of this enjoyment comes from eating and drinking with friends.

By law, every eating establishment must display a written menu including prices. Bread will automatically be put on your table and usually costs between €0.30 and €0.90, depending on the restaurant's category.

Where to Eat

Tavernas The taverna is usually a traditional place with a rough-and-ready ambience, although some are more upmarket, particularly in Athens, resorts and big towns. In simple tavernas, a menu is usually displayed in the window or on the door, but you may instead be invited into the kitchen to peer into the pots and point to what you want. This is not merely a privilege for tourists; Greeks also do it because they want to see the taverna's version of the dishes on offer. Some tavernas don't open until 8pm, and then stay open until the early hours. Some are closed on Sunday.

Greek men are football (soccer) and basketball mad. If you happen to be eating in a taverna on a night when a big match is being televised, expect indifferent service.

Psistaria These places specialise in spit roasts and charcoal-grilled food – usually lamb, pork or chicken.

Restaurants A restaurant *(estiatorio)* is normally more sophisticated than a taverna or psistaria – damask tablecloths, smartly attired waiters and printed menus at each table with an English translation. Ready-made food is usually displayed in a *bain-marie* and there may also be a charcoal grill.

Ouzeria An *ouzeri* serves ouzo. Greeks believe it is essential to eat when drinking alcohol so, in traditional establishments, your drink will come with a small plate of titbits or *mezedes* (appetisers) – perhaps olives, a slice of feta and some pickled octopus. Ouzeria are becoming trendy and many now offer both appetisers and main courses.

Phone numbers listed incorporate changes due in Oct 2002; see p83

Galaktopoleia A *galaktopoleio* (literally meaning 'milk shop') sells dairy produce including milk, butter, yogurt, rice pudding, cornflour pudding, custard, eggs, honey and bread. It may also sell home-made ice cream in several flavours. Look for the sign '*pagoto politiko*' displayed outside. Most have seating and serve coffee and tea. They are inexpensive for breakfast and usually open from very early in the morning until evening.

Zaharoplasteia A *zaharoplasteio* (patisserie) sells cakes (both traditional and Western), chocolates, biscuits, sweets, coffee, soft drinks and, possibly, bottled alcoholic drinks. They usually have some seating.

Kafeneia The kafeneia are often regarded by foreigners as the last bastion of male chauvinism in Europe. With bare light bulbs, nicotine-stained walls, smoke-laden air, rickety wooden tables and raffia chairs, they are frequented by middle-aged and elderly Greek men in cloth caps who while away their time fiddling with worry beads, playing cards or backgammon, or engaged in heated political discussion.

It was once unheard of for women to enter a kafeneio but in large cities this situation is changing. In rural areas, Greek women are rarely seen inside kafeneia. When a female traveller enters one, she is inevitably treated courteously and with friendship if she manages a few Greek words of greeting. If you feel inhibited about going into a kafeneio, opt for outside seating. You'll feel less intrusive.

Kafeneia originally only served Greek coffee but now most also serve soft drinks, Nescafe and beer. Most kafeneia are open all day every day, but some close during the siesta time (which is roughly from 3pm to 5pm).

Other Eateries You'll find plenty of pizzerias, creperies and *gelaterias* (which sell Italian-style ice cream in various flavours), but international restaurants are rare outside Athens – and expensive.

Meals

Breakfast There's some truth in the apocryphal story about the restaurant that serves a cup of coffee and two cigarettes as its Greek breakfast. Greeks are not big morning eaters; most have coffee and perhaps a cake or pastry for breakfast. Budget hotels and pensions offering breakfast provide it continental-style (rolls or bread with jam, and tea or coffee) and upmarket hotels serve breakfast buffets (Western and continental-style). Otherwise, restaurants and galaktopoleia serve bread with butter, jam or honey; eggs; and the budget travellers' favourite, yogurt *(yiaourti)* with honey. In tourist areas, many menus offer an 'English' breakfast – which means bacon and eggs.

Lunch This is eaten late – between 1pm and 3pm – and may be either a snack or a complete meal. The main meal can be lunch or dinner – or both. Once into their stride, Greeks enjoy eating and often have two large meals a day.

Dinner Greeks also eat dinner late. Many people don't start to think about food until about 9pm, which is why some restaurants don't bother to open their doors until after 8pm. In tourist areas dinner is often served earlier.

A full dinner in Greece begins with appetisers and/or soup, followed by a main course of either ready-made food, grilled meat, or fish. Only very posh restaurants or those pandering to tourists include Western-style desserts on the menu. Greeks usually eat cakes separately in a galaktopoleio or zaharoplasteio.

Greek Specialities

Snacks Favourite Greek snacks include pretzel rings sold by street vendors, *tyropitta* (cheese pie), *bougatsa* (custard-filled pastry), *spanakopitta* (spinach pie) and *sandouits* (sandwiches). Street vendors sell various nuts and dried seeds such as pumpkin for €0.60 or €1.50 a bag. You will often see chestnuts roasted on the roadsides in winter.

Mezedes In a simple taverna, possibly only three or four *mezedes* (appetisers) will be offered – perhaps *taramasalata* (fish-roe dip), *tzatziki* (yogurt, cucumber and garlic dip), olives and feta (sheep- or goat's-milk) cheese. Ouzeria and restaurants usually offer wider selections.

Mezedes include *ohtapodi* (octopus), *garides* (shrimps), *kalamaria* (squid), dolmades (stuffed vine leaves), *melitzanosalata* (aubergine or eggplant dip) and *mavromatika* (black-eyed beans). Hot mezedes include *keftedes* (meatballs), *fasolia* (white haricot beans), *gigantes* (lima beans), *loukanika* (little sausages), tyropitta, spanakopitta, *bourekaki* (tiny meat pie), *kolokythakia* (deep-fried zucchini), *melitzana* (deep-fried aubergine) and *saganaki* (fried cheese).

It is quite acceptable to make a full meal of these instead of a main course. Three plates of mezedes are about equivalent in price and quantity to one main course. You can also order a *pikilia* (mixed plate).

Soups Generally soup is a satisfying starter or, indeed, an economical meal in itself with bread and a salad. *Psarosoupa* is a filling fish soup with vegetables, while *kakavia* (Greek bouillabaisse) is laden with seafood and more expensive. *Fasolada* (bean soup) is also a meal in itself. *Avgolemano soupa* (egg and lemon soup) is usually prepared from a chicken stock. If you're into offal, don't miss the traditional Easter soup *mayiritsa* at this festive time.

Salads The ubiquitous (and no longer inexpensive) Greek or village salad, *horiatiki salata*, is a side dish for Greeks, but many euro-conscious tourists make it a main dish. It consists of peppers, onions, olives, tomatoes and feta cheese, sprinkled with oregano and dressed with olive oil and lemon juice. A tomato salad often comes with onions, cucumber and olives, and, with bread, makes a satisfying lunch. In winter, try the cheaper *radikia salata* (dandelion salad).

Main Dishes The most common main courses are *mousakas* (layers of eggplant or zucchini, minced meat and potatoes topped with cheese sauce and baked), *pastitsio* (baked cheese-topped macaroni and bechamel, with or without minced meat), dolmades and *yemista* (stuffed tomatoes or green peppers). Other main courses include *giouvetsi* (casserole of lamb or veal and pasta), *stifado* (meat stewed with onions), *soutzoukakia* (spicy meatballs in tomato sauce, also known as Smyrna sausages) and *salingaria* (snails in oil with herbs). *Melizanes papoutsakia* is baked eggplant stuffed with meat and tomatoes and topped with cheese, which looks, as its Greek name suggests, like a little shoe. Spicy *loukanika* (sausage) is a good budget choice and comes with potatoes or rice. Lamb fricassee, cooked with lettuce, *arni fricassée me maroulia*, is usually filling enough for two to share.

Fish is usually sold by weight in restaurants, but is not as cheap nor as widely available as it used to be. Calamari (squid), deep-fried in batter, remains a tasty option for the budget traveller at €3.55 to €4.70 for a generous serve. Other reasonably priced fish (about €3.55 a portion) are *marides* (whitebait), sometimes cloaked in onion, pepper and tomato sauce, and *gopes*, which are similar to sardines. More expensive are *ohtapodi* (octopus), *bakaliaros* (cod), *xifias* (swordfish) and *glossa* (sole). Ascending the price scale further are *synagrida* (snapper) and *barbounia* (red mullet). *Astakos* (lobster) and *karabida* (crayfish) are top of the range at about €44 per kilo.

Fish is mostly grilled or fried. More imaginative fish dishes include shrimp casserole and mussel or octopus *saganaki* (fried with tomato and cheese). Greece has few rivers and lakes, so freshwater fish are not widely available, although reasonably priced *pestrofa* (trout) can be found in parts of northern Greece – Lake Pamvotis in Ioannina, the Aoös River in Zagoria, and also from the Prespa Lakes.

Desserts Greek cakes and puddings include *baklava* (layers of filo pastry filled with honey and nuts), *loukoumades* (puffs or fritters with honey or syrup), *kataïfi* (chopped nuts inside shredded wheat pastry or filo soaked in honey), *rizogalo* (rice pudding), *loukoumi* (Turkish delight), *halva* (made from semolina or sesame seeds) and *pagoto* (ice cream). Tavernas and restaurants usually only have a few of these on the menu. The best places to go for these delights are galaktopoleia or zaharoplasteia.

Regional Dishes

Greek food is not all mousakas and souvlaki. Every region has its own specialities and it need not be an expensive culinary adventure to discover some of these. Corfu, for example, which was never occupied by the Turks, retains traditional recipes of Italian, Spanish and ancient Greek derivations. Corfiot food is served in several restaurants and includes *sofrito* (lamb or veal with garlic, vinegar and parsley), *pastitsada*, (beef with macaroni, cloves, garlic, tomatoes and cheese) and *burdeto* (fish with paprika and cayenne). Look for poultry and rabbit in the Peloponnese; game is inevitably on the menu in Thessaly and Macedonia.

Santorini's baby tomatoes flavour distinctive dishes, not least a rich soup as thick and dark as blood. The *myzithra* (soft ewe's-milk cheese) of Ios is unique, and the lamb pies of Kefallonia and Crete are worth searching for. Andros' speciality, *froutalia* (spearmint-flavoured potato and sausage omelette), is good value. Rhodes turns out a baked omelette loaded with meat and zucchini.

Vegetarian Food

Greece has few vegetarian restaurants. Unfortunately, many vegetable soups and stews are based on meat stocks. Fried vegetables are safe bets as olive oil is always used – never lard. The Greeks do wonderful things with artichokes *(aginares)*, which thrive in Greece. Stuffed, served as a salad, as a meze, (particularly with *raki* in Crete) and as the basis of a vegetarian stew, the artichoke warrants greater discovery by visitors. Vegetarians who eat eggs can rest assured that an economical omelette can be whipped up anywhere. Salads are cheap, fresh, substantial and nourishing. Other options are yogurt, rice pudding, cheese and spinach pies, and nuts. Creperies also offer tasty vegetarian selections.

Lent, incidentally, is quite a good time for vegetarians because the meat is missing from many dishes.

Fast Food

Western-style fast food has arrived in Greece in a big way. 'Mac' fans will find their favourite burger at a number of locations in Athens and other major towns, but McDonald's has found Greece a hard market to conquer. Patriotic Greeks seem to prefer the local chain Goody's, which has a better salad bar than most of its rivals. The big international chicken and pizza chains are also around.

It's hard, though, to beat eat-on-the-street Greek offerings. Foremost among them are the *gyros* and the souvlaki. The gyros is a giant skewer laden with slabs of seasoned meat which grills slowly as it rotates and the meat is trimmed steadily from the outside; souvlaki are small individual kebab sticks. Both are served wrapped in pitta bread, with salad and lashings of tzatziki.

Another favourite is *tost*, which is a bread roll cut in half, stuffed with the filling(s) of your choice, buttered on the outside and then flattened in a heavy griddle iron. It's the speciality of the Everest fast-food chain, which has outlets nationwide.

Fruit

Greece grows many varieties of fruit. Most visitors will be familiar with *syka* (figs), *rodakina* (peaches), *stafylia* (grapes), *karpouzi* (watermelon), *milo* (apples), *portokalia* (oranges) and *kerasia* (cherries).

Many will not, however, have encountered the *frangosyko* (prickly pear). Also known as the Barbary fig, it is the fruit of the opuntia cactus, recognisable by the thick green spiny pads that form its trunk. The fruit are borne around the edge of the pads in late summer and autumn and vary in colour from pale orange to deep red. They are delicious but need to be approached with extreme caution because of the thousands of tiny prickles (invisible to the naked eye) that cover their skin. Never pick one up with your bare hands. They must be peeled before you can eat them. The simplest way to do this is to trim the ends off with a knife and then slit the skin from end to end.

Another fruit that will be new to many people is the *mousmoula* (loquat). These small orange fruit are among the first of summer, reaching the market in mid-May. The flesh is juicy and pleasantly acidic.

Self-Catering

Eating out in Greece is as much an entertainment as a gastronomic experience, so to self-cater is to sacrifice a lot. But if you are on a low budget you will need to make the sacrifice – for breakfast and lunch at any rate. All towns and villages of any size have supermarkets, fruit and vegetable stalls and bakeries.

Only in isolated villages and on remote islands is food choice limited. There may only be one all-purpose shop – a *pantopoleio*, which will stock meat, vegetables, fruit, bread and tinned foods.

Markets Most larger towns have huge indoor *agora* (food markets) which feature fruit and vegetable stalls, butchers, dairies and delicatessens, all under one roof. They are lively places that are worth visiting for the atmosphere as much as for the shopping. The markets at Hania (Crete) and Kalamata are good examples.

Smaller towns have a weekly *laïki agora* (street market) with stalls selling local produce.

DRINKS
Nonalcoholic Drinks

Coffee & Tea Greek coffee is the national drink. It is a legacy of Ottoman rule and, until the Turkish invasion of Cyprus in 1974, the Greeks called it Turkish coffee. It is served with the grounds, without milk, in a small cup. Connoisseurs claim there are at least 30 variations of Greek coffee, but most people know only three – *glyko* (sweet), *metrio* (medium) and *sketo* (without sugar).

The next most popular coffee is instant, called Nescafe (which it usually is). Ask for Nescafe *me ghala* (pronounced 'me **ga**-la') if you want it with milk. In summer, Greeks drink Nescafe chilled, with or without milk and sugar – this version is called *frappé*.

Espresso and filtered coffee, once sold only in trendy cafes, are now also widely available.

Tea is inevitably made with a tea bag.

Fruit Juice & Soft Drinks Packaged fruit juices are available everywhere. Fresh orange juice is also widely available, but doesn't come cheap. The products of all the major soft-drink multinationals are available everywhere in cans and bottles, along with local brands.

Milk Fresh milk can be hard to find on the islands and in remote areas. Elsewhere, you'll have no problem. A litre costs about €1.20. UHT milk is available almost everywhere, as is condensed milk.

Water Tap water is safe to drink in Greece, although sometimes it doesn't taste too good because of the chlorination levels. Many tourists prefer bottled spring water, sold widely in 500mL and 1.5L plastic bottles. If you're happy with tap water, fill a container with it before embarking on ferries or you'll wind up paying through the nose for bottled water. Sparkling mineral water is rare.

Alcoholic Drinks

Beer Greek beers are making a strong comeback in a fast-growing market long dominated by the major northern European breweries. The most popular beers are still Amstel and Heineken, both brewed locally under licence and available everywhere, but many consumers are switching to local beers like Mythos, Alpha and Vergina. Mythos has claimed a healthy share of the market since it was launched in 1997 and is the most widely available. It has proved popular with drinkers who find the northern European beers a bit sweet.

Imported lagers, stouts and beers are found in tourist spots such as music bars and discos. You might even spot Newcastle Brown, Carlsberg, Castlemaine XXXX and Guinness.

Wine + Pine = Retsina

A holiday in Greece would not be the same without a jar or three of *retsina*, the famous – some might say notorious – resinated wine that is the speciality of Attica and neighbouring areas of central Greece.

Your first taste of retsina may well leave you wondering whether the waiter has mixed up the wine and the paint stripper, but stick with it – it's a taste that's worth acquiring. Soon you will be savouring the delicate pine aroma, and the initial astringency mellows to become very moreish. Retsina is very refreshing consumed chilled at the end of a hot day, when it goes particularly well with tzatziki.

Greeks have been resinating wine, both white and rosé, for millennia. The ancient Greeks dedicated the pine tree to Dionysos, also the god of wine, and held that land that grew good pine would also grow good wine.

No-one seems quite sure how wine and pine first got together. The consensus is that it was an inevitable accident in a country with so much wine and so much pine. The theory that resin entered the wine-making process because the wine was stored in pine barrels does not hold water, since the ancients used clay amphora rather than barrels. It's more likely that it was through pine implements and vessels used elsewhere in the process. Producers discovered that wine treated with resin kept for longer, and consumers discovered that they liked it.

Resination was once a fairly haphazard process, achieved by various methods such as adding crushed pine cones to the brew and coating the insides of storage vessels. The amount of resin also varied enormously. One 19th-century traveller wrote that he had tasted a wine 'so impregnated with resin that it almost took the skin from my lips'. His reaction was hardly surprising; he was probably drinking a wine with a resin content as high as 7.5%, common at the time. A more sophisticated product awaits the modern traveller, with a resin content no higher than 1% – as specified by good old EU regulations. That's still enough to give the wine its trademark astringency and pine aroma.

The bulk of retsina is made from two grape varieties, the white *savatiano* and the red *roditis*. These two constitute the vast majority of vine plantings in Attica, central Greece and Evia. Not just any old resin will do; the main source is the Aleppo pine *(Pinus halepensis)*, which produces a resin known for its delicate fragrance.

Retsina is generally cheap and it's available everywhere. Supermarkets stock retsina in a variety of containers ranging from 500mL bottles to 5L casks and flagons. Kourtaki and Cambas are both very good, but the best (and worst) still flows from the barrel in traditional tavernas. Ask for *heema*, which means 'loose'.

Supermarkets are the cheapest place to buy beer, and bottles are cheaper than cans.

Wine According to mythology, the Greeks invented or discovered wine and it has been produced in Greece on a large scale for more than 3000 years.

The modern wine industry, though, is still very much in its infancy. Until the 1950s, most Greek wines were sold in bulk and were seldom distributed any farther afield than the nearest town. It wasn't until industrialisation (and the resulting rapid urban growth) that there was much call for bottled wine. Quality control was unheard of until 1969, when appellation laws were introduced as a precursor to applying for membership of the European Community. Wines have improved significantly since then.

Don't expect wines of Greece to taste like French wines. The varieties that are grown in Greece are quite different. Some of the most popular and reasonably priced labels include Rotonda, Kambas, Boutari, Calliga and Lac des Roches. Boutari's Naoussa is worth looking out for. It's a dry red wine from the Naoussa area of northwest Macedonia.

More expensive, but of good quality, are the Achaïa-Clauss wines from Patras. The most expensive wines are the Kefallonian Robola de Cephalonie, a superb dry white, and those produced by the Porto Carras estate in Halkidiki. Good wines are produced on Rhodes (famous in Greece for its champagne) and Crete. Other island wines worth sampling are those from Samos (immortalised by Lord Byron), Santorini, Kefallonia and Paros. *Aspro* is white, *mavro* is red and *kokkinelli* is rosé.

Spirits Ouzo is the most popular aperitif in Greece. Distilled from grape stems and flavoured with anise, it is similar to the Middle Eastern *arak*, Turkish *raki* and French Pernod. Clear and colourless, it turns white when water is added. A 700mL bottle of a popular brand like Ouzo 12, Olympic or Sans Rival costs about €4.40 in supermarkets. In an ouzeri, a glass costs from €0.90 to €1.50. It will be served neat, with a separate glass of water to be used for dilution.

The second-most popular spirit is Greek brandy, which is dominated by the Metaxa label. Metaxa comes in a range of grades, starting with three star – a high-octane product without much finesse. You can pick up a bottle in a supermarket for about €4.40. The quality improves as you go through the grades: five star, seven star, VSOP, Golden Age and finally top-shelf Grand Olympian Reserve (€18). Other reputable brands include Cambas and Votrys. The Cretan speciality is raki, a fiery clear spirit that is served as a greeting (regardless of the time of day).

If you're travelling off the beaten track, you may come across *chipura*, a moonshine version of ouzo that packs a formidable punch. You'll most likely encounter chipura in village kafeneia or private homes.

ENTERTAINMENT
Cinemas
Greeks are keen movie-goers and almost every town of consequence has a cinema. English-language films are shown in English with Greek subtitles. Admission ranges from €4.10 in small-town movie houses to €5.90 at plush big-city cinemas.

Discos & Music Bars
Discos can be found in big cities and resort areas, though not in the numbers of a decade ago.

Most young Greeks prefer to head for the music bars that have proliferated to fill the void. These bars normally specialise in a particular style of music – Greek, modern rock, 60s rock, techno and, very occasionally, jazz.

Ballet, Classical Music & Opera
Unless you're going to be spending a bit of time in Athens or Thessaloniki, you're best off forgetting about ballet, classical music and opera while in Greece. See the Entertainment section of the Athens chapter for information on venues.

Theatre
The highlight of the Greek dramatic year is the staging of ancient Greek dramas at the Theatre of Herodes Atticus in Athens during the Athens Festival from late June to early September. Performances are also staged at the amazing Theatre of Epidaurus. See the Special Events section of the Athens chapter and the Epidaurus section of the Peloponnese chapter for more information.

Rock
Western rock music continues to grow in popularity, but live music remains a rarity outside Athens and Thessaloniki.

Traditional Music
Most of the live music you hear around the resorts is tame stuff laid on for the tourists. If you want to hear music played with a bit of passion, the *rembetika* clubs in Athens are strongly recommended.

Folk Dancing
The pre-eminent folk dancers in Greece are the ones who perform at the Dora Stratou Theatre on Filopappos Hill in Athens, where performances take place nightly in summer. Another highly commendable place is the Old City Theatre in Rhodes City, where the Nelly Dimoglou Dance Company performs during the summer

months. Folk dancing is an integral part of all festival celebrations and there is often impromptu folk dancing in tavernas.

SPECTATOR SPORTS

Soccer (football) remains the most popular spectator sport, although basketball is catching up fast following the successes of Greek sides in European club competition in recent years. Greek soccer teams, in contrast, have seldom had much impact on the European club competition, and the national team is the source of constant hair-wrenching. The side's only appearance in the World Cup finals, in the USA in 1994, brought a string of heavy defeats. The two glamour clubs of Greek soccer are Olympiakos of Piraeus and Panathinaikos of Athens. The capital supplies a third of the clubs in the first division (see Spectator Sports in the Athens chapter for more information).

The season lasts from September to mid-May; cup matches are played on Wednesday night and first division games on Sunday afternoon. Games are often televised. Entry to a match costs around €5.90 for the cheapest terrace tickets, or €15 for a decent seat. Fixtures and results are given in the *Athens News*.

Olympiakos and Panathinaikos are also the glamour clubs of Greek basketball. Panathinaikos was European champion in 1996, and Olympiakos followed suit in 1997. Entry costs around €5.80 to €8.80 a game.

SHOPPING

Greece produces a vast array of handicrafts. The Centre of Hellenic Tradition, at Pandrossou 36, Plaka, Athens, has a good range.

Antiques

It is illegal to buy, sell, possess or export any antiquity in Greece (see Customs earlier in this chapter). However, there are antiques and 'antiques'; a lot of items only a century or two old are regarded as junk, rather than part of the national heritage. These items include hand-made furniture and odds and ends from rural areas in Greece, ecclesiastical ornaments from churches and items brought back from far-flung lands. Good hunting grounds for this 'junk' are Monastiraki and the flea market in Athens, and the Piraeus market held on Sunday morning.

Ceramics

You will see ceramic objects of every shape and size – functional and ornamental – for sale throughout Greece. The best places for high-quality, hand-made ceramics are Athens, Rhodes and the islands of Sifnos and Skyros.

There are a lot of places selling plaster copies of statues, busts, grave stelae and the like.

Leather Work

There are leather goods for sale throughout Greece; most are made from leather imported from Spain. The best place for buying leather goods is Hania on Crete. Bear in mind that the goods are not as high quality nor as good value as those available in Turkey.

Jewellery

You could join the wealthy North Americans who spill off cruise ships onto Mykonos to indulge themselves in the high-class, gold jewellery shops. But although gold is good value in Greece, and designs are of a high quality, it is priced beyond the capacity of most tourists' pockets. If you prefer something more reasonably priced, go for filigree -silver jewellery. Ioannina is the filigree jewellery centre of Greece.

Bags

Tagari bags are woven wool bags – often brightly coloured – which hang from the shoulder by a rope. Minus the rope, they make attractive cushion covers.

Getting There & Away

AIR

Most travellers arrive in Greece by air, the cheapest and quickest way to get there.

Airports & Airlines

Greece has 16 international airports, but only those in Athens, Thessaloniki and Iraklio (Crete) take scheduled flights.

Athens handles the vast majority of the flights, including all intercontinental traffic. Thessaloniki has direct flights to Amsterdam, Belgrade, Berlin, Brussels, Cyprus, Dusseldorf, Frankfurt, İstanbul, London, Milan, Moscow, Munich, Paris, Stuttgart, Tirana, Vienna and Zürich. Most of these flights are with Greece's national airline, Olympic Airways, or whichever flag carrier of the country concerned. Iraklio's sole scheduled connection is to Amsterdam with Transavia.

Greece's other international airports are found at Mykonos, Santorini (Thira), Hania (Crete), Kos, Karpathos, Samos, Skiathos, Hrysoupolis (for Kavala), Aktion (for Lefkada), Kefallonia and Zakynthos. These airports are used exclusively for charter flights, mostly from the UK, Germany and Scandinavia. Charter flights also fly to all of Greece's other international airports.

Olympic Airways is the country's national airline. Olympic has been through dire times in recent years, and was for sale at the time of research. The government decided to put the beleaguered airline on the market following the expiry of a two-year management deal with British Airways.

Olympic is no longer Greece's only international airline. Cronus Airlines flies direct from Athens to London, Paris and Rome, and via Thessaloniki to Cologne, Dusseldorf, Frankfurt, Munich and Stuttgart.

Buying Tickets

World aviation has never been so competitive, making air travel better value than ever. But you have to research the options carefully to make sure you get the best deal.

The Internet is an increasingly useful resource for checking air fares.

Full-time students and people under 26 years (under 30 in some countries) have access to better deals than other travellers. You have to show a document proving your date of birth or a valid International Student Identity Card (ISIC) when buying your ticket and boarding the plane.

Generally, there is nothing to be gained by buying a ticket direct from the airline. Discounted tickets are released to selected travel agents and specialist discount agencies, and these are usually the cheapest deals going.

One exception to this rule is the expanding number of 'no-frills' carriers, which mostly sell only direct to travellers. Unlike the 'full-service' airlines, no-frills carriers often make one-way tickets available at around half the return fare, meaning that it is easy to put together an open-jaw ticket when you fly to one place but leave from another.

The other exception is booking on the Internet. Many airlines, full-service and no-frills, offer some excellent fares to Web surfers. They may sell seats by auction or simply cut prices to reflect the reduced cost of electronic selling.

Online ticket sales work well if you are doing a simple one-way or return trip on specified dates. However, online super-fast fare generators are no substitute for a travel agent who knows all about special deals, has strategies for avoiding layovers and can offer advice on everything from which airline has the best vegetarian food to the best travel insurance to bundle with your ticket.

You may find the cheapest flights are advertised by obscure agencies. Most such firms are honest and solvent, but there are some rogue fly-by-night outfits around. Paying by credit card generally offers protection, as most card issuers provide refunds if you can prove you didn't get what you paid for. Similar protection can be obtained by

Air Travel Glossary

Alliances Many of the world's leading airlines are now intimately involved with each other, sharing everything from reservations systems and check-in to aircraft and frequent-flyer schemes. Opponents say that alliances restrict competition. Whatever the arguments, there is no doubt that big alliances are the way of the future.

Courier Fares Businesses often need to send urgent documents or freight securely and quickly. Courier companies hire people to accompany the package through customs and, in return, offer a discount ticket which is sometimes a bargain. However, you may have to surrender all your baggage allowance and take only carry-on luggage.

Fares Airlines traditionally offer 1st class (coded F), business class (coded J) and economy class (coded Y) tickets. These days there are so many promotional and discounted fares available that few passengers pay full fare.

Lost Tickets If you lose your airline ticket, an airline will usually treat it like a travellers cheque and, after inquiries, issue you with another one. Legally, however, an airline is entitled to treat it like cash and if you lose it then it's gone forever. Take very good care of your tickets.

Onward Tickets An entry requirement for many countries is that you have a ticket out of the country. If you're unsure of your next move, the easiest solution is to buy the cheapest onward ticket to a neighbouring country or a ticket from a reliable airline which can later be refunded if you do not use it.

Open-Jaw Tickets These are return tickets where you fly out to one place but return from another. If available, this can save you backtracking to your arrival point.

Overbooking Since every flight has some passengers who fail to show up, airlines often book more passengers than they have seats. Usually excess passengers make up for the no-shows, but occasionally somebody gets 'bumped' onto the next available flight. Guess who it is most likely to be? The passengers who check in late. If you do get 'bumped', you are normally offered some form of compensation.

Reconfirmation Some airlines require you to reconfirm your flight at least 72 hours prior to departure. Check your travel documents to see if this is the case

Restrictions Discounted tickets often have various restrictions on them – such as needing to be paid for in advance and incurring a penalty to be altered or cancelled. Others are restrictions on the minimum and maximum period you must be away.

Round-the-World Tickets RTW tickets give you a limited period (usually a year) in which to circumnavigate the globe. You can go anywhere the carrying airlines go, as long as you don't backtrack. The number of stopovers or total number of separate flights is decided before you set off and they usually cost a bit more than a basic return flight.

Ticketless Travel Airlines are gradually waking up to the realisation that paper tickets are unnecessary encumbrances. On simple one-way or return trips, reservations details can be held on computer and the passenger merely shows ID to claim their seat.

Transferred Tickets Airline tickets cannot be transferred from one person to another. Travellers sometimes try to sell the return half of their ticket, but officials can ask you to prove that you are the person named on the ticket. On an international flight, tickets are compared with passports.

buying a ticket from a bonded agent, such as one covered by the Air Travel Organiser's Licence (ATOL) scheme in the UK (more details available at Ⓦ www.atol.org.uk). Agents who accept only cash should hand over the tickets straight away and not tell you to 'come back tomorrow'. After you've made a booking or paid your deposit, call the airline and confirm that the booking was made. It's generally not advisable to send money (even cheques) through the post unless the agent is very well established – some travellers have reported being ripped off by fly-by-night mail-order ticket agents.

If you purchase a ticket and later want to make changes to your route or get a refund, you need to contact the original travel agent. Airlines issue refunds only to the purchaser of a ticket – usually the travel agent who bought the ticket on your behalf. Many travellers change their routes halfway through their trips, so think carefully before you buy a ticket which is not easily refunded.

If you are buying a ticket to fly out of Greece, Athens is one of the major centres in Europe for budget airfares.

In Greece, as everywhere else, always remember to reconfirm your onward or return bookings by the specified time – usually 72 hours before departure on international flights. If you don't, there's a risk you'll turn up at the airport only to find you've missed your flight because it was rescheduled, or that the airline has given the seat to someone else.

Charter Flights

Charter flight tickets are vacant seats on flights which have been block-booked by package companies. Tickets are cheap but conditions apply on charter flights to Greece. A ticket must be accompanied by an accommodation booking. This is normally circumvented by travel agents issuing accommodation vouchers not meant to be used – even if the hotel named on the voucher actually exists. The law requiring accommodation bookings was introduced in the 1980s to prevent budget travellers flying to Greece on cheap charter flights and sleeping rough on beaches or in parks. It hasn't worked.

Charter flight tickets are valid for up to four weeks, and usually have a minimum-stay requirement of at least three days. Sometimes it's worth buying a charter return even if you think you want to stay for longer than four weeks. The tickets can be so cheap that you can afford to throw away the return portion.

The travel section of major newspapers is the place to look for cheap charter deals. More information on charter flights is given later in this chapter under specific point-of-origin headings.

Courier Flights

Another budget option (sometimes even cheaper than a charter flight) is a courier flight. This deal entails accompanying freight or a parcel that will be collected at the destination. The drawbacks are that your time away may be limited to one or two weeks, your luggage is usually restricted to hand luggage (the parcel or freight you carry comes out of your luggage allowance), and you may have to be a resident of the country that operates the courier service and apply for an interview before they'll take you on.

Travel Agents

Many of the larger travel agents use the travel pages of national newspapers and magazines to promote their special deals. Before you make a decision, there are a number of questions you need to ask about the ticket. Find out the airline, the route, the duration of the journey, the stopovers allowed, any restrictions on the ticket and – above all – the price. Ask whether the fare quoted includes all taxes and other possible inclusions.

You may discover when you start ringing around that those impossibly cheap flights, charter or otherwise, are not available, but the agency just happens to know of another one that 'costs a bit more'. Or the agent may claim to have the last two seats available for Greece for the whole of July, which they will hold for a maximum of two hours only. Don't panic – keep ringing around.

If you are flying to Greece from the USA, South-East Asia or the UK, you will most likely find the cheapest flights are being advertised by obscure agencies whose names haven't yet reached the telephone directory – the proverbial bucket shops. Many such firms are honest and solvent, but there are a few rogues who will take your money and disappear, only to reopen elsewhere under a new name. If you feel suspicious about a firm, don't give them all the money at once – leave a small deposit and pay the balance when you get the ticket. If they insist on cash in advance, go somewhere else or be prepared to take a big risk. Once you have booked the flight with the agency, ring the airline to check you have a confirmed booking.

It can be easier on the nerves to pay a bit more for the security of a better-known travel agent. Firms such as STA Travel, with offices worldwide, Council Travel in the USA or Travel CUTS in Canada offer good prices to Europe (including Greece), and are unlikely to disappear overnight.

The fares quoted in this book are intended as a guide only. They are approximate and are based on the rates advertised by travel agents at the time of writing.

Travel Insurance

The kind of cover you get depends on your insurance and type of ticket, so ask both your insurer and your ticket-issuing agency to explain where you stand. Ticket loss is usually covered.

Buy travel insurance as early as possible. If you buy it just before you fly, you may find you're not covered for such problems as delays caused by industrial action. Make sure you have a separate record of all your ticket details – preferably a photocopy.

Paying for your ticket with a credit card sometimes provides limited travel insurance, and you may be able to reclaim the payment if the operator doesn't deliver. In the UK, for instance, credit card providers are required by law to reimburse consumers if a company goes into liquidation and the amount in contention is more than UK£100.

Travellers with Special Needs

If they're warned early enough, airlines can often make special arrangements for travellers such as wheelchair assistance at airports or vegetarian meals on the flight. Children under two years travel for 10% of the standard fare (or free on some airlines) as long as they don't occupy a seat. They don't get a baggage allowance. 'Skycots', baby food and nappies should be provided by the airline if requested in advance. Children aged between two and 12 can usually occupy a seat for half to two-thirds of the full fare, and do get a baggage allowance.

The disability-friendly Web site W www .everybody.co.uk has an airline directory that provides information on the facilities offered by various airlines.

Departure Tax

The airport tax is €12 for passengers travelling to destinations within the EU, and €22 for other destinations. It applies to travellers aged over five, and is paid when you buy your ticket, not at the airport.

Passengers aged over two departing from Athens are liable for a further €10.30 as a contribution to facilities at the new airport, and a security charge of €1.29. These charges also are paid when you buy your ticket.

The USA

Discount travel agents in the USA are known as consolidators (although you won't see a sign on the door saying Consolidator). San Francisco is the ticket consolidator capital of America, although some good deals can be found in Los Angeles, New York and other big cities.

America's largest student travel organisation, Council Travel (☎ 800-226 8624, W www.counciltravel.com), has around 60 offices in the USA. Contact it for the office nearest you. STA Travel (☎ 800-777 0112, W www.statravel.com) has offices in Boston, Chicago, Miami, New York, Philadelphia, San Francisco and other major cities. Contact it for office locations.

Ticket Planet (W www.ticketplanet.com) is a leading ticket consolidator in the USA and is recommended.

New York has the widest range of options to Athens. The route to Europe is very

ompetitive and there are new deals almost
very day. At the time of research, Virgin
Atlantic led the way, offering Athens for
US$944 return in high season via London,
alling to US$740 at other times. Olympic
Airways flies direct at least once a day, and
Delta Airlines flies direct three times a
week. Apex fares with Olympic range from
US$730 to US$1015, depending on the sea-
on. These fares don't include taxes.

Boston is the only other east-coast city
with direct flights to Athens – on Saturday
with Olympic Airways. Fares are the same
s for flights from New York.

There are no direct flights to Athens from
he west coast. There are, however, con-
ecting flights to Athens from many US
ities, either linking with Olympic Airways
n New York or flying with one of the Euro-
ean national airlines to their home country,
nd then on to Athens. At the time of re-
earch, Virgin Atlantic was offering Los
Angeles–Athens for US$982 return in high
eason, falling to US$879 at other times.

Courier flights to Athens are occasionally
advertised in the newspapers, or you could
ontact air-freight companies listed in the
hone book. You may even have to go to
he air freight company to get an answer – the
ompanies aren't always keen to give out in-
ormation over the phone. Travel Unlimited
PO Box 1058, Allston, MA 02134, USA) is
 monthly travel newsletter from the USA
hat publishes many courier flight deals from
estinations worldwide. A 12-month sub-
cription to the newsletter costs US$25, or
US$35 for residents outside the US. Another
ossibility (at least for US residents) is to join
he International Association of Air Travel
Couriers (IAATC). The membership fee of
45 gets members a bimonthly update of air-
ourier offerings, access to a fax-on-demand
ervice with daily updates of last-minute spe-
ials and the bimonthly newsletter the Shoe-
tring Traveler. For more information,
ontact IAATC (☎ 561-582-8320, W www
courier.org). However, be aware that joining
his organisation does not guarantee that
ou'll get a courier flight.

If you're travelling from Athens to the
USA, the travel agents around Syntagma

offer the following one-way fares (prices do
not include airport tax): Atlanta €340,
Chicago €340, Los Angeles €380 and New
York €265.

Canada
Canadian discount air ticket sellers are also
known as consolidators and their air fares
tend to be about 10% higher than those sold
in the USA. The *Globe and Mail*, the
Toronto Star, the *Montreal Gazette* and the
Vancouver Sun carry travel agents' ads and
are a good place to look for cheap fares.

Canada's national student travel agency
is Travel CUTS (☎ 800-667-2887, W www
.travelcuts.com) which has offices in all
major cities.

Olympic Airways has two flights weekly
from Toronto to Athens via Montreal.
There are no direct flights from Vancouver,
but there are connecting flights via Toronto,
Amsterdam, Frankfurt and London on
Canadian Airlines, KLM, Lufthansa and
British Airways. You should be able to get
to Athens from Toronto and Montreal for
about C$1150/950 in high/low season or
from Vancouver for C$1500/1300.

For courier flights originating in Canada,
contact FB On Board Courier Services in
Montreal (☎ 514-631 7929). It can get you
to London for C$760 return.

At the time of writing, budget travel
agencies in Athens were advertising flights
to both Toronto and Montreal for €330,
plus airport tax.

Australia
Two well-known agents for cheap fares are
STA Travel and Flight Centre. STA Travel
(☎ 03-9349 2411, Australia-wide ☎ 131
776, W www.statravel.com.au) has its main
office at 224 Faraday St, Carlton, in Melbourne, but also has offices in all major
cities and on many university campuses.
Call for the location of your nearest branch.
Flight Centre (Australia-wide ☎ 131 600,
W www.flightcentre.com.au) has a central
office at 82 Elizabeth St, Sydney, and there
are dozens of offices throughout Australia.

Olympic Airways has two flights weekly
from Sydney and Melbourne to Athens.

Return fares normally cost from about A$1799 in low season to A$2199 in high season.

Thai International and Singapore Airlines also have convenient connections to Athens, as well as a reputation for good service. If you're planning on doing a bit of flying around Europe, it's worth checking around for special deals from the major European airlines. Alitalia, KLM and Lufthansa are three likely candidates with good European networks.

If you're travelling from Athens to Australia, a one-way ticket to Sydney or Melbourne costs about €550, plus airport tax.

New Zealand

Round-the-World (RTW) and Circle Pacific fares are usually the best value, often cheaper than a return ticket. Depending on which airline you choose, you may fly across Asia, with possible stopovers in India, Bangkok or Singapore, or across the USA, with possible stopovers in Honolulu, Australia or one of the Pacific islands.

The New Zealand Herald has a travel section in which travel agents advertise fares. Flight Centre (☎ 09-309 6171) has a central office in Auckland at National Bank Towers (corner Queen and Darby Sts) and many branches throughout the country. STA Travel (☎ 09-309 0458, W www.sta.travel.co.nz) has its main office at 10 High St, Auckland, and has other offices in Auckland as well as in Hamilton, Palmerston North, Wellington, Christchurch and Dunedin.

The UK

Airline ticket discounters are known as bucket shops in the UK. Despite the somewhat disreputable name, there is nothing under-the-counter about them. Discount air travel is big business in London. Advertisements for many travel agents appear in the travel pages of the weekend broadsheets, such as the *Independent* on Saturday and the *Sunday Times*. Look out for the free magazines, such as *TNT*, which are widely available in London – start by looking outside the main train and underground stations.

For students or travellers under 26, popular travel agencies in the UK include STA Travel (☎ 08701 600 599, W www .statravel.co.uk), which has an office at 86 Old Brompton Rd, London SW7, and other offices in London and in Manchester. Usit Campus Travel (☎ 0870 240 1010 W www.usitcampus.co.uk), 52 Grosvenor Gardens, London SW1W, has branches throughout the UK. Both of these agencies sell tickets to all travellers but cater especially to young people and students. Charter flights can work out as a cheaper alternative to scheduled flights, especially if you do not qualify for the under-26 and student discounts.

Other recommended bucket shops include: Trailfinders (☎ 020-7937 1234), 194 Kensington High St, London W8 7RG; Bridge the World (☎ 0870 444 7474), 4 Regent Place, London W1R 5FB; and Flightbookers (☎ 020-7757 2000), 177–178 Tottenham Court Rd, London W1P 9LF.

British Airways, Olympic Airways and Virgin Atlantic operate daily flights between London and Athens. Pricing is very competitive, with all three offering return tickets for around UK£220 in high season, plus tax. At other times, prices fall as low at UK£104, plus tax. British Airways has flights from Edinburgh, Glasgow and Manchester.

Cronus Airlines (☎ 020-7580 3500) flies the London-Athens route five times weekly for £210, and offers connections to Thessaloniki on the same fare. Most scheduled flights from London leave from Heathrow.

The cheapest scheduled flights are with EasyJet (☎ 0870 6 000 000, W www.easyjet .com), the no-frills specialist, which has two Luton-Athens flights daily. One-way fares range from UK£52 to UK£112 in high season, and from a bargain UK£17 to UK£42 at other times.

There are numerous charter flights between the UK and Greece. Typical London-Athens charter fares are around UK£99/149 one way/return in the low season and UK£119/209 in the high season. These prices are for advance bookings, but even in high season it's possible to pick up last-minute deals for as little as UK£69/109.

There are also charter flights from Birmingham, Cardiff, Glasgow, Luton, Manchester and Newcastle.

If you're flying from Athens to the UK, budget fares start at €75 to London or €90 to Manchester, plus airport tax.

Continental Europe

Athens is linked to every major city in Europe by either Olympic Airways or the flag carrier of each country.

London is the discount capital of Europe, but Amsterdam, Frankfurt, Berlin and Paris are also major centres for cheap airfares.

Across Europe many travel agencies have ties with STA Travel, where cheap tickets can be purchased and STA-issued tickets can be altered (usually for a US$25 fee). Outlets in major cities include: Voyages Wasteels (☎ 08 03 88 70 04 (this number can only be dialled from within France), fax 01 43 25 46 25), 11 rue Dupuytren, 756006 Paris; STA Travel (☎ 030-311 0950, fax 313 0948), Goethestrasse 73, 10625 Berlin; and Passaggi (☎ 06-474 0923, fax 482 7436), Stazione Termini FS, Galleria Di Tesla, Rome.

France has a network of travel agencies which can supply discount tickets to travellers of all ages. They include Usit Connect Voyages (☎ 01 42 44 14 00), 14 rue de Vaugirard, 75006 Paris, with branches across the country; and OTU Voyages (☎ 01 40 29 12 12, W www.otu.fr), 39 ave Georges-Bernanos, 75005 Paris, with branches across the country. Both companies are student and young person specialist agencies. Other recommendations include Voyageurs du Monde (☎ 01 42 86 16 00), 55 rue Ste-Anne, 75002 Paris, and Nouvelles Frontières (nationwide number ☎ 08 25 00 08 25, Paris ☎ 01 45 68 70 00, W www.nouvelles-frontieres.fr), 87 blvd de Grenelle, 75015 Paris, with branches across the country.

In Germany, recommended agencies include STA Travel (☎ 030-311 0950), Goethestrasse 73, 10625 Berlin, as well as branches in major cities all across the country. Usit Campus (call centre ☎ 01805 788336, Cologne ☎ 0221 923990, W www .usitcampus.de) also has several offices in Germany (you'll find the details on the Web site), including one at 2a Zuelpicher Strasse, 50674 Cologne.

In the Netherlands, there's NBBS Reizen (☎ 020-620 5071, W www.nbbs.nl), 66 Rokin, Amsterdam, plus branches in most cities, and Budget Air (☎ 020-627 1251, W www.nbbs.nl), 34 Rokin, Amsterdam. Another agency, Holland International (☎ 070-307 6307), has offices in most cities.

If you're travelling from Athens to Europe, budget fares to a host of European cities are widely advertised by the travel agents around Syntagma. Following are some typical one-way fares (not including airport tax):

destination	one-way fare
Amsterdam	€170
Copenhagen	€175
Frankfurt	€165
Madrid	€220
Milan	€145
Munich	€165
Paris	€165
Rome	€125

Turkey

Olympic Airways and Turkish Airlines share the İstanbul-Athens route, with at least one flight a day each. The full fare is US$330 one way. Students qualify for a 50% discount on both airlines.

There are no direct flights from Ankara to Athens; all flights go via İstanbul.

Cyprus

Olympic Airways and Cyprus Airways share the Cyprus-Greece routes. Both airlines have three flights daily from Larnaca to Athens, and there are five flights weekly to Thessaloniki. Cyprus Airways also flies from Pafos to Athens once a week in winter, and twice a week in summer.

Asia

Most Asian countries offer fairly competitive air-fare deals with Bangkok, Singapore and Hong Kong the best places to shop around for discount tickets. Hong Kong's travel market can be unpredictable, but some excellent bargains are available if you are lucky.

Khao San Rd in Bangkok is the budget travellers' headquarters. Bangkok has a number of excellent travel agents, but there are also some suspect ones; ask the advice of other travellers before handing over your cash. STA Travel (☎ 02-236 0262), 33 Surawong Rd, is a good and reliable place to start.

In Singapore, STA Travel (☎ 65-737 7188, W www.statravel.com.sg), 35a Cuppage Road, Cuppage Terrace, offers competitive discount fares for most Asian destinations and beyond. Singapore, like Bangkok, has hundreds of travel agents, so it is possible to compare prices on flights. Chinatown Point shopping centre on New Bridge Rd has a good selection of travel agents.

Hong Kong has a number of excellent, reliable travel agencies and some that are not-so-reliable. A good way to check on a travel agent is to look it up in the phone book: fly-by-night operators don't usually stay around long enough to get listed. Phoenix Services (☎ 2722 7378, fax 2369 8884) Room B, 6th floor, Milton Mansion, 96 Nathan Rd, Tsimshatsui, is recommended. Other agencies to try are Shoestring Travel (☎ 2723 2306), Flat A, 4th floor, Alpha House, 27–33 Nathan Rd, Tsimshatsui, and Traveller Services (☎ 2375 2222), Room 1012, Silvercord Tower 1, 30 Canton Rd, Tsimshatsui.

LAND
Turkey

Bus The Hellenic Railways Organisation (OSE) operates Athens-İstanbul buses (22 hours) daily except Wednesday, leaving the Peloponnese train station in Athens at 7pm and travelling via Thessaloniki and Alexandroupolis. One-way fares are €67.50 from Athens, €44 from Thessaloniki and €15 from Alexandroupolis. Students qualify for a 20% discount and children under 12 travel for half-fare. See the Getting There & Away sections for each city for information on where to buy tickets.

Buses from İstanbul to Athens leave the Anadolu Terminal (Anatolia Terminal) at the Topkapı *otogar* (bus station) at 10am daily except Sunday.

See Alexandroupolis in the Norther Greece chapter for alternative public trans port options to Turkey.

Train There are daily trains between Athen and İstanbul (€58.70) via Thessalonik (€39) and Alexandroupolis (€19.50). Th service is incredibly slow and the train get uncomfortably crowded. There are ofte delays at the border and the journey ca take much longer than the supposed 2 hours. You'd be well advised to take th bus. Inter-Rail Passes are valid in Turkey but Eurail passes are not.

Car & Motorcycle If you're travellin between Greece and Turkey by private ve hicle, the crossing points are at Kipi, 43km north-east of Alexandroupolis, and at Kas tanies, 139km north-east of Alexandroupo lis. Kipi is probably more convenient i you're heading for İstanbul, but the rout through Kastanies goes via the fascinatin towns of Soufli and Didymotiho, i Greece, and Edirne (ancient Adrianople) i Turkey.

Bulgaria

Bus The OSE operates two Athens-Sofi buses (15 hours, €45.50) leaving at 7am and 5pm daily, except Monday. It also op erates Thessaloniki-Sofia buses (7½ hours €19, four daily). There is a private bus ser vice to Plovdiv (six hours, €32.50) an Sofia (seven hours, €32.50) from Alexan droupolis at 8.30am on Wednesday an Sunday.

Train There is an Athens-Sofia train dail (18 hours, €30.65) via Thessaloniki (nin hours, €15.60). From Sofia, there are dail connections to Budapest (€48.10) and con nections to Bucharest (€81) on Wednesda and Sunday.

Car & Motorcycle The Bulgarian borde crossing is located at Promahonas, 145km north-east of Thessaloniki and 50km from Serres.

Albania

Bus There is a daily OSE bus between Athens and Tirana (€35.20) via Ioannina and Gjirokastra. The bus departs Athens Peloponnese train station) at 7pm arriving n Tirana the following day at 5pm. It leaves oannina at 7.30am and passes through Gjirokastra at 10.30am. On the return trip, the bus departs Tirana at 7am. There are uses from Thessaloniki to Korça (Korytsa Greek) at 8am and noon daily. The fare ; €19.

Car & Motorcycle If travelling by car or notorcycle, there are two crossing points etween Greece and Albania. The main one s 60km north-west of Ioannina. Take the nain Ioannina-Konitsa road and turn left at Kalpaki. This road leads to the border town f Kakavia. The other border crossing is at Krystallopigi, 14km west of Kotas on the lorina-Kastoria road. Kapshtica is the losest town on the Albanian side. It is pos-ible to take a private vehicle into Albania, lthough it's not a great idea, because of se-urity concerns and problems with obtain-ng spare parts. Always carry your passport areas near the Albanian border.

Former Yugoslav Republic of Macedonia

Train There is a daily train from Thes-aloniki to Skopje (three hours, €12.50) t 6.15am, crossing the border between lomeni and Gevgelija. It continues from kopje to the Serbian capital of Belgrade 2 hours, €28.50).

There are no trains between Florina and YROM, although there may be some ains to Skopje from the FYROM side of he border.

Car & Motorcycle There are two border rossings between Greece and FYROM. ne is at Evzoni, 68km north of Thessa-oniki. This is the main highway to Skopje 'hich continues to Belgrade. The other order crossing is at Niki, 16km north of lorina. This road leads to Bitola, and con-nues to Ohrid, once a popular tourist re-ort on the shores of Lake Ohrid.

Western Europe

Overland travel between Western Europe and Greece is almost a thing of the past. Airfares are so cheap that land transport cannot compete. Travelling from the UK to Greece through Europe means crossing various borders, so check whether any visas are required before setting out.

Bus There are no bus services to Greece from the UK, nor from anywhere else in northern Europe. Bus companies can no longer compete with cheap airfares.

Train Unless you have a Eurail pass or are aged under 26 and eligible for a discounted fare, travelling to Greece by train is prohibi-tively expensive. Indeed, the chances of anyone wanting to travel from London to Athens by train are considered so remote that it's no longer possible to buy a single ticket for this journey. The trip involves travelling from London to Paris on the Euro-star (UK£105 to UK£165 one way), fol-lowed by Paris to Brindisi (UK£102.50 one way), then a ferry from Brindisi to Patras – and finally a train from Patras to Athens.

Greece is part of the Eurail network. Eu-rail passes can only be bought by residents of non-European countries and are sup-posed to be purchased before arriving in Europe. They can, however, be bought in Europe as long as your passport proves that you've been there for less than six months. In London, head for the Rail Europe Travel Centre (☎ 08705 848 848), 179 Piccadilly, W1. Sample fares include US$420 for an adult Eurail Selectpass, which permits eight days 1st-class travel in two months, and US$294 for the equivalent youth pass for 2nd-class travel. Check the Eurail Web site (**W** www.eurail.com) for full details of passes and prices.

If you are starting your European travels in Greece, you can buy your Eurail pass from the Hellenic Railways Organisation offices at Karolou 1 and Filellinon 17 in Athens, and at the station in Patras and Thessaloniki.

Greece is also part of the Inter-Rail Pass system, available to residents in Europe

Warning

The information in this chapter is particularly vulnerable to change: Prices for international travel are volatile, routes are introduced and cancelled, schedules change, special deals come and go, and rules and visa requirements are amended. Airlines and governments seem to take a perverse pleasure in making price structures and regulations as complicated as possible. You should check directly with the airline or a travel agent to make sure you understand how a fare (and ticket you may buy) works. In addition, the travel industry is highly competitive and there are many lurks and perks.

The upshot of this is that you should get opinions, quotes and advice from as many airlines and travel agents as possible before you part with your hard-earned cash. The details given in this chapter should be regarded as pointers and are not a substitute for your own careful, up-to-date research.

for six months or more. A one-month Global Pass (all zones) costs UK£319 for travellers over 26, and UK£229 for under 26. See the Inter-Rail Web site (**W** www .interrailnet.com) for details.

Car & Motorcycle Before the troubles in the former Yugoslavia began, most motorists driving from the UK to Greece opted for the direct route: Ostend, Brussels, Salzburg and then down the Yugoslav highway through Zagreb, Belgrade and Skopje and crossing the border to Evzoni.

These days most people drive to an Italian port and get a ferry to Greece. Coming from the UK, this means driving through France, where petrol costs and road tolls are exorbitant.

SEA
Turkey

There are five regular ferry services between Turkey's Aegean coast and the Greek islands. Tickets for all ferries to Turkey must be bought a day in advance. You will almost certainly be asked to turn in your

passport the night before the trip but don't worry, you'll get it back the next day before you board the boat. Port tax for departures to Turkey is €8.80.

See the relevant sections under individual island entries for more information about the following services.

Rhodes to Marmaris There are daily ferries from Rhodes to Marmaris (approximately €47 one way) between April and October and less frequent services in winter. Prices vary, so shop around.

The hydrofoils are cheaper. There are daily services to Marmaris (provided the weather permits) from April to October for €32.30/39.70 one way/return, plus port tax

Chios to Çeşme There are daily Chios-Çeşme boats from July to September, dropping steadily back to one boat a week in winter. Tickets cost €38.50/50 one way/ return, plus port taxes.

Kos to Bodrum There are daily ferries in summer from Kos to Bodrum (ancient Halicarnassus) in Turkey. Boats leave at 8.30am and return at 4pm. The one-hour journey costs €30 to €38 return, including port taxes.

Lesvos to Ayvalık There are up to four boats weekly on this route in high season. Tickets cost €38/47 one way/return.

Samos to Kuşadası There are two boats daily to Kuşadası (for Ephesus) from Samos in summer, dropping to one or two boats weekly in winter. Tickets cost around €41 return, plus taxes.

Italy

There are ferries to Greece from the Italian ports of Ancona, Bari, Brindisi, Trieste and Venice. For more information about these services, see the Patras, Igoumenitsa, Corfu and Kefallonia sections.

The ferries can get very crowded in summer. If you want to take a vehicle across it's a good idea to make a reservation beforehand. In the UK, reservations can be made n almost all of these ferries at Viamare Travel Ltd (☎ 020-7431 4560, fax 7431 5456, e ferries@viamare.com), 2 Sumatra Rd, London NW6 IPU.

You'll find all the latest information about ferry routes, schedules and services on the Internet. For a good overview try W www.ferries.gr. Most of the ferry companies have their own Web sites, including the following:

ANEK Lines: W www.anek.gr
Blue Star Ferries: W www.bluestarferries.com
Hellenic Mediterranean Lines:
W www.ferries.gr/hml
Italian Ferries: W www.italianferries.it
Minoan Lines: W www.minoan.gr
Superfast: W www.superfast.com
Ventouris: W www.ventouris.gr

The following ferry services are for high season (July and August), and prices are for one way deck class. Deck class on these services means exactly that. If you want a reclining, aircraft-type seat, you'll be up for another 10% to 15% on top of the listed fares. Most companies offer discounts for return travel. Prices are about 30% less in the low season.

Ancona to Patras This route has become increasingly popular in recent years. There can be up to three boats daily in summer, and at least one a day year-round. All ferry operators in Ancona have booths at the *stazione marittima* (ferry terminal) off Piazza Candy, where you can pick up timetables and price lists and make bookings.

Superfast Ferries (☎ 071-207 0218) provides the fastest and most convenient service. It has boats to Patras daily (19 hours, €78.10), and also accepts Eurail passes. Passengers pay port taxes and a high-season loading of €8.80 in July and August. ANEK Lines (☎ 071-207 2275) and Blue Star Ferries (☎ 071-207 1068) are about 20% cheaper and take a couple of hours longer. Both have daily services to Patras via Igoumenitsa. Minoan travels the route daily except Tuesday.

Bari to Corfu, Igoumenitsa & Patras Superfast Ferries (☎ 080-521 1416) operates daily to Patras (15½ hours, €51.40) via Igoumenitsa (9½ hours). It also accept Eurail passes.

Ventouris (☎ 080-521 7609) has daily boats to Corfu (10 hours, €45) and Igoumenitsa (11½ hours), and two or three boats a week to Patras (17½ hours, €46).

Brindisi to Corfu, Igoumenitsa, Patras & Paxi The route from Brindisi to Patras is the cheapest and most popular of the various Adriatic crossings. There can be up to five boats daily in high season. Most travel via Corfu and Igoumenitsa.

Companies operating ferries from Brindisi to Greece are: Blue Star Ferries (☎ 0831-548 115), Costa Morena; Five Star Lines (☎ 0831-524 869), represented by Angela Gioia Agenzia Marittima, Via F Consiglio 55; Fragline (☎ 0831-590 196), Corso Garibaldi 88; Hellenic Mediterranean Lines (☎ 0831-528 531), Corso Garibaldi 8; Med Link Lines (☎ 0831-548 116/7), represented by Discovery Shipping, Costa Morena; and Ventouris (☎ 0831-521 614), Corso Garibaldi 56.

The cheapest crossing is with Five Star Lines, which charges €42 to either Igoumenitsa (8½ hours) or Patras (15½ hours); Med Link sails the same route for €44; Blue Star Ferries has services direct to Patras (13 hours, €48.15) as well as services to Corfu (seven hours, €48.15) and Igoumenitsa (8½ hours). Hellenic Mediterranean travels to Patras (15 hours, €47) three times a week. Fragline and Ventouris Ferries have daily services to Corfu and Igoumenitsa. Most lines charge about €50 for a car, and €100 for campervans.

Blue Star Ferries and Hellenic Mediterranean accept Eurail passes, although you will still have to pay the port tax of €6.45 and a high-season loading of €8.80 in July and August. Hellenic Mediterranean issues vouchers for travel with Med Link on days when there is no Hellenic Mediterranean service.

Ventouris Ferries (see above) and Italian Ferries (☎ 0831-590 305), Corso Garibaldi 96, operate high-speed catamarans to Corfu (3¼ hours, €65). Between them, there's at least one service a day from May until early

September. From 27 July to September, both companies continue to Paxi three times a week (4¾ hours, €82.20).

Brindisi to Kefallonia Med Link stops at Sami (11 hours, €44) on its Brindisi-Patras run during August and early September.

Trieste to Patras ANEK Lines (☎ 040-322 0561), Stazione Marittima di Trieste, has daily boats to Patras (31 hours, €71.30) travelling via Igoumenitsa.

Venice to Patras Minoan Lines (☎ 041-240 7101), Stazione Marittima 123, has boats travelling from Venice to Patras (37 hours, €72.30) via Corfu and Igoumenitsa. Blue Star Ferries (☎ 041-277 0559), Stazione Marittima 123, operates to Patras (34 hours, €61.40) via Igoumenitsa four times weekly.

Albania
Much less popular than the Italy-bound ferries is the twice-daily ferry between Corfu and Agiou Saranda in Albania (one hour, €11.80). Most travellers to Albania need a visa, so it's best to investigate this before you leave home. Alternatively, Petrakis Lines (☎ 031 649) offers regular day trips to the historical areas around Agiou Saranda for around €52.80. No visa is required for this trip.

Cyprus & Israel
Two companies ply the route between Piraeus and the Israeli port of Haifa, via Lemesos (Limassol) on Cyprus. These boats also stop at Rhodes and various other Greek islands.

Salamis Lines (W www.viamare.com/Salamis) leaves Haifa at 7pm on Sunday and Lemesos at 4pm on Tuesday, reaching Rhodes at 11am on Wednesday and Piraeus at 9.30am on Thursday. The return service departs Piraeus at 7pm on Thursday, and stops at Patmos on the way to Rhodes, Lemesos and Haifa. Bookings in Haifa are handled by Rosenfeld Shipping (☎ 04-861 3670), 104 Ha'Atzmaut St, and in Lemesos by Salamis Tours (☎ 05-355 555), Salamis House, 28 October Ave.

Poseidon Lines (W www.ferries.gr/poseidon) has two services. The *Sea Serenade* sail from Haifa at 8pm on Friday and Lemesos a 2pm on Saturday, reaching Rhodes at 8am o Sunday and Piraeus at 6.30am on Monday. leaves Piraeus at 7pm on Monday, stoppin at Patmos on the way to Rhodes, Lemeso and Haifa. It switches to a different timetabl in late July and August, leaving Haifa at 8p on Thursday, and making additional stops a Iraklio (Crete) and Santorini on the way Piraeus. On the way back, it skips Patmo but calls at Mykonos, Santorini and Iraklio

Poseidon's *FB Olympia* leaves Haifa a 8pm on Monday and Lemesos at 2pm o Tuesday, reaching Rhodes at 6.30am o Wednesday and Piraeus at 7am on Thurs day. It departs Piraeus at 7pm on Thursda and stops at Patmos on the way to Rhode Lemesos and Haifa. Bookings in Haifa ar handled by Caspi Travel (☎ 04-867 4444 76 Ha'Atzmaut St, and in Lemesos by P seidon Lines Cyprus (☎ 05-745 666), 12 Franklin Roosevelt St.

Salamis and Poseidon charge the sam fares. Deck-class from Haifa costs €97 Rhodes, Iraklio and Santorini, and €10 to Piraeus. Fares from Lemesos are €62 Rhodes, Iraklio and Santorini, and €70.5 to Piraeus. Aircraft-type seats cost abo 10% more, while a berth in the cheape cabin costs about 50% more.

ORGANISED TOURS
If a package holiday of sun, sand and se doesn't appeal to you, but you would like t holiday with a group, there are several com panies that organise special-interest holiday

UK-based Explore Worldwide (☎ 012 234 4161, W www.explore.co.uk) organise reasonably priced small-group holidays whic include visits to many of Greece's ancie sites. Island Holidays (☎ 0176-477 010 specialises in cultural holidays on Crete.

There are lots of UK companies specia ising in package holidays to unspoilt are of Greece, including Laskarina (☎ 0162 824 881, W www.laskarina.co.uk), Gree Islands Club (☎ 020-8232 9780), Gree Options (☎ 020-7233 5233) and Simpl Ionian (☎ 020-8995 9323).

Getting Around

Greece is an easy place to travel around thanks to a comprehensive public transport system.

Buses are the mainstay of land transport, with a network that reaches out to the smallest villages. Trains are a good alternative, where available. To most visitors, though, travelling in Greece means island-hopping on the multitude of ferries that crisscross the Adriatic and the Aegean. If you're in a hurry, Greece also has an extensive domestic air network.

The information in this chapter was for the 2001 high season. You'll find lots of travel information on the Internet. The Web site W ellada.com is a useful site with lots of links, including airline timetables.

AIR
Domestic Air Services
Olympic Airways The vast majority of domestic flights are handled by the country's much-maligned national carrier, Olympic Airways, together with its offshoot, Olympic Aviation.

Olympic has offices wherever there are flights (see the tables below), as well as in other major towns. The head office (☎ 21 0966 6666) is at Leoforos Syngrou 96 in Athens. The toll-free number (within Greece) for reservations is ☎ 0801 44444.

The prices listed in this book are for full-fare economy, and include domestic taxes and charges (see the following Domestic Departure Tax section for details). Olympic also offers cheaper options between Athens and some of the more popular destinations such as Corfu, Iraklio, Lesvos, Rhodes and Thessaloniki. There are discounts for return tickets for travel between Monday and Thursday, and bigger discounts for trips that include a Saturday night away. You'll find full details on the Internet at W www.olympic-airways.gr, as well as information on timetables.

The baggage allowance on domestic flights is 15kg, or 20kg if the domestic

flight is part of an international journey. Olympic offers a 25% student discount on domestic flights, but only if the flight is part of an international journey.

Other Airlines Crete-based Aegean Airlines is the sole survivor of the many new airlines that emerged to challenge Olympic following the 1993 decision to end Olympic's monopoly on domestic flights.

While other airlines have come and gone, Aegean appears to have settled in for the long run following its merger with international operator Cronus Airlines in June 2001. It offers flights from Athens to Alexandroupolis, Corfu, Hania, Ioannina, Iraklio, Kavala, Lesvos, Rhodes, Santorini and Thessaloniki; from Thessaloniki to Iraklio, Lesvos, Rhodes and Santorini; and from Iraklio to Rhodes.

Full-fare economy costs slightly more than Olympic, but Aegean often has special deals. It offers a 20% youth discount for travellers under 26, and a similar discount for the over-60s.

You'll find details of prices and timetables on the Internet at W www.aegeanair.com. Aegean's toll-free number for reservations is ☎ 0801 20000.

Mainland Flights
Athens is far and away the busiest of the nine airports on the Greek mainland. The only mainland route that doesn't involve Athens is the daily Olympic Airways Thessaloniki-Ioannina service (50 minutes, €50.50). See the accompanying table for details of all Olympic flights to mainland cities from Athens (fares are one-way).

Mainland to Island Flights
Olympic Airways operates a busy schedule to the islands, particularly in summer. Athens has flights to 22 islands, with services to all the island groups as well as to three destinations on Crete – Hania, Iraklio and Sitia. Thessaloniki also has flights to all

Olympic Airways Services Within Greece

Flights from Athens to the Greek Islands (High Season)

destination	flights/week	duration	price
Astypalea	5	65 mins	€74.55
Chios	35	50 mins	€67.50
Corfu	26	50 mins	€92.45
Crete (Hania)	25	50 mins	€85.10
Crete (Iraklio)	42	60 mins	€78.95
Crete (Sitia)	3	85 mins	€83.95
Ikaria	6	50 mins	€70.30
Karpathos	3	120 mins	€96.85
Kefallonia	10	60 mins	€74.10
Kos	21	55 mins	€85.10
Kythira	6	45 mins	€61
Leros	7	65 mins	€77.50
Lesvos	29	50 mins	€80.15
Limnos	21	60 mins	€64
Milos	7	45 mins	€61.30
Mykonos	43	45 mins	€78.65
Naxos	7	45 mins	€75.45
Paros	21	45 mins	€74
Rhodes	38	60 mins	€92.45
Samos	35	60 mins	€71.60
Santorini	56	50 mins	€83.35
Skiathos	8	40 mins	€65.45
Skyros	2	50 mins	€55.50
Syros	9	35 mins	€62.80
Zakynthos	7	35 mins	€72.20

Flights from Thessaloniki to the Greek Islands (High Season)

destination	flights/week	duration	price
Chios	3	50 mins	€76.30
Corfu	3	50 mins	€73.40

the island groups except the Sporades. See the tables of summer flights (between 14 June and 26 September) from Athens and Thessaloniki to the Greek islands for details (fares given are one-way). Aegean Airlines offers cheaper fares on some of the more popular routes, so check around.

In spite of the number of flights, it can be hard to find a seat during July and August. Early bookings are recommended. Flight schedules are greatly reduced in winter, especially to Mykonos, Paros, Skiathos and Santorini.

Inter-Island Flights

Olympic and Aegean Airlines both fly the Iraklio-Rhodes route; all other flights are operated by Olympic. See the accompanying table for details.

Domestic Departure Tax

The airport tax for domestic flights is €12, paid as part of the ticket. It applies to all passengers aged over five. Passengers aged over two departing from Athens must pay an additional €7.21 for the privilege of using the facilities at the new Eleftherios

Olympic Airways Services Within Greece

Crete (Hania)	2	75 mins	€103.30
Crete (Iraklio)	3	110 mins	€97
Lesvos	6	60 mins	€76.30
Limnos	6	50 mins	€56
Mykonos	3	75 mins	€91.30
Rhodes	2	115 mins	€105.40
Samos	3	80 mins	€88

Mainland Flights from Athens

destination	flights/week	duration	price
Alexandroupolis	14	65 mins	€87.75
Ioannina	14	70 mins	€77.80
Kalamata	4	50 mins	€55.80
Kastoria	4	75 mins	€75.15
Kavala	13	60 mins	€67.20
Kozani	3	70 mins	€68.70
Preveza	5	60 mins	€60.45
Thessaloniki	70	55 mins	€92.15

Inter-Island Flights

destination	flights/week	duration	price
Chios – Lesvos	1	30 mins	€41.40
Iraklio – Rhodes	4	45 mins	€79.50
Iraklio – Santorini	2	40 mins	€56.05
Karpathos – Kasos	3	15 mins	€23.50
Karpathos – Rhodes	14	40 mins	€44.30
Kasos – Rhodes	3	40 mins	€44.30
Kastellorizo – Rhodes	7	45 mins	€35.80
Lesvos – Limnos	4	35 mins	€48.50
Mykonos – Rhodes	2	60 mins	€78.10
Mykonos – Santorini	6	30 mins	€54
Rhodes – Santorini	6	60 mins	€76.90

Venizelos International Airport, plus a security charge of €1.29. These charges also are paid as part of the ticket.

All prices quoted in this book include these taxes and charges where applicable.

BUS

All long-distance buses, on the mainland and the islands, are operated by regional collectives known as KTEL (Koino Tamio Eispraxeon Leoforion). Every prefecture on the mainland has a KTEL, which operates local services within the prefecture and services to the main towns of other prefectures. Most can be found on the Internet at W www .ktel.org. Fares are fixed by the government.

The network is comprehensive. With the exception of towns in Thrace, which are serviced by Thessaloniki, all the major towns on the mainland have frequent connections to Athens. The islands of Corfu, Kefallonia and Zakynthos can also be reached directly from Athens by bus – the fares include the price of the ferry ticket.

Most villages have a daily bus service of some sort, although remote areas may have only one or two buses a week. They operate for the benefit of people going to town to shop, rather than for tourists. They normally leave the villages very early in the morning and return early in the afternoon.

On islands where the capital is inland rather than a port, buses normally meet the boats. Some of the more remote islands have not yet acquired a bus, but most have some sort of motorised transport – even if it is only a bone-shaking, three-wheeled truck.

Larger towns usually have a central, covered bus station with seating, waiting rooms, toilets, and a snack bar selling pies, cakes and coffee. Big cities like Athens, Iraklio, Patras and Thessaloniki have several bus stations, each serving different regions.

In small towns and villages the 'bus station' may be no more than a bus stop outside a *kafeneio* or taverna which doubles as a booking office. In remote areas, the timetable may be in Greek only, but most booking offices have timetables in both Greek and Roman script. The timetables give both the departure and return times – useful if you are making a day trip. Times are listed using the 24-hour clock system.

When you buy a ticket you will be allotted a seat number, which is noted on the ticket. The seat number is indicated on the back of each seat of the bus, not on the back of the seat in front; this can cause confusion among Greeks and tourists alike. You can board a bus without a ticket and pay on board, but on a popular route, or during the high season, this may mean that you have to stand. Keep your ticket for the duration of the journey; it will be checked several times en route.

It's best to turn up at least 20 minutes before departure to make sure you get a seat. Buses have been known to leave a few minutes before their scheduled departure time – another reason to give yourself plenty of time. Check the destination with the driver before you board the bus, and ensure your luggage has been placed in the hold.

Buses do not have toilets on board and they don't have refreshments available, so make sure you are prepared on both counts. Buses stop about every three hours on long journeys. Smoking is prohibited on all buses in Greece; only the drivers dare to ignore the no-smoking signs.

Bus fares are reasonably priced, with a journey costing approximately €4 per 100km. Fares and journey times on some of the major routes are: Athens-Thessaloniki, 7½ hours, €26.40; Athens-Patras, three hours, €11.75; Athens-Volos, five hours, €17; and Athens-Corfu, 11 hours, €26.70 (including ferry).

TRAIN

The Greek Railways Organisation, OSE (Organismos Sidirodromon Ellados), is gradually getting its act together and modernising its creaky rolling stock; but train travel in Greece is still viewed by most people as a poor alternative to road travel.

For starters, the rail system is not huge. There are essentially two main, standard-gauge lines: Athens to Thessaloniki and Thessaloniki to Alexandroupolis. The Peloponnese system uses a narrow-gauge track.

There are also two very distinct levels of service: the slow, stopping-all-stations services that crawl around the countryside, and the faster, modern intercity trains that link most major cities.

The slow trains represent the country's cheapest form of public transport: 2nd-class fares are absurdly cheap, and even 1st class is cheaper than bus travel. The downside is that the trains are painfully slow, uncomfortable and unreliable. There seems to be no effort to upgrade the dilapidated rolling stock on these services. Unless you are travelling on a very tight budget, they are best left alone – except on shorter runs. Sample journey times and fares on these trains include Athens-Thessaloniki, 7½ hours, €21/14 (1st/2nd class); Athens-Patras, five hours, €7.95/5.30; and Thessaloniki-Alexandroupolis, seven hours, €14.60/9.70.

The intercity trains which link the major Greek cities are a much better way to travel. The services are not necessarily express – the Greek terrain is far too mountainous for that – but the trains are modern and comfortable. Available are 1st- and 2nd-class smoking/non-smoking seats and there is a cafe-bar on board. On some services, meals can be ordered and delivered to your seat.

Ticket prices for intercity services are subject to a distance loading charged on top of the normal fares. Seat reservations should be made as far in advance as possible, especially during summer. Sample journey times and fares include Athens-Thessaloniki, six hours, €37.30/27.60 (1st/2nd class); Thessaloniki-Alexandroupolis, 5½ hours, €21.90/16.20; and Athens-Patras, 3½ hours, €13.80/10.

A comfortable night service runs between Athens and Thessaloniki, with a choice of couchettes (from €5.90), two-bed compartments (€19) and single compartments (€29.35).

Eurail and Inter-Rail cards are valid in Greece, but it's not worth buying one if Greece is the only place you plan to use it. The passes can be used for 2nd-class travel on intercity services without paying the loading.

Another option if you're planning on using the trains a lot is to buy a tourist rail pass, which is available for individual passengers, as well as for families and groups of up to five people. Passes are valid for 10, 20 or 30 days and entitle the holder to make an unlimited number of journeys on all the rail routes. An individual pass costs €43.15 for 10 days, €72.20 for 20 days and €92.30 for 30 days. Whatever pass you have, you must have a reservation. You cannot board a train without one.

Senior cards are available to passengers over 60 years of age on presentation of their IDs or passports. They cost €82.50 for 1st-class travel and €54.90 for 2nd class, and are valid for one year from the date of issue. Cardholders get a 50% reduction on train travel, plus five free journeys per year.

Tickets can be bought from OSE booking offices in a few major towns, otherwise from train stations. There is a 30% discount on return tickets, and a 30% discount for groups of 10 or more.

You'll find information on fares and schedules on the Hellenic Railways Organization Web site, W www.ose.gr.

CAR & MOTORCYCLE

No-one who has travelled on Greece's roads will be surprised to hear that the country's road fatality rate is the highest in Europe. More than 2000 people die on the roads every year, with overtaking listed as the greatest cause of accidents. Ever-stricter traffic laws have had little impact on the toll; Greek roads remain a good place to practise your defensive-driving techniques.

Heart-stopping moments aside, your own car is a great way to explore off the beaten track. The road network has improved enormously in recent years; many roads marked as dirt tracks on older maps have now been asphalted – particularly in remoter parts of Epiros and the Peloponnese. It's important to get a good road map (see the Maps section in the Facts for the Visitor chapter).

Greece is not the best place to initiate yourself into motorcycling. There are still a lot of gravel roads – particularly on the islands. Novices should be very careful; dozens of tourists have accidents every year.

There are seven stretches of highway in Greece where tolls are levied. They are Athens-Corinth, Corinth-Patras, Corinth-Tripolis, Athens-Lamia, Lamia-Larisa, Larisa-Thessaloniki and Thessaloniki-Evzoni. Sample tolls include €1.50 from Athens to Corinth and €1.80 from Corinth to Patras.

Almost all islands are served by car ferries, but they are expensive. Sample prices for small vehicles include Piraeus-Mykonos, €57.25; Piraeus-Crete (Hania and Iraklio), €61.65; and Piraeus-Rhodes, €76.30. The charge for a large motorbike is about the same as the price of a 3rd-class passenger ticket.

Petrol in Greece is expensive, and the farther you get from a major city the more it costs. Prices vary from petrol station to petrol station. Super can be found as cheaply as €0.70 per litre at big city discount places, but €0.75 to €0.85 is the normal range. You may pay closer to €0.90 per litre in remote areas. The price range for unleaded – available everywhere – is from €0.75 to €0.85 per litre. Diesel costs about €0.60 per litre.

Phone numbers listed incorporate changes due in Oct 2002; see p83

See the Visas & Documents section in the Facts for the Visitor chapter for information on licence requirements.

See Useful Organisations in the Facts for the Visitor chapter for information about the Greek automobile club (ELPA).

Warning If you are planning to use a motorcycle or moped, check that your travel insurance covers you for injury resulting from a motorbike accident. Many insurance companies don't offer this cover, so check the fine print!

Road Rules

In Greece, as throughout Continental Europe, you drive on the right and overtake on the left. Outside built-up areas, traffic on a main road has right of way at intersections. In towns, vehicles coming from the right have right of way. Seat belts must be worn in front seats, and in back seats if the car is fitted with them. Children under 12 years of age are not allowed in the front seat. It is compulsory to carry a first-aid kit, fire extinguisher and warning triangle, and it is forbidden to carry cans of petrol. Helmets are compulsory for motorcyclists if the motorbike is 50cc or more.

Outside residential areas the speed limit is 120km/h on highways, 90km/h on other roads and 50km/h in built-up areas. The speed limit for motorbikes up to 100cc is 70km/h and for larger motorbikes, 90km/h.

Drivers exceeding the speed limit by 20% are liable to receive a fine of €58.70; and by 40%, €147. In practice, most tourists escape with a warning. Other offences and fines include:

illegal overtaking: €293.50
going through a red light: €293.50
driving without a seat belt: €147.75
motorcyclist not wearing a helmet: €147.75
wrong way down one-way street: €147.75
illegal parking: €29.35

The police have also cracked down on drink-driving laws – at last. A blood-alcohol content of 0.05% is liable to incur a fine of €147.75, and over 0.08% is a criminal offence.

If you are involved in an accident and no-one is hurt, the police will not be required to write a report, but it is advisable to go to a nearby police station and explain what happened. A police report may be required for insurance purposes. If an accident involves injury, a driver who does not stop and does not inform the police may face a prison sentence.

Rental

Car If the deadly driving has not put you off getting behind a wheel in Greece, then perhaps the price of hiring a car will. Rental cars are widely available, but they are more expensive than in most other European countries. Most of the big multinational car-hire companies are represented in Athens and large towns, on large islands and at international airports. The smaller islands often have only one car-hire outlet.

The multinationals are, however, the most expensive places to hire a car. High-season weekly rates with unlimited mileage start at about €380 for the smallest models, such as a Fiat Seicento. The rate drops to about €300 per week in winter. To these prices must be added VAT of 18%, or 13% on the islands of the Dodecanese, the North-Eastern Aegean and the Sporades. Then there are the optional extras, such as a collision damage waiver of €10.30 per day (more for larger models), without which you will be liable for the first €4400 of the repair bill (much more for larger models). Other costs include a theft waiver of at least €4.40 per day and personal accident insurance. It all adds up to an expensive exercise. The major companies offer much cheaper prebooked and prepaid rates.

You can find much better deals at some of the local companies. Their advertised rates can be up to 50% cheaper, and they are normally more open to negotiation, especially if business is slow.

If you want to take a hire car to another country or onto a ferry, you will need advance written authorisation from the hire company. Unless you pay with a credit card, most hire companies will require a minimum deposit of €120 per day. See the

Road Distances (km)

	Alexandroupolis	Athens	Corinth	Edessa	Florina	Igoumenitsa	Ioannina	Kalamata	Kastoria	Kavala	Lamia	Larisa	Monemvasia	Nafplio	Patra	Pyrgos	Sparta	Thessaloniki	Trikala	Tripolis	Volos
Alexandroupolis	---																				
Athens	464	---																			
Corinth	884	84	---																		
Edessa	441	569	596	---																	
Florina	497	592	251	353	---																
Igoumenitsa	816	473	393	380	353	---															
Ioannina	716	447	364	298	320	96	---														
Kalamata	1064	284	175	767	763	501	467	---													
Kastoria	535	489	519	108	67	286	204	690	---												
Kavala	177	682	655	250	320	615	525	878	358	---											
Lamia	643	214	244	355	360	353	263	415	274	466	---										
Larisa	503	361	389	218	309	305	209	561	239	323	151	---									
Monemvasia	1156	350	266	869	855	613	579	156	756	976	505	655	---								
Nafplio	947	165	63	659	664	482	427	163	582	770	307	455	215	---							
Patra	844	220	138	567	513	281	247	220	483	664	193	341	332	201	---						
Pyrgos	944	320	234	636	643	367	347	119	542	747	284	432	275	208	96	---					
Sparta	1060	225	145	737	759	517	483	60	660	848	385	533	96	119	236	180	---				
Thessaloniki	349	513	544	89	159	452	362	715	220	169	303	154	807	610	488	584	711	---			
Trikala	346	330	356	227	233	247	148	520	159	377	115	62	597	419	310	400	501	216	---		
Tripolis	964	194	110	713	681	457	430	90	639	820	324	472	157	81	176	155	61	624	466	---	
Volos	556	326	355	278	293	371	271	518	301	383	115	62	620	417	308	408	524	214	124	435	---

Getting Around sections of cities and islands for details of places to rent cars.

The minimum driving age in Greece is 18 years, but most car-hire firms require you to be at least 21 – or 23 for larger vehicles.

Motorcycle Mopeds and motorcycles are available for hire wherever there are tourists to rent them. In many cases their maintenance has been minimal, so check the machine thoroughly before you hire it – especially the brakes: you'll need them!

Motorbikes are a cheap way to travel round. Rates range from €10 to €15 per day for a moped or 50cc motorbike to €25 per day for a 250cc motorbike. Out of season these prices drop considerably, so use our bargaining skills. By October it is sometimes possible to hire a moped for as little as €5 per day. Most motorcycle hirers include third-party insurance in the price, but it's wise to check this. This insurance will not include medical expenses.

BICYCLE

Cycling has not caught on in Greece, which isn't surprising considering the hilly terrain. Tourists are beginning to cycle in Greece, but you'll need strong leg muscles. You can hire bicycles in most tourist places, but they are not as widely available as cars and motorbikes. Prices range from €5.90 to €12 per day, depending on the type and age of the bike. Bicycles are carried free on ferries.

HITCHING

Hitching is never entirely safe in any country in the world, and we don't recommend it. Travellers who decide to hitch should understand that they are taking a small but potentially serious risk. People who do choose to hitch will be safer if they travel in pairs and should let someone know where they are planning to go. Greece has a reputation for being a relatively safe place for women to hitch, but it is still unwise to do it alone. It's better for a woman to hitch with a companion, preferably a male one.

Some parts of Greece are much better for hitching than others. Getting out of major cities tends to be hard work, and Athens is notoriously difficult. Hitching is much easier in remote areas and on islands with poor public transport. On country roads, it is not unknown for someone to stop and ask if you want a lift even if you haven't stuck a thumb out.

WALKING

Unless you have come to Greece just to lie on a beach, the chances are you will do quite a bit of walking. You don't have to be a trekker to start clocking up the kilometres. The narrow, stepped streets of many towns and villages can only be explored on foot, and visiting the archaeological sites involves a fair amount of legwork. See the What to Bring, Health and Trekking sections in the Facts for the Visitor chapter for more information about walking.

BOAT
Ferry

For most people, travel in Greece means island-hopping. Every island has a ferry service of some sort, although in winter services to some of the smaller islands are fairly skeletal. Services start to pick up again from April onwards, and by July and August there are countless services crisscrossing the Aegean. Ferries come in all shapes and sizes, from the giant 'superferries' that work the major routes to the small, ageing open ferries that chug around the backwaters.

Routes The hub of Greece's ferry network is Piraeus, the port of Athens. Ferries leave here for the Cyclades, Dodecanese, the North-Eastern Aegean Islands, Saronic Gulf Islands and Crete. Athens' second port is Rafina, 70km east of the city and connected by an hourly bus service. It has ferries to the northern Cyclades, Evia, Lesvos and Limnos. The port of Lavrio, in southern Attica, is the main port for ferries to the Cycladic island of Kea. There are regular buses from Athens to Lavrio.

Ferries for the Ionian Islands leave from the Peloponnese ports of Patras (for Kefallonia, Ithaki, Paxi and Corfu) and Kyllini (for Kefallonia and Zakynthos); from Astakos (for Ithaki and Kefallonia) and Mytikas (for Lefkada and Meganisi), both in Sterea Ellada; and from Igoumenitsa in Epiros (for Corfu).

Ferries for the Sporades leave from Volos, Thessaloniki, Agios Konstantinos, and Kymi on Evia. The latter two ports are easily reached by bus from Athens.

Some of the North-Eastern Aegean Islands have connections with Thessaloniki as well as Piraeus. The odd ones out are Thasos, which is reached from Kavala, and Samothraki, which can be reached from Alexandroupolis year-round and also from Kavala in summer.

Schedules Ferry timetables change from year to year and season to season, and ferries can be subject to delays and cancellations at short notice due to bad weather, strikes or the boats simply conking out. No timetable is infallible, but the comprehensive weekly list of departures from Piraeus put out by the EOT in Athens is as accurate as is humanly possible. The people to go to for the most up-to-date ferry information are the local port police *(limenarheio)*, whose offices are usually located on or near the quay side.

There's lots of information about ferry services available on the Internet. Try W www.ferries.gr, which has a useful search program and links. Many of the larger ferry companies have their own sites, including:

ANEK: W www.anek.gr
Minoan Lines: W www.minoan.gr
Strintzis: W www.strintzis.gr
Superfast: W www.superfast.com
Ventouris: W www.ventouris.gr

Throughout the year there is at least one ferry a day from a mainland port to the major island in each group, and during the high season (from June to mid-September) there are considerably more. Ferries sailing from one island group to another are not so

GREECE - MAIN FERRY ROUTES

requent, and if you're going to travel in his way you'll need to plan carefully, otherwise you may end up having to back-rack to Piraeus.

Travelling time can vary considerably from one ferry to another, depending on how many islands are called in at on the way to your destination. For example, the Piraeus-Rhodes trip can take between 15 and 18 hours depending on which route is taken. Before buying your ticket, check how many stops the boat is going to make, and its estimated arrival time. It can make a big difference.

Costs Prices are government fixed, and determined by the distance travelled rather than by the facilities of a particular boat. There can be big differences in the size, comfort and facilities of boats offering rival services on a given route, but the fares will be the same.

The small differences in price you may find at ticket agencies are the results of some agents sacrificing part of their designated commission to qualify as a 'discount service'. The discount is seldom more than €0.30. Ticket prices include embarkation tax, a contribution to NAT (the seamen's union) and 8% VAT.

Phone numbers listed incorporate changes due in Oct 2002; see p83

Classes The large ferries usually have four classes: 1st class has air-con cabins and a posh lounge and restaurant; 2nd class has smaller cabins and sometimes a separate lounge; tourist class gives you a berth in a shared four-berth cabin; and 3rd (deck) class gives you access to a room with 'airline' seats, a restaurant, a lounge/bar and, of course, the deck.

Deck class remains an economical way to travel, while a 1st-class ticket can cost almost as much as flying on some routes. Children under four travel for free, while children between four and 10 pay half fare. Full fares apply for children over 10. Unless you state otherwise, when purchasing a ticket, you will automatically be given deck class. Prices quoted in this book are for deck class as this is the most popular with tourists.

Ticket Purchase Given that ferries are prone to delays and cancellations, it's best not to purchase a ticket until it has been confirmed that the ferry is leaving. If you need to reserve a car space, however, you may need to pay in advance. If the service is then cancelled you can transfer your ticket to the next available service with that company.

Agencies selling tickets line the waterfront of most ports, but rarely is there one that sells tickets for every boat, and often an agency is reluctant to give you information about a boat they do not sell tickets for. This means you have to check the timetables displayed outside each agency to find out which ferry is next to depart – or ask the port police.

In high season, a number of boats may be due at a port at around the same time, so it is not beyond the realms of possibility that you might get on the wrong boat. The crucial thing to look out for is the name of the boat; this will be printed on your ticket, and in large English letters on the side of the vessel.

If for some reason you haven't purchased a ticket from an agency, makeshift ticket tables are put up beside a ferry about an hour before departure. Tickets can also be purchased on board the ship after it has sailed. If you are waiting at the quayside for a delayed ferry, don't lose patience and wander off. Ferry boats, once they turn up can demonstrate amazing alacrity – blink and you may miss the boat.

Ferry Travel Once on board, the fun really begins. It can be absolute chaos in high season. No matter how many passengers are already on the ferry, more will be crammed on. Bewildered, black-shrouded grannies are steered through the crowd by teenage grandchildren, children get separated from parents and people stumble over backpacks and overloaded suitcases as everyone rushes to grab a seat.

Greeks travelling deck class usually make a beeline for the indoor lounge/snack bar, while tourists make for the deck where they can sunbathe. Some ferry companies have allegedly attempted to capitalise on this natural division by telling backpackers and non-Greeks that they are barred from the deck-class saloon and indoor-seating area, directing them instead to the sun deck. There is no such thing as 'deck only' class on domestic ferries, although there is on international ferries.

All ferries now provide nonsmoking areas, although they are often next to smoking areas – or right in the middle of them.

On overnight trips, backpackers usually sleep on deck in their sleeping bags – you can also roll out your bag between the 'airline' seats. If you don't have a sleeping bag, claim an 'airline' seat as soon as you board. Leave your luggage on it – as long as you don't leave any valuables in it. The noise on board usually dies down around midnight so you should be able to snatch a few hours of sleep.

The food sold at ferry snack bars ranges from mediocre to inedible, and the choice is limited to packets of biscuits, sandwiches, very greasy pizzas and cheese pies. Most large ferries also have a self-service restaurant where the food is OK and reasonably priced, with main courses starting at around €5. However, if you are budgeting, have special dietary requirements, or are at all fussy about what you eat, take your own food with you.

Inter-Island Boat

In addition to the large ferries which ply between the large mainland ports and island groups, there are smaller boats which link islands within a group, and occasionally, an island in one group with an island in another.

In the past these boats were always caiques – sturdy old fishing boats – but gradually these are being replaced by new purpose-built boats, which are usually called express or excursion boats. Tickets tend to cost more than tickets for the large ferries, but the boats are very useful if you're island-hopping.

Hydrofoil

Hydrofoils offer a faster alternative to ferries on some routes, particularly to islands close to the mainland. They take half the time, but cost twice as much. They do not take cars or motorbikes. Most routes operate only during high season, and according to demand, and all are prone to cancellations if the sea is rough. The ride can be bumpy at the best of times.

The biggest operator is Minoan Flying Dolphin, which runs the busy Argosaronic network linking Piraeus with the Saronic Gulf Islands and the ports of the eastern Peloponnese (plus occasional services south to the Ionian island of Kythira). Minoan also operates hydrofoils from Piraeus and Rafina to the eastern Cyclades, and from Agios Konstantinos, Thessaloniki and Volos to Evia and the Sporades.

Hydrofoil services in the eastern and south Cyclades are operated by Speed Lines out of Santorini. These Santorini Dolphins operate daily between Santorini, Ios, Naxos, Paros, Tinos and Syros, with services to Folegandros, Sikinos and Milos once or twice weekly – and occasional services to Iraklio on Crete.

The Dodecanese has its own network, centred on Rhodes, and connections to the North-Eastern Aegean islands of Ikaria and Samos. Other routes are between Kavala and Thasos in the North-Eastern Aegean, and from Alexandroupolis to Samothraki and Limnos.

Tickets cannot be bought on board hydrofoils – you must buy them in advance from an agent. You will be allocated a seat number.

Catamaran

High-speed catamarans have rapidly become an important part of the island travel scene. They are just as fast as the hydrofoils – if not faster – and much more comfortable. They are also much less prone to cancellation in rough weather.

Minoan again is the major player. It operates giant, vehicle-carrying, Highspeed cats from Piraeus and Rafina to the Cyclades, and smaller Flying Cats from Rafina to the central and northern Cyclades and on many of the routes around the Saronic Gulf.

Strintzis Lines uses its Seajet catamarans on the run from Rafina to Syros, Paros, Naxos, Ios and Santorini. It also operates to Tinos and Mykonos, stopping once a week at Andros, Syros, Paros, Naxos and Amorgos.

These services are very popular; book as far in advance as possible, especially if you want to travel on weekends.

Taxi Boat

Most islands have taxi boats – small speedboats which operate like taxis, transporting people to places that are difficult to get to by land. Some owners charge a set price for each person, others charge a flat rate for the boat, and this cost is divided by the number of passengers. Either way, prices are usually quite reasonable.

Yacht

Despite the disparaging remarks among backpackers, yachting is *the* way to see the Greek islands. Nothing beats the experience of sailing the open sea, and the freedom of being able to visit remote and uninhabited islands.

The free EOT booklet *Sailing the Greek Seas*, although long overdue for an update, contains lots of information about weather conditions, weather bulletins, entry and exit regulations, entry and exit ports and guidebooks for yachties. You can pick up the booklet at any GNTO/EOT office either abroad or in Greece.

If your budget won't cover buying a yacht, there are several other options open to you. You can hire a bare boat (a yacht without a crew) if two crew members have a sailing certificate. Prices start at US$1300 per week for a 28-footer that will sleep six. It will cost an extra US$800 per week to hire a skipper. Some yacht-charter companies operating in and around Athens and Piraeus are listed here (contact the EOT for others).

Aegean Tourism (☎ 21 0346 6229,
　fax 21 0342 2121, W www.aegeantours.gr)
　Kadmias 8, Athens
Alpha Yachting (☎ 21 0968 0486,
　fax 21 0968 0488, e mano@otenet.gr)
　Poseidonos 67, Glyfada
Amphitrion Yachting (☎ 21 0411 2045, fax 21
　0417 0742, e amphitship@travelling.gr,
　W www.amphitrion.gr/yachting) Merarchias 3,
　Piraeus
Ghiolman Yachts & Travel (☎ 21 0323 3696,
　fax 21 0322 3251, e ghiolman@travelling.gr)
　Filellinon 7, Athens
Hellenic Charters (☎/fax 21 0988 5592,
　e hctsa@ath.forthnet.gr) Poseidonos 66,
　Alimos

LOCAL TRANSPORT
To/From Airports
Olympic Airways operates buses to a few domestic airports (see individual entries in the appropriate chapters). Where the service exists, buses leave the airline office about 1½ hours before departure. In many places, the only way to get to the airport is by taxi. Check-in is an hour before departure for domestic flights. Transport to international airports in Greece is covered in the Getting Around section of the relevant city.

Bus
Most Greek towns are small enough to get around on foot. The only places where you may need to use local buses are Athens, Piraeus and Thessaloniki. The procedure for buying tickets for local buses is covered in the Getting Around section for each city.

Metro
Athens is the only city in Greece large enough to warrant the building of an underground system. See the Athens chapter for news of the latest developments in the metro extension program.

Taxi
Taxis are widely available in Greece except on very small or remote islands. They are reasonably priced by European standards, especially if three or four people share costs.

Yellow city cabs are metered. Flagfall is €0.74, followed by €0.24 per kilometre (€0.44 per kilometre outside town). These rates double between midnight and 5am. Costs additional to the per-kilometre rate are €1.18 from an airport, €0.59 from a bus, port or train station and €0.30 for each piece of luggage over 10kg. Grey rural taxis do not have meters, so you should always settle on a price before you get in.

The taxi drivers of Athens are legendary for their ability to part locals and tourists alike from their money – see the 'Dangers & Annoyances' boxed text in the Athens chapter. If you have a complaint about a taxi driver, take the cab number and report your complaint to the tourist police. Taxi drivers in other towns in Greece are, on the whole, friendly, helpful and honest.

ORGANISED TOURS
Tours are worth considering only if your time is very limited, in which case there are countless companies vying for your money. The major players are CHAT, GO Tours, Hop In Sightseeing and Key Tours, all based in Athens and offering almost identical tours. They include day trips to Delphi (€72) and Mycenae and Epidaurus (€72). They also offer longer trips such as a four-day tour calling at Mycenae, Nafplio, Epidaurus, Olympia and Delphi (€90 per day). These prices include twin share accommodation and half-board. See Organised Tours in the Athens chapter.

Organised Treks
Trekking Hellas (☎ 21 0331 0323-6, fax 21 0324 4548, e info@trekking.gr, W www .trekking.gr), at Filellinon 7, Athens 105 57, is a well-established company which specialises in doing treks and other adventure

activities for small groups. It offers a wide range of treks lasting from four to nine days and graded from introductory to challenging. It has fairly easy introductory walks in the foothills of Taygetos Mountains in the Peloponnese, on the Ionian island of Ithaki and on the Cycladic islands of Andros and Tinos.

The treks around Meteora and the Pelion Peninsula are a bit more demanding, while only fit, experienced walkers should attempt the challenging treks in the Pindos Ranges and to the summits of Mt Olympus. Other activities include canoeing, river-rafting (available January–April), canyoning and cycling. Information is available about these and other activities as well as the range of prices on the Trekking Hellas Web site.

Athens Αθήνα

postcode 102 00 (Omonia),
103 00 (Syntagma) • pop 3.7 million

The perpetual 'high' that novelist Henry Miller experienced during his travels in Greece did not flag when he came to the capital. In *The Colossus of Maroussi*, Miller waxed lyrical about the extraordinary quality of the city's light and rhythm. Few visitors today, however, share his bubbling enthusiasm. Most beat a hasty retreat after the obligatory visit to the Acropolis and the National Archaeological Museum. Despite its glorious past and its enduring influence on Western civilisation, it is a city that few fall in love with. Modern Athens is a vast concrete urban sprawl that suffers badly from the curse of the modern age: pollution.

To appreciate Athens (in Greek, Athina), it's important to be aware of the city's traumatic history. Unlike most capital cities, Athens does not have a history of continuous expansion; it is one characterised by glory, followed by decline and near annihilation, and then resurgence in the 19th century – when it became the capital of independent Greece.

The historical event that, more than any other, shaped the Athens of today was the compulsory population exchange between Greece and Turkey that followed the signing of the Treaty of Lausanne in July 1923. The population of Athens virtually doubled overnight, necessitating the hasty erection of concrete apartment blocks to house the newcomers.

The expansion of Athens in all directions began at this time, and accelerated during the 1950s and '60s when the country began the transition from an agricultural to an industrial nation. Young people began to flock to the city from the islands and rural areas, and this trend has continued ever since.

Athens has many redeeming qualities. The city is bounded on three sides by Mt Parnitha (1413m), Mt Pendeli (1109m) and Mt Hymettos (1026m). The latter was once

Highlights

- The inspirational Acropolis (and outdoor dining below it)
- The treasures of the National Archaeological Museum
- Panoramic views from Lykavittos Hill
- The lively rembetika clubs
- Sunset over the sea at Cape Sounion

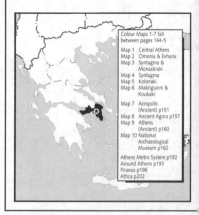

Colour Maps 1-7 fall between pages 144-5

Map 1 Central Athens
Map 2 Omonia & Exharia
Map 3 Syntagma & Monastiraki
Map 4 Syntagma
Map 5 Kolonaki
Map 6 Makrigianni & Koukaki
Map 7 Acropolis (Ancient) p151
Map 8 Ancient Agora p157
Map 9 Athens (Ancient) p160
Map 10 National Archaeological Museum p162
Athens Metro System p192
Around Athens p193
Piraeus p196
Attica p202

famed for its violet sunsets – these days normally obliterated by the city's appalling pollution. At least one of these mountains can be glimpsed from almost every street in Athens.

Within the city there are no less than eight hills, of which the most prominent are Lykavittos (277m) and the Acropolis (156m). These hills are a pleasant escape from the traffic-congested streets. Athens improves considerably when viewed from a height, and there are stunning views over the city to the glistening waters of the Saronic Gulf – its boundary to the south.

Perhaps most significant of all is the fact that wherever you are in the centre of the city, the Acropolis, with its transcendent and compelling aura, stands proudly on the skyline. It serves as a constant reminder that whatever trials and tribulations might have befallen the city, its status as the birthplace of Western civilisation is beyond doubt.

SUGGESTED ITINERARIES
One Week

Combine a walking tour of Plaka with a visit to the Acropolis (one day); visit the National Archaeological Museum (one day); day-trip to Cape Sounion (one day); climb up Lykavittos Hill in the early morning followed by visits to the Goulandris Museum of Cycladic & Ancient Greek Art and the Byzantine Museum (one day); day-trip to Elefsina, stopping at Moni Dafniou on the way (one day); visit the Ancient Agora and the Keramikos (one day); day-trip to Moni Kaissarianis (one day). Evening activities to schedule in include the Dora Stratou folk dancers on Filopappos Hill; summer performances of ancient Greek drama at the Theatre of Herodes Atticus; and a visit to a rembetika club.

HISTORY
Early History

The early history of Athens is inextricably interwoven with mythology, making it impossible to disentangle fact from fiction. What is known, though, is that the hilltop site of the Acropolis, endowed with two bounteous springs, drew some of Greece's earliest Neolithic settlers. When a peaceful agricultural existence gave way to the war-orientated city-states, the Acropolis provided an ideal defensive position: its steep slopes formed natural defences on three sides and it was an excellent vantage point from which to spot danger approaching from land or sea.

By 1400 BC, the Acropolis had become a powerful Mycenaean city. Unlike the cities of Mycenae, Pylos and Tiryns, it survived the Dorian assault on Greece in 1200 BC. It couldn't, however, escape the dark age that enveloped Greece for the next 400 years, and very little is known of this period.

After its emergence from the dark age in the 8th century BC, a period of peace followed, both for Athens and the surrounding united towns. During this time the city became the artistic centre of Greece, excelling

Athena & the Olive Tree

According to mythology, Cecrops, a Phoenician, came to Attica, where he founded a city on a huge rock near the sea. The gods of Olympus proclaimed that the city should be named after the deity who could produce the most valuable legacy for mortals. Athena (goddess of wisdom) and Poseidon (god of the sea) contended. Athena produced an olive tree, symbol of peace and prosperity. Poseidon struck a rock with his trident and a horse sprang forth, which symbolised all the qualities of strength and fortitude for which he was renowned. Athena was the victor, for the gods proclaimed that her gift would better serve the citizens of Athens than the arts of war personified by Poseidon's gift.

in ceramics. The geometric designs of vases from the dark ages evolved into a narrative style, depicting scenes from everyday life and mythology. This pottery subsequently became known as the Proto-Attic style.

By the 6th century BC, Athens was ruled by aristocrats, generals and the *arhon* (chief magistrate). A person's position in the hierarchy depended on their wealth, which was gained either from commerce or agriculture. Labourers and peasants had no say at all in the functioning of the city – until the reform-oriented Solon became arhon in 594 BC.

Solon did much to improve the lot of the poor and is regarded as the harbinger of Athenian democracy. His most significant reforms were the annulment of all debts and the implementation of trial by jury. Continuing unrest over the reforms created the pretext for the tyrant Peisistratos, formerly head of the military, to seize power in 560 BC.

Peisistratos built up a formidable navy, much to the consternation of other city-states, and extended the boundaries of Athenian influence on land. He was a patron of the arts as well as a general, inaugurating the Festival of the Great Dionysia, which was the precursor of Attic drama, and commissioning many splendid sacred and secular buildings – most of which were

Phone numbers listed incorporate changes due in Oct 2002; see p83

destroyed by the Persians on the eve of the Battle of Salamis in 480 BC.

Peisistratos was succeeded by his son Hippias, who was very much a tyrant. Athens managed to rid itself of this oppressor in 510 BC only by swallowing its pride and accepting the help of Sparta. Hippias wasn't finished, however, heading off to Persia to stir up trouble and returning with Darius 20 years later to be defeated at the Battle of Marathon.

Athens' Golden Age

After Athens had finally repulsed the challenge of the Persian Empire at the battles of Salamis and Plataea (again, with the help of Sparta), its power knew no bounds.

In 477 BC Athens established a confederacy on the sacred island of Delos and demanded tributes from the surrounding islands to protect them from the Persians. It was little more than a standover racket because the Persians were no longer much of a threat. The treasury was moved to Athens in 461 BC and Pericles (ruler from 461 to 429 BC) used the money to transform the city. The period has become known as Athens' golden age, the pinnacle of the classical era.

Most of the monuments on the Acropolis today date from this time. Drama and literature flourished in the form of the tragedies written by Aeschylus, Sophocles and Euripides. The sculptors Pheidias and Myron and the historians Herodotus, Thucydides and Xenophon also lived at this time.

Rivalry with Sparta

Arch rival Sparta wasn't prepared to sit back and allow Athens to revel in its newfound glory. The increasing jockeying for power between the two led to the outbreak of the Peloponnesian Wars in 431 BC. The warring dragged on until 404 BC, when Sparta gained the upper hand. Athens was never to return to its former glory. The 4th century BC did, however, produce three of the West's greatest orators and philosophers: Socrates, Plato and Aristotle. The degeneracy into which Athens had fallen was perhaps epitomised by the ignominious death sentence passed on Socrates for the crime of corrupting the young with his speeches.

Athens' days of glory were now numbered. In 338 BC, along with the other city-states of Greece, Athens was conquered by Philip II of Macedon. After Philip's assassination, his son Alexander the Great, a cultured young man, favoured Athens over other city-states. After his untimely death, Athens passed in quick succession through the hands of several of his generals.

Roman & Byzantine Rule

Athens continued to be a major seat of learning under Roman rule, and many wealthy young Romans attended Athens' schools. Anybody who was anybody in Rome at the time spoke Greek. The Roman emperors, particularly Hadrian, graced Athens with many grand buildings.

After the subdivision of the Roman Empire into east and west, Athens remained an important cultural and intellectual centre until Emperor Justinian closed its schools of philosophy in AD 529. The city then declined into nothing more than an outpost of the Byzantine Empire.

Between 1200 and 1450, Athens was continually invaded – by Franks, Catalans, Florentines and Venetians, all opportunists preoccupied only with grabbing for themselves principalities from the crumbling Byzantine Empire.

Ottoman Rule & Independence

Athens was captured by the Turks in 1456, and nearly 400 years of Ottoman rule followed. The Acropolis became the home of the Turkish governor, the Parthenon was converted into a mosque and the Erechtheion was used as a harem.

In the early stages of the War of Independence (1821–27), fierce fighting broke out in the streets of Athens, with the city changing hands several times between Turks and Greek liberators. In 1834 Athens superseded Nafplio as the capital of independent Greece and King Otho set about transforming the sparsely populated, war-scarred town into something worthy of a capital. Bavarian architects created a city of imposing neoclassical buildings, tree-lined boulevards, flower gardens and squares. Sadly, many of these buildings have been demolished. The best surviving examples are on Vasilissis Sofias.

The 20th Century

Athens grew steadily throughout the latter half of the 19th and early 20th centuries, and enjoyed a brief heyday as the 'Paris of the eastern Mediterranean'. This came to an abrupt end in 1923 with the Treaty of Lausanne. The treaty resulted in nearly a million refugees from Turkey descending on Athens – an event which marked the beginning of its much-maligned concrete sprawl.

Athens, along with the rest of Greece, suffered appallingly during the German occupation of WWII. During this time more Athenians were killed by starvation than by the enemy. This suffering was perpetuated in the civil war that followed.

The industrialisation program that was launched during the 1950s, with the help of US aid, brought another population boom as people from the islands and mainland villages headed to Athens in search of work.

The colonels' junta (1967–74), with characteristic insensitivity, tore down many of the crumbling old Turkish houses of Plaka and the imposing neoclassical buildings of King Otho's time. The junta failed, however, to take any action on the chronic infrastructural problems resulting from such rapid and unplanned growth. The elected governments that followed in the late 70s and 80s didn't do much better, and by the end of the 80s the city had developed a sorry reputation as one of the most traffic-clogged and polluted in Europe.

The 1990s appear to have been a turning point in the city's development, with politicians finally accepting the need for radical solutions. Inspired initially by the failed bid to stage the 1996 Olympics, authorities embarked on an ambitious program to prepare the city for the 21st century. Two key elements in this program have been a major expansion of the metro network, and the construction of a new international airport at Spata, east of Athens.

These projects played an important role in the city's successful bid to stage the 2004 Olympics. The Olympics have now created a momentum of their own; confidence is riding high and billions are being poured into city-centre redevelopment. The city will look very different by the time the construction hoardings finally disappear. See the boxed text 'The Rocky Road to 2004' for more information.

The '90s ended on a disastrous note when the city was struck by a major earthquake on 7 September 1999, leaving 139 dead and 100,000 homeless. Registering 5.9 on the Richter Scale, it was the most powerful earthquake to hit the Greek capital for almost 200 years. Its epicentre was about 20km north of Athens near Mt Parnitha, and most of the fatalities occurred in the northern suburbs of Menidi, Nea Eritrea and Metamorphosi, where dozens died in a factory collapse. The effects were felt throughout the city and Piraeus, and many buildings still carry the scars.

It dislodged fragments of marble from the pillars of the Parthenon, which has survived many quakes in the course of its 2500-year history, and smashed pottery in the National Archaeological Museum. The pottery collection remained closed at time of research. See the Geology section in the Facts about the Country chapter for more information.

ORIENTATION
City Centre (Map 1)

Although Athens is a huge, sprawling city, nearly everything of interest to travellers is located within a small area surrounding Plateia Syntagmatos (Syntagma Square). This area is bounded by the districts of Plaka to the south, Monastiraki to the west, Kolonaki to the east and Omonia to the north.

The city's two major landmarks, the Acropolis and Lykavittos Hill, can be seen from just about everywhere and are useful for getting one's bearings. The streets are clearly signposted in Greek and English.

Here's a brief introduction to the main suburbs:

Phone numbers listed incorporate changes due in Oct 2002; see p83

ATHENS

Syntagma This is the central business district surrounding Plateia Syntagmatos, heart of the modern city of Athens. The square is flanked by luxury hotels, banks, airline offices and expensive coffee shops, and is dominated by the old royal palace. It was from the palace balcony that the constitution *(syntagma)* was declared on 3 September 1843. The building has housed the Greek parliament since 1935.

Syntagma is a pleasant introduction to the city, despite the manic speed at which the traffic zooms around it. At its centre is a large, paved square, planted with orange, oleander and cypress trees.

Amalias is the main street heading south from the eastern side of Plateia Syntagmatos. Next to it are the National Gardens, with subtropical trees and ornamental ponds, and the more formal Zappeio Gardens. Amalias skirts the Arch of Hadrian and the Temple of Olympian Zeus and leads into Syngrou, which runs all the way to the coast at Faliro. Buses from the airport and Piraeus approach Syntagma along Amalias.

If you're arriving by bus and want to stay in Plaka, get off at Syntagma. The stop is opposite the National Gardens on Amalias.

Plaka South of Syntagma, Plaka is the old Turkish quarter of Athens and virtually all that existed when Athens was declared the capital of independent Greece. Its narrow, labyrinthine streets nestle into the northeastern slope of the Acropolis, and most of the city's ancient sites are close by. Plaka is touristy in the extreme. Its main streets, Kydathineon and Adrianou, are packed solid with restaurants and souvenir shops. It is the most attractive and interesting part of Athens and most visitors make it their base. The most convenient trolleybus stop is on Filellinon, near the junction with Kydathineon.

Monastiraki Centred on busy Plateia Monastirakiou, Monastiraki lies just west of Syntagma and is the city's market district. The famous Athens flea market is southwest of the square on Ifestou, while the central meat and fish market is to the north on Athinas, opposite the fruit and vegetable market. Shops along the streets bordering the markets sell cheeses, nuts, herbs, honey, dried fruits and cold meats. On Eolou most shops sell cut-price clothing and street vendors offer items such as sheets, towels, tablecloths and underwear.

Kolonaki Chic is the best way to describe the smart residential district of Kolonaki, east of Syntagma. Tucked beneath Lykavittos Hill, it has long been the favoured address of Athenian socialites; its streets are full of trendy boutiques and private art galleries, as well as dozens of trendy cafes and international restaurants.

Vasilissis Sofias, on its southern flank, was laid out by the Bavarian architects brought in by King Otho and is one of Athens' most imposing streets. Its neoclassical buildings now house museums, embassies and government offices.

Omonia Chic is not a word that springs readily to mind when describing the district of Omonia, north of Syntagma. Once one of the city's smarter areas, Omonia has gone to the dogs in recent years and is better known for its pickpockets and prostitutes than its architecture.

This can be expected to change though, with a number of high-profile projects scheduled in the lead-up to the 2004 Olympics. The main square, Plateia Omonias, is due to be transformed from a traffic hub into an expanse of formal gardens. It will become pedestrian only, with traffic bypassing the square.

Beyond the City Centre (Map 1)
To get a glimpse of how today's Athenians live, it's well worth exploring the streets beyond the city centre.

South of the Acropolis Plaka dwellers who want to escape the hurly burly of souvenir shops and tourist restaurants need walk no more than a few hundred metres to find relief in the quiet suburbs south of the Acropolis.

The first area you come to is Makrigianni, a trendy residential suburb occupying the southern slope of the Acropolis between Filopappos Hill and Syngrou. It has a smattering of upmarket hotels and restaurants, and is also home to the city's main gay area - occupying the belt between Makrigianni (the street) and Syngrou.

South of Makrigianni is the less risque residential district of Koukaki. To the east, on the other side of Syngrou, is the district of Mets, which has some delightful old Turkish houses. North-east of Mets is Pangrati, another pleasant residential neighbourhood.

West of Monastiraki The suburbs west of Monastiraki have undergone a remarkable transformation during the 1990s.

Thisio, to the south-west, led the way in the early 90s when young professionals started buying up the run-down area's cheap housing. It's now a thriving area full of music bars and cafes, particularly around the junction of Apostolou Pavlou and Iraklidon. Places like Stavlos, at Iraklidon 8, were pioneers of the Athens retro style of renovation – ripping out modern finishings to expose and highlight old stonework and chunky timber beams.

This style is now being taken a step further in nearby Psiri, north-west of Monastiraki. As recently as 1997, Psiri rated as Athens at its most clapped-out'; it still looks that way from the outside, but the maze of narrow streets within are now brimming with dozens of stylish restaurants and bars. Some sit incongruously alongside old-style shops with their bizarre arrays of bric-a-brac overflowing onto the pavements.

A new Asian quarter has emerged just north of Psiri, in the blocks west of Plateia Eleftherias. There are several Bangladeshi shops as well as cheap Asian restaurants.

North of Omonia The area to the north-west of Plateia Omonias probably rates as the sleaziest part of Athens, particularly the streets around Plateia Vathis – notorious for prostitutes. The city's main red-light area is actually farther north on Filis, near Plateia Viktorias.

Generally, though, the seediness gradually recedes as you head north from Plateia

Vathis, giving way to a respectable, if characterless, neighbourhood. Athens' two train stations are at the western edge of this area, on Deligianni. The National Archaeological Museum is on the eastern side, on 28 Oktovriou-Patission.

Just south of the National Archaeological Museum is the Athens Polytehnio. This establishment has university status, with faculties of fine arts and engineering. It also has a long tradition of radical thinking and alternative culture, and led the student sit-in of 1973 in opposition to the junta.

Squashed between the Polytehnio and Strefi Hill is the student residential area of Exarhia. It's a lively area with graffiti-covered walls and lots of cheap restaurants catering for Bohemian-looking professors and crowds of rebellious-looking students.

Maps
The free map handed out by the tourist office is fine for central Athens, which is all that most visitors get to see. If you want to get serious about exploring Athens beyond the city centre, buy yourself a copy of the Athens-Piraeus *Proasteia* (street directory).

INFORMATION
Tourist Offices
Athens' main EOT tourist office (☎ 21 0331 0561/0562, fax 21 0325 2895, e info@gnto.gr) is close to Syntagma at Amerikis 2. It has information sheets and brochures on just about every topic you care to mention, including a very useful timetable of the week's ferry departures from Piraeus and information about public transport prices and schedules from Athens. It also has a useful, free map of Athens, which has most of the places of interest, and the main trolleybus routes, clearly marked. The office is open 9am to 4pm Monday to Friday.

The EOT office at the airport (☎ 21 0353 0445, 21 0354 5101) is open 9am to 9pm daily.

Tourist Police
The tourist police's head office (☎ 21 0924 2700) is at Dimitrakopoulou 77, in Koukaki. It is open 24 hours a day, but it's quite a trek

from the city centre – take trolleybus No 1, 5 or 9 from Syntagma. The tourist police also have a 24-hour information service (☎ 171) for general tourist information or for emergency help – someone who speaks English is always available.

They will also act as interpreters for any dealings you might have with the crime police (☎ 21 0770 5711/5717), Leoforos Alexandras 173, or the traffic police (☎ 21 0528 4000), Deligianni 24-26, near Omonia.

Money

Most of the major banks have branches around Plateia Syntagmatos, open 8am to 2pm Monday to Thursday and 8am to 1.30pm Friday. The National Bank of Greece on Karageorgi Servias, Syntagma, is open extended hours for foreign exchange dealings only: 3.30pm to 6.30pm Monday to Thursday, 3pm to 6.30pm on Friday, 9am to 3pm Saturday, and 9am to 1pm Sunday. It also has a 24-hour automatic exchange machine outside on Stadiou.

American Express (☎ 21 0322 3380, 21 0324 4979), Ermou 7, Syntagma, is open 8.30am to 4pm Monday to Friday and 8.30am to 1.30pm Saturday. It's open longer hours in summer.

Eurochange has a couple of branches around the city centre. The Syntagma office (☎ 21 0322 0155), Karageorgi Servias 4, is open 8am to 8pm Monday to Friday and 10am to 6pm weekends, while the Plaka office (☎ 21 0324 3997), Filellinon 22, is open 8am to 8pm Monday to Friday, 9am to 7pm on Saturday and 10am to 7pm on Sunday. Eurochange changes Thomas Cook travellers cheques without commission.

Also in Plaka, Acropole Foreign Exchange (☎ 21 0331 2765), Kydathineon 23, is open 9am to midnight daily.

The banks at the airport are open 7am to 9pm.

Post

Athens' central post office (☎ 21 0321 6023) is at Eolou 100, Omonia (postcode 102 00), just east of Plateia Omonias. Unless specified otherwise, poste restante will be sent here.

If you're staying in Plaka, it's far more convenient to get your mail sent poste restante to the large post office on Plateia Syntagmatos (postcode 103 00), on the corner of Mitropoleos.

Both are open 7.30am to 8pm Monday to Friday and 7.30am to 2pm Saturday.

Parcels for abroad that weigh over 2kg must be taken to the parcel post office (☎ 21 0322 8940), Stadiou 4, Syntagma. The office is in the arcade that runs between Amerikis and Voukourestiou. Parcels should be taken along unwrapped for inspection.

Business communications specialist Mail Boxes Etc (☎ 21 0324 5060, fax 21 0324 5070, @ mbeathens@interfranchise.gr), Leka 14, Syntagma, hires out private mail boxes.

Telephone

The OTE office at 28 Oktovriou-Patission 85, Omonia, is open 24 hours a day. There is another office at Athinas 50, south of Omonia, next to Klaoudatos department store, open 7.30am to 2pm. Some useful telephone numbers include:

General telephone information	☎ 134
Numbers in Athens and Attica	☎ 131
Numbers elsewhere in Greece	☎ 132
International telephone information	☎ 161 or 162
International telegrams	☎ 165
Domestic operator	☎ 151 or 152
Domestic telegrams	☎ 155
Wake-up service	☎ 182

Mobile Phones Greek Travel Phones (☎ 21 0322 4932, fax 21 0324 9104, @ blakjohn@athena.compulink.gr), Voulis 31–33, Plaka, specialises in providing mobile phones for English-speaking visitors. It charges €167.30, and provides a phone that is fully charged, programmed in English and ready to use. You can sell the phone back (for €55.80) at the end of your stay, or just hang on to it until your next trip. Greek Travel Phones operates from the same shop as Acropolis Rugs.

Fax

You can send faxes from the post office, but you'll find better service and better prices at

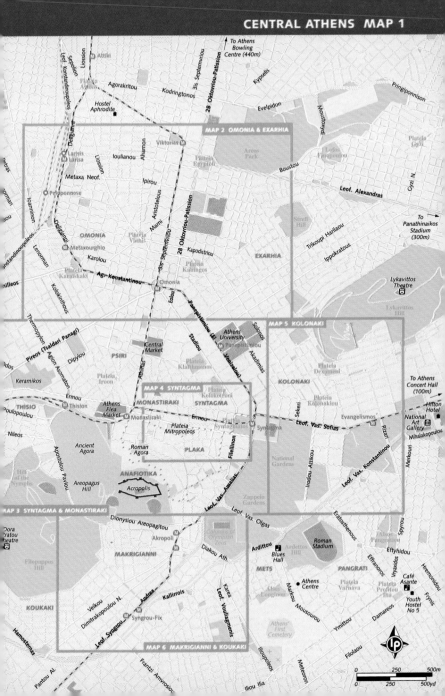

MAP 2 OMONIA & EXARHIA

PLACES TO STAY
3 Zorba's Hotel
8 Novotel Athens
19 Athens International
 Youth Hostel
26 Hotel Dryades
27 Hotel Orion
41 Titania Hotel

PLACES TO EAT
5 Dafni Taverna
7 O Makis Pistaria
16 Restaurant Arheon Gefsis
28 Taverna Barbargiannis
29 Ouzeri I Gonia
34 Neon Cafeteria
36 Marinopoulos
38 Bazaar Discount Supermarket
40 Vegetarian Fast Food

OTHER
1 Mavromateon Bus Terminal (Marathon & Rafina)
2 OTE main office
4 Mavromateon Bus Terminal (Southern Attica)
6 Trolley Stop for Train
9 Museum Internet Café
10 USIT-ETOS Travel
11 Flocafe
12 Rodon Club
13 Buses to Mt Parnitha
14 Public Toilets
15 Traffic Police
17 Sun Laundry
18 Laundry Self Service
20 OSE Office
21 National Theatre
22 Bus No 051 to Bus Terminal A
23 Astor Internet Café
24 Athens Polytechnio
25 National Archaeological Museum
30 AN Club
31 Fairytale
32 The Web Café
33 Bus A7 to Kifissia; 224 to Moni Kaissarianis
35 Bus No 049 to Piraeus
37 Central Post Office
39 Titania Cinema
42 Ideal (Cinema)
43 Bits & Bytes Internet Café
44 Olympia Theatre
45 Road Editions
46 French Institute of Athens

MAP 3 SYNTAGMA & MONASTIRAKI

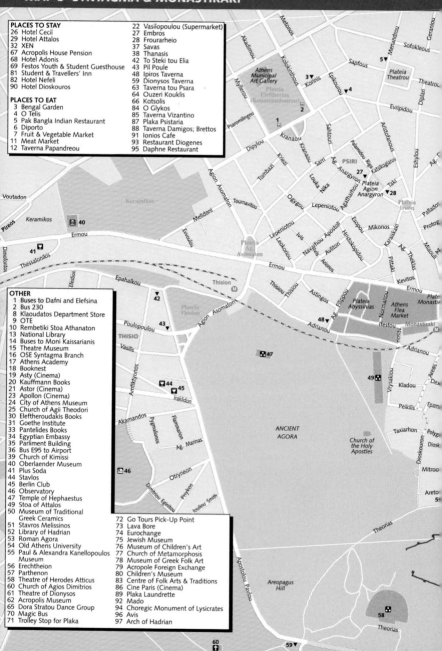

PLACES TO STAY
26 Hotel Cecil
29 Hotel Attalos
32 XEN
67 Acropolis House Pension
68 Hotel Adonis
69 Festos Youth & Student Guesthouse
81 Student & Travellers' Inn
82 Hotel Nefeli
90 Hotel Dioskouros

PLACES TO EAT
3 Bengal Garden
4 O Telis
5 Pak Bangla Indian Restaurant
6 Diporto
7 Fruit & Vegetable Market
11 Meat Market
12 Taverna Papandreou
22 Vasilopoulou (Supermarket)
27 Embros
28 Frourarheio
37 Savas
38 Thanasis
42 To Steki tou Elia
43 Pil Poule
48 Ipiros Taverna
59 Dionysos Taverna
63 Taverna tou Psara
64 Ouzeri Kouklis
66 Kotsolis
84 O Glykos
85 Taverna Vizantino
87 Plaka Psistaria
88 Taverna Damigos; Brettos
91 Ionios Cafe
93 Restaurant Diogenes
95 Daphne Restaurant

OTHER
1 Buses to Dafni and Elefsina
2 Bus 230
8 Klaoudatos Department Store
9 OTE
10 Rembetiki Stoa Athanaton
13 National Library
14 Buses to Moni Kaissarianis
15 Theatre Museum
16 OSE Syntagma Branch
17 Athens Academy
18 Booknest
19 Asty (Cinema)
20 Kauffmann Books
21 Astor (Cinema)
23 Apollon (Cinema)
24 City of Athens Museum
25 Church of Agii Theodori
30 Eleftheroudakis Books
31 Goethe Institute
33 Pantelides Books
34 Egyptian Embassy
35 Parliment Building
36 Bus E95 to Airport
39 Church of Kimissi
40 Oberlaender Museum
41 Plus Soda
44 Stavlos
45 Berlin Club
46 Observatory
47 Temple of Hephaestus
49 Stoa of Attalos
50 Museum of Traditional
   Greek Ceramics
51 Stavros Melissinos
52 Library of Hadrian
53 Roman Agora
54 Old Athens University
55 Paul & Alexandra Kanellopoulos
   Museum
56 Erechtheion
57 Parthenon
58 Theatre of Herodes Atticus
60 Church of Agios Dimitrios
61 Theatre of Dionysos
62 Acropolis Museum
65 Dora Stratou Dance Group
70 Magic Bus
71 Trolley Stop for Plaka
72 Go Tours Pick-Up Point
73 Lava Bore
74 Eurochange
75 Jewish Museum
76 Museum of Children's Art
77 Church of Metamorphosis
78 Museum of Greek Folk Art
79 Acropole Foreign Exchange
80 Children's Museum
83 Centre of Folk Arts & Traditions
86 Cine Paris (Cinema)
89 Plaka Laundrette
92 Mado
94 Choregic Monument of Lysicrates
96 Avis
97 Arch of Hadrian

Dimarhio

Plateia Kotzia

Stavrou Georgiou

Arsaki

Asklipiou

Akadimias

Massalias

Solonos

Kapi'anon

Kratinou

Streit

Athinas

Klisthenous

9

8

Pesmazoglou

13

14

Riga Fereou

Athens University

Sofokleous

modiou uit & etable arket

7

10

Meat Market

11

12

Aristidou

Praxitelous

Evripidou

Dragatsaniou

Panepistimiou

M

Korab

19

Vissarionos

15

Sina

Sina

geitonos

26

da

Vlahava

Polyklitou

Ag. Markou

Miltiadou

Ag. Filotheis

Plateia Karamanou

Kalir

Agathonos

Nikiou

Leoharous

Panepistimiou (El. Venizelou)

18

Plateia Klafthmonos

25

P. Patron Germanou

Papangopoulou

Panisasiou

20

21

24

22

23

SYNTAGMA

Edouardou Lo.

Stadiou

Omirou

16

17

31

Akadimias

32

33

30

Amerikis

Valaoritou

Voreou

Vyssis

Hrysospiliotissis

Ag. Kary

Karytsi

Gazi Anthimou

Kolokotroni

National Historical Museum

MAP 4 SYNTAGMA

Amerikis

Avramiotou

Karori

Flower Market

Skouze

Klitiou

Thiseos

Leka

Plateia Kolokotroni

Irinis

Athinaidos

Katanaliotou

Evangelistrias

Romvis

Perikleous

MONASTIRAKI

Eolou

Kiena

Komnaou

Diomias

Axailian

Karageorgi Servias

Vassileos Georgiou

34

Leof. Vas. Sofias

37

Korai'leou

Plateia Dimoprafilon

Fokionos

Stadiou

Ermou

Syntagma

Mitropoleos

Pandrosou

Kapinikarea

Plateia Mitropoleos

Athens Cathedral

Petraki

Ipatias

Patrovu

Pendelis

Plateia Syntagmatos

35

Plateia Agoras

Adrianou

Mnisikleous

Apollonos

Othonos

36

Eolou

Diogenous

Voulis

Ipitou

Skoufou

Nikis

Xenofontos

Leof. Vas. Amalias

Markou Aureliou

Kyrristou

PLAKA

Navarhou Apostoli

Iperidou

National Gardens

Roman Agora

Lyssiou

Flessa

Thoukididou

66

Plateia Rallou Manou

svoulou

54

Erotokritou

63

Pratiniou

Kekropos

67

68

Lamahou

69

70

75

72

ANAFIOTIKA

65

Hill

82

83

Plateia Satoris

76

77

71

74

73

Sholiou

Hatzimihali Angelikis

80

81

86

85

84

Plateia Filomouson Eterias

78

ACROPOLIS

64

87

88

89

Dedalou

90

Tsatsou K.

Simonidou

62

Rangavi

Thespidos

Shelley

92

94

91

Afroditis

Thalou

Zappeio Gardens

93

Epimenidou

95

Galanou

Goura

90

61

Vyronos

Vakhou

Lysikratous

96

97

Frynihou

Ehinou

Leof. Vas. Olgas

0   125   250m

0   125   250yd

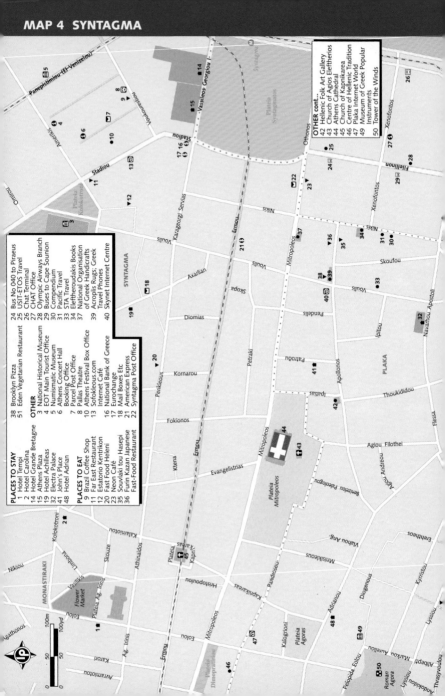

MAP 4 SYNTAGMA

PLACES TO STAY
1 Hotel Tempi
2 Hotel Carolina
14 Hotel Grande Bretagne
15 Athens Plaza
19 Hotel Achilleas
32 Electra Palace
41 John's Place
48 Hotel Adrian

PLACES TO EAT
9 Brazil Coffee Shop
11 Far East Restaurant
12 Estiatorio Kentrikon
20 Fast Food Heleni
23 Neon Café
35 Souvlaki tou Hasepi
36 Furin Kazan Japanese
    Fast-Food Restaurant
38 Brooklyn Pizza
51 Eden Vegetarian Restaurant

OTHER
3 National Historical Museum
4 EOT Main Tourist Office
5 Numismatic Museum
6 Athens Concert Hall
7 Parcel Post Office
8 Pallas Theatre
10 Athens Festival Box Office
13 Sofokleous.com
16 Internet Café
17 National Bank of Greece
18 Eurochange
21 Mail Boxes Etc
22 American Express
22 Syntagma Post Office
24 Bus No 040 to Piraeus
25 USIT-ETOS Travel
26 Chat Terminal
27 CHAT Office
28 Olympic Airways Branch
29 Buses to Cape Sounion
30 Compendium
31 Pacific Travel
33 STA Travel
34 Eleftheroudakis Books
37 National Organisation
    of Greek Handicrafts
39 Acropolis Rugs; Greek
    Travel Phones
40 Skynet Internet Centre

OTHER cont...
42 Hellenic Folk Art Gallery
43 Church of Agios Eleftherios
43 Athens Cathedral
45 Church of Kapnikarea
46 Centre of Hellenic Tradition
47 Plaka Internet World
49 Museum of Greek Popular
    Instruments
50 Tower of the Winds

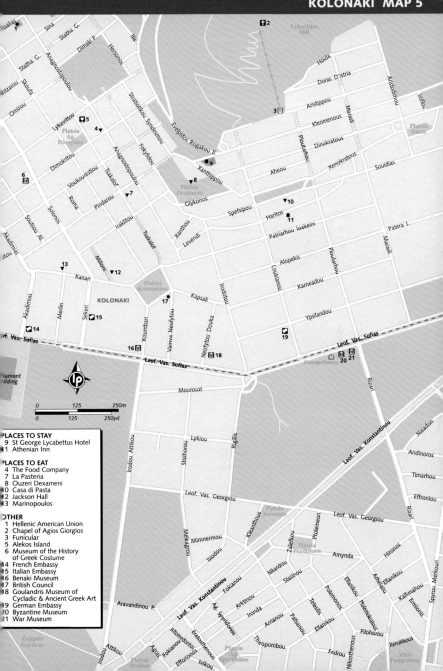

PLACES TO STAY
9 St George Lycabettus Hotel
11 Athenian Inn

PLACES TO EAT
4 The Food Company
7 La Pasteria
8 Ouzeri Dexameni
10 Casa di Pasta
12 Jackson Hall
13 Marinopoulos

OTHER
1 Hellenic American Union
2 Chapel of Agios Giorgios
3 Funicular
5 Alekos Island
6 Museum of the History
of Greek Costume
14 French Embassy
15 Italian Embassy
16 Benaki Museum
17 British Council
18 Goulandris Museum of
Cycladic & Ancient Greek Art
19 German Embassy
20 Byzantine Museum
21 War Museum

MAP 6 MAKRIGIANNI & KOUKAKI

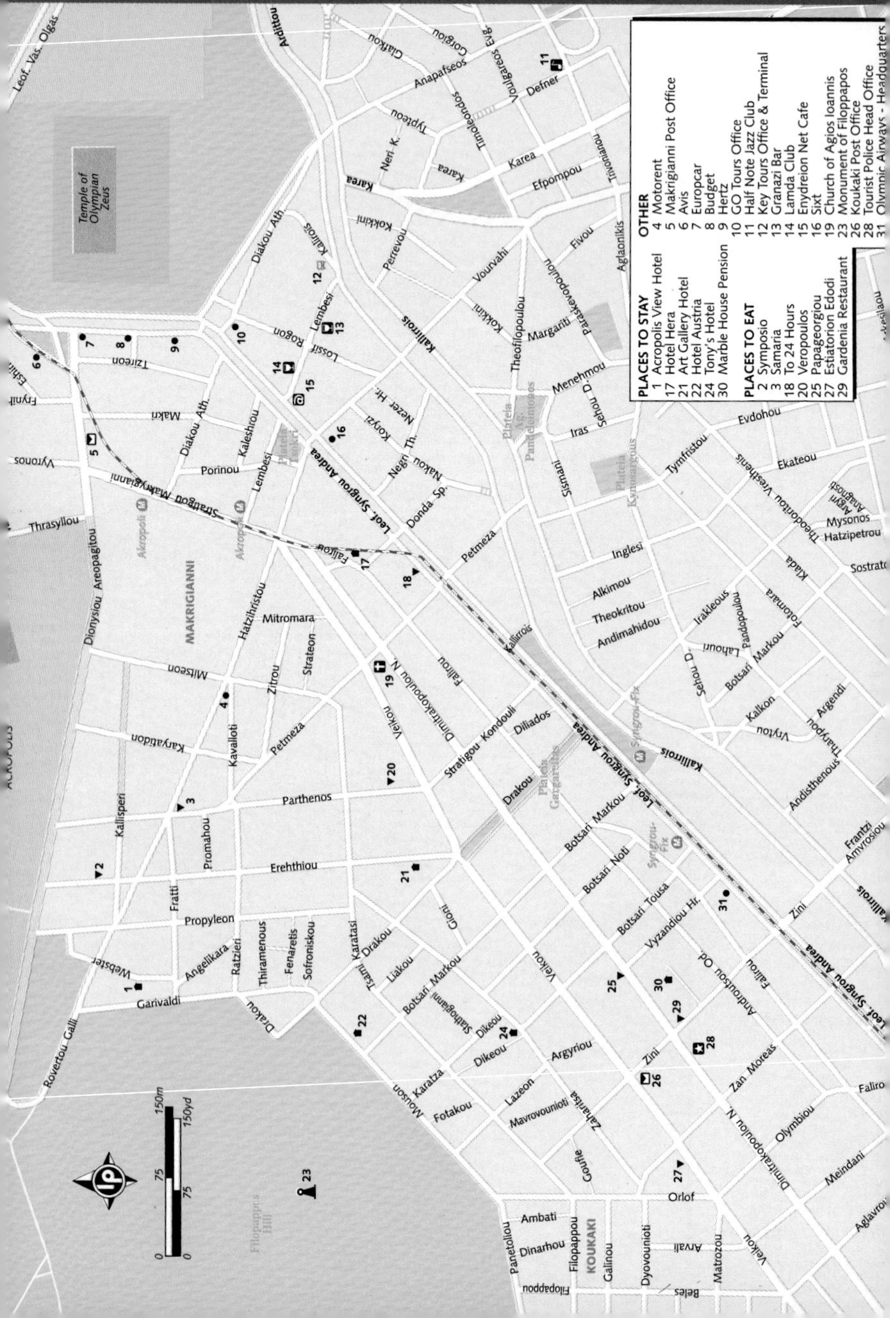
PLACES TO STAY
1 Acropolis View Hotel
17 Hotel Hera
21 Art Gallery Hotel
22 Hotel Austria
24 Tony's Hotel
30 Marble House Pension
PLACES TO EAT
2 Symposio
3 Samaria
18 To 24 Hours
20 Veropoulos
25 Papageorgiou
27 Estiatorion Edodi
29 Gardenia Restaurant
OTHER
4 Motorent
5 Makrigianni Post Office
6 Avis
7 Europcar
8 Budget
9 Hertz
10 GO Tours Office
11 Half Note Jazz Club
12 Key Tours Office & Terminal
13 Granazi Bar
14 Lamda Club
15 Enydreion Net Cafe
16 Sixt
19 Church of Agios Ioannis
23 Monument of Filoppapos
26 Koukaki Post Office
28 Tourist Police Head Office
31 Olympic Airways - Headquarters
Temple of Olympian Zeus
MAKRIGIANNI
KOUKAKI
Filopappou Hill
Leof Syngrou Andrea
Kallirrois
Dionysiou Areopagitou
Leof. Vas. Olgas
Platela Ag. Panteleimonos
Platela Kynosargous
Platela Gargarettas
150m
150yd

Mail Boxes Etc, just west of Syntagma at Leka 14. A fax to the UK costs €2.35 for the first page and €2.05 for each subsequent page. To the US it's €3.25/2.65 and to Australia and New Zealand €4.40/3.70.

Email & Internet Access

Internet cafes are popping up like mushrooms all over Athens. Most charge from €4.40 to €5.90 per hour of computer time, whether you're on the Net or not. The following is a list of places around the city centre:

Astor Internet Café Oktovriou-Patission 27, Omonia; open 10am to 10pm daily

Bits and Bytes Internet Café Akadimias 78, Exarhia; open 9am to midnight daily

Enydreion Net Café Syngrou 13, Makrigianni; open 7am to midnight Monday to Saturday

Museum Internet Café Oktovriou-Patission 46, Omonia, next to National Archaeological Museum; open 9am to 3am daily

Plaka Internet World Pandrosou 29, Monastiraki; open 11am to 11pm daily

Skynet Internet Centre Corner Voulis & Apollonos, Plaka; open 9am to 11pm Monday to Saturday

Sofokleous.com Internet Café Stadiou 5, Syntagma, behind Flocafé; open 10am to 10pm Monday to Saturday, 1pm to 9pm Sunday

The Web Café George 10, off Plateia Kaningos, Exarhia; open 10am to 2am daily

Travel Agencies

The bulk of the city's travel agencies are round Plateia Syntagmatos, particularly just south of it on Filellinon, Nikis and Voulis. Many of these agencies employ touts to roam the area looking for customers. Give them a miss – these places are responsible for most of the rip-offs described under Travel Agents in the 'Dangers and Annoyances' boxed text later in this chapter.

Reputable agencies include STA Travel (☎ 21 0321 1188, 21 0321 1194, e statravel@robissa.gr), Voulis 43; and USIT-ETOS Travel (☎ 21 0324 0483, fax 21 0322 8447, e usit@usitetos.gr), Filellinon 7. USIT-ETOS has another branch (☎ 21 0522 2228, e etosath@usitetos.gr) opposite the National

Archaeological Museum at Oktavriou-Patission 53A & Marni.

Both STA Travel and USIT-ETOS also issue International Student Identity Cards (ISIC).

Magic Bus (☎ 21 0323 7471, e magic25@attglobal.net), Filellinon 20, has some very good last-minute deals on charter flights.

Bookshops

Athens has several good English-language bookshops. You'll find the largest selection of books at Eleftheroudakis (☎ 21 0331 4180), Panepistimiou 17, Syntagma. Eleftheroudakis has a chain of stores around Athens, including a Syntagma branch (☎ 21 0322 9388) at Nikis 20.

Compendium (☎ 21 0322 1248), upstairs at Nikis 28, Plaka, has a second-hand section as well as a good selection overall. The English-language notice board outside has information about jobs, accommodation and courses in Athens.

Pantelides Books (☎ 21 0362 3673), Amerikis 11, Syntagma, stocks a range of feminist books as well as paperbacks, travel guides, maps etc.

Booknest (☎ 21 0323 1703), on the mezzanine level of the arcade at Panepistimiou 25–29, stocks books in French, German, Italian, Spanish and Russian as well as English. Kauffmann (☎ 21 0322 2160), Stadiou 28, stocks books in English and French. Map specialists Road Editions (☎ 21 0361 3242) have a shop at Ippokratous 39, Exarhia. You'll find a wide range of travel literature as well as their complete selection of maps. All these shops stock Lonely Planet guides.

International newspapers reach the *periptera* (kiosks) on Syntagma on the same day as they are published at 3pm on weekdays and 7pm on weekends.

Cultural Centres

Following is a list of international cultural centres located in Athens:

British Council (☎ 21 0369 2314,
  e library@britishcouncil.gr) Plateia
  Kolonakiou 17, Kolonaki
French Institute of Athens (☎ 21 0362 4301,
  e ifa@ifa.gr) Sina 31, Kolonaki

Phone numbers listed incorporate changes due in Oct 2002; see p83

Goethe Institute (☎ 21 0360 8114,
ⓔ gi@athen.goethe.org) Omirou 14–16,
Kolonaki
Hellenic-American Union (☎ 21 0362 9886,
ⓔ vioannou@hau.gr) Massalias 22, Kolonaki

These cultural centres hold concerts, film
shows and exhibitions from time to time.
Major events are listed in various English-
language newspapers and magazines.

Laundry
Plaka has a convenient laundrette at Angelou Geronta 10, just off Kydathineon near
the outdoor restaurants. It charges €7.35 to
wash and dry 5kg. Laundry Self Service,
Psaron 9, near Plateia Karaïskaki, and Sun
Laundry, Kolokinthous 41, both charge
€7.95.

Toilets
Public toilets are a rarity in Athens – and
those that do exist are so primitive that they
are best avoided except in an absolute emergency. Fortunately there are fast-food outlets everywhere in Central Athens; very
handy in an emergency. Failing that, head
to a cafe, although you'll be expected to buy
something for the privilege of using the
facilities.

Left Luggage
Many of Athens' hotels will store luggage
free for guests, although a lot of them do no
more than pile the bags in a hallway. Pacific
Travel (☎ 21 0324 1007), Nikis 26, Plaka,
charges €1.50 per day, €4.40 per week and
€8.80 per month. Opening hours are 8am to
8pm Monday to Saturday, 8am to 2pm Sunday and holidays.

Emergency
The police emergency number is ☎ 100. For
the fire brigade ring ☎ 199. For emergency
medical treatment ring the tourist police
(☎ 171) and they will tell you the location
of the nearest hospital. Hospitals give free
emergency treatment to tourists. For hospitals with outpatient departments on duty,
call ☎ 106; for the telephone number of an
on-call doctor, ring ☎ 105 (2pm to 7am); for

a pharmacy open 24 hours call ☎ 107; and
for first-aid advice phone ☎ 166. US citizens can ring ☎ 21 0721 2951 for emergency medical aid.
    Some travellers have recommended SOS
Doctors (☎ 21 0322 0046/0015), a 24-hour
call-out service employing doctors who
speak English and a range of other languages. They charge about €58.70 for a
call.

WALKING TOUR
This walk takes in most of Plaka's main sites.
It involves about 45 minutes' walking, but
can take up to four hours if you linger and
allow yourself to be lured into a few detours.
Plaka is a fascinating place to explore, full of
surprises tucked away in the labyrinthine
streets that weave over the undulating terrain.
The route is marked on Maps 3 and 4.
    The walk begins at **Plateia Syntagmatos**.
This square has been a favourite place for
protests and rallies ever since the rally that
led to the granting of a constitution on 3
September 1843, declared by King Otho
from the balcony of the royal palace. In
1944 the first round of the civil war began
here after police opened fire on a rally organised by the communists. Known as the
Dekembriana (events of December), it was
followed by a month of fierce fighting between the communist resistance and the
British forces. In 1954 the first demonstration demanding the *enosis* (union) of
Cyprus with Greece took place here. At
election time, political parties stage their
rallies in the square and most protest
marches end up here.
    Flanking the eastern side of Plateia Syn-
tagmatos is the former royal palace, now the
parliament building. The palace, designed
by the Bavarian architect Von Gartner, was
built in 1836–42. The building remained the
royal palace until 1935, when it became the
seat of the Greek parliament. (The royal
family moved to a new palace on the corner
of Vasileos Konstantinou and Herod Atticus, which became the presidential palace
upon the abolition of the monarchy in 1974.)
    The parliament building is guarded by
the much-photographed *evzones* (guards

raditionally from the village of Evzoni in Macedonia). Their somewhat incongruous uniform of short kilts and pom-pom shoes s the butt of much mickey-taking by sight-eers. Their uniform is based on the attire worn by the *klephts*, the mountain fighters who battled so ferociously in the War of Independence. Every Sunday at 11am the vzones perform a full changing-of-the-guard ceremony.

Standing with your back to the parliament building you will see ahead of you, to the right, the **Hotel Grande Bretagne**. This, the grandest of Athens' hotels, was built in 862 as a 60-room mansion to accommodate visiting dignitaries. In 1872 it was converted into a hotel and became the place where the crowned heads of Europe and minent politicians stayed. The Nazis made it their headquarters during WWII. The hotel was the scene of an attempt to blow up the British prime minister Winston Churchill on Christmas Eve 1944 while he was in Athens to discuss the Dekembriana fighting. A bomb was discovered in the hotel sewer.

Use the metro underpass to cross from the parliament building to the centre of Plateia Syntagmatos. The route takes you through the upper hall of Syntagma metro station, showpiece of the city's swish new metro system. Glass cases at the southern end of this huge marble hall display finds uncovered during construction, while the western wall has been preserved like a trench at an archaeological dig. It provides a fascinating look back through the ages.

The central square would be a pleasant place to sit and contemplate were it not for the roar of the passing traffic. Head for the south-western corner of the square and cross Filellinon at the junction with Othnos, then continue west along Mitropoleos and take the first turn left into Nikis. Walk south up Nikis for about 300m to the crossroads with Kydathineon, which is a pedestrian walkway and one of Plaka's main thoroughfares.

Turn right and a little way along you will come to the **Church of Metamorphosis** on Plateia Satiros; opposite is the **Museum of Greek Folk Art**. Continue along here, and after Plateia Filomousou Eterias (usually known as Plateia Plakas), the square with the outdoor tavernas, turn left into Adrianou, another of Plaka's main thoroughfares. At the end, turn right, and this will bring you to the square with the **Choregic Monument of Lysicrates**. (The name *choregos* was given to the wealthy citizens who financed choral and dramatic performances.) This monument was built in 334 BC to commemorate a win in a choral festival. An inscription on the architrave states:

Lysicrates of Kykyna, son of Lysitheides, was choregos; the tribe of Akamantis won the victory with a chorus of boys; Theon played the flute; Lysiades of Athens trained the chorus; Euainetos was arhon.

The reliefs on the monument depict the battle between Dionysos and the Tyrrhenian pirates, whom the god had transformed into dolphins. It is the earliest known monument using Corinthian capitals externally. It stands in a cordoned-off archaeological site which is part of the **Street of Tripods**. It was here that winners of ancient dramatic and choral contests dedicated their tripod trophies to Dionysos.

In the 19th century, the monument was incorporated into the library of a French Capuchin convent, in which Lord Byron stayed in 1810–11 and wrote *Childe Harold*. The convent was destroyed by fire in 1890. Recent excavations around the monument have revealed the foundations of other choregic monuments.

Facing the monument, turn left and then right into Epimenidou. At the top of the steps, turn right into Stratonos, which skirts the Acropolis. A left fork after 150m leads to the highest part of Plaka, an area called **Anafiotika**. The little whitewashed cube houses are the legacy of the people from the small Cycladic island of Anafi who were used as cheap labour in the building of Athens after Independence. It's a beautiful spot, with brightly painted olive-oil cans brimming with flowers bedecking the walls of the tiny gardens in summer.

Dangers & Annoyances

Athens is a big city, and it has its fair share of the problems found in all major cities. Fortunately, violent street crime remains very rare, but travellers should be alert to the following traps.

Pickpockets

Pickpockets have become a major problem in Athens. Their favourite hunting grounds are the metro system and the crowded streets around Omonia, particularly Athinas. The Sunday market on Ermou is another place where it pays to take extra care of your valuables. There have been numerous reports of thefts from day-packs and bags.

Taxi Drivers

Many Athens residents will tell you that their taxi drivers are the biggest bunch of bastards in the world. It seems that they have as much trouble getting a fair deal as tourists do.

Most (but not all) rip-off stories involve cabs picked up late at night from the taxi ranks at the city's main arrival and departure points: the airport, the train stations, the two bus terminals – particularly Terminal A at Kifissou – and the port of Piraeus. Paying by the meter, the fare from any of the above places to the city centre shouldn't be more than €7.50 at any time of day.

The trouble is that the cabbies who work these ranks don't like to bother with the meter, especially after midnight when most public transport stops. They prefer to demand whatever they think they can get away with. If you insist on using the meter, many will simply refuse to take you. You can either negotiate a set fare, or attempt to find a taxi elsewhere.

CLINT CURE

Every now and again, the police conduct well-publicised clampdowns. One such purge turned up an airport cabby who was well prepared for tourists who want to see the meter working – he was equipped with a handy remote-controlled device that could make the meter spin round at mind-boggling speed!

A more common trick is to set the meter on night rate (tariff 2) during the day. Between 6am and midnight the day rate (tariff 1) should be charged. If there is a dispute over the fare, take the driver's number and report them to the tourist police.

The path winds between the houses and comes to some steps on the right, at the bottom of which is a curving pathway leading downhill to Pratiniou. Turn left at Pratiniou and veer right after 50m into Tholou. The yellow-ochre building with brown shutters at No 5 is the old university, built by th Venetians. The Turks used it as public o fices and it housed Athens University fro 1837 to 1841.

At the end of Tholou, turn left int Panos. At the top of the steps on the left

Dangers & Annoyances

Taxi Touts

Taxi drivers working in league with some of the overpriced C-class hotels around Omonia are another problem. The scam involves taxi drivers picking up late-night arrivals, particularly at the airport and Bus Terminal A, and persuading them that the hotel they want to go to is full – even if they have a booking. The taxi driver will pretend to phone the hotel of your choice, announce that it's full and suggest an alternative. Ask to speak to your chosen hotel yourself, or simply insist on going where you want.

Taxi drivers frequently attempt to claim commissions from hotel owners even if they have just gone where they were told. If the taxi driver comes into the hotel, make it clear to hotel staff that there is no reason to pay a commission.

Bar Scams

Lonely Planet continues to hear from readers who have been taken in by one of the various bar scams that operate around central Athens, particularly around Syntagma.

The basic scam runs something like this: friendly Greek approaches solo male traveller and discovers that the traveller knows little about Athens; friendly Greek then reveals that he, too, is from out of town. Why don't they go to this great little bar that he's just discovered and have a beer? They order a drink, and the equally friendly owner then offers another drink. Women appear, more drinks are provided and the visitor relaxes as he realises that the women are not prostitutes, just friendly Greeks. The crunch comes at the end of the evening when the traveller is presented with an exorbitant bill and the smiles disappear. The con men who cruise the streets playing the role of the friendly Greek can be very convincing: some people have been taken in more than once.

Other bars (see under Bars in the Entertainment section) don't bother with the acting. They target intoxicated males with talk of sex and present them with outrageous bills.

Travel Agents

Several travel agents in the Plaka/Syntagma area employ touts to patrol the streets promoting 'cheap' packages to the islands. These touts like to hang out at the bus stops on Amalias, hoping to find naive new arrivals who have no idea of prices in Greece.

Potential customers are then taken back to the agency, where slick salespeople then pressure them into buying outrageously overpriced packages. Lonely Planet regularly hears complaints from victims of this scam.

There is no need to buy a package; you will always be able to negotiate a better deal yourself when you get to the island of your choice. If you are worried that everywhere will be full, select a place from the pages of this guide and make a booking.

Slippery Surfaces

Many of Athens' pavements and other surfaces underfoot are made of marble and become incredibly slippery when wet, so if you are caught in the rain, tread carefully.

a restored 19th-century mansion which is now the **Paul & Alexandra Kanellopoulos Museum** (☎ 21 0321 2313, Panos 2; admission €1.50; open 8am-2.30pm Tues-Sun). It houses the family's eclectic private collection.

Retracing your steps, go down Panos to the ruins of the **Roman Agora**, turn left into Polygnotou and walk to the crossroads. Opposite, Polygnotou continues to the **Ancient Agora**. (Further details of these agora, or markets, are given later in this chapter.)

Phone numbers listed incorporate changes due in Oct 2002; see p83

At the crossroads, turn right and then left into Peikilis, then immediately right into Areos. On the right are the remains of the **Library of Hadrian** and next to it is the **Museum of Traditional Greek Ceramics** (*☎ 21 0324 2066, Areos 1; admission €1.50; open 10am-2pm Wed-Mon*). The museum is housed in the Mosque of Tzistarakis, built in 1759. After Independence it lost its minaret and was used as a prison.

Ahead is **Plateia Monastirakiou**, named after the small church. To the left is the metro station and the **flea market**. Plateia Monastirakiou is Athens at its noisiest, most colourful and chaotic. It teems with street vendors selling nuts, coconut sticks and fruit.

Turn right just beyond the mosque into Pandrosou. This street is a relic of the old Turkish bazaar. Today it is full of souvenir shops, selling everything from cheap kitsch to high-class jewellery and clothes. The street is named after King Cecrops' daughter, Pandrosos, who was the first priestess of Athens. At No 89 is Stavros Melissinos, the 'poet sandal-maker' of Athens who names the Beatles, Rudolph Nureyev and Jackie Onassis among his past customers. Fame and fortune have not gone to his head, however – he still makes the best-value sandals in Athens, costing €8.80 to €14.70 per pair.

Pandrosou leads to **Plateia Mitropoleos** and the **Athens Cathedral**. The cathedral has little architectural merit, which isn't surprising considering that it was constructed from the masonry of over 50 razed churches and from the designs of several architects. Next to it stands the much smaller, and far more appealing, **Church of Agios Eleftherios**, which was once the cathedral. Turn left after the cathedral, and then right into Mitropoleos and follow it back to Syntagma.

THE ACROPOLIS (MAP 7)

Athens exists because of the Acropolis, the most important ancient monument in the Western world. Crowned by the Parthenon, it stands sentinel over Athens, visible from almost everywhere within the city. Its monuments of Pentelic marble gleam white in the

midday sun and gradually take on a honey hue as the sun sinks. At night they are floodlit and seem to hover above the city. No matter how harassed you may become in Athens, a sudden unexpected glimpse of this magnificent sight cannot fail to lift your spirits.

Inspiring as these monuments are, they are but faded remnants of Pericles' city, and it takes a great leap of the imagination to begin to comprehend the splendour of his creations. Pericles spared no expense – only the best materials, architects, sculptors and artists were good enough for a city dedicated to the cult of Athena, tutelary goddess of Athens. The city was a showcase of colossal buildings, lavishly coloured and gilded, and of gargantuan statues, some of bronze, others of marble plated with gold and encrusted with precious stones.

Visiting the Site

There is only one entrance to the Acropolis archaeological site (*☎ 21 0321 0291; adult/student €5.90/2.95 site & museum; site open 8am-6.30pm daily, museum open 8am-6.30pm Tues-Sun, noon-6.30pm Mon Apr-Oct; site & museum open 8am-4.30pm daily Nov-Mar*), but there are several approaches to this entrance. The main approach from the north is along the path that is a continuation of Dioskouron in the south-west corner of Plaka. From the south, you can either walk or take bus No 230 along Dionysiou Areopagitou to just beyond the Theatre of Herodes Atticus, where a path leads to the entrance.

The crowds that swarm over the Acropolis need to be seen to be believed. It's best to get there as early in the day as possible. You need to wear shoes with good soles because the paths around the site are uneven and very slippery.

History

The Acropolis (high city) was first inhabited in Neolithic times. The first temples were built during the Mycenaean era in homage to the goddess Athena. People lived on the Acropolis until the late 6th century BC, but in 510 BC the Delphic oracle declared that it should be the province of the gods.

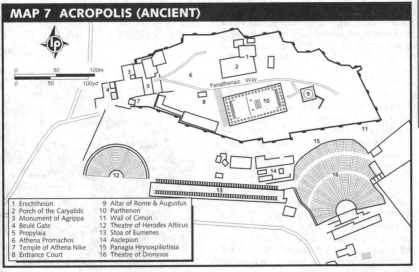

MAP 7 ACROPOLIS (ANCIENT)

Panathenaic Way

1 Erechtheion
2 Porch of the Caryatids
3 Monument of Agrippa
4 Beulé Gate
5 Propylaia
6 Athena Promachos
7 Temple of Athena Nike
8 Entrance Court
9 Altar of Rome & Augustus
10 Parthenon
11 Wall of Cimon
12 Theatre of Herodes Atticus
13 Stoa of Eumenes
14 Asclepion
15 Panagia Hrysospiliotissa
16 Theatre of Dionysos

After all the buildings on the Acropolis were reduced to ashes by the Persians on the eve of the Battle of Salamis (480 BC), Pericles set about his ambitious rebuilding program. He transformed the Acropolis into a city of temples which has come to be regarded as the zenith of classical Greek achievement.

All four of the surviving monuments of the Acropolis have received their fair share of battering through the ages. Ravages inflicted upon them during the years of foreign occupation, pilfering by foreign archaeologists, inept renovation following independence, visitors' footsteps and earthquakes have all taken their toll. The year 1687 was a particularly bad one. The Venetians attacked the Turks and opened fire on the Acropolis, causing an explosion in the Parthenon, where the Turks were storing gunpowder. The resulting fire blazed for two days, damaging all the buildings.

However, the most recent menace, acid rain, caused by industrial pollution and traffic fumes, is proving to be the most irreversibly destructive. It is dissolving the very marble of which the monuments are built. Major renovation work is taking place

in an effort to save the monuments for future generations, and the site now boasts a World Heritage Site listing.

Beulé Gate & Monument of Agrippa

Once you've bought your ticket for the Acropolis and have walked a little way along the path, you will see on your left the Beulé Gate, named after the French archaeologist Ernest Beulé, who uncovered it in 1852. The 8m pedestal on the left, halfway up the zigzag ramp leading to the Propylaia, was once topped by the Monument of Agrippa, a bronze statue of the Roman general riding a chariot. It was erected in 27 BC to commemorate victory in a chariot race at the Panathenaic games.

Propylaia

The Propylaia formed the towering entrance to the Acropolis in ancient times. Built by Mnesicles in 437–432 BC, its architectural brilliance ranks with that of the Parthenon. It consists of a central hall, with two wings on either side. Each section had a gate, and in ancient times these five gates were the only entrances to the 'upper city'. The middle gate (which was the largest) opened onto the Panathenaic Way. The western portico of the Propylaia must indeed have been imposing, consisting of six double columns, Doric on the outside and Ionic on the inside. The fourth column along has been restored. The ceiling of the central hall was painted with gold stars on a dark blue background. The northern wing was used as a picture gallery (*pinakotheke*) and the south wing was the antechamber to the Temple of Athena Nike.

The Propylaia is aligned with the Parthenon – the earliest example of a building designed in relation to another. It remained intact until the 13th century when various occupiers started adding to it. It was badly damaged in the 17th century when a lightning strike set off an explosion in a Turkish gunpowder store. Heinrich Schliemann paid for the removal of one of its appendages – a Frankish tower – in the 19th century. Reconstruction took place between 1909 and 1917 and there was further restoration after WWII. Once you're through the Propylaia, there is a stunning view of the Parthenon ahead.

Panathenaic Way

The Panathenaic Way, which cuts across the middle of the Acropolis, was the route taken by the Panathenaic procession. The procession was the climax of the Panathenaia, the festival held to venerate the goddess Athena. The origins of the Panathenaia are uncertain. According to some accounts it was initiated by Erichthonius; according to others, by Theseus. There were two festivals: the Lesser Panathenaic Festival took place annually on Athena's birthday, and the Great Panathenaic Festival was held on every fourth anniversary of the goddess' birth.

The Great Panathenaic Festival began with dancing and was followed by athletic, dramatic and musical contests. The Panathenaic procession, which took place on the final day of the festival, began at the Keramikos and ended at the Erechtheion. Men carrying animals sacrificed to Athena headed the procession, followed by maidens carrying *rhytons* (horn-shaped drinking vessels). Behind them were musicians

playing a fanfare for the girls of noble birth who followed, proudly holding aloft the sacred *peplos* (a glorious saffron-coloured shawl). Bringing up the rear were old men bearing olive branches. The grand finale of the procession was the placing of the peplos on the statue of Athena Polias in the Erechtheion.

Temple of Athena Nike

On the right after leaving the Propylaia, there is a good view back to the exquisitely proportioned little Temple of Athena Nike (which is closed to visitors). It stands on a platform perched atop the steep south-west edge of the Acropolis, overlooking the Saronic Gulf. The temple, designed by Callicrates, was built of Pentelic marble in 427–424 BC.

The building is almost square, with four graceful Ionic columns at either end. Its frieze, of which only fragments remain, consisted of scenes from mythology on the east and south sides, and scenes from the Battle of Plataea (479 BC) and Athenians fighting Boeotians and Persians on the other sides. Parts of the frieze are in the

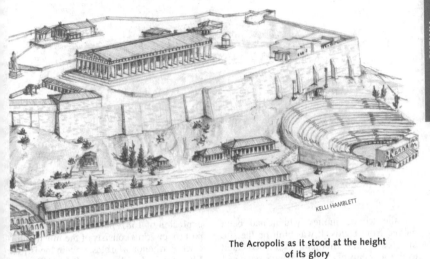

KELLI HAMBLETT

The Acropolis as it stood at the height
of its glory

Acropolis Museum. The platform was surrounded by a marble parapet of relief
sculptures; some of these are also in the
museum, including the beautiful sculpture
of Athena Nike fastening her sandal.

The temple housed a statue of the goddess Athena. In her right hand was a pomegranate (symbol of fertility) and in her left,
a helmet (symbol of war). The temple was
dismantled in 1686 by the Turks, who positioned a huge cannon on the platform. It
was carefully reconstructed between 1836
and 1842, but was taken to pieces again in
1936 because the platform was crumbling.
The platform was reinforced and the temple
rebuilt.

Statue of Athena Promachos

In ancient times, only the pediment of the
Parthenon was visible from the Propylaia;
the rest was obscured by numerous statues
and two sacred buildings.

Continuing ahead along the Panathenaic
Way you will see, to your left, the foundations of pedestals for the statues which once
lined the path. One of them, about 15m beyond the Propylaia, is the foundation of the

gigantic statue of Athena Promachos (*promachos* means 'champion'). The 9m-high
statue was the work of Pheidias, and symbolised Athenian invincibility against the
Persians. The helmeted goddess held a shield
in her left hand and a spear in her right. The
statue was carted off to Constantinople by
Emperor Theodosius in AD 426. By 1204 it
had lost its spear, so the hand appeared to
be gesturing. This led the inhabitants to believe
that the statue had beckoned the crusaders to
the city, so they smashed it to pieces.

Parthenon

You have now reached the Parthenon, the
monument which more than any other epitomises the glory of ancient Greece. The
name Parthenon means 'virgin's apartment'. It is the largest Doric temple ever
completed in Greece, and the only one to be
built completely (apart from its wooden
roof) of Pentelic marble. It is built on the
highest part of the Acropolis, halfway between the eastern and western boundaries.

The Parthenon had a dual purpose – to
house the great statue of Athena commissioned by Pericles, and to serve as a treasury

KELLI HAMBLETT

The Parthenon c.400 BC

for the tribute money which had been moved from Delos. It was built on the site of at least four earlier temples, all dedicated to the worship of Athena. It was designed by Ictinus and Callicrates, under the surveillance of Pheidias, to be the pre-eminent monument of the Acropolis. Building began in 447 BC and was completed in time for the Great Panathenaic Festival of 438 BC.

The temple consisted of eight fluted Doric columns at either end and 17 on each side. To achieve perfect form, its lines were ingeniously curved in order to counteract inharmonious optical illusions. As a result the foundations are slightly concave and the are columns slightly convex, to make both look straight. Supervised by Pheidias, the sculptors Agoracritos and Alcamenes worked on the pediments and the sculpted sections of the frieze (metopes). All of the sculptures they created were brightly coloured and gilded. There were 92 metopes, 44 statues and a frieze, which went all the way around.

The metopes on the eastern side depicted Athenians fighting giants (gigantions), and on the western side they showed Theseus leading the Athenians into battle against the Amazons. Those on the southern side represented the contest of the Lapiths and Centaurs at the marriage feast of Pierithoös. An Ionic frieze 159.5m long ran all around the Parthenon. Much of it was damaged in the

explosion of 1687, but the greatest existing part (over 75m) consists of the much publicised Parthenon Marbles, now in the British Museum in London. The British Government continues to scorn Greek requests for their return.

The ceiling of the Parthenon, like that of the Propylaia, was painted blue and gilded with stars. At the eastern end was the cella (inner room of a temple), the holy of holies, into which only a few privileged initiates could enter.

Here stood the statue for which the temple was built – the **Athena Polias** (Athena of the City), which was considered one of the wonders of the ancient world. The statue was designed by Pheidias and completed in 432 BC. It was made of gold plate over an inner wooden frame, and stood almost 12m high on its pedestal. The face, hands and feet were made of ivory, and the eyes were fashioned from jewels. The goddess was clad in a long dress of gold with the head of Medusa carved in ivory on her breast. In her right hand, she held a statuette of Nike – the goddess of victory – and in her left a spear; at the base of the spear was a serpent. On her head she wore a helmet, on top of which was a sphinx with griffins in relief at either side.

In AD 426 the statue was taken to Constantinople, where it disappeared. There is a Roman copy (the Athena Varvakeion) in the National Archaeological Museum.

Erechtheion

Although the Parthenon was the most impressive monument of the Acropolis, it was more of a showpiece than a sanctuary. That role fell to the Erechtheion, built on the part of the Acropolis that was held most sacred. It was here that Poseidon struck the ground with his trident and that Athena produced the olive tree. The temple is named after Erichthonius, a mythical king of Athens. It housed the cults of Athena, Poseidon and Erichthonius.

If you follow the Panathenaic Way around the northern portico of the Parthenon, you will see the Erechtheion to your left. It is immediately recognisable by the six larger-than-life maidens who take the place of columns to support its southern portico, its much-photographed **Caryatids**. They are so called because the models for them were women from Karyai (modern-day Karyes) in Lakonia.

The Erechtheion was part of Pericles' plan for the Acropolis, but the project was postponed after the outbreak of the Peloponnesian Wars, and work did not start until 421 BC, eight years after his death. It is thought to have been completed in 406 BC.

The Erechtheion is architecturally the most unusual monument of the Acropolis. Whereas the Parthenon is considered the supreme example of Doric architecture, the Erechtheion is considered the supreme example of Ionic. Ingeniously built on several

levels to counteract the unevenness of the ground, it consists of three basic parts – the main temple, northern porch and southern porch – all with different dimensions.

The main temple is of the Ionic order and is divided into two cellae, one dedicated to Athena, the other to Poseidon. Thus the temple represents a reconciliation of the two deities after their contest. In Athena's cella stood an olive-wood statue of Athena Polias holding a shield on which was a gorgon's head. The statue was illuminated by a golden lantern placed at its feet. It was this statue on which the sacred peplos was placed at the culmination of the Panathenaic Festival.

The northern porch consists of six graceful Ionic columns; on the floor are the fissures supposedly cleft by Poseidon's trident. This porch leads into the **Temenos of Pandrossos**, where, according to mythology, the sacred olive brought forth by Athena grew. To the south of here was the **Cecropion** – King Cecrops' burial place.

The southern porch is that of the Caryatids, which prop up a heavy roof of Pentelic marble. The ones you see are plaster casts – the originals (except for one removed by Lord Elgin) are in the site's museum.

Acropolis Museum

The museum at the south-east corner of the Acropolis houses a collection of sculptures and reliefs from the site. The rooms are organised in chronological order, starting with finds from the temples predating the Parthenon and destroyed by the Persians. They include the pedimental sculptures of Heracles slaying the Lernaian Hydra and of a lioness devouring a bull, both in Room I.

The Kora (maiden) statues in Room IV are regarded as the museum's prize exhibits. Most date from the 6th century BC and were uncovered from a pit on the Acropolis, where the Athenians buried them after the Battle of Salamis. The statues were votives dedicated to Athena, each once holding an offering to the goddess. The earliest of these Kora statues are quite stiff and formal in comparison with the later ones, which have flowing robes and elaborate headdresses.

KELLI HAMBLETT

The Caryatids of the Erechtheion

Phone numbers listed incorporate changes due in Oct 2002; see p83

Room VIII contains the few pieces of the Parthenon's frieze that escaped the clutches of Lord Elgin. They depict the Olympians at the Panathenaic procession. It also holds the relief of Athena Nike adjusting her sandal. Room IX is home to four of the five surviving Caryatids, safe behind a perspex screen. The fifth is in the British Museum.

SOUTHERN SLOPE OF THE ACROPOLIS (MAP 3)

All the attractions on the southern slope of the Acropolis are covered at this site (☎ 21 0322 4625, entrance on Dionysiou Areopagitou; admission €1.50; open 8am-7pm daily July-Oct, 8.30am-3pm Tues-Sun Nov-Jan).

Theatre of Dionysos

The importance of theatre in the life of the Athenian city-state can be gauged from the dimensions of the enormous Theatre of Dionysos on the south-eastern slope of the Acropolis.

The first theatre on this site was a timber structure erected sometime during the 6th century BC, after the tyrant Peisistratos had introduced the Festival of the Great Dionysia to Athens. This festival, which took place in March or April, consisted of contests where men clad in goatskins sang and performed dances. Everyone attended, and the watching of performances was punctuated by feasting, revelry and generally letting rip.

During the golden age in the 5th century BC, the annual festival had become one of the major events on the calendar. Politicians would sponsor the production of dramas by writers such as Aeschylus, Sophocles and Euripides, with some light relief provided by the bawdy comedies of Aristophanes. People came from all over Attica, their expenses met by the state – if only present-day governments were as generous to the arts!

The theatre was reconstructed in stone and marble by Lycurgus between 342 and 326 BC. The auditorium had a seating capacity of 17,000, spread over 64 tiers of seats, of which about 20 survive. Apart from the front row, the seats were built of Piraeus limestone and were occupied by

ordinary citizens, although women were confined to the back rows. The front row consisted of 67 thrones built of Pentelic marble, which were reserved for festival officials and important priests. The grandest was in the centre and reserved for the Priest of Dionysos, who sat shaded from the sun under a canopy. The seat can be identified by well-preserved lion-claw feet at either side. In Roman times, the theatre was also used for state events and ceremonies, as well as for performances.

The reliefs at the rear of the stage, mostly of headless figures, depict the exploits of Dionysos and date from the 2nd century BC. The two hefty, hunched-up guys who have managed to keep their heads are *selini*. Selini were worshippers of the mythical Selinos, the debauched father of the satyrs, whose chief attribute seems to have been an outsized phallus. His favourite pastime was charging up mountains in lecherous pursuit of nymphs. He was also Dionysos' mentor.

Asclepion & Stoa of Eumenes

Directly above the Theatre of Dionysos, wooden steps lead up to a pathway. On the left at the top of the steps is the Asclepion, which was built around a sacred spring. The worship of Asclepius, the physician son of Apollo, began in Epidaurus and was introduced to Athens in 429 BC at a time when plague was sweeping the city.

Beneath the Asclepion is the Stoa of Eumenes, a long colonnade built by Eumenes II, King of Pergamum (197–159 BC), as a shelter and promenade for theatre audiences.

Theatre of Herodes Atticus

The path continues west from the Asclepion to the Theatre of Herodes Atticus, built in AD 161. Herodes Atticus was a wealthy Roman who built the theatre in memory of his wife Regilla. It was excavated in 1857–58 and completely restored in 1950–61. There are performances of drama, music and dance here during the Athens Festival. The theatre is open to the public only during performances.

Panagia Hrysospiliotissa

If you retrace your steps back to the Theatre of Dionysos, you will see an indistinct rock-strewn path leading to a grotto in the cliff face. In 320 BC, Thrasyllos turned the grotto into a temple dedicated to Dionysos. Now it is the tiny Panagia Hrysospiliotissa (Chapel of our Lady of the Cavern). It is a poignant little place with old pictures and icons on the walls. Above the chapel are two Ionic columns, the remains of Thrasyllos' temple.

ANCIENT AGORA (MAP 8)

Athens' meeting place in ancient times was the agora (market; ☎ 21 0321 0185, western end of Adrianou; admission €3.55; open 8.30am-3pm Tues-Sun). It was the focal point of administrative, commercial and political life, not to mention social activity. All roads led to the Agora, and it was a lively, crowded place. Socrates spent a lot of time here expounding his philosophy, and in AD 49 St Paul disputed daily in the Agora, intent upon winning converts to Christianity.

The site was first developed in the 6th century BC. It was devastated by the Persians in 480 BC, but a new agora was built in its place almost immediately. It was flourishing by Pericles' time and continued to do so until AD 267, when it was destroyed by the Herulians, a Gothic tribe from Scandinavia. The Turks built a residential quarter on the site, but this was demolished by archaeologists after Independence. If they'd had their way the archaeologists would have also knocked down the whole of Plaka, which was also Turkish. The area has been excavated to classical and, in parts, Neolithic levels.

The main monuments are the Temple of Hephaestus, the Stoa of Attalos and the Church of the Holy Apostles.

The site is bounded by Areopagus Hill in the south, the Athens-Piraeus metro line to the north, Plaka to the east and Leoforos Apostolou Pavlou to the west. There are several entrances, but the most convenient is the northern entrance from Adrianou.

Stoa of Attalos

The Agora Museum in the reconstructed Stoa of Attalos is a good place to start if you want to make any sense of the site. The museum has a model of the Agora upstairs as well as a collection of finds from the site.

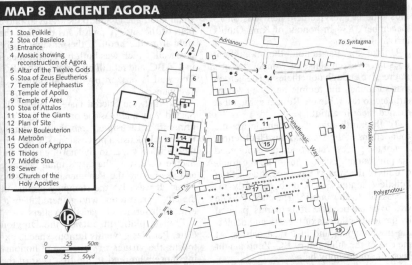

MAP 8 ANCIENT AGORA

1 Stoa Poikile
2 Stoa of Basileios
3 Entrance
4 Mosaic showing reconstruction of Agora
5 Altar of the Twelve Gods
6 Stoa of Zeus Eleutherios
7 Temple of Hephaestus
8 Temple of Apollo
9 Temple of Ares
10 Stoa of Attalos
11 Stoa of the Giants
12 Plan of Site
13 New Bouleuterion
14 Metroön
15 Odeon of Agrippa
16 Tholos
17 Middle Stoa
18 Sewer
19 Church of the Holy Apostles

The original stoa was built by King Attalos II of Pergamum (159–138 BC). It was two storeys high with two aisles, and housed expensive shops. A popular stamping ground for wealthy Athenians, people also gathered here to watch the Panathenaic procession, which crossed in front of the stoa.

It was authentically reconstructed in 1953–56 by the American School of Archaeology. The reconstruction deviates from the original in only one detail: the facade has been left in natural Pentelic marble, but it was originally painted red and blue. The stoa has a series of 45 columns which are Doric on the ground floor and Ionic on the upper gallery.

Temple of Hephaestus

This temple on the western edge of the Agora was surrounded by foundries and metalwork shops, and was dedicated to Hephaestus, god of the forge. It was one of the first buildings of Pericles' rebuilding program and is the best preserved Doric temple in Greece. Built in 449 BC by Ictinus, one of the architects of the Parthenon, it has 34 columns and a frieze on the eastern side depicting nine of the Twelve Labours of Heracles. In AD 1300 it was converted into the **Church of Agios Georgios**. The last service held here was on 13 December 1834 in honour of King Otho's arrival in Athens.

Unlike the Parthenon, the monument does not evoke a sense of wonder, but it's impressive enough nonetheless. The garden that surrounds the temple has been reconstructed to resemble the Roman garden that existed there in antiquity.

To the north-east of the temple are the foundations of the **Stoa of Zeus Eleutherios**, one of the places where Socrates expounded his philosophy. Farther north are the foundations of the **Stoa of Basileios** and the **Stoa Poikile** (Painted Stoa), both currently inaccessible to the public. The Stoa Poikile was so called because of its murals, painted by the leading artists of the day and depicting mythological and historical battles. At the end of the 4th century BC, Zeno taught his Stoic philosophy here.

To the south-east of the Temple of Hephaestus was the **New Bouleuterion**, or council house, where the Senate (originally created by Solon) met. To the south of here was the circular **Tholos** where the heads of government met.

Church of the Holy Apostles

This charming little church, which stands near the southern entrance, was built in the early 11th century to commemorate St Paul's teaching in the Agora. In 1954–57 it was stripped of its 19th-century additions and restored to its original form. It contains some fine Byzantine frescoes.

THE KERAMIKOS (MAP 3)

The city's cemetery from the 12th century BC to Roman times was the Keramikos (☎ 21 0346 3552, entrance at Ermou 148; admission €1.50; open 8am-3pm Tues-Sun). It was discovered in 1861 during the construction of Pireos, the street which leads to Piraeus. Despite its location on the seedier part of Ermou, beyond Monastiraki, it is one of the most green and tranquil of Athens' ancient sites.

Sacred & Dipylon Gates

Once you have entered the site, head for the small knoll ahead and to the right, to find a plan of the site. A path leads down to the right from the knoll to the remains of the city wall, which was built by Themistocles in 479 BC, and rebuilt by Konon in 394 BC. The wall is broken by the foundations of two gates.

The first, the Sacred Gate, spanned the Sacred Way and was the one by which pilgrims from Eleusis entered the city during the annual Eleusian procession. The second, the Dipylon Gate, to the north-east of the Sacred Gate, was the city's main entrance and was where the Panathenaic procession began. It was also the stamping ground of the city's prostitutes, who gathered there to offer their services to jaded travellers.

From a platform outside the Dipylon Gate, Pericles gave his famous speech extolling the virtues of Athens and honouring those who died in the first year of the

Peloponnesian Wars. The speech stirred many more to battle – and to their deaths.

Between the Sacred and the Dipylon gates are the foundations of the **Pompeion**. This building was used as a dressing room for participants in the Panathenaic procession.

Street of Tombs

The Street of Tombs leads off the Sacred Way to the left as you head away from the city. This avenue was reserved for the tombs of Athens' most prominent citizens. The surviving stelae are now in the National Archaeological Museum, and what you see are replicas. They consist of an astonishing array of funerary monuments, and their bas-reliefs warrant more than a cursory examination.

Ordinary citizens were buried in the areas bordering the Street of Tombs. One very well-preserved stele shows a little girl with her pet dog. You will find it by going up the stone steps on the northern side of the Street of Tombs. The site's largest stele, that of sisters Demetria and Pamphile, is on the path running from the south-east corner of the Street of Tombs. Pamphile is seated beside a standing Demetria.

Oberlaender Museum (Map 3)

The site's Oberlaender Museum *(Open 8am-3pm Tues-Sun)* is named after its benefactor, Gustav Oberlaender, a German-American stocking manufacturer. It contains stelae and sculpture from the site, as well as an impressive collection of vases and terracotta figurines. The museum is to the left of the site entrance and admission is included in the Keramikos entrance fee.

ROMAN ATHENS

All the sites covered in this section appear on Map 7 (Ancient Athens), as well as on individual maps as indicated here.

Tower of the Winds & Roman Agora (Map 4)

This archaeological site *(☎ 21 0324 5220, Cnr Pelopida Eolou & Markou Aureliou; admission €1.50; open 8.30am-3pm Tues-Sun)* comprises the Tower of the Winds and the Roman Agora, next to one another to the

east of the Ancient Agora and north of the Acropolis.

The well-preserved Tower of the Winds was built in the 1st century BC by a Syrian astronomer named Andronicus. The octagonal monument of Pentelic marble is an ingenious construction which functioned as a sundial, weather vane, water clock and compass. Each side represents a point of the compass, and has a relief of a figure floating through the air, which depicts the wind associated with that particular point. Beneath each of the reliefs are the faint markings of sundials. The weather vane, which disappeared long ago, was a bronze Triton that revolved on top of the tower. The Turks, not ones to let a good building go to waste, allowed dervishes to use the tower.

The entrance to the Roman Agora is through the well preserved **Gate of Athena Archegetis**, which is flanked by four Doric columns. It was erected sometime in the 1st century AD and financed by Julius Caesar.

The rest of the Roman Agora appears to the layperson as little more than a heap of rubble. To the right of the entrance are the foundations of a 1st-century public latrine. In the south-east area are the foundations of a propylon and a row of shops.

Arch of Hadrian (Map 3)

The Roman emperor Hadrian had a great affection for Athens. Although, like all Roman emperors, he did his fair share of spiriting its classical artwork to Rome, he also embellished the city with many monuments influenced by classical architecture. Grandiose as these monuments are, they lack the refinement and artistic flair of their classical predecessors.

The Arch of Hadrian is a lofty monument of Pentelic marble, now blackened by the effluent of exhausts, which stands where traffic-clogged Vasilissis Olgas and Amalias meet. It was erected by Hadrian in AD 132, probably to commemorate the consecration of the Temple of Olympian Zeus (see the following section). The inscriptions show that it was also intended as a dividing point between the ancient city and the Roman city. The north-west frieze

MAP 9 ATHENS (ANCIENT)

1 Acharnian Gate	12 Library of Hadrian	23 Gymnasium	32 South Gate
2 North-East Gate	13 Roman Agora	24 Baths	33 Halade Gate
3 Eriai Gate	14 Tower of the Winds	25 Hippades Gate	34 Itonian Gate
4 Dipylon Gate	15 Pantheon	26 Temple of Olympian	35 Hadrian's Gymnasium
5 Sacred Gate	16 Diochares Gate	Zeus	36 Diomeian Gate
6 Pompeion	17 Lyceum	27 Arch of Hadrian	37 Kallirhoë Fountain
7 Stoa Poikile	18 Demian Gate	28 Dipylon above Gate	38 Agrai Metroön
8 Peiraic Gate	19 Melitides Gate	29 Northern Long Wall to	39 Artemis Agrotera
9 Temple of Hephaestus	20 Pnyx	Piraeus	40 Poseidon Heliconios
10 Metroön	21 Odeon of Pericles	30 Southern Long Wall	41 Ardettos Hill
11 Stoa of Attalos	22 Monument of Lysicrates	31 Monument of Filopappos	

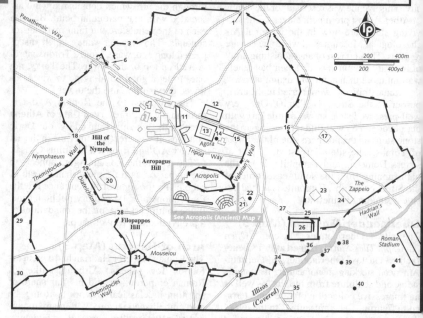

bears the inscription 'This is Athens, the Ancient city of Theseus'; while the southeast frieze states 'This is the city of Hadrian, and not of Theseus'.

Temple of Olympian Zeus (Map 6)

This is the largest temple in Greece (☎ 21 0922 6330; admission €1.50; open 8.30am -3pm Tues-Sun). It took over 700 years to build. The temple was begun in the 6th century BC by Peisistratos, but was abandoned for lack of funds. Various other leaders had stabs at completing the temple,

but it was left to Hadrian to complete the work in AD 131.

The temple is impressive for the sheer size of its 104 Corinthian columns (17m high with a base diameter of 1.7m), of which 15 remain – the fallen column was blown down in a gale in 1852. Hadrian put a colossal statue of Zeus in the cella and, in typically immodest fashion, placed an equally large one of himself next to it.

Library of Hadrian (Map 3)

This library is to the north of the Roman Agora. The building, which was of vast dimensions, was erected in the 2nd century AD and included a cloistered courtyard bordered by 100 columns. As well as books, the building housed music and lecture rooms and a theatre. The library is at present inaccessible to visitors.

Roman Stadium (Map 1)

The last Athenian monument with Roman connections is the Roman Stadium, which lies in a fold between two pine-covered hills between the neighbourhoods of Mets and Pangrati. The stadium was originally built in the 4th century BC as a venue for the Panathenaic athletic contests. A thousand wild animals are said to have been slaughtered in the arena at Hadrian's inauguration in AD 120. Shortly after this, the seats were rebuilt in Pentelic marble by Herodes Atticus.

After hundreds of years of disuse the stadium was completely restored in 1895 by wealthy Greek benefactor Georgios Averof. The following year the first Olympic Games of modern times were held here. It is a faithful replica of the Roman Stadium, comprising seats of Pentelic marble for 70,000 spectators, a running track and a central area for field events.

BYZANTINE ATHENS

Byzantine architecture in Athens is fairly thin on the ground. By the time of the split in the Roman Empire, Athens had shrunk to little more than a provincial town and Thessaloniki had become the major city. The most important Byzantine building is the **monastery** at Dafni, 10km west of the city, which is covered in the Around Athens section later in this chapter.

Central Athens has a number of churches, of which the 11th-century **Church of Agios Eleftherios** (Map 4) on Plateia Mitropoleos, Plaka, is considered the finest. It is built partly of Pentelic marble and decorated with an external frieze of symbolic beasts in bas-relief. It was once the city's cathedral, but now stands in the shadows of the much larger new cathedral.

The **Church of Kapnikarea** (Map 4), halfway down Ermou, in Monastiraki, is

another small 11th-century church. Its dome is supported by four large Roman columns. The **Church of Agii Theodori** (Map 3), just off Plateia Klafthmonos on Stadiou, has a tiled dome and walls decorated with a terracotta frieze of animals and plants.

Other churches worth peering into are the **Church of the Holy Apostles** (see Ancient Agora, earlier) and the **Church of Agios Dimitrios** (see the Hills of Athens section, later).

NEOCLASSICAL ATHENS (MAP 3)

Athens also boasts a large number of fine neoclassical buildings dating from the period after independence. Foremost among these are the buildings of the celebrated **neoclassical trilogy** on Panepistimiou, halfway between Omonia and Syntagma, which draw heavily on the monuments of the ancient city for their inspiration.

The centrepiece is the splendid **Athens University**, designed by the Danish architect Cristian Hansen and completed in 1864. It still serves as the university's administrative headquarters, although the main campus has moved east to Zografou. It is flanked to the south by the **Athens Academy**, designed by Hansen's brother Theophile and completed in 1885. The Ionian-style entrance mimics the eastern entrance to the Erechtheion. Neither is open to the general public.

The trilogy is completed by the **National Library** (☎ 21 0360 8185, Panepistimiou 32; admission free; open 9am-8pm Mon-Thur, 9am-2pm Fri & Sat), north of the university. Completed in 1902, the main feature is the corridor leading to the reading room, which is flanked by a row of Doric columns influenced by the Temple of Hephaestus in the Ancient Agora.

NATIONAL ARCHAEOLOGICAL MUSEUM (MAP 9)

Opened in 1874, and standing supreme among the nation's finest is the National Archaeological Museum (☎ 21 0821 7717, Oktovriou-Patission 44; adult/student

MAP 10 NATIONAL ARCHAEOLOGICAL MUSEUM

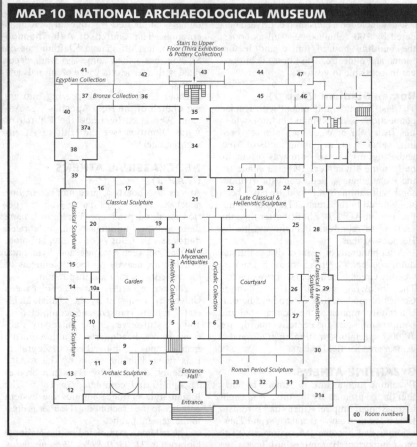

Stairs to Upper Floor (Thira Exhibition & Pottery Collection)

41 *Egyptian Collection*
42
43
44
47

37 *Bronze Collection* 36
45
46

40

37a

35

38

34

39

16 17 18
22 23 24
Late Classical & Hellenistic Sculpture

21

Classical Sculpture

20 19

25 28

3 *Hall of Mycenaen Antiquities*

Classical Sculpture

15

Neolithic Collection

Cycladic Collection

Late Classical & Hellenistic Sculpture

14 10a

Garden

Courtyard

26 29

10

5 4 6

27

Archaic Sculpture

9

30

11 8 7

13 *Archaic Sculpture*

Entrance Hall

Roman Period Sculpture

33 32 31

12

31a

1

Entrance

00 *Room numbers*

€5.90/2.95; open 12.30pm-7pm Mon, 8am-7pm Tues-Sun Apr-Oct, 10.30am-5pm Mon, 8am-5pm Tues-Sun Nov-Mar). Despite all the pilfering by foreign archaeologists in the 19th century, it still has the world's finest collection of Greek antiquities – in particular, the magnificent Hall of Mycenaean Antiquities and the Thira Exhibition, which contains the celebrated collection of Minoan frescoes unearthed at Akrotiri on the island of Santorini (Thira).

The museum highlights are described here, and there are comprehensive explanations given in English in each room.

Guidebooks on sale in the foyer provide more information.

To reach the museum from Plaka, catch trolleybus No 5 or 15 from outside the National Gardens on Amalias. The walk takes about 30 minutes.

Map 9 features a floor plan of the museum; see Map 3 for the museum's location. At the time of research, the museum's first floor was closed for renovation following damage sustained in the 1999 earthquake. Some of the displays from this floor have been relocated to the Temporary Exhibitions room on the ground floor.

Mycenean Antiquities: Rooms 3 & 4

The museum's *tour de force* is the Hall of Mycenaean Antiquities, straight ahead from the entrance foyer. Gold gleams at you from everywhere. The chief exhibits are finds from the six shaft graves of Grave Circle A at Mycenae. Graves one to five were excavated by Heinrich Schliemann in 1874–76 and the sixth by Panagiotes Stamatakis in 1886–1902. The star attraction is the golden **Mask of Agamemnon**, housed in case 3. (It has subsequently been proven to belong to a king who died three centuries before Agamemnon.)

In the centre of the hall, cases 28 and 29 contain gold sheets that covered the bodies of two royal babies. On the left, cases 5 and 6 contain finds from Grave Circle B (from 1650 to 1550 BC), which was outside the citadel at Mycenae. Case 5 has an unusual rock-crystal vase in the shape of a duck: its head and neck are gracefully turned back to form a handle. Case 30, also in the centre, contains miscellaneous finds from Mycenae, including a delightful ivory carving of two voluptuous women and a child, who may represent Demeter, Persephone and Iacchus.

On the right, just beyond here, is the famous **Warrior Vase** which, along with the Mask of Agamemnon, Schliemann rated as one of his greatest finds. It depicts men leaving for war and a woman waving them goodbye.

The rest of the hall is devoted to other Mycenaean sites. Case 9 features tablets with inscriptions in Cretan Linear B script, while case 15 contains objects from Tiryns, including the famous **Tiryns Treasure**. The treasure is believed to have been looted by a tomb robber, who then reburied it and failed to retrieve it. Back in the centre, case 32 contains the famous gold cups from the beehive-shaped tomb at Vaphio, which depict the taming of wild bulls. These magnificent cups are regarded as among the finest examples of Mycenaean art.

Room 3 contains Mycenaean finds from Central Greece, Thessaly and the island of Skopelos.

Neolithic Collection: Room 5

To the left of the Hall of Mycenaean Antiquities, Room 5 contains Neolithic finds – mainly from Thessaly. There is also a case of pottery, figurines and jewellery from Troy, including a beautiful necklace of delicate gold beads. These finds were presented to the museum by Sophie Schliemann, wife of Heinrich.

Cycladic Collection: Room 6

The collection includes the largest Cycladic figurine ever found. It is almost life-size and was discovered on the island of Amorgos.

Cases 56, 57 and 58 contain ceramic 'frying pans' from early Cycladic cemeteries on Syros. They are black with intricate inlaid patterns in white. In case you're wondering why on earth these people took frying pans to the grave with them, they are so called merely because of their shape.

Archaic Sculpture: Rooms 7 to 14

The huge sepulchral amphora (a jar with two handles and a narrow neck) in room 7 is considered the best example of the geometric style of pottery. It dates from 760 BC and was found in the Keramikos.

The chief exhibit in room 8 is the huge *kouros* dating from 600 BC. This was a votive offering found in the Temple of Poseidon at Cape Sounion.

Room 10 contains gravestones from the 6th century and two well-preserved sphinxes, one from Piraeus (540 BC) and the other from Sparta (570 BC).

Room 11 features the torso of another colossal kouros (540 BC), found at Megara in Attica.

Room 13 is dominated by the sepulchral kouros named Croesus. To the left of this sculpture is the base of a kouros found in the Keramikos. It has reliefs on three sides: one shows four clothed youths provoking a fight between a cat and dog; another shows naked youths wrestling; and the third shows youths playing a ball game.

Room 14 is devoted to provincial stele monuments. The gravestone by Alxenor is one of the finest in the room and bears an endearing, if egocentric, inscription by the artist: 'Alxenor the Naxian made me. Admire me'.

Classical Sculpture: Rooms 15 to 20

The bronze statue of **Poseidon of Artemision** (450 BC) in room 15 is another of the highlights of the museum. The statue was hauled out of the sea off Cape Artemision in 1928, and shows Poseidon poised to hurl his trident (now missing). More than any other statue of Poseidon, it conveys the god's strength and unlimited power.

Just within the door of this room is a beautiful relief from Eleusis (440 BC). It depicts Demeter, accompanied by her daughter Persephone, giving Triptolemos an ear of wheat to sprout.

Room 16 contains classical grave monuments, most of which were found in Attica. Rooms 17 and 19 contain classical votive sculpture. Room 20 consists mostly of Roman copies of classical Greek statues. At the far end is the statue of Athena Varvakeion, which was made in about 200 BC. It is the most famous copy – much reduced in size – of the statue of Athena Polias by Pheidias that once stood in the Parthenon. Room 18 contains late-5th- and early-4th-century sepulchral monuments.

Late Classical & Hellenistic Sculpture: Rooms 21 to 30, 34 & 35

Room 21, the central hall, is dominated by the remarkable 2nd-century bronze statue of the **Horse and Jockey of Artemision**, so named because it was found with the statue of Poseidon. It is a wonderfully animated sculpture – check out the worried look on the jockey's face.

There is an unusual grave monument (540 BC) in the centre of room 24 consisting of a floral column which supports a cauldron decorated with griffins.

Room 25 is mostly devoted to charming diminutive reliefs of nymphs. They are not individually labelled, but there is an explanation in English of their role. On the left, just before room 26, is a highly unusual votive relief of a snake and a huge sandal on which is carved a worshipping figure. It dates from 360 BC and is believed to depict the Hero of the Slipper, who was worshipped near the Theatre of Dionysos.

Room 28 contains some extremely realistic funerary monuments, particularly the Grave Monument of Aristonautes (330 BC), found in the Keramikos. The large sepulchral relief of a boy attempting to restrain a frisky horse is a powerful and unprecedented piece of realist sculpture, especially the leg muscles of both the horse and boy, and the magnificent drapery. It was found near Larisis Station in 1948, and dates from the second half of the 3rd century.

The famous **Ephebos of Antikythira** (340 BC) stands in the centre of the room. The amazingly lifelike eyes are almost hypnotic. Behind this statue, to the right, is the head of a bronze statue – probably of the Elean boxer Satyros. He certainly looks a nasty piece of work in contrast to the calm 'other world' expressions on the faces surrounding him.

Room 29 is dominated by the statue of Themis (the goddess of justice). Behind her is a head of Alexander the Great sporting graffitied cheeks (added later), and a head of the orator Demosthenes looking very perplexed.

The comic masks on the right in room 30 provide some light relief, although some of their expressions are as menacing as they are funny. A little way down, in the middle of the room, is a delightful and sensitive sculpture of a naked boy with his hand on a goose – note his gentle smile and the apparent softness of his skin.

Dominating the room is yet another statue of the sea god, Poseidon (140 BC), which was found on Milos in 1877. Behind this statue is the bronze head of a melancholic-looking guy; it was found on Delos. To the right is an amusing sculpture of Pan making amorous advances towards Aphrodite, who is about to clobber him with her sandal.

Room 34 is built to simulate an open-air sanctuary and displays objects from the **Sanctuary of Aphrodite** which existed near Dafni.

oman Period Sculpture: ooms 31 to 33

1ese rooms house sculptures produced
Greece during the period of the Roman
cupation from the 1st to the 5th cen-
ries AD.

ronze Collection: ooms 36 & 37

1e highlight of these rooms is the **Kara-
anos Collection** of bronzes (room 36)
und at the celebrated Sanctuary of Zeus at
odoni in Epiros. It includes a chariot from
e Roman period. Room 37 was the first
onze room to be opened. A case on the
ft shows casting techniques; another
ows burial offerings. In the middle is a
onze statue of a youth (337 BC), which
as found in the Bay of Marathon.

gyptian Collection: ooms 40 & 41

1e main point of interest is the collection
elaborately decorated mummy cases in
om 40.

emporary Exhibitions: oom 45

oom 45 has become the temporary home
r a mixture of pieces drawn from the
1ira Exhibition and the pottery collection,
ormally found on the first floor.

hira Exhibition: Room 48a

1e rear section of the hall at the top of the
airs houses the celebrated frescoes un-
rthed by Spyridon Marinatos at the Min-
an settlement of Akrotiri on Santorini
hira) in the late 1960s.

The frescoes are better preserved than the
inoan frescoes found on Crete. Extremely
eautiful and harmonious in both colour and
rm, they give a comprehensive insight into
e everyday life of the Minoans. Scenes de-
cted in the frescoes include two boxing
ouths, a youth holding two strings of fish,
d women performing religious rites. The
ost unusual is one which shows a flotilla of
ips sailing from one coastal town to an-
her. The frescoes will remain here until a
itable museum has been built on Santorini.

Pottery Collection: Rooms 48 to 56

These rooms house the world's most comprehensive collection of ancient Greek pottery. The collection traces the development
from the Bronze Age (room 48), through the
Protogeometric and Geometric periods, to
the beginning of simple decorative motifs.

Flora, fauna and human figures first featured on pottery in the 8th century BC, and
mythical scenes appeared a century later.
The 6th century BC saw the emergence of
the famous Attic black-figured pottery. By
the middle of the 5th century BC, the pots
with black figures had been superseded by
red-figured pottery, which reached the peak
of perfection during Pericles' rule.

OTHER MUSEUMS

The National Archaeological Museum
might steal the show, but Athens has lots
more in store for keen museum-goers with
time on their hands. The following selection
has been drawn from a list of 28 (available
from the tourist office), covering everything
from Byzantine art to old theatre props. See
the following Free Museums in Athens section for more information on museums.

Benaki Museum (Map 5)

This museum (☎ 21 0367 1000, Cnr Vasilissis Sofias & Koumbari 1, Kolonaki;
adult/student €5.90/2.95; open 9am-5pm
Mon, Wed, Fri & Sat, 9am-midnight Thur,
9am-3pm Sun) contains the sumptuous collection of Antoine Benaki, accumulated during 35 years of avid collecting in Europe and
Asia. In 1931 he turned the family house
into a museum and presented it to the Greek
nation. The collection includes Bronze Age
finds from Mycenae and Thessaly; two early
works by El Greco; ecclesiastical furniture
brought from Asia Minor; pottery, copper,
silver and woodwork from Egypt, Asia
Minor and Mesopotamia; and a stunning
collection of Greek regional costumes.

Goulandris Museum of Cycladic & Ancient Greek Art (Map 5)

This private museum (☎ 21 0801 5870, Cnr
Vasilissis Sofias & Neofytou Douka,

Kolonaki; adult/student €2.95/1.50; open 10am-4pm Mon, Wed-Fri, 10am-3pm Sat) houses a collection of Cycladic art second in importance only to that displayed at the National Archaeological Museum. The museum was custom-built for the collection and the finds are beautifully displayed and well labelled. Although the exhibits cover all periods from Cycladic to Roman times, the emphasis is on the Cycladic from 3000 to 2000 BC. The 230 exhibits include the marble figurines with folded arms which inspired many 20th-century artists with their simplicity and purity of form.

The museum has now taken over the 19th-century mansion next door, which it uses for temporary exhibitions. The entrance is on Neofytou Douka.

Byzantine Museum (Map 5)

A large collection of Christian art, dating from the 4th to 19th century, is housed in the Villa Ilissia, an attractive, mock-Florentine mansion now a museum (*☎ 21 0723 1570, Vasilissis Sofias 22, Kolonaki; admission €1.50; open 8.30am-3pm Tues-Sun).*

Unfortunately, the museum appears to be operating permanently at half-capacity with no evidence of progress towards reopening the wing to the right of the courtyard. This wing housed many of the finest frescoes and icons; some are in storage, others have been moved temporarily to Thessaloniki.

The downstairs rooms in the surviving wing are given over to re-creations of churches, starting with a very solemn basilica from the 5th to the 7th centuries. The reconstruction of an 11th-century Byzantine church is beautiful in its simplicity, in contrast to the elaborate decorations of the post-Byzantine church next door. The bishop's throne in this room was brought to Athens by refugees from Asia Minor. The upstairs rooms contain icons and frescoes.

Numismatic Museum (Map 4)

This collection is housed in a magnificent neoclassical mansion (*☎ 21 0821 7769, Panepistimiou 12, Syntagma; admission €2.35; open 8am-2.30pm Tues-Sun).* It comprises 400,000 coins from ancient

Greek, Hellenic, Roman and Byzantine times. The building was once the home of the celebrated archaeologist Heinrich Schliemann.

Museum of Greek Folk Art (Map 3)

A superb collection of secular and religious folk art, mainly from the 18th and 19th centuries, is housed in this museum (*☎ 21 032 9031, Kydathineon 17, Plaka; admission €1.50; open 10am-2pm Tues-Sun).* On the 1st floor is embroidery, pottery, weaving and puppets. On the 2nd floor is a reconstructed traditional village house with paintings by the primitive artist Theophilos of Lesvos (Mytilini). Greek traditional costumes are displayed on the 3rd and 4th floors.

National Art Gallery (Map 1)

The emphasis in this gallery (*☎ 21 0723 5857, Vasileos Konstantinou 50, adult/student €2.95/1.50; open 8.30am-7pm Tues-Sun July-Oct; 9am-3pm Mon-Sat, 6pm-9pm Mon & Wed, 9am-2pm Sun Nov-June),* opposite the Hilton Hotel, is on Greek painting and sculpture from the 19th and 20th centuries. There are also 16th-century works and a few works by European masters, including paintings by Picasso, Marquet and Utrillo and Magritte's sculpture *The Therapist.*

Paintings by the primitive painter Theophilos are displayed on the mezzanine floor and 20th-century works are on the 1st floor. The 2nd floor has mostly 19th-century paintings, with one room of earlier works. It has four El Greco paintings, including *The Crucifixion* and *Symphony of the Angels.*

Greek sculpture of the 19th and 20th centuries is effectively displayed in the sculpture garden and sculpture hall, reached from the lower floor. There are several works by Giannolis Halepas (1851–1937), one of Greece's foremost sculptors.

National Historical Museum (Map 4)

This museum (*☎ 21 0323 7617, Stadiou 13, adult/student €2.95/0.60; open 9am-2pm Tues-Sun)* specialises in memorabilia from the War of Independence, including Byron's helmet and sword. There is also a series of paintings depicting events leading up to the war, Byzantine and medieval exhibits and a collection of photographs and royal portraits.

The museum is housed in the old parliament building at Plateia Kolokotroni, Stadiou, in Syntagma. Theodoros Deligiannis, who succeeded Trikoupis as prime minister of Greece, was assassinated on the steps of the building in 1905.

City of Athens Museum (Map 3)

Occupying the palace where King Otho and his consort Amalia lived for a few years during the 1830s is this museum (☎ 21 0324 5164, Paparigopoulou 7, Syntagma; admission €1.50; open 9am-1.30pm Mon, Wed, Fri & Sat). It contains some of the royal couple's furniture, costumes and personal mementoes, as well as paintings, prints and models of Athens in the 19th century.

Jewish Museum (Map 3)

This museum (☎ 21 0322 5882, Nikis 39, Plaka; admission €1.50; open 9am-2.30pm Mon-Fri, 10am-2pm Sun), housed in a 19th-century mansion, traces the history of the Jewish community in Greece back to the 3rd century BC through an impressive collection of religious and folk art, and documents. It includes a reconstruction of a synagogue.

Theatre Museum (Map 3)

Aspiring thespians may be interested in visiting this museum (☎ 21 0362 9430, Akadimias 50; admission €1.50; open 9am-2.30pm Mon-Fri). It contains memorabilia from the 19th and 20th centuries. Exhibits include photographs, costumes, props and reconstructions of the dressing rooms of Greece's most celebrated 20th-century actors.

Free Museums

Athens also has some interesting free museums. A favourite, near the Tower of the Winds, is the Museum of Greek Popular Instruments (Map 4; ☎ 21 0325 4119, Diogenous 1-3, Plaka; open 10am-2pm Tues, Thur-Sun, noon-6pm Wed). It has displays and recordings of a wide selection of traditional instruments.

A good display of costumes, embroideries, pottery and musical instruments can be seen at the Centre of Folk Arts & Traditions (Map 3; ☎ 21 0324 3987, Angelika Hatzimihali 6, Plaka; open 9am-1pm & 5pm-9pm Tues-Fri, 9am-1pm Sat & Sun).

Displays are shown from a different region of Greece every year at the Museum of the History of Greek Costume (Map 5; ☎ 21 0362 9513, Dimokritou 7, Kolonaki).

Next to the Byzantine Museum in Kolonaki, is the War Museum (Map 5; ☎ 21 0729 0543/0544, Cnr Vas Sofias & Rizari 2; open 9am-2pm Tues-Fri, 9.30am-2pm Sat & Sun). It is a relic of the colonels' junta as well as being an architectural statement of the times. Greece seems to have been at war since time immemorial, and a look around helps to get the country's history in perspective. All periods from the Mycenaean to the present day are covered, and displays include weapons, maps, armour and models of battles.

HILLS OF ATHENS
Lykavittos Hill (Map 5)

The name Lykavittos means 'hill of wolves' and derives from ancient times when the hill was surrounded by countryside and its pine-covered slopes were inhabited by wolves. Today, it is no longer surrounded by countryside nor inhabited by wolves, but rises out of a sea of concrete to offer the finest views in Athens. Pollution permitting, there are panoramic views of the city, the Attic basin, the surrounding mountains and the islands of Salamis and Aegina. A path leads to the summit from the top of Loukianou. Alternatively, you can take the funicular railway (€1.50/2.95 single/return, 9.15am-11.45pm daily) from the top of Ploutarhou.

There is a cafe halfway up the path and another at the top, as well as a restaurant with a spectacular view over the Acropolis. Also on the summit is the little Chapel of Agios Giorgios. The chapel is floodlit at night and from the streets below looks like a vision from a fairy tale. The open-air Lykavittos Theatre (Map 1), to the northeast of the summit, is used for performances of jazz and rock during the Athens Festival.

West of the Acropolis

The low **Areopagus Hill (Map 3)** lies between the Acropolis and the Ancient Agora. According to mythology, it was here that Ares was tried by the council of the gods for the murder of Halirrhothios, son of Poseidon. The council accepted his defence of justifiable deicide on the grounds that he was protecting his daughter, Alcippe, from unwanted advances.

The hill became the place where murder trials were heard before the Council of the Areopagus, whose jurisdiction by the 4th century had been extended to cover treason and corruption. In AD 51, St Paul delivered his famous 'Sermon to an Unknown God' from Areopagus Hill and gained his first Athenian convert, Dionysos, who became patron saint of the city.

Areopagus Hill is linked to the Acropolis by a saddle and can be climbed by steps cut into the rock. There are good views of the Ancient Agora from the summit. The rock is very, very slippery, so wear suitable shoes and be careful.

Filopappos Hill (Map 6), also called the Hill of the Muses, is clearly identifiable to the south-west of the Acropolis by virtue of the Monument of Filopappos at its summit. The monument was built in AD 114–16 in honour of Julius Antiochus Filopappos, who was a prominent Roman consul and administrator.

There are small paths all over the hill, but the paved path to the top starts next to the Dionysos Taverna on Dionysiou Areopagitou. The pine-clad slopes are a pleasant place for a stroll and offer good views of the plain and mountains of Attica and of the Saronic Gulf. After 250m, the path passes the **Church of Agios Dimitrios**, which contains some fine frescoes. It was sensitively restored in 1951–57.

North of here is the rocky **Hill of the Pnyx (Map 3)**. This was the meeting place of the Democratic Assembly in the 5th century BC. Among the great orators who addressed assemblies here were Aristides, Demosthenes, Pericles and Themistocles.

To the north-west of the Hill of the Pnyx is the **Hill of the Nymphs**, on which stands

an observatory built in 1842. It is open t visitors on the last Friday of each month.

PARKS

Athens is sadly lacking in parks. Only thre are large enough to be worth a mention.

National Gardens (Map 3)

For a delightful, shady refuge during th summer months try these gardens (Entrance on Vasilissis Sofias & Amalias; admissio free). They are the favourite haunt of Athen many stray cats, and were formerly the roy gardens designed by Queen Amalia.

The gardens contain subtropical trees, o namental ponds with waterfowl, and **botanical museum** (Admission free; ope 9am-3pm Tues-Sun). This museum house some interesting old photographs of 19th century Athens as well as botanical info mation about gardens. The gardens als contain a large children's playground.

Zappeio Gardens (Map 3)

These gardens (Entrances on Amalias Vasilissis Olgas; admission free) are lai out in a network of wide walkways aroun the Zappeio, which was built in the 187(with money donated by the wealthy Gree Romanian benefactor Konstantinos Zappa Until the 1970s, the Zappeio was use mainly as an exhibition hall. It was used fo Council of Europe meetings durin Greece's presidency of the EC.

Areos Park (Map 2)

North of the National Archaeological Mu seum is a pleasant park (Entrances on Lec foros Alexandras & Mavromateon; admissio free). It's large with wide, tree-lined a enues, one of which has a long line of sta ues of War of Independence heroes.

Athens' First Cemetery (Map 1)

Athens' First Cemetery (Proto Nekr tafeion Athinon; Mets; open 7.30am-6p daily) is not strictly a park, but in the al sence of real parks, any patch of greenery welcome. Athenian families who come t attend the graves of loved ones certain seem to take this attitude, turning duty in

n outing by bringing along a picnic. It's a
eaceful place to stroll around and is the
esting place of many famous Greeks and
hilhellenes.

The cemetery is well kept and most of the
ombstones and mausoleums are lavish in the
xtreme. Some are kitsch and sentimental,
thers are works of art created by the fore-
ost Greek sculptors of the 19th century,
uch as the *Sleeping Maiden* by Halepas,
vhich is the tomb of a young girl. Someone
laces a red rose in her hand every day.

Among the cemetery's famous residents
re the writers Rangavis (1810–92) and
outsos (1800–68); the politician Harilaos
rikoupis (1832–96); the archaeologists
leinrich Schliemann (1822–90) and Adolph
urtwängler (1853–1907); the benefactors
ntoine Benaki, Georgios Averof and Theo-
oros Syngros; and War of Independence
eroes Sir Richard Church (1784– 1873),
olokotronis (1770–1843), Makrygiannis
nd Androutsos. Schliemann's mausoleum
s decorated with scenes from the Trojan
Var. Located near the entrance is a memo-
ial – poignant in its simplicity – to the
0,000 citizens who died of starvation dur-
1g WWII.

The cemetery is 600m south-east of the
emple of Olympian Zeus at the end of
Anapafseos in Mets. You'll know you're
etting close when you see all the stone-
1asons and flower shops. Other shops sell
emetery paraphernalia, ranging from life-
ize figures of Christ to miniature picture
rames – used to put photographs of the de-
eased on the gravestones.

ACTIVITIES
Beaches
Most tourists forget that Athens is a coastal
ity, and there are some good beaches
vithin easy distance of the city centre. The
est beaches are around the resort district of
Glyfada, about 12km south-east of Syn-
agma. See the Around Athens section later
n this chapter for details.

Skiing
The nearest ski fields to Athens are at Mt
Parnassos, three hours north-west, where

the season lasts from mid-December to
March or April. Excursions to the resort of
Kelaria are organised by the ski department
at the big department store of **Klaoudatos**
(☎ 21 0324 1915, *Kratinou 3–5 & Athinas;
bus €8.80, skis, bindings, boots & poles
€8.80, snowboards €11.75, toboggans
€5.90*). Its buses leave from the stadium in
Athens every morning at 4.50am and get to
Kelaria just after 8.30am. They leave the resort at 4pm.

Golf
Near the airport, is Athens' only course the
Glyfada Golf Club (☎ 21 0894 6820, *End of
Pronois; green fees €41.10/52.85 weekdays/
weekends & public holidays, clubs €20.55,
buggy €5.90*).

Tennis
Visitors are welcome to use the courts at the
Glyfada Golf Club (*see above; €8.80 per
hour; open 1pm-sunset Mon, 7.30am-sunset
Tues-Sun*).

There are public courts at the beaches
south of Glyfada. The beaches at Voula,
Vouliagmeni and Varkiza all have courts.
They cost €4.40 an hour during the day and
€6.45 an hour with lights. All are open 8am
to 8pm daily.

Tenpin Bowling
The **Athens Bowling Centre (off Map 1)**
(☎ 21 0867 3645, *Oktovriou-Patission 177;
games €4.40/5.30 weekdays/weekends;
open 10am-2am daily*) is 100m north of
Plateia Amerikis.

LANGUAGE COURSES
If you are serious about learning Greek, an
intensive course at the start of your stay is
a good way to go about it.

The Athens Centre (☎ 21 0701 2268, *fax
21 0701 8603,* e *athenscr@compulink.gr,*
w *www.athenscentre.gr, Arhimidous 48*)
Map 1 In the quiet residential suburb of
Mets, this centre has a very good reputation.
Its courses cover five levels of proficiency
from beginners to advanced. There are eight
immersion courses a year for beginners,
packing approximately 60 hours of class

time into three weeks for €4.40. The centre occupies a fine neoclassical building.

Hellenic American Union (☎ 21 0362 9886, fax 21 0363 3174, [e] *vioannou@hau .gr*, [W] *www.hau.gr, Massalias 22, Kolonaki)* **Map 5** Prices from €295. This is another place offering courses, with courses lasting between one and three months covering all levels of proficiency.

Private lessons are sometimes advertised on the notice board outside the Compendium Bookshop, Nikis 28, Plaka.

Language courses on the islands are covered under Courses in the Facts for the Visitor chapter.

CHILDREN'S ACTIVITIES (MAP 3)

More of a play group than a museum is the **Children's Museum** (☎ 21 0331 2995, *Kydathineon 14, Plaka; admission free; open 9.30am-1.30pm Mon & Wed, 9.30am-1.30pm & 5pm-8pm Fri, 10am-1pm Sat & Sun)*. It has a games room and a number of 'exhibits', such as a mock-up of a metro tunnel, for children to explore. Parents have to stay and supervise their children.

Nearby is the **Museum of Children's Art** (☎ 21 0331 2621, *Kodrou 9, Plaka; admission free; open 10am-2pm Tues-Sat, 11am-2pm Sun)*. It has a room set aside where children can let loose their creative energy. Crayons and paper are supplied. A €0.60 fee applies only to children attending special programs.

ORGANISED TOURS

There are four main companies running organised tours around Athens: *Hop In Sightseeing* (☎ 21 0428 5500, *Zanni 29, Piraeus), CHAT* (☎ 21 0322 3137, *Xenofontos 9), GO Tours* (☎ 21 0921 9555, *Athanassiou 20)* and *Key Tours* (☎ 21 0923 3166/3266, *Kaliroïs 4)*.

They include a half-day sightseeing tour of Athens (€29.35), which does nothing more than point out all the major sights, and Athens by Night (€40), which takes in the *son et lumière* (sound-and-light show) before a taverna dinner with folk dancing.

The companies also have one-day tours to Cape Sounion (€22.30); Delphi (€52.85

with lunch); the Corinth Canal, Mycenae, Nafplio and Epidaurus (same prices); and one-day cruises to Aegina, Poros and Hydra (€65 including lunch).

You will find brochures for the tour companies everywhere; all the hotels listed in the following Places to Stay chapter act as a booking agent for at least one tour company. The hotels often offer substantial discounts on the official tour prices as a service to their customers – discounts that aren't available if you book directly.

CHAT tours begin from the company's terminal at the Amalias Hotel, Amalias 10; GO Tours leave from outside the peripteron at the junction of Amalias and Souri; and Key Tours begin from the combined office and terminal at Kaliroïs 4. If you are staying nearby, you can walk to the terminal of the respective company. If not, when you make your booking, you will be informed of the time and location of a pick-up point close to your hotel; a company bus will then collect you and transport you to its terminal.

Hop-In Tours works differently. For city tours, its buses work a set route with a number of specified pick-up points. You can get on, or off, wherever you choose – and go around as many times as you like. For tours outside Athens, Hop-In will inform you of the time and location of your pick-up point and then keep going with the tour.

HELLENIC FESTIVAL

The annual Hellenic Festival is the city's most important cultural event, running from mid-June to late September. It features a line-up of international music, dance and theatre at the Theatre of Herodes Atticus. The setting is superb, backed by a floodlit Acropolis.

The festival has been going from strength to strength in recent years. Recent performers include the renowned Vienna Boys' Choir, the Moscow Philharmonic Orchestra, super tenor Placido Domingo, rock star Elton John, flamenco wizard Joaquim Cortes and Jean Michel Jarre, as well as a mix of opera, modern dance and theatre both ancient and modern.

The festival also features performances of ancient Greek drama at the famous heatre of Epidaurus in the Peloponnese, ½ hours west of Athens. There are performances in Epidaurus every Friday and Saturday night during July and August. See pidaurus in the Peloponnese chapter for ore information.

The festival program should be available om the beginning of February on the festival Web site: W www.greekfestival.gr.

Tickets sell out quickly, so try to buy ours as soon as possible. They can be ought at the festival box office (Map 4; 21 0322 1459, fax 21 0323 5172, Stadiou , Syntagma). The box office is open 30am to 4pm Monday to Friday, three eeks before the start of the festival. There e student discounts for most performances n production of an ISIC card.

Tickets may also be bought on the day of e performance at the theatre box offices, ut queues can be very long.

LACES TO STAY

thens is a noisy city and Athenians keep te hours, so an effort has been made to sect hotels in quiet areas, pedestrian recincts or side streets. Except where specfied, the prices quoted here were for the 001 high season. Most places offer conderable discounts in the off season.

The enormous influx of refugees from e troubles in neighbouring Albania (in articular) and other Balkan nations has had major impact on the budget accommodaon scene. Many cheap hotels and hostels at once were popular with travellers have ow become little more than refugee amps. The budget places recommended in is section all attempt to ensure a secure vironment for their guests.

Plaka is the most popular place to stay. ost of the sights are close by and it's conenient for every transport connection other an the train station. It has a choice of acommodation right across the price specum, from travellers hostels to smart id-range hotels and pensions. Not surprisgly, rooms fill up quickly in July and Auust, so it's wise to make a reservation. If ou haven't booked, a telephone call can ve a fruitless walk.

The other main hotel area is around Plateia Omonias, but the options are not very attractive. They all seem to be either cheap bordellos, where you won't get a wink of sleep, or characterless modern C-class places. An added drawback to the Omonia region is the general seediness, although this can be expected to change in the lead-up to the Olympics.

There are also some good pensions and mid-range hotels in the suburbs south of the Acropolis.

If you arrive in the city late and cannot find a place to stay, don't be tempted to sleep out. It is illegal and could be dangerous.

Hotel Touts

Many of the budget hotels and hostels in Athens employ touts to meet tourists who arrive by train, particularly the late train from Patras. Some of the hostels recommended in this chapter do this, and it often saves a lot of hassle to take up an offer. Before doing so, however, ask to see the hostel leaflet. This will have a picture of the hostel, information about the facilities offered and (very importantly) a map showing its location. Be very suspicious of a tout who cannot show you a leaflet.

PLACES TO STAY – BUDGET
Camping

There are no camping grounds in central Athens. The EOT's *Camping in Greece* brochure lists all 17 sites in Attica.

Athens Camping (☎ 21 0581 4114, fax 21 0582 0353, Leoforos Athinon 198) **Around Athens map** Adult/tent €4.70/3.55. Open year-round. This place is 7km west of the city centre on the road to Corinth, making it the nearest camping ground to the city centre. It has reasonable facilities but nothing else going for it.

There are better camp sites at Shinias Beach, east of Athens, and near Cape Sounion (see the Attica section later in this chapter).

Hostels

Athens International Youth Hostel (☎ 21 0523 4170, fax 21 0523 4015, Victor Hugo

16) **Map 2** Members €8.40, joining fee €12.35, daily stamp €2.05. Situated in Omonia, the location isn't overly salubrious, but otherwise this is an excellent HI-affiliated place which is almost too good to be true. It occupies the former C-class Hotel Victor Ougo, which has been completely renovated – it even has double-glazed windows. The spotless rooms, with bathroom, sleep two to four people and include sheets and pillow cases. Facilities include a guest kitchen, laundry and free safety-deposit boxes. There is no curfew and the reception staff speak English.

Youth Hostel No 5 (☎ 21 0751 9530, fax 21 0751 0616, e y-hostel@otenet.gr, Damareos 75) **Map 1** Dorm beds €5.90, stays over 6 nights €5.30 per night. This place is very basic, and a long way from anything else of interest. To get there, take trolleybus No 2 or 11 from Syntagma to the Filolaou stop on Frinis, just past Damareos.

XEN (YWCA; ☎ 21 0362 4291, fax 21 0362 2400, e xene7@hol.gr, Amerikis 11) **Map 3** Singles/doubles with bathroom €29.35/35.20, stays over 2 nights €26.40/32.30 per night. The XEN is an option for women only. There are laundry facilities and a snack bar which charges €2.35 for continental breakfast. Annual membership costs €2.95.

Hotels – Plaka & Syntagma
Festos Youth & Student Guesthouse (☎ 21 0323 2455, fax 21 0321 0907, e consolas@hol.gr, Filellinon 18) **Map 2** Dorm beds €11.75, doubles/triples €26.40/38.15. This place has long been popular with travellers despite being on one of the noisiest streets in Athens. It tends to cram beds into the rooms in summer. A popular feature is the bar on the 1st floor, which also serves meals, including several vegetarian items.

Student & Travellers' Inn (☎ 21 0324 4808, fax 21 0321 0065, e students-inn@ath.forthnet.gr, Kydathineon 16) **Map 2** Dorm beds €11.75-17.60, singles/doubles €30.85/39.65, with bathroom €35.25/49.90. The Student Inn occupies a converted nursing home, and is a veritable maze of rooms large and small – some with fine old timber

floors. The dorms here are good value, especially in the quieter months. All dorms share communal bathrooms and facilities include a courtyard with big-screen TV, Internet access and a travel service. Rooms are heated in winter.

Hotel Dioskouros (☎ 21 0324 816, e consolas@hol.gr, Pittakou 6) **Map** Doubles/triples/quads €29.35/44/58.7 Tucked away on a quiet side street on the edge of Plaka, the Dioskouros is an old-sty place with timber floors and very high ceilings. The shady courtyard at the back has snack bar serving breakfast and light meal

John's Place (☎ 21 0322 9719, Patröc 5) **Map 4** Singles/doubles/triples €23.5 32.30/47. This small, old-fashioned, family run place is ideally situated just west Syntagma.

Hotels – Monastiraki (Map 4)
Hotel Tempi (☎ 21 0321 3175, fax 21 032 4179, e tempihotel@travelling.gr, Eolc 29) Singles €22, singles/doubles/triple with bathroom €27.90/37/44. This friendl family-run place was named one of th world's top 50 budget hotels by Britain's *I* *dependent* newspaper. Yiannis and Kateri keep the place spotless, and the rooms at th front have balconies overlooking prett Plateia Agia Irini with its flower market ar church – not to mention views to the Acro olis. There is also a communal kitchen wi a refrigerator and facilities for preparing h drinks and snacks. Credit cards are accepte – unusual for a budget hotel.

Hotels – Koukaki (Map 6)
Marble House Pension (☎ 21 0923 405 fax 21 0922 6461, Zini 35A) Singles/double triples €23.50/41.10/44, with bathroo €29.35/47/49.90. This isn't exactly back packer territory, but this pension, on a quie cul-de-sac off Zini, is one of Athens' bett budget hotels. All rooms have a bar fridge ceiling fans and safety boxes for valuable and air-con is available for an extra €8.8 There's a book exchange in the receptic area. To get there, catch trolleybus No 1, 9 or 22 from Syntagma to the Zini stop c Veïkou.

Tony's Hotel (☎ *21 0923 0561, fax 21 0923 6370, Zaharitsa 26*) Singles/doubles/ triples with bathroom €35.20/41.10/51.40. This is a clean, well-maintained pension. There is a small communal kitchen downstairs for tea/coffee and breakfast. Tony also has well-equipped studio apartments nearby for long- or short-term rental. Short-term prices are the same as for rooms at the pension.

Hotels – Omonia & Surrounds

This section includes the area around the train stations as well as Omonia. There are dozens of hotels around Omonia, but most of them are either bordellos masquerading as cheap hotels or uninspiring, overpriced C-class hotels. There are very few places worthy of a mention.

Zorba's Hotel (☎ *21 0823 4239, fax 21 0823 4239*, e *zorbashotel@hotmail.com, Gilfordiou 10*) **Map 2** Dorm beds €11.75, singles/doubles/triples with bathroom €26.40/35.20/44. This hotel occupies a quaint old building 100m east of Plateia Viktorias. Facilities include Internet access and a laundry service. Breakfast is available in the 1st-floor bar.

Hostel Aphrodite (☎ *21 0881 0589, fax 21 0881 6574*, e *hostel-aphrodite@ath .forthnet.gr, Einardou 12*) **Map 1** Dorm beds €11.75, singles/doubles/triples €27.90/ 35.20/39.70, with bathroom €30.80/38.15/ 42.55. Open 16 Feb-21 Oct. This place is definitely worth checking out. It's 10 minutes' walk from the train stations, and has very clean, good-sized rooms – many with balconies. It seems to be party time every night at the downstairs bar. In the morning, the bar becomes the breakfast room. Facilities include Internet access. You can get there on trolleybus No 1, which travels north up Mihail Voda, although the route is not shown on the EOT map. Get off at the Proussis stop, just south of Einardou. The nearest metro station is Viktorias, five minutes' walk south-east at Plateia Viktorias.

Hotels – Exarhia (Map 2)

Exarhia is off the beaten track as far as hotels go, but there are a couple of good places tucked away at the base of Strefi Hill.

Hotel Orian (☎ *21 0382 7362, fax 21 0380 5193*, e *orion-dryades@lycosmail .com, Emmanual Benaki 105*) Singles/doubles €23.50/29.35. This clean and well-kept hotel is managed by a friendly guy who speaks English. This and Hotel Dryades are to the left at the top of the steps leading off Emmanual Benaki at the junction with Kalidromiou. You can save yourself a long uphill trek by catching bus No 230 from Amalias to the Kalidromiou stop on Harilaou Trikoupi.

Hotel Dryades (*same contact details as Hotel Orian, Dryades 4*) Singles/doubles with bathroom €35.20/44. The co-managed Dryades is just 50m from Hotel Orian. The main difference is that the rooms here have private bathrooms.

PLACES TO STAY – MID-RANGE

All rooms in this category come with private bathroom.

Plaka & Syntagma

Acropolis House Pension (☎ *21 0322 2344, fax 21 0324 4143, Kodrou 6-8)* **Map 3** Singles/doubles €47.70/57.25. This is a beautifully preserved, 19th-century house which retains many original features. It also boasts undoubtedly the most complex pricing structure in Athens, with discounts for stays of three days or more, supplements for air-conditioning etc, etc. All the rooms are heated in winter. Breakfast costs €4.95 per person.

Hotel Adonis (☎ *21 0324 9737, fax 21 0323 1602, Kodrou 3*) **Map 3** Singles/ doubles with breakfast €33.75/60.20. Opposite the Acropolis House Pension, this comfortable modern hotel represents one of the best deals around. All the rooms come with air-con and TV. There are good views of the Acropolis from the 4th-floor rooms, and from the rooftop bar.

Hotel Nefeli (☎ *21 0322 8044, fax 21 0322 5800, Iperidou 16*) **Map 3** Singles/ doubles with breakfast €58.70/67.50. The Nefeli has a quiet location and comfortable air-con rooms.

Hotel Achilleas (☎ *21 0323 3197, reservations* ☎ *21 0322 2706, fax 21 0322 2412,* e *achilleas@tourhotel.gr, Leka 21)* **Map 4** Singles/doubles with breakfast €73.40/ 82.20. The rooms at the Achilleas are large and airy – and those on the top floor open onto garden terraces. This place is a real bargain in winter.

Hotel Adrian (☎ *21 0322 1553, fax 21 0325 0461,* e *douros@otenet.gr, Adrianou 74)* **Map 4** Singles/doubles €76.30/93.90, with Acropolis view €88.05/108.60. This hotel is smart and modern boasting well-appointed rooms. Prices include breakfast.

Monastiraki

Hotel Cecil (☎ *21 0321 7909, fax 21 0321 8005,* e *cecil@netsmart.gr, Athinas 39)* **Map 3** Singles/doubles/triples with breakfast €39.65/52.85/69. If there were a prize for the best restoration job, it should go to the owners of Hotel Cecil. They have done a magnificent job in reviving this fine old hotel, with its beautiful high, moulded ceilings and polished timber floors. The rooms are tastefully furnished and equipped with air-con and TV.

Hotel Attalos (☎ *21 0321 2801, fax 21 0324 3124,* e *atthot@hol.gr, Athinas 29)* **Map 3** Singles/doubles/triples €44.60/ 55.80/66.90. This is a comfortable (if characterless) modern hotel. Its best feature is the rooftop bar which offers wonderful views of the Acropolis by night. All rooms have air-con and TV. Breakfast costs €5.90.

Hotel Carolina (☎ *21 0324 3551/3552, fax 21 0324 3550,* e *hotelcarolina@ galaxynet.gr, Kolokotroni 55)* **Map 4** Singles/ doubles/triples €44/47/52.85, plus €8.80 air-con charge. The owners of the Carolina have spent a lot of money upgrading the place in the last couple of years, including a fine job on the facade. All rooms have air-con which incurs an additional charge. There are also cheaper rooms with shared bathroom. Breakfast costs an extra €3.55 per person.

Makrigianni (Map 6)

Hotel Austria (☎ *21 0923 5151, fax 21 0924 7350,* e *austria@hol.gr, Mouson 7)* Singles/doubles/triples including breakfast €62.80/80.70/98.60. The Austria occupies a quiet spot on the slopes of Filopappos Hill, with good views over the city from its roof garden.

Acropolis View Hotel (☎ *21 0921 7303/7304/7305, fax 21 0923 0705, Webster 10)* Singles/doubles/triples with buffet breakfast €85.10/114.45/137.95. The Acropolis View has one of the quietest settings around, nestled below Filopappos Hill just south of the Theatre of Herodes Atticus. There are indeed views of the Acropolis from many of the rooms, although the best views are from the roof terrace. Other rooms look out over Filopappos Hill. All the rooms have air-con and TV.

Hotel Hera (☎ *21 0923 6682, fax 21 0924 7334,* e *hhera@hol.gr, Falirou 9)* Singles/doubles/triples with buffet breakfast €85.10/114.45/143.50. The Hera has comfortable air-con rooms with TV and bathroom.

Koukaki (Map 6)

Art Gallery Hotel (☎ *21 0923 8376, fax 21 0923 3025,* e *ecotec@otenet.gr, Erehthiou 5)* Singles/doubles/triples €44/52.25/62.50. This is a small, friendly place that's full of personal touches – like fresh flowers. It's run by the brother-and-sister team of Ada and Yannis Assimakopoulos, who are full of information about the city. The rooms are heated in winter, when cheaper long-term rates are available. A generous breakfast costs €5.

Around Omonia (Map 2)

Omonia is not really the place to be looking for upmarket accommodation – you can do much better for your money elsewhere, but there are a couple of exceptions.

Titania Hotel (☎ *21 0330 0111, fax 21 0330 0700,* e *titania@titania.gr, Panepistimiou 52)* Singles/doubles with breakfast €86/116. With its imposing facade, this is a comfortable modern hotel with large rooms, all with satellite TV. There are great views over the city from the rooftop bar at night.

Novotel Athens (☎ *21 0820 0700, fax 21 0820 0700,* e *H0866@accor-hotels.com, Mihail Voda 4-6)* Singles/doubles with breakfast €146.75/164.35. This hotel, 150m north-west of Plateia Vathis, has jumped the gun a bit in anticipating the desleazing of this area. The hotel itself, though, is a typical representative of this international chain. There are views over the city to the Acropolis from the rooftop pool and bar area.

Kolonaki (Map 5)

Athenian Inn (☎ 21 0723 8097/9552, fax 21 0724 2268, Haritos 22) Singles/doubles with breakfast €66.25/99.40. This posh area has the B-class Athenian Inn. It's a small but distinguished place on a quiet street in the heart of Kolonaki that was reputably a favourite of writer Lawrence Durrell. It has a cosy intimacy which is often lacking in hotels of this category. The rooms are unpretentious but comfortable with air-con and pretty pictures of island scenes on the walls.

PLACES TO STAY – TOP END

Hotel Grande Bretagne (☎ 21 0333 0000, fax 21 0322 8034, e gbhotel@otenet.gr, Vassileos Georgiou 1, Plateia Syntagmatos) **Map 4** Singles/doubles from US$305, suites from US$650. If you are wealthy, *the* place to stay in Athens is – and always has been – the deluxe Hotel Grande Bretagne. Built in 1862 to accommodate visiting heads of state, it ranks among the grand hotels of the world. No other hotel in Athens can boast such a rich history (see the Walking Tour section earlier). It has undergone much expansion since it first became a hotel in 1872, but still has an old-world grandeur. The elegantly furnished rooms have air-con, mini-bar, satellite TV and video.

Athens Plaza (☎ 21 0325 5301, fax 21 0323 5856, e njv@grecotel.gr) **Map 4** Singles/doubles from €220.10/250, suites from €470. Next door to the Grande Bretagne, the Athens Plaza isn't far behind in the luxury stakes following a complete refit and a change of name – it was formerly the Meridien.

St George Lycabettus Hotel (☎ 21 0729 0711/0719, fax 21 0729 0439, e info@ sglycabettus.gr, Kleomenous 2, Kolonaki)

Map 5 Singles/doubles from €140.90/ 171.70, with Acropolis view €213.35/ 244.50. This hotel has a prime position at the foot of Lykavittos Hill. No hotel in Athens offers better views, and the rooms are priced accordingly.

Hilton (☎ 21 0725 0201, fax 21 0725 3110, e fom_athens@hilton.com, Vasilissis Sofias 46, Ilissia) **Map 1** Singles/doubles US$285/315 plus tax, suites from US$550. Hilton-hoppers will find their favourite opposite the National Art Gallery. The Athens version is a vast concrete edifice. From the outside, it looks more like a 1950s housing project than a luxury hotel, but inside, no expense has been spared. It has lashings of marble and bronze, public areas with enormous chandeliers and carpets which were especially designed by eminent Greek artists.

Electra Palace (☎ 21 0337 0000, fax 21 0324 1875, Navarhou Nikodimou 18) **Map 4** Singles/doubles from €140.30/169.65. Plaka's smartest hotel is this A-class property. The best feature is the rooftop pool with views over the Acropolis. There are often special deals.

Pentelikon Hotel (☎ 21 0808 0311, fax 21 0801 0314, Deligianni 66) Singles/ doubles €264/308.15, suites from €381.50. The posh leafy northern suburb of Kifissia has a number of luxury hotels. The pick of them is this deluxe property. It's an exquisite place built in traditional style with a swimming pool and a lovely garden. All of the beautifully furnished rooms have mini-bar and satellite TV.

PLACES TO EAT

Plaka is the part of town where most visitors wind up eating. The streets are lined with countless restaurants, tavernas, cafes, patisseries and souvlaki stalls.

There's more to Athens eating than Plaka, though. Every neighbourhood in Athens has its own good eating places, often small unpretentious tavernas tucked away on side streets. Monastiraki is great for souvlaki and cheap eats, and Exarhia also has lots of places with prices in tune with the average student's pocket. The

Phone numbers listed incorporate changes due in Oct 2002; see p83

waiters may not speak any English, but you'll find tasty food and reasonable prices.

International cuisine is harder to find, as is vegetarian food. Both categories are listed separately at the end of this section.

PLACES TO EAT – BUDGET
Plaka

For most people, Plaka is the place to be. It's hard to beat the atmosphere of dining out beneath the floodlit Acropolis. You do, however, pay for the privilege – particularly at the outdoor restaurants around the square on Kydathineon.

Most hotels serve breakfast, but if you're not happy with what's on offer you'll find breakfast advertised at many of the Plaka restaurants. Prices start at around €2.35 for continental breakfast.

Taverna Vizantino (☎ 21 0322 7368, Kydathineon 18) **Map 3** Mains €3.25-11.30. This place is the best of this lot. It prices its menu realistically and is popular with locals year-round. The daily specials are good value, with dishes like stuffed tomatoes (€4.25), *pastitsio* (baked macaroni with cheese; €2.95) and baked fish (€5.60).

Plaka Psistaria (☎ 21 0324 6229, Kydathineon 28) **Map 3** Plaka Psistaria has a range of gyros and souvlaki to eat there or take away. The dash of paprika and extra-garlic tzatziki gives this place the edge over dozens of similar places around town. Try the chicken souvlaki wrapped in pitta bread (€1.35) or pork gyros (€1.20), and ask for *apola* – with the lot!

Ouzeri Kouklis (☎ 21 0324 7605, Tripodon 14) **Map 3** Mezedes €2.05-4.10. Ouzeri Kouklis is an old Plaka institution that's worth seeking out. It's an old-style ouzeri with an oak-beamed ceiling, marble tables and wicker chairs. It serves only mezedes, which are brought round on a large tray for you to take your pick. It gets very busy later in the evening. Flaming sausages and cuttlefish costs €4.10, as well as the usual dips at €2.05. The whole selection, enough for four hungry people, costs €35.20. A litre of draught red wine costs €2.95 and a 250ml serving of ouzo is €2.95.

Taverna Damigos (☎ 21 0322 5084, Kydathineon 41) **Map 3** Mains €3.85-6.45. Open Sept-Jun. Opened by the Damigos family in 1865, Taverna Damigos claims to be the oldest taverna in Plaka. It calls itself a *bakaliarakia*, which means that the house speciality is *bakalarios* (cod), fried in a crisp batter. It should be eaten with lashings of *skordalia* (garlic dip) and washed down with plenty of house retsina.

O Glykos (☎ 21 0322 3925, Angelou Geronta 2) **Map 3** Mezedes €2.65-4.40. Tucked away on a quiet side street between two of the busiest streets in Plaka, O Glykos seems a million miles away from all the tourist hustle and bustle. There's outdoor seating beneath a large jacaranda tree, wine by the litre and a good selection of mezedes – all at prices that are very reasonable by Plaka standards.

Syntagma (Map 4)

Fast food is the order of the day at busy Syntagma.

Neon Café (☎ 21 0324 6873, Mitropoleos 3) Mains €3.40-5.75. Neon Café is a stylish and modern cafeteria with a good selection of meals, as well as coffee and cakes. You'll find spaghetti or fettuccine napolitana for €3.40 and bolognese or carbonara for €4.40. Main dishes include mousakas (€4.25), roast beef with potatoes (€4.70) and pork kebab (€5.75). It's located in the south-west corner of Plateia Syntagmatos.

Fast Food Heleni (☎ 21 0323 7361, Perikleos 30-32) Mains €2.95-3.85. This place has fast-food favourites like toasted sandwiches and souvlaki as well as a daily selection of taverna dishes. In season, you'll find tasty artichoke stew (€2.65).

Souvlaki tou Hasepi (The Butcher's Souvlaki; Apollonos 3) Open 10am-4pm Mon-Fri. Meat is the only item on the menu at the tiny Souvlaki tou Hasepi. There's a choice of pork souvlakis for €0.60, or grilled *bifteki* (beef patties) for €0.75. A large, cold beer costs €1.05.

Brazil Coffee Shop (☎ 21 0323 5463, Voukourestiou 1) It's very hard to ignore the delicious aromas emanating from the

Brazil Coffee Shop. It offers a range of coffees, including Greek coffee (€1.50), cappuccino and filter coffee (both €1.80). Cakes and croissants are priced from €1.05.

Monastiraki (Map 3)

There are some excellent cheap eats around Plateia Monastirakiou, particularly for gyros and souvlaki fans.

Thanasis (☎ 21 0324 4705, Mitropoleos 59) Thanasis is famous for its special souvlaki, made using a traditional house recipe that combines minced lamb, minced beef and seasonings. The place is always packed out and the service is pure theatre – at times the waiters have to run to keep up with the demand. Thanasis charges €1.05 for takeaway wrapped in a small pitta, or €4.10 to sit down to a plate of four souvlaki and a large pitta.

Savas (☎ 21 0324 5048, Mitropoleos 86) Pork, beef gyros €0.90, chicken €1.05. Savas specialises in gyros. It has a takeaway stall and a restaurant (there's a shop in between) with seating in the square opposite.

Diporto (Cnr Theatrou & Sofokleous) Eating places don't get any more low key than Diporto. There's not even a sign, just a smell of cooking wafting up from the cellar beneath the olive shop west of the fruit and vegetable markets. There's no menu: Diporto serves only half a dozen dishes, and they haven't changed in years. The house speciality is *revythia* (chick peas); try a bowl (€2.35), followed by a plate of grilled fish (€2.95) and a salad (€1.80). This should be washed down with a jug of retsina from one of the giant barrels lining the wall.

Taverna Papandreou (☎ 21 0321 4970, Aristogeitonos 1) Mains €4.10-6.45. This place is inside the central meat market, which might sound like a strange place to come for a meal, but the market tavernas are important part of Athens life, turning out tasty, traditional taverna dishes 24 hours a day. The clientele ranges from hungry market workers in search of a solid meal, to elegant couples emerging from the local clubs and bars at 5am in search of a bowl of steaming *patsas* (tripe soup) – or *podarakia* pig-trotter soup).

Ipiros Taverna (☎ 21 0324 5572, Filippou 16) Mains €3.25-7.35. There are a few places to eat in the flea market, including this taverna which has cheap, tasty food. The outdoor tables are great in summer for watching the market's hustle and bustle.

Thisio (Map 3)

To Steki tou Elia (☎ 21 0345 8052, Epahalkou 5) Mains €4.40-5.90. To Steki tou Elia specialises in lamb chops (€11.75/kg). Locals swear that they are the best chops in Athens, and the place has achieved some sort of celebrity status. Eat here with Greek friends, and they will constantly be pointing out famous personalities rolling up their sleeves to tuck into great piles of chops and a few jars of retsina. There are pork chops (€5.90) and steaks (€4.40) for those don't eat lamb, as well as dips, chips and salads.

Psiri (Map 3)

O Telis (☎ 21 0324 2775, Evripidou 86) Chops & chips €5.30. This busy psistaria, on the corner with Epikourou near Plateia Eleftherias, is famous for its only dish – pork chops and chips. A huge pile of chips comes topped by three or four chops.

Makrigianni (Map 6)

To 24 Hours (☎ 21 0922 2749, Syngrou 44) Mains €4.10-5.90. Open 24 hours. This is something of an institution among Athenian night owls. The place never closes, except on Easter Sunday, and seems to be at its busiest in the wee small hours. The customers are as much of an attraction as the food: you'll be rubbing shoulders with an assortment of hungry cabbies, middle-aged couples dressed for the opera, and leather-clad gays from the area's many bars – all tucking into steaming bowls of the house speciality, *patsas* (tripe soup). It also has a constantly changing choice of other popular taverna dishes.

Samaria (☎ 21 0923 7260, Rovertou Galli 17) Mains €6.45-12.65. Samaria is the reincarnation of Socrates Prison, an old Athens favourite recently forced to shift from its long-time home on Mitseon. Socrates (the philosophical owner) didn't have to move far, and has brought his collection of 19th-century Parisian posters with him – as well as his imaginative selection of mezes and main dishes. The new location has a rooftop terrace with Acropolis views.

Koukaki (Map 6)

Gardenia Restaurant (☎ 21 0922 5831, Zini 31) Mains €2.65-3.85. The Gardenia is a typical old-fashioned neighbourhood place turning out solid taverna food at old-fashioned prices. Cheerful owners Nikos and Gogo reckon they have the cheapest prices in Athens.

Omonia (Map 2)

The Omonia area is a place where people clutch at their wallets for safety, not a place to relax over a meal. You'll have to run the gauntlet of junkies and pimps if you want to eat at any of the fast-food outlets around Athinas and Pireos on the southern side of Plateia Omonias.

Neon Cafeteria (☎ 21 0522 3201, Dorou 1, Plateia Omonias) Mains €3.55-6. This place is an exception to the normal chaos of this area; it's an oasis of calm occupying a beautiful neoclassical building on the corner of Dorou, on the opposite side of the square. It is a stable mate of the Neon at Syntagma and serves the same fare.

Around the Train Stations (Map 2)

Wherever you choose to eat in this area you will find the lack of tourist hype refreshing – it's a million miles from the strategically placed menus and restaurant touts of Plaka.

O Makis Psistaria (☎ 21 0825 3988, Psaron 48) Mains €3.55-8.25. Located opposite the Church of Agios Pavlos on Psaron, this is a lively place serving hunks of freshly grilled pork or beef, plus chips. It also does delicious grilled chicken with lemon sauce for €4.70.

Dafni Taverna (☎ 21 0821 3914, Ioulianou 65) Mains €3.25-5.90. This taverna offers good value with very tasty gigantes beans for €2.65 or baked fish with potatoes for €4.40. In summer, there's outdoor seating in the small courtyard.

Exarhia (Map 2)

Exarhia has lots of small ouzeria and tavernas to choose from, and prices are tailored to suit the pockets of the district's student clientele. It's quite a long hike to the area from Syntagma; or you can catch a No 230 bus from Amalias or Panepistimiou to Harilaou Trikoupi and walk across from there. It is, however, only a short walk from the National Archaeological Museum to lively Plateia Exarhion. The square (triangle actually) is lined with cafes and snack bars, many with seating under shade. Most of the better eating places are south of Plateia Exarhion or Emmanual Benaki.

Ouzeri I Gonia (☎ 21 0363 9947, Cnr Emmanual Benaki & Arahovis) Mezedes €1.80-5.30. I Gonia is typical of the many small ouzeria in this area. It has a good range of tasty mezedes and draught wine as well as ouzo.

Taverna Barbargiannis (☎ 21 0330 0185, Emmanual Benaki 94) Mains €2.80-5.30. This is an excellent place, on the corner of Dervenion, with a blackboard list of daily specials. Your best bet is to line up at the counter and ask to have a look. There's a delicious thick chicken soup for €3.40 that comes with a generous portion of chicken on the side. Draught retsina is €2.05 for a litre.

Kolonaki (Map 5)

Cheap eats are hard to find around Kolonaki, but not impossible.

Ouzeri Dexameni (☎ 21 0729 2578, Plateia Dexameni) Mains €4.10-7.05. This ouzeri, in the middle of shady Plateia Dexameni, is a good spot to stop for a bite. It has a choice of mezedes, and a good selection of cold drinks. Keep an eye out for the neighbourhood rooster, who struts around challenging the cats for scraps.

The Food Company (☎ 21 0363 0373, Anagnostopoulou 47) Mains €4.70-5.90. The Food Company turns out an interesting range of salads and pasta dishes at prices well below the Kolonaki norm. The house wine is an excellent red from Nemea (€8.80).

PLACES TO EAT – MID-RANGE

Eating out in Athens remains fairly cheap, especially if you're eating Greek food. The few places that do charge a bit extra tend to be doing so because of their location rather than the excellence of their cuisine. This is particularly the case in Plaka, where many restaurants charge way over the odds for very average food. A sure way to end up with a large bill is to eat fresh seafood at any of the restaurants on Kydathineon. Psiri is a good place to look if you're happy to pay a bit more for something interesting.

Two people can expect to pay from €29.35 to €35.20, plus wine, for a meal at most places in this category.

Plaka (Map 3)
Taverna tou Psara (☎ 21 0321 8734, Eretheos 16) Mains €5.30-17.35. Tucked away from the main hustle and bustle of Plaka, Taverna tou Psara is a cut above the Plaka crowd. The menu includes a fabulous choice of mezedes – the *melizanakeftedes* (aubergine croquettes, €5.30) are particularly good. You'll need to get in early to secure a table on the terrace, which has views out over the city.

Restaurant Diogenes (☎ 21 0322 4845, Plateia Lysikratous 3 & Sellev 3) Mains €10.90-25.25. The main attraction of the Diogenes is the outdoor seating right next to the Monument of Lysicrates. In winter, it moves indoors to Sellev 3.

Kotsolis (☎ 21 0322 1164, Adrianou 112) Cakes from €2.50. This is a smart pastry shop with a mouth-watering array of goodies. They include such traditional Greek favourites as *galaktoboureko* (€2.65), *baklava* and *kataifi* (both €2.50).

Syntagma (Map 4)
Estiatorio Kentrikon (☎ 21 0323 2482, Kolokotroni 3) Mains €5.60-17.60. Open noon-6pm Mon-Fri. The Kentrikon is a favourite with local businessmen – a cool, air-conditioned retreat tucked away in a quiet arcade off Kolokotroni. The menu is upmarket taverna with a few international touches.

Psiri (Map 3)
The maze of narrow streets that make up the newly trendy district of Psiri are lined with dozens of small restaurants and ouzeris, particularly the central area between Plateia Agion Anargyron and Plateia Iroön. Most places are open 8pm until late Monday to Saturday, and for Sunday lunch.

Embros (☎ 21 0321 3285, Plateia Agion Anargyron 4) Meze €3.50-11.15. If none of the places grabs your attention as you wander around, try Embros. It's a popular spot with seating in the square, and a choice of about 20 mezedes. They include delicious cheese croquettes (€3.40) and chicken livers wrapped in bacon (€4.70).

PLACES TO EAT – TOP END
The following is a selection of Athens' top-end, blow-the-budget restaurants. The prices quoted do not include wine. Reservations are strongly recommended, sometimes essential.

Estiatorion Edodi (☎ 21 0921 3013, Veikou 80) **Map 6** Mains €17.35-20.55. Tucked away in quiet, suburban Koukaki, the tiny Estiatorion Edodi turns out probably the most exciting food in central Athens. Brothers Giorgos and Michalis have come up with a winning combination of clever, creative food and wonderful, stylish presentation. There's no menu as such, just a daily selection of eight or nine starters followed by a similar choice of main courses. Lobster and crayfish feature prominently, as do other delicacies like foie gras, pheasant and ostrich. Dessert eaters face an impossible choice from a mouth-watering line-up (€9.40). Coffee drinkers can choose between six types of sugar. This is food, and service, to make you smile. Perfect for a romantic night out.

Daphne Restaurant (☎ 21 0322 7971, Lysikratous 4, Plaka) **Map 3** Mains €11.75-17. Open from 7pm nightly. This is where then US First Lady Hillary Clinton and daughter Chelsea dined during their one-night stopover in 1996 on their way to light the Olympic flame at Olympia. It's an exquisitely restored, 1830s neoclassical mansion decorated with frescoes from

Greek mythology. The menu includes regional specialities like rabbit cooked in mavrodaphne wine.

Pil Poule (☎ *21 0342 3665, Apostolou Pavlou 51, Thisio*) **Map 3** Mains €20.25-47. Open from 8pm Mon-Sat. Style is all important at Pil Poule, which occupies a beautifully restored, 1920s neoclassical mansion. Snappily clad waiters in black suits and bow ties are obviously used to serving a cast of wealthy business people and foreign dignitaries. The menu is modern Mediterranean with a strong French presence, dotted with extravagances like warm foie gras (€24.95) and Beluga caviar (€73.40). In summer, seating moves to the restaurant's rooftop terrace, which boasts fabulous views across to the floodlit Acropolis. It even has a private VIP terrace.

Symposio (☎ *21 0922 5321, Erehthiou 46, Makrigianni*) **Map 6** Mains €18.80-40. Open 8pm until late Mon-Sat. Symposio is one of Athens' most elegant restaurants, occupying a restored 1920s house in the quiet streets south of the Acropolis. The menu is loaded with regional specialities from the Epiros region of north-western Greece, where the restaurant owners raise wild boar and pasture-fed yearling beef. In season, the menu features such delicacies as wild asparagus, wild mushrooms, freshwater crayfish and – occasionally – Lake Ioannina frogs' legs. Symposio's signature dish is fish baked in a salt crust (€55.80/kg).

Restaurant Arheon Gefsis (☎ *21 0523 9661, fax 21 0520 0372,* ⓔ *adamis@arxaion .gr, Kodratou 22, Metaxourgio*) **Map 2** Mains €10.30-17.30. The Arheon Gefsis is a fun place where the clock has been turned back 2500 years to the days of ancient Greece – to a time before the advent of potatoes, rice, tomatoes and many other staples of the modern Greek diet. Diners will notice a few other differences, too, as they are seated at their solid wooden tables by waiting staff dressed in flowing red robes. There are no glasses – the ancients used earthenware cups, and spoons instead of forks. Small portions must also be a modern idea, because the servings here are huge. Not surprisingly, roast meats and fish

dominate the menu, served with purees of peas or chick peas and vegetables. Try the pork stuffed with plums (€13.25), served with a sweet plum sauce, pea puree and artichoke hearts. Wine, from the barrel, is €7.95 a litre. Bookings are essential.

Frourarheio (☎ *21 0321 5220, Agion Anargyron 6, Psiri*) **Map 3** Mains €13.25-19.10. Psiri's finest takes its name from the old army barracks it occupies. It has an interesting Mediterranean menu and courtyard seating.

PLACES TO EAT – INTERNATIONAL

International cuisine remains something of a rarity in Athens, although the choice is steadily improving. Most of the non-Greek restaurants that do exist are located in far outer suburbs like Kifissia and Glyfada, but there are a few good places around the city centre. Here are a few suggestions.

American

Jackson Hall (☎ *21 0361 6098, Milioni 4, Kolonaki*) **Map 5** Mains €9.70-17.30. If you can't get no satisfaction from the burgers at the fast-food places around town, head here. It has a selection of sit-down burgers, all with chips and salad. It also has huge steaks. Milioni is the pedestrian precinct on the south-western edge of Plateia Kolonakiou, off Kanari.

Curries

Until very recently, curries were virtually unobtainable in Athens. Suddenly there's a cluster of tiny curry restaurants in the streets between Plateia Eleftherias and Plateia Omonias. It's hardly the most salubrious part of town, but it's the place to go for a good cheap curry. All these place are open 9am to about 10pm daily.

Bengal Garden (☎ *21 0325 3060, Korinis 12*) **Map 3** Mains €2.35-4.10. This is one of the cheapest places to eat in Athens, turning out a large plate of curry and rice for just €2.35. There's no menu: just walk up to the serving counter and check out what's on offer (but don't look at the kitchen too closely!). The day's dishes normally include either chick peas or dhal (€1.50) as well as a choice of chicken curry (€1.80) or beef curry (€2.35). It also has chapatis and delicious spicy vegetable pakhoras (both €0.30). Takeaways are available.

Pak Bangla Indian Restaurant (☎ 21 0321 9412, Menandrou 13) **Map 3** Mains €7.35-11.75. This is the most upmarket of this neighbourhood's cluster of curry restaurants, but still a bargain.

Italian (Map 5)

La Pasteria (☎ 21 0363 2032, Tsakalof 18) Mains from €5.60. Kolonaki is the area to go to for good Italian food. This is a popular spot, offering a choice of pasta served a dozen different ways.

Casa di Pasta (☎ 21 0723 3348, Spefsipou 30) Meal plus wine around €26.40. This is rated by many as having the city's best Italian food – meaning that bookings are essential.

Oriental (Map 4)

Furin Kazan Japanese Fast-Food Restaurant (☎ 21 0322 9170, Apollonos 2, Syntagma) Mains €4.70-15.25. Open 11am- 11pm Mon-Sat. It's reassuring to see that the Furin Kazan is always full of Japanese visitors, obviously enjoying the food at the cheapest and best Japanese restaurant in town. There's a selection of rice and noodle dishes as well as old favourites like chicken yakitori, but it's the sashimi and sushi trays that steal the show.

Far East Restaurant (☎ 21 0323 4996, Stadiou 7, Syntagma) Mains €13.20-23.35. Open 1pm-1am daily. This is a cool, elegant retreat tucked away at the back of an arcade. It serves a selection of Chinese and Korean food.

Pizza

Brooklyn Pizza (☎ 21 0323 2727, Voulis 31-33) **Map 4** Mains €2.80-14.70, takeaway slices from €1.35. Brooklyn Pizza was opened by a local guy who wanted pizza just like he'd eaten in New York, and set about doing just that. You'll find pizzas to eat in or take away, as well as calzones, hot dogs and other favourites.

PLACES TO EAT – VEGETARIAN

Eden Vegetarian Restaurant (☎ 21 0324 8858, Lyssiou 12, Plaka) **Map 4** Mains €4.70-8.50. Open Wed-Mon. The Eden is unchallenged as the best vegetarian restaurant in Athens. It's been around for years, substituting soya products for meat in tasty vegetarian versions of mousakas (€4.70), and other Greek favourites. You'll also find vegie burgers (€5.30), mushroom stifado (€8.50), as well as organically produced beer and wine.

Vegetarian Fast Food (☎ 21 0321 0361, Panepistimiou 57, Omonia) **Map 2** Buffet €3.10. Here you are offered a choice of three dishes from the buffet, as well as portions of wholemeal pizza and pies. You can wash your meal down with a range of fresh fruit or vegetable juices (from €1.50). There is also a health-food shop, which carries a small range of biodynamic produce.

PLACES TO EAT – SELF-CATERING
Markets (Map 3)

You'll find the widest range of whatever's in season and the best prices at the central markets on Athinas, halfway between Plateia Omonias and Plateia Monastirakiou. The *fruit and vegetable market* is on the western side of Athinas, and the *meat market* opposite on the eastern side. The stretch of Athinas between the meat market and Plateia Monastirakiou is the place to shop for nuts and nibblies.

Supermarkets

You can find the following supermarkets in central Athens: *Marinopoulos (Kanari 9, Kolonaki)* **Map 5**; *Vasilopoulo (Stadiou 19, Syntagma)* **Map 3**; *Marinopoulos (Athinas 60, Omonia)* **Map 2**; *Bazaar Discount Supermarket (Eolou 104, Omonia)* **Map 2**; *Papageorgiou (Dimitrakopoulou 72, Veikou)* **Map 6**; and *Veropoulos (Parthenos 6, Koukaki)* **Map 6**.

ENTERTAINMENT

The best source of entertainment information is the weekly listings magazine *Athenorama*, but you'll need to be able to read some Greek to make much sense of it. It costs €1.50 and is available from periptera all over the city.

English-language listings appear daily in the *Kathimerini* supplement that accompanies the *International Herald Tribune*, while the *Athens News* carries a weekly entertainment guide.

Another useful source of information is the quarterly magazine *Welcome to Athens*, available free from the tourist office. It has details of theatre, dance, classical music concerts and art exhibitions.

Bars (Map 3)
Brettos (☎ *21 0323 2110, Kydathineon 41*) Open 10am-midnight daily. This is a delightful place right in the heart of Plaka. Very little has changed here in years, except that being old-fashioned has suddenly become very fashionable. It's a family-run business which acts as a shop-front for the family distillery and winery in Kalithea. Huge barrels line one wall, and the shelves are stocked with a colourful collection of bottles that is backlit at night. Shots of Brettos brand spirits (ouzo, brandy and many more) cost €1.80, as does a glass of wine.

Most bars in Athens have music as a main feature. Thisio is a good place to look, particularly on Iraklidon.

Stavlos (☎ *21 0345 2502, Iraklidon 10*) This place occupies an amazing old rabbit warren of a building. It has a rock bar playing mainly alternative British music, and more mellow sounds in the cafe/ brasserie outside.

Berlin Club (☎ *21 0671 5455, Iraklidon 8*) Cafe by day and rock'n'roll bar by night, Berlin is known for its special theme nights, which you'll see advertised around town.

See the Piraeus section later in this chapter for information about the Hard Rock Café.

Gay Bars
The greatest concentration of gay bars is to be found around Makrigianni, south of the Temple of Olympian Zeus. All the places listed below open about 11pm, but you

won't find much of a crowd until after midnight. Popular spots include the following.

Granazi Bar (☎ *21 0924 4185, Lembes 20, Makrigianni*) **Map 6** The Granazi has long been at the forefront of the gay scene. These days, the ambience is Pet Shop Boys – played at a volume that permits only body language. It's popular with the under-35 crowd, who come to party.

Lamda Club (☎ *21 0922 4202, Lembes 15, Makrigianni*) **Map 6** The Lamda is the most risqué of Makrigianni's bars, with chunky chains adorning the walls and murals of well-muscled guys strutting their stuff. There's a dance floor upstairs, playing a mixture of Greek and mainstream Western rock, and various other rooms.

Alekos Island (☎ *21 0364 0249, Tsakalof 42, Kolonaki*) **Map 5** Alekos is a long-standing feature of the gay scene, drawing a sedate, older crowd of gays.

Fairytale (☎ *21 0330 1763, Kolleti 25, Exarhia*) **Map 2** This intimate, hole-in-the-wall bar is a favourite haunt of young lesbians.

Discos
Discos operate in Athens only between October and April. In summer, the action moves to the coastal suburbs of Ellinikon and Glyfada. Many of the big names operate in both locations. Admission at most places ranges from €2.95 Monday to Thursday to €8.80 on Friday and Saturday nights. The price often includes one free drink. Subsequently, expect to pay about €2.35 for soft drinks, €2.95 for a beer and €4.40 for spirits. Discos don't start to get busy until around midnight.

Lava Bore (☎ *21 0324 5335, Filellinon 25*) **Map 3** Admission €6. Open 10pm-5pm daily. The Lava Bore is one city-centre disco that stays open all year, although Filellinon 25 is its third address in five years. The formula remains much the same: a mixture of mainstream rock and techno and large beers for €2.95. The admission fee includes one free drink.

Plus Soda (*winter* ☎ *21 0345 6187, Ermou 161, Thisio; summer* ☎ *21 0894 0205, Eurualis 2, Glyfada*) **Map 3** Plus Soda is glamorous with a cast of chic DJs turning out a diet of techno, trance and psychedelia for an energetic crowd of under-25s.

Live Music

Rock *Rodon Club (☎ 21 0524 7427, Marni 24, Omonia)* **Map 2** The Rodon, north of Plateia Omonias, is the city's main rock venue. It has bands most Fridays and Saturdays.

AN Club (☎ 21 0330 5056, Solomou 13-15, Exarhia) **Map 2** The small AN Club is worth checking out. It hosts lesser-known international bands, as well as some interesting local bands.

Top-name international acts play at a variety of venues, including the spectacular *Lykavittos Theatre* on Lykavittos Hill and the *Panathinaïkos football stadium* on Leoforos Alexandras.

Jazz *Half Note Jazz Club (☎ 21 0921 3310, Trivonianou 17, Mets)* **Map 6** The Half Note, opposite the Athens Cemetery, is the principal jazz venue. It hosts an interesting array of international names.

Café Asante (☎ 21 0756 0102, Damareos 78, Pangrati) **Map 1** The Asante features a mixture of modern jazz and African music.

Blues *Blues Hall (☎ 21 0924 7448, Ardiou 44, Mets)* **Map 1** The name says it all!

Traditional Music Tavernas (Map 4)

There is a cluster of tavernas on the upper reaches of Mnissikleous in Plaka that feature live Greek music, occasionally accompanied by folk dancing.

Rembetika Clubs

Athens has a good number of rembetika clubs, but most close down from May to September. Performances in these clubs start at around 11.30pm; most places do not have a cover charge but drinks are expensive.

Rembetiki Stoa Athanaton (☎ 21 0321 4362, Sofokleous 19) **Map 3** Open 3pm-6pm & midnight-6am Mon-Sat. The best known club is the almost legendary Stoa

Athanaton, which occupies a hall above the central meat market. Despite its strange location, it features some of the biggest names on the local rembetika scene. Access is by a lift in the arcade at Sofokleous 19.

Boemissa (☎ 21 0384 3836, Solomou 19) Open 11pm-4am. Purists criticise the modern interpretation of rembetika found here, but the Boemissa certainly knows how to pull a crowd – particularly on Friday and Saturday.

Cinema

Athenians are avid cinema-goers. Most cinemas show recent releases from Britain and the USA in English. The two areas with the highest concentration of cinemas are the main streets running between Syntagma and Omonia, and the Oktovriou-Patission and Plateia Amerikis area. Admission costs between €4.70 and €5.90.

The major cinemas in central Athens are *Apollon (☎ 21 0323 6811, Stadiou 19)*, *Astor (☎ 21 0323 1297, Stadiou 28)*, *Asty (☎ 21 0322 1925, Koraï 4)*, *Cine Paris (☎ 21 0322 0721, Kydathineon)*, *Elly (☎ 21 0363 2789, Akadimias 64)*, *Ideal (☎ 21 0382 6720, Panepistimiou 46)* and *Titania (☎ 21 0381 1147, Cnr Panepistimiou & Themistokleous)*. The Asty shows mostly avant-garde films; the others show mostly first-run films (usually from Britain or the USA with Greek subtitles).

Theatre

Athens has a dynamic theatre scene, but, as you'd expect, most performances are in Greek. If you're a theatre buff you may enjoy a performance of an old favourite, provided you know the play well enough. The listings mention when a performance is in English – which happens occasionally. The *National Theatre (☎ 21 0522 3243, Agiou Konstantinou 22-24)* **Map 2** is one of the city's finest neoclassical buildings.

Greek Folk Dancing

Dora Stratou Dance Company (☎ 21 0921 6650, Dora Stratou Theatre, Filopappos Hill) **Map 1** Adult/student €11.75/5.90. Performances 10.15pm daily, 8.15pm Wed

The Rocky Road to 2004

The eyes of the world will be upon Athens for 17 days in August 2004 when athletes from some 200 countries descend on the city for the 29th Olympiad.

It will be the end of a dramatic seven years of what is turning into an emotional roller coaster ride for the people of Athens. Back in 1997, when the city won the right to host the games, there was jubilation that the games were coming home to Greece after 108 years. Slowly but surely the magnitude of the task ahead began to sink in – and jubilation gave way to anxiety. Anxiety was replaced by alarm after Sydney raised the organisational standard to new heights in 2000. It quickly developed into despondency amid a series of dire warnings from the International Olympic Committee (IOC) about the lack of progress.

At the time of writing, the IOC appeared sufficiently satisfied with recent developments to issue an assurance that Athens would not be stripped of the Games, leading to a huge sense of relief. Doubtless there will be many more ups and downs before the ride comes to an end.

Many people have questioned the sanity of staging the games in August in one of Europe's hottest and most polluted capitals. The environmental watchdog Greenpeace has expressed concerns over the possible effects of traffic fumes on the health of athletes. Organisers argue that August is normally a quiet traffic month, because most Athenians have enough sense to abandon the city for the coast and the islands. It remains to be seen if this exodus is repeated in Olympic year.

The Olympics seem sure to be a source of constant anxiety right up until the opening ceremony, but Greece is deeply committed – both emotionally and financially – to making them work.

Olympic Venues

The centrepiece is the 80,000-seat Olympic Stadium (see the Around Athens map), in the northern suburb of Maroussi, which will stage the athletic events as well as the opening and closing ceremonies. The stadium has doubled as the city's No 1 soccer venue since it was completed in 1996.

& Sun May-Oct. In summer, performances of Greek folk dances are given by this company at its own theatre on the western side of Filopappos Hill. The company was formed many years ago and has gained an international reputation for authenticity and professionalism. Tickets can be bought at the door. The theatre is signposted from the western end of Dionysiou Areopagitou. The company also runs folk dancing workshops in summer – see Courses in the Facts for the Visitor chapter.

Classical Music, Opera & Ballet

Athens Concert Hall (Megaron Mousikis; ☎ 21 0728 2333, W www.megaron.gr, Vasilissis Sofias & Kokkali 1, Ilissia) The Megaron is the city's premier concert venue, hosting performances by local and international artists. You'll find a program of upcoming events at the Megaron's city-centre

box office, 26 Stoa Spyrou Milou, which is the arcade between Voukourestiou and Amerikis. The box office is open 10am to 4pm Monday to Friday.

Pallas Theatre (☎ 21 0322 4434, Voukourestiou 1, Syntagma) **Map 3** The Pallas has performances of classical music.

Olympia Theatre (☎ 21 0383 0404, Akadimias 59, Exarhia) **Map 4** The Olympia has performances by the National Opera (Ethniki Lyriki Skini). It also stages ballet.

Son et Lumière

Hill of the Pnyx Theatre (☎ 21 0322 1459, Hill of the Pnyx) Bus No 230 from Syntagma. Adult/child €8.80/4.40. English shows 9pm nightly; French shows 10pm Wed, Thur, Sat-Mon; German shows 10pm Tues & Fri. This 'sound and light' spectacle can be seen from April to the end of October. It is not one of the world's best, but it i

The Rocky Road to 2004

The stadium is part of the Athens Olympic Sports Complex, next to Irini metro station, which also includes an indoor sports hall for gymnastics and basketball, a swimming complex with diving pool, a velodrome and a tennis centre. The rhythmic gymnastics, table tennis and water polo will take place 4km south of the stadium at the Galatsi Olympic Indoor Hall.

The other main area of Olympic activity is in the costal suburb of Faliro. Karaïskaki Stadium, home ground for the Olympiakos soccer (football) club, will host the preliminary rounds of – what else – soccer (the semifinals and finals will take place at the Nea Philadelphia Stadium, 3km west of the Olympic Stadium), while the nearby Peace and Friendship Stadium will be used for handball and basketball. The yachting will be held in Faliro Bay, and the beach volleyball at Faliro Beach. The Faliro Ippodromo, Athens' premier horse-racing track, will host the judo, boxing and taekwondo.

Naturally enough, the marathon will start from Marathon – the town which gave the race its name. It will finish at the Panathenaic Stadium – the home of the first modern Olympic Games. The stadium will also host the archery.

Other venues include the Markopoulo Olympic Shooting and Equestrian Centre, 10km south of Peania; the Ano Liossia Olympic Indoor Hall, in northern Athens, which will stage the wrestling; the Nikea Olympic Hall, in western Athens, where the weightlifting will take place; a new Olympic Centre at Ellinikon, the old international airport, which will hold the baseball, softball, hockey and badminton events; as well as the Vouliagmeni Olympic Triathlon Centre, 8km south of Glyfada, and the Goudi Olympic Modern Pentathlon Centre, west of central Athens. The cycling road race will be raced through Athens' historical centre and the mountain biking event will be staged at Mt Parnitha. The rowing and kayaking events look certain to be held at a new Olympic Rowing Centre at Shinias, near Marathon, despite continuing controversy about the destruction of coastal wetlands.

Soccer is the only event that will be staged outside Attica, with Iraklio, Patras, Thessaloniki and Volos to host group and quarterfinal matches.

For updated details on Olympic venues and news, log on to the official Athens 2004 Web site at ⓦ www.athens.olympic.org.

an enduring and integral part of the Athens tourist scene. During the performance, the monuments of the Acropolis are lit up in synchronisation with accompanying music, sound effects and historical narration. The lights are the most exciting part of the performance. The Hill of the Pnyx is west of the Acropolis off Dionysiou Areopagitou.

SPECTATOR SPORTS
Soccer

Athens and Piraeus supply seven of the 18 teams in the Greek first division. They are AEK, Ionikos, Panathinaïkos and Panionios from Athens; and Ethnikos, Olympiakos and Proödeftiki from Piraeus. Two other Athenian clubs, Apollon and Athinaikos, fluctuate between the first and second divisions.

Greek soccer (football) is dominated by the intense rivalry between Olympiakos and Panathinaïkos, which are the nation's two best-supported teams. Both have enthusiastic supporters' clubs nationwide. Olympiakos has dominated on the domestic front; its success in the 2000/2001 Greek championship was its fifth straight and 30th in 76 years. Panathinaïkos, however, has enjoyed the greater success on the European stage, reaching the semifinals of the European club championship in 1996 – the best result achieved by a Greek team. The supremacy of the big two is occasionally challenged by AEK Athens, another club to perform well in Europe.

Olympiakos normally plays its home matches at the Karaiskaki stadium in Piraeus, but the stadium was closed for Olympic upgrading at the time of writing. Home games had been transferred to the Olympic Stadium in Maroussi, five minutes' walk from Irini metro station.

Panathinaïkos plays the majority of its home games at the Panathinaïkou stadium on Leoforos Alexandras, five minutes' walk from Ambelokopi metro station. Games likely to draw huge crowds are transferred to the Olympic Stadium. AEK plays at the Nikos Goumas Stadium in Nea Philadelphia; Panionios at Nea Smyrni; and Proödeftiki at the Korydalos Stadium in Piraeus. First division matches are played on Sunday and cup matches on Wednesday. They are often televised. The soccer season lasts from September to the middle of May.

Basketball

Olympiakos, Panathinaïkos and AEK also feature prominently on the local basketball scene. All three were upstaged in 2001 by Maroussi (from northern Athens), which reached the final of the European club championships.

Basketball receives no pre-match publicity in the English-language papers, so you'll need to ask a local for information about fixtures.

Horse Racing

Faliro Ippodromos (☎ 21 0941 7761, Cnr Syngrou & Poseidonos) **Around Athens Map** Bus No 126 from Syntagma. Admission from €1.50. Horse races are held three times a week, usually 2pm Monday, Wednesday and Friday, at this track, at the southern end of Syngrou.

SHOPPING
Flea Market (Map 3)

This market is the first place which springs to most people's minds when they think of buying things in Athens. The flea market is the commercial area which stretches west of Plateia Monastirakiou and consists of shops selling goods running the whole gamut from high quality to trash. These shops are open every day during normal business hours.

However, when most people speak of the Athens flea market, they are referring to the Sunday morning outdoor flea market *(Open 7am-2pm)*. This market spills over into Plateia Monastirakiou and onto Ermou.

A visit to Athens isn't complete without a visit to the flea market. All manner of things – from new to fourth-hand – are on sale. There's everything from clocks to condoms, binoculars to bouzoukis, tyres to telephones, giant evil eyes to jelly babies, and wigs to welding kits to be found. Wandering around the market, you'll soon realise that Greece is top of the league of European countries when it comes to mass-produced kitsch. If you're looking for a plastic jewellery box with a psychedelic picture of the Virgin Mary on the lid, which plays 'Never on a Sunday' when you open it, you might just be in luck at the flea market.

Traditional Handicrafts

Hellenic Folk Art Gallery (☎ 21 0325 0524, Cnr Apollonos & Ipatias, Plaka) **Map 4** Open 9am-8pm Tues-Fri, 9am-3pm Mon & Sat. Run by the National Welfare Organisation, this is a good place for purchasing handicrafts. It has top-quality merchandise and the money goes to a good cause – the preservation and promotion of traditional Greek handicrafts. It has a wide range of knotted carpets, kilims, flokatis, needle-point rugs and embroidered cushion covers, as well as a small selection of pottery, copper and woodwork.

Acropolis Rugs (☎ 21 0322 4932, Voulis 31-33, Plaka) **Map 4** Acropolis Rugs specialises in oriental carpets, but also has a large selection of flokati rugs.

Centre of Hellenic Tradition (☎ 21 0321 3023, Pandrosou 36, Plaka) **Map 4** This centre has a display of traditional and modern handicrafts from each region of Greece. Most of the items are for sale.

Mado (☎ 21 0322 3628, Sellev 6, Plaka) **Map 3** Next to the Lysicrates monument, this workshop turns out beautiful, hand-woven wall hangings. Many depict island scenes.

Stavros Melissinos (☎ 21 0321 9247, Pandrosou 89) **Map 3** Athens' famous sandalmaker/poet is still turning out good-quality leather sandals (see the Walking Tour section earlier in this chapter).

GETTING THERE & AWAY
Air
Athens is served by Eleftherios Venizelos International airport at Spata, 21km east of Athens.

Facilities at the new airport, named in honour of the country's leading 20th-century politician, are immeasurably better than at the city's former airport at Ellnikon. Where Ellnikon was shabby and outdated, the new airport gleams. Built by a German consortium, everything is absolutely state of the art. In addition to standard facilities like cafes, restaurants, shops and banks, the new airport also has a hotel for transit passengers – although the Sofitel was still unfinished at the time of research.

For Olympic Airways flight information ring ☎ 21 0936 3363, and for all other airlines ring ☎ 21 0969 4466/4467. The head office of Olympic Airways (☎ 21 0926 7251/7254) is at Leoforos Syngrou 96. The most central Olympic Airways branch office (☎ 21 0926 7444, international ☎ 21 0926 7489) is at Filellinon 13, just off Plateia Syntagmatos. For information about domestic flights from Athens see the Getting Around chapter.

Athens is one of Europe's major centres for buying discounted air tickets. There are dozens of travel agents on Filellinon, Nikis and Voulis that sell low-priced air tickets to Europe and the USA. See the Travel Agencies section under Information at the beginning of this chapter for some recommendations.

Airline offices in Athens include:

Aeroflot (☎ 21 0322 0986)
Air Canada (☎ 21 0615 5321)
Air France (☎ 21 0353 0110)
Air India (☎ 21 0360 2001)
Alitalia (☎ 21 0353 1304)
American Airlines (☎ 21 0325 5061)
British Airways (☎ 21 0890 6666, 21 353 0453)
Continental Airlines (☎ 21 0324 9300)
Cyprus Airways (☎ 21 0322 6413/6414)
Delta Airlines (☎ 21 0331 1660, 21 0353 1134)
EasyJet (☎ 21 0967 0000)
Egypt Air (☎ 21 0353 1272)
El Al (☎ 21 0677 4029, 21 353 1003)
Garuda Indonesia (☎ 21 0679 5600)
Gulf Air (☎ 21 0322 9544)

Iberia (☎ 21 0323 4523/4526)
Japan Airlines (☎ 21 0324 8211)
KLM (☎ 21 0353 1133)
Lufthansa (☎ 21 0617 5200)
Malaysian Airlines (☎ 21 0921 2470)
Qantas Airways, see British Airways
SAS (☎ 21 0361 3910)
Singapore Airlines (☎ 21 0324 4113, 21 0353 1259)
Thai Airways (☎ 21 0353 1237)
Turkish Airlines (☎ 21 0322 1035)
TWA (☎ 21 0921 3400)
United Airlines (☎ 21 0924 2645)
Virgin Atlantic (☎ 21 0690 5300)

Bus
Athens has two main intercity bus stations. Terminal A is about 7km north-west of Plateia Omonias at Kifissou 100 and has departures to the Peloponnese, the Ionian Islands and western Greece. Terminal B is about 5km north of Plateia Omonias off Liossion and has departures to central and northern Greece as well as to Evia. The EOT gives out an intercity bus schedule.

Terminal A Terminal A is not a good introduction to Athens – particularly if you arrive between midnight and 5am when there is no public transport. See the following Getting Around section for details of fares, and the boxed text 'Dangers & Annoyances' earlier in this chapter for information on avoiding rip-offs. The only public transport to the city centre is bus No 051, which runs between the terminal and the junction of Zinonos and Menandrou, near Omonia. Buses run every 15 minutes from 5am to midnight. Don't bother visiting the Tourist Information office at the terminal. It's a booking agency. See the accompanying Departures table for more information.

Terminal B Terminal B is much easier to handle than Terminal A, although again there is no public transport from midnight to 5am. The EOT information sheet misleadingly lists the address of the terminal as being Liossion 260, which turns out to be a small car repair workshop. Liossion 260 is where you should get off the No 024 bus that runs from outside the main gate of the National Gardens on Amalias. From Liossion 260, turn right onto Gousiou and you'll see the terminal at the end of the road on Agiou Dimitriou Oplon. A taxi from the terminal to Syntagma should cost no more than €4.40 at any time. See the accompanying Departures table for more information.

Mavromateon Terminal Buses for destinations in Attica leave from the Mavromateon terminal at the junction of Alexandras and 28 Oktovriou-Patission, 250m north of the National Archaeological Museum and next to Areos Park. Buses for southern Attica leave from this terminal, while buses to Rafina and Marathon leave from the bus stops 150m north on Mavromateon.

Train
Athens also has two train stations (Map 4), located a few hundred metres apart about 1km north-east of Plateia Omonias.

Larisis station, on Deligianni, handles trains on the standard-gauge lines to central and northern Greece. It also handles all international services, which travel via Thessaloniki. Selected destinations, journey times, fares and frequency are listed in the accompanying table (see the Getting There & Away chapter for information on international trains).

The 7am service from Athens runs express right through to Alexandroupolis, arriving at 7pm. Couchettes are available on overnight services to Thessaloniki, priced from €5.90 in 2nd class and €19 in 1st class.

The Peloponnese train station, on Sidirodromon, handles services on the narrowgauge line to the Peloponnese, including the port of Patras. Selected destinations, journey times, fares and frequency are listed in the accompanying table.

The easiest way to get to the stations is to catch the metro to the Larisa stop on Line 2, which is right outside Larisis station. To get to the Peloponnese train station, cross over the metal bridge at the southern end of Larisis train station. You can also get to the stations on trolleybus No 1.

There is baggage storage at Larisis train station, open 6.30am to 9.30pm, and the cost is €3.25 per piece, or €1.65 if you have a train ticket.

More information on services is available from the OSE offices at Karolou 1 (☎ 21 0524 0647), Omonia, and at Sina 6 (☎ 21 0362 4402), near Syntagma. Both offices also handle advance bookings. The Karalou office is open 8am to 6pm Monday to Friday and 8am to 3pm Saturday, while the Sina office is open 8am to 3.30pm Monday to Friday and 8am to 3pm Saturday.

Car & Motorcycle
National Road 1 is the main route north from Athens. It starts at Nea Kifissia. To get there from central Athens, take Vasilissis Sofias from Syntagma. National Road 8 which begins beyond Dafni, is the road to the Peloponnese. Take Agiou Konstantinou from Omonia.

The northern reaches of Syngrou, situated just south of the Temple of Olympian Zeus, are packed solid with car-rental firms. Local companies offer better deals than international ones. International outlets include:

Avis (☎ 21 0322 4951) Amalias 48
Budget (☎ 21 0921 4771) Syngrou 8
Europcar (☎ 21 0924 8810) Syngrou 36–38
Hertz (☎ 21 0922 0102) Syngrou 12
Sixt (☎ 21 0922 0171) Syngrou 23

It's also possible to rent mopeds and motorcycles. Motorent (☎ 21 0923 4939, Ⓦ www.motorent.gr), Rovertou Galli 1, Makrigianni 117 41, has a choice of machines ranging from 50cc to 250cc. Prices for a Honda C50 start at €14.70 per day in high season (16 June to 15 October), or €88.05 per week. Rates are about 15% cheaper for the rest of the year.

Hitching
Athens is the most difficult place in Greece to hitchhike from. Your best bet is to ask the truck drivers at the Piraeus cargo wharves for a ride. Otherwise, for the Peloponnese, take bus No 860 or 880 from Panepistimiou to Dafni, where National Road 8 begins

For northern Greece, take the metro to Kifissia, then a bus to Nea Kifissia and walk to National Road 1.

GETTING AROUND
To/From the Airport

Bus There are two special express bus services operating between the airport and the city as well as a service between the airport and Piraeus.

Service E94 operates between the airport and the eastern terminus of Metro line 3 at Ethniki Amyna. There are departures every 16 minutes, according to the official timetable, between 6am and midnight. The journey takes about 25 minutes.

Service E95 operates between the airport and Plateia Syntagmatos. This line operates 24 hours with services approximately every 30 minutes. The bus stop is outside the National Gardens on Amalias on the eastern side of Plateia Syntagmatos. The journey takes between an hour and 90 minutes, depending on traffic conditions.

Service E96 operates between the airport and Plateia Karaiskaki in Piraeus. This line also operates 24 hours, with services approximately every 40 minutes.

Tickets for all these services cost €2.95. The tickets are valid for 24 hours, and can be used on all forms of public transport in Athens – buses, trolleybuses and the metro.

Taxi The move from Ellinikon to Spata has done nothing to mend the ways of the notorious airport cabbies. It's still virtually impossible to catch a cab from the airport without getting involved in an argument about the fare. See the boxed text 'Dangers & Annoyances' earlier in this chapter for the full run-down on the scams operated by the city's notorious cabbies.

Whatever happens, make sure that the meter is set to the correct tariff (see the following Taxi section for details). You will also have to pay a €0.90 airport surcharge and a €0.60 toll for using the tollroad connecting the airport to the city. Fares vary according to the time of day and level of traffic, but you should expect to pay €14.70 to €20.55 from the airport to the city centre, and €17.60 to €23.50 to Piraeus, depending on traffic conditions. Both trips should take no longer than an hour. If you have any problems, do not hesitate to threaten to involve the tourist police.

Bus & Trolleybus

Since most of Athens' ancient sites are within easy walking distance of Syntagma, and many of the museums are close by on Vasilissis Sofias near Syntagma, the chances are that you won't have much need for public transport.

The blue-and-white buses that serve Athens and the suburbs operate every 15 minutes from 5am until midnight. There are two types of service. Regular services, which stop every few hundred metres, are indicated by a three-figure number – such as bus 224 from Akadimias to Moni Kaissarianis. Express buses are indicated by a letter followed by a one- or two-figure number – such as bus A2 from Panepistimiou to Glyfada, and the E95 between the airport and Syntagma.

There are special buses operating 24 hours a day between the city centre and Piraeus – every 20 minutes from 6am until midnight and then hourly. Bus No 040 runs from Filellinon to Akti Xaveriou in Piraeus, and No 049 runs from the northern end of Athinas to Plateia Themistokleous in Piraeus.

Trolleybuses also operate from 5am until midnight. The free map handed out by EOT shows most of the routes.

There is a flat fare of €0.45 throughout the city on both buses and trolleybuses. Tickets must be purchased before you board, either at a transport kiosk or at most periptera. They can be bought in blocks of 10, but there is no discount for bulk buying. The same tickets can be used on either buses or trolleybuses and must be validated using the red ticket machine as soon as you board. Plain-clothed inspectors make spot checks, and the penalty for travelling without a validated ticket is €17.60.

Metro

The opening of the first phase of the long-awaited new metro system has transformed travel around central Athens. Athenians can

ATHENS

Bus & Train Departures from Athens

Bus Terminal A

destination	duration	price	frequency
Argos	2 hours	€7.35	hourly
Astakos	5 hours	€17.20	2 daily
Corfu	11 hours	€26.70	2 daily
Corinth	1½ hours	€5.45	half-hourly
Epidaurus	2½ hours	€7.80	2 daily
Gythio	4¼ hours	€14.30	5 daily
Igoumenitsa	8½ hours	€27.15	4 daily
Ioannina	7½ hours	€23.80	8 daily
Kalamata	3½ hours	€13.65	9 daily
Kalavryta	3½ hours	€10.45	1 daily
Kavala	10 hours	€35.80	3 daily
Kefallonia	8 hours	€21.90	4 daily
Lefkada	5½ hours	€20.55	4 daily
Loutraki	1½ hours	€5.45	9 daily
Monemvasia	5½ hours	€17.75	4 daily
Nafplio	2½ hours	€8.25	hourly
Olympia	5½ hours	€18.20	4 daily
Patras	3 hours	€11.75	half-hourly
Pylos	5½ hours	€16.75	2 daily
Pyrgos	5 hours	€16.90	10 daily
Sparta	3¼ hours	€12.05	11 daily
Thessaloniki	7½ hours	€26.40	8 daily
Tripolis	2¼ hours	€10	12 daily
Zakynthos	7 hours	€20.85	8 daily

Bus Terminal B

destination	duration	price	frequency
Agios Konstantinos	2½ hours	€9.85	hourly
Delphi	3 hours	€9.70	6 daily
Edipsos	3¼ hours	€8.50	3 daily
Halkida	1 hour	€4.30	half-hourly
Karpenisi	5 hours	€15.45	3 daily
Kymi	3½ hours	€8.70	3 daily
Lamia	3 hours	€12.80	hourly
Larisa	4½ hours	€19.40	6 daily

hardly believe their luck. Journeys that once took more than an hour above ground can now be completed in a matter of minutes.

Coverage is still largely confined to the city centre, but that's good enough for most visitors. The following is a brief outline of the three lines that make up the network:

Line 1 This is the old Kifissia-Piraeus line. Until the opening of lines 2 and 3, this was the metro system. It is indicated in green on maps and signs. Useful stops include Piraeus (for the port), Monastiraki and Omonia (city centre), Plateia Viktorias (National Archaeological Museum) and Irini

Bus & Train Departures from Athens

Livadia	2 hours	€9.40	hourly
Thiva	1½ hours	€5	hourly
Trikala	5½ hours	€17.60	8 daily
Volos	5 hours	€17	9 daily

Mavromateon Terminal

destination	duration	price	frequency
Cape Sounion (via coast road)	1½ hours	€3.70	hourly
Cape Sounion (via Lavrio)	1½ hours	€3.55	hourly
Lavrio	1¼ hours	€2.95	half-hourly
Marathon	1 hour	€2.35	hourly
Rafina	¾ hour	€1.50	half-hourly

Trains for northern Greece, Evia & Europe from Larisis train station

destination	duration	price	frequency
Alexandroupolis	15 hours	€24	1 daily
(Intercity)	12¼ hours	€43.30	2 daily
Halkida *	1½ hours	€3.55	17 daily
Larisa	5 hours	€10	8 daily
(Intercity)	4 hours	€18.80	5 daily
Litohoro *	6 hours	€11.15	3 daily
Thessaloniki	7½ hours	€14	4 daily
(Intercity)	6 hours	€27.60	5 daily
Volos	6 hours	€10.60	1 daily
(Intercity)	5 hours	€19.40	2 daily

Trains for the Peloponnese from Sidirodromon

destination	duration	price	frequency
Corinth	1¾ hours	€2.95	10 daily
(Intercity)	1½ hours	€5.30	5 daily
Kalamata *	6½ hours	€7.35	4 daily
Nafplio *	3½ hours	€4.70	2 daily
Patras	4½ hours	€5.30	4 daily
(Intercity)	3½ hours	€10	4 daily
Pyrgos	6½ hours	€7.20	4 daily
(Intercity)	5 hours	€16.15	3 daily
Tripolis *	4 hours	€5.30	4 daily

* Intercity service not available

Olympic Stadium). Omonia and Attiki are transfer stations with connections to Line 2; Monastiraki will eventually become a transfer station with connections to Line 3.

Line 2 This line runs from Sepolia in the north-west to Dafni in the south-east. It is indicated in red on maps and signs. Useful stops include Larisa (for the train stations), Omonia, Panepistimiou and Syntagma (city centre) and Akropoli (Makrigianni). Attiki and Omonia are transfer stations for Line 1, while Syntagma is the transfer station for Line 3.

Phone numbers listed incorporate changes due in Oct 2002; see p83

ATHENS METRO SYSTEM

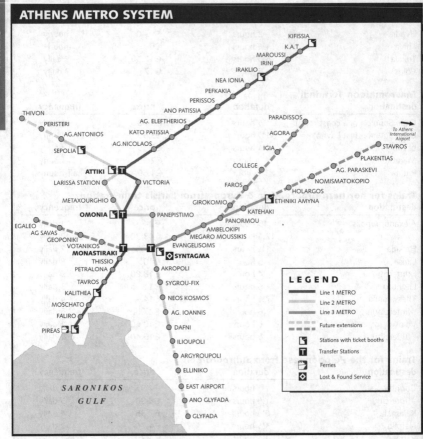

Line 3 This runs north-east from Syntagma to Ethniki Amyna. It is indicated in blue on maps and signs. Useful stops are Evangelismos (for the museums on Vasilissis Sofias) and Megaro Musikis (Athens Concert Hall). Syntagma is the transfer station for Line 2. This line is scheduled to be extended south-west to Monastiraki, and north-east to Stavros. Eventually, according to the master plan, Stavros will have rail service to the airport.

Tickets The ticket pricing is unnecessarily complicated. Travel on lines 2 and 3 costs €0.75, while Line 1 is split into three sections: Piraeus-Monastiraki, Monastiraki-Attiki and Attiki-Kifissia. Travel within one section costs €0.60, and a journey covering two or more sections costs €0.75. The same conditions apply everywhere, though: tickets must be validated at the machines at platform entrances before travelling. The penalty for travelling without a validated ticket is €23.50.

The trains operate between 5am and midnight. They run every three minutes during peak periods, dropping to every 10 minutes at other times.

CHRISTINE COSTE

The ruins of the Acropolis still dominate Athens and remain one of Greece's most important sites.

GEORGE TSAFOS

Athens has the hustle and bustle of a modern city.

RICK GERHARTER

Syntagma Square, Athens

JULIET COOMBE

The old and the new vie for space in the cosmopolitan city of Athens.

Harbourside shopping – Hania, Crete

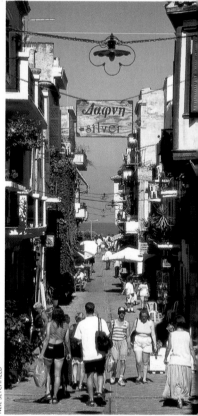
Picturesque, but hard on the feet – Hania, Crete

The traffic is manic in Syntagma Square, Athens.

Plaka's local shops sell a mind-boggling array of weird and wonderful produce for Athens' tourists.

Car & Motorcycle

Appalling traffic, confusing signposting and the one-way system that operates on most streets in the city centre combine to make Athens a nightmarish place to try to drive in. The traffic jams do at least offer an opportunity to work out where you're going!

Athenian drivers have a cavalier attitude towards driving laws. Contrary to what you will see, parking *is* illegal alongside kerbs marked with yellow lines, where street signs prohibit parking and on pavements and in pedestrian malls.

Athens has numerous small car parks, but these are totally insufficient for the number of cars in the city. There is an underground car park beneath the fruit and vegetable market on Athinas, with entry from Sokratous.

For details of car- and motorcycle-rental agencies in Athens, see the preceding Getting There & Away section.

Taxi

Athens' taxis are yellow. If you see an Athenian standing in the road bellowing and waving their arms frantically, the chances are they will be trying to get a taxi

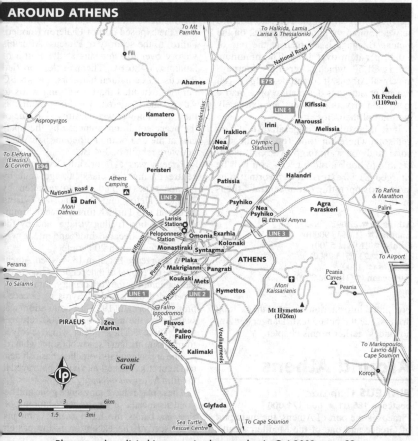

AROUND ATHENS

Phone numbers listed incorporate changes due in Oct 2002; see p83

at rush hour. Despite the large number of taxis careering around the streets of Athens, it can be incredibly difficult to get one.

To hail a taxi, stand on a pavement and shout your destination as they pass. If a taxi is going your way the driver may stop even if there are already passengers inside. This does not mean the fare will be shared: each person will be charged the fare shown on the meter. If you get in one that does not have other passengers, make sure the meter is switched on.

The flag fall is €0.75, with a €0.60 surcharge from ports and train and bus stations, and a €0.90 surcharge from the airport. After that, the day rate (tariff 1 on the meter) is €0.23/km. The rate doubles between midnight and 5am (tariff 2 on the meter). Baggage is charged at the rate of €0.30 per item over 10kg. The minimum fare is €1.50, which covers most journeys in central Athens. It sometimes helps if you can point out your destination on a map – many taxi drivers in Athens are extremely ignorant of their city.

If it is absolutely imperative that you get somewhere on time (eg, to the airport), and you want to go by taxi, it is advisable to book a radio taxi – you will be charged €1.80 extra, but it's worth it. The radio taxis operating out of central Athens include:

Athina 1 (☎ 21 0921 7942)
Enotita (☎ 21 0645 9000)
Ermis (☎ 21 0411 5200)
Ikaros (☎ 21 0515 2800)
Kosmos (☎ 1300)
Parthenon (☎ 21 0532 3300)

For more information about Athens' taxi drivers, see the boxed text 'Dangers & Annoyances' earlier in this chapter.

Around Athens

PIRAEUS Πειραιάς
postcode 185 01 • pop 171,000
Piraeus is the port of Athens, the main port of Greece and one of the Mediterranean's major ports. It's the hub of the Aegean ferry network, centre for Greece's maritime export-import and transit trade and base for its large merchant navy. Nowadays, Athens has expanded sufficiently to meld imperceptibly into Piraeus. The road linking the two passes through a grey, urban sprawl of factories, warehouses and concrete apartment blocks. Piraeus is as bustling and traffic-congested as Athens. It's not a place many visitors want to linger; most come only to catch a ferry.

History
The histories of Athens and Piraeus are inextricably linked. Piraeus has been the port of Athens since classical times, when Themistocles transferred his Athenian fleet from the exposed port of Phaleron (modern Faliro) to the security of Piraeus. After his victory over the Persians at the Battle of Salamis in 480 BC, Themistocles fortified Piraeus' three natural harbours. In 445 BC Pericles extended these fortifying Walls to Athens and Phaleron. The Long Walls, as they were known, were destroyed as one of the peace conditions imposed by the Spartans at the end of the Peloponnesian Wars, but were rebuilt in 394 BC.

Piraeus was a flourishing commercial centre during the classical age, but by Roman times it had been overtaken by Rhodes, Delos and Alexandria. During medieval and Turkish times Piraeus diminished to a tiny fishing village, and by the time Greece became independent, it was home to fewer than 20 people.

Its resurgence began in 1834 when Athens became the capital of independent Greece. By the beginning of the 20th century, Piraeus had superseded the island of Syros as Greece's principal port. In 1923 its population was swollen by the arrival of 100,000 refugees from Turkey. The Piraeus which evolved from this influx had a seedy but somewhat romantic appeal with its bordellos, hashish dens and rembetika music – all vividly portrayed in the film *Never on a Sunday*.

These places have long since gone and beyond its facade of smart, new shipping offices and banks, much of Piraeus is now just plain seedy. The exception is the eastern quarter around Zea Marina and Mikrolimano, where the seafront is lined with seafood restaurants, bars and discos.

Orientation

Piraeus is 10km south-west of central Athens. The largest of its three harbours is the Great Harbour (Megas Limin), on the western side of the Piraeus peninsula. All ferries leave from here. Zea Marina (Limin Zeas), on the other side of the peninsula, is the port for hydrofoils to the Saronic Gulf Islands (except Aegina) as well as being the place where millionaires moor their yachts. North-east of here is the picturesque Mikrolimano (small harbour), brimming with private yachts.

The metro line from Athens terminates at the north-eastern corner of the Great Harbour on Akti Kalimassioti. Most ferry departure points are a short walk from here. A left turn out of the metro station leads after 250m to Plateia Karaïskaki, which is the terminus for buses to the airport. Jutting out into the harbour behind the square is Akti Tzelepi with its mass of ticket agencies.

South of Plateia Karaïskaki, the waterfront becomes Akti Poseidonos, which leads into Vasileos Georgiou beyond Plateia Themistokleous. Vasileos Georgiou is one of the two main streets of Piraeus, running south-east across the peninsula; the other main street is Iroön Polytehniou, which runs south-west along the ridge of the peninsula, meeting Vasileos Georgiou by the main square, Plateia Korai.

Information

Tourist Offices Thanks to some kind of bureaucratic bad joke, the Piraeus EOT (☎ 21 0452 2586/2591) is at Zea Marina. Why it should be here and not at the Great Harbour defies imagination. The office is open 8am to 3pm Monday to Friday. The telephone number of Piraeus' port police is ☎ 21 0412 2501.

Money There are lots of places to change money at Great Harbour, including virtually all the ticket and travel agencies. The Emporiki Bank, just north of Plateia

Themistokleous on the corner of Antistaseos and Makras Stoas, has a 24-hour automatic exchange machine. The National Bank of Greece has a Great Harbour branch at the corner of Antistaseos and Tsamadou, and another branch above the naval museum at Zea Marina.

Post & Communications The main post office is on the corner of Tsamadou and Filonos, just north of Plateia Themistokleous. It's open 7.30am to 8pm Monday to Friday and 7.30am to 2pm Saturday. The OTE is just north of here at Karaoli 19 and is open 24 hours.

You can check your email at the Surf Internet Café at Platanos 3, off Iroön Polytehniou. It's open 8am to 9pm Monday to Friday and 8am to 3pm Saturday. Another possibility is the Dios Internet Café, Androutsou 170, open 9.30am to midnight daily.

Archaeological Museum

If you have time to spare in Piraeus, the archaeological museum (☎ 21 0452 1598, Harilaou Trikoupi 31; admission €1.50; open 8.30am-3pm Tues-Sun) is a good place to spend it. It's well laid out and contains some important finds from classical and Roman times. These include some very fine tomb reliefs dating from the 4th to the 2nd century BC. The star piece of the museum, however, is the magnificent statue of Apollo, the Piraeus Kouros. It is the oldest larger-than-life, hollow bronze statue yet found. It dates from about 520 BC and was discovered, buried in rubble, in 1959.

Hellenic Maritime Museum

The maritime museum (☎ 21 0451 6822, Akti Themistokleous; admission €1.20; open 9am-2pm Tues-Sat) has a collection spanning the history of the Greek navy from ancient times to the present day, with drawings and plans of battles, models of ships, battle scenes, uniforms and war memorabilia. There are various nautical oddments in the small park outside the museum, including a submarine conning tower which children love to climb. The museum is at Zea Marina, very close to the hydrofoil quay.

PIRAEUS

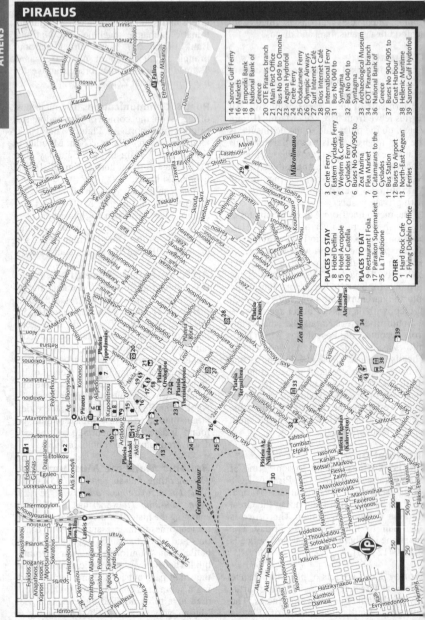

PLACES TO STAY
8   Hotel Delfini
15 Hotel Acropole
29 Hotel Castella

PLACES TO EAT
9   Restaurant I Folia
17 Pairaikon Supermarket
35 La Tradizione

OTHER
1   Hard Rock Cafe
2   Flying Dolphin Office
3   Crete Ferry
4   Eastern Cyclades Ferry
5   Western & Central
    Cyclades Ferry
6   Buses No 904/905 to
    Zea Marina
7   Flea Market
10 Catamarans to the
    Cyclades
11 Bus Station
12 Buses to Airport
13 North-East Aegean
    Ferries
14 Saronic Gulf Ferry
16 Markets
18 Emporiki Bank
19 National Bank of
    Greece
20 OTE Piraeus branch
21 Main Post Office
22 Bus No 049 to Omonia
23 Aegina Hydrofoil
24 Crete Ferry
25 Dodacanese Ferry
26 Olympic Airways
27 Surf Internet Café
28 Dios Internet Café
30 International Ferry
31 Bus No 040 to
    Syntagma
32 Bus No 040 to
    Syntagma
33 Archaeological Museum
34 EOT Piraeus branch
36 National Bank of
    Greece
37 Buses No 904/905 to
    Great Harbour
38 Hellenic Maritime
39 Saronic Gulf Hydrofoil

Places to Stay
There's no reason to stay at any of the shabby cheap hotels around Great Harbour when Athens is so close. The cheap hotels are geared more towards accommodating sailors than tourists. Whatever happens, don't attempt to sleep out – Piraeus is the most dangerous place in Greece to do so.

Hotel Acropole (☎ 21 0417 3313, fax 21 0988 2726, Gounari 7) Dorm beds €10.30, singles/doubles €17.60/26.40. This hotel has plain rooms. Gounari is the main thoroughfare running inland from Plateia Karaïskaki.

Hotel Delfini (☎ 21 0412 9779, fax 21 0417 3110, Leoharous 7) Singles/doubles with bathroom €26.40/35.20. This C-class hotel is a bit smarter than the Acropole. Make sure you don't get taken there by one of the touts who hang around the port or you will wind up inflated prices.

Hotel Castella (☎ 21 0411 4735, fax 21 0417 5716, Vasileos Pavlou) Singles/doubles with breakfast €70.45/108.60. This is the pick of the hotels on Vasileos Pavlou, which runs around the hillside above the Mikrolimano. It has good views of the harbour.

Places to Eat
Great Harbour There are dozens of cafes, restaurants and fast-food places along the waterfront.

Restaurant I Folia (☎ 21 0421 0781, Akti Poseidonos 30) Dishes €2.45-4.20. This tiny restaurant, opposite Plateia Karaïskaki, is perfect for a quick bite before you board a ferry.

If you want to stock up on supplies before a ferry trip, head for the area just inland from Poseidonos. You'll find fresh fruit and vegetables at the *markets* on Demosthenous. Opposite the markets is *Pairaikon supermarket* (☎ 21 0411 7177), open 8am to 8pm Monday to Friday, 8am to 4pm Saturday.

Zea Marina *La Tradizione* (☎ 21 0451 7519, Akti Moutsoupoulou 12) Mains €4.10-6.75. The choice is more limited over at Zea Marina. You'll find pasta dishes and pizzas at this Italian restaurant next to the Flying Dolphin office.

Mikrolimano The setting around the Mikrolimano is rather more relaxed, with a string of *seafood restaurants* right on the waterfront.

Entertainment
Hard Rock Café (☎ 21 0413 6750, e hard-rock@united-hellas.com, Etolikou 28) Open 11am-3am Sun-Thur, 11am-4am Fri, 11am-5am Sat. The location isn't the greatest, but this is the place to come for aficionados in search of Hard Rock Café Piraeus T-shirts and other souvenirs. As well as beers, the bar menu also a choice of burgers, priced from €4.40 to €7.35, and salads.

Shopping
Piraeus flea market (Alipedou & Skilitsi) Open Sun morning. Many locals will tell you that the Piraeus flea market is infinitely better than its famous counterpart in Athens. As well as stalls selling junk, there are small shops selling high-quality jewellery, ceramics and antiques. The market is on Alipedou and Skilitsi, near Plateia Ippodamias, which is behind the metro station.

Getting There & Away
Air Olympic Airways (☎ 21 0926 7560) has an office at Akti Miaouli 27.

Bus Special buses (Nos 040 and 049) operate 24 hours a day between Piraeus and central Athens; they run every 20 minutes from 6am until midnight and then hourly. No 040 runs between Akti Xaveriou in Piraeus and Filellinon in Athens and is the service that goes closest to Zea Marina; the most convenient stop is outside Hotel Savoy on Iroön Polytehniou. No 049 runs between Plateia Themistokleous in Piraeus and Plateia Omonias in Athens. The fare is €0.45 on each service.

E96 buses to the airport leave from the south-western corner of Plateia Karaïskaki. Departure times are listed under To/From the Airport in Athens' Getting Around section.

There are no intercity buses to or from Piraeus.

Ferries from Piraeus

destination	duration	price	frequency
Cyclades			
Amorgos	10 hours	€15	2 daily
Anafi	11 hours	€19.70	4 weekly
Folegandros	6-9 hours	€14.70	4 weekly
Ios	7½ hours	€15.80	4 daily
Kimolos	6 hours	€13.20	2 weekly
Kythnos	2½ hours	€9.10	daily
Milos	7 hours	€14.70	2 daily
Mykonos	5½ hours	€15.10	3 daily
Naxos	6 hours	€14.70	6 daily
Paros	5 hours	€14.70	6 daily
Santorini	9 hours	€18	4 daily
Serifos	4½ hours	€11.45	daily
Sifnos	5½ hours	€12.60	daily
Sikinos	8-10 hours	€17	daily
Syros	4 hours	€12.90	3 daily
Tinos	4½ hours	€13.80	daily
Dodecanese			
Astypalea	12 hours	€21.40	3 weekly
Halki	22 hours	€29.50	2 weekly
Kalymnos	10-13 hours	€21.80	daily
Karpathos	18½ hours	€24.40	4 weekly
Kasos	17 hours	€24	4 weekly
Kos	12-15 hours	€23.20	2 daily
Leros	11 hours	€19.70	daily

Train Piraeus also has train stations for both northern Greece and the Peloponnese. Piraeus' train station is one block north of the metro. All the railway services to the Peloponnese (see Getting There & Away under Athens) actually start and terminate at Piraeus, although most schedules don't mention it. There are about 15 trains daily to Athens.

The single service from the northern line train station (via Larisis train station) is of purely academic interest, leaving at 1.30pm and taking more than seven hours to crawl to Volos, stopping all stations. The station for northern Greece is at the western end of Akti Kondyli.

Metro The metro is the fastest and easiest way of getting from the Great Harbour to central Athens (see Athens' Getting Around section). The station is at the northern end of Akti Kalimassioti. Travellers should take extra care of valuables on the metro; the section between Piraeus and Monastiraki is notorious for pickpockets (see the Dangers & Annoyances section earlier in this chapter).

Ferry – Domestic Piraeus is the busiest port in Greece with a bewildering array of departures and destinations, including daily services to all the island groups except the Ionians and the Sporades.

The following table lists all the destinations that can be reached by ferry. The information is for the high season – from mid-June to September.

Ferries from Piraeus

Lipsi	16 hours	€28	1 weekly
Nisyros	13-15 hours	€23.20	2 weekly
Patmos	9½ hours	€21	daily
Rhodes	15-18 hours	€26.70	2 daily
Symi	15-17 hours	€21.20	2 weekly
Tilos	15 hours	€21.80	2 weekly
North-Eastern Aegean Islands			
Chios	8 hours	€17	5 weekly
Fourni	10 hours	€17.60	3 weekly
Ikaria	9 hours	€17	daily
Lesvos	12 hours	€22.50	daily
Limnos	13 hours	€21	4 weekly
Samos	13 hours	€20.50	2 daily
Crete			
Agios Nikolaos	12 hours	€22.60	3 weekly
Hania	10 hours	€19.90	daily
Iraklio	10 hours	€21.10	2 daily
Kastelli-Kissamou	12 hours	€17.10	2 weekly
Rethymno	10-12 hours	€19.90	daily
Sitia	14½ hours	€23.40	3 weekly
Saronic Gulf Islands (*most from Zea Marina)			
Aegina	1¼ hours	€4.40	hourly
Hydra*	3½ hours	€7.35	2 daily
Poros*	2½ hours	€6.45	4 daily
Spetses*	4½ hours	€10	daily

For the latest departure information, pick up a weekly ferry schedule from the tourist office in Athens. See the Getting There & Away sections for each island for specific details, and the Getting Around chapter for general information about ferry travel.

The departure points for ferry destinations are shown on the map of Piraeus. Note that there are two departure points for Crete. Ferries for Iraklio leave from the western end of Akti Kondyli, but ferries for other Cretan ports occasionally dock there as well. It's a long way to the other departure point for Crete on Akti Miaouli, so check where to find your boat when you buy your ticket.

Tickets Ferry prices are fixed by the government. All ferries charge the same for any given route, although the facilities on board differ – quite radically at times. The small differences in prices charged by agents are the result of them sacrificing part of their allotted commission to increase sales (allowing them to call themselves 'discount' agencies). These discounts seldom amount to more than €0.15. Agents cannot charge more than the fixed price.

If you want to book a cabin or take a car on board a ferry, it is advisable to buy a ticket in advance in Athens. Otherwise, you should wait until you get to Piraeus; agents selling ferry tickets are thick on the ground around Plateia Karaïskaki. If you're running short of time, you can buy your ticket at the quay from the tables set up next to each ferry. It costs no more to buy your

Hydrofoils from Piraeus

destination	duration	price	frequency
Cyclades (*from Zea Marina)			
Kythnos	1¾ hours	€17.60	5 weekly
Milos	4½ hours	€28.80	daily
Mykonos	3½ hours	€29.65	2 daily
Naxos	3¼ hours	€27.30	2 daily
Paros	2½ hours	€28.80	2 daily
Serifos	2¾ hours	€22.30	daily
Sifnos	3½ hours	€24.95	daily
Syros	2½ hours	€25.25	2 daily
Tinos	3 hours	€27	daily
Peloponnese (*most from Zea Marina)			
Ermioni*	2 hours	€15.85	4 daily
Gerakas*	3½ hours	€23.80	daily
Kyparissi*	3 hours	€22.30˙	daily
Leonidio*	2½ hours	€21.15	daily
Monemvasia*	2½ hours	€26.15	daily
Porto Heli*	2 hours	€17	6 daily
Saronic Gulf Islands (*most from Zea Marina)			
Aegina	35 mins	€8.50	hourly
Hydra*	1¼ hours	€13.80	7 daily
Poros*	1 hour	€12.35	6 daily
Spetses*	2 hours	€19.10	7 daily
Ionian Islands (from Zea Marina)			
Kythira	5 hours	€30.80	daily

ticket at the boat, contrary to what some agents might tell you.

Ferry – International There are two ferries weekly in summer to Lemesos (Limassol) in Cyprus and Haifa in Israel, and one a week in winter. Salamis Lines operates the F/B *Nissos Kypros* year-round via Rhodes. It leaves Piraeus at 7pm on Thursday and Rhodes at 8pm on Friday, arriving at Lemesos at 2.30pm on Saturday and Haifa at 6am on Sunday. In summer, Poseidon Lines operates the F/B *Sea Armony* via Rhodes, leaving Piraeus at 8pm on Thursday.

Deck-class fares from Piraeus to Lemesos are €47/58.70 in low/high season, and €76.30/85.15 to Haifa. Both lines offer 20% student (up to 28 years), youth (up to 24 years) and return-ticket discounts.

Hydrofoil Minoan Lines operates its Flying Dolphin hydrofoil services from Piraeus to the Saronic Gulf Islands, the Peloponnese and a growing range of destinations in the Cyclades. Services to the Cyclades leave from Great Harbour, while other departures are split between Great Harbour and Zea Marina – check when you buy your ticket.

The information in the hydrofoil timetable is for the high season, from mid-June to September.

For more information about hydrofoil services, see the Getting Around chapter and the Getting There & Away sections of the island chapters.

Tickets Although it is often possible to buy tickets at Minoan's quayside offices at both Great Harbour and Zea Marina, reservations are strongly recommended – especially at weekends. You can book seats, and pay by credit card, by phoning Minoan's bookings centre (☎ 042 8001).

Getting Around

Piraeus has its own network of buses and trams, but the only services likely to be of much interest to travellers are the buses (No 904 or 905) which run between Zea Marina and the bus stop next to the metro.

MONI KAISSARIANIS
Μονή Καισσαριαής

Five kilometres east of Athens, set amid pines, plane and cypress trees on the slopes of Mt Hymettos, is this 11th-century monastery (☎ 21 0723 6619, Mt Hymettos; admission €2.35; buildings open 8am-2.30pm Tues-Sun, grounds open to sunset). The air is permeated with the aroma of herbs which grow on the mountain.

The source of the river Ilissos is on the hill above the monastery. Its waters were once believed to cure infertility and were sacred to Aphrodite; a temple dedicated to her stood nearby. The spring feeds a fountain on the eastern wall of the monastery, where the water gushes from a marble ram's head (this is a copy – the 6th-century original is in the National Archaeological Museum).

Surrounding the courtyard of the monastery are a mill, bakery, bathhouse and refectory. The church is dedicated to the Presentation of the Virgin and is built to the Greek-cross plan. Four columns taken from a Roman temple support its dome. The 17th-century frescoes in the narthex are the work of Ioannis Ipatos. Those in the rest of the church date from the 16th century, and were painted by a monk from Mt Athos.

The monastery is best visited during the week – it's swarming with picnickers at weekends. To get to the monastery take bus No 224 from Plateia Kaningos (at the north end of Akadimias), or from the junction of Akadimias and Sina, to the terminus. From here it's a walk of about 30 minutes to the monastery.

Attica Αττική

Attica, a *nomos* of Sterea Ellada, contains more than just the capital and its port of Piraeus. Although no longer dominated by Athens, until the 7th century it was home to a number of smaller kingdoms such as those at Eleusis (Elefsina), Ramnous and Brauron (Vravrona). The remains of these cities remain among the region's main attractions, although they pale alongside the superb Temple of Poseidon at Cape Sounion.

Attica also has some fine beaches, particularly around Glyfada and at Shinias, near Marathon.

Many of these places can be reached by regular city buses; others can be reached by the orange buses from the Mavromateon bus terminal north of the National Archaeological Museum.

GLYFADA Γλυφάδα

Glyfada, 12km south-east of Athens, is Attica's principal resort. It marks the beginning of a stretch of coastline known as the Apollo Coast, a string of fine beaches running south to Cape Sounion. Unfortunately, the region is fast falling victim to overdevelopment.

These days, Glyfada is virtually part of Athens, although local residents are quick to tell you otherwise. In summer, half of Athens descends on Glyfada, anyway, drawn by its beaches, bars and restaurants – not to mention sea breezes.

Most things are located within easy distance of the main square, Plateia Katriki Vasos.

Beaches

The main beaches are just south of Glyfada at **Voula**, **Vouliagmeni** and **Varkiza**. All are run by the Greek National Tourist Organisation (EOT) and charge admission (adults/children €1.80/0.90). They are open 8am to

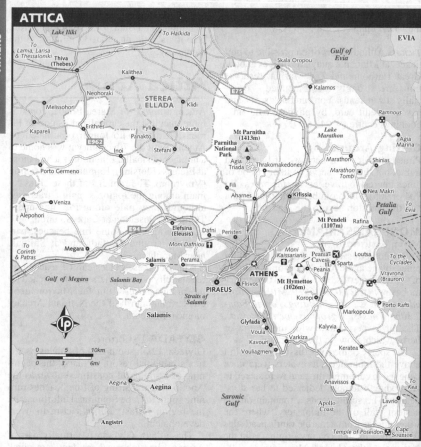

ATTICA

Lake Iliki
To Halkida
EVIA
To Lamia, Larisa & Thessaloniki
Thiva (Thebes)
Gulf of Evia
Skala Oropou
Kalithea
Kalamos
Neohoraki
STEREA ELLADA
Klidi
Melissohori
E75
Ramnous
Pyli
Skourta
Mt Parnitha (1413m)
Lake Marathon
Agia Marina
Erithres
Panakto
Parnitha National Park
Kaparelli
E962
Inoi
Stefani
Agia Triada
Thrakomakedones
Marathon
Shinias
Porto Germeno
Fili
Marathon Tomb
Veniza
Aharnes
Nea Makri
Kifissia
Petalia Gulf
Alepohori
E94
Elefsina (Eleusis)
Dafni
Peristeri
Mt Pendeli (1107m)
Rafina
To Evia
To Corinth & Patras
Megara
Moni Dafniou
Moni Kaissarianis
Peania Caves
Loutsa
To the Cyclades
Salamis
Perama
Sparta
Peania
ATHENS
Vravrona (Brauron)
Gulf of Megara
Salamis Bay
PIRAEUS
Flisvos
Mt Hymettos (1026m)
Koropi
Porto Rafti
Straits of Salamis
Salamis
Glyfada
Markopoulo
Voula
Kalyvia
Kavouri
Varkiza
Keratea
Vouliagmeni
Aegina
Aegina
Saronic Gulf
Anavissos
To Kea
Lavrio
Apollo Coast
Angistri
Temple of Poseidon
Cape Sounion

0   5   10km
0   3   6mi

8pm daily and offer facilities like children's playgrounds, tennis courts and changing rooms.

Vouliagmeni Beach also hires individual cabins for €5.90 to lounge about in for the day.

Third Beach, at the south-eastern end of Varkiza Beach, is a popular gay spot.

All these beaches can be reached by buses travelling south from Plateia Katriki Vasos.

Sea Turtle Rescue Centre

One good reason to stop here is to check out the work of the Sea Turtle Rescue Centre

(☎/fax 21 0898 2600, ℮ stps.rescue@compulink.gr, Third Marina; admission free; open 10am-2pm & 5pm-7pm daily), about 500m from the bus stops on Glyfada's main square, Plateia Katriki Vasos.

The centre is housed in old freight carriages donated by the Greek railways, and cares for injured turtles found in Greek waters – mainly leatherbacks (Caretta caretta). Some of the injuries are quite heartbreaking.

Diving

The **Aegean Dive Centre** (☎ 21 0894 5409, fax 21 0898 1120, ℮ dive@adc.gr,

W *www.adc.gr, Cnr Zamanou & Pandoras; Beginners course from €251, dives €50 Sat & Sun, night dives €53 Sat)* offers dives at a variety of sites between Vouliagmeni and Cape Sounion – although not at Cape Sounion itself, where diving is strictly forbidden. Prices include all equipment.

Places to Stay

Hotel Ilion (☎ 21 0894 6011, Kondyli 4) Singles/doubles with bathroom €24.95/ 30.80. The cheapest rooms in Glyfada are at the gloomy Hotel Ilion, which are hard to recommend on any ground other than price.

Hotel Zina (☎ 21 0960 3872, fax 21 0960 4004, Evangelistras 6) Apartments €73.40-82.20. If your budget permits, a good choice is this quiet hotel, 500m north-east of Plateia Vyzaniou. It has spacious, well-equipped apartments with kitchen, lounge and TV.

Places to Eat

The streets around Glyfada's main square are filled with representatives of every fast-food chain operating in Greece. Konstantinopoleos, which runs inland from the main square, is packed solid with bars and tavernas.

Tzavelas Taverna (☎ 21 0894 4125, Konstantinopoleos 16) Meals €4.70-11.75. This taverna, away from the main pack, has the best prices.

The Sushi Bar (☎ 21 0894 2200, Konstantinopoleos 15) Mains €3.85-6.45. The popular Sushi Bar is great value. There is plenty of variety on offer including an excellent range of vegetarian rolls, soups and sashimi dishes.

The Garden of Eden (☎ 21 0898 0754, Zerva 12) Mains €2.95-8.25. For authentic Lebanese head straight to the Garden of Eden. Try the delicious *makdous* (eggplant stuffed with walnuts and spices; €2.50) or the *hommos snouber* (hummus with pine nuts; €3.55).

JJ's Pub (☎ 21 0898 3600, Maragou 8) Beers from €4.40. This is the favourite haunt of the expatriate community and has a large range of imported British and continental beers.

Getting There & Away

The quickest way to get to Glyfada is on express bus A2, A3 or E2 from Plateia Syntagmatos in Athens. The A2 continues to Voula and Vouliagmeni.

CAPE SOUNION

Ακρωτήριο Σούνιο

Temple of Poseidon

The ancient Greeks chose their temple sites carefully, with the prime considerations being a site's natural beauty and its appropriateness to the god in question. Nowhere is this more evident than at Cape Sounion, 70km south of Athens, where the Temple of Poseidon *(☎ 2292 039 363; admission €2.35; open 8am-sunset summer, 10am-sunset winter)* stands on a craggy spur that plunges 65m down into the sea. The temple was built in 444 BC at the same time as the Parthenon. It is constructed of local marble from Agrilesa and its slender columns – of which 16 remain – are Doric. It is thought that the temple was built by Ictinus, the architect of the Temple of Hephaestus in Athens' Ancient Agora.

The temple looks gleaming white when viewed from the sea and is discernible from a long distance. It gave great comfort to sailors in ancient times; they knew they were nearly home. The views from the temple are equally impressive. On a clear day, you can see Kea, Kythnos and Serifos to the south-east, and Aegina and the Peloponnese to the west. The site also contains scanty remains of a propylon, a fortified tower and, to the north-east, a 6th-century temple to Athena.

Visit early in the morning before the tourist buses arrive if you wish to indulge the sentiments of Byron's lines from *Don Juan*:

Place me on Sunium's marbled steep,
Where nothing save the waves and I,
May hear our mutual murmurs sweep...

Byron was so taken by Sounion that he carved his name on one of the columns – many others have followed suit.

Places to Stay & Eat

Camping Bacchus (☎ 2292 039 571/572, fax 2292 039 572, e linosP@panafonnet .gr, 4.5km east of Temple of Poseidon) Adult/tent €4.70/4.10. Camping Bacchus' is well located and its facilities include a mini market and a laundry service. The bus to Sounio stops at the site.

Hotel Saron (☎ 2292 039 144, fax 2292 039 045, 4km east of Temple of Poseidon) Singles/doubles €38.15/41.10. Set amid pines, the friendly Hotel Saron has well-priced, comfortable rooms. It also has a pool.

Taverna Akrogiali (☎ 2292 039 107) Mains €5.60-14.70. This small family-run taverna oozes with charm and history. Dating from 1887, it boasts such famous guests as Jackie Kennedy – ask to see the framed letter of thanks sent from the White House – and Sophia Loren. The taverna is on the seafront below Temple of Poseidon, next to the Aegeon Hotel.

Getting There & Away

You can take either the inland or coastal bus to Cape Sounion. The *paraliako* (coastal) buses leave Athens hourly, on the half-hour (two hours, €3.70), from the Mavromateon bus terminal (see Athens' Getting There & Away section for details). These buses also stop on Filellinon, on the corner of Xenofontos, 10 minutes later, but by this time they're usually very crowded. The *mesogiaki* (inland) buses take 2¼ hours (€3.55) and travel via Peania, Koropi, Markopoulo and Lavrio (see the Mesogeia).

THE MESOGEIA

The Mesogeia (middle land) covers the central heartland of the Attic Peninsula. Until the building of Athens' new international airport, the region was best known for the fine olives and grapes grown on its red soil. The arrival of the airport marks the beginning of the end for this once tranquil region.

Peania, a village 18km east of Athens in the eastern foothills of Mt Hymettos, was the birthplace of the orator Demosthenes (384–322 BC). Little remains of the ancient town, but visitors come today not for the ruins, but to look around the **Vorres**

Museum (☎ 21 0664 2520, Plateia Vasileos Konstantinou; admission €2.95; open 10am-2pm Sat & Sun), which houses folkloric items, prints and pictures, and an impressive collection of contemporary Greek paintings. Modern sculptures stand in the courtyard. The museum is a fair hike from the bus stop on Peania's main square. Walk down Demosthenous (which has the New Democracy building on the corner and the post office next to it) and turn right onto Dimihounta at the bottom. Walk to the top of Dimihounta, and turn left onto Diadohou Konstantinou – where you'll soon find a sign pointing straight ahead to the museum.

The **Peania Caves** (☎ 21 0664 2108; admission €4.40; open 9am-4.30pm daily), 4km west of Peania on the slopes of Mt Hymettos, have an impressive array of stalactites and stalagmites that are very effectively lit. The caves were discovered in 1926 when a shepherd saw a lamb disappear down the tiny crevice that is the only natural entrance. The temperature inside the caves is a constant 17°C all year, making them a pleasant retreat from the heat of summer. The caves are signposted from Peania, but there is no public transport.

The largest of the villages of Mesogeia is **Koropi**, a lively market town 7km south of Peania. Its Church of the Transfiguration, on the road to Markopoulo, is one of the oldest churches in Attica and contains the remains of 10th-century frescoes.

The road continues to **Markopoulo** – home of the Kourtaki company, producer of Greece's most popular bottled retsina. The road south continues to Lavrio and Cape Sounion.

Getting There & Away

The *mesogiaki* (inland) buses from the Mavromateon terminal in Athens to Cape Sounion (2¼ hours, €3.55) stop at both Peania and Koropi and continue south via Markopoulo and Lavrio.

LAVRIO Λαύριο

postcode 195 00 • pop 2500

Lavrio is an unattractive industrial town on the east coast of Attica, 10km north of

Sounion. It is only worth a mention because it is the departure point for ferries to the islands of Kea and Kythnos. The town has definitely seen better days. In ancient times its silver mines, worked by slaves, helped to finance Pericles' building program.

The island of Makronisos, opposite the port, was used as a place of exile during the civil war.

Getting There & Away

Bus Buses run every 30 minutes to Lavrio from the Mavromateon terminal in Athens (1½ hours, €2.95).

Ferry Goutos Lines runs the F/B *Myrina Express* from Lavrio to Kea (€5.15) and Kythnos (€7.35). From mid-June, there are ferries to Kea every morning and evening Monday to Friday, and up to six daily at weekends. Three ferries weekly continue to Kythnos. In winter there are ferries to Kea every day except Monday, returning every day except Wednesday. One service a week continues to Kythnos. The EOT in Athens gives out a timetable for this route. The ticket office at Lavrio is opposite the quay.

VRAVRONA (BRAURON)
Βραυρώνα
The ruins of the ancient city of Brauron (☎ 2299 027 020; admission €1.50; site & museum open 8am-3pm Tues-Sun) lie just outside the small village of Vravrona (vrah-vro-nah), 40km east of Athens. Brauron belonged to King Cecrops' league of 12 cities (King Cecrops was the mythical founder of Athens). Remains dating back to 1700 BC have been found at the site, but it is best known for the **Sanctuary of Artemis**.

According to mythology, it was to Brauron that Iphigenia and Orestes brought the *xoanon* (sacred image) of Artemis that they removed from Tauris. The site became a sanctuary to Artemis during the time of the tyrant Peisistratos, who made the worship of Artemis the official religion of Athens.

The cult centred around a festival, held every five years, at which girls aged between five and 10 performed a ritual dance

that imitated the movements of a bear. The ruins of the dormitories where the girls stayed can be seen at the site.

The sanctuary's Doric temple, of which only a small section still stands, was built in the 5th century BC on the site of an earlier temple that was destroyed by the Persians. The site's **museum** houses finds from the sanctuary and the surrounding area.

Getting There & Away
Extremely early risers can follow the tourist office's advice and catch the 5.50am bus from the Mavromateon terminal in Athens to Cape Sounion as far as Markopoulo, where you take the 6.50am bus to Vravrona. A less painful option is to catch the metro to Ethniki Amyna at the end of Line 2. There are buses to Vravrona (€0.45) from here every 20 minutes.

RAFINA Ραφήνα
postcode 190 09 • pop 10,000
Rafina, on Attica's east coast, is Athens' main fishing port and second-most important port for passenger ferries. The port is much smaller than Piraeus and less confusing – and fares are about 20% cheaper, but you have to spend an hour on the bus and €1.80 to get there.

The port police (☎ 2294 022 888) occupy a kiosk near the quay, which is lined with fish restaurants and ticket agents. The main square, Plateia Plastira, is at the top of the ramp leading to the port.

Places to Stay
There's no reason to hang about in Rafina and there are frequent bus connections with Athens. If, however, you want to stay the night and catch an early ferry or hydrofoil, there are a couple of reasonable hotels.

Hotel Koralli (☎ 2294 022 477, Plateia Plastira) Singles/doubles €16.15/23.50. This is a D-class hotel.

Hotel Avra (☎ 2294 022 781, fax 2294 023 320) Singles/doubles €44/76. The Avra is a comfortable C-class hotel that overlooks the port opposite Plateia Plastira. It has large rooms with sea views and prices include breakfast.

Getting There & Away

Bus There are frequent buses from the Mavromateon terminal in Athens to Rafina (one hour, €1.50) between 5.45am and 10.30pm. The first bus leaves Rafina at 5.50am and the last at 10.15pm.

Ferry Blue Star Ferries operates a daily service at 8am to Andros (two hours, €7.35), Tinos (3½ hours, €11.15) and Mykonos (4½ hours, €12.65). It also has a 7.30pm daily ferry to Andros, continuing to Tinos and Mykonos on Friday.

The Maritime Company of Lesvos has four boats weekly to Limnos (10 hours, €17).

There are also ferries to the ports of Karystos and Marmari on the island of Evia. There are four daily to Marmari (1¼ hours, €3.80) and two to Karystos (1¾ hours, €5.60).

Catamaran Blue Star Ferries and Minoan Lines operate high-speed catamarans to the Cyclades.

Blue Star has three services daily to Tinos (1¾ hours, €22.30) and Mykonos (2¼ hours, €25.25), departing at 7.40am, noon and 5.30pm. The 7.40am service continues to Paros (three hours, €25.55); on Tuesday it goes to Amorgos (five hours, €29.05).

Minoan operates giant vehicle-carrying catamarans on a daily run to Syros (1¾ hours, €21.15), Mykonos (two hours, €25.25) and Paros (three hours, €25.55). They continue to Santorini (4¾ hours, €29.35) six times weekly, stopping at Ios (four hours, €25.55) four times weekly.

Minoan operates smaller catamarans on the daily 7.55am route to Tinos (1½ hours, €22.30), Mykonos (two hours, €25.25) and Paros (2¾ hours, €25.55). The Wednesday morning service also calls at Andros (one hour, €14.70), and continues from Paros to Amorgos (4½ hours, €29.05) and Ios (5½ hours, €25.55). Minoan operates an additional 3pm service to Tinos and Mykonos five times weekly.

MARATHON REGION
Marathon Μαραθώνας

The plain surrounding the unremarkable small town of Marathon, 42km north-east of Athens, is the site of one of the most celebrated battles in world history. In 490 BC, an army of 9000 Greeks and 1000 Plataeans defeated the 25,000-strong Persian army, proving that the Persians were not invincible. The Greeks were indebted to the ingenious tactics of Miltiades, who altered the conventional battle formation so that there were fewer soldiers in the centre, but more in the wings. This lulled the Persians into thinking that the Greeks were going to be a pushover. They broke through in the centre, but were then ambushed by the soldiers in the wings. At the end of the day, 6000 Persians and only 192 Greeks lay dead. The story goes that after the battle a runner was sent to Athens to announce the victory. After shouting *'Enikesame!'* ('We won!') he collapsed in a heap and never revived. This is the origin of today's marathon foot race.

Marathon Tomb

This burial mound (☎ 2294 055 462, 350m from Athens-Marathon road; site & museum €1.50; open 8.30am-3pm Tues-Sun) is 4km before the town of Marathon. In ancient Greece, the bodies of those who died in battle were returned to their families for private burial, but as a sign of honour the 192 men who fell at Marathon were cremated and buried in this collective tomb. The mound is 10m high and 180m in circumference. The tomb site is signposted from the main road. The site **museum** (☎ 2294 055 155) is nearer to the town.

Lake Marathon

This huge dam, 8km west of Marathon, was Athens' sole source of water until 1956. The massive dam wall, completed in 1926, is faced with the famous Pentelic marble that was used to build the Parthenon. It's an awesome sight, standing over 50m high and stretching for more than 300m.

Ramnous Ραμνούς

The ruins of the ancient port of Ramnous (☎ 2294 063 477; admission €1.50; open 8.30am-3pm daily) are 15km north-east of Marathon. It's an evocative, overgrown and secluded little site, standing on a plateau overlooking the sea. Among the ruins are the remains of a Doric **Temple of Nemesis** (435 BC), which once contained a huge statue of the goddess. Nemesis was the goddess of retribution and mother of Helen of Troy. There are also ruins of a smaller 6th-century temple dedicated to Themis, goddess of justice.

Shinias Σχοινιάς

The long, sandy, pine-fringed beach at Shinias, south-east of Marathon, is the best in this part of Attica. It's also very popular, particularly at weekends.

   Camping Ramnous (☎ 2294 055 855, fax 2294 055 244, e ramnous@otenet.gr, Leoforos Poseidonos 174) Adult/tent €5/4.10. The well-maintained Camping Ramnous is on the way to the beach. Its shared shower and kitchen facilities are kept spotlessly clean. The camp site also has a children's playground and waterslide (adult/child €5/2.95 per half hour). The bus to Marathon stops at the entrance to the site.

Getting There & Away

There are hourly buses from Athens' Mavromateon terminal to Marathon (1¼ hours, €2.35). The tomb, the museum and Shinias Beach are all within short walking distance of bus stops (tell the driver where you want to get out). There are no buses to Lake Marathon or Ramnous; you need your own transport.

DAFNI Δαφνί
Moni Dafniou

This 11th-century monastery *(☎ 21 0581 1558, Leoforos Athinon; admission €2.35; normally open 8.30am-3pm daily)*, 10km north-west of Athens along the busy road to Corinth, is Attica's most important Byzantine monument, and is on Unesco's World Heritage list. The history of the site dates back more than 2500 years. The monastery stands on the site of an ancient Sanctuary of Apollo along the route of the Sacred Way which ran from Elefsina (ancient Eleusis) to the Acropolis in Athens. Its name derives from the daphne laurels which were sacred to

Apollo. The temple was destroyed by the Goths in AD 395, although a single Ionic column survives in the narthex of the church.

   The church contains some of Greece's finest **mosaics**, created at a time when the artistic and intellectual achievements of Byzantium had reached unprecedented heights. The monastery was sacked in 1205 by the renegades of the Fourth Crusade who had earlier captured Constantinople. It was rebuilt and occupied by monks until the time of the War of Independence, after which it was used as army barracks and as a hospital for the mentally ill.

   The mosaics on the church walls depict saints and monks, while the ones on the dome depict apostles, prophets and guardian archangels. Exquisite though these mosaics are, they fade into insignificance once the visitor has gazed upon the Christos Pantokrator (Christ in Majesty) which occupies the centre of the dome.

   Unfortunately the monastery was badly damaged by the earthquake that struck Athens on 14 September, 1999. It was cloaked in scaffolding at the time of research, and unlikely to reopen before the beginning of 2002.

Getting There & Away

Bus No A16 from Plateia Eleftherias, north of Monastiraki, can drop you at the Venzini stop right outside the monastery. The buses run every 20 minutes and take about 30 minutes in reasonable traffic.

ELEFSINA (ELEUSIS) Ελευσίνα

The ruins of ancient Eleusis *(☎ 21 0554 6019; admission €1.50; site & museum open 8.30am-3pm Tues-Sun)* lie beside the modern industrial town of Elefsina, 12km further along the road from Moni Dafniou and on the same bus route.

   Modern Elefsina is one of the least attractive towns in Greece. It has become an industrial extension of Athens, surrounded by oil refineries and factories. It's hard to imagine how Eleusis must have been in ancient times. Doubtless, like all the great spiritual centres of ancient Greece, the place had a special feel about it, nestled on the slopes of a low hill close to the shore of the Saronic Gulf. The modern setting is far from inspiring, surrounded by heavy industry – which encroaches on the western edge of the site.

The ancient city of Eleusis was built around the **Sanctuary of Demeter**. The site dates back to Mycenaean times, when the cult of Demeter began. The cult became one of the most important in ancient Greece. By classical times it was celebrated with a huge annual festival, which attracted thousands of pilgrims wanting to be initiated into the Eleusian mysteries. They walked in procession from the Acropolis to Eleusis along the Sacred Way, which was lined with statues and votive monuments. Initiates were sworn to secrecy on punishment of death, and during the 1400 years that the sanctuary functioned its secrets were never divulged. The sanctuary was closed by the Roman emperor Theodosius in the 4th century AD.

A visit to the site's **museum** first will help to make some sense of the scattered ruins. The museum has models showing how the city looked in classical times and in Roman times.

MT PARNITHA

Mt Parnitha National Park lies just 20km north of the city centre and is a popular weekend escape for Athenians.

Mt Parnitha itself comprises a number of smaller peaks, the highest of which is Mt Karavola at 1413m – high enough to get snow in winter. The park is crisscrossed by numerous walking trails, marked on the Road Editions trekking map of the area. Most visitors access the park by cable car from the outer Athens suburb of Thrakomakedones. The cable car drops you below *Casino Mt Parnes* (☎ 21 0246 9111) gaming and hotel complex. Room prices here start at €55.80/76.30 for singles/doubles.

Peloponnese Πελοπόννησος

The Peloponnese (pel-o-**pon**-ih-sos in Greek) is the southernmost section of the Balkan Peninsula. The construction of the Corinth Canal through the Isthmus of Corinth in the late 19th century effectively severed it from the mainland, and now the only links are the bridges that span the canal. Indeed, the Peloponnese has every attraction of an island – and better public transport.

It's a region of outstanding natural beauty, with lofty, snow-crested mountains, valleys of citrus groves and cypress trees, cool springs and many fine beaches. The landscape is diverse and dotted with the legacies of the many civilisations which took root in the region: ancient Greek sites, crumbling Byzantine cities, Frankish and Venetian fortresses. The best-known attraction is the ancient site at Olympia. Less well known is that the beaches of the Messinian Mani, south of Kalamata, are some of the finest in Greece. The rugged Mani Peninsula has additional attractions – the remnants of fortified tower houses built from the 17th century onwards.

With your own transport, two weeks is sufficient to visit the major attractions. On public transport, allow at least three weeks, or be selective about your destinations. Ideally, the Peloponnese warrants a month's wandering, such is the variety of its natural and ancient splendours.

SUGGESTED ITINERARIES
One week
Travel from Athens to Nafplio (two days) and use it as a base for side trips to Epidaurus and Mycenae; head south to Sparta for a visit to Mystras (one day); travel across the Taygetos Mountains to Kalamata and continue west to Pylos (one day); head up the west coast to Ancient Olympia (one day); visit the site early and continue north around the coast through Patras to Diakofto and ride the rack-and-pinion railway up to Kalavryta (one day); travel back to Diakofto and take the train back to Athens (one day).
Two weeks
Follow the above itinerary to Sparta/Mystras, and then head south-east to Monemvasia (one day).

Highlights

- The charming Venetian town of Nafplio
- Ancient Olympia in springtime
- Trekking in the hills above Kardamyli
- The historic tower settlements of the Mani
- The train ride up the spectacular Vouraïkos Gorge from Diakofto to Kalavryta
- Kalavryta's splendid Cave of the Lakes

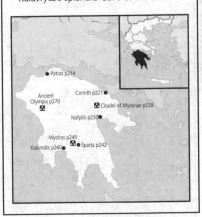

Patras p214
Corinth p221
Ancient Olympia p270
Citadel of Mycenae p228
Nafplio p230
Mystras p245
Kalamata p260
Sparta p242

From here, travel west through Gythio to Aeropoli and use it as a base for exploring the Lakonian Mani (two days) before moving up the coast to Kardamyli (two days). Head west via Kalamata to Pylos (one day), and north to Olympia (one day). Visit the site early and continue to Tripolis (one day), and then take the bus north through the mountains to Kalavryta (one day). From Kalavryta, ride the rack-and-pinion railway to Diakofto via Zahlorou and catch a train to Athens.

HISTORY & MYTHOLOGY
The name Peloponisos means 'island of Pelops', and derives from the mythological hero Pelops, and from the Greek word for island, *nisos*. The region's medieval name

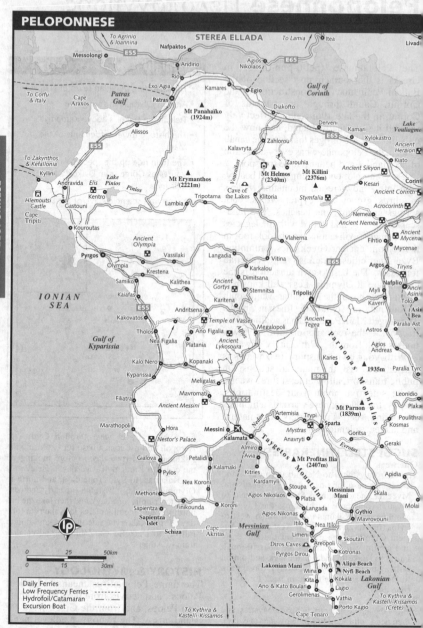

PELOPONNESE

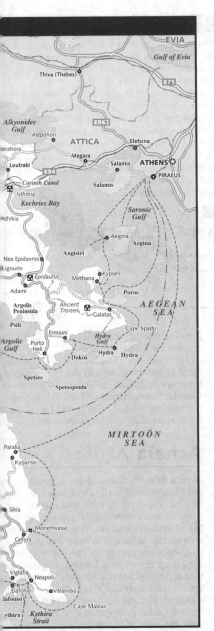

PELOPONNESE

was 'Morea' (*mouria* means mulberry tree), perhaps because mulberry trees grow so well in the area.

The deities may have resided on Mt Olympus, but they made frequent jaunts to the Peloponnese. It is a region rich in myths, and Pelops features in many of them.

Since ancient times, the Peloponnese has played a major role in Greek history. When the Minoan civilisation declined after 1450 BC, the focus of power in the ancient Aegean world moved from Crete to the hill-fortress palaces of Mycenae and Tiryns in the Peloponnese. As elsewhere in Greece, the 400 years following the Dorian conquests in the 12th century BC are known as the dark age. When the region emerged from it in the 7th century BC, Sparta, Athens' arch rival, had surpassed Mycenae as the most powerful city in the Peloponnese. The period of peace and prosperity under Roman rule (146 BC to around AD 250) was shattered by a series of invasions by Goths, Avars and Slavs.

The Byzantines were slow to make inroads into the Peloponnese, and did not become firmly established until the 9th century. In 1204, after the fall of Constantinople to the crusaders, the crusader chiefs William de Champlitte and Geoffrey de Villehardouin divided the region into 12 fiefs, which they parcelled out to various barons of France, Flanders and Burgundy. These fiefs were overseen by de Villehardouin, the self-appointed Prince of Morea (as the region was called in those days).

The Byzantines gradually won back the Morea. Although the empire as a whole was now in terminal decline, a glorious renaissance took place in the Morea, centred on Mystras, which the Byzantine emperor Michael VIII Paleologus made the region's seat of government.

The Morea fell to the Turks in 1460 and hundreds of years of power struggles between the Turks and Venetians followed. The Venetians had long coveted the Morea and succeeded in establishing profitable trading ports at Methoni, Pylos, Koroni and Monemvasia.

The War of Independence began in the Peloponnese, when bishop Germanos of

The Wily Pelops

Pelops was the son of the conniving Tantalos, who invited the gods to a feast and served up the flesh of his son to test their power of omniscience. Of course, the all-knowing gods knew what he had done and refrained from eating the flesh. However, Demeter, who was in a tizz over the abduction of her daughter, Persephone, by Hades, accidentally ate a piece of Pelops' shoulder.

Fortunately, the gods reassembled Pelops, and fashioned another shoulder of ivory. Tantalos was suspended from a fruit tree overhanging a lake, and was punished with eternal tantalising thirst.

Pelops took a fancy to the beautiful Hippodameia, daughter of Oinomaos, king of Elia. Oinomaos, a champion chariot racer, was told by an oracle that his future son-in-law would bring about his death. Oinomaos announced that he would give his daughter in marriage to any suitor who defeated him in a chariot race, but that he would kill those who failed – a fate which befell many suitors. Pelops took up the challenge and bribed the king's charioteer, Myrtilos, to take a spoke out of a wheel of the king's chariot. The chariot crashed during the race and Oinomaos was killed, so Pelops married Hippodameia and became king of Elia. The couple had two children, Atreus and Thyestes. Atreus became king of Mycenae and was the father of that kingdom's greatest king, Agamemnon. Pelops' devious action has been blamed for the curse on the Royal House of Atreus, which ultimately brought about its downfall.

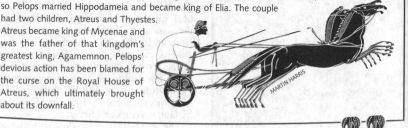

MARTIN HARRIS

Patras raised the flag of revolt near Kalavryta on 25 March 1821. The Egyptian army, under the leadership of Ibrahim Pasha, brutally restored Turkish rule in 1825.

In 1827, the Triple Alliance of Great Britain, France and Russia, moved by Greek suffering and the activities of philhellenes (Byron's death in 1824 was particularly influential), came to the rescue of the Greeks by destroying the Egyptian-Turkish fleet at the Battle of Navarino, ending Turkish domination of the area.

The Peloponnese became part of the independent state of Greece, and Nafplio in Argolis became the first national capital. When Kapodistrias, Greece's first president, was assassinated on the steps of Nafplio's Church of St Spyridon in October 1831, the new king, Otho, moved the capital to Athens in 1834.

Like the rest of Greece, the Peloponnese suffered badly during WWII. The town clock of Kalavryta, in the central north, is forever stopped at 2.34, the time at which, on 13 December 1943, the Germans began a massacre of all the males aged over 15 in reprisal for resistance activity.

The civil war (1944–49) brought widespread destruction and, in the 1950s, many villagers migrated to Athens, Australia, Canada, South Africa and the USA. More recently, the towns of Corinth and Kalamata have suffered devastating earthquakes.

Achaïa Αξαία

Achaïa owes its name to the Achaeans, an Indo-European branch of migrants who settled on mainland Greece and established what is more commonly known as the Mycenaean civilisation. When the Dorians arrived, the Achaeans were pushed into this north-western corner of the Peloponnese, displacing the original Ionians. Legend has it that the Achaeans founded 12 cities, which later developed into the powerful Achaean Federation that survived until Roman times. Principal among these cities were the ports of Patras and Egio.

The coast of modern Achaïa consists of a string of resorts more popular with Greeks than with tourists. Inland are the high peaks of Mt Panahaïko, Mt Erymanthos (where Heracles captured the Erymanthian boar) and Mt Helmos.

The village of Diakofto, 55km east of Patras, is the starting point for a ride on the fantastic rack-and-pinion railway to Zahlorou and Kalavryta. Overnight stops at Zahlorou and Kalavryta are highly recommended.

PATRAS Πάτρα
postcode 260 01 • pop 153,300

Achaïa's capital Patras (in Greek, Patra), is Greece's third-largest city and the principal port for boats travelling to and from Italy and the Ionian Islands. It is named after King Patreas, who ruled Achaïa in about 1100 BC. Despite a history stretching back 3000 years, Patras is not wildly exciting. Few travellers today stay around any longer than it takes to catch the next boat, bus or train.

The city was destroyed by the Turks during the War of Independence and rebuilt on a modern grid plan of wide, arcaded streets, large squares and ornate neoclassical buildings. Many of these old buildings were being restored at the time of research in preparation for the city's role as Europe's City of Culture for 2006.

The higher you climb up the steep hill behind the teeming, somewhat seedy waterfront, the better Patras gets.

Orientation

Patras' grid system means easy walking. The waterfront is known as Iroön Polytehniou at the north-eastern end, Othonos Amalias in the middle and Akti Dimeon to the south. Customs is at the Iroön Polytehniou end, and the main bus and train stations are on Othonos Amalias. Most of the agencies selling ferry tickets are on Iroön Polytehniou and Othonos Amalias. The main thoroughfares of Agiou Dionysiou, Riga Fereou, Mezonos, Korinthou and Kanakari run parallel to the waterfront. The main square is Plateia Vasileos Georgiou, up from the waterfront along Gerokostopoulou.

Information

Tourist Offices The EOT (☎ 2610 620 353) is outside the international arrivals terminal at the port. In theory, it's open 8am to 10pm Monday to Friday; in practice, it's invariably closed. The most useful piece of information is an arrow pointing to the helpful tourist police (☎ 2610 451 833), upstairs in the embarkation hall, who are open 7.30am to 11pm daily.

Money The National Bank of Greece is on Plateia Trion Symahon, opposite the train station. It's open 8am to 2pm (8am to 1.30pm on Friday) and 6pm to 8.30pm Monday to Friday. On weekends, in summer only, it is open 11am to 1pm and 6pm to 8.30pm for foreign exchange only.

Post & Communications The main post office is on the corner of Zaïmi and Mezonos. It is open 7.30am to 8pm Monday to Friday, 7.30am to 2pm Saturday, and 9am to 1.30pm Sunday. The main OTE office is on the corner of Gounari and Kanakari in the western part of the city. There's another office opposite the tourist office at the port.

For Internet access, head inland. There are several places around the upper reaches of Gerokostopoulou. Netp@rk (☎ 2610 279 699), Gerokostopoulou 37, and the co-managed Netrino Internet Café (☎ 2610 623 344), Karaiskaki 133, are both open 10am to 2am daily and charge €2.35 per hour.

Bookshops Discover (☎ 2610 624 916), Mezonos 58, is better known as the city's leading music shop – on the ground floor. The first floor has English-language books. Most of them are of the coffee table variety, but there's a travel section with Lonely Planet guides and a useful selection of maps. News Stand (☎ 2610 273 092), Agiou Andreou 77, has a small selection of novels, as well as international newspapers and magazines. You'll also find international newspapers at the *periptera* (kiosks) on Plateia Trion Symahon.

Laundry The laundrette on Zaïmi, just uphill from Korinthou, charges €6.75 to wash

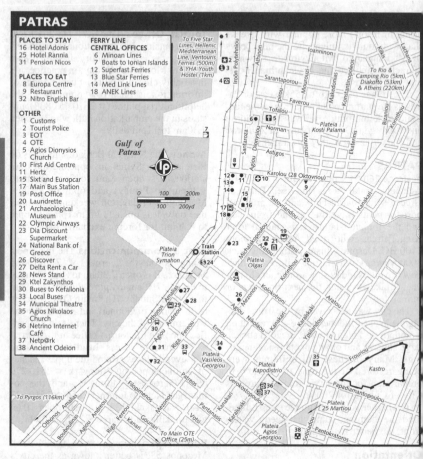

PATRAS

PLACES TO STAY
16 Hotel Adonis
25 Hotel Rannia
31 Pension Nicos

PLACES TO EAT
8 Europa Centre
9 Restaurant
32 Nitro English Bar

OTHER
1 Customs
2 Tourist Police
3 EOT
4 OTE
5 Agios Dionysios Church
10 First Aid Centre
11 Hertz
15 Sixt and Europcar
17 Main Bus Station
19 Post Office
20 Laundrette
21 Archaeological Museum
22 Olympic Airways
23 Dia Discount Supermarket
24 National Bank of Greece
26 Discover
27 Delta Rent a Car
28 News Stand
29 Ktel Zakynthos
30 Buses to Kefallonia
33 Local Buses
34 Municipal Theatre
35 Agios Nikolaos Church
36 Netrino Internet Café
37 Netp@rk
38 Ancient Odeion

FERRY LINE CENTRAL OFFICES
6 Minoan Lines
7 Boats to Ionian Islands
12 Superfast Ferries
13 Blue Star Ferries
14 Med Link Lines
18 ANEK Lines

and dry a load. It's open 9am to 3pm and 5.30pm to 9pm Monday to Friday, 9am to 3pm on Saturday, closed Sunday.

Left Luggage The left-luggage office at the train station charges €3.25 per item per day, or €1.65 if you have a train ticket – so buy your ticket before you drop off your bags.

Emergency There is a first-aid centre (☎ 2610 277 386) at the corner of Karolou and Agiou Dionysiou. Patras' port police are on ☎ 2610 341 002.

Kastro

The medieval Venetian kastro, built on the ruins of an ancient acropolis, dominates the city. Set in an attractive pencil-pined park, it is reached by climbing the steps at the end of Agiou Nikolaou. Great views of the Ionian islands of Zakynthos and Kefallonia are the reward.

Archaeological Museum

The small museum (☎ 2610 275 070, Mezonos 42; admission free; open 8.30am-2.30pm Tues-Sun), houses a collection of finds from the Mycenaean, Hellenic and

Roman periods. It's well laid out and exhibits are labelled in English.

Patras Carnival

Patras is noted for the exuberance with which its citizens celebrate the city's annual carnival. The carnival program begins in mid January, and features a host of minor events leading up to a wild weekend of costume parades, colourful floats and celebrations at the end of February or early March. The event draws big crowds, so hotel reservations are essential if you want to stay overnight. Contact the Greek National Tourist Organisation for dates and details (see Tourist Offices in the Facts for the Visitor chapter).

Places to Stay

The shortage of decent budget accommodation in Patras is one of the reasons few travellers stick around.

Camping Rion (☎ 2610 991 585, fax 2610 993 388, Rio) Adult/tent €4.10/3.55. Open year-round. This small family-run site, 9km north-east of Patras at Rio Beach, is the closest camping ground. It's right on the beach 500m west of Rio's port. You can get to the port on Bus No 6 from Plateia Agios Georgios.

YHA Youth Hostel (☎ 2610 427 278, Iroön Polytehniou 62) Dorm beds €5.90. It's hard to recommend this rundown place, which belongs to the Greek-run Youth Hostels Association – not Hostelling International. It's also a fair haul from the city centre, 1km north of the customs building.

Pension Nicos (☎ 2610 623 757, Cnr Patreos & Agiou Andreou) Singles/doubles/triples with bath €14.70/23.50/41.10. Nicos is easily the best budget choice in town. The sheets are clean, the water is hot and it's close to the waterfront. There are also cheaper rooms with shared bathroom.

Hotel Rannia (☎ 2610 220 114, fax 2610 220 537, Riga Fereou 53) Singles/doubles with bath €29.35/44. This C-class hotel, facing Plateia Olgas, has comfortable aircon rooms with TV.

Hotel Adonis (☎ 2610 224 213, fax 2610 226 971, Zaïmi 9) Singles/doubles with bath €42/48.50. A step up from the Hotel Rannia is this place, behind the bus station. Rooms have good views out over the port and breakfast is included.

Places to Eat

Europa Centre (☎ 2610 437 006, Othonos Amalias 10) Mains €3-5.30. This convenient cafeteria-style place is close to the international ferry dock. It has taverna dishes, spaghetti and a choice of vegetarian meals.

Restaurant Tzorou Erimioni (☎ 2610 271 487, Riga Fereou 3) Mains €2.95-4.70. Locals prefer this family-run restaurant, which specialises in traditional dishes like *patsas* (tripe). Travellers will probably be happier with a large bowl of fish soup (€4.10) or roast chicken with potatoes (€3.55).

Nitro English Bar (☎/fax 2610 279 357, e nitrobar@hotmail.com, Pantanasis 9) Mains €7.35-8.80. This is the perfect spot for Brits pining for a taste of the Old Dart. You'll find daily specials like steak and kidney pie or shepherd's pie, Sunday roasts and a choice of English beers. It's also well set up for travellers with a shower room and Internet access.

Dia Discount Supermarket (Agiou Andreou 29) is not the largest supermarket in town, but it's ideally located for travellers planning to buy a few provisions and keep moving.

Getting There & Away

Many first-time visitors to Greece assume the best way to get from Patras to Athens is by bus. The bus is faster than the train, but is more expensive and drops you off a long way from the centre of Athens at Terminal A on Kifissou. This is a real hassle if you're arriving in Athens after midnight, when there are no connecting buses to the city centre, leaving newcomers at the mercy of the notorious Terminal A taxi drivers.

The train takes you close to the city centre, with easy connections to the metro system. If you arrive after midnight, you're within easy walking distance of good accommodation.

Bus The main bus station located on Othonos Amalias has buses to Athens (three hours, €11.75, half-hourly) via Corinth (1½ hours, €7.65); Pyrgos (two hours, €5.90, 10 daily); four daily to Ioannina (4½ hours, €14) and Kalavryta (two hours, €4.95); three daily to Thessaloniki (9½ hours, €27.80) via Amfissa (for Delphi, three hours, €8.10); and two daily to Kalamata (four hours, €13.35) via Tripolis (four hours, €10.30) and Megalopoli.

Buses to the Ionian islands of Lefkada (€9.70, two daily) and Kefallonia leave from the KTEL Kefallonia bus station (☎ 277 854) at the corner of Othonos Amalias and Gerokostopoulou. Services to Kefallonia travel by ferry to Poros (€7.95) and continue by road to Argostoli (€10). Buses to Zakynthos (3½ hours, €8.80) leave from the KTEL Zakynthos bus station (☎ 220 219) at Othonos Amalias 58. They also travel via the port of Kyllini.

Train There are at least eight trains daily to Athens. Half of them are slow trains, which take five hours and cost €5.30. They travel via Diakofto (one hour, €2.05) and Corinth (2½ hours, €3.55). The intercity trains to Athens take 3½ hours and cost €10. The last intercity train leaves Patras at 6.30pm. Holders of Eurail passes can travel free, but will need a reservation.

There are also trains to Pyrgos (two hours, €2.95, seven daily) and Kalamata (six hours, €5.30, two daily).

Ferry – Domestic There are daily ferries from Patras to the Ionian islands of Kefallonia (2½ hours, €10), Ithaki (3¾ hours, €10.90) and Corfu (7 hours, €17.90).

Ferries between Rio, 5km north-east of Patras, and Andirio (for Lefkada) operate every 15 minutes between 7am and 11pm, and every 30 minutes through the night (10 minutes, €0.35, car €5.30).

Ferry – International Patras is Greece's main port for ferry services to Italy. The most popular crossing is from Brindisi. Crossing times and fares vary a lot between companies. In summer, there are up to five boats daily on this route. One-way, deck-class fares range from €42 with Five Star

Lines to €48.15 with Blue Star Ferries. Hellenic Mediterranean is the only company to accept Eurail passes, although you will still have to pay the port tax of €6.45. From mid-June to the end of September there is a high-season loading of €8.80.

Of the boats to Ancona, Superfast is the fastest, doing the trip in 19 hours for €78.10. Others operating on this route are Blue Star Lines (20 hours, €61.35), Minoan (20 hours, €71.65) and ANEK Lines (21 hours, €63.40).

Superfast has a daily service to Bari (15½ hours, €51.40) while Ventouris (17½ hours, €45.50) has three boats weekly. Minoan has daily boats to Venice (37 hours, €71.65). ANEK Lines has three boats weekly to Trieste (32 hours, €71.40).

With the exception of the express services to Ancona, most of these ferries stop at Igoumenitsa and Corfu. Some allow a free stopover on Corfu – ask when you buy your ticket. See the Getting There & Away chapter for more details of services.

The contact details of the central offices or representatives and routes of the ferry lines operating out of Patras are:

ANEK Lines (☎ 2610 226 053) Othonos Amalias 25: Ancona and Trieste via Corfu and Igoumenitsa

Five Star Lines (☎ 2610 422 102) Cnr Iroön Polytehniou and Naum Ellas: Brindisi via Igoumenitsa

Hellenic Mediterranean (☎ 2610 452 521) Cnr Iroön Polytehniou and Pente Pigadion: Brindisi via Kefallonia and Corfu

Med Link Lines (☎ 2610 623 011) Giannatos Travel, Othonos Amalias 15: to Brindisi direct or via Kefallonia and Igoumenitsa

Minoan (☎ 2610 421 500) Cnr Norman 1 and Athinon: Ancona via Igoumenitsa; Venice via Igoumenitsa and Corfu

Blue Star Ferries (☎ 2610 634 000) Othonos Amalias 12-14: Brindisi direct; Ancona and Venice via Igoumenitsa and Corfu

Superfast Ferries (☎ 2610 622 500) Othonos Amalias 12: Ancona direct or via Igoumenitsa Bari via Igoumenitsa

Ventouris Ferries (☎ 2610 454 873/874) Iroön Polytehniou 44-46: Bari direct

Getting Around

Local buses leave from north-western corner of Plateia Vasileos Georgiou. Car rental outlets include Budget (☎ 2610 455 190), Iroön Polytehniou 36; Delta Rent a Car (☎ 2610 272 764, fax 2610 220 532), Othonos Amalias 44; Europcar (☎ 2610 621 360), Agiou Andreou 6; Hertz (☎ 2610 220 990), Karolou 2; and Sixt (☎ 2610 275 577), Agiou Andreou 10b.

DIAKOFTO Διακοφτό
postcode 251 00 • pop 2250

Diakofto (dih-ah-kof-to), 55km east of Patras and 80km north-west of Corinth, is a serene village, tucked between steep mountains and the sea amid lemon and olive groves.

Orientation & Information

Diakofto's layout is easy to figure out. The train station is in the middle of the village. To reach the waterfront, cross the railway track and walk down the road ahead. After 1km you will come to pebbly Egali Beach.

There is no EOT or tourist police. The post office, OTE and the National Bank of Greece are all on the main street that leads inland from the station.

Things to Do

The main reason people come to Diakofto is to ride the rack-and-pinion railway up the Vouraïkos Gorge to Kalavryta (see the boxed text 'Diakofto-Kalavryta Railway').

If you want to relax by the sea, the best section of Egali Beach is on the western side of town; turn right when you reach the seafront on the road from the station.

Places to Stay & Eat

Hotel Lemonies (☎ 2691 041 229/820) Singles/doubles with bath €23.50/35.20. This quiet, old-fashioned hotel is 500m north of the train station on the road leading to the beach.

Chris Paul Hotel (☎ 2691 041 715/855, fax 2691 042 128, e chris-pa@otenet.gr) Singles/doubles/triples €27.90/51.40/61.65. This modern C-class hotel has Diakofto's best rooms with bath, air-con and TV, and also has a swimming pool, bar and restaurant. It's conveniently situated near the train station, and well signposted. Breakfast costs €4.

Costas (☎ 2691 043 228) Mains €2.95-7.35. This popular taverna/psistaria, opposite the National Bank on the main street heading inland from the train station, is the pick of the restaurants. It's run by a friendly Greek-Australian family and has a good choice of taverna-style dishes alongside the usual grilled meats.

People heading up to Kalavryta on the train can stock up for the trip at the shops opposite the station, which include *Elvar Supermarket* (☎ 2691 043 361).

Getting There & Away

Bus There's not much point in catching a bus to/from Diakofto – the trains are much more convenient. Patras-Athens buses bypass the village on the New National Road.

Train Diakofto is on the main Athens-Patras line and there are frequent trains in both directions.

There are trains on the rack-and-pinion line to Kalavryta (one hour, 1st/2nd class €4.40/3.70, four daily) via Zahlorou (€4/3.25) departing 8am, 10.30am, 1.15pm and 3.45pm Monday to Friday; and 9am, 11.35am, 2.10pm and 4.48pm on the weekend. The 1st class compartments are at the front and rear of the train and have the best views.

ZAHLOROU Ζαχλωρού
postcode 250 01 • pop 50

The picturesque and unspoilt settlement of Zahlorou, the halfway stop on the Diakofto-Kalavryta train line, straddles both sides of the river and railway line. Many people take the train to this point and walk back to Diakofto.

Moni Mega Spileou Μονή Μεγάλου Σπηλαίου

A steep path (signposted) leads up from Zahlorou to the Moni Mega Spileou (Monastery of the Great Cavern). The original monastery was destroyed in 1934 when

Diakofto–Kalavryta Railway

The railway from Diakofto to Kalavryta takes travellers on an unforgettable ride through the dramatic Vouraïkos Gorge. The train climbs over 700m in 22.5km, using a rack-and-pinion (cog) system for traction on the steep sections. Built by an Italian company between 1885 and 1895, the railway was a remarkable feat of engineering for its time.

The opening section of the journey is fairly sedate, climbing gently through the lush citrus orchards that flank the lower reaches of the Vouraïkos River. The ascent begins in earnest about 5km south of Diakofto, and the section from here to Zahlorou is spectacular as the line switches back and forth across the gorge in search of a foothold. As the gorge narrows, the train disappears into a long curving tunnel and emerges clinging to a narrow ledge that seems to overhang the river. This stretch is quite awesome in spring when the waters are swollen by snowmelt from the surrounding mountains.

South of the charming village of Zahlorou, the line follows the river beneath a leafy canopy of plane trees, before meandering through open country for the final run to Kalavryta.

The journey takes just over an hour, stopping en route at Zahlorou. Second class fares are €3.25 to Zahlorou and €3.70 to Kalavryta, but spending €4/4.40 for a 1st class compartment at the front or rear of the train is well worth the extra €0.70 – they have the best views.

The line was commissioned by Greece's great railway building prime minister, Harilaos Trikoupis, who had the romantic notion of using the new train technology of the time to provide access to the birthplace of the modern Greek nation – Moni Agias Lavras, near Kalavryta. It was at this monastery that Bishop Germanos of Patras raised the flag of revolt that launched the War of Independence on 25 March, 1821.

The original steam engines that first plied the route were replaced in the early 1960s by diesel cars, but the old steam engines can still be seen outside Diakofto and Kalavryta stations.

See the Diakofto and Kalavryta Getting There & Away sections for information on train departure times.

gunpowder stored during the War of Independence exploded. The new monastery houses illuminated gospels, relics, silver crosses, jewellery and the miraculous icon of the Virgin Mary which, like numerous icons in Greece, is said to have been painted by St Luke. It was supposedly discovered in the nearby cavern by St Theodore and St Simeon in AD 362. A monk will show visitors around. Modest dress is required of both sexes – no bare arms or legs. The 3km walk up to the monastery takes about an hour.

Places to Stay & Eat

Hotel Romantzo (☎/fax 2692 022 758) Singles/doubles/triples with bath €23.50/35.20/44. This quaint D-class hotel is one of Greece's more eccentric little hotels. It stands right next to the railway line at the end of the platform. You can almost reach out and touch the trains from the windows of its seven rooms. It's a wonderful place

with old timber floors and old-fashioned furnishings – and not a square edge in sight. It's advisable to book at weekends. During the week, the manager uses one triple room as a dorm where hikers can roll out their sleeping bags (€5.90). The hotel has a good restaurant with outdoor seating on the opposite side of the railway. It also serves breakfast.

Getting There & Away

All Diakofto-Kalavryta trains stop at Zahlorou. You can drive to Zahlorou on a dirt road leading off the Diakofto-Kalavryta road. The turn-off is 7.5km north of Kalavryta.

KALAVRYTA Καλάβρυτα

postcode 250 01 • pop 2200

At an elevation of 756m, Kalavryta (kah-lah-vrih-tah) is a cool mountain resort with copious springs and shady plane trees. Two relatively recent historical events have assured the town a special place in the hearts of all Greeks. The revolt against the Turks began here on 25 March 1821 when Bishop Germanos of Patras raised the banner of revolt at the monastery of Agias Lavras, 6km from Kalavryta. Also, on 13 December 1943, in one of the worst atrocities of WWII, the Nazis set fire to the town and massacred all its male inhabitants over 15 years old as punishment for resistance activity. The total number killed in the region was 1436. The hands of the old cathedral clock stand eternally at 2.34, the time the massacre began.

Orientation & Information

Most people arrive at the train station, on the northern edge of town. Opposite is a large building that will eventually become the Municipal Museum of the Kalavryta Holocaust. Kalavryta is the founding member of the Union of Martyred Towns. To the right of the museum-to-be is Syngrou, a pedestrian precinct. After one block, it becomes 25 Martiou. To the left of the museum is Konstantinou.

The central square, Plateia Kalavrytou, is between these two streets, two blocks up from the train station.

The bus station is on Kapota. From the train station, walk up Syngrou and turn right at Hotel Maria onto Kapota, cross Ethnikis Antistassis and you'll see the buses parked outside at the bottom of the hill on the left. Kalavryta has neither EOT nor tourist police. The post office is on the main square and the OTE is on Konstantinou. The National Bank of Greece is on 25 Martiou, just before the central square.

Martyrs' Monument

A huge white cross on a cypress-covered hillside just east of town marks the site of the 1943 massacre. Beneath this imposing monument is a poignant little shrine to the victims. It is signposted off Konstantinou.

Places to Stay

Kalavryta does not have a lot of accommodation. Peak season here is the ski season, from late November to April. Reservations are essential at this time, and at weekends throughout the year when Athenians come to enjoy the cool mountain air. The prices listed below are slashed by as much as 50% at other times.

There are no budget hotels, but there are several **domatia** on the streets behind the train station.

Hotel Maria (☎ 2692 022 296, fax 2692 022 686, Syngrou 10) Singles/doubles with bath €41.10/52.85. Conveniently located opposite the museum, this small family-run hotel has cosy rooms with TV. Breakfast, served in the cafe downstairs, costs €4.40.

Hotel Anesis (☎ 2692 023 070, @ anesis@ otenet.gr, Plateia Kalavrytou) Singles/ doubles/triples with bath €44/55.80/66. This smart modern hotel is run by Greek-Australian brothers Nikos and Dimitris Mihalopoulos, who have quickly established the Anesis as the best hotel in town. The rooms are stylishly furnished and well-appointed; the best room has its own fireplace. In summer, prices drop to just €23.50/29.35/38.15, making it also the best deal in town. Breakfast costs €5.90, served in the restaurant downstairs.

Hotel Filoxenia (☎ 2692 022 422, fax 2692 023 009, @ filoxenia@otenet.gr, Ethnikis Antistaseos 10) Singles/doubles/triples with bath €62.25/79.25/98.65. The Filoxenia is another safe choice. It's an old-fashioned place where not much has changed in years, except that the rooms now have a minibar and safe as well as TV. Prices include breakfast. Like the Anesis, big discounts are available in summer.

Places to Eat

Most places to eat in Kalavryta are on 25 Martiou.

Taverna O Australos (☎ 2692 023 070, Plateia Kalavrytou) Mains €3.85-6.45. Located below the Hotel Anesis, this taverna has built up a strong local following with specialities like rabbit stifado (€5.30) and goat in lemon sauce (€5.90).

To Tzaki Taverna (☎ 2692 022 609, 25 Martiou & Plateia Kalavrytou) Prices €4.10-8.25. This is another popular spot with a good choice of daily specials.

Entertainment

Air Music Club About 1km north of town on the road to Diakofto, this club is housed in one of the original Boeing 720-68 planes bought by Aristotle Onassis for the launch of Olympic Airways in the 60s. It was transported here in pieces and reassembled *in situ*.

Getting There & Away

There are buses to Patras (€4.85, four daily) via Diakofto (€2.50), Athens (€10.50, two daily) and Tripolis (€5.15, one daily).

Trains leave Kala Vryta for Diakofto (via Zahlorou) at 9.15am, 11.45am, 2.30pm and 5pm Monday to Friday, as well as 10.12am, 12.45pm, 3.20pm and 6pm on weekends.

Kalavryta's taxi rank (☎ 2692 022 127) is on the central square.

AROUND KALAVRYTA
Moni Agias Lavras

The original 10th-century monastery was burnt by the Nazis. The new monastery has a small museum where the banner standard is displayed along with other monastic memorabilia. Buses heading south from Kalavryta to Klitoria or Tripolis can drop you a short walk from the monastery, or take a taxi.

Cave of the Lakes

The remarkable Cave of the Lakes (☎ 2692 031 633, W www.kastriacave.gr; adult/child €5.90/2.95; open 9.30am-4.30pm Mon-Fri, 9am-6pm Sat & Sun) lies 16.5km south of Kalavryta near the village of Kastria. The cave features in Greek mythology and is mentioned in the writings of the ancient traveller Pausanias, but its whereabouts remained unknown in modern times until 1964, when locals noticed water pouring from the roof of a smaller, lower cave after heavy rain and decided to investigate. They found themselves in a large bat-filled cavern at the start of a winding 2km-long cave carved out by a subterranean river.

The cavern is now reached by an artificial entrance, which is the starting point for a 350m raised walkway that snakes up the riverbed. It passes some wonderfully ornate stalactites, but they are mere sideshows alongside the lakes themselves. The lakes are actually a series of 13 stone basins formed by mineral deposits over the millennia. In summer, the waters dry up to reveal a curious lace work of walls, some up to 3m high.

Getting to the cave is difficult without your own transport. The daily bus from Kalavryta to Kastria isn't much help. A taxi from Kalavryta will cost about €17.60 return.

Ski Centre

The ski centre (elevation 1650m to 2100m), with nine pistes and one chairlift, is 14km east of Kalavryta on Mt Helmos. It has a cafeteria and first-aid centre but no overnight accommodation. The ski centre also has an office (☎ 2692 022 661, fax 2692 022 415, 25 Martiou, Kalyvryta; open 7am-3pm Mon-Fri). Several outlets on Konstantinou rent skis. **Ski Time Center** (☎ 2692 022 030, Agiou Alexiou 11) charges €8.80 per day for skis, poles and bindings, €17.60 for snowboards and €5.90 for toboggans.

There is no transport to the centre from Kalavryta, so you will need to organise your own. A taxi costs about €17.60 return. The season lasts from November to February, snow permitting.

Corinthia Κορινθία

Corinthia occupies a strategic position adjoining the Isthmus of Corinth. The region was once dominated by the mighty, ancient city of Corinth, now one of the main attractions. Few travellers opt to linger long, although there are several minor sites in the pretty hinterland west of Corinth that are worth a detour if you have your own transport.

CORINTH Κόρινθος
postcode 201 00 • pop 27,400

Modern Corinth (in Greek, Korinthos; **ko-rin-thoss**), 6km west of the Corinth Canal, is the dull administrative capital of Corinthia prefecture. It was rebuilt here after the old

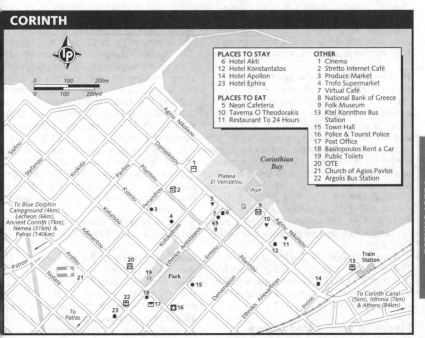

CORINTH

0   100   200m
0   100   200yd

Corinthian Bay

Plateia El Venizelou

Port

To Blue Dolphin Campground (4km), Lecheon (6km), Ancient Corinth (7km), Nemea (31km) & Patras (140km)

Park

Train Station

To Patras

To Corinth Canal (5km), Isthmia (7km) & Athens (84km)

PLACES TO STAY
6 Hotel Akti
12 Hotel Konstantatos
14 Hotel Apollon
23 Hotel Ephira

PLACES TO EAT
5 Neon Cafeteria
10 Taverna O Theodorakis
11 Restaurant To 24 Hours

OTHER
1 Cinema
2 Stretto Internet Café
3 Produce Market
4 Trofo Supermarket
7 Virtual Café
8 National Bank of Greece
9 Folk Museum
13 Ktel Korinthos Bus Station
15 Town Hall
16 Police & Tourist Police
17 Post Office
18 Basilopoulos Rent a Car
19 Public Toilets
20 OTE
21 Church of Agios Pavlos
22 Argolis Bus Station

PELOPONNESE

town was destroyed by an earthquake in 1858. The new town was wrecked by another, equally violent, earthquake in 1928 and badly damaged again in 1981.

The modern town is dominated by concrete buildings built to withstand future earthquakes, but it has a pleasant harbour, friendly people, tasty food and warrants an overnight stay because of its proximity to ancient Corinth and Nemea. Old Corinth is a mere village near the ancient site.

Orientation & Information

It is not difficult to negotiate Corinth, which is laid out on a grid of wide streets stretching back from the waterfront. Social activity centres around the large square by the harbour, Plateia El Venizelou, while transport and administrative activity is based around the small park 200m inland on Ethnikis Antistaseos.

There is no EOT in Corinth. The tourist police (☎ 2741 023 282), located next to the

park at Ermou 51, are open 8am to 2pm and 5pm to 8pm daily between May and October. The regular police (☎ 2741 022 143) are in the same building. The National Bank of Greece is one of several banks on Ethnikis Antistaseos, the post office is on the edge of the park at Adimantou 33, and the OTE is nearby on the corner of Kolokotroni and Adimantou.

You can check email at the Virtual Café (☎ 2741 080 355), Ethnikis Antistaseos 3, open 10am to 1am daily, or at Stretto Internet Café (☎ 2741 025 570), Pilarinou 70, open 8am to midnight Monday to Saturday and 11am to midnight Sunday. Both charge €2.95 per hour with a minimum of €1.50.

Folk Museum

The Folk Museum (☎ 2741 025 352, Ermou 1; admission €1.50; open 8.30am-1.30pm Tues-Sun), to the south of the wharf, focuses on bridal and festive costumes from the past three centuries. There are costumes from the islands and the mainland, as well as metalwork, embroidery, gold and silver objects, and carvings, both secular and ecclesiastical.

Places to Stay – Budget
Blue Dolphin Campground (☎ 2741 025 766/767, fax 2741 085 959, ℮ skoupos@ otenet.gr) Adult/tent €4.55/2.80. This camping ground is about 4km west of town just beyond the ruins of the ancient port of Lecheon. It's a well-organised site with its own stretch of Gulf of Corinth pebble beach. Buses from Corinth to Lecheon can drop you there.

Hotel Akti (☎ 2741 023 337, Ethnikis Antistaseos 1) Singles/doubles with bath €11.75/23.50. The rooms aren't the greatest, but the Akti represents reasonable value for the price.

Hotel Apollon (☎ 2741 022 587, fax 2741 083 875, Pirinis 18) Singles/doubles with bath €23.50/35.20. The Apollon is the best budget option in town. All the rooms are equipped with air-con & TV.

Places to Stay – Mid-Range
Hotel Ephira (☎ 2741 024 021, fax 2741 024 514, Ethnikis Antistaseos 52) Singles/doubles/triples with bath €29.35/49.90/55.80. Architecturally it's probably the most boring building in town, but it houses the best rooms – comfortably furnished with air-con rooms and TV. Breakfast costs €3.55.

Hotel Konstantatos (☎ 2741 022 120, fax 2741 085 634, Cnr Damaskinou & Derve-nakion) Singles/doubles with bath €47/52.85. The Konstantos exists in some sort of 50s timewarp, a quaint, old-fashioned place with stuffed foxes in the foyer. The rooms are clean and comfortable, and the rates negotiable.

Places to Eat
Taverna O Theodorakis (☎ 2741 022 578, Seferi 8) Mains €2.95-8.80, fresh fish €20.55 per kg. Open year-round. Just back from the waterfront near the Folk Museum, this is a lively place specialising in fresh grilled fish. You can have a plate of sardines for €2.95, a large Greek salad for

€2.95 and a litre of retsina for €2.35. It has outdoor seating in summer.

Restaurant To 24 Hours (☎ 2741 083 201, Agiou Nikolaou 19) Mains €3.25-7.35. As the name suggests, this place never closes, turning out an ever changing selection of taverna favourites 24 hours a day.

Neon Cafeteria (☎ 2741 084 950, Cnr Damaskinou & Ethnikis Antistaseos) Mains €4.10-5.60. This is a popular cafeteria with a good range of daily specials like macaroni with octopus (€4.25) or veal with rice (€4.85) as well as a salad bar (€3.25).

Trofo supermarket (☎ 2741 085 281, Kolokotroni 8) Open 8am-9pm Mon-Fri, 8am-6pm Sat. This is another option for self-caterers.

The main *produce market* is on the corner of Kyprou and Periandrou.

Getting There & Away
Bus Buses to Athens (1½ hours, €5.45) leave every half-hour from the KTEL Korinthos bus station (☎ 2741 0754 24), Dimocratias 4, opposite the railway station. This is also the departure point for buses to ancient Corinth (20 minutes, €0.80, hourly), Lecheon and to Nemea (one hour, €2.80, seven daily).

Buses to Argos (one hour, €2.95) and Nafplio (1¼ hours, €3.70) leave from the Argolis bus station on the corner of Aratou and Ethnikis Antistaseos. They also stop at Fihtio (45 minutes, €2.20), on the main road 2km from Mycenae.

Catching a bus to other parts of the Peloponnese is a hassle. Buses to Patras don't come into town. They can be picked up from the bus stop on the Athens side of the Corinth Canal – which means you'll have to get there on one of the frequent buses to Loutraki. You're better off catching the train. The Corinth Canal stop is also the spot for buses south to Tripolis (1½ hours, €4.25), Sparta (three hours, €6.60) and Kalamata (four hours, €8.25).

Train There are 15 trains daily to Athens (1¾ hours, €2.95). Four of them are intercity services, but they are only 15 minutes faster. The Peloponnese rail network divides t Corinth, with eight trains daily heading long the north coast to Diakofto, Patras and eyond. It's worth checking the timetable efore you set out – journey times to Patras ange from under two hours on intercity rains to 3½ hours on the slowest slow train. ix trains continue down the west coast rom Patras to Pyrgos, five go to Kyparissia nd one takes 8½ hours to crawl all the way o Kalamata.

If Kalamata is your destination, you're etter off taking the inland line. It has trains o Kalamata (4½ hours, €5.75, four daily), ia Argos (one hour, €2.05) and Tripolis 2¼ hours, €2.65). There are also trains on he branch line to Nafplio (1¼ hours, €2.95, three daily).

Car There are several car rental outlets around the city centre, including Baslopoulos Rent a Car (☎ 2741 025 573), Adimantou 39.

ANCIENT CORINTH & ACROCORINTH

The ruins of ancient Corinth lie 7km southwest of the modern city, surrounded by the attractive village of Ancient Corinth. Towering 575m above them is the Acrocorinth, a massive limestone outcrop that was the finest natural fortification in ancient Greece.

Most visitors come on whirlwind guided tours from Athens, but there's enough to see to warrant spending at least a full day. The village has a choice of restaurants and tavernas, and is a great alternative to staying in modern Corinth. The tour groups disappear in the evening, and overnighters are left pretty much with the place to themselves.

History During the 6th century BC, Corinth was one of ancient Greece's richest cities. It owed its wealth to its strategic position on the Isthmus of Corinth, which meant it was able to build twin ports, one on the Aegean Sea (Kenchreai) and one on the Ionian Sea (Lecheon), and it traded throughout the Mediterranean. It survived the Peloponnesian Wars and flourished under Macedonian rule, but it was sacked by the Roman consul Mummius in 146 BC

for rebelling against Roman rule. In 44 BC, Julius Caesar began rebuilding the city and it again became a prosperous port.

During Roman times, when Corinthians weren't clinching business deals, they were paying homage to the goddess of love, Aphrodite, in a temple dedicated to her (which meant they were having a rollicking time with the temple's sacred prostitutes, both male and female). St Paul, perturbed by the Corinthians' wicked ways, spent 18 fruitless months preaching here.

Ancient Corinth

In the centre of the village lies the site of Ancient Corinth (☎ 2741 031 207; site & museum €3.55; open 8am-7pm summer, 8am-5pm winter).

Earthquakes and sackings by a series of invaders have left little standing in the ancient Greek city. The remains are mostly from Roman times. An exception is the 5th century BC Doric **Temple of Apollo**, the most prominent ruin on the site. To the south of this temple is a huge **agora**, or forum, bounded at its southern side by the foundations of a **stoa**. This was built to accommodate the bigwigs summoned here in 337 BC by Philip II to sign oaths of allegiance to Macedon. In the middle of the central row of shops is the **bema**, a marble podium from which Roman officials addressed the people.

At the eastern end of the forum are the remains of the **Julian Basilica**. To the north is the **Lower Peirene fountain** – the Upper Peirene fountain is on Acrocorinth. According to mythology, Peirene wept so much when her son Kenchrias was killed by Artemis that the gods, rather than let all the precious water go to waste, turned her into a fountain. In reality, it's a natural spring which has been used since ancient times and still supplies old Corinth with water. The water tanks are concealed in a fountain house with a six-arched facade. The remains of frescoes can be seen through the arches.

West of the fountain, steps lead to the **Lecheon road**, once the main thoroughfare to the port of Lecheon. On the east side of the road is the **Peribolos of Apollo**, a courtyard

Phone numbers listed incorporate changes due in Oct 2002; see p83

PELOPONNESE

flanked by Ionic columns, some of which have been restored. Nearby is a **public latrine**. Some seats remain. The site's **museum** houses statues, mosaics, figurines, reliefs and friezes.

Acrocorinth Ακροκόρινθος

Earthquakes and invasions compelled the Corinthians to retreat to Acrocorinth (admission free; open 8am-7pm Tues-Sun summer, 8am-2.30pm winter). This sheer bulk of limestone was one of the finest natural fortifications in Greece. The original fortress was built in ancient times, but it has been modified many times over the years by a string of invaders. The ruins are a medley of imposing Roman, Byzantine, Frankish, Venetian and Turkish ramparts, harbouring remains of Byzantine chapels, Turkish houses and mosques.

On the higher of Acrocorinth's two summits is the **Temple of Aphrodite** where the sacred courtesans, who so raised the ire of St Paul, catered to the desires of the insatiable Corinthians. Little remains of the temple, but the views are tremendous.

Places to Stay & Eat

There are several places in the village advertising rooms to rent.

Shadow Rooms to Rent (☎ 2741 031 232, fax 2741 031 481) Singles/doubles with bath €23.50/38.15. The rooms are on the north-western edge of the village on the road to Corinth and have wonderful views across the village to Acrocorinth. A hearty breakfast costs an extra €4.40.

Rooms to Rent Tasos (☎ 2741 031 225/183, above Taverna O Tasos) Singles/doubles with bath €17.60/26.40. These rooms are closer to the centre of the village on the road into town from Corinth, next to the ruins of a so-called Turkish nunnery. Tasos describes them as deluxe, which they're not. But they are clean and bright and convenient.

Taverna O Tasos (☎ 2741 031 225/183) Mains €2.95-5.90. O Tasos is a small family-run place with outdoor seating in the shade of a couple of large walnut trees. It's primarily a psistaria serving grilled meats and salads, but it also offers a small selection of taverna dishes.

CORINTH CANAL

The concept of cutting a canal through the Isthmus of Corinth to link the Ionian and Aegean seas was first proposed by the tyrant Periander, founder of ancient Corinth. The magnitude of the task defeated him, so he opted instead to build a paved slipway across which sailors dragged small ships on rollers – a method used until the 13th century.

In the intervening years, many leaders, including Alexander the Great and Caligula, toyed with the canal idea, but it was Nero who actually began digging in AD 67. In true megalomaniac fashion, he struck the first blow himself using a golden pickaxe. He then left it to 6000 Jewish prisoners to do the hard work. The project was soon halted by invasions by the Gauls. Finally, in the 19th century (1883–93), a French engineering company completed the canal.

The Corinth Canal, cut through solid rock, is over 6km long and 23m wide. The vertical sides rise 90m above the water. The canal did much to elevate Piraeus' status as a major Mediterranean port. It's an impressive sight, particularly when a ship is passing through it.

Getting There & Away

The canal is reached by Loutraki bus from modern Corinth to the canal bridge. Any bus or train between Corinth and Athens will pass over the canal. Exadas Travel (☎ 2741 080 028, fax 2741 074 820, e exadastrv@yahoo.gr), Damaskinou 39, offers cruises through the canal on Sundays for €20.55.

ISTHMIA Ισθμία

At the south-eastern end of the canal is the site of ancient Isthmia (☎ 2741 037 244; site & museum €1.50; open 8.30am-3pm Tues-Sun). The remains of the **Sanctuary of Poseidon**, a defensive wall, and **Roman theatre** are mainly of interest to archaeology buffs. As with Nemea, Delphi and Olympia, ancient Isthmia was one of the sites of the Panhellenic Games, and the

My other donkey is a Ferrari!

George, the octopus fisherman – Paros

Whitewashed streetscape on Santorini

Young boy sets out for school on Hydra.

Tomb of the Unknown Soldier, Syntagma Square

This Cretan woman wears the traditional black outfit still seen in many parts of Greece.

Baking a feast fit for the village in an outdoor communal oven – Olymbos village, Karpathos

Time stands still for three Greek friends, from the Lasithi Plateau on the island of Crete.

site's **museum** contains various ancient athletic exhibits. The site is south-west of the modern village of Isthmia, signposted off the main road.

The Old National Road to Athens crosses the canal at Isthmia by a submersible bridge, which is lowered to allow ships to pass over it.

LOUTRAKI Λουτράκι
population 7000
Loutraki, 6km north of the Corinth Canal, lounges between a pebbled beach and the tall cliffs of the Gerania Mountains. Once a traditional spa town patronised by elderly and frail Greeks, it's best known these days as the home of the country's biggest casino. It remains a major producer of bottled mineral water. The town was devastated by the 1981 earthquake, and subsequent reconstruction has resulted in its reincarnation as a tacky resort with dozens of modern, characterless hotels along the seafront. Loutraki hardly warrants an overnight stay.

Getting There & Away
Buses run from Corinth to Loutraki (20 minutes, €0.90) every half-hour, and there are nine buses daily from Athens (1½ hours, €4.70).

NEMEA Νεμύα
Ancient Nemea (☎ 2746 022 739; site & museum €1.50; open 8.30am-3pm Tues-Sun), 31km south-west of Corinth, lies 4km north-east of the modern village of the same name. According to mythology, it was here that Heracles carried out the first of his labours – the slaying of the lion that had been sent by Hera to destroy Nemea. The lion became the constellation Leo (each of the 12 labours is related to a sign of the zodiac).

Like Olympia, Nemea was not a city but a sanctuary and venue for the biennial Nemean Games, held in honour of Zeus. These games became one of the great Panhellenic festivals. Remarkably, three columns of the 4th century BC Doric **Temple of Zeus** remain. Other ruins include a bathhouse and hostelry. The site's **museum** has a model of the site and explanations in English.

At the **stadium** (☎ 2746 022 739; admission €1.50; open 8.30am-3pm Tues-Sun), 500m back along the road, you can see the athletes' starting line and distance markers.

Getting There & Away Buses to Nemea (one hour, €2.80, seven daily) from Corinth travel past the site. There are also buses to Nemea from Argos (€1.90).

Argolis Αργολίδα

The Argolis Peninsula, which separates the Saronic and Argolic gulfs in the north-east, is a veritable treasure trove for archaeology buffs. The town of Argos, from which the region takes its name, is thought to be the longest continually inhabited town in Greece. Argolis was the seat of power of the Mycenaean Empire that ruled Greece from 1600 to 1200 BC. The ancient cities of Mycenae, Tiryns, Argos and Epidaurus are the region's major attractions.

ARGOS Αργος
postcode 212 00 • pop 22,300
Argos may well be the oldest continuously inhabited town in Greece, but most vestiges of its past glory lie buried beneath the uninspiring modern town. Although the town itself is of minor interest, it is a convenient base from which to explore the sites of Argolis and has a refreshing lack of tourist hype. It is also a transport hub for buses.

Orientation & Information
Argos' showpiece and focal point is the magnificent central square, Plateia Agiou Petrou, with its Art Nouveau street lights, citrus and palm trees and the impressive Church of Agios Petros. Beyond, Argos deteriorates into an unremarkable working town.

The main bus station is just south of the central square on Kapodistriou, while the train station is on the south-eastern edge of town by the road to Nafplio.

There is no tourist office or tourist police. The regular police can be contacted on ☎ 100. The post office and OTE are both close to Plateia Agiou Petrou. The post office is clearly signposted on Kapodis-triou, and the OTE office is on Nikitara, which leads off the square next to the National Bank of Greece. Travellers can check email at Café Net (☎ 2751 029 677), 28th Oktavriou 4. It charges €3.55 per hour.

Archaeological Museum

Even if you're only passing through Argos, try to pause long enough to visit the archaeological museum (☎ 2751 068 819; admission €1.50; open 8.30am-3pm Tues-Sun), on the edge of the central square. The collection includes some outstanding Roman mosaics and sculptures; Neolithic, Mycenaean and Geometric pottery; and bronze objects from the Mycenaean tombs.

Roman Ruins

There are Roman ruins (admission free; open 8.30am-3pm) on both sides of Tripolis, which is the main Argos-Tripolis road. To get there from the central square, head south along Danaou for about 500m and then turn right onto Theatrou. Theatrou joins Tripolis opposite the star attraction, the enormous **theatre**, which could seat up to 20,000 people (more than at Epidaurus). It dates from classical times but was greatly modified by the Romans. Nearby are the remains of a 1st century AD **odeion** (indoor theatre) and **Roman baths**.

It is a 45-minute hard slog by footpath from the theatre up to the **Fortress of Larissa**, a conglomeration of Byzantine, Frankish, Venetian and Turkish architecture, standing on the foundations of the city's principal ancient citadel. There is also a road to the top, signposted from the centre of town.

Places to Stay

Hotel Apollon (☎ 2751 068 065, Papaflessa 13) Singles/doubles €14.70/20, with bath €16.15/23.50. This is the best budget choice, tucked away on a quiet side street behind the National Bank of Greece, close to the main square. The rooms come with TV.

Hotel Mycenae (☎ 2751 068 754, fax 2751 068 332, Plateia Agiou Petrou 10) Singles/doubles with bath €29.35/38.15,

apartments €64.60. This C-class hotel on the central square has large, comfortable rooms and a four-bed 'apartment'. All rooms come with air-con and TV and are centrally heated in winter. Breakfast costs €5.90 per person.

Hotel Telesilla (☎ 2751 068 317, fax 2751 066 249, Plateia Agiou Petrou & Danaou 2) Singles/doubles with bath €29.35/47. The hotel has been transformed following a complete refit. It offers smart, modern rooms with air-con and TV.

Places to Eat

Restaurant Aigli (☎ 2751 067 266, Plateia Agiou Petrou 6). Mains €2.65-5.30. The Aigli is a good place to check out. It offers pasta from €2.65, pizzas from €4.70, burgers from €4.10 as well as traditional favourites like mousakas (€3.85). With outdoor seating opposite the church in the main square, it's also perfect for people watching.

Self-caterers can check out Argos' **food market** in the neoclassical agora on Tsokri. There are several supermarkets around the town centre.

Getting There & Away

Bus Most services of interest to travellers are operated by KTEL Argolida (☎ 2751 067 324) from its office at Kapodistriou 8, just south of the main square. It has buses to Nafplio (20 minutes, €0.85, half-hourly), Mycenae (30 minutes, €1.25, five daily) and Nemea (one hour, €1.90, two daily). There are also buses to Athens (two hours, €7.35, hourly) via Corinth (€2.95); and Tripolis (1¼ hours, €3.40, eight daily).

Services south to Astros (one hour, €1.90) and Leonidio (2¼ hours, €4.85) are operated by KTEL Arcadias from the Kafeneion Christos Klisaris (☎ 2751 023 162), Theatrou 40. There are three services a day on this route, leaving at 10am, 1pm and 6pm.

Train There are seven trains daily to Athens (three hours, €3.85), also stopping at Fihtio, near Mycenae (20 minutes, €1) and Corinth (one hour, €2.05). There are four trains daily to Kalamata (3½ hours, €4.40) via Tripolis (one hour, €2.35).

MYCENAE Μυκήνες
postcode 212 00 • pop 450

The modern village of Mycenae (in Greek, Mikines; mih-**kee**-ness) is 12km north of Argos, just east of the main Argos-Corinth road. The village is geared towards the hordes of package tourists visiting ancient Mycenae, and has little to recommend it other than its proximity to the ancient site, 2km to the north. There is accommodation along its single street. There's no bank, but the mobile post office at the ancient site has a currency exchange service.

Ancient Mycenae

In the barren foothills of Mt Agios Ilias (750m) and Mt Zara (600m) stand the sombre and mighty ruins of ancient Mycenae (☎ 2751 076 585; citadel & Treasury of Atreus €4.40; open 8am-7pm summer, 8am-5pm winter). For 400 years (1600–1200 BC) this vestige of a kingdom was the most powerful in Greece, holding sway over the Argolid (the modern-day prefecture of Argolis) and influencing the other Mycenaean kingdoms.

History & Mythology Mycenae is synonymous with Homer and Schliemann. In the 9th century BC, Homer told in his epic poems, the *Iliad* and the *Odyssey*, of 'well-built Mycenae, rich in gold'. These poems were, until the 19th century, regarded as no more than gripping and beautiful legends. But in the 1870s, the amateur archaeologist Heinrich Schliemann (1822–90), despite derision from professional archaeologists, struck gold, first at Troy then at Mycenae.

In Mycenae, myth and history are inextricably linked. According to Homer, the city of Mycenae was founded by Perseus, the son of Danae and Zeus. Perseus' greatest heroic deed was the killing of the hideous snake-haired Medusa, whose looks literally petrified the beholder. Eventually, the dynasty of Perseus was overthrown by Pelops, a son of Tantalus. The Mycenaean Royal House of Atreus was

probably descended from Pelops, although myth and history are so intertwined, and the genealogical line so complex, that no-one really knows. Whatever the bloodlines, by Agamemnon's time the House of Atreus was the most powerful of the Achaeans (Homer's name for the Greeks). It eventually came to a sticky end, fulfilling the curse which had been cast because of Pelops' misdeeds.

The historical facts are that Mycenae was first settled by Neolithic people in the 6th millennium BC. Between 2100 and 1900 BC, during the Old Bronze Age, Greece was invaded by people of Indo-European stock who had crossed Anatolia via Troy to Greece. The invaders brought an advanced culture to the then-primitive Mycenae and other mainland settlements. This new civilisation is now referred to as the Mycenaean, named after Mycenae, its most powerful kingdom. The other kingdoms included Pylos, Tiryns, Corinth and Argos in the Peloponnese. Evidence of Mycenaean civilisation has also been found at Thiva (Thebes) and Athens.

The city of Mycenae consisted of a fortified citadel and surrounding settlement. Due to the sheer size of the walls of the citadel (13m high and 7m thick), the ancient Greeks believed they must have been built by a Cyclops, one of the giants described by Homer in the *Odyssey*.

Archaeological evidence indicates that the palaces of the Mycenaean kingdoms were destroyed around 1200 BC. It was long thought that the destruction was the work of the Dorians, but later evidence indicates that the decline of the Mycenaean civilisation was symptomatic of the general turmoil around the Mediterranean at the time. The great Hittite Empire in Anatolia, which had reached its height between 1450 and 1200 BC, was now in decline, as was the Egyptian civilisation.

The Mycenaeans, Hittites and Egyptians had all prospered through their trade with each other, but this had ceased by the end of the 1200s. Many of the great palaces of the Mycenaean kingdoms were destroyed 150 years before the Dorians arrived.

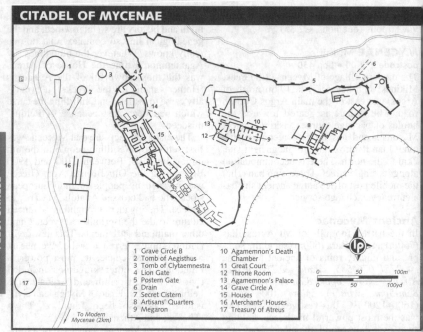

CITADEL OF MYCENAE

1 Grave Circle B
2 Tomb of Aegisthus
3 Tomb of Clytaemnestra
4 Lion Gate
5 Postern Gate
6 Drain
7 Secret Cistern
8 Artisans' Quarters
9 Megaron
10 Agamemnon's Death Chamber
11 Great Court
12 Throne Room
13 Agamemnon's Palace
14 Grave Circle A
15 Houses
16 Merchants' Houses
17 Treasury of Atreus

To Modern Mycenae (2km)

Whether the destruction was the work of outsiders or due to internal division between the various Mycenaean kingdoms remains unresolved.

The site was added to the World Heritage list in 1999.

Exploring the Site The Citadel of Mycenae is entered through the Lion Gate, so called because of the relief above the lintel of two lionesses supporting a pillar. This motif is believed to have been the insignia of the Royal House of Atreus.

Inside the citadel, you will find Grave Circle A on the right as you enter. This was the royal cemetery and contained six grave shafts. Five were excavated by Schliemann in 1874–76 and the magnificent gold treasures he uncovered are in the National Archaeological Museum in Athens. In the last grave shaft, Schliemann found a well-preserved gold death mask with flesh still clinging to it. Fervently, he sent a telegram

to the Greek king stating, 'I have gazed upon the face of Agamemnon'. The mask turned out to be that of an unknown king who had died some 300 years before Agamemnon.

To the south of Grave Circle A are the remains of a group of houses. In one was found the famous Warrior Vase which Schliemann regarded as one of his greatest discoveries.

The main path leads up to Agamemnon's palace, centred around the Great Court. The rooms to the north were the private royal apartments. One of these rooms is believed to be the chamber in which Agamemnon was murdered. Access to the throne room, west of the Great Court, would originally have been via a large staircase. On the south-eastern side of the palace is the megaron (reception hall).

On the northern boundary of the citadel is the Postern Gate through which, it is said, Orestes escaped after murdering his other. In the far north-eastern corner of the citadel is the **secret cistern**. It can be explored by torchlight, but take care – the steps are slippery.

Until the late 15th century BC, the Mycenaeans put their royal dead into shaft graves. They then devised a new form of burial – the tholos tomb, shaped like a beehive. The approach road to Mycenae passes to the right of the best preserved of these, the **Treasury of Atreus** or tomb of Agamemnon. A 40m-long passage leads to this immense beehive-shaped chamber. It is built with stone blocks that get steadily smaller as the structure tapers to its central point. Farther along the road on the right is **Grave Circle B**, and nearby are the **tholos tombs of Aegisthus and Clytaemnestra**.

Places to Stay & Eat

Camping Mycenae (☎ 2751 076 121, fax 2751 076 850, e dars@arg.forthnet.gr, off Christou Tsounta) Adult/tent €4.10/3.25. Open year-round This small camping ground is conveniently located right in the middle of Mycenae village, opposite the Hotel Belle Helene.

There are several signs advertising rooms on the Fihtio side of the village, and half a dozen hotels.

Hotel Belle Helene (☎ 2751 076 225, fax 2751 076 179, Christou Tsounta 15) Singles/doubles €26.40/38.15. The Belle Helene is a curious mixture of ancient and modern: a tiny old-fashioned hotel with a large modern restaurant tacked on the front. The renowned archaeologist Heinrich Schliemann stayed in room 3, now marked with a plaque, while excavating at ancient Mycenae.

La Petit Planete (☎ 2751 076 240, fax 2751 076 610, 500m north-west of Mycenae) Singles/doubles/triples with bath €44/58.70/73.40. This comfortable modern B-class hotel stands on a hillside overlooking orange groves between the village and the ancient site. It has a swimming pool, restaurant and bar.

Getting There & Away

There are buses to Mycenae from Nafplio (one hour, €1.90, three daily) and Argos (30 minutes, €1.25, five daily). The buses stop in the village and at the ancient site.

Other bus services, such as Athens-Nafplio, advertise a stop at Mycenae but they actually go no closer than the village of Fihtio on the main road, leaving you 3km from the village.

NAFPLIO Ναύπλιο
postcode 211 00 • pop 11,900
Nafplio, 12km south-east of Argos on the Argolic gulf, is one of Greece's prettiest towns. The narrow streets of the old town are filled with elegant Venetian houses and gracious neoclassical mansions. The setting is dominated by the towering Palamidi Fortress.

Nafplio was the first capital of Greece after independence and has been a major port since the Bronze Age. So strategic was its position that it had three fortresses – the massive principal fortress of Palamidi, the smaller Akronafplia and the diminutive Bourtzi on an islet west of the old town.

Removed from the spotlight as capital of Greece after Kapodistrias' assassination by the Maniot chieftains Konstantinos and Georgos Mavromihalis, Nafplio has settled into a more comfortable role as a peaceful seaside resort. With good bus connections, the city is an absorbing base from which to explore many ancient sites.

Orientation
The old town occupies a narrow promontory with the Akronafplia fortress on the southern side and the promenades of Bouboulinas and Akti Miaouli on the north side. The principal streets of the old town are Amalias, Vasileos Konstantinou, Staïkopoulou and Kapodistriou. The old town's central square is Plateia Syntagmatos (Syntagma Square), at the western end of Vasileos Konstantinou.

The bus station is on Syngrou, the street separating the old town from the new. The main street of the new town, known to locals as Neapolis, is 25 Martiou – an easterly continuation of Staïkopoulou.

Information
Nafplio's municipal tourist office (☎ 2752 024 444) is on 25 Martiou. It's open 9am to

PELOPONNESE

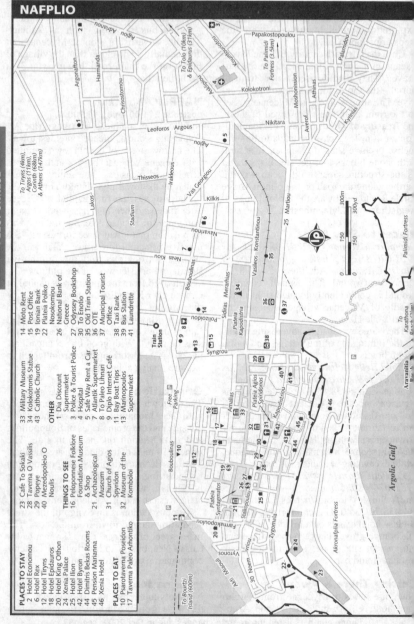

NAFPLIO

PLACES TO STAY
2 Hotel Economou
6 Hotel Rex
12 Hotel Tiryns
18 Hotel Epidauros
20 Hotel King Othon
24 Xenia Palace
25 Hotel Ilion
42 Hotel Byron
44 Dimitris Bekas Rooms
45 Pension Marianna
46 Xenia Hotel

PLACES TO EAT
10 Psarotaverna Poseidon
17 Taverna Paleo Arhontiko
23 Cafe To Sokaki
28 Taverna O Vassilis
29 Popeye
40 Mezedopoleio O Noulis

THINGS TO SEE
16 Peloponnese Folklore Foundation Museum & Shop
21 Archaeological Museum
31 Church of Agios Spyridon
32 Museum of the Komboloi
33 Military Museum
34 Kolokotronis Statue
43 Catholic Church

OTHER
1 Dia Discount Supermarket
4 Hospital
5 Police & Tourist Police
7 Safe Way Rent a Car
8 Atlantik Supermarket
9 Diplo Internet Café
11 To Paleo Lihnari
13 Bay Boat Trips
13 Marinopoulos Supermarket
14 Moto Rent
15 Post Office
19 Ionian Bank
22 Plateia Poliko Nosokomiou
26 National Bank of Greece
27 Odyssey Bookshop
30 To Enotio
35 Old Train Station
36 OTE
37 Municipal Tourist Office
38 Taxi Rank
39 Bus Station
41 Laundrette

m and 4pm to 8pm daily. The tourist po-
ce (☎ 2752 028 131) can be found behind
e hospital at Kountouridou 16, sharing an
fice with the regular police (☎ 2752 022
0). The post office is on Syngrou, and the
TE is on 25 Martiou opposite the tourist
fice. All the major banks have branches in
wn, including the National Bank of
reece on Plateia Syntagmatos and the Ion-
n Bank at the western end of Amalias.

The laundrette at 22 Papanikolaou is
en 9.30am to 1.30pm and 5.30pm to
30pm Monday to Saturday. It charges
10.30 to wash and dry a 6kg load.

For Internet access, head to the Diplo
ternet Café (☎ 2752 021 280), Boubouli-
s 43. It's open 9am to midnight daily and
arges €4.40 per hour.

Odyssey (☎ 2752 023 430), Plateia Syn-
gmatos, stocks international newspapers,
aps, and a small selection of novels in
nglish, French and German.

alamidi Fortress
his vast citadel (☎ 2752 028 036; admission
2.35; open 8am-6.45pm summer, 8am-5pm
nter) stands on a 216m-high outcrop of
ck. Within its walls stand three separate
enetian fortresses, built between 1711 and
14, but seized by the Turks only a year
ter completion. Above each of the gates of
e citadel is the Venetian emblem, the
on of St Mark. During the War of Inde-
ndence, the Greeks, under the leadership of
e venerable klepht (mountain fighter) chief,
eodoros Kolokotronis, besieged the citadel
r 15 months before the Turks surrendered.

In the new town, north of the OTE, stands
splendid equestrian statue of Kolokotronis,
ho was known as the Grand Old Man of
e Morea.

The fortress affords marvellous views.
he energetic can tackle the seemingly end-
ss 999 steps that begin south-east of the
s station. Climb early and take water.
here's also a road to the fortress. A taxi
sts about €3.50 one way.

kronafplia Fortress
e Akronafplia fortress, which rises above
e old part of town, is the oldest of Naf-

plio's three castles. The lower sections of
the walls date back to the Bronze Age. Up
until the arrival of the Venetians, the town
was restricted to within its walls. The Turks
called it İç Kale (meaning 'inner castle'). It
was used as a political prison from 1936-56.
It now houses a hotel complex built by the
government-run Xenia group.

There's a lift up to the fortress from
Plateia Poliko Nosokomiou at the western
edge of town – look for the flags at the entrance of the tunnel leading to the lift. The
old gateway to the fortress, crowned with a
fine Venetian lion emblem, is at the top of
Potamianou, the stepped street that heads
uphill off Plateia Agios Spridonos.

Bourtzi
This small island fortress lies about 600m
west of the port. Most of the existing structure was built by the Venetians. Boats to the
island leave from the north-eastern end of
Akti Miaouli, provided there are at least
four passengers. The trip costs €1.50.

Museums
Nafplio's **Peloponnese Folklore Foundation
Museum** (☎ 2752 028 947, fax 2752 027 960,
ⓔ pff@otenet.gr, Ⓦ www.pfi.gr, Vasileos
Alexandros 1; adult/student €2.95/1.50;
open 9am-3pm Wed-Mon, closed Feb) has
displays of traditional textile-producing techniques (with in-depth explanations in English) and folk costumes.

The **archaeological museum** (☎ 2752
027 502, Plateia Syntagmatos; admission
€1.50; open 8.30am-3pm Tues-Sun) is
housed in an impressive stone building constructed as an arsenal by the Venetians at
the beginning of the 18th century. The collection includes pottery from Neolithic to
classical times, and finds from Mycenae
and Tiryns. The prize piece is a suit of
bronze Mycenaean armour from Tiryns that
is virtually intact.

The **military museum** (Amalias 22; admission free; open 9am-2pm Tues-Sat,
9.30am-2pm Sun) traces Greece's military
history from the War of Independence onwards through a collection of photographs,
paintings, uniforms and assorted weaponry.

PELOPONNESE

Museum of the Komboloi (*☎/fax 2752 021 618,* ℮ *arisevag@otenet.gr,* ⓦ *www .komboloi.gr, Staïkopoulou 25; admission €1.50*) This is really more of a shop than a museum. It sells a wide range of *komboloi* (worry beads), evil eye charms and amulets. The upstairs museum has a collection of ancient beads assembled by owner Aris Evangelinos.

Beaches

Aravanitia Beach is a small pebble beach just 10 minutes' walk south of town, tucked beneath the Palamidi Fortress.

If you're feeling energetic, you can follow a path east around the coast to sandy **Karathona Beach**, at the far side of the Palamidi Fortress. The walk takes about an hour. It's also possible to walk around the base of the Akronafplia Fortress.

Special Events

Nafplio hosts a classical music festival in late May and early June featuring both Greek and international performers. Venues include the Palamidi Fortress and the Bourtzi.

The town is also a good base for visits to Epidaurus for performances of ancient Greek dramas at the famous theatre during the Hellenic Festival in July and August. The local bus syndicate operates special buses to the festival, leaving Nafplio at 7.30pm. Theatre tickets are no longer sold in Nafplio; buy them at the theatre.

Places to Stay – Budget

The closest camping grounds are at the beach resorts, including Tolo, east of Nafplio (see Beaches in the Around Nafplio section).

Hotel Economou (*☎ 2752 023 955, Argonafton 22*) Dorm beds €7.35, doubles/triples with bath €29.35/35.20. Owner George Economou offers special deals for backpackers at this D-class hotel. He was once the manager of the town's youth hostel (opposite), which closed years ago due to lack of funding, and he keeps a couple of shared rooms aside for budget travellers. The hotel is about 15 minutes' walk from

the bus station off Leoforos Argous. Th street sign for Argonafton went missin during the building of the new Dia Discou Supermarket, on the corner.

Most people prefer to stay in the ol town, which is the most interesting place t be. Unfortunately, there is very little budg accommodation.

Dimitris Bekas (*☎ 2752 024 59 Efthimiopoulou 26*) Singles/doubles/triple €14.70/19/22. Dimitris Bekas is the on good budget option. Rooms are top value fo a great location above the Catholic church o the slopes of the Akronafplia. The roofto terrace has great views over the old town.

Hotel Epidauros (*☎/fax 2752 027 54 Kokinou 2*) Doubles with bath €35.20. Th hotel is a good fallback, with a selection o rooms here and at the co-owned *Hote Tiryns* (*☎ 2752 021 020, fax 2752 027 54* nearby.

Places to Stay – Mid-Range

Pension Marianna (*☎ 2752 024 256, fo 2752 021 783,* ℮ *petros4@otenet.g* ⓦ *marianna8K.com, Potamianou 9*) Single doubles/triples with bath €35.20/41.10/4 For a large room with a view, head to th place, perched high above the town. It's family business run by brothers Panos, Pe ros and Takis. A generous breakfast cos an extra €3.55, served on the terrace ove looking the town. According to season, yo can look forward to fresh orange juice fro the family farm or home-made lemonade.

Hotel Byron (*☎ 2752 022 351, fax 275 026 338,* ℮ *byronhotel@otenet.gr,* ⓦ *ww .otenet.gr/byronhotel, Platanos 2*) Single from €38.15, doubles €52.85-70.50, triple €64.60-76.30, all with bathroom. For man years it was the stylish Byron that set th standard for the city's hotel operators. It re mains a class act: a fine old building bea tifully furnished in traditional style. It worth paying more for a room with a view The hotel is up the steps opposite the chur of Agios Spyridon on Kapodistriou. Brea fast costs €5.90.

Hotel King Othon (*☎/fax 2752 027 59 Farmakopoulou 4*) Singles/doubles €4 64.60, 4-bed family room €85.10. Th otel has come up looking a treat after a hange of ownership and a complete refit. Prices include breakfast.

Hotel Rex (☎ 2752 026 907, fax 2752 028 106, Bouboulinas 21) Singles/doubles €48.50/75. This is another place that has been transformed following a change of ownership. It has large, comfortable rooms with air-con, TV and fridge. Prices include buffet breakfast.

Places to Stay – Top End

Hotel Ilion (☎ 2752 025 114, fax 2752 024 497, e ilionhot@otenet.gr, W www .ilionhotel.gr, Kapodistriou 6). Doubles with bath €64.60-114.50. The Ilion is the latest addition to Nafplio's range of luxury accommodation, aimed at well-heeled Athenian couples looking for a romantic weekend away. Housed in a renovated mansion, the 15 rooms carry names like the Room of Passion and the Suite of Dreams. The best room, the Suite of Love and Soul, has a jacuzzi. Hotel services include a hair stylist and an aesthetician – to ensure that guests look and feel their best! Breakfast costs €7.35.

Xenia Palace (☎ 2752 028 981-5, fax 2752 028 783, e palace@nafplionhotels. gr, W www.nafplionhotels.gr, Akronafplia) Singles/doubles with bath €188/235, bungalows from €141, suites €470. Formerly part of the government-run Xenia chain, this place has lifted its game considerably under private ownership – but not enough to justify these prices.

The city's original *Xenia Hotel*, controversially built atop the Akronafplia's historic Castel di Toro bastion, was closed at the time of research while new owners pondered the building's future. A demolition team would be the kindest choice for this pile of crumbling concrete and rusting iron rods. It's an eyesore of embarrassing proportions.

Places to Eat

The streets of the old town are filled with dozens of restaurants. Staïkopoulou, in particular, is one long chain of restaurants; it would take weeks to eat at all of them. Most of these places close down in winter, and the choice shrinks to a few long-standing favourites.

Taverna Paleo Arhontiko (☎ 2752 022 449, Cnr Ypsilandou & Sofroni) Mains €4.40-7.65. Top of the list is this excellent taverna. Owner Tassos runs the place like a party, and it's very popular with locals. There is live music every night from 10pm in summer, and on Friday and Saturday night in winter. Reservations are essential on weekends.

Mezedopoleio O Noulis (☎ 2752 025 541, Moutzouridou 21) Meze €1.50-7.35. This is another popular spot. It serves a fabulous range of *mezedes* (snacks) which can easily be combined to form a meal. Check out the *saganaki flambé* (€3.55), ignited with Metaxa (brandy) as it reaches your table.

Taverna O Vassilis (☎ 2752 025 334, Staikopoulou 20-24) Mains €3.85-7.65. O Vassilis is a popular family-run place at the heart of the restaurant strip on Staikopoulou. It has a large choice of starters, and a good selection of main dishes – including a very tasty rabbit stifado for € 4.85.

The restaurants along the promenade on Bouboulinas specialise in seafood.

Psarotaverna Poseidon (☎ 2752 027 515, Bouboulinas 77) Calamari €4.70, fish from €23.50/kg. This is the territory of Kostas Bikakis, once acclaimed by a French travel magazine as 'the greatest *kamaki* (womaniser) in the Argolid'. That was back in the 1950s. You can read about his exploits and study photos of a youthful Kostas with a bevy of glamorous girls while you munch on a plate of calamari or fresh fish.

Popeye (Staïkopoulou 32) Breakfast €2.35-4.40. Popeye has a good selection of breakfast menus and reasonable prices.

Self-caterers will find a choice of *supermarkets* in the new town, including *Marinopoulos* (Cnr Syngrou & Flessa) and *Atlantik* (☎ 2752 026 438, Bouboulinas 24).

Entertainment

Nafplio seems to have almost as many nightclubs and bars as it has restaurants. Most of them are on Bouboulinas – just cruise along until you find a sound that you like at a volume you can handle.

PELOPONNESE

To Paleo Lihnari (☎ 2752 022 041, Bouboulinas 39) You'll find live Greek music here on Friday and Saturday night.

Shopping
To Enotio (☎ 2752 021 143, Staïkopoulou 40) Traditional and modern Greek shadow puppets are produced and sold here. Prices start at €5.90.

Getting There & Away
Bus The bus station (☎ 2752 027 323) is at Syngrou 8. There are buses from Nafplio to Athens (2½ hours, €8.25, hourly), Argos (30 minutes, €0.85, half-hourly), Tolo (15 minutes, €0.85, hourly), Porto Heli (two hours, €4.85, three daily); and three daily to Mycenae (one hour, €1.90), Epidaurus (40 minutes, €1.90) and Galatas (two hours, €5.15). Other destinations include Tripolis (1½ hours, €4.10) and Corinth (1¼ hours, €3.70).

Train Train services from Nafplio are of little more than academic interest. There are trains to Athens (three hours, €4.70) leaving at 6.10am and 6.30pm daily. The station is by the port on Bouboulinas. An old train has been converted into the ticket office (☎ 2752 026 400) and kafeneio.

Getting Around
There are several car hire places in town, so it pays to shop around. Two places worth checking out are Auto Europe (☎ 2752 024 160/161, fax 2752 024 164), Bouboulinas 51, and Safe Way Rent a Car (☎ 2752 022 155, fax 2752 025 738), Agiou 2. Moto Rent (☎ 2752 021 407, fax 2752 025 642), Polizoidou 8, also has a motorcycles.

AROUND NAFPLIO
Tiryns Τίρυνθα
The ruins of Homer's 'wall-girt Tiryns' (☎ 2752 022 657, Nafplio-Argos road; admission €1.50; open 8am-8pm summer, 8am-2.30pm winter) are 4km north-west of Nafplio. The walls of Tiryns are the apogee of Mycenaean architectural achievement (or paranoia), being even more substantial than those at Mycenae. In parts, they are 20m

thick. The largest stones are estimated weigh 14 tons. Within the walls there a vaulted galleries, secret stairways, and sto age chambers. Frescoes from the palace a in Athens' National Archaeological M seum. Tiryns' setting is less awe-inspiri than Mycenae's and much less visited, b the two share equal billing on the Wor Heritage list. The ruins stand to the right the Nafplio-Argos road. Any Nafplio-Arg bus can drop you outside the site.

EPIDAURUS Επίδαυρος
Epidaurus (eh-pee-dahv-ross; ☎ 2753 0. 006; admission €4.40), 30km east of Na plio, is one of the most renowned Greece's ancient sites, as reflected by i World Heritage listing. Epidaurus was sanctuary of Asclepius, the god of med cine. The difference in the atmosphere her compared with that of the war-orientate Mycenaean cities, is immediately obviou Henry Miller wrote in The Colossus Maroussi that Mycenae 'folds in on itsel but Epidaurus is 'open, exposed… devote to the spirit'. Epidaurus seems to emana joy, optimism and celebration.

History & Mythology
Legend has it that Asclepius was the son Apollo and Coronis. While giving birth Asclepius, Coronis was struck by a thunde bolt and killed. Apollo took his son to N Pelion where the physician Chiron i structed the boy in the healing arts.

Apollo was worshipped at Epidaurus i Mycenaean and Archaic times but, by th 4th century BC, he had been superseded b his son. Epidaurus became acknowledge as the birthplace of Asclepius. Althoug there were sanctuaries to Asclepius throug out Greece, the two most important were Epidaurus and on the island of Kos. Th fame of the sanctuary spread, and when plague was raging in Rome, Livy and Ov came to Epidaurus to seek help.

It is believed that licks from snakes we one of the curative practices at the sanctu ary. Asclepius is normally shown with serpent, which – by renewing its skin symbolises rejuvenation. Other treatmen

ovided at the sanctuary involved diet in-
ruction, herbal medicines and occasion-
ly even surgery. The sanctuary also
rved as an entertainment venue. Every
ur years the Festival of Asclepieia took
ace at Epidaurus. Dramas were staged and
hletic competitions were held.

heatre

oday, it's the 3rd-century theatre, not the
nctuary, that pulls the crowds to Epidau-
s. It is one of the best-preserved classical
reek buildings, renowned for its amazing
oustics. A coin dropped in the centre can
e heard from the highest seat. Built of
mestone, the theatre seats up to 14,000
ople. Its entrance is flanked by restored
orinthian pilasters. It's used for perform-
ces of ancient drama during the annual
ellenic Festival (see the following Enter-
inment section for details).

Museum

he museum, between the sanctuary and
e theatre, houses statues, stone inscrip-
ns recording miraculous cures, surgical
struments, votive offerings and partial
constructions of the sanctuary's once-
aborate tholos. After the theatre, the
olos is considered to have been the site's
ost impressive building and fragments of
eautiful, intricately carved reliefs from its
iling are also displayed.

anctuary

he ruins of the sanctuary are less crowded
an the theatre. In the south is the huge kat-
gogeion, a hostelry for pilgrims and pa-
ents. To the west is the large banquet hall
which the Romans built an odeum. It was
ere that the Festival of Asclepieia took
lace. Opposite is the stadium, venue for
e festival's athletic competitions.

To the north are the foundations of the
emple of Asclepius and next to them is the
baton. The therapies practised here seemed
have depended on the influence of the
ind upon the body. It is believed that pa-
ents were given a pep talk by a priest on the
owers of Asclepius then put to sleep in the
baton to dream of a visitation by the god.

The dream would hold the key to the healing process.

East is the **Sanctuary of Egyptian Gods**,
which indicates that the cult of Asclepius
was an adaptation of the cult of Imhotep,
worshipped in Egypt for his healing powers. To the west of the Temple of Asclepius
are the remains of the **tholos**, built in
360–320 BC; the function of which is unknown.

Set among the green foothills of Mt
Arahneo, the air redolent with herbs and
pine trees, it's easy to see how the sanctuary would have had a beneficial effect upon
the ailing. Considering the state of Greece's
current health system, perhaps the centre
should be resurrected.

Places to Stay & Eat

There was no accommodation at the site at
the time of research following the closure of
the Xenia Hotel. The closest hotels are in
Ligourio, 4km north of Epidaurus.

Hotel Koronis (☎ *2753 022 267, fax
2753 022 450, Nafplio-Epidaurus road)*
Singles/doubles with bath €23.50/26.40.
This small family-run hotel is the best bet
for the independent traveller. It's conveniently situated in the middle of town on the
main street.

There are several *restaurants* on the
main street.

Entertainment

The theatre at Epidaurus is used to stage
performances of ancient Greek dramas during the annual Hellenic Festival in July and
August. Performances are held at 9pm on
Friday and Saturday. Tickets can be bought
in Epidaurus at the *site office* (☎ *2753 022
006)* Open 9.30am-1pm & 6pm-9pm Thur,
Fri & Sat. They can also be bought from the
Athens Festival box office (see under Hellenic Festival in the Athens chapter). Prices
vary according to seating. Student discounts
are available. There are special buses from
Athens and Nafplio.

Getting There & Away

There are buses from Nafplio to Epidaurus
(40 minutes, €1.90, four daily) via Ligourio

(also €1.90), and two buses daily to Athens (2½ hours, €7.80).

Arcadia Αρκαδία

The picturesque rural prefecture of Arcadia occupies much of the central Peloponnese. Its name evokes images of grassy meadows, forested mountains, gurgling streams and shady grottoes. It was a favourite haunt of Pan, who played his pipes, guarded herds and frolicked with nymphs in this sunny, bucolic idyll.

Almost encircled by high mountains, Arcadia was remote enough in ancient times to remain largely untouched by the battles and intrigues of the rest of Greece. It was the only region of the Peloponnese not conquered by the Dorians. It remains a backwater, dotted with crumbling medieval villages, remote monasteries and Frankish castles, visited only by determined tourists. It also has 100-odd kilometres of unspoilt coastline on the Argolic Gulf, running south from the pretty town of Myli to Leonidio.

TRIPOLIS Τρίπολη
postcode 221 00 • pop 25,000

The violent recent history of Arcadia's capital, Tripolis (**tree**-po-lee), is in stark contrast with the surrounding rural idyll. In 1821, during the War of Independence, the town was captured by Kolokotronis and its 10,000 Turkish inhabitants massacred. The Turks retook the town three years later, and burnt it to the ground before withdrawing in 1828.

Tripolis itself is not a place you may want to linger long in, but it's a major transport hub for the Peloponnese. It also has some impressive neoclassical buildings and Byzantine churches.

Orientation

Tripolis can be a bit confusing at first. The streets radiate out from the central square, Plateia Vasileos Georgiou, like an erratic spider's web. The main streets are Washington, which runs south from Plateia Georgiou to Kalamata; Ethnikis Antis-

taseos, which runs north from the square and becomes the road to Kalavryta; and Vasileos Georgiou, which runs east from the square to Plateia Kolokotroni. El Venizelou runs east from Plateia Kolokotroni, leading to the road to Corinth.

The main Arkadias bus station is conveniently central on Plateia Kolokotroni. The city's other bus station is opposite the train station, about a 10-minute walk away, at the south-eastern end of Lagopati – the street that runs behind the Arkadias bus terminal.

Information

There's a tourist information office (☎ 2710 231 844) in the town hall, about 250m north of Plateia Vasileos Georgiou at Ethniki Antistaseos 43. It's open 7am to 2pm Monday to Friday. The tourist police (☎ 2710 222 265) cohabit with the regular police at Plateia Petrinou, which is the square between Plateia Georgiou and the town hall. The police station is next to the ornate Malliaropoulio Theatre.

The post office is just off Plateia Vasileos Georgiou, behind Hotel Galaxy at the junction of Athanasiadou and Nikitara. The OTE is nearby on 28 Oktovriou. Internet access is available at the Pacman Net Cafe (☎ 2710 226 407), Deligianni 3 – the cafepacked pedestrian precinct near Hotel Anactoricon. It's open 10am until late every day. It charges €3.55 per hour, with a €1.80 minimum.

Tripolis has branches of all the major banks. The National Bank of Greece is on the corner of 28 Oktovriou and Ethnikis Antistaseos. The bookshop on the northern side of Plateia Vasileos Georgiou sells English-language newspapers.

Archaeological Museum

The city's archaeological museum (☎ 2710 242 148, Evangistrias 2; admission €1.50, open 8.30am-3pm Tues-Sun) occupies a neoclassical mansion and is clearly signposted off Vasileos Georgiou next to Hotel Alex. The museum houses finds from the surrounding ancient sites of Megalopoli, Gortys, Lykosoura and Mantinea.

Places to Stay & Eat

Hotel Alex (☎ *2710 223 465, fax 2710 223 466, Vasileos Georgiou 26*) Singles/doubles/triples with bath €23.50/38.15/44. The Alex had just completed a radical refit at the time of research. It's top value for spacious rooms with air-con and TV.

Hotel Anactoricon (☎ *2710 222 545, fax 2710 222 021, Ethnikis Antistaseos 48*) Singles/doubles/triples with bath €44/58.70/70.50. This friendly, family-run hotel is beyond the town hall. It has comfortable rooms with air-con and TV, and discounts can normally be negotiated.

Estiatorio Ioniko (☎ *2710 222 908, Plateia Vasileos Georgiou*) Mains €2.95-5.30. A good no-nonsense taverna with a good range of dishes, speedy service and bargain prices.

Taverna Piterou (☎ *2710 222 058, Kalavrytou 11A*) Mains €3.55-7.05. For something a shade more upmarket, try this popular taverna on Kalavrytou – the northern extension of Ethnikis Antistaseos – beyond the park with the old steam train.

There are numerous supermarkets around town, including a large *Atlantik* (☎ *2710 223 412, Cnr Atlantis & Lagopati*).

Getting There & Away

Bus The Arkadias bus station (☎ 2710 222 560) on Plateia Kolokotroni is the city's main terminal. There are 12 buses daily to Athens (2¼ hours, €10), via Corinth (one hour, €5). There are also at least two buses daily west to Olympia (2½ hours, €7.65) and Pyrgos (three hours, €8.80), and three east to Argos (one hour, €3.40) and Nafplio (1½ hours, €4.10).

Regional services include buses to Megalopoli (40 minutes, €2.05, eight daily) and Stemnitsa (one hour, €2.35, three daily). There are also two daily to Dimitsana (1½ hours, €3.10), Andritsena (1½ hours, €4.85) via Karitena (€3.25), and Leonidio (2½ hours, €5.75).

Buses to Tegea (20 minutes, €0.80, hourly) leave from the stop outside Hotel Arkadia on Plateia Kolokotroni.

The bus station on Lagopati (☎ 2710 242 086) handles departures to Achaïa, Lakonia and Messinia. They include buses to Sparta (one hour, €3.25, nine daily), Kalamata (two hours, €5, six daily), Kalavryta (2¼ hours, €5.15, one daily) and Patras (3½ hours, €.7.50).

Train Tripolis lies on the main Athens-Kalamata line. There are four trains daily to Athens (four hours, €5.30), via Argos (1¼ hours, €2.35) and Corinth (2¼ hours, €3.25). There are also trains to Kalamata (2½ hours, €3.10, four daily).

MEGALOPOLI Μεγαλόπολη
postcode 222 00 • pop 4700

Despite its name, there's little left of Megalopoli (great city) that reflects its former grandeur. It was founded in 371 BC as the capital of a united Arcadia. In those days, it was nestled in a leafy valley on the banks of the Elisson river. These days, the ruins lie in the shadow of an enormous power station, fuelled by coal strip-mined from the surrounding plains. It looks strangely out of place, surrounded by rolling orchard country, belching great plumes of grey smoke into the blue sky.

Megalopoli is an important transport hub on the main route from Tripolis to Kalamata and Pyrgos.

Places to Stay & Eat

There are six modest hotels to choose from, but most of them are booked out long-term by power station workers.

Hotel Paris (☎ *2791 022 410, Agiou Nikolaou 9*) Singles/doubles with bath €20.55/32.30. The Paris is the best bet for tourists, with clean comfortable rooms close to the large central square, Plateia Polyvriou.

Psistaria O Meraklis (☎ *2791 022 789, Papanastasiou 8*) Mains €2.95-5.30. There are several restaurants around Plateia Polyvriou, but this very popular psistaria is the best place to start. It's just off the square on Papanastasiou – the road to Tripolis. It has a range of grilled food, starting with souvlaki sticks for €0.50, as well as salads and vegetable dishes. It's run by an extended Greek-Canadian family.

PELOPONNESE

Getting There & Away

There are bus services to Athens (three hours, €11.30, eight daily), via Tripolis (40 minutes, €2.05); Kalamata (one hour, €3.40, eight daily); and Andritsena (1¼ hours, €2.95, two daily).

CENTRAL ARCADIA

The area to the west of Tripolis is a tangle of medieval villages, precipitous ravines and narrow winding roads, woven into valleys of dense vegetation beneath the slopes of the Menalon Mountains. This is the heart of the Arcadia prefecture, an area with some of the most breathtaking scenery in the Peloponnese. The region is high above sea level and nights are chilly, even in summer. Snow is common in winter.

You need your own transport to do the area justice, but the three most important villages – Karitena, Stemnitsa and Dimitsana – are within reach of Tripolis by public transport. Stemnitsa and Dimitsana are on the 37km stretch of road that cuts through the mountains from the Pyrgos-Tripolis road in the north to the Megalopoli-Andritsena road in the south.

Karitena Καρίταινα
postcode 222 07 • pop 320

High above the Megalopoli-Andritsena road is the splendid medieval village of Karitena (kar-**eet**-eh-nah). A stepped path leads from the central square to the village's 13th-century **Frankish castle** which is perched atop a massive rock. The castle was captured by Greek forces under Kolokotronis early in the War of Independence, and thus became a key stronghold as the war unfolded.

Before the advent of the euro, Karitena was known as the home of the wonderful old arched stone bridge over the River Alphios that adorned the old 5000 dr note. The bridge remains, although it now sits beneath a large modern concrete bridge.

Activities Athens-based adventure specialists **Alpin Club** (☎ 21 0729 5486, fax 21 0721 2773, e alpinclub@internet.gr, w www .alpinclub.gr) uses Karitena as its base in the Peloponnese. It offers an interesting line-up of activities, starting with whitewater rafting (€44) on the nearby Lousios and Alphios rivers. Other possibilities include kayaking (€44), hot dogging in inflatable canoes (€44), canyoning (€23.50), and mountain biking around Karitena (€23.50, including bike). The Alpin club base is on the main road, just north of the Alphios bridge.

Places to Stay & Eat *Christos Papadopoulos Rooms to Rent* (☎ 2791 031 203) Singles/doubles/triples €17.60/23.50/ 29.35. Christos and family are to be found 200m north of town on the road to Gortys. The three rooms are clean but basic, with one shared bathroom.

Vrenthi Rooms (☎ 2791 031 650) Doubles/ triples with bath €35.20/44. Vrenthi has the best accommodation in the village. The rooms at the front have fabulous views over the Alphios Valley. The Café Vrenthi, 100m up the road, doubles as reception for the rooms.

Taverna To Konaki (☎ 2791 031 600). Mains €2.65-4.40. To Konaki is the only taverna in town. The food is not as inspiring as the views of the Alphios Valley below.

Getting There & Away Buses between Tripolis to Andritsena call at Karitena. A few will leave you on the main road, from where it's an arduous uphill walk to the village. The staff at the bus station you leave from will be able to tell you where the bus will stop.

Stemnitsa Στεμνίτσα
postcode 220 24 • pop 550

Stemnitsa, 15km north of Karitena, is a spectacular village of stone houses and Byzantine churches. North of the village, signposts point the way to **Moni Agiou Ioannitou Prodromou**. The monastery is about 20-minutes' walk beyond the carpark. A monk will show visitors the chapel's splendid 14th- and 15th-century frescoes. From here, paths lead to the deserted monasteries of **Paleou** and **Neou Philosophou**, and also south along the riverbank to the site of ancient Gortys. The monks at Prodromou can direct you.

Places to Stay & Eat *Hotel Triokolonion* (☎ 2795 081 297, fax 2795 081 483) Singles/doubles/triples with bath €23.50/34.95/41.10. The rooms are no better than average, but this is Stemnitsa's only hotel. The prices are nothing to complain about, and they include breakfast.

Taverna Klinitsas (☎ 2795 081 518/438) Mains €3.55-5.90. Named after the highest peak in the surrounding hills, the Klinitsas makes no great claims to culinary heights. It's so low key that it doesn't have a menu, just a selection of daily specials. It's on the main street, on the Dimitsana side of the central square.

Getting There & Away There are three buses daily between Stemnitsa and Tripolis (one hour, €3.10).

Dimitsana Διμιτσάνα
postcode 220 07 • pop 650

Built amphitheatrically on two hills at the beginning of the Lousios Gorge, Dimitsana (dih-mit-**sah**-nah), 11km north of Stemnitsa, is a lovely medieval village. Despite its remoteness, Dimitsana played a significant role in the country's struggle for self-determination. Its Greek school, founded in 1764, was an important spawning ground for the ideas leading to the uprisings against the Turks. Its students included Bishop Germanos of Patras and Patriarch Gregory V, who was hanged by the Turks in retaliation for the massacre in Tripolis. The village also had a number of gunpowder factories and a branch of the secret Filiki Eteria (friendly society) where Greeks met to discuss the revolution (see History in the Facts about the Country chapter for more details on the Filiki Eteria).

From the heady days before independence, Dimitsana has become a sleepy village where the most exciting event is the arrival of the daily bus from Tripolis.

Open Air Water Power Museum This museum (☎ 2785 031 630, admission €1.20; open 10am-2pm & 5pm-7pm Wed-Mon 11 Apr-10 Oct, 10am-4pm Wed-Mon 11 Oct-10 Apr) offers a fascinating insight into the region's pre-industrial past. It occupies the old Agios Yiannis mill complex about 1.5km south of town, signposted off the road to Stemnitsa, where the waters of a spring-fed stream once supplied power for a succession of mills spread down the hillside. A flour mill, a gunpowder mill and a fulling tub (for treating wool) have been restored to working order. There's also an old leather factory.

A feature of this place is the high standard of the explanations (in Greek and English), and the use of videos (subtitled in English) to explain the processes of gunpowder and leather production.

Trekking The best way to appreciate these magnificent surroundings is on foot. There are some wonderful walks in the Dimitsana area, particularly along the Lousios River. The principal walks are outlined in the *Walker's Map of the River Lousios Valley* (€2.95), available at the Open Air Water Power Museum.

Places to Stay You'll see several signs for *domatia* in the middle of town (Plateia Agia Kyriaki).

Tsiapas Rooms to Rent (☎ 2795 031 583). Doubles with bath €35.20. These very comfortable rooms are signposted off Plateia Agia Kyriaki. All the rooms are equipped with fridge and facilities for tea and coffee making. There's also a communal living room with a fireplace – perfect for a cold evening.

Hotel Dimitsana (☎ 2795 031 518, fax 2710 239 061) Doubles with bath €41.10. Dimitsana's only hotel was temporarily closed for renovations at the time of research. It's 1km south of the village on the road to Stemnitsa and has great views of the Lousios Valley. Room rates include breakfast.

Getting There & Away There are buses from Tripolis to Dimitsana (1½ hours, €3.10, two daily).

PELOPONNESE

KYNOURIA Κψνουρια

Kynouria is the name of the coastal region of Arcadia. It covers a narrow strip of territory that stretches south from the tiny village of Kaveri, 41km east of Tripolis, to Kosmas, perched high in the Mt Parnon ranges close to the Lakonian border. Much of the land is incredibly rugged, with a narrow coastal plain and very little fertile ground.

In ancient times, the region was contested by Argos and Sparta – the Argives held sway in the north, and the Spartans controlled the south. Although modern Kynouria is part of Arcadia, the best access is from Argos.

Kaveri to Leonidio

Kaveri is no more than a blip on the map, but it's the meeting point of the main roads east from Tripolis and south from Argos, 12km to the north. From here, the main road hugs the coast for most of the 64km south to Leonidio, curving above a succession of tiny pebble-beached villages.

The first town of consequence is **Astros**, perched in the hills 28km south of Argos. The main attraction around here is the **Villa of Herodes Atticus**, in the hills 2km west of Astros. It was built in the 2nd century AD for the wealthy Roman founder of the celebrated Theatre of Herodes Atticus in Athens. This was his modest country retreat, spread out over a small plateau with views over the Argolic Gulf. Recent excavations have uncovered a stunning spread of more than 10,000 sq m of mosaics. They have been left *in situ*, and will be put on display once a roof has been built to protect them from the elements.

Astros overlooks **Paralio Astros**, an unattractive modern resort full of multi-storey concrete apartment blocks

Apart from some magnificent coastal scenery, there's very little to see between Astros and the minor resort of **Paralia Tyrou**, 29km further south. Also known as **Tyrosapounakia**, it appears to be doing its best to emulate Paralio Astros. Development at this stage is limited to a smattering of hotels and tavernas.

Leonidio Δεϖνίδιο

postcode 223 00 ● pop 3800

The small town of Leonidio, 76km south of Argos, has a dramatic setting at the mouth of the Badron Gorge. Its tiny Plateia 25 Martiou is an archetypal, unspoilt, white-washed Greek village square, surrounded by shady trees. The OTE is visible from the square, and the police (☎ 2757 022 222) are close at hand on Kiloso. Many of the older people around here still speak *chakonika*, the language of ancient Sparta, in preference to Greek.

There are some excellent, unspoilt beaches to be found at the nearby seaside villages of **Plaka** and **Poulithra**. Plaka – which is no more than a cluster of buildings around a small square – is Leonidio's port. The fertile alluvial river flats between Leonidio and the coast are intensively farmed.

Places to Stay & Eat There are apartments for rent in town, but most people head for the beach at Plaka where there are several *domatia*.

Hotel Dionysos (☎ 2757 023 455, *opposite the port*) Doubles with bath €38.15. Plaka's only hotel is a good spot to unwind and do nothing for a few days.

Taverna Michel & Margaret (☎ 2757 022 379, *overlooking the port*) Mains €4.40-5.30, fresh fish from €14.70. This is top spot for a long, lazy lunch. It has good food, friendly service and a great location overlooking Plaka's picturesque little port.

Getting There & Away There are buses down the coast from Argos (2¼ hours, €4.85, three daily) and Tripolis (2½ hours, €5.75, two daily).

Hydrofoil Leonidio's port of Plaka is part of the Flying Dolphin circuit around the Saronic Gulf and the eastern Peloponnese. In summer, there is a daily service to Zea Marina at Piraeus (2½ hours, €22), travelling via Spetses (45 minutes), and Hydra (80 minutes). There are also daily services south to Monemvasia (80 minutes).

South of Leonidio

The road south from Leonidio over the rugged Parnon Mountains to the town of Geraki in Lakonia, 48km away, is one of the most scenic in the Peloponnese. For the first 12km, the road snakes west up the Badron Gorge, climbing slowly away from the river until at times it is no more than a speck of silver far below. The road then leaves the Badron and climbs rapidly through a series of dramatic hairpin bends towards Kosmas.

Just before the top of the climb, there's a dirt road to the left leading to **Moni Profitas Ilonas**, an amazing little monastery perched precariously on the mountainside. Visitors are welcome providing they are suitably dressed. Almost as amazing as the monastery is the cardphone outside.

It's another 14km from the monastery to the peaceful, beautiful mountain village of **Kosmas**. There are no hotels, but there are several domatia (see Places to Stay). Even if you don't stay overnight, it's worth pausing for a cold drink beneath the huge plane trees in the square.

After Kosmas, the road descends – more gently this time – to the village of Geraki in Lakonia. From here you can head 40km west to Sparta, or continue south through **Vlahiotis**, **Molai** and **Sikia**, in Lakonia, to Monemvasia.

Places to Stay & Eat

Maleatis Apollo (☎ *2757 031 494, main square*) Singles/doubles/triples with bath €29.35/35.20/41.10. Named after an unusual brass statue of Apollo that was found nearby, these comfortable rooms all come with TV and kitchen. The cozy co-owned taverna downstairs is open for meals at lunch and dinner.

Kosmas Studios (☎ *2757 031 483*) Doubles with bath €29.35. The rooms are smaller, but equally well equipped. The owners have been very busy on the sign-writing front; there are signs everywhere on the approaches to town.

There is a weekly bus service to Leonidio on Thursday, but otherwise no public transport is available.

Lakonia Λακωνία

The modern region of Lakonia occupies almost identical boundaries to the powerful kingdom ruled by King Menelaus in Mycenaean times. Menelaus ruled from his capital at Sparta, which was later to achieve much greater fame as the arch rival of Athens in classical times. The Spartans who fought Athens were the descendants of the Dorians, who had arrived in about 1100 BC after the decline of the Mycenaean empire.

Little remains of ancient Sparta, but the disappointment is more than compensated for by the glorious Byzantine churches and monasteries at Mystras, just to the west. Another place not to be missed is the evocative medieval town of Monemvasia, in the south-east.

English-speakers can thank the Lakonians for the word 'laconic' – brief of speech – which many Lakonians still are.

SPARTA Σπάρτη
postcode 231 00 • pop 14,100

Modern Sparta (in Greek, Sparti) is an easy-going town of wide, tree-lined streets that is very much in contrast with the ancient image of discipline and deprivation (see boxed text 'A Spartan Existence' in this chapter). The town lies at the heart of the Evrotas Valley, an important citrus and olive growing region. The Taygetos Mountains, snow-capped until early June, provide a stunning backdrop to the west.

Orientation

You won't get lost in Sparta. It was constructed in 1834 on a grid system, and has two main thoroughfares. Palaeologou runs north-south through the town, and Lykourgou east-west. They intersect in the middle of town. The central square, Plateia Kentriki, is a block west of the intersection. The bus station is at the eastern end of Lykourgou.

Information

The tourist information office (☎ 2731 024 852) in Sparta is on the 1st floor of the town hall on the main square. It's open 8am to

PELOPONNESE

SPARTA

To Taverna Acrolithi (50m) &
& Sanctuary of Artemis Orthia (200m)

To Acropolis (100m)

To Tripoli (57km),
Corinth (145km)
& Athens (225km)

Approximate Scale
0   100   200
0   100   200yd

PLACES TO STAY & EAT
6 Hotel Cecil
7 Hotel Apollo
8 Psistaria Rihia
10 Restaurant Elysse
13 Hotel Menelaion
15 Hotel Maniatis;
   Zeus Restaurant

THINGS TO SEE
1 Ancient Theatre
3 Statue of King
   Leonidas
4 Sanctuary of
   Leonidas
9 John Coumantarios
   Art Gallery
21 Archaeological
   Museum
25 Court House
26 Sparta Cathedral

OTHER
2 Soccer Stadium
5 Basilopoulou Supermarket
11 Bus Station
12 Market
14 National Bank of Greece
16 OTE
17 Buses to Mystras
18 Aerodromio (Internet)
19 Post Office
20 Tourist Police
22 Libro Bookshop
23 Tourist Information &
   Town Hall
24 Buses to Mystras
27 Cosmos Club Internet Cafe

To Mystras (5km)
& Kalamata (58km)

To Gythio (42km)

2.30pm Monday to Friday. The tourist police (☎ 2731 020 492) are at Hilonos 8, one block east of the museum.

The post office is signposted off Lykourgou on Archidamou, and the OTE is between Lykourgou and Kleomvrotou, one block east of Palaeologou. For Internet access, try the Cosmos Club Internet Café (☎ 2731 021 500), Palaeologou 34. It's open 8.30am to 11pm daily and charges €3.55 per hour. Aerodromio (☎ 2731 029 268), Lykourgou 55, is open 10am to midnight and charges €4.70.

The National Bank of Greece has branches at Palaeologou 84 and 106. Both have ATMs.

Foreign newspapers are available from Libro Bookshop (☎ 2731 089 233), Palaeologou 52.

Exploring Ancient Sparta

If the city of the Lacedaemonians were destroyed, and only its temples and the foundations of its buildings left, remote posterity would great[ly] doubt whether their power were ever equal [to] their renown.

Thucydide[s]

A wander around ancient Sparta's meag[re] ruins bears testimony to the accuracy o[f] Thucydides' prophecy. Head north alon[g] Palaeologou to the statue of a belligeren[t] King Leonidas, standing in front of a socce[r] stadium. West of the stadium, signs point th[e] way to the southern gate of the **acropolis**.

A dirt path leads off to the left (west[) through olive groves to the 2nd or 3rd cen[-] tury BC **ancient theatre**, the site's most dis[-] cernible ruin. You'll find a reconstructe[d] plan of the theatre on the wall at th[e] Restaurant Elysse (see Places to Eat).

The main cobbled path leads north to th[e] acropolis, passing the ruins of the **Byzantin[e] Church of Christ the Saviour** on the way t[o] the hilltop **Sanctuary of Athena Halkioitou[**] Some of the most important finds in th[e] own's archaeological museum were unearthed here.

The history of the **Sanctuary of Artemis Orthia**, on the north-eastern side of town, is more interesting than the site itself. Like most of the deities in Greek mythology, the goddess Artemis had many aspects, one of which was Artemis Orthia. In the earliest times, this aspect of the goddess was honoured through human sacrifice. The Spartans gave this activity away for the slightly less gruesome business of flogging young boys in honour of the goddess. The museum houses a collection of clay masks used during ritual dances at the sanctuary. The sanctuary is signposted at the junction of Odos Ton 118 and Orthias Artemidos.

Museum & Gallery

Just east of the town centre, Sparta's **archaeological museum** (☎ 2731 028 575, Lykourgou & Agios Nikolaos; admission €1.50; open 8.30am-3pm Tues-Sat, 8.30am-2.30pm Sun). Exhibitions include votive sickles which Spartan boys dedicated to Artemis Orthia, heads and torsos of various deities, a statue of Leonidas, masks and a stele.

The **John Coumantarios Art Gallery** (☎ 2731 081 557, Palaeologou 123; admission free; open 9am-3pm Tues-Sat, 10am-2pm Sun) has a collection of 19th- and 20th-century French and Dutch paintings. There are also changing exhibitions of works by contemporary Greek painters.

Places to Stay

There is no budget accommodation in Sparta following the overdue closure of the crumbling Hotel Panellinion. The closest camping grounds are in nearby Mystras (see the following Mystras section).

Hotel Cecil (☎ 2731 024 980, fax 2731 081 318, Palaeologou 125) Singles/doubles with bath €23.50/29.35. Most travellers head for the small, family-run Cecil. It's good value for clean, comfortable rooms with TV.

Hotel Apollo (☎ 2731 022 491/492/493, fax 2731 023 936, Thermopylon 84) Singles/doubles with bath €23.50/29.35. The Apollo is a reasonable alternative.

A Spartan Existence

The bellicose Spartans sacrificed many things in life for military expertise. Male children were examined at birth by the city council and those deemed too weak to become good soldiers were left to die of exposure. Those fortunate enough to survive infancy were taken from their mothers at the age of seven to undergo rigorous military training.

Training seems to have consisted mainly of beatings and appalling deprivations. Would-be soldiers were forced to go barefoot, even in winter, and were starved so that they would have to steal food for survival. If discovered, they were punished not for the crime, but for allowing themselves to be caught.

Although girls were allowed to stay with their mothers, they also underwent tough physical training so they would give birth to healthy sons.

TAMSIN WILSON

Hotel Maniatis (☎ 2731 022 665, fax 2731 029 994, Palaeologou 72-76) Singles/doubles/triples with bath €52.85/70.50/88, including breakfast. The rooms are spotless and the service is friendly and efficient, but the atmosphere is a little on the sterile side.

Hotel Menelaion (☎ 2731 022 161-5, fax 2731 026 332, Palaeologou 91) Singles/doubles/triples with bath €52.85/70.50/88, including breakfast. When it comes to nominating the best hotel in town, the presence of a swimming pool gives the Menelaion the edge over the Maniatis. It also has one of the finest neoclassical facades in town.

Places to Eat

There are lots of restaurants to be found along Palaeologou.

Restaurant Elysse (☎ 2731 029 896, Palaeologou 113) Mains €4.40-8.50. This is a popular place run by a helpful Greek-

PELOPONNESE

Canadian family. The menu features a couple of Lakonian specialities: *chicken bardouniotiko* (€4.85) – chicken cooked with onions and feta cheese, and *arni horiatiki* (€5.30) – lamb baked with bay leaves and cinnamon.

Psistaria Rihia (☎ 2731 027 350, *Thermopylon 93*) Chicken €2.95, pork €3.55, lamb €3.85. Owner Theodoros is another Spartan restaurateur who has spent time in Canada. His speciality is spit roast meats and salads.

Zeus Restaurant (☎ 2731 022 665, *Palaeologou 72-76*) Mains €3.10-10.10. Prices at this elegant restaurant, next to Hotel Maniatis, are much more reasonable than the decor suggests. The air-conditioning is welcome on a hot day.

Basilopoulou (☎ 2731 081 751, *Cnr Thermopylon & Gortsologlou*) Self-caterers will find a super-abundance of supermarkets in Sparta. This one, opposite the Sparta Inn, is bigger and better stocked than most.

Getting There & Away

Sparta's well organised, modern bus station (☎ 2731 026 441) is at the east end of Lykourgou. Departures are displayed in English on a large information board above the entrance outside. They include 10 buses daily to Athens (3¼ hours, €12.05) via Corinth (two hours, €8.25), five daily to Gythio (one hour, €2.50), four to Neapoli (three hours, €8.25) and Tripolis (1¼ hours, €3.25), and three to Geraki (45 minutes, €2.35) and Monemvasia (2½ hours, €5.90).

There is a service to Kalamata (2½ hours, €3.25, two daily), which involves changing buses at Artemisia (€1.90) on the Messinian side of the Langada Pass.

Departures to the Mani Peninsula include buses to Gerolimenas (three hours, €6, two daily) via Areopoli (two hours, €4.10) and a 9am service to the caves at Pyrgos Dirou (2¼ hours, €4.70).

There are also 12 buses daily to Mystras (30 minutes, €0.80). You can catch these on their way out to Mystras, at the stop next to the OTE building on Lykourgou or at the stop on Leonidou.

MYSTRAS Μυστράς

The captivating ruins of the once-awesome town of Mystras (miss-**trahss**), crowned by an imposing fortress, spills from a spur of Mt Taygetos.

History

The fortress of Mystras was built by Guillaume de Villehardouin in 1249. When the Byzantines won back the Morea from the Franks, Emperor Michael VIII Paleologus made Mystras its capital and seat of government. It soon became populated by people from the surrounding plains seeking refuge from the invading Slavs. From this time until the last despot, Dimitrios, surrendered to the Turks in 1460, a despot of Morea (usually a son or brother of the ruling Byzantine emperor) lived and reigned at Mystras.

While the empire plunged into decline elsewhere, Mystras enjoyed a renaissance under the despots. A school of humanistic philosophy was founded by Gemistos Plethon (1355–1452). His enlightened ideas attracted intellectuals from all corners of Byzantium. After Mystras was ceded to the Turks, Plethon's pupils moved to Rome and Florence where they made a significant contribution to the Italian Renaissance. Art and architecture also flourished, seen in the splendid buildings and vibrant frescoes of Mystras.

Mystras declined under Turkish rule. It was captured by the Venetians in 1687 and thrived again with a flourishing silk industry and a growing population of 40,000. It was recaptured by the Turks in 1715, and from then on it was downhill all the way. Mystras was burned by the Russians in 1770, by the Albanians in 1780 and by Ibrahim Pasha in 1825. By the time of independence, it was in a very sorry state, virtually abandoned and in ruins. Much restoration has taken place since the 1950s, and Mystras was added to the World Heritage list in 1989.

Exploring the Site

A whole day is needed to do justice to the ruins of Mystras (☎ 2731 0 83 377; *admission €3.55; open 8am-6pm summer, 8am-3.30pm winter*). Wear sensible shoes, bring

MYSTRAS

Agios
Theodoros

Aphentiko

Evangelistria

Episcopal
Palace

Vrontokhion
Monastery

Museum

Nafplio
Gate

Palace of
the Despots

Lower
Entrance

Upper
Entrance

Small
Palace

Mitropolis
(Cathedral of
Agios Dimitrios)

LOWER
TOWN

Vaulted
Passage

Agia
Sofia

Agios
Hristoforos

Agios
Nikolaos

Monemvasia
Gate

Laskaris
Mansion

Marmara
Fountain

UPPER
TOWN

Agios
Georgios

Convent of
Pantanassa

Kastro
(621m)

Taxiarhes

House of
Frangopoulos

Monastery
of Perivleptos

To Nea Mystras
& Sparta

0   50   100m
0   50   100yd

plenty of water and begin at the upper entrance to the site to walk down, rather than
uphill. The site is divided into three sections – the **kastro** (the fortress on the summit), the **upper town** (hora) and the **lower
town** (kato hora).

Kastro & Upper Town From opposite the
upper entrance ticket office, a path (signposted 'kastro') leads up to the fortress. The
fortress was built by the Franks and extended by the Turks. The path descending
from the ticket office leads to **Agia Sofia**,
which served as the palace church – some

frescoes survive. Steps descend from here to
a T-junction. A left turn leads to the **Nafplio
Gate**, which was the main entrance to the
town. Near the gate is the huge **Palace of the
Despots**, a complex of several buildings
constructed at different times. The vaulted
audience room, the largest of the palace's
buildings, was added in the 14th century. Its
facade is painted, and its window frames are
very ornate, but hundreds of years of neglect
have robbed it of its former opulence.

From the palace, a winding, cobbled path
leads down to the **Monemvasia Gate**, the
entrance to the lower town.

Lower Town Through the Monemvasia gate, turn right for the well-preserved, 14th-century **Convent of Pantanassa**. The nuns who live here are Mystras' only inhabitants. The building has beautiful stone-carved ornamentation on its facade and the capitals of its columns. It's an elaborate, perfectly proportioned building – never overstated. Exquisite, richly coloured, 15th-century frescoes are among the finest examples of late Byzantine art. There is a wonderful view of the pancake-flat and densely cultivated plain of Lakonia from the columned terrace on the northern facade.

The path continues down to the **Monastery of Perivleptos**, built into a rock. Inside, the 14th-century frescoes equal those of Pantanassa and have been preserved virtually intact. Each scene is an entity, enclosed in a simple symmetrical shape. The overall effect is of numerous icons, placed next to one another, relating a visual narrative. The church has a very high dome. In the centre is the Pantokrator, surrounded by the apostles, and the Virgin flanked by two angels.

As you continue down towards the Mitropolis, you will pass **Agios Georgios**, one of Mystras' many private chapels. Farther down and above the path on the left is the **Laskaris Mansion**, a typical Byzantine house where the ground floor was used as stables and the upper floor was the residence.

The **Mitropolis** (Cathedral of Agios Dimitrios) consists of a complex of buildings enclosed by a high wall. The original church was built in the 13th century but was greatly altered in the 15th century. The church stands in an attractive courtyard surrounded by stoas and balconies. Its impressive ecclesiastical ornaments and furniture include a carved marble iconostasis, an intricately carved wooden throne and a marble slab in the floor in which is carved a two-headed eagle (symbol of Byzantium) – located exactly on the site where Emperor Constantine XI was crowned. The church also has some fine frescoes. The adjoining **museum** houses fragments of sculpture and pottery taken from Mystras' churches.

Beyond the Mitropolis is the **Vrontokhion Monastery**. This was once the wealthiest monastery of Mystras, the focus of cultural activities and the burial place of the despots. Of its two churches, **Agios Theodoros** and **Aphentiko**, the latter is the most impressive, with striking frescoes.

Outside the lower entrance to Mystras is a *kantina* (mobile cafe) selling snacks and fresh orange juice.

Places to Stay
Camping Paleologio Mystras *(☎ 2731 022 724, fax 2731 025 256, 2km west of Sparta)* Adult/tent €3.55/3.25. Open year-round. This friendly, well-organised site, with a swimming pool, is west of Sparta on the road to Mystras. Buses to Mystras can drop you off there.

Castle View Camping *(☎ 2731 083 303, fax 2731 020 028, 3km west of Sparta)* Adult/tent €4.70/2.65. Open Apr-Oct. This is another good option, located 1km closer to Mystras on the road from Sparta.

Hotel Byzantion *(☎ 2731 083 309, fax 2731 020 019)* Singles/doubles/triples with bath €29.35/44/52.80. Right in the centre of Mystras on the road from Sparta, this place looks all the better for a recent facelift, and offers rooms equipped with air-con and TV.

There are also several *domatia* around the village.

Getting There & Away
Frequent buses go to Mystras from Sparta (see the Getting There & Away section for Sparta). A taxi from Sparta to Mystras' lower entrance costs €5.90, or €7.35 to the upper entrance.

ANAVRYTI Ανάβρυτι
postcode 231 00 • pop 300
The pretty little mountain village of Anavryti, 12km south-west of Sparta, stands in magnificent isolation on a small plateau hidden away in the foothills of the Taygetos Range. At an altitude of more than 900m, the air is delightfully cool and fresh, and the high peaks of the surrounding mountains are so close that you can almost reach out and touch them.

It was once a substantial town of more than 3000 people, but it suffered badly at the hands of the Germans during WWII and during the subsequent years of the Greek civil war, prompting most residents to pack their bags for the US or Canada.

Most visitors come to Anavryti for the trekking. The E4 trans-European trail passes through the village on the way from Mystras to the EOS Taygetos shelter, farther up the mountain at an altitude of 1650m. The section above Anavryti should only be attempted by properly equipped, experienced trekkers. But the Anavryti–Mystras section is relatively straightforward and clearly marked with the E4's distinctive black-on-yellow signs. You'll need a decent pair of hiking boots and drinking water.

The best approach is to catch a bus up to Anavryti from Sparta (40 minutes, €1.35) and walk back down. There are buses from Sparta at 6.30am and 1.55pm on Monday, Thursday and Saturday. The walk back to Mystras takes about two hours.

Places to Stay & Eat
Hotel Anavryti (☎ 2731 021 788) Singles/doubles with bath €14.70/20.55. The owner of this hotel speaks English and can help with trekking directions. The hotel also has a restaurant.

LANGADA PASS
The 59km Sparta-Kalamata road is one of the most stunning routes in Greece, crossing the Taygetos Mountains by way of the Langada Pass.

The climb begins in earnest at the village of **Trypi**, 9km west of Sparta, where the road enters the dramatic **Langada Gorge**. To the north of this gorge is the site where the ancient Spartans threw babies too weak or deformed to become good soldiers.

From Trypi, the road follows the course of the Langada River for a while before climbing sharply through a series of hairpin bends to emerge in a sheltered valley. This is a good spot to stop for a stroll among the plane trees along the river bank. The road then climbs steeply once more to the high point of 1524m – crossing the boundary

from Lakonia into Messinia on the way. You can stop overnight here (see the Places to Stay section).

The descent to Kalamata is equally dramatic, although the area will take a long time to recover from the devastating forest fires of 1998.

Travelling this route by bus involves changing buses at Artemisia, the closest Messinian settlement to the summit.

Places to Stay & Eat
Pandoheio Canadas (☎ 2721 099 281, 2721 022 436, 22km from Sparta) Singles/doubles/triples with bath €14.70/20.55/23.50. This small guest house is perched on the upper slopes of the Taygetos mountains at an altitude of 1250m. As the name suggests, it's run by a Greek-Canadian couple. The restaurant is a major attraction, turning out delicious bean soup (€2.35). Specialities include the home-cured smoked pork (€3.85) and the home-made pork sausages (€2.35).

Hotel Taygetos (☎ 2721 099 236, fax 2721 098 198, 24km from Sparta) Singles/doubles with bath €23.50/29.35. The Taygetos has a superb location at the very top of the Langada Pass. It also boasts a good restaurant with specialities like rooster with red wine (€4.70), roast goat (€5.30) and rabbit stifado (€5.60).

GEFYRA & MONEMVASIA
Γέφυρα & Μονεμβασία
postcode 230 70 • pop 900
Monemvasia (mo-nem-vah-**see**-ah), 99km south-east of Sparta, is the Gibraltar of Greece – a massive rock rising dramatically from the sea just off the east coast. It is reached by a causeway from the mainland village of Gefyra (also called Nea Monemvasia). In summer, Gefyra and Monemvasia brim with tourists, but the extraordinary impact of the first encounter with the medieval town of Monemvasia – and the delights of exploring it – override the effects of mass tourism. The poet Yiannis Ritsos, who was born and lived for many years in Monemvasia, wrote of it: 'This scenery is as harsh as silence'.

PELOPONNESE

From Gefyra, Monemvasia is a huge rock topped by a fortress with a few buildings scattered at sea level. But cross the causeway and follow the road that curves around the side of the rock and you will come to a narrow tunnel in a massive fortifying wall. The tunnel is L-shaped so you cannot see the other side until you emerge, blinking, into the magical town of Monemvasia, concealed until that moment. Unlike Mystras, Monemvasia's houses are inhabited, mostly by weekenders from Athens.

History
The island of Monemvasia was part of the mainland until it was separated by an earthquake in AD 375. Its name means 'single entry' (*moni* – single, *emvasia* – entry), as there is only one way to the medieval town.

During the 6th century, barbarian incursions forced inhabitants of the surrounding area to retreat to this natural rock fortress. By the 13th century, it had become the principal commercial centre of Byzantine Morea – complementary to Mystras, the spiritual centre. It was famous throughout Europe for its highly praised Malvasia (or Malmsey) wine.

Later came a succession of invasions from Franks, Venetians and Turks. During the War of Independence, its Turkish inhabitants were massacred on their surrender following a three month siege.

Orientation & Information
All the practicalities are located in Gefyra. The main street is 23 Iouliou, which runs south around the coast from the causeway, while Spartis runs north up the coast and becomes the road to Molai. Malvasia Travel, just up from the causeway on Spartis, acts as the bus stop. The post office and the National Bank of Greece are opposite. The OTE is at the top of 28 Oktovriou, which runs inland off 23 Iouliou. The police (☎ 2732 061 210) are at 137 Spartis.

Medieval Town
You can find everything you want in this city – except water.

18th-century Turkish traveller

The narrow, cobbled main street is lined with souvenir shops and tavernas, flanked by winding stairways that weave between a complex network of stone houses with walled gardens and courtyards. The main street leads to the central square and the **Cathedral of Christ in Chains**, dating from the 13th century. Opposite is the **Church of Agios Pavlos**, built in 956. A new **museum** was under construction next door at the time of research. Farther along the main street is the **Church of Mirtidiotissa**, virtually in ruins, but still with a small altar and a defiantly flickering candle. Overlooking the sea is the recently restored, whitewashed 16th-century **Church of Panagia Hrysaphitissa**.

The path to the **fortress** and the upper town is signposted up the steps to the left near the entrance to the old town. The upper town is now a vast and fascinating jumbled ruin, except for the **Church of Agia Sophia**, which perches on the edge of a sheer cliff.

Monemvasia Archaeological Museum
This small museum (☎ *2732 061 403, admission free, 8.30am-3pm Tues-Sun*) houses finds unearthed in the course of excavation and building around the old town. The star turn is the *templon* (chancel screen) from an 11th-century church near the sea gate. Other pieces of note include a marble door frame from the Church of Hagia Sofia.

Places to Stay – Budget
Camping Paradise (☎ *2732 061 123, fax 2732 061 680,* e *paradise@otenet.gr*) Adult/tent €4.30/2.80. This pleasant, well-shaded camping ground is on the coast 3.5km south of Gefyra. It's right next to a beach and it has its own minimarket, bar and disco as well as big screen cable TV. The site is open all year.

The best places are in Monemvasia but there is no budget accommodation. There are plenty more hotels and numerous *domatia* in Gefyra.

Hotel Akrogiali (☎ *2732 061 360*) Singles/ doubles with shower €17.60/26.40. This basic hotel, next to the National Bank of

Greece on Spartis, has the cheapest rooms in town.

Hotel Monemvasia (☎ *2732 061 381, fax 2732 061 707)* Singles/doubles with bath €23.50/35.20. This small modern hotel is 500m north of town on the road to Molai. It has large balconies looking out to sea to Monemvasia, and prices include breakfast.

Places to Stay – Mid-Range & Top End
If you've got money to spend, Monemvasia is a good place to spend it. There's a range of impeccably restored traditional settlements to choose from. Bookings are recommended, especially at weekends.

Malvasia Hotel (☎ *2732 061 113/323, fax 2732 061 722)* Singles €32.30, doubles with bath €38.15-47, triples €52.85-102.70. The Malvasia has some beautifully furnished rooms spread around several locations in the old town. All prices include a generous breakfast. It has an inquiries office on the main 'street'.

Byzantino (☎ *2732 061 254, fax 2732 061 331)* Doubles with/without view from €58.70/41.10. The set-up here is similar to the Malvasia, with rooms (all with private bath) spread around the old town. It also has an inquiries office on the main street.

Kellia (☎ *2732 061 520, fax 2732 061 767)* Singles/doubles/triples/quads with bathroom €35.20/79.25/93.95/123.25. The Kellia occupies a converted monastery down by the sea next to the Church of Panagia Hrysaphitissa. Formerly run by EOT, this place has now been transferred to private ownership – and looks all the better for the change. Breakfast is €5.90.

Places to Eat
Taverna O Botsalo (☎ *2732 061 486, 23 Iouliou 46, Gefyra)* Mains €3.85-6.45. This taverna has a good location overlooking Gefyra's small port, and tasty, reasonably priced dishes.

T'Agnantio Taverna (☎ *2732 061 754, Gefyra)* Mains €3.85-11.75. T'Agnantio is a small place on the southern edge of town with a strong local following.

To Kanoni (☎ *2732 061 387, main street, Monemvasia)* Mains €4.70-15.20. To Kanoni boasts an imaginative and extensive menu. Its specialities include *stamna* (stew with cheese baked in a clay pot, €6.75) and hearty fish soup (€5.30).

Self-caterers will find most things at the *Lefkakis Supermarket* (☎ *2732 061 167)* behind the post office in Gefyra. It also stocks international newspapers.

Getting There & Away
Bus Buses leave from outside Malvasia Travel (☎ 2732 061 752), which also sells tickets. There are four buses daily to Athens (5½ hours, €17.75) via Sparta (two hours, €5.90), Tripolis and Corinth. The 4.10am departure is an express service (4½ hours, €13.20).

Hydrofoil In summer, there is at least one Flying Dolphin service daily to Zea Marina at Piraeus (four hours, €27.60), travelling via Leonidio, Spetses and Hydra. There are also four services a week south to Kythira (three hours). Buy tickets from Angelakos Travel (☎ 2732 061 219), by the petrol station on the Monemvasia side of the causeway.

Getting Around
The medieval town of Monemvasia is inaccessible to cars and motorcycles, and cars are not allowed across the causeway between June and September. Parking is available outside the old town at other times. A free shuttle bus operates between the causeway and old Monemvasia 7.30am and 10pm from June to September.

Cars can be hired from Christos Rent Car & Moto (☎ 2732 061 581, fax 2732 071 661) on 23 Iouliou. Brother Mihailis (☎ 2732 061 173), opposite, rents motorcycles.

NEAPOLI Νεάπολη
postcode 230 70 • pop 2500
Neapoli (neh-**ah**-po-lih), 42km south of Monemvasia, lies close to the southern tip of the eastern prong of the Peloponnese. It's a fairly uninspiring town, in spite of its location on a huge horseshoe bay. The western

flank of the bay is formed by the small island of Elafonisi. Few travellers make it down this far, but the town is popular enough with local holiday-makers to have three seafront hotels and several domatia. Most travellers come here only to catch a ferry to the island of Kythira, clearly visible across the bay.

Getting There & Away

Bus There are four buses daily from Neapoli to Sparta (three hours, €8.25) via Molai (1¼ hours, €4), which is the place to change buses for Monemvasia.

Ferry There are daily ferries going from Neapoli to Agia Pelagia on Kythira (one hour, €4.70). Tickets are sold at Alexandrakis Shipping (☎ 2734 022 940, fax 2734 023 590), Akti Voiou 160, opposite the ferry quay.

GYTHIO Γύθειο
postcode 232 00 • pop 4900

Once the port of ancient Sparta, Gythio (**yee**-thih-o) is the gateway to the Lakonian Mani. It's an attractive fishing town with a bustling waterfront of pastel-coloured, 19th-century buildings, behind which crumbling old Turkish houses clamber up a steep, wooded hill.

Orientation

Gythio is not too hard to figure out. Most things of importance to travellers are along the seafront on Akti Vasileos Pavlou. The bus station is at the north-eastern end, next to the small triangular park known as the Perivolaki – meaning 'tree-filled'.

Vasileos Georgiou runs inland past the main square, Plateia Panagiotou Venetzanaki, and becomes the road to Sparta.

The square which is at the south-western end of Akti Vasileos Pavlou is Plateia Mavromihali, the hub of the old quarter of Marathonisi. The ferry quay is situated opposite this square. Beyond it, the waterfront road becomes Kranais, which leads south to the road to Areopoli. A causeway leads out to Marathonisi Islet at the southern edge of town.

Information

The EOT tourist office (☎/fax 2733 024 484) is about 500m north of the waterfront at Vasileos Georgiou 20. Apart from a couple of brochures, it's fairly information-free, even by EOT's own lamentable standards. For the record, it's open 11am to 3pm Monday to Friday. The tourist police (☎ 2733 022 271) and regular police (☎ 2733 022 100) share offices on the waterfront between the bus station and Plateia Mavromihali.

The post office is on Ermou, two blocks north of the bus station, and the OTE office is between the two at the corner of Irakleos and Kapsali. Travellers can access email at Electron Computers (☎ 2733 022 120), Kapsali 5. It charges €4.40 per hour, with a minimum of €0.90. Despite being opposite the OTE, poor lines are a major problem here – as everywhere in Gythio. Open 8am to 9pm Monday to Saturday.

International newspapers are available from Hassanakos Bookstore (☎ 2733 022 064), Vasileos Pavlou 39, below the Hotel Aktaion.

The Sea Turtle Protection Society runs an information tent next to the ferry quay from mid-June until the end of September. It has films and displays about turtle nesting sites on the beaches of the Lakonian Gulf east of Gythio.

Marathonisi Islet

According to mythology, tranquil pine-shaded Marathonisi is ancient Cranae where Paris (prince of Troy) and Helen (wife of Menelaus) consummated the affair that sparked the Trojan Wars. The 18th-century Tzanetakis Grigorakis tower at the centre of the island houses a small **museum** (☎ 2733 024 484; admission €1.50; open 9am-7pm) which relates Maniot history through the eyes of European travellers who visited the region between the 15th and 19th centuries. The top floor has a fascinating collection of plans of Maniot towers and castles.

Ancient Theatre

Gythio's small but well-preserved ancient theatre is next to an army camp on the northern edge of town. It's signposted off Plateia Panagiotou Venetzanaki along Arheou Theatrou. You can scramble up the hill behind the theatre to get to the **ancient acropolis**, now heavily overgrown. Most of ancient Gythio lies beneath the nearby Lakonian Gulf.

Beaches

There's safe swimming off the 6km of sandy beaches which extend from the village of **Mavrovouni**, 2km south of Gythio.

Places to Stay – Budget

Camping Meltemi (☎ 2733 022 833, fax 2733 023 833, 3km south-west of Gythio) Adult/tent €4.40/3.85. Open year-round. This very well organised place is the pick of the three camping grounds at Mavrovouni, south-west of Gythio. It's right behind the beach and sites are set among 3000 olive trees. Buses to Areopoli stop outside.

Camping Porto Ageranos (☎ 2733 093 469, fax 2733 093 239; Vathy, 8km south-west of Gythio) Adult/tent €4.40/3.25. This camping ground is harder to get to without your own transport. It offers good shady sites on an excellent beach, and is signposted off the road to Aeropolis.

Xenia Karlaftis Rooms to Rent (☎ 2733 022 719) Singles/doubles/triples with bath €20.55/26.40/29.35. This is the best budget option in town, situated opposite Marathonisi Islet on Kranais. There's a communal kitchen area upstairs with a fridge and small stove for making tea and coffee. Manager Voula (daughter of Xenia) is a wonderful host, full of suitably laconic observations about life. Voula also has studios for rent 3km west of town, beyond Mavrovouni.

Koutsouris Rooms to Rent (☎ 2733 022 321) Singles/doubles with bath €14.70/20.55, family room €23.50. This quaint old-style place is run by a retired merchant navy captain and his wife. It's a long-standing favourite with independent travellers. To get there, walk up Tzannibi Gregoraki from Plateia Mavromihali, turn right at the church with the clock tower onto Moretti and the rooms are on the left.

Saga Pension (☎ 2733 023 220, fax 2733 024 370, 150m from the port on Kranais) Singles/doubles with bath €20.55/29.35. The French-run Saga is also good value for comfortable rooms with air-con and TV.

Places to Stay – Middle & Top End

Hotel Kranai (☎/fax 2733 024 394, @ kranai@forthnet.gr, Akti Vasileos Pavlou 17). Singles with bath €35.20, doubles with bath €38.15-47. The Kranai is an attractive older-style place with rooms overlooking the port.

Hotel Aktaion (☎ 2733 023 500/501, fax 2733 022 294, Akti Vasileos Pavlou 39) Doubles with bath €58.70, suites €73.40. This beautifully restored neoclassical building boasts the finest facade in town. It also has the best rooms. Breakfast is €5.

Places to Eat

Seafood is the obvious choice, and the waterfront is lined with numerous fish tavernas – especially on Kranais, where tourists walk the gauntlet of waiters touting for custom.

Psarotaverna I Kozia (☎ 2733 024 086, Akti Vasileos Pavlou 11) Mains €4.40-5.90. There are no touts at this place, between Rozakis Travel and the Hotel Kranai, just lots of locals tucking into plates of grilled octopus (€4.40), calamari (€3.55) and other treats over a glass or two of ouzo.

Taverna Petakou (☎ 2733 022 889, beside stadium on Xanthaki) Mains €2.65-5.30. The Petakou is another favourite with locals. There are no frills here. The day's menu is written down in an exercise book in Greek. It may include a hearty fish soup (€5.30), which comes with a large chunk of fish on the side.

Oinomagereion O Potis (☎ 2733 024 253, Moretti 5) Mains €2.95-8.25. This cheerful place is a welcome addition to the restaurant scene. It has an interesting menu with a good selection of salads. It's just uphill from Plateia Mavromihali, at the corner of Tzannibi Gregoraki and Moretti.

General Store & Wine Bar (☎ 2733 024 113, Vasileos Georgiou 67) Mains €5.30-10.30. For something completely different,

PELOPONNESE

head inland to this tiny restaurant run by the Greek-Canadian Thomakos family. You'll find an unusually varied and imaginative menu featuring dishes like orange and pumpkin soup (€2.95) and fillet of pork with black pepper and ouzo (€10.30).

There are several supermarkets, including *Kourtakis*, around the corner from the bus station on Irakleos, and *Karagiannis (Cnr Vasileos Georgiou & Orestou)*.

The *laïki agora* (street market) is along Ermou on Tuesday and Friday morning.

Getting There & Away

Bus Bus station (☎ 2733 022 228). There are buses heading south to Areopoli (30 minutes, €1.65, four daily); Athens (4¼ hours, €14.10, five daily) via Sparta (one hour, €2.50); Gerolimenas (two hours, €3.55, two daily); the Diros Caves (one hour, €2.20, one daily); and Vatheia (1¼ hours, €4, one daily). Getting to Kalamata can be hard work, and involves changing buses at Itilo (45 minutes, €2.35). There are only two buses daily (6am and 1pm) to Itilo.

Ferry ANEK Lines operates services from Gythio to Kastelli-Kissamou on Crete, travelling via Kythira, between June and September. The schedule is subject to constant change, so check with Rozakis Travel (☎ 2733 022 207, fax 2733 022 229, ℮ rosakigy@otenet.gr), on the waterfront near Plateia Mavromihali, before coming here to catch a boat.

Getting Around

Rozakis Travel (see Ferry earlier) hires cars. Mopeds and scooters are available from Moto Makis (☎ 2733 022 950) on Kranais.

The Mani Η Μάνη

The region referred to as the Mani covers the central peninsula in the south of the Peloponnese. For centuries, the Maniots were a law unto themselves, renowned for their fierce independence and resentment of any attempt to govern them.

Today, the Maniots are regarded by other Greeks as independent, royalist and right-wing. But don't be deterred from visiting the region by descriptions of the Maniots as hostile, wild and hard people. Contact with the outside world and lack of feuding have mellowed them. The Maniots are as friendly and hospitable as Greeks elsewhere, despite the fierce appearance of some older people who dress like the Cretans and offer fiery *raki* (a spirit) as a gesture of hospitality.

The Mani is generally divided into the Messinian Mani (also called the outer Mani) and the Lakonian (or inner) Mani. The Messinian Mani starts south-east of Kalamata and runs south between the coast and the Taygetos Mountains, while the Lakonian Mani covers the rest of the peninsula south of Itilo. Such was the formidable reputation of the inhabitants of the remote inner Mani that foreign occupiers thought they were best left alone.

The Mani has no significant ancient sites, but it well compensates with medieval and later remains, bizarre tower settlements – particularly in the inner Mani – built as refuges from clan wars from the 17th century on, and magnificent churches, all enhanced by the distant presence of the towering peaks of the Taygetos Mountains. The Diros Caves in the south are also a major attraction.

History

The people of the Mani regard themselves as direct descendants of the Spartans. After the decline of Sparta, citizens loyal to the principles of Lycurgus, founder of Sparta's constitution, chose to withdraw to the mountains rather than serve under foreign masters. Later, refugees from occupying powers joined these people who became known as Maniots, from the Greek word *mania*.

The Maniots claim they are the only Greeks not to have succumbed to foreign invasions. This may be somewhat exaggerated but the Maniots have always enjoyed a certain autonomy and a distinctive lifestyle. Until independence, the Maniots lived in clans led by chieftains. Fertile land was so scarce that it was fiercely fought over.

blood feuds were a way of life and families constructed towers as refuges.

The Turks failed to subdue the Maniots, who eagerly participated in the War of Independence. But, after 1834, although reluctant to relinquish their independence, they became part of the new kingdom.

For background reading, try *Mani* by Patrick Leigh Fermor, *Deep into Mani* by Eliopoulis & Greenhold and *The Architecture of Mani* by Ioannis Saïtis.

The Mani by long-time Stoupa resident Bob Barrow is worth seeking out in local shops if you're planning on doing any exploring. Bob manages Thomeas Travel in Stoupa, and spends all his spare time exploring the Mani. His self-published guide is full of little gems of information about the region's villages, towers and churches.

LAKONIAN MANI

Grey rock, mottled with defiant clumps of green scrub, characterises the bleak mountains of inner Mani. Land that's suitable for cultivation is at a premium, and even that is incapable of supporting much more that a few stunted olives and figs. A curious anomaly is the profusion of wild flowers which mantle the valleys in spring, exhibiting nature's resilience by sprouting from the rocks.

The indented coast's sheer cliffs plunge into the sea and rocky outcrops shelter pebbled beaches. This wild and barren landscape is broken only by austere and imposing stone towers, mostly abandoned, but still standing sentinel over the region. Restoration of Maniot buildings is increasing and many refugee Albanians, who are fine stonemasons, have been engaged on these projects.

Equipped with your own vehicle, you can explore the Mani by the loop road that runs down the west coast from the main town, Areopoli, to Gerolimenas, and returns via the east coast. Public transport is effectively limited to the west coast.

Areopoli Αρεόπολη
postcode 230 62 • pop 980

Areopoli (ah-reh-o-po-lih), capital of the Mani, is aptly named after Ares, the god of war. Dominating the central square is a statue of Petrobey Mavromihalis, who proclaimed the Maniot insurrection against the Turks. Konstantinos and Georgos Mavromihalis, who assassinated Kapodistrias, belonged to the same family. The town retains many other reminders of its rumbustious past.

In the narrow, cobbled streets of the old town, grim tower houses stand proudly vigilant. Stroll around during siesta time when the heat and silence make it especially evocative.

Also have a look at the unusual reliefs above the doors of the Church of Taxiarhes, on Kapetan Matapan, which depict feuding archangels and signs of the zodiac.

Orientation & Information The bus stop is in front of the Europa Grill on Plateia Athinaton, the central square. There is no tourist office or tourist police. The post office and OTE are on the corner of the square and Kapetan Matapan, the main thoroughfare through the old town that leads downhill from the square. The National Bank of Greece is on P Mavromihali – turn right at the first church on Kapetan Matapan and the bank is on the left after 150m. It's open normal banking hours in July and August, and 9am to noon on Tuesday and Thursday for the rest of the year. There's an ATM outside.

Foreign newspapers and a small selection of books are available from Konstantinakos (☎ 2733 051 253) on the main square.

Places to Stay – Budget *Tsimova Rooms* (☎ 2733 051 301, Kapetan Mapetan) Singles/doubles with bath €20.55/35.20, apartment €44. The rooms, behind the Church of Taxiarhes, are housed in a beautiful old renovated tower behind the church. Owner George Versakos has cosy rooms, filled with ornaments, family photos and icons, and a two-room apartment with kitchen. George loves to show off his private collection of daggers and pistols. You'll see a sign at the Church of Taxiarhes pointing the way.

Pyrgos Kapetanakas (☎ 2733 051 233, fax 2733 051 401) Singles/doubles/triples with

Phone numbers listed incorporate changes due in Oct 2002; see p83

PELOPONNESE

bath €29.35/41.10/49.90. This excellent place, signposted at the bottom of Kapetan Matapan, occupies the tower house built by the powerful Kapetanakas family in the 18th century. The architecture is austerely authentic, in keeping with the spirit of the Mani, but rooms are comfortably furnished and equipped with air-con. Breakfast is €3.55.

Hotel Kouris (☎ 2733 051 340, fax 2733 051 331, Plateia Athanaton) Singles/doubles with bath €29.35/41.40. The Kouris is a fairly characterless modern hotel, but a useful fallback.

Places to Stay – Top End *Londas Pension* (☎ 2733 051 360, fax 2733 051 012, ℮ londas@otenet.gr) Doubles/triples with bath €70.50/88, plus breakfast. The most stylish rooms are in this 200-year-old tower signposted right off Kapetan Matapan at the Church of Taxiarhes. The rooms have whitewashed stone walls and beamed ceilings.

Places to Eat *Nicola's Corner Taverna* (☎ 2733 051 366, Plateia Athanaton) Mains €2.95-6.45. Nicola's is a popular spot on the central square with a good choice of tasty taverna staples.

Barbar Petros (☎ 2733 051 205) Prices €2.95-5.30. This is primarily a psistaria serving grilled steak and chops, but it also has daily specials like eggplant and potato pie – €3.55 for an enormous serving.

There is a small *Koilakos supermarket* (☎ 2733 051 221, Kapetan Matapan), near the Plateia Athanaton.

Getting There & Away The bus office (☎ 2733 051 229) is inside the Europa Grill on Plateia Athinaton. There are five buses daily to Gythio (30 minutes, €1.65); three to Itilo (20 minutes, €0.80) via Limeni; two to Gerolimenas (45 minutes, €1.80) and the Diros Caves (15 minutes, €0.80); one daily to Lagia (40 minutes, €2.20) via Kotronas; and three weekly (Monday, Wednesday and Friday) to Vathia (one hour, €2.50).

Diros Caves Σπήλαιο Διρού
These extraordinary caves (☎ 2733 052 222; admission €10.90 including tour;

open 8am-5.30pm June-Sept; 8am-3p Oct-May) are 11km south of Areopoli, ne the village of Pyrgos Dirou – notable for i towers (signposted to the left off the roa down to the caves).

The natural entrance to the caves is on tl beach, and locals like to believe the leger that they extend as far north as Spar (speleologists have so far traced the cav inland for 5km). They were inhabited Neolithic times, but were abandoned aft an earthquake and weren't rediscovere until 1895. Systematic exploration began 1949. The caves are famous for their stala tites and stalagmites, which have fitting poetic names such as the Palm Forest, Cry tal Lily and the Three Wise Men.

Unfortunately, the guided tour throu the caves is disappointingly brief. It cove only the lake section, and bypasses the d section that features the most spectacul formations. The 20-minute tour isn't goc enough to justify the admission charge.

Finds from the caves are housed in tl nearby **Neolithic Museum** (☎ 2733 0. 223; admission €1.50; open 8.30am-3p Tues-Sun).

Places to Stay *To Panorama* (☎ 27. 052 280) Singles/doubles with ba €20.55/26.40. This small family-run ho is 1km south of the caves on the road Pyrgos Dirou. The comfortable rooms ha air-con and TV.

Pyrgos Dirou to Gerolimenas
Πύργος Διρού το Γερολιμένας
Journeying south down Mani's west coa from Pyrgos Dirou to Gerolimenas, the ba ren mountain landscape is broken only I deserted settlements with mighty towers. right turn 9km south of Pyrgos Dirou lea down to the **Bay of Mezapos**, sheltered the east by the frying pan shaped Tiga Peninsula. The ruins on the peninsula a those of the **Castle of Maina**, built by tl Frankish leader Guillaume de Vill hardouin in 1248, and subsequently adapte by the Byzantines.

Kita, 13km south of Pyrgos Dirou, po itively bristles with the ruins of its wa wers and fortified houses. It was the setting for the last great inter-family feud corded in the Mani. It erupted in 1870 d required the intervention of the army, mplete with artillery, to force the sides come to a truce.

laces to Stay *Tsitsiris Castle Guest ouse* (☎ *2733 056 297, fax 2733 056 296, avri*) Singles/doubles with bath €41.10/ 1.90, buffet breakfast included. Although 7km separates Pyrgos Dirou and Geroli-enas, this is the only place to stay in be-veen. The 'castle' is a restored tower use on the edge of the village. The castle us its own restaurant with home-cooked eals at standard taverna prices. The guest-use is signposted off the main road 4km rth of Gerolimenas.

erolimenas Γερολιμένας
stcode 230 71 • pop 250
erolimenas (yeh-ro-lih-**meh**-nahss) is a anquil fishing village built around a small, eltered bay at the south-western tip of the ninsula.

laces to Stay & Eat *Hotel Akrotenari-
s* (☎ *2733 054 205*) Singles/doubles with th €14.70/29.35. This is a good budget tion. All the rooms are equipped with air-n, and some have views over the harbour. also has a restaurant.

Hotel Akrogiali (☎ *2733 054 204, fax 733 054 272*) Singles/doubles with bath 23.50/35.20, apartments €47. Hotel krogiali has a great setting overlooking e bay on the way into town. It has a good oice of rooms, all with air-conditioning, nging from standard doubles in the orig-al hotel building to 'superior' rooms set a new wing, beautifully crafted from cal stone. The owners also rent out four-rson apartments nearby. Breakfast costs 3.55.

There is a small *supermarket* facing the rbour on the road into town.

etting There & Away There are buses om Gerolimenas to Sparta (2¼ hours, 6), Gythio (1¼ hours, €3.55) and Are-

opoli (45 minutes, €1.80). The Hotel Akrotenaritis acts as the bus station.

Gerolimenas to Porto Kagio
Γερολιμένας to Πόρτο Κάγιο
South of Gerolimenas, the road continues 4km to the small village of Alika, where it divides. One road leads east to Lagio and the other goes south to Vathia and Porto Kagio. The southern road follows the coast, passing pebbly beaches. It then climbs steeply inland to **Vathia**, the most dramatic of the traditional Mani villages, comprising a cluster of closely packed tower houses perched on a rocky spur.

A turn-off to the right 9km south of Alika leads to two sandy beaches at Marmari, while the main road cuts across the penin-sula to the tiny east coast fishing village of **Porto Kagio**, set on a perfect horseshoe bay.

Places to Stay & Eat *Akroteri Domatia* (☎/*fax 2733 052 013, Porto Kagio*) Doubles with bath €29.35-38.15. This is a great place to hang for a few days. The rooms are large and have balconies overlooking the bay. The only decision to make is whether to eat at the Akroteri's own restaurant, or at one of its two rivals on the beachfront. Not surprisingly, all specialise in fish.

Vathia Towers The magnificent towers at Vathia were once part of a government-run traditional hotel, which closed several years ago for renovation. Sadly, the place remains closed – with no indication of reno-vation work in progress and no clues as to when it might reopen.

Lagio to Kotronas Λάγια to
Κότρωνας
Lagio was once the chief town of the south-eastern Mani. Perched 400m above sea level, it's a formidable looking place, espe-cially when approached from Alika.

From Lagio, the road winds down with spectacular views of the little fishing har-bour of **Agios Kyprianos** – a short diversion from the main road. The next village is **Kokala**, a busy, friendly place with two pebbled beaches. The bus stop is in front of Synantisi Taverna.

PELOPONNESE

Once through Kokala, the road climbs again. After 4km, there are more beaches at the sprawling village of **Nyfi**. A turn-off to the right leads to the sheltered beach of **Alipa**. Continuing north, a turn-off beyond Flomohori descends to Kotronas.

Places to Stay & Eat Accommodation on the east coast is disappointing – there is nothing that can be recommended with enthusiasm. Lagio has nothing, but there are possibilities in Kokala.

Pension Kokala (☎ 2733 021 107) Singles/doubles with bath €17.60/23.50. Open May-Oct. This small modernish pension is conveniently located on the main street in the middle of the village.

To Kastro Pension (☎ 2733 021 090) Doubles from €29.35. You'll see signs promoting this pension, formerly *Papa's Rooms*, all the way down the east coast. The place is perched high above the village, reached by a steep concrete road leading up the hill next to Hotel Soleteri.

Marathos Taverna (*North of Kokala*) Mains €2.95-7.35, fresh fish from €26.40. Open May-Oct. The Marathos is the best thing in Kokala, with good food and a great setting right on the beach. The road down to the taverna is signposted on the northern edge of the village.

Kotronas Κοτρώνας
pop 600
Around Kotronas the barrenness of the Mani gradually gives way to relatively lush hillsides, with olive groves and cypress trees. Kotronas bustles compared with the Mani's half-deserted tower villages. Its main thoroughfare leads to the waterfront where the bus turns around. To the left is a bay with a small, sandy beach. The post office is on the right of the main thoroughfare as you face towards the sea. The islet off the coast is linked by a causeway. Walk inland along the main thoroughfare and turn left at the fork. Take the first left and walk to a narrow road, which soon degenerates into a path, leading to the causeway. On the island are ruins surrounding a small, well-kept church.

Places to Stay & Eat There are two place of note in Kotronas.

Adelfia Pension (☎ 2733 021 209) Single doubles €14.70/17.60. This small family run pension is on the right of the main road as you head towards the sea.

Kotronas Bay Bungalows (☎ 2733 02 340, fax 2733 021 402) Bungalows €9 These bungalows are 500m east of the village on the road that skirts the bay. The can accommodate up to four people an come with fully equipped kitchens.

There are two *minimarkets* and a *baker* on the main street.

Kotronas to Skoutari
The upgrading of the coast road from Kotronas to Skoutari, 14km to the north east, means that it's now possible to com plete a circuit of the Mani without doublin back to Areopoli.

Skoutari is a quiet little village over looking pretty Skoutari Bay, which term nates in a long sandy beach with a sma summer *psarotaverna*. There are *domati* in the village. There's a good sealed roa from Skoutari to the Gythio-Areopoli roac about 5km to the north.

Limeni Λιμένι
The tiny village of Limeni is 3km north c Areopoli on the southern flank of beautif Limeni Bay.

Places to Stay & Eat The village prope has *domatia* and a *taverna*.

Limeni Village Bungalows (☎ 2733 05 111, fax 2733 051 182, south side of Limer Bay) Singles/doubles with bath €55/7(There are spectacular views over the bay Itilo from this complex of replica Mani towers overlooking the village. Facilitie include a pool, bar and restaurant.

Itilo & Nea Itilo Οίτυλο & Νέο Οίτυλο
postcode 230 62 • pop 550
Itilo (**eet**-ih-lo), 11km north of Areopol was the medieval capital of the Mani. T travel between Lakonian and Messini Mani, you must change buses at Itilo.

The village is now a crumbling and tranquil backwater, perched on the northern edge of a deep ravine traditionally regarded as the border between outer and inner Mani. Above the ravine is the massive 17th-century **Castle of Kelefa** from which the Turks attempted to constrain the Maniots. It's on a hill above the road from Nea Itilo. Nearby, the **Monastery of Dekoulou** has colourful frescoes in its church. Nea Itilo, 4km before, lies at the back of secluded Limeni Bay.

Places to Stay Apart from a few *domatia* down by Limeni Bay in Nea Itilo, there is no budget accommodation to be found around here.

Hotel Itilo (☎ 2733 059 222, fax 2733 059 234, Limeni Bay) Singles/doubles with bath €35.20/47, including breakfast. This plush, C-class hotel is right by the beach in Nea Itilo.

Getting There & Away There are three buses daily to Areopoli (20 minutes, €0.80) and Kalamata (two hours, €4.10). Areopoli–Itilo buses go via Nea Itilo and Limeni.

MESSINIAN MANI

The Messinian Mani, or outer Mani, lies to the north of its Lakonian counterpart, sandwiched between the Taygetos Mountains and west coast of the Mani Peninsula. Kalamata lies at the northern end of the peninsula. The rugged coast is scattered with numerous small coves and beaches backed by mountains that remain snow-capped until late May. There are glorious views along the way, particularly on the descent from Stavropigi to Kardamyli and farther south around the small village of Agios Nikon.

Stoupa Στούπα
postcode 240 54 • pop 730

Stoupa, 10km south of Kardamyli, has undergone a rapid transformation from fishing village to upmarket resort. Tourist development remains fairly low-key; it's billed as a resort for discriminating package tourists intent on discovering the unspoilt Greece. Although not as picturesque as Kardamyli, it does have two lovely beaches.

Celebrated author Nikos Kazantzakis lived here for a while and based the protagonist of his novel *Zorba the Greek* on Alexis Zorbas, a coal mine supervisor in Pastrova, near Stoupa.

Orientation & Information Stoupa is 1km west of the main Areopoli-Kalamata road, connected by link roads both north and south of town. Both roads lead to the larger of Stoupa's main beaches – a glorious crescent of golden sand.

Stoupa's development has been so rapid that its amenities have yet to catch up. Katerina's supermarket, on the coast road behind the main beach, doubles as both the post office and the OTE. It sells stamps, accepts mail for delivery, changes money and sells phonecards.

There is no tourist office, but most tourists treat Thomeas Travel (☎ 2721 077 689, fax 2721 077 571, e antthom@otenet.gr) as if it were one. Manager Bob Barrow is a keen student of Mani history and a mine of information about local attractions. He can also change money, organise hire cars and advise on accommodation.

Places to Stay & Eat Stoupa's growing band of pensions and custom-built domatia all seem to be block-booked by package tour operators. Thomeas Travel may know of vacancies.

Camping Ta Delfinia (☎ 2721 077 237, fax 2721 077 318) Adult/tent €3.85/2.95. Open Mar-Oct. If you want to escape the crowds, try this site, near Kaminia Beach, 2km away on the Kardamyli side of Stoupa.

Hotel Lefktron (☎ 2721 077 322, fax 2721 077 700, e info@lefktron-hotel.gr) Singles/doubles with bath €38.15/44. The Lefktron, signposted off the southern approach road to Stoupa, is a comfortable modern hotel 150m from the beach. Rooms are equipped with fridge and air-con.

Stoupa has lots of restaurants and tavernas, none particularly cheap.

Taverna Akrogiali (☎ 2721 077 335) Mains €3.55-6.15. This taverna has a top location at the southern end of the beach, and good food.

PELOPONNESE

Katerina's Supermarket (☎ 2721 077 777, on the waterfront) carries a remarkable range of stock for a small-town supermarket. Ouzo fans will be pleased to find their favourite tipple promoted as a health food.

Getting There & Away Stoupa is on the main Itilo-Kalamata bus route. There are bus stops at the junctions of both the southern and northern approach roads, but the buses don't go into town.

Kardamyli Καρδαμύλη
postcode 240 22 • pop 350

The tiny village of Kardamyli (kah-dah-mee-lih) has one of the prettiest settings in the Peloponnese, nestled between the calm waters of the Messinian Gulf and the Taygetos Mountains. The deep Vyros Gorge, which emerges just north of town, runs straight up to the foot of Mt Profitas Ilias (2407m), the highest peak of the Taygetos. The gorge and surrounding areas are very popular with trekkers.

Kardamyli was one of the seven cities offered to Achilles by Agamemnon.

Orientation & Information Kardamyli is on the main Areopoli-Kalamata road. The bus stops at the central square, Plateia 25 Martiou 1821, at the northern end of the main thoroughfare. The post office is towards Stoupa on the main street. Koursaros Internet Café (☎ 2721 073 963) is on the street opposite the post office. It's open daily 10am to 2am, and charges €5.30 per hour with a minimum of €2.95 for 30 minutes.

Kardamyli's main pebble-and-stone beach is off the road to Kalamata; turn left beyond the bridge on the northern edge of town. The road up to Old (or Upper) Kardamyli is on the right before the bridge.

Trekking This has become Kardamyli's biggest drawcard. The hills behind the village are crisscrossed with an amazing network of colour-coded trails. All the accommodation places in the village will be able to supply you with a map that explains the routes. Most of the treks are strenuous, but

Strong footwear is essential to support your ankles on the rough ground, particularly if you venture into the boulder-strewn gorge itself. You will also need to carry plenty of drinking water.

Many treks pass through the mountain village of **Exohorio**, perched on the edge of the Vyros Gorge at an altitude of 450m. The village is also accessible by road, and it's a good place for non-trekkers to do a spot of more gentle exploration. The turn-off to Exohorio is 3km south of Kardamyli.

Places to Stay There are plenty of domatia signs along the main road. The street down to the sea opposite the post office is a good place to look.

Melitsina Camping (☎ 2721 073 461, fax 2721 073 334) Adult/tent €4/3.25. Open May-Sept. This camping ground has good shady sites at the northern end of Kardamyli's main beach. The beachfront road terminates at the gates.

Olympia Koumounakou rooms (☎ 2721 073 623/021 026) Singles/doubles with bath €17.60/26.40. This place, on the left after 150m, has double rooms with bathroom and a communal kitchen.

Stratis Bravacos rooms (☎ 2721 073 326) Doubles €35.20. Stratis has spotless studio apartments with kitchen facilities. The rooms are opposite Olympia Koumounakou.

Lela's Rooms (☎ 2721 073 541) Doubles with bath €32.30. Lela, who is the former housekeeper of author Patrick Leigh Fermor, has a great location overlooking the sea at the end of the street opposite the post office.

Anniska Apartments (☎ 2721 073 600, fax 2721 073 000) Studios/apartments from €49.90/73.40. This place, by the sea 200m north of Lela's, has a range of spacious, well-appointed studios and apartments, all with kitchen facilities. The studios sleep two people, while the larger apartments accommodate up to four people.

Vardia (☎ 2721 073 513, fax 2721 073 156) Studios/apartments from €58.70/79.25. The views are a major attraction at Vardia, which has a wonderful setting on the hillside overlooking Old Kardamyli. Like Anniska, it offers a range of fully equipped studios and apartments. Contact Dimitreas Supermarket (see Places to Eat following) for information and directions. Breakfast costs €5.90.

Places to Eat There are nine tavernas in the village, so there's no shortage of eating options.

Lela's Taverna (☎ 2721 073 541) Mains €2.95-5.90. Lela's has a fabulous setting with a terrace overlooking the sea, and taverna favourites like *gemista* (stuffed tomatoes and peppers, €3.25).

Taverna Perivolis (☎ 2721 073 713) Mains €3.55-7.35. This popular taverna is run by a friendly Greek-Australian family. It's on the left as you head towards Anniska Apartments from the main road.

Taverna Dioskouroi (☎ 2721 073 236) Mains €2.95-4.70. The Dioskouri is another local favourite, overlooking the seas from the hillside just south of town.

Dimitreas Supermarket (☎ 2721 073 513) is one of two supermarkets side by side at the northern edge of the village. It's open 7am to 9.30pm daily.

Getting There & Around Kardamyli is on the main bus route from Itilo to Kalamata (one hour, €2.20).

Early birds can catch the sole bus to Exohorio at 6.15am; most prefer to take a cab (€4.40).

Messinia Μεσσηνία

Messinia occupies the south-western corner of the Peloponnese. Its boundaries were established in 371 BC following the defeat of Sparta by the Thebans at the Battle of Leuctra. The defeat ended more than 350 years of Spartan domination of the Peloponnese, during which time Messinian exiles founded the city of Messinia in Sicily, and the Messinians were left free to develop their kingdom in the region stretching west from the Taygetos Mountains. Their capital was ancient Messini, about 25km northwest of Kalamata on the slopes of Mt Ithomi.

Few travellers make it to Messinia, which is a shame. Finikounda has one of the best beaches in the country, and the old Venetian towns of Koroni and Methoni are delightful little hideaways that have yet to feel the weight of package tourism.

KALAMATA Καλαμάτα
postcode 241 00 • pop 44,000

Kalamata is Messinia's capital and the second-largest city in the Peloponnese. 'Calamitous Kalamata' aptly sums up this hapless city. The old town was almost totally destroyed by the Turks during the War of Independence and rebuilt unimaginatively by French engineers in the 1830s. On 14 September 1986, Kalamata was devastated by an earthquake measuring 6.2 on the Richter scale. Twenty people died, hundreds were injured and more than 10,000 homes were destroyed.

Orientation
The old town around the kastro is quite picturesque, and the waterfront along Navarinou is lively – but it's a very long, hot walk between the two. The main streets linking the old town with the waterfront are Faron and Aristomenous. The city centre is situated around Plateia Georgiou on Aristomenous.

The main bus station is on the northwestern edge of town on Artemidos, while local buses leave from Plateia 25 Martiou – the No 1 goes to the waterfront. The train station is on Frantzi, near Plateia Georgiou.

Information
Tourist Offices The town is dotted with arrowed 'tourist information' signs. Most of them are directing people to the unusually helpful tourist police (☎ 2721 095 555), close to the port on Miaouli opposite the Lambos supermarket. They are open 8am until 9pm Monday to Friday. Other signs point to the old EOT tourist office (now closed) by the yachting marina. None of them point to the new EOT office (☎ 2721 022 059, ℮ detak@compulink.gr) at Polyvriou 5 in the town centre, open 8am to 2pm Monday to Friday.

PELOPONNESE

PELOPONNESE

KALAMATA

To Sparta (58km)

Kastro

River Nedon

Nedontos

OLD TOWN

0   200   400m
0   200   400yd

Artemidos

Athinon

To Megalopoli (56km),
Corinth (90km) &
Athens (284km)

Plateia
Eleftherias

Nedontos

Ypapantis

Plateia
Ypapantis

Polyvriou

Plateia
25 Martiou

Stadiou

Mavromhali

Kolokotroni

Dimakopoulou

Iatropoulou S
Stathmou

Katsari

Georgouli

Plateia Georgiou

Franzi

Dagre

Palama

Train
Station

Vas Georgiou

Aristodimou

Solonos

Makedonias

To Airport (10km)
& Messini (12km)

Idras

Psaron

Aristomenous

Filellinon

Kanari

Lykourgou

Kritis

Mezonos

Bouboulinas

Miaouli

Faron

Methonis

Koronis

Vyronos

Santa Rosa

Ariti

To Marina

Port

Navarinou

Messinian Gulf

To Maria's Sea & Sun Camping (4km)
& Kardamyli (35km)

PLACES TO STAY & EAT
8   Hotel Rex
15 Psitaria O Ilias
17 O Fotis Taverna
18 Hotel George
26 Hotel Hibiscus
28 Hotel Nevada
29 Pension Avra

OTHER
1   Bus Station
2   Food Market
3   Cathedral
4   Archaeological
    Museum
5   Local Bus Terminal
6   Children's Playground
7   EOT
9   Town Hall
10 Diktyo Internet Café
11 OTE
12 Olympic Aviation
13 National Bank of
    Greece
14 Avis
16 Post Office
19 Police
20 Trofos Supermarket
21 OSE Park
22 Spyros Maniatis Travel
23 Tourist Police
24 Laundrette
25 Lambos Supermarket
27 Verga Rent a Car
30 Hertz
31 Alpha Rent a Bike
32 National Bank of
    Greece

Post & Communications The post office is near the train station at Iatropoulou 4, and the OTE is on the north-western side of Plateia Georgiou. Diktyo Internet Café (☎ 2721 097 282), Nedontos 75, is open 10am to midnight daily and charges €2.95 per hour with a €1.50 minimum.

Money There are branches of all the major banks, including the National Bank of Greece, opposite the OTE on Aristomenous. There's another branch on the waterfront on the corner of Ariti and Navarinou.

Laundry The laundrette near the waterfront at Methonis 3 charges €5.30 to wash and dry 6kg. It's open 9am to 2pm and 6pm to 9pm Monday to Friday and 9am to 3pm Saturday.

Kastro
Looming over the town is the 13th-century kastro (off Vileardouinou; admission free; open 10am-1.30pm Mon-Fri). Remarkably, it survived the 1986 earthquake. The arched entry gate is its most impressive feature. There's not much else to see, but there are good views from the battlements.

Archaeological Museum
The Archaeological Museum of Kalamata (☎ 2721 026 209, e protocol@zepka .culture.gr, Papazoglou 6; admission €1.50; open 8am-2.30pm Tues-Sat, 8.30am-3pm Sun) is just north of Plateia 25 Martiou, signposted off Ypapantis. It's one of the best local museums around. The first floor prehistoric displays are particularly good, with comprehensive explanations in English.

OSE Park
The leafy park at the southern end of Aristomenous is home to a collection of old steam locomotives and carriages, parked next to the city's quaint old station.

Places to Stay – Budget
Maria's Sea & Sun Camping (☎ 2721 041 314, fax 2721 041 251, Verga) Adult/tent €4.40/2.95. Maria's is the pick of the city's many camping grounds, located right on the

beach 4km east of town. It has a minimarket, bar, restaurant and two-person bungalows. Buses to Avias from the main bus station can drop you close by.

Hotel Nevada (☎ 2721 082 429, Santa Rosa 9) Singles/doubles/triples €13.50/19.40/26.75. This small old-fashioned hotel is the best value in town, especially outside July and August when prices drop 25% on the listed rates – already a bargain. It's tucked away one block back from the waterfront.

Pension Avra (☎ 2721 082 759, Santa Rosa 10) Singles/doubles €17.60/29.35. This pension is almost opposite the Nevada. A big attraction is the communal kitchen.

Hotel George (☎ 2721 027 225, Cnr Frantzi & Dagre) Singles/doubles with bath €20.55/26.40. The George has the best budget rooms in the city centre. All rooms come with TV. Ask for one away from the street.

Places to Stay – Mid-Range & Top End

The waterfront east of Faron is lined with characterless C-class hotels that are best avoided.

Hotel Hibiscus (☎ 2721 062 511, fax 2721 082 323, Faron 196) Singles/doubles with bath €58.70/88.05. The Hibiscus is a welcome addition to the accommodation scene, occupying a beautifully restored, neoclassical building at the seafront end of Faron. Beautifully polished timber floors and elegant furnishings make this place a real treat. Breakfast costs €5.90.

Hotel Rex (☎ 2721 094 440, fax 2721 023 293, e rex@galaxynet.gr, Aristomenous 26) Singles/doubles with bath €80.70/113. The Rex has reclaimed its title as the best hotel in town following a major renovation program that has restored one of the city's finest neoclassical buildings to its former glory. Room rates include buffet breakfast.

Places to Eat

O Fotis Taverna (☎ 2721 028 925, Sidirodromikou Stathmou 15) Mains €2.95-5.30. O Fotis is a cheery place with a good choice of dishes and a loyal local following.

Psistaria O Ilias (Sidirodromikou Stathmou 22) Mains €2.65-4.70. This busy place specialises in grilled food, but also has a small selection of taverna dishes, like boiled goat with vegetables (€3.85) and tripe (€3.55).

Down by the seafront, Navarinou is lined with countless cafes, fast-food restaurants and seafood tavernas.

Self-caterers should visit Kalamata's large *food market*, across the bridge from the bus station. Kalamata is noted for its olives, olive oil, figs, raki and *mastica* (a surprisingly smooth mastic-based liqueur).

There are dozens of supermarkets around town. *Trofos (☎ 2721 092 811, Kritis 13)* is the biggest and the best.

Getting There & Away

Air There are three flights weekly to Athens (€47.55). The Olympic Aviation office (☎ 2721 022 724, fax 2721 027 868) is at Giatrakou 3 in the centre of town.

Bus Heading north, there are buses to Athens (4¼ hours, €13.65, nine daily) via Tripolis (1¼ hours, €5) and Corinth (2½ hours, €9.70); Kyparissia (1¼ hours, €4.10, five daily); and Patras (four hours, €13.35, two daily) via Pyrgos (two hours, €7.65). Heading west, there are buses to Koroni (1½ hours, €2.95, nine daily) and Pylos (1¼ hours, €2.95, nine daily). Five of the buses to Pylos continue to Methoni (1¾ hours, €3.55) and three keep going to Finikounda (2¼ hours, €4.70). Heading east, there are buses to Sparta (1½ hours, €3.25, two daily) via Artemisia (€1.50), and to Itilo (2¼ hours, €4.10, three daily) via Kardamyli and Stoupa.

Train Kalamata is the end of the line for both branches of the Peloponnese railway. There are four trains daily to Athens (6½ hours, €7.35) on the inland line via Tripolis (2½ hours, €3.10); Argos (3½ hours, €4.40) and Corinth (4½ hours, €4.85). There are two trains daily to Patras (six hours, €5.30) on the west-coast line via Kyparissia (1¾ hours, €2.35) and Pyrgos (3¼ hours, €3.25).

Kalamata Olives

Kalamata is the capital of Messinia, the region occupying the south-western corner of the Peloponnese and famous as the home of the prized Kalamata olive.

While not all olives grown around here are the Kalamata variety, it is this plump, purple-black variety that is found in delicatessens around the world. They are also grown extensively in neighbouring Lakonia and on the islands of Crete and Lesvos.

Locals insist, though, that the finest olives are grown on Messinian soil, particularly in the Pamisos Valley, north of Messini. The region's reliable winter rains and hot summers make for perfect olive-growing conditions.

The Kalamata tree can be distinguished from the common olive, grown for oil, by the size of its leaves. Like its fruit, the leaves of the Kalamata are twice the size of other varieties – and greener. Another important difference is that the Kalamata is alternate bearing – which means a heavy crop one year followed by a light crop.

Unlike other varieties, Kalamata olives cannot be picked green. They ripen in late November, and must be hand-picked to avoid bruising. The olives are then graded according to size and brine-cured.

You can check out a selection of these famous olives at the markets in Kalamata.

Ferry ANEK Lines operates ferry services from Kalamata to Kastelli-Kissamos on Crete via Kythira. Contact Spyros Maniatis Travel (☎ 2721 020 704), by the port on Psaron, for the latest information.

Getting Around

To/From the Airport Kalamata's airport is 10.5km west of the city near Messini. There is no airport shuttle bus. A taxi costs about €7.35.

Bus Local buses leave from Plateia 25 Martiou. The most useful service is bus No 1, which goes south along Aristomenous to the seafront, and then east along Navarinou

to Filoxenia Hotel. The flat fare is €0.60 Buy tickets from the kiosk on Ypapantis just north of Plateia 25 Martiou.

Car & Motorcycle Kalamata is a good place to hire due to hot competition between the agencies at the waterfront end of Faron. The possibilities include Hertz (☎ 2721 088 268), Faron 235; Avis (☎ 2721 020 352) Katsari 2; Budget (☎ 2721 027 694, fax 2721 028 136), Iatropoulou 1; and Verga (☎ 2721 095 190, fax 2721 041 753), Faron 202.

Alpha Rent a Bike (☎ 2721 093 423, fax 2721 025 370), Vyronos 156, hires a range of bikes from 50cc to 500cc.

MAVROMATI (ANCIENT MESSINI)

postcode 240 04 • pop 350

The ruins of ancient Messini lie scattered across a small valley below the picturesque village of Mavromati, 25km north-west of Kalamata. The village takes its name from the fountain in the main square; the water gushes from a hole in the rock that looks like a black eye – *mavro mati* in Greek.

History

Ancient Messini was founded in 371 BC after the Theban general Epaminondas defeated Sparta at the Battle of Leuctra, freeing Messinians from almost 350 years of Spartan rule.

Built on the site of an earlier stronghold, the new Messinian capital was one of a string of defensive positions designed to keep watch over Sparta. Epaminondas himself helped to plan the fortifications, which were based on a massive wall that stretched 9km around the surrounding ridges and completely enclosed the town.

Apart from its defensive potential, the site was also favoured by the gods. According to local myth, Zeus was born here – not Crete – and raised by the nymphs Neda and Ithomi, who bathed him in the same spring that gives the modern village its name.

Exploring the Site

The best views of the site are from Mavromati's main square, and it's worth spending a few minutes examining the layout before heading down for a closer look. Access is by a couple of steep paths leading downhill either side of the museum, about 300m north-west of the square.

The **museum** *(☎ 2721 051 201; admission €1.50; open 8.30am-3pm Tues-Sun)* houses finds from the site – but not the splendid statue of Hermes unearthed in the gymnasium.

Before heading down to the site, it's worth continuing another 800m along the road past the museum to view the celebrated **Arcadian Gate**. This unusual circular gate guarded the ancient route to Megalopoli – now the modern road north to Meligala and Zerbisia, which runs through the gate, dodging an enormous fallen stone slab on the way. Running uphill from the gate is the finest surviving section of the mighty defensive wall built by Epaminondas. It remains impressive, studded with small, square forts. It's well worth the gentle uphill walk from the village.

The site itself *(admission free)* remained unexplored until very recent times, and is slowly emerging from the valley floor. Much of the land is still covered with olive trees and small patches of vineyard, fenced off using sections of the ancient columns that lie scattered everywhere.

Excavation so far has concentrated on the **asklepion** complex that lay at the heart of the ancient city. This extensive complex was centred on a **Doric temple** which once housed a golden statue of Ithomi. The modern awning west of the temple protects the **artemision**, where fragments of an enormous statue of Artemis Orthia were found. The structures to the east of the asklepion include the **ekklesiasterion**, which once acted as an assembly hall.

The site's main path leads downhill from the asklepion to the **stadium**, still largely intact although all the seats have subsided and settled at disconcerting angles. The stadium is surrounded by the ruins of an enormous **gymnasium**.

Places to Stay & Eat

Rooms to Rent Zeus *(☎ 2721 051 025/005)* Doubles €38.15. The territory of Zeus

covers just two cozy double rooms with a communal kitchen and shared bathroom. The rooms overlook the site from above the family jewellery shop on the main square.

Rooms to Rent Lykourgos *(☎ 2721 051 297)* Singles/doubles with bath €26.40/ 35.20. Lykourgos offers large rooms with private bath. The rooms are signposted next to the Taverna/Psistaria Ithomi, opposite the spring.

Taverna/Psistaria Ithomi *(☎ 2721 051 298)* Mains €4.10-5.90. This is a typical village psistaria specialising in grilled food and salads. The small selection of taverna dishes has normally gone by the evening. It's opposite the spring in the middle of the village.

Getting There & Away

There are two buses daily to Mavromati (one hour, €1.80) from Kalamata, leaving at 5.40am and 2.05pm.

KORONI Κορώνη
postcode 240 04 • pop 1420

Koroni (ko-**ro**-nih) is a delightful old Venetian town on the coast 43km southwest of Kalamata. Its narrow streets lead up to the old castle, most of which is occupied by the **Timios Prodromos Convent**. The small promontory beyond the castle is a tranquil place for a stroll with lovely views over the Messinian Gulf to the Taygetos Mountains. Koroni's main attraction is **Zaga Beach**, a long sweep of golden sand just south of the town.

Orientation & Information

Buses will drop you in the main square outside the Church of Agios Dimitrios, one block back from the harbour. There is no tourist office, but you'll find all the information you need on the large map of town on the church wall. It shows the location of the post office, OTE and both banks, all of which are nearby. There are no tourist police. The main street runs east from the square, one block back from the sea. Most locals appear unaware that it has a name, Perikli Ralli.

It takes about 20 minutes to walk to Zaga Beach. To get there, take the road that leads up to the castle from above the square; turn right at the top of the hill and follow the road that curves uphill around the castle. You'll see a sign to the beach on the left after 500m.

Places to Stay & Eat

Camping Koroni (☎ 2725 022 119, fax 2725 022 884) Adult/tent €4.70/3.55. This small camping ground is 500m north of town on the road from Kalamata. It's a friendly place, although the grounds look badly in need of maintenance. Buses stop outside.

Koroni does not have a lot of accommodation. Most of the rooms are spread around a cluster of *domatia* by the sea at the eastern end of the main street. Expect to pay around €20.55/26.40 for singles/doubles with bathroom. There are more domatia overlooking Zaga Beach, but they are often block-booked in summer.

Hotel Diana (☎/fax 2725 022 312, ℮ dhotel@hol.gr) Singles/doubles with bath €24.95/39.65. The Diana represents top value for good rooms with TV, fridge and air-con. It's off the main square on the way to the seafront. Some rooms also have sea views. Breakfast (€3.55) is available.

Symposium Restaurant (☎ 2725 022 385, main street) Mains €3.55-7.35. This place is about as traveller-friendly as you could ever want a restaurant to be. Years of New York living have taught George, the amiable Greek-American owner, all about keeping the customer satisfied. He has seafood and grills as well as a daily selection of taverna staples. Vegetarians will find at least six dishes to choose from.

Psarotavera Ifigenia (☎ 2725 022 097) Mains €2.95-8.80. This is a great spot to munch a plate of fresh calamari (€4.40).

Self-caterers will find everything they need at the shops around the main square.

Getting There & Away

There are nine buses daily to Kalamata (1½ hours, €2.95).

FINIKOUNDA Φοινικούντα

postcode 240 06 • pop 650

The fishing village of Finikounda, midway between Koroni and Methoni, is a popular place for backpackers to hang out. The attraction is the string of fine beaches that stretch either side of the village. The area has a reputation for good windsurfing.

Finikounda has spread steadily along the beach over the years. All the shops and facilities are in the old village around the port. The bus stop is outside Hotel Finikountas, 100m from the port on the way to Methoni.

Places to Stay & Eat

Camping Anemomilos (☎ 2723 071 360, fax 2723 071 121) Adult/tent €4.40/2.65. Most young campers head to this place by the beach, 3km west of Finikounda off the road to Methoni.

Akti Studios (☎ 2723 071 316) Doubles/ triples with bath €35.20/41.10. This small family-run place has comfortable studios with kitchen facilities. It's set back from the beach road about 250m east of the port.

Hotel Korakakis Beach (☎ 2723 071 221, fax 2723 071 232, ℮ korakaki@otenet.gr) Singles/doubles with bath €26.40/€49,90. The Korakakis is a comfortable modern hotel at the eastern end of the main town beach. It also has studios nearby. Breakfast costs €4.40.

Getting There & Away

There are three buses daily to Kalamata (2¼ hours, €4.70) via Methoni (30 minutes, €1.20) and Pylos.

METHONI Μεθώνη

postcode 240 06 • pop 1200

Methoni (meh-**tho**-nih), 12km south of Pylos, was another of the seven cities offered to Achilles by Agamemnon. Homer described it as 'rich in vines'. Today, it's a pretty seaside town, with a sandy beach that's crowded in summer, and a magnificent 15th-century Venetian fortress.

This vast fortification is built on a promontory south of the modern town, surrounded on three sides by the sea and separated from the mainland by a moat. The medieval port town, which stood within the fortress walls, was the Venetians' first and longest-held possession in the Peloponnese, and a stopover point for pilgrims en route to the Holy Land. In medieval times, the twin fortresses of Methoni and Koroni were known as 'the Eyes of the Serene Republic'.

Orientation & Information

The road from Pylos forks on the edge of town to create Methoni's two main streets, which then run parallel through town to the fortress. As you come from Pylos, the fork to the right is the main shopping street. It has shops, a supermarket and a National Bank of Greece. The left fork leads directly to the fortress car park, passing the post office on the way. Turn left at the fortress end of either street onto Miaouli, which leads to Methoni Beach. The small square by the beach is surrounded by fairly characterless C-class hotels and several seafood restaurants.

There is no tourist office and no tourist police. The regular police (☎ 2723 031 203) are signposted near the post office.

Fortress

This splendid fortress (admission free; open 8.30am-5pm Tues-Sat, 9am-5pm Sun), a supreme example of military architecture, is vast and romantic. It's easy to spend half a day wandering around. Within the walls are a Turkish bath, cathedral, house, cistern, parapets and underground passages. See how many Lion of St Mark insignias you can spot. A short causeway leads from the fortress to the diminutive octagonal Bourtzi castle on an adjacent islet. Bring a torch to explore the interior.

Places to Stay & Eat

Camping Methoni (☎ 2723 031 228) Adult/tent €3.25/2.05. This camping ground has a good location right behind the beach, but could use a few shade trees.

Rooms to Rent Giorgos (☎ 2723 031 640/426) Singles/doubles with bath €20.55/23.50. You'll see several signs for domatia in the streets near the fortress, including this one, above Cafeteria George at the fortress end of the main shopping street.

Hotel Castello (☎ 2723 031 300/280, fax 2723 031 300, Miaouli) Singles/doubles/triples with bath €36.70/44/51.40. This

hotel, facing the fortress, has beautifully furnished rooms. Breakfast costs €4.40.

Hotel Albatros (☎ 2723 031 160, fax 2723 031 114) Singles/doubles with bath €38.15/45.40. This friendly hotel, next to the post office has comfortable air-con rooms with refrigerator. Breakfast is €4.70.

Taverna Nikos (☎ 2723 031 282) Mains €2.65-5. This no-frills taverna, halfway along Miaouli near the fortress, is always full of locals and stays open all year.

Restaurant Kali Karthia (☎ 2723 031 260) Mains €3.55-9.50. The Kali Karthia is a small family-run place halfway along the shopping street with good food and good wine.

Café La Mare (☎ 2723 031 311) Pizzas from €4.70. This popular local hangout on the small square near Methoni Beach has a range of pizzas as well as ice creams and snacks.

Getting There & Away

Buses leave from the fork at the Pylos end of town where the two main streets meet. You'll find a timetable pinned to the door of the adjacent Assimakis Food Market. There are seven buses daily to Kalamata (1¼ hours, €3.55) and Pylos (15 minutes, €0.80), and three to Finikounda (30 minutes, €1.20).

PYLOS Πύλος
postcode 240 01 • pop 2500

Pylos (pee-loss), on the coast 51km southwest of Kalamata, presides over the southern end of an immense bay. On this bay on 20 October 1827, the British, French and Russian fleets, under the command of Admiral Codrington, fired at point-blank range on Ibrahim Pasha's combined Turkish, Egyptian and Tunisian fleet, sinking 53 ships and killing 6000 men, with negligible losses on the Allies' side.

It was known as the Battle of Navarino (the town's former name) and was decisive in the War of Independence, but it was not meant to have been a battle at all. The Allied fleet wanted to achieve no more than to persuade Ibrahim Pasha and his fleet to leave, but things got out of hand. George IV,

PELOPONNESE

on hearing the news, described it as a 'deplorable misunderstanding'.

With its huge natural harbour almost enclosed by the Sfaktiria Islet, a delightful tree-shaded central square, two castles and surrounding pine-covered hills, Pylos is one of the most picturesque towns in the Peloponnese.

Orientation & Information

Everything of importance is within a few minutes' walk of the central square, Plateia Trion Navarhon, down by the seafront. The bus station is on the inland side of the square. There is no tourist office. The post office is on Nileos, which runs uphill from the bus station towards Arviniti Hotel. The police station (☎ 2723 022 316) and the National Bank of Greece are on the square, while the main Kalamata-Methoni road runs around it.

Castles

There are castles on each side of Navarino Bay. The more accessible of them is the **Neo Kastro** (☎ 2723 022 010; admission €2.35; open 8.30am-3pm Tues-Sun), on the hilltop at the southern edge of town off the road to Methoni. It was built by the Turks in 1573 and was later used as a launching pad for the invasion of Crete. It remains in good condition, especially the formidable surrounding walls. Within its walls are a citadel, a mosque converted into a church and a courtyard surrounded by dungeons (it was used as a prison until the 1900s). The road to Methoni from the central square goes past the castle.

The ancient **Paleokastro**, 6km north of Pylos, is covered in the following Around Pylos section.

Boat Tours

You can ask around the waterfront for fishing boats to take you around the Bay of Navarino and the island of Sfaktiria. The price will depend on the number of passengers, but reckon on about €10 each for a group of four or more. On the trip around the island, stops can be made at memorials to admirals of the Allied ships. Boats may pause

so you can see wrecks of sunken Turkish ships, discernible in the clear waters.

Places to Stay & Eat

Navarino Beach Camping (☎ 2723 022 761, fax 2723 023 512) Adult/tent €4.10/2.95. This camping ground, 8km north of Pylos on Gialova Beach, is the closest. Take a Kyparissia bus from Pylos.

Rooms to Rent Stavroula Milona (☎ 2723 022 724) Doubles €17.60. This charming little place is right on the seafront to the south of the harbour above the Café-Bar En Plo. The rooms are small, but clean and comfortable. There's a communal kitchen and TV room.

12 Gods (dodeka theoi; ☎ 2723 022 179, 022 324, 022 878, fax 2723 022 878, e a12gods@otenet.gr) Doubles with bath €19.10. These rooms are perched high above the harbour about 1km south of the main square on Kalamatas – which becomes the main road to Kalamata. Rooms are named after the gods of the ancient Greek pantheon. Appropriately enough, Poseidon has superb views over Navarino Bay.

Hotel Miramare (☎ 2723 022 751, fax 2723 022 226) Singles/doubles/triples with bath €41.10/58.70/64.60, including breakfast. The town's finest is a comfortable midrange seafront hotel, 150m north of harbour, with views over Navarino Bay.

Places to Eat

Psarotaverna 4 Epohes (☎ 2723 022 739) Mains €2.65-7.35, fresh fish from €29.35/kg. On the seafront beyond Hotel Miramare, this popular family-run place has taverna favourites like stuffed tomatoes (€2.95) and mousakas (€3.20) as well as a good selection of fresh seafood.

Restaurant 1930 (☎ 2723 022 032). Mains €3.55-11.75, seafood €35.20/kg. The decor here is an amusing recreation of scenes from the 1930s; the menu is a mix of traditional fare like spetsofai (sausages in spicy sauce, €4.10) and modern Mediterranean dishes like pork fillet in roquefort (€11.75).

There is an *Atlantik supermarket* on the main square.

Getting There & Away

There are buses to Kalamata (1¼ hours, €2.95, nine daily); Kyparissia (1¼ hours, €3.55, five daily) via Nestor's Palace (30 minutes, €1.50) and Hora (35 minutes); Methoni (20 minutes, €0.80, five daily); Finikounda (45 minutes, three daily). On weekends, there are two buses a day to Athens (five hours, €16.75).

AROUND PYLOS

Paleokastro

The ruins of this ancient castle lie on Ko-yphasio Hill at the northern side of Navarino Bay. It was built at the end of the 13th century, and occupies the site of the acropolis of ancient Pylos. It was captured in 1361 by Spanish invaders from Navarra, after whom the bay is named.

The site is best approached by the track leading south from the village of Petrohori, about 12km north of modern Pylos off the road to Hora. The track ends at **Voidokilias Beach**, a beautiful, sandy horseshoe bay presumed to be Homer's 'sandy Pylos' – where Telemachus was warmly welcomed when he came to ask wise old King Nestor the whereabouts of his long-lost father, Odysseus, King of Ithaca.

The path up to the castle passes **Nestor's Cave**. According to mythology, this is the cave where Hermes hid the cattle he stole from Apollo. It boasts some impressive stalactites.

Nestor's Palace

The palace (☎ 2763 031 437; admission €1.50; open 8.30am-3pm Tues-Sun summer, 8am-2.30pm winter), originally a two-storey building, is the best preserved of all Mycenaean palaces. Its walls stand 1m high, giving a good idea of the layout of a Mycenaean palace complex. The main palace, in the middle, was a building of many rooms. The largest, the **throne room**, was where the king dealt with state business. In the centre was a large, circular hearth surrounded by four ornate columns which supported a 1st floor balcony. Some of the fine frescoes discovered here are in the museum in the nearby village of Hora

(see following). Surrounding the throne is the sentry box, pantry, waiting room, a vestibule and, most fascinating, a bathroom with a terracotta tub still in place.

The most important finds were about 1200 Linear B script tablets, the first discovered on the mainland. Some are in Hora's museum. The site was excavated later than the other Mycenaean sites, between 1952 and 1965. An excellent guidebook by Carl Blegen, who led the excavations, is sold at the site.

Nestor's Palace is 17km north of modern Pylos.

Hora Χώρα

Hora's fascinating little **archaeological museum** (☎ 2763 231 358; admission €1.50; open 8.30am-3pm Tues-Sun), 3km north-east of Nestor's Palace, houses finds from the site and other Mycenaean artefacts from Messinia. The prize pieces are the frescoes from the throne rooms at Nestor's Palace.

Getting There & Away

Buses from Pylos to Kyparissia stop at Nestor's Palace and Hora.

Elia Ηλία

The western prefecture of Elia is home to some of the best farming country in Greece. The main agricultural areas are along the broad valley of the River Alfios, the 'Sacred Alph' of Samuel Taylor Coleridge's Kubla Khan, and in the north-west around Gastouni and Andravida. The rich alluvial flats around here are watered by the River Pinios, which has been dammed upstream to create Lake Pinios, the largest water storage facility in the Peloponnese.

Ancient Elia took its name from the mythical King Helios. Its capital was the city of Elis, now a forgotten ruin on the road from Gastouni to Lake Pinios. When the Franks arrived, they made Andravida the capital of their principate of Morea. Pyrgos is the dull modern capital. Most people come to Elia for one reason: to visit ancient Olympia.

PELOPONNESE

THOLOS TO PYRGOS

Heading north into Elia from Messinia, the mountains to the east give way to interrupted plains fringed by golden sand beaches. Interspersed by pebbled shores and rocky outcrops, these beaches stretch right around Elia's coastline. The best beaches in the south are at **Tholos**, **Kakovatos** and **Kouroutas**. There's seaside accommodation in each village, but most of it is in uninspiring concrete buildings.

A sign outside Tholos points to the mountain village of **Nea Figalia**, 14km inland. From here, it's a further 21km to reach the tranquil site of **ancient Figalia** which is set high above the River Neda almost at its source. Laurels, cypresses and citrus trees are clustered around the ruins of this ancient Arcadian marketplace, with towers, a small acropolis, an agora, and a temple to Dionysos, the wine pourer. A rough road leads east from Nea Figalia to Andritsena (see the Andritsena section later in this chapter).

PYRGOS Πύργος
postcode 271 00 • pop 28,700

Pyrgos, 98km south-west of Patras and 24km from Olympia, is an agricultural service town with little of interest except its municipal theatre and market. It is, however, the capital of Elia prefecture and all forms of public transport pass through here, including buses and trains to Olympia. The bus and train stations are about 400m apart, the former in the town centre on Manolopoulou and the latter at the northern edge of town on Ypsilantou.

Places to Stay

If you need to stay overnight there are several hotels on the streets leading into town off Ypsilantou.

Hotel Pantheon (☎ 2621 029 746, fax 2621 037 791, Themistokleous 7) Singles/doubles with bath €38.15/57.85. The Hotel Pantheon is nothing special, but it's clean and centrally located. Normally, you should be able to bargain the price for a double down to €30. Breakfast is available for €4.10.

Getting There & Away

Bus There are 16 buses daily to Olympia (30 minutes, €1.35) on weekdays, 14 on Saturday, and nine on Sunday. There are 10 buses daily to Athens (five hours, €16.90) and Patras (two hours, €5.90); and three daily to Kyllini (50 minutes, €3.40), Kyparissia (1¼ hours, €4.70), Tripolis (3½ hours, €8.80), Kalamata (two hours, €7.65) and Andritsena (1½ hours, €5.45).

Train Heading north, there are eight trains daily to Patras (two hours, €2.95), seven of which continue to Athens (6½ hours, €7.20). Three of these trains are intercity, which take five hours to Athens. Heading south, there are five trains daily to Kyparissia (1¼ hours, €2.20), two of which continue to Kalamata (3¼ hours, €3.25). There are also five trains daily on the branch line to Olympia (35 minutes, €1.20).

OLYMPIA Ολυμπία
postcode 270 65 • pop 1000

The modern village of Olympia (o-lim-bee-ah) panders unashamedly to the hundreds of thousands of tourists who pour through here each year on their way to ancient Olympia, 500m south on the road to Tripolis. The main street is lined with countless overpriced souvenir shops, coffee shops and restaurants.

Orientation

The modern village lies along the main Pyrgos-Tripolis road, known as Praxitelous Kondyli, through town. The bus stops for Pyrgos and Tripolis are opposite one another by the tourist office towards the southern end of Praxitelous Kondyli, and the train station is close to the centre on Douka.

Information

Olympia's helpful municipal tourist office (☎ 2624 023 100/173) on Praxitelous Kondyli comes as a pleasant surprise after dealing with government-run EOT offices elsewhere. The friendly staff offer a good map of the village, have comprehensive information on bus, train and ferry schedules (from Kyllini and Patras) and can change currency. The office is open 9am to 9pm daily June to September. The rest of the year it's open 8am to 2.45pm Monday to Saturday. The tourist police (☎ 2624 022 550) are behind the tourist office on Spiliopoulou 5, which runs parallel to Praxitelous Kondyli one block up the hill.

The post office is up the first street to the right as you walk along Praxitelous Kondyli towards ancient Olympia from the tourist office. The OTE is on Praxitelous Kondyli, beyond the turn-off for the post office. The National Bank of Greece is on the corner of Praxitelous Kondyli and Stefanopoulou. Travellers can check email at the Café-Bar Ailolos (☎ 2624 022 914) at the corner of Spiliopoulou and Stefanopoulou. It's open 10.30am to 3am daily and charges €4.10 per hour.

Historical Museum of the Olympic Games

This museum (☎ 2624 022 544, opposite junction of Agerinai & Kosmopoulou; admission €1.50; open 8.30am-3.30pm Mon-Sat, 9am-4pm Sun) is two blocks west of Praxitelous Kondyli. Although most of the labelling is in French, the collection of commemorative stamps and literature needs little explanation.

Ancient Olympia

Ancient Olympia (☎ 2624 022 517; admission €3.55, free Sun & public holidays; open 8am-7pm) was a complex of temples, priests' dwellings and public buildings. It was also the venue of the Olympic Games, which took place every four years. During the games the city-states were bound by ekeheiria (a sacred truce) to stop beating the hell out of one another, and compete in races and sports instead.

History & Mythology The origins of Olympia date back to Mycenaean times. The Great Goddess, identified with Rea, was worshipped here in the 1st millennium BC. By the classical era, Rea had been superseded by her son Zeus. A small regional festival, which probably included athletic events, was begun in the 11th century BC.

The first official quadrennial Olympic Games were declared in 776 BC by King Iphitos of Elis. By 676 BC, they were open to all male Greeks, reaching their height of prestige in 576 BC. The games were held in honour of Zeus, popularly acclaimed as their founder. They took place at the time of the first full moon in August.

The athletic festival lasted five days and included wrestling, chariot and horse racing, the pentathlon (wrestling, discus and javelin throwing, long jump and running), and the pancratium (a vicious form of fisticuffs).

Originally only Greek-born males were allowed to participate, but later Romans were permitted. Slaves and women were not allowed to enter the sanctuary as participants or spectators. Women trying to sneak in were thrown from a nearby rock.

The event served purposes besides athletic competition. Writers, poets and historians read their works to a large audience, and the citizens of various city-states got together. Traders clinched business deals and city-state leaders talked in an atmosphere of festivity that was conducive to resolving differences through discussion, rather than battle.

The games continued during the first years of Roman rule. By this time, however, their importance had declined and, thanks to Nero, they had become less edifying. In AD 67, Nero entered the chariot race with 10 horses, ordering that other competitors could have no more than four. Despite this advantage, he fell and abandoned the race. He was still declared the winner by the judges.

The games were held for the last time in 394, before they were banned by Emperor Theodosius I as part of a purge of pagan festivals. In 426, Theodosius II decreed that the temples of Olympia be destroyed.

The modern Olympic Games were instituted in 1896 and, other than during WWI and WWII, have been held every four years in different cities around the world ever since. The Olympic flame is lit at the ancient site and carried by runners to the city where the games are held.

The site was added to the World Heritage list in 1989.

ANCIENT OLYMPIA

To Museum (200m)

To Olympia Village (500m)

Kladeos River

1	Entrance
2	Gymnasium
3	East Portico of the Gymnasium
4	Prytaneum
5	Philippeion
6	Temple of Hera
7	Nymphaeum
8	Metroön
9	Treasuries
10	Stadium
11	Pelopion
12	Palaestra (Wrestling School)
13	Theokoleon (Priest's House)
14	Pheidias' Workshop
15	Temple of Zeus
16	Hippodrome
17	Bouleuterion (Council House)
18	Altar of Oaths
19	Leonidaion

Altis (Sacred Precinct of Zeus)

0   50   100m
0   50   100yd

Exploring the Site Ancient Olympia is signposted from the modern village. The entrance is beyond the bridge over the Kladeos River (a tributary of the Alfios). Thanks to Theodosius II and various earthquakes, little remains of the magnificent buildings of ancient Olympia, but enough remains to sustain an absorbing visit in an idyllic, leafy setting. The first ruin encountered is the **gymnasium**, which dates from the 2nd century BC. South of here is the partly restored **palaestra**, or wrestling school, where contestants practised and trained. The next building was the **theokoleon** (the priests' house). Behind it was the **workshop** where Pheidias sculpted the gargantuan ivory-and-gold Statue of Zeus, one of the Seven Wonders of the Ancient World. The workshop was identified by archaeologists after the discovery of tools and moulds. Beyond the theokoleon is the **leonidaion**, an elaborate structure which accommodated dignitaries.

The **altis**, or **Sacred Precinct of Zeus**, lies to the left of the path. Its most important building was the immense 5th-century Doric **Temple of Zeus** in which stood Pheidias' statue. The 12m-high statue was later

removed to Constantinople by Theodosius II, where it was destroyed by fire in 475 BC. The temple consisted of 13 lateral columns and six at either end. None is still standing.

South of the Temple of Zeus is the **bouleuterion** (council house), where competitors swore to obey the rules decreed by the Olympic Senate.

The **stadium** lies to the east of the altis and is entered through an archway. The start and finish lines of the 120m sprint track and the judges' seats still survive. There are normally plenty of athletic types weaving through the tourists as they time themselves over the distance. The stadium could seat at least 30,000 spectators. Slaves and women spectators had to be content to watch from the Hill of Cronos. South of the stadium was the **hippodrome**, where the chariot contests thrilled the crowds.

To the north of the Temple of Zeus was the **pelopion**, a small, wooded hillock with an altar to Pelops. It was surrounded by a wall and the remains of its Doric portico can be seen. Many artefacts, now displayed in the museum, were found on the hillock.

Further north is the 6th-century Doric **Temple of Hera**, the site's most intact structure. Hera was worshipped along with Rea until the two were superseded by Zeus.

To the east of this temple is the **nymphaeum**, erected by the wealthy Roman banker Herodes Atticus from AD 156 to 160. Typical of buildings financed by Roman benefactors, it was grandiose, consisting of a semicircular building with Doric columns flanked at each side by a circular temple. The building contained statues of Herodes Atticus and his family. Despite its elaborate appearance, the nymphaeum had a practical purpose: it was a fountain house supplying Olympia with fresh spring water.

From the nymphaeum, a row of 12 **treasuries** stretched to the stadium. These looked like miniature temples. Each was erected by a city-state for use as a storehouse. These buildings marked the northern boundaries of the altis. The remains are reached by ascending a flight of stone steps.

At the bottom of these steps are the scant remains of the 5th century BC **metroön**, a temple dedicated to Rea, the mother of the gods. Apparently the ancients worshipped Rea in this temple with orgies.

To the west of the Temple of Hera are the foundations of the **philippeion**, a circular construction with Ionic columns built by Philip of Macedon to commemorate the Battle of Khaironeia (338 BC), where he defeated a combined army of Athenians and Thebans. The building contained statues of Philip and his family.

North of the philippeion was the **prytaneum**, the magistrate's residence. Here, winning athletes were entertained and feasted.

Museum The museum (*☎/fax 2624 022 529; admission €3.55; open 8am-7pm Tues-Sun, noon-7pm Mon*) is 200m north of the site, on the opposite side of the road. The star piece is the 4th-century Parian marble statue of **Hermes of Praxiteles**, a masterpiece of classical sculpture from the Temple of Hera. Hermes was charged with taking the infant Dionysos to Mt Nysa.

Other important exhibits are a sculptured **Head of Hera** and the pediments and metopes from the Temple of Zeus. The eastern pediment depicts the chariot race between Pelops and Oinomaos. The western pediment shows the fight between the Centaurs and Lapiths, and the metopes depict the Twelve Labours of Heracles.

Places to Stay – Budget

Camping Diana (*☎ 2624 022 314, fax 2624 022 425*) Adult/tent €5/3.85. Open year-round. This friendly, well-run place is nestled on a leafy hillside clearly signposted just 250m west of the village.

Camping Alphios (*☎/fax 2624 022 950*) Adult/tent €4.40/2.35. Open Apr-end Oct. This ground shares a million-dollar view with the neighbouring Hotel Europa in the hills 1km south-west of town.

Youth Hostel (*☎ 2624 022 580, Praxitelous Kondyli 18*) Dorm beds €5.30. Conditions aren't deluxe, but this youth hostel is much better than the Greek average. Rates include hot showers and there's no curfew. Breakfast is available for €2.05.

Pension Achilleys (*☎ 2624 022 562, Stefanopoulou 4*) Singles/doubles/triples €14.70/23.50/29.35. This small family-run pension is just uphill from the National Bank of Greece. Breakfast costs €4.40.

Pension Posidon (*☎ 2624 022 567, Stefanopoulou 9*) Singles/doubles with bath €17.60/26.40/35.20. The Posidon represents great value for bright, spotless and airy rooms with balcony. It's just up the hill from the Achilleys. Breakfast costs €2.95.

Place to Stay – Middle & Top End

Hotel Pelops (*☎/fax 2624 022 543, e hotel_pelops@hotmail.com, Cnr Kosmopoulou & Vas Varela*). Singles/doubles/triples with bath €39.60/57.25/72.20. The Pelops is a comfortable family-run place on the western side of town. The Greek-Australian owners are full of ideas for further exploration in the area. Prices include a generous buffet breakfast.

Best Western Hotel Europa International (*☎ 2624 022 650, fax 2624 023 166, e hoteleuropa@hellasnet.gr*) Singles €57.25-66, doubles €82.20-100, triples €96.85-114.45, including buffet breakfast.

Phone numbers listed incorporate changes due in Oct 2002; see p83

PELOPONNESE

If you want a bit of style, this excellent A-class hotel is the place to go. It has sensational views from its hilltop location south-west of the village. Facilities include a bar, restaurant, swimming pool and tennis court.

Places to Eat

With so many one-off customers passing through, Olympia's restaurants have little incentive to strive for excellence – and they don't.

Taverna To Anesi (*☎ 2624 022 644, Cnr Avgerinou & Spiliopoulou*) Mains €3.85-5.30. This busy psistaria is a favourite with locals, who come here to feast on portions of succulent roast chicken (€3.55) or pork (€4.70), washed down with a local red wine.

Taverna To Steki tou Vangeli (*☎ 2624 022 530, Stefanopoulou 13*) Mains €3.85-6.15. Vangeli is another place that stands out from the crowd with hearty servings of tasty food.

Self-caterers will find **supermarkets** along Praxitelous Kondyli.

Getting There & Away

There are four buses daily to Athens (5½ hours, €18.20), via Pyrgos and the coast, as well as numerous services to Pyrgos (30 minutes, €1.35). Three buses daily also go east to Tripolis (3½ hours, €7.65).

There are five trains daily to Pyrgos (36 minutes, €1.05).

ANDRITSENA Ανδρίτσαινα
postcode 270 61 • pop 900

The village of Andritsena, 65km south-east of Pyrgos, is perched on a hillside overlooking the valley of the River Alfios. Crumbling stone houses with rickety wooden balconies flank its narrow cobbled streets and a stream gushes through its central square, Plateia Agnostopoulou. Look out for the fountain emerging from the trunk of a huge plane tree.

The post office, OTE and bank are near the central square. Travellers can check email at the Café Club Mylos (*☎ 2624 022 301*), open 2pm to 2am daily. It charges €3.55 per hour. Most people come to Andritsena to visit the World Heritage listed Temple of Vasses, 14km away.

Temple of Vasses

The Temple of Vasses (*☎ 2626 022 254, admission €1.50; open 8am-5pm daily*) 14km south of Andritsena, stands at an altitude of 1200m on a hill overlooked by Mt Paliavlakitsa. The road from Andritsena climbs steadily along a mountain ridge through increasingly dramatic scenery, to Greece's most isolated temple.

The well-preserved temple was built in 420 BC by the people of nearby Figalia, who dedicated it to Apollo Epicurus (the Helper) for delivering them from pestilence. Designed by Ictinus, the architect of the Parthenon, it combines Doric and Ionic columns and a single Corinthian column – the earliest example of this order.

At the time of research, the temple was enclosed by a giant tent and was undergoing a much-needed restoration program.

There are no buses to Vasses. In summer, it's usually possible to find people in the square to share a taxi for about €17.50 return.

Places to Stay

Hotel Theoxenia (*☎/fax 2624 022 219*) Singles/doubles/triples with bath €29.35/41.10/47. The Theoxenia is one of the last of the Xenia hotels – a relic of a bygone era. Once a famously shoddy chain of government-run hotels, most Xenias have now been transferred to private enterprise. It features many of the Xenia trademarks, which guests laugh about afterwards. There's a receptionist who's always watching sitcoms in the bar, door handles that fall off in your hand, showers that explode when the water is turned on, and guests bumping around a labyrinth of corridors trying to locate their rooms in the dark. It's on the main road on the eastern side of town.

Epikourios Apollon (*☎ 2624 022 840, Plateia Agnostopoulou*) Doubles with bath & breakfast €35.20. This smart new place has cheerful rooms overlooking the main square, complete with an enthusiastic owner who's keen to please.

There are half a dozen small restaurants spread along the main street.

Getting There & Away
There are two buses daily to Andritsena from Athens Bus Terminal A (four hours, €13.95). There are also services to Pyrgos (1½ hours, €5.45), and to Tripolis (two hours, €4.70) via Karitena and Megalopoli (1¼ hours, €2.95).

KYLLINI Κυλλήνη
The tiny port of Kyllini (kih-**lee**-nih), 78km south-west of Patras, warrants a mention only as the jumping-off point for ferries to Kefallonia and Zakynthos. Most people pass through Kyllini on buses from Patras that board the ferries. If you get stuck in Kyllini, the tourist/port police (☎ 2623 092 211) at the quay can suggest accommodation.

Stretching south from Kyllini is a succession of excellent beaches.

Getting There & Away
Bus There are between three and seven buses daily to Kyllini (1¼ hours, €4.40) from the Zakynthos bus station in Patras, as well as at least three buses daily from Pyrgos (50 minutes, €3.40).

Ferry There are boats to Zakynthos (1½ hours, €4.40, up to five daily) and to Poros (1¼ hours, €6.15, three daily) and Argostoli (2¼ hours, €8.80, two daily) on Kefallonia.

Central Greece Κεντρική Ελλάδα

Steeped in history, central Greece is a land of contrasts. From the rugged mountains of the South Pindos to densely populated Attica, from the sleepy wetlands of the southwest to the verdant Pelion, central Greece covers a wide range of varied landscapes.

Three major attractions draw travellers to this ancient land – the oracle of Delphi, the amazing rock forest of Meteora and its monasteries, and the lush Pelion Peninsula with its traditional stone houses.

SUGGESTED ITINERARIES
One week
Central Greece offers two main sightseeing areas for short-term visitors: the Meteora and Pelion Peninsula. Start at Volos and spend two days exploring the Pelion Peninsula. Then head southwards across the mountains via Karditsa, Lamia and Amfissa and visit the oracle of Delphi. Allow two days for this magical place. If time and patience allow, head along the north coast of the Gulf of Corinth from Delphi and visit Messolongi in Etolo-Akarnania. Take along some of Byron's poetry to get in the mood. Otherwise you may prefer Galaxidi, a seaside town on the north Gulf of Corinth, 27km from Delphi.

Two weeks
Start at Volos but allow an extra two to three days to visit the villages of the Pelion Peninsula, overnighting in perhaps Tsangarada and Vyzitsa. From Volos traverse Thessaly – including a short visit to workaday Larisa – before halting at Meteora. A stay of at least two to three days should be allowed for Meteora, especially if you wish to visit all the monasteries at walking pace. With more time on your hands you might detour slightly to the Monastery of Osiou Loukas in Central Greece before resuming the one week itinerary at Delphi. From Messolongi you might care to loop back to Central Greece via the little-visited mountains of the Agrafa and the capital of Greece's 'little Switzerland', Karpenisi.

Sterea Ellada
Στερεά Ελλάδα

Sterea Ellada is bordered by Thessaly and Epiros to the north and the narrow gulfs of

Highlights °

- The spectacular rock-pillar monasteries of Meteora
- The ancient oracle of Delphi and Sanctuary of Apollo
- The lush, green mountain villages of the Pelion Peninsula
- The superb Byzantine monastery of Osiou Louka

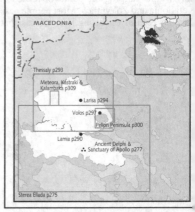

Corinth and Patras in the south. The regio acquired the name Sterea Ellada (mainlan Greece) in 1827, because it was the onl continental portion of the newly forme Greek state – the Peloponnese was classe as an island. To the west is the prefecture Etolo-Akarnania where England's most fa mous philhellene bard, Lord Byron, died Messolongi while assisting in the Gree War of Independence.

To the east is the large island of Evi which is separated from the mainland by narrow gulf, and is a jumping-off point f the Sporades islands.

ATHENS TO THIVA
If you want to travel from Athens to Delph you have a choice of two routes: the mai

STEREA ELLADA

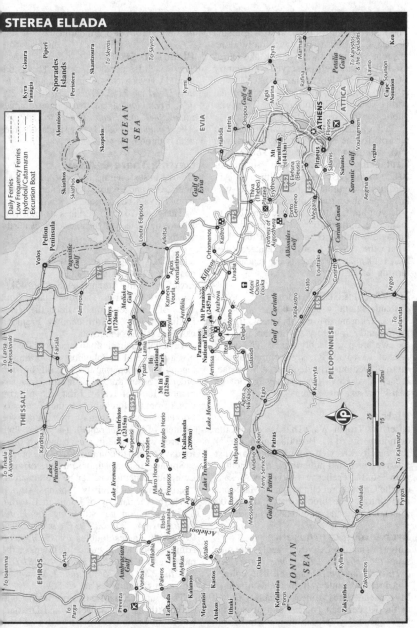

highway or the old mountain road to Thiva. The latter is a turn inland west of Elefsina (Eleusis), and buses run twice daily along this route. Along the way you can take a turn-off left to the well-preserved 4th-century BC **Fortress of Aigosthena**, and have a swim at **Porto Germeno**, a low-key resort on the north coast of the Gulf of Corinth. There is no public transport to Porto Germeno.

Back on the Thiva road, 2km beyond the turn-off for the Fortress of Aigosthena, you will see the less impressive **Fortress of Eleutherai** to the right, standing at the entrance to the pass over Mt Kythairon. According to mythology, baby Oedipus was left to perish on this mountain.

If you are a battle buff you may like to make the 5km detour to the remains of **Plataea**, which once overlooked the plain where the famous Battle of Plataea (479 BC) took place. The ruins are reached by turning left at Erythres.

THIVA (THEBES) Θήβα
postcode 322 00 • pop 19,000
Thiva, 87km north-west of Athens, figures prominently in history and mythology, and the two are inextricably linked. The tragic fate of its royal dynasty, centred on the myth of Oedipus, rivalled that of Mycenae. Present-day Thiva has few vestiges of its past glory as a city state.

History
After the Trojan War, Thebes became the dominant city of the Boeotia region. In 371 BC the city was victorious in battle against Sparta, which had hitherto been invincible.

In 336 BC, Thebes was sacked by Alexander the Great for rebelling against Macedonian control. The bloody battle saw 6000 Thebans killed and 30,000 taken prisoner.

Archaeological Museum
Thiva has an impressive archaeological museum (☎ 2262 027 913; admission €1.50; open 8.30am-3pm Tues-Sun). The collection includes pottery from prehistoric and Mycenaean times, Linear B tablets found in the Mycenaean palaces and also some Mycenaean clay coffins, unique to mainland

Greece. The museum is at the southern end of the main street of Pindarou.

Places to Stay
There is little need to stay in Thiva, but should you wish to there are two hotels: *Meletiou Hotel* (☎ 2262 027 333, fax 2262 223 334, Epaminondou 58) has singles/doubles for €29/47, and *Neobe Hotel* (☎ 2262 027 949, Epaminondou 63) has singles/doubles with bathroom for €29/35.

Getting There & Away
Hourly buses operate to both Athens (1½ hours, €5) and Livadia (45 minutes, €2.80) from Thiva's bus station.

There are 10 train services to and from Athens daily, as well as nine services northwards.

LIVADIA Λειβαδιά
postcode 321 00 • pop 18,000
Livadia is on the Athens-Delphi road, 45km north-west of Thiva. The town flanks both sides of a gorge through which the River Erkinas flows. A 14th-century Frankish castle overlooks the town.

Livadia's main claim to fame is as the site of the oracle of Trophonios. According to legend, the ordeal one had to go through in order to consult this oracle resulted in a permanent look of fright. First, the pilgrim drank from the fountain of Lethe (Waters of Forgetfulness) and then of the Mnemosyne (Waters of Remembrance). They were then lowered into a hole in a cave and left there for days on end to commune with the oracle.

Springs that are supposedly the original Lethe and Mnemosyne can be seen in an attractive park; look for the 'Springs' sign.

There is a paucity of hotels in Livadia, but should you get stuck try the *Hotel Philippos* (☎ 2261 024 931, fax 2261 024 934) with singles/doubles for €35/53, on Athinon, on the Thiva side of town, or the more central *Levadia Hotel* (☎ 2261 023 611, fax 2261 028 266, Plateia L Katsoni 4) where singles/doubles are €67/94.

There are frequent buses run from Livadia to Athens, Thiva, Delphi and Distomo (for Moni Osiou Louka). There are 13 train

ANCIENT DELPHI & SANCTUARY OF APOLLO

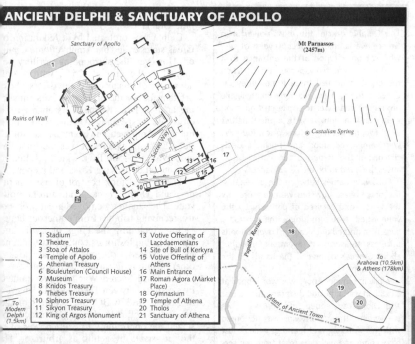

1	Stadium	13	Votive Offering of
2	Theatre		Lacedaemonians
3	Stoa of Attalos	14	Site of Bull of Kerkyra
4	Temple of Apollo	15	Votive Offering of
5	Athenian Treasury		Athens
6	Bouleuterion (Council House)	16	Main Entrance
7	Museum	17	Roman Agora (Market
8	Knidos Treasury		Place)
9	Thebes Treasury	18	Gymnasium
10	Siphnos Treasury	19	Temple of Athena
11	Sikyon Treasury	20	Tholos
12	King of Argos Monument	21	Sanctuary of Athena

ervices to and from Athens daily, as well
s services to most destinations in the north.

ELPHI Δελφοί

ostcode 330 54 • pop 2400
the ancient Greeks hadn't chosen Delphi
lel-**fee**) as their navel of the earth and built
e Sanctuary of Apollo here, someone else
ould have thought of a good reason to
ake this eagle's eyrie village a tourist at-
action. Its location on a precipitous cliff
dge is spectacular and, despite its overt
ommercialism and the constant passage of
ur buses through the modern village, it
ill has a special feel. Modern Delphi is
78km north-west of Athens and is the base
r exploring one of Greece's major tourist
tes. The site and museum are on the left
00m back along the Delphi-Arahova road.

Orientation & Information

lmost everything you'll need in Delphi is
n Vasileon Pavlou & Friderikis. The bus

station is here next to Taverna Castri at the
Itea side of town. The post office, OTE and
banks are also on this street. Ancient Delphi
is 1.5km along the main road to Arahova.

Delphi's municipal tourist office (☎ 2265
082 900) is at the Arahova end of Vasileon
Pavlou & Friderikis. Opening times are
7.30am to 2.30pm Monday to Friday.

Delphi's other through road is Apollonos, which runs north of and parallel to
Vasileon Pavlou & Friderikis.

Ancient Delphi Αρχαιοι Δελφοι

To the majority of people, Delphi (☎ 2265
082 312; adult €3.55/5.90 site/site & museum, EU/non-EU student free/€1.80, free
Sun & public holidays 1 Nov-31 Mar; open
7.30am-6.45pm Mon-Fri, 8.30am-2.45pm
Sat & Sun), of all the ancient sites in Greece,
is the one with the most potent 'spirit of
place'. Built on the slopes of Mt Parnassos,
overlooking the Gulf of Corinth and extending into a valley of cypress and olive trees,

The Delphic Oracle

The Delphic oracle, the most powerful in Greece, was a priestess over 50 years of age, who sat on a tripod at the entrance to a chasm which emitted vaporous fumes. When the priestess inhaled these fumes, they induced a frenzy. Her seemingly unintelligible utterances in answer to a pilgrim's question were translated into verse by a priest. Battles were fought, marriages took place, journeys were embarked upon and business deals clinched on the strength of the oracle's utterances, believed to be divine guidance.

Following battles between the city-states, the oracle was showered with treasures by the victors and accused of partiality by the vanquished. Not surprisingly, the sanctuary became a hotbed of chicanery, coveted for its priceless treasures. It eventually brought about Greece's demise at the hands of the Macedonians.

While in summer Apollo was worshipped at Delphi, in winter he and the oracle took a rest and Dionysos stepped into his place. As everywhere, the god of wine was honoured with merrymaking and feasting, which must have come as a welcome relief from the serious business of trying to comprehend the cryptic messages of the oracle.

this World Heritage-listed site's allure lies both in its stunning setting and its awe-inspiring ruins. The ancients regarded Delphi as the centre of the world, for according to mythology Zeus released two eagles at opposite ends of the world and they met here.

History During early Mycenaean times, the earth goddess, Gaea, was worshipped at Delphi, and it is believed the oracle originated at that time. Later Delphi became a sanctuary to Themis, then Demeter and later Poseidon, but by the end of the Mycenaean period, Apollo had replaced the other deities.

Delphi reached its height in the 4th century BC, when multitudes of pilgrims bearing expensive votive gifts came to ask advice of its oracle, believed to be Apollo's mouthpiece (see the boxed text 'The Delphic Oracle').

Delphi was protected by a federation of Greek states called the Amphyctionic Council. However, the surrounding territory belonged to the city of Krisa, which took advantage of this by charging visitors an exorbitant fee for the privilege of disembarking at its port of Kirrha. This angered the city-states, especially Athens, who called upon the Amphyctionic Council to do something about it. The result was the First Sacred War (595–586 BC), which resulted in the council destroying Krisa and its port.

The council took control of the sanctuary, and Delphi became an autonomous state. The sanctuary enjoyed great prosperity, receiving tributes from numerous benefactors, including the kings of Lydia and Egypt. Struggles for its control ensued, and Delphi passed from one city-state to another, resulting in further sacred wars.

The Third Sacred War was precipitated by a dispute between Thebes and the district of Phocis, in 356 BC, over control of the sanctuary. Philip II, the king of Macedon, seized the opportunity to exert power over the city-states by acting as arbitrator. He brought an end to the conflict and, in 346 BC, the sanctuary again came under the protection of the Amphyctionic Council. Philip took Phocis' place in the council, which had probably been his intention all along.

The Fourth Sacred War broke out in 339 BC when the Amphyctionic Council declared war on Amfissa because it had staked a claim to the sanctuary. The council appealed to Philip for help. Philip saw this as an opportunity to bring his formidable army into Greece and, in so doing, not only destroyed Amfissa, but fought, and defeated, a combined army of Athenians, Thebans and their allies in the Battle of Khaironeia, in Boeotia (north-west of Athens). Philip had achieved his ambition – control of Greece.

In 191 BC, Delphi was taken by the Romans and the oracle's power dwindled. It was consulted on personal, rather than political issues. Along with the country's other pagan sanctuaries, it was abolished by Theodosius in the late 4th century AD.

Exploring the Site The **Sanctuary of Apollo** is on the left of the main road as you walk towards Arahova. In summer try to visit the site early. Otherwise not only will you have to share the site with bus loads of other tourists, but you might find the heat too much.

From the main entrance, at the site of the old **Roman agora**, steps lead to the **Sacred Way**, which winds up to the foundations of the Doric **Temple of Apollo**.

Once you have entered the site, you will pass on your right the pedestal which held the statue of a bull dedicated by the city of Corfu (Kerkyra). Farther along are the remains of monuments erected by Athenians and Lacedaemonians. The semicircular structures on either side of the Sacred Way were erected by the Argives (people of Argos). The one to the right was the **King of Argos Monument**, built in the 4th century BC.

In ancient times the Sacred Way was lined with treasuries and statues given by grateful city-states, including Thebes, Siphnos, Sikyon, Athens and Knidos, in thanks to Apollo for helping them win battles. The **Athenian treasury** has been reconstructed. To the north of this treasury are the foundations of the **bouleuterion** (council house).

The 4th century BC Temple of Apollo dominated the entire sanctuary. Inside the cella was a gold statue of Apollo and a hearth where an eternal flame burned. On the temple architrave were inscriptions of the wise utterings of Greek philosophers, such as 'Know Thyself' and 'Nothing in Excess'. The chasm from which the priestess inhaled the intoxicating vapours has not been found; all that is known is that it was somewhere within the temple.

Above the temple is the well-preserved 4th century BC **theatre**, which was restored by the Romans. From the top row of seats here are magnificent views. Plays were performed here during the Pythian Festival, which, like the Olympic Games, was held every four years. From the theatre the path continues to the **stadium**, the best-preserved in all of Greece.

From the Sanctuary of Apollo, walk towards Arahova along the paved path which runs parallel to the main road and you will come to the **Castalian spring** on the left, where pilgrims had to cleanse themselves before consulting the oracle. Opposite is the **Sanctuary of Athena** *(admission free)*, where Athena Pronaia was worshipped. This is the site of the 4th century BC **tholos**, the most striking of Delphi's monuments. It was a graceful circular structure comprising 20 columns on a three-stepped podium – three of its columns have been re-erected. The purpose of the tholos is unknown.

Museum Ancient Delphi managed to amass a considerable treasure-trove, and this is reflected in its magnificent museum collection *(☎ 2265 082 312; adult €3.50/5.90 museum/museum & site, EU/non-EU student free/€1.80, free Sun & public holidays 1 Nov-31 Mar; open noon-6.15pm Mon, 8.30am-2.45pm Tues-Fri, 8.30am-2.45pm Sat, Sun & public holidays)*. On the landing is a copy of the **omphalos**, a sculpted cone that once stood at what was considered the centre of the world – the spot where the eagles released by Zeus met. In the first room to the right are displayed parts of the frieze from the Siphnian treasury, which depicts the battle between the gods and the giants, and the gods watching the fight over the corpse of Patroclus during the Trojan War. Also in this room is the **Sphinx of the Naxians**, dating from 550 BC. In the room straight ahead are two fine examples of 6th century BC **kouroi**.

In the rooms to the left are fragments of metopes from the Athenian treasury depicting the Labours of Hercules, the Exploits of Theseus and the Battle of the Amazons. Farther on you can't miss the large **Acanthus Column**, with three women dancing around it. In the end room is the celebrated life-size **Bronze Charioteer**, which commemorates a victory in the Pythian Games of 478 or 474 BC.

Places to Stay

Apollon Camping (☎ 2265 082 750, fax 2265 082 888) Adult/tent €3.50/1.80. This is Delphi's nearest and best camping ground, 1.5km west of modern Delphi. It

CENTRAL GREECE

has good facilities including a restaurant, minimarket, swimming pool and barbecue.

Hotels are plentiful in Delphi but it is advisable to ring ahead in peak season and during public holidays. Most of Delphi's hotels have some rooms with views down to the Gulf of Corinth from the balconies.

Hotel Tholos (☎ 2265 082 268, fax 2265 083 268, Apollonos 31) Singles/doubles with bathroom €17.60/29.40. This hotel is a good option for budget travellers. The rooms are clean and nicely furnished.

Hotel Pan (☎ 2265 082 294, fax 2265 083 244, Vasileon Pavlou & Friderikis 53) Singles/doubles with bathroom €25.60/32.35. This refurbished hotel has comfortable, nicely furnished rooms; some have bathrooms. A co-owned hotel, Hotel Artimis, was due to open in mid-2001 – it promised to be one of the best hotels in Delphi.

Hotel Parnassos (☎ 2265 082 321, fax 2265 082 621, Vasileon Pavlou & Friderikis 32) Singles/doubles with bathroom & breakfast €23.50/29.40. This hotel has immaculate, stylishly furnished rooms.

Hotel Hermes (☎ 2265 082 318, fax 2265 082 639, Vasileon Pavlou & Friderikis 29) Singles/doubles with breakfast €32.40/38.20. If it's a spacious and tastefully furnished room with a view you're after, this hotel probably has the edge.

Hotel Olympic (☎ 2265 082 793, fax 2265 082 780, Vasileon Pavlou & Friderikis 59) Singles/doubles with breakfast €44.10/52.90. After a tiring day at Ancient Delphi you can relax in a cosy traditional-style lounge at this hotel. The rooms are immaculate and attractively furnished.

Hotel Amalia (☎ 2265 082 101, fax 2265 082 290, Apollonos 1) Singles/doubles €88/117. This establishment is Delphi's most luxurious hotel. Rooms have all the amenities commensurate with a place in this price bracket and there is a bar, restaurant and swimming pool. The hotel is at the Itea end of the village.

Places to Eat
Eating places in Delphi tend to be mediocre and cater for the passing tourist traffic. The following are exceptions.

Taverna Vakhos (☎ 2265 083 186, Apollonos 31) Mains €4.70-10.30. This excellent taverna serves reasonably priced ready-made food. A generous plate of lamb in lemon sauce with rice and potatoes only €5.60. More expensive dishes include shrimp saganaki and grilled swordfish, both €9.70. There are great views down to the Corinthian Gulf from its terrace.

Taverna H Skala (☎ 2265 082 442, Isaia 11) Mains €4.60-10.50. This unpretentious place has wood-panelled walls adorned with kitsch pictures. It serves a range of tasty ready-made food, grills and delicious homemade mezedes, such as cheese and spinach pies and fried cheese and eggplant salad, for around €2. To reach the taverna, climb the steps opposite Hotel Castellia.

Getting There & Away
Bus There are seven buses daily from Delphi to Amfissa (30 minutes, €1.30), Itea (30 minutes, €1.10) and Arahova (20 minutes, €0.80); six to Athens (three hours, €9.70); one direct bus to Patras (€8.10), three to Lamia (two hours, €5.60) and two to Nafpaktos (three hours, €6.60).

For Kalambaka and Meteora (4½ hours, €13.90) there is a daily bus at 10.15am (3.15pm on Friday and Sunday) to Larisa where you must change buses. If you take the 3.15pm bus you will not be able to get a bus from Larisa until 11pm. This means very late arrival in Kalambaka, so if you intend taking this bus it is advisable to ring ahead and book accommodation. For Thiva take a bus to Livadia, from where there are frequent buses. The bus to and from Athens gets very crowded in the summer, so turn up early to buy a ticket.

Train The nearest train station to Delphi in Livadia (47km away), on the Athens-Thessaloniki line.

MT PARNASSOS
Παρνασσός Όρος

Parnassos National Park was established 1938. With the Fterolakkas ski centre grazing its north-eastern flanks it's hardly a remote wilderness; but despite this, inadequa nservation measures and overgrazing, ekkers on Parnassos are rewarded with lendid vistas and an array of wildflowers spring.

The 3600 hectare park, to the north of elphi and Arahova, has three peaks over 00m: Liakoura (the highest), Geronvrakhos and Kotrona.

Between 800m and 1800m the slopes of arnassos support Kefallonian fir and juper, interspersed with yellow-flowered rubs and the rare purple-flowered *Daphne sminea*. Above the treeline are meadows fescue grass and wild plum trees. Spring owers including crocuses, squills, tulips, chids and irises sprout from the limestone cks. Greece's most common mammals – x, hare, squirrels and jackals, may be otted – as well as hawks, passerines and ltures.

The most popular ascent on Parnassos is the Liakoura peak. The route begins at e Greek Alpine Club's Parnassos refuge 1900m, 20km north of Arahova and 5km south of Amfiklia.

There are two ski centres on Mt Parnas-s, both with overnight accommodation. he largest is the EOT centre at Fterolakkas 750m), which also has facilities higher up Kelaria (1950m). For more information ntact the municipal tourist office in Del-i or the EOT in Athens, or the **ski centre** ☎ 2267 022 689). The centre is 24km from rahova and 17km from Amfiklia. The thens department store Klaoudatos organ-es trips to this ski centre. For more infor-ation, see the Activities section of the thens chapter. There is also a branch of laoudatos (☎ 2267 032 553) on Delphon Arahova where you can get information out the centre.

The second centre is at Gerondovrahos. or more information contact **Athens Ski-vers Club** (☎ *21 0643 3368, Sarantapi-u 51, Athens)*. The centre is 25km from rahova and 34km from Delphi.

etting There & Away
here is no public transport to either centre you'll need to take a taxi or hitch from elphi, Arahova or Amfiklia.

ARAHOVA Αράχωβα
postcode 320 04 • pop 4000
Arahova (ah-**ra**-ho-vah) is built on a rocky spur of Mt Parnassos at an altitude of 960m. It's only 12km from Delphi on the main Athens-Delphi road and so is an alternative base from which to visit the ancient site. The main street is flanked by shops selling embroidery, hand-woven goods, flokati rugs and various other souvenirs. The town is also noted for its cheese, honey, *hilopittes* (dried pasta) and a pleasant red wine.

Despite this overt flaunting of its assets to passing tourists, Arahova is essentially a rugged mountain town and to appreciate its charm you need to explore its stepped alley-ways.

The **Festival of Agios Georgios** is held in the town on 23 April (if this date falls dur-ing Lent, the festival is postponed until Easter Tuesday). It's a joyous celebration of feasting and folk dancing.

Arahova is primarily an accommodation resort for skiers, and for Greeks it is very much the 'in' place to be seen during the skiing season. Prices in winter reflect this trend and some restaurants close in summer.

Orientation & Information
The town's main thoroughfare is Delphon, which snakes its way through three squares. The bus station is at Celena Café opposite the central square of Plateia Lakka. The EOT office (☎ 2267 031 630, ☎/fax 2267 029 170) is on Plateia Xenias, one block west of the central square. Opening hours are 8am to 10pm (winter) and 8am to 8.30pm (summer) daily. The helpful staff can assist in finding accommodation. The post office and OTE are also on Plateia Xenias.

Places to Stay
All the prices given here are for high (win-ter) season. During low season there are substantial reductions.

Hotel Parnassos (☎ *2267 031 307/189)* Singles/doubles €23.50/32.40. This hotel at the eastern end of Delphon is Arahova's best budget choice. The unadorned rooms are clean and comfortable and the hotel has a small bar.

Apollon Inn (☎/fax 2267 031 057, Delphon 106) Singles/doubles with bathroom €20.60/29.40. This is a pleasant and comfortable hotel and good value, except at Easter when prices, astonishingly, almost treble.

Studios Celena (☎ 2267 031 990, fax 2267 031 256) 3-bed studios €88.20. These lovely split-level studios above Celena Café on Delphon are tastefully furnished, well equipped and have log fires in winter.

Pension Nostos (☎ 2267 031 385, fax 2267 031 765, e nostos@otenet.gr) Doubles/triples €76.50/96.50. This homey and characterful place on Plateia Xenias has comfortable rooms that are kept spotless, and a good buffet breakfast is included in the price. In chilly weather you can enjoy a drink in front of a roaring log fire in the snug little bar. The Beatles visited here in the 1960s – look for their photos on the wall.

Anemolia Hotel (☎ 2267 031 640, fax 2267 031 642, e bwgreece@travelling.gr) Doubles €117. Arahova's most luxurious, this hotel has a swimming pool, small gym and a sauna. It stands on a hill above the Arahova-Delphi road, 1.5km from Arahova.

Places to Eat

Restaurant Parnassos (☎ 2267 032 569) Mains €2.60-5.90. You can tuck into a bowl of hearty soup at this welcoming restaurant on Plateia Xenias, or choose from a range of ready-made food and grilled meats.

Restaurant Fterolaka (☎ 2267 032 556) Mains €5.90-8.60. This restaurant serves generous portions of succulent grilled meats in a pleasant, relaxed atmosphere. It's in the middle of Arahova, and reached through an archway from Delphon.

Restaurant Roumeli (☎ 2267 032 245) Mains €4.40-10.30. You can enjoy a generous portion of grilled meat surrounded by folksy wall hangings and cushions in this cosy little restaurant with a wood-beamed ceiling. It's at the eastern end of Delphon, on the left as you go towards Delphi.

Kaplanis Restaurant (☎ 2267 031 891) Mains €3.50-12.40. For a change of scenery, clamber up to this restaurant on Plateia

Tropeou, which in addition to grilled meat offers a large range of mezedes, soups and other ready-made foods. A speciality i zucchini flowers. The interior has split level dining rooms and gilded chandelier and there's also an outdoor terrace. Fron Delphon, turn right at the Apollon Inn an when the road bends left, go straight ahea up the stepped street. Follow it as it bend right, and take the second turn on the righ Continue ahead and turn left at the nex two T-junctions, and the taverna is on th left.

Getting There & Away

The five buses daily that run betwee Athens and Delphi stop at Arahova. In ad ition there are some local buses to Delph (20 minutes, €0.80).

AROUND ARAHOVA
Moni Osiou Louka

Μονή Οσίου Λουκά

The Moni Osiou Louka (Monastery of . Luke Stiris; ☎ 2267 022 797; admissio €2.40; open 8am-7pm, closed 2pm-4p May-Sept) is 8km east of the village of Dis tomo, which lies just south of the Athens Delphi road. Its principal church contain some of Greece's finest Byzantine frescoe Modest dress is required (no shorts).

The monastery is dedicated to a local her mit who was canonised for his healing an prophetic powers. The monastic comple includes two churches. The interior c **Agios Loukas**, the main one, is a gloriou symphony of marble and mosaics. Ther are also icons by Michael Damaskinos, th 16th-century Cretan painter.

In the main body of the church, the ligh is partially blocked by the ornate marbl window decorations. This creates strikin contrasts of light and shade, which greatl enhance the atmosphere. The crypt where : Luke is buried also contains fine frescoes.

The other church, **Panagia** (Church of th Virgin Mary), built in the 10th century, ha a less impressive interior as none of its fre coes have survived.

This World Heritage-listed monastery in an idyllic setting, with breathtaking vista from its leafy terrace, where *Café Bar Yannis* (☎ 2267 021 255) sells local produce and serves good coffee – just in case you're one of those people who can't go anywhere outside hissing distance of an espresso machine.

Distomo Δίστομο
postcode 320 05 • pop 2156
The only thing worth seeking out in Distomo is the **war memorial**, which commemorates the slaying of over 200 Distomo villagers by the Nazis in 1944 in reprisal for a guerrilla attack. The large, white marble slab on the memorial wall with an inscription in both Greek and German is an official German government apology for the atrocity. Look for the 'mausoleum' sign.

Places to Stay Moni Osiou Louka is a hassle to get to by public transport, so if you get stuck, Distomo has two hotels.

Hotel America (☎/fax 2267 022 079, *Kasriti 1*) Singles/doubles with bathroom €20/40. This hotel has clean and tidy rooms.

Hotel Koutriaris (☎ 2267 022 268, fax 2267 022 267, *Plateia Ethnikis Antistasis 6*) Singles/doubles €30/40. This comfortable hotel has carpeted, nicely furnished rooms with telephone and TV.

Getting There & Away You can take the Delphi bus from Athens and ask the driver to stop at the turn-off for Distomo, from where you should be able to flag down a taxi for the 12km to the monastery (€7.90). Otherwise it's a 3km walk to the taxi stand at Distomo. From Livadia there are 11 buses daily to Distomo (45 minutes, €1.50) and one to the monastery at 1pm (one hour, €2.20). There are hourly buses to Athens from Livadia (two hours, €7.60).

GALAXIDI Γαλαξίδι
postcode 330 52 • pop 1200
Galaxidi is the prettiest of the low-key resorts on the north coast of the Corinthian Gulf. If you have your own transport it makes a pleasant base from which to visit Delphi.

Galaxidi's most prosperous period was between 1830 and 1910 when it was a major caique-building centre. Some fine stone mansions survive from this time.

Galaxidi is reasonably tranquil except during high season and holiday weekends when its narrow streets become choked with carloads of Athenians.

Orientation & Information
Galaxidi's central square is Plateia Iroön Manoisakia, from where the main street of Nikolou Mama leads to the larger of Galaxidi's two harbours, and Str Kammenoi leads to the smaller harbour. The post office and a bank are on Nikolou Mama. There is no OTE but there are several cardphones.

A forested headland, opposite the waterfront, is fringed by a series of pebbled coves.

Things to See
The **ethnographical museum** (☎ 2265 041 910; admission €1.40; open 9.30am-1.30pm daily) has displays of embroidery and costumes. Galaxidi also has a **naval museum** (☎ 2265 041 795). It was closed for refurbishment at the time of research.

The wood-carved iconostasis in the **Church of Agios Nikolaos** is one of Greece's finest. Follow the signs for the museums and church.

The little 13th-century **Moni Metamorfosis** stands amid olive groves and cypresses, 7km inland from Galaxidi. From this vantage point there are terrific views down to the Gulf of Corinth. To reach it go under the flyover and take the road opposite. A lone nun lives in the cloister.

Places to Stay
Hotel Ganimede (☎ 2265 041 328, fax 2265 042 160, ⓦ gsp.gr/ganimede.gr, *Nik Gourgouri 16*) Singles/doubles €35/50. This Italian-owned hotel in a 19th-century captain's house is an absolute gem. The impeccable rooms have subtle harmonious tones with patterned rugs and wood-panelled ceilings and floors. Excellent gut-busting breakfasts (€7.30) are served in the gorgeous flower-filled courtyard, which has a fountain. Walk 20m down Nikolou Mama and look for the sign pointing right.

CENTRAL GREECE

Hotel Arhontiko (☎ 2265 042 292, fax 2265 042 492) Doubles/triples €79/82.50. The advertising about this beautiful and idiosyncratic stone mansion at the small harbour states 'the extremely uncommon rooms here will astonish you' – and well they might! The 'honeymoon room' has a four-poster bed with white diaphanous drapes, another has a rather bizarre boat-style bed. The hotel has a lovely garden and sea views.

Hotel Argo (☎ 2265 041 996, fax 2265 041 878, Str Kammenoi 17-19) Singles/doubles €44/70.50. Housed in a beautiful neo-classical mansion near the small harbour, this hotel has immaculate, well-equipped rooms with pretty pastel decor.

Places to Eat

Cafes and tavernas line the waterfront of Galaxidi's larger harbour.

Albatross (☎ 2265 042 233, Constadinou Satha 36) Mains €3.50-10.30. You could write the menu of this little place, near the Church of Agios Nicholaos, on the back of a postage stamp, but offerings (usually ready-made food) are always tasty and cheap. Look for the sign on Nikolou Mama.

Taverna Il Posto (☎ 2265 041 328, Nik Gourgouri 21) Mains €4.70-13.20. This romantic taverna with a fountain serves authentic Italian food. The oven-baked fish dishes are especially delectable.

Taverna Porto (☎ 2265 041 182, Akti Oianthis 41) Mains €4.50-14.70. Locals give the thumbs up to this waterfront taverna. You can tuck into a huge plate of gavros or whitebait for €4.50. More expensive options include seabream and mullet (€23.50/kg).

Getting There & Away

The bus station is on Plateia Iroön Manoisakia. There are three buses to Patras and Athens. You can also take the Thessaloniki bus from Agrino (€7.90). This bus will drop you off on the highway from where it's a short walk to Galaxidi.

AROUND GALAXIDI

From the market town and burgeoning holiday resort of Itea, 19km north-east of Galaxidi and 10km from Delphi, a road branches left for 2km to **Kira**. This was ancient Kirrha, the port of Delphi, which was destroyed by the Amphyctionic Council in the First Sacred War (595–586 BC). Kira is today a quiet suburb of Itea, and has a long sand-and-pebble beach, very clean sea and two excellent camping grounds nearby (see Places to Stay).

West of Galaxidi the coastal highway passes a number of seaside towns and villages before meeting the important ferry-boat link at **Andirio**. Boats here run every 15 minutes between 6.45am and 10.45pm to Rion. **Nafpaktos**, 9km east of Andirio, has an attractive harbour, a good beach and well-preserved Venetian castle. Nafpaktos was known as Lepanto in medieval times and it was here in 1571 that the famous naval battle of Lepanto took place.

Places to Stay

There are two camping grounds near Kira on the Itea-Distomo road. In summer a frequent bus from Itea passes them.

Kaparelis Camping (☎ 2265 032 330) Adult/tent €4.50/2.70. This is a good, well-shaded ground with well-maintained facilities, a restaurant, bar and minimarket. It's opposite the beach 2km east of Kira.

Ayannis Camping (☎ 2265 032 555, fax 0265 233 870) Adult €3.80, car €2.30, small/large tent €2.40/2.90. This site has good shade, well-kept toilet and shower facilities, a restaurant, minimarket and beachside bar. It's next to a nice pebble beach and there are several small coves nearby.

Between Nafpaktos and Andirio there are several hotels as well as two camping grounds.

Doric Camping (☎ 2266 031 722) Adult/tent €3.80/2.90. This camping ground on the inland side of the road at Agio Nikolaos, is well maintained with restaurant, bar and minimarket.

Platanitis Beach Camping (☎ 2634 03 555) Adult/tent €3.80/2.90. This well maintained site is on the seaward side of the coast road is just 2km from the ferry crossing at Andirio. It has a restaurant, bar and minimarket.

Getting There & Away

The Delphi-Patras bus goes along this stretch of coast. There are five buses daily from Itea to Nafpaktos and vice versa, stopping at the coastal towns along the way.

MESSOLONGI Μεσολόγγι
postcode 302 00 • pop 13,000

Most people come to Messolongi for historical or sentimental reasons, rather than to seek a lively holiday spot. It is Messolongi's connection with the War of Independence and the role played by Britain's philhellene bard Lord Byron that gives the town its historic reputation.

Messolongi is as flat as a pancake and skirts a murky-looking lagoon, so does not sound very promising. However, recent efforts to beautify it have paid off. Harilaou Trikoupi, which runs from the central square; Athanasiou Razikotsika, which is parallel to it; and the pedestrian lanes between them are now appealing and atmospheric with good bars and tavernas. As one hotel owner put it: Messolongi could only get better'.

History

During the War of Independence, the strategically important town of Messolongi was chosen by the Phanariot Mavrordatos to be the western centre of resistance, in order to inhibit Turkish communications with the Peloponnese. Lord Byron arrived in Messolongi in 1824, already a famous international philhellene, with the intention of lending his weight, reputation and money to the independence cause. After months of vainly attempting to organise the motley Greek forces, who spent much time squabbling among themselves, Byron's efforts came to naught. He contracted a fever, no doubt brought on by the unsanitary conditions of what was, at the time, a miserable outpost, and died on 19 April 1824, his immediate aims unfulfilled.

Ironically, Byron's death spurred on internationalist forces to precipitate the end of the War of Independence and he became a Greek national hero. One hundred years after his death, many male children, now in their seventies, were christened with the name Byron (Vyronas in Greek), and most Greek towns have a street named after him.

Messolongi was captured by the Turks in April 1826, after their year-long siege of the city drove 9000 men, women and children to escape on the night of 22–23 April 1826 through what is now called the Gate of Exodus. Most took refuge on Mt Zygos, only to be caught and killed by a nearby Albanian mercenary force. This self-sacrificial exodus is recognised as one of the most heroic deeds of the war and was immortalised in Dionysios Solomos' epic poem *I Eleftheri Poliorkimeni* (The Free Besieged).

Orientation & Information

Messolongi is the capital of the prefecture of Etolo-Akarnania. The town is laid out in a roughly rectangular grid with the main square, Plateia Markou Botsari, in the middle. The square is dominated by the town hall on its eastern side. The OTE is on Spyrou Trikoupi and the post office is on Spyrou Moustakli, both of which are just east of the central square. Internet access is available at Star Light Internet Club on the central square. It's open 10am to 11pm Monday to Saturday.

Messolongi does not have an EOT. The tourist police (☎ 2631 027 220) are at Spyro Trikoupi 29.

Things to See

All arrivals to Messolongi enter via the aforementioned **Gate of Exodus**. The gate is narrow and dangerous for traffic, so beware if you are entering by car.

Just beyond the gate, to the right, is the **Garden of the Heroes** *(open 9am-8pm, closes earlier in winter)*, translated incorrectly as Heroes' Tombs on the road sign. This memorial garden was established on the orders of the then governor of Greece, Yiannis Kapodistrias, who in May 1829 issued the following decree:

...within these walls of the city of Messolongi lie the bones of those brave men, who fell bravely while defending the city...it is our duty to gather together, with reverence, the holy remains of these men and to lay them to rest in a memorial where our country may, each year, repay its debt of gratitude.

CENTRAL GREECE

You will find the Greek text of this decree on the marble slab to the right as you enter the garden. Within the leafy grounds of the garden you will find memorials to many other philhellenes as well. Beneath the **statue of Lord Byron**, which features prominently in the garden, the heart of the poet is buried. A much larger and more modern bronze statue of Byron outside the garden now overshadows the smaller sculpted one inside.

The **museum** (☎ *2631 022 134; town hall, Plateia Markou Botsari; admission free; open 9am-1.30pm & 4pm-7pm daily*) is dedicated to the revolution and has a collection of Byron memorabilia. Bone up on your War of Independence history beforehand in order to get a full feel for the importance of these historic events.

Places to Stay & Eat

Messolongi has three hotels.

Avra (☎/fax *2631 022 284, Harilaou Trikoupi*) Singles/doubles with bathroom €25.50/41.50. The rooms are modern, bright and clean at this hotel, which is right in the centre of things, overlooking Plateia Markou Botsari.

Theoxenia (☎ *2631 022 493, fax 2631 022 230, Tourlidos 2*) Singles/doubles €41.50/65. This hotel's modern, spacious rooms are well equipped. It overlooks the lagoon and is well signposted.

Liberty (☎ *2631 024 831, fax 2631 024 832, Iroön Polytechniou 41*) Singles/doubles €41.50/53. This massive hotel has spacious rooms but looks as though it is need of refurbishment. On the plus side it is near the Garden of Heroes, which some of its balconies overlook.

Unlike the accommodation situation, you're spoilt for choice when it comes to eating in Messolongi.

Poseidon Restaurant (☎ *2631 022 223, Athanasiou Razikotsika 4*) Mains €5-8.80. At this characterful little place you can eat low-priced, tasty, filling meals. Tzatziki, chips and gavros, for instance, is €5.

Karvelis Taverna (☎ *2631 051 532, Dimitris Makri 7*) Mains €7.30-14.70. This fine taverna with a serene green-and-white interior and pictures of old Messolongi, serves

very tasty oven-cooked meat dishes. Tak the second turn left from Harilaou Trikou and it's on the right.

Ouzeri Proton Voithion (☎ *2631 02 707, Vironos 19*) Mains €4.50-8.80. you'd like to try Messolongi's speciality eels from the lagoon – head for this roug and-ready little ouzeri. Turn right one bloc along Harilaou Trikoupi, and look for th eels hanging in the window.

Entertainment

Versus bar (☎ *2631 022 068, Dimitr Makri 5*) You can hear jazz and tradition Greek music – sometimes live – at this ba As well as alcoholic drinks it serves tea milk shakes, chocolate fondues and sorbe in many different flavours.

Getting There & Away

The bus station is on Mavrokordatou 5, ju off the central square. Buses go to Athen Patras and most destinations north, thoug you may need to change at Agrinio.

SOUTH-WEST COASTAL RESORTS

Amfilohia Αμφιλοχία

This attractive little place at the south eastern corner of the Gulf of Ambracia a tracts a small holiday crowd. Most visito are merely passing through, as it is on th main highway between Epiros and th south. It is a lively town and an amenabl enough stopover point. Swimming is touc and go, despite the town touting an officia beach, as the water is stagnant. You mig want to try a bit farther north up the gulf t wards Menidi. There is a long, curvin promenade with many restaurants and cafe If you are here in August or Septembe look out for the strange luminescence of th water at night. The town has five hotels an one camping ground.

Vonitsa Βόνιτσα

The town of Vonitsa is popular with loc holiday-makers, but doesn't have any re beach scene to speak of, since it is on th still waters of the Gulf of Ambracia. It quiet and pleasant, and conveniently locate or the town of Preveza and the Aktio airport. Its waterfront is being developed and here are a number of modern cafes and restaurants. The route through Vonitsa from Preveza is a quicker way through to the main north-south highway to the Peloponnese. There are five hotels to choose from.

Mytikas Μύτικας
The small village of Mytikas is built on the gulf of the same name. This place has yet to feel the effect of mass tourism. It's an oddly pleasant kind of place, though, with its palm trees and houses built right up to the water's edge. The beach is pebbly and uncommercialised, but is being gradually developed. There are only a couple of hotels, a few domatia and a scattering of tavernas. You can take a local caique to the isolated islands of Kalamos, looming over Mytikas, or Kastos tucked away on the other side.

Astakos Αστακός
Slightly more upmarket and bigger than Mytikas, Astakos is another place for a quiet holiday, though it lacks Mytikas' cosiness. It can be used as a more convenient stepping stone for access to the Ionian Islands, via the daily ferry to and from Ithaki in summer. There is one hotel and some domatia in summer.

Getting There & Away
Public transport to these locations is by bus from either Agrinio or Vonitsa.

KARPENISI Καρπενήσι
**postcode 361 00 • pop 10,000
elevation 960m**
Karpenisi is in the foothills of Mt Tymfristos (2315m), 82km west of Lamia. Beyond the Ypati turn-off the Lamia-Karpenisi road is relatively flat and runs along the valley of the River Sperhios. After Makri, it begins to climb through forested hills and really climbs at the village of Tymfristos, winding slowly upwards to enter the prefecture of Evrytania. You then enter Karpenisi via the new 1.5km Mt Tymfristos tunnel. There are many opportunities for trekking and, if you have your own transport, you can explore

some delightful mountain villages. Karpenisi sees tourists all year round and the skiing centre, 17km away, is popular with Greeks. The town itself is not especially attractive but lies in a beautiful, well-wooded region the EOT brochures tout as the 'Switzerland of Greece'.

Orientation & Information
The central square is in the north-west of the town. The thoroughfares of Zinopoulou, Athanasion Karpenisioti and Spyridon Georgiou Tsitsara run downhill from this square; Ethnikis Antistaseos runs northwest from it. Karpenisi's tourist office (☎/fax 2237 021 016) is on the central square indicated by a folksy sign in Greek. (Folksy signs seem to be all the rage in Karpenisi – even the public toilet has one.) The English-speaking staff can help you find accommodation, and has information on adventure sports in the area. The office is open 9am to 2pm and 5pm to 8pm Monday to Friday, 10am to 2pm and 5pm to 8pm Saturday, 10am to 2pm Sunday.

Several banks around the central square have ATM machines. The post office is on Agiou Nikolaou Kaprienisiotou. To get there walk 150m down Athanasou Karpenisioti and turn left. The OTE is just off the central square on Ethnikis Antistaseos.

Activities
Trekking Hellas (☎/fax 2237 025 940, *Zinopoulou 19*) This outfit organises adventure sport activities including group activities in trekking, kayaking, canoeing and rafting.

Places to Stay
The following are some of the most central accommodation options.

Konstantinos Koutsikos domatia (☎ 2237 021 400) Doubles with bathroom €35.30. These attractive domatia are high up (51 steps), just south of the bus station.

Hotel Galini (☎ 2237 022 914, fax 2237 025 623, *Riga Fereou 3*) Singles/doubles with bathroom €26.50/41. The Galini is a good budget choice. The furniture might be circa 1960, but rooms are comfortable and spotless and it's on a quiet street. To reach it, walk down Spyridon Georgiou Tsitsara and take the first right.

Anesis Hotel (☎ 2237 022 840, fax 2237 022 305, Zinopoulou 50) Singles/doubles €73.50/88. This beautiful, but expensive, hotel has spacious and tastefully furnished rooms, and the price includes breakfast.

Places to Eat

Three Stars Restaurant (☎ 2237 024 222, Athanasiou Karpenisioti 35) Mains €3.50-7.95. This American-style restaurant is Karpenisi's cheapest eatery. Choose from well-prepared pasta dishes, pizza and grills, or tuck into a bowl of hearty goat stew (€4.10). Tasty but cholesterol-raising breakfasts also feature.

Taverna H Folia (☎ 2237 024 405) Mains €4.30-7.25. This pleasant taverna has a 'museumy' ambience, with a display of ancient-looking cooking utensils and other paraphernalia. Generous portions of grilled meats are served with a range of mezedes. Walk one block down Athanasiou Karpenisioti and look for the restaurant's folksy sign on the left.

Klimataria (☎ 2237 022 230, Kosma Etolou 25) Mains €5.30-7.20. Hare in oregano and rooster in red wine sauce are among the specialities here. To get there, walk 50m down Athanasiou Karpenisioti and turn right onto Kosmo Etolou.

Panorama (☎ 2237 025 976, Riga Fereou 18) Mains €3.85-8.25. Locals like the family ambience of this place, with its outdoor eating area – somewhat marred by a ghastly unfinished hotel complex overlooking it. There's a comprehensive menu featuring ready-made food and grilled meats. It is 100m past Hotel Galini.

Entertainment

Mousikes Epafe Club (☎ 2237 025 555, Kosma Etolou 17) Open Fri, Sat & public holidays. You might want to catch some late-night, authentic live Greek music here. Things don't get going until after midnight.

Getting There & Away

Karpenisi's bus station is just beyond the central square. There are three buses daily to Athens (five hours, €15.45) and four to Lamia (1¾ hours, €4.40). There are also two buses daily to and from Agrinio in Etolo-Akarnania (3½ hours, €6.60). For Mikro and Megalo Horio there are three buses daily (20 minutes, €0.90) and for Proussos, two weekly on Monday and Friday (45 minutes, €2.10).

AROUND KARPENISI

From Karpenisi, a scenic mountain road leads south for 37km to the village of **Proussos**. Along the way you'll pass several picturesque villages. The charming village of **Koryshades**, 5km south-west of Karpenisi, has well-preserved mansions and is reached by a right turn-off along the Proussos road. **Mikro Horio** and **Megalo Horio** are 12km farther along the road. Megalo Horio, the more attractive of the two, has many traditional stone houses. One of these is the well-signposted **folklore museum** *(☎ 223 041 245; admission free; open 10.30am-3pm Fri, Sat & Sun Oct-May; 10am-3pm, 6pm-8pm daily June-Oct).*

Megalo Horio is the starting point for the trek up Mt Kaliakouda. To reach the path veer left onto Soilou 25m beyond the central square; the route is marked with red spots. If you fancy something more sedate, you can take a pleasant stroll along the banks of the River Karpenisotis along a footpath which begins opposite the bus terminal.

The **Monastery of the Virgin of Proussi otissa** *(☎ 2237 080 705),* just before the village of Proussos, has a miracle-working icon. There are more icons and ecclesiastical ornaments in the monastery's 18th-century church. There are several resident monks, and pilgrims flock there in August for the Feast of the Assumption.

Places to Stay

Hotel Antigone (☎ 2237 041 395, fax 223 041 450, Megalo Horio) Singles/doubles with bathroom €35.30/44. The rooms of this hotel on the central square are prettily furnished and most have balconies with mountain views.

Domatia Agnanti (☎/fax 2237 041 303, Megalo Horio) Singles/doubles €23.50/35.30

vith bathroom. This welcoming place has mmaculate and stylish rooms and balcony iews with a high 'wow!' factor. It's on the eft before the bus terminal.

Agathidis Pension (☎ *2237 080 813, Proussos*) Singles/doubles with bathroom €23.50/41. This hotel in Proussos is nothing to write home about, but is the village's only option.

KARPENISI TO AGRINIO
Two buses daily ply this tortuous (but sealed) road across the mountains and villages of the Agrafa to Agrinio in Etolo-Akarnania. During the Tourkokratia (the period of Turkish occupation of Greece), the villages of this region were considered too remote to be recorded for taxation purposes, so they were classified as *agrafa* (unrecorded). The bus covers the distance in a low 3½ hours and there is no rest stop on the journey, so make sure you go to the toilet before you board, or forever hold your pees.

It's a spectacular drive through remote and beautiful countryside. The road climbs and twists downwards as far as the first main centre of habitation, the twin villages of Anatoliki and Dytiki Frangista. The road then crosses the long bridge over the artificial Lake Kremasta into Etolo-Akarnania, climbs high over the last ridge and eventually winds down through small farm holdings into Agrinio. If you suffer from motion sickness, think twice before making this trip.

LAMIA Λαμία
postcode 351 00 • pop 44,000
Lamia is the capital of the prefecture of Fthiotida and is an attractive town at the western end of the Maliakos Gulf, built on the foothills of Mt Orthys. Lamia rarely figures on people's itineraries, but it deserves a look-in. Like most towns that are not dependent on tourism for their livelihood, Lamia is a vibrant and lively place year-round. It is famous for its lamb on the spit, its *kourabiedes* (almond shortcake) and its *cynogala* (sour milk).

To the east of Lamia is the narrow pass of Thermopylae, where, in 480 BC, Leonidas and 300 Spartans managed to temporarily

halt the Persian advance of Xerxes and his 30,000-strong army.

Orientation & Information
The main cluster of activity in Lamia is centred on Plateia Eleftherias, Plateia Laou and Plateia Parkou. Confusingly, there are six bus terminals, all serving different destinations (see Getting There & Away later). The local train station is south of the centre on Konstantinoupoleos.

The EOT office is at Plateia Laou 3 (☎ 2231 030 065, fax 2231 030 066) and is open 7am to 2.30pm Monday to Friday. The OTE is on Plateia Eleftherias and the post office is on Athanasiou Diakou. Random Games Internet Café is at Rozaki Angeli 40. It is open 9am to midnight Monday to Saturday.

You will find most banks on, or near, Plateia Parkou. The police station is on Patroklou.

Things to See & Do
Lamia's **frourio**, or fort, is worth the hike just for the views. Within it is the **archaeological museum** (☎ *2231 029 992; admission €1.47; open 8.30am-2.30pm daily*). This museum has finds from Neolithic to Roman times.

The **Gorgopotamos railway bridge**, 7km from Lamia, is a fairly famous landmark in recent Greek history. It was blown up by the united national forces on 25 November 1944 to delay the German advance, this was considered one of the greatest acts of sabotage of the time. If you are heading south by train to Athens, you will have to cross the reconstructed bridge which spans over a deep ravine, shortly after leaving Lianokladi station.

Thermopylae (Thermopyles in modern Greek) is 18km from Lamia on the main Athens highway. A large statue of Leonidas marks the spot where the Persian army was delayed on its way to Thessaly, but where Leonidas and his brave Spartans ultimately perished.

Today the pass is much wider than it was in antiquity because of a gradual silting up of the land on the sea side.

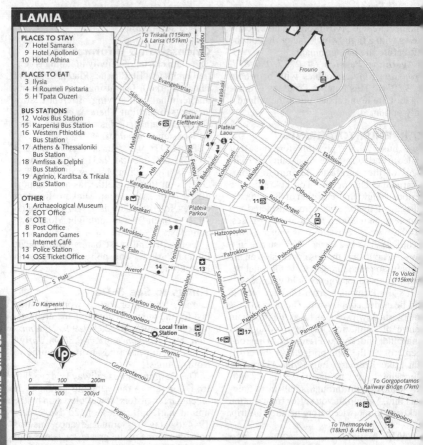

LAMIA

PLACES TO STAY
7 Hotel Samaras
9 Hotel Apollonio
10 Hotel Athina

PLACES TO EAT
3 Ilysia
4 H Roumeli Psistaria
5 H Tpata Ouzeri

BUS STATIONS
12 Volos Bus Station
15 Karpenisi Bus Station
16 Western Fthiotida
   Bus Station
17 Athens & Thessaloniki
   Bus Station
18 Amfissa & Delphi
   Bus Station
19 Agrinio, Karditsa & Trikala
   Bus Station

OTHER
1 Archaeological Museum
2 EOT Office
6 OTE
8 Post Office
11 Random Games
   Internet Café
13 Police Station
14 OSE Ticket Office

Places to Stay & Eat

As it does not figure in most tourists itineraries, Lamia does not have an abundance of hotels.

Hotel Athina (☎ 2231 027 700, *Rozaki Angeli 47*) Singles/doubles with bathroom €25/38.30. Although somewhat lacklustre, the rooms at the Athina are clean and comfortable and have air-con and TV.

Hotel Apollonio (☎ 2231 022 668, *fax 2231 023 032*) Singles/doubles with bathroom €29.40/38.25. This hotel has a nice location overlooking Plateia Parkou and the rooms are modern and well maintained.

Hotel Samaras (☎ 2231 028 971, fax 223 042 704, *Athanasiou Diakou 14*) Singles doubles €41.20/53. This smart hotel with lashings of black-and-white marble has styl ish blue-and-white decorated rooms with TV and air-con.

Central Greece's proclivity for grille meats reaches its apotheosis in Lamia. The pedestrianised southern end of Karaïskaki i full of psistarias with the rather grotesque sight of whole roast lamb in their windows

H Roumeli Psistaria (☎ 2231 025 793 *Karaïskaki 23*) Mains €5.85-10.30. All the psistarias on Karaïskaki serve good lamb but the Roumeli is the only one that gives more than a passing nod to ambience.

Ilysia (☎ *2231 027 006, Kalyva Bakogianni 10)* Mains €2.65-4.45. This large, no-frills taverna serves a huge range of tasty, ready-made dishes.

H Tpata ouzeri (☎ *2231 043 883, Androutsou 14)* Mains €3.25-7.35. This is one of a cluster of ouzeria on Androutsou. Outdoor eating is under a canopy surrounded by copious greenery. 'Tpata' means trawler and, appropriately, the fish dishes are especially good here.

Plateia Eleftherias, with its swish cafeterias, attracts the younger set, whereas Plateia Laou, shaded by large plane trees, is more sedate, with traditional kafeneia.

There's a bustling *street market* on Riga Fereou and its side streets every Saturday.

Getting There & Away

Bus The terminal for Athens and Thessaloniki buses is on Papakyriazi, which runs off Satovriandou. There are almost hourly buses for Athens (three hours, €12.80) and two daily (three weekends) for Thessaloniki (four hours, €15.60). There is a bus for Patras on Friday and Sunday (3½ hours, €14.40).

Farther down the hill on the corner of Konstantinoupoleos is the bus station for western Fthiotida, which includes the village of Ypati.

The terminal for Karpenisi is at Markou Botsari 3. There are four buses daily to Karpenisi (1¾ hours, €4.40). There are another two stations on Thermopylon, 100m south of the railway line: one for Agrinio, Karditsa and Trikala (€5.90) and the other for Amfissa and Delphi. Finally, buses for Volos leave from a station on Rozaki Angeli.

Train Lamia has a very inconveniently located main train station 7km west of the town centre at Lianokladi. Most intercity trains stop at Lianokladi. Train tickets can be prepurchased in Lamia from the OSE office at Averof 28. Bus No 6 (to Stavros) links the Lianokladi station with the Lamia town centre and passes the OSE ticket office.

The small train station in town has only two trains daily linking Lamia with

Lianokladi from the branch line terminus at Stylida (14km east of Lamia) – hardly a reliable transport option, though the train does go on to Athens.

ITI NATIONAL PARK

The village of **Ypati**, 22km west of Lamia and 8km south of the Karpenisi-Lamia road, has the remains of a fortress and is the starting point for treks on Mt Iti (2125m). This mountain is the focus of the Iti National Park. It's a verdant region with forests of fir and black pine. According to mythology, Mt Iti was the place where the dying Hercules built his own funeral pyre and was burned to death. While the mortal elements in Hercules perished, the immortal Hercules joined his divine peers on Mt Olympus.

Ypati is untouched by tourism, reminiscent of the Greece of thirty years ago before it became prettified, sanitised and 'Eurofied'. The hub of the village is the tree-shaded, central square of Plateia Ainianon, flanked by traditional kafeneia. From here it's a four-hour walk to the **Trapeza Refuge** (1850m) on Mt Iti. To reach the path, walk uphill along 25 Martiou and turn right at the T-junction. The route is marked with red spots and red squares. For information about the refuge contact the Lamia EOS (☎ 2231 026 786), Ipsilandou 20, Lamia.

If you forgot to pack your hiking boots, Ypati has plenty of nothing to do – it's a great place to chill out. You could indulge in a spot of people-watching from one of the kafeneia – there are some quirky characters among the locals!

Places to Stay & Eat

Hotel Panorama (☎ *2231 098 222/337, 25 Martiou)* Singles/doubles with bathroom €17.60/2.10. Current trends in decor have passed this hotel by, much as they have the entire village. However, this is more than compensated for by its cleanliness and comfort, peaceful terrace and welcoming owners.

Eleni Karyampa Ouzeri (☎ *2231 098 335, Plateia Ainianon)* Mains €4.70-5.90. This modest place serves tasty salads, souvlaki and *kokoretsi* (spit-roast lamb offal) in the evening.

CENTRAL GREECE

To Steki Ouzeri (☎ *2231 098 462, Plateia Ainianon)* Mains €4.70-5.90. Salads, grilled meats and delicious crispy fried gavros are specialities offered at this little eatery.

AGIOS KONSTANTINOS
Άγιος Κωνσταντίνος
postcode 350 06 • pop 2360
Agios Konstantinos, which is on the main Athens-Thessaloniki route, is one of the three mainland ports that serve the Sporades Islands (the others are Thessaloniki and Volos).

With judicious use of buses from Athens to the port, you will not need to stay overnight before catching a Sporades-bound ferry or hydrofoil. However, if you get stuck there are around ten hotels and a camping ground to choose from.

Places to Stay
Hotel Poulia (☎ *2235 031 663, Thermopolou 4)* Singles/doubles with bathroom €20.60/29.30. This hotel, with plain but clean and comfortable rooms with balconies, is the town's cheapest.

Hotel Olga (☎ *2235 031 766, fax 2235 033 266, Eivoilou 6)* Singles/doubles €22/31.40. Most of the town's hotels, including the Olga, are situated right on the seafront. The spacious rooms here are pleasant and clean and have TV, telephone and air-con.

Getting There & Away
Bus Buses depart hourly for Agios Konstantinos from Athens Terminal B bus station (2½ hours, €9.85).

Ferry There are one or two daily ferries from Agios Konstantinos to Skiathos (3½ hours, €9.90) and one or two to Skopelos Town (4½ hours, €11.80) and Alonnisos (six hours, €13.30).

Hydrofoil Hydrofoils depart up to four times daily for Skiathos (1½ hours, €20.30) and four times daily for Skopelos Town (2½ hours, €23.50) and Alonnisos (three hours, €25.60).

Thessaly Θεσσαλία

Thessaly is the proud possessor of two of Greece's most extraordinary natural phenomena: the giant rock pinnacles of Meteora and the riotously fertile Pelion Peninsula.

On a more modest scale, it also has the beautiful Vale of Tembi. Travelling north through Thessaly to Macedonia, you will pass through this 12km-long valley, which is a narrow passageway between Mt Olympus and Mt Ossa. The road and railway line share the valley with a river, whose richly verdant banks contrast dramatically with the sheer cliffs on either side. There are viewpoints at the most scenic spots. The valley has also been a favoured place for invaders of Greece. The Persian king Xerxes gained access to central Greece via Tembi in 480 BC, as did the Germans in 1941.

LARISA Λάρισα
postcode 410 00 • pop 112,777
Larisa is the kind of place you would normally bypass on your travels through Greece, but it is worth more than a fleeting glance. Larisa is an important transport hub and it is likely that you will find yourself at least passing through here on the train heading either north or south.

Larisa is a lively and sophisticated town, almost bereft of tourists, and is a very important service centre for the whole of the vast agricultural plain of Thessaly. It is a vibrant student town, as the bustling cafeterias in the centre testify, and has a military and air-force base.

Larisa has been inhabited for over 8000 years and its multifarious and fascinating past is only gradually being uncovered, since in recent years fast-growing residential development has tended to disguise what historical remains lie beneath the modern city.

Orientation
Larisa occupies the east bank of the River Pinios, which eventually flows through the Vale of Tembi to the sea. Its main square is

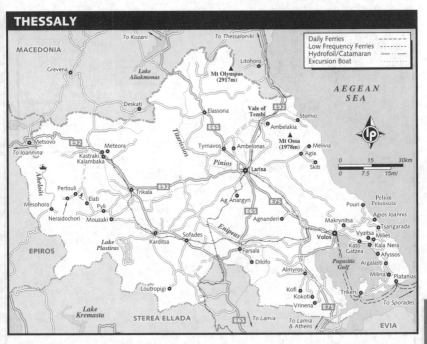

THESSALY

Daily Ferries
Low Frequency Ferries
Hydrofoil/Catamaran
Excursion Boat

MACEDONIA

To Kozani

To Thessaloniki

Grevena

Lake
Aliakmonas

Litohoro

Mt Olympus
(2917m)

Deskati

Elassona

Vale of
Tembi

Stomio

AEGEAN
SEA

Metsovo

To Ioannina

Meteora

Kastraki
Kalambaka

Pertouli

Elati
Pyli

Mesohora

Neraidochori
Mouzaki

Trikala

Ambelakia

Mt Ossa
(1978m)

Tyrnavos

Ambelonas

Pinios

Larisa

Ag Anargyri

Agnanderi

Melivia

Agia

Skiti

Pouri

Pelion
Peninsula

Agios Ioannis

Makrynitsa

Tsangarada

Volos

Vyzitsa
Milies

Kato
Gatzea

Kala Nera

Afyssos

Sofades

Karditsa

Enipeas

Farsala

Dilofo

Almyros

Pagasitic
Gulf

Argalasti

Milina

Platanias

Lake
Plastiras

Loutropigi

Lake
Kremasta

STEREA ELLADA

To Lamia

Kofi

Kokoti

Vrinena

To Lamia
& Athens

To Sporades

EVIA

0   15   30km
0   7.5   15mi

CENTRAL GREECE

Plateia Laou. The train station is on the southern side of town and the main bus station on the northern side. To get to the town centre from the train station, bear left onto Paleologou outside the station. This runs towards a busy intersection; turn right at the intersection into Alex Panagouli. This street leads north to Plateia Laou.

Kyprou and Nikitara run across the south end of Plateia Laou, and Eleftheriou Venizelou and 31 Avgoustou across the town's north end. Plateia Ethnarhou Makariou and Plateia Mihail Sapka are the other two squares around which most of the social life revolves. The streets around these squares are mainly pedestrianised.

To get to Plateia Laou from the main bus station, walk south along Olympou.

Information

The Larisa EOT office is at Koumoundourou 18 (☎ 241 0250 919, fax 241 0534 369); opening hours are 7am to 2.30pm Monday to Friday. The post office is on the corner of A Papanastasiou and Athanasiou Diakou. The OTE office is on Filellinon, just north of Plateia Mihail Sapra. There are ATMs at the train station and several banks on Platiea Mihail Sapra. The police station is located on A Papanastasiou.

Greece's first Internet cafe, the Planet Café, opened in Larisa in 1996. It is at Skarlatou Soutsou 20, and is open 8am to midnight daily.

Things to See

The **Acropolis** on Agios Ahillios Hill has archaeological evidence that indicates this area has been settled since the Neolithic Age (6000 BC), and that it was used as the ancient settlement's Acropolis during classical times, when the temple of **Polias Athina** once existed. The Acropolis is now the site of the **kastro**. Nearby are the excavations of a newly discovered **ancient theatre** which, when fully excavated, could

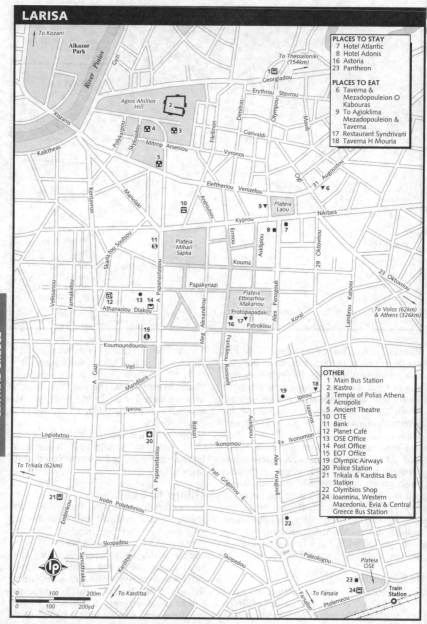

LARISA

PLACES TO STAY
7 Hotel Atlantic
8 Hotel Adonis
16 Astoria
23 Pantheon

PLACES TO EAT
6 Taverna & Mezadopouleion O Kabouras
9 To Agioklima Mezadopouleion & Taverna
17 Restaurant Syndrivani
18 Taverna H Mouria

OTHER
1 Main Bus Station
2 Kastro
3 Temple of Polias Athena
4 Acropolis
5 Ancient Theatre
10 OTE
11 Bank
12 Planet Café
13 OSE Office
14 Post Office
15 EOT Office
19 Olympic Airways
20 Police Station
21 Trikala & Karditsa Bus Station
22 Olymbios Shop
24 Ioannina, Western Macedonia, Evia & Central Greece Bus Station

rival that at Epidaurus. The excavation site is on the corner of A Papanastasiou and Eleftheriou Venizelou. It is not particularly impressive at the moment, and to fully uncover it will mean demolishing a good section of the neighbouring streets.

When we were there it seemed everything in Larisa, except the Acropolis and park, was on the move. The following museums and art gallery were closed, pending moves to larger premises, and new addresses were not available – inquire at the EOT as to whether they have reopened.

The **archaeological museum** (☎ *241 028 8515; admission free; open 8am-2.30pm Tues-Sun)* contains Neolithic finds and grave stelae from the region.

The **ethnographical and historical museum** (☎ *241 0239 446; admission free; open 10am-2pm Mon-Sat)* comprises a collection of tools and utensils from the pre-industrial age, traditional costumes and bronze ware from Tyrnavos, a nearby town.

The **Art Gallery of Larisa** (☎ *241 062 120; admission free; open 10.30am-2.30pm & 5pm-8.30pm Tues-Thur, 10.30am-2.30pm Sat & Sun)* houses a superb collection of contemporary Greek art second only to the National Art Gallery in Athens.

Alkazar Park, just across the river, is a nice place to relax and cool down. Larisa, along with Agrinio, shares the unenviable record of being the hottest place in Greece. The grandly titled **sculpted river** is a set of marble sculptures on Plateia Ethnarhou Makariou, with gushing, running water. If nothing else, it is a refreshing sight on a hot day.

Activities
For adventure sports fans, the **Olymbios Shop** (☎ *241 0553 521,* e *OLIMPPRO@ x-treme.gr, Panagouli 99)* is very good and able to cater for your hiking, climbing, windsurfing and skiing needs.

Places to Stay
As Larisa is not a tourist centre you should have no difficulty finding a room, even though there are not many hotels.

Pantheon (☎ *241 0236 726, Plateia OSE 4)* Singles/doubles €17.60/23.40, with bathroom €23.40/29.40. The best of the three hotels opposite the train station, this one has clean and tidy rooms.

Hotel Adonis (☎ *241 0534 648, fax 241 0536 628, Alex Panagouli 8)* Singles/doubles €29.40/35.30. This pleasant hotel has carpeted rooms with modern furniture and bathrooms with bath tubs.

Hotel Atlantic (☎ *241 0287 711, fax 241 0230 022, Alex Panagouli 1)* Singles/doubles €26.50/35.30. Although this hotel is showing signs of wear and tear, the drab rooms are comfortable and spotless.

Hotel Astoria (☎ *241 0252 941, fax 241 0536 486, Protopapadaki 4)* Singles/doubles €54.40/73.50. The rooms are modern, tasteful and spacious at this hotel. It's as central as you can get and the nightlife in the immediate area is lively.

Places to Eat
There's no shortage of food places in Larisa, although many are of the fast variety.

Restaurant Syndrivani (☎ *241 0535 933, Protopapadaki 8)* Mains €3.50-5.90. This place is one of those long-established, no-nonsense restaurants that every sizable Greek town seems to have. It's open all day and always packed. Excellent ready-made food and roast meats are available.

To Agioklima Mezadopopouleion & Taverna (☎ *241 0254 858, Olympou 9)* Mains €4.40-5.90. This quietly sophisticated little taverna with stone walls and subdued lighting overlooks Plateia Laou. Grilled meats and a range of tasty mezedes are served.

Taverna H Mouria (☎ *241 0281 320, Ipirou 109)* Mains €3.50-8.80. This agreeable neighbourhood taverna serves generous portions of grilled meat with rice and potatoes. It has several small wood-panelled dining areas and is popular with the over-30s; ideal for a quiet evening meal.

Taverna & Mezadopouleion O Kabouras (☎ *241 0238 496, 31 Augoustou 12)* Mains €3.50-5.90. This unexpectedly pristine little place in a drab area of town has pretty green-and-cream decor. As well as the ubiquitous grilled meats it has 15 mezedes to choose from.

CENTRAL GREECE

Getting There & Away

Bus Buses leave from Larisa's main bus station on Georgiadou for many destinations, including six travelling daily to Athens (4½ hours, €19.40), 13 to Thessaloniki (two hours, €10.30) and 12 to Volos (one hour, €3.50). Buses run regularly to and from Karditsa and Trikala from a separate bus station south of the city centre on Iroön Polytehniou, near the junction with Embirikou.

There is a third bus station opposite the train station. Buses for Ioannina, towns in western Macedonia, Evia, central Greece, the Peloponnese and even Crete leave from here.

Train Larisa is on the main train line to and from Thessaloniki (two hours, €4.70) and Athens (five hours, €10), and five intercity trains pass daily through Larisa. In addition to these services, there are also two intercity services to Athens that originate in Volos, travelling through Larisa, and another intercity service to and from Kozani in Northern Greece. These better-appointed trains attract a supplementary charge. There are also 15 local trains to Volos (one hour, €2.90) and Kalambaka. You can buy tickets at the OSE office in town at Papakyriazi 41. Luggage storage is available at the train station.

VOLOS Βόλος

postcode 380 01 • pop 112,000

Volos is a large and bustling city on the northern shores of the Pagasitic Gulf. According to mythology, Volos was the ancient Iolkos from where Jason and the Argonauts set sail on their quest for the Golden Fleece. The name Volos is believed to be a corruption of the original Iolkos.

Volos is not a holiday destination in its own right: the lure of the Pelion Peninsula or the Sporades islands draws people to the city while they are in transit. It is nonetheless a pleasant place to spend a night or two, or even as a base for touring the Pelion.

Much of Volos was rebuilt after the disastrous 1955 earthquake. The city is home to the University of Thessaly and its students give the city a vibrant and youthful feel.

Orientation

The waterfront street of Argonafton is, for half its length, a pedestrian area; running parallel to it are the city's main thoroughfares of Iasonos, Dimitriados and Ermou. The central section of Ermou and its side streets is, in fact, a very lively pedestrian precinct. Heading north-east out of the town centre towards the hills and at right angles to the main thoroughfares are K Kartali and Eleftheriou Venizelou: this latter street is known to the locals as Iolkou. The central square of Plateia Riga Fereou is at the north-western end of the main waterfront. To the west of this square is the train station. The bus station is 500m farther along Grigoriou Lambraki.

Magic Net Café, Iasonos 141, is Volos' largest Internet cafe. It is open 9am to 4am daily.

Information

The EOT (☎ 2421 023 500, fax 2421 024 750 ℮ eotm@hol.gr) is on the northern side of Plateia Riga Fereou. The multilingual staff gives out town maps, information on bus, ferry and hydrofoil schedules, and has a list of hotels for all of Thessaly. Opening hours are 7.30am to 2.30pm and 6pm to 8.30pm Monday to Friday, 9.30am to 1.30pm weekends and public holidays. In low season (September to June), opening hours are 7.30am to 2.30pm Monday to Friday. The tourist police (☎ 2421 039 065) are at 28 Oktovriou 179.

The city's post office is presently at Pavlou Mela 45 but is due to move. The OTE is at Eleftheriou Venizelou 22.

There are several banks with ATMs found on Argonafton. Volos' General Hospital (☎ 2421 027 531-5) is near the archaeological museum.

Archaeological Museum

On the waterfront in the south-east of town is this excellent museum (☎ 2421 025 285, Athanasaki 1; admission €1.50; open 8.30am-3pm Tues-Sat, 9.30am-2.30pm Sun & public holidays). It houses a comprehensive collection of finds found in the area – especially impressive is the large collection

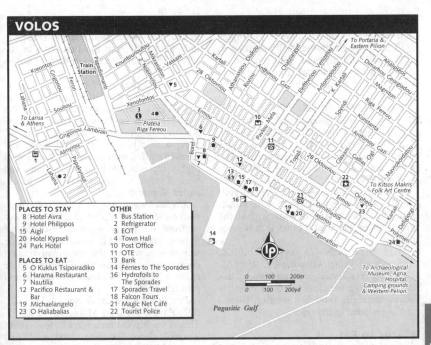

VOLOS

PLACES TO STAY	OTHER
8 Hotel Avra	1 Bus Station
9 Hotel Philippos	2 Refrigerator
15 Aigli	3 EOT
20 Hotel Kypseli	4 Town Hall
24 Park Hotel	10 Post Office
	11 OTE
PLACES TO EAT	13 Bank
5 O Kuklus Tsipoiradiko	14 Ferries to The Sporades
6 Harama Restaurant	16 Hydrofoils to
7 Nautilia	The Sporades
12 Pacifico Restaurant &	17 Sporades Travel
Bar	18 Falcon Tours
19 Michaelangelo	21 Magic Net Café
23 O Haliabalias	22 Tourist Police

Pagasitic Gulf

CENTRAL GREECE

of painted grave stelae from the nearby Hellenistic site of Dimitrias.

Kitsos Makris Folk Art Centre

Housing the superb collection of the late Kitsos Makris, a folk art historian is this outstanding museum (☎ *2421 037 119, Kitsos Makris 38; admission free; open 8.30am-2pm Mon-Fri*). Makris lived here with his wife, Kyveli, from 1955 till his death in 1988. The centre now belongs to the university. The items, collected from the Pelion, include 25 paintings by Theophilos Hatzimichael. Other highlights are the Makris' study and living room, which has a beautiful 18th-century carved-wood ceiling and a delightful frieze of the Pelion painted by Makris. You will be given a guided tour by one of the knowledgeable staff.

Places to Stay

The nearest camping grounds to Volos are at Kato Gatzea, 20km away, on the west

coast of the Pelion Peninsula. The buses to Milies and Platanias pass all three grounds.

Camping Hellas (☎ *2423 022 267, fax 2423 022 492*) Adult/tent €3.80/2.90. This camping ground is the best of the bunch on this stretch of road. It has a restaurant, minimarket and bar. Book if you plan to come in July or August.

Sikia Fig Tree Camping (☎ *2423 022 279*) Adult/tent €3.80/2.90. This ground has a restaurant and all the usual good camping facilities. It is next to Camping Hellas and shares the same beach.

Volos has many hotels, so you should not miss out on a bed.

Hotel Avra (☎ *2421 025 370, fax 2421 028 980*, ℮ *avra@internet.gr, Solonos 3*) Singles/doubles with bathroom €29.40/47.50. The shabby Avra that weary backpackers used to stumble into after a long boat, train or bus journey has been refurbished and now has comfortable and attractive rooms with TV and telephone.

Hotel Kypseli (☎ *2421 024 420, fax 2421 026 020, Agiou Nikolaou 1*) Singles €23.55, singles/doubles with bathroom €29.40/47.05. This hotel with a prime location on the waterfront has nicely furnished, clean rooms with TV, fridge and balcony.

Hotel Philippos (☎ *2421 037 607, fax 2421 039 550,* e *info@philoppos.gr, Solonos 9*) Singles/doubles/triples €36.70/52.25/62.80. The Philoppos has bright, modern rooms with TV and air-con. There's a spacious bar where breakfast and drinks are served.

Park Hotel (☎ *2421 036 511, fax 2421 028 645,* e *amhotels@ote.gr, Deligiorgi 2*) Singles/doubles €44.70/69.15 with breakfast. The Park has stylish rooms with all the amenities expected of a hotel in this price bracket.

Aigli (☎ *2421 024 471, fax 2421 033 006, Argonafton 24*) Singles/doubles €52.95/83.65. This long-established, top-end hostelry has an impressive neoclassical facade and a warm, tastefully furnished interior. Breakfast is included in the price.

Places to Eat

Since Volos is considered the ouzeri capital of Greece, it would be a shame not to eat and drink as the locals do. Some typical mezedes are *spetsofaï* (chopped sausages and peppers in a rich sauce), *ohtapodi* (octopus), *htypiti* (a mixed feta cheese and hot pepper dip) and fried calamari.

Nautilia (☎ *2421 025 340, Borel 4*) Mezedes €1.80-6.50. Excellent mezedes at this old-style ouzeri include squid (€3.80), shrimp saganaki (€6.50) and spetsofaï (€4.70). If you can't stand traffic fumes, or the pong from the harbour opposite, join the weather-beaten old fishers in the cavernous interior, with bare walls and ancient TV.

O Kuklus Tsipoiradiko (☎ *2421 020 872, Mikrasiaton 85*) Baked potatoes €0.90, mezedes €0.90-5.90. This atmospheric place with wood-vaulted ceiling and flagstone floors is a favourite student hangout. The speciality is potatoes baked in a traditional wood-fired oven.

Harama Restaurant (☎ *2421 038 402, Dimitriados 49*) Mains €1.90-4.10. This rough-looking place serves excellent, low-priced, ready-made food. Plants on the patio hide the traffic, and the twittering of the local bird population almost drowns out its noise.

O Haliabalias (☎ *2421 020 234, Orpheos 8*) Mains €5.90-11.95. This charming taverna on a pedestrian street offers well-prepared traditional Greek dishes. Rabbit with fresh tomatoes and carrots, pork with white wine and lemon, and chicken stuffed with cheese and ham are all highly recommended, and the organic red wine is excellent. Note that Orpheos is also called Kontaratou.

Michaelangelo (☎ *2421 037 140, Argonafton 46*) Mains €5.90-13.25. This classy seafront restaurant, with state-of-the-art lighting and tasteful frescoes, offers a huge selection of starters and imaginative main courses with an Italian bias. Deserts include such calorific shockers as tiramisu and profiteroles.

Pacifico Restaurant & Bar (☎ *2421 020 002, Pavlou Mela 7*) Mains €6.45-13.25. This is the hippest restaurant in town, with a stylish decor featuring stone walls and subdued lighting. The international cuisine includes meat and fish dishes served with fresh vegetables. Over 60 wines are available. Early in the evening jazz is played, and although the music becomes more eclectic later, it's a strictly heavy metal-free zone.

Entertainment

For a wild night of dancing head for Lahana – a street lined with discos. These are winter-only discos; in summer things get even wilder, with dancing on the tables at the outdoor discos at Alikes, a beach suburb 1.5km from the city centre.

Refrigerator (☎ *2421 038 757, Lahana 32*) Most discos on Lahana cater for heavy metal fans, but at this very popular place, Greek music is also played.

Getting There & Away

Bus From the bus station there are nine buses daily to Athens (five hours, €17), 12 to Larisa (one hour, €3.50), five to Thessaloniki (three hours, €11.80), and four to

The Ouzeri

An *ouzeri* (strictly speaking, a *tsipouradiko*), if you have not already come across one, is a type of small restaurant where you eat from various plates of *mezedes* and drink bottles of *tsipouro*. Tsipouro is a distilled spirit similar to ouzo, but stronger. You can dilute it with water if you prefer it weaker, or want it to last a little longer. When you have finished one round of mezedes or tsipouro, you order another and so on, until you are full, or can't stand up.

Volos is famous throughout Greece for the quality and quantity of its ouzeria. The institution came about as a result of refugees from Asia Minor who established themselves in Volos after the exchange of populations in 1923, when Greeks and Turks were forced to swap homelands. Most of the refugees who came to Volos were seafarers who would gather on the harbour at lunchtime and drink tsipouro accompanied by various mezedes. As this eating and drinking routine flourished, demand for more exotic mezedes grew and so too did the repertoire of the establishments serving them. Seafood mezedes were the mainstay of the Volos ouzeri.

Kalambaka (three hours, €9.90) and Ioannina (six hours, €14.30). The Ioannina bus continues to Igoumenitsa.

Buses to the major villages of the Pelion Peninsula are as follows: 11 daily to Kala Nera and five daily to Afyssos, 10 daily to Makrynitsa (via Portaria), seven to Vyzitsa (via Milies), six to Milina (via Argalasti and Horto), and three daily to Platanias, Zagora (via Hania) and Agios Ioannis (via Tsangarada). Buses run to many of the smaller villages, but often only two or three times daily. Check the board at the bus station and bear in mind possible seasonal changes.

Train There are 15 trains daily to Larisa (1¼ hours, €2.10). Two direct intercity trains daily go to Athens (the *Trikoupis* at 6.25am and the *Thessalia* at 7pm, €19.40) and three local trains go to Thessaloniki,

with a connection at Larisa. However, there are many connections daily to both Thessaloniki and Athens from Larisa. You can make reservations for these connections and the Athens or Thessaloniki intercity trains from Volos station's booking office.

Ferry There are two ferries daily to Skiathos (three hours, €8.50), Glossa (Skopelos, 3½ hours, €9.70), Skopelos Town (4½ hours, €10.30) and Alonnisos (five hours, €11.50). Buy tickets from Sporades Travel (☎/fax 2421 035 846), Argonafton 33.

Hydrofoil In summer, there are five or six daily hydrofoils to Skiathos (1½ hours, €17.10), Glossa (1¾ hours, €19.10), Skopelos Town (two hours, €20.90) and Alonnisos (three hours, €22.60). Additional services operate to Evia and some of the Sporades services stop at Trikeri Island, Agia Kyriaki and Platanias. Tickets are available from Falcon Tours (☎ 2421 021 626, 2421 033 586, ☎/fax 2421 025 688).

Getting Around

Cars can be rented from European Car Rental (☎ 2421 024 381, fax 2421 024 192), at Iasonos 79, and from Avis (☎ 2421 020 849, fax 2421 032 360), at Argonafton 41.

PELION PENINSULA

Πήλιον Ορος

The well-watered Pelion Peninsula lies to the east and south of Volos. It consists of a mountain range, of which the highest peak is Mt Pliassidi (1651m). The inaccessible eastern flank consists of high cliffs which plunge dramatically into the sea. The gentler western flank coils around the calm sea of the Pagasitic Gulf. The interior is a green wonderland where trees heavy with fruit vie with wild olive groves, forests of horse chestnut, oak, walnut, eucalyptus and beech trees to reach the light of day.

The villages tucked away in this profuse foliage are characterised by whitewashed, half-timbered houses with overhanging balconies, grey slate roofs and cobbled paths winding around their vibrant gardens.

CENTRAL GREECE

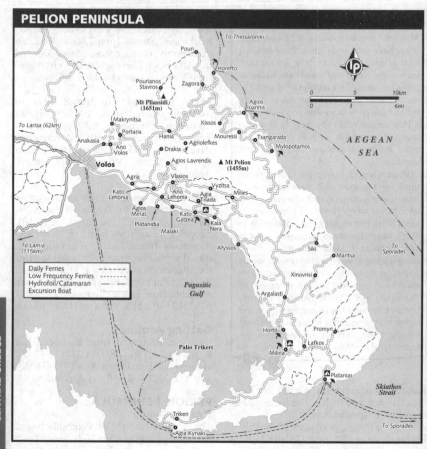

PELION PENINSULA

To Thessaloniki

Pouri
Horefto
Zagora
Pourianos
Stavros
▲ Mt Pliassidi
(1651m)
Agios
Ioannis
Makrynitsa
Kissos
Portaria
Hania
Mouressi
Tsangarada
Anakasia
Agriolefkes
Mylopotamos
Ano
Volos
Drakia
Volos
Agios Lavrendis
▲ Mt Pelion
(1455m)
To Larisa (62km)

AEGEAN
SEA

Agria
Vlasios
Kato
Lehonia
Ano
Lehonia
Vyzitsa
Milies
Agios
Minas
Agia
Triada
Platanidia
Kato
Gatzea
Kala
Nera
Malaki

To Lamia
(115km)
Afyssos
Siki
Maritsa

Xinovrisi

Daily Ferries
Low Frequency Ferries
Hydrofoil/Catamaran
Excursion Boat

*Pagasitic
Gulf*

Argalasti

Horto
Promyri
Lafkos
Milina

Palio Trikeri

Platanias

*Skiathos
Strait*

Trikeri

Agia Kyriaki

To Sporades

To Sporades

0   5   10km
0   3   6mi

With your own transport you can see much of the peninsula in one day, but bear in mind that the roads here are tortuous and driving can be an ordeal. If you're travelling by bus, allow for two or three days: no single bus route covers the whole peninsula.

The Pelion is a lovely region in which to walk. The only book on this in English is *Walks in the Pelion* by Lance Chilton, available from Marengo Publishers (☎/fax 01485 53 2710, 17 Bernard Cres, Hunstanton, PE 36 6ER, UK) and from the Old Silk Store (see Places to Stay in the Tsangarada section).

Many of the places to stay in the Pelion are traditional mansions tastefully converted into pensions. They are wonderful places, but rather pricey.

The Pelion has an enduring tradition of regional cooking. Be sure to try some of the local specialities, such as *fasolada* (bean soup), *kouneli stifado* (rabbit stew), spetsofaï and *tyropsomo* (cheese bread).

History & Mythology

In mythology the Pelion was inhabited by centaurs – reprobate creatures who took delight in deflowering virgins.

The Turkish occupation did not extend into the inaccessible central and eastern parts of the Pelion, and as a result the western coastal towns were abandoned in favour of mountain villages. In these remote settlements culture and the economy flourished; silk and wool were exported to many places in Europe. Like other remote areas in Greece, the Pelion became a spawning ground for ideas that culminated in the War of Independence.

Getting There & Away

Buses to the villages of the Pelion leave from the Volos bus station (see Getting There & Away in the Volos section).

Volos to Makrynitsa

Taking the north-eastern route from Volos, the road climbs to the villages of **Anakasia** and **Ano Volos**. The former is 4km north-east of Volos; on its central square the **Theophilos museum** (☎ 2421 049 109; admission free; open 8am-2pm Mon-Fri) features the works of the primitive painter Theophilos (1866–1934), who lived in Volos.

Portaria, the next village, is 13km north-east of Volos. True to form, its plateia has a splendid old plane tree, and the little 13th-century **Church of Panagia of Portaria** has fine frescoes. A fork to the left in the village leads to Makrynitsa.

Makrynitsa Μακρυνίτσα
postcode 370 11 • pop 650
• elevation 750m

Clinging to a mountainside, Makrynitsa is aptly called the Balcony of Pelion. The traditional houses were built with three storeys at the front and one at the back, giving the impression they are stacked on top of one another. It is one of the loveliest of the Pelion villages, and the most touristy; however, as it is closed to traffic, it remains tranquil. There's a car park at the entrance to the village; the bus terminus is a little farther back along the road. To get to the central square walk straight along the cobbled main street of 17 Martios 1878. The square has an old hollow plane tree, a marble fountain and the little church of Agios Ioannis.

Places to Stay & Eat There are several places to choose from.

Leonidas Domatia (☎ 2428 099 071) Doubles €35. This reasonably priced place has clean and simply furnished rooms. It's on the right side of 17 Martios 1878.

Archontiko Diomidi (☎ 2428 099 430, fax 2428 099 114) Doubles/triples €56/71. This traditional-style mansion, which overlooks the central square, features lots of wall hangings and brass and ceramic ornaments.

Archontiko Routsou (☎ 2428 099 090, fax 2428 099 114) Doubles/triples €56/71. This attractive mansion has cosy rooms with wooden floors, low ceilings and white walls bedecked with weavings. Coming from the car park it's on the right of 17 Martios 1878.

Archontiko Karamarli (☎ 2428 099 570, fax 2428 099 779) Doubles/4-person suites €88/176. This stunning stone mansion has rooms dreamed up by a theatre designer. It's richly decorated with furniture, frescoes and ornaments influenced by ancient Greece and Pelion folk art, combined with modern luxury. The pension is on the left of 17 Martios 1878.

Restaurant Galini (☎ 2428 099 355) Mains €5.50-6.50. This is the best of the central square's restaurants. Its well-prepared Pelion dishes include spetsofaï and kouneli stifado.

Taverna A-B (☎ 2428 099 355) Mains €5-8.85. You can enjoy a bowl of lamb soup (€7.60), pork in wine (€5) or octopus and onions (€7.50) while enjoying the view from this taverna's peaceful terrace. Follow the signs from the central square.

Makrynitsa to Tsangarada

Back on the main Volos-Zagora route the road continues to the modern village of **Hania**. Some 16km uphill from here is the ski resort of **Agriolefkes**, where there is a ski centre, information about which can be obtained from the EOT in Volos.

From Hania the road zigzags down through chestnut trees to a road junction. The left turn leads to **Zagora**, the largest of the Pelion villages and a major fruit-growing centre. Zagora is a long, strung-out village,

CENTRAL GREECE

as the approach along the main road testifies, and is not as dependent on tourism as other villages in the area. The very successful Zagora agricultural cooperative was founded in 1916 and has been instrumental in promoting the growing and export of fruit (mainly apples) as a means of sustaining growth in the village region. The cooperative has its own restaurant, cafeteria and mini-market complex in a town called **Milon tis Eridos** (Apple of Discord). Just down past the turn-off to Horefto, you will pass, on the left, the **Ellinomousio** (admission €0.90; open 9.30am-1.30pm & 5.30pm-8.30pm daily), a museum dedicated to Rigas Fereos, one of the intellectual instigators of the War of Independence.

Horefto, 8km downhill from Zagora, is a popular resort with a long sandy beach. The main beach is OK, but there are a couple of better beaches within walking distance, north and south of the main village. There is a reasonable camping ground here. North of Zagora, **Pouri**, another charming village, spills down a steep mountainside and is worth the detour from Zagora.

Back at the road junction, the right turn-off takes you through a series of villages to Tsangarada. This route is one of the most scenically spectacular in the Pelion.

The delightful village of **Kissos** is built on steep terraces. Its 18th-century Church of Agia Marina has fine frescoes. From Kissos, a 6km road leads down to the coastal resort of **Agios Ioannis**, which is popular, though not one of the best. It is connected to Thessaloniki and the Sporades by a summer hydrofoil service.

Tsangarada Τσαγκαράδα
postcode 370 12 • pop 4950

Tsangarada (tsang-ah-**rah**-dah), nestling in oak and plane forests, is an extremely spread-out village comprising the four separate communities of Agii Taxiarhes, Agia Paraskevi, Agios Stefanos and Agia Kyriaki. The largest is Agia Paraskevi, which is just north of the main Volos-Milies-Tsangarada road. The bus stops near the central square of Plateia Paraskevis. The plane tree on this square is reputedly

the largest and oldest in Greece – locals claim it is 1500 years old. No doubt this is an exaggeration, but whatever its age it's a magnificent specimen with a girth of 14m

The small seaside resort of **Mylopotamos**, which has a lovely pebble beach, is 8km down the road from Tsangarada, and the agricultural village of **Mouressi** is just 2km further along the main road.

Places to Stay & Eat There are several domatia on the main road near Plateia Paraskevis and also along the roads to Mylopotamos.

Paradisos Pension (☎ 2426 049 209, fax 2426 049 551, @ info@paradisoshotel.gr, Agia Paraskevi) Doubles/triples/quads €88/102/118. This is a lovely place run by the friendly and enthusiastic Rigakis brothers. The rooms are cosy and immaculate, and breakfast is included. It's on the right travelling south, between the two turn-offs for Mylopotamos.

Lost Unicorn (☎ 2426 049 930, fax 2426 049 931, Agia Paraskevi) Singles/doubles €80/100. Persian carpets, ornaments and antique furniture grace the dining room, salon and well-stocked library of this exquisite British-owned mansion found on Plateia Paraskevis. The library's resident myna bird has a very limited vocabulary, despite its habitat. Room rates also include breakfast.

The Old Silk Store (☎ 2426 049 086, fax 2426 049 565, Mouressi) Doubles/triples €47/50. This pension, housed in a 19th-century neoclassical building, has simple but delightful traditional-style rooms. The British owner, Jill Sleeman, leads walks in the Pelion in the spring and autumn. The pension is 150m down the road to Mouressi from the main Tsangarada-Zagora road.

Paradisos Restaurant (☎ 2426 049 209) Mains €6.30-11.70. The roast kid and local retsina are top-notch at this restaurant at Paradisos Pension, and its home-made preserves are ambrosia to anyone with a sweet tooth.

There are plenty of other restaurants to choose from, and in summer there's a **taverna** at Mylopotamos.

Volos to Milies & Vyzitsa

After leaving Volos, the west-coast road passes through the touristy villages of **Agria**, **Kato Lehonia** and **Ano Lehonia**. Several roads off to the left lead to one of the most beautiful areas of Pelion; the road from Ano Lehonia to **Vlasios** is particularly lovely. A right turn leads to the seaside resorts of **Platanidia**, **Malaki** and **Kato Gatzea**. After the tortuous and narrow roads of the eastern Pelion villages, this stretch of road is a blessing.

Farther along the coast road just past Kala Nera, 22km from Volos, there is a turn-off to the left for Tsangarada. A little way along here, another turn-off to the left leads through apple orchards to the photogenic villages of Milies and Vyzitsa.

Milies Μηλιές
postcode 370 10 • pop 952

Established in the late 16th century, Milies (mih-lih-**ess**) was a rich agricultural centre, prospering on olive oil, fruit and silk production. Like most of the Pelion it enjoyed semi-autonomy and, largely due to its excellent school, it played a major role in the intellectual and cultural awakening that led to Greek independence.

Milies was the birthplace of Anthinos Gazis (1761–1828), the man who raised the Thessalian revolt in 1821. Shortly after independence a railway line was built between Volos and Milies and the town became a prosperous centre of commerce. **To Trenaki** (€5.90), the steam train that used to chug along this route, retired formally long ago, but has recently been revived as a weekend tourist attraction. It currently runs a limited route from Milies to Ano Lehonia; it's unlikely that its route will be extended to Volos, as it would mean some serious realignment of the old track, which is clearly visible under the surface of the main Volos-Gatzea road.

The train stations at Milies and Ano Lehonia have been renovated and you can take a delightful walk along the track between the two stations. To reach the station from Milies' central square, descend the cobbled path by the post office. If you are

approaching under your own steam from Kala Nera, look for the left turn-off to the station just before you reach the main village turn-off. Close to the station is a memorial to the 29 residents of Milies who were executed by the Germans in 1942.

Just beyond the central square, the **Milies folk museum** (☎ 2423 086 602; admission free; open 10am-2.30pm & 6.30pm-9.30pm Tues-Sun 16th June-14th Sept; 10am-2pm Tues-Fri, 10am-5pm Sat & Sun 15th Sept-15th June). It houses a display of local crafts.

Places to Stay & Eat *Palios Stathmos* (☎ 2423 086 425, fax 2423 086 736) Doubles €45. This pension, in an idyllic setting by the station in Milies, is an old stone house with traditional furnishings. Rates include breakfast.

Palios Stathmos Restaurant (☎ 2423 086 425) Mains €4-8. This restaurant at Palios Stathmos pension serves tasty traditional Pelion dishes. The rabbit and goat stifados are recommended.

Panorama Psistaria (☎ 2423 086 128) Mains €5.80-11.70. Beyond the central square on the road to Vyzitsa, this psistaria offers a range of local foods including goat soup and roast sausages.

Tournos Bakery Cheese pies €1.80. The gastronomic highlight of Milies is the scrumptious *tyropsomo* (cheese pie). You can buy it at this bakery on the main Volos-Tsangarada road, just before the Milies turn-off.

Vyzitsa Βυζίτσα
postcode 370 10 • pop 295
• elevation 555m

Just 2km beyond Milies is the lovely little village of Vyzitsa. Proclaimed a state heritage village by EOT, this is a model Pelion community. Cobbled pathways wind between its traditional slate-roof houses. To reach Vyzitsa's shady central square, walk up the cobbled path by Thetis Café, near the main parking area.

Places to Stay & Eat As in the rest of the Pelion, accommodation in Vyzitsa is pricey.

Phone numbers listed incorporate changes due in Oct 2002; see p83

CENTRAL GREECE

Thetis Xenonas (☎ 2423 086 111) Doubles €41. This place near the car park has very pleasant, good-value rooms.

Rooms Kaiti (☎ 2423 086 447, 2423 038 765) Doubles €58. This homey little place has rooms with wood ceilings, stained glass windows and pretty embroidered curtains. It's on the right of the road as you come from Milies.

Karagiannopoulos Mansion (☎ 2423 086 717, fax 2423 086 878) Doubles €68. This handsome, traditionally furnished mansion on the road coming from Milies has a magnificent 18th-century carved-wood ceiling in the salon.

Mansion Vafiadis (☎ 2423 086 765, fax 2423 086 045) Doubles/triples €62/78. This 17th-century mansion is the loveliest of all, featuring stone floors and beautiful ornate wood furniture. To reach it from Vizitsa's central square, take the cobbled path by the fountain.

Thetis Café (☎ 2423 086 111) Breakfast & snacks €1.20-3.50. This serene place with a pleasant shady patio is at Thetis Xenonas.

Georgaras Restaurant (☎ 2423 086 359) Mains €5-7. In the evening you can enjoy some unusual Greek dishes at this restaurant on the Vizitsa-Milies road. They include lamb cooked with tomatoes, peppers and cheese, and pork stuffed with cheese, carrots and egg.

South to Platanias Πλατανιάς

Continuing south from Kala Nera, the bus goes as far as Platanias. Although not as fertile as the northern part of the peninsula, the southern part of the Pelion is still attractive, with pine-forested hills and olive groves. Before heading inland after Kala Nera, the road skirts the little coastal village of **Afyssos**, winds upwards through to the large, unexceptional inland farming community of **Argalasti**, and then forks – the left fork continues inland, the right goes to the coastal resorts of Horto and Milina. From Milina the road heads inland and then south to Platanias. You can take a twice-daily bus from Volos all the way to the end of the desolate-looking peninsula to Trikeri and finally to Agia Kyriaki.

Horto & Milina (Χόρτο & Μηλίνα These are the next two villages down that you will meet, if you take the right fork after Argalasti at Metohi. Horto is very low key and small, while Milina is larger and offers a better balance of amenities. Both are on a quiet part of the peninsula with clear water but no spectacular beaches. There are domatia at both villages and two camp sites nearby.

Trikeri (Τρικέρι) The road from Milina to Trikeri now becomes more and more desolate and the vegetation more stunted as rock takes over. Apart from one or two small sections, the road is sealed all the way and is wide and fast, with little to distract your attention other than the odd house-cum-taverna or goat pen. There is an end-of-the-world feel about this part of the Pelion and Trikeri may come as a surprise when you discover this lively and historically important little community perched on the hilltop keeping guard over the straits that separate the mainland from Evia.

Donkeys outnumber cars here and the residents pride themselves on their tradition as seafarers, fighters against the Turks in the War of Independence and as upholders of traditional customs and dress. The week following Easter is one of continual revelry as dancing takes place every day and women try to outdo each other in their local costume finery.

Agia Kyriaki (Αγία Κυριακή) This is the last stop on the Pelion Peninsula, a winding 5km drive down the hill, or a fast 15-minute walk down a stone path. This is a fishing village without tourist trappings and most people only see it during a five-minute stopover on the Flying Dolphin to or from the Sporades. Here you will find bright, orange-coloured fishing boats put to good use by a lively, hard-working population of 285.

Lambis Domatia (☎ 2423 091 587, Mylos) Singles/doubles/triples with bathroom €17.60/23.70/52.80. These clean simply furnished rooms are in a peaceful setting in the tiny coastal hamlet of Mylos just 20 minutes' walk from Agia Kyriaki

From the hydrofoil quay turn left, and follow the road around the bay and up the hill. Turn left at the sign for Mylos, and left again at the sign for the rooms. If you arrive by bus, ask to be let off at the Mylos turnoff.

Anchor Taverna (☎ *2423 091 228; waterfront, Agia Kyriaki*) Mains €2.50-4.80. This excellent taverna is the first of a row of three at Agia Kyriaki. It specialises in fish; prices are given per kilo – lobster is €35.20 and red mullet €29.30. A large range of starters and some meat dishes are also offered. Veal cutlet, beefsteak and chicken are all €3.80.

Palio Trikeri (Παλιό Τρικέρι) If you really must go that one step further to get away from it all, then head for this little island with a population of only 91, just off the coast and inside the Pagasitic Gulf. The hydrofoil is supposed to stop here four times weekly, but you may have to ask to make sure. Alternatively, you can twist someone's arm at Agia Kyriaki to take you down a farm track to the end of the headland, where they will whistle or shout to get someone to come from the island to take you over on a caique.

At the time of research there was no accommodation for tourists at Palio Trikeri. Inquire at the EOT in Volos to find out if this is still the case. Wild camping is possible on the island and there is a taverna.

Platanias Πλατανιάς
postcode 370 06 • pop 171

Platanias (plah-tah-nih-**ahs**) is a popular resort with a good sand-and-pebble beach. It's a fun place to spend a day or two, although it's quite developed. **Les Hirondelles Travel Agency** (☎ *2423 071 231*) on the waterfront rents various water sports equipment.

Places to Stay & Eat *Louisa Camping* (☎ *2423 071 260*) Adult/tent €4/2. This ground, on the approach road to Platanias, is well shaded and has reasonable facilities.

Hotel Platanias (☎ *2423 065 565*) Singles/doubles/4-bed apartments €21/35/47. This

pleasant waterfront hotel, above the co-owned To Steki Restaurant, has bright, well-kept rooms and well-equipped apartments.

Hotel des Roses (☎ *2423 071 268,* ☎*/fax 2423 071 230*) Doubles/triples with bathroom €26.50/29.50. This long-established hotel by the bus stop is an agreeable budget option. The owner, Madame Tulla, may show you her collection of guestbooks which date back to the 1950s when she had a hotel in Egypt.

To Steki Restaurant (☎ *2423 065 565*) Dishes €6-10. There are six eating places in Platanias, including this seafront restaurant with a large choice of well-prepared dishes.

Getting There & Away See Getting There & Away in the Volos section for bus services between there and Platanias.

There is a daily caique running to Skiathos in the summer. At least two hydrofoils call by Platanias from 1 June onwards on their way to Skiathos (€8.20), Skopelos Town (€11.80) and Alonnisos (€11.80), and there are five weekly to Volos. Tickets can be purchased from Les Hirondelles Travel Agency.

Getting Around Les Hirondelles Travel Agency rents motorbikes. There are ad hoc excursion boats to Skiathos in addition to the regular caique service. Other caiques run daily to local, but less accessible, beaches.

TRIKALA Τρίκαλα
postcode 421 00 • pop 48,000

Trikala (tree-kah-lah) is ancient Trikki, the reputed birthplace of Asclepius, the god of healing. It's a bustling agricultural town, through which flows the River Litheos, and is a major hub for buses. While Trikala's attractions hardly warrant a special trip, the chances are if you're exploring central Greece you'll eventually pass through here.

Orientation & Information
Trikala's main thoroughfare is Asklipiou, the northern end of which is a pedestrian precinct. Facing the river, turn left from the bus station to reach Plateia Riga Fereou at

the northern end of Asklipiou. The train station is at the opposite end of Asklipiou, 600m from Plateia Riga Fereou.

To reach the central square of Plateia Iroön Polytehniou cross the bridge over the river, opposite Plateia Riga Fereou.

Trikala does not have an EOT or tourist police; the regular police (☎ 2431 032 777) are 1km from the town centre on Sidiras Merarchias, a left turn off the road to Larisa. The National Bank of Greece is on the central square. The post office is at Saraphi 13; turn left at the central square and it's a little way along on the left. The OTE is on 25 Martiou, to reach it take the second turning left from the central square.

Greek Paradise Holidays (☎ 2431 079 680, fax 2431 079 682), Stournara 7, is an independent travel company based in Trikala. It specialises in winter holidays in Thessaly, which focus on archaeological sites and places of natural beauty.

Things to See

The River Litheos bisects the town. The **Fortress of Trikala** is currently closed for restoration, but it's worth a wander up to the gardens which surround it for the views. The **Fouri Trikala Café Bar** (☎ 2431 038 637), which has pleasant seating in the garden, has remained open. Walk 400m up Saraphi from the central square and look for the sign pointing right. Just before the turn for the fortress are the remains of the **Sanctuary of Asclepius**. To get to the old Turkish quarter of **Varousi**, take a sharp right at the sign for the fortress. It's a fascinating area of narrow streets and fine old houses with overhanging balconies. If you keep on walking through Varousi and up the hill, you will come to the chapel of **Profitis Ilias**. It is a pleasant, tree-lined walk, and you will eventually reach a small **zoo**. Entry is free.

At the other side of town is the **Koursoun Tzami**, a Turkish mosque built in the 16th century by Sinan Pasha, the same architect who built the Blue Mosque in İstanbul. EU-funded restoration work has just been completed. From the bus station, turn right, follow the river and you'll reach the mosque after 300m.

Places to Stay

Trikala isn't a tourist centre, so hotels are unlikely to be full.

Hotel Palladion (☎ 2431 028 091, Vyronos 4) Singles/doubles €29.50/38. This hotel, Trikala's only budget option, has clean and tidy rooms. It is behind Plateia Riga Fereou's Hotel Achillion.

Hotel Panellinio (☎ 2431 073 545, 2431 073 035, fax 2431 027 350, Plateia Fereou 2) Singles/doubles €41/52. This neo-classical hostelry dates from 1914. Once a luxury hotel with an illustrious past, it eventually became so run down that even budget backpackers turned up their noses. It has now been restored to its former splendour; the spacious rooms have elegant traditional furniture and exquisite Persian carpets.

Hotel Dina (☎ 2431 074 777, fax 29490, Karanasiou 1) Singles/doubles €32/44. This hotel has well-kept modern rooms with air-con, telephone and balconies. It's 100m along Asklipiou from Plateia Riga Fereou

Places to Eat

Trikala's cafe life is centred on the northern end of Askipilon. Traditional kafeneia are mostly in the little streets to the north of 25 Martiou.

Taverna Archontissa (☎ 2431 033 603, Gregoriou Patriarhoi 16) Mains €5.80-11.70. Greek peasant meets gothic, with a touch of 1960s anarchy thrown in, at this funky taverna. Well-prepared grilled meats and mezedes and delicious home-made ice cream are offered. To reach it, walk north along the left side of Plateia Iroön Polytehniou and take the first left after the square.

Pliatsikas Restaurant (☎ 2431 028 445, Ioulietas Adam 16) Mains €5.90-11.80. This elegant taverna serves reasonably priced meat, fish and mezedes, which are all appetisingly displayed in a glass cabinet. The eggplant and blackeye bean salads are especially tasty. To get there from Askiplou, turn right at Dina Hotel and take the first left.

Getting There & Away

Bus From Trikala's bus station there are 20 buses daily to Kalambaka (30 minutes,

€1.30), almost half-hourly buses to Larisa (one hour, €3.50), eight daily to Athens (5½ hours, €17.60), six to Thessaloniki (5½ hours, €10.60), four to Volos (2½ hours, €7) and two to Ioannina (3½ hours, €9.55).

Train From Trikala's station there are trains to Kalambaka (one daily), Larisa (three daily), Athens (10 daily) and Thessaloniki (seven daily).

AROUND TRIKALA
Pyli
About 18km from Trikala is the village of Pyli, which means 'gate' – and rightly so, for just beyond Pyli is a spectacular gorge leading into one of Greece's more attractive wilderness areas. A vigorous ecological debate has erupted here, as industrial progressives, despite the protests of the ecological lobby and the local inhabitants, build a large, 135m-high dam near Mesohora village on the upper Aheloös River. Once completed, the area behind the dam, which includes two villages and three settlements, will be flooded, thereby destroying the area's native flora and fauna. The dam builders also want to divert part of the flow of the Aheloös River to the plain of Thessaly, thus radically reducing the natural water flow of the river to the wetlands of Messolongi in Etolo-Akarnania. This, it is claimed, would result in the destruction of the natural habitat of the bird life in the region.

At the entrance to the gorge, 1.5km from Pyli, is the 13th-century **Church of Porto Panayia**. It has an impressive mosaic and a marble iconostasis. To reach the church, you'll need to cross the footbridge over the river and turn left.

The 16th-century **Mono Agios Vissariou** stands on a slope of Mt Koziakis, 5km from Pyli. To get there, cross the road bridge over the river and follow the sign.

Places to Stay & Eat *Hotel Babanara* (☎ 2434 022 325, fax 2434 022 242) Doubles with bathroom €53. This hotel, opposite the bus stop, has comfortable rooms. At quiet times you should be able to negotiate a substantially lower price.

Fancy a Flokati?

There are few better souvenirs of a visit to Greece than the luxuriant woollen flokati rugs produced in the mountain areas of central and northern Greece, which make beautiful, cosy floor coverings.

The process by which these rugs are produced has changed little over the centuries. The first step is to weave a loose woollen base. Short lengths of twisted wool are then looped through it, leaving the two ends on top to form the pile – the more loops, the denser the pile.

At this point, the rug looks like a scalp after stage one of a hair transplant – a series of unconvincing little tufts. The twisted threads can easily be pulled through.

A transformation takes place during the next stage, the 'waterfall treatment'. The rugs are immersed in fast-running water for between 24 and 36 hours, unravelling the twisted wool and shrinking the base so that the pile is held fast. They can then be dyed.

The main production areas are the villages of Epiros, around the town of Tripolis in the Peloponnese and around the towns of Trikala and Karditsa in Thessaly. All these villages have plenty of the running water required for the waterfall treatment.

The rugs are sold by weight. A rug measuring 150 x 60cm will cost from €45 to €140, depending on the length and density of the pile.

Taverna O Thodora (☎ 2434 022 217) Mains €3-8.90. The humble appearance of this little taverna belies the excellence of its food. The mousakas, stuffed eggplant and fried zucchini are all recommended. It's next to the Agricultural Bank on Ermou.

Beyond Pyli
The area beyond Pyli is gradually being opened up to tourism. From Pyli the 40km road north to the village of **Neraidochori** climbs steadily through breathtaking alpine scenery, passing through the villages of **Elati** and **Pertouli**. All three villages have

Phone numbers listed incorporate changes due in Oct 2002; see p83

CENTRAL GREECE

domatia and tavernas. There is a small but locally popular skiing centre near Pertouli, 30km beyond Pyli. Skis can be hired and the centre has a cosy, family atmosphere. These villages are served by buses from Trikala.

Kayaking enthusiasts come to the **Tria Potamia** area, 30km north of Mesohora, to ride the waters of the Aheloös River. The sport is not as organised as in Konitsa in northern Epiros, but nonetheless attracts a growing number of white-water jockeys. How long this activity will last once the dam is built is anyone's guess.

If you have your own transport, you can drive on a very scenic, almost completely sealed road from Pyli to Arta (three hours), via Stournareïka and Mesohora and the disputed upper Aheloös dam. Buses do not cover this route.

METEORA Μετέωρα

Meteora (meh-**teh**-o-rah) is an extraordinary place. The massive pinnacles of smooth rocks with holes in them like Swiss cheese are ancient and yet could be the setting for a futuristic science fiction story. The monasteries atop them are the icing on the cake in this already strange and beautiful landscape, which is listed as a World Heritage Site.

Each monastery is built around a central courtyard surrounded by monks' cells, chapels and a refectory. In the centre of each courtyard stands the *katholikon* (main church).

History

The name Meteora derives from the adjective *meteoros*, which means 'suspended in the air'. The word 'meteor' is from the same root. Many theories have been put forward as to the origins of this rock forest, but it remains a geological enigma.

From the 11th century, solitary hermit monks lived in the caverns of Meteora. By the 14th century, Byzantine power was on the wane and incursions into Greece were on the increase, so monks began to seek peaceful havens away from the bloodshed. The inaccessibility of the rocks of Meteora

made them an ideal retreat, and the greater the threat to the monks, the higher they climbed, until eventually they were living on top of the rocks.

The earliest monasteries were reached by climbing articulated, removable ladders. Later, windlasses were used so monks could be hauled up in nets; this method was used until the 1920s. A story goes that when apprehensive visitors asked how frequently the ropes were replaced, the monks' stock reply was 'when the Lord lets them break'.

These days, access to the monasteries is by steps hewn into the rocks. Some windlasses can still be seen (you can have a good look at one at Agia Triada), but they are now used for hauling up provisions.

Monasteries

The monasteries are linked by asphalt roads, but the area is best explored on foot on the old paths (where they still exist). You could walk around all the monasteries in one day, but you would need an early start and plan at least a two hour break from 1pm to 3pm when most monasteries close. They are only all open at the same time on weekends, and opening times and closure days do vary from season to season. Walking and climbing around the rocks can be thirsty work, but there are mobile canteens selling drinks and snacks at most monastery car parks.

Entry to all monasteries is currently €1.50 unless you are Greek, or can convince the ticket seller that you are, in which case entry is free. Strict dress codes are enforced. Women must wear skirts below their knees, men must wear long trousers and arms must be covered. Skirts, which you can wear over your trousers, are often provided for women upon entering the monastery.

The **Moni Agiou Nikolaou Anapafsa** (☎ 2432 022 375; open 9am-5pm daily) is a 15-minute walk from Kastraki (see the Kastraki section later). From Kastraki's main square walk north, passing Villa San Giorgio. This road peters out to a dirt track. After about 10 minutes the track crosses a stream (which may be dry in summer). Almost immediately after the stream, scramble up a steep slope towards the monastery

METEORA, KASTRAKI & KALAMBAKA

PLACES TO STAY
- 7 Dupiani House
- 8 Boufidis Camping
- 9 Villa San Giorgio
- 10 Hotel Tsileli
- 18 Hotel Astoria
- 22 Koka Roka Rooms & Taverna
- 24 Hotel Meteora
- 31 Hotel Helvetia
- 33 Sydney Hotel
- 35 Vrachos Camping
- 36 Camping Meteora Garden

PLACES TO EAT
- 11 Taverna Gardenia
- 12 Philoxenia Restaurant
- 17 Taverna O Skaros
- 27 Restaurant Meteora

OTHER
- 1 Moni Ypapanti (closed to the public)
- 2 Moni Megalou Meteorou (Grand Meteora)
- 3 Moni Varlaam
- 4 Moni Agiou Nikolaou Anapafsa
- 5 Moni Agias Varvaras Rousanou
- 6 Psaropetra
- 13 Agiou Antoniou (closed to the public)
- 14 Panagia
- 15 Moni Agias Triados (Holy Trinity)
- 16 Moni Agiou Stefanou
- 19 Tourist Services Office
- 20 Bank
- 21 Post Office
- 23 Church of the Assumption of the Virgin
- 25 Hobby Shop
- 26 Bus Stop for Megala Meteora & Kastraki
- 28 Bus Station
- 29 OTE
- 30 Tourist Police
- 32 All Time Café
- 34 Bus Station
- 37 Hospital

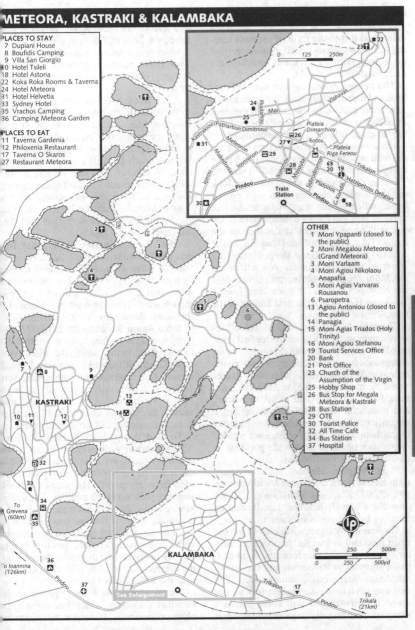

CENTRAL GREECE

which you will see perched on a rock high up on your left. You will come out on the main road just to the right of the path leading to the monastery. A slightly longer but more straightforward route is to follow the main road from Kastraki.

The monastery was built in the 15th century, and the superlative frescoes in its katholikon were painted by the monk Theophanes Strelizas from Crete. Especially beautiful is the fresco of Adam naming the animals.

On leaving the monastery, turn left onto the road and five minutes along, just before it begins to wind, take a path off to the left. The start of the path is not marked, so look out for a white chevron road sign on the bend, indicating the start. After about five minutes turn left onto a cobbled path. Soon you will come to a fork at the base of the rocks. Take the right fork (keeping on the cobbled path) and after a steep, zigzagging climb of about 20 minutes you will reach the **Moni Megalou Meteorou** (*Grand Meteora;* ☎ 2432 022 278; *open 9am-1pm & 3pm-6pm Wed-Mon*), the best known of the monasteries.

The majestic and imposing Megalou Meteorou monastery is built on the highest rock, at 613m above sea level. Founded by St Athanasios in the 14th century, it became the richest and most powerful monastery thanks to the Serbian emperor Symeon Uros, who turned all his wealth over to the monastery and became a monk. Its katholikon has a magnificent 12-sided central dome. Its striking, although gory, series of frescoes entitled *Martyrdom of Saints* depicts the persecution of Christians by the Romans.

From Megalo Meteoro make a sharp right turn to reach the nearby **Moni Varlaam** (☎ 2432 022 277; *open 9am-1pm & 3.30pm-6pm Sat-Thur*). It has fine late-Byzantine frescoes by Frangos Kastellanos.

On leaving Varlaam walk back to the main road and veer right. In about 15 minutes you will come to a fork: the right path has a signpost to Rousanou and the left to the Agiou Stefanous Nannery (sic). The best approach is to take the left fork and in about 10 minutes you will come across a signpost pointing right to the Rousanou

monastery. A 10-minute walk along a pa will lead to the **Moni Agias Varvaras Ro sanou** (☎ 2432 022 649; *open 9am-1pm 3.30pm-5pm in winter, 9am-6pm in summe Thur-Tues*); access is across a vertiginou bridge. The katholikon features more go frescoes.

After Rousanou you can either take short walk down the steps to the Agic Nikolaos-Metamorphosis road or go bac along the path and continue along the roa to Moni Agias Triados. If you do the latt you will reach the Agia Triada monastery i about 45 minutes (you may be able to hitc a lift on this stretch). A path leads down t Kalambaka from this monastery. If yo want to take this path it is better to visit th Agiou Stefanou monastery first and the backtrack to Agia Triada.

Of all the monasteries, **Moni Agias Tria dos** (*Holy Trinity;* ☎ 2432 022 290; *ope 9am-12.30pm & 3pm-5pm in winter, 9am 5pm in summer, Fri-Wed*) has the most re mote feel about it. It gained meteoric though short-lived, fame when it featured i the James Bond film *For Your Eyes Only.*

Moni Agiou Stefanou (☎ 2432 022 27 *open 9am-1pm & 3pm-5pm*) is another 10 minute walk farther along the road. Afte Agia Triados it feels like returning to civi isation, with business-like nuns selling sou venirs and even videotapes of Meteora Among the exhibits in the monastery's mu seum is an exquisite embroidered Epitaphio (a picture on cloth of Christ on his bier).

To find the path to Kalambaka from Agias Triados, walk straight ahead whe you leave the monastery; the path is off t the left. The first part is a dirt path but i soon becomes paved. The monks will tel you this walk takes 10 minutes, but unles you're James Bond or have the agility of mountain goat, it'll take you around 30 minutes. On the walk there are tremendou views of the rocks at close quarters, wher you see not only their dramatic contours bu the details of their strata, too. The path end near the Koka Roka Taverna.

For your lunch break try to picnic on the **Psaropetra** lookout, which has some grea photo opportunities. It is along the road to the

gios Triados and Agiou Stefanou monas-
ries, close to the point where the track down
the Rousanou monastery begins.

Be wary of walking along the paths in
gh winds as walkers have reported being
t by falling rocks at such times.

ctivities

Ieteora is a mecca for rock climbers and if
ou are one of those people whose feet are
rmly planted on terra firma, you will be
nazed at the spectacle of fly-like climbers
iching their way up almost vertical pillars
f rock.

The Kalambaka branch of Trekking Hel-
s, which ran a rock-climbing school and
ck-climbing packages in the Meteora re-
ion, has now closed. Inquire at its branch
Trikala (☎ 2977 451 953), Sokratous 1,
see if it has any such courses. Otherwise
e owners at Vrachos Camping can put you
touch with local instructors.

ALAMBAKA Καλαμπάκα
ostcode 422 00 • pop 12,000

.alambaka is almost entirely modern, hav-
ig been devastated by the Nazis in WWII.
s chief claim to fame is its proximity to
Ieteora. It takes a whole day to see all of
e monasteries of Meteora, so you'll need
spend the night either in Kalambaka or
e village of Kastraki, which is closer to the
cks. First-time visitors to Kalambaka will
e amazed at the vertical rocks that guard
e northern flank of the town. Apart from
e rocks the only other thing in Kalambaka
orth a glance is the old cathedral, the
hurch of the Assumption of the Virgin
dmission €1.20; open 8am-1pm & 4pm-
pm daily) a 7th-century, three-aisle basilica
ith frescoes dating from the 14th century.

Orientation & Information

he central square is Plateia Dimarchiou and
e main thoroughfares of Rodou, Trikalon,
anninon, Kastrakiou and Vlahavas radiate
rom it. Kalambaka's other large square is
lateia Riga Fereou – Trikalon connects the
vo. The bus station is on Ikonomou. Most
1coming buses stop on Plateia Dimarchiou
let passengers alight.

Tourist Services Office (☎ 2432 075 306,
fax 2432 024 343) at Kondyli 38 has a wide
range of information on all aspects of
tourism. Its opening times are 8am to
3.30pm Monday to Friday. A municipal
tourist office was due to open in the town
hall on Plateia Dimarchiou in mid-2001.
The tourist police (☎ 2432 076 100) are at
the junction of Ipirou and Pindou.

The National Bank of Greece, on Plateia
Riga Fereou, has an ATM and an automatic
exchange machine. The post office is
Trikalon 24 and the OTE is at Ioanninon 13.

Places to Stay

There are several camping grounds strung
along Pindou road.

Camping Meteora Garden (☎ 2432 022
727, fax 2432 023 119) Adult/tent €4.40/2.
This is the nicest of the camping grounds. It
is flat and shaded and has a well-kept, modern toilet and shower block, washing machine, restaurant and swimming pool. The
site is 2km west of Kalambaka.

Rooms are plentiful in Kalambaka and
you may well be approached as you arrive
by bus. Choose with care, and look for the
EOT-approved sign. You might find that
the rooms offered by a Mr Tottis are not as
good value as the others.

Koka Roka Rooms (☎ 2432 024 554,
🖂 kokaroka@yahoo.com, Kanari 21) Doubles with bathroom €26.50. The estate
agent's mantra of 'location, location, location' aptly sums up this tranquil place
below the rocks, near the path to Agia Triada monastery. It's a bit of an institution
among travellers. The few rooms are clean
and nicely furnished. Internet usage for
guests is €3 an hour. From Plateia Dimarchiou, walk to the top of Vlahavas, and continue ahead along Kanari.

Hotel Astoria (☎ 2432 022 213, G
Kondili 93) Singles/doubles €15/21, with
bathroom €24/29. This budget hotel has
clean, pine-furnished rooms.

Hotel Meteora (☎ 2432 022 367, fax 2432
075 550, 🖂 gekask@otenet.gr, Ploutarhou
14) Singles/doubles €18/24. This lovely
hotel is a cosy place with welcoming owners.
The immaculate rooms have air-con, and

breakfast is included. Internet usage for guests is €3 an hour. The hotel is at the top of a quiet cul-de-sac below the rocks. From Plateia Dimarchiou walk along Kastrakiou, and take the second turn right.

Hotel Helvetia (☎ *2432 023 041, fax 2432 025 241, Kastrakiou 45*) Singles/doubles €35/56. This hotel has very pleasant, unadorned modern rooms with TV, telephone and air-con.

Places to Eat

Restaurant Meteora (☎ *2432 022 316, Ikonomou 2*) Mains €5.90-8.90. Never mind the kitsch interior and the coachloads of tourists who stop off here – this long-established restaurant dishes up excellent, reasonably priced look-and-point fare.

Koka Roka Taverna (☎ *2432 024 554, Kanari 21*) Mains €5.90-6.80. This taverna below Koka Roka Rooms serves tasty, low-priced food in a warm environment. Grills prepared on the open hearth are its speciality and its home-made white wine is splendid.

Taverna O Skaros (☎ *2432 024 152*) Mains €5.70-7.80. Locals like this taverna for its enormous helpings of high-quality grilled meat. Also commendable are the homemade eggplant and cheese salads and tzatziki. It's at the eastern end of Trikalon.

Getting There & Away

Bus There are frequent buses to Trikala (30 minutes, €1.30) and surrounding villages, two buses to both Ioannina (three hours, €7.65) and Grevena (1¼ hours, €4.50) and four buses to Volos (three hours, €9.90).

Frequent buses for Kastraki (€0.70) leave from Plateia Dimarchiou and two of these, at 9am and 1.30pm Monday to Friday and 8.20am and 1.20pm on Saturday and Sunday, continue to Moni Megalou Meteorou. Buses to other major destinations depart from Trikala.

Train At the time of writing, the train station had only recently reopened after upgrading of the line and a regular timetable had not been established. Trains run to Athens and to Volos (change at Farsala) and to Thessaloniki (change at Larisa).

Getting Around

Motorbikes and bicycles can be hired fro the Hobby Shop (☎/fax 2432 025 262), P triarhou Dimitriou 28.

KASTRAKI Καστράκι
postcode 422 00 • pop 1500

The village of Kastraki is about 2km fro Kalambaka. Its location right under t rocks is most impressive and the view around the village has an otherworldly fe about it. Despite its small size, more th a million people pass through here eve year, so it can feel a bit crowded at time If you want a base for exploring the Met ora monasteries, or for climbing the roc themselves, Kastraki is a better choice th Kalambaka.

Surprisingly, Kastraki has an Intern cafe, All Time Café, on the main road, op 9am to 3pm daily.

There is a nice walk from Kastraki Kalambaka along the base of the rock From the children's playground by the ma square, descend the steps and follow t road opposite up the hill. Turn right at t top and follow the road until you join with the main road, from where Kalamba is a 15-minute walk away.

Places to Stay

Vrachos Camping (☎ *2432 022 293, f 2432 023 134,* @ *camping-kastraki@kn .forthnet.gr*) Adult & tent/car €3.50/0.9 This outstanding camping ground on t Kalambaka-Kastraki road has spotless toi and shower blocks, a swimming pool, covered, communal eating area, a restaura in summer and a barbecue for self-cateret

Boufidis Camping (☎/fax *2432 024 80* Adult/tent €2.95/1.80. This small campi ground below the rocks is quite basic but clean and shaded and has a swimming po The ground is on the right, 300m beyon Philoxenia Restaurant.

Sydney Hotel (☎ *2432 023 079, fax 24 077 861,* @ *gekask@otenet.gr*) Single doubles €26/29. From the options along t Kalambaka-Kastraki road this hotel is th best choice. It is run by a welcoming Gree Australian and the very comfortable room

kept immaculate; the price includes a
ge breakfast.

Villa San Giorgio (☎ *2432 022 289, mobile
097 229 5553*) Doubles/triples €35/44.
is domatia has tastefully furnished, carted rooms and bathrooms with bathtubs.
s on a quiet road near the path to Mete-
. Guests may use the swimming pool at
 co-owned Boufidis Camping.

Hotel Tsileli (☎ *2432 022 438, fax 2432
7 872*) Singles/doubles with bathroom
9/44. This place has comfortable, nicely
nished rooms and a pleasant front gar-
. Take the road to Meteora and look for
 hotel sign on the left.

Dupiani House (☎/fax *2432 075 326,
 Dupianihouse@kmpforthnet.gr*) Singles/
bles/triples €29/44/52. This guesthouse
ncomparably set in its own grounds just
tside the village. The balconied rooms

are clean and tastefully furnished. From the
attractive garden there are splendid views of
the village and rocks. The turn-off to the
guesthouse is to the left, 300m along the
Kastraki-Meteora road.

Places to Eat

There is no shortage of food places to be
found in Kastraki.

Taverna Gardenia (☎ *2432 022 504*)
Mains €5.30-8.25. This taverna near the
main square is a good place to meet both locals and other travellers. Well-prepared
mousakas, stuffed peppers and tomatoes, as
well as grilled meats, fish and mezedes are
offered.

Philoxenia Restaurant (☎ *2432 023 514*)
Mains €5.90-10.30. The speciality at this
restaurant on the main road to Meteora is
mousakas, but grills are also served.

CENTRAL GREECE

Northern Greece Βόρεια Ελλάδα

Northern Greece comprises the regions of Epiros, Macedonia and Thrace. With thickly forested mountains and tumbling rivers, these areas resemble the Balkans more than other parts of Greece. Northern Greece offers great opportunities for trekking, but it is an area where you don't have to go into the wilds to get away from well-worn tourist tracks, because its towns are little visited by foreign holiday makers. Unlike the unglamorous and noisy towns of the Peloponnese and central Greece, many of which serve as transport hubs to get out of quickly, most towns in northern Greece have considerable appeal, with atmospheric old quarters of narrow streets and wood-framed houses.

SUGGESTED ITINERARIES
One week
Start in Epiros and use Ioannina as your base to visit Ioannina, Vikos Gorge and the Zagoria villages. Head eastwards to Macedonia via Konitsa and make for Florina via the Prespa Lakes basin. Move on to Thessaloniki via the waterfalls of Edessa. Spend at least two days in Thessaloniki and visit the impressive Archaeological Museum and Vergina treasures. If you have time (and are male), complete your stay with a couple of nights on Mt Athos. If you are female, perhaps take in the sites of Vergina itself and nearby Pella.
Two weeks
Allow at least four to five days to visit Vikos Gorge and the Zagoria villages, and if walking is your cup of tea then base yourself at Papingo or Konitsa. Include the Vlach village of Metsovo as a side trip from Ioannina then head east via Konitsa to western Macedonia. In addition to the sights listed in the one-week itinerary you could perhaps head east to the Dadia Forest Reserve in Thrace, the home of Europe's few remaining birds of prey. From Alexandroupolis you can head to Turkey or take the weekly ferry as far down as Rhodes.

Epiros Ηπειρος

Epiros occupies the north-west corner of the Greek mainland. To the north is Albania, to

Highlights

- The fairy-tale slate and stone villages of the Zagorohoria
- Greece's natural wonder, the Vikos Gorge
- The solitude and spiritual peace in the monastic community of Mt Athos
- Thessaloniki, the dynamic, bustling capital of northern Greece
- Vergina, site of the majestic royal tombs of Philip II of ancient Macedonia
- The lonely beauty of the Prespa Lakes
- Climbing Mt Olympus, and being at one with the gods of ancient Greece
- The lush forest and bird life of the Dadia Forest Reserve

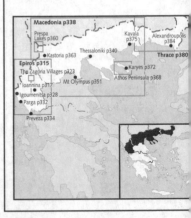

Macedonia p338
Prespa Lakes p360
Kavala p375
Alexandroupolis p384
Thessaloniki p340
Kastoria p363
Thrace p380
Epiros p315
The Zagoria Villages p323
Karyes p372
Mt Olympus p351
Athos Peninsula p368
Ioannina p317
Igoumenitsa p328
Parga p332
Preveza p334

the west is the Ionian Sea and Corfu. Its po of Igoumenitsa is a jumping-off point fo ferries to Corfu and Italy. The high Pind Mountains form the region's eastern bour ary, separating it from Macedonia a Thessaly.

The road from Ioannina to Kalamba cuts through the Pindos Mountains and one of the most scenically spectacular Greece, particularly the section betwe

EPIROS

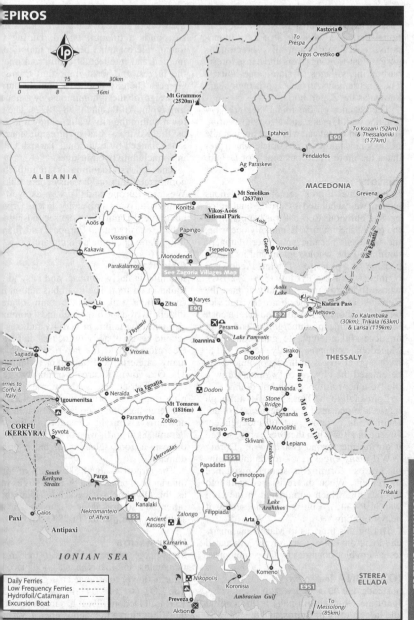

Phone numbers listed incorporate changes due in Oct 2002; see p83

Metsovo and Kalambaka, called the Katara Pass. In northern Epiros the Vikos-Aoös National Park is a wilderness of lofty mountains, cascading waterfalls, precipitous gorges, fast-flowing rivers and dense forests harbouring villages of slate-stone houses. These settlements, in the Zagoria region, are known as the Zagorohoria.

The beaches on the Ionian Sea are very popular with Greeks, and also with visiting Italians and Germans, while the ancient site of Dodoni is known for its oracle which predates the more illustrious oracle of Delphi.

History

In early times Epiros' remote mountainous terrain was inhabited by tribes unaffected by, and oblivious to, what was happening in the rest of the country. Eventually one tribe, the Molossi, became so powerful that it dominated the whole region, and its leader became king of Epiros. The most renowned of these was King Pyrrhus (319–272 BC), whose foolhardy fracas in Italy against the Romans gave rise to the phrase 'Pyrrhic victory' – a victory achieved at too great a cost.

Pyrrhus came to an undignified end. After unsuccessful attempts to gain control of Macedonia and parts of Italy, he decided to have a go at Argos in the Peloponnese. As he entered the city, an old woman threw a tile from her rooftop which killed him.

Epiros fell to the Turks in 1431, although its isolation ensured it a great degree of autonomy. It became part of independent Greece in 1913 when the Greek army seized it during the second Balkan War. During WWII many Greeks took to the mountains of Epiros, forming a strong resistance movement. When the resistance split into the factions which culminated in the civil war (1944–45), Epiros was the scene of heavy fighting.

During this time, as in Macedonia, many children from Epiros were forcibly evacuated to Eastern bloc countries by the communists.

IOANNINA Ιωάννινα
postcode 450 00 • pop 56,700

Ioannina (ih-o-**ah**-nih-nah) is the capital and largest town of Epiros, and the gateway to the Vikos-Aoös National Park. It lies the western shore of Lake Pamvotis, wh surrounds a tranquil island. During toman rule Ioannina became a major co mercial and intellectual centre and one the largest and most important towns Greece. The city reached its height dur the reign of the ignominious, swashbu ling tyrant Ali Pasha (1788–1822). The town within the city walls – known loca as the Kastro – has picturesque narr lanes flanked by traditional Turkish bu ings, including two mosques.

These days, Ioannina is an import commercial hub on the busy route link Western Europe and Turkey as well being a thriving university town. Driv take note: Ioannina has the second-high vehicle density rate in Europe after Mila Italy. Parking can be a nightmare.

Orientation

Ioannina is fairly compact and easy to round in on foot. The main bus station i five-minute walk from the main squar Plateia Pyrrou – from which most comm cial and entertainment activity radiates second centre of activity focuses on Pla Georgiou next to the lakefront. Here many cafeterias and upmarket restaura The Old Town (Kastro) is primarily a r dential district, but is also home to Io nina's main historical sights. Hotels clustered near the main bus station, thou new arrivals might consider heading Perama, 8km north-west of Ioannina, wh there is a good selection of better-pri domatia.

The airport is about 5km north of Io nina and can be reached by local bus as w as the Olympic Airways bus. Ioannin other bus station is at Vizaniou 28, southerly continuation of 28 Oktovriou.

Information

Most people come to Epiros to trek in mountains, and Ioannina is a good place information or to arrange an organised tr The EOT (☎ 2651 041 142, fax 2651 (139) is at Dodonis 39. It has information the Vikos Gorge trek and is open 7.30am

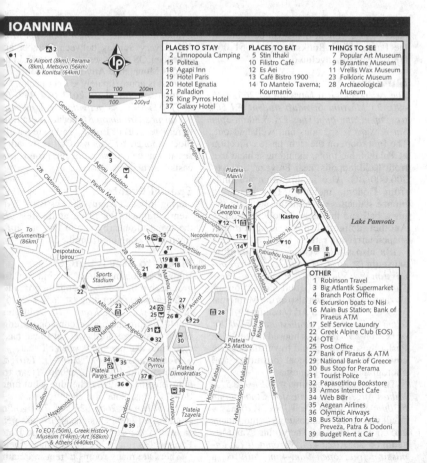

IOANNINA

To Airport (8km), Perama (8km), Metsovo (56km) & Konitsa (64km)

0   100   200m
0   100   200yd

PLACES TO STAY
2 Limnopoula Camping
15 Politeia
18 Agapi Inn
19 Hotel Paris
20 Hotel Egnatia
21 Palladion
26 King Pyrros Hotel
37 Galaxy Hotel

PLACES TO EAT
5 Stin Ithaki
10 Filistro Cafe
12 Es Aei
13 Café Bistro 1900
14 To Manteio Taverna; Kourmanio

THINGS TO SEE
7 Popular Art Museum
9 Byzantine Museum
11 Vrellis Wax Museum
23 Folkloric Museum
28 Archaeological Museum

Georgiou Papandreou

To Igoumenitsa (86km)

28 Oktovriou

Agiou Nikolaou

Pavlou Mela

Despotatou Ipirou

Sina

Sports Stadium

Mihail Trikoupi

Spyrou Lambrou

Harilaou

Angelou

Dodonis

Soulioui

Napoleonda

Plateia Pargis

Plateia Pyrrou

Plateia Dimokratias

Plateia Tzavela

Plateia 25 Martiou

Averof

Markou Botsari

Anexartisias

Neopoleumou

Koundounotou

Plateia Georgiou

Plateia Mavili

Stratigou Papagou

Karamanli

Noutsou

Dionysiou

Kastro

Lake Pamvotis

Paleologou 1st

Patriarhou Ioasf

Ethnikis Andistasis

Garivaldi Ritsioti

Akti Miaouli

Hristou Katsari

Arhiepiskopou Makariou

Plateia Tzavela

To EOT (50m), Greek History Museum (14km), Art (68km) & Athens (440km)

OTHER
1 Robinson Travel
3 Big Atlantik Supermarket
4 Branch Post Office
6 Excursion boats to Nisi
16 Main Bus Station; Bank of Piraeus ATM
17 Self Service Laundry
22 Greek Alpine Club (EOS)
24 OTE
25 Post Office
27 Bank of Piraeus & ATM
29 National Bank of Greece
30 Bus Stop for Perama
31 Tourist Police
32 Papasotiriou Bookstore
33 Armos Internet Cafe
34 Web B@r
35 Aegean Airlines
36 Olympic Airways
38 Bus Station for Arta, Preveza, Patra & Dodoni
39 Budget Rent a Car

2.30pm and 5.30pm to 8.30pm Monday to Friday, and 9am to 1pm Saturday year-round.

The tourist police (☎ 2651 025 673) are opposite the post office on 28 Oktovriou. The OTE and post office are on 28 Oktovriou. There is a branch post office on Georgiou Papandreou, about a 10-minute walk from Limnopoula Camping. Most banks are clustered around the central square and along the southern end of Averof. The Bank of Piraeus has an ATM in the main bus station as well as a branch and ATM on Averof.

There are now around 10 Internet cafes scattered around the central district. Two easy ones to find are the Armos Internet Cafe (☎ 2651 071 488) at Harilaou Trikoupi 40 (€2.10 per hour) and Web B@r (☎ 2651 083 21) in the Stoa Saka – (€1.75 per hour). Both include a free coffee and are open 10am until very late.

There's a Self Service Laundry (☎ 2651 025 542) on Tsirigoti, close to the main bus station. It is open 9.30am to 2.30pm and 6pm to 9pm Monday to Friday and 9.30am to 2.30pm Saturday. A full wash costs €7.30.

Phone numbers listed incorporate changes due in Oct 2002; see p83

NORTHERN GREECE

English-language books, magazines, newspapers and excellent maps can be found at the Papasotiriou Bookstore (☎ 2651 064 000) at Mihail Angelou 6.

Museums

The **Archaeological Museum** (☎ 2651 025 490, 25 Martiou 6; adult/student €1.50/ free; open 8am-6pm Tues-Fri, 8.30am-3pm Sat & Sun) is spacious and well laid out. The first room on the right has a collection of Palaeolithic tools, including a hand axe from Kokkinopolis, near Preveza, dated to 200,000 BC. Also in this room are finds from Dodoni, including two charming bronze statuettes of children; one is throwing a ball and the other is holding a dove. Another delightful piece is a tortoise-shaped terracotta rattle.

It's also worth visiting the **Byzantine Museum** (☎ 2651 039 692, To Kastro; admission €1.50; open 8.30am-3pm Tues-Sun), which has a good collection of Byzantine art. Known also as the Municipal Museum, the **Popular Art Museum** (☎ 2651 026 356, To Kastro; adult/student €2/0.90; open 8am-8pm daily) is housed in the Aslan Pasha mosque in the old town. Its eclectic collection includes local costumes and photographs of old Ioannina.

The **Folkloric Museum** (☎ 2651 020 515, Mihail Angelou 42; admission €0.60; open 5.30pm-8pm Mon, 10am-1pm Wed) has a small display of local costumes, embroidery and cooking utensils. The **Vrellis Wax Museum** (☎ 2651 022 414, Karamanli 15; admission free; open 9am-4pm daily) is a showcase of the wax exhibits that can be viewed in greater detail at the grandiose **Greek History Museum** (☎ 2651 092 128, Bizani; adult/student €5/2.50; open 7.30am-5pm). This is a mini Madame Tussaud's, but with an emphasis on modern Greek history. The museum is at Bizani, 14km out of Ioannina on the road to Athens. Take bus No 5 (four daily) from the main square to get there.

Trekking

If you wish to trek in more remote areas than the Vikos Gorge, then talk to someone at the **EOS** (Greek Alpine Club; ☎ 2651 022 138, Despotatou Ipirou 2; open 7pm-9pm Mon Fri). Every Sunday between October and June the EOS organises a one-day trek in the Pindos Mountains. Anyone is welcome and the cost is approximately €7 per person.

Robinson Travel (☎ 2651 074 989, fa. 2651 025 071, e activities@robinson.gr Merarhias Grammou 8) specialises in trek to remote areas of Epiros. Treks are usually block-booked by groups. Call or email to see if you can join one of the groups as casual participant.

Special Events

During July and August the Festival of Ancient Drama takes place at the restored theatre at the nearby site of Dodoni. Information is available from the EOT.

Places to Stay – Budget

Budget accommodation is thin on the ground, but there is one camping ground.

Limnopoula Camping (☎ 2651 025 265 fax 2651 038 060, Kanari 10) Adult/ten €4.40/3. This camping ground on the edg of the lake, 2km north-west of town, has restaurant and bar and is open all year.

Hotel Paris (☎ 2651 020 541, Tsirigo 6) Singles/doubles €19/29.50. Near the main bus station, this rather dingy but func tional D-class hotel has clean rooms.

Agapi Inn (☎ 2651 020 541, Tsirigoti 6 Doubles €17.60. This cheap, E-class pen sion is in the same alleyway as the Hote Paris and is run by the same management

There are many rooms to rent in Perama at a decent price.

Rooms to Rent (☎ 2651 081 786, Spileo 76, Perama) Singles/doubles €17.60/23.50 Rooms are on the small size but clean and pleasant, and have private bathrooms.

Nearby are more **domatia** (☎ 2651 08 633, I Petrohilou 2, Perama) Doubles/triple €26.50/29.50. Rooms have private bath, TV and a shared kitchen.

Places to Stay – Mid-Range

Hotel Egnatia (☎ 2651 025 667, fax 265 075 060, Cnr Dangli & Aravantinou Singles/doubles €38.20/55.80. This C-clas otel near the main bus station has somewhat spartan rooms, but is OK.

King Pyrros Hotel *(☎ 2651 027 652, fax 2651 029 980, e kpyrros@eol.gr, Gounari 3)* Singles/doubles €41/55.80. This is a comfortable C-class hotel right in the centre of Ioannina.

Galaxy Hotel *(☎ 2651 025 432, fax 2651 030 724, Plateia Pyrrou)* Singles/doubles €44/58.70. On the south side of the main square is this pleasant and modern C-class hotel. Most rooms have fine views over the lake.

Hotel Persa *(☎ 2651 081 151, fax 2651 063 179, Agiou Haralambous 62, Perama)* Doubles €47. This is a neat and breezy hostel in Perama, 8km from Ioannina. Rooms are spacious with TV, kitchenette and balcony. There is ample parking for guests with vehicles. Look for the sign along Spileou, the main street.

Places to Stay – Top End

Politeia *(☎ 2651 030 090, fax 2651 022 235, e etip@etip.gr, Anexartisias 109)* Doubles/triples/suites €61.65/76.50/146.75. Next to the main bus station is this excellent place to stay. Each studio has a kitchenette, TV, telephone, heating and air-conditioning. The four-person luxury suite is very spacious.

Palladion *(☎ 2651 025 856, fax 2651 074 034, e palladion@otenet.gr, Noti Botari 1)* Singles/doubles €60.20/81.60. This modern B-class hotel has very well-appointed rooms with satellite TV, phone and air-conditioning.

Places to Eat

Filistro Cafe *(☎ 2651 072 429, Andronikou Paleologou 20)* Breakfast €4.50. For a wide choice of teas, coffee and liqueurs, visit this small but very atmospheric cafe inside the kastro. It is also a good place for breakfast on weekends.

To Manteio Taverna *(☎ 2651 025 452, Plateia Neomartyros Georgiou 16)* Mains €3-5. Dishes range from *mayirefta* (prepared food) to grills and are filling and well prepared. The mousakas (€4.40) is recommended.

Kourmanio *(☎ 2651 038 044, Plateia Neomartyros Georgiou 16)* Grills €3.50-4. Next door to the Manteio Taverna is this more intimate and slightly cheaper place, with excellent home cooking as well as the usual grills.

Stin Ithaki *(☎ 2651 073 012, Stratigou Papagou 20a)* Mains €5.60. This is a well-recommended lakeside restaurant. Its imaginative menu includes *aïvaliotiko*, a Lesvos speciality made from aubergines and pork, and *bekri mezes Thrakiotikos*, a tasty dish of beef cubes in a spicy sauce.

Es Aei *(☎ 2651 034 571, Koundouriotou 50)* Mains €8.80. For a touch of arty, rustic funk visit this wine bar-cum-bistro under a glass-roofed courtyard. It serves up exquisite mezedes with a Cretan bent. Try also the vegetarian platter and rabbit with wild greens.

Café Bistro 1900 *(☎ 2651 033 131, Neoptolemou 9)* Mains €10, wine from €11.50. This is the best restaurant in town and oozes style and class. One of the house specialities is pork fillet in plum sauce. The *Syllogi Kondyli* red wine goes down well with most dishes. Background music ranges from jazz to cubano.

Shopping

For a long time Ioannina has been a centre for the manufacture of filigree silver. Shops selling this type of jewellery line Averof and Karamanli. Prices start at around €8.80 for rings and earrings.

You can also buy woodcarvings and other souvenirs in the same area. Epiros is famous for its flokati rugs, also known as *velentzes*.

Getting There & Away

Air Olympic Airways *(☎ 2651 026 518)*, Kendriki Plateia, has two flights daily to Athens (€69.55) and one to Thessaloniki (€50.50). Aegean Airlines *(☎ 2651 064 444, fax 2651 065 202)*, Pyrsinella 11, has two flights daily to Athens (€70.75).

Bus From Ioannina's main bus station *(☎ 2651 026 404)* there are buses to Igoumenitsa (2½ hours, €5.60, nine daily),

NORTHERN GREECE

Athens (7½ hours, €23.80, nine daily), Konitsa (two hours, €3.70, 11 daily), Thessaloniki (seven hours, €19.50, five daily with one weekly via Kozani) and Metsovo (1½ hours, €3.50, four daily). There are also two buses daily to Trikala (3½ hours, €9.55) and Kozani (4½ hours, €13.40), and one daily in summer to Parga (three hours, €5.90).

From the other bus station (☎ 2651 025 014) at Vizaniou 28 there are buses to Arta (2½ hours, €4.25, 10 daily) and Patras (4½ hours, €14, two daily). Buses also leave here for Preveza and Dodoni here (see the Dodoni Getting There & Away section for details).

To/From Albania There are buses from Ioannina to the Greek border post of Kakavia (one hour, €3.70, nine daily) from where you can cross into Albania and seek onward transport – usually taxi – to the nearest town of Gjirokastra.

Getting Around
To/From the Airport Ioannina's airport is 5km north-west of town on the road to Perama. Take bus No 7, which runs every 20 minutes from the bus stop just south of Averof near the clock tower. Bus Nos 1 and 2 run less frequently, but they also go past the airport.

Bus & Taxi The local bus service covers most parts of Ioannina. Buses from the lakefront usually take you up to the main square. Buy your ticket before you board the bus; there is a kiosk near the Olympic Airways office. Within the central area a single-trip ticket costs €0.60.

Taxis (☎ 2651 046 777) can be found around the main square and by the lake.

Car Budget Rent a Car (☎/fax 2651 043 901) is at Dodonis 109, and it has a booth at Ioannina airport to meet all incoming flights.

AROUND IOANNINA
The Island Το Νησί
This traffic-free island (To Nisi) in Lake Pamvotis is a serene place to wander around. It has four monasteries and a whitewashed village built in the 17th century by refugees from the Mani in the Peloponnese. It is now a permanent home to about 90 families.

The **Moni Pandeleïmonos**, where Ali Pasha was killed in 1822, houses a small **museum** (admission €0.45). It was rebuilt using the original stones after a tree fell on it in a storm. The museum is usually open as long as the ferry is running.

The Moni Pandeleïmonos is signposted as are all the other monasteries on the island.

Places to Eat There are a number of restaurants on the island and they make popular Sunday lunch destinations for people from Ioannina and visitors alike.

Gripos Mains €7-8. For a memorable meal in a lakeside setting, head for this restaurant, to the right as you disembark from the ferry. The grilled trout served is exquisite.

Pamvotis Mains €7-8. This restaurant to the left of the quay, is owned by the same proprietor as Gripos. It is equally good, and more likely to be open in the low season. The trout is excellent.

Getting There & Away There are regular boats to the island (10 minutes, €0.75). They usually run every hour in winter and every half-hour in summer, leaving from near the gate to the fortress, 50m west of Plateia Mavili.

Perama Cave Σπήλαιο Περάματος
Four kilometres from Ioannina is Perama Cave (☎ 2651 081 521, Perama; adult/student €4.40/2.65; open 8am-8pm daily). It is one of the largest caves in Greece. It was discovered in 1940 by locals searching for a hiding place from the Nazis, and explored by speleologists Ioannis and Anna Petrohilos, who also explored the Diros Caves in the Peloponnese. The cave at Perama is second in Greece only to the Diros Caves in its array of stalactites and stalagmites. It consists of many chambers and passageways and is 1100m long.

Ali Pasha

Ali Pasha, one of the most flamboyant characters of recent Greek history, was born in 1741 in the village of Tepeleni in Albania. In 1787 the Turks made him Pasha (governor) of Trikala and by 1788 he ruled Ioannina. His life was a catalogue of brigandage, murder, warfare and debauchery.

Tales abound about Ali. He supposedly had a harem of 400 women, but as if that were not enough he was also enamoured of Kyra Frosyni, his eldest son's mistress. When she rejected his amorous overtures, she and 15 other women were put into sacks and tipped into the lake.

Ali's sons seem to have taken after their father: one was a sex maniac who was in the habit of raping women; the other had the more innocuous hobby of collecting erotic literature.

Ali's lifelong ambition was to break away from the Ottoman Empire and create an independent state. In 1797 he collaborated with Napoleon, but in 1798 he wrested Preveza from the French. In 1817 he courted the British, who rewarded him with Parga.

In 1822 Sultan Mahmud II decided he had had enough of Ali's opportunistic and fickle alliances and sent his troops to execute him. The 82-year-old Ali took refuge on the 1st floor of the guesthouse of Agios Pandeleimon monastery on the island, but was killed when the troops fired bullets at him through the ceiling from below. Ali was then beheaded, and his head paraded around Epiros before being buried in Constantinople (İstanbul) – the rest of his body was buried in Ioannina.

Bus No 8 runs every 20 minutes from near the clock tower to the village of Perama, 50m south of the cave.

Dodoni Δωδώνη

In a fertile valley at the foot of Mt Tomaros, 21km south-west of Ioannina, is Epiros' most important ancient site, the **Theatre of Dodoni** (☎ 2651 082 287; adult/EU student €1.50/free; open 8am-5pm daily).

History An earth goddess was worshipped here as long ago as 2000 BC. She spoke through an oracle, reputedly the oldest in Greece. By the 13th century BC Zeus had taken over and it was believed he spoke through the rustling of leaves from a sacred oak tree. Around 500 BC a temple to Zeus was built, but only the foundations and a few columns of this and other smaller temples remain. The oracle was the most important in Greece until superseded by the Delphic oracle in the 6th century BC.

Exploring the Site The site's colossal 3rd-century BC **theatre**, an ambitious project overseen by King Pyrrhus, has been restored, and is now the site of the Festival of Ancient Drama (see Special Events in the Ioannina section for details). To the north of the theatre a gate leads to the **acropolis**; part of its once-substantial walls are still standing. To the east of the theatre are the foundations of the **bouleuterion** (council house) and a small temple dedicated to Aphrodite. Close by are the scant remains of the **Sanctuary of Zeus**. This sacred precinct was the site of the oracle of Zeus and the sacred oak.

Christianity also left its mark on Dodoni, as evident from the remains of a 6th-century Byzantine basilica, built over the remains of a sanctuary dedicated to Hercules.

Places to Stay & Eat *Pension Andromahi* (☎/fax 2651 082 296) Doubles €41. This pension is in the village of Dodoni, near the site.

Restaurant Andromachi (☎ 2651 082 296) Roasts €7-8. Open year-round. This restaurant does great pot-roast lamb (€7.30) which goes down well with a drop of Zitsa wine.

Getting There & Away The bus service to Dodoni is pretty abysmal considering it's Epiros' major ancient site. Buses leave from the bus station on Vizaniou in Ioannina at 6.30am and 4.30pm on Monday, Tuesday, Wednesday, Friday and Saturday. There are no buses on Thursday and only

NORTHERN GREECE

one on Sunday at 6pm, which returns at 6.45pm.

Buses return to Ioannina at 7.30am and 5.30pm. An alternative is to get a Zotiko bus, which stops 1.5km from the site. This bus leaves the Vizaniou station on Monday, Wednesday and Friday at 5.30am and 2pm, and returns at 7.15am and 4.30pm. A taxi will cost around €18 return plus €2.30 per hour of waiting time.

THE ZAGORIA VILLAGES

The region of Zagoria, north of Ioannina, offers some breathtaking vistas and is drawing more and more visitors. The 44 villages in the area are collectively known as the Zagorohoria (Ζαγοροχώρια). As with many inaccessible mountainous areas in Greece, the Zagorohoria maintained a high degree of autonomy in Turkish times, so the economy and culture flourished.

An outstanding feature of the villages is the architecture. The houses are built entirely of slate from the surrounding mountains – a perfect blending of nature and architecture. With winding, cobbled and stepped streets, the villages could have leapt straight out of a Grimm's fairy tale. Some are sadly depopulated, with only a few elderly inhabitants, while others, like Papingo, Monodendri and Tsepelovo, are beginning to thrive on the new-found tourism in the area.

There are three main destinations in the Zagorohoria of interest to travellers: the Papingo villages to the north; central Monodendri; and Tsepelovo farther east. Good roads connect most of the villages, and with a car you can see many of them in one day.

The **Vikos-Aoös National Park** encompasses much of the area. Within the park is the Tymfi Massif, part of the north Pindos Range which comprises Mt Astraka (2436m), Mt Gamila (2497m) and Mt Smolikas (2637m), the Vikos Gorge and the Aoös River Gorge. It's an area of outstanding natural beauty which is becoming popular with trekkers.

The area is thickly forested; hornbeam, maple, willow and oak predominate, but there are also fir, pine and cedar trees. Bears, wolves, wild boars, wild cats and wild goats roam the mountains. Vlach and Sarakatsani shepherds still live a semi nomadic existence, taking their flocks up to high grazing ground in the summer and returning to the valleys in the autumn.

Monodendri is 38km north of Ioannina and is reached by turning right off the main Ioannina-Konitsa road near the village of Karyes.

Farther north are the twin villages of **Megalo Papingo** and **Mikro Papingo**. The view is awe-inspiring as you approach these villages by road from the bed of the **Voïdomatis River**, after you have passed through **Aristi**, the last village before Papingo. There are no fewer than 15 hairpin bends that switchback in rapid succession up to the ledge where the Papingo villages nestle under the looming hulk of Mt Astraka. As you wind your way up, there are spectacular views into the Vikos Gorge on your right.

Papingo is popular with well-heeled urban Greeks, so be prepared to pay for services accordingly. Trekkers of less lavish means can buy some food items, though it might be a good idea to stock up on provisions in Ioannina, since there are limited supplies in the Papingo villages.

After a strenuous hike to Papingo you might want to cool off in the natural rock pools, which are exquisitely refreshing on a hot day. The 300m path to the pools starts at a bend in the road between Megalo and Mikro Papingo.

The village of **Vikos**, 5km beyond Aristi is a good starting point for the gorge trek and it is a shorter hike to Monodendri, or vice versa, than from the Papingo villages. The view from the panoramic platform in Vikos is stunning.

Tsepelovo is a delightful Zagoria village 51km north of Ioannina. There are many opportunities for scenic day walks from here. There is a post office and public phone as well as comfortable places to stay and very good restaurants.

Vikos Gorge Χαράδρα του Βίκου

The focal point of the region is the 10km long Vikos Gorge, which begins at the village of **Monodendri** (1090m), situated the southern end of the gorge.

THE ZAGORIA VILLAGES

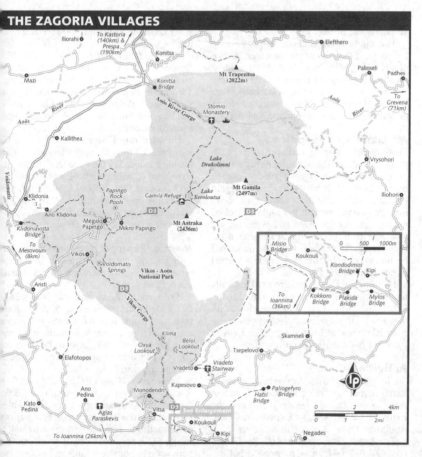

The Vikos Gorge is the most trekked gorge in Greece after the Samaria Gorge on Crete. It doesn't require any special expertise, but it is a strenuous walk of around 7½ hours, ending at either of the twin villages of **Megalo Papingo** or **Mikro Papingo**. Stout walking boots are recommended. You can tackle the gorge from either end, but if you have come by car, you will have to arrange a lift back to your vehicle via the long road route.

Before you come to Monodendri, visit the Ioannina EOT or EOS. The staff there will give you a map of the gorge, and

answer any questions. Whatever you do, come prepared for serious walking; this is no Sunday afternoon stroll in the park.

At the far end of Monodendri there is a spectacular view down into the gorge from the 15th-century **Moni Agias Paraskevis**. The descent into the gorge is a steep, marked path between the village and the monastery. Once in the gorge, it's a four-hour walk to the end, from where a trail up to the right leads to the settlement of Mikro Papingo (2½ hours). The larger settlement of Megalo Papingo is a farther 2km west, but the track splits into two at the base of

NORTHERN GREECE

the climb. You can also terminate your trek at the village of **Vikos**.

The **Klima Spring**, about halfway along the gorge, is the only source of water, so take plenty along with you. Probably the most breathtaking view of the gorge for the less energetic is from the **Oxya Lookout**, 5km beyond Monodendri. You will have to hitch or walk since there is no public transport.

Mt Gamila to Tsepelovo

From Mikro Papingo there is a good, marked path to the **Gamila Refuge** (also called Rodovoli Refuge) at 1950m, owned by the EOS (☎ 2653 041 115) in Megalo Papingo, which you must contact for bookings (€8.80 per person per night). Cooked meals, soft drinks, beer and wine are all available from the refuge at somewhat inflated prices. If it is fully booked you should be able to camp by the dry lake *(xeroloutsa)* on the next valley floor.

From this refuge there are marked trails to Drakolimni, or 'Dragon Lake' (one hour), and to the village of Tsepelovo (six to seven hours). For rock climbers there are over 20 routes up Mt Astraka. The EOS in Ioannina has a leaflet detailing these.

Activities

So far the region is untouched by mass tourism, but several companies organise treks in the Zagoria region, including the British-based Exodus Expeditions and Robinson Travel Agency in Ioannina.

The latter also runs an **Activity Centre** (☎ 2653 071 041, e activities@robinson. gr; open May-Oct), located in the village of Kipi. The staff organise a whole range of activities in the area, including walking, rock climbing, paragliding, canyoning and mountain biking.

Places to Stay & Eat

Monodendri There is a good range of accommodation here and it is not as expensive, or hard to book, as that in the Papingo villages.

To Kalderimi (☎ 2653 071 510, mobile 09-4521 1241, w www.epirus.com) Doubles/triples €35/41. This is one of the neatest

places to stay in. All rooms are cosy an spacious, have wooden floors, TV and heat ing for winter.

Rooms Ladia (☎/fax 2653 071 48* Doubles/triples €38.20/44. This tradition* hostel nearby has very comfortable room* Two have their own fireplace and a grea valley view. Request one when booking.

There is a brace of eateries on the upp* road, all offering a wide range of pittes.

Haradra tou Vikou (☎ 2653 071 55* Pittes €3-4. Enjoy the very friendly and hos pitable service. Try the excellent cheese pie *(tyropitta)* or wild greens pies *(hortopitta)*.

O Dionysos (☎ 2653 071 366) Pittes €* 4. Try the original lentil pie *(fakopitta)* c go for the spare ribs (€20.20/kg). Ask for shot of *tsipouro* to liven up your palate.

Megalo Papingo Accommodation an* eating tends to be a bit pricier in the P* pingo villages and there are no really buc get options.

Xenonas tou Kouli domatia (☎/fax 265* *041 115)* Doubles/triples €38.20/47. Xer onas tou Kouli has six rooms in variou combinations. There is a minimarket an* cafe-bar as well. It is best to book in ac vance. The owners also serve as offici* EOS tour guides.

Xenonas Kalliopi (☎/fax 2653 041 08* Rooms €32.30-47. On the southern side c the village (look out for the purple and blu gate), this place has eight rooms, in variou combinations ranging from singles t triples. There is also a small restaurant-ba here serving home cooking and pittes.

O Nikos (☎ 2653 041 893) Mains €5-6 This place serves good food such as veal i red wine sauce (€5.60), or trout (€5.30). offers local pittes along with other regula fare, and has a good wine selection. Try th white *Velando Zitsas* from Zitsa.

Ioannides (☎ 2653 041 125) Pitte €3.50-4. Near O Nikos, this is a little stor* cottage-cum-restaurant and serves tasty, if little pricey, home-cooked meals.

Mikro Papingo *Xenonas Dias* (☎ 265* *041 257, fax 2653 041 892)* Doubles/triple €35.50/38. Open year-round. This pleasa* lace has 12 rooms. There is also a little restaurant for breakfast and excellent meals.

Vikos *Sotiris Karpouzas Domatia* (☎ 2653 41 176, fax 2651 093 576) Doubles/triples with bathroom €41/50. This place has modern rooms. Food is also available.

Ioannis Dinoulis Rooms (☎ 2653 042 12, mobile 69-3279 5180) Doubles/triples €47/56. This stone inn's five rooms are neat and clean. It's a little more expensive than Karpouzas, but perhaps a better choice.

Restaurant H. Tsoumanis (☎ 2653 042 70) Pittes €3. All the usual pittes are available, but the gamey wild boar (€13.20) should be tried. Dishes are hearty and filling.

Tsepelovo *Domatia Erasmias Deligianni* (☎ 2653 081 232) Doubles/triples €32/38. There are a few domatia in the village. Try this one, on the main square.

Gouris Pension (mobile ☎ 69-4478 9909) Doubles €35, breakfast €3. This place is immaculate.

Hagiati Hotel (☎/fax 2653 081 301, glinavos@otenet.gr) Double studios with breakfast €44. This hotel is just back from the main square. Winter prices are higher.

Gerasimos Stavrou Taverna (☎ 2653 81 088) Pittes €3. This homely taverna is on the main square.

O Giorgos (☎ 2653 081 341) Meals around €7. This place is on the right of the main road as you approach from Ioannina.

Getting There & Away

There are buses from Ioannina to Megalo and Mikro Papingo (two hours, €3.50, 6am and 2.30pm Monday, Wednesday and Friday, with the Wednesday bus calling in at Vikos in summer), Tsepelovo (1½ hours, 3, 6am and 3.15pm Monday, Wednesday and Friday) and Monodendri (one hour, 2.40, 7.30am and 5pm daily).

All buses return to Ioannina almost immediately upon arrival in the villages.

KONITSA Κόνιτσα

Postcode 441 00 • pop 2858

Konitsa (ko-nit-sah), 64km north of Ioannina, is the largest settlement in the area.

It's a lively market town and a good base from which to explore the northern Zagorohoria. In recent times it has become a centre of sorts for kayaking and trekking in the Vikos-Aoös National Park.

Konitsa is built amphitheatrically on a hillside, and the view over the Voïdomatis-Aoös Valley as the sun sets over the mountains in Albania is quite a sight. A serpentine road leads to the town centre from the main Ioannina-Kozani road.

Information

The bus station (☎ 2655 022 214) is just off the central square, where you will also find a post office and a Commercial Bank with an ATM. There is no EOT or tourist police. Check your email at Odeon Internet Cafe (☎ 2655 023 797) on the central square. It's open 10am until late and charges €3.20 per hour.

Activities

The scenic walk to **Stomio Monastery** (Moni Stomiou) along the Aoös River Gorge takes about 1½ hours. Cross the stone bridge at the beginning of the town (coming from Ioannina), turn left and follow the Aoös River to the waterfall. Cross the bridge and follow the path up to the monastery. The last 15 minutes walking is very steep. Occasionally there is a lone monk in residence here who shows visitors around, but even if you find the monastery locked, the walk is worthwhile for the tremendous views.

Paddler (☎ 2655 023 102, fax 2655 023 101, Averof 16) organises kayaking, rafting, canyoning, paragliding and trekking expeditions. Ask for Nikos Kyritsis.

Places to Stay & Eat

There is limited but good accommodation in Konitsa.

To Dendro Guesthouse (☎/fax 2655 022 055, W www.epirus.com/todendro) Doubles/triples with bath €31/41. Most travellers head for this popular inn on the last bend of the road coming up from Ioannina. Look for the bright orange exterior. English-speaking owner Ioannis Mourehidis can advise on

NORTHERN GREECE

local walks and will be opening a new upper-market, traditional guesthouse by 2002.

Kougias Hotel (☎ 2655 023 830, fax 2655 023 960, Kendriki Plateia) Singles/ doubles €28/35. This tastefully furbished hotel is a good choice. It offers exquisite rooms, each decorated with a different floral colour scheme. There is a bar and cafeteria, and favoured guests get to taste the owner's award-winning cabernet sauvignon wine.

To Dendro Restaurant (☎ 2655 022 055) Mains €5. Part of the Dendro Guesthouse, this is the best restaurant in town. Pot-roast goat or lamb is a good bet and trout is equally satisfying, or try the speciality of grilled feta with chilli and tomato.

Zourloukas Psistaria (☎ 2655 022 915, Kendriki Plateia) Grills €4-5. This reasonable psistaria is on the main square. *Kokoretsi* is spit-grilled offal (€4.40) and is a local speciality.

Spitiko (☎ 2655 023 697) Snacks €2-3. Spitiko is great for a quick snack. See what pittes are on offer. Try a *lahonopitta* (cabbage pie) if it is available.

Getting There & Away

On weekdays there are eight buses to Ioannina (two hours, €3.70); there are five on weekends. Two daily Ioannina-Kozani buses (four hours, €9.70) pass through Konitsa. If you want to go farther, go to Kozani first, then take an onward bus. There are also buses from Ioannina to Thessaloniki that pass through Konitsa on Monday in winter (six hours, €16.70) and on Monday and Friday in summer.

METSOVO Μέτσοβο

postcode 442 00 • pop 2917

The village of Metsovo (**met-so-vo**), 58km north-east of Ioannina and 90km from Trikala and at an altitude of 1156m, sprawls down a mountainside just south of the Katara Pass, at the junction of Epiros, Thessaly and Macedonia. The inhabitants are descendants of Vlach shepherds, most of whom have hung up their crooks to make a living in the tourist trade.

Metsovo has much tourist appeal: loca dressed in traditional costumes, local hand crafts, regional cuisine, stone mansions, i vigorating air, a superb mountain settin and good skiing. Some find the village tw and artificial while others are enamoured its considerable charm.

Despite its peasant origins, Metsovo a tracts an urban set and there is a wid choice of quality hotels and restaurants. you are on your way by road across the Pi dos Range, stop for a day or two and sar ple the ambience.

History

Originally a small settlement of shepherd Metsovo was granted many privileges Ottoman times as reward for guarding t pass upon which the village stands. Th pass was the only route across the Pind Range, and Metsovite vigilance facilitate the passage of Ottoman troops. These pri ileges led to Metsovo becoming an impo tant centre of finance, commerce, handicraf and sheep farming. A school was esta lished in 1659, at a time when Gree language schools were not allowed in oth parts of the country.

Metsovo's privileges were abolished 1795 by that spoilsport Ali Pasha, and 1854 it suffered considerable damage fro Ottoman troops. But Metsovo was ve lucky in its many prosperous benefactors: l cals who had gone on to achieve national ar international recognition. The most famou of them were Georgios Averof (1815–9 and Mihail Tositsas (1885–1950). Both b queathed large amounts of money Metsovo, which was used to restore the tow to its former glory and to finance sever small industries.

Orientation & Information

From Kalambaka, turn left after the Kata Pass to reach Metsovo. Orientation Metsovo is easy as there is only one ma thoroughfare, which loops down to the ce tral square, passing many restaurants, hote and souvenir shops. A maze of stone pat ways winds between the fine, tradition houses.

The bus stop is on the central square. here is no EOT or tourist police. The regular police (☎ 2656 041 233) are on the ght, along the road opposite the bus stop.

The post office is on the right side of the main thoroughfare as you leave the central quare. The OTE is a couple of blocks back om the main square. The Commercial ank, Agricultural Bank and National Bank f Greece are all near the main square and ll have ATMs.

For some useful information on the own, check out the Web site **W** www netsovo.com.

hings to See
he **Tositsas mansion** has been restored as folk museum (☎ 2656 041 084; admission €1.50; open 9.30am-1.30pm & 4pm-6pm ri-Wed). It is a faithful reconstruction of a ealthy 19th-century Metsovite household, ith exquisitely handcrafted furniture, artects and utensils. It's about halfway up the ain street – look for the wooden sign. Vait at the door until the guide lets you in very half hour).

The 14th-century **Moni Agiou Nikolaou** ands in a gorge below Metsovo. Its chapel as post-Byzantine frescoes and a beautiful arved wooden iconostasis. The monastery a 30-minute walk from Metsovo and is ignposted to the left, just before Hotel thens.

The **Averof Gallery** (adult/student €1.50/ .90; open 10am-7pm Wed-Mon) was financed by Georgios Averof's three chilren. It houses a permanent collection of 9th- and 20th-century works by Greek ainters and sculptors. Turn left at the far de of the central square – the gallery is on e right.

kiing
s you come from Kalambaka, Metsovo's ki centre (☎ 2656 041 211) is on the rightand side of the main Kalambaka-Ioannina ighway, just before the turn-off for the wn. There is a taverna and an 82-seat ski ft, two downhill runs and a 5km crossountry run. Ski hire is available in letsovo.

Places to Stay – Budget
There is no shortage of accommodation, with no fewer than 14 hotels and abundant domatia. The hotels, predictably, have a folksy ambience.

Hotel Athens (☎ 2656 041 332, fax 2656 042 009) Doubles with bathroom €23.50. This E-class hotel is just off the central square, It's old but clean, and the woven rugs on the floors add a homely touch.

Filoxenia Domatia (☎ 2656 041 021, fax 2656 042 009) Singles/doubles €26.50/30, 4-person suite €44. These domatia, just behind the central park area, close to the art gallery, are allied to the Hotel Athens. The suite has one of the most spectacular views in town.

Hotel Acropolis (☎ 2656 041 672) Doubles €32.50/44. This D-class hotel has traditional furniture, wooden floors and ceilings, and colourful wall hangings. Look out for it on the right at the beginning of the road to Metsovo.

Places to Stay – Mid-Range & Top End
Hotel Galaxias (☎ 2656 041 202, fax 2656 041 124) Singles/doubles €35.50/47. This is the closest hotel to the bus stop. Rooms are very comfortable.

Hotel Egnatia (☎ 2656 041 263, fax 2656 041 485, **W** www.metsovo.com/ egnatia) Singles/doubles €44/52. This C-class hotel has cosy rooms with balcony and wood-panelled walls. It's on the right side of the main road as you approach the central square.

Hotel Bitouni (☎ 2656 041 217, fax 2656 041 545, **e** bitounis@net.forthnet.gr) Singles/doubles/suites €42.50/56/76.50. Opposite the Hotel Egnatia, farther up the hill, is this C-class establishment. It has immaculate rooms and a charming lounge with a flagstone floor, brass plates, embroidered cushions and carved wooden coffee tables.

Hotel Apollon (☎ 2656 041 844, fax 2656 042 110) Singles/doubles €44/56. This is Metsovo's best hotel. The carpeted rooms are gorgeous. Walk along the road opposite the bus station and look for the sign pointing right.

Phone numbers listed incorporate changes due in Oct 2002; see p83

Places to Eat

Hotel Athens Restaurant (☎ 2656 042 332) Meals €5-6. This restaurant has tasty, reasonably priced food with many local specialities.

Restaurant Galaxias (☎ 2656 041 202) Meal plus wine €7-8. Next to its associated hotel, this is a very good choice. Try the local pittes and *hilopittes* (pasta with veal), accompanied by fine rosé wine.

To Koutouki tou Nikola (☎ 2656 041 732) Mains €4.20. Here you can enjoy a good selection of pittes. Try also the meatballs with leek. All dishes are generally cheap and filling.

Shopping

Craft shops selling both quality stuff and kitsch are ubiquitous. The old-fashioned food shop opposite the bus stop sells the famous local cheeses.

Getting There & Away

There are six direct buses to Ioannina (€3.50) and two or three to Trikala (€5). In summer there is also a direct bus to Athens (€23). To catch a Thessaloniki bus you will have to walk up to the main road and wave the bus down – these buses normally come from Ioannina.

In winter the Katara Pass is occasionally blocked by snow and buses and vehicles may not be able to get through to Thessaly. The eventual completion of the Via Egnatia which will bypass Metsovo will solve this problem.

IGOUMENITSA Ηγουμενίτσα

postcode 461 00 • pop 6807

Once a sleepy little outpost, the west-coast port of Igoumenitsa (ih-goo-meh-**nit**-sah), 100km from Ioannina, is where you get ferries to Corfu and Italy. It is growing quickly thanks to its strategic position as an important port to Western Europe from the southern Balkans and Middle East. There is little of interest, but if you are travelling by ferry and using Igoumenitsa as your Greek entry or exit point, then you are likely to be spending some time here, if only to have a meal or wait for a boat or bus. Ferries leave

IGOUMENITSA

To Post Office (1.5km),
Drepanos (6km), Ioannina
(86km) & Sagiada (20km)

Zoumadon

Mihala

Vyronos

Kyprou

Evangelistrias

Ethnikis Andistasis

Zalongou

Eryrthrou Stavrou

Kyras Vasilikis

Elinas

Evias

Pargas

Ionian Sea

To Camping Kalami
Beach (8km),
Hotel Oscar,
Minoan Lines,
Superfast Ferries,
Alfa Travel,
Syvota (18km) &
Parga (45km)

Agiou Apostolon

H Trikoupi

Xanthou

PLACES TO STAY
10 Egnatia
20 Hotel Aktaion
23 Rooms to Rent

PLACES TO EAT
1 Alekos
15 To Koutoukaki
18 O Salonikios

OTHER
2 Cafe Planet
3 Blue Star Ferries Agency
4 OTE
5 Chris Travel
6 Bus Station
7 Marlines Agency
8 Agoudimos Lines
9 Olympic Airways
11 Alpha Bank & ATM
12 National Bank & ATM
13 EOT
14 Eurobank & ATM
16 Commercial Bank & ATM
17 Old Port Ferry Terminal
19 Police
21 Ferries to Corfu
22 Dimas Supermarket
24 New Port Ferry Terminal; Port Police

in the morning and evening, so you may not have to stay overnight.

There is a very pleasant beach and taverna at **Drepanos**, about 6km north of town, if you feel like a relaxing swim and a meal. Take a cab or walk there.

Orientation

Ferries for Italy and Corfu leave from three separate quays quite close to one another on the waterfront of Ethnikis Andistasis. Ferries to Ancona and Venice (in Italy) depart from the new port on the south side of town; those for Brindisi and Bari (in Italy) use the d port in front of the main shipping offices; and ferries for Corfu (Kerkyra) and axi depart from just north of the new port.

The bus station is on Kyprou, two blocks ack from the waterfront

nformation

he main EOT office (☎ 2665 022 227), in he old port area, is open 7am to 2.30pm aily. There is also an EOT booth just outide the arrivals area of the new port. The ost office is 1.5km out of town toward oannina. The OTE is on Evangelistrias. urrency exchange machines and ATMs re available at the Alpha Bank, National ank, Eurobank and Commercial Bank all ext to each other on Ethnikis Andistasis. dditional exchange booths are at the New ort. Internet access is available at Cafe lanet at Ethnikis Andistasis 76. It is open 0am to 2pm. Olympic Airways (☎ 2665 22 359) is at Zalongou 2.

The tourist police and regular police ☎ 2665 022 222) are together on the main oad near the port entrance. The port police re beside the ferry quays.

laces to Stay

Not many people linger in Igoumenitsa but ampers have two decent choices.

Camping Kalami Beach (☎ 2665 071 11, fax 2665 071 245, Plataria) Adult/tent €4.40/2.90. The shady site is 8km south of goumenitsa on a small, secluded cove with rystal-clear water.

Drepanos Camping (☎ 2665 024 442, ax 2665 028 767, Drepanos) Adult/tent €3.80/2.40. On wide Drepanos Beach, this rassy and shady site is a good option.

Rooms to Rent (☎ 2665 023 612, Xanhou 12) Rooms without bath €23.50, mini tudio €23.30. These rooms are decent nough and very handy for the ferry.

Egnatia (☎ 2665 023 648, fax 2665 023 33, Eleftherias 2) Singles/doubles with athroom €29.40/38.15. This D-class hotel as comfortable rooms. Turn right from the us station and walk 100m. You will see it cross the square on your left.

Hotel Oscar (☎ 2665 023 338, fax 2665 23 557, Agion Apostolon 149) Singles/

doubles €29.40/44. This C-class hotel, opposite the new port arrivals area, has reasonable rooms.

Hotel Aktaion (☎/fax 2665 022 330, Agion Apostolon 27) Singles/doubles €44/58.70. This C-class hotel is on the waterfront between the Corfu ferry quay and the old port.

Places to Eat

O Salonikios (☎ 2665 026 695, Pargas 5) Breakfast €4.40. For breakfast and good Greek coffee try this little place in the backstreets near the Corfu ferry terminal.

To Koutoukaki (☎ 2665 021 063, Kosti Palama 9) Mezedes €2.35 a serve. For good Italian coffee and mezedes visit this place.

Alekos (☎ 2665 023 708, Ethnikis Andistasis 84) Mains €3.50-5.50. Enjoy excellent Greek cuisine here. Two recommended dishes are mousakas (€3.80) and veal with aubergines (€5.20). Alekos is very popular with locals.

Dimas Supermarket (Tsakalof 8) This is the best place for your travel and picnic supplies.

Getting There & Away

Bus From the bus station (☎ 2665 022 309) at Kyprou 29 there are buses to Ioannina (two hours, €5.90, nine daily), Parga (one hour, €3.65, five daily), Athens (eight hours, €27.15, four daily), Preveza (2½ hours, €6.75, two daily) and Thessaloniki (eight hours, €25.25, one daily).

Ferry – Corfu There are ferries to Corfu Town hourly between 5am and 10pm (1¾ hours, €4.10). Ferries also go to Lefkimmi in southern Corfu (one hour, €2.50, six daily) and Paxi (1¾ hours, €5, three weekly). Agency booths opposite the quay sell tickets. Boats are a mixture of closed-hull ferries and smaller landing-craft-type ferries.

Most of the ferries to/from Italy also stop at Corfu. There are also weekly passenger and car ferries to Corfu from Sagiada (40 minutes, €3.50), 20km north of Igoumenitsa (see the Sagiada section later in this chapter).

NORTHERN GREECE

There is a hydrofoil service to and from Corfu (35 minutes, €8.80) and Paxi (one hour, €10.30) on Monday, Tuesday and Friday in summer. Call Milano Travel (☎ 2665 026 670) for further details.

Ferry – Italy There are many options for getting to Italy from Igoumenitsa. You can usually just turn up and buy an onward passenger ticket, although demand is high in summer and securing a vehicle spot may be trickier. Phoning and booking ahead is always advisable at these times. There are different prices for low, middle and high seasons, and return tickets are 30% cheaper than two one-way tickets.

There are ferries to Brindisi (11 hours, six to eight daily), Bari (13 hours, two to four daily), Ancona (24 hours, two or three daily), Venice (33 hours, nine weekly) and Trieste (28 hours, six weekly). Some go to Italy direct, but most go via Corfu (two hours), where some lines allow you to stop over free of charge. Boats leave between 6am and 8am, and between 6pm and 9pm, but timetables are subject to change. You should turn up at the port at least two hours before departure and check in at the shipping agent's office.

Travellers with campervans should note that on board 'camping' is allowable on a number of services – check with the individual ferry lines.

The following table shows one-way passenger fares, based on high-season deck rates.

The quality of service varies from compan to company, but it should be noted th Superfast Ferries and Minoan Ferries pric are higher because the transit times are a preciably faster and the fleet is noticeab more modern and streamlined. Blue St Ferries have smaller but comfortable a well-appointed boats and offers the be overall deals.

For a comprehensive brochure of fer options, go to Chris Travel (☎ 2665 02 351, fax 2665 025 350) at Ethnikis Andi tasis 60. You can also book most ferry cor panies at Alfa Travel (☎ 2665 022 797, fa 2665 026 330) at Agion Apostolon 167 o posite the new port.

There are quite a number of shipping c fices on Ethnikis Andistasis and anoth brace over on Agion Apostolon opposite th new port.

The main ferry offices are:

Agoudimos Lines (☎ 2665 025 682, fax 2665 024 960, e nztrv@otenet.gr) Ethnikis Andistasis 32
ANEK Lines (☎ 2665 022 104, fax 2665 025 421) Revis Travel Tourism & Shipping, Ethnikis Andistasis 34
Blue Star Ferries (☎ 2665 023 970, fax 2665 022 348) Agion Apostolon 145
Fragline (☎ 2665 027 906, fax 2665 028 172, e fragline@fragline.gr) Revis Travel Touris & Shipping, Ethnikis Andistasis 34
Hellenic Mediterranean (☎ 2665 022 180, 2665 025 682, e hml@otenet.gr) Ethnikis Andistasis 30
Marlines (☎ 2665 023 301, fax 2665 025 428, e info@barkbas.gr) Ethnikis Andistasis 42
Minoan Lines (☎ 2665 022 952, fax 2665 022 101, e minoanig@compulink.gr) Ethnikis Andistasis 58a
Superfast Ferries (☎ 2665 028 150, fax 2665 028 156, e info.igoumenitsaport@ superfast.com) Pitoulis & Co Ltd, Agion Apostolon 147
Ventouris Ferries (☎ 2665 023 565, fax 2665 024 880) Milano Travel, Agion Apostolon 1

SAGIADA Σαγάδα

Sagiada (sah-**yiah**-dah) is a sleepy fishin village 20km north of Igoumenitsa favoure by day-tripping yachties from Corfu, a well as the passengers on the weekly ferr

destination	company	price
Ancona	ANEK Lines	€63.40
Ancona	Minoan Lines	€72.30
Ancona	Blue Star Ferries	€61.40
Bari	Superfast Ferries	€51.40
Bari	Ventouris Ferries	€45
Brindisi	Agoudimos Lines	€30
Brindisi	Fragline	€43.80
Brindisi	Blue Star Ferries	€48.20
Brindisi	Ventouris Ferries	€45
Trieste	ANEK Lines	€71.30
Venice	Minoan Lines	€72.30
Venice	Blue Star Ferries	€61.40

rvice to/from Corfu (40 minutes, €3.50, am Tuesday). Aside from the five tavernas ad few bars that crowd its waterfront, there not much activity. With transport you can sit the little coves of Strovili and eramidi beaches, 3km and 4km north of agiada respectively.

You can now officially cross from agiada to Albania via a rather rough road axi, or bus from Igoumenitsa) to the Mavromati border post. Cross on foot to the Ibanian side. A new vehicle road is slowly eing constructed via a more northerly route.

Sagiada can accommodate up to 40 visirs at any one time in the various *domatia*. verage prices in high season are around 30 for two people. The village is linked by vo daily buses to both Igoumenitsa and iliates farther inland.

For a fish lunch seek out *Alekos (☎ 2664 51 244)*. It's the first of the restaurants ong the harbour; mullet costs €20.50 per ilogram. For an ouzo or a beer, head for e *Skala Cafe*.

YVOTA Σψβοτα

yvota is another sleepy little village, this me 18km south of Igoumenitsa. Its reverie disturbed for about six weeks each year hen it becomes a busy little holiday entre for Greeks and a few foreign packageur companies. There is a good yacht harour, a sprinkling of restaurants and small otels or domatia and even a Commercial ank ATM booth.

For accommodation try the neat studios f *Villa Emily (☎ 2665 093 033)* with ooms for €30 for two persons. For a hearty eal drop in to *Georgeos Family Restaurnt (☎ 2665 093 266)* where mains cost 3.80. Open all year, Georgeos' speciality lobster with spaghetti (€52.80 for four ersons).

ARGA Πάργα

ostcode 480 60 ● pop 1669

arga, 48km south of Igoumenitsa and 7km north of Preveza, spills down to a ocky bay flanked by coves and islets. Add Venetian kastro and the long pebblend-sand Valtos Beach, and you have

somewhere truly alluring. So it will come as no surprise that it's overrun with tourists in midsummer and that hotels, domatia and travel agents have swamped this once-serene fishing village.

Nonetheless, if you choose your time carefully it is still a very attractive place to spend a day or two and is Epiros' number one tourist resort. Try to visit in early or late summer; if you're travelling along this coast, be sure to stop by.

Orientation & Information

There is a Municipal Tourist Office (☎ 2684 032 107, fax 2684 032 511, e parga@ otenet.gr, W www.parga.gr) with helpful and friendly staff, and also a computerised Tourist Information Booth opposite the OTE and the main taxi stand (mobile ☎ 09-4591 9237 or 09-4619 2337). The tourist police have an office in the same building as the regular police (☎ 2684 031 222), which is shared with the post office at Alexandrou Baga 18. The bus stop is on the main loop road on the east side of the village.

There are ATMs at the National Bank of Greece, the Commercial Bank and the Agricultural Bank. Internet access is available at the Terra Internet Cafe (☎ 2684 032 408) on the waterfront for €4.40 per hour; it's open 8am to 2am.

Nekromanteio of Afyra

Just about every travel agent in Parga advertises trips to the Nekromanteio of Afyra *(☎ 2684 041 206; adult/student €1.45/0.90; open 8.30am-3pm daily)*. This involves a boat ride down the coast to the Aherondas River and then up the navigable river as far as the Nekromanteio itself, which you approach on foot. The day trip costs about €10.30. If you have your own transport, take the Preveza road as far as the village of Mesopotamos and look out for the sign to the Nekromanteio, 1km off the main road.

The Nekromanteio was the ancients' venue for the equivalent of a modern séance. They believed this to be the gate of Hades, god of the underworld, and so it became an oracle of the dead and a sanctuary to Hades and Persephone. Pilgrims made offerings of

NORTHERN GREECE

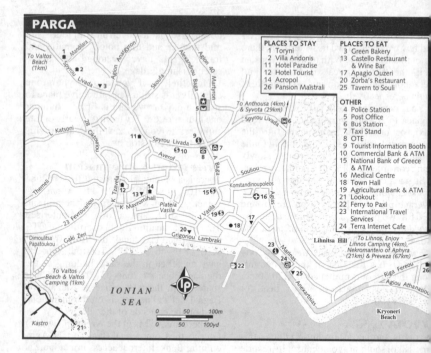

PARGA

PLACES TO STAY
1 Toryni
2 Villa Andonis
11 Hotel Paradise
12 Hotel Tourist
14 Acropol
26 Pansion Maïstrali

PLACES TO EAT
3 Green Bakery
13 Castello Restaurant & Wine Bar
17 Apagio Ouzeri
20 Zorba's Restaurant
25 Tavern to Souli

OTHER
4 Police Station
5 Post Office
6 Bus Station
7 Taxi Stand
8 OTE
9 Tourist Information Booth
10 Commercial Bank & ATM
15 National Bank of Greece & ATM
16 Medical Centre
18 Town Hall
19 Agricultural Bank & ATM
21 Lookout
22 Ferry to Paxi
23 International Travel Services
24 Terra Internet Cafe

milk, honey and the blood of sacrificed animals in the hope that the spirits of the departed would communicate with them.

The labyrinth of buildings was only discovered in 1958, revealing not only the Nekromanteio itself, but also the monastery of Agios Ioannis Prodromos and a graveyard. The eerie underground vault, the purpose of which is still not known, could easily have been the meeting place for the dead and the living.

There is a good, colour guidebook written in English by Professor Sotiris Dakaris of the University of Ioannina. It's available at the sanctuary entrance for €4.40.

The Kastro

The Venetian Castle (to kastro) dominates the town and separates Valtos Beach from Parga proper. A reminder of 400 years of Venetian presence in Epiros, the kastro is a bit overgrown, but its ramparts provide some lovely rambling, as well as superb views of the coastline. At the time of writing, it was undergoing extensive renovation with a hostel and conference centre being built in what was once the French armoury.

Activities

If you like scuba diving, contact **International Travel Services** (see Places to Stay). It will put you in touch with the diving school, where a one-day beginner's course costs about €35.50. ITS also organises Aheron River cruises for about €10.30; cruises with a beach barbecue and unlimited drinks cost around €28.

Places to Stay – Budget

Avoid mid-July to the end of August as accommodation availability is very tight. For accommodation help try International Travel Services (☎ 2684 031 833, fax 2684 031 834, ⓔ zigourisco@otenet.gr), Anexartisias 37–39 on the main waterfront.

Enjoy Lihnos Beach Camping (☎ 2684 031 371, fax 2684 032 076, Lihnos Beach) Adult/tent €5/3. The site is well shaded and quite extensive and boasts a small super-market and restaurant. The beach is sandy and the water is very clean. There are also fully equipped two-person apartments for €52.80.

Valtos Camping (☎ 2684 031 287, Valtos Beach) Adult/tent €4.90/3. This camping ground at Valtos Beach is a good choice.

Parga Camping (☎ 2684 031 161, Kryoneri) Adult/tent €4.50/2.90. This site is closer to Parga than Valtos Camping but is less appealing.

Domatia are best found by heading up to-wards the kastro and walking along Di-moulitsa Papatoukou, the street to your right at the top of Gaki Zeri. There are sev-eral possibilities here.

Places to Stay – Mid-Range

Pansion Maïstrali (☎/fax 2684 031 275, Riga Fereou 4) Doubles/triples €35.25/41. This pension on the south side of town, up from Kryoneri Beach, is very clean and convenient. Rooms have TV and air-con.

Villa Andonis (☎ 2684 031 540, fax 2684 031 340, Spyrou Livada 200) Doubles/triples €38.20/47. This is a neat set of domatia which deals with package groups as well as individuals, and offers modern rooms.

Toryni (☎ 2684 031 219, fax 2684 032 376, Mandilara 1) Singles/doubles €35.20/ 41. Toryni is a small, traditional-style hotel that deals mainly with individual travellers.

Hotel Paradise (☎ 2684 031 229, fax 2684 031 266, e hotelpar@otenet.gr, W www.epirus.com/hotel-paradise, Spyrou Livada 23) Singles/doubles €36.70/50. This is a neat C-class hotel.

Acropol (☎ 2684 031 239, fax 2684 031 236, e zigourisco@otenet.gr, Agion Apos-tolon 6) Singles/doubles €56.70/73.40. Radically upgraded in 2001, these eight spacious rooms have TV, minibar, spa bath and air-conditioning.

Hotel Tourist (☎ 2684 031 239, fax 2684 031 236, e zigourisco@otenet.gr, Kitsou Tzavela 6) Double studios €61.70. This comfortable pension is affiliated to the Acropol. Each room has a fridge and kitchenette.

Places to Eat

Not surprisingly, there are plenty of places to eat, many of them touting tourist menus and English breakfasts. In high sea-son prices can be a bit high, so choose carefully.

Green Bakery (☎ 2684 031 400, Spyrou Livada 40) Breakfast €4.40. Have a full English, or a 'diet' breakfast, among other choices. Try also its Parga bagels (€0.45), or the scrumptious pittes (€0.75).

Taverna to Souli (☎ 2684 031 658, Anexartisias 45) Mezedes €2-3. Great for a sunset ouzo and appetisers, or a full meal. Try the *feta Souli* (grilled feta cheese served with tomatoes and herbs; €2.40) or the fried zucchini for appetisers, or the *kleftiko* (slow, oven-baked lamb or goat; €4.40) for a filling main course.

Zorba's Restaurant (☎ 2684 032 545) Grills €4-5.50. Open year-round. This restaurant caters for locals as well as visi-tors, offering good food and draught wine. Sample the excellent stuffed (vegetarian) aubergines (€2.95).

Apagio Ouzeri (☎ 2684 032 791) Mezedes €3.50. Try this homely ouzeri, in a little alley just off the promenade. All food is home-made and the very tasty mari-nated sardines (€3.60) are highly recom-mended. Wash your meal down with the excellent draught Zitsa wine.

Castello Restaurant & Wine Bar (☎ 2684 031 239, Agion Apostolon 6) Mains €7-9. This is a smart, well-run restaurant, with professionally prepared food and a wide wine selection including Australian and Chilean vintages. The chef recommends pork a la Veneta (€8.80).

Shopping

Irida (☎ 2684 032 562, e iridacri@ otenet.gr, W www.iridaweb.com, Frouriou 4) Top-class leatherware and blown glass candelabras can be found here. Prices range from the very reasonable to the pretty steep, for designer Italian leather bags.

NORTHERN GREECE

Getting There & Away

Bus From the small bus station (☎ 2684 031 218) there are buses to Igoumenitsa (one hour, €3.70, five daily), Preveza (two hours, €3.80, five daily), Ioannina (three hours, €7.35, one daily in summer) and Athens (seven hours, €25.40, three daily). The ticket office is open 6.30am to 2pm.

Excursion Boat The small Ionian islands of Paxi and Antipaxi lie just 20km off the coast. In summer there is a scheduled passenger-only service (€3.80) at 9.30am daily. Excursion boats offer various cruise options to and around the islands for between €19 and €22.

PREVEZA Πρέβεζα

postcode 481 00 ● pop 13,341

Preveza (**preh**-veh-zah), built on a peninsula between the Ionian Sea and the Ambracian Gulf, is primarily a port from which ferries cross the narrow strait to Aktion, but it is also a popular holiday destination for Greeks. Most people coming to Preveza are either heading out to the resorts at Parga, or to the beach resorts north of the town. Preveza is a pleasant town in its own right and a leisurely stroll through its narrow, pedestrian-only central streets is a great pleasure.

Orientation & Information

The bus station is at the northern end of Preveza, a five-minute walk to the main hotel and restaurant strip. Arrivals by ferry from Aktion will arrive at the new port 400m north of the centre. When the new underwater tunnel is completed (in late 2001) Aktion will be linked to Preveza by road. The tunnel entrance is on the south side of Preveza. Banks, most with ATMs, are clustered along Ethnikis Andistasis, the main shopping thoroughfare.

For Internet access try Net Cafe (☎ 2682 027 230) at Spiliadou 10 or NetcafeAscot (☎ 2682 027 746, ⓔ netcafeascot@mail .com) at Balkou 6. Access is about €2 per hour. Both open from early until late.

For good maps, foreign magazine and newspapers visit News Stand (☎ 2682 022

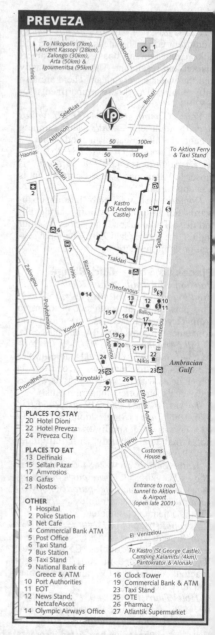

PREVEZA

To Nikopolis (7km), Ancient Kassopi (28km), Zalongo (30km), Arta (50km) & Igoumenitsa (95km)

To Aktion Ferry & Taxi Stand

Kastro (St Andrew Castle)

Ambracian Gulf

Customs House

Entrance to road tunnel to Aktion & Airport (open late 2001)

El Venizelou

To Kastro (St George Castle), Camping Kalamitsi (4km), Pantokrator & Alonaki

PLACES TO STAY
20 Hotel Dioni
22 Hotel Preveza
24 Preveza City

PLACES TO EAT
13 Delfinaki
15 Seitan Pazar
17 Amvrosios
18 Gafas
21 Nostos

OTHER
1 Hospital
2 Police Station
3 Net Cafe
4 Commercial Bank ATM
5 Post Office
6 Taxi Stand
7 Bus Station
8 Taxi Stand
9 National Bank of Greece & ATM
10 Port Authorities
11 EOT
12 News Stand; NetcafeAscot
14 Olympic Airways Office
16 Clock Tower
19 Commercial Bank & ATM
23 Taxi Stand
25 OTE
26 Pharmacy
27 Atlantik Supermarket

370) at Balkou 10. There is a pharmacy at Karyotaki 5.

Special Events
In July each year there is an International Choral Festival with up to 20 or more choirs taking part – Preveza's own choir has won considerable international acclaim. For festival details look around for street posters.

At the beginning of August you may come across a mildly whimsical sardine festival. The Nikopolia Festival is an umbrella event for various musical and theatrical presentations held in August at Nikopolis to the north-west of town. Look out for posters with details.

Places to Stay
Camping Kalamitsi (☎ *2682 022 192, fax 2682 028 660, Kalamitsi*) Adult/tent €4.50/3. The best of four camping grounds is this place, which has 116 grassed sites with ample shade, a large pool, restaurant, laundry facilities, communal fridges and a minimarket. It's 4km along the main Preveza-Igoumenitsa road.

Hotel Preveza (☎ *2682 021 230, fax 2682 026 454, Eleftheriou Venizelou 19*) Singles/doubles €35.50/47. Rooms are smallish, but this hotel is the best of the town-centre options and enjoys a harbour view.

Preveza City (☎ *2682 027 370, fax 2682 023 872, Irinis 81*) Singles/doubles €38.20/48.50. This C-class place has clean, modern rooms and is a five-minute walk from the bus station.

Hotel Dioni (☎ *2682 027 381, fax 2682 027 384, Plateia Theofilou Papageorgiou*) Singles/doubles €44/58.70. This is a reasonable choice, but its jaded rooms are overpriced and could do with some renovation.

Places to Eat
Sardines are a popular local dish in Preveza. They can be found on the menu from May to September.

Amvrosios (☎ *2682 027 192, Grigoriou E 9*) Mains €4-5. For a no-nonsense, unadorned sardine and wine meal (€6.20) in a low-ceilinged room lined with functioning wine barrels, head here.

Gafas (☎ *2682 028 309, Tsakalof 2*) Mains €4-5. Next to Amvrosios, this place offers similar fishy fare, but you can sit outside.

Delfinaki (☎ *2682 026 130, Sapountzaki 4*) Mains €5-6. This is a tastefully modern but touristy taverna. It serves some excellent home-made specialities, such as baked peppers stuffed with cheese and fried zucchini balls (€5.50).

Seïtan Pazar (☎ *2682 060 863, Kondou 18*) Mezedes €3.20. Busy, lively and atmospheric, this small traditional kafeneio spills out onto the vehicle-free street and serves up enticing mezedes such as mussels with rice, or potato rissoles – both worth ordering.

Nostos (☎ *2682 060 363, Parthenagogiou 9*) Mains €6-7. It's rather expensive, but worth the investment for this restaurant's exceptionally well-prepared seafood and salads. Grilled octopus or squid (€6.75) is recommended. Nostos is open all year and gets busy, so get in early for a seat.

Atlantik Supermarket (*Karyotaki 15*) Get your camping and picnic provisions right here.

Getting There & Away
Air Preveza airport, 7km south of the town, is sometimes called Lefkada or Aktion. The Olympic Airways bus to the airport costs €1.75, plus the ferry fare.

There are at least five flights weekly to Athens in the low season and daily flights in the high season (20 minutes, €52.25). The Olympic Airways office (☎ 2682 028 343) is at Irinis 37.

Bus From the bus station (☎ 2682 022 213) there are buses to Ioannina (two hours, €6.30, 10 daily), Parga (two hours, €4.60, four daily), Arta (one hour, €3.25, five daily), Igoumenitsa (2½ hours, €6.75, two daily), Athens (six hours, €24, three daily) and Thessaloniki (eight hours, €25.25, one daily).

Ferry The Preveza-Aktion ferry departs every half-hour (€0.30 per person, €2.65 per car) from the new harbour, to the north of town.

NORTHERN GREECE

AROUND PREVEZA
Nikopolis Νικόπολη

In 31 BC, Octavian (later the Roman emperor Augustus) defeated the allies Mark Antony and Cleopatra in the famous naval Battle of Actium (present-day Aktion). To celebrate, Octavian built Nikopolis (*City of Victory;* ☎ *2682 041 336; adult/EU student €3/free including museum; museum open 8.30am-3pm daily*). He populated it by forcible resettlement of people from surrounding towns and villages. It was plundered by Vandals and Goths in the 5th and 6th centuries AD, but was rebuilt by Justinian. It was sacked again by the Bulgars in the 11th century, after which nobody bothered to rebuild it.

Little is left of the Roman walls, but the Byzantine walls and a theatre survive, and there are remains of temples to Mars and Poseidon (an appropriate choice of gods for the warmongering Octavian), an aqueduct, Roman baths and a restored Roman odeum. The immense site sprawls over both sides of the Preveza-Arta road.

There is an **archaeological museum** at the site with exhibits from the ancient citadel. Other exhibits from Nikopolis are displayed in Ioannina's Archaeological Museum.

Preveza-Arta buses stop at Nikopolis.

Zalongo & Kassopi
Ζάλογγο & Κασσώπη

Although historically unrelated, these two sites lie close to each other some 30km north of Preveza near the village of Kamarina. **Zalongo** is the craggy spot where the women and children of the mountain villages of Souli jumped to their death rather than be captured by the Turks during the prelude to the Greek War of Independence. Their brave act of sacrifice is marked by a rather striking monument perched on the summit and which can be seen from far away. Access to the monument is via a steep but manageable path from the car park at the foot of the hill. The views, if nothing else, are stunning, especially on a clear day.

Kassopi is the site of an ancient settlement built in the first half of the 4th century

BC. It is located in a naturally fortified panoramic location at an altitude of 650m. It was abandoned after the Battle of Actium, after the Romans built Nikopolis and forced the inhabitants of Kassopi to resettle in the new city on the lowlands. The site is fairly well preserved and little visited; access is free.

Beaches

Just north of Preveza, beaches are strung out for some 30km along the **Bay of Nikopolis**. Those at **Monolithi**, 10km from Preveza, and **Kastrosykia**, 15km away, are particularly popular. They are accessible on Parga-bound buses.

ARTA Αρτα
postcode 471 00 • pop 19,087

Arta, the second-largest town of Epiros, is 76km south of Ioannina and 50km northeast of Preveza. It's easy to miss if you're speeding to Athens or locations farther south, which is a pity, because it's worth a visit. After the barren agricultural scenery of Ioannina and the north, it's refreshing to come across groves of citrus plantations as you leave the Louros Valley and reach the open plains and wetlands of the north Ambracian Gulf.

The town is built over ancient Ambracia, which King Pyrrhus of Epiros made his capital in the 4th century BC. In the 14th century AD the Frankish despot of Epiros made it his seat of government. The town has a wealth of Byzantine monuments of which the locals are justifiably proud.

Today, Arta is a bustling supply centre for the north Ambracia region and is a pleasant place to stroll around.

Orientation & Information

The main bus station is on the Ioannina-Athens road on the eastern side of town, just outside the town walls. From the bus station, walk about 200m to your right and look for Krystalli, which will lead to Nikiforou Skoufa, the main street. Half of this street is for pedestrians only.

The OTE is on the main square, Plateia Ethnikis Andistasis, which is halfway along

Skoufa. The post office is on Amvrakias, about five minutes from the OTE in the general direction of the fortress walls.

Things to See

The most distinguished feature is its fine 18th-century **Bridge of Arta**, which spans the Arahthos River. This bridge, made famous in Greek demotic poetry, is probably Arta's most photographed monument. Legend has it that the master builder had difficulty in preventing the bridge from being washed away every time he tried to complete it, and was advised to entomb his wife in the stonework of the central arch. The bridge is still standing, although it has had a facelift or two in recent times and is now used by pedestrians.

The **Folkloric Museum** (☎ 2681 022 192; admission €0.60; open 8.30am-2.30pm daily) was originally a Turkish guard post. Located on the north side of the Bridge of Arta, it contains a small but interesting collection of religious, agricultural and domestic artefacts including ouzo and candle-making equipment.

Arta also has several churches of note. The 13th-century **Church of Panagia Parigoritissa**, overlooking Plateia Skoufa just south of Plateia Kilkis, is a well preserved and striking building. The churches of **Agios Vasilios** and **Agia Theodora** have attractive ceramic decorations on their exterior walls. Both of these churches are just west of Pyrrou, the main thoroughfare which runs south from the fortress to Plateia Kilkis.

Places to Stay & Eat

Hotel Cronos (☎ 2681 022 211, fax 2681 073 795, Plateia Kilkis) Singles/doubles with bathroom €41/50. This is a reasonable if rather bland C-class hotel.

Hotel Amvrakia (☎ 2681 028 311, fax 2681 078 544, Priovolou 13) Singles/doubles with bathroom €42.90/52.90. This C-class hotel is one block east of Pyrrou.

There are several restaurants situated on Plateia Kilkis, and you can always get a snack at the cafeterias on Plateia Ethnikis Andistasis.

Protomastoras (☎ 2681 075 686, Thiakogianni 17) Mains €6-7. On the south side of the Bridge of Arta, Protomastoras is open for lunch and dinner daily, all year. The stuffed pork fillet (psaronefri; €6.50) is a good bet.

Getting There & Away

From Arta's bus station (☎ 2681 027 348) there are buses to Ioannina (2½ hours, €4.25, 10 daily), Preveza (one hour, €3.25, five daily), Athens (five hours, €20, eight daily) and Thessaloniki (7½ hours, €23, one daily).

Macedonia
Μακεδονία

Macedonia (mah-keh-do-**nee**-ah) is the largest prefecture in Greece, and its capital, Thessaloniki, is the country's second city. With abundant and varied attractions, it's surprising that more travellers don't find their way here. Tucked in the north-western corner are the beautiful Prespa Lakes, home to one of Europe's most important bird sanctuaries. To the south, Mt Olympus, Greece's highest peak at 2917m, rises from a plain just 6km from the sea.

The unsung towns of Veria, Edessa and Florina unfold their charms to only the occasional visitor. For archaeology buffs there is Alexander the Great's birthplace of Pella; the sanctuary of Dion, where he sacrificed to the gods; Vergina, where the Macedonian kings (apart from Alexander) were buried; and Philippi, where the battle which set the seal on the future of the Western world was fought. Macedonia is also the site of the Monastic Republic of Athos.

THESSALONIKI Θεσσαλονίκη
postcode 541 00 • pop 750,000

Thessaloniki (thess-ah-lo-**nee**-kih) was the second city of Byzantium and is the second city of modern Greece. However, being second does not mean Thessaloniki lies in the shadow of, or tries to emulate, the capital. It is a sophisticated city with its own

MACEDONIA

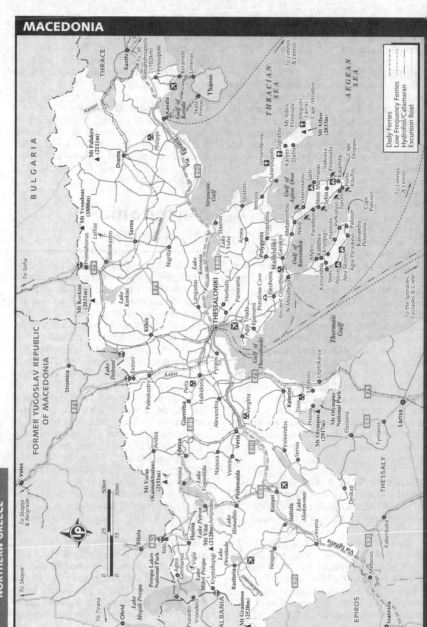

listinct character. It has a lively nightlife, good restaurants and, although without the impressive monuments of the capital, it has several museums, a scattering of Roman ruins and superlative Byzantine churches.

Thessaloniki sits at the top of the wide Thermaic Gulf. The oldest part of the city is the kastro, the old Turkish quarter, whose narrow streets huddle around a Byzantine fortress on the slopes of Mt Hortiatis.

Thessaloniki is best avoided during festival time (September to October), as accommodation is almost impossible to find and rates are at a premium. Finding a room at other times should not be a problem.

History

Like almost everywhere in Greece, Thessaloniki has had not only its triumphs but more than its fair share of disasters. As with Athens, an awareness of these helps greatly in one's appraisal of the city.

The city was named in 316 BC by the Macedonian general Kassandros, after his wife, a daughter of Philip II and half-sister of Alexander the Great, who was born when Philip was successfully expanding his territory in Thessaly. When he arrived home, Philip announced that the child would be called Thessaloniki, 'Victory in Thessaly'.

After the Roman conquest in 168 BC, Thessaloniki became the capital of the province of Macedonia. Thessaloniki's location on the Thermaic Gulf and its position on the Via Egnatia helped to promote its development. It was also an important staging post on the trade route to the Balkans.

The Roman emperor Galerius made it the eastern imperial capital, and after the empire officially divided it became the second city of Byzantium, flourishing as both a spiritual and economic centre. Inevitably, its strategic position brought attacks and plundering by Goths, Slavs, Muslims, Franks and Epirots. In 1185 it was sacked by the Normans, and in 1204 was made a feudal kingdom under Marquis Boniface of Montferrat, but was reincorporated into the Byzantine Empire in 1246. After several sieges it finally capitulated to Ottoman rule when Murad II staged a successful invasion in 1430.

Along with the rest of Macedonia, Thessaloniki became part of Greece in 1913. In August 1917 a fire broke out in the city and, as there was no fire brigade, the flames spread quickly, destroying 9500 houses and rendering 70,000 inhabitants homeless. The problem of homelessness was exacerbated by the influx of refugees from Asia Minor after the 1923 population exchange. During the late 1920s the city was carefully replanned and built on a grid system with wide streets and large squares.

In 1978 Thessaloniki experienced a severe earthquake. Most of the modern buildings were not seriously damaged, but the Byzantine churches suffered greatly and most are still in the process of being restored. Thessaloniki was Europe's 'Cultural Capital' in 1997.

Orientation

Thessaloniki's waterfront, Leoforos Nikis stretches from the port in the west to the White Tower (Lefkos Pyrgos) in the east. North of the White Tower are the exhibition grounds where the annual International Trade Fair is held. The university is to the north.

The other principal streets of Mitropoleos, Tsimiski and Ermou run parallel to Nikis. Egnatia, the next street up, is the main thoroughfare and most of the Roman remains are between here and Agiou Dimitriou. The two main squares, both abutting the waterfront, are Plateia Eleftherias, which is one of the local bus terminals, and Plateia Aristotelous. Kastra, the old Turkish quarter, is north of Athinas and just within the ramparts.

The central food market is between Egnatia, Irakliou, Aristotelous and Dragoumi. The train station is on Monastiriou, a westerly continuation of Egnatia. The main bus terminal is at Plateia Dikastirion. The city does not have one general intercity bus station, but several terminals for different destinations (see Getting There & Away).

Information

Tourist Offices The EOT (☎ 231 022 2935), Plateia Aristotelous 8, is open 8.30am to 8pm Monday to Friday and 8.30am to 2pm Saturday.

NORTHERN GREECE

THESSALONIKI

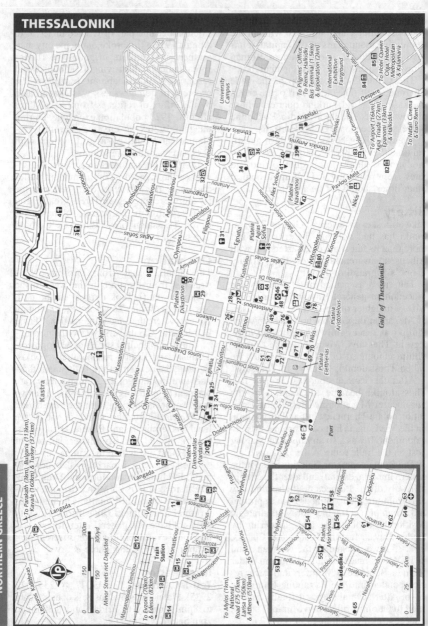

THESSALONIKI

PLACES TO STAY
11 Capsis Hotel
21 Hotel Acropol
22 Hotel Atlantis
24 Hotel Averof
25 Hotel Atlas
37 ABC Hotel
40 GYHA Hostel
73 Hotel Tourist
75 Electra Palace Hotel

PLACES TO EAT
23 Ta Nea Ilysia
26 O Loutros Fish Taverna
28 Ta Spata Psistaria
41 Hryso Pagoni
42 Taverna Ta Aderfia tis
   Pyxarias
48 Ouzeri Aristotelous
50 Babel Snack Bar
58 Ouzeri Taverna 1901
59 Iatros Tis Pinas
60 Zythos
61 Ta Bakaliarakia tou Aristou
62 Ta Bakaliarakia sto Limani
74 Ouzeri Toumbourlika
79 Ta Nisia Restaurant

THINGS TO SEE
2 Church of Agia Ekaterini
3 Church of Osios David
4 Monastery of Vlatadon
5 Church of Nikolaos Orfanos

6 Atatürk's House
8 Church of Agios Dimitrios
9 Church of the Dodeka
   Apostoli
30 Roman Agora
31 Church of Panagia Ahiropiitos
33 Rotonda
34 Arch of Galerius
43 Church of Agia Sofia
80 Museum of the Macedonian
   Struggle
82 White Tower
84 Archaeological Museum
85 Museum of Byzantine
   Culture

OTHER
1 Kavala Bus Station
7 Turkish Consulate
10 Langadas Bus Station
12 Alexandroupolis Bus Station
13 Airport Bus Terminal
14 Ioannina Bus Station
15 Athens & Trikala Bus Station
16 Florina Bus Station
17 Pella, Kastoria, Volos &
   Edessa Bus Station
18 Katerini Bus Station
19 Veria Bus Station
20 Tourist Police
27 Main Post Office
29 Local Bus Station
32 Xnet
35 Bianca Laundrette

36 Link Internet
38 Budget Rent a Car
39 En Chordais
44 OTE
45 Train Tickets Office (OSE)
46 Shopping Complex
47 US Consulate
49 Malliaris Kaisia Bookshop
51 National Bank of Greece
52 Midas Exchange
53 Rendezvous Club
54 Cargo
55 Very Koko
56 Xyladiko
57 Balkonaki
63 First-Aid Centre
64 Karaharisis Travel & Shipping
   Agency
65 Olympic Airways
66 Makedonia Passenger
   Terminal (Ferries & Hydrofoil)
67 Customs House
68 Ferries to Lesvos, the
   Sporades, Cyclades and Crete
69 Aegean Airlines
70 Axon Airlines
71 Doucas Tours; UK Consulate
72 Molho Bookshop
76 Foreign Newspapers Kiosk
77 Olympian Cinema
78 EOT
81 Cinema Pallas
83 Aristotelion Cinema

The tourist police (☎ 231 055 4871), at 5th floor, Dodekanisou 4, are open 7.30am to 11pm daily all year.

Money Most banks around town are equipped with credit card-friendly ATMs. You will find most banks along central Tsimiski. The National Bank of Greece at Tsimiski 11 opens on weekends for the benefit of people wishing to change currency. There is an exchange machine and an ATM at the train station.

Midas Exchange, at the western end of Tsimiski close to the Ladadika district, is a reasonably efficient exchange bureau open 8.30am to 8.30pm Monday to Friday, 8.30am to 2pm Saturday and 9am to 1.30pm Sunday. It's handy for people using the ferry terminal.

Post & Communications The main post office is at Aristotelous 26 and is open 7.30am to 8pm Monday to Friday, 7.30am to 2.15pm Saturday and 9am to 1.30pm Sunday. The OTE, open 24 hours, is at Karolou Dil 27.

The most central Internet cafes are Xnet (☎ 231 096 0161) at Manolaki Kyriakou 5, open daily from 10am to 6am (€2.35 per hour), and Link (☎ 231 020 7953) at Dimitriou 50, open 9am to 3am (€1.50 to €2 per hour).

Bookshops Molho, at Tsimiski 10, has a comprehensive stock of English-language books, magazines and newspapers. Malliaris Kaisia, at Aristotelous 9, also has many English-language publications including a reasonable selection of LP titles and good

NORTHERN GREECE

Phone numbers listed incorporate changes due in Oct 2002; see p83

maps of Greece by Road Editions and Emvelia Publications

Foreign-language newspapers and magazines can be obtained from a kiosk on the corner of Polytehniou and Aristotelous.

Laundry Bianca Laundrette, on Antoniadou, has a utilitarian ambience. Walk up D Gournari from the Arch of Galerius and Antoniadou is off to the right. It's open 8am to 8.30pm Monday to Friday, and charges around €5 for a decent-sized load.

Mt Athos Permits Permits for the monastic region of Mt Athos may be obtained from the Pilgrims' Office (☎ 231 083 3733, fax 231 086 1811), Leoforos Karamanli 14. For further information, see under Mt Athos in the Halkidiki section later in this chapter.

Emergency There is a first-aid centre (☎ 231 053 0530) at Navarhou Koundourioti 6, near the port. The largest public hospital is the Ippokration (☎ 231 083 7921), Papanastasiou 50, 2km east of the city centre.

Archaeological Museum

In 1977 one of Greece's most eminent archaeologists, Professor Manolis Andronikos, was excavating at Vergina near Thessaloniki when he found an unlooted tomb which turned out to be that of King Philip II of Macedon. The spectacular contents of this tomb, comparable to the grave treasures of Mycenae, are now on display in this museum (☎ 231 083 0538, fax 231 0861 306, Manoli Andronikou 6; admission €4.40, €5.90 including Museum of Byzantine Culture; open 8.30am-3pm daily).

Among the exhibits are exquisite gold jewellery; bronze and terracotta vases; tiny, intricately detailed ivory reliefs; and a solid gold casket with lion's feet, embossed with the sunburst symbol of the royal house of Macedonia, which contained the bones of Philip II. The most mind-boggling exhibit is that of the bones themselves, which are carefully laid out to reconstruct an almost complete skeleton. There is something very strange about looking at someone who has been just a name in a history book.

The museum is opposite the entrance to the exhibition grounds; either walk east along Tsimiski or take bus No 3.

White Tower

This 15th-century tower is both the city's symbol and most prominent landmark. During the 18th century it was used as a prison for insubordinate janissaries, the elite troops of forcibly converted Christian boys who became servants of the sultan. In 1826, at the order of Mahmud II, many of the janissaries were massacred in the tower and thereafter it was known as the 'bloody tower'. After independence it was whitewashed as a symbolic gesture to expunge its Turkish function. The whitewash has now been removed and it has been turned into a very fine **Museum of History and Art of Thessaloniki** (☎ 231 026 7832, Lefkos Pyrgos; admission free; open 8am-3pm Tues-Sun). Here you will find splendid frescoes and icons.

In the pleasant museum cafe, a 30-minute audiovisual is shown every hour between 10am and 2pm.

Other Museums

The **Museum of the Macedonian Struggle** (☎ 231 022 9778, Proxenou Koromila 23; admission free; open 9am-2pm Tues-Fri, 6pm-8pm Wed, 11am-2pm Sat & Sun) outlines the story of the liberation of Macedonia from the Ottomans and the threat of Bulgarian nationalism. The museum is housed in what was the Greek consular building when Macedonia was still part of the Ottoman Empire. Proxenou Koromila runs parallel to, and between, Mitropoleos and Nikis.

Kemal Atatürk, the founder of the Republic of Turkey, was born in Thessaloniki in 1880. The Turkish timber-framed house where he was born and spent his childhood has been faithfully restored and is now a museum called **Atatürk's House** (☎ 231 024 8452, Agiou Dimitriou 151; admission free; open 2pm-6pm daily). Visiting is a bit of a cloak-and-dagger affair, but is worth the effort: you ring the bell of the Turkish Consulate building (around the corner on Agiou Dimitriou), produce your passport, and then someone will show you around.

The **Museum of Byzantine Culture** (☎ 231 086 8570, fax 231 083 8597, e protocol@mbp.culture.gr, Leoforos Stratou 2; admission €3; open 8am-7pm Tues-Sun, 12.30pm-7pm Mon) opened in 1994 and currently houses three permanent exhibitions: 'Early Christian Churches', 'Early Christian Cities and Dwellings' and another entitled 'From the Elysian Fields to the Christian Paradise'.

Roman & Byzantine Thessaloniki

Thessaloniki has few remaining Roman ruins, but its churches represent every period of Byzantine art and architecture, once the city's foremost glory, and enjoy World Heritage Site status. Notwithstanding the extensive damage from fire and earthquakes and conversion to mosques, a visit to the most renowned ones is still worthwhile. The circular walk described here takes you around the Roman ruins and the major churches.

The **Roman agora**, in the upper part of Plateia Dikastirion, is reached by crossing Egnatia from Aristotelous. Excavations began in the 1970s and are still going, so the site is cordoned off from the public. So far, the odeum and two stoas have come to light.

From the north-east corner of this site, walk up Agnostou Stratioti, cross Olympou, and straight ahead you will see the 5th-century **Church of Agios Dimitrios** (☎ 231 027 0008, Agiou Dimitriou 97; admission free; open 7am-10pm daily, crypt 8am-8pm daily) across the road. Dimitrios was born in the city in the 3rd century and became an eminent scholar and Christian convert. He was martyred on the orders of Galerius, not a Christian and ruthless in persecuting those who were. There are several claims that Dimitrios' ghost appeared in warrior-like guise at apposite moments during sieges, causing the enemy to flee in terror. This, coupled with claims of miraculous cures at the site of his martyrdom, gained him sainthood.

The church is Greece's largest and was built on the site where he was martyred. It was converted into a mosque by Turks who plastered over the interior walls. When it was restored to the Christians, it was discovered to have the finest mosaics of all the city's churches. The frescoes and the buildings were extensively damaged in the 1917 fire. However, five 8th-century mosaics have survived and can be seen on either side of the altar.

Turn left from Agios Dimitrios and walk along Agiou Dimitriou till you come to Dragoumi, which leads off to the right. Here you'll reach Filippou, with the 3rd-century AD **Rotonda** (☎ 231 021 8720, Plateia Agiou Georgiou; admission free) ahead. It is the oldest of Thessaloniki's churches. The Roman brick rotunda was originally intended as a mausoleum for Galerius, but never fulfilled this function; Constantine the Great transformed it into a church. The minaret, erected during its days as a mosque, remains. Opening hours are unpredictable as the rotonda was closed for restoration at the time of research.

Walk a little way around the church and turn right into D Gounari, where you'll see the imposing **Arch of Galerius**, erected in AD 303 to celebrate the emperor's victories over the Persians in 297. Its eroded bas-reliefs depict battle scenes with the Persians. Turn right into Egnatia, and then left to reach the 8th-century **Church of Agia Sofia** on Agias Sofias, which emulates its renowned namesake in İstanbul. The dome has a striking mosaic of the Ascension.

On leaving the Church of Agia Sofia, retrace your steps back to Egnatia, cross the road, and continue a little way up Agias Sofias to the **Church of the Panagia Ahiropiitos**, on the right. This 5th-century church is an early example of basilica form; some mosaics and frescoes remain. The name means 'made without hands' and derives from the 12th century, when an icon miraculously appeared in the church.

Several of the smaller churches are also worth a look, including the 13th-century **Church of Agia Ekaterini**, the **Church of the Dodeka Apostoloi** (Twelve Apostles) and the 4th-century **Church of Nikolaos Orfanos**, which has exquisite frescoes. The little 5th-century **Church of Osios David** in Kastra was allegedly built to commemorate Galerius' daughter, Theodora, who was clandestinely baptised while her father was on one of his campaigns.

NORTHERN GREECE

Kastra & the Ramparts

The Turkish quarter of Kastra is all that is left of 19th-century Thessaloniki. The original ramparts of Kastra were built by Theodosius (379–475), but were rebuilt in the 14th century.

Kastra's streets are narrow and steep, with lots of steps, flanked by timber-framed houses with overhanging upper storeys and tiny, whitewashed dwellings with shutters. From Kastra there are stunning views of modern Thessaloniki and the Thermaic Gulf. Take bus No 22 or 23 from Plateia Eleftherias, or walk north along Agias Sofias, which becomes Dimadou Vlatadou after Athinas, and turn right into Eptapyrgiou at the top.

Organised Tours

Doucas Tours (☎ 231 026 9984, fax 231 028 6610, ⒠ info@doucas.gr, El Venizelou 8). Doucas organises a wide range of half- and full-day tours around Thessaloniki and Halkidiki. Prices range from €26 for a half-day Thessaloniki City tour to €41 for a full-day eco-trekking tour of the Sithonian Peninsula in Halkidiki.

Special Events

Thessaloniki hosts a string of festivals in the exhibition grounds during September and October. The first is the International Trade Fair, followed by a cultural festival, which includes film shows and Greek song performances and culminates in the celebration of St Dimitrios' Day on 26 October. This is followed by military parades on Ohi Day on 28 October. Ask the EOT what is currently on.

Places to Stay – Budget

There are no close camping grounds; the nearest ones are EOT camps listed below.

Agia Triada campsite (☎ 2392 051 360, Agia Triada) Adult/tent €3.50/2.30. Open 1 June-end Aug. This ground is 27km away on the crowded beach at Agia Triada. Take bus No 67 or 72 from Plateia Dikastirion.

Epanomi (☎ 2392 041 378, Epanomi 575 00). Adult/tent €3.30/2.30. Open 1 Apr-end Aug. This site is 33km out of town at Epanomi. Take bus No 69.

GYHA hostel (☎ 231 022 5946, fax 231 026 2208, Alex Svolou 44) Dorm beds €7.40. The dormitories here are open all day. It's not part of the HI organisation, but an HI, VIP Backpacker or ISIC card will get you a 10% discount.

Hotel Acropol (☎ 231 053 6170, Tandalidou 4) Singles/doubles €17.60/26.50 This D-class establishment, just beyond the central police station, is Thessaloniki's best budget hotel. It's clean, quiet and owned by a friendly English-speaking family and there is a small courtyard for bicycle storage.

Hotel Atlantis (☎ 231 054 0131, fax 231 053 6185, Egnatia 14) Doubles/triples €20.50/26.50. This E-class hotel has pokey but clean rooms.

Hotel Averof (☎ 231 053 8498, fax 231 054 3194, Leontos Sofou 24) Singles/doubles €20.50/29.50. This D-class hotel is a quiet option, with attractive pine-furnished rooms.

Hotel Atlas (☎/fax 231 053 7046, ⒠ h-atlas@hol.gr, Egnatia 40) Singles/doubles €23.50/32.30, doubles with bathroom €41. This D-class property has clean, carpeted rooms. The hotel is quite reasonable, but the rooms at the front get a lot of traffic noise.

Hotel Tourist (☎ 231 027 0501, fax 231 022 6865, Mitropoleos 21) Singles/doubles €53/67.50. The D-class Hotel Tourist has a spacious lounge with comfortable armchairs and a TV. Rooms are pleasant but prices are on the high side for its category.

Places to Stay – Mid-Range

All of the hotels in this category have bars and restaurants, and include breakfast in the room rate.

Hotel Queen Olga (☎ 231 082 4621, fax 231 086 8581, Vasilissis Olgas 44) Singles/doubles €67.50/91. This modern B-class hotel has cosy rooms with warm decor and bathroom, radio, colour TV, minibar and air-con. This hotel also has a car park (€4.40); if you're travelling east, it's on the right.

Hotel Metropolitan (☎ 231 082 4221, fax 231 084 9762, ⒠ metropolitan@metropolitan .gr, Ⓦ www.metropolitan.gr, Vasilissis Olgas 65) Singles/doubles €68.80/87.50. A little farther along from the Queen Olga is the B-class Metropolitan, where rooms are attractively furnished and have bathroom, telephone and radio.

ABC Hotel (☎ *231 026 5421, fax 231 027 6542, Angelaki 41*) Singles/doubles €85/111.20. This B-class hotel, at the eastern end of Egnatia, has 102 rooms, all with bathroom, telephone and balcony.

Places to Stay – Top End

Capsis Hotel (☎ *231 052 1321, fax 231 051 0555,* e *capsis@spark.net.gr, Monastiriou 18*) Doubles €88-118. Close to the train station is this well-appointed A-class property. Capsis is a smart business hotel with good facilities. Rates vary according to season and demand.

Electra Palace Hotel (☎ *231 023 2221, fax 231 023 5947,* e *electrapalace@ the.forthnet.gr, Plateia Aristotelous 5a*) Singles/doubles in July & Aug €88/97, other times €114/140. This A-class hotel has an impressive facade in the style of a Byzantine palace. It also has two restaurants and a bar.

Places to Eat

You'll never go hungry in Thessaloniki since you're spoiled with a very good selection of eating places. There are lots of fast-food places and snack bars where you can get gyros, pizza or a cheese pie for around €1.80.

Ta Nea Ilysia (☎ *231 053 6996, Leondos Sofou 17*) Mayirefta €4-5. This is a popular place near the west-end hotel strip with reasonably priced Greek staples including good mousakas (€4.40).

Hryso Pagoni (☎ *231 026 5338, Alex Svolou 40*) Mains €3.50. Opposite the youth hostel is this simple, clean and green (in colour) place which is popular with locals. The restaurant is best known for its roast chicken.

O Loutros Fish Taverna (☎ *231 022 8895, M Koundoura 5*) Fish €6-9. For a lively evening out you could try this venerable taverna. This place has a cult following and you'll be rubbing shoulders with politicians, professors and actors. The fish is excellent. The taverna is always crowded and there are often spontaneous renderings of rembetika music.

Ta Spata Psistaria (☎ *231 027 7412, Aristotelous 28*) Mains €4.50-6. At this popular psistaria, you choose from the dishes on display – a simple meal of beans, feta cheese and half a litre of retsina is a good and inexpensive choice. Service is smart and business-like.

Taverna Ta Aderfia tis Pyxarias (☎ *231 026 6432, Plateia Navarinou 7*) Grills €4-5. This is a popular place. It has a pleasing ambience, with enlarged pictures of old Thessaloniki on the walls; the kebabs (€4) are very tasty.

Ouzeri Toumbourlika (☎ *231 028 2174, Kalapothaki 11*) Mezedes €2.20-3.80. This ouzeri is apparently little more than a hole in the wall but has tables aplenty inside. It's on a pedestrian street off Plateia Aristotelous. It has tasty mezedes to be washed down with ouzo or draught wine.

Ouzeri Aristotelous (☎ *231 023 3195, Aristotelous 8*) Mains €7. Open to late Mon-Sat, to 6pm Sun. This ouzeri in the Vosporion Megaron arcade off Aristotelous has first-rate mezedes including cuttlefish stuffed with cheese, grilled eggplant with garlic and prawns in red sauce. The restaurant has a Parisian ambience with marble-topped tables.

Ta Nisia Restaurant (☎ *231 028 5991, Proxenou Koromila 13*) Mains €7-8. This is a wonderful place with white stucco walls, a wood-beamed ceiling, lots of plants, and pretty plates on the walls. The unusual, imaginative mezedes include cuttlefish and spinach in wine, and little triangles of pastry filled with eggplant.

To Rema (☎ *231 090 1286, I Passalidi 2*) Mezedes €2.50-3.50. Graze on a huge range of excellent mezedes with very original names. Try the *Colossus of Rhodes* (aubergine croquettes), *Perestroika* (chargrilled mushrooms), or *Beri* (Florina peppers stuffed with cheese). The food is particularly appealing to vegetarians. Take a cab to get there. It's about five to ten minutes from the city centre.

Parakath (☎ *231 065 3705, Konstandinoupoleos 114*) Pontian dishes €4-12. This is Thessaloniki's only Pontian restaurant and is worth it for the fine food and electric

NORTHERN GREECE

atmosphere. Try *syrou* if there are four of you (€11.70), or *yvrishto* (€4.40) if fewer – both are rich, traditional pasta-based dishes. There is live music (11.30pm onwards) on Friday and Saturday nights and no one goes home until the sun is up. Take a cab (€6) along the main Kavala road to get there. Bookings are essential on weekends.

Ta Ladadika This is a small area consisting of a few blocks of formerly derelict warehouses and small shops close to the ferry terminal. Over the last few years the area has been gradually restored and is now the focus of a number of tavernas, music bars and pubs.

Iatros tis Pinas (☎ 231 054 6304, Katouni 7) Mezedes €3. A cheap place to start is this small place, which doubles as a snack bar and ouzeri.

Ta Bakaliarakia sto Limani (☎ 231 054 2906, Fasianou 4) Fish & chips €3.50. Open to 6pm. On Fasianou, a short street leading to the seafront, this unassuming fish and chip joint does a reasonable job of this staple Anglo dish.

Ta Bakaliarakia tou Aristou (☎ 231 054 2906, Fasianou 1) Fish & chips €4.10. Open to 6pm. This is the other popular places on Fasianou doing good fish and chips.

Ouzeri Taverna 1901 (☎ 231 055 3141, Katouni 9) Mains €4.40. Housed in an old pink building is this ever-popular eatery. A couple of its specialities are prawns and baked pasta (*garidoyiouvetsi*) and the spicy aubergine dip. It's open for lunch and dinner daily; closed 15 July to 15 August.

Zythos (☎ 231 054 0284, Plateia Katouni) Mains €6-7. Zythos does an admirable pint of Murphy's stout (€3.50) and offers an imaginative lunch and dinner menu, albeit on the slightly pricey side.

Entertainment
Discos & Music Bars *Mylos* (☎ 231 052 5968, Andreou Georgiou 56) Admission free. This is a huge old mill which has been converted into an entertainment complex with an art gallery, restaurant, bar and live music club (classical and rock). Walk down

26 Oktovriou from Plateia Vardari to Andreou Georgiou, which is off to the right, next to the petrol station at 26 Oktovriou 36. Mylos is a spruce cream and terracotta building, 250m on the right.

Music bars abound in the Ladadika area, with the main emphasis on music and all kinds of draught and bottled beer.

Very Koko (☎ 231 054 4554, Plateia Morihovou) Drinks €7.30. Very Koko (a pun on the Greek for 'apricot') is big, bouncy and loud and very Greek.

Cargo (Orvilou 16) Drinks €5.90. Close to the main Ladadika action, Cargo is a classy and popular club.

Xyladiko (☎ 231 055 5243, Loudia 1) Drinks €7.30. With mainly Greek music, this crowded place is supposedly good for meeting people.

Balkonaki (☎ 231 053 2098, Egyptou 10) Drinks €3.80-6.75. In a similar vein to Xyladiko and drawing its own clientele is this lively nightspot.

Rendezvous Club (☎ 231 054 1454, Cnr Polytehniou & Lykourgou) Drinks €5.30-7.30. This place offers Greek dance music and a 'Ladies' Night' three times a week.

Cinema First-run English-language films are shown at the revamped *Olympion* (☎ 231 027 7113, Plateia Aristotelous), *Aristotelion* (☎ 231 026 2051, Ethnikis Amynis 2), opposite the White Tower, and *Cinema Pallas* (☎ 231 027 8515, Nikis 73).

There is also an open-air summer cinema, *Natali* (☎ 231 082 9457, Stasi Stratigou).

Shopping
Thessaloniki's women have a reputation for being the most chic in Greece so, to supply the demand, there are many shops selling ultra-fashionable clothes and shoes. Bargains can be found along Egnatia and the shops around the indoor food market, and there's high-quality, expensive stuff on Tsimiski. Also on Tsimiski, look out for trendy, handmade jewellery at reasonable prices. A large shopping complex has opened on Tsimiski below the American Embassy. Here you'll find multiplex cinemas, cafes and all the brand-name stores.

En Chordais (☎ *231 028 2248, Plateia Ip-podromiou 3*) If you are seriously interested in Greek or Middle Eastern music, you can buy some genuine traditional instruments at this shop. Kyriakos Kalaïtzidis, the owner, is also an accomplished musician and runs a music school, should you have a burning desire to learn the *oud*, the *toumberleki* (lap drum) or Byzantine choral music.

Getting There & Away

Air The airport (☎ 231 047 3212) is 16km south-east of the city. The Olympic Airways office (☎ 231 036 8666) is at Navarhou Koundourioti 1–3. Aegean Airlines (☎ 231 028 0050) is at Venizelou 2. The Axon Airlines office (☎ 231 025 2535) is at the corner of Komninon & Nikis.

Air – Domestic Olympic has flights to Athens (€58.40, seven daily), Limnos (€56, one daily), Ioannina (€58.80, one daily), Mytilini (€73.40, six weekly), Corfu (€73.40, three weekly), Iraklio (€97, three weekly), Mykonos (€91.30, three weekly), Hania (€103.30, two weekly), Chios (€76.30, two weekly) and Samos (€88, two weekly).

Aegean Airlines has flights to Athens (€75.40, seven daily), Iraklio (€90, two daily), Mytilini (€81, one daily), Rhodes (€107.50) and Santorini (€104.50, one daily).

Axon Airlines has flights to Athens (€75.40, three daily).

Air – International There are international flights between Thessaloniki and a wide number of European destinations. For full details see Thessaloniki's Makedonia Airport Web page: **W** users.otenet.gr/~cpnchris/skg.html.

Bus – Domestic Most of Thessaloniki's bus terminals are close to the train station.

destination	terminal
Alexandroupolis	Koloniari 17 (☎ 231 0514 111)
Athens	Monastiriou 65 (☎ 231 051 0834)
Edessa	Anageniseos 22 (☎ 231 052 5100)
Florina	Anageniseos 42 (☎ 231 052 2161)
Ioannina	Giannitson 19 (☎ 231 051 2444)
Kastoria	Anageniseos 22 (☎ 231 052 2162)
Katerini	Promitheos 10 (☎ 231 051 9101)
Pella	Anageniseos 22
Trikala	Monastiriou 67 (☎ 231 051 7188)
Veria	26 Oktovriou 10 (☎ 231 052 2160)
Volos	Anageniseos 22 (☎ 231 053 4087)

Kavala (☎ 231 052 5530) buses leave from Langada 59, the main road north out of Thessaloniki starting at Plateia Vardari. All buses for the Halkidiki Peninsula (☎ 231 092 4445) leave from Karakasi 68, which is in the eastern part of the city. Take bus No 10 to the Botsari stop (near Markou Botsari) from either the train station or anywhere along Egnatia.

Bus – International Greek Railways (OSE; ☎ 231 059 9100) runs buses to Sofia (seven hours, €19 but 20% discount for persons under 26 years, 7.30am, 2pm, 4pm and 10pm daily), İstanbul (12 hours, €44, 2.30am daily, except Monday) and Korça (Korytsa) in Albania (six hours, €19, 8am and noon daily). Buses leave from the station forecourt and tickets can be bought in the station. These services, however, are subject to change, so check beforehand.

Train – Domestic All domestic trains leave from the station on Monastiriou (☎ 231 051 7517). There are four regular trains daily to Athens (7½ hours, €14) and Kozani (four hours, €5.30) with connections to Florina (3¼ hours, €4.70), and three daily to Alexandroupolis (eight hours, €9.70) and Larisa with connections to Volos (4½ hours, €6.80).

There are five additional express intercity services to Athens (six hours, €27.60) – one is nonstop with a meal included in the ticket price; two to Alexandroupolis (5½ hours, €16.20) and one to Kozani (3¼ hours, €6.50). Note that tickets to all destinations and intermediate stations using the intercity services attract a supplement which is worked out on a sliding scale, determined by the distance travelled. There are also a couple of overnight sleepers to Athens.

NORTHERN GREECE

Tickets are available from the train station or the OSE office (☎ 231 059 8120), Aristotelous 18.

The station also has a National Bank of Greece, a post office, a couple of ATMs, an OTE and a restaurant which is open 6am to 10pm. Luggage storage is €3.50 per item per day, or €1.60 if you have a train ticket.

Train – International There are currently four international services operating out of Thessaloniki. There is one train daily to Belgrade at 6.15pm (€28.50). At 10pm there is a service to Sofia (€15.60) with a connection to Budapest (€65). On Wednesday and Sunday there is an additional connection to Bucharest (€32.60). There is a daily service at 7.25am to İstanbul (€39). This is in practice the Intercity IC90 service to Orestiada; passengers for İstanbul change at Pythio. These times are subject to seasonal changes, so do check before making plans.

Ferry A ferry to Chios (18 hours, €25.50) via Limnos (eight hours, €16.50) and Lesvos (13 hours, €25.50) sails on Sunday throughout the year. In summer there are three to six boats weekly to Iraklio on Crete (€36.70), via Skiathos, Syros, Paros and Santorini.

There are also additional boats just to Skiathos three times weekly (5½ to seven hours, €13.20) in July and August, and one weekly to Rhodes (21 hours, €45) via Samos and Kos throughout the year.

Ferry tickets are available from Karaharisis Travel & Shipping Agency (☎ 231 052 4544, fax 231 053 2289), Koundourioti 8. The telephone number of Thessaloniki's port police is ☎ 231 053 1504.

Hydrofoil & Catamaran In summer there are more or less daily hydrofoils and a catamaran service to the Sporades islands of Skiathos (3¼ hours, €26), Skopelos (four hours, €25.50) and Alonnisos (4½ hours, €25.50), via Nea Moudania (one hour, €13.20) in Halkidiki. Tickets can be purchased from Karaharisis Travel & Shipping Agency (see Ferry).

Getting Around

To/From the Airport There is no Olympic Airways shuttle, but bus No 78 plies the airport route; it leaves from in front of the train station and stops in front of the ferry terminal (€0.50). A one-way taxi costs around €7.50.

Bus Orange articulated buses operate within the city, and blue and orange buses operate both within the city and out to the suburbs. The local bus station is found on Filippou.

On the articulated buses you must buy a ticket from the conductor who sits next to the door; driver-only buses have ticket machines. Make sure you have change before you board the bus. There are three different ticket zones: €0.30 within the city, €0.40 for the suburbs and €0.50 for outlying villages.

Car The ELPA (Greek Automobile Club; ☎ 231 042 6319) is at Vasilissis Olgas 228 in Kalamaria. Cars can be hired from Budget Rent a Car (☎ 231 022 9519), Angelaki 15, and Euro Rent (☎ 231 082 6333), G Papandreou 5, among others.

Drivers arriving in Thessaloniki would be best advised to head for Plateia Eleftherias, where there is a decent-sized pay car park. Parking elsewhere in the streets can be extremely difficult. The signposting to and from the main access roads to Thessaloniki can be very deficient or just plain misleading. Follow your map very carefully.

Taxi Thessaloniki's taxis are blue and white, and the procedure for hailing one is the same as in Athens: stand on the edge of the pavement and bellow out your destination as they pass. There are five taxi companies available:

Alfa – Lefkos Pyrgos (☎ 231 024 9100)
Omirou 12, Sykies
Makedonia (☎ 231 055 0500) Karyofylli 4
Megas Alexandros (☎ 231 086 6866)
Omega (☎ 231 051 1855)
Terma Giannitson 179
Thessaloniki (☎ 231 055 1525) Giannitson 140

AROUND THESSALONIKI
Langadas Λαγκαδάς

The village of Langadas, 12km north-east of Thessaloniki, is famous for the *anastenaria* fire-walking ritual which takes place on 21 May, the feast day of St Constantine and his mother, St Helena.

The fire walkers, or *anastenarides* (groaners), believe that the ritual originated in the village of Kosti (an abbreviation of Konstantinos) in eastern Thrace. The story is that in AD 1250 the Church of St Constantine caught fire and the villagers, hearing the icons groan, entered the church, rescued them, and escaped unscathed.

The icons were kept by the families concerned, and their descendants and other devotees honoured the saint each year by performing the ritual. In 1913, when the village was occupied by Bulgarians, the families fled to the villages of Serres, Drama and Langadas, taking the icons with them.

The anastenarides step barefoot onto burning charcoal. Holding the icons and waving coloured handkerchiefs, they dance while emitting strange cries, accompanied by drums and lyres. They believe they will not be burned because God's spirit enters into them. New fire walkers are initiated each year.

The Church condemns the ritual as pagan, and indeed the celebration seems to have elements of the pagan worship of Dionysos. If you would like to see this overtly commercial but intriguing spectacle, it begins at 7pm – turn up early to get a ringside seat. Frequent buses leave for Langadas from the Thessaloniki terminal at Irinis 17, near Langada.

PELLA Πέλλα

Pella (☎ 2382 031 160; admission €2.50; open 7am-7pm daily), most famous as the birthplace of Alexander the Great, lies on the Macedonian plain astride the Thessaloniki-Edessa road. Its star attraction is its marvellous mosaics. King Archelaos (who ruled from 413–399 BC) moved the Macedonian capital from Aigai (Vergina) to Pella, although Aigai remained the royal cemetery.

The mosaics, which mainly depict mythological scenes, are made from naturally

---

Who are the Pontians?

Prior to the forced exchange of populations between Greece and Turkey in 1922, there lived a vibrant Greek community along the shores of the Black Sea and in the Black Sea hinterland. These were the Pontians (*pontos* means 'sea' in Ancient Greek). This proud and warrior-like Greek people have lived along the Black Sea littoral ever since Ancient Greeks travelled far and wide colonising the region. Jason and his Argonauts may even have contributed to their settlement since the fabled Golden Fleece was supposed to have been kept in Kolchis, in present-day Georgia in the Eastern Black Sea region. In one fell swoop virtually the whole Pontian population was relocated to Greece and spread out across northern Greece resettling large tracts of Thrace and Macedonia. Many even settled in Epiros. Some of the major population centres today are Kilkis, Serres and Thessaloniki.

The Pontians consider themselves as quite distinct from their fellow Greek brethren. Their language, a dialect of Modern Greek relying heavily on Ancient Greek lexicon and syntax, is virtually impenetrable to non-Pontians. Their dancing is considered the most visually exciting to watch: it is both warlike and sweet and almost always accompanied by a strident Pontian lyre (*pontiaki lyra*), a large goatskin drum (*daouli*), flute (*flogera*) and a bagpipe (*angio*) made from animal skin. The food is almost unknown outside of the Pontian community. Some of the most famous dishes are *perek*, a griddle-grilled flat pitta, *yvrishto*, oven-dried pasta, and *syrou*, a filling yogurt and pasta concoction that is a meal in itself. Try some of these dishes and others at one of the few Pontian restaurants in Greece (see Places to Eat in the Thessaloniki section).

Considered by native Greeks to be the 'Greek Irish', the Pontians are nonetheless a successful, colourful and vibrant part of the Greek cultural scene. Catch up with them if you can: *s'kots!*

coloured stones; the effect is one of subtle and harmonious blends and contrasts. They were discovered in the remains of houses and public buildings, on the northern side of the road. Some are *in situ* and others are housed in the museum. Also on this side is a courtyard laid out with a black and white geometric mosaic and six re-erected columns.

On the southern side, is one of Greece's best site **museums** *(admission €1.50; open 8am-7pm Tues-Fri, 7am-3pm Sat & Sun, noon-7pm Mon)*. Room 1 has a reconstruction of a wall from a house at Pella, and a splendid circular table inlaid with intricate floral and abstract designs, thought to have belonged to Philip II. Room 2 houses mosaics which have been removed from the site.

There is a drinking fountain outside the museum, and a *kafeneio* near the northern side of the site.

Getting There & Away
There are frequent buses from Thessaloniki (40 minutes, €3). If you wish to visit Pella and Vergina by bus in one day, first see Pella, then take a Thessaloniki bus back along the main road and get off at Halkidona, where you can pick up a bus to Vergina.

MT OLYMPUS Ολυμπω Ορος
Mt Olympus, chosen by the ancients as the abode of their gods, is Greece's highest and most awe-inspiring mountain. It has around 1700 plant species, some of which are rare and endemic. The lower slopes are covered with forests of holm oak, arbutus, cedar and conifers; the higher ones with oak, beech, black and Balkan pine. The mountain also maintains varied bird life. In 1937 it became Greece's first national park.

In August 1913, Christos Kakalos, a native of Litohoro, and the Swiss climbers Frederic Boissonas and Daniel Baud-Bovy, were the first mortals to reach the summit of Mytikas (2918m), Olympus' highest peak.

Litohoro Λιτόχωρο
postcode 602 00 • pop 6600
The village of Litohoro (lih-**to**-ho-ro, 305m) is the place to go if you wish to climb

Olympus. The village was developed in the 1920s as a sanatorium for the tubercular; later it settled comfortably into its role as 'base camp' for climbers. The approach to Litohoro along the main road is picture-postcard stuff on a fine day. Directly in front as you make the final approach to the village, the gorge of the Enipeas River parts to reveal the towering peaks of Olympus.

In recent years Litohoro has once again begun to promote its health-resort image. This has resulted in difficulties in finding a hotel room in July and August, particularly at weekends.

Orientation The main road is Agiou Nikolaou, which, from Thessaloniki or Katerini, is the road by which you enter the village; it leads up to Plateia Kendriki, the central square. On the right side of this road is a large army camp. The road to Prionia, where the main trail up Olympus begins, is on the right, just before the central square. Uphill to the left of the main square is 28 Oktovriou, where most of the provision stores are.

The bus terminal is on Plateia Kendriki, on the right as you face the sea.

Information The EOT information booth is in a little white building with wooden eaves on Agiou Nikolaou, just before the Prionia turn-off.

The EOS' (☎ 2352 084 544) English-speaking staff give out information about Olympus and a free pamphlet which details some of the treks. Face inland on Agiou Nikolaou, turn left opposite Myrto Hotel and follow the signs. The office is open 9am to 1pm and 6pm to 8.30pm Monday to Friday, and 9am to 1pm Saturday (closed Sunday). The EOS runs three refuges on Olympus.

The SEO (Association of Greek Climbers; ☎ 2352 084 200) also gives information, but you are more likely to find someone who speaks English at the EOS. To reach the SEO, walk along the road to Prionia and take the first turn left and first left again. The office is open 6pm to 10pm daily, and runs one refuge on Olympus.

MT OLYMPUS

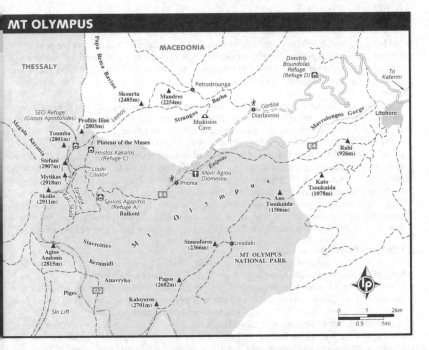

The post office is on 28 Oktovriou. The OTE is on Agiou Nikolaou, diagonally opposite the EOT booth. The National Bank of Greece is on Plateia Kendriki; both this and the nearby Commercial Bank sport ATMs.

The police station (☎ 2352 081 100) is on the corner of the road to Prionia. There is a health centre (☎ 2352 022 222) 5km away, at the Litohoro turn-off from the main coastal highway.

Places to Stay There's a plethora of camping grounds along the coast around the Litohoro turn-off. They all have good facilities and a taverna, snack bar and minimarket. A couple of the better ones are *Olympios Zeus* (☎ 2352 022 115, fax 2352 022 117, e bgo/rens@otenet.gr, Plaka Litohorou), charging €4.40/3 per adult/tent, and *Olympos Beach* (☎ 2352 022 112, Plaka Litohorou), at €4.30/2.90 per adult/tent.

There are some rooms to rent around town – look for signs – but the supply is not great.

Hotels are your safest option. Book beforehand if you know when you are arriving.

Hotel Markisia (☎ 2352 081 831, fax 2352 061 862, Dionysou 5) Singles/doubles with bathroom €20.50/23.50. Open all year. This clean, well-kept D-class hotel is the cheapest. Face inland from Plateia Kendriki, turn left into 28 Oktovriou, and the hotel is on the left.

Hotel Enipeas (☎ 2352 084 328, fax 2352 081 328, Enipeos 2) Doubles/triples €32.30/38.20. This hotel, on the corner of the main square, is bright, breezy and spotlessly clean. The rooms have balconies, and probably the best views of Mt Olympus in town.

Hotel Aphrodite (☎ 2352 081 415, fax 2352 083 646, Enipeos 3) Singles/doubles with bathroom €35.20/50. Directly opposite the Enipeas is this C-class property, with tidy, colour-coded rooms.

Myrto Hotel (☎ 2352 081 398, fax 2352 082 298) Singles/doubles €38/44. This

Mt Olympus Trails

The following trails by no means exhaust the possibilities on Olympus, but they are the ones which (between June and September) can be tackled by any fit person – no mountaineering experience or special equipment are required. It takes two days to climb Olympus, with one night spent in a refuge. However, if you are a keen trekker you'll want to take longer exploring the mountain – it really deserves more than a couple of days.

You will need to take warm clothing as it can become very cold and wet, even in August. Sunblock cream is also essential because much of the climbing is above the tree line. Climbing boots are the most suitable footwear, but sturdy shoes or trainers will suffice.

The 1:50,000 *Olympus* map by Road Editions (☎ 21 0929 6541, ℮ road@enet.gr) is considered – even by locals – to be the best available. It contains detailed route descriptions in English, as well as information about the Enipeas Gorge trek. The similar 1:50,000 *Mt Olympus* map from Anavasi (☎/fax 21 0729 3541, ℮ info@mountains.gr) is also very good. They are available for €5.40 and €4.40 respectively and are best obtained in Athens or Thessaloniki.

Do your homework before you begin by talking with someone at the EOS or SEO (see Information in the Litohoro section). Let them know how long you plan to trek and when you will return. Bear in mind that Olympus is a high and challenging mountain – it has claimed its share of lives.

Litohoro to Prionia

The most popular trail up Olympus begins at **Prionia** (Πριόνια), a tiny settlement 18km from Litohoro. It has a car park, basic taverna and water, but no telephone or bus service.

The EOS **Dimitris Boundolas Refuge** *(Refuge D; ☎ 2352 084 519)* is halfway along the Litohoro-Prionia road at Stavros (940m). It is open from April to November. If you plan to do the six-hour trek from Diastavrosi to the SEO refuge, you might wish to stay here.

Most people opt to drive, hitch or take a taxi (€19) to Prionia, but if you have sufficient stamina, you can trek there along an 11km marked trail, which follows the course of the Enipeas River. The strenuous 4½-hour trek is over sharply undulating terrain but offers glorious views. It begins beyond the cemetery in Litohoro and ends just before the taverna at Prionia. One kilometre before Prionia is the ruined **Moni Agiou Dionysiou**, built at the beginning of the 16th century and blown up by the Turks in 1828. It was rebuilt, only to be blown up again in 1943 by the Nazis who believed that resistance fighters were using it as a hideout.

Prionia to Spilios Agapitos

The trail begins just beyond the taverna in Prionia. You'll have to fill up with water here as it is the last source before Refuge A at **Spilios Agapitos** (Σπήλαιος Αγαπητός). The trail is well maintained and well used – there is no chance of getting lost and you will meet other trekkers along the way. The steep trail passes first through thick deciduous forests, then conifers. It takes around 2½ hours to reach the refuge.

Refuge A *(☎ 2352 081 800)* accommodates up to 140 people. It has cold showers and serves good meals (breakfast 6am to 9am, lunch to order, dinner 6pm to 8pm) to guests and people just popping in. Lights out and bed for all is 10pm. The warden, Kostas Zolotas, speaks fluent English, and is an experienced mountaineer who can answer any questions. The refuge is open from May to October, and costs €11.50 a night (€9 for Alpine Club members). During July and August it is advisable to make a reservation either through the EOS in Litohoro or Thessaloniki, or by telephoning the refuge.

C-class property is Litohoro's poshest hotel. It's near the central square. Rooms have air-con, telephone, minibar and satellite TV.

Places to Eat There is a selection of places to eat on both the main square and the approach road from the army barracks, with the choice ranging from fast food to traditional.

Mt Olympus Trails

Spilios Agapitos to Mytikas (via Kaki Skala)

The path to **Mytikas** (Μύτικας) begins just behind Refuge A. Fill up your water bottles because there is no water beyond here. The last of the trees thin out rapidly; the path is still marked by red slashes and once again it is easy to follow. After one to 1½ hours you will come to a sign pointing right towards the SEO refuge. Continue straight ahead for Mytikas. The path now zigzags over the scree for another hour before reaching the summit ridge. From the ridge there is a 500m drop into the chasm of **Kazania** (the cauldron).

Just before the drop, in an opening to the right, is the beginning of **Kaki Skala** (Κακή Σκάλα, meaning Bad Stairway), which leads, after 40 minutes of rock scrambling, to the summit of Mytikas. The route is marked by red slashes on the rocks. The route now keeps just below the drop into Kazania, although at a couple of places you can look down into the cauldron – a dramatic sight.

If you have never done rock scrambling before, look at Kaki Skala and decide then and there whether you want to tackle it. Many turn back here, but just as many novices tackle Kaki Skala. If you decide against it, all is not lost, for if you turn left at the summit ridge, an easy path leads in 15 to 20 minutes to **Skolio** (Σκολιό, 2911m), Mt Olympus' second-highest peak.

Mytikas to Giossos Apostolides (SEO Refuge)

After you've admired the breathtaking views from Mytikas, signed the summit book and said a prayer of thanks to the gods for helping you up (and another asking them to help you down), you face the choice of returning to Refuge A via Kaki Skala, or continuing on to the SEO **Refuge of Giosos Apostolides** (Γιόσος Αποστολίδης). At 2720m, this is the highest refuge in the Balkans, with a stunning panorama of the major peaks of Olympus. The refuge has 90 beds and serves meals. It has no showers or natural drinking water, but bottled water is sold. The EOS **Refuge C Hristos Kakalos** (Χρήστος Κάκαλος) is nearby with 18 beds, but is open only during July and August. Both refuges are more exposed to the weather than Refuge A and are not as popular.

Neither of these refuges has a telephone. To reach them you can return via Kaki Skala to the Zonaria (Ζωνάρια) path signposted to the SEO Refuge; this leads to the refuge in one hour. Alternatively, you can descend Mytikas via **Louki Couloir**, which begins just north of the summit and is another 45-minute rock scramble. A few experienced climbers claim that Louki Couloir is easier than Kaki Skala, but the general consensus is that it's more difficult. It is certainly more sheer and prone to rock falls – more of a danger to those climbing up than to those descending. At the bottom of Louki Couloir you meet the Zonaria path. Turn left and the SEO lodge is 20 minutes away.

SEO Refuge to Diastavrosi

The refuge is on the edge of the Plateau of the Muses and from here a well-maintained path leads, in 4½ hours, to **Diastavrosi** (Διασταύρωση), on the Prionia-Litohoro road. From the plateau the path goes along a ridge called **Lemos** (Λαιμός), meaning Neck), with the Enipeas Ravine on the right and the Papa Rema Ravine on the left. After one hour you arrive at **Skourta** summit (2485m), from which it is 1½ hours to **Petrostrounga** (Stony Sheepfold). The next stretch of path leads through woodland to a small meadow known as **Barba**; from here it is 40 minutes to Diastavrosi, 14km from Litohoro.

Olympus Taverna (☎ *2352 084 288,* *Kendriki Plateia)* Mains €3-5.50. On the main square itself, this taverna serves tasty mezedes and ready-made food. Make a point of trying the unusual red retsina (€1.80) and grilled wild boar (€5.30). Owner Christos Kakalos is the grandson of one of the first three men to climb Mt Olympus.

Phone numbers listed incorporate changes due in Oct 2002; see p83

To Pazari (☎ 2352 082 540, Plateia 3 Martiou) Fish dishes €6-8. Just down from Hotel Markisia, this place specialises in fish, but also dishes up steaks and mayirefta.

Damaskinia (☎ 2352 081 247, Vasileos Konstandinou 4) Mains €4.5. Not 50m from To Pazari is this place popular with the locals, with a garden at the back and known for its homemade mousakas and *kokoretsi* (spit-roast lamb offal).

Getting There & Away From the bus station (☎ 2352 081 271), there are buses to Katerini (25 minutes, €1.50, 16 daily), Thessaloniki (1½ hours, €5.60, 10 daily) and Athens (5½ hours, €23.50, three daily via Katerini). Buses from Thessaloniki to Athens or Volos will drop you off on the main highway, where you can catch the Katerini-Litohoro bus.

Litohoro is situated on the Athens-Volos-Thessaloniki line (10 trains daily), but the station is 9km from town.

Ancient Dion Δίον

At the foot of Mt Olympus, just north of Litohoro and 16km south of Katerini, lies Ancient Dion *(Dion Archaeological Park; ☎ 2352 053 276, Dion; adult/student €2.35/1.20; open 8am-7pm daily, 8am-6pm daily in winter)* An extensive, well-watered site, it was the sacred city of the Macedonians, who worshipped the Olympian gods here. Alexander the Great sacrificed here before setting off to conquer the world.

Dion's origins are unknown, but there is evidence that an earth goddess of fertility was first worshipped here. Later, other gods were worshipped, including Asclepius, the god of medicine. The most interesting discovery so far is the evocative Sanctuary to Isis, the Egyptian goddess, in a lush, low-lying part of the site. Its votive statues were found virtually intact with traces of colour remaining. Copies have been placed in the positions of the originals, which are now in the site museum. Also worth seeking out is the magnificent, well-preserved mosaic floor, dating from AD 200, which depicts the Dionysos Triumphal Epiphany.

During the Olympus Festival, which takes place during August, plays are performed at the site's reconstructed theatre.

There is also a **museum** (☎ 2351 053 206; adult/student €2.35/1.20; open 8am-7pm Tues-Fri, 12.30pm-7pm Mon), with a well-laid-out, large collection of statues and offerings from Ancient Dion, labelled in English and Greek.

Places to Stay Because it is a bit of a hassle to get to Dion, you may wish to stay overnight in the modern village.

Dion Hotel (☎ 2351 053 222, fax 2351 031 202, Dion) Singles/doubles with bathroom €29.30/35.20. This pleasant C-class hotel is on the main road in (modern) Dion near the bus stop.

Getting There & Away There are no buses from Litohoro, but there is a direct road and taking a cab is the best way to get there. It shouldn't cost more than €6.50. There are also regular buses from Katerini

VERIA Βέροια
postcode 591 00 • pop 60,000

Most people merely pass through Veria 75km west of Thessaloniki, en route to the ancient site of Vergina. But Veria, capital of the prefecture of Imathia, is a fascinating town with over 70 churches – some call it 'Little Jerusalem'. There are many rather dilapidated houses from the Turkish era, but a government preservation order is in force and most of them are now undergoing gradual restoration. Mineral springs are located all over the town and the local tap water is said to be very good. Veria is also the centre of a vast peach-growing industry and wines made from grapes grown on the escarpment from Veria to Edessa are among Greece's most famous exports. The local Boutaris vineyards produce some of Greece's best wines.

Orientation & Information

The town's two main squares, Plateia Andoniou and Plateia Raktivan, are 1km apart linked by the town's two main thoroughfares: Venizelou which becomes Mitropoleo halfway along, and the traditional Vasileos Konstandinou (also called Kendrikis). The bus station is one block from Venizelou. The train station is 3km from the town centre on the old road to Thessaloniki.

The Municipal Culture Office (☎ 2331 062 548, fax 2331 027 914, ⓔ city@veria-art.gr) on the corner of Pavlou Mela and Bizaniou is responsible for tourism promotion in Veria. It produces some useful brochures on Veria. See also its Web site Ⓦ www.veria-art .gr for more information.

The post office is at Dionysiou Solomou 4 (off Mitropoleos). The OTE is at Mitropoleos 53. The police (☎ 2331 022 391) are on Mitropoleos, next to the post office. The National Bank of Greece is on the corner of Mitropoleos and Ippokratous while the Eurobank is at Mitropoleos 44, opposite the OTE. Both banks have ATMs.

The Internet Meeting Center (☎ 2331 063 394) is at Kondogiorgaki 7; it's open 11am to late (€3 per hour). Taxis can be called on ☎ 2331 063 394.

Things to See

The most interesting part of Veria is the old Turkish quarter called Barbouta. For a short tour around this area, begin by walking down Vasileos Konstandinou from Plateia Andoniou. The narrow, winding Vasileos Konstandinou is the commercial street of old Veria, flanked by old-fashioned tailor shops, bookbinders, kafeneia and antique shops.

Halfway along on the right is a huge, ancient plane tree where in 1430 the Turks, after taking Veria, hanged Archbishop Arsenios. Directly opposite is the dilapidated **old cathedral**, which dates from the 12th century. A rather incongruous and now decapitated minaret bears testament to the cathedral's conversion to a mosque during the Turkish era.

The **archaeological museum** (☎ 2331 024 972, Leoforos Anixeos 45; admission €1.50; open 8.30am-3pm Tues-Sun) is in this part of town on Leoforos Anixeos, which snakes its way to the left across the escarpment from the end of Elias. It contains some finds from the tombs of Vergina and Levkadia.

St Paul the Apostle visited Veria on both his second and third voyages (AD 49–52 and 53–58). Veria was referred to as Beroea in the New Testament, and there is now a **shrine** at Mavromihali 1 where Paul is believed to have preached. Mavromihali runs off Plateia Raktivan.

Places to Stay

Hotel Veroi (☎ 2331 022 866, fax 2331 023 566, Plateia Raktivan 10) Singles/doubles with balcony & bathroom €35.50/45.50. This is the best value among the few hotels. Rooms are very clean, large, and comfortably furnished.

Hotel Villa Elia (☎ 2331 026 800, fax 2331 021 880, Elias 16) Singles/doubles €41/50. This is a comfortable business hotel with large, air-conditioned rooms.

Hotel Macedonia (☎ 2331 066 902, fax 2331 066 902, Kondogiorgaki 50) Singles/doubles €42.50/57. This B-class property is the best in town. Rooms are spacious and tastefully furnished. Walk along Venizelou, turn left into Elias and then right into Paster at the Bull's Family Restaurant. Kondogiorgaki is the continuation of Paster.

Places to Eat

Veria is famous for its *revani*, a sweet syrupy cake found throughout most of the town. It's also known for the infamous bean concoction, *fasolada*, usually cooked in an oven.

Ouzeri ton Angelon (☎ 2331 027 705, Angelon 4) Fish dishes €4.50-6. This is a neat little ouzeri-style restaurant. One of the house specialities is *mydopilafo tis yiayias* – 'grandma's rice and mussels'.

Menou (☎ 2331 072 788, Plateia Raktivan 14) Ladera €2.70. This place is good for *ladera* (oil-based) dishes. Try *fasolia* (beans), or *imam baïldi* (aubergines in oil with herbs). Great for vegetarians.

Within 200m of Plateia Raktivan is a little leafy square called Papakia. Look out for two places to eat.

Saroglou (☎ 2331 061 162, Afroditis 2) Grills €5. It is slightly pretentious, but very popular locally.

Kostalar (☎ 2331 061 801, Afroditis 4) Mezedes €4-5. A traditional eatery, which has been in business since 1939. Good for grills and mezedes.

Getting There & Away

Bus Frequent buses leave from the bus station (☎ 2331 022 342) on Trembesinas for Thessaloniki (1¼ hours, €4.25), Athens (seven hours, €27.60), Edessa (one hour, €3) and Vergina (20 minutes, €0.90). Buses for Kozani (1¼ hours, €3.50) depart from a separate bus station on Pierion 1km west of the town centre (take a taxi). Bus for Ioannina (six hours, €13.50) also stop here.

Train There are eight trains daily in both directions on the Thessaloniki-Kozani-Florina line. Additional intercity services to/from Kozani pass through Veria twice daily – one goes to Athens and the other to Thessaloniki. The train station's phone number is ☎ 2331 024 444.

VERGINA Βεργίνα
postcode 590 31 • pop 1255

The ancient site of Vergina (*ver-yee-nah;* ☎ 2331 092 347; admission €3.50; open 8am-7pm Tues-Sun, 12.30pm-7pm Mon), 11km south-east of Veria, is ancient Aigai, the first capital of Macedon. The capital was later transferred to Pella, but Aigai continued to be the royal cemetery. Philip II was assassinated here in 336 BC at the wedding of his daughter Cleopatra.

To fully appreciate the significance of the discoveries, you need to visit Thessaloniki's archaeological museum, where the magnificent finds of Philip II's tomb are displayed, along with Philip II himself! Unfortunately, the actual tomb is off limits to visitors as it is still being excavated.

The ruins are spread out, but well signposted from the modern village of the same name. The **Macedonian tomb**, 500m uphill from the village, has a facade of four Ionic half-columns and a marble throne inside. Continue 400m farther up the road to reach the ruins of an extensive **palatial complex**, built as a summer residence for Antigonos Gonatas (king from 283–240 BC). The focal point is a large Doric peristyle which was surrounded by pebble mosaic floors.

One of the mosaics, with a beautiful floral design, is well preserved *in situ*. A large oak tree on the highest point of the site affords some welcome shade. The site has been World Heritage listed.

Places to Stay & Eat

Ikos (☎ 2331 092 366, Vergina) Singles/doubles €22/33. These small domatia are on the same road as the tombs. Look for the red-tiled roof.

Pension Vergina (☎ 2331 092 510, fax 2331 092 511, Vergina) Singles/doubles €23.50/35. This neat-looking pension is 300m past the tombs. Rooms have bath and a large communal balcony.

There is a *cafe* opposite the Macedonian tomb.

EDESSA Εδεσσα
postcode 582 00 • pop 16,000

Edessa (**ed**-eh-sah) is the capital of the prefecture of Pella. Extolled by Greeks for its many waterfalls, it is little-visited by foreign tourists. Little streams and bridges, and cool and shady parks, dot the whole of Edessa which, being a small town, is very easy and pleasant to explore on foot. The town is perched precariously on a ledge overlooking the seemingly endless agricultural plain, and is the most northern of the Mt Vermion escarpment centres.

Until the discovery of the royal tombs at Vergina, Edessa was believed to be the ancient Macedonian city of Aigai.

Orientation

The bus station (☎ 2381 023 511) is on the corner of Filippou and Pavlou Mela. To reach the town centre, cross over Filippou and walk straight ahead along Pavlou Mela to the T-junction, and turn right into Egnatia where the road forks almost immediately. The left branch continues as Egnatia, and the right is Dimokratias. These two streets, along with Filippou, are the main thoroughfares.

The train station (☎ 2381 023 510) is opposite the end of 18 Oktovriou. To reach the town centre, walk up 18 Oktovriou for 400m to a major junction; the biggest waterfall is signposted sharp left, or veer right for Dimokratias.

Information
There is a helpful and well-stocked Tourist Information Office (☎ 2381 020 300, fax 2381 024 359) in a kiosk at the falls themselves, with a handy map of Edessa and surrounding tourist attractions. See the official Edessa Web site at W www.edessacity.gr.

The National Bank of Greece is at Dimokratias 1 and has an ATM. The post office is at Dimokratias 26. The OTE is on Agiou Dimitriou – turn right from Pavlou Mela (by Hotel Pella) and it's off to the left. The taxi stand (☎ 2381 022 904) is next to the National Bank of Greece.

There is no tourist police; the regular police (☎ 2381 023 333) are on Iroön Polytehniou, which runs between Filippou and Dimokratias.

Things to See & Do
Edessa's main attraction is its **waterfalls**. There are a number of little ones (usually artificial) dotted around the town, but the biggest waterfall, called **katarraktes** (waterfalls), plunges dramatically down a cliff to the agricultural plain below. There are actually two falls: one drops more or less vertically, and another, a little way to the left, tumbles and twirls, zigzagging down the cliff face.

The area surrounding Edessa lends itself to a wide range of year-round **outdoor activities** including rafting, kayaking, parapente, trekking, rappelling, canyoning and archery, to name but a few of those promoted by the Tourist Information Office. See its Web site for the full low-down.

Places to Stay
Hotel Elena (☎ 2381 023 218, fax 2381 023 951, Plateia Timenidon) Singles/doubles with bathroom & TV €26.50/35. This D-class hotel has light and airy rooms. From the bus station turn right at Filippou, walk three blocks to the junction signposted to the waterfalls and Florina, turn right into Pandeleimonos, and the hotel is a little way along on the left.

Hotel Katarraktes (☎ 2381 022 300, fax 2381 027 237, Karanou 18) Singles/doubles €41/55. The comfortable rooms are traditionally furnished and have bathroom and balcony. Follow the signposts for the waterfalls, and look for the hotel on the left.

Hotel Alfa (☎ 2381 022 221, fax 2381 024 777, Egnatia 28) Singles/doubles €44/70.50. This renovated C-class property is the best hotel in town. It has double-glazed and sound-proofed rooms with TV, telephone and air-con. There is also Internet access for guests.

Places to Eat
Estiatorion Omonia (☎ 2381 029 231, Egnatia 20) Mains €4.50-6. Close to the bus station on the same street as Hotel Alfa is this long-established eatery. Food is cheap and good, with mayirefta dishes to choose from.

Taverna-Psistaria (☎ 2381 027 959, Filippou 26) Grills €4-5.50. Diagonally opposite the bus station, this taverna is convenient for through-travellers. Roast chicken (€4.50) is a safe bet for hungry travellers.

You'll pay more to eat at the waterfalls, where there are at least five places to eat.

Katarraktes Edessas (☎ 2381 027 810, Kapetan Gareti-Perdika 1) Specialities around €5.50. This is a publicly owned institution with the prime spot next to the falls. Try the specialities of tsoblek kebab, or kleftiko; both are delicious dishes made with veal and various vegetables.

Bar and cafe life is centred on the little brick-paved Angeli Gatsou, which starts just opposite the post office by the little bridge.

Getting There & Away
Bus From the main bus station (☎ 2381 023 511) at Pavlou Mela 13 there are buses to Thessaloniki (one hour 40 minutes, €5, hourly), Veria (one hour, €3, six daily) and Athens (eight hours, €28.50, three daily). Four buses daily go to Florina (1¼ hours, €5.20) and Kastoria (1¾ hours, €5.20) from a second bus stop at Filippou 15, outside a pitta shop.

Train There are eight trains daily both ways on the Thessaloniki-Kozani/Florina line,

Phone numbers listed incorporate changes due in Oct 2002; see p83

NORTHERN GREECE

plus an additional two intercity services, one of which goes direct to Athens. The stretch between Edessa and Amyndeo skirts the western shore of Lake Vegoritida and is particularly beautiful.

FLORINA Φλώρινα
postcode 531 00 • pop 12,500

The northern town of Florina (**flo**-rih-nah) is the capital of the prefecture of the same name. Tourists used to come to Florina only because it was the last Greek town before the border with the former Yugoslavia. Now its economy is somewhat slower, but has picked up again in recent times thanks to its burgeoning student population which gives the town a lively, lived-in feel. It's a convenient and pleasant enough place to spend the night if you are touring the area.

Florina is the only place from which you can take a bus to the Prespa Lakes and there is also a low-key ski resort at Vigla, just west of Florina on the Prespa Lakes road.

Orientation & Information

Florina is laid out in a long curve, much like a boomerang, and is divided by the river that flows along the length of the town. The main street is Pavlou Mela, which leads to Plateia Georgiou Modi, the central square. Half of Pavlou Mela is a pedestrian mall. From the train station, walk straight ahead, keeping the archaeological museum to your left. Bear left and you are on Pavlou Mela.

From Plateia Georgiou Modi, turn right into Stefanou Dragoumi for the intercity bus station, 250m up the street. Bear right at the end of the street, cross the road and look for the KTEL bus office. Turn left from Plateia Georgiou Modi into 25 Martiou for the river.

There is no EOT or tourist police. The National Bank of Greece is about 50m up Megalou Alexandrou on the right, and the Commercial Bank is just behind it. Both banks have ATMs. The post office is at Kalergi 22; walk along Stefanou Dragoumi towards the bus station and Kalergi is off to the left. The OTE is at Tyrnovou 5.

The telephone number of the police is ☎ 2385 022 100.

Things to See & Do

Housed in a modern building near the train station is the **archaeological museum** (☎ 2385 028 206, *Sidirodromikou Stathmou 3; admission free; open 8.30am-3pm Tues-Sun*). It is well laid out, but only the downstairs labels are in English. Downstairs there is pottery from the Neolithic, early Iron and Bronze Ages, and Roman grave stelae and statues. Upstairs there are some Byzantine reliefs and fragments of frescoes, and finds from an as yet unidentified town built by Philip II, discovered on the nearby hill of Agios Pandeleimonas.

Old Florina occupied both river banks, and many Turkish houses and neoclassical mansions survive. The town has a thriving artistic community, and the Society for the Friends of Art of Florina has restored one of the neoclassical mansions on the river bank, now the **Museum of Modern Art** (☎ 2385 029 444, *Leoforos Eleftherias 103; admission free; open 5pm-8pm Mon-Sat, 10am-1pm Sun*). The museum houses a permanent collection of works by contemporary Greek artists and hosts frequent exhibitions. Walk down 25 Martiou, cross the bridge over the river and turn right; walk for about 200m. Even if you are not interested in art, this is a pleasant walk along the river bank.

Places to Stay

Budget accommodation is thin on the ground. Be prepared to pay extra to stay in Florina.

Hotel Ellenis (☎ 2385 022 671, fax 2385 022 815, e ellinis@line.gr, Pavlou Mela 31) Singles/doubles with bathroom €41/53. This C-class property is the nearest hotel to the train station. The renovated rooms have digital phones and TV. As you come from the train station, it's on the left.

King Alexander (☎ 2385 023 501, fax 2385 029 643, e naidis@otenet.gr, Konstandinou Karamanli 68) Singles/doubles €45.50/62. This B-class hotel, a little out of town along the road to Prespa, has comfortable, renovated rooms. The views over Florina from the front rooms are particularly attractive.

Hotel Antigone (☎ *2385 023 180, fax 2385 045 620, Arianou 1)* Singles/doubles €47/65. This C-class place has pleasant, if pricey, rooms. Turn right into Stefanou Dragoumi from Plateia Georgiou Modi, and the hotel is 200m along on the left, close to the bus station.

Hotel Lingos (☎ *2385 028 322, fax 2385 029 643,* e *lingos@line.gr, Tagmatarhou Naoum 1)* Singles/doubles €50/73. This B-class hotel, just north of Plateia Georgiou Modi, has comfortable, refurbished rooms.

Places to Eat

There's an array of eating places, from fast-food to traditional. Florina is famous for its *piperies Florinis* – large, sweet red peppers served pickled. Pavlou Mela hosts a swathe of fast-food joints and buzzing cafeterias.

Restaurant Olympos (☎ *2385 022 758, Megalou Alexandrou 22)* Lunch with wine €6. Open for lunches Mon-Sat. Close to Plateia Modi, this old-fashioned, traditional mayirio has a good choice of well-cooked, low-priced pre-prepared food.

Tria Adherfia (☎ *2385 029 447, Makedonomahon 14)* Mains €5-6. About 70m to the left as you exit the bus station ticket office is this unpretentious, clean and convenient place.

Restaurant Park (☎ *2385 022 430, Makedonomahon 8)* Mains €5.50-7. This restaurant does good omelettes, schnitzel and ouzo mezedes. It's near the bus station.

High (☎ *2385 022 905, Plateia Modi 5)* Meals €6-7. In the centre of town, High does pizzas, pasta and grills. A filling baked spaghetti with cheese and mushrooms and a large Dab beer is a good choice.

To Steki tou Pavlara (☎ *2385 023 543, 25 Martiou 18)* Meals with salad & wine €7. This is one of the few traditional restaurants left in town. It does good roast chicken.

Getting There & Away

Bus – Domestic From the bus station (☎ 2385 022 430) buses go to Athens (nine hours, €31, 8.30am daily), Thessaloniki (three hours, €9.70, six daily), Kozani (1¾ hours, €5.30, seven daily) and, for the Prespa Lakes, to Agios Germanos (1½ hours,

€3.20, three weekly). For Kastoria, you have to take a bus to Amyndeo and change there.

Bus – International If you are planning to enter the Former Yugoslav Republic of Macedonia from Florina, there are three buses daily to the border town of Niki (30 minutes, €1.10).

For Albania, there are two buses daily to the border post near Krystallopigi (1½ hours, €3.30). There's also a Greek Railways (OSE) bus to Korça (Korytsa) in Albania; it operates on Monday, Tuesday, Wednesday, Friday and Saturday. The bus, which originates in Thessaloniki, leaves Florina train station between 11.30am and 12.30pm (three hours, €10.30). See also the Getting There & Away chapter earlier in this book for details on travel to Albania.

Train Florina's train station (☎ 2385 022 404) is at the end of the Thessaloniki-Edessa-Amyndeo line. There are five to seven trains daily (depending on the season) in both directions. The approximate journey time from Thessaloniki is 3½ hours and tickets costs €4.70. You can also take the train to Kozani (1¾ hours, €2.70), via Amyndeo. There is a surcharge for the intercity service from Amyndeo to Athens or Thessaloniki.

Taxi Some of the Florina taxi drivers can take passengers directly to Bitola in the Former Yugoslav Republic of Macedonia. It's very convenient, though a little pricey for one person – at around €30 one way. Call ☎ 2385 022 800, or ask any of the taxi drivers near the bus station.

PRESPA LAKES Πρέσπα

In the mountainous north-west corner of Greece at an altitude of 850m are the two lakes of Megali Prespa and Mikri Prespa, separated by a narrow strip of land. The area is one of outstanding natural beauty and is little-visited by foreign tourists. The road from Florina crosses the Pisoderi Pass and winds its way through thick forests and lush meadows with grazing cattle; if you have your own transport, there are lots of picnic tables.

NORTHERN GREECE

Mikri (little) Prespa has an area of 43 sq km and is located almost entirely in Greece, except for the south-western tip, which is in Albania. Megali Prespa is the largest lake in the Balkans; the majority (1000 sq km) is in the Former Yugoslav Republic of Macedonia – 38 sq km is in Greece and a small south-western part is in Albania. Much of the Megali Prespa shore is precipitous rock which rises dramatically from the chilly blue water. The Prespa area became a national park in 1977. There is an excellent information centre in Agios Germanos.

Mikri Prespa is a wildlife refuge of considerable interest to ornithologists. It is surrounded by thick reed beds where numerous species of birds, including cormorants, pelicans, egrets, herons and ibis, nest.

The islet of **Agios Ahillios** has Byzantine remains. The island is linked to the mainland by a 1km-long floating pontoon and there is even a comfortable place to eat and stay for visitors who really like to get away from it all – the *Agios Ahillios Hostel* (☎ 2385 046 601), where doubles cost €33.

Incidentally, one of the best places for viewing the lake's wildlife is the top of the sizable hillock overlooking the beginning of

MARTIN HARRIS

Mikri Prespa is home to species such as the Dalmation pelican

the pontoon bridge – but it is often swarming with school groups on field trips.

Agios Germanos Αγιος Γερμανός
postcode 530 77 • pop 267
This little village serves as the main transport hub for the Prespa region and, although it is a little way from the lakes themselves, it is an attractive and convenient base. There are some good walks to be made from the village, and there is always a taxi handy should you need to move farther afield.

The village is primarily an agricultural settlement renowned for its bean crops. The mounds of cut cane you will see in springtime as you enter the village are used for supporting the beanstalks.

Orientation & Information Agios Germanos has a bus terminus and the only post office in the Prespa basin. There are no banking facilities, but you can change money at the post office. The phone number of the local police is ☎ 2385 051 202 and of the local community clinic ☎ 2385 046 284.

Things to See There are two churches that may be of interest to admirers of Byzantine ecclesiastical art: **Agios Athanasios** and

PRESPA LAKES

FORMER YUGOSLAV REPUBLIC OF MACEDONIA

Lake Megali Prespa

ALBANIA

Ljubojno

askitiria

Psarades
Koula Beach

Hotel Psarades

Miliona

Agios Germanos

Lemos

Prespa Information Centre

Platy

Pontoon

Agios Ahillios

Kallithea

Pyli

Lefkonas

Lake Mikri Prespa

Karyes

Vrondero

PRESPA LAKES NATIONAL PARK

Mikrolimni

To Florina

0   2.5   5km
0   1.5   3mi

To Kastoria

NORTHERN GREECE

Agios Germanos, named after the village's patron saint.

For friends of nature, there is a very well-presented display and resource centre for the Prespa National Park in the **Information Centre** (*☎/fax 2385 051 452; open 9.30am-2.30pm daily*). There is some excellent material in Greek, but not too much in English. Nonetheless, the photos, maps and diagrams are pretty self-explanatory.

Places to Stay & Eat *Agios Germanos Hostel* (*☎ 2385 051 320*) Doubles/triples €30/32.50. This well-run and comfortable hostel, managed by the local Women's Cooperative, is at the top end of the village – follow the signs.

Rooms Pelekanos (*☎ 2385 051 442*) Singles/doubles €28/32.50 This comfortable place has EOT-approved domatia, and is just below the main square.

Lefteris Taverna (*☎ 2385 051 418*) Meal €7-8. This cosy taverna is opposite the Agios Germanos Hostel and is one of the better places to eat.

Women's Cooperative Taverna (*☎ 2385 051 320*) Meals €5-6. The Women's Co-op runs this taverna, serving pittes, *trahanas* (crushed wheat boiled in milk then dried) and fasolada that can be washed down with local wine.

Getting There & Away Florina is the only town with a direct bus link to the lakes. There are three buses on weekdays to Lemos, 14km east of Psarades.

Psarades Ψαράδες
postcode 530 77 • pop 95

The village of Psarades, 70km from Florina, is a revelation. It's positioned within a small inlet of Megali Prespa and is the last Greek village before the tri-national border on Megali Prespa Lake. Psarades is a little village with traditional stone houses which are subject to a National Trust preservation order, old fishing boats made of cedar and oak, and some of the most unusual miniature cows in Greece.

According to the latest estimates, only 95 permanent residents remain from a prewar population of 770 – many emigrated to the USA and Australia. A large lakefront marble memorial from the Macedonian Association of Chicago attests to the strong bonds between Psarades and its emigrants.

Orientation & Information Psarades village consists of an attractive, landscaped lakefront lined with numerous modern restaurants and fish tavernas.

There is no bank or post office, but Philippos Papadopoulos, the owner of the grocery shop on the village square, will exchange cash. There is no OTE, but there is a cardphone and most restaurants have metered phones. Mobile phones pick up all three Greek networks.

Things to See & Do It will be hard to resist a boat trip out onto Megali Prespa, since Psarades is the only Greek village with anchorage on this lake. More specifically, you should strive to be taken to the three **askitiria** (places of solitary worship) that can only be visited by boat.

All three are out past the Roti headland to the left. The first one, **Metamorfosi**, dates from the 13th century. There are only a few remnants of the rich painting that once decorated this site and two sections from the woodcarved *temblon* (votive screen), the rest of which is in the Florina museum. The second is called **Mikri Analipsi** and is from the 14th or 15th century. Access to this one is a little difficult. The third and probably the best is **Panagia Eleousa**.

A trip will cost you about €3 for a short tour to the rock paintings and one of the askitiria, or €6 for the full tour to all of them, assuming there are at least four people per boat.

More or less opposite the village are rock paintings of **Panagia Vlahernitsa** (1455–56) and of **Panagia Dexiokratousa** (1373), along with some inscriptions. These are included in the boat tours mentioned above.

The church of **Kimisis Theotokou** in the village itself dates from 1893 and is decorated on the outside with the double-headed eagle of the Byzantine Empire. There is also an inscription that refers to the old name of the village, Nivitsa.

NORTHERN GREECE

Places to Stay & Eat If you plan on arriving in July or August without making a reservation, think twice, as the region is becoming very popular and accommodation is limited. There are at least four places to stay in Psarades.

There is no official camping ground, but you can *camp* freelance at Koula Beach on the southern shore of Megali Prespa, 5km east of Psarades.

Rooms Arhondiko (☎ *2385 046 260*) Singles/doubles €25/35. This place has comfortable, clean rooms right on the lakefront.

Hotel Psarades (☎ *2385 046 015*) Singles/doubles €28/35. This hotel is right opposite the village. It has excellent rooms, all with views over Psarades, as well as a bar and restaurant.

Five tavernas line the waterfront at Psarades. They all dish up excellent fish, straight from the lake.

Paradosi (☎ *2385 046 013*) Trout €5. This is probably the best of the waterfront tavernas, and is possibly the only one open out of season. The fasolada is very filling.

Getting There & Away You will need your own transport to get to Psarades, or you can take a taxi from either Lemos or Agios Germanos.

There are three buses a week to and from Florina and Lemos (€3.80, Monday, Wednesday and Friday). The Wednesday bus has a connection to Psarades.

From Lemos you have the choice of either hitching the long uphill then downhill road to Psarades, or calling for a taxi (☎ 2385 051 247, 2385 051 207 or mobile 09-4270 4496). Approximate taxi fares from Psarades are €7.50 to Lemos (to pick up the bus to Florina), and €28 to either Florina or Kastoria.

KASTORIA Καστοριά
postcode 521 00 • pop 17,000

Kastoria (kah-sto-rih-**ah**) lies between Mt Grammos and Mt Vitsi in western Macedonia, 200km west of Thessaloniki. It is regarded by many Greeks as their most beautiful town. Indeed, its setting is exemplary, occupying the isthmus of a promontory which projects into the tree-fringed Lake Orestiada, surrounded by mountains.

Its architecture is also outstanding, featuring many Byzantine and post-Byzantine churches and many 17th- and 18th-century mansions, known as *arhondika* because they were the homes of the *arhons* – the town's leading citizens. In Kastoria the arhondika were the dwellings of rich fur merchants.

The town has a long tradition of fur production. Jewish furriers (refugees from Europe) came to Kastoria because of the large numbers of beavers (*kastori* in Greek) around the lake. They carried out their trade with such zeal that by the 19th century the beaver was extinct in the area. Since then the furriers have worked with imported fur.

Orientation

The main bus station is one block inland from the southern lakeside, on 3 Septemvriou. Here also is a large park, the main taxi stand and a large car park for travellers with their own wheels. Most services – banks, hotels and tourist information – are at the western end of town. The older part of town with its arhondika and churches lies up the hill to the east side. Walking Kastoria's hilly streets can be tiring.

Information

The Municipal Tourist Office (☎/fax 2467 026 777) is in the town hall on Ioustinianou – a five-minute walk from the bus station. The staff are helpful and give out lots of brochures, maps and information.

The National Bank of Greece is on 11 Noemvriou and the Credit Bank is on Grammou. Both banks have ATMs. The post office is at the northern end of Leoforos Megalou Alexandrou, which skirts the lake. The OTE is on Agiou Athanasiou, which runs off Plateia Davaki, just north of Mitropoleos. The police (☎ 2467 083 214) is near the bus station. There is a decent-sized car park on the lake shore, near the bus station.

Things to See & Do

Many of the numerous **Byzantine churches** in Kastoria were originally private chapels

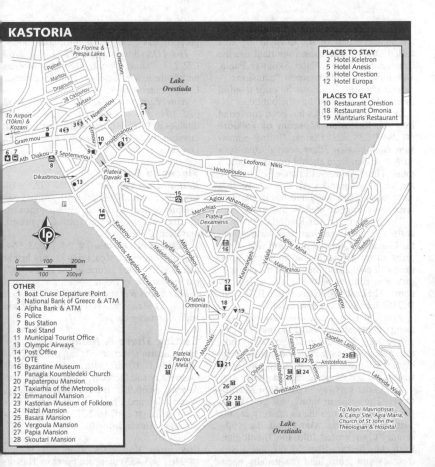

KASTORIA

PLACES TO STAY
2 Hotel Keletron
5 Hotel Anesis
9 Hotel Orestion
12 Hotel Europa

PLACES TO EAT
10 Restaurant Orestion
18 Restaurant Omonia
19 Mantziaris Restaurant

OTHER
1 Boat Cruise Departure Point
3 National Bank of Greece & ATM
4 Alpha Bank & ATM
6 Police
7 Bus Station
8 Taxi Stand
11 Municipal Tourist Office
13 Olympic Airways
14 Post Office
15 OTE
16 Byzantine Museum
17 Panagia Koumbledeki Church
20 Papaterpou Mansion
21 Taxiarhia of the Metropolis
22 Emmanouil Mansion
23 Kastorian Museum of Folklore
24 Natzi Mansion
25 Basara Mansion
26 Vergoula Mansion
27 Papia Mansion
28 Skoutari Mansion

attached to arhondika. Almost all of the churches are locked, and gaining access to them is something of a Byzantine experience in itself. Ask around the kafeneia on the square for the person who has the keys. Another possibility is the Byzantine Museum's curator, who may be able to contact someone who can show you some of the churches.

Even if you don't manage to get a look inside any churches, all is not lost, for some of them have external frescoes. One such church is the **Taxiarhia of the Metropolis**, on Plateia Pavlou Mela, south of Plateia Omonias, which has a 13th-century fresco of the Madonna and Child above the entrance. Inside is the tomb of Pavlos Melas, a Macedonian hero killed by Bulgar terrorists during the struggles that culminated in the 1912–13 Balkan Wars. Melas' life is documented in Thessaloniki's Museum of the Macedonian Struggle. Many Macedonian streets are named Pavlou Mela in his memory.

The **Byzantine Museum** (☎ 2467 026 781, Plateia Dexamenis; admission free; open 8.30am-3pm Tues-Sun) houses outstanding icons from many of the town's churches. Visiting this museum first will help you to appreciate the churches.

NORTHERN GREECE

Most of the surviving **arhondika** are in the southern part of the town in the area called Doltso. The most important are the Emmanouil, Basara, Natzi, Skoutari, Papia, Vergoula and Papaterpou mansions – named after the families who once lived in them. These are closed to the public.

One of the arhondika has been converted into the **Kastorian Museum of Folklore** (☎ 2467 028 603, Plateia Doltso; admission €0.60; open 10am-noon & 3pm-6pm daily). A visit here should be considered a must. The 530-year-old house belonged to the wealthy Nerantzis Aïvazis family. It is sumptuously furnished and has displays of ornaments, kitchen utensils and tools.

The Municipality of Kastoria runs **boat cruises** around Lake Orestiada starting from the Psaradika Quay on the north side of the promontory. Departing at noon and 6pm, the small boat circumnavigates the promontory and returns to the quay, taking 1¼ hours. The cost is €3 (students €1.50). Call ☎ 2467 026 777 for more details.

You can take a relaxing **lakeside walk** along a pretty, shaded 9km road that skirts the promontory. The lake is fringed with reeds, the habitat of frogs, turtles and many species of birds. On the lake are many species of water fowl and the great crested grebe.

Just under halfway is the **Moni Mavriotissas**. The resident monk will give you a guided tour. Next to the monastery are the 11th-century **Agia Maria** and the 16th-century **Church of St John the Theologian**. Both churches are liberally festooned with frescoes and icons, and are usually open. Beside the monastery there is a reasonably priced restaurant, the only source of refreshment on the walk. To begin the walk, take the road to the hospital.

Places to Stay

There is a free *camping ground* in the grounds of the Moni Mavriotissas.

Hotel Keletron (☎ 2467 022 676, 2467 023 262, 11 Noemvriou 52) Singles/doubles with bathroom €23.50/35. This vaguely seedy C-class hotel has reasonable rooms.

Hotel Anesis (☎ 2467 083 908, fax 2467 083 768, Grammou 10) Singles/doubles with bathroom €35/47. This neat C-class property has clean and comfortable rooms.

Hotel Orestion (☎ 2467 022 257, fax 2467 022 258, Plateia Davaki 1) Singles/doubles with bathroom €35.50/44. This is a superior C-class hotel with very pleasant rooms.

Hotel Europa (☎ 2467 023 826, fax 2467 025 154, Agiou Athanasiou 12) Singles/doubles €35/45.50. In a similar vein to the Orestion is this place, just up from Plateia Davaki.

Places to Eat

Restaurant Orestion (☎ 2467 022 853, Ermou 27) Meals €5.50-6.50. Closed Sat evening & Sun. This is an unpretentious little place which dishes up tasty, low-priced, mayirefta dishes.

Restaurant Omonia (☎ 2467 023 964, Plateia Omonias) Meals €6-7. This bright and modern place is one of the better budget restaurants in town.

Mantziaris Restaurant (☎ 2467 029 492, Valala 8) Meals €6-7. This place is good and reasonably cheap.

Getting There & Away

Air Kastoria's Aristotelis airport (☎ 2467 042 515) is 10km south of Kastoria. Between May and October, there are flights to Athens (€66.95) on Sunday, Tuesday, Wednesday and Friday. The Olympic Airways office (☎ 2467 022 275) is at Leoforos Megalou Alexandrou 15.

Bus From Kastoria's main bus station (☎ 2467 083 455) there are buses to Thessaloniki (four hours, €12, six daily), Kozani (two hours, €5.80, five daily) and Athens (nine hours, €31.30, two daily). The 6.30am and 3.30pm Thessaloniki buses go via Kozani and Veria. There are more buses in summer.

Taxi Taxis can be found 100m east of the bus station, or can be called on ☎ 2467 082 100.

HALKIDIKI Χαλκιδική

The Halkidiki Peninsula is a large blob to the south-east of Thessaloniki, from which three long 'fingers' extend into the Aegean.

The two large lakes of Koronia and Volvi separate the peninsula from the rest of Macedonia.

Halkidiki boasts 500km of coastline, with superb sandy beaches surrounded by calm, aquamarine sea. Unfortunately, many of these assets have been ruthlessly exploited and while the 'finger' of Kassandra consists either of luxurious holiday complexes for the rich and famous, or package-tourist ghettos, the middle finger of Sithonia has escaped most of the excesses and you can still find some of the most magical beaches in the whole of Greece, if you are prepared to look. The easternmost promontory of Halkidiki is the Monastic Republic of Mt Athos (Agion Oros) and most of it is open only to male pilgrims

Halkidiki is not a place for budget or independent travellers as virtually all accommodation can be booked solid throughout summer. If you are camping, however, a visit is more practicable: Halkidiki has around 30 camping grounds which, even if they are bursting at the seams, are unlikely to turn you away.

Northern Halkidiki

Polygyros As the capital of Halkidiki, Polygyros is the main town in the peninsula. It is a pleasant, thriving agricultural and administrative town of some 4500 inhabitants, set among verdant hills of pine trees. Polygyros makes a good base for touring the whole Halkidiki region.

Housing finds from the peninsula's ancient sites is the **archaeological museum** (☎ 2371 022 148; admission €1.50; open 8.30am-3pm Tues-Sun). It includes the Sanctuary of Zeus at Aphytis and the ancient city of Acanthos.

Every year on 14 and 15 August, the feast of the Panagia is celebrated in the nearby village of **Vrastama**, 14km east of Polygyros in the guise of the **arbute berry festival**. The arbute berry, known as *koumaro* in Greek, is made into a potent spirit which is given away freely to all and sundry along with plates of mezedes. Live music begins at about 10pm on the evening of 14 August and goes on all night. The festival takes places at the small church of the Panagia, a few hundred metres north of the village centre.

The municipality of Polygyros each year organises the **Olynthos Olive Festival** (☎ 2371 021 312) which takes place at the site of **Ancient Olynthos**, 17km south-west of Polygyros. The four-day festival consists of music, theatre, dancing and talks and is usually finished off with a concert by one or more of Greece's best-known singers.

Ancient Olynthos (Nea Olynthos; admission €1.50; open 8am-7pm Tues-Sun), a fairly important archaeological site in Halkidiki, dates to the 7th century BC when the site, distinguished by two rounded hills, was settled by inhabitants from central Macedonia. The Persians destroyed the original city in 479 BC, but Olynthos regained its status 45 years later as the capital of Halkidiki. In 348 BC, Philip II, king of Macedonia, razed the city to the ground, a disaster from which Olynthos never raised its head.

The Petralona Cave In northern Halkidiki, the Petralona Cave (☎ 0373 071 671, ⓔ aee@vip.gr, ⓦ www.aee.gr/index_english.html, Petralona; adult/student €4.40/2.40; open 9am-7pm daily, 9am-5pm daily in winter), 56km south-east of Thessaloniki, has stalactites and stalagmites and is where a 700,000-year-old human skull (evidence of one of Europe's earliest inhabitants) was found. The cave is well presented with an illuminated walkway taking visitors around what is in effect only a small section of a huge cave.

The prevailing theory held by the resident archaeologist Professor Aris Poulianos is that finds in Petralona irrefutably establish that archaic homo sapiens (archanthropos) arose in Europe, not Africa, as is hitherto widely believed. Displays in the museum next door confidently uphold this controversial view. Doucas Tours (see Organised Tours in the Thessaloniki section earlier in this chapter) sometimes takes tours to the caves.

Places to Stay & Eat *Maria Kastretsiou Rooms* (☎ 2371 023 360, Doubiotou 7, Polygyros) Doubles €35.20. Housed in a

NORTHERN GREECE

restored wood-and-stone family home, the six rooms are neat and homely. Bathrooms are shared and there is a fridge in each room. Enjoy the leafy communal garden under the shade of a laurel tree.

Filoxenio Morfeas (☎ *2371 024 039, Doubiotou 8, Polygyros*) Doubles/triples €35.20/44. In a restored stone home and on a quiet pedestrian street, these four cosy rooms are an option for visitors to Polygyros.

Exi Vryses (☎ *2371 022 725, Poly-tehniou, Polygyros*) Grills €4.10-6.20. Set in a large tree-studded garden, Exi Vryses is restaurant, bar and cafeteria all in one. From its wide menu try *kaloyeros* (€4.70) – a dish of veal, eggplant and cheese in a piquant tomato sauce cooked in a clay pot. Breakfast can also be had for €1.50 to €2.90.

Getting There & Away A bus from Thessaloniki goes to Petralona Cave (one hour, €3.25) at 1.15pm every day except Sunday and public holidays, and continues on to the village of Krini from where it immediately heads back to Thessaloniki. This hardly leaves time to see the cave, so to get back to Thessaloniki you must walk or hitch 5km south to the village of Eleohoria, where you can pick up a regular Nea Moudania bus to Thessaloniki.

There are nine buses each day between Polygyros and Thessaloniki (1¼ hours, €3.80), four to/from Moudania (one hour, €2.20) and six to/from Sarti in Sithonia (2½ hours, €7.50). The phone number of Polygyros' bus station is ☎ 2371 022 309.

Kassandra Peninsula

The Kassandra Peninsula is less beautiful than the Sithonian Peninsula. Its commercialism is horrendous and even if you're not averse to package tourists, roaring motorbikes, fast-food joints and discos, you're unlikely to easily find independent accommodation. However, if you have a tent, there are lots of well-advertised camping grounds. Freelance camping is prohibited and there are signs alerting you to that fact.

For what it's worth, the western side of the 'finger' is somewhat quieter, with a couple of almost get-away-from-it-all camping

grounds at Posidi and Nea Skioni. The little resort of Siviri, also on this side, has a sandy beach, but has been taken over by the luxurious private apartments of Thessaloniki's elite. Kassandra's only saving grace is the little traditional seaside village of **Afytos** which, to its inhabitants' credit, has made an effort to remain pleasant and mostly concrete-free. Its pedestrian-friendly streets and laid-back ambience make Afytos a worthwhile stop in an otherwise humdrum set of options.

Clubbers and nightbirds will of course find singular solace in Kassandra. The peninsula has a very active bar and disco scene centred on the village of **Kallithea** on the east side of the peninsula. If it's peace and quiet you are looking forward to, look across the bay farther east to Sithonia.

Getting There & Away There are 13 buses daily from Thessaloniki to Kallithea (1½ hours, €5) on the east coast; 11 to Pefkohori (two hours, €6.50), also on the east coast, via Kryopigi and Haniotis; seven to Paliouri (two hours, €7.30) and three to Agia Paraskevi (2½ hours, €7.20), both on the southern tip. All the buses leave from the terminal at Karakasi 68 in Thessaloniki.

Sithonian Peninsula

West Coast Sithonia is a vast improvement on Kassandra. The landscape en route is spectacular with sweeping vistas of thickly forested hills. The southern end and eastern coastline are the least touristed and the best destinations for independent travellers.

An undulating road makes a loop around Sithonia, skirting wide bays, climbing into the pine-forested hills and dipping down to the resorts. Down the west coast are good stretches of sandy, very popular, beaches between **Nikiti** and **Paradisos**, with **Kalogria Beach** and **Lagomandra Beach** worth a special mention. Beyond, **Neos Marmaras** is Sithonia's largest resort, with a very crowded beach, but lots of places to stay in the form of domatia. Look out for the big information boards on both waterfronts.

Beyond Neos Marmaras the road climbs into the hills where roads (some of them dirt) lead down to several beaches and camping grounds. Development along here is less noticeable and if you have a rented motorbike you can find some very pleasant spots by the sea.

Toroni and **Porto Koufo** are small resorts at the south-western tip. The latter is a picturesque little yacht harbour sheltered in a deep bay and has a decent enough beach. There are several fish tavernas for lunch and domatia, should you decide to stay on. The southern tip of Sithonia is still relatively isolated and is the most spectacular region of Halkidiki (excluding the Athos Peninsula) – rocky, rugged and dramatic. As the road rounds the south-eastern tip, Mt Athos comes into view across the gulf, further adding to the spectacular vistas.

The minuscule and almost hidden settlement of **Kalamitsi** is the most delightful corner of the Sithonian Peninsula. This little enclave has a gorgeous sandy beach, a sprinkling of tavernas, some domatia, a couple of reasonable camping grounds and boat-hire facilities. Not yet commercialised, it's one of the Sithonian Peninsula's hidden treasures.

Places to Stay Kalamitsi is the place of choice, if you plan to stay in the far south of Sithonia. Campers have at least two choices.

Porto Camping (☎ *2375 041 346, Kalamitsi)* Adult/tent €2.30/3.50. This camping ground is on the main beach at Kalamitsi.

Camping Kalamitsi (☎ *2375 041 411, Kalamitsi)* Adult/tent €2.50/3.70. This site is around the headland to the west and is close to the beach.

O Giorgakis (☎ *2375 041 338, fax 2375 041 013, Kalamitsi)* Studios €50. Just above the restaurant of the same name, this place is a stone's throw from the beach at Kalamitsi. Studios sleep five and are fully equipped.

Ennea Mouses (☎ *2375 041 704, Kalamitsi)* Apartments €35-44. On the main road, set back in a spacious garden with fruit and olive trees are these nine smallish, but well-equipped, self-contained apartments for up to four persons.

East Coast Continuing up the east coast, you can make a short 2km detour inland to the pleasant village of **Sykia**, which has less tourist hype than the coastal resorts. The beach (3½km from the village) is a little wide and exposed, but if you follow the road along the south side of the wide bay you will find a couple of secluded smaller beaches with turquoise water and golden sand just before **Skala Sykias**. Discreet beach tavernas complete the scene.

Back on the coast, the resort of **Sarti** is next along the route. This sizable village has not succumbed entirely to the package tourist industry and has a good, laid-back atmosphere. From its excellent, long, sandy beach there are splendid views of the startling, pyramid-like hulk of Mt Athos. The town is compact and pleasant enough and tends to cater for local tourism, though groups from Europe occasionally filter in. The beach is OK, though it's rather exposed, but there is more choice in nightlife and eating options. There is a bank, but no ATM. It's a good compromise between the get-away-from-it-all view and the let's-have-*some*-comfort approach. There are usually boat excursions across to Mt Athos from Sarti. Ask at local travel agents.

Between Sarti and Panagia where the loop roads meet up again, things get interesting for the independent travellers. There are some of the better-equipped camping grounds along here as well as some of the best, and least frequented, beaches in Sithonia. With a motorbike or reasonably powered scooter you can get to explore in depth. Look out for the turn-off to **Kavourotrypes** (Crab Holes) – a series of small rocky coves which are great for swimming, about 6km north of Sarti.

A further 13km north you will come across the locally popular and spread-out settlement of **Vourvourou** with a couple of camping grounds and lots of private domatia and studios. The best beach is not an obvious one, but it is **Karydi** reached by a short dirt road from the centre of Vourvourou. Backed by shady pine trees, Karydi Beach is an ideal mix of sand, rocks and solitude.

ATHOS PENINSULA

MONASTERIES
1 Esfigmenou
2 Hiliandariou
3 Zografou
4 Vatopediou
5 Konstamonitou
6 Dohiariou
7 Xenofondos
8 Pandokratoros
9 Stavronikita
10 Iviron
11 Koutloumousiou
12 Agiou Pandeleimonos
13 Xiropotamou
14 Filotheou
15 Karakallou
16 Simonos Petras
17 Osiou Grigoriou
18 Dionysiou
19 Agiou Pavlou
20 Megistis Lavras

SKITES
21 Agias Annis
22 Kerasia
23 Agias Triados
24 Timiou Prodromou

Daily Ferries
Low Frequency Ferries
Hydrofoil/Catamaran
Excursion Boat

At **Ormos Panagias** with a long, sandy beach 1km to the north you can take day excursions by catamaran to Mt Athos.

Places to Stay & Eat *Sarti Beach Camping* (☎ 2375 094 450, fax 2375 044 269, Sarti) Adult/tent €2.50/3.80. This place is not only a camping ground, but a holiday complex with a variety of accommodation. The ground is shaded, but offers little greenery. From the south it's on the right side of the main approach road – buses stop outside.

Armenistis Camping (☎ 2375 091 497, fax 2375 091 487, W www.armenistis.com.gr) Adult/tent €2.70/4. Open 15 May-10 Oct. This is one of the best camping grounds along the coast. There's a great beach and lots of facilities. It's 11km north of Sarti.

Ta Asteria (☎ 2375 094 370, Sarti) 3-/4-person apartments €38/47. In Sarti, this small studio complex has smallish but modern apartments. It is about 100m inland and to the right from the kiosk by the bus stop.

There are also many *domatia* to rent. Just look for the signs around the centre of the village.

Kivotos (☎ 2375 094 143, Sarti). This is the longest-running and perhaps prettiest restaurant in Sarti. It's right in the middle of the waterfront; you can't miss its blue and white facade and cane chairs. Fish is the best deal, though the owner also recommends his fish soup (€5.90).

Getting There & Away Buses leave from the bus terminal at Karakasi 68 in Thessaloniki for Neos Marmaras (2½ hours, €7.70, four daily) and Sarti (3½ hours, €10.30, three daily). Most of the Sarti buses loop around the Sithonian Peninsula, enabling you to see its magnificent southern tip.

Athos Peninsula (Secular Athos)

Most of the easternmost portion of the three prongs of the Halkidiki Peninsula is occupied by the Athonite monasteries. You will probably only want to pass through secular Athos on your way to see the monasteries. The beaches are admittedly very fine in parts, but they have long been developed for the package-tour industry. Soulless resorts based on large hotels with neither interest in, nor of interest to, independent travellers are dotted along the short, southern stretch of the Athos coast. Ierissos is one of the few real towns, notable mainly as the terminus for the boat serving the east-coast monasteries.

The canal dug across the peninsula by the Persian king Xerxes in the 5th century BC for his invading fleet is featured proudly on most maps, but was filled in centuries ago so there's precious little for the untrained eye to see.

The small jetty at Trypiti is the jumping-off point for ferries (three to four daily) to the off-shore island of Amoliani where there are more fine beaches, domatia, camping, tavernas and far fewer people.

Ouranoupolis (Ουρανούπολη) The village of Ouranoupolis is at the northern end of secular Athos. The most prominent feature is the 14th-century tower built to guard what was then a dependency of Vatopediou monastery. A building housing a pharmacy in a side street, one block back from the waterfront, is, despite appearances, actually early 20th century. It once housed a monastic copper works. Most of the village was founded in 1922–23 by refugees from Asia Minor.

As well as the ferry for pilgrims to Athos, boats run tourist trips along the coast of Mt Athos for those unwilling or unable (because of their gender) to set foot there.

Places to Stay & Eat There are a few options in Ouranoupolis, including a good selection of *domatia* (look for signs) and a few budget (ie pilgrim) hotels.

Ouranoupolis Camping (☎ 2377 071 171, fax 2377 071 396) Adult/tent €2.40/3.50. Open 20 May-30 Oct. This shaded site is on the north side of the village next to the beach and is fairly reasonable.

Hotel Galini (☎ 2377 071 217) Singles/doubles €23.50/29.50. This tidy D-class

hotel is located one block back from the main street.

Petrino Spiti (☎ 2377 071 121) Singles/doubles €26.50/35. On the north side of the village is this place; it is hard to miss its stone facade. Rooms are comfortable, though perhaps a little functional.

Hotel Akrogiali (☎ 2377 071 201, fax 2377 071 310) Singles/doubles €29.50/38.20. This D-class hotel is on the waterfront.

Paralia (☎ 2377 071 355) Meals with wine €9. There are a number of 'tourist' restaurants on the beach facing the sea; this is among the better ones, with its fetching blue and white decor.

Mt Athos (Agion Oros)
Αγιον Ορος
This semi-autonomous monastic area, known in Greek as the 'Holy Mountain', occupies most of the Athos Peninsula, and is listed as a World Heritage Site. To enter is to step back in time – literally by 13 days because the Athonite community still uses the Julian calendar, and metaphorically by 500 years as this is a remnant of the Byzantine Empire, which otherwise ended with the fall of Constantinople in 1453.

Setting foot here, however, is not straightforward. Foreign men are allowed to stay in the monasteries for four nights (extendible to six) after completing some formalities – see Obtaining a Permit. Visitors walk from monastery to monastery, enjoying the landscape (Athos is also called the Garden of the Virgin Mary), experiencing a little of the ascetic life of the monks. Despite the rigours associated with a visit to the Holy Mountain, this unique experience can be a very enriching one.

Women may not enter the area at all, unfortunately. The closest they may approach the monasteries is to view them from one of the round-trip cruises from Ouranoupolis. Boats carrying women must stay at least 500m offshore.

History Hermits gravitated to Mt Athos from the very early years of the Byzantine Empire. The first monastery on Athos, Megistis Lavras, was founded between 961 and 963 by St Athanasios with support from Emperor Nikephoros II Phokas. The next emperor, Ioannis Tsimiskis, gave Athos its first charter.

The Athonite community flourished under the continuing support of the Byzantine emperors, whose decrees reinforced its status. The most notorious was that made under Constantine IX Monomahos barring access to women, beardless persons and female domestic animals. This is still in force, except that beards are no longer mandatory and hens (for eggs) are tolerated.

Monasteries continued to be founded, particularly when Christians from outside the area came in during the first crusades. By 1400 there were said to be 40 monasteries, including foundations by Bulgarian, Russian and Serbian princes. The Athos community submitted to Turkish rule after the fall of Constantinople, but managed to retain its semi-independent status. The last monastery to be founded was Stavronikita, in 1542. The community declined over the centuries and today there are 20 ruling monasteries.

In the Greek War of Independence (1821–29) many monasteries were plundered and entire libraries burned by Turkish troops. The present constitution of Athos dates from 1924. It was guaranteed by the 1975 Greek Constitution, and recognises Athos as a part of Greece (all the monks, regardless of their origin, must become Greek nationals), with the Iera Synaxis (holy council, composed of one representative from each of the 20 monasteries) responsible for all the internal administration.

Obtaining a Permit Only 10 foreign adult males may enter Mt Athos per day and 100 Orthodox men may enter. Males under the age of 18 must be accompanied by their father. Males under 18 visiting with a group leader or guardian will need written permission from their father. Start the procedure early, particularly for summer visits, when you may have to wait weeks for a place – make a reservation. Athos can get quite crowded at weekends.

You can start the process from outside Thessaloniki, but you'll have to pass through Thessaloniki anyway in order to pick up your written reservation confirmation. Ordained clergymen should have an introduction from their bishop, and need permission to visit Athos from the Ecumenical Patriarchate of Constantinople – apply at the Metropolis of Thessaloniki (☎ 231 022 7677) Vogatsikou 5.

You must first book a date for your visit. This is handled by the Mount Athos Pilgrims' Office (☎ 231 083 3733, fax 231 086 1811) at Leoforos Karamanli 14, just east of the Thessaloniki Exhibition Site. This office is open 8.30am to 1.30pm and 6pm to 8pm weekdays, excluding Wednesday. Make a telephone booking first. The phone number given above is for English speakers; Greek speakers may phone ☎ 231 086 1611.

The Ecclesiastic Authorities require that you declare your intention to be a pilgrim. Letters of recommendation are no longer required, but you will be asked to mail a photocopy of your passport details and, if you are Orthodox, a photocopied certificate showing your religion (a baptismal certificate will suffice). You must then call in to the Pilgrims' Office to collect your booking confirmation.

Once you have secured a reservation and written confirmation from the Pilgrims' Office, you may now proceed to Ouranoupolis to obtain your *diamonitirion* (permit).

Entering Athos When you arrive in Ouranoupolis, you must first call in at the Pilgrims' Office (☎ 2377 071 422, fax 2377 071 450), on a street to the right, just before a Jet Oil petrol station, as you enter the village. Look for the black and yellow Byzantine flag. The Pilgrims' Office is open 8.10am to 2pm daily.

Officials will check your passport and booking confirmation and issue a diamonitirion for €23.50 (€11.80 for students) to actually enter Athos. Both diamonitirion and passport will be checked as you board the ferry for Athos. Make sure you get to Ouranoupolis early as there may be queues, especially on weekends. Leave video cameras behind – they're prohibited on Athos. Cameras are OK.

A Survival Guide to Mt Athos

If the idea of a peaceful and spiritually enlightening three days on Mt Athos appeals to you, then read on. With a little bit of preparation and foresight you can make your stay as satisfying as possible. If you are female though, forget it. With the exception of a few chickens, all female beings are banned to a distance of 500m from the coastline of Mt Athos. For male visitors, being in the company of males only for three or more days can be a sobering experience. Bear in mind that you are visiting Mt Athos as a pilgrim not a tourist. The lifestyle of Mt Athos has been created for the benefit of its inhabitants not for secular visitors.

Your dress is important. It is politically correct to wear conservative clothing such as long shirts and trousers. Your behaviour is also important. Refrain from being loud or from playing music that will disturb others. You may use a camera but use it discreetly and never photograph a monk without his permission. Should you decide to swim, do so out of sight of a monastery.

When travelling between monasteries make sure that you arrive at your destination before sunset otherwise you may well be locked out. Upon arrival make for the guest quarters (arhondariki) where you will be welcomed by the monk in charge of guests. You will normally be offered a coffee or tsipouro and some loukoumi and then be shown to a guest dormitory which is shared by up to 10 persons.

Unless you travel exclusively by boat, you need to be reasonably fit and prepared to walk for several hours daily in the heat. Carry water and, as food often becomes an obsession among visitors, extra supplies such as biscuits and dried fruit. You will need a map; the best by far is the Road Editions 1:50,000 Mt Athos map showing all the paths and roads in considerable detail. This is not available in Ouranoupolis, so get it in Athens or Thessaloniki before you arrive. It costs €4.40.

Other useful items to take with you include a torch (flashlight), compass, whistle (in case you get lost), small shaving mirror (not all monastic washrooms have mirrors) and mosquito coils. Take extra food since monastic meal times may not always coincide with your activities.

You can only spend one night in each monastery. Some of the heavily visited ones near Karyes request that you phone in advance to be sure of a place (the numbers are listed here, and there will always be an English speaker to take bookings), but this can be frustrating as the telephone is often not answered during daily periods of rest and meditation. You could alternatively fax your request (where available), but you should follow it up with a phone call to confirm your booking.

The Mount Athos timetable is rather out of kilter with the rest of the world – the 'day' begins at sunset – so be prepared for Athos-lag. Many religious services take place at night or early morning and it is considered good form to participate whenever possible. Adjust your body clock to that of the monks and you will cope better. Approach your stay on Mt Athos with an open mind; leave behind your secular cares and worries for a while and unwind spiritually. You will be rewarded.

The boat leaves Ouranoupolis at 9.45am for the small port of Dafni (€2.90). The journey takes about two hours; some intermediate stops are made for monks and other residents, and if you are not heading directly to Karyes you may alight earlier. Once you arrive in Dafni, a bus takes you to Karyes for €1.80.

Alternatively, you can depart from Ierissos at 8am or from Nea Roda at about 9am. This service operates daily between 1 July and 12 September, and daily except Tuesday and Wednesday the rest of the year. This ferry drops you off at Iviron. There is no land access from secular Greece. The morning bus from Thessaloniki connects with the boat departure at Nea Roda from where you can also obtain your diamonitirion without having to visit the main Pilgrims' Office in Ouranoupolis.

Once in the main square of Karyes you are free to start walking to the monastery of your choice for the first night. The monasteries will not expect any further donations

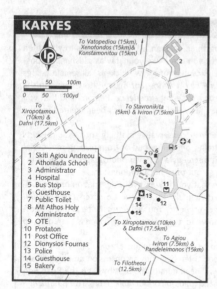

KARYES

To Vatopediou (15km),
Xenofondos (15km) &
Konstamonitou (15km)

To
Xiropotamou
(10km) &
Dafni (17.5km)

To Stavronikita
(5km) & Iviron (7.5km)

1 Skiti Agiou Andreou
2 Athoniada School
3 Administrator
4 Hospital
5 Bus Stop
6 Guesthouse
7 Public Toilet
8 Mt Athos Holy
   Administrator
9 OTE
10 Protaton
11 Post Office
12 Dionysios Fournas
13 Police
14 Guesthouse
15 Bakery

To Xiropotamou (10km)
& Dafni (17.5km)

To Agiou
Iviron (7.5km) &
Pandeleimonos (15km)

To Filotheou
(12.5km)

for accommodating you, but technically you're supposed to spend only one night in each. You might get two nights if you ask politely. The diamonitirion can be extended for another two days in Karyes at the end of the initial four days.

Orientation & Information Dafni, the small port of Athos, has a port authority, police, customs, post office, a couple of general stores selling food and religious artefacts made on Athos, and a cafe. There is no OTE office, but there are cardphones.

The only other town is Karyes, the administrative capital, which includes the headquarters of the Holy Epistasia (council), an inn, bank, post office, OTE, doctor and a couple of shops. The remaining settlements are the 20 monasteries plus 12 scattered *skites* – the isolated dwellings of hermits. The total population of monks and resident laymen is about 1600.

There are no tourist police, but there is a regular police station (☎ 2377 023 212) in Karyes. In addition to Karyes and Dafni, there are police at Agiou Pandeleimonos, Megistis Lavras, Agias Annis, Zografou and Hiliandariou.

The landscape is dominated in the south by the white peak of Mt Athos; the northern part is densely wooded. Wildlife abounds, the small population and absence of industry (apart from some logging) have virtually turned the area into a nature reserve.

Exploring Athos With a diamonitirion, you are free to roam. There is a reasonable network of unsealed roads, used primarily by service vehicles. You normally get around on foot, following the old paths or, given the sometimes considerable distances involved, by local taxi (☎ 2337 023 266) or by boat.

A caique leaves Agias Annis every day at 9.45am for Dafni, serving intermediate west-coast monasteries or their *arsanas* (landing stage for inland monasteries) and returning from Dafni every afternoon. A less-regular caique serves the east coast (theoretically three times weekly, weather permitting) between Ierissos and Mandraki, the harbour for Megistis Lavras. Another service around the south connects Mandraki and Agias Annis. The caiques are inexpensive (€1).

In **Karyes** you should see the 10th-century **Protaton**, the basilican church opposite the Holy Epistasia, which contains a number of treasures including paintings by Panselinos, the master of the Macedonian School. Karyes itself is a strange place – a ghost town with many derelict buildings testifying to a former, grander era. If you've had a long day, you may decide to stay at the monastery of **Koutloumousiou** (☎ 2377 023 226, fax 2377 023 731) in Karyes. Otherwise, you should decide on your itinerary now.

A popular route is to head for one of the east-coast monasteries, and then to continue to Megistis Lavras, returning to Dafni on the west coast. This can involve some lengthy walks unless you use the caiques, but these can be unreliable.

From Karyes, you can walk to either **Stavronikita** (☎ 2377 023 255) or **Iviron** ☎ 2377 023 248, fax 3377 023 248) on the coast, to continue by caique or coastal paths (easier to follow than the inland paths). Alternatively, you can walk to **Filotheou** (☎ 2377 023 256, fax 2377 023 674) along a pleasant shady path (spring water available) in about

½ hours. About 30 minutes farther on is arakallou (☎ 2377 023 225, fax 2377 023 46). Beyond, the old Byzantine path has een converted into a road, and you face a ½-hour walk (unless a monastic vehicle ives you a lift) to **Megistis Lavras** (☎ 2377 22 586, fax 2377 023 762).

Not only is this the oldest monastery on thos, it is also the only one to remain un-amaged by fire. Its 10th-century structure rotects a number of treasures, including escoes by Theophanes of Crete and the omb of St Athanasios, the founder.

A caique leaves Megistis Lavras at about pm for the skiti of **Agias Annis**. Alterna-vely, you can follow the path around the vilderness of the southern end of the penin-ula. You first approach the skiti of **Timiou rodromou**, then **Agias Triados** on the coast off the main track), then **Kerasia**, and sub-equently Agias Annis, either of which can e used as a base for climbing Mt Athos, al-hough Agias Annis has a better reputation or hospitality.

The climb up **Mt Athos** (2033m) should ot be undertaken lightly, and it is wise not o attempt it alone. It also wouldn't hurt to nform someone of your plans before set-ng off. Remember that it will be cold at the op, and you will need to take food and vater. Water is available from a well at the hapel of Panagia (Virgin Mary), a short istance below the summit. You can return o Dafni from Agias Annis by caique.

An alternative is to head from Karyes to ee the architecturally interesting west-coast nonasteries, including Simonos Petras, linging to a cliff like a Tibetan lamasery. rom Karyes you climb over the central spine f the hills and head down again. **Xiropota-nou** (☎ 2377 023 251, fax 2377 023 733) is ne first you'll come to, with comfortable uest rooms (still lit by oil lamps) and good ood and wine served to guests separately rom the monks. A path leads from here to Dafni; you can follow the coastal path or ake the daily caique which leaves for Agias Annis at 12.30pm, calling at Simonos Pe-ras, Grigoriou, Dionysiou and Pavlou. Or rom Karyes you could head for Filotheou nd then take a path to Simonos Petras.

Simonos Petras (☎ 2377 023 254, fax 2377 023 707), also called Simopetra, is an awesome sight from its arsanas, from which it's a stiff climb to the monastery. The monastery's outside walls are surrounded by wooden balconies – as you walk along these from the guest rooms to the wash-room, you can see the sheer drop beneath your feet. You can't normally get outside the monasteries to experience Athos at night – standing on these balconies in the dark, listening to the swallows and staring down towards the light of a solitary fishing boat is a magical experience.

From Simonos Petras you can descend to a coastal path which branches off the path to the arsanas at a small shrine. The path brings you to **Osiou Grigoriou** (☎ 2377 023 218, fax 2377 023 671), which has a very pleasant position by the sea, and a comfort-able guesthouse by the harbour outside the main monastery building. This has electric light and the rare luxury of showers.

The coastal path from here onwards is quite strenuous as it climbs and descends three times before reaching **Dionysiou** (☎ 2377 023 687, fax 2377 023 686), another cliff-hanger monastery resembling Simonos Petras. One of the treasures of its *katholikon* (main church) is an age-blackened icon claimed as the oldest in Athos, housed in a separate chapel. It is said to have been car-ried round the walls of Constantinople to in-spire its successful defence against a combined Persian and Avar siege in 626. The coastal path continues to **Agiou Pavlou** and Agias Annis.

A road less travelled covers the monaster-ies north of Karyes. Your first stop could be the slightly out-of-the-way **Pandokratoros** (☎ 2377 023 253, 2377 023 685) monastery with its own harbour, or you can keep going to **Vatopediou** (☎ 2377 023 219, fax 2377 023 781), also on the coast. This picturesque monastery is an oddity in that it keeps to the Gregorian (Western) calendar. When Athos was at its height, Vatopediou had a cele-brated school, now in ruins. A coastal path leads to **Esfigmenou** (☎ 2377 023 796, fax 2377 023 938); farther on, little-visited be-cause of its isolation, is **Hiliandariou**

NORTHERN GREECE

(☎ 2377 023 797, 2377 023 129), a Serbian foundation still inhabited by Serbs and noted for its hospitality.

The somewhat hard-to-get-to and humble **Konstamonitou** (☎ 2377 023 228) monastery might be worth a visit if you are really keen, but farther north between the east and west coasts is the Bulgarian monastery, **Zografou** (☎ 2377 023 247). Its name, meaning 'Painter', comes from a miraculous icon not painted by human hands. The northernmost west-coast monastery is **Dohiariou** (☎ 2377 023 245), considered to have some of the best architecture on Athos.

Coming south on the coastal path you reach **Xenofondos** (☎ 2377 023 249, fax 2377 023 631) and then **Agiou Pandeleimonos** (☎ 2377 023 252, fax 2377 023 682), the Russian monastery which welcomes visitors with tea. This enormous building used to accommodate over 1000 monks, who came from Russia in droves in the 19th century. Most of the distinctive Russian-style buildings date from that period and many are now derelict. The monastery was once renowned for the quality of its singing, which has been through a low point in the recent past, but is happily picking up again. Note that accommodation may not be available here. These west-coast monasteries are served by the Ouranoupolis-Dafni ferry.

Many alternative routes are possible using the network of old Byzantine paths – most of which have been recently marked by the Thessaloniki Mountaineering Club, but unmarked logging tracks make it amazingly easy to get lost in the woods. Monks' paths, which cross vehicle tracks and lead directly to and from monasteries, are marked by small roadside crosses.

Getting There & Away Entry to Athos is usually by boat from Ouranoupolis, which is accessible by bus from Thessaloniki's Halkidiki terminal at Karakasi 68 (☎ 231 092 4445). There are seven buses daily (2½ hours, €6.50). The first bus (6am) from Thessaloniki arrives just in time for the boat, but leaves you little time to organise your diamonitirion; otherwise, you need to stay overnight in Ouranoupolis. This gives you a chance to buy easily carried food, and find somewhere to store unwanted gear (probably for a fee). Take only the bare minimum to Athos, as you'll have to lug it round all the time.

You may prefer to store unneeded baggage in Thessaloniki – when you return from Athos to Ouranoupolis, the Thessaloniki bus will be waiting, and you may miss it while recovering luggage. Also, you might want to leave Athos via the east coast boat to Ierissos – no good if all your worldly goods are in Ouranoupolis.

The daily boat from Athos to Ouranoupolis leaves Dafni at noon – there is a fairly rigorous customs check to ensure that you're not taking off with any antiquities (even visiting clerics have been known to snaffle valuable relics).

The morning caique from Agias Annis arrives in Dafni in ample time for the Ouranoupolis boat. The irregular east-coast caique provides an alternative exit to Ierissos.

KAVALA Καβάλα
postcode 655 00 • pop 60,000
Kavala, 163km east of Thessaloniki, is one of the most attractive of Greece's large cities. It spills gently down the foothills of Mt Symvolon to a commodious harbour. The old quarter of Panagia nestles under a massive Byzantine fortress.

Modern Kavala is built over ancient Neopolis, which was the port of Philippi. Mehmet Ali (1769–1849), who became Pasha of Egypt and founder of its last royal dynasty, was born in Kavala. Like Athens and Thessaloniki, its population was almost doubled by the 1923 population exchange with Asia Minor.

Orientation
Kavala's focal point is Plateia Eleftherias. The two main thoroughfares, Eleftheriou Venizelou and Erythrou Stavrou, run west from here parallel with the waterfront Ethnikis Andistasis. The old quarter of Panagia occupies a promontory to the south-east of Plateia Eleftherias. Walk south-east along Eleftheriou Venizelou from Plateia Eleftherias, turn left at the T-junction and

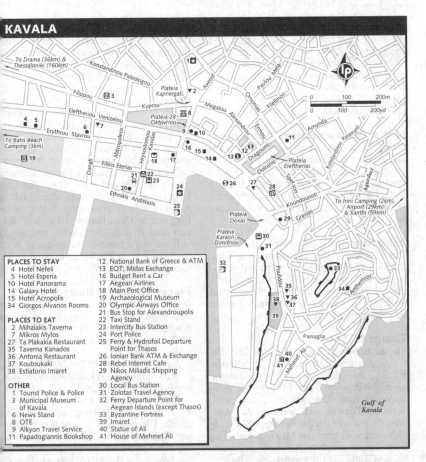

KAVALA

To Drama (36km) & Thessaloniki (160km)

To Batis Beach Camping (3km)

To Irini Camping (2km), Airport (29km) & Xanthi (59km)

Plateia Doxas

Plateia Karaoli-Dimitriou

Gulf of Kavala

Panagia

PLACES TO STAY
4 Hotel Nefeli
5 Hotel Esperia
10 Hotel Panorama
14 Galaxy Hotel
15 Hotel Acropolis
34 Giorgos Alvanos Rooms

PLACES TO EAT
2 Mihalakis Taverna
7 Mikros Mylos
27 Ta Plakakia Restaurant
35 Taverna Kanados
36 Antonia Restaurant
37 Koutoukaki
38 Estiatorio Imaret

OTHER
1 Tourist Police & Police
3 Municipal Museum of Kavala
6 News Stand
8 OTE
9 Alkyon Travel Service
11 Papadogiannis Bookshop

12 National Bank of Greece & ATM
13 EOT; Midas Exchange
16 Budget Rent a Car
17 Aegean Airlines
18 Main Post Office
19 Archaeological Museum
20 Olympic Airways Office
21 Bus Stop for Alexandroupolis
22 Taxi Stand
23 Intercity Bus Station
24 Port Police
25 Ferry & Hydrofoil Departure Point for Thasos
26 Ionian Bank ATM & Exchange
28 Rebel Internet Cafe
29 Nikos Miliadis Shipping Agency
30 Local Bus Station
31 Zolotas Travel Agency
32 Ferry Departure Point for Aegean Islands (except Thasos)
33 Byzantine Fortress
39 Imaret
40 Statue of Ali
41 House of Mehmet Ali

ake the first right (signposted to Panagia and the Castle).

The intercity bus station is on the corner of Hrysostomou Kavalas and Filikis Eterias, near the Thasos ferry quay.

One of the town's most prominent landmarks is an imposing aqueduct built during the reign of Süleyman the Magnificent (1520–66).

Information

Tourist Offices The EOT (☎ 251 022 2425) is on the western side of Plateia Eleftherias. The helpful staff have a map of the town, provide transport information and have lists of the town's hotels and prices. They also have information on the summer drama festivals at Philippi and Thasos. Opening times are 8am to 2pm Monday to Friday.

The City of Kavala Tourism and Development Enterprise (Detak; ☎ 251 083 1388, fax 251 083 1378, e detakav@otenet.gr, w www.detakav.gr) is also responsible for the promotion of tourism to the city.

The tourist police (☎ 251 022 2905) are in the same building as the regular police at Omonias 119.

NORTHERN GREECE

Money The National Bank of Greece is on the corner of Megalou Alexandrou and Dragoumi and has an exchange machine and ATM. There is a 24-hour Ionian Bank exchange machine and ATM on the harbour front, and the Midas Exchange office next to the EOT is open 8.30am to 8pm Monday to Friday and 9am to 8pm Saturday.

Post & Communications The main post office is on the corner of Hrysostomou Kavalas and Erythrou Stavrou. The OTE is on the northern side of Plateia 28 Oktovriou. Access your email at Rebel Internet Cafe (☎ 251 022 0460) at Eleftheriou Venizelou 8; it's open 9am to 1am (€3 per hour).

Bookshops The Papadogiannis Bookshop, Omonias 46 (on the corner with Amynda), stocks a wide range of international newspapers and magazines. It also has a few English-language paperbacks. News Stand at Erythrou Stavrou 32 also sells foreign newspapers and magazines.

Things to See
The **archaeological museum** (☎ 251 022 2335, Erythrou Stavrou 17; admission €1.50, free Sun & public holidays; open 8.30am-3pm Tues-Sun) houses well-displayed finds from ancient Amphipolis, between Thessaloniki and Kavala. Amphipolis was an Athenian colony, and a gold-rush town with mines on Mt Pangaeum. The finds include sculpture, jewellery, grave stelae, terracotta figurines and vases. The museum entrance is at the western end of Ethnikis Andistasis.

Also worth a visit is the **Municipal Museum of Kavala** (☎ 251 022 8689, Filippou 4; admission €1.50; open 8am-2pm Mon-Fri, 9am-1pm Sat). On the ground floor are pictures and sculptures by contemporary Greek artists, including a large collection of works by Polygnotos Vagis (1894–1965), who was born in Potamia on Thasos, and emigrated to the US where he gained an international reputation. On the upper floor is a superb folk-art collection with costumes, jewellery, handcrafts, household items and tools.

Panagia (Παναγία) The pastel houses the narrow, tangled streets of the Panagia quarter are less dilapidated than those of Thessaloniki's Kastra and the area is less commercialised than Athens' Plaka.

The most conspicuous building is the **Imaret**, a huge structure with 18 domes which overlooks the harbour from Poulidou. In Turkish times the Imaret was a hotel for theology students. It has been restored and is now a pleasant cafe and restaurant (see Places to Eat). Within the cafe are some cabinets displaying memorabilia from Mehmet Ali's time. The carefully restored **Turkish house** where Mehmet Ali was born is now open to the public. Ring the bell and the caretaker will show you around; along with other rooms, you will see Ali's harem. The house is at the southern end of Poulidou, near an equestrian statue of Ali.

Places to Stay – Budget
Irini Camping (☎ 251 022 9785, fax 251 022 9748, Perigiali Kavala) Adult/tent €3.80/2.60. This is the military-looking EOT camping ground 2km east of Kavala on the coast road.

Batis Beach (☎ 251 024 3051, Batis Beach) Adult/tent €3.60/2.60. This small site is 3km west of Kavala.

Giorgos Alvanos Rooms (☎ 251 022 8412, Anthemiou 35) Singles/doubles €13/ 20.50. The best deal available for budget travellers and perhaps the cosiest environment in Kavala are the homely domatia in this beautiful 300-year-old house in Panagia.

Hotel Acropolis (☎ 251 022 3543, fax 251 083 2291, Eleftheriou Venizelou 29) Singles €22, doubles with bathroom €50. This C-class property is the closest thing to a budget hotel. Take the lift to reception as you enter the building.

Places to Stay – Mid-Range & Top End
Always bear in mind that the prices listed here may be heavily discounted out of season, sometimes by as much as 50%.

Hotel Panorama (☎ 251 022 4205, fax 251 022 4685, Eleftheriou Venizelou 26 C) ingles/doubles €44/56. This C-class hotel as reasonable rooms.

Hotel Nefeli (☎ 251 022 7441, fax 251 22 7440, Erythrou Stavrou 50) Singles/oubles with bathroom €47/59. Near the aterfront, this C-class hotel has pleasant ooms.

Hotel Esperia (☎ 251 022 9621, fax 251 22 0621, ℮ esperiakav@otenet.gr, Erythrou avrou 44) Singles/doubles €56/73.50. This a tastefully renovated B-class hotel.

Galaxy Hotel (☎ 251 022 4811, fax 251 22 6754, ℮ galaxy@hol.gr, Eleftheriou enizelou 27) Singles/doubles €56/73. his B-class property is Kavala's best hotel, ith spacious, attractively furnished rooms. ll rooms have air-con, refrigerator, tele-hone, radio and bathroom.

laces to Eat

avala's restaurant scene is a vast im-rovement on its accommodation.

Mikros Mylos (☎ 251 022 8132, Dangli) Wholemeal bread €1.50. You can get reat bread and cakes at this modern bakery, ne block south of the Municipal Museum.

Ta Plakakia Restaurant (☎ 251 083 761, Doïranis 4) Mezedes €3. This estaurant, near Plateia Eleftherias, is a con-eniently located place with a huge choice f low-priced mezedes (or *binelikia* as it is nown locally). Turkey in red wine sauce €4.70) is another good bet.

Mihalakis Taverna (☎ 251 022 1185, assandrou 3) Meals €7-8. On Plateia apnergati, this taverna is rather upmarket. he house speciality is *fileto Mihalis* – fil-t steak cooked in a savoury sauce.

Taverna Kanados (☎ 251 083 5172, oulidou 27) Mains €5-7. There are at least nree popular restaurants on Poulidou, op-osite the Imaret. The first is this taverna, hich has a wide-ranging fish menu and ther seafood specialities – try the mussels n tomato sauce.

Antonia Restaurant (☎ 251 022 1711, oulidou 29) Mains €5-7. Next door to anados, this place is recommended by lo-als and is well patronised.

Koutoukaki (☎ 251 083 8583, Poulidou 1) Mains €5-7. Farther along the street

from Antonia, this place also pulls in its fair share of the clientele.

Estiatorio Imaret (☎ 251 083 6286, Poulidou 32) Mains €4.50-7. For a unique eating environment, try this place in the Imaret itself. This is probably Kavala's most atmospheric eating location. Ask for its speciality – *Al Halili cheese,* a tasty hot dip of cheese, tomato and onion. Also scrumptious are the baked mushrooms and baked potato salad.

If you don't want a meal, then the *cafe* in the Imaret is in a lovely serene setting around a courtyard of fruit trees, where you can while away an hour or so playing backgammon or other board games.

Getting There & Away

Air Kavala shares the Hrysoupolis airport, 29km east of town, with Xanthi. There are three flights daily to Athens with Olympic Airways and Aegean Airlines (€60.45). Both airlines also fly twice a week to Düs-seldorf and Stuttgart in Germany. Tickets cost around €214 one way.

Bus From the intercity bus station (☎ 251 022 3593) buses go to Athens (9½ hours, €36, three daily), Xanthi (one hour, €3.40, half-hourly), Keramoti (one hour, €2.80, hourly) and Thessaloniki (two hours, €9.30, hourly). For Philippi, take one of the frequent Drama buses and ask to be let off at the ancient site (20 minutes, €1.10).

Buses for Alexandroupolis (2½ hours, €9.50), which originate in Thessaloniki, depart from outside the 7-11 Snack Bar at Hrysostomou Kavalas 1, opposite the KTEL office. Get departure times and tick-ets from inside the store.

To/From Turkey OSE buses that originate in Thessaloniki depart from Kavala at 4.30am daily except Thursday (€38.20/69 single/return). Student and youth discounts apply to student card-holders.

The buses depart from Alkyon Travel Service (☎ 251 023 1096, fax 251 083 6251, ℮ alkyon-trv@kav.forthnet.gr) at Elefthe-riou Venizelou 26d, next door to Hotel Panorama, where you can also buy tickets.

NORTHERN GREECE

Ferry There are ferries to Skala Prinou on Thasos (1¼ hours, €2.65/13.50 per person/car, hourly). There is also a service running every hour or so during summer from the small port of Keramoti, 46km east of Kavala, to Limenas (40 minutes, €1.20/8.50 per person/car).

In summer there are ferries to Samothraki (four hours, €9.70). Times and frequency vary month by month. Buy tickets and check the latest schedule at Zolotas Travel Agency (☎ 251 083 5671) near the entrance to the Aegean Islands ferry departure point.

There are ferries to Limnos (four to five hours, €9.70), Agios Efstratios (6¾ hours, €11.80) and Lesvos (10 hours, €17). Some services also go through to Rafina (in Attica) and Piraeus via Chios and Samos. Tickets and the latest schedules are available from Nikos Miliadis Shipping Agency (☎ 251 022 6147, fax 251 083 8767), Karaoli-Dimitriou 36.

Hydrofoil There are about nine hydrofoils daily to Limenas (30 minutes, €5) and two to Potos (€8) via Kallirahi, Maries and Limenaria. Purchase tickets at the departure point at the port.

Both hydrofoil and ferry schedules are posted in the window of the port police near the hydrofoil departure point.

Getting Around
To/From the Airport There is no Olympic Airways bus to the airport, but Aegean Airlines runs buses for its own passengers only (€3) from in front of its office (☎ 251 022 9000, fax 251 022 9400), Erythrou Stavrou 1. A taxi to the airport will cost around €16.

Car Budget Rent a Car (☎ 251 022 8785) is on the 1st floor of Eleftheriou Venizelou 35, opposite Hotel Panorama. You can also rent a car from the Europcar agency at Alkyon Travel Service.

Taxi Kavala's bright orange taxis congregate outside the bus station and can be ordered on ☎ 251 083 1600.

PHILIPPI Φίλιπποι
The ancient site of Philippi (fee-lih-pi ☎ 251 051 6470; adult/student €2.30/1.20 open 8am-6.30pm daily) lies 15km inland from Kavala astride the Kavala-Dram road. The original city was called Krenide Philip II seized it from the Thasians in 35 BC because it was in the foothills of M Pangaion, and there was 'gold in them tha hills', which he needed to finance his ba tles to gain control of Greece.

During July and August the Philippi Fe tival is held at the site's theatre. Informatio can be obtained from the EOT in Kavala.

History
A visit to Philippi is worthwhile more f the significance of the events that happene there than for what can actually be seen, s some knowledge of its history is essentia Philippi is famous for two reasons: it wa the scene of one of the most decisive battle in history, and it was the first European cit to accept Christianity.

By mid-1st century BC, Greece had be come the battleground of the Roman Re public, and Philippi was coveted for i strategic position on the Via Egnatia. Afte Julius Caesar's assassination in 44 BC, th assassins (or Liberators, as they calle themselves), led by Brutus and Cassius, as sumed command of the armies stationed i Macedonia and the surrounding province In 42 BC they were confronted at Philip by the combined forces of Mark Anton Caesar's experienced lieutenant, and th 19-year-old Octavian, the dead dictator great-nephew and heir.

In fact, two battles were fought at Philip in the space of three weeks. Initially, Ca sius was defeated by Antony (and commi ted suicide in a fit of despair) while Brut was victorious over Octavian's wing. Late Brutus himself was defeated by Antony, an also chose suicide over surrender. The re of the Republican forces capitulated. Th set the stage for the inevitable conflict be tween Antony and Octavian, which ende 11 years later with Antony's defeat at A tium and subsequent suicide in Egypt, lea ing Octavian the undisputed ruler of Rom

Neopolis (modern Kavala), the port of Philippi, was the European landing stage for travellers from the Orient. And so it was here that St Paul came in AD 49 to embark on his conversion of the pagan Europeans. His overzealous preaching landed him in prison – a misadventure which would be repeated many times in the future.

Exploring the Site

Despite Philippi being the first Christian city in Europe, its people didn't have much luck in their church-building endeavours. The 5th-century **Basilica A** was the first church built in the city, but it was wrecked by an earthquake shortly after completion. The remains can be seen on the northern side of the site (on the right coming from Kavala), near the road, to the west of the theatre.

Their next attempt was the 6th-century **Basilica B**, on the southern side of the site, next to the large and conspicuous forum. This was an ambitious attempt to build a church with a dome, but the structure was top-heavy and collapsed before it was dedicated. In the 10th century its sole remaining part, the narthex, was made into a church – several of its Corinthian columns can be seen.

Philippi's best-preserved building is the **theatre**, which isn't Roman but was built by Philip II. Also in good nick are 50 marble latrines at the southern end of the forum. The site's **museum**, on the north side, houses Roman and Christian finds, and also Neolithic finds from the nearby Dikili Tach site. It was closed for renovation in 1997, but should be up and running again now.

Getting There & Away

Kavala-Drama buses will let passengers off at Philippi (20 minutes, €1.10).

Thrace Θράκη

Thrace (**thrah**-kih) is the north-eastern region of Greece and the backwater of the mainland. If you ask Greeks from elsewhere what it has to offer, chances are most will reply 'nothing', and some will add words to the tune of 'and Turks live there'.

The Turkish population of Thrace, along with the Greek population of Constantinople and the former Greek islands of Imvros (Gökçeada) and Tenedos (Bozcaada), were exempt from the 1923 population exchange. This phenomenon alone sets Thrace apart.

The landscape is dotted with the slender minarets of mosques and villages of Turkish-style, red-roofed houses. There is also a more pronounced Turkish influence in the food, and a greater proliferation of eastern-style bazaars and street vendors.

Besides being of ethnographical interest, the region has some picturesque towns and a varied landscape. It has a long coastline interspersed with wetlands and a hinterland of mountains (the Rodopi Range) covered in thick forest and undergrowth. The mountains are punctuated by valleys through which flow several rivers. The most important is the Evros River, which marks the boundary with Turkey.

Between the coast and the mountains is a fertile plain where sunflowers, grown for oil, create a pretty foreground to the mountainous backdrop. Tobacco is also grown to supply a thriving industry – although the rest of Europe is giving up the noxious weed, smoking among Greeks is increasing at an alarming rate. Another feature of the area is the large number of storks. Look out for their huge, untidy nests on high extremities of buildings.

History

The earliest Thracian tribes were of Indo-European extraction, and the ethnic and cultural origins of the region have a greater affinity with Bulgaria and Turkey than Greece. During the 7th century BC, the Thracian coast was conquered by the most powerful Greek city-states, but in the 6th and 5th centuries BC it was subjugated by the Persians.

After the Persian defeat at the Battle of Plataea, Thrace was governed by Athens. In 346 BC, Philip II of Macedon gained control. During Roman times it was an insignificant backwater, but after the empire split, the region developed culturally and economically, because of its strategic position on the Via Egnatia. Later, its fate was

Phone numbers listed incorporate changes due in Oct 2002; see p83

NORTHERN GREECE

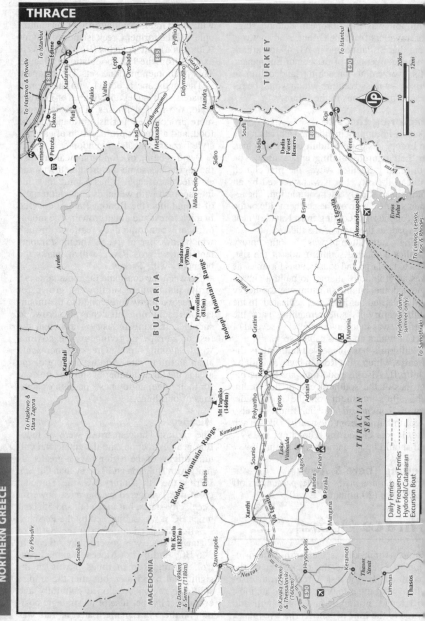

THRACE

NORTHERN GREECE

similar to that of pretty much everywhere else in Greece: invaded by Goths, Huns, Vandals and Bulgars, and finally by the Turks in 1361.

In 1920 the Treaty of Sèvres decreed that all of Thrace should become part of the modern Greek state, but after the 1923 population exchange, eastern Thrace was ceded to Turkey.

XANTHI Ξάνθη
postcode 671 00 • pop 34,889

If you're travelling east from Thessaloniki or Kavala, Xanthi is the first Thracian town you will encounter. The old town has many beautiful, well-maintained 19th-century Turkish dwellings. Xanthi is a lively and flourishing town where Turkish-speaking Muslims make up 10% of the population, and live amicably with Greeks. The town is the centre of Thrace's tobacco-growing industry. The areas to the north, though you technically can visit them, are subject to military control and a pass is usually required.

Orientation & Information
The main thoroughfare is 28 Oktovriou, which runs north-south. Halfway along is Plateia Eleftherias, just west of which on Iroön is a huge, fascinating indoor food market. The bus station is 800m south of the main square at Dimokritou 6. The train station is 2km from town, just off the main Kavala-Xanthi road.

If you continue up 28 Oktovriou from Plateia Eleftherias, you will come to the central square of Plateia Kendriki, with a prominent clock tower on the western side. To reach the old town, continue north along Vasileos Konstandinou, a picturesque cobbled street.

Walk one block up Vasileos Konstandinou, turn right and you'll see the National Bank of Greece on the left. The post office is at A Giorgiou 16, and the OTE is at Michael Vogdou 2; both streets lead west from Plateia Kendriki.

There is no tourist office or tourist police, but the regular police (☎ 2541 022 100), at 28 Oktovriou 223, will do what they can to help.

Old Xanthi
Old Xanthi was built on a hillside overlooking the modern town. The narrow, winding streets have some lovely neoclassical mansions which once belonged to wealthy tobacco merchants. The more modest dwellings also have considerable charm; most are pastel, with overhanging timber-framed floors. Many houses have been restored and many are under restoration. The whole neighbourhood is very photogenic and is worth an idle hour or two just to wander at random.

Places to Stay
Budget hotels are more or less non-existent, so be prepared to fork out a bit extra for accommodation. Prices listed here are usually quite flexible, so be prepared to negotiate a better deal.

Hotel Dimokritos (☎ 2541 025 111, fax 2541 025 537, 28 Oktovriou 41) Singles/doubles €38/53. This fully renovated C-class hotel is near Plateia Kendriki and is very comfortable. Computer users have dedicated modem connections in the rooms.

Hotel Xanthippion (☎ 2541 077 061, fax 2541 077 076, 28 Oktovriou 212) Singles/doubles around €44/53. This is a clean and comfortable C-class option. This hotel has a car park, and is at the southern end of town.

Hotel Nestos (☎ 2541 027 531, fax 2541 027 535, Terma 28 Oktovriou) Singles/doubles €47/55.50. This modern B-class property used to be Xanthi's best hotel. The hotel is 1km south of the town centre. Coming from Kavala by road, it's on the right as you enter the town.

Places to Eat
Klimataria Restaurant (Plateia Kendriki) Meals €7.50-8. This is a long-time local favourite (since 1952). It has a large selection of ready-made food – a healthy lunch of beans, Greek salad and retsina is recommended.

At the top end of Vasileos Konstandinou is a clutch of atmospheric eateries in the Old Town.

Arhontissa (☎ 2541 073 161, Paleologou 1) Mezedes €3.80-4.20. Recommended are

Phone numbers listed incorporate changes due in Oct 2002; see p83

its mince sausages *(soudzoukakia)* and kaseri cheese balls *(kaserokroketes)*.

Myrovolos *(☎ 2541 072 720, Plateia Hristidi)* Mezedes €2.30-4. Open daily all year. It has a wide selection of 'tsipouro mezedes' *(tsipouromezedes)*. Recommended are the garlic aubergines. There's live rembetika music Friday and Saturday.

To Palio Meraki *(☎ 2541 076 581, Plateia Andika)* Mains €5.60. Zucchini balls *(kolokythokeftedes)* are a good vegetarian mezes, while *kokoretsi* (spit-roasted offal) is a good non-vegie bet, as is *yiouvetsi* (pot-baked pasta and beef).

Getting There & Away

Air Xanthi shares the Hrysoupolis airport, 47km away, with Kavala in Macedonia (see the Kavala section for flight details). The Olympic Airways office (☎ 2541 022 944) is at Michael Vogdou 4, near the OTE.

Bus From the bus terminal (☎ 2541 022 684) buses go to Komotini (45 minutes, €3.40, eight daily), Thessaloniki (four hours, €10.30, seven daily) and Athens (10 hours, €38.20, two daily). Thessaloniki buses go via Kavala (one hour, €3.40). There are no direct buses to Alexandroupolis; you must change at Komotini.

Train Trains go to Alexandroupolis (1½ hours, €2.70, six daily) and Thessaloniki (four hours, €6.60, six daily). Thessaloniki-bound intercity services leave Xanthi at 8.49am and 7.12pm. The equivalent services to Alexandroupolis depart at 11.32am and 6.35pm. The 11.32am intercity service connects at Pythio with the train to Istanbul. These intercity trains attract an additional ticket supplement. A taxi to the train station will cost about €2.90.

Getting Around

There are no Olympic Airways buses to Hrysoupolis; a taxi costs €23.50. Alternatively, take a Kavala-bound bus to Hrysoupolis, then a taxi 12km to the airport.

KOMOTINI Κομοτινή
postcode 691 00 • pop 37,036

Komotini (ko-mo-tih-**nee**), 52km east of Xanthi, is the capital of the prefecture of Rodopi. Its population is half Greek and half Turkish-speaking Muslims. It lacks the character of Xanthi and is a generally unremarkable place, but its otherwise ordinariness is compensated for nonetheless by an active student population and the accompanying cafe and bar scene.

Orientation & Information

Komotini is a somewhat disorienting town for first-time arrivals, but everything is within easy walking distance. The bus station is a five-minute walk south of the main square which is the main point of reference. Banks with ATMs, the post office restaurants and places to stay are all within earshot of the central square. Check your email at Zita Net (☎ 2531 037 972) at Apostolou Souzou 14, one block south of the central square; it's open 9am to 3am (€3 per hour).

Things to See

Visit Komotini's outstanding **archaeological museum** *(☎ 2531 022 411, Simeonidi 4; admission free; open 9am-5pm daily)*, which houses well-displayed finds taken from little-known ancient sites in Thrace, most notably from Abdera and Maronia.

The latter was Homer's Ismaros, where Odysseus obtained the wine which he used to intoxicate the Cyclops Polyphemus who

CLINT CURÉ

NORTHERN GREECE

ad imprisoned him. While in this drunken tate, Polyphemus was blinded by Odysseus nd his men, enabling their escape. (The cant remains of the site are near the modern illage of Maronia, 31km south-east of Komotini.) The museum is well signposted.

Have also a look in the **Museum of Folk ife & History** (☎ *2531 025 975, fax 2531 37 145, Agiou Georgiou 13; admission ee; open 10am-1pm daily*). It's worth a isit if you're between buses. Housed in the 'eïdi Mansion, the display has samples of ome wares, manuscripts and costumes. The ore important displays are also labelled in nglish. Turn right from the bus station, alk 100m along Agiou Georgiou Mameli, irn left onto Agiou Georgiou and after another 100m you'll find it on your right.

Places to Stay & Eat

Fanari Komotinis Camping (☎ *2535 031 17, Fanari*) Adult/tent €3.80/2.80. This is he nearest camping ground to Komotini. It s by the sea near the village of Fanari, bout 26km south-east of Komotini.

If you get stuck in Komotini, finding a lace to stay shouldn't be too much of a roblem. Most hotel prices are negotiable.

Hotel Hellas (☎ *2531 022 055, Dimokriou 31*) Singles/doubles €15/20.50. This is basic but OK E-class hotel.

Democritos Hotel (☎ *2531 022 579, fax 2531 023 396, Plateia Vizynou 8*) Singles/ oubles with bathroom €47/65. Renovated n 2001 and close to the central square, ooms here have TV, telephone and air-con.

Hotel Astoria (☎ *2531 035 054, fax 2531 022 707, Plateia Irinis*) Singles/doubles €59/78. This snazzy hotel has neat, modern ooms with air-con.

Psistaria to KTEL (☎ *2531 024 094, Agiou Georgiou Mameli 13*) Gyros with pitta €1.50. This is cheap and easy to find for bus ravellers as it is opposite the bus station.

Ta Adelfia (☎ *2531 020 201, Orfeos 25*) Mayirefta €4.50-50. Komotini's students nay well gorge themselves on fast food and izza, but travellers should seek out the old raditional restaurants such as this one. There is a wide range of mayirefta on offer as well as a la carte dishes.

Getting There & Away

Bus There are frequent departures from Komotini's bus station (☎ 2531 022 912) to Xanthi (45 minutes, €3.40) and Alexandroupolis (70 minutes, €3.80). There are also buses to Thessaloniki (4½ hours, €14.40, eight daily), stopping at Kavala (1½ hours, €6), and to Athens (11 hours, €41.20, one daily).

Train There are six trains daily to both Alexandroupolis (one hour, €1.90) and Thessaloniki (4½ hours, €7.60). The Thessaloniki-bound intercity trains leave Komotini in the morning and early evening. The equivalent services to Alexandroupolis depart at about noon and mid-evening. These trains attract a ticket supplement. The noon eastbound intercity train connects at Pythio with a service to İstanbul.

For further information call the train station on ☎ 2531 022 650. The station is at the end of Pangi Tsaldari in an oddly unmarked cream building.

ALEXANDROUPOLIS
Αλεξανδρούπολη
postcode 681 00 • pop 36,994

Alexandroupolis (ah-lex-an-**droo**-po-lih), the capital of the prefecture of Evros, is a modern and prosaic town with a lively student atmosphere supplemented by a considerable population of young soldiers. Most travellers come here simply in transit heading east to Turkey, or to catch ferries to Samothraki or to the Dodecanese Islands. The maritime ambience of this town, and its year-round liveliness, make it a pleasant stopover.

Alexandroupolis' hotels get surprisingly full, since Greek holiday-makers from northern Evros flock here in July and August. Their numbers are swelled by overlanders who pass through the town en route to Turkey. During these months try to continue your journey to Samothraki, other islands farther south or Turkey; otherwise, reserve accommodation in advance.

Orientation
The town is laid out roughly on a grid system, with the main streets running east-west,

NORTHERN GREECE

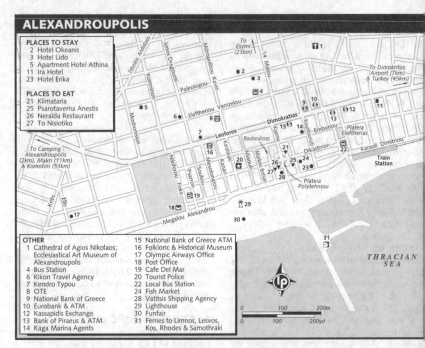

ALEXANDROUPOLIS

PLACES TO STAY
2 Hotel Okeanis
3 Hotel Lido
5 Apartment Hotel Athina
11 Ira Hotel
23 Hotel Erika

PLACES TO EAT
21 Klimataria
25 Psarotaverna Anestis
26 Neraïda Restaurant
27 To Nisiotiko

OTHER
1 Cathedral of Agios Nikolaos;
  Ecclesiastical Art Museum of
  Alexandroupolis
4 Bus Station
6 Kikon Travel Agency
7 Kendro Typou
8 OTE
9 National Bank of Greece
10 Eurobank & ATM
12 Kassapidis Exchange
13 Bank of Piraeus & ATM
14 Kaga Marina Agents
15 National Bank of Greece ATM
16 Folkloric & Historical Museum
17 Olympic Airways Office
18 Post Office
19 Cafe Del Mar
20 Tourist Police
22 Local Bus Station
24 Fish Market
28 Vatitsis Shipping Agency
29 Lighthouse
30 Funfair
31 Ferries to Limnos, Lesvos,
   Kos, Rhodes & Samothraki

parallel with the waterfront, where the lively evening *volta* (promenade) takes place. Karaoli Dimitriou is at the eastern end of the waterfront, with Megalou Alexandrou at the western end.

The town's most prominent landmark is the large 19th-century lighthouse in the middle of the waterfront. The two main squares are Plateia Eleftherias and Plateia Polytehniou, both just one block north of Karaoli Dimitriou.

The train station is on the waterfront just south of Plateia Eleftherias and east of the port where boats leave for Samothraki. The intercity bus station is at Eleftheriou Venizelou 36, five blocks inland. The local bus terminal is on Plateia Eleftherias, just outside the train station.

Information

Official tourist information is handled by the Municipal Tourist Information office at Camping Alexandroupolis (see Places to Stay). The tourist police (☎ 2551 037 424) are at Karaïskaki 6.

The main post office is on the waterfront on the corner of Nikiforou Foka and Megalou Alexandrou. The OTE is on the corner of Mitropolitou Kaviri and Eleftheriou Venizelou.

The Bank of Piraeus and the Eurobank are diagonally opposite each other or Dimokratias and both have ATMs. Other banks with ATMs can be found along the same street. Kassapidis Exchange (☎ 2551 080 910), at Dimokratias 209, changes money and arranges money transfers to and from overseas via Western Union. It is open 8am to 9.30pm Monday to Saturday and 10am to 2pm on Sunday.

For Internet access Cafe Del Mar (☎ 2551 081 187) at Psarron 1 is the best bet. It is open all day and charges around €3 per hour. Foreign newspapers and magazines can be purchased at the Kendro Typou on Dimokratias diagonally opposite the Folkloric and Historical Museum.

Local produce at the Glyfada market

Greek bread, a local speciality – Hania, Crete

Pirean pulses for purchase

It doesn't get any fresher! Rethymno, Crete

Fresh, ripe watermelons for sale – Rhodes

A dazzling variety in Athens' central markets

Fresh fish is a popular choice on Naxos island

Grapes from Corinth at the Glyfada market

Local cafes still pull the crowds.

A welcome respite from the wonders of Crete

Lively outdoor taverna in what was once Athens' old Turkish district, now the touristy Plaka district

Eating and drinking are national pastimes – Iraklio, Crete.

Fresh produce market – Corfu

The phone number for the port police is ☎ 2551 226 468.

Things to See

The outstanding **Ecclesiastical Art Museum of Alexandroupolis** (☎ 2551 026 359, *Plateia Agiou Nikolaou; admission free; 9am-2pm Tues-Fri, 10am-1pm Sat*) is one of the best in the country. It contains a priceless collection of icons and ecclesiastical ornaments brought to Greek Thrace by refugees from Asia Minor. The museum is in the grounds of the Agios Nikolaos Cathedral.

The **Folkloric and Historical Museum** (☎ 2551 028 926, *Cnr Dimokratias & Kanari; admission free; 10.30am-1.30pm, 6.30pm-9.30pm Tues-Sat, by appointment Sun & holidays*) is organised by the Society of the Friends of Antiquities of the Evros Prefecture. The displays offer an insight into the life and culture of Eastern Thrace.

Children will be pleased to learn that there is a lively **funfair** just off the promenade in front of the lighthouse.

Places to Stay

Camping Alexandroupolis (☎/fax 2551 028 735, *Leoforos Makris*) Adult/tent €3.50/2.60. This spacious but rather characterless ground is on the beach 2km west of town. It's nonetheless a clean, well-run site with good facilities. Take a local bus from Plateia Eleftherias to reach the site.

Hotel Lido (☎ 2551 028 808, *Paleologou 15*) Singles/doubles €16.20/22, with bathroom €22/27. This is an outstanding D-class hotel with comfortable rooms, one block north of the bus station.

Hotel Okeanis (☎ 2551 028 830, *fax 2551 034 118, Paleologou 20*) Singles/doubles €40/50. This C-class hotel, almost opposite the Lido, has very comfortable rooms. You can connect your laptop to the Internet from the rooms.

Hotel Erika (☎ 2551 034 115, *fax 2551 034 117, Karaoli Dimitriou 110*) Singles/doubles €44/50. This is a very superior D-class hotel. All rooms have bathroom, telephone, TV and balcony.

Ira Hotel (☎ 2551 023 941, *fax 2551 034 *Dimokratias 179*) Singles/doubles €47/59. The C-class Ira, close to the train station like Hotel Erika, has rather pricey, but small rooms.

Apartment Hotel Athina (☎ 2551 034 492, *fax 2551 037 301, Paleologou 53*) Doubles/suites €80/97. This is an excellent option for groups of two or more. Rooms are self-contained with air-con and modern kitchen facilities. Suites sleep three to four people. Prices are often negotiable.

Places to Eat

Neraïda Restaurant (☎ 2551 022 867, *Plateia Polytehniou*) Main dishes €4.70-6.50. This restaurant is a good choice and has a range of standard fare and some local specialities.

Klimataria (☎ 2551 026 288, *Plateia Polytehniou*) Mayirefta €4. In a similar vein to Neraïda and with similar prices, is this basic place, diagonally opposite Neraïda.

Psarotaverna Anestis (☎ 2551 027 037, *Athanasiou Diakou 5*) Mezedes €5. Opposite the fish market and where freshness is guaranteed is this place, one street east of Kyprou. It looks very unassuming, but has a fine choice of mezedes, especially those with fish. *Mydia saganaki* (chilli mussels) are highly recommended.

To Nisiotiko (☎ 2551 020 202, *Bouboulinas 2*) Fish dishes €7.50. This cosy option with its tasteful blue and white decor has a selection of very tasty and reasonably priced mezedes.

Platanos (☎ 2551 071 772, *Makri*) Fish dishes €6-8. Head out here for a special treat. Platanos is 11km west of Alexandroupolis by the sea in Makri. Dine on excellent fresh fish and other specialities. Try the squid stuffed with cheese. Go by bus (€1.20), every 30 minutes, or taxi (€3.50).

Getting There & Away

Air Alexandroupolis' domestic Dimokritos airport, 7km east of town and near the village of Loutra, does receive occasional international charter flights. Olympic Airways (€79.55) and Aegean Airlines offer about four flights a day to and from Athens and usually extra flights in summer. The Olympic Airlines office (☎ 2551 026 361) is at Ellis 6 while the Aegean Airlines office (☎ 2551 089 150) is at the airport.

Bus From Alexandroupolis' bus station (☎ 2551 026 479) there are frequent buses to Soufli (1½ hours, €3.70), Didymotiho (1¾ hours, €5.30), Orestiada (two hours, €6.40) and Komotini (70 minutes, €3.90). There are buses to Thessaloniki (six hours, €19, six daily) via Xanthi and Kavala.

For what it's worth, there is one bus daily to Athens (12 hours, €41) though it's cheaper and probably more fun to take the boat to Rafina, near Athens.

To/From Turkey There is a daily OSE bus to İstanbul, leaving at 8.30am (five to seven hours, €15). There are currently no private buses running to Turkey. Otherwise, you can take a bus from the intercity bus station to the border town of Kipi (€2.50, three daily), 43km from Alexandroupolis. You cannot walk across the border but it is easy enough to hitch across – you may be lucky and get a lift all the way to İstanbul. Otherwise, take a bus to Ipsala (5km beyond the border) or Keşan (30km beyond the border) from where there are many buses to İstanbul.

To/From Bulgaria There is a private bus service to Plovdiv (six hours, €32.50) and Sofia (seven hours, €32.50) departing from Alexandroupolis on Wednesday and Sunday at 8.30am. Return dates and times from Bulgaria are the same. Contact Kikon Travel Agency (☎ 2551 025 455, fax 2551 034 755), Eleftheriou Venizelou 68 for details.

Train There are trains to Thessaloniki (seven hours, €10, five daily), including one which continues on to Athens and intermediate stations (14 hours, €24). Two of these trains are intercity services; the *Alexandros* terminates in Thessaloniki and the *Vergina* terminates in Athens – both attract a ticket supplement. There are also several trains daily to Dikea via Pythio, Didymotiho, Orestiada (2½ hours, €3.30) and Kastanies for the Turkish border crossing. Note that the border closes at 4pm. For further information call the train station on ☎ 2551 026 395.

To/From Turkey There is one train daily to İstanbul, which currently leaves Alexandroupolis daily at 1pm. This is the IC90 intercity service with a connection to Üzunköpru in Turkey at Pythio. Tickets cost €19.50 and the journey can take 10 hours. The train is hot and crowded in summer – the OSE bus is a marginally better choice.

To/From Bulgaria There is one service daily to Svilengrad (four hours, €8.80) with an ongoing connection to Plovdiv and Sofia. The train currently leaves Alexandroupolis at 5.15am. Double-check with OSE in case of any changes.

Ferry In July and August there are two to three sailings daily to Samothraki. In spring and autumn there are two sailings and in winter, one. Tickets for the *Saos* ferry and the latest departure details may be obtained from Vatitsis Shipping Agency (☎ 2551 026 721, fax 2551 032 007, e saos@orfeasnet.gr), Kyprou 5 (opposite the port). Tickets cost €7.50, a car costs an exorbitant €33 and the trip takes two hours.

There is a weekly ferry to Rhodes, via five other islands en route. Sample base prices are: Limnos (five hours, €12), Lesvos (11½ hours, €16.50) and Rhodes (18 hours, €35). It currently leaves on Tuesday. On Friday there is a ferry to Limnos, Agios Efstratios and Rafina (17¼ hours, €24). Contact Kikon Travel Agency (see Bus) for tickets and reservations.

Hydrofoil Hydrofoil services operate mainly during the summer months, linking Alexandroupolis with Samothraki (one hour, €14.70), Limnos (three hours, €23.50) and mainland ports to the west. Contact Kaga Marina Agents (☎/fax 2551 081 700) at Emboriou 70 for current timetables and tickets.

Getting Around
There is no airport shuttle bus. Take a Loutra-bound bus from Plateia Eleftherias. A taxi (☎ 2551 028 358) to the airport will cost about €4.50.

EVROS DELTA Δέλτα Εβρου

The Evros Delta, 20km south-east of Alexandroupolis, is ecologically one of Europe's most important wetlands. Three hundred species of birds have been recorded, including the last 15 surviving pairs of royal eagles, and more than 200,000 migrating waterfowl spend part of their winter here. Unfortunately, the wetlands are in a highly sensitive area due to their proximity to Turkey, and permission from the security police in Alexandroupolis is technically required in order to visit.

Contact Kikon Travel Agency (☎ 2551 025 455) or the tourist police (☎ 2551 037 424) in Alexandroupolis, or the Feres municipal tourist office (☎ 2555 022 211) for further information on organised tours.

ALEXANDROUPOLIS TO DIDYMOTIHO

North-east of Alexandroupolis the road, railway line and Evros River run close together, skirting the Turkish border. This is a highly sensitive area with many signs prohibiting photography. It's also a lush and attractive region with fields of wheat and sunflowers, and forests of pine trees. In the far north near the village of Petrota there are even a few vineyards.

Feres, 29km north-east of Alexandroupolis, has the interesting 12th-century Byzantine Church of Panagia Kosmosotira. It is signposted from the main road.

Soufli Σουφλί

Farther north, the little town of Soufli, 67km north-east of Alexandroupolis and 31km south of Didymotiho, has lots of character. It has retained a number of its Turkish wattle-and-daub houses and is renowned in Greece for its production of silk. This is because the mulberry tree, upon which the silkworms feed, used to thrive in the region. Unfortunately, most of the mulberry trees have been chopped down to make way for crops, but the town still has one silk factory.

Soufli nonetheless has a fascinating **silk museum** (☎ 2551 023 700, *Eleftheriou Venizelou 73; admission €1.20; open*

10am-5pm Sun-Fri). It has a display of silk-producing equipment and many interesting photographs illustrating the silk-making process. The yellow and brown museum – formerly the Konstandinos Kourtidis mansion – is 400m back from the town's main through road and is clearly signposted.

There is also an Agricultural Bank and a National Bank of Greece in Soufli, both with an ATM.

Places to Stay The only two hotels in town are on the busy and noisy main road. Avoid front rooms if at all possible.

Egnatia Hotel (☎ 2554 024 124, *Vasileos Georgiou 225*) Singles/doubles €18/26.50. If you decide to spend the night, try this D-class hotel.

Hotel Orpheas (☎ 2554 022 922, fax 2554 022 305, *Tsimiski 1*) Singles/doubles with bathroom €35/53. This C-class hotel is on a corner with Vasileos Georgiou.

Getting There & Away Soufli is on the Alexandroupolis-Orestiada bus and train routes. There are six trains daily in either direction and many bus departures.

Dadia Forest Reserve
Δάσος Δαδιάς

Some 8km off the main Alexandroupolis-Orestiada highway is the little-known but highly recommendable Dadia Lefkimmi Soufli Forest, to use its full title. Created in 1980, it consists of a protected zone of some 7290 hectares and a buffer zone of

The grey wolf survives in small numbers in northern Greece & the Dadia Forest area

NORTHERN GREECE

TRUDI CANAVAN

The Story of Silk

The production of silk was first developed in about 2640 BC by the Chinese emperor Hsi Ling Shi. The canny Chinese, knowing they were on to a good thing, kept the secret to themselves for 3000 years until it was finally leaked to the West. The eastward campaigns of Alexander the Great in the 4th century BC were instrumental in bringing the production of silk to the West and in particular to several key centres in Greece. Soufli in eastern Thrace was found to be very favourable thanks to the abundance of mulberry trees in the region, an essential requirement for the production of silk.

Silk is produced from the fine threads of the cocoon of the silkworm before it has had time to metamorphose into a butterfly. Silkworm eggs are first hatched to produce the actual white-coloured silkworms. These are fed a diet that consists entirely of mulberry tree leaves. A box containing 25g of silkworm eggs will require 1000kg of mulberry leaves in order to produce silk-producing worms. After five stages of development during which the growing and increasingly voracious silkworms are meticulously tended to by the silkworm cultivators – or serologists as they are known – the silkworms climb into specially prepared branches to weave a silken cocoon around themselves in preparation for hatching as butterflies. It is at this point that the hapless worms are asphyxiated and the delicate task of unwinding the silken thread begins. This is a labour-intensive process that once involved many hands. Today the job is done mechanically.

Soufli still produces fine and affordable silks but production is nowhere near the levels it was at between 1920 and 1940 when Soufliote silk was exported in large quantities all over Europe. From worms to royal robes, the story of silk is a fascinating one.

35,170 hectares. Here are some of Europe's last remaining breeding and feeding grounds of rare raptors (birds of prey). Of the 38 known species of European raptors, 36 can be found here, making this site quite unique.

There is an informative **Ecotourist Centre** (☎ 2554 032 209, e ecodadia@otenet.gr, *Dadia; open 10am-4pm daily Dec & Jan, 9am-7pm daily Mar-May & Sept-Nov, 8.30am-8.30pm387 daily June-Aug*) with detailed bilingual wall displays and free slide shows. Visitors can take a minibus to a well-constructed bird hide (€2.20), hire a mountain bike (€3 an hour) and ride up, or opt to take the free walking track and hike up. The track is marked orange for the upward leg and yellow for the (different) downward leg. It takes about an hour to walk up. Binoculars are usually provided at the hide and there is a tripod available for photographers. But you will need at least a 500mm telephoto lens to get any serious joy out of photographing the vultures or other raptors commonly visible at the feeding grounds across the wooded valley.

Places to Stay & Eat *Ecotourist Hostel of Dadia* (☎ 2554 032 263, fax 2554 032 463, *Dadia*) Singles/doubles with breakfast €25/35. You can stay the night in this smart, well-appointed hotel. Snacks can be had in the cafeteria next door, or in the village of Dadia , a 1km walk from the Ecotourist Centre.

Traditional Family Taverna Mains €3.50-4. The best place for hearty grills. Ask for the hot (!) pickled peppers for starters; quench the sting with icy draught retsina.

Getting There & Away Three buses go daily from Soufli to Dadia, leaving at 7.30am, 11.30am and 1.50pm, and returning from Dadia some 15 or 20 minutes later (€0.90).

DIDYMOTIHO Διδυμότειχο
postcode 683 00 • pop 8336
Didymotiho (dih-dih-**mo**-tih-ho) is the most interesting of the towns north of Alexandroupolis, although few tourists venture here. The town's name derives from the double walls that once enclosed it (*didymo* 'twin', *tihos* 'wall').

In Byzantine times it was an important town. When it fell to the Turks in 1361,

Murad I made it the capital. In 1365 he transferred the capital to Adrianople (modern Edirne). The town's most prominent landmark is a large mosque, with a pyramid-shaped roof, on Plateia Kendriki.

Turkish-speaking Muslims comprise 15% of the town's population, and there are also Roma (Gypsies).

Orientation & Information

Almost everything you need is on or near Plateia Kendriki, the central square, which you can't miss because of the mosque.

To get to Plateia Kendriki from the bus station, take the road leading in the direction of the visible minaret and mosque, and turn right into Venizelou, the town's main thoroughfare – the square is at the end. From the rather inconveniently located train station turn left, keep walking to 25 Maïou, and continue along here to Venizelou.

There is no tourist office or tourist police. The OTE and the National Bank of Greece and its ATM are on Plateia Kendriki and the post office is just north of here. Walk along Vasileos Alexandrou, and take the first left into Kolokotroni, and it's on the right.

Things to See

Didymotiho is yet another place to wander in. With the mosque on your left, walk straight ahead from Plateia Kendriki to the picturesque, tree-shaded Plateia Vatrahou (Frog Square), so named because of its frog-shaped fountain. Continue straight ahead up Metaxa. In this area there are many Turkish timber-framed houses. Continue uphill to the **Cathedral of Agios Athanasios**. Next to the cathedral are some well-preserved sections of the town's Byzantine walls.

Back down Metaxa, and left into Vatatzi, sees the **folk museum** (☎ 2553 022 154, Vatatzi 24; admission €0.90; open 5pm-8pm Wed & Thur, 10am-2pm Sat & Sun) on the right. This outstanding museum has displays of Thracian costumes, 19th- and early 20th-century agricultural equipment and household implements, and a reconstructed 1920s kitchen. Call if you wish to visit out of hours.

Construction of the **mosque** on Plateia Kendriki was started by Murad I and finished

by his son, Bayazıt, in 1368. It is the oldest and largest mosque in Europe. Its minaret, which has two intricate ornate balconies, has lost its top, the windows are smashed and the walls are crumbling, but it is still obvious that it must once have been a fine building.

Places to Stay & Eat

Hotel Anesis (☎ 2553 024 850, Vasileos Alexandrou 51) Singles/doubles with bathroom €29.50/41. This is a tidy but rather drab-looking D-class property. Vasileos Alexandrou runs off Plateia Kendriki.

Hotel Plotini (☎ 2553 023 400, fax 2553 022 251, Agias Paraskevis 36) Singles/doubles €35.50/59. This renovated B-class hotel is 1km south of town on the road to Alexandroupolis. If you're coming from Alexandroupolis, it's on the left.

There are fast-food and cheap souvlaki places on Venizelou.

Zythestiatorio Kypselaki (Ypsilantou 10) Lunch with wine €6.50. Open to 5.30pm. Opposite the OTE, this is about the only place resembling a traditional eatery within the central area.

Getting There & Away

There are many buses daily from Alexandroupolis (two hours, €3.50). There are also trains to/from Alexandroupolis (three hours, €2.50, seven daily).

NORTH OF DIDYMOTIHO

From Didymotiho the road continues for another 20km to **Orestiada** (population 14,700). This town was built in the 1920s to house refugees who came from Turkey during the population exchange. It's a modern town with little character. Despite its apparent backwater status, Orestiada has been given a magnificent train station, better than most in Greece. It is the terminus for one intercity train from Thessaloniki.

If you get stuck, there are a couple of budget hotels – see Places to Stay. You can access the Internet at the Komvos Internet Cafe (☎ 2552 082 342) at Lohagou Diamandi 17, round the corner from the Hotel Electra (see Places to Stay & Eat). ATM-equipped banks are clustered around the main square.

NORTHERN GREECE

It's another 19km to **Kastanies**, Greece's northern road border point into Turkey. Unless you're planning to continue to Turkey, there's little point coming here. If you cross the Turkish border, the first town you'll arrive at is the Turkish Thracian town of **Edirne** (Adrianoupolis in Greek), 9km from Kastanies. The town is overlooked by most tourists and retains much of its traditional character.

If you want to cross the border here, bear in mind that the crossing is only open 9am to 4pm, so time your arrival accordingly. However, the only reason anyone would want to cross here is to visit Edirne, since it's way off the Alexandroupolis-İstanbul axis. The morning trains will get you to the border in time for the crossing (see the Alexandroupolis section earlier in this chapter).

Places to Stay & Eat

Hotel Acropolis (☎ 2552 022 277, *Vasileo. Konstandinou 48*) Singles/doubles with bathroom €12/19. This D-class hotel is the cheapest in Orestiada.

Hotel Electra (☎ 2552 023 540, fax 2552 023 133, *A Pantazinou 52*) Singles/doubles €32/42. The best hotel in the area is this rather gaudy-looking hotel. Rooms here have air-con and TV.

Hotel Vienna (☎ 2552 022 578, fax 2552 022 258, *Orestou 50*) Singles/doubles €35/48.50. Somewhat better than Hotel Acropolis is this C-class hotel.

There are plenty of decent places to eat

O Mylos tou Saki (☎ 2552 027 542, *Lohagou Diamandi 8*) Pizzas €4.50. Head to this place for good pizza and pasta meals.

Saronic Gulf Islands
Νησιά του Σαρωνικού

The five Saronic Gulf Islands are the closest group to Athens. The closest, Salamis, is little more than a suburb of the sprawling capital. Aegina is also close enough to Athens for people to commute to work. Along with Poros, the next island south, it is a popular package-holiday destination. Hydra, once famous as the rendezvous of artists, writers and beautiful people, manages to retain an air of superiority and grandeur. Spetses, the most southerly island in the group, is a favourite with British holiday-makers.

Spetses has the best beaches, but these islands are not the place to be if you want long stretches of golden sand. And with the exception of the Temple of Aphaia, on Aegina, the islands have no significant archaeological remains.

Nevertheless, the islands are a popular escape for Athenians. Accommodation can be impossible to find between mid-June and mid-September, and weekends are busy all year round. If you plan to go at these times, it's a good idea to reserve a room in advance.

The islands have a reputation for high prices, which is a bit misleading. What is true is that there are very few places for budget travellers to stay – no camping grounds and only a couple of cheap hotels. There is plenty of good accommodation available if you are happy to pay €45 or more for a double. Mid-week visitors can get some good deals. Food is no more expensive than anywhere else.

The Saronic Gulf is named after the mythical King Saron of Argos, a keen hunter who drowned while pursuing a deer that had swum into the gulf to escape.

SUGGESTED ITINERARIES
One Week
Starting from Athens, head to Aegina (two days), visiting the Temple of Aphaia and exploring the ruins of Paleohora; Poros warrants no more than a brief stopover on the way to tranquil Hydra (three days); continue to Spetses (two days). From Spetses, you can either return to Athens or continue by hydrofoil to one of the ports of the eastern Peloponnese.

Highlights

- The rambling ruins of the old town of Paleohora on Aegina
- Views over the Saronic Gulf from the Temple of Aphaia on Aegina
- Staying in Hydra's gracious old stone mansions
- Exploring the back roads of Spetses by motorcycle

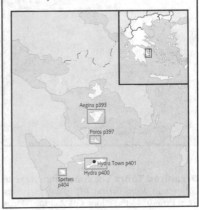

Aegina p393

Poros p397

Hydra Town p401
Hydra p400

Spetses p404

Getting To/From the Saronic Gulf Islands

Ferry At least 10 ferries daily sail from Piraeus' Great Harbour to Aegina Town (1½ hours, €4.40). Four continue to Poros (2½ hours, €6.45), two keep going to Hydra (3½ hours, €7.35) and one goes all the way to Spetses (4½ hours, €10).

Hydrofoil & Catamaran Minoan Lines operates a busy schedule to the islands and nearby Peloponnesian ports with its Flying Dolphin hydrofoils. Services to Aegina leave from Piraeus' Great Harbour, while services to Hydra, Poros and Spetses leave from both the Great Harbour and Zea Marina – be sure to take note of the departure point.

SARONIC GULF ISLANDS

of the Saronic Gulf. It began to emerge as a commercial centre in about 1000 BC. By the 7th century BC, it was the premier maritime power in the region and amassed great wealth through its trade with Egypt and Phoenicia. The silver 'turtle' coins minted on the island at this time are thought to be the first coins produced in Europe. Aegina's fleet made a major contribution to the Greek victory over the Persian fleet at the Battle of Salamis in 480 BC.

Athens, uneasy about Aegina's maritime prowess, attacked the island in 459 BC. Defeated, Aegina was forced to pull down its city walls and surrender its fleet. It did not recover.

The island's other brief moment in the spotlight came during 1827–29, when it was declared the temporary capital of partly liberated Greece. The first coins of the modern Greek nation were minted here.

Aegina has since slipped into a more humble role as Greece's premier producer of pistachio nuts.

Aegina was named after the daughter of the river god, Asopus. According to mythology, Aegina was abducted by Zeus and taken to the island. Her son by Zeus, Aeacus, was the grandfather of Achilles of Trojan War fame.

Organised Tours The cruise ships *Aegean Glory* and *King Saron* offer daily cruises from Piraeus to the islands of Aegina, Poros and Hydra. The cruises leave Piraeus at 9am, returning at about 7pm. Passengers get to spend about an hour on shore at each island – long enough to buy a souvenir and take the obligatory 'been there, done that' photo.

See the Organised Tours section of the Athens chapter for more information about these tours. The official price is €65, including buffet lunch, but tickets are often heavily discounted.

Aegina Αίγινα

postcode 180 10 • pop 11,000
Unassuming Aegina (**eh**-yee-nah) was once a major player in the Hellenic world, thanks largely to its strategic position at the mouth

Getting To/From Aegina

Ferry In summer there are at least 10 ferries daily from Aegina Town to Piraeus (1½ hours, €4.40) as well as services from Agia Marina (1½ hours, €3.25) and Souvala (1¼ hours, €3.10). There are at least three boats daily to Poros (one hour, €3.85) via Methana (40 minutes, €3.25), two daily to Hydra (two hours, €4.70), and one to Spetses (three hours, €7.35). The ferry companies have ticket offices at the quay, where you'll find a full list of the day's sailings.

Hydrofoil These operate almost hourly from 7am to 8pm between Aegina Town and the Great Harbour at Piraeus (35 minutes, €8.50), but there are no services south to Poros, Hydra or Spetses. Tickets are sold at the quay in Aegina Town.

AEGINA

To Piraeus (30km)

To Piraeus (23km)

Saronic Gulf

Souvala

Cape Plakakia

Livadi

Kypseli

Vathy

Agii

Vaia

Cape Tourlos

Temple of Apollo

Aegina

Mt Paliomyli (300m) ▲

Haldeika

Temple of Aphaia 🏛

To Angistri (6.5km) (See Inset)

Moni Agiou Nektariou 🏛

Paleohora

Mesagros

Agia Marina

To Piraeus (28km)

AEGINA

Alones

Moni Hrysoleontissas 🏛

Gianakides

Marathonas

▲ Mt Nikolaki (451m)

Saronic Gulf

Pahia Rahi

● Hellenic Wildlife Rehabilitation Centre

Portes

Daily Ferries	– – – – –
Low Frequency Ferries	- - - - -
Hydrofoil/Catamaran	– · – · –
Excursion Boat	· · · · · ·

Anitseo

▲ Mt Oros (532m)

Perdika

MONI

Vlahides

Sfendouri

0   1   2km
0   0.5   1mi

Cape Pyrgos

To Methana (20km), Poros (27km), Hydra (56km) & Spetses (84km)

To Aegina Town (6.5km)

Angistri ● Metohi

ANGISTRI

Limenaria

Same Scale as Main Map

Services from Piraeus to Agia Marina (30 minutes) and Souvala (25 minutes) are operated by Sea Falcon Lines. Both trips cost €6.75 one way, €11.15 return.

Getting Around Aegina

There are frequent buses running from Aegina Town to Agia Marina (30 minutes, €1.40), via Paleohora and the Temple of Aphaia. Other buses go to Perdika (15 minutes, €0.80) and Souvala (20 minutes, €1.10). Departure times are displayed outside the ticket office which is on Plateia Ethnegersias.

There are numerous places in Aegina to hire motorcycles. Their advertised prices start from around €10.30 per day for a 50cc machine.

AEGINA TOWN

Aegina Town, which is located on the west coast, is the island's capital and main port. The town is a charming and bustling, if slightly ramshackle, place; its harbour is lined with colourful caiques. Several of the town's crumbling neoclassical buildings survive from its glory days as the Greek capital.

Phone numbers listed incorporate changes due in Oct 2002; see p83

Orientation & Information

The ferry dock and nearby small quay used by hydrofoils are on the western edge of town. A left turn at the end of the quay leads to Plateia Ethnegersias, where you'll find the bus terminal and post office. The town beach is 200m farther along. A right turn at the end of the quay leads to the main harbour.

Aegina doesn't have an official tourist office. The 'tourist offices' you'll see advertised on the waterfront are booking agencies, which will do no more than add a 25% commission to the price of whatever service you care to nominate. The tourist police (☎ 2297 027 777) are on Leonardou Lada, opposite the hydrofoil quay. The port police (☎ 2297 022 328) are next to the hydrofoil ticket office at the entrance to the hydrofoil quay.

The OTE is off Aiakou, which heads inland next to the port authority building. The National Bank of Greece is on the waterfront just past Aiakou, and the Credit Bank is 150m farther around the harbour. You can check your email at the Nesant Internet Cafe, Afeas 13, open 10am to 2am daily.

Kalezis Bookshop (☎ 2297 025 956), on the waterfront, has foreign newspapers and books.

Temple of Apollo

'Temple' is a bit of a misnomer for the one Doric column which stands at this site (☎ 2297 022 637; admission €1.50; open 8.30am-3pm Tues-Sun). The column is all that's left of the 5th-century Temple of Apollo, which once stood on the Hill of Koloni. The hill was the site of the ancient acropolis, and there are remains of a Helladic (early) settlement. The site, on the far side of the town beach, also has a **museum**.

Water Park

Aegina's Water Park (☎ 2297 022 540; adult/child €10.30/5.90; open 10am-8pm daily May-Oct), on the coast 1.5km south of Aegina Town, is a big hit with kids.

Places to Stay

Aegina Town doesn't have a huge choice of accommodation.

Hotel Plaza (☎ 2297 025 600, fax 2297 028 404) Singles/doubles with bathroom €20.55/23.50. The Plaza, on the waterfront 100m north of Plateia Ethnegersias, is a long-standing favourite with travellers. It has some good rooms overlooking the sea.

There are several *domatia* at the top of Leonardou Lada with singles/doubles for around €20.55/29.35.

Xenon Pavlou Guest House (☎ 2297 022 795, Aiginitou 21) Singles/doubles with bathroom €26.40/35.20. The Xenon Pavlou is a small family-run guesthouse tucked away behind the Church of Panagytsa on the south-eastern side of the harbour.

Hotel Artemis (☎ 2297 025 195, fax 2297 028 466, e pipinis@otenet.gr, Kanari 20) Singles/doubles with bathroom €29.35/47; air-con extra €5.90. This hotel, north of Plateia Ethnegersias, has a wide range of rooms and offers good discounts for midweek visitors.

Eginitiko Arhontiko (☎ 2297 024 968, fax 2297 024 156, e fotisvoulgarakis@aig .forthnet.gr, Cnr Thomaïdou & Agios Nikoloau) Singles/doubles/triples with bathroom €44/58.70/69, suite €88.05. This fine 19th-century sandstone *arhontiko* (mansion once belonging to an *arhon*, a leading town citizen) has the most interesting rooms in town, particularly the ornate two-room suite.

Places to Eat

The harbour front is lined with countless cafes and restaurants – good for relaxing and soaking up the atmosphere, but not particularly good value.

Locals prefer to head for the cluster of *ouzeria* and restaurants around the fish markets at the eastern side of the harbour.

Mezedopoleio To Steki (☎ 2297 023 910, Pan Irioti 45) Seafood mezedes €3.55-7.35. This tiny place, tucked away behind the fish markets, must be the most popular restaurant in town. It's always packed with people tucking into the local speciality, barbecued octopus (€3.55), over a glass or two of ouzo.

Taverna I Synantasis (☎ 2297 024 309, Afeas 40) Mains €4.70-5.90. This place comes to life on Friday and Saturday night when there's live music from 10pm.

Kritikos Supermarket (☎ *2297 027 772, Pan Irioti 53*) Self-caterers will find most things at this supermarket behind the fish markets.

Delicious local pistachio nuts are on sale everywhere, priced from €3.25 for 500g.

Entertainment

There are dozens of music bars dotted around the maze of small streets behind the waterfront.

One For the Road (☎ *2297 022 340, Afeas 3*) This lively bar draws a young crowd with a mixture of modern Greek and rock music.

Avli (☎ *2297 026 438, Pan Irioti 17*) Avli attracts an older audience with a mixture of '60s music and Latin.

Mousiki Skini (☎ *2298 022 922, Thomaïdou 4*) Mousikini Skini is for serious night owls, with rembetika music on Wednesday, Friday, Saturday and Sunday night from midnight until 5am.

AROUND AEGINA
Temple of Aphaia

The splendid, well preserved Doric Temple of Aphaia (☎ *2297 032 398; admission €2.35; open 8.30am-7pm Mon-Fri, 8.30am-3pm Sat & Sun*), a local deity of pre-Hellenic times, is the major ancient site of the Saronic Gulf Islands. It was built in 480 BC when Aegina was at its most powerful.

The temple's pediments were decorated with outstanding Trojan War sculptures, most of which were spirited away in the 19th century and eventually fell into the hands of Ludwig I (father of King Otho). They now have pride of place in Munich's Glyptothek. The temple is impressive even without these sculptures. It stands on a pine-covered hill and commands imposing views over the Saronic Gulf as far as Cape Sounion.

Aphaia is 10km east of Aegina Town. Buses to Agia Marina (20 minutes, €1.20) stop at the site. A taxi from Aegina Town costs about €5.90.

Paleohora Παλαιοχώρα

The ruins of Paleohora, on a hillside 6.5km east of Aegina Town, are fascinating to explore. The town was the island's capital from the 9th century to 1826 when pirate attacks forced the islanders to flee the coast and settle inland. It didn't do them much good when the notorious pirate Barbarossa arrived in 1537, laid waste the town and carried the inhabitants off into slavery.

The ruins are far more extensive than they first appear. The only buildings left intact are the churches. There are more than two dozen of them, in various states of disrepair, dotted around the hillside. Remnants of frescoes can be seen in some.

In the valley below Paleohora is **Moni Agiou Nektariou**, an important place of pilgrimage. The monastery contains the relics of a hermit monk, Anastasios Kefalas, who died in 1920. When his body was exhumed in 1940 it was found to have mummified – a sure sign of sainthood in Greek Orthodoxy, especially after a lifetime of performing miracle cures. Kefalas was canonised in 1961 – the first Orthodox saint of the 20th century. The enormous new church that has been built to honour him is a spectacular sight beside the road to Agia Marina. A track leads south from here to the 16th-century **Moni Hrysoleontissas**, in a lovely mountain setting.

The bus from Aegina Town to Agia Marina stops at the turn-off to Paleohora.

Hellenic Wildlife Rehabilitation Centre

If you want to get an idea of the kind of toll that hunting takes on the nation's wildlife, pay a visit to the Hellenic Wildlife Rehabilitation Centre (☎ *2297 028 367,* **e** *hlcwfhos@ otenet.gr ,* **w** *www.ekpaz.gr; admission free but donations appreciated; open 11am-1pm daily*), known in Greek as the Elliniko Kentro Perithalifis Agrion Zoon.

At the time of research, the centre was preparing to move from the old jail in Aegina Town to new, custom-built premises about 10km to the south-west, near Pahia Rahi. The centre is on the left about 1km west of Pahia Rahi on the road to Mt Oros.

It is designed to handle the 4000-odd animals and birds that are brought here every year. They come from all over Greece; the majority have been shot.

Volunteers are welcome: the need is greatest in the winter months. The new centre has accommodation for volunteer workers. There is no public transport.

Perdika

The small fishing village of Perdika, 21km south of Aegina Town, is popular for its fish tavernas, with half-a-dozen places overlooking the harbour.

Beaches

Beaches are not Aegina's strong point. The east-coast town of **Agia Marina** is the island's premier tourist resort, but the beach is not great – if you can see it for package tourists. There are a couple of sandy patches that almost qualify as beaches between Aegina and Perdika, at the southern tip of the west coast.

MONI & ANGISTRI ISLETS

Ναμονα & Νααγκίστρι

The Moni and Angistri Islets lie off the west coast of Aegina, opposite Perdika. Moni, the smaller of the two, is a 10-minute boat ride from Perdika – frequent boats (10 minutes, €0.60) make the trip in summer.

Angistri is much bigger with around 500 inhabitants. There's a sandy beach at the port and other smaller beaches around the coast. Both package-holiday tourists and independent travellers find their way to Angistri, which is served by regular boats from Aegina Town and Piraeus.

Poros Πόρος

postcode 180 20 • pop 4000

The island of Poros is little more than a stone's throw from the mainland. The slender passage of water that separates it from the Peloponnesian town of Galatas is only 360m wide at its narrowest point.

Poros was once two islands, Kalavria and Sferia. These days they are connected by a narrow isthmus, cut by a canal for small boats and rejoined by a road bridge. The vast majority of the population lives on the small volcanic island of Sferia, which is more than half-covered by the town of Poros. Sferia hangs like an appendix from the southern coast of Kalavria, a large, well-forested island that has all the package hotels. The town of Poros is not wildly exciting, but it can be used as a base for exploring the ancient sites of the adjacent Peloponnese.

Getting To/From Poros

Ferry There are at least eight ferries daily to Piraeus (2½ hours, €6.45), via Methana and Aegina (one hour, €3.85), two daily to Hydra (one hour, €3.25), and one to Spetses (two hours, €5). Ticket agencies are opposite the ferry dock.

Small boats shuttle constantly between Poros and Galatas (five minutes, €0.30) on the mainland. They leave from the quay opposite Plateia Iroön in Poros Town. Car ferries to Galatas leave from the dock on the road to Kalavria.

Hydrofoil There are six services daily from Piraeus (one hour, €12.95), one from Great Harbour and five from Zea Marina. There are also six hydrofoils south to Hydra (30 minutes, €6.15), two of which continue to Spetses (one hour, €10.60).

The Flying Dolphin agency is on Plateia Iroön, and has a timetable of departures posted outside.

Getting Around Poros

The Poros bus operates almost constantly along a route that starts near the hydrofoil dock on Plateia Iroön in Poros Town. It crosses to Kalavria and goes east along the south coast as far as Moni Zoödohou Pigis (10 minutes, €0.60), then turns around and heads west as far as Neorion Beach (15 minutes, €0.60).

Some of the caiques operating between Poros and Galatas switch to ferrying tourists to beaches in summer. Operators stand on the waterfront and call out their destinations.

There are several places on the road to Kalavria offering bikes for hire, both motorised and pedal-powered. Prices start at €4.40 per day for bikes and €10.30 for 50cc mopeds.

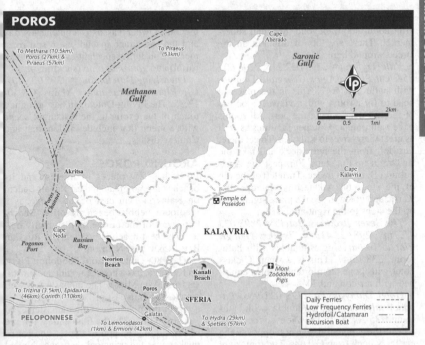

POROS

Cape Aherado

Saronic Gulf

To Methana (10.5km), Poros (27km) & Piraeus (57km)

To Piraeus (53km)

Methanon Gulf

Cape Kalavria

Akritsa

Temple of Poseidon

Cape Neda

KALAVRIA

Pogonos Port

Russian Bay

Neorion Beach

Moni Zoödohou Pigis

Kanali Beach

Poros

To Trizina (3.5km), Epidaurus (46km) Corinth (110km)

SFERIA

PELOPONNESE

Galatas

To Lemonodasos (1km) & Ermioni (42km)

To Hydra (29km) & Spetses (57km)

Daily Ferries	-------
Low Frequency Ferries	---------
Hydrofoil/Catamaran	— · — ·
Excursion Boat	··········

POROS TOWN

Poros Town is the island's main settlement. It's a pretty place of white houses with terracotta-tiled roofs, and there are wonderful views over to the mountains of Argolis. It is a popular weekend destination for Athenians as well as for package tourists and cruise ships.

Orientation & Information

The main ferry dock is at the western tip of Poros Town, overlooked by the striking blue-domed clock tower. A left turn from the dock puts you on the waterfront road leading to Kalavria. The OTE building is on the right after 100m. A right turn at the ferry dock leads along the waterfront facing Galatas. The first square (triangle actually) is Plateia Iroön, where the hydrofoils dock. The bus leaves from next to the kiosk at the eastern end of the square.

The next square along is Plateia Karamis, which is where you'll find the post office.

Coconuts Internet Café (☎ 2298 025 407), on the waterfront, charges €5.90 per hour with a €1.50 minimum. It's open daily 10am to 2pm and 5pm to 11pm.

The National Bank of Greece is 500m farther along the waterfront. There are branches of the Alpha Bank and the Bank Emporiki on Plateia Iroön.

Poros does not have a tourist office. The tourist police (☎ 2298 022 462/256) are at Dimosthenous 10 – behind the Poros high school. Dimosthenous runs inland from the road to Kalavria, starting just beyond the small supermarket.

Suzi's Laundrette Service, next to the OTE, charges €8.80 to wash and dry a 5kg load.

Places to Stay

Poros has very little cheap accommodation.

If things are not too hectic, you may be offered a room by one of the *domatia* owners when you get off the ferry. Otherwise, head left along the waterfront and turn right after about 400m, beyond the small supermarket. There are lots of domatia on the streets around here.

Villa Tryfon (☎ 2298 022 215, 2298 025 854, Off Plateia Agios Georgiou) Doubles with bathroom €47. This is the place to head to for a room with a view. It's on top of the hill overlooking the port. All rooms have bathroom and kitchen facilities as well as great views over to Kalavria. To get there, turn left from the ferry dock and take the first right up the steps 20m past the Agricultural Bank of Greece. Turn left at the top of the steps on Aikaterinis Hatzopoulou Karra, and you will see the place signposted up the steps to the right after 150m.

The Seven Brothers Hotel (☎ 2298 023 412, fax 2298 023 413, e 7brothrs@hol.gr, Plateia Iroön) Singles/doubles with bathroom €38.15/47. This is a smart C-class hotel with large, comfortable rooms equipped with air-con and TV.

Hotel Dionysos (☎ 2298 023 953, Papadopoulou 78) Singles/doubles with bathroom €35.20/58.70. The Dionysos occupies a beautifully restored mansion opposite the car ferry dock from Galatas. The rooms are comfortably furnished with air-con and TV. Breakfast is €4.40.

Places to Eat

Poros has some excellent restaurants.

Taverna Karavolos (☎ 2298 026 158) Mains €3.25-5.90. Open from 7pm. Karavolos means 'big snail' in Greek and is the nickname of cheerful owner Theodoros. Sure enough, snails are a speciality of the house – served in a delicious thick tomato sauce. You'll find a range of imaginative mezedes like *taramokeftedes* (fish roe balls), and a daily selection of main courses like pork stuffed with garlic (€5). Bookings are advisable because Theodoros has only a dozen tables – and a strong local following. The restaurant is signposted behind Cinema Diana on the road to Kalavria.

Taverna Platanos (☎ 2298 024 249, Plateia Agios Georgiou) Mains €4.10-7.35. The Platanos is another popular spot, with seating beneath a large old plane tree

in the small square at the top of Dimosthenous. Owner Tassos is a butcher by day and the restaurant specialises in spit-roast meats. You'll find specialities like *kokoretsi* (offal) and *gouronopoulo* (suckling pig).

The Flying Dutchman (☎ 2298 025 407, Off Plateia Karamanos) Mains €8.50-17.35. The Flying Dutchman has brought a touch of the exotic to the restaurant scene with a menu that includes Indonesian and Chinese dishes.

AROUND POROS

Poros has few places of interest and its beaches are no great shakes. **Kanali Beach**, on Kalavria 1km east of the bridge, is a mediocre pebble beach. **Neorion Beach**, 3km west of the bridge, is marginally better. The best beach is reputedly at **Russian Bay**, 1.5km past Neorion.

The 18th-century **Moni Zoödohou Pigis**, on Kalavria, has a beautiful gilded iconostasis from Asia Minor. The monastery is well signposted 4km east of Poros Town.

From the road below the monastery you can strike inland to the 6th-century **Temple of Poseidon**. The god of the sea and earthquakes was the principal deity worshipped on Poros. There's very little left of this temple, but the walk is worthwhile for the scenery on the way. From the site there are superb views of the Saronic Gulf and the Peloponnese. The orator Demosthenes, after failing to shake off the Macedonians who were after him for inciting the city-states to rebel, committed suicide here in 322 BC.

From the ruins you can continue along the road, which eventually winds back to the bridge. The road is drivable, but it's also a fine 6km walk that will take around two hours.

PELOPONNESIAN MAINLAND

The Peloponnesian mainland opposite Poros can easily be explored from the island.

The celebrated citrus groves of **Lemonodassos** (Lemon Forest) begin about 2km south-east of **Galatas**. There's no public transport, but it's an easy walk.

The ruins of ancient **Troizen**, legendary birthplace of Theseus, lie in the hills near the modern village of Trizina, 7.5km west of Galatas. There are buses to Trizina (15 minutes, €0.80) from Galatas, leaving a walk of about 1.5km to the site.

Getting There & Around

Small boats run between Galatas and Poros (five minutes, €0.30) every 10 minutes. A couple of buses daily depart for Nafplio (two hours, €5.15) and can drop you off at the ancient site of Epidaurus (see the Peloponnese chapter for details on this site).

The district around Galatas is ideal for exploring by bicycle. These can be hired on the seafront in Galatas.

Hydra Υδρα

postcode 180 10 • pop 3000

Hydra (ee-drah) is the Saronic Gulf island with the most style. The gracious white and pastel stone mansions of Hydra Town are stacked up the rocky hillsides that surround the fine natural harbour. Film-makers were the first foreigners to be seduced by the beauty of Hydra. They began arriving in the 1950s when the island was used as a location for the film *Boy on a Dolphin*, among others. The artists and writers moved in next, followed by the celebrities, and nowadays it seems the whole world is welcomed ashore.

If you've been in Greece for some time you may fall in love with Hydra for one reason alone – the absence of kamikaze motorcyclists. Hydra has no motorised transport except for sanitation and construction vehicles. Donkeys (hundreds of them) are the only means of transport.

The name Hydra suggests the island once had plenty of water. Legend has it that the island was once covered with forests, which were destroyed by fire. Whatever the real story, these days the island is virtually barren and imports its water from the Peloponnese.

History

Like many of the Greek islands, Hydra was ignored by the Turks, so many Greeks from the Peloponnese settled on the island to escape Ottoman suppression and taxes. The population was further boosted by an influx of Albanians. Agriculture was impossible, so these new settlers began building boats. By the 19th century, the island had become a great maritime power. The canny Hydriots made a fortune by running the British blockade of French ports during the Napoleonic Wars. The wealthy shipping merchants built most of the town's grand old arhontika from the considerable profits. It became a fashionable resort for Greek socialites, and lavish balls were a regular feature.

Hydra made a major contribution to the War of Independence. Without the 130 ships supplied by the island, the Greeks wouldn't have had much of a fleet with which to blockade the Turks. It also supplied leadership in the form of Georgios Koundouriotis, who was president of the emerging Greek nation's national assembly from 1822 to 1827, and Admiral Andreas Miaoulis, who commanded the Greek fleet. Streets and squares all over Greece are named after these two.

A mock battle is staged in Hydra harbour during the Miaoulia Festival held in honour of Admiral Miaoulis in late June.

Getting To/From Hydra

Ferry There are two ferries daily to Piraeus (3½ hours, €7.35), sailing via Poros (one hour, €3.25), Methana (1½ hours, €4.40) and Aegina (two hours, €4.70). There's also a daily boat to Spetses (one hour, €3.55). Departure times are listed on a board at the ferry dock.

You can buy tickets from Idreoniki Travel (☎ 2298 054 007), next to the Flying Dolphin office overlooking the port.

Hydrofoil Hydra is well served by the Flying Dolphin fleet with up to nine services daily to Piraeus (€13.50) – two to the Great Harbour, the rest to Zea Marina. Direct services take 1¼ hours, but most go via Poros (30 minutes, €5.90) and take 1½ hours. There are also frequent services to Spetses (30 minutes, €6.75), some of which

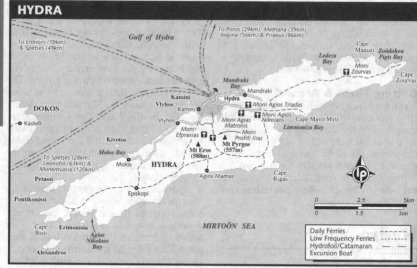

HYDRA

call at Ermioni, adding 20 minutes to the trip. Many of the services to Spetses continue on to Porto Heli (50 minutes, €7.35). There is a daily service to Leonidio, Kyparissi, Gerakas and Monemvasia. This service also continues to Kythira four times weekly.

The Flying Dolphin office (☎ 2298 053 814) is on the waterfront opposite the ferry dock.

Getting Around Hydra

In summer, there are caiques from Hydra Town to the island's beaches. There are also water taxis (☎ 2298 053 690) which will take you anywhere you like. A water taxi to Kamini costs €4.70, and €7.35 to Mandraki and Vlyhos.

The donkey owners clustered around the port charge around €7.35 to transport your bags to the hotel of your choice.

HYDRA TOWN

Most of the action in Hydra Town is concentrated around the waterfront cafes and shops, leaving the upper reaches of the narrow, stepped streets virtually deserted – and a joy to explore.

Orientation

Ferries and hydrofoils both dock on the eastern side of the harbour. The town's three main streets all head inland from the waterfront at the back of the harbour. Walking around from the ferry dock, the first street you come to is Tombazi, at the eastern corner. The next main street is Miaouli, on the left before the clock tower, which is the town's main thoroughfare. The third is Lignou, at the western extreme. It heads inland and links up with Kriezi, which runs west over the hills to Kamini. Lignou is best reached by heading up Votsi, on the left after the clock tower, and taking the first turn right.

Information

There is no tourist office, but Saitis Tours (☎ 2298 052 184, fax 2298 053 469), on the waterfront near Tombazi, puts out a useful free guide called *Holidays in Hydra*. You can find information about the island on the Internet at Ⓦ www.compulink.gr/hydranet.

Most things of importance are close to the waterfront. The post office is on a small side street between the Commercial (Emporiki) Bank and the National Bank of

Greece. The tourist police (☎ 2298 052 205) can be found at the police station opposite the OTE on Votsi from mid-May until the end of September.

You can check your email at the Flamingo Internet Café (☎ 2298 053 485) on Tombazi. It's open noon to 11pm daily and charges €7.35 per hour with a €1.50 minimum.

There's a laundry service in the small market square near the post office. It's open 10am to 1.30pm and 5pm to 8.30pm daily and charges €10.30 to wash and dry a load.

Things to See

The **Historical Archives Museum of Hydra** (☎ 2298 052 355; admission €1.50; open 10am-4.30pm Tues-Sun) is close to the ferry dock on the eastern side of the harbour. It houses a collection of portraits and naval oddments, with an emphasis on the island's role in the War of Independence.

The **Byzantine Museum** (☎ 2298 054 071; admission €1.50; open 10am-5pm Tues-Sun), upstairs at the Monastery of the Assumption of Virgin Mary, houses a collection of icons and assorted religious paraphernalia. The entrance is through the archway beneath the clock tower on the waterfront.

Places to Stay

Accommodation in Hydra is generally of a very high standard, and you pay accordingly. The prices listed here are for the high season, which in Hydra means every weekend as well as July and August.

Places to Stay – Budget

Hotel Dina (☎ 2298 052 248, Stavrou Tsipi) Singles/doubles with bathroom €29.35/35.20. The cheapest rooms are found at this small, cheery place. The high location means great views over the town and harbour.

Pension Theresia (☎ 2298 053 984, fax 2298 053 983, Tombazi) Singles/doubles with bathroom €29.35/44. This popular place is about 300m from the waterfront, and has clean, comfortable rooms with bathroom and a small communal kitchen.

Pension Alkionides (☎/fax 2298 054 055, Off Oikonomou) Singles/doubles with bathroom €35.20/44. The Alkionides is a good budget choice, tucked away about 250m from the port. All rooms have a fridge.

Hotel Hydra (☎/fax 2298 052 102, @ hydrahotel@aig.forthnet.gr, Sahini) Singles/doubles with bathroom €35.20/49.90. This hotel has a great setting overlooking the town from the west. It has large, comfortable rooms. It's a fair haul to get there – more than 100 steps up Sahini from Lignou – but the views over the town and harbour are worth it.

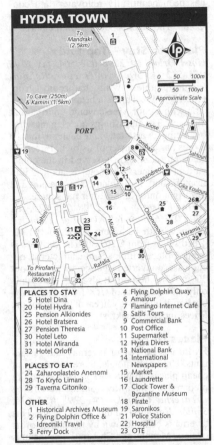

HYDRA TOWN

To Mandraki (2.5km)

To Cave (250m) & Kamini (1.5km)

PORT

Tombazi

Sahtoun

Papandreou

Gika Kouloura

Oikonomou

S Haramis

Sahini

Lignou

Vois

Maouli

Rafalla

To Pirofani Restaurant (800m)

0   50   100m
0   50   100yd
Approximate Scale

PLACES TO STAY	
5	Hotel Dina
20	Hotel Hydra
25	Pension Alkionides
26	Hotel Bratsera
27	Pension Theresia
30	Hotel Leto
31	Hotel Miranda
32	Hotel Orloff

PLACES TO EAT	
24	Zaharoplasteio Anenomi
28	To Kryfo Limani
29	Taverna Gitoniko

OTHER	
1	Historical Archives Museum
2	Flying Dolphin Office & Idreoniki Travel
3	Ferry Dock
4	Flying Dolphin Quay
6	Amalour
7	Flamingo Internet Café
8	Saitis Tours
9	Commercial Bank
10	Post Office
11	Supermarket
12	Hydra Divers
13	National Bank
14	International Newspapers
15	Market
16	Laundrette
17	Clock Tower & Byzantine Museum
18	Pirate
19	Saronikos
21	Police Station
22	Hospital
23	OTE

Places to Stay – Mid-Range

Hotel Leto (☎ 2298 053 385, fax 2298 053 806, Off Miaouli) Doubles with bathroom €64.60-80.70. The Leto is a stylish place with beautiful polished timber floors. Prices include buffet breakfast. It's hidden away in the maze of streets behind the port, but signposted to the left off the first square on Miaouli.

Hotel Miranda (☎ 2298 052 230, fax 2298 053 510, e mirhydra@hol.gr, Miaouli) Doubles with bathroom €52.85-102.75, triples €117.40. Originally the mansion of a wealthy Hydriot sea captain, the Miranda has been beautifully renovated and converted into a very smart hotel. Breakfast is €7.35. The hotel is 300m from the port.

Places to Stay – Top End

Hotel Orloff (☎ 2298 052 564, fax 2298 053 532, e orloff@internet.gr, Rafalia) Singles/doubles with bathroom from €82.20/93.90. This is a beautiful old mansion with a cool, vine-covered courtyard at the back. The furnishings are elegant without being overstated, and each of the 10 rooms has a character of its own. Prices include buffet breakfast, served in the courtyard in summer. The hotel is about 250m from the port; head inland from the port and turn right onto Rafalia after the square.

Hotel Bratsera (☎ 2298 053 971, fax 2298 053 626, e tallos@hol.gr, Tombazi) Doubles with bathroom €102.70-161.40, 4-bed suites from €167.30. The Bratsera is another place with loads of character. It occupies a converted sponge factory about 300m from the port. It also has the town's only swimming pool. It's for guests only, but you'll qualify if you eat at its restaurant. Prices include breakfast.

Places to Eat

Hydra has dozens of tavernas and restaurants. Unlike the hotels, there are plenty of cheap places around – especially if you're prepared to head away from the waterfront.

Taverna Gitoniko (☎ 2298 053 615, Spilios Haramis) Mains €2.95-8.80. This taverna is better known by the names of its owners, Manolis and Christina. The menu is nothing special, but they have built up an enthusiastic local following through the simple formula of turning out consistently good traditional taverna food. Try the beetroot salad – a bowl of baby beets and boiled greens served with garlic mashed potato. The flavours complement each other perfectly. Get in early or you'll have a long wait.

To Kryfo Limani (The Secret Port; ☎ 2298 052 585) Meals €3.55-8.50. Tucked away on a small alleyway is this charming spot with seating beneath a large lemon tree and delicious specials like hearty fish soup (€4.70).

Pirofani Restaurant (☎ 2298 053 175) Mains €5.90-8.80. For something special, head out to this excellent restaurant at Kamini. Owner Theo specialises in desserts – so be sure to leave room for a slice of lemon meringue pie or chocolate and pear cake. The restaurant is at the base of the steps on the inland route between Kamini and Hydra Town; to get there, follow Kriezi over the hill from Hydra Town.

Entertainment

Hydra boasts a busy nightlife. The action is centred on the bars on the south-western side of the harbour where places like *Pirate* (☎ 2298 052 711) and *Saronikos* (☎ 2298 052 589) keep going until almost dawn. Pirate plays Western rock while Saronikos plays Greek.

Amalour (mobile ☎ 69-7746 1357, Tombazi) This sophisticated cafe-bar, 100m from the port, sells a wide range of fresh juices as well as alcohol.

AROUND HYDRA

It's a strenuous but worthwhile one-hour walk up to **Moni Profiti Ilias**, starting from Miaouli. Monks still live in the monastery, which has fantastic views down to the town. It's a short walk from here to the convent of **Moni Efpraxias**.

The beaches on Hydra are a dead loss, but the walks to them are enjoyable. **Kamini**, about 20 minutes walk along the coastal path from town, has rocks and a very small pebble beach. **Vlyhos**, 20 minutes farther on, is an attractive village with a slightly larger pebble beach, two tavernas and a ruined 19th-century stone bridge.

From here, walkaholics can continue to the small bay at **Molos**, or take a left fork before the bay to the inland village of **Episkopi**. There are no facilities at Episkopi or Molos.

An even more ambitious walk is the three-hour stint from Hydra Town to **Moni Zourvas**, in the north-east of the island. Along the way you will pass **Moni Agias Triadas** and **Moni Agios Nikolaos**.

A path leads east from Hydra Town to the pebble beach at **Mandraki**.

Walking Tours

A range of guided walks around the island in spring and autumn is offered by **Lisa Bartsiokas** (☎ 2298 053 836, fax 2298 053 842, e hydragr@otenet.gr; €14.70 per person). The walks take between five and eight hours, including breaks. There must be a minimum of four people.

Diving

Hydra Divers (☎ 2298 053 900, e diveinst@ x-treme.gr, w www.divingteam.gr) is a new business offering dives at a range of locations around the nearby Peloponnese coast. It has introductory dives for €58.70, and packages for experienced divers such as four dives for €123.30. These prices include equipment.

Spetses Σπέτσες

postcode 180 50 ● pop 3700

Pine-covered Spetses, the most distant of the group from Piraeus, has long been a favourite with British holiday-makers.

Spetses' history is similar to Hydra's. It became wealthy through shipbuilding, ran the British blockade during the Napoleonic Wars and refitted its ships to join the Greek fleet during the War of Independence. Spetsiot fighters achieved a certain notoriety through their pet tactic of attaching small boats laden with explosives to the enemy's ships, setting them alight and beating a hasty retreat.

The island was known in antiquity as Pityoussa (meaning 'pine-covered'), but the original forest cover disappeared long ago. The pine-covered hills that greet the visitor today are a legacy of the far-sighted and wealthy philanthropist Sotirios Anargyrios.

Anargyrios was born on Spetses in 1848 and emigrated to the USA, returning in 1914 an exceedingly rich man. He bought two-thirds of the then largely barren island and planted the Aleppo pines that stand today. He also financed the island's road system and commissioned many of the town's grand buildings, including the Hotel Possidonion. He was a big fan of the British public (ie, private) school system, and established Anargyrios & Korgialenios College, a boarding school for boys from all over Greece. British author John Fowles taught English at the college in 1950–51, and used the island as a setting for his novel *The Magus*.

Getting To/From Spetses

Ferry There is one ferry daily to Piraeus (4½ hours, €10), via Hydra (one hour, €3.55), Poros (two hours, €5) and Aegina (three hours, €7.35). Two companies operate the service on alternate days. You'll find departure times on the waterfront outside Alasia Travel (☎ 2298 074 098), which sells tickets. The port police (☎ 2298 072 245) are opposite the quay.

There are also water taxis to Kosta (€10.30), just 15 minutes away on the Peloponnese mainland. There are three buses daily from Kosta to Nafplio (2¼ hours, €5).

Hydrofoil There are up to nine Flying Dolphins daily to Piraeus (2½ hours, €19.10). Most services travel via Hydra (30 minutes, €7.05) and Poros (70 minutes, €10). There are also daily connections to Leonidio (one hour, €7.35) and Monemvasia (1½ hours, €12.65).

Getting Around Spetses

Spetses has two bus routes. There are three or four buses daily from Plateia Agias Mamas in Spetses Town to Agioi Anargyri (40 minutes, €1.40), via Agia Marina and

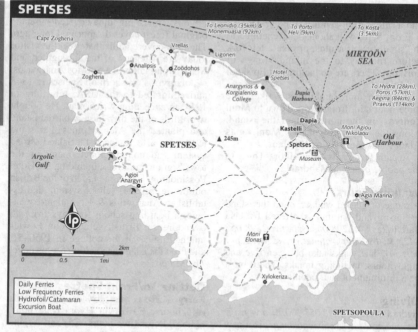

SPETSES

Xylokeriza. Departure times are displayed on a board by the bus stop. There are hourly buses to Ligoneri (€0.60) departing from in front of the Hotel Possidonion.

No cars are permitted on the island. Unfortunately this ban has not been extended to motorbikes, resulting in there being more of the critters here than just about anywhere else.

The colourful horse-drawn carriages are a pleasant but expensive way of getting around. Prices are displayed on a board where the carriages gather by the port.

Boat Water taxis (☎ 2298 072 072) go anywhere you care to nominate from opposite the Flying Dolphin office at Dapia Harbour. Fares are displayed on a board. Sample one-way fares include €17.60 to Agia Marina and €35.20 to Agioi Anargyri. In summer, there are caiques from the harbour to Agioi Anargyri (€5.30 return) and Zogheria (€3.55 return).

SPETSES TOWN

Spetses Town sprawls along almost half the north-east coast of the island. This is a good reflection of the way in which the focal point of settlement has changed over the years.

There's evidence of an early Helladic settlement near the old harbour, about 1.5km east of the modern commercial centre and port of Dapia. Roman and Byzantine remains have been unearthed in the area behind Moni Agios Nikolaos, halfway between the two.

The island is thought to have been uninhabited for almost 600 years before the arrival of Albanian refugees fleeing fighting between the Turks and the Venetians in the 16th century. They settled on the hillside just inland from Dapia, the area now known as Kastelli.

The Dapia district has a few impressive arhontika, but the prettiest part of town is around the old harbour.

Orientation & Information

The quay at Dapia Harbour serves both ferries and hydrofoils. A left turn at the end of the quay leads east along the waterfront on Sotirios Anargyris, skirting a small square where the horse-drawn carriages wait. The road is flanked by a string of uninspiring, concrete C-class hotels, and emerges after 200m on Plateia Agias Mamas, next to the town beach. The bus stop for Agioi Anargyri is next to the beach. The post office is on the street running behind the hotels; coming from the quay, turn right at Hotel Soleil and then left.

The waterfront to the right of the quay is also called Sotirios Anargyris. It skirts Dapia Harbour, passes the grand old Hotel Possidonion and continues west around the bay to Hotel Spetses and becomes the road to Ligoneri.

The main road inland from Dapia is N Spetson, which runs south-west off the small square where horse-drawn carriages wait. It soon becomes Botassi, which continues inland to Kastelli. These two streets are among the few on Spetses with street signs.

There is no tourist office on Spetses. The tourist police (☎ 2298 073 100) are based in the police station – on the well-signposted road to the museum – from mid-May to September.

The OTE is behind Dapia Harbour, opposite the National Bank of Greece. Internet access is available at Delfinia Net Café (☎ 2298 075 051) on Plateia Agias Mamas, open daily 9am to 2am.

Things to See

The **old harbour** is a delightful place to explore. It is ringed by old Venetian buildings, and filled with boats of every shape and size – from colourful little fishing boats to sleek luxury cruising yachts. The shipbuilders of Spetses still do things the trad_itional way and the shore is dotted with the hulls of emerging caiques. The walk from Dapia Harbour takes about 20 minutes. **Moni Agios Nikolaos** straddles a headland at the halfway mark.

The **museum** (☎ 2298 072 994; admission €1.50; open 8.30am-2.30pm Tues-Sun)

Lascarina Bouboulina

Spetses contributed one of the most colourful figures of the War of Independence, the dashing heroine Lascarina Bouboulina. Her exploits on and off the battlefield were the stuff of legend. She was widowed twice by the time the war began – both her shipowning husbands had been killed by pirates, leaving her a very wealthy woman – and she used her money to commission her own fighting ship, the *Agamemnon*, which she led into battle during the blockade of Nafplio.

Bouboulina was known for her fiery temperament and her countless love affairs, and her death was in keeping with her flamboyant lifestyle – she was shot during a family dispute in her Spetses home. Bouboulina featured on the old 50 drachma note, depicted directing cannon fire from the deck of her ship.

---

is housed in the arhontiko of Hadzigiannis Mexis, a shipowner who became the island's first governor. While most of the collection is devoted to folklore items and portraits of the island's founding fathers, there is also a fine collection of ships' figureheads. The museum is hidden away in the back streets of Evangelistras, but is clearly signposted from Plateia Orologiou.

The mansion of Lascarina Bouboulina (see the boxed text), behind the OTE building, has now been converted into a **museum** (☎ *2298 072 416; adult/child €2.95/0.90; open 9am-5pm Tues-Sun*). Billboards around town advertise the starting times for tours in English.

Places to Stay – Budget

The prices listed here are for the high season in July and August. Travellers should be able to negotiate substantial discounts at other times – particularly for longer stays.

Orloff Apartments (☎ *2298 072 246, fax 2298 074 470,* e *orloff_christos@hotmail .com*) Singles/doubles with bathroom €23.50/35.20. Manager Christos has a dozen or so well-equipped studio rooms set in the gardens of the family home on the road leading out to Agioi Anargyri, above the old harbour about 1.5km from the port. All the rooms come with fridge and facilities for making tea and coffee.

Villa Marina (☎ 2298 072 646, Off Plateia Agias Mamas) Singles/doubles with bathroom €29.35/47. This small, friendly place is just off this square beyond the row of restaurants. It has good rooms with bathrooms looking out onto a delightful little garden full of fresh flowers. All rooms have refrigerators and there is a well-equipped communal kitchen downstairs.

Hotel Kamelia (☎ 2298 072 415) Singles/doubles with bathroom €35.20/41.10. This hotel is signposted to the right at the supermarket, 100m past Plateia Agias Mamas on the road that leads inland to Agioi Anargyri. It is almost hidden beneath a sprawling burgundy bougainvillea. Rooms have bathrooms and are spotless.

Otherwise, you might be forced to fall back on one of the uninspiring C- and D-class places that line the waterfront between the ferry dock and Plateia Agias Mamas, or seek help from one of the travel agents.

Places to Stay – Mid-Range & Top End

Hotel Possidonion (☎ 2298 072 308, fax 2298 072 208) Singles/doubles/triples with bathroom €49.90/64.60/73.40. The Possidonion is a wonderful old Edwardian-style hotel that overlooks the seafront just south of the Dapia harbour. It has seen better days, but it remains an imposing building with wide wrought-iron balconies looking out to sea. Prices include breakfast.

Nisia (☎ 2298 075 000, fax 2298 075 012, ✉ nissia@otenet.gr) Doubles around €135. Nisia, about 200m west of Hotel Possidonion, represents the luxury end of the market with apartment-style rooms clustered around a large swimming pool.

Places to Eat

Restaurant Stelios (☎ 2298 073 748) 3 courses from €8.25. The Stelios, between Plateia Agias Mamas and the post office, is a good option with a series of set menus.

Taverna O Lazaros (☎ 2298 072 600) Mains €3.55-6.15. This taverna is in the district of Kastelli, about 600m inland at the top end of Spetson. Treat yourself to a plate of *taramasalata* (€2.35); its homemade version of this popular fish-roe dip is utterly different from the mass-produced muck served at many restaurants. The speciality of the house is baby goat in lemon sauce (€4.70).

Restaurant Patralis (☎ 2298 072 134) Mains €4.10-7.65, fresh fish from €32.30/kg. Fish fans should head out to the Patralis, about 1.5km west of Dapia on the road to Ligoneri. It has a great setting, a good menu and the fish are supplied by the restaurant's own boat. The fish a la Spetses (€7.05), a large tuna or swordfish steak baked with vegetables and lots of garlic, goes down perfectly with a cold beer.

Orloff (☎ 2298 075 255) Mains €4.70-7.05. If character is what you want, you won't find a better place than this, 600m from Plateia Agios Mamas on the coast road to the old harbour. The early-19th century port-authority building has been converted into a stylish restaurant specialising in mezedes.

Kritikos Supermarket (☎ 2298 074 361, Kentriki Agora) Self-caterers can head to this supermarket which is next to Hotel Soleil on the waterfront near Plateia Agias Mamas.

Entertainment

Bar Spetsa (☎ 2298 074 131) For a quiet beer and a great selection of music from the '60s and '70s, try this bar, 50m beyond Plateia Agias Mamas on the road to Agioi Anargyri.

I Vouli (☎ 2298 074 179) Call into this classic old-fashioned wine bar at 10am and you'll realise why nothing very much ever happens on Spetses. It's always busy with locals gossiping over a morning tumbler of wine (€0.90), poured from one of the giant barrels that line the walls. Come along equipped with a few snacks to share around. It overlooks the old harbour about 800m from Plateia Agias Mamas.

AROUND SPETSES

Spetses' coastline is speckled with numerous coves with small, pine-shaded beaches. A 24km road (part sealed, part dirt) skirts the entire coastline, so a motorcycle is the ideal way to explore the island.

The beach at **Ligoneri**, west of town, has the attraction of being easily accessible by bus. **Agia Marina**, to the south of the old harbour, is a small resort with a crowded beach. **Agia Paraskevi** and **Agioi Anargyri**, on the south-west coast, have good, albeit crowded, beaches; both have water sports of every description. A large mansion between the two beaches was the inspiration for the Villa Bourani in John Fowles' *The Magus*.

The small island of **Spetsopoula** to the south of Spetses is owned by the family of the late shipping magnate Stavros Niarchos.

Cyclades Κυκλαδες

The Cyclades (kih-**klah**-dez) are the quint-essential Greek islands – rugged outcrops of rock dotted with brilliant-white buildings offset by vividly painted balconies and bright-blue church domes, all bathed in dazzling light and fringed with golden beaches lapped by aquamarine seas.

Goats and sheep are raised on the mountainous, barren islands, as well as some pigs and cattle. Naxos is the most fertile island, producing potatoes and other crops for export to Athens and neighbouring islands. Many islanders still fish, but tourism is becoming the dominant source of income.

Some islands, especially Mykonos, Santorini (Thira) and Ios, have eagerly embraced tourism – their shores are spread with sun lounges, umbrellas and water-sports equipment. Other islands, such as Andros, Syros, Kea, Serifos and Sifnos, are less visited by foreigners but, thanks to their proximity to the mainland, are popular weekend and summer retreats for Athenians.

To Greek people, Tinos is not a holiday island but the country's premier place of pilgrimage – a Greek Lourdes. Other islands, such as Anafi and the Little Cyclades east of Naxos, are little more than clumps of rock with tiny, depopulated villages.

The Cyclades are so named because they form a circle *(kyklos)* around the island of Delos, one of the country's most significant ancient sites.

SUGGESTED ITINERARIES
One Week
Spend two days on Naxos, exploring the hilltop Kastro and backcountry, lush Tragaea region and villages of Halki, Filoti and Apiranthos. Catch a ferry to Santorini and spend three or four days here, staying in Fira or Oia to view the spectacular sunsets, and visit Ancient Akrotiri and Fira's museums. Take a trip to Thirasia and the volcanic islets. Spend at least one day lazing by the sea. Head to Syros to explore the graceful neoclassical city of Ermoupolis and the hilltop village of Ano Syros for a day, or head to Ios and dance the night away and then recover on the beach.

Highlights

- Spectacular sunsets over Santorini's submerged volcano

- Walks though the verdant countryside of Naxos and Andros, and the drier landscape of Folegandros

- Unspoilt, whitewashed villages on Amorgos, Folegandros and Sifnos

- Ouzo and freshly grilled fish at beachside tavernas

- Uncrowded island beaches and bays with crystal-clear water

- The island-sized archaeological site of ancient Delos

- Hedonistic nightlife on Mykonos, Santorini and Ios

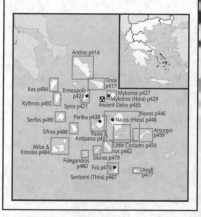

Two Weeks
Spend a day and night on Syros and explore Ermoupolis and Ano Syros. On Mykonos, sample the nightlife, and take an excursion to Ancient Delos. Then follow the one-week itinerary for Naxos and Santorini. Head to Folegandros for a day or two. Soak up the atmosphere of the lovely Hora, and visit one of the beaches. On the way back to Athens, stop off at Sikinos for a couple of days if you like quiet, or at Ios, if you feel the need to party. Amorgos would make a good

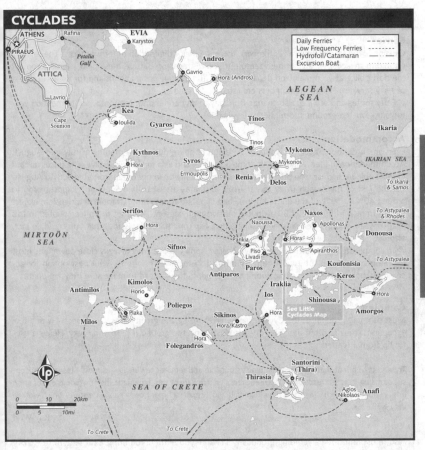

CYCLADES

CYCLADES

Daily Ferries	- - - - -
Low Frequency Ferries	- - · - - ·
Hydrofoil/Catamaran	———
Excursion Boat	· · · · · · · ·

AEGEAN SEA

IKARIAN SEA

MIRTOÖN SEA

MEDITERRANEAN

SEA OF CRETE

alternative to Folegandros. From Amorgos you can make a side trip to the cute little island of Koufonisia before heading back to Athens.

History

The Cyclades have been inhabited since at least 7000 BC, and there is evidence that the obsidian (hard, black volcanic glass used for manufacturing sharp blades) on Milos was exploited as early as 7500 BC. Around 3000 BC, the Cycladic civilisation, a culture famous for its seafarers, appeared. During the Early Cycladic period (3000–2000 BC) there were settlements on Keros, Syros, Naxos, Milos, Sifnos and Amorgos. It was during this time that the famous Cycladic marble figurines were sculpted.

In the Middle Cycladic period (2000–1500 BC), many of the islands were occupied by the Minoans – at Akrotiri, on Santorini, a Minoan town has been excavated. At the beginning of the Late Cycladic period (1500–1100 BC), the Cyclades passed to the Mycenaeans. The Dorians followed in the 8th century BC, bringing Archaic culture with them.

Most of the Cyclades joined the Delian League in 478 BC, and by the middle of the 5th century the islands were members of a

Getting it Straight – Things You Should Know Before You Go

Ferries

Outside high season (June to September), there is a major diminution of ferry services. The services quoted in this chapter are for high season. If you're travelling outside these peak periods, contact the port police at your mainland departure point and at your destination island for an accurate list of ferry services. Telephone numbers are listed in the guide.

Ferry routes and services also change from day to day and month to month, not to mention year to year – on-the-ground information is invaluable.

Accommodation

Everyone in Europe, it seems, wants to go island hopping during the months of July and August. Accommodation in the Cyclades at this time is scarce – and also mighty expensive. The prices quoted in this book are high season prices that will generally only be in operation from mid-July to August. For the rest of the season (May to early-July and late-August to late-September), prices drop to around 40% to 50% of the quoted price. For a standard room with bathroom in a pension, expect to pay from €14.50 to €23.30 a double outside high season. Don't let the prices quoted in this chapter scare you off – or cause you to pass up a trip (or a particular island) that you could, in fact, afford.

To complicate things further, from November to April, the Cyclades virtually close down, and most people involved with the tourist industry return to Athens. Pensions are your best option for accommodation if you're travelling during this period, but call ahead to make sure they are open.

Camping

Most camping grounds in the Cyclades are unlikely to be the green oases you expect – with a few exceptions, they're often desolate, dry and dusty, and the ground is hard and rocky. Here's a useful tip from a reader:

Try and take a tent that is as free-standing as possible and requires few pegs – as most sites seem to consist of mainly crushed road stone. We met Greeks who, aware of this, had made their own pegs out of ankle iron. I ended up purchasing some nine-inch nails and a small hammer from a hardware store, which worked very well.

Ray West

Also, most, but not all, camping grounds will charge you extra if you bring a car (€2.10 to €3.50) or motorbike (€1.50 to €2.10) on site.

Car Hire

Car hire costs €20.30 to €49.30 depending on the island and the season. Expect to pay less from May to June. Some destinations such as Ios, Santorini and Kea charge high prices throughout the tourist season, while others such as Tinos and Paros are far more reasonable.

The Meltemi

The Cyclades are more exposed to the north-westerly *meltemi* wind than other island groups, making for some literally hair-raising, exhausting wind-battered days. The winds can often play havoc with ferry schedules (especially on smaller vessels that ply the Little Cyclades routes). Take this into consideration if you're travelling on a tight schedule.

ully fledged Athenian empire. In the Hellenistic era (323–146 BC) the islands fell under the control of Egypt's Ptolemies and, later, the Macedonians. In 146 BC, the islands became a Roman province and trade links were established with many parts of the Mediterranean, bringing prosperity.

After the division of the Roman Empire into western and eastern entities in AD 395, the Cyclades were ruled from Byzantium (Constantinople). Following the fall of Byzantium in 1204, the Franks gave the Cyclades to Venice, which parcelled the islands out to opportunistic aristocrats. The most powerful was Marco Sanudo (self-styled Duke of Naxos), who acquired Naxos, Paros, Ios, Santorini, Anafi, Sifnos, Milos, Amorgos and Folegandros.

The islands came under Turkish rule in 1537. Neglected by the Ottomans, they became backwaters prone to pirate raids, hence the labyrinthine, hilltop character of their towns – the mazes of narrow lanes were designed to disorientate invaders. Nevertheless, the impact of piracy led to massive depopulation; in 1563 only five out of 16 islands were still inhabited.

In 1771 the Cyclades were annexed by the Russians during the Russian-Turkish War, but were reclaimed by the Ottomans a few years later.

The Cyclades' participation in the Greek War of Independence was minimal, but they became havens for people fleeing islands where insurrections against the Turks had led to massacres. During WWII the islands were occupied by the Italians.

The fortunes of the Cycladics have been revived by the tourism boom that began in the 1970s. Until then, many islanders lived in abject poverty and many more gave up the battle and headed for the mainland in search of work.

Getting To/From & Around the Cyclades

For information on travel within the Cyclades, see the individual island entries.

Air Olympic Airways links Athens with Naxos, Syros, Santorini, Mykonos, Paros

and Milos. Santorini has direct flights to/from Mykonos, Thessaloniki, Iraklio (Crete) and Rhodes, and Mykonos has flights to/from Thessaloniki and Rhodes (see individual island sections for prices).

Ferry Ferry routes tend to separate the Cyclades into western, northern, central and eastern subgroups. Most ferries serving the Cyclades connect one of these subgroups with Piraeus, Lavrio or Rafina on the mainland. The central Cyclades (Paros, Naxos, Ios and Santorini) are the most visited and have the best links with the mainland, usually Piraeus.

The northern Cyclades (Andros, Tinos, Syros and Mykonos) also have very good connections with the mainland. The jumping-off point for Andros is Rafina, but it's possible to access it from Piraeus by catching a ferry to Syros, Tinos or Mykonos and connecting from there.

The western Cyclades (Kea, Kythnos, Milos, Serifos, Sifnos, Folegandros and Sikinos) have less frequent connections with the mainland. Lavrio is the mainland port for ferries serving Kea.

The eastern Cyclades (Anafi, Amorgos, Iraklia, Shinousa, Koufonisia and Donousa) are the least visited and have the fewest links with the mainland. They are best visited from Naxos and Santorini.

There are usually relatively good connections within each of the subgroups, but infrequent connections between them. When you plan your island-hopping, it pays to bear this pattern of ferry routes in mind. However, Paros is the ferry hub of the Cyclades, and connections between different groups are usually possible via Paros if not direct.

The following table gives an overview of high-season ferry services to the Cyclades from the mainland and Crete.

Fast Boats & Catamaran Large high-speed boats and cats are now major players on Cyclades routes. The travel time is usually half that of regular ferries. Seats fill fast in July and August, especially on weekends, so it's worth booking your ticket a day or so in advance.

Ferry Connections to the Cyclades

origin	destination	duration	price	frequency
Agios Nikolaos (Crete)	Milos	7 hours	€14.80	3 weekly
Iraklio (Crete)	Mykonos	9 hours	€18.80	3 weekly
Iraklio	Naxos	7½ hours	€16.15	2 weekly
Iraklio	Paros	7-8 hours	€16.15	2 weekly
Iraklio	Santorini	3¾ hours	€12.05	3 weekly
Iraklio	Syros	10 hours	€17.60	1 weekly
Iraklio	Tinos	10¼ hours	€20	2 weekly
Lavrio	Kea	1¼ hours	€5.30	2 daily
Lavrio	Kythnos	3½ hours	€7	4 weekly
Lavrio	Syros	3½ hours	€10.80	2 weekly
Piraeus	Amorgos	10 hours	€13.10	15 weekly
Piraeus	Anafi	11 hours	€20.10	4 weekly
Piraeus	Donousa	7 hours	€14.20	3 weekly
Piraeus	Folegandros	6-9 hours	€14.80	4 weekly
Piraeus	Ios	7 hours	€15.70	4 daily
Piraeus	Iraklia	6¾ hours	€14	4 weekly
Piraeus	Kimolos	6 hours	€13.40	2 weekly
Piraeus	Koufonisia	8 hours	€13.70	4 weekly
Piraeus	Kythnos	2½ hours	€9.10	3 daily
Piraeus	Milos	5-7 hours	€14.80	2 daily
Piraeus	Mykonos	6 hours	€15.40	3 daily
Piraeus	Naxos	6 hours	€14.80	6 daily
Piraeus	Paros	5 hours	€15.10	6 daily
Piraeus	Santorini	9 hours	€17.70	4 daily
Piraeus	Serifos	4½ hours	€11.60	1 daily
Piraeus	Sifnos	5 hours	€12.80	1 daily
Piraeus	Sikinos	10 hours	€17.40	9 weekly
Piraeus	Syros	4 hours	€13.10	3 daily
Piraeus	Tinos	5 hours	€14	2 daily
Rafina	Amorgos	10¾ hours	€14.70	2 weekly
Rafina	Andros	2 hours	€7.35	2 daily
Rafina	Mykonos	4½ hours	€12.65	2 daily
Rafina	Paros	7 hours	€21.20	3 daily
Rafina	Syros	5 hours	€11	1 daily
Rafina	Tinos	3¾ hours	€11	2 daily
Sitia (Crete)	Milos	9 hours	€16	3 weekly
Thessaloniki	Mykonos	14 hours	€29.05	3 weekly
Thessaloniki	Naxos	15 hours	€27.30	1 weekly
Thessaloniki	Paros	15-16 hours	€28.70	2 weekly
Thessaloniki	Santorini	17¾ hours	€29.05	3 weekly
Thessaloniki	Syros	12 hours	€26.40	1 weekly
Thessaloniki	Tinos	13 hours	€28.50	2 weekly

Andros Ανδρος

postcode 845 00 • pop 8781

Andros is the northernmost island of the Cyclades and the second largest after Naxos, with a coastline of 110km. It is also one of the most fertile, producing citrus fruit and olives, and is unusual in that it has retained its pine forests and mulberry woods. There is plentiful water – indeed, Andros is famous for its water, which is bottled at Sariza spring in the village of Apikia.

More distinctive features are its dovecotes (although Tinos has more of them) and elaborate stone walls. Many of the old water mills and oil mills are now being restored. If you have a sweet tooth, seek out the island's walnut and almond sweets: *kalsounia*, *amygdolota*, and *karidaki*, a deliciously sticky treat of whole, unripe walnuts in a syrup of cinnamon, cloves, nutmeg and honey.

Getting To/From Andros

Ferry At least two ferries daily leave Andros' main port of Gavrio for Rafina (two hours, €7.30). Daily ferries run to Tinos (1½ hours, €5.60) and Mykonos (2½ hours, €7.80); allowing daily connections to Syros and Paros in the high season. Services run direct to Syros three times a week (two hours, €5.80). There is a weekly service to Paros (3½, €10.80), Naxos (4½, €12.20), Kythnos (€11.70) and Kea (€13.20).

Catamaran One catamaran weekly goes to Rafina (one hour, €14.70), Tinos (35 minutes, €10.80), Mykonos (1¼ hours, €15.70), Paros (two hours, €16.80), Amorgos (three hours, €27.50) and Ios (4½, €26).

Getting Around Andros

Around nine buses daily (fewer on weekends) link Gavrio and Hora (30 minutes, €2.50) via Batsi (15 minutes, €1); schedules are posted at the bus stop in Gavrio and Hora and outside Andros Travel in Batsi; otherwise, call ☎ 2282 022 316 for information. A taxi (☎ 2282 022 171) from Batsi

to Hora costs €17.60. Caiques from Batsi go to some of the island's nicest beaches.

GAVRIO Γαύριο

Gavrio, on the west coast, is the main port of Andros. Nothing much happens in Gavrio, but there are lovely beaches nearby.

Orientation & Information

The ferry quay is in the middle of the waterfront and the bus stop is next to it. Turn left from the quay and walk along the waterfront for the post office. The tourist office opposite the quay is rarely open. The port police (☎ 2282 071 213) are on the waterfront.

Places to Stay & Eat

If you decide to stay in town, look for *domatia* signs along the waterfront.

Hotel Galaxy (☎/fax 2282 071 228) Doubles €34.80. This hotel with reasonable rooms is to the left of the quay.

Andros Holiday Hotel (☎ 2282 071 384, fax 2282 071 097) Singles/doubles with aircon €68.40/85.50. Overlooking the beach, this hotel has a restaurant, bar and tennis court. Breakfast is included in the price.

Veggera (☎ 2282 071 077) Dishes €2.30-8.80, plus seafood by the kilo. This is a nice eatery, serving excellent meat dishes, with tables on a large plateia one block back from the waterfront. Turn right from the quay and take the first right after the Batsi road.

To Konaki (☎ 2282 071 733) Dishes €1.50-7.40. On the waterfront, this relaxed ouzeria has local specialities such as *fourtalia* (omelette with savoury sausage and potato).

BATSI Μπατσί
postcode 845 03

Batsi, 8km south of Gavrio, is Andros' major resort. The attractive town encircles a bay with a fishing harbour at one end and a nice sandy beach at the other. There is no EOT, but Andros Travel (☎ 2282 041 252, fax 2282 041 608, e androstr@otenet.gr), near the car park, and Greek Sun Holidays (☎ 2282 041 198, fax 2282 041 239,

CYCLADES

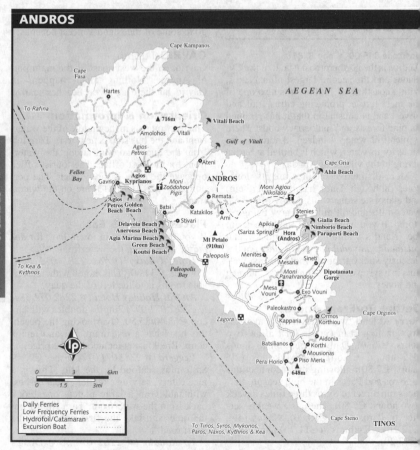

ANDROS

Cape Kampanos

Cape Fasa

Hartes

To Rafina

AEGEAN SEA

▲ 716m

Amolohos   Vitali

↗ Vitali Beach

Agios Petros

Gulf of Vitali

Ateni

Cape Gria

↗ Ahla Beach

ANDROS

Fellos Bay

Gavrio

Agios Kyprianos

Moni Zoödohou Pigis

Remata

Moni Agiou Nikolaou

Agios Petros Beach   Golden Beach

Batsi

Katakilos

Arni

Stenies

Apikia (Sariza Spring)

Hora (Andros)

↗ Gialia Beach
↗ Nimborio Beach
↗ Paraporti Beach

Delavoia Beach ↗
Anerousa Beach ↗
Agia Marina Beach ↗
Green Beach ↗
Koutsi Beach ↗

Stivari

Mt Petalo (910m)

Paleopolis

Menites

Aladinou

Mesaria

Sineti

Dipotamata Gorge

Moni Panahrandou

Paleopolis Bay

To Kea & Kythnos

Mesa Vouni

Exo Vouni

Paleokastro

Zagora

Kapparia

Ormos Korthiou

Cape Orginos

Aidonia

Batsilianos

Korthi

Mousionas

Pera Horio   Piso Meria

▲ 648m

Cape Steno

TINOS

Daily Ferries	– – – – –
Low Frequency Ferries	- - - - - -
Hydrofoil/Catamaran	— ⋅ —
Excursion Boat	⋅⋅⋅⋅⋅⋅⋅⋅⋅

0   3   6km
0   1.5   3mi

*To Tinos, Syros, Mykonos,
Paros, Naxos, Kythnos & Kea*

e greeksun@travelling.gr) are helpful and can handle everything from accommodation to sightseeing and ferry tickets. Car hire is available at Auto Europe (☎ 2282 041 995, fax 2282 041 239) based at Greek Sun Holidays. Bike hire is available on the waterfront for €14.70.

The post office is near the large car park. The taxi rank, bus stop and National and Alpha banks (with ATMs) are all on the main square near the fishing boats. A stepped path leads up from behind the square through lush vegetation sprouting along a watercourse.

Organised Tours

Andros Travel organises island tours from May to October (€17.60 to €23.50) tha take in Menites, Apikia, Moni Agiou Niko laou, Korthi and Paleopolis. Small-group guided half- and full-day walks following old paths through beautiful countryside range from €13.20 to €23.50.

Places to Stay & Eat

Scan the waterfront and the side streets be hind Hotel Chryssi Akti for *domatia* signs

Cavo d'Oro (☎ 2282 041 776, fax 2282 042 706) Doubles €40.80. At the beach end f the waterfront, above the taverna, all ooms here have telephone, TV and air-con.

Karanasos Hotel *(☎ 2282 041 480)* ingles/doubles €40.80/46.60. This hotel, 0m from the beach, has pleasant rooms /ith telephones.

Hotel Chryssi Akti *(☎ 2282 041 237)* ingles/doubles €43.70/52.50. Right on the each, and towering over the domatia be-ind it, this hotel has a pool, and rooms ave TV, phone and balcony.

Likio Studios *(☎ 2282 041 050, fax 2282 42 000)* Double/family studios €52.50/ 2.50. Open year-round. This relaxing lace is set back from the beach amid asses of greenery and geraniums. The pacious studios, with kitchen, TV, phone nd balcony, are spotless. Likio is about 50m past Dino's Rent a Bike.

There are a few decent tavernas along the aterfront. ***Cavo d'Oro*** does a fine clay-pot ousakas; ***Kandouni***, next door, spe-ialises in dishes baked in a wood-fired ven. There's also ***Oti Kalo*** and ***Stamatis*** y the main square.

Entertainment

here are several lively bars on the water-ront, including ***Nameless*** *(☎ 2282 041 88)* by the Avro Hotel, which attracts all e young things, and ***Capricio Music Bar*** *☎ 2282 041 770)*, which plays a Greek and aternational sound mix.

HORA (ANDROS) Χώρα (Ανδρος)

Iora is on the east coast, 35km east of javrio, and is strikingly set along a narrow eninsula. It's an enchanting place full of arprises, and there are some fine old neo-lassical mansions.

Orientation & Information

he bus station is on Plateia Goulandri. To he left as you face the sea is a tourist infor-nation office *(☎ 2282 025 162)*, which op-rates only in July and August, and the main edestrian thoroughfare where the post of-ice, OTE and National Bank of Greece with ATM) are found. Walk along here to-vards the sea for Plateia Kaïri, the central quare, beyond which is the headland. Steps

descend from the square to Paraporti and Nimborio Beaches. The street leading along the promontory ends at Plateia Riva, where there is a bronze statue of an unknown sailor. The ruins of a Venetian fortress stand on an island joined to the tip of the headland by an old, steeply arched bridge.

Museums

Hora has two outstanding museums; both were endowed by Vasilis Goulandris, a wealthy ship owner and Andriot. Contents at the **archaeological museum** *(☎ 2282 023 644, Plateia Kaïri; adults/students €1.50/ free; open 8.30am-3pm Tues-Sun)* include the 2nd century BC Hermes of Andros and finds from the ancient cities of Zagora and Paleopolis.

The **museum of modern art** *(☎ 2282 022 650; adult/student €5.90/3 June-Sept, €3/1.50 Oct-May; open 10am-2pm daily & 6pm-10pm Sat-Mon June-Sept, 10am-4pm daily Oct-May)* has special international ex-hibitions held over June and September. It's down the stairs, to the left of the archaeo-logical museum.

There is also a **nautical museum** *(☎ 2282 022 275; open 10am-2pm & 6pm-9pm Mon-Sat, 10am-2pm Sun)* near the end of the promontory.

Places to Stay & Eat

Karaoulanis Rooms *(☎/fax 2282 024 412, ⓔ riva@otenet.gr)* Doubles/self-contained apartments €30.20/72.50. Run by a young couple, the rooms are in an atmospheric spot in Plakoura, near Nonnas restaurant. Follow the steps down from the museum of modern art to reach it.

Alcioni Inn *(☎ 2282 024 533, Nimbo-rio)* Doubles from €46.60. Located on the waterfront, most rooms in this place are self-contained, some come with balconies with ocean views. Cheaper rooms are also available.

Hotel Egli *(☎ 2282 022 303)* Doubles with shared/private bathroom €30.20/59. This recently renovated hotel is between the two squares, off the right side of the main road as you head towards the sea. Breakfast is included.

CYCLADES

Parea Taverna (☎ *2282 023 721, Plateia Kaïri*) Dishes €1.50-5. Parea has commanding water views and reasonable food.

Nonnas (☎ *2282 023 577*) Dishes €3.50-10.30. This is a lovely *mezedes* place in the old port area known as Plakoura, on the way to Nimborio Beach; to get there continue down the steps past the museum of modern art.

Ta Delfinia (☎ *2282 024 179, Nimborio*) Dishes €2-5.60. On the waterfront, Delfinia has excellent home-cooked fare.

Cabo del Mar (☎ *2282 025 001*) Dishes €3-14.50. Del Mar, at the far end of Nimborio, has a lovely setting and a good reputation.

There are also several good fish tavernas at Gialia, the next beach from Nimborio, including *Balas* and *Ta Gialia*.

AROUND ANDROS

About 2.5km from Gavrio, the **Agios Petros tower** is an imposing circular watchtower dating from Hellenistic times – possibly earlier. Look for the signpost for Agios Petros, also the name of a village.

Along the coast road from Gavrio to Batsi is a turn-off left leading 5km to the 12th-century **Moni Zoödohou Pigis**, where a few nuns still live (open to visitors before noon only). Between Gavrio and Paleopolis Bay are several nice beaches: **Agios Kyprianos** (where a former church is now a beachfront **taverna**), **Delavoia** (nudist), **Green Beach** and **Anerousa**.

An old path running between the villages of **Arni** and **Remata**, both east of Batsi, passes water mills. In Remata, a renovated 19th-century olive-oil mill now houses a **museum**. **Paleopolis**, 9km south of Batsi on the coast road, is the site of Ancient Andros, where the Hermes of Andros was found. There is little to see, but the mountain setting is lovely. **Menites**, southwest of Hora, has springs and a row of drinking fountains with spouts shaped like lions' heads.

From the pretty village of **Mesaria**, it's a strenuous two-hour walk to the 12th-century **Moni Panahrandou**, the island's

largest and most important monastery. **Apikia**, north-west of Hora, is famous for its mineral springs. Near **Sineti**, the wild **Dipotamata Gorge** and its water mills are EU-protected. An old cobbled path, once the main route from Korthi to Hora, leads along the gorge.

The pretty blue-green bay and holiday hamlet at **Ormos Korthiou**, in the south east, has a lot of faded charm and several good restaurants. The Korthi Nautical Club (☎ noka@andros.gr) holds swimming lessons (€14.70 per week) and group windsurfing courses (€23.50 per week) during July and August.

Places to Stay & Eat

Anerousa Beach Hotel (☎ *2282 041 044, fax 2282 041 444*) Singles/doubles with breakfast €60.50/72.30. Just around the bay from Batsi, this plush hotel has its own private bay.

Hotel Korthion (☎ *2282 061 218, fax 2282 061 118*) Singles/doubles €30.50/34.90 with bath. This hotel is on the shore at Ormos Korthiou.

Asimoleyka (☎ *2282 024 150, Ipsilou Syrapouries*) Meals €10.30. Five kilometres from Nimborio Beach, this taverna has views of the hora and makes excellent traditional dishes.

Tinos Τήνος

postcode 842 00 • pop 7747

Tinos is green and mountainous, like nearby Andros. The island is a Greek Orthodox place of pilgrimage, so it's hardly surprising that churches feature prominently among the attractions. The celebrated Church of Panagia Evangelistria dominates the uninteresting capital, while unspoilt hill villages and ornate white-washed dovecotes are rural attractions.

Tinos also has a large Roman Catholic population – the result of its long Venetian occupation. The Turks didn't succeed in wresting the island from the Venetians until 1715, long after the rest of the country had surrendered to Ottoman rule.

shing boat in Sitia, Crete

Where's the rest of the boat? Iraklio, Crete

JON DAVISON

JON DAVISON

GEORGE TSAFOS

ows of colourful wooden fishing boats moored in the old harbour on Kasos island.

The mesmerising blue around Cape Tigani and the rocky islet of Gramvousa – Hania Province, Crete

Rethymno's harbourfront makes the perfect place for a meal and a drink (or two) – Crete.

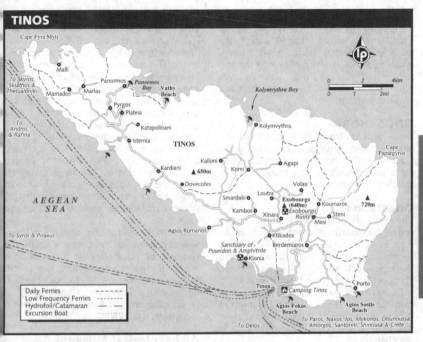

TINOS

Cape Fyra Myti
Malli
To Skyros, Skiathos & Thessaloniki
Mamados
Marlas
Panormos
Panormos Bay
Vathy Beach
Pyrgos
Plateia
To Andros & Rafina
Katapolioani
Isternia
Kolymvythra Bay
Kolymvythra
TINOS
Kalloni
Komi
Agapi
Cape Papargyros
Kardiani
▲ 650m
Volax
Dovecotes
Smardaki
Loutra
Exobourgo ▲ (640m)
Exobourgo Ruins
Koumaros
▲ 729m
AEGEAN SEA
Kambos
Xinara
Mesi
Steni
Agios Romanos
Ktikados
To Syros & Piraeus
Sanctuary of Poseidon & Amphitrite
Berdemiaros
Kionia
Tinos
▲ Camping Tinos
Porto
Agios Fokas Beach
Agios Sostis Beach
To Paros, Naxos, Ios, Mykonos, Dounoussa, Amorgos, Santorini, Shinousa & Crete
To Delos

Daily Ferries
Low Frequency Ferries
Hydrofoil/Catamaran
Excursion Boat

0   2   4km
0   1   2mi

CYCLADES

Getting To/From Tinos

Ferry At least six ferries daily go to Mykonos (30 minutes, €3.50), and one daily to Rafina (3½ hours, €11.15) and Andros (1½ hours, €5.30). There is at least two daily to Syros (50 minutes, €3.70) and Piraeus (six hours, €14).

Four weekly ferries go to Ikaria (3½ hours, €9.60).

Three ferries weekly go to Thessaloniki (14 hours, €28.50), and daily services to Paros (2½ hours, €5.30) and Santorini (5 hours, €5.50).

Two weekly services run to Naxos (4¼ hours, €6) and Iraklio on Crete (10¼ hours, €20).

There is one weekly ferry to Donousa (2½ hours, €10.30), Amorgos (3½ hours, €8.80), Ios (5½ hours, €9) and Skiathos (7½ hours, €17.60).

Fast Boat & Catamaran There are at least three services daily to Mykonos (15 minutes, €5.90) and Rafina (1½ hours, €22.30).

There are daily services to Paros (1¼ hours, €10.50), five weekly to Piraeus (three hours, €28.50), one weekly to Andros (35 minutes, €10.80), daily to Syros (two hours, €6.90) and two weekly to Ios (3 hours, €18). There are also weekly services to Amorgos (2¾ hours, €18.60) and Shinousa (3 hours, €14).

Excursion Boat Excursion boats run daily to Delos (€17.60) 10am Tuesday to Saturday and 9am Sunday June to September.

Getting Around Tinos

There are frequent buses from Tinos (Hora) to Kionia and several daily to Panormos via Pyrgos and Kambos, and to Porto. Buses leave from the station on the waterfront, opposite the National Bank of Greece. The travel agent next to the bank has a timetable in its front window.

However, by far the best way to explore the island is by motorcycle (prices start at €8.80 a day) or car (€20.50 a day); the roads are generally pretty good. Motorcycles and cars can be hired along the waterfront at Hora; try Koulis Rent-a-Car & Moto (☎ 2283 023 955), at the southern end of the waterfront.

TINOS (HORA)

Tinos, also known as Hora, is the island's rather shabby capital and port. The waterfront is lined with cafes and hotels, while the little streets behind have shops and stalls catering to pilgrims and tourists.

Orientation

The new ferry quay is at the north-western end of the waterfront, about 300m from the main harbour, but there are two other, more central, quays where catamarans and smaller ferries dock. When you buy your ticket, check which quay your boat departs from.

Leoforos Megaloharis, straight ahead from the main harbour, is the route pilgrims take to the church. The narrow Evangelistria, to the right facing inland, also leads to the church.

Information

There are many travel agencies supplying information as well as accommodation and car hire services. Windmills Travel & Tourism (☎ 2283 023 398, fax 2283 023 398, e windmills@travelling.gr), at Kionion 2 above the new ferry quay, and Malliaris Travel (☎ 2283 024 241, fax 2283 024 243, e malliaris@thn.forthnet.gr), on the waterfront near Hotel Posidonion, are helpful.

The post office is located at the south-eastern end of the waterfront, just past the bus station and the Agricultural Bank of Greece (with ATM), next door to Hotel Tinion – turn right from the quay. The OTE is situated on Megaloharis, not far from the church. The pebbled town beach of Agios Fokas is a 10-minute walk south from the waterfront.

The port police (☎ 2283 022 348) are on the waterfront, near the Hotel Oceanis.

Church of Panagia Evangelistria

This surprisingly small church (open 8am-8pm daily) is a neoclassical marble confection of white and cream, with a high bell tower. The ornate facade has white, graceful upper and lower colonnades. The final approach is up carpeted steps, doubtless a relief to pious souls choosing to crawl. Inside, the miraculous icon is draped with gold, silver, jewels and pearls, and surrounded by gifts from the hopeful.

A lucrative trade in candles, icon copies, incense and evil-eye deterrents is carried out on Evangelistria. The largest candles, which are about 2m long, cost €3; after an ephemeral existence burning in the church, the wax remains are gathered, melted and resold.

Within the church complex, several museums house religious artefacts, icons and secular artworks. Below the church, a crypt marks the spot where the icon was found. Next to it is a memorial to the sailors killed on the Elli, a Greek ship torpedoed by an Italian submarine in Tinos' harbour on Assumption Day, 1940.

Archaeological Museum

This somewhat disappointing museum (☎ 2283 022 670, Leoforos Megaloharis; admission €1.50; open 8am-3pm Tues-Sun), below the church, has a small collection that includes impressive clay pithoi (large storage jars), a few Roman sculptures and a 1st-century sundial.

Places to Stay

Avoid Tinos on 25 March (Annunciation), 15 August (Feast of the Assumption) and 15 November (Advent), unless you want to join the huddled masses who sleep on the streets at these times.

Camping Tinos (☎ 2283 022 344, fax 2283 025 551) Adult/tent €4.40/2.70, bungalows with/without bathroom €17.40/13.30. This is a lovely site with good facilities south of the town, near Agios Fokas. It also has comfortable bungalow rooms shaded by bursts of bougainvillea. A minibus meets ferries. The camping ground is about a five-minute walk from the ferry

Beware the Evil Eye

When travelling through Greece – particularly in rural areas – you may notice that some bus drivers keep a chain bearing one or two blue stones dangling over the dashboard. Or you may spot a small, plastic blue eye attached to the cross hanging around someone's neck.

Puzzle no longer. The Greeks are not sporting colours in support of their favourite soccer team or to show a particular political leaning. No – they are warding off the evil eye.

The evil eye is associated with envy, and can be cast – apparently unintentionally – upon someone or something that is praised or admired (even secretly). So those most vulnerable to the evil eye include people, creatures or objects of beauty, rarity and value. Babies are particularly vulnerable, and those who admire them will often spit gently on them to repel any ill effects. Adults and older children who are worried about being afflicted by the evil eye will wear blue.

Who then is responsible for casting the evil eye? Well, most culprits are those who are already considered quarrelsome or peculiar in some way by the local community. And folk with blue eyes are regarded with extreme suspicion – no doubt more than partly because being blue-eyed is a trait Greeks associate with Turks. All these quarrelsome, peculiar or blue-eyed folk have to do is be present when someone or something enviable appears on the scene – and then the trouble starts.

If, during your travels, someone casts the evil eye on you, you'll soon know about it. Symptoms include dizziness, headaches, a feeling of 'weight' on the head or tightening in the chest. Locals will point you in the direction of someone, usually an old woman, who can cure you.

The cure usually involves the curer making the sign of the cross over a glass of water, praying silently and, at the same time, dropping oil into the glass. If the oil disappears from the surface, it proves you have the evil eye – but also cures it, for the 'blessed' water will be dabbed on your forehead, stomach and at two points on your chest (at the points of the crucifix).

Apparently, the cure works. But you know the old adage about prevention being better than cure. If you're worried about the evil eye, don't take any chances – wear blue.

quay and is clearly signposted from the waterfront; head towards the Oceanic Hotel.

Look for domatia signs along Evangelistria and other streets leading inland from the waterfront, especially behind Rooms to Rent Yiannis.

Rooms to Rent Yiannis (☎ 2283 022 575) Doubles with/without bathroom €34.90/23.50, apartments €43.50. On the waterfront next to Hotel Oceanis and five minutes from the beach, is this clean, homey place. Its shared balcony is a perfect place to chill and watch the sun set.

Hotel Posidonion (☎ 2283 023 121, fax 2283 025 808) Singles/doubles €49/67.90. This hotel on the waterfront opposite the bus station has bright rooms with balcony.

Hotel Tinion (☎ 2283 022 261, fax 2283 024 754) Doubles €49. At the southern end of the waterfront near the roundabout, rooms at this grand old place have balconies, TV and air-con.

Places to Eat & Drink

The waterfront is lined with places serving the usual fare – none of them outstanding.

Pallada Taverna (☎ 2283 023 516) Dishes €1.70-5.60, seafood by the kilo. Just off the waterfront, at the rear of the Hotel Lito, Pallada serves hearty, if somewhat oily, traditional dishes; the wine is poured from huge barrels overhead.

Mixhalis Taverna (☎ 2283 023 498) Dishes €2-8.80, seafood by the kilo. In the narrow first lane to the right off Evangelistria, Mixhalis is noted for high-quality meat.

To Epilekto (☎2283 025/024 619) On the waterfront, Epilekto is one of the better choices for a generous breakfast. It also has rooms.

Koursaros (☎ 2283 023 963) Near the Hotel Lito on the waterfront, this darkly-lit music bar plays a mix of Greek and world music.

CYCLADES

AROUND TINOS

Unless you've come solely to visit the church, you'll need to explore the countryside and its 42 villages to make the most of Tinos. Most of the island is still farmed in one way or another, and you should look out for livestock (including piglets, goats and donkeys) wandering onto roads.

Kionia, 3km north-west of Hora, has several small beaches, the nearest overlooked by Tinos Beach Hotel. The site of the **Sanctuary of Poseidon & Amphitrite**, before the hotel, dates from the 4th century BC. Poseidon was worshipped because he banished the snakes that once infested the island.

At **Porto**, 6km east of Hora, there's a sandy, uncrowded beach. **Kolymvythra Bay**, beyond Komi, has two beautiful sandy beaches; a lovely road leads through reed beds and vegetable gardens to the bay.

Further along the coast there's a small beach at **Panormos** from where distinctive green marble quarried in nearby **Marlas** was once exported. **Pyrgos** is a picturesque village where marble is still carved. There's a marble sculpture school, **Dellatos Marble Sculpture Studio** (☎ 2283 023 164, fax 2283 023 460, W www.tinosmarble.com) open to both novice and experienced sculptors for two-week terms year-round. The village also has several little workshops with traditional items such as lintels and plaques (which both adorn houses around the village) and figurines for sale. About three buses per day run to Pyrgos; from there it's a pleasant 2km walk to Panormos.

The ruins of the Venetian fortress of **Exobourgo**, atop a 640m-high hill, stand sentinel over a cluster of unspoilt villages. At the fortress, built on an ancient acropolis, the Venetians made their last stand against the Turks in 1715. The ascent can be made from several villages; the shortest route is from Xinara. It's a steep climb, but the views are worth it.

The famous basket weavers of Tinos are based in the tiny, lime-washed traditional village of **Volax**, nestled on a spectacular rocky plain in the centre of the island. You can usually buy direct from the workshops, but if they're shut for siesta, a small souvenir shop sells baskets. There is a small **folkloric museum** (ask at the souvenir shop for someone to open it for you) and an attractive Catholic chapel; follow the path beyond the amphitheatre, opposite O Rokos taverna. Buses to Volax are rare indeed, so hire a car or motorcycle to get there.

O Rokos (☎ 2283 041 989, Volax) Dishes €1.50-7.40. This is one of the best tavernas on the island, serving fresh produce. Everything is delicious, right down to the olives and capers in the Greek salad.

Syros Σύρος

postcode 841 00 • pop 19,870

Many tourists come to Syros merely to change ferries. This is a pity because the capital, Ermoupolis (named after Hermes, god of trade, messengers and thieves) is a beautiful city with inhabitants who have not become tourist-weary.

Syros' economy depends little on tourism, and though its ship-building industry (once the most vigorous in Greece) has declined, it has textile factories, dairy farms and a horticultural industry that supplies the rest of the Cyclades with plants and flowers.

If you have a sweet tooth, don't miss the famous *loukoumia* (Turkish delight) and *halvadopites* (nougat).

History

Excavations of an Early Cycladic fortified settlement and burial ground at Kastri in the island's north-east, dating from 2800-2300 BC, reveal that the inhabitants farmed, fished and had close connections with other communities.

In the Middle Ages, Syros was the only Greek island with an entirely Roman Catholic population, the result of conversions by the Franks who took over the island in 1207. This gave it the support and protection of the west (particularly the French) during Turkish rule.

Syros remained neutral during the War of Independence and thousands of refugees from islands ravaged by the Turks fled here

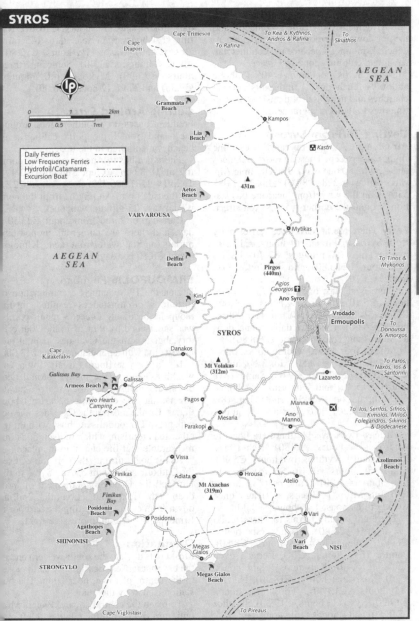

SYROS

Cape Trimeson

To Kea & Kythnos,
Andros & Rafina

To Skiathos

To Rafina

Cape Diapori

Cape Diapori

AEGEAN
SEA

Grammata
Beach

Kampos

Lia
Beach

Kastri

Daily Ferries
Low Frequency Ferries
Hydrofoil/Catamaran
Excursion Boat

0   1   2km
0   0.5   1mi

Aetos
Beach

431m

VARVAROUSA

Mytikas

AEGEAN
SEA

Delfini
Beach

Pirgos
(440m)

To Tinos &
Mykonos

Kini

Agios
Georgios

Ano Syros

Vrodado

Ermoupolis

To Donoussa
& Amorgos

SYROS

Danakos

Mt Volakas
(312m)

Cape Katakefalos

Lazareto

To Paros,
Naxos, Ios &
Santorini

Galissas Bay
Armeos Beach

Galissas

Pagos

Manna

Two Hearts
Camping

Mesaria

Ano
Manno

To Ios, Serifos, Sifnos,
Kimolos, Milos,
Folegandros, Sikinos
& Dodecanese

Parakopi

Vissa

Finikas

Adiata

Hrousa

Atelio

Azolimnos
Beach

Finikas
Bay

Mt Axachas
(319m)

Posidonia
Beach

Agathopes
Beach

Posidonia

SHINONISI

Vari

STRONGYLO

Megas
Gialos

Vari
Beach

NISI

Megas Gialos
Beach

Cape Viglostasi

To Pireaus

CYCLADES

Phone numbers listed incorporate changes due in Oct 2002; see p83

bringing the Orthodox religion. They built a new settlement (now called Vrodado), and the port town of Ermoupolis. After independence, Ermoupolis became the commercial, naval and cultural centre of Greece.

Today, Syros' population is 40% Catholic and 60% Orthodox. Ermoupolis' ornate churches and neoclassical mansions are testimonies to its former grandeur.

Getting To/From Syros

Air Olympic Airways operates at least one flight daily except Tuesday to/from Athens (€54.30/62.80 one way). The Olympic Airways office (☎ 2281 088 018, fax 2281 083 536) is on the waterfront, near the bus station, around the corner from Naxou street.

Ferry There are at least three ferries daily from Syros to Piraeus (4 hours, €13.10), two to Tinos (50 minutes, €3.70), Lavrio (3½ hours €10.80) and Mykonos (1¼ hours, €5.10).

There is at least one daily to Paros (1½ hours, €5.10), Iraklio (7½ hours, €17.60), Rafina (5¾ hours, €10.50) and Naxos (three hours, €6.60). There are daily connections to Andros via Tinos (2¾ hours, €8.80).

At least four ferries weekly go to Amorgos (4½ hours, €10.50), Ios (2¾ hours, €11), Ikaria (2½ hours, €9.60), Samos (five hours, €15.40) and Santorini (5¼ hours, €12.50); and one weekly serves Crete (8½ hours, €17.20) and Rafina (5 hours, €10.55).

At least twice weekly there are boats to Andros (1¾ hours, €5.80), Kea (three hours, €8.20), Kythnos (two hours, €5.90), Sifnos (5½ hours, €6.40), Serifos (three to five hours, €6.90), Kimolos (five hours, €9) and Milos (6 hours, €9) and once weekly to Donousa (3½ hours, €8.20).

There are weekly ferries to Thessaloniki (12 hours, €26.40), Sikinos (six hours, €8.40), Folegandros (six hours, €8.80), Patmos (five hours, €14), Leros (seven hours, €15.40), Kalymnos (eight hours, €16), Kos (nine hours, €18.30), Nisyros (11 hours, €13.40), Tilos (12 hours, €17.20), Symi (13 hours, €19.50), Skiathos (€18.80) and Rhodes (15½ hours, €22).

Fast Boat & Catamaran Services depart daily for Piraeus (2½ hours, €26.40), Rafina (1¾ hours, €21.15), Paros (45 minutes, €9.50), Naxos (1½ hours, €12.40), Ios (2¼ hours, €21.40), Santorini (three hours, €25.90), Mykonos (30 minutes €9.50) and Tinos (2 hours, €6.90).

Getting Around Syros

Frequent buses do a southern loop around the island from Ermoupolis, calling at all beaches mentioned in the text.

There is a bus to Ano Syros every morning at 10.30am, except Sunday (€0.90) Taxis (☎ 2281 086 222) charge about €2.50 for the ride up to Ano Syros from the port it's an easy 25-minute walk back.

Cars can be hired from about €23.50 day, and there are numerous moped-hire outlets on the waterfront near Kimolo (from €8.80 per day).

ERMOUPOLIS Ερμούπολη

During the 19th century, a combination of fortuitous circumstances resulted in Ermoupolis becoming Greece's major port. It was superseded by Piraeus in the 20th century, but is still the Cyclades' capital and largest city, with a population of over 13,000

It's a very affluent, lively town; its wealth evident in the many restored neoclassical mansions, the marble-paved streets, and the chic little backstreet boutiques. Unlike most of the Cyclades, the occupants of Ermoupolis are busy with things other than tourism, which in itself adds immeasurable real-life charm to the place.

As the boat sails into the port you will see the Catholic settlement of Ano Syros to the left, and the Orthodox settlement of Vrodado to the right, both set on hills. Spilling down from each and skirting the harbour is Ermoupolis – it's an impressive sight.

Orientation

Most boats dock at the south-western end of the bay, but ferries occasionally berth close to the centre of town, near Hiou. The bus station is also by the quay.

To reach the central square, Plateia Miaouli, turn right from the quay, and left into

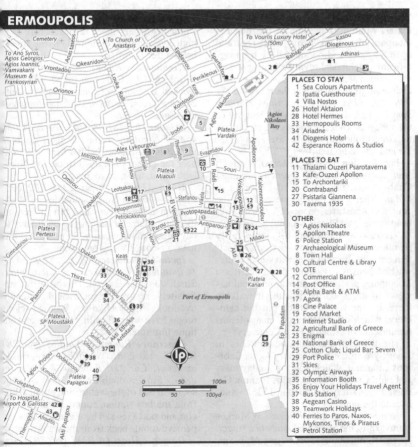

ERMOUPOLIS

PLACES TO STAY
1 Sea Colours Apartments
2 Ipatia Guesthouse
4 Villa Nostos
26 Hotel Aktaion
28 Hotel Hermes
33 Hermopoulis Rooms
34 Ariadne
41 Diogenis Hotel
42 Esperance Rooms & Studios

PLACES TO EAT
11 Thalami Ouzeri Psarotaverna
13 Kafe-Ouzeri Apollon
15 To Archontariki
20 Contraband
27 Psistaria Giannena
30 Taverna 1935

OTHER
3 Agios Nikolaos
5 Apollon Theatre
6 Police Station
7 Archaeological Museum
8 Town Hall
9 Cultural Centre & Library
10 OTE
12 Commercial Bank
14 Post Office
16 Alpha Bank & ATM
17 Agora
18 Cine Palace
19 Food Market
21 Internet Studio
22 Agricultural Bank of Greece
23 Enigma
24 National Bank of Greece
25 Cotton Club; Liquid Bar; Severn
29 Port Police
31 Skies
32 Olympic Airways
35 Information Booth
36 Enjoy Your Holidays Travel Agent
37 Bus Station
38 Aegean Casino
39 Teamwork Holidays
40 Ferries to Paros, Naxos,
   Mykonos, Tinos & Piraeus
43 Petrol Station

CYCLADES

El Venizelou. There are public toilets around the bay to the east, and off Antiparou.

Information

In summer there is an information booth on the waterfront, near the corner of Nikolaou Filini, about 100m north-east of the quay. The travel agents Enjoy Your Holidays (☎ 2281 087 070, fax 2281 082 739, ℓ enjoy-holidays.gr), opposite the bus station on the waterfront, can help with accommodation and ferry tickets.

The post office is on Protopapadaki and the OTE is on the eastern edge of Plateia Miaouli. Internet Studio (☎/fax 2281 081 653), on the waterfront, provides Internet access during the summer months at reasonable rates.

There are ATMs at the Alpha Bank on El Venizelou, the Commercial Bank on Vokotopoulo, the National Bank of Greece on Protopapadaki and the Agricultural Bank of Greece on El Venizelou at the waterfront.

The police station (☎ 2281 082 610) is beside the Apollon Theatre, just north of the OTE. Syros' port police (☎ 2281 082 690, 2281 088 888) are on the eastern side of the waterfront.

Phone numbers listed incorporate changes due in Oct 2002; see p83

Things to See

Plateia Miaouli is the hub of bustling Ermoupolis. It's flanked by palm trees and open-air cafes and dominated by the magnificent neoclassical **town hall**, designed by the German architect Ernst Ziller. The small **archaeological museum** at the rear (☎ 2281 088 487; admission €1.50; open 8.30am-3pm Tues-Sun), founded in 1834 and one of the oldest in Greece, houses a tiny collection of ceramic and marble vases, grave stelae and Cycladic figurines.

The **Apollon Theatre** (*Plateia Vardaki*) was designed by the French architect Chabeau and is a replica of La Scala in Milan. There are terrific views from the church of **Anastasis**, on top of Vrodado Hill; head north from Plateia Miaouli to get there.

Vrodado and Ermoupolis merge fairly seamlessly, but **Ano Syros** – a medieval settlement with narrow alleyways and whitewashed houses – is quite different. It's a fascinating place to wander around and has views of neighbouring islands. If walking there, on the way up check out the **cemetery**, which has ostentatious mausoleums reminiscent of Athens' First Cemetery.

The finest of the Catholic churches in Anos Syros is the 13th-century **Agios Georgios** cathedral, which holds a Sunday mass at 11am. Close by is the **Agios Ioannis** Capuchin monastery, founded in 1535 to minister to the poor.

Ano Syros was the birthplace of Markos Vamvakaris, the celebrated *rembetika* singer. A small **museum** (*10am-1pm Mon-Sat; July-August only*) on Piatsa, the town's main thoroughfare, houses his personal effects and records.

Organised Tours & Activities

The *MS Esperors II* sails to the southern beaches and to a small offshore island. Book through *Teamwork Holidays* (☎ 2281 083 400, fax 2281 083 508, ⓔ teamwork@otenet.gr) 3-hour cruises €11.75.

Cyclades Sailing (☎ 2281 082 501, fax 2281 082 536, ⓔ csail@otenet.gr) can organise yachting charters, as can *Nomikos Sailing* (☎ 2281 088 527); call direct or book through Enjoy Your Holidays.

Places to Stay

Domatia owners meet ferries. There is a high concentration of domatia in the streets behind the waterfront.

Hermopoulis Rooms (☎ 2281 087 475) Doubles €46.60. On Naxou, the bougainvillea cloaked balconies of these compact, self-contained rooms offer snatched glimpses of the water.

Ariadne (☎ 2281 080 245, fax 2281 080 454, 9 Nikolaou Filini) Singles/doubles €30.20/49. Ariadne, behind the waterfront near the corner of Agios Proiou and Nikolaou Filini, has nice rooms.

Hotel Aktaion (☎/fax 2281 082 675, Plateia Kanari) Singles/doubles €52/64. Aktaion has been renovated, but still retains its rustic character (although you'll have to pay much more to enjoy it now). Rooms have air-con, TV and telephone.

Ipatia Guesthouse (☎/fax 2281 083 575, ⓔ ipatiaguest@yahoo.com, 3 Babagiotou) Singles/doubles €42/64. This beautiful, exquisitely restored neoclassical mansion overlooks Agios Nikolaos Bay. Spacious rooms have original ceiling frescoes and antique furniture.

Esperance Rooms & Studios (☎ 2281 081 671, fax 2281 085 707, ⓔ espernik@otenet.gr; Cnr Akti Papagou & Folegandrou) Singles/doubles €52/64. At the southern end of the waterfront, about 100m from the bus station, rooms have TV, air-con and port views. There are also less expensive rooms back from the waterfront.

Diogenis Hotel (☎ 2281 086 301) Singles/doubles €55/70. A few doors away from the Esperance, rooms here have TV and minibar.

Villa Nostos (☎ 2281 084 226, 2 Spartiaton) Doubles with/without bathroom €42.80/54.60. This old mansion west of the Agios Nikolaos church has spacious, simple rooms.

Hotel Hermes (☎ 2281 083 011, fax 2281 087 412, Plateia Kanari) Double from €82.50. This spiffy B-class hotel on the waterfront has comfortable rooms. Breakfast is included in the price.

Sea Colours Apartments (☎ 2281 083 400, fax 2281 083 508, ⓔ teamwork@otenet.gr)

Studios/apartments €56.50/110. Open year-round. North-east of the port, this modern mansion has nice apartments. To find it, descend the steps after Agios Nikolaos church; it's on the right, perched above lovely Agios Nikolaos Bay.

Vourlis Luxury Hotel (☎/fax 2281 088 440, Mavrokordatou 5) Doubles from €94.25. Vourlis is a beautifully restored neoclassical mansion about 150m beyond Spatia Guesthouse. Suites have antique furniture and many have spectacular sea views. Make sure you book well in advance.

Places to Eat

The waterfront and the southern edge of Plateia Miaouli are lined with restaurants and cafes.

Psistaria Giannena (☎ 2281 082 994, Plateia Kanari) Dishes €1.70-19.80, seafood by the kilo. This *psistaria* specialises in *kokoretsi* (spit-roasted lamb's entrails) and spiced rolled pork.

Contraband (☎ 2281 081 028) Dishes €1.70-8.80. In a narrow walkway behind the waterfront, this small cafe has delicious seafood and generous dishes.

Taverna 1935 Dishes €2-8.80. One of the better waterfront places, with moderately priced traditional fare, including fresh fish.

Kafe-Ouzeri Apollon (☎ 2281 088 461) Dishes €1.70-4.40. On Stefanou, this ouzeri is a great place to sample octopus and fish grilled over hot coals.

To Archontariki (☎ 2281 081 744, 8 Em Roidi) Dishes €1.50-8.80. One block south-east of Plateia Miaouli, off Vikela, Archontariki is deservedly popular. Its extensive menu features the regular fare plus delicious dishes such as parsley salad (€2.35) and fennel pie (€3.80). The wine list includes regional favourites from all over Greece.

Thalami Ouzeri Psarotaverna (☎ 2281 085 331) Dishes €2.35-18.60, seafood by the kilo. On Souri, Thalami overlooks Agios Nikolaos Bay. The food is pretty good and *kakavia*, a local fish soup, is available. To get there, follow Souri (which runs off the southern side of Plateia Miaouli) east to its end.

Frankosyriani (☎ 2281 084 888, Piatsa) Dishes €2.35-4. Up in Ano Syros near the Vamvakaris museum, Frankosyriani is a great place to stop for a drink and mezedes, although food is only served in the evening. The view from the terrace is superb and you can sing along with Vamvakaris as you sup.

There are several other good *cafes* in Ano Syros that take in the views and atmosphere.

The best place for fresh produce is the *food market* on Hiou.

Entertainment

There are plenty of bars around Plateia Miaouli and along the waterfront.

Agora (☎ 2281 088 329, Plateia Miaouli) Adjacent to Piramatiko Bakery, this restaurant-bar is very subdued and positively glows with Syros style.

The Cotton Club, next door to Hotel Aktaion, is the hub of waterfront nightlife. Androu, the narrow lane to The Cotton Club's left is door-to-door bars, including *Enigma*, a metal hang-out with an interesting, edgy atmosphere.

If you're looking for something a little more hip, head to *Liquid Bar (☎ 2281 082 284)*, nearby, where the resident DJ plays a House and Greek mix. *Severn*, next door, is also a hot spot for a drink.

If bouzouki is your thing, there are quite a few places. Try *Skies*, on the waterfront near Taverna 1935.

Cine Palace (☎ 2281 082 313, Plateia Miaouli) Admission €5.60. Open 9.30pm June-Sept. This outdoor cinema screens mainstream new release English- and French-language films subtitled in Greek.

GALISSAS Γαλησσψς

The west coast resort of Galissas has one of the island's best beaches: a 900m crescent of dark sand, shaded by tamarisk trees. **Armeos**, a walk round the rocks to the left of the bay, is an official nudist beach. There are two travel agents, including Galissas Tours (☎ 2281 042 801, fax 2281 042 801, ℮ galtours@syr.forthnet.gr) at the main intersection.

CYCLADES

Places to Stay

Two Hearts Camping (☎ 2281 042 052, fax 2281 043 290, e etta@otenet.gr) Adult/tent €5.30/2.70. Set in a pistachio orchard about a kilometre from the village, this camping ground has most facilities; turn right at Galissas Tours and follow the signs. A minibus meets ferries in high season.

There are plenty of domatia available, mostly much of a muchness in standard concrete box style.

Rooms P Sicala (☎ 2281 042 643) Doubles €25.30. On the way to Two Hearts Camping, this is a cute little traditional place shaded by flowering vines; book early.

Karmelina Rooms (☎ 2281 042 320) Doubles €26. On the right of the main road, not far from the branch road to the beach, Karmelina's has clean rooms and a communal kitchen.

Pension Blue Sky (☎ 2281 043 410, fax 2281 043 411) Doubles/apartments €52/64. This popular pension is close to Karmelina Rooms.

Hotel Benois (☎/fax 2281 042 833, e h-benois@otenet.gr) Singles/doubles with breakfast €46.50/67.90. This modern hotel is close to the beach. Rooms have TV and air-con.

Dolphin Bay Resort (☎ 2281 042 924, fax 2281 042 843, e dbh@otenet.gr) Doubles with breakfast €107. This A-class property is a large, white cluster of buildings left of the beach as you face the sea. Rooms have satellite TV.

Places to Eat

Markos O Psilos (☎ 2281 043 924) Dishes €1.50-7.10. Next to the minimarket, this place serves good-value meals, as do most of the other tavernas.

Argo Café Bar (☎ 2281 042 819) Dishes €3-7.30. This colourful bar-cafe, around the corner from Hotel Benois is a nice relaxing place to hang out, with comfy cushions and deck chairs on the patio.

AROUND SYROS

The beaches south of Galissas all have domatia and some have hotels. The first is **Finikas**, with a nice, tree-lined beach and a shop selling interesting old things as well as local crafts. The next, **Posidonia**, has a sand-and-pebble beach shaded by tamarisk trees

Further south, **Agathopes** has a nice tree-bordered sandy beach. On the south coast, tranquil **Megas Gialos** has two sandy beaches.

Vari, the next bay, has a sandy beach, but is more developed. **Azolimnos**, the next beach along, has a few **fish tavernas**. Kini is fast becoming popular – it has a long stretch of beach and many new hotels.

Places to Stay

Vari has a few places to stay.

Hotel Domenica (☎ 2281 061 216, fax 2281 061 289) Doubles with/without sea view €59/49. Some rooms in this hotel have the sea have kitchen and TV.

Hotel Kamelo (☎ 2281 061 217, fax 2281 061 117, Vari) Singles/doubles €34.90/59. This modern hotel has rooms with air-con and TV.

Mykonos Μκονος

postcode 846 00 • pop 6170

Mykonos is perhaps the most visited and expensive of all Greek islands (although these days Santorini runs a pretty close second) and it has the most sophisticated nightlife, as well as uninhibited beach raves. Despite its reputation as the gay capital of Greece, that shouldn't – and doesn't – deter others. The days when Mykonos was the favourite rendezvous for the world's rich and famous may be over, but the island probably still has more poseurs per square metre than any other Mediterranean resort.

Depending on your temperament, you'll either be captivated or take one look and stay on the ferry. Barren, low-lying Mykonos would never win a beauty contest, but it has some decent beaches and is the jumping-off point for the sacred island of Delos.

Getting To/From Mykonos

Air There are at least five flights daily to/from Athens (€70.15/78.65 one way), and

MYKONOS

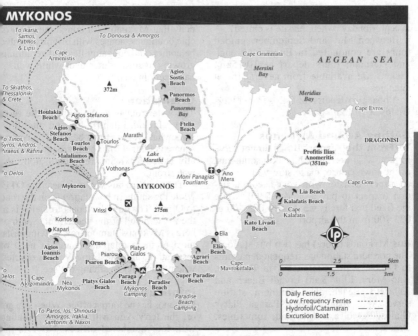

Map labels:
To Ikaria, Samos, Patmos & Lipsi; Cape Armenistis; To Donousa & Amorgos; Cape Grammata; AEGEAN SEA; Mersini Bay; 372m; Agios Sostis Beach; Panormos Beach; Panormos Bay; Meridias Bay; Cape Evros; To Skiathos, Thessaloniki & Crete; Houlakia Beach; Agios Stefanos; Ftelia Beach; DRAGONISI; To Tinos, Syros, Andros, Piraeus & Rafina; Agios Stefanos Beach; Tourlos Beach; Tourlos; Marathi; Lake Marathi; Malaliamos Beach; Profitis Ilias Anomeritis (351m); To Delos; Vothonas; Moni Panagias Tourlianis; Ano Mera; MYKONOS; Mykonos; Cape Goni; Lia Beach; Kalafatis Beach; Cape Kalafatis; Vrissi; 275m; Korfos; Kato Livadi Beach; Kapari; Elia; Elia Beach; Ornos; Agios Ioannis Beach; Psarou; Platys Gialos; Agrari Beach; Super Paradise Beach; Cape Mavrokefalas; Cape Alogomandra; Nea Mykonos; Platys Gialos Beach; Psarou Beach; Paraga Beach; Mykonos Camping; Paradise Beach; Paradise Beach Camping; To Paros, Ios, Shinousa, Amorgos, Iraklia, Santorini & Naxos

Legend:
Daily Ferries; Low Frequency Ferries; Hydrofoil/Catamaran; Excursion Boat

Scale: 0 — 2.5 — 5km; 0 — 1.5 — 3mi

CYCLADES

well as flights to Santorini (€54 one way, daily except Friday), Thessaloniki (€91.30, three weekly) and Rhodes (two weekly, €78.10).

Ferry Mykonos has daily services to Rafina (4½ hours, €12.65) via Tinos (30 minutes, €3.50) and Andros (2½ hours, €7.80); to Piraeus (six hours, €16.50) via Tinos and Syros (1½ hours, €5), Paros (two hours, €6.10); connect at Paros for Naxos. Daily ferries also run to Ios (four hours, €9.60).

There are three ferries a week to Thessaloniki (14 hours, €29.05).

There are two ferries weekly to Santorini (six hours, €10.50), and four weekly to Amorgos (2½ hours, €9.30), Iraklia (five to eight hours, €8.80), Shinousa (six hours, €8.80) and Crete (nine hours, €14.80).

One weekly runs to Donousa (two hours, €8.80), Patmos (nine hours, €15.70), Lipsi (ten hours, €15.40) and Skiathos (8½ hours, €80.80). One daily goes to Samos (5 hours, €15.40) and Ikaria (2¾ hours, €9.60).

Fast Boat & Catamaran There are two daily services connecting Mykonos with Andros (1¼ hours, €15.70) and three daily to Tinos (15 minutes, €5.90). Five daily services go to Rafina (2 hours, €25.25) and two daily go to Piraeus (three hours, €30.80) and Syros (30 minutes, €9.50). There are three daily services to Paros (45 minutes, €10.30), which connect with services to Naxos (1½, €11.75), Santorini (three to four hours, €16.90) and Ios (2¾, €14.70). One service weekly goes directly to Ios (1¾ hours, €16) and Shinousa (2½ hours, €13). One weekly service goes to Amorgos (2¼ hours, €18.60).

Excursion Boat Boats for Delos (20 to 30 minutes, €5.60 return) leave at 9am, 9.30am, 10.15am, 11am, 11.40pm and 12.50pm, from the quay at the western end of the port, returning between 12.20pm and 3pm daily except Monday (when the site is closed).

Between May and September, guided tours are conducted in English, French and German; tours depart at 10.15am. Tickets are available from several travel agencies.

A boat also departs for Delos from Platys Gialos at 10.15am daily.

Getting Around Mykonos

To/From the Airport Buses do not serve Mykonos' airport, which is 3km south-east of the town centre; make sure you arrange an airport transfer with your accommodation (expect to pay around €5.90); while the fixed taxi fare is €5. Call ☎ 022 400 or 023 700 from the airport.

Bus Mykonos (Hora) has two bus stations. The northern station has frequent departures to Ornos, Agios Stefanos (via Tourlos), Ano Mera, Elia, Kato Livadi Beach and Kalafatis Beach. The southern station serves Agios Ioannis Beach, Paraga, Platys Gialos, Paradise Beach, and, sometimes, Ornos.

Car & Motorcycle Most car and motorcycle rental firms are around the southern bus station. Expect to pay around €29 for car hire.

Caique Services leave Mykonos (Hora) for Super Paradise Beach, Agrari and Elia Beaches (June to September only) and from Platys Gialos to Paradise (€2.35), Super Paradise (€3), Agrari (€3.50) and Elia (€3.50) Beaches.

MYKONOS (HORA)

Mykonos, the island's port and capital, is a warren-like Cycladic village turned toy town. It can be very hard to find your bearings – just when you think you've got it worked out, you'll find yourself back at square one. Throngs of pushy people add to the frustration. Familiarise yourself with the three main streets that form a horseshoe behind the waterfront and you'll have a fighting chance of finding your way around.

Even the most disenchanted could no deny that Mykonos – a conglomeration o chic boutiques, houses with brightly painte balconies, and bougainvillea and geranium growing against whiter-than-white walls has a certain charm.

Orientation

The waterfront is to the right of the ferr quay (facing inland), beyond the tiny somewhat grubby, town beach. The centra square is Plateia Manto Mavrogenous (usu ally called Taxi Square), south along th waterfront.

The northern bus station is near the OTE while the southern bus station is on the roa to Ornos. The quay for boats to Delos is a the western end of the waterfront. South o here is Mykonos' famous row of windmills most of them dilapidated and in need o restoration, and the Little Venice quarter where balconies overhang the sea.

Information

Mykonos has no tourist office. When you ge off the ferry, you will see a low building with four numbered offices. No 1 is the Hoteliers Association of Mykonos (☎ 2289 024 540, fax 2289 024 760, ⓦ www .mykonosgreece.com), open 8am to mid night daily; No 2 is the Association o Rooms, Studios & Apartments (☎ 2289 020 860), open 10am to 6pm daily; No 3 ha camping information (☎ 2289 022 852), bu is rarely open; and No 4 houses the touris police (☎ 2289 022 482), with variable open ing times. Mykonos Accommodation Cente (☎ 2289 023 408, fax 2289 024 137, ⓦ www .mykonos-accommodation.com), 1st floor 10 Enoplon Dinameon, provides the mos comprehensive tourist information and car find mid-range to top-end accommodation as well as gay-friendly accommodation.

The Olympic Airways office is by the southern bus station (☎ 2289 022 490, fax 2289 023 366).

The National Bank of Greece (with ATM is on the waterfront (and there are also sev eral banks by the ferry quay). Two door away, Delia Travel (☎ 2289 022 322, fax 2289 024 440) represents American Express

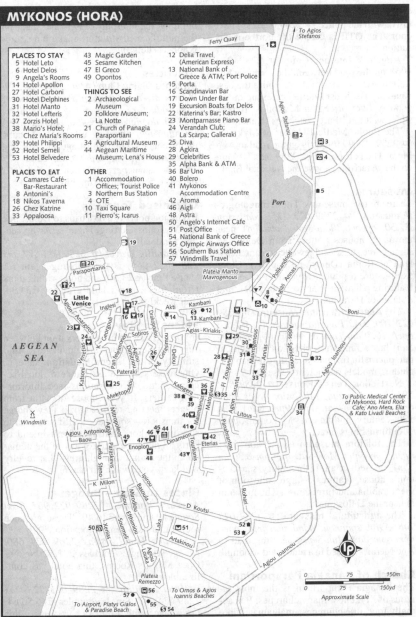

MYKONOS (HORA)

PLACES TO STAY
5 Hotel Leto
6 Hotel Delos
9 Angela's Rooms
14 Hotel Apollon
27 Hotel Carboni
30 Hotel Delphines
31 Hotel Manto
32 Hotel Lefteris
37 Zorzis Hotel
38 Mario's Hotel;
 Chez Maria's Rooms
39 Hotel Philippi
52 Hotel Semeli
53 Hotel Belvedere

PLACES TO EAT
7 Camares Café-
 Bar-Restaurant
8 Antonini's
18 Nikos Taverna
26 Chez Katrine
33 Appaloosa

43 Magic Garden
45 Sesame Kitchen
47 El Greco
49 Opontos

THINGS TO SEE
2 Archaeological
 Museum
20 Folklore Museum;
 La Notte
21 Church of Panagia
 Paraportiani
34 Agricultural Museum
44 Aegean Maritime
 Museum; Lena's House

OTHER
1 Accommodation
 Offices; Tourist Police
3 Northern Bus Station
4 OTE
10 Taxi Square
11 Pierro's; Icarus

12 Delia Travel
 (American Express)
13 National Bank of
 Greece & ATM; Port Police
15 Porta
16 Scandinavian Bar
17 Down Under Bar
19 Excursion Boats for Delos
22 Katerina's Bar; Kastro
23 Montparnasse Piano Bar
24 Verandah Club;
 La Scarpa; Galleraki
25 Diva
28 Agkira
29 Celebrities
35 Alpha Bank & ATM
36 Bar Uno
40 Bolero
41 Mykonos
 Accommodation Centre
42 Aroma
46 Aigli
48 Astra
50 Angelo's Internet Cafe
51 Post Office
54 National Bank of Greece
55 Olympic Airways Office
56 Southern Bus Station
57 Windmills Travel

CYCLADES

Phone numbers listed incorporate changes due in Oct 2002; see p83

The post office is in the southern part of town, with the police (☎ 2289 022 235) next door. The OTE is beside the northern bus station.

Angelo's Internet Cafe (☎ 2289 024 106), on the road between the southern bus station and the windmills, provides the best email access. Most Internet cafes are outrageously over-priced in Mykonos; if possible, wait until Paros or Syros to email.

The Public Medical Center of Mykonos (☎ 2289 023 994/996) is on the road to Ano Mera. The port police (☎ 2289 022 716) are on the waterfront, above the National Bank.

Museums

There are five museums. The **archaeological museum** (☎ 2289 022 325; admission €1.50; open 8.30am-3pm Tues-Sun), near the quay, houses pottery from Delos and some grave stelae and jewellery from the island of Renia (Delos' necropolis). Chief exhibits are a pithos (Minoan storage jar), featuring a Trojan War scene in relief, and a statue of Heracles.

The **Aegean Maritime Museum** (☎ 2289 022 700, Tria Pigadia; admission €1.50; open 10.30am-1pm & 6.30pm-9pm Tues-Sun) has a fantastic collection of nautical paraphernalia from all over the Aegean, including models of ancient vessels.

Next door, **Lena's House** (☎ 2289 022 591; Tria Pigadia; admission free; open 6pm-9pm Mon-Sat, 7pm-9pm Sun) is a 19th-century, middle class Mykonian house with furnishings intact.

The **folklore museum** (admission free; open 7pm-9pm Mon-Sat, 6.30pm-8.30pm Sun), housed in an 18th-century sea captain's house, features a large collection of memorabilia and furnishings. The museum is near the Delos quay.

The **agricultural museum** (☎ 2289 022 748, Agiou Ioannou; admission free; open 4pm-6pm daily Jun-Sept), near the road to Ano Mera, is housed in a renovated windmill.

Church of Panagia Paraportiani

The Panagia Paraportiani is the most famous of Mykonos' many churches. It is actually four little churches amalgamated into one beautiful, white, lumpy, asymmetrical building; the interplay of light and shade on the multifaceted structure make it a photographer's delight.

Activities

Mykonos Diving Club (☎/fax 2289 026 539; W www.diveadventures.gr, Paradise Beach; 2 introductory dives €105, snorkelling €23.50, diving course €406, plus €59 certification fee) offers a full range of scuba diving courses with multi-lingual instructors.

Planet Windsurfing (☎/fax 2289 072 345, W www.pezi-huber.com, Kalafatis Beach) offers windsurfing hire.

Organised Tours

Excursion boats run day trips to Delos. See the Mykonos Getting There & Away section for details.

Windmills Travel (☎ 2289 023 877, fax 2289 022 066) is the booking agent for snorkelling (€23.50) and horse-riding tours (from €29), and island cruises (€34.90, four weekly).

Places to Stay

If you arrive without a reservation between July and September and manage to find suitably priced accommodation, take it. Otherwise seek the assistance of local accommodation organisations (see Information earlier). If you choose domatia from owners meeting ferries, ask if they charge for transport – some do; and if you plan to stay in the hora and you don't intend to party all night, be wary of any of the domatia on the main thoroughfares – bar revelry will keep you awake till dawn.

Places to Stay – Budget

Angela's Rooms (☎ 2289 022 967, Taxi Square) Doubles €46.40. These are nice rooms in a very central location.

Mario's Hotel (☎/fax 2289 024 680, Kalogera) Singles/doubles €32/52. Next to Chez Maria's Rooms, this hotel has comfortable rooms.

Hotel Apollon (☎ 2289 022 223, fax 2289 024 237) Singles/doubles €46.50/64. For a place with a bit of character, try this old-world hotel. It's been around since 1930 and most of the furniture looks older, but it's very well kept and the owner is sweet.

Hotel Delphines (☎ 2289 024 505, fax 2289 027 307, Mavrogenous) €38/59. This hotel is also run by friendly people; rooms have TV.

Hotel Philippi (☎ 2289 022 294, 2289 024 680, Kalogera) Doubles €46.60. Philippi has an agrarian feel; the garden out the back has fruit trees and flowers.

Chez Maria's Rooms (☎ 2289 022 480, 27 Kalogera) Doubles/triples €43.50/59. Next door to Hotel Philippi is this pretty place with potted geraniums out the front and lovely rooms.

Hotel Lefteris (☎ 2289 027 117, 9 Apollonos) Singles/doubles €46.50/61. This hotel is in the residential backstreets away from the hubbub. Some of the rooms have a balcony. Signs point from Taxi Square.

Hotel Carboni (☎ 2289 022 217, fax 2289 023 264) Doubles/triples €49/61. This D-class hotel on Andronikou Matogianni has plain but clean rooms with TV.

Places to Stay – Mid-Range
Hotel Delos (☎ 2289 022 517, fax 2289 022 312) Doubles/triples €72.50/88. This C-class hotel is in a great location, right on the waterfront by the town beach.

Hotel Manto (☎ 2289 022 330, fax 2289 026 664) Singles/doubles €61/85.50. This hotel is just off Mavrogenous, and has simple rooms, some with balcony.

Zorzis Hotel (☎ 2289 022 167, fax 2289 024 169, e zorzis@otenet.gr, 30 Kalogera) Doubles €81. This rather smart hotel is in a central location, but is reasonably sheltered from bar noise.

Places to Stay – Top End
Hotel Leto (☎ 2289 022 207, fax 2289 023 985) Singles/doubles/studios with breakfast €197/255/290. Even with a recent facelift, the hotel's rooms are looking outdated, but it does have a chic poolside area and balcony views facing the town beach.

Hotel Belvedere (☎ 2289 025 122, fax 2289 025 126, e reservations@belvederehotel.com) Doubles from €218. Much better value can be found at the Belvedere, away from the town centre, in the Rohari area. The Belvedere has jacuzzis, a massage therapist, fitness studio, DVD and Internet corner. Rooms have balconies with town views, and the hotel has a pool, bar and lounge area.

Hotel Semeli (☎ 2289 027 466, fax 2289 027 467, e semeliht@otenet.gr, Rohari) Doubles with breakfast €160. Adjacent to the Belvedere, Semeli is run by the same family. The hotel is built around the old family house and old-world charm is combined with modern comforts.

For more top-end listings, see the Beaches and Ano Mera sections.

Places to Eat
The high prices charged in many eating establishments in the area are not always indicative of quality. The fish served in most of the tavernas is likely to be cheap frozen stuff imported from Asia, which often tastes like warmed up old boots. If you want good fish, you're best off trying another island.

Antonini's (☎ 2289 022 319, Taxi Square) Dishes €2.50-12.20. This is where the locals go for reliably good Greek food.

Nikos Taverna (☎ 2289 024 320, Porta) Dishes €2.70-13.20, seafood by the kilo. Up from the Delos quay, the food at Nikos is nothing great, but it's better than what's on offer in a lot of the other 'traditional' places.

Camares Cafe-Bar-Restaurant (☎ 2289 028 570). Dishes €2.35-13.20. On the waterfront by Taxi Square, expect to dine on what you'd likely find in a cafe at home – risotto, salads and seafood.

Magic Garden (☎ 2289 026 217) Dishes €7.30-13.20. Formerly Gatsby's, it has retained the same slightly refined atmosphere and still serves some interesting food, including shrimp with spinach and green apple in a hot black sauce (€13.20).

Appaloosa (☎ 2289 027 086) Dishes €2-13.40. This Mexican-inspired place on Mavrogeneous has guacamole and nachos, as well as more substantial burgers and pasta dishes.

CYCLADES

El Greco (☎ 2289 022 074, Tria Pigadia) Dishes €4.20-18.90, seafood by the kilo. El Greco offers dishes such as, zucchini stuffed with Mykonos cheese and fennel (€5.70) and *sofrito* (Corfu-style veal with parsley, garlic and vinegar; €9.30). Some of their fish is local.

Sesame Kitchen (☎ 2289 024 710, Tria Pigadia) Dishes €5.30-20.10. A few doors up from El Greco, this restaurant serves innovative fare, much of it vegetarian, including Delos salad with *arugula*, Mykonos goat's cheese and sesame seeds (€11).

Chez Maria's Garden (☎ 2289 027 565) Set menu €17.40. There's a lovely outdoor candle-lit setting at Maria's, and the food is always good, if pricey.

Chez Katrine (☎ 2289 022 169, Gerasimou at Nikou) Meal with wine from €52.50. Probably the classiest restaurant on Mykonos, Katrine serves Greek food with a French twist. It's been open since 1971 and has diligent service and a relaxed, unfussy atmosphere.

There's a cluster of cheap fast-food outlets and creperies in the centre of town; *Opontos* serves gyros for €1.50. There are also several *supermarkets* and *fruit stalls*, particularly around the southern bus station area.

Entertainment

The Little Venice quarter has dreamy sunset bars perched right on the water's edge, some with glowing candle-lit tables. The music leans towards smooth soul sounds and lounge easy-listening gems. Head to *Katerina's Bar* (☎ 2289 023 084), *Verandah Club* (☎ 2289 026 262), *Galleraki* (☎ 2289 027 188) and *La Scarpa* (☎ 2289 023 294).

Aroma (☎2289 027 148, Kalogera) is open for coffee and breakfast by day, and by night transforms into an exclusive bar, complete with face-and-fashion police on the door – watch out!

On Enaplon Dinameon there is a cluster of large bars playing a mix of dance and lounge music, depending on the crowd, including *Astra* (☎ 2289 024 767). Opposite El Greco, *Aigli* (☎ 2289 027 265) has a huge outdoor

area. *Agkira* (☎ 2289 024 273) and the tragically named *Celebrities* (☎ 2289 022 333), both on Matogianni, are in a similar vein, but rather more chic.

Bar Uno (☎ 2289 022 689, Kalogera), near Alpha Bank, is less straightjacket chic and far more fun – raucous evenings are the go here. *Bolero* (☎ 2289 024 877, Malamatenias) plays world music.

The *Scandinavian Bar* (☎ 2289 022 669) and the *Down Under Bar* nearby, have less fashionista, less edge and the drinks are cheaper – so if that suits head on over.

Hard Rock Cafe (☎ 2289 072 162), about 4km along the Ano Mera road, has the usual Hard Rock gimmickry and a restaurant and nightclub. A shuttle bus runs from the 24-hour down-at-heel *Yacht Club* (☎ 2289 023 430), by the port, to the Hard Rock every half-hour between noon and 4am.

By the folk museum, *La Notte* is the place to go for an authentic Greek night of clubbing – bouzouki and contemporary Greek dance music is on the play list.

Gay Bars Mykonos is a gay travel destination in danger of being overrun by heterosexuals *(quelle horreur!)*, but bastions of gay nightlife survive year after year. *Kastro* (☎ 2289 023 072) in Little Venice is the place to kick start the night with cocktails as the sun sets. Around 11pm, things get a bit livelier at *Porta* (☎ 2289 027 807), which is reputably the best bar to cruise and gets full to overflowing late in the evening. Afterwards head to *Pierro's* (☎ 2289 022 177), a dance club, playing heavy-beat house, that also has raucous drag shows. Adjoining it, *Icarus* has several different spaces, a bar, rooftop terrace and 'darkrooms'. And then there's *Diva* (☎ 2289 027 271), which is where the gals like to hang, but it generally has a mixed crowd.

Cinemas *Cinemanto* (☎ 2289 027 190) Admission €5.90. Sessions 9pm & 11pm. If you're tired of partying, this outdoor cinema and taverna could provide some welcome respite; it screens new films every two days.

AROUND MYKONOS
Beaches
The nearest beaches to Hora are **Malaliamos** and the tiny, crowded **Tourlos**, 2km to the north. **Agios Stefanos**, 2km beyond, is larger, but just as crowded. To the south, beyond Ornos, is **Agios Ioannis**, where *Shirley Valentine* was filmed. **Psarou**, east of Ornos, is a pretty little cove. **Platys Gialos**, on the south-west coast, is bumper to bumper sun lounges backed by very ordinary package tour hotels – really not nice at all.

From Platys Gialos, caiques call at the island's best beaches further south: **Paradise**, **Super Paradise**, **Agrari** and **Elia**. Nudism is accepted on all these beaches. **Elia** is the last caique stop, so is the least crowded.

The next beach along, **Kato Livadi**, is relatively quiet. North-coast beaches are exposed to the meltemi, but **Panormos** and **Agios Sostis** are sheltered and uncrowded.

Places to Stay Mykonos has two camping grounds; minibuses from the camping grounds meet ferries.

Paradise Beach Camping (☎ 2289 022 852, fax 2289 024 350) Camp sites €21.80, single/double bungalows €55/72.50. This site on Paradise Beach is close to the action but has overpriced facilities and readers have complained of lecherous staff, dirty toilets and overcrowding.

Mykonos Camping (☎/fax 2289 024 578; [W] www.mycamp.gr) Adult/tent €7/3.50; 2-person bungalows €23.50 per person. This cosy camping ground is on quieter Paraga Beach (a 10-minute walk from Platys Gialos) and has good facilities.

There are many top-end places around the coast.

Villa Katerina (☎ 2289 023 414, fax 2289 022 503) Double studios €82.50. This quiet, romantic place, 300m up the hill above Agios Ioannis, has a garden and pool.

Princess of Mykonos (☎ 2289 023 806, fax 2289 023 031) Doubles with/without sea view €177/142. At Agios Stefanos, this A-class place was once a Jane Fonda hangout. Breakfast is included.

Aphrodite Beach Hotel (☎ 2289 071 367, fax 2289 071 525) Doubles/triples with

---

The Paradise Club Scene
Paradise has a buzzing clubbing scene. After 3pm, the *Beach Bar* and the *Tropicana Bar*, crank out the dance tunes, and the long arc of beach, swamped from headland to headland by sun lounges, becomes filled with dancing bodies.

For big-name international DJs head to *Cavo Paradiso (☎ 027 205/026 124)*, 300m above Paradise Beach. Admission is from €17.40 and it opens at 3am July to August.

To whet your dancing appetite, check out [W] www.cavopardiso.gr for a line-up of upcoming DJs.

---

breakfast €188.50/230. On Kalafatis Beach, this A-class hotel has masses of facilities including water sports.

Ornos Beach Hotel (☎ 2289 023 216, fax 2289 022 483, [W] www.ornosbeach.com.gr) Doubles €130.50. This hotel has great sea views and a swimming pool.

Ano Mera Ανω Μέρα
The village of Ano Mera, 7km east of Hora, is the island's only inland settlement. On its central square is the 6th-century **Moni Panagias Tourlianis** *(☎ 2289 071 249; visits by prior arrangement)*, which has a fine carved marble bell tower, an ornate wooden iconostasis carved in Florence in the late 1700s, and 16th-century icons painted by members of the Cretan School. Speakers, turned up to 11, blast out beautiful Orthodox hymns, which makes for a powerful experience.

Ano Mera Hotel (☎ 2289 071 215, fax 2289 071 276) Singles/doubles/triples €78/88/117.50. This A-class hotel has a pool, restaurant and disco. Breakfast is included in the price.

The central square is edged with *tavernas*. Near the bus stop, *O Apostolis* has decent traditional food.

Delos Δύλος

Despite its diminutive size, the World Heritage-listed Delos *(☎ 2289 022 259;*

CYCLADES

site & museum €3.50; open 9am-3pm Tues-Sun) is one of the most important archaeological sites in Greece, and certainly the most important in the Cyclades. Lying a few kilometres off the west coast of Mykonos, this sacred island is the mythical birthplace of the twins Apollo and Artemis.

History

Delos was first inhabited in the 3rd millennium BC. In the 8th century BC, a festival in honour of Apollo was established; the oldest temples and shrines on the island (many donated by Naxians) date from this era. For a long time, the Athenians coveted Delos, seeing its strategic position as one from where they could control the Aegean. By the 5th century BC, it had come under their jurisdiction.

Athens' power grew during the Persian Wars, and in 478 BC it established an alliance known as the Delian League that kept its treasury on Delos. Athens carried out a number of 'purifications', decreeing that no-one could be born or die on Delos, thus strengthening its control over the island by removing the native population.

Delos reached the height of its power in Hellenistic times, becoming one of the three most important religious centres in Greece and a flourishing centre of commerce. It traded throughout the Mediterranean and was populated with wealthy merchants, mariners and bankers from as far away as Egypt and Syria. These inhabitants built temples to the various gods worshipped in their homelands, although Apollo remained the principal deity.

The Romans made Delos a free port in 167 BC, which brought even greater prosperity – due largely to a lucrative slave market that sold up to 10,000 people a day. Later, Delos was prey to pirates and to looters of antiquities.

Getting To/From Delos

See Excursion Boats in the Mykonos section for schedules and prices of services from Mykonos. Boats also operate to Delos from Tinos and Paros.

ANCIENT DELOS
Orientation & Information

The quay where excursion boats dock is south of the tranquil Sacred Harbour. Many of the most significant finds from Delos are in the National Archaeological Museum in Athens. The site museum has an interesting collection, and it now also houses the lions from the Terrace of the Lions (those on the terrace itself are plaster-cast replicas).

Overnight stays on Delos are forbidden and boat schedules allow a maximum of six or seven hours there. Bring water and food as the cafeteria's offerings are poor value for money. Wear a hat and sensible shoes. If you hire a guide once you get to Delos you'll need to fork out more cash.

Exploring the Site

Following is an outline of some significant archaeological remains on the site. For further details, buy a guidebook at the ticket office, or – even better – take a guided tour.

If you have the energy, climb Mt Kythnos (113m), which is south-east of the harbour, to see the layout of Delos. There are terrific views of the surrounding islands on clear days. The path to Mt Kythnos is reached by walking through the **Theatre Quarter**.

It was in this quarter that Delos' wealthiest inhabitants built their houses. These houses surrounded peristyle courtyards, with mosaics (a status symbol) the most striking feature of each house. These colourful mosaics were exquisite art works, mostly representational and offset by intricate geometric borders. The most lavish dwellings were the **House of Dionysos** (named after the mosaic depicting the wine god riding a panther) and the **House of Cleopatra** (where headless statues of the owners were found). The **House of the Trident** was one of the grandest. The **House of the Masks**, probably an actors' hostelry, has another mosaic of Dionysos resplendently astride a panther, and the **House of the Dolphins** has another exceptional mosaic.

The **theatre** dates from 300 BC and had a large cistern, the remains of which can be seen. It supplied much of the town with water. The houses of the wealthy had their

ANCIENT DELOS

1 Stadium	15 Stoa of Antigonas	31 Agora of the Delians
2 Gymnasium	16 Sanctuary of Dionysos	32 House of Dionysos
3 Sanctuary of Archegetes	17 Tourist Pavillion	33 House of Cleopatra
4 Lake House	18 Museum	34 Wall of the Triarus
5 House of Diadumenos	19 Monument of the Bulls	35 House of the Trident
6 House of Comedians	20 Temple of Apollo	36 Cistern
7 Hill House	21 Temple of the Athenians	37 Theatre
8 Institution of the	22 Poros Temple	38 House of the Masks
Poseidoniasts	23 Temple of Artemis	39 House of the Dolphins
9 Palaestra	24 Keraton	40 Shrine to the Samothracian
10 Roman Wall	25 Stoa of the Naxiots	Great Gods
11 Agora of the Italians	26 House of the Naxiots	41 House of Hermes
12 Terrace of the Lions	27 Ferries to Mykonos	42 Sanctuary of the Syrian Gods
(Replicas Only)	28 Agora of the Competialists	43 Shrine to the Egyptian Gods
13 Stoa of Poseidon	29 Stoa of Philip V	44 Sacred Cave
14 Dodekatheon	30 South Stoa	45 Warehouses

CYCLADES

Sacred Lake

AEGEAN SEA

To Mykonos

0   0.5   1km

See Main Map

Renia

Mt Kynthos (113m)

Ekati

Delos

SANCTUARY OF APOLLO

Sacred Harbour

Ancient Breakwater

Commercial Harbour

Sacred Way

THEATRE QUARTER

HARBOUR QUARTER

SANCTUARIES OF THE FOREIGN GODS

Mt Kynthos (113m)

0   100   200m

0   100   200yd

own cisterns – essential as Delos was almost as parched and barren then as it is today.

Descending from Mt Kythnos, explore the **Sanctuaries of the Foreign Gods**. Here, at the **Shrine to the Samothracian Great Gods**, the Kabeiroi (the twins Dardanos and Aeton) were worshipped. At the **Sanctuary of the Syrian Gods** there are the remains of a theatre where an audience watched ritual orgies. There is also an area where Egyptian deities, including Serapis and Isis, were worshipped.

The **Sanctuary of Apollo**, to the north of the harbour, contains temples dedicated to him. It is the site of the much-photographed **Terrace of the Lions** (although the originals, now tucked away inside the site museum, are difficult to view). These proud beasts, carved from marble, were offerings from the people of Naxos, presented to Delos in the 7th century BC to guard the sacred area. To the north-east is the **Sacred Lake** (dry since it was drained in 1925 to prevent malarial mosquitoes breeding) where, according to legend, Leto gave birth to Apollo and Artemis.

Paros & Antiparos
Πάρος & Αντίπαρος

PAROS
postcode 844 00 • pop 9591
Paros is an attractive island with softly contoured, terraced hills culminating in Mt Profitis Ilias (770m). The island is famous for the pure-white marble from which it prospered from the Early Cycladic period onwards – the *Venus de Milo* was carved from Parian marble, as was Napoleon's tomb.

Paros is now the main ferry hub for the Greek islands. The port town of Parikia is the busiest on the island, largely because of the volume of people waiting for ferry connections. The hubbub surrounding the ferry quay is countered by the charming and peaceful old hora that lies one block back from the waterfront. The other major settlement, Naoussa, on the north coast, is a

pretty resort with a colourful fishing village at its core.

The relatively unspoilt island of Antiparos, 1km south-west of Paros, is easily accessible by car ferry and excursion boat.

Getting To/From Paros
Air Olympic has daily flights to/from Athens (€65.45/74 one way). The Olympic Airways office (☎ 2284 021 900, fax 2284 022 778) is on Plateia Mavrogenous in Parikia.

Ferry Paros offers a comprehensive array of ferry connections. It has frequent links to all of the Cyclades, and is also a regular stop for boats en route from the mainland to the Dodecanese, the North-Eastern Aegean islands of Ikaria and Samos, and Crete.

There are around six boats daily to Piraeus (five hours, €15.10), Naxos (one hour, €4), three daily to Ios (2½ hours, €7.40), Santorini (three to four hours, €9.90) and Mykonos (1¾ hours, €5.30). There are daily services to Syros (1½ hours, €5.10), Tinos (2½ hours, €5.30) and Amorgos (three to 4½ hours, €8.40).

Six weekly go to Koufonisia (4½ hours, €8.40) and Sikinos (three to four hours, €5.40), and five to Anafi (six hours, €10.50).

Four weekly go to Astypalea (six hours, €15.40) and Samos (7½ hours, €13.20).

There are three ferries weekly to Folegandros (3½ hours, €5.90), Ikaria (4 hours, €10), Samos (six to seven hours, €13.50) and Crete (seven to eight hours, €15.40).

There are two weekly to Thessaloniki (15 to 16 hours, €29.05), Iraklio (7½ hours, €16.15), Serifos (three hours, €6.30), Sifnos (two hours, €5.70), Milos (4½ hours, €8.40), Kimolos (4½ hours, €6.90), Shinousa (four hours, €6.40) and Donousa (two to four hours, €7).

There is one boat weekly to Skiathos (10 hours, €18.70), Rhodes (12 to 15 hours, €20), Kos (six to eight hours, €13.20), Patmos (four hours, €12.20), Leros (5½ hours, €13.70), Megisti (20 hours, €25), Nissyros (9½ hours, €13.70), Tilos (10½ hours, €15.70), Andros (3½, €10.80) and Symi (11 hours, €18.60).

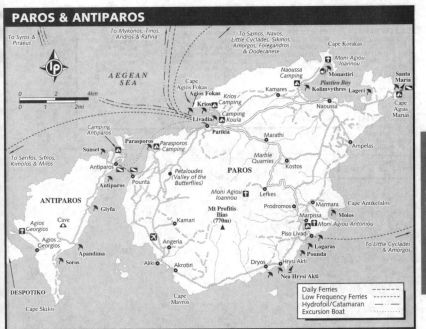

PAROS & ANTIPAROS

There is also a half-hourly car ferry available which runs from Pounta on the west coast of Paros to Antiparos (10 minutes, €0.60 one way, €5.30 car); the first ferry departs for Antiparos at around 7am, and the last boat returning leaves Antiparos at 1.30am.

Fast Boat & Catamaran There are three daily catamarans to Rafina (2½ hours, €25.55), at least two daily catamarans to Naxos (30 minutes, €8.20), Tinos (1¼ hours, €10.50), Syros (45 minutes, €9.60), Mykonos (one hour, €10.30), Ios (1½ hours, €14.30) and Santorini (2¼ hours, €17.70). There are ten services weekly to Piraeus (2½ hours, €30.25) and two weekly to Andros (two hours, €16.80) and Amorgos (1½ to 2 hours, €16.90).

Excursion Boat In summer, frequent excursion boats depart for Antiparos from Parikia.

Getting Around Paros

Bus There are around seven buses daily from Parikia to Naoussa via Dryos, Hrysi Akti, Marpissa, Marmara, Prodromos, Kostos, Marathi and Lefkes, and frequent buses to Pounta (for Antiparos), Aliki (via Petaloudes and the airport). Around 12 buses daily link Parikia and Naoussa directly.

Car, Motorcycle & Bicycle There are numerous rental outlets along the waterfront and all around the island. Paros Rent-a-Car (☎ 2284 024 408) shares an office with Santorineos Travel Services and has models from €20.30.

Taxi Boat Taxi boats leave from the quay for beaches around Parikia. Tickets are available on board.

Parikia Παροικία
The island's capital and port is Parikia. The waterfront conceals an attractive and

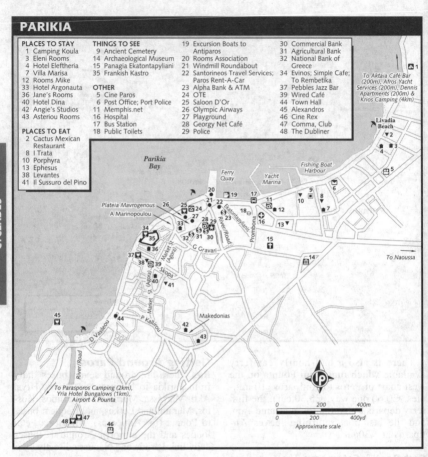

PARIKIA

PLACES TO STAY
1 Camping Koula
3 Eleni Rooms
4 Hotel Eleftheria
7 Villa Marisa
12 Rooms Mike
33 Hotel Argonauta
36 Jane's Rooms
40 Hotel Dina
42 Angie's Studios
43 Asteriou Rooms

PLACES TO EAT
2 Cactus Mexican Restaurant
8 I Trata
10 Porphyra
13 Ephesus
38 Levantes
41 Il Sussuro del Pino

THINGS TO SEE
9 Ancient Cemetery
14 Archaeological Museum
15 Panagia Ekatontapyliani
35 Frankish Kastro

OTHER
5 Cine Paros
6 Post Office; Port Police
11 Memphis.net
16 Hospital
17 Bus Station
18 Public Toilets

19 Excursion Boats to Antiparos
20 Rooms Association
21 Windmill Roundabout
22 Santorineos Travel Services; Paros Rent-A-Car
23 Alpha Bank & ATM
24 OTE
25 Saloon D'Or
26 Olympic Airways
27 Playground
28 Georgy Net Café
29 Police

30 Commercial Bank
31 Agricultural Bank
32 National Bank of Greece
34 Evinos; Simple Cafe; To Rembetika
37 Pebbles Jazz Bar
39 Wired Café
44 Town Hall
45 Alexandros
46 Cine Rex
47 Comma, Club
48 The Dubliner

typically Cycladic old quarter with a 13th-century Venetian kastro.

Orientation & Information The main square, Plateia Mavrogenous, is straight ahead from the quay. The road on the left leads around the northern waterfront to the beach at Livadia and is lined with modern hotels. On the left, heading inland from the quay, Prombona leads to the famous Panagia Ekatontapyliani, which lies within a walled courtyard. The road to the right follows the cafe-lined south-western waterfront, a pedestrian precinct in high season.

Market St (Agora in Greek, but also known by other names) is the main commercial thoroughfare running south-west from Plateia Mavrogenous through the old town, which is all narrow pedestrian streets.

Kiosks on the quay give out information on domatia and hotels (see Places to Stay). By the bay, Santorineos Travel Services (☎ 2284 024 245, fax 2284 023 922, ℮ santorineos-travel@ticketcom.gr) can help with accommodation, ferry tickets and tours. Santorineos is also the representative for American Express and MasterCard.

The National Bank of Greece, the Commercial Bank of Greece and police (☎ 2284 023 333) are all on Plateia Mavrogenous. The bus station is 50m left of the quay (looking inland), and the post office is 300m further along. The OTE is on the waterfront, to the right of the ferry quay (facing inland). The cosy Wired Café (☎ 2284 022 003), on Market St, Memphis.net, near the bus station, and Georgy Net Café (☎ 2284 022 543), near the Commercial Bank, all provide Internet access, with Georgy Net offering the best rates and new machines.

The port police (☎ 2284 021 240) are back from the northern waterfront, near the post office.

Afros Yacht Services (☎ 2284 023 625), next door to Aktaia Cafe Bar at Livadia Beach, is a yacht chandlery and does sail and boat repairs.

Things to See The **Panagia Ekatontapyliani** (☎ 2284 021 243; open 8am-1pm & 4pm-9pm daily), which dates from AD 326, is one of the most splendid in the Cyclades. The building is actually three distinct churches: Agios Nikolaos, the largest, with lovely columns of Parian marble and a carved iconostasis, is in the east of the compound; the others are the Church of Our Lady and the Baptistery. The name translates as Our Lady of the Hundred Gates, although only 99 doors have been counted. It is said that when the 100th is found, İstanbul will return to Greek jurisdiction.

Next to a school behind the Panagia Ekatontapyliani, the **Archaeological Museum** (☎ 2284 021 231; admission €1.50; open 8.30am-3pm Tues-Sun) has some interesting reliefs and statues, including a Gorgon, but the most important exhibit is a fragment of the 4th-century Parian Chronicle, which lists the most outstanding artistic achievements of ancient Greece. It was discovered in the 17th century by the Duke of Arundel's cleric, and most of it ended up in the Ashmolean Museum, Oxford. Typically, some of the most exquisite pieces are only plaster casts – the originals having long since been displaced to museums in New York and Germany.

North along the waterfront there is a fenced **ancient cemetery** dating from the 7th century BC; it was excavated in 1983. Roman graves, burial pots and sarcophagi are floodlit at night. Photographs and other finds are exhibited in an attached building, but it's rarely open.

The **Frankish Kastro** was built on the remains of a temple to Athena by Marco Sanudo, Venetian Duke of Naxos, in AD 1260. Not much remains, save an impressively large wall with cross-sectional chunks of columns from the temple embedded in it. To find it, head west along Market St and take the first right.

Activities & Organised Tours *Eurodivers Club* (☎/fax 2284 092 071, W www .eurodivers.gr) PADI open-water certification course €377. Down the coast at Pounta, this club offers scuba diving courses and dives for all levels and interests.

Aegean Diving School (☎ 2284 041 778, fax 2284 041 978, mobile ☎ 69 7484 0084, W www.ageandiving.gr) PADI open-water certification €375. Based at New Golden Beach, this school also offers a range of scuba courses from beginners to advanced.

Marel Tours (☎ 2284 021 258, fax 2284 024 181) has a trip to Lefkes and the quarries at Marathi (from €18.90); book through travel agents.

Places to Stay All camping grounds have minibuses that meet the ferries.

Camping Koula (☎ 2284 022 081, fax 2284 022 740, e koula@otenet.gr) Adult/tent €5.90/2.35. This site, 1km along the northern waterfront at Livadia, is the most central.

Parasporos Camping (☎/fax 2284 022 268) Adult/tent €5.90.50. This site is 2km south of Parikia and 300m from the beach, and gets the thumbs up from readers. A minibus meets ferries.

Krios Camping (☎ 2284 021 705,) Adult/tent €5.90.50. This site is on Krios Beach, beyond Livadia Beach. It runs a taxi boat across the bay to Parikia every 10 minutes for €1.50 per person (return). It also has a restaurant and minimarket.

The Rooms Association (☎/fax 2284 024 528, *after hours* ☎ 2284 022 220) on the quay has information on domatia; otherwise domatia owners meet ferries. For hotel details, call ☎ 2284 024 555 (Parikia) or ☎ 2284 041 333 (around the island).

Rooms Mike (☎ 2284 022 856) Doubles/triples €30.20/43.50, self-contained studios €43.50/46.60. Mike's place is deservedly popular; rooms have TV, shared kitchen and a roof terrace. To get there, walk 50m left from the quay – it's next to Memphis.net.

Jane's Rooms (☎ 2284 021 338) Doubles €46.60. In the atmospheric old Kastro, rooms have sea views and balconies; apartments are also available nearby. To reach it, facing the town, follow the road right for 200m. It's up the next set of stairs beyond the signpost for the Frankish Kastro; or Jane will meet you at the port if you book ahead.

Villa Marisa (☎ 2284 022 629, fax 2284 023 286) Doubles/triples €43.50/29. This friendly pension has nice rooms.

Elini Rooms (☎ 2284 022 714, fax 2284 024 170, ℮ roomelen@otenet.gr) Singles/doubles €49/52. Rooms don't have views, but there's a pretty bougainvillea-covered courtyard area. Turn right at Hotel Argo by Livadia Beach to reach Elini's; transfer to/from the port is available.

Hotel Eleftheria (☎ 2284 022 047) Doubles €43.50. This welcoming hotel nearby Livadia Beach has a rooftop terrace, and breakfast is available. Turn right at Taverna Katerina on the waterfront.

Angie's Studios (☎ 2284 023 909, fax 2284 024 346) Singles/doubles €61/69.60. These studios are out in the back blocks, but it's a nice walk there from the centre of town. They are dripping with bougainvillea and have a pleasant patio and lawn.

Hotel Dina (☎ 2284 023 325, Market St) Singles/doubles €46.50/52.50. This hotel is in the old town and all rooms have balconies.

Hotel Argonauta (☎/fax 2284 021 440) Singles/doubles €52/64. This lovely, central C-class hotel, on the main square, has sparkling rooms with air-con and balcony.

Dennis Apartments (☎/fax 2284 022 466) Doubles €49. For something a bit more rural and quiet, head to these spacious apartments, near Livadia. Take the first major road on the right after Camping Koula to get there, or telephone in advance to be picked up from the boat.

There are also plenty of run-of-the-mill hotels to choose from along the waterfront at Livadia, near Camping Koula.

Yria Hotel Bungalows (☎ 2284 024 154, fax 2284 021 167, ℮ yria1@otenet.gr) Singles/doubles with breakfast €127/168. This fine A-class property, 2.5km south of Parikia, overlooks pretty Parasporos Beach. It has a restaurant, bar, pool and tennis courts.

Places to Eat *Trata* Meals €2.35-11.75. Near the ancient cemetery, Trata has very good seafood, not least its shrimp *saganaki*, and a stimulating array of mezedes, fresh fish and salads.

Porphyra Dishes €2.35-11.75. On the opposite side of the cemetery, Porphyra (named after a shellfish famed for its purple dye and ability to drill a hole into its prey) specialises in unusual seafood delicacies, including raw shellfish. Tamer offerings include fresh fish, calamari and prawns cooked to perfection.

Ephesus Dishes €1.50-8.80. This Anatolian place behind the hospital has delicious, herb-laden home-made dips and appetisers, a large selection of kebabs, and stuffed pizzas cooked in a wood-fired oven.

Levantis (☎ 2284 023 613, Market St) Dishes €3.20-7.70. This is an interesting place in a garden setting with creative international cuisine.

Il Sussuro del Pino Dishes €1.90-11.75, seafood by the kilo. This place earns a big zero for friendliness, but has fresh fish and unusual dishes such as artichokes with calamari. Follow the signs from Skopa, which runs off Market St.

Cactus Mexican Restaurant (☎ 2284 024 164) Dishes €2.10-9.30. By the beach at Livadia, this restaurant has Mexican as well as Greek and international fare.

Entertainment Most bars are along the south-western waterfront, including some busy rooftop bars, like ***Evinos*** and ***Simple***

Cafe. Below the Simple Cafe is *To Rembetika*, which has rembetika music most nights.

Perched above the waterfront, *Pebbles Jazz Bar* (☎ 2284 022 283) plays classical music by day and jazz in the evenings, and has occasional live music.

Alexandros (☎ 2284 023 133) Open 5pm. This restored windmill right on the water's edge is a dreamy spot for a quiet drink.

Aktaia Cafe Bar (☎ 2284 069 7039) Meals €2-8.80. At the northern end of Livadia Beach, this is *the* chilled place for a drink. It's popular with visiting yachties and serves cafe fare at lunch and in the evening, including laksa and risotto.

Saloon D'Or (☎ 2284 022 176) Most big nights out start with warm-up drinks on the waterfront here, and then carry on to the cluster of rowdy nightclubs, further south.

The Dubliner (☎ 2284 021 113) Admission €3. The Dubliner houses the Down Under Bar, the Scandinavian Bar and Paros Rock, all theme bars. If you want to drink, get drunk and dance on tables – get on down. The lamely named *Comma, Club* is nearby.

Avoid any bars offering very cheap cocktails (invariably made from the local *bombes* (moonshine). See the boxed text 'Bombes Beware!' later.

Cinemas Popular open-air cinemas are *Cine Paros*, in Livadia's backstreets, and *Cine Rex* nearby The Dubliner at the southern end of the waterfront. Admission is €5.90 for both places and screening times are 9pm and 11pm.

Around Paros *Punda Beach Club* (☎ 2284 041 717, ⓦ www.pundabeach.gr) This all-day clubbing venue at Punda is a huge complex with a swimming pool, bar, restaurant and, as a matter of necessity, an in-house tattooist and Cuban cigar maker.

Naoussa Ναουσσα

Naoussa, on the north coast, has metamorphosed in twenty years from a peaceful and pristine fishing village into a popular tourist resort. For many visitors, Naoussa *is* Paros; its popularity is due in part to its proximity

to nice beaches and to its slightly upmarket, French Riviera feel. It's certainly a lot less hectic than Parikia. Despite an incursion by package tourists, Naoussa remains relaxed.

Naoussa is still a working harbour with piles of yellow fishing nets, bright caiques, and little ouzeria with rickety tables and raffia chairs, although smart music bars are making inroads here. Behind the central square (where the bus terminates) is a picturesque village, with narrow alleyways whitewashed with fish and flower motifs.

Naoussa Information (☎ 2284 052 158) is an exceptionally helpful information booth near the bus station. It can book accommodation and also has mud maps of the village. *Nissiotissa Tours* (☎ 2284 051 480), left off the main square, can book accommodation and tours, and also has a book exchange.

The post office is a tedious uphill walk from the central square. An Alpha Bank (with ATM) is by the bus station.

Things to See In July and August, Naoussa Paros (ⓔ *parafolk@otenet.gr*), a nationally known folk-dancing group based in Naoussa, performs every Sunday (€7.30); book at Naoussa Information.

Naoussa's **Byzantine museum** *(admission €1.50; open 11am-1.30pm & 7pm-9pm Tues, Thur, Sat & Sun)* is housed in the blue-domed church, about 200m uphill from the town centre. A small **folklore museum** *(admission €1.50; open 7pm-9pm daily)* and the **folklore collection of Naoussa** (☎ 2284 052 284), which focuses on regional costumes, are both signposted from the post office.

The best beaches are **Kolimvythres**, which has interesting rock formations; and **Monastiri**, which has a *clubbing venue* above water and some good snorkelling underwater. Low-key **Lageri** is also worth seeking out. **Santa Maria**, on the other side of the eastern headland, is good for windsurfing. From Naoussa, caiques go to Kolimvythres, Monastiri, Lageri and Santa Maria.

Activities & Organised Tours Scuba diving courses are offered by the *Santa Maria Diving Club* (☎/fax 2284 053 007,

W *www.isdc.gr/santamaria)* Introductory dive €52.50, diploma courses €377. Limited English is spoken here; snorkelling gear is available for hire.

Naoussa Paros Sailing Center *(☎ 2284 052 646,* **e** *sailing@par.forthnet.gr)* Full day €43.50 per person. Departs 9.30am. This company offers sailing tours to Naxos, Delos or Iraklia; half-day tours and yacht charters are also available.

Kokou Riding Centre 1/2/3 hours €20.50/ 29/40.80. Morning and evening horse rides are operated by Kokou. Rides start from the central square; book with any of the travel agents.

Nissiotissa Tours can organise excursions to Naxos, Delos, Mykonos, Santorini and Amorgos.

Places to Stay There are two camping grounds. Minibuses from both meet ferries.

Naoussa Camping *(☎ 2284 051 595)* Adult/tent €5.30/3. This shady camping ground is at Kolimvythres. It has a small taverna and lovely bays nearby.

Surfing Beach *(☎ 2284 052 491, fax 2284 051 937,* **e** *info@surfbeach.gr)* Adult/ tent €5.30/3. This camping ground, at Santa Maria, has a windsurfing and water-ski school (windsurfing courses €14.70 per hour, water-skiing from €17.40 per hour). The staff are decidedly surly, though it has reasonable facilities.

Anna's Rooms *(☎ 2284 051 538)* Doubles €40.80. Anna's has simple, clean rooms with patio. To get there, turn right off the main road into town at Hotel Atlantis (just before the main square).

Hotel Gallini *(☎/fax 2284 051 210)* Doubles €40.80. Directly behind the blue dome of the local church, this small hotel has nice rooms.

Hotel Madaky *(☎ 2284 051 475, fax 2284 052 968)* Singles/doubles €49/53.70. This decent E-class hotel is off the central square.

Hotel Stella *(☎ 2284 051 317, fax 2284 053 617,* **e** *hotelstella@usa.net)* Singles/ doubles €36.30/56.50. In the heart of town, this pension has a shady garden. To reach it, turn left from the central square at Café

Naoussa, then take the first right; continue past a small church on the left.

You'll find there is no shortage of good self-contained accommodation.

Sunset Studios & Apartments *(☎/fax 2284 052 060,* **e** *sunsetmm@otenet.gr)* Doubles/apartments €53.70/69.60,. Nice rooms and 2-bedroom apartments with telephone and air-con are on offer. Face inland from the main square, follow the one-way street uphill, and turn right at the T-junction – it's on the left.

Katerina's *(☎ 2284 051 642)* 2-bedroom apartments €59. This is a stunning place with red shutters and a beautiful patio with views over town and beach. As you come into town, Katerina's is off the main road to the right, behind the OTE.

Spiros Apartments *(☎/fax 2284 052 327, Kolimvythres)* Doubles/triples €46.50/49. These attractive apartments are right on the beach.

Hotel Fotilia *(☎ 2284 052 581, fax 2284 052 583)* Doubles with breakfast €72.50. This elegant B-class hotel, near the big church 200m uphill from the town centre, has spacious, traditional rooms. There is an old windmill in its courtyard, as well as a jacuzzi and pool.

Places to Eat ***Moshonas Ouzeri*** *(☎ 2284 051 623)* Dishes €2.50-8.80, seafood by kilo. Pronounced 'Moskonas', this ouzeria at the harbour serves great fish, supplied by their own fishing boat.

Papadakis Dishes €2.50-8.80. Don't miss Papadakis, on the waterfront near the caiques. The food is traditional, but inventive. The octopus and onion stew is luscious, and there are refreshing salads with fennel, soft local cheese and an assortment of olives and greens.

Perivolaria Dishes €5.30-16. Open from 7pm. This garden restaurant, on the left, along from the bus stop, is a fine, upmarket place. It serves Greek and Italian cuisine and has a take-away pizza bar.

Taverna Christos *(☎ 2284 051 901)* Dishes €2.70-10.30. Open from 7pm. On the way to the post office, Christos is another good option; it's just behind Avra Tours.

Around Paros
Marathi Maraqi In antiquity Parian marble was considered the world's finest. The **marble quarries** have been abandoned, but it's exciting to explore the area. Take the Lefkes bus and get off at Marathi village, where you'll find a signpost to the quarries.

Lefkes (Λεκες) **to Moni Agiou Antoniou** (Μονή Αγίου Αντωνίου) Lefkes, 12km south-east of Parikia, is the island's highest and loveliest village, and was its capital during the Middle Ages. It boasts the magnificent **Agias Trias** cathedral, with it's shaded entrance of olive trees, as well as the **Museum of Popular Aegean Civilisation**, an amphitheatre and an interesting library.

From the central square, a signpost points to a well-preserved Byzantine paved path, which leads to the village of **Prodromos**. Just below the village the path takes a sharp left, which is easy to miss because there isn't a sign – don't take the wider route straight ahead. The walk through beautiful countryside takes about an hour.

From Prodromos, it's a short walk to either **Marmara** or **Marpissa**. From Marmara, it's a stroll to the sandy beach at **Molos**; from Marpissa you can puff your way up a steep, paved path to the 16th-century **Moni Agiou Antoniou** atop a 200m-high hill. On this fortified summit, the Turks defeated Paros' Venetian rulers in 1537. Although the monastery and its grounds are generally locked, there are breathtaking views to neighbouring Naxos.

After this exertion, you'll probably feel like having a swim at the nice little beach at **Piso Livadi**. This pretty fishing village is well on the way to becoming a resort.

Candaca Travel (☎ *2284 041 449, fax 041 449,* e *candaca@otenet.gr) can arrange accommodation and car rental, and also has Internet access.

Places to Stay & Eat There are some *domatia* on the road into Lefkes, including *Studio Calypso* (☎ *2284 041 583).*

Hotel Pantheon (☎*/fax 2284 041 700)* Doubles €42. The only mid-range hotel

accommodation in Lefkes, it has comfortable rooms with balconies. This is a great place to base yourself for a walking holiday.

There are plenty of places to stay and eat overlooking the harbour in Piso Livadi and *Stavros Taverna* is recommended. There's a *camping ground* on the outskirts of town.

Petaloudes Πεταλοδες In July and August, butterflies almost enshroud the copious foliage at Petaloudes *(Valley of the Butterflies; admission €1.20; open 9am-7pm Mon-Sat, 9am-1pm & 4pm-8pm Sun July & Aug).* It's 8km south of Parikia. The butterflies are actually tiger moths, but spectacular all the same. Travel agents organise tours from both Parikia and Naoussa; or take the Aliki bus and ask to be let off at the Petaloudes turn-off.

Beaches Apart from the beaches already mentioned, there is a good beach at **Krios**, accessible by taxi boat (€2 return) from Parikia. Paros' most talked about beach, **Hrysi Akti** (Golden Beach), on the southeast coast, is nothing spectacular, but it's popular with windsurfers. Equipment for various **water sports**, including catamaran sailing, water-skiing and windsurfing, is available from the **Fanatic Fun Centre** (☎ *69-3830 7671,* w *www.fanatic-paros .com; board hire from €11.75 per hour, one-week courses €160).*

The coast between Piso Livadi and Hrysi Akti has some decent, empty beaches, although there are newish beach resorts springing up and swallowing up the coastline all the time, such as those at **Nea Hrysi Akti** (New Golden Beach).

ANTIPAROS
postcode 840 07 • pop 819
Antiparos was once regarded as the quiet alternative to Paros, but development is increasing. The permanent inhabitants live in an attractive village (also called Antiparos) that is rapidly becoming obscured by tourist accommodation. It's still a very pleasant place and is a popular holiday spot for families with young kids. No cars are allowed in the village, which makes it even nicer.

CYCLADES

CYCLADES

Getting To/From Antiparos

For details on boats from Paros, see Getting There & Away under Paros.

The only bus service on Antiparos runs to the cave in the centre of the island (€3). In summer, this bus continues to Soros and Agios Georgios.

Orientation & Information

To reach the village centre if you've come from Pounta, turn right from the quay, walk along the waterfront and turn left into the main street at Anarghyros restaurant. If you've come by excursion boat, walk straight ahead from the quay.

The post office is a fair way down on the left. The OTE, with currency exchange and ferry information, is just beyond. The central square is left at the top of the main street and then right, behind Smiles Cafe.

There are several travel agencies, including Antiparos Travel Agency (☎ 2284 061 300, fax 2284 061 465), by the waterfront, which can organise accommodation.

To reach the kastro, another Marco Sanudo creation, go under the stone arch that leads north off the central square.

Beach bums will direct you to the decent beaches. Nudism is only permitted at Camping Antiparos.

Cave of Antiparos

Despite previous looting of stalactites and stalagmites, this cave (*admission €3; open 10am-3.30pm daily summer*) is still awe-inspiring. In 1673, the French ambassador, Marquis de Nointel, organised a Christmas Mass (enhanced by a large orchestra) inside the cave for 500 Parians.

There are buses every hour from the village of Antiparos (€1.20 one way) or you can take an excursion boat (high season only) from Antiparos village (€3.50) or Parikia (€7.40); the price includes the 1.5km bus ride from the landing stage to the cave.

Activities & Organised Tours

Blue Island Divers (☎/fax 2284 061 493, ⓦ *www.blueisland-divers.gr*) 4-day PADI open-water course €290, advanced course €246, snorkelling day trip €17.40/8.80

adult/child. Based on the main pedestrian thoroughfare, Blue Island has a wide range of dive options and can organise accommodation.

The **MS Thiella** tours around the island daily, stopping at several beaches. The tour includes lunch; book at travel agents.

Places to Stay & Eat

Camping Antiparos (☎/fax 2284 061 221) Adult/tent €4.40/2.30. This well-equipped camping ground, planted with bamboo, is on a beach 1.5km north of the quay; signs point the way.

Domatia are prevalent, especially in the area behind Kouros Village, and there are several hotels.

Argo (☎ 2284 061 419, fax 2284 061 186) Singles/doubles €30.20/49, double studios €82.50. On the road to Camping Antiparos, this small friendly place is recommended by readers, and also has a very good *taverna*. Breakfast is included in the price.

Anarghyros (☎ 2284 061 204) Singles/doubles €34.9/43.50. Rooms have air-con and TV and overlook the fishing harbour.

Hotel Mantalena (☎ 2284 061 206, fax 2284 061 550, ⓔ *mantalenahotel1@par .forthnet.gr*) Doubles/triples €59/64. This hotel is further along from Anarghyros, to the left. All rooms have air-con and a balcony overlooking the port and there's a nice terrace.

The main street has many cafes and tavernas, including the popular *Taverna Yorgis* on the right, which serves Greek family staples and specialises in fish. *Taverna Klimataria* on the path to Fanari is also worth seeking out.

Maki's (☎ 2284 061 616) Dishes €2-8.20. Maki's has two tavernas, one on the waterfront, and the better of the two opposite the OTE. Try the very generous prawn souvlaki with calamari (€8.20).

Stillwaters Restaurant (☎ 2284 024 537, ⓔ *stillwatersap@aol.com, Apandima Beach*) Dishes €4.40-10.30. Only a step away from the water, Stillwaters is a British-run operation which serves modern international cuisine.

Agios Georgios, in the south, has several *tavernas*.

Entertainment

Signposted left off Market St, *Yam Bar Cafe* is an open-air chill-out bar, with views of the sea. It plays a mix of Latin and House music.

The casual *Time Marine Beach Club* (☎ 2284 061 575), about five minutes' walk from the port at Fanari Beach, is a great spot for a game of backgammon and a beer after a swim.

Naxos Ναξος

postcode 843 00 • pop 18,000

According to legend, it was on Naxos that Theseus abandoned Ariadne after he helped him find his way out of the Cretan labyrinth. She didn't pine long – she was soon ensconced in the arms of Dionysos, the god of wine and ecstasy and the island's favourite deity. Ever since, Naxian wine has been considered a fine remedy for a broken heart.

The island is the Cyclades' largest and most fertile, producing olives, grapes, figs, citrus, corn and potatoes. Rugged mountains and lush green valleys also make it one of the most beautiful. Mt Zeus (1004m; also known as Mt Zas or Zefs) is the archipelago's highest peak.

Naxos was an important Byzantine centre and boasts about 500 churches and monasteries, many containing interesting frescoes. Some of the early Christian basilicas were originally ancient temples.

The island is a wonderful place to explore on foot and walking is now a major draw for many visitors, especially Germans. Many old paths linking villages, churches and other sights still survive. For detailed route information, consult Christian Ucke's excellent *Walking Tours on Naxos*, available from local bookshops.

Getting To/From Naxos

Air There is at least one flight daily to/from Athens (€66.90/75.45 one way). Olympic

Airways is represented by Naxos Tours, who also sell ferry tickets.

Ferry Naxos has around six ferry connections daily with Piraeus (six hours, €14.80), Paros (one hour, €4), Ios (1¼ hours, €6.10) and Santorini (three hours, €9); and four daily with Mykonos (three hours, €6).

There is one daily boat to Tinos (4¼ hours, €6.60), Syros (three hours, €6.60), Iraklia (1¼ to 5¼ hours, €4.50), Shinousa (1¾ to five hours, €4.80), Koufonisia (2½ to 4¼ hours, €4.80), Amorgos (two to 5¾ hours, €7) and Donousa (one to four hours, €5).

There are four ferries weekly to Anafi (four hours, €10.30) and Samos (4¾ to 7½ hours, €15.40).

There are three ferries weekly to Fourni (four hours, €11.20), Samos (five to six hours, €15.50) and Ikaria (3½ hours, €9).

There are two boats weekly to Astypalea (5½ hours, €12.90), Rhodes (10 hours, €17.90), Sikinos (three hours, €5.10) and Folegandros (three hours, €7.40).

One goes weekly to Thessaloniki (15 hours, €27.30), Kos (15 hours, €13.50), Iraklio (7 hours, €16.15), Andros (4½ hours, €12.20) and, late in the season, to Skiathos (8½ hours, €21.80).

Fast Boat & Catamaran There are at least two catamarans daily to Paros (30 minutes, €8.20), Mykonos (1½ hours, €11.75) and Piraeus (3¼ hours, €30.20); four weekly to Syros (1½ hours, €12.40); two weekly to Santorini (1½ hours, €19.20); and one weekly to Ios (50 minutes, €12.20).

Excursion Boat There are daily excursions to Mykonos (€26) and frequent excursions to Delos; book through travel agents.

Getting Around Naxos

To/From the Airport There is no shuttle bus, but buses to Agios Prokopios Beach and Agia Anna pass close by. A taxi costs €7.40.

Bus Frequent buses run to Agia Anna (€0.90) from Hora. Five buses daily serve Filoti

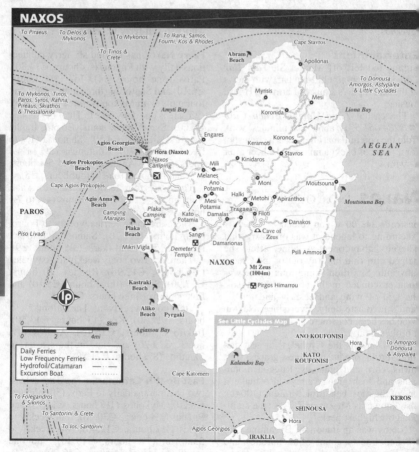

NAXOS

To Piraeus
To Delos & Mykonos
To Mykonos
To Ikaria, Samos, Fourni, Kos & Rhodes
To Tinos & Crete
Cape Stavros
Abram Beach
Apollonas
To Mykonos, Tinos, Paros, Syros, Rafina, Pireaus, Skiathos & Thessaloniki
To Donousa Amorgos, Astypalea & Little Cyclades
Myrisis
Mesi
Amyti Bay
Koronida
Liona Bay
Engares
Koronos
Keramoti
AEGEAN SEA
Agios Georgios Beach
Hora (Naxos)
Naxos Camping
Kinidaros
Stavros
Agios Prokopios Beach
Mili
Melanes
Moni
Moutsouna
Cape Agios Prokopios
Ano Potamia
Halki
Metohi
Apiranthos
Moutsouna Bay
Agia Anna Beach
Plaka Camping
Mesi Potamia
Tragaea
Filoti
PAROS
Camping Maragas
Kato Potamia
Damalas
Danakos
Piso Livadi
Plaka Beach
Sangri
Cave of Zeus
Mikri Vigla
Demeter's Temple
Damarionas
Psili Ammos
NAXOS
Mt Zeus (1004m)
Kastraki Beach
Pirgos Himarrou
Aliko Beach
Pyrgaki
Agiassou Bay

See Little Cyclades Map

ANO KOUFONISI
Hora
To Amorgos Donousa & Asypalea
KATO KOUFONISI
Kalandos Bay
Cape Katomeri

Daily Ferries	– – – – –
Low Frequency Ferries	– · – · –
Hydrofoil/Catamaran	—— ——
Excursion Boat	· · · · ·

0   4   8km
0   2   4mi

To Folegandros & Sikinos
To Santorini & Crete
To Ios, Santorini

SHINOUSA
Hora
KEROS
Agios Georgios
IRAKLIA

(€1.20) via Halki (€1), four serve Apiranthos (€1.70) via Filoti and Halki, at least three serve Apollonas (€3.20), Pyrgaki (€1.20) and Melanes (€0.90). There are less frequent departures to other villages.

Buses leave from the end of the wharf; timetables are posted outside the bus station and the Naxos Tourist Information Centre in Hora.

Car, Motorcycle & Bicycle You can hire cars and motorcycles as well as 21-speed all-terrain bicycles from the waterfront outlets in Hora. Bicycle hire starts at €4.40. You'll need all the gears – the roads are steep, winding and not always in good condition. Remember that this is a relatively large island. It's 35km from Naxos to Apollonas.

HORA

Hora, on the west coast, is the island's port and capital. It's a large town, divided into two historic neighbourhoods – Bourgos, where the Greeks lived, and Kastro, on the hill above, where the Venetian Catholics lived.

A causeway to the north of the port leads to the Palatia Islet and the unfinished emple of Apollo, Naxos' most famous andmark. Legend has it that when İstanbul s returned to Greece, the temple door will niraculously appear.

There are some good swimming areas long the waterfront promenade below the emple. The town's northern shore, called Grotta – nicknamed Grotty by some tourists is not good for swimming as it's very ex->osed, rocky and riddled with sea urchins. outh-west of the town is the sandy beach f Agios Georgios.

Orientation

The ferry quay is at the northern end of the vaterfront, with the bus terminal in front. The busy waterfront is lined with cafes and estaurants and is the focus of most of the ac-ion. Behind the waterfront, a warren of lit-le laneways and steps leads up to the Kastro.

Information

Information booths on the quay give out in-ormation about hotels and domatia. The rivately owned Naxos Tourist Information Centre (NTIC; ☎ 2285 025 201, emergency ☎ 2285 024 525, fax 2285 025 200, e apollon-hotel@naxos-island.com), op->osite the quay, provides in-depth advice on ccommodation, excursions and rental cars; uggage storage is available (€1.50). Note hat the NTIC does not sell ferry tickets.

Zas Travel (☎ 2285 023 330, fax 2285 •23 419) and Naxos Tours (☎ 2285 022 •95, 2285 023 043, e naxostours@ naxos-island.com) are both helpful travel gencies that sell boat tickets and organ-se accommodation, tours and rental cars.

There are at least three ATMs on the wa-erfront. The OTE is 150m further south. 'or the post office, continue past the OTE, ross Papavasiliou and take the left branch vhere the road forks. Internet access is vailable from Matrix Cyber Café (☎/fax 25 •27, e enquiries@matrixnaxos.com, W www matrixnaxos.com) and Zoom (☎ 2285 023 •75) on the waterfront.

The police are south-east of Plateia Pro-odikiou (☎ 2285 022 100). The port police ☎ 2285 023 300) are in the town hall, south f the quay.

The island is endowed with many springs; look for public taps and drinking fountains where you can refill your water bottle.

Things to See & Do

After leaving the waterfront, turn into the winding backstreets of Bourgos. The most alluring part of Hora is the residential Kastro, with winding alleyways and whitewashed houses. Marco Sanudo made the town the capital of his duchy in 1207, and there are some handsome Venetian dwellings, many with well-kept gardens and the insignia of their original residents. Take a stroll around the Kastro during siesta to experience its hushed, medieval atmosphere.

The archaeological museum (☎ 2285 022 725, admission €3; open 8.30am-3pm Tues-Sun) is in the Kastro, housed in a for-mer school where Kate Nikos Kazantzakis was briefly a pupil. The contents include Hellenistic and Roman terracotta figurines. There are also, more interestingly, some early Cycladic figurines.

Close by, the crumbling Della Rocca-Barozzi Venetian Museum (☎ 2285 022 387; open 10am-3pm & 7pm-10pm daily; multilingual guided tours €4.40/1.50 adult/student, Kastro tours €10.30/5.90), is within the Kastro ramparts by the north-west gate. It was, until recently, still a resi-dence; a visit is a brief, voyeuristic journey back in time. Sunset concerts are held here several times a week.

The Roman Catholic cathedral (open 6.30pm daily), also in the Kastro, is worth visiting (tours at 6pm) as well. The Naxos Cultural Centre nearby has exhibitions over summer.

Organised Tours

NTIC offers day tours of the island by bus (€17.60) or caique (€38, including barbe-cue). One-day walking tours (€43.50 for two people) are offered three times weekly.

Cruises run to different destinations daily run from Agia Anna. Cruises head either to Iraklia and Koufonisia, Shinousa and Kou-fonisia, or Antiparos; book at travel agents.

Small-group mountain-biking tours for €5.90 per person are also on offer; contact

CYCLADES

CYCLADES

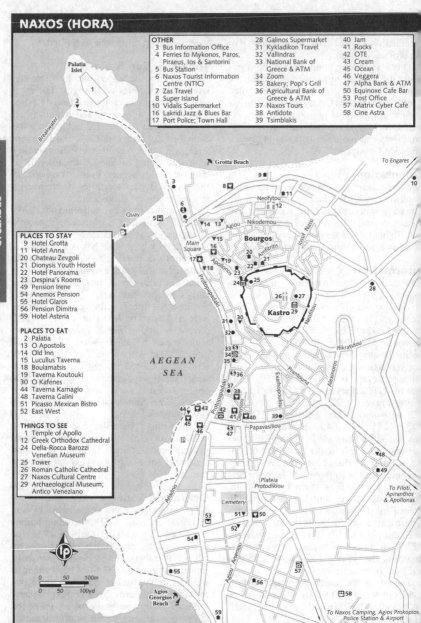

NAXOS (HORA)

OTHER
3 Bus Information Office
4 Ferries to Mykonos, Paros, Piraeus, Ios & Santorini
5 Bus Station
6 Naxos Tourist Information Centre (NTIC)
7 Zas Travel
8 Super Island
10 Vidalis Supermarket
16 Lakridi Jazz & Blues Bar
17 Port Police; Town Hall
28 Galinos Supermarket
31 Kykladikon Travel
32 Vallindras
33 National Bank of Greece & ATM
34 Zoom
35 Bakery; Popi's Grill
36 Agricultural Bank of Greece & ATM
37 Naxos Tours
38 Antidote
39 Tsimblakis
40 Jam
41 Rocks
42 OTE
43 Cream
45 Ocean
46 Veggera
47 Alpha Bank & ATM
50 Equinoxe Cafe Bar
53 Post Office
57 Matrix Cyber Cafe
58 Cine Astra

PLACES TO STAY
9 Hotel Grotta
11 Hotel Anna
20 Chateau Zevgoli
21 Dionysis Youth Hostel
22 Hotel Panorama
23 Despina's Rooms
49 Pension Irene
54 Anemos Pension
55 Hotel Glaros
56 Pension Dimitra
59 Hotel Asteria

PLACES TO EAT
2 Palatia
13 O Apostolis
14 Old Inn
15 Lucullus Taverna
18 Boulamatsis
19 Taverna Koutouki
30 O Kafenes
44 Taverna Karnagio
48 Taverna Galini
51 Picasso Mexican Bistro
52 East West

THINGS TO SEE
1 Temple of Apollo
12 Greek Orthodox Cathedral
24 Della-Rocca Barozzi Venetian Museum
25 Tower
26 Roman Catholic Cathedral
27 Naxos Cultural Centre
29 Archaeological Museum; Antico Veneziano

Palatia Islet

Breakwater

Grotta Beach

To Engares

Quay

Neofytou

Main Square

Bourgos

Agiou Nikodemou

Iosif Nassa

Amfitritis

Apollonos

Kastro

Protopapadaki

Neofitou

AEGEAN SEA

Ifikratidou

Prantouna

Alexinoros

Exathopoulou

Protopapadaki

Dionissou

Papavasiliou

Ariadnis

Plateia Protodikiou

Cemetery

Agiou Arseniou

Plateia Protodikiou

To Filoti, Apiranthos & Apollonas

Agios Georgios Beach

To Naxos Camping, Agios Prokopios Police Station & Airport

0   50   100m
0   50   100yd

ain (☎ 2285 024 641, e *eastwest@naxos -island.com*), or drop into the East West restaurant.

Places to Stay – Budget

There are several camping grounds near Hora. All have good facilities and some offer walking tours. Minibuses meet the ferries.

Naxos Camping (☎ 2285 023 500) €4.65 per person. This place is 1km south of Agios Georgios Beach and has a swimming pool.

Camping Maragas (☎/fax 2285 024 552) €4.65 per person. This site is at Agia Anna Beach.

Plaka Camping (☎ 2285 042 700, fax 2285 042 701) €4.65 per person. This site is 6km from town at Plaka Beach.

Dionysos Youth Hostel (☎ 2285 022 331) Dorm beds €5.90, singles/doubles €14.70/17.60. Open year-round. This is a good place to meet other travellers, and has dorm beds and simply furnished rooms. The hostel is signposted from Agiou Nikodemou, Bourgos' main street.

Many domatia owners meet ferries.

Despina's Rooms (☎ 2285 022 356) Singles/doubles from €23.20/34.90. This 400-year-old family home is on the edge of the Kastro, nearby Chateau Zevgoli. The views here are impressive and rooms are comfortable.

Pension Dimitra (☎ 2285 024 922) Doubles/triples €30.20/49. This pension is right on Agios Georgios Beach; rooms have a balcony.

Pension Irene (☎ 2285 023 169, e *irenepension@hotmail.com*) Doubles around €29. This pension is south-east of the town centre and has cooking facilities.

Hotel Anna (☎ 2285 025 213) Singles/ doubles €29/34.90, triples €43.50 with kitchenette. This is a nice place near the Orthodox cathedral.

Anemos Pension (☎ 2285 025 098) Doubles €40.60. This pension is near the post office.

Hotel Panorama (☎/fax 2285 024 404) Doubles €46.60. This hotel near the Kastro has a roof garden with superb views; rooms are lovely and quiet.

Places to Stay – Mid-Range

Hotel Grotta (☎ 2285 022 215, fax 2285 022 000, e *grotta@naxos-island.com*) Singles/doubles €49/61. This friendly hotel has splendid sea views from its dining room (though only a limited number of rooms have views).

Chateau Zevgoli (☎ 2285 026 123, fax 2285 025 200) Doubles €46.60-72.50. In Bourgos, Zevgoli has traditionally furnished rooms.

Hotel Argo (☎ 2285 025 330, fax 2285 024 910) Singles/doubles with air-con €38/52.50. This hotel is on Agios Georgios Beach and rooms all have balcony with either sea or mountain view, TV and kitchenette.

Hotel Glaros (☎ 2285 023 101, fax 2285 024 877) Singles/doubles with breakfast €43.50/56.50. Rooms here have a sea view.

Hotel Asteria (☎ 2285 023 002, fax 2285 022 334) Singles/doubles €46.40/75.40. Down by the beach at Agios Georgios and run by friendly staff, Asteria a good midrange option.

Places to Eat

Naxos seems to be overflowing with good restaurants, popular local favourites include *Taverna Koutouki*, *Boulamatsis*, *Popi's Grill* (the best place for souvlaki), and *Taverna Galini*.

O Apostolis (☎ 2285 026 777) Dishes €0.90-20.50. Apostolis is a great place for mezedes, fresh fish and grilled octopus (a local speciality); Follow the path from the Old Inn, past Arali and turn right.

The Old Inn (☎ 2285 026 093) Dishes €3.50-11. The Old Inn has German fare with the occasional Greek influence. On offer are dishes, such as home-made sausages with beer sauce, potatoes and salad.

Lucullus Taverna (☎ 2285 022 569) Dishes €1.70-11.30. Lucullus is one of the oldest tavernas in Naxos, operating since 1905, and has a relaxed dining area cloaked in grape vines.

Taverna Karnagio (☎ 2285 023 057) Dishes €1.70-5.80, seafood by the kilo. Owned by an eccentric fisherman, Karnagio has limited, but excellent, choices on offer.

CYCLADES

Palatia (☎ 2285 026 588) Dishes €1.50-8.80, seafood by the kilo. At the end of the promenade, Palatia is a lovely spot with tables right on the water's edge. It serves light meals and seafood.

Picasso Mexican Bistro (☎ 2285 025 408) Mains €3.50-9.30. Open 7pm-midnight. Arrive early and nab a table – Picasso and its *burritos*, *fajitas* and *quesadillas* are very popular.

East West (☎ 2285 024 641, *off Arseniou*) Mains €5.60-9.90. If you're hankering for Chinese, Indian or Thai favourites, head to East West. It's not as good as the real thing – but it's still good.

Immediately adjacent to Zoom bookshop is the town's best *bakery*. The cheapest *supermarkets* are Galinos and Vidalis, both a little way out of town.

Naxian specialities include *kefalotyri* (hard cheese), honey, *kitron* (a liqueur made from the leaves of the citron tree), *raki*, ouzo, and fine white wine. Head to *Tsimblakis* on Papavasiliou, a fascinating, cavernous old place selling local produce.

Entertainment
Sunset Concerts Evening concerts, featuring traditional instruments, are held several times weekly in the outdoor grounds of the *Venetian Museum* (☎ 2285 022 387).

Bars Arseniou St, nearby Picasso, is buzzing early in the evening. *Equinoxe Cafe Bar* (☎ 2285 025 839) is a fine place to take in all the energy and atmosphere of the street. It plays a mix of Spanish, Mojo, disco and Latino grooves.

One block back from the waterfront, *Rocks* is a popular late-night bar, while *Jam* is a small, dark low-key place that plays rock and assorted odd-bod sounds.

Antidote has at least 55 different types of beer from around the world, while *Lakridi Jazz & Blues Bar*, on the way to the Kastro, is a nice, laid-back little place.

Nightclubs For clubbing, head to *Cream*, *Ocean* and *Veggera Bar* (☎ 2285 023 567), all at the end of the waterfront near the OTE. Expect to hear a mix of House, techno

and electronica. On Saturday night, Veggera has a fun '70s- and '80s-inspired night.

Super Island, right on the waterfront, at Grotta Beach, is a huge dance space and *the* late-night venue.

Cinemas *Cine Astra* (☎ 2285 025 381, Admission €5.90. Sessions 9pm & 11pm. About a five-minute walk from Plateia Protodikiou, Cine Astra shows new release mainstream films and has a bar.

Shopping
At *Vallindras* (☎ 2285 022 227) on the waterfront, you can find kitron liqueur in beautiful French and Italian bottles, as well as ouzo.

In the streets heading up to the Kastro you can find beautiful embroidery and hand-made silver jewellery.

Antico Veneziano, an upmarket antique store and gallery, in a restored home in the Kastro, makes for a fascinating visit.

AROUND NAXOS
Beaches
Agios Georgios is just a typical town beach but you can windsurf here and the water is so shallow that it seems you could wade to Paros, visible in the distance (the beach becomes so crowded that you may develop an uncontrollable desire to do so).

Flisvos Sport Club (☎/fax 2285 024 308 @ *flisvos@otenet.gr*) holds a free windsurfing trial lesson every Saturday at 4pm. The club also rents out catamarans and mountain bikes.

The next beach south is **Agios Prokopios**, a sheltered bay. This is followed by **Agia Anna**, a lovely long arc of sand. Sandy beaches continue down as far as **Pyrgaki**. There are *domatia* and *tavernas* aplenty along this stretch, and any of these beaches would make a good spot to stop for a few days. Other worthy beaches are **Plaka**, **Aliko**, **Mikri Vigla** and **Kastraki**. **Abram**, north of Hora, is also a nice spot.

Tragaea Τραγαία
The lovely Tragaea region is a vast plain of olive groves and unspoilt villages harbouring

Glory Days of the Citron

The citron *(Citrus medica)* looks like a very large, lumpy lemon. It has a thick rind and an interior yielding little juice. This seemingly useless fruit was introduced to the Mediterranean area in about 300 BC, probably by Alexander the Great, and up until the Christian era it was the only citrus fruit cultivated in Europe. In antiquity the citron was known for its medicinal qualities and was also a symbol of fertility and affluence. The ancient Greeks called it the 'median' apple (from Media, the ancient Greek name for Persia).

Citron trees are fussy about where they'll grow – they need abundant water and do not tolerate any wind or cold – but they have been happy on Naxos for centuries. Although the fruit is barely edible in its raw state, the Naxians discovered that the rind becomes quite exquisite when preserved in syrup. They also put the aromatic leaves to good use by creating *kitroraki*, a raki distilled from grape skins and citron leaves. By the late-19th century the preserved fruit and a sweet version of kitroraki, known as *kitron*, had cult followings outside Greece and were popular exports to Russia, Austria, France and the USA. Kitron was so much in demand that it became the mainstay of the island's economy and, by the early 20th century, Naxos was carpeted with citron orchards.

Alas, kitron went out of vogue after WWII; even the islanders abandoned it, seduced by the invasion of exotic alcohols from the outside world. In the 1960s most citron trees were uprooted to make way for more useful, more profitable crops.

This might seem like a sad story but fear not, the citron is on the rise. On Naxos, Vallindras distillery in Halki still distils citron the old-fashioned way, using leaves collected from the orchards in the autumn and winter. The harvesting of leaves is an arduous, time-consuming task, due to the trees' thorns, and if too many leaves are taken the tree can be destroyed. The leaves are laid out in a dry room, dampened with water and then placed with alcohol and water in a boiler fuelled by olive wood. The distillate is added to water and sugar, and citron is born.

These days approximately 13,000 to 15,000L of kitron are produced each year at Vallindras. Still, this is nowhere near enough to meet current demand, and nothing can be done about this until more citron trees are planted. It is nearly impossible to get hold of kitron outside Greece, so make sure you track some down while visiting its island home. It comes in three strengths and degrees of sweetness: The green is the traditional Naxian liqueur and has the most sugar and least alcohol; the yellow has little sugar, more aroma and more alcohol; the white falls somewhere in between and resembles Cointreau. Kitron is very good after dinner, especially after fish.

If you want to see citron trees in action, look for orchards around Hora and in Engares, Melanes, Halki and Apollonas.

CYCLADES

numerous little Byzantine churches. **Filoti**, on the slopes of Mt Zeus, is the region's largest village. On the outskirts of the village (coming from Hora), an asphalt road leads off right into the heart of the Tragaea. This road brings you to the isolated hamlets of **Damarionas** and **Damalas**.

From Filoti, you can also reach the **Cave of Zeus**. From the end of the signposted road, a path leads past a small spring and a handful of goats. Follow the markers to the cave – a steep and strenuous half-hour walk. The cave is best explored with a torch. The path is also an excellent spot to view the peak of Mt Zeus; a stark and strikingly barren rocky peak.

The picturesque village of **Halki** has several tower houses built by aristocratic families as refuges and lookouts in the days of pirate raids and feuds between the islanders and the Venetians and Turks. The best preserved is the **Gratsia Pyrgos**; to reach it turn right at **Panagia Protothronis**, which is itself worth checking out for its fine frescoes. It is on the main road near the bus stop.

The **Vallindras distillery** (☎ *2285 031 220)*, housed in a lovely old building in the centre of Halki, offers kitron tastings and impromptu tours. A few steps away is *L'O-livier* (☎ 2285 032 829), a ceramic studio and craft gallery that specialises in detailed crockery ceramics focused around that most sacred of plants, the olive tree. Olive products from candles to oil are also on sale.

Agii Apostoli (Holy Apostles) church in Metohi is famous for its odd triple-storey architecture, while **Agios Mamas**, near Potamia, is known for its early 'cross in a square' layout. The **Panagia Drosiani**, at **Moni** north of Halki, is one of the oldest and most important churches in the Balkans. Successive layers of frescoes have been uncovered, some dating back to the 7th century. If it's locked, seek out the priest's wife and ask for the key.

South-west of the Tragaea, near **Sangri**, an impressive **Temple to Demeter** (also known as Dimitra's Temple) has been restored. The small church next to the temple was originally built from remnants of the temple and was recently demolished and rebuilt so that the temple material could be salvaged. Signs point the way from Sangri.

Melanes Μέλανες

Near the hillside villages of Melanes and Mili, there is a 2m-high, unfinished 6th-century BC **kouros** (male statue), abandoned in a quarry that is now encircled by orchards. The Kondylis family, who own the land, are the official guardians.

Next to the site is a little *cafe* of sorts where an old lady serves Greek coffee, wine, omelettes and salads. Another, less famous, kouros was found nearby a few years ago; ask at the cafe for directions.

From Melanes you can walk down to **Kato Potamia**, **Mesi Potamia** and **Ano Potamia**, where there are more orchards and lovely tavernas. From there, it's not far to Halki, where you can catch the bus back to town.

Places to Eat *Taverna Xenakis* (☎ 2285 062 374) Dishes €1.50-5.50. In Melanes, Xenakis has delicious rabbit and free-range chicken; if you order an hour in advance, you will be served a feast.

Yanni's in Halki in the main square, serves perfect village salads (€4.40) with lashings of *myzithra*, the local cheese; one salad is enough for two.

Pirgos Himarrou Πύργος Χειμάρρου

South of Filoti, in the island's remote southeast, the Pirgos Himarrou is a well preserved cylindrical marble tower dating from Hellenistic times. It is three storeys high with an internal spiral staircase. One theory holds that it was a lookout post used to warn of approaching pirates, but the position of the tower in a place with limited views discounts this. It was more likely a fortified house on a prosperous farmstead – the marble base of a large olive or wine press lies nearby.

After checking out the tower, continue south for a swim at **Kalandos Bay**. Take food and water as there are no shops or tavernas.

Apiranthos Απείρανθος

Apiranthos is a handsome village of stone houses and marble-paved streets. Its inhabitants are descendants of refugees who fled Crete to escape Turkish repression. The village is known for its communist tendencies – its most famous son is Manolis Glezos, the resistance fighter who during WWII replaced the Nazi flag atop the Acropolis with the Greek one. He later became the parliamentary representative for the Cyclades.

Right of the village's main thoroughfare (coming from the Hora-Apollonas road) is a **museum of natural history** *(open 8.30am-3pm Tues-Sun)*. Just before the museum a path on your left leads to the centre of town, the **geology museum** *(open 8.30am-3pm Tues-Sun)* and the **archaeology museum** *(admission €3; open 8.30am-3pm Tues-Sun)*. The museums are sometimes open later in summer.

Just before the beautiful main square dominated by a huge plane tree is *Lefteris* where you can eat in the garden overlooking the valley. It has a selection of delicious home-made sweets and baklava. Apiranthos has no accommodation.

Moutsouna Μουτσούνα

The road from Apiranthos to Moutsouna winds through spectacular mountain scenery,

Formerly a busy port shipping the emery mined in the region, Moutsouna is now something of a ghost town. It feels peaceful rather than spooky and there are some nice beaches with superbly clear water. There are a few pensions and *tavernas* here.

Apollonas Απολλωνας

Apollonas, on the north coast, was once a tranquil fishing village, but is now a popular resort. It has a small sandy beach and a larger pebble one.

Hordes of day-trippers come to see the gargantuan 7th century BC **kouros**, which lies in an ancient quarry a short walk from the village. The largest of three on the island (the other two are in the Melanes region), it is signposted to the left as you approach Apollonas on the main inland road from Hora. This 10.5m statue was apparently abandoned unfinished because it cracked. Apollonas has several *domatia* and *tavernas*.

The inland route from Hora to Apollonas winds through spectacular mountains – a worthwhile trip. With your own transport you can return to Hora via the west-coast road, passing through wild and sparsely populated country with awe-inspiring sea views. Several tracks branch down to secluded beaches.

Little Cyclades
Μικρές Κυκλάδες

The chain of small islands between Naxos and Amorgos is variously called the Little Cyclades, Minor Islands, Back Islands and Lesser Islands. Only four – Donousa, Koufonisia (comprising Ano Koufonisia and Kato Koufonisia), Iraklia and Shinousa – have permanent populations.

All were densely populated in antiquity, as is evident from the large number of graves found. In the Middle Ages, the islands were uninhabited except by pirates and goats. After independence, intrepid souls from Naxos and Amorgos began to reinhabit them, and now each island has a

small population. Until recently, their only visitors were Greeks returning to their roots. These days they receive a few tourists, mostly backpackers looking for splendid beaches and a laid-back lifestyle.

Donousa is the northernmost of the group and farthest from Naxos. The others are clustered near the south-east coast of Naxos. Each has a public telephone and post agency. Money can usually be changed at the general store or post agency, but rates are lousy – bring cash with you .

Getting To/From the Little Cyclades

Links with the Little Cyclades are regular but tenuous, so make sure you have plenty of time before embarking on a visit – these islands do not make a convenient last stop a few days before you're due to fly home!

At least a few times a week the Fast Boat *Express Skopelitis* provides a lifeline service between Naxos and Amorgos via the Little Cyclades (see the Naxos and Amorgos sections for details), but it's small, extremely slow, and susceptible to bad weather (make sure you're wearing warm, wet-weather gear on board – expect to get wet!). In high season it operates several routes, with regular runs from Amorgos to Koufonisia (one hour, €4.40), Shinousa (1½ hours, €5.90) Iraklia and Naxos, returning by the same route, and a run from Amorgos to Donousa. There is also one weekly ferry from Donousa to Syros (3½ hours, €8.20) and Tinos (2½ hours, €10.30); 2 weekly to Mykonos (2 hours, €8.80) and Paros (two to four hours, €7); one weekly catamaran from Shinousa to Tinos (three hours, €14) and Mykonos (2½ hours, €13). Two weekly ferries go to Paros (four hours, €6.40). One daily ferry goes to Naxos (1¾ to five hours, €4.80), Iraklia and Naxos, returning by the same route; and Naxos to Paros (Piso Livadi) to Iraklia, Shinousa, Koufonisia, Donousa and Amorgos.

Once a week the Fast Boat *Express Apollon* sails from Piraeus to each of the Little Cyclades via Naxos, continuing to Amorgos. A few other large ferries call at the islands in high season, often at ungodly hours.

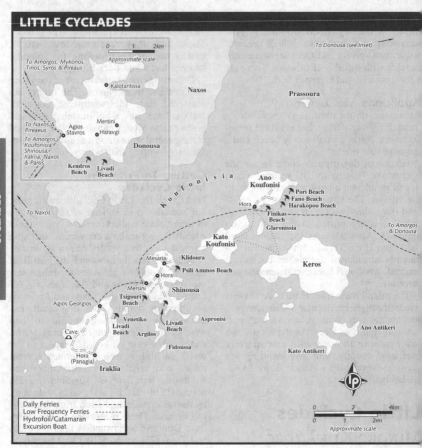

LITTLE CYCLADES

To Donousa (see Inset)

To Amorgos, Mykonos, Tinos, Syros & Pireaus

0   1   2km
Approximate scale

Kalotaritissa

Naxos

Prassoura

To Naxos & Pireaeus

Mersini

Agios Stavros

Haravgi

To Amorgos, Koufonisia, Shinousa, Iraklia, Naxos & Paros

Donousa

Kendros Beach   Livadi Beach

K o u f o n i s i a

Ano Koufonisi

Hora

Pori Beach
Fano Beach
Harakopou Beach

Finikas Beach
Glaronissia

To Naxos

Kato Koufonisi

To Amorgos & Donousa

Keros

Mesaria

Klidoura

Hora

Psili Ammos Beach

Mersini

Shinousa

Agios Georgios

Tsigouri Beach

Cave

Venetiko Livadi Beach

Argilos

Livadi Beach

Aspronisi

Ano Antikeri

Fidoussa

Kato Antikeri

Hora (Panagia)

Iraklia

Daily Ferries
Low Frequency Ferries
Hydrofoil/Catamaran
Excursion Boat

0   2   4km
0   1   2mi
Approximate scale

Because of its northerly position, it is sometimes easier to get to Donousa from Mykonos than from Naxos.

IRAKLIA Ηρακλεια
postcode 843 00 • pop 110

This rather barren island has a couple of tiny villages, a nice beach and not much else, save a small clique of Germans who return each year. The island's only sight as such is a **cave** with fine stalactites. Tourism is increasing, but amenities (including rooms) are few. The port and main village is **Agios Georgios**. It's very quiet and not

particularly scenic, although the deep cove-like harbour is rather pretty. The way into town is to the right, around the port beach and then left up the hill. From here the town's two main roads fork around a cactus-filled ravine.

The right fork leads to Melissa, the general store that sells ferry tickets. Melissa also has a cardphone, serves as the island's post office and has domatia. The left fork leads past the second minimarket (which is also Perigiali restaurant) and more domatia. You can exchange money at Melissa and at Maistrali bar-cafe.

A new sealed road leads off to the left (as you face inland from the harbour). This runs to **Livadi** – the island's nicest beach, and the stomping ground of a picturesque herd of goats. Farther on is the tiny village of **Hora**, also known as Panagia.

Places to Stay & Eat

All domatia and tavernas are in Agios Georgios, although a few spring up on the beach at Livadi in high season. Domatia owners meet the boats, but the shortage of rooms makes it a sellers' market – take whatever you can get and don't bother looking for bargains. In high season doubles go for around €29. If possible, call ahead.

The most central rooms are near the port and include: *Melissa* (☎ *2285 071 539, fax 2285 071 561*) with doubles from €43.50; *Anthi & Angelo's* (☎ *2285 071 486*) with doubles for €34.90; and *Manolis* (☎ *2285 071 569, fax 071 561*) which has doubles for €34.90 (open high season only).

Alexandra (☎ *2285 071 482, fax 2285 071 545*) Doubles €34.90. Up on the windy hill on the way to Livadi, rooms here have nice patios and are just a stone's throw from the beach.

Anna's Place (☎/fax *2285 071 145*) Doubles €34.90. This swish place also has deluxe apartments with a view.

Marietta (☎ *2285 071 252*) Doubles €29. Marietta has nice rooms right on the beach at Livadi.

There are three tavernas in Agios Georgios, all serving fresh fish and the usual fare. *Perigiali*, a popular place, has a large marble table encircling an old pine tree. *O Pevkos*, also known as Dimitri's, is more traditional and shaded by an even larger pine. You'll be led into the kitchen to choose your meal; for breakfast try the yogurt served with the local thyme honey.

Maistrali (☎ *2285 071 807*), opposite Pevkos, is the local cafe-bar; it also sells ferry tickets and has *rooms*.

SHINOUSA Σχοινοσα
postcode 843 00 • pop 120
Shinousa (skih-**noo**-sah) is a little gem of an island with a lively **hora** and smiling residents. The hora (also known as Panagia) has sweeping views of the sea and neighbouring islands on all sides, and nestles inconspicuously into the rolling golden landscape. Although a recent spate of building on the outskirts of the hora and by the beaches has taken place, there's still a very pastoral feeling about the island, which has its share of happy cows, chickens, donkeys and goats.

Ferries pull in at the harbour in **Mersini**, home to the island's fishing boats. The hora is 1km uphill, so try to get a lift with one of the locals offering rooms. Dirt tracks lead from the hora to numerous beaches around the coast; take food and water, because, with the exception of **Tsigouri**, there are no shops or tavernas at the beaches.

There's a public telephone in the main square and a couple of general stores sell stamps. The first among these sells ferry tickets. Tickets are also sold at the port a few minutes before boats arrive. There is a travel agency at Grispos Tsigouri Beach Villas in Tsigouri, which has ferry information and tickets.

Places to Stay
There are a few rooms down at Mersini, but if you want to see the rest of the island you're much better off staying in the hora.

Kyra Pothiti (☎ *2285 071 184*) Doubles €29. In the centre of the village on the main street, Pothiti has nice, cosy rooms with balcony.

Anna Domatia (☎ *2285 071 161, fax 2285 071 948*) Singles/doubles €26.10/32. On the road to Mesaria, Anna's has good, clean rooms.

Hotel Sunset (☎ *2285 071 948, fax 2285 071 948*) Singles/doubles €32/43.50. This is a brand new, comfortable but impersonal complex. It's run by the folk at Anna Domatia.

Grispos Tsigouri Beach Villas (☎ *2285 071 930, fax 2285 071 176*, e *grispos@ nax.forthnet.gr*) Doubles with breakfast €55. This is a crazy family affair about 500m away from the hora, down by the beach at Tsigouri. It's close to the beach, but if you want to pop into the hora

CYCLADES

occasionally, you're faced with a long walk uphill.

Panorama (☎ *2285 071 160*) Doubles €38, with kitchen €43.50. By the beach at Livadi, Panorama is similarly isolated.

Places to Eat

You're unlikely to have any very uplifting culinary adventures on Shinousa, an island where you might want to do a bit of self-catering. Outside high season the only establishment open for lunch is ***Kyra Pothiti***. All drinks and meals come with obligatory serves of home-made *myzithra*. Steer clear of the greasy-spoon *giouvetsi* (meat with macaroni) and stick to fish and baked vegetables. *Panorama* has good salads and char-coal-grilled fish, and ***tavernas*** at the port serve freshly caught fish and lobster. The ***bakery*** just past Anna Domatia on the road to Mesaria is a good place to have breakfast.

To Kentro Kafeneio is the most popular and nicest looking bar, but is pretty much a male-only domain; brave women may wish to transgress its boundaries.

Cafe-Pub Margarita, down the steps just around the corner, is the only other bar.

KOUFONISIA Κουφονήσια
postcode 843 00 • pop 284

Koufonisia is the only one of the Little Cyclades that's anywhere near the tourist trail, and it has a lot to offer. It's really two islands, Ano Koufonisi and Kato Koufonisi, but only the latter is permanently inhabited.

Despite being the smallest of the Little Cyclades, Koufonisia is the most densely populated, which adds quite a bit of life to its hora. Every family is involved with fishing – the island boasts the largest fishing fleet in Greece in proportion to its population. And because it's so attractive, it hasn't suffered from an exodus of young people to the mainland and the consequent ghost-town effect seen on many of the Cyclades; in fact, it's brimming with happy children and teenagers.

The beaches are picture-perfect swathes of golden sand lapped by crystal-clear turquoise waters; the locals are hospitable and friendly; and food and accommodation options are far more plentiful and refined than on neighbouring islands.

A caique ride away, **Kato Koufonisi** has beautiful beaches and a lovely church. Archaeological digs on **Keros**, the large lump of rock that looms over Koufonisia to the south, have uncovered over 100 Early Cycladic figurines, including the famous harpist and flautist now on display in Athens' archaeological museum. There are no guides at the site.

Orientation & Information

Koufonisia's only settlement extends behind the ferry quay and around the pretty harbour filled with the island's fishing flotilla. The older part of town, the hora, is on the low hill behind the quay.

From the quay head right towards the town beach, and take the first road to the left. Continue to the crossroads, then turn left onto the village's main pedestrian thoroughfare, decorated with flower motifs.

Along here you'll find a small mini-market and an inconspicuous ticket agency (look for the dolphins painted above the door). Also here is the tiny OTE. The post office is on the first road to the left as you come from the ferry quay.

Koufonisia Tours (see Organised Tours later) sells ferry tickets and can organise accommodation on the island.

The town beach sees a few swimmers, but mostly serves as a football field (fishing nets are strung up on the goal posts) for the local kids. Cars and pedestrians heading to the south coast road also traverse it.

Beaches

Koufonisia is blessed with some outstanding beaches and a wild coastal landscape of low sand dunes punctuated by rocky coves and caves. The dunes are covered in wild flowers and hardy shrubs.

A walk along the south coast road is the nicest way to access the island's beaches. The road extends a couple of kilometres from the eastern end of the town beach to **Finikas**, **Harakopou** and **Fano** Beaches.

However, the best beaches and swimming places are farther along the path that follows the coast from Fano to the superb stretch of sand at **Pori**. A *cantina* operates in high season selling delicious cheese pies and cold drinks. Pori can also be reached by an inland road that heads east from the crossroads in the hora.

Organised Tours

Koufonisia Tours (☎ 2285 071 671, fax 2285 074 091, Villa Ostria), can organise caique trips to Keros and Kato Koufonisi.

Places to Stay

Koufonisia Camping (☎/fax 2285 071 683) Camp sites €9.30 for 2. This site is by the beach at Harakopou; though there's not much shade, it's adequate.

Rooms Maria (☎ 2285 071 778) Apartments €34.90. At the western end of the village, Maria's has cute two-person apartments overlooking the small fishing harbour. To get there, walk along the main pedestrian street and take the first left after Scholeio bar.

Rooms to Let Akrogiali (☎ 2285 071 685) Doubles €35.70. Akrogiali has nice rooms with sea views at the eastern end of the beach.

Lefteris Rooms (☎/fax 2285 071 458) Doubles/triples/quads €30.20/34.90/46.60. These rooms are on the town beach.

Katerina's (☎ 2285 071 670) Doubles €40.80. On the road leading from the port to the hora, Katerina's has nice clean doubles with balcony and shared kitchen.

Villa Ostria (☎/fax 2285 071 671) Doubles with/without breakfast €59/52.50. This is a cosy little hotel with very comfortable rooms with telephone and veranda. To get there, walk along the town beach and take the first left.

Keros Hotel (☎ 2285 071 600, fax 2285 071 601) Doubles €59-69.60. This hotel, near the post office, has nice rooms.

Hotel Finikas (☎ 2285 071 368, fax 2285 071 744) Doubles €23.20-43.50. On the beach at Finikas, this hotel has both simple and swish rooms; all rooms have a balcony.

Places to Eat

Giorgos At the eastern end of the waterfront on the road to the beaches, Giorgos has

excellent fish and good wines from all over Greece.

Everything at *Captain Nikolas* is delicious, but the grilled fresh fish, is hard to beat. The restaurant looks out over the small harbour at the western end of the village; to get there, follow the main pedestrian street (past signage for another unrelated Captain Nikolas taverna) to the end and turn left. *Nikitouri*, past the Keros Hotel, also has good fish.

Below the rooms of the same name *Lefteris* has fine, reasonably priced Greek standards and is one of the few places open for lunch.

Next to the windmills above the quay, *Fanari* has good wood-fired pizzas, *pastitsio* and gyros. *Scholeio* is a cosy little bar and creperie occupying an old schoolhouse at the far end of the main pedestrian street.

Out of town, there's a *taverna* by the beach at Finikas and an excellent fish taverna, *Taverna Giannis* (☎ 2285 074 074) on Kato Koufonisi.

DONOUSA Δονούσα
postcode 843 00 • pop 110

Donousa is the least accessible of the Little Cyclades because it's too far north to be a convenient stop for ferries en route to more popular islands. The main attraction here, as on Iraklia, is that there is nothing much to do except lie on the beach.

Agios Stavros is the main settlement and the island's port. It has a reasonably nice beach, which also serves as a thoroughfare for vehicles and foot traffic. Behind the beach there are lush vegetable gardens and vineyards.

Kendros, over the hill to the west, is a sandy and secluded beach. **Livadi**, the next beach along, sees even fewer visitors. As on many of the other small islands, a frenzy of road construction is currently under way on Donousa, making many of the walks, which used to be so pleasurable, a lot less attractive.

There is one public telephone, up the hill two streets back from the waterfront; look for the large satellite dish above the OTE shack. Stamps are sold at the minimarket on the street running behind the beach.

CYCLADES

There is a ticket agency, Roussos Travel (☎ 2285 051 648, fax 2285 051 649) on the waterfront.

Places to Stay & Eat
Camping is tolerated at Kendros, although there are no facilities and you'll need to hike into town for food and water.

Spiros Skopelitis Rooms (☎ 2285 051 586) Doubles €32. Halfway along the town beach, are these nice bungalows, decorated with oriental rugs, set in a shady garden.

Nikitas Markoulis Rooms Doubles around €32. These rooms can be found near the *kafeneio*.

To Ilio Vasilema (☎ 2285 051 570) Doubles €32. At the far end of the town beach, Ilio also has reasonable *rooms*; all have bathrooms and some have a kitchen.

Aposperitis, next to Spiros Skopelitis, serves the usual fare, as does *To Ilio Vasilema*.

The hub of village life is *Kafeneio To Kyma* by the quay. Everyone seems to pass through here at least once a day and in the evenings it gets rather lively.

Amorgos Αμοργος

postcode 840 08 • pop 1630

Elongated Amorgos (ah-mor-**goss**) is the most easterly Cycladic island. With rugged mountains and an extraordinary monastery clinging to a cliff, Amorgos is an enticing island for those wishing to venture off the well-worn Mykonos-Paros-Santorini route. It also offers excellent walking.

Amorgos has two ports, Katapola and Aegiali; boats from Naxos usually stop at Katapola first. The beautiful, unspoilt capital, Hora (also known as Amorgos), is up high, north-east of Katapola.

Getting To/From Amorgos
Ferry Most ferries stop at both Katapola and Aegiali, but check if this is the case with your ferry. There are daily boats to Naxos (two to 5¾ hours, €7), Koufonisia (one hour, €4.40), Shinousa (1½ hours, €5.90), Iraklia (two hours, €6.10) and

Paros (three hours, €8.40), but some of these go to the resort of Piso Livadi (three to 4½ hours, €8) rather than Parikia, and Piraeus (10 hours, €15.40).

Ferries also serve Mykonos (2½ hours, €9.30, four weekly), Donousa (30 minutes, €4.65, four weekly), Astypalea (2½ hours, €8.40, two weekly) and Syros (4½ to 9½ hours, €10.50, four weekly). There is a twice-weekly boat to Rafina (10¾ hours, €14.70) via Tinos and Andros.

Fast Boat & Catamaran Weekly services run from Katapola to Rafina (five hours, €29.05), Paros (1½ to 2½ hours, €16.90), Mykonos (2¼ to four hours, €18.60), Ios (1½ hours, €12.80), Tinos (2¾ hours, €18.60) and Andros (3½ to 6¼ hours, €27.50). Several services will also stop at Aegiali.

Getting Around Amorgos
Regular buses go from Katapola to Hora (15 minutes, €0.70), Moni Hozoviotissis (15 minutes, €0.70), Agia Anna Beach (20 minutes, €0.70) and less frequent services go to Aegiali (30 minutes, €1.30); however there are fewer services on weekends. There are also buses from Aegiali to the picturesque village of Langada. Schedules are posted on bus windscreens.

Cars and motorcycles are available for rent from Travel Agency N. Synodinos in Katapola and Aegialis Tours (☎ 2285 073 107, fax 2285 073 394, W www .amorgos-aegialis.com) in Aegiali.

KATAPOLA Καταπολα
Katapola, the principal port, is a pretty town occupying a large, dramatic bay in the most verdant part of the island. A smattering of remains from the ancient Cretan city of Minoa, as well as a Mycenaean cemetery, lie above the port. Amorgos has also yielded many Cycladic finds; the largest figurine in the National Archaeological Museum in Athens was found in the vicinity of Katapola.

Boats dock either in front of the central square or to the right (facing inland). The bus station is on the waterfront, near the square.

AMORGOS

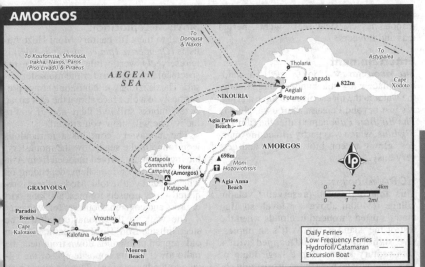

Travel Agency N. Synodinos (☎ 2285 071 201, fax 2285 071 278, **e** synodinos@ nax.forthnet.gr) is very helpful (and is open year-round). Ferry tickets, money exchange and car rental are available.

The port police (☎ 2285 071 259) and regular police (☎ 2285 071 210) are on the central square. There is a post office on the square, and limited Internet access is available at Hotel Minoa. A bank (with ATM) is on the waterfront nearby the travel agency. There is a bookshop opposite Idiston cafe.

Places to Stay & Eat

Katapola Community Camping (☎ 2285 071 802) Adult/tent €3.70/2.30. This shady site is back from the northern end of the waterfront. It doesn't pick up from the ferry wharf. Turn left from the quay (as you face inland) and continue past the turn-off for the Hora. Turn right at the next paved road and walk about 100m.

Domatia owners usually meet ferries.

Pension Amorgos (☎ 2285 071 013, fax 2285 071 214) Singles/doubles €30.20/ 34.90. Rooms at this pension, on the waterfront near the square, are spotless.

Diosmarini (☎ 2285 071 636, **e** diosmarini @yahoo.com) Doubles/triples €30.20/ 52, apartments €88. This new pension is tucked away to the left, up the steps behind the northern end of the harbour. Rooms are pleasant and most have balconies.

Villa Katapoliani (☎/fax 2285 071 064) Doubles/studios €49/59. Just before Panagia Katapoliani, this renovated Cycladic building has nice rooms, all with balcony and a view of the garden.

Hotel Minoa (☎ 2285 071 480, fax 2285 071 003) Doubles with breakfast €67.90. This C-class hotel on the square has comfortable double rooms with air-conditioning and telephone. It also has a reasonable taverna *Mythos*.

Vitsenzos (☎ 2285 071 518) Dishes €2.10-7.80, seafood by the kilo. At the northern end of the waterfront beyond Pension Maroussa, this cafe has good, reasonably priced daily specials. Traditional *Psaropoula*, nearby, is the best taverna for seafood, and *Mouragio* on the waterfront near the square, is also a good traditional place.

Idiston (☎ 2285 074 165) Dishes €0.80-5.80. Idiston, a smart little cafe in the laneway around the corner from Hotel Minoa, has classic Greek sweets, herbal teas and liqueurs.

Entertainment

The Moon Bar (☎ 2285 071 598) This laid-back place with tables under a large tree by the water is the nicest place to have a drink; it's just beyond Pension Maroussa. Nearby *The Big Blue Pub*, named after the film *The Big Blue*, which was partly filmed in Amorgos, glows a neon blue at night and gets very busy.

HORA Αμοργος

This amazingly well-preserved Cycladic village is 400m above sea level, so high that it's often shrouded in clouds when the rest of the island is sunny. It's an impressive sight, all white and capped with a 13th-century kastro atop a large lump of rock. The village has some surprisingly sophisticated bars and cafes.

The bus stop is on a square at the edge of town. The post office is on the main square, reached by a pedestrian laneway from the bus stop. The OTE is in a new building on the main road near the high school.

The **archaeology museum** *(open 9am-1pm & 6pm-8.30pm Tues-Sun)* is on the main pedestrian thoroughfare, near Cafe Bar Zygol.

Places to Stay & Eat

There are no hotels, but domatia are available.

Rooms to Rent (☎ 2285 071 216) Singles/doubles €17.40/23. This nice little domatia on the main pedestrian thoroughfare has good value rooms. By the main bus square, *Pension Ilias (☎ 2285 071 277)* and *Pension Panorama (☎ 2285 071 606)*, both with doubles for €43.50, have views over the valley.

Kastanis Dishes €1.90-5.30. On the main pedestrian thoroughfare, Kastanis is a staunchly traditional place; try the chicken with peppers (€4.40).

Cafe Bar Zygol (☎ 2285 071 359) Open 8am-3am daily. Zygol's rooftop terrace is a fine spot to take in the Hora.

MONI HOZOVIOTISSIS

Μονή Χωζοβιοτίσσις

A visit to the 11th-century Moni Hozoviotissis *(Open 8am-1pm & 5pm-7pm daily)* is unreservedly worthwhile, as much for the spectacular scenery as for the monastery itself. The dazzling white building clings precariously to a cliff face above the east coast. A few monks still live there and, if you're lucky, one will show you around.

The monastery contains a miraculous icon found in the sea below the monastery, having allegedly arrived unaided from Asia Minor, Cyprus or Jerusalem, depending on which legend you're told. Modest dress is required – long trousers for men, and long skirt or dress and covered shoulders for women.

The walk to the monastery down the steep hillside from Hora is breathtaking; an old stepped path winds down from near the radio tower (at the opposite end of the village to the bus station). There's also a bus; the monastery bus stop is at the Agia Anna road junction, about 500m uphill from the monastery itself.

AEGIALI Αιγιαλη

Aegiali is Amorgos' other port. The atmosphere is much more laid-back than Katapola – a leftover hippy vibe from the free camping days of the 70s is discernible – and there is a good beach stretching left of the quay.

Internet access is available at Amorgos Net Cafe, next to Aegialis Tours. Nautilus Travel Agent (☎ 2285 073 032) opposite Aegialis Tours sells ferry tickets and provides general tourist information.

Organised Tours

Aegialis Tours (see Getting Around earlier) Island tours €17.60. Departs 10am-4pm. Aegialis organises a bus outing around the island with stops at Agia Pavlos, Moni Hozoviotissis, Hora and Mouron. Afternoon donkey-riding expeditions cost €14.70 per hour.

Places to Stay

As in Katapola, domatia owners meet the ferries.

Aegialia Camping, a pleasant and shaded site, is on the road behind Lakki Village; go left from the port and follow the signs.

Rooms in the Garden (☎ 2285 073 315) Definitely worth investigating, these small bungalows, with verandahs, have a rural setting. They're at the far end of the beach; a path leads from the beach to the studios.

Rooms Irini (☎ 2285 073 237) Doubles €45. This pretty place is at the top of the steps after the terrace restaurants.

Lakki Village (☎ 2285 073 253, fax 2285 072 344) Singles/doubles €43.50/49; 2-person/4-person apartments €78.30/110. Right on the beach, Lakki has immaculate rooms and apartments. There are also luxury two-person apartments with air-con, view and traditional furniture for €75.40. The pension has a delightful garden, a taverna and a bar. Breakfast is included.

Pension Poseidon (☎ 2285 073 453, fax 2285 073 007) Singles/doubles/studios €30.20/46.50/52. At the base of the hill behind the waterfront, Poseidon has nice rooms, some with views. The studios have kitchens.

Grispos Hotel (☎ 2285 073 502, fax 2285 073 557) 2-person/4-person studios €52/82.50. This hotel, up a witheringly steep hill behind the waterfront, has spacious studios.

Aegialis Hotel (☎ 2285 073 393, fax 2285 073 395, ⓔ aegialis@hotmail.com) Singles/doubles €68.20/101.50. This hotel sits above two sandy beaches and is the classiest place around. It has a seawater pool, two bars and a restaurant.

Places to Eat & Drink

To Limani (☎ 2285 073 269) Dishes €1.50-5.80, seafood by the kilo. Expect good traditional fare prepared with home-grown produce at Limani, behind Aegialis Tours. Its walls also double as an exhibition space for local artists.

To Koralli Dishes €1.60-7.30. Up a flight of stairs beyond the cluster of cafes by the windmill, this fish taverna has tasty seafood *meze* platters.

Restaurant Lakki (☎ 2285 073 253) Dishes €2.35-8.80. Home-grown ingredients make all the difference here – the food

is simple yet fragrant and delicious. Interesting wines are also available.

Disco The Que (☎ 2285 073 212) The hippy vibe is alive and well at this sandy beachside cafe run by an alternative clique. The play list is eclectic, and any opportunity to celebrate the wax and wane of the moon in the form of a party is embraced.

AROUND AMORGOS

Pebbled **Agia Anna Beach**, on the east coast south of Moni Hozoviotissis, is the nearest decent beach to both Katapola and Hora. The setting is stunning, with a vista of rocky granite islets just offshore. It gets very busy in the high season, and there's a small cantina on the cliff top selling food and drinks.

Langada and **Tholaria** are the most picturesque of the villages inland from Aegiali.

Ios Ιος

postcode 840 01 • pop 2000

Ios – the apogee of sun, sea and sex – is the *enfant terrible* of the Greek islands. There's no denying that most visitors come to party hard, but for those who are looking for a more relaxing stay, the island also offers plenty to explore: beautiful beaches, a pretty capital and an interesting rocky, Mars-like landscape. Ios also has a tenuous claim to being Homer's burial place; his tomb is in the island's north.

Getting To/From Ios

Ferry There are at least four daily connections with Piraeus (seven hours, €16.30), Paros (2½ hours, €7.40) and Naxos (1¼ hours, €6.40). There are daily boats to Mykonos (four hours, €9.60) and Santorini (1¼ hours, €5.60), five weekly to Sikinos (30 minutes, €3.20) and Folegandros (1½ hours, €4.65), four weekly to Anafi (three hours, €6.10) and Syros (2¾ hours, €11).

There are weekly boats to Crete (six hours, €13.20), Kimolos (2½ hours, €5.90), Milos (3½ hours, €8.80), Sifnos (five hours, €7.80), Serifos (six hours, €8.80), Tinos (5½ hours, €9) and Kythnos (seven hours, €10.50).

CYCLADES

HORA, ORMOS & MILOPOTAS

Ios has three population centres, all very close together on the west coast: the port (Ormos); the capital, Hora (also known as the 'village'), 2km inland from the port; and Milopotas, the beach 1km downhill from Hora. Gialos Beach stretches west of the port.

Orientation

The bus terminal in Ormos is right of the ferry quay on Plateia Emirou. If you want to walk from the port to Hora, turn left from Plateia Emirou, then immediately right and you'll see the stepped path leading up to the right after about 100m. The walk takes about 15 minutes.

In Hora, the church is the main landmark. It's opposite the bus stop, across the car park. To reach the central square of Plateia Valeta from the church, head in to the village and turn left at the junction. There are public toilets up the hill behind the main square. The road straight ahead from the bus stop leads to Milopotas Beach.

Information

Amiridakis Travel (☎ 2286 091 252, fax 2286 091 067), in front of the ferry quay, is very helpful; Acteon Travel (☎ 2286 091 343, fax 2286 091 088, ⓔ acteon@otenet .gr), on the square near the quay, is the American Express representative, and has branches in Hora and Milopotas. There is a hospital (☎ 2286 091 227) 250m north-west of the quay, on the way to Gialos, and there are several doctors in Hora. The port police (☎ 2286 091 264) are at the southern end of the waterfront, just before Ios Camping.

In Hora, the National Bank of Greece, behind the church, and the Commercial Bank nearby both have ATMs. To get to the post office from the church, continue uphill along the edge of the village, past the bakery, and take the second left.

The OTE is in Hora, along the street that leads right (east) from the top of the port steps; a signpost points the way.

Things to See & Do

Hora itself is a very lovely Cycladic village with myriad laneways and cute houses and

Fast Boat & Catamaran There are daily catamarans to Santorini (30 minutes, €9.60), Naxos (50 minutes, €12.20), Paros (1½ hours, €14.30), Syros (2¼ hours, €22.40) and Rafina (four hours, €25.55). Services travel twice a week to Tinos (three hours, €18); and also once a week to Amorgos (two hours, €16.60), Mykonos (1¾ hours, €14.70) and Andros (4½ hours, €26).

Getting Around Ios

In summer, crowded buses run between Ormos, Hora (€0.80) and Milopotas Beach (€0.80) about every 15 minutes. Private excursion buses go to Manganari Beach (€4.40, 10.30am and 12.30am) and Agia Theodoti Beach (€0.80).

Caiques travelling from Ormos to Manganari cost €7.34 per person for a return trip (departings 11am daily). Ormos and Hora both have car and motorcycle rental firms.

shops. Its charm is most evident during daylight hours when the bars are shut and the locals come out of the woodwork.

The only real 'cultural' attraction is the **archaeological museum** (*admission free; open 8.30am-3pm Tues-Sun*) in Hora. The building is immaculately decked out, but the exhibits are a tad disappointing. It's in the yellow building by the bus stop.

The views from the top of the hill in Hora are worth the climb, especially at sunset. On the way, pause at **Panagia Gremiotissa**, the large church next to the palm tree.

Activities

Snorkel gear, windsurfers and canoes can be hired from **Mylopotas Water Sports Center** (*☎ 2286 091 622, fax 2286 091 451, e iossport@otenet.gr; windsurfing rental €16/46.50 per hour/day*). It's based at Milopotas. Waterskiing is also an option (€17.40/52 per hour/day).

Worthwhile sailing and snorkelling options around Ios or to Sikinos, with hands-on sailing involved, are available from **Frog's Sails** (*mobile ☎ 69-4563 5590, e frogs@otenet.gr; cruises €43.50, book 2 days in advance*). You should be able to find the captain down at the port or ask at Cafe Cyclades (also by the port); you can also book at travel agents.

Places to Stay

Ormos *Ios Camping* (*☎ 2286 092 035, fax 2286 092 101*) €5.90 per person. This camping ground is well set up, with a pool with sea vista and a restaurant. Sleeping bunks (slabs of concrete) are available for those without a tent. Turn right at Plateia Emirou and walk along the waterfront to find it.

Zorba's Rooms (*☎ 2286 091 871*) Singles/doubles €11.75/34.90, 3-4 person apartments €61. Straight ahead from the quay in Ormos, Zorba's has neat rooms.

Hotel Poseidon (*☎ 2286 091 091, fax 2286 091 069*) Singles/doubles/triples €47.90/59/72.50. There are stunning views from the swimming pool at this hotel, which is very good value outside July and August. From the waterfront, turn left at Enigma Bar and climb the steps on the left.

Sun Club (*☎ 2286 092 140, fax 2286 092 140, e acteon@otenet.gr*) Rooms €93.10. Sun Club, on the road to Hora, has immaculate rooms with bath, TV, phone and sea view. There's also a pool and bar.

Gialos Beach *Pension O Kampos* (*☎ 2286 091 424*) Doubles with/without bath €34.90/29. Set back a bit from the beach, this is a great, old-fashioned pension.

Galini Pension (*☎/fax 2286 091 115*) Doubles/triples €52/59. Next door to Pension O Kampos, this pension has a lovely shady garden.

Hotel Glaros (*☎/fax 2286 091 876*) Rooms with breakfast €59. This is a relaxed, family-run place on the beach.

Hotel Yialos Beach (*☎ 2286 091 421, fax 2286 091 866*) Rooms €64. This is a friendly place with nicely designed Cycladic-style units around a pool. Rooms have air-con, phone and balcony.

Hora to Milopotas *Fiesta Rooms* (*☎ 2286 091 766*) Doubles €38. On the Ormos-Hora road, run by the same family who run Fiesta taverna, these basic rooms are clean and comfortable.

Markos Village (*☎ 2286 091 059, fax 2286 091 060, e markovlg@otenet.gr*) Dorm beds/doubles €11.75/43.50. Popular Markos Village is 50m from the bus stop. Nice double rooms have air-con, TV and balcony and there's a swimming pool.

Francesco's (*☎/fax 2286 091 223, e fragesco@otenet.gr*) Dorm beds €10.30; doubles with/without bathroom €34.90/26. Francesco's is a lively meeting place for backpackers, with a bar and terrace and a wonderful view of the bay.

Rooms Helena (*☎ 2286 091 595*) Singles/doubles €23/29. This is an old-style place with a bit of character; it's on the left, halfway between Hora and the beach.

There are lots of domatia signs on the route towards Milopotas Beach from the Hora bus stop.

Hermes Rooms (*☎ 2286 091471*) and *Pelagos* (*☎ 2286 091 112*) and *Petradi* (*☎ 2286 091 510, fax 2286 091 660*) all have doubles with terrace views for €59.

Katerina Rooms to Let (☎ 2286 091 614, fax 2286 092 049) Doubles €46.60. Farther along from Hermes, Katerina's is set in a lovely garden and breakfast is served on its terrace.

Milopotas *Far Out Camping* (☎ 2286 091 468, fax 2286 092 303, Ⓦ www.faroutclub .com) Adult/tent €5.90/1.50, small/ large bungalows €8.80/14.70. This site is a slick, over hyped but super-popular operation. It has a 24-hour bar, restaurant and two swimming pools (open to everyone on the beach). The basic 'bungalows' look like dog kennels; the larger ones are decent and have double and single beds. There's little tree cover and roofed areas provide most of the shade.

Stars Camping (☎ 2286 091 302, fax 2286 091 612, ⓔ purplepigios@hotmail .com) Camp sites €5.90, dorm beds €14.70, bungalows €17.60 per person. Shaded by tall trees, Stars is a smaller and less hard-sell place than Far Out. It has a swimming pool and bar.

Nissos Ios Hotel (☎ 2286 091 610, fax 2286 091 306) 3-bed dorms/singles/doubles €23/52/59. On the beach, Nissos has kooky '70s-style murals in all of its well-kept rooms.

Drakos Twins (☎/fax 2286 091 626) Singles/doubles €30.20/34.90 Also known as Elpis, this taverna has nice rooms right on the beach.

Hotel Ios Plage (☎/fax 2286 091 301, ⓔ contact@iosplage.com) Doubles/triples €59/76.90. This French-run hotel situated at the far end of Milopotas Beach has simply decorated rooms, with large mosquito nets draped over the beds. There is a lively bar here and an excellent *French restaurant*.

Ios Palace Hotel (☎ 2286 091 269, fax 2286 091 082, ⓔ ios@matrix.kapatel.gr) Singles/doubles €93/107, suites €246. This plush hotel consists of a cluster of traditional Cycladic cubes rising up the hill at the Hora end of Milopotas Beach. The four-person suites have a private pool. Breakfast is included in the room rate.

Places to Eat

Ormos *Ciao Café* (☎ 2286 028 581) Dishes from €1.90. Right by the ferry quay, this smart little cafe has filled baguettes and *ciabatta*; there's a small Internet cafe situated next door.

Gialos Beach   *To Coralli* (☎ 2286 091 272, fax 2286 091 552) Dishes €3.50-11 Coralli has the reputation (and there's a lot of competition in carbohydrate-hungry Ios) as the best place for wood-fired pizza.

Hora *Pithari Taverna* (☎ 2286 091 379) Dishes €2.35-8.80. Behind the large church, Pithari serves cheap, traditional Greek dishes.

Lord Byron (☎ 2286 092 125) Dishes €2.70-14. Close to Pithari Taverna this *mezedopolion* has a very cosy atmosphere augmented by rembetika music; different mezedes are served every day.

Pinocchio Ristorante (☎ 2286 091 470) Dishes €4.10-12.80. This pizzeria has good pizza, *calzone* and pasta, and *panna cotta* for dessert. Look for the signs and Pinocchio standing outside.

La Buca (☎ 2286 091 447) Dishes €4.10-10.30. Next to the bus stop, La Buca has reasonably authentic Italian food, including wood-fired pizza, calzone, pasta and nice salads.

Fiesta (☎ 2286 091 766) Breakfast €1-4.65, dishes €1.70-8.80. Fiesta, on the Ormos-Hora road, has good Greek food as well as wood-fired pizzas – all made with fresh produce in generous portions (authentic English-style fish and chips is also an option!).

Saini's (☎ 2286 091 106) Dishes €2.35-6.70 Open year-round, until 5am July-August. Saini's serves fine Greek originals and wine by the barrel and bottle; expect occasional live music as well. To find it, go past Ali Baba's and turn left; it's down a dark alley.

There are also numerous *gyros stands* where you can get a cheap bite.

Koumbara In Koumbara head to *Taverna Polydoros* (☎ 2286 091 132), or to *Filippos* for spectacular seafood.

Milopotas *Drakos Taverna* (☎ 2286 091 281) Dishes €1.70-7.30, seafood by the kilo. This legendary taverna at the southern end of the beach is not to be missed.

Hotel Ios Plage (☎ 2286 091 301) Dishes €4.40-11.75. Ios Plage serves French cafe fare, such as *croque monsieur* and Roquefort salad, during the day and more elaborate meals after 8pm.

Harmony (☎ 2286 091 613) Dishes €4.40-12.80. At the village end of Milopotas beyond the Ios Palace, Harmony restauant-bar has a lovely terrace dotted with deckchairs and hammocks. Tex-Mex food is the main attraction, although pizza, pasta, grills and breakfasts are also pretty good.

Entertainment

Ios nightlife can be fairly well summarised by the advertising flier for one of its bars, the Blue Note. It reads: 'You wanna have fun? Dance on the bar? Get drunk?' And, that in essence, is what Ios is all about.

At night Hora's tiny central square is transformed into a noisy, crowded open-air party. The crowd is mostly made up of alcohol-swilling backpackers in their teens and early twenties – if you're older, the fun wears thin quite quickly.

Popular bars and clubs on the square include: *Disco 69* (with a 'stylish' logo) which is generally full of crash-and-burn types; *Slammer Bar* (☎ 2286 092 119), infamous for it's 'Tequila Slammer with the Hammer'; and *Red Bull* (☎ 2286 091 019) which is everyone's favourite. The neon-lit *Flames Bar* just off the square is also a popular spot.

A gauntlet of themed bars are scattered about the Hora, drawing on tenuous links between international hard-drinking nations. 'Scandinavian' bars include places such as the ever-crowded *Blue Note* (☎ 2286 092 271). For a touch of the Irish, you can visit *Sweet Irish Dream* (☎ 2286 091 141; admission €5.90; free before 2am), whose only Celtic connection is the Guinness on tap. *The Little Irish Bar*, on the path up from the Hora, is a low-key spot for an early evening drink.

The Jungle Bar – Down Under Aussie & Kiwi Bar (☎ 2286 092 702), opposite the bus stop, revels in the sport of drinking.

Ios Club (☎ 2286 091 410) is one of the island's oldest bars, and provides sweeping views and a relaxed place for a drink. Head there for a cocktail to watch the sunset. To find it, walk right along the pathway by the Sweet Irish Dream.

Ali Baba's (☎ 2286 091 558) is a relaxed place to kick back and wait for the evening to begin, and plays movies between 8pm and 10pm. From the bus stop, keep the church on your left, continue past the jewellery shops, then turn right.

Orange Bar, 150m beyond the central square, is a laid-back escape hatch, as is *Cafe Click* (☎ 2286 092 477), which makes excellent top-shelf cocktails. *Cafe Astra* (☎ 2286 921 830) is a dark little bar that attracts an older, less desperate-to-drink crowd. It's above the Hora branch of Acteon Travel.

For Greek music, head to *Fantastico* (☎ 2286 091 539) by the Hora bus stop, or to the sleek dance bar *Di Porto* (☎ 2286 091 685, Gliaros Beach), near Coralli. *Marina Bar* (☎ 2286 091 557), overlooking Gialos Beach, also plays good Greek music.

There are a couple of big dance clubs on the Milopotas road, but they don't open until July. *Mojo Club* (info ☎ mobile 69-7275 9318; admission €11.75) brings in international DJs from Moscow, the UK and Amsterdam. *Scorpion's* is another late-night dance venue.

AROUND IOS

Apart from the nightlife, the beaches are what lure travellers to Ios. From Ormos, it's a 10-minute walk past the little church of Agia Irini for **Valmas Beach**. **Kolitzani Beach**, south of Hora, down the steps by Scorpion's, is also nice. **Koubara**, a 30-minute walk north-west of Ormos, is the official nudist beach. **Tsamaria**, nearby, is nice and sheltered when it's windy elsewhere.

Vying with Milopotas for best beach is **Manganari**, a long swathe of fine white sand on the south coast, reached by bus or by excursion boat in summer. There are several domatia; see Places to Stay & Eat.

CYCLADES

Bombes Beware!

Unfortunately, there's no such thing as a free cocktail – don't expect top-shelf (or even bottom-shelf) spirits. The cheap local moonshine used in mixed drinks and cocktails is bad news, as one reader pointed out:

There is a huge black market for alcohol distilled from rubbing alcohol – drinks made with this strange brew are called *bombes* and leave you with a nasty hangover (a lot of people say you can go blind from drinking too much of this). Most bars basically serve a mix of 'clean' and 'dirty' cocktails – but the really sketch bars serve all *bombes*. I've heard that on some islands some bars even advertise with billboards that say: BOMBES 1000dr – CLEAN DRINKS 2000dr

Cemile Kavountzis

Ios is notorious for this practice (but not alone) – so watch out. The safest (and usually cheaper) drinks are ouzo, bottled beer and the premixed bottled drinks like Gordon's Space and Rigo.

Agia Theodoti, **Psathi** and **Kalamos** Beaches, all on the north-east coast, are more remote. **Moni Kalamou**, on the way to Manganari and Kalamos, stages a huge religious festival in late August and a festival of music and dance on 7 September.

Places to Stay & Eat
Dimitri's (☎ 2286 091 483, Manganari) Doubles €43.50. Dimitri's, behind Antonio's Restaurant, has lovely rooms.

Hotel Manganari (☎ 2286 091 200, fax 2286 091 204) Villas €113. This very private hotel is accessible only by boat and has villas for two people. Breakfast, dinner and port transfer are included.

Antonio's Restaurant (☎ 2286 091 483, Manganari) Dishes €2.10-5.30. This restaurant has incredibly fresh fish and good grills; make sure you sample the different homemade cheeses.

Cristos Taverna (☎ 2286 092 286) Dishes €1.70-10.30, doubles €29. Christos

has excellent fresh fish at Manganari *Rooms* are also available.

Santorini (Thira)
Σαντορίνη (Θα)

postcode 847 00 • pop 9360
Santorini, officially known as Thira, is regarded by many as the most spectacular o all the Greek islands. Thousands visit annually to gaze in wonder at the submerged caldera, a vestige of what was probably the biggest volcanic eruption in recorded history. Although it gets crowded and is overly commercial, Santorini is unique and should not be missed. The caldera is a real spectacle – it's worth arriving by ferry rather than catamaran or hydrofoil if you want to experience the full dramatic impact. The main port is Athinios. Buses (and taxis) meet all ferries and cart passengers to Fira the capital, which teeters on the lip of the caldera, high above the sea.

History
Greece is susceptible to eruptions and earth quakes – mostly minor – but on Santorin these have been so violent as to change the shape of the island several times.

Dorians, Venetians and Turks occupied Santorini, as they did all other Cycladic is lands, but its most influential early inhab itants were the Minoans. They came from Crete some time between 2000 and 1600 BC, and the settlement at Akrotiri dates from the height of their great civilisation.

The island then was circular and called Strongili (the Round One). Around 1650 BC, a colossal volcanic eruption caused the centre of Strongili to sink, leaving a caldera with high cliffs – one of the world's most dramatic geological sights. Some archaeologists have speculated that this catastrophe destroyed not only Akrotiri but the whole Minoan civilisation as well. Another theory that has fired the imaginations of writers artists and mystics since ancient times, postulates that the island was part of the mythical lost continent of Atlantis. See the boxed

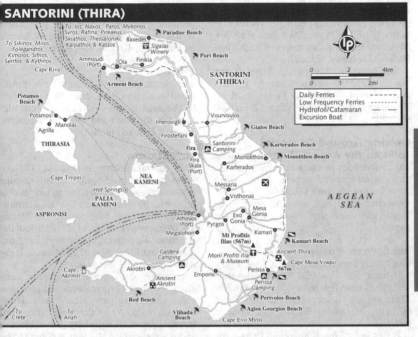

SANTORINI (THIRA)

To Ios, Naxos, Paros, Mykonos,
Syros, Rafina, Pireaeus,
Skiathos, Thessaloniki, Baxedes
Karpathos & Kassos

To Sikinos, Milos,
Folegandros,
Kimolos, Sifnos,
Serifos & Kythnos

Paradise Beach
Ammoudi (Port)
Oia
Finikia
Sigalas Winery
Pori Beach

Cape Riva
Armeni Beach

SANTORINI (THIRA)

Potamos Beach
Potamos
Manolas
Agrilla

THIRASIA

Vourvoulos

Imerovigli
Firostefani
Fira
Fira Skala (Port)

Gialos Beach

Santorini Camping
Karterados Beach
Monolithos
Karterados
Monolithos Beach

Daily Ferries
Low Frequency Ferries
Hydrofoil/Catamaran
Excursion Boat

Cape Trypiti

NEA KAMENI

Hot Springs
PALIA KAMENI

ASPRONISI

Messaria
Vothonas

AEGEAN SEA

Athinios (Port)
Pyrgos
Megalohori
Exo Gonia
Mesa Gonia

Caldera Camping

Mt Profitis Ilias (567m)
Kamari
Kamari Beach

Cape Akrotiri
Akrotiri
Ancient Akrotiri

Moni Profiti Ilia & Museum
Ancient Thira
567m
Cape Mesa Vouno
Perissa

Perissa Camping

Red Beach
Emporio

To Crete
To Anafi
Vlihada Beach
Cape Evo Mytis

Perivolos Beach
Agios Georgios Beach

CYCLADES

ext 'Santorini's Unsettling Past' later in
his section for more details on the volcano.

Getting To/From Santorini
Air Olympic Airway operates at least six
flights daily to/from Athens (€74.85/83.35
one way), six weekly to Rhodes (€76.90)
and Mykonos (€54), daily flights to Thessaloniki (€103) and two weekly to Iraklio
(€56). The Olympic Airways office (☎ 2286
22 493) is in Fira, on the road to Kamari,
one block east of 25 Martiou. Several other
small airlines offer flights to/from Athens
and Thessaloniki. Maria's Tours & Travel
sell tickets for the small operators and for
Olympic airlines.

Ferry Santorini is the southernmost island
of the Cyclades, and as a major tourist destination it has good connections with Piraeus
and Thessaloniki on the mainland, as well as
with Crete. Santorini also has useful services to Anafi, Folegandros and Sikinos.

There are at least four boats daily to
Naxos (three hours, €9.30), Paros (three to
four hours, €9.90), Ios (1¼ hours, €5.60),
Piraeus (nine hours, €18.60) and Tinos
(five hours, €12.50), and two weekly for
Kythnos (eight hours, €10.30) and Folegandros (1½ to 2½ hours, €5.30). Change
at Naxos for Amorgos.

Three boats weekly go to Anafi (one
hour, €5.90), Sifnos, (six hours, €9.30),
Thessaloniki (18 to 19½ hours, €31.15),
Sikinos (2½ hours, €5.60), Iraklion on
Crete (3¾ hours, €12.05) and also
Skiathos (13½ hours, €25).

There are two weekly ferries running to
Mykonos (six hours, €10.50), Crete (four
hours, €11.75), Milos (four hours, €10.80),
Kimolos (3½ hours, €9.30) and Syros (5¼
hours, €12.50), Kythnos (eight hours,
€10.30).

One weekly ferry goes to Serifos (seven
hours, €10.50), Karpathos (€14.80) and
Kassos (€12.50).

Phone numbers listed incorporate changes due in Oct 2002; see p83

Fast Boat & Catamaran Daily services go to Ios (30 minutes, €10.30), Naxos (1½ hours, €19.20), Paros (2¼ hours, €17.70), Mykonos (three to four hours, €16.90) and Rafina (5¼ hours, €30.20).

Six boats weekly run to Syros (three hours, €25.90). Services run to Piraeus daily, except Wednesday (4 hours, €36) Twice weekly boats go to Sifnos (2½ hours, €15.40).

Getting Around Santorini

To/From the Airport There are frequent bus connections in summer between Fira's bus station and the airport. A taxi from Athinios to Fira costs €7.30 (set fare). Enthusiastic hotel and domatia staff meet flights and some also return guests to the airport.

Bus In summer, buses leave Fira's bus station hourly for Akrotiri (€1.20) and every half-hour for Oia (€0.90), Monolithos (€0.80), Kamari (€0.80) and Perissa (€1.30). There are less frequent buses to Exo Gonia (€0.80), Perivolos (€1.30) and Vlihada (€1.50).

Buses leave Fira, Kamari and Perissa for the port of Athinios (€1.20) 1½ hours before most ferry departures. Buses for Fira meet all ferries, even late at night.

Boat From the seafront at Ancient Akrotiri, you can catch a caique to Red Beach, White Beach and Black Beach for around €4.40. Caiques also run regularly from Perissa to Red Beach.

Car, Motorcycle & Bicycle Fira has many car-, motorcycle- and bicycle-rental firms. Hired wheels are the best way to explore the island as the buses are intolerably overcrowded in summer and you'll usually be lucky to get on one at all; be very patient and cautious when driving – the narrow roads, especially in Fira, can be a nightmare.

Taxi There is a taxi stand in the main square. Call a taxi on ☎ 2286 023 951 or 2286 022 555.

Cable Car & Donkey Cable cars shun cruise-ship and excursion-boat passengers up to Fira from the small port below, known as Fira Skala. Tickets cost €3 one way.

FIRA Φα

The commercialism of Fira has not diminished its all-pervasive, dramatic aura. Walk to the edge of the caldera for spectacular views of the cliffs and their multicoloured strata of lava and pumice.

Orientation

The central square is Plateia Theotokopoulou. The main road, 25 Martiou, runs north-south, intersecting the square and is lined with travel agencies. The bus station is on 25 Martiou, 50m south of Plateia Theotokopoulou. West of 25 Martiou the streets are old pedestrian laneways; Erythrou Stavrou, one block west of 25 Martiou, is the main commercial thoroughfare.

Another block west, Ypapantis runs along the crest of the caldera and provides some staggering panoramic views. Head north on Nomikou for the cable car station. If you keep walking along the caldera – and it's well worth it – you'll come to the Nomikos Convention Centre and, eventually, the cliff-top villages of Firostefani and Imerovigli. Keep going and you'll reach Oia.

Information

Fira doesn't have an EOT or tourist police. It's best to seek out the smaller travel agents in Fira, where you'll generally receive more helpful service. Readers have recommended Maria's Tours (☎ 2286 024 701, fax 2286 023 848) and Pelican Tours & Travel (☎ 2286 022 220, fax 2286 022 570), both can book accommodation and ferry tickets, and Maria's has reasonably priced car rental (from €29).

The National Bank of Greece is between the bus station and Plateia Theotokopoulou, on the caldera side of the road. American Express is represented by Alpha Bank on Plateia Theotokopoulou. Both banks have ATMs. The post office is about 150m south of the bus station.

Santorini's Unsettling Past

Santorini's violent volcanic history is visible everywhere – in black sand beaches, raw lava-layered cliffs plunging into the sea, earthquake-damaged dwellings and in the soil's fertility, which supports coiled-up grape vines. The volcano may be dormant, but it's not dead. Santorini's caldera ('cauldron'), which often has a surface as calm and glassy as a backyard fish pond, could start to boil at any moment...

Santorini first appeared when the landmass known as Aegis, which joined the European and Asian continents, was gradually flooded around one million years ago, leaving only the highest peaks above water. Profitis Ilias and Monolithos are both ancient rocks dating back to this time. At some point a complex of submarine, overlapping shield volcanoes began to toil and trouble, eventually erupting and filling in the area between Santorini's mountains with lava. This process continued for thousands of years and over time the island took on a conical shape.

Eventually the volcanoes became dormant, and vegetation established itself in the fertile ash. Around 3000 BC the first human settlers arrived and, from evidence found at Akrotiri, it appears that they led very idyllic lives and fashioned a highly evolved culture.

But the peace and harmony didn't last, and around 1650 BC a chain of earthquakes and eruptions culminated in one of the largest explosions in the history of the planet. Thirty cubic kilometres of magma spewed forth and a column of ash 36km high jetted into the atmosphere. So much magma was ejected that the magma chambers of the volcano gave way and the centre of the island collapsed, producing a caldera that the sea quickly filled. It's hard to imagine the magnitude of the explosion, but it is often compared to thousands of atomic bombs detonating simultaneously. The event sent ash all over the Mediterranean, and it also generated huge tsunamis (tidal waves) that travelled with dangerous force all the way to Crete and Israel. Anafi was hit by a wave 250m high. The fallout from the explosion was more than just dust and pumice – it's widely believed that the catastrophe was responsible for the demise of Crete's Minoan culture, one of the most powerful civilisations in the Aegean at that time. After the Big One, Santorini once again settled down for a time and allowed plants, animals and humans to recolonise it. In 236 BC the rumbles from the deep resumed and volcanic activity separated Thirasia from the main island. Further changes to the landscape continued intermittently. In 197 BC the islet now known as Palia Kameni appeared in the caldera, and in AD 726 there was a major eruption that catapulted pumice all the way to Asia Minor. The south coast of Santorini collapsed in 1570, taking the ancient port of Eleusis with it. In 1650 earthquakes and explosions caused tsunamis and killed and blinded many people on the island. An eruption of lava in 1707 created Nea Kameni Islet next to Palia Kameni, and further eruptions in 1866–70, 1925–6, 1928, 1939-41 and 1950 augmented it. A major earthquake measuring 7.8 on the Richter scale savaged the island in 1956, killing scores of people and destroying most of the houses in Fira and Oia. If you walk around the laneways of Fira, you will see many abandoned mansions.

Volcanic activity has been pretty low-key since 1956, but minor tremors are quite common and the ground shakes, usually imperceptibly, almost every day. A major earthquake is due at any moment, but the locals don't seem worried – they seem to like living on the edge. For lovers of impermanence, precariousness and drama, no other place even comes close.

PC World (☎ 2286 025 551), above Santo Volcano Tours & Travel on the main square, has the best value Internet (€3 for a one-hour card). Lava Internet Cafe (☎ 2286 025 551), up from the main square, has a better atmosphere, but a minimum of 20 minutes only is possible at more expensive rates.

There is a laundrette and dry cleaner 200m north of Plateia Theotokopoulou, underneath Pension Villa Maria, and another laundrette next to Pelican Hotel; locked luggage storage is also possible at this laundrette (€1.50).

The hospital (☎ 2286 022 237) is on the road to Karterados, near the Olympic

Phone numbers listed incorporate changes due in Oct 2002; see p83

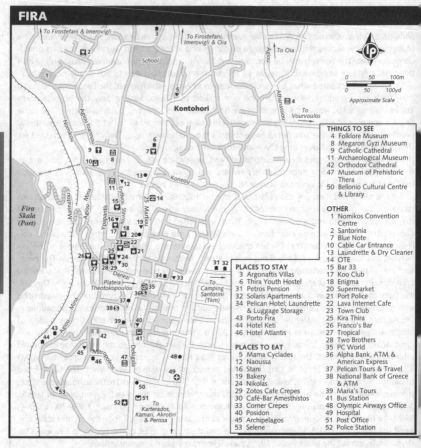

FIRA

To Firostefani & Imerovigli

To Firostefani,
Imerovigli & Oia

To Oia

School

To Vourvoulos

Kontohori

Fira
Skala
(Port)

To
Camping
Santorini
(1km)

Plateia
Theotokopoulou

To
Karterados,
Kamari, Akrotiri
& Perissa

0   50   100m
0   50   100yd
Approximate Scale

THINGS TO SEE
4   Folklore Museum
8   Megaron Gyzi Museum
9   Catholic Cathedral
11 Archaeological Museum
42 Orthodox Cathedral
47 Museum of Prehistoric
    Thera
50 Bellonio Cultural Centre
    & Library

OTHER
1   Nomikos Convention
    Centre
2   Santorinia
7   Blue Note
10 Cable Car Entrance
13 Laundrette & Dry Cleaner
14 OTE
15 Bar 33
17 Koo Club
18 Enigma
20 Supermarket
21 Port Police
22 Lava Internet Cafe
23 Town Club
25 Kira Thira
26 Franco's Bar
27 Tropical
28 Two Brothers
35 PC World
36 Alpha Bank, ATM &
    American Express
37 Pelican Tours & Travel
38 National Bank of Greece
    & ATM
39 Maria's Tours
41 Bus Station
48 Olympic Airways Office
49 Hospital
51 Post Office
52 Police Station

PLACES TO STAY
3   Argonaftis Villas
6   Thira Youth Hostel
31 Petros Pension
32 Solaris Apartments
34 Pelican Hotel; Laundrette
    & Luggage Storage
43 Porto Fira
44 Hotel Keti
46 Hotel Atlantis

PLACES TO EAT
5   Mama Cyclades
12 Naoussa
16 Stani
19 Bakery
24 Nikolas
29 Zotos Cafe Crepes
30 Café-Bar Amesthistos
33 Corner Crepes
40 Posidon
45 Archipelagos
53 Selene

Airways office. The police station (☎ 2286 022 649) is south of Plateia Theotokopoulou; the port police (☎ 2286 022 239) are north of the square.

Museums

The **Museum of Prehistoric Thera** (☎ 2286 022 217; admission free; 8.30am-3pm Tues-Sun) is a new museum near the bus station. It houses extraordinary finds which were excavated from Akrotiri (where to date only 5% of the area has been excavated). Most impressive is the glowing gold ibex figurine, measuring around 10cm

in length and dating from the 17th century BC, which was discovered in mint condition in 1999.

Megaron Gyzi Museum (☎ 2286 022 244; admission €3; open 10.30am-1pm & 5pm-8pm Mon-Sat, 10.30am-4.30pm Sun) behind the Catholic cathedral, has local memorabilia, including fascinating photographs of Fira before and immediately after the 1956 earthquake.

The **archaeological museum** (☎ 2286 022 217; adult/students €2.35/1.20; open 8.30am-3pm Tues-Sun), opposite the cable car station, houses finds from Akrotiri and ancient Thira, some Cycladic figurines, and Hellenistic and Roman sculpture.

There is a small **folklore museum** (admission €3) on the road to Oia, notable for its *canava* (wine-making cellar).

For the past few years the **Nomikos Convention Centre** (☎ 2286 023 016; adult/student €3/1.50; open 10am-9pm daily), also known as the Thera Foundation, has displayed three-dimensional photographic reproductions of the Akrotiri frescoes. To get there, follow the old Byzantine path along the caldera, past the cable-car station.

The **Bellonio Cultural Centre & Library** (admission free; open 9am-2pm daily & 6pm-9pm Tues-Sun), next to the post office, has a large collection of books and occasional exhibitions about Santorini.

Organised Tours

Four agencies operate trips to Thirasia, the volcanic island of Nea Kameni, Palia Kameni's hot springs and Oia; book at travel agencies.

Places to Stay – Budget

Camping Santorini (☎ 2286 022 944, fax 2286 025 065, e santocam@otenet.gr) Adult/tent €5.90/2.70, basic bungalows €26. This camping ground has some shade and modest facilities, but it's a long way from the nearest beach. There's a self-serve restaurant and a pool (though a reader's letter reported staff hassling people to buy drinks when lounging by the pool). It's 400m east of Plateia Theotokopoulou – look for the sign.

The fairly aggressive owners of accommodation who greet boats and buses are now confined to 'official' information booths. Some owners of rooms in Karterados (3km south-east of Fira) claim that their rooms are in town; ask to see a map showing the location. If you're looking for a caldera view, expect to pay at least double the prices elsewhere.

Thira Youth Hostel (☎ 2286 023 864) Dorm beds from €10.30, beds on roof €5.90, doubles with bathroom €34.90. This massive hostel, 300m north of Plateia Theotokopoulou, is a dilapidated, grubby old place that was formerly part of the Catholic monastery. Some of the double rooms have remnants of antique furniture.

Petros Pension (☎ 2286 022 573, fax 2286 022 615) Doubles €30.20. On the pension-filled road to Santorini Camping, this is a fine place close to the main square; pick up and drop off to the port and airport is possible.

Hotel Keti (☎ 2286 022 324, fax 2286 022 380) Doubles €52.50. This is a real gem with lovely traditional rooms dug into the cliffs.

Argonaftis Villas (☎ 2286 022 055) Doubles €59, 2-person/4-person apartments €61/85.50. Folksy paintings decorate many of the rooms, and one of the apartments is a traditional cave house.

Kafieris Hotel (☎ 2286 022 189) Doubles €49. This hotel, on the path up to Firostefani, not far from the convention centre, has lovely rooms on the caldera.

Apartments Gaby (☎/fax 2286 022 057) Doubles €52.50, 4-person apartments €117. This great place is near Kafieris Hotel.

Hotel Sofia Sigala (☎ 2286 022 802) Doubles €59. Farther up the hill, near Firostefani's main square, are these nice rooms.

Ioaniss Roussos Rooms (☎ 2286 022 611, fax 2286 028 186) Doubles €40.80. These rooms are near Hotel Sofia Sigala.

Places to Stay – Mid-Range & Top End

Pelican Hotel (☎ 2286 023 113) Singles/doubles/triples €67.90/80.40/96. Open year-round. This gloomy hotel, right in the centre of town, has comfortable rooms and breakfast is available.

Solaris Apartments (☎ 2286 022 631, fax 2286 028 581, e zefksi00@otenet.gr) Singles/doubles €69.60/99. Open year-round. Solaris is centrally located and has a pool, spa and gym, but no caldera views.

Porto Fira (☎ 2286 022 849, fax 2286 023 098) Singles/doubles €88.50/110. Hotels perched on the caldera's edge in Fira are naturally a bit more expensive, but this one's worth it.

Hotel Atlantis (☎ 2286 022 232, fax 2286 022 821, e atlantis@atlantishotel.gr)

CYCLADES

Singles/doubles with breakfast €122/183. This spacious, airy A-class hotel offers all comforts. Rooms have incredible views over the caldera.

Eterpi Villas (☎ 2286 022 541) 2-person studios €133, 3-person apartments €160. Up in Firostefani, Eterpi has traditional abodes dug into the caldera.

Spiliotica Apartments (☎ 2286 022 637, fax 2286 023 590, e spiliot@san.forthnet .gr) Doubles/triples €117/145. In Imerovigli, these are traditional abodes dug into the caldera. Spiliotica has a nice little cafe-bar and a small swimming pool.

Skaros Villas (☎ 2286 023 153) Doubles €88. Nearby Spiliotica, Skaros (also a traditional dwelling) is furnished in the traditional way, and has views, views, views.

Places to Eat

Fira has many terrible tourist-trap eateries, so it's worth being picky.

Nikolas (☎ 2286 024 550) Dishes €2.10-11.75. Opposite the Kira Thira bar, Nikolas has tasty traditional food and friendly service.

Naoussa (☎ 2286 024 869) Dishes €2.10-17.20. This upstairs eatery (not to be confused with the very average establishment at ground level), beyond Bar 33, serves excellent, reasonably priced Greek classics, with new specials daily.

Stani (☎ 2286 023 078) Dishes €2-9.60. Upstairs next to Koo Club, the roof-top restaurant Stani has good home-cooked food.

Posidon (☎ 2286 025 480) Dishes €2.35-12.80. Below the bus station, Poseidon has reasonable, inexpensive food and stays open late.

Archipelagos (☎ 2286 023 673) Dishes €3.80-22. This is a classy place with simple dishes like octopus cooked with eggplant and potatoes (€14).

Selene (☎ 2286 022 249, w www.selene .gr) Mains €17.20-18.30. This is one of the best restaurants in town and has a lovely, romantic atmosphere and creative dishes.

Among the best places for juices, coffee, cake and crepes are *Zotos Cafe Crepe* and *Café-Bar Amesthistos* (Erythrou Stavrou) where dishes are €2.35 to €5.90. Good

breakfast places include *Mama Cyclades* near Thira Youth Hostel, and *Corne Crepes* near the Museum of Prehistori Thera.

There are several gyros stands up from the main square where you can grab quick bite.

Firostefani & Imerovigli *To Aktaio* (☎ 2286 022 336) Dishes €2.10-8.80. O the main square in Firostefani, this is a nic little taverna serving traditional food.

Skaros Fish Tavern (☎ 2286 023 616 Dishes €2.35-11.75. Farther up the calder in Imerovigli, Skaros has excellent mezede and fish as well as a spectacular view.

Entertainment

Kira Thira (☎ 2286 022 770) This is th oldest bar in Fira and a favourite haunt c both locals and travellers. It's a funky littl candle-lit dive with an eclectic selection o sounds and occasional live music.

Tropical (☎ 2286 023 089) In an envi able position, Tropical is another long established bar with a loyal clientele; i plays a mix of music from disco to rock.

Franco's Bar (☎ 2286 024 428) Franco' is the place to watch the sun set with cock tail in hand, although expect to pay for th privilege. There's also a sublime bar in doors, carved into the caldera.

After midnight Erythrou Stavrou is th place to head for a sweaty but sleek knees up – unless you want to feel uncomfortabl out of place, make sure you frock up i style. The five bars at *Koo Club* (☎ 228 022 025) attract a Greek fashionista crow and play the occasional Greek hit. The su perkitsch *Town Club* (☎ 2286 022 820) is smaller space playing a more even mix o Greek and international music. Shin *Enigma* (☎ 2286 022 466) plays pure an unadulterated mainstream dance music.

Not far from the cable car station and th convention centre, *Santorinia* (☎ 2286 02 777) is popular with the young local crow and has traditional live music, includin rembetika and *laïko*.

Bar 33 (☎ 2286 023 065), just past Ko Club, is a lively bouzouki place.

Two Brothers (☎ 2286 023 061) is an old rock bar that's worth stopping by for a drink, soaking up the Greek atmosphere, and then moving on.

Just by Thira Youth Hostel, *Blue Note* (☎ 2286 024 888) has an outdoor area and plays a mix of music – and there's no need to frock up – style is irrelevant here.

Shopping

Grapes thrive in Santorini's volcanic soil, and the island's wines are famous all over Greece and beyond. Local wines are widely available in Fira and elsewhere. Try the pricey 50-50 (so-called because 50% of the grapes are from the mainland and 50% are grown on Santorini) from Canava Nomikos, or the wines from Oia.

Cava Sigalas in Firostefani sells local fava beans, capers, caper leaves (a delicacy), wines and thyme honey.

AROUND SANTORINI

Ancient Akrotiri Παλαισ Ακρωτα

Ancient Akrotiri (☎ 2286 081 366; adult/student €5.30/1.7; open 8.30am-3pm Tues-Sun) was a Minoan outpost; excavations begun in 1967 have uncovered an ancient city beneath the volcanic ash. Buildings, some three storeys high, date to the late 16th century BC. The absence of skeletons and treasures indicates that inhabitants were forewarned of the eruption and escaped.

The actual site is a disappointment. At the time of writing it resembled a haphazard construction zone as a new roof was being built over the excavations. It's advisable to go with a guide to get the most out of the site.

The most outstanding finds are the stunning frescoes and ceramics, many of which are now on display at the Museum of Prehistoric Thera in Fira (there are none on display at the excavation site). Accurate fresco replicas are on display at the Nomikos Convention Centre also.

On the way to Akrotiri, pause at the enchanting traditional settlement of **Megalochori**. The winegrowers cooperative, **Santo Wines** (☎ 2286 022 596, ℮ santowines@san.forthnet.gr), has a showcase selection

here of regional produce taken from all over Greece.

Places to Stay & Eat *Caldera View Camping* (☎ 2286 082 010, fax 2286 081 889, ℮ caldera@hol.gr) Adult/tent €5.90/3.80; 2-person/4-person bungalows €93/125. This camping ground, near Akrotiri, doesn't have a view over the caldera, although it does have views across to the sea. It's a long way from any nightlife in a semi-rural area, but the facilities are very good and there's a swimming pool and free transfer to/from the port. Breakfast is included.

On the beach below the archaeological site there are some nice little fish *tavernas*, and *Hotel Akrotiri* (☎ 2286 081 375, fax 2286 081 377, ℮ hotelakrotiri@yahoo.com) which is a nice place to stay, with doubles including breakfast for €69.60.

Ancient Thira Αρχαία Θα

First settled by the Dorians in the 9th century BC, Ancient Thira (Admission free; open 8.30am-3pm Tues-Sun), consists of Hellenistic, Roman and Byzantine ruins. These include temples, houses with mosaics, an agora, a theatre and a gymnasium. The site has splendid views.

It takes about 45 minutes to walk to the site along the path from Perissa on rocky, difficult ground. If you're driving, take the road from Kamari.

Moni Profiti Ilia Μοναπροφαηλία

This monastery crowns Santorini's highest peak, Mt Profitis Ilias (567m). Although it now shockingly shares the small peak with radio and TV pylons and a military radar station, it's worth the trek for the stupendous views. The monastery has an interesting **folk museum**. You can walk there from Pyrgos (1½ hours) or from Ancient Thira (one hour).

Oia Οία

The village of Oia (**ee**-ah) was devastated by the 1956 earthquake and has never fully recovered, but it is dramatic, striking and quieter than tourist-frenzied Fira, although it's streets are also filled with expensive

CYCLADES

jewellery boutiques. Built on a steep slope of the caldera, many of its dwellings nestle in niches hewn into the volcanic rock. Oia is famous for its dramatic sunsets and its narrow passageways get crowded in the evenings. The most popular spot to watch the sunset is by the Kastro walls, and towards 7pm, everyone is jockeying for the best position.

From the bus turnaround, go left (following signs for the youth hostel), turn immediately right, take the first left, ascend the steps and walk across the central square to the main street, Nikolaou Nomikou, which skirts the caldera. There is an Alpha Bank (with ATM) on the main street.

You can get information, book hotels, cars and bikes, and use the Internet at Ecorama (☎/fax 2286 071 507, ⓔ ecorama@otenet.gr, ⓦ www.santorinitours.com), by the bus turnaround. Kargounas Tours (☎ 071 290) on Nikolaou Nomikou is also helpful.

The last bus for Fira leaves Oia at 11.20pm in summer. After that, three to four people can bargain for a shared taxi for about €8.80. Six buses daily connect Oia with Baxedes beach.

The **maritime museum** (☎ 2286 071 156; *adult/student €3/1.50; open 10am-2pm, 5pm-8pm Tues-Sun*) is housed in an old mansion and pays homage to Santorini's maritime history.

You can swim at breathtaking **Ammoudi**, the tiny port with excellent *fish tavernas* and colourful fishing boats that lies 300 steps below. If you turn left at the bottom of the stairs and go south around the headland, you'll find a lovely rocky swimming spot. In summer at least two boats and tours go from Ammoudi to Thirasia daily; check travel agents for departure times.

The traditional settlement of **Finikia**, just east of Oia, is a beautiful, quiet place to wander around.

Places to Stay *Oia Youth Hostel* (☎/fax 2286 071 465) Dorm beds with breakfast €11.75. Open summer only. Oia's exceptional hostel has a whitewashed rooftop terrace and bar with great views; laundry facilities and family rooms are available. If it's a toss up between here and Fira's youth hostel – head here.

A little farther on there are several domatia with reasonable prices.

Irini Halari (☎ 2286 071 226) Singles/doubles/triples €23/29/38. On the main road near the pink church, Irini's has great views to the north-east. Next door, *Antoni* has similar rooms and prices.

Lauda Traditional Pension (☎ 2286 071 204, fax 2286 071 274) Singles/doubles €34.90/43.50, double/triple studios €52/69.60. This pension is on the main pedestrian thoroughfare overlooking the caldera.

Hotel Anemones (☎ 2286 071 342, fax 2286 071 220) Singles/doubles €29/43.50. On the main thoroughfare, near Thalami taverna, this hotel has nice rooms with balconies and caldera views.

Hotel Museum (☎ 2286 071 515, fax 2286 071 516) Studios/double apartments €105/119. This restored mansion is now a rather grand hotel with a pool by a landscaped garden.

Chelidonia (☎ 2286 071 287, fax 2286 071 649, ⓦ www.chelidonia.com) studios €130.50, 2-person/4-person apartment €113/157. If you can afford to splurge, Oia is the place to do it. For lovingly restored traditional cave dwellings, contact Chelidonia. The office is in the centre of town.

Zoe-Aegeas (☎/fax 2286 071 466) Studios with shared/private courtyard €101.50/130.50. Zoe-Aegeas has lovely two-person studios in traditional houses.

Katikies (☎ 2286 071 401, fax 2286 071 129, ⓔ katikies@otenet.gr) Doubles €203, suites from €267, honeymoon suite €435. This is one of the most beautiful hotels on the island and has a spectacular pool filled to the brim and balanced on the lip of the caldera.

Perivolas (☎ 2286 071 308, perivolas@san.forthnet.gr) Doubles €313.20. Perivolas is also a knockout.

Places to Eat & Drink *Thomas Grill* (☎ 2286 071 769) Dishes €1.50-6.40. Thomas Grill is very popular with locals due to its good, inexpensive food and excellent service. It's between the bus station and the church, down a small laneway.

Skala (☎ *2286 071 562*) Dishes €2.70-13. There is no shortage of restaurants with a view; Skala, on the caldera, has excellent lamb, salads and hors d'oeuvres.

1800 (☎ *2286 071 485*) Mains €13-23. Open from 7.30pm. In a restored sea captain's house complete with original furniture is this upmarket place serving contemporary Greek cuisine.

Strogili (☎ *2286 071 415*) Dishes €2.70-29. This rooftop cafe-restaurant perched high above caldera is an excellent spot to watch the sun set.

Kastro (☎ *2286 071 045*) Dishes €5.90-13. On the path down to Ammoudi, Kastro is another fine spot to marvel at the sunset. Dine on ravioli with spinach, fresh cream and shavings of roasted hazelnut (€9.30).

Karterados Καρτεραδος

There's not a lot to see here, and the old village with houses dug into a ravine is very neglected now that new apartments have been built on its periphery. However, accommodation is cheaper than in Fira and it makes a good base, providing you don't mind the 20-minute walk to town.

Pension George (☎/fax 2286 022 351, e *pensiongeorge@san.forthnet.gr,* W *www .pensiongeorge.com*) Singles €34.90, doubles €46.50-59. Run by a friendly Englishman, the pension has a swimming pool and views across to the sea. Rooms have balcony and some have air-con; call ahead to be picked up from Fira, the port or airport. Otherwise, walk or take a bus to the village turn-off. Follow the road and turn right after the church on your left. The pension is on the left.

Messaria Μεσσαρια

Situated at a shady junction between Karterados and Kamari, Messaria has a few tavernas and domatia. The main attraction is the **Arhontiko Argirou** (☎ *2286 031 669, fax 2286 033 064; open 9am-2pm & 4.30pm-7.30pm daily*), a sumptuously restored neoclassical mansion that dates from 1888. You can also overnight here: Doubles are €52.50, while apartments with kitchen are €69.60.

Santorini Wines

Santorini's two lauded wines are its crisp, clear dry whites, and the amber-coloured, unfortified dessert wine *vinsanto*, both produced from the ancient indigenous cultivar *assyrtiko*. Most vineyards hold tastings and tours, and there are also two fascinating wine museums.

There are several wineries that hold tastings in summer:

Antoniou (☎/fax 023 557) in Megalohori
Boutari (☎ 081 011, W www.boutari.gr) in Megalohori
Canava Roussos (☎/fax 031 349) on the way to Kamari
Hatzidakis (☎ 032 552, e hatzidakiswinery@ san.forthnet.gr) Call before you visit this small organic winery based in the village of Pyrgos Kallistis Thera, near Moni Profiti Ilia.
Santo Wines (☎ 022 596, e santowines@san.forthnet.gr) near Pyrgos
Sigalas (☎/fax 071 644) off the beach road near Oia.
Volcano Wine Museum (☎ 031 322, W www .waterblue.gr), also known as Lava, on the way to Kamari

Antoniou winery was designed early this century by a winemaker with his eye on the export market. Built into the cliffs directly above Athinios port, the *canava* (wine cellar) is a masterpiece of free-form ingenuity: wine was once piped down to waiting boats. Wine is no longer made at this site, but it's a fascinating place to visit.

Santo Wines is the local vine growers' cooperative and is well worth supporting.

The atmospheric Volcano Wine Museum (admission €1.70, includes three tastings), housed in a traditional canava, has some interesting displays, including a 17th-century wooden wine press.

Kamari

Kamari is a long strand covered by beach umbrellas and backed by package tour hotels, bars and nightclubs. Patches of tall pistachio orchards in the streets give some idea of how pretty Kamari once must have been.

Lios Tours (☎ 2286 033 765, fax 2286 033 661), on the main road into Kamari, is very helpful and can book accommodation.

Volcano Diving Centre (☎ 2286 033 177, W www.scubagreece.com) on the beach, offers dives and courses for beginners (from €59) and certified divers (from €88). Snorkel trips are also available (€18).

Lava Trails (☎ 2286 031 165, e simosvog@ yahoo.com; bike tour €23.20) full-day mountain-bike tour goes from Kamari to Exo Gonia, Vothonas, Messaria and Monolithos.

Cinema Kamari (☎ 2286 031 974, W www .cinekamari.gr; admission €5.90; sessions 9pm & 11.15pm daily), on the main road coming into Kamari, is a great open-air theatre set in a thicket of trees and showing recent releases. In July it hosts the three-day **Santorini Jazz Festival** (☎ 2286 033 452, W www.jazzfestival.gr), featuring lively performances by Greek and foreign musicians.

Just outside Kamari, make sure you visit **Art Space** (☎ 2286 032 774, Exo Gonia), at one of the oldest wineries on the island. Inside the cavernous rooms, there are some hauntingly beautiful pieces on display, including sculpture carved from lava rock. Wine making is in the owner's blood, so a tasting of his *vinsanto* adds to the whole experience.

Other Beaches

Santorini's black-sand beaches become so hot that a mat is essential. The nicest beaches are on the east coast.

The beach at the village of **Perissa** gets quite busy. Wreck and volcano dives are offered here by **Mediterranean Dive Club** (☎ 2286 083 080, e mdc@diveclub.gr; certified dive €43.50, PADI open-water certification €377, snorkelling cruise/hire €32/8.80).

Perivolos and **Agios Georgios**, farther south, are more relaxed.

Monolithos Beach, farther along again, near an abandoned tomato cannery, is less crowded and there are sometimes sizable waves to splash about in.

North of Monolithos, the beaches are almost deserted. **Red Beach**, near Ancient Akrotiri, is breathtaking – high red cliffs and hand-size pebbles submerged under clear water. **Vlihada**, also on the south coast, is much nicer. On the north coast near Oia, **Paradise** and **Pori** are both worth a stop.

At **Armeni** and **Ammoudi**, down the cliffs below Oia, you can plunge right into the caldera. If you're interested in exploring the depths, contact **Atlantis Diving** (☎ 2286 071 507, mobile 69 3222 3064, e ecorama@ otenet.gr, Ammoudi).

Places to Stay *Perissa Camping* (☎ 2286 081 343, Perissa Beach) Adult/tent €5.90/ 2.35. This camping ground is right on the foreshore, which is rare in the Cyclades. It has reasonable shade and stunning, rocky mountain views. There's a beach bar next door.

Plenty of *domatia* are available in Perissa and at Perivolos.

Hostel Anna (☎ 2286 082 182, fax 2286 081 943, e annayh@otenet.gr) Dorm beds €6.10; doubles/quads with pool €29/59. Also in Perissa, this hostel has kitchen facilities, Internet and a swimming pool; a minibus picks up guests from the port.

Stelio's Place (☎ 2286 081 860, fax 2286 081 707) Doubles €29. A minute from Perissa beach, is this popular place attracting a regular stream of backpackers; pick up (no drop off) to the port is possible.

Places to Eat *Leonidas* (☎ 2286 082 170, Agios Georgios) Dishes €2.35-11.75. Leonidas is a nice place to kick-back and have a relaxing ouzo or raki and a bite to eat.

There are several good tavernas near Perissa, including *The Nets* (☎ 2286 082 818), which serves exquisite, delicate mezedes and seafood, and *Perivolos* (☎ 2286 082 007) nearby. On the beachfront in Perissa, *Taverna Lava* (☎ 2286 081 776) is a low-key place with excellent, unfussy traditional food.

There are a few *domatia* in the backstreets of Kamari, and one or two good tavernas away from the beach. Colourful *Ouzeria Pontios*, near the football ground, and *Taverna the Fat Man* (☎ 2286 034 025), on the road into Kamari, are worth seeking out if you're in the area.

Mythos Mezedopoleio Dishes €2.35-1.75, fish by the kilo. In Monolithos, with tables on a stone wall overlooking the beach, this is a good stop for ouzo and a nibble.

Paradissos (☎ 2286 071 583) Dishes €2.10-7.30 On the Oia coast road near Sigalas winery, Paradissos is known for its home-style dishes.

THIRASIA (Θηρασιά) & VOLCANIC ISLETS

Unspoilt Thirasia was separated from Santorini by an eruption in 236 BC. The cliff-top hora, **Manolas**, has *tavernas* and *domatia*. It's a pretty place that gives some idea of what Santorini was like before tourism took over.

The *Nisos Thirasia* leaves Athinios port for Thirasia on Monday and Friday at the inconveniently early hour of 7am, returning at 2pm. On Wednesday it leaves Athinios at 7.45pm but does not return to Santorini. Tickets are available only at the port. There are also morning and afternoon boats to Thirasia from Oia's port of Ammoudi.

The islets of **Palia Kameni** and **Nea Kameni** are still volcanically active and can be visited on half-day excursions from Fira Skala and Athinios. Two-hour trips to Nea Kameni are also possible. A day's excursion taking in Nea Kameni, the hot springs at Palia Kameni, Thirasia and Oia is about €20.50. A tour around the caldera by glass-bottomed boat costs €20.50. Tours that include Ancient Akrotiri as well are available. Shop around Fira's travel agencies for the best deals and the nicest boats.

The very bella *Bella Aurora*, an exact copy of an 18th-century schooner, scoots around the caldera every afternoon on a sunset buffet dinner tour (€29), stopping for sight-seeing at Nea Kameni and for ouzo at Thirasia.

Anafi Αναφη

postcode 840 09 • pop 250

Unpretentious Anafi is a one-hour ferry ride east of Santorini. The main attractions are the beaches, the slow-paced, traditional lifestyle and the lack of commercialism – it's an ideal place to unwind. In mythology, Anafi emerged at Apollo's command when Jason and the Argonauts were in dire need of refuge during a storm. The island's name means 'no snakes'.

Its little port is **Agios Nikolaos**. The main town, the **hora**, is a 10-minute bus ride or steep 30-minute walk from the port. To get to the hora's main pedestrian thoroughfare, head up the hill behind the ouzeria at the first bus stop. This street has most of the domatia, restaurants and minimarkets, and there is also a post office that opens occasionally.

There are several lovely beaches near Agios Nikolaos; palm-lined **Klissidi**, a 10-minute walk east of the port, is the closest and most popular.

Anafi's main sight, **Moni Kalamiotissas**, is a three-hour walk from the hora in the extreme east of the island, near the meagre remains of a sanctuary to Apollo. **Monastery Rock** (584m) is the highest rock formation in the Mediterranean Sea. There is also a ruined Venetian kastro at **Kastelli**, east of Klissidi.

Jeyzed Travel (☎ 2286 061 253, fax 2286 061 352), down at the port, organises Monastery Rock climbs, sells ferry tickets, exchanges money and can help with accommodation.

Getting To/From Anafi

There are four ferries weekly to Ios (three hours, €6.10), Naxos (four hours, €10.30) and Paros (6 hours, €10.50). Seven ferries weekly go to Santorini (one hour, €5.90)

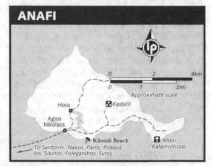

ANAFI

0   2   4km

0   1   2mi

Approximate scale

Hora   ◼ Kastelli

Agios
Nikolaos

◼ Klissidi Beach   🏠 Moni
To Santorini, Naxos, Paros, Pireaus,   Kalamiotissas
Ios, Sikinos, Folegandros, Syros

CYCLADES

and four go to Piraeus (11 hours, €20.10), and one goes to Syros (eight hours, €12.80), two go to Folegandros (five hours, €7.60) and Sikinos (four hours, €5.90). Twice weekly there's a post boat to Santorini (3½ hours, €6.40).

Getting Around Anafi

An undersized bus carts passengers from the port up to the hora. Caiques serve various beaches and nearby islands.

Places to Stay & Eat

Camping is tolerated at Klissidi Beach, but the only facilities are at nearby tavernas.

Rooms in the hora are overpriced and pretty much of a muchness. Shop around if you can, but be careful not to miss out altogether. Domatia owners are looking for long stays – if you're only staying one night you should take whatever you can get. In high season, contact Jeyzed Travel in advance to be sure of a room; places at Klissidi fill fast, so book well in advance.

Rooms Rent Paradise (☎ 2286 061 243, fax 2286 061 253) Doubles €29. Paradise, on the main street, has clean rooms with a nice view.

Panorama (☎ 2286 061 292) Doubles €29. Next door to Rooms Rent Paradise, Panorama has similar rooms for the same price.

Anafi Rooms (☎ 2286 061 271) Doubles €38. These rooms are near Panorama.

Villa Apollon (☎ 2286 061 237, fax 2286 061 287, ⓔ vapollon@panafonet.gr) Doubles/studios €116/140.70. This villa at Klissidi Beach is the nicest and priciest. It has traditional rooms all with sea views.

Rooms to Let Artemis (☎ 2286 061 235) Rooms €38. Artemis is also at Klissidi.

Tavernas in the hora are all reasonably priced and have nice views. These include *Alexandra's* (☎ 2286 061 212), *Astrakan* (☎ 2286 061 249) and *To Steki* (☎ 2286 061 380). *Taverna Armenaki* (☎ 2286 061 234), below the main street, past To Steki, has a lively atmosphere and a menu that includes Cretan tacos, local greens and cheeses, and lamb. It also has raki with honey. Klissidi has a few *tavernas* as well.

Sikinos Σίκινος

postcode 840 10 • pop 287

If a quiet, unspoilt island is what you'r looking for, Sikinos fits the bill. It has som nice beaches and a beautiful terraced lan scape that drops dramatically down to th sea. The port of Alopronia, and the contigu ous villages of Hora and Kastro that togeth comprise the hilltop capital, are the onl settlements. Hora/Kastro has a combine post office and OTE, but no banks. Ferr tickets are sold at Koundouris Travel (☎/fa 2286 051 168) in Hora/Kastro and at a boot at the port before departures. If you're brin ing a car or motorcycle, bring petrol too there's no petrol station on the island.

Getting To/From Sikinos

Seven ferries weekly go to Piraeus (1 hours, €17.90) and five weekly to Ios (3 minutes, €3.20), two to Naxos (three hour €5) and Syros (six hours, €8.40), six t Paros (four hours, €5.40), and four to Fole gandros (45 minutes, €3.80). The ferrie run to Santorini (2½ hours, €5.60), Kimc los (2½ hours, €5.30), Milos (three hour €8.80) and Sifnos (five hours, €5.90). On weekly runs to Serifos (five hours, €5.90 and Thirasia (2½ hours, €5.60), and tw run to Anafi (four hours, €5.90) and Kyth nos (seven hours, €9.30).

Getting Around Sikinos

The local bus meets all ferries and runs be tween Alopronia and Hora/Kastro ever half hour in August and less frequently a other times of the year. A timetable i sometimes posted near the minimarket.

Things to See & Do

The **Kastro** is a cute and compact place wit some lovely old houses and friendly locals In the centre there's a pretty square that wa created in the '40s by the occupying Ital ians, who apparently planned to stay. Th fortified **Moni Zoödohou Pigis** stands on hill above the town.

Sikinos' main excursion is a one-hou scenic trek (or five-minute drive along

SIKINOS

Daily Ferries	------
Low Frequency Ferries	--------
Hydrofoil/Catamaran	---·---·---
Excursion Boat	·············

AEGEAN SEA

Moni Zoödhochou Pigis
Malta Beach
Kastro
Agios Georgios Beach
Hora
▲552m
Alopronia
Agios Nikolaos Beach
SIKINOS
Katergo
Episkopi
To Ios & Santorini

Kalogeri
▲432m

Kardiotissa

Karra Beach

To Ios, Thirassia & Santorini

0   2   4km
0   1   2mi

To Folegandros, Kimolos, Milos, Naxos, Paros, Syros, Sifnos, Serifos, Kythnos & Pireaus

rather silly new road) south-west to **Episkopi**. When ruins there were investigated by 19th-century archaeologists, the Doric columns and inscriptions led them to believe it had originally been a shrine to Apollo, but the remains are now believed to be those of a 3rd century AD Roman mausoleum. In the 7th century the ruins were transformed into a church, which was extended in the 17th century to become **Moni Episkopis** *(Open 6.30pm-8.30pm daily)*. From here it's possible to climb up to a little church and ancient ruins perched on a precipice to the south, from where the views are spectacular.

Caiques run to nice beaches at **Agios Georgios, Malta** – with ancient ruins on the hill above – and **Karra**. **Katergo**, a swimming place with interesting rocks, and **Agios Nikolaos Beach** are both within easy walking distance of Alopronia.

Places to Stay & Eat

Alopronia has the bulk of accommodation.

Lucas Rooms to Let (☎ 2286 051 075) Doubles/apartments €32/43.50. Near the restaurant of the same name and recommended by readers, Lucas has doubles, and three- to four-person apartments.

Tasos Rooms (☎ 2286 051 005) Doubles €34.90. These bougainvillea-covered rooms are past the Rock Café.

Porto Sikinos (☎/fax 2286 051 220) Doubles with breakfast €69.60. This stylish B-class spot is on the port beach. A traditional Cycladic-style establishment, it has a bar and restaurant.

In Hora/Kastro, *To Steki tou Garbi* is a good grill house. There are also good *tavernas* at Agio Georgios. Down at the port, *Lucas* serves the best food. In high season a lovely *bar* opens over the water at the northern end of Alopronia's bay; at other times the *Rock Café*, above the quay, suffices.

Folegandros
Φολέγανδρος

The happiest man on earth is the man with fewest needs. And I also believe that if you have light, such as you have here, all ugliness is obliterated.
Henry Miller

postcode 840 11 • pop 650

Folegandros (fo-**leh**-gan-dross) is one of Greece's most enticing islands, bridging the gap between tourist traps and small, under-populated islands on the brink of total abandonment. The number of visitors is increasing, but most locals still make a living from fishing and farming.

Tourists come in search of unspoilt island life and, except for July and August, the island is uncrowded and blissful. The island has several good beaches – be prepared for strenuous walking to reach some of them – and a striking landscape of cultivated terraces that give way to precipitous cliffs.

The capital is the concealed cliff-top Hora, one of the prettiest capitals in the Cyclades. Boats dock at the small harbour of Karavostasis, on the east coast. The only other settlement is Ano Meria, 4km north-west of Hora.

Getting To/From Folegandros

Ferry There are four services weekly to Piraeus (six to nine hours, €15.40), Santorini (1½ to 2½ hours, €5.30), Ios (1½ hours,

CYCLADES

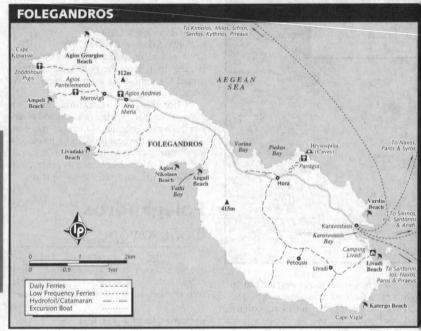

FOLEGANDROS

To Kimolos, Milos, Sifnos,
Serifos, Kythnos, Pireaus

Cape Kiparissi

Agios Georgios Beach

Zoödohous Pigis

Agios Pantelemonos

Merovigli

312m

Agios Andreas

Ano Meria

Ampeli Beach

AEGEAN SEA

Livadaki Beach

FOLEGANDROS

Agios Nikolaos Beach

Angali Beach

Vathi Bay

Vorina Bay

Pinkas Bay

Hrysospilia (Caves)

Panagia

Hora

To Naxos, Paros & Syros

415m

Vardia Beach

To Sikinos, Santorini & Anafi

Karavostasis

Karavostasis Bay

Camping Livadi

Petousis

Livadi

Livadi Beach

To Santorini, Ios, Naxos, Paros & Piraeus

Katergo Beach

Cape Vigla

Daily Ferries
Low Frequency Ferries
Hydrofoil/Catamaran
Excursion Boat

0   1   2km
0 0.5   1mi

CYCLADES

€4.65), Paros (four hours, €5.90), Naxos (three hours, €7.40) and Sikinos (40 minutes, €3.80).

Three weekly services go to Syros (six hours, €8.80), Milos (2½ hours, €5.30), Sifnos (four hours, €5.30) and Serifos (five hours, €4.65).

Two weekly ferries go to Kimolos (1½ hours, €3.50) and Anafi (five hours, €7.60).

Once weekly there are ferries to Thirasia (1½ hours, €5.30) and Kythnos (six hours, €9).

Getting Around Folegandros

The local bus meets all boats and takes passengers to Hora (€0.80). From Hora there are buses to the port one hour before all ferry departures, even late at night. Buses from Hora run hourly to Ano Meria (€1), stopping at the road leading to Angali Beach. The bus stop for Ano Meria is on the western edge of town, next to the Sottovento Tourism Office. There is one overworked

taxi (☎ 2286 041 048, mobile 69 4469 3957) on the island, and motorbikes, not cars, are the only form of transport available for hire.

In July and August, excursion boats make separate trips from Karavostasis to Kartergo, Angali and Agios Nikolaos and from Angali to Livadaki Beach.

KARAVOSTASIS Καραβοστασις
This port town lacks charm but makes a convenient base from which to explore the island's beaches.

Places to Stay & Eat
Camping Livadi (☎ 2286 041 204) Adult/tent €4.10/2. This site is at Livadi Beach, 1.2km from Karavostasis. It has a kitchen, minimart, bar, restaurant and laundry. Turn left on the cement road skirting Karavostasis Beach.

There are several domatia and hotels – look for the signs as you get off the ferry.

Aeolos Beach Hotel (☎ 2286 041 205) Singles/doubles/suites €32/49/67.90. This

C-class hotel, on the beach, has clean rooms and a pretty garden.

Vrahos (☎ *2286 041 450, fax 2286 041 92,* e *vrahos@tee.gr)* Doubles with breakfast €75.40. Built in traditional Cyladic style, Vrahos has an outdoor bar and breakfast area with views of the surrounding islands. It's at the far end of the beach beyond the Aeolos Beach Hotel.

Restaurant Kati Allo (☎ *2286 041 272)* Dishes €1.70-4.65, seafood by the kilo. Part of the Poseidon Hotel, this restaurant has one of the best reputations for top-quality traditional food and fresh fish.

The cafe-bars *Evangelos* and *Sirma* (☎ *2286 041 527)* are both on the beach, so you'll be face-to-face with fishermen working on their nets and kids playing; both serve snacks, sandwiches and meze. *Two Hearts* is also a nice place to eat, and Hotel Vrahos has a small, quiet bar with marvellous views.

HORA Χώρα
The captivating Hora, complete with a medieval kastro filled with little houses draped in bougainvillea, is perhaps the most beautiful capital in the Cyclades.

Orientation & Information
From the bus turnaround, facing away from the port, turn left and follow the curving road. An archway on the right leads to the kastro, where the walls have been incorporated into dwellings. A left turn leads to a row of three shady squares. The third is the central plateia.

There is no tourist police. The post office is 200m downhill from the bus turnaround, on the port road.

There is no bank, but all three travel agencies exchange travellers cheques, and Diaplous General Tourism Office can provide VISA cash advances. Note that, except for a couple of boutiques, credit cards are not usually accepted on Folegandros.

Maraki Travel (☎ 2286 041 273, fax 2286 041 149), by the first square, has a monopoly on the sale of ferry tickets, and provides limited Internet access; it also has a ticket booth at the port. It's open 10.30am to 12.15pm and 5.30am to 9.15pm.

The police (☎ 2286 041 249) are beyond the third plateia, past Nikos' Restaurant.

Things to See
The Hora is a well-preserved village with white churches, sugar-cube houses and shady squares. The medieval **Kastro**, a tangle of narrow streets spanned by low archways, dates from when Marco Sanudo ruled the island in the 13th century. The houses' wooden balconies blaze with bougainvillea and hibiscus.

The newer village, outside the kastro, is just as pretty. From the first bus stop, a steep path leads up to the large church of the **Panagia** *(open 6pm-8pm)*, which is perched on a cliff top above the town.

Courses
The *Cycladic School* (☎ *2286 041 137,* e *a-f-pap@otenet.gr)*, founded on Folegandros in 1984, offers one and two-week courses in drawing, painting, Greek cookery, folk and modern dancing and Hatha yoga. Accommodation is included.

Organised Tours
Sottovento Tourism Office *(☎ 2286 041 444, fax 2286 041 430,* e *sottovento94@hotmail .com)* Adult/child €18.90/10.30, including lunch. Departs 10am Mon, Wed, Fri summer. Day trips by caique to hidden bays and beaches are offered by this company. It's by the bus stop for Ano Meria and Angali; if you have snorkelling gear, take it along. The office also organises accommodation.

Places to Stay
In July and August most domatia and hotels are booked solid; unless you're happy to join the homeless overspill down at Camping Livadi, make sure you book well in advance. Diaplous General Tourism Office (☎ 2286 041 158, fax 2286 041 159, e diaplous@x-treme.gr), by the port-Hora bus stop books accommodation.

Spyridoula Rooms (☎ *2286 041 078, fax 2286 041 034)* Doubles €43.50. This is one of numerous, reasonably priced domatia near the police station.

Artemis (☎ *2286 041 313)* Doubles €49. Open year-round. Artemis is by the port-

CYCLADES

Hora bus station above its cosy cafe. Some rooms have sea views.

Hotel Polikandia (☎ 2286 041 322, fax 2286 041 323) Doubles €55. By the port-Hora bus stop, this new hotel has a lovely garden area to hang out in. Rooms have telephone, radio, fan and balcony.

Hotel Odysseus (☎ 2286 041 276, fax 2286 041 366) Doubles €59. This new hotel has a swimming pool and rooms have a balcony. It's next to Spyridoula Rooms.

Hotel Castro (☎/fax 2286 041 230) Doubles/triples with bathroom €55/78.30. Some of the cosy rooms at this atmospheric hotel have incredible views straight down the cliffs to the sea. Walk straight ahead from the kastro entrance and you'll find the hotel on the left. Breakfast is available.

Folegandros Apartments (☎ 2286 041 239, fax 2286 041 166, e foleaps@ath .forthnet.gr) Studios from €75.40. This C-class establishment can be found where the port bus terminates. It has well-equipped apartments and a swimming pool.

Anemomilos Apartments (☎ 2286 041 309) Doubles from €90. Views don't come any better than from this top-of-the-range property by the bus station, although snooty reception staff don't come any worse either. Apartments are furnished with antiques, and there is one unit for the disabled.

Kallista (☎ 2286 041 555, fax 2286 041 554) Singles/doubles €64/81. This A-class hotel has a swimming pool and views of the sea in the distance. The beds are a novelty – they have a traditional stone base. Kallista is on the street behind Sottovento Tourism Office.

Places to Eat

Punta (☎ 2286 041 063) Dishes €2.35-6.40. Punta, at the port-Hora bus turn-around, has tables in a wild garden area. Excellent breakfast, spanakopitta, rabbit *stifado* (stew), lamb and vegetarian dishes are served at very reasonable prices in striking crockery made by one of the owners.

Apanemos Dishes €2-5. Next to the Sottovento Tourism Office, this friendly place is run by the same crew as Punta. It serves crepes, pasta and traditional dishes.

Melissa (☎ 2286 041 067) Dishes €1.50-5.50. Melissa, on the main square under an umbrella of pepper trees, has good home-cooked food.

Piatsa Restaurant (☎ 2286 041 274) Dishes €2.50-8.20. This is one of the best restaurants on the island and has interesting daily specials, as well as vegetarian dishes. It's on the second square past the kastro.

O Kritikos (☎ 2286 041 219) Dishes €2-6.40. On the third square past the kastro (and with a rotisserie in front), O Kritikos serves succulent grilled meat.

Entertainment

On the main square, *Astarti* is a good place to go after dinner for Greek music. Opposite Punta, *Kellari* (☎ 2286 041 119) is a moody little wine bar where regional Greek wines are available by the glass.

Arajo (☎ 2286 041 463) is the place to go for a late-night drink and some Latin, jazz and hip hop; it's on the road that leads west off the third square towards the Ano Meria bus stop and the Sottovento Tourism Office.

Next door to Sottovento, the vivid wall murals in *Greco Café Bar* (☎ 2286 041 456) provide some promise for a colourful night out, while *Laoumi*, left of Sottovento, is a tiny, atmospheric ouzeria.

In an idyllic setting a few minutes' walk from the Hora, *Rakendia Sunset Bar* has a fabulous view over the terraced dry-stone walls that lead down to the ocean. It's open early in the afternoon until late and is sign posted off the road to Ano Meria.

AROUND FOLEGANDROS
Ano Meria Ανω Μερια

The settlement of Ano Meria stretches for several kilometres because small farms surround most of the dwellings. Agriculture is still very much alive at this end of the island and you'll see haystacks, market gardens, goats and donkeys.

The folklore museum (admission €1.50, open 5pm-8pm daily) is on the eastern outskirts of the village. Ask the bus driver to drop you off nearby.

There are several excellent tavernas in Ano Meria, including *I Synantisi* (☎ 2286

41 208) and ***Mimi's*** *(☎ 2286 041 377),* which specialise in *matsada* – a type of handmade pasta served with rabbit or rooster.

The very old and authentic kafeneio ***Barakosta*** frequented by locals, is well worth a stop, as is the local ***bakery*** nearby, which makes excellent almond biscuits and the local sweet *karpouzenia*, a baked, soft melange of watermelon chunks, honey and sesame seeds.

Beaches

Karavostasis has a pretty white-pebbled beach. For **Livadi Beach**, follow the signs for Camping Livadi. The sandy and pebbled **Angali Beach** has a lovely aspect. There are several *domatia* here and two reasonable *tavernas*.

There are other good beaches at **Agios Nikolaos** and **Livadaki**, both west of Angali. The steep path to the beach at Agios Nikolaos is exhausting, but it's worth it if you plan to have lunch here. Don't miss the octopus in wine sauce at ***Taverna Papalagi***. **Agios Georgios** is north of Ano Meria. A path from Agios Andreas church in Ano Meria leads to Agios Georgios Beach. The walk takes about an hour.

Most of the beaches have no shops or tavernas, so make sure you take food and water.

Milos & Kimolos
Μήλος & Κίμωλος

MILOS
postcode 848 00 • pop 4390

Volcanic Milos (**mee**-loss), the most westerly island of the Cyclades, is overlooked by most foreign tourists. While not as visually dramatic as the volcanic islands of Santorini and Nisyros, it does have some mesmerising rock formations, hot springs and pleasant beaches. Flowers seem to grow in abundance on the island, and it appears wildly verdant and green when compared with its near neighbour Folegandros.

A boat trip around the island allows you to visit most of Milos' stunning beaches

(many inaccessible by road), coves and geologically interesting places.

Filakopi, an ancient Minoan city in the island's north-east, was one of the earliest settlements in the Cyclades. During the Peloponnesian Wars, Milos remained neutral, and was the only Cycladic island not to join the Athenian alliance. It paid dearly in 416 BC when avenging Athenians massacred the adult males and enslaved the women and children.

The island's most celebrated export, the beautiful *Venus de Milo* (a 4th century BC statue of Aphrodite) is far away in the Louvre (apparently having lost its arms on the way to Paris in the 19th century).

Since ancient times, the island has been quarried for minerals, resulting in huge gaps and fissures in the landscape. Obsidian was mined on the island and exported throughout the Mediterranean.

Getting To/From Milos

Air There is a daily flight to/from Athens (€52.85/61.30 one way). The Olympic Airways office (☎ 2287 022 380, fax 2287 021 884) is in Adamas, just past the main square, on the road to Plaka (and is worth going into just for the original '70s decor).

Ferry The *Nissos Kimolos* departs five times daily from Pollonia for Kimolos at 9am, 11am, 2.15pm, 6.30pm, 10.40pm (20 minutes, €1.70/1.30/7.80 per person/ motorbike/car).

There are at least two ferries daily to Piraeus (five to seven hours, €16). There is at least one daily ferry to Sifnos (1¼ hours, €5.30), Serifos (two hours, €5.60) and Kythnos (3½ hours, €5.30). Six weekly ferries go to Kimolos (one hour, €4.65).

Five times weekly the *Vitsentsos Kornaros* sails to the Cretan ports of Agios Nikolaos (seven hours, €14.80) and Sitia (nine hours, €16), sometimes continuing on to Kassos (11 hours, €18.30), Karpathos (12 hours, €22) and Rhodes (13 hours, €25.90).

There are three weekly ferries to Folegandros (2½ hours, €5.30) and Sikinos (three hours, €8.80), and two weekly to Paros (4½ hours, €8.40). Services also run regularly to Milos.

Phone numbers listed incorporate changes due in Oct 2002; see p83

CYCLADES

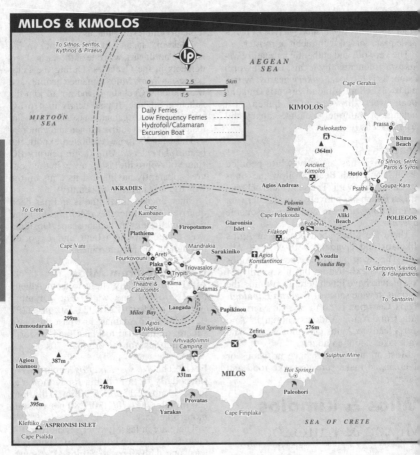

MILOS & KIMOLOS

AEGEAN SEA

Daily Ferries	— — — —
Low Frequency Ferries	- - - - -
Hydrofoil/Catamaran	— · — ·
Excursion Boat	· · · · · · ·

MIRTOÖN SEA

To Sifnos, Serifos, Kythnos & Piraeus

Cape Gerahia

KIMOLOS

Paleokastro

Prassa

Klima Beach

(364m)

Ancient Kimolos

Horio

To Sifnos, Serifos, Paros & Syros

Agios Andreas

Psathi

Goupa-Kara

To Crete

AKRADIES

Cape Kambanes

Polonia Strait

Cape Pelekouda

Pollonia

Aliki Beach

POLIEGOS

Firopotamos

Glaronisia Islet

Filakopi

Plathiena

Mandrakia

Sarakiniko

Agios Konstantinos

Voudia *Voudia Bay*

To Santorini, Sikinos & Folegandros

Cape Vani

Fourkovouni Areti

Plaka

Triovasalos

Trypiti

Ancient Theatre & Catacombs Klima

Adamas

To Santorini

299m

Langada

Papikinou

Milos Bay

Agios Nikolaos

Hot Springs

Zefiria

276m

Ammoudaraki

Arhivadolimni Camping

Agiou Ioannou 387m

Sulphur Mine

331m

MILOS

Hot Springs

749m

395m

Paleohori

Provatas

Yarakas

Cape Firiplaka

SEA OF CRETE

Kleftiko **ASPRONISI ISLET**

Cape Psalida

There is one weekly ferry to Santorini (four hours, €9.60), Ios (5½ hours, €8.80) and Syros (6 hours, €9).

Fast Boat & Catamarans One weekly service goes to Santorini (1¾, €19.20), and one daily to Sifnos (1¾, €7.70), Serifos (1¼, €8.80) and at least one daily to Piraeus (3¾ hours, €30).

Getting Around Milos

There are no buses to the airport, so you'll need to take a taxi (☎ 2287 022 219) for €3.80 from Adamas.

Buses leave Adamas for Plaka and Trypi (both €1.10) every hour or so. Buses ru daily to Pollonia (€0.80, nine daily), Paleo hori (€1, eight daily), and Provatas (€1.1(eight daily), Milos Camping (eight daily) an Sarakiniko (two daily). Taxis can be ordere on ☎ 2287 022 219. Cars, motorcycles an mopeds can be hired along the waterfront.

Adamas Αδαμας
postcode 848 01

Although Plaka is the capital, the rathe plain port of Adamas has most of the ac commodation.

To get to the town centre from the quay, urn right at the waterfront. The central quare, with the bus stop, taxi rank and out-oor cafes, is at the end of this stretch of vaterfront. Just past the square is a road to 1e right that skirts the town beach. Straight 1ead is the town's main thoroughfare and 1e road to Plaka.

Milos' municipal tourist office (☎ 2287 22 445, W www.milostravel.com), opposite 1e quay, is one of the most helpful in the 'yclades, although it's open 10am-4pm in 1mmer only. Terry's Travel (☎ 2287 022 40, fax 2287 022 261, e teristur@otenet.gr), ; up the steps from the quay and organises 1urs and pricey windmill accommodation. For the post office, turn right just after the quare and take the third street on the left. 1here are ATMs on the main square. The 1lice (☎ 2287 021 378) are on the main quare, next to the bus stop; the port police ☎ 2287 022 100) are on the waterfront.

1ining Museum This museum (☎ 2287 22 481; admission free; open 9am-2pm & 1m-9pm daily) has some interesting geo-1gical exhibits and traces the island's long 1ining history. To get there, take the first ght after the central square and continue long the waterfront for about 500m.

ctivities Dive courses are offered by 1ilos Diving Center (☎/fax 2287 041 296, 1 www.marras.gr/milosdiving). Based at 1llonia, Milos Diving is a member of the 1ternational Association for Handicapped 1ivers.

Milos Yachting (☎ 2287 022 079, fax 287 023 723) has yachts and skippers for 1arter.

1rganised Tours *Milos Round 1 & 2* ☎ 2287 023 411) Tours €17.40. Departs 1m. These tour boats stop at beaches 1ound the island and Kleftiko, pausing at imolos for lunch; tickets are available on 1e waterfront.

Andromeda Yachts (☎ 2287 023 680) 1iling trips €45 per person, sailing tours 240 per tour. Oct-Nov. Andromeda has iling trips to the island's nicest beaches and coves; they feature a seafood lunch, ouzo and sweets. Sailing tours take place in the south-west Cyclades. Book through travel agencies or visit Andromeda on the waterfront.

Special Events The Milos Festival, a well-orchestrated event, is held in early July and features traditional dancing, cooking and jazz.

Places to Stay *Arhivadolimni (Milos) Camping* (☎ 2287 031 410, fax 2287 031 412, W www.miloscamping.com, Arhiva-dolimni) Adult/tent €4.80/3.50, bungalows €61. This camping ground has excellent fa-cilities, including a restaurant, bar and bike rental. It's 6.5km east of Adamas; to get there, follow the signs along the waterfront from the central square.

In summer, lists of domatia are given out at the tourist office on the quay, but decent accommodation is quite thin on the ground – make sure you call ahead.

Ethelvina's Rooms (☎ 2287 022 169) Singles/doubles/triples €20.50/43.50/52.50. These excellent rooms are uphill from the bakery on the main square.

Langada Beach Hotel (☎ 2287 023 411, fax 2287 023 416) Singles/doubles/triples €30.20/49/61. Left of the ferry quay, be-hind Langada Beach, this is a huge complex with a pool.

Hotel Delfini (☎ 2287 022 001, fax 2287 023 409) Doubles €29/52.50 with shared/ private bathroom. Behind Langada Beach Hotel, Delfini has friendly owners and nice simple rooms.

Hotel Dionysis (☎ 2287 022 117 fax 2287 022 118) Double/triple studios €61/ 78.30. Just up from the square near Olym-pic Airways, Dionysis has comfortable stu-dios with TV and air-con.

Portiani Hotel (☎ 2287 022 940, fax 2287 022 766, e sirmalen@otenet.gr) Singles/ doubles from €67.90/88. On the waterfront at the square, the rooms have TV, air-con, phone, balcony and terrace. Rates include a buffet breakfast featuring fresh figs, comb honey, cheeses and home-made jams.

Villa Helios (☎ 2287 022 258, fax 2287 023 974, e heaton.theologitis@utanet.gr)

CYCLADES

Apartments €72.50. On the hill behind the quay, Helios has beautifully furnished two-person apartments with phone, TV and air-con.

Places to Eat *Aragosta* (☎ 2287 022 292) Mains €10.30-26. This upmarket Italian eatery, on the first staircase up from the port as you head into town, serves duck, lobster, turkey and pasta dishes.

O Kinigos (☎ 2287 022 349) Dishes €2.10-25.90, fish by the kilo. Superb Greek staples are on offer at this waterfront taverna, which is refreshingly crowded with locals.

Navagio (☎ 2287 023 392) beyond the Portiani Hotel is an excellent fish taverna.

Entertainment *Akri* (☎ 2287 022 064) is an overflowing, up-beat bar opposite Aragosta, up the first staircase by the port.

Vipera Lebetina, beyond Akri and named after the island's breed of poisonous snake, plays deafeningly loud rock and summer-loving hits, which is just what the young crowd of locals want.

Malion is a local bouzouki bar with live music, nearby Navagio.

Plaka & Trypiti Πλακα & Τρυπητα

Plaka, 5km uphill from Adamas, is a typical Cycladic town with white houses and labyrinthine laneways. It merges with the settlement of Trypiti to the south.

The **Milos Folk & Arts Museum** (☎ 2287 021 292; admission €1.50; open 10am-2pm, 6pm-8pm Tues-Sat, 10am-2pm Sun) is in a 19th-century house in Plaka. It's signposted at the bus turnaround in Plaka.

At the bus turnaround, turn right for the path to the **Frankish Kastro** built on the ancient acropolis. The 13th-century church, **Thalassitras**, is inside the walls. The final battle between ancient Melians and Athenians was fought on this hill. The kastro offers panoramic views of most of the island.

The **archaeology museum** (☎ 2287 021 629; admission €1.50; open 8.30am-3pm Tues-Sun) is in Plaka, near the junction with the road leading to the much signposted catacombs. Don't miss the perfectly preserved terracotta figurine of Athena (unlabelled) in

the middle room. The room on the left ha charming figurines from Filakopi.

Plaka is built on the site of Ancien Milos, which was destroyed by the Atheni ans and rebuilt by the Romans. Ther are some Roman ruins near Trypiti, includ ing Greece's only Christian **catacomb** (☎ 2287 021 625; open 8am-3pm Tues Sun). On the road to the catacombs, a sig points right to the well-preserved **ancier theatre**, which hosts the **Milos Festiva** every July. On the track to the theatre, sign points to where a farmer found th **Venus de Milo** in 1820. Opposite are re mains of massive Doric walls. Fifty metre farther along on the cement road is a sig to the 1st-century catacombs. A passag leads to a large chamber flanked by tunne that contained the tombs.

Places to Stay & Eat Both Plaka an Trypiti have *domatia*; ask at tavernas.

Arhontoula (☎ 2287 021 384) Dishe €2-8.20. Left from the bus turnaround i Plaka, Arhontoula has a large selection c meze, including cod with *skordalia* (garli sauce) and interesting salads.

Alisahni (☎ 2287 023 485) Mains €5 11.30. Just around the corner from Arhor toula, this voguish place is also very goo with creative starters, such as tzatziki wit pine nuts and almonds.

Utopia Cafe (☎ 2287 023 678) The vie from this smart little cafe-bar is breath taking. Utopia is open till late and signposte down a laneway opposite Arhontoula.

Erghina's (☎ 2287 022 524) Dishe €2.10-11.75. On the main 'road' throug Trypiti to the left, local's describe Erghina creations as 'dream food'. Try deliciou dishes such as *pitaraki* (hard-cheese pie) an young wild goat with potatoes. *Methysmer Politia* on the road to the catacombs, is als worth seeking out.

Around Milos

Klima, once the port of ancient Milos, now a charming, unspoilt fishing villag skirting a narrow beach below Trypiti an the catacombs. Whitewashed building with bright blue, green and red doors an alconies, have boat houses on the ground loor and living quarters on the first floor.

Plathiena is a lovely sandy beach below 'laka. On the way to Plathiena you can de-ur to the fishing villages of **Areti** and **Fourovouni**. The beaches of **Provatas** and aleohori, on the south coast, are long and andy, and there are hot springs at Paleoori. *Deep Blue* (☎ 2287 031 158) in Pale-hori is an atmospheric terraced music cafe uilt into the surrounding rocks.

Pollonia, on the north coast, is a fishing illage-cum-resort with a small beach and *omatia*. It serves as the jumping-off point or the boat to Kimolos. **Mandrakia** is a ovely fishing hamlet north-east of Plaka.

The Minoan settlement of **Filakopi** is km inland from Pollonia. Three levels of ities have been uncovered here – Early, Middle and Late Cycladic.

The islet of **Glaronisia**, off the north oast, is a rare geological phenomenon omposed entirely of hexagonal volcanic tone bars.

Places to Stay & Eat *Hotel Panorama* (☎ 2287 021 623, fax 2287 022 112)* Doubles vith breakfast €59. This is Klima's only otel. It's 2km from the village. There's lso a restaurant.

KIMOLOS

'his small island lies just north-east of Milos. It receives few visitors, although here are *domatia*, *tavernas*, *bars* and de-ent beaches. Domatia owners meet ferries.

Those who do make the effort tend to be ay-trippers arriving on the boat from Pol-onia, on the north-eastern tip of Milos. The oat docks at the port of **Psathi**, from where 's 3km to the pretty capital of **Horio**. Seek ut promising *To Kyma* (☎ 2287 051 001) or a meal.

There's no petrol station on Kimolos – if ou're bringing a car or moped from Milos, ake sure you've got enough fuel. Donkeys re still the principal mode of transport, and ere are tracks all around the island.

There are thermal springs at the settle-ent of **Prassa** on the north-east coast. eaches can be reached by caique from

Psathi. At the centre of the island is the 364m-high cliff on which sits the fortress of **Paleokastro**.

Day-trippers should try the local special-ity, *ladenia*, a pizza-like pie with tomato, onion and olives.

Getting To/From Kimolos

Ferry Boats go daily to/from Pollonia on Milos, departing from Kimolos at 8am, 10am, 1.15pm, 5.30pm and 10pm (see the Milos Getting There & Away section for details).

There are three ferries weekly to Adamas (one hour, €3.80), Folegandros (1½ hours, €4.20) and Sikinos (2½ hours, €5.30).

There are four weekly to Sifnos (1½ hours, €4.40) and Serifos (two hours, €5.90).

Two weekly services go to Kythnos (three hours, €7.40), Syros (five hours, €9), Paros (4½ hours, €6.90), Santorini (3½ hours, €9.30) and Piraeus (seven hours, €13.40).

Sifnos Σίφνος

postcode 840 03 • pop 2900

Sifnos coyly hides its assets from passing ferry passengers. At first glance it looks barren, but the port is in the island's most arid area. Explore and you'll find an abun-dantly attractive landscape of terraced olive groves and almond trees, with oleanders in the valleys and hillsides covered in wild ju-niper, which used to fuel potters' kilns. There are numerous dovecotes, white-washed houses and chapels. Plenty of old paths link the villages, which makes it an ideal island for walking.

During the Archaic period the island was very wealthy due to its gold and silver re-sources. To protect their loot the islanders constructed an elaborate communications network of watchtowers that used fire and smoke signals to warn of attack. The ruins of 55 towers have been located to date. By the 5th century BC the mines were exhausted and Sifnos' fortunes were reversed – the is-land became so poor that it was the butt of endless jokes in Athens and elsewhere.

CYCLADES

SIFNOS

AEGEAN SEA

Daily Ferries	-----
Low Frequency Ferries	-----
Hydrofoil/Catamaran	---
Excursion Boat	·····

Cape Heronisos

Heronisos

To Serifos, Paros,
Syros, Kythnos
& Piraeus — Agios Dimos

476m

Kamares
Bay

Camping
Makis

SIFNOS

Kamares

Ano Petali — Artemonas

To Kimolos, Milos,
Santorini, Sikinos,
Folegandros & Piraeus

Apollonia

Kastro
Seralia
Kato Petali

Katavati — Exambelas

680m — Moni
Profiti Ilia

Faros

Platys
Gialos

Vathi

Camping
Platys Gialos

Fasolou
Beach
Moni
Hrysopigis

Hrysopigis
Beach

Vathi
Bay

201m

Platys Gialos
Bay

To Santorini

Cape Kondou

KITRIANI

0   2   4km
0   1   2mi

(five hours, €5.90) and Santorini (six hours, €9.30), and two weekly to Paros (two hours, €5.70) and Syros (5½ hours, €6.40).

Fast Boat & Catamaran There is a daily catamaran to Piraeus (2¾ hours, €26.40), four weekly to Kythnos (1¼ hours, €9.90) and one daily to Serifos (20 minutes, €7.30) and Milos (¾ hour, €7.70). There are five weekly catamarans to Santorini (2½ hours, €15.40).

Getting Around Sifnos

Frequent buses link Apollonia with: Kamares (€0.80), with some services continuing onto Artemonas; Kastro (€0.80), Vathi (€1.50), Faros (€0.80) and Platy Gialos (€1.50).

I Meropi Taverna runs a taxi-boat service to anywhere on the island. Taxis (☎ 228-031 347) hover around the port and Apollonia's main square. Cars can be hired from Hotel Kamari (☎ 2284 033 383), in Kamares, and from Apollo Rent a Car (☎ 228-032 237), in Apollonia from €29.

KAMARES Καμαρες

Unlike most villages on the island, the port of Kamares is a newish resort-style town. It has a nice enough 'holiday' feel about it with lots of waterfront cafes and tavernas and a reasonable sandy beach. The bus stop is the stand of tamarisk trees outside the municipal tourist office.

Opposite the quay, the very helpful municipal tourist office (☎ 2284 031 977) can find accommodation anywhere on the island (open until midnight). It also offers free luggage storage and has copies of the bus schedule.

Places to Stay & Eat

Camping Makis (☎/fax 2284 032 366) Adult/tent €4.20/2.35, rooms from €23.20. This site is just behind the beach, 600m north of the port. It's a nice place with an outdoor cafe area to hang out, a barbecue area, laundry and shaded sites.

Domatia owners rarely meet boats, and in high season it's best to book ahead.

The island has a long history of producing superior pottery because of the quality of its clay, and many shops sell local ceramics. Some potters' workshops are open to the public – it's quite mesmerising to watch them work.

Sifniot olive oil is highly prized throughout Greece, which might have something to do with the island's reputation for producing some of the country's best chefs. Local specialities include *revithia* (baked chickpeas), *revithokeftedes* (falafel-like vegetable balls), *xynomyzithra* (a sharpish fresh cheese) and almond sweets flavoured with orange flowers.

Getting To/From Sifnos

Ferry There are daily ferries to Milos (two hours, €4.65), Piraeus (five hours, €13.40) via Serifos (one hour, €4.40) and Kythnos (2½ hours, €5.90). There are three ferries weekly to Kimolos (1½ hours, €4.40), Folegandros (four hours, €5.30), Sikinos

Hotel Afroditi (☎ *2284 031 704, fax 284 031 622,* e *hotel_afroditi@hotmail. om)* Doubles with mountain/sea view €46.50/49. Beyond Hotel Boutaris, and opposite the beach, Hotel Afroditi is a popular place; breakfast is available.

Stavros Hotel (☎ *2284 031 641, fax 2284 031 709)* Doubles €40.80. In the middle of the waterfront, Stavros has basic, clean rooms.

Hotel Kamari (☎ *2284 033 383, fax 2284 031 709)* Doubles €49. This hotel, about 100m up the road to Apollonia, has attractive rooms.

There are several reasonably priced waterfront eateries serving good Greek staples, including *O-Simos*, *I Meropi*, *Ouzeri Kamares* and *Captain Andreas*, which is the best place for fish.

APOLLONIA Απολλώνια

The capital is situated on a plateau 5km uphill from the port.

The bus stop for Kamares is on the lively central square where the post office and OTE are located; all other buses stop outside Hotel Anthousa. The main pedestrian thoroughfare – with jewellery and clothes shops, restaurants and bars – is to the right behind the museum. There is an Alpha Bank (with ATM) next to Hotel Sofia and the National Bank of Greece (with ATM), is about 50m out on the road to Artemonas; the police are another 50m beyond.

The interesting little **Museum of Popular Art** (☎ *2284 033 730; admission €0.90; open 10am-2pm & 6pm-10pm Tues-Sun)*, on the central square and just opposite the post office, contains old costumes, pots and textiles.

Places to Stay & Eat

Hotel Sofia (☎ *2284 031 238)* Singles/doubles €23/38. This C-class hotel, north of the central square, has basic rooms and TV.

Hotel Sifnos (☎/fax *2284 031 624)* Singles/doubles/triples €49/59/69.60. This C-class hotel, on the main pedestrian street that leads off to the right behind the museum, has immaculate rooms. It also has an excellent *taverna*.

Peristeronas Apartments (☎ *2284 071 288)* Doubles/quads €72.50/90. This Sifnos-style house overlooking terraced fields is downhill from Hotel Anthousa.

Hotel Petali (☎/fax *2284 033 024)* Doubles/triples €99/110. This newer, more upmarket hotel is about 100m along the footpath to Artemonas. It has spacious rooms with air-con, TV and telephone.

Apostoli tou Koutouki (☎ *2284 031 186)* Dishes €2.20-10.30, fish by the kilo. Open 7pm. This eatery on the main pedestrian street serves excellent meat dishes – try the veal cooked with oregano in a clay pot (€7.30).

Shopping

As well as fine ceramics and jewellery (there are a few workshops here), you can also find beautiful hand-woven textiles. On the main pedestrian thoroughfare, Margarita Baki has a tiny workshop.

AROUND SIFNOS

The pretty village of **Artemonas** is a short walk or bus ride north of Apollonia. Not to be missed is the walled cliff-top village of **Kastro**, 3km from Apollonia. The former capital, it is a magical place of buttressed alleys and whitewashed houses. It has a small **archaeological museum** (☎ *2284 031 022; admission free; open 8.30am-3pm Tues-Sun)*.

The pretty downhill walk along old paths from Apollonia to Kastro takes under an hour and you can return by bus. The path begins at the junction of the roads to Exambelas, Kastro and Kamares. The serene village of **Exambelas**, south of Apollonia, is said to be the birthplace of most of Sifnos' accomplished chefs.

The resort of **Platys Gialos**, 10km south of Apollonia, has a long sandy beach. The spectacularly situated **Moni Hrysopigis**, near Platys Gialos, was built to house a miraculous icon of the Virgin found in the sea by two fishermen. A path leads from the monastery to **Hrysopigis Beach**, although most people find a space in the rocks below the church and sunbathe and swim there. There is a taverna on the watch. **Vathi**, on

CYCLADES

the west coast, is a gorgeous sandy bay with several *tavernas*. **Faros** is a cosy little fishing hamlet with a couple of nice beaches nearby, such as the sweet little beach of **Fasolou**, up the stairs and over the headland from the bus stop.

Places to Stay & Eat
Platys Gialos has quite a few accommodation options, most of them oriented towards package tourists.

Camping Platys Gialos (☎ 2284 071 286) Adult/tent €3.50/2.20. This site is in an olive grove 700m from the beach.

Angeliki Rooms (☎/fax 2284 071 288) Doubles/triples €46.50/55. These rooms are right on the beach.

Platys Gialos Beach Hotel (☎ 2284 071 324, fax 2284 071 325) Doubles with breakfast €130.50. Rooms at this lodge-like hotel have air-con, TV, minibar and sea views.

There are quite a few rooms for rent in Faros right by the beach: Try *Margarita* (☎ 2284 071 438), *Aristi Pension* (☎ 2284 071 443) or *Villa Maria* (☎ 2284 071 421).

Fabrika (☎ 2284 071 427, Faros) Rooms €46.50. Fabrika has rooms in an atmospheric old flour mill.

In Artemonas, on the main square, *Liotrivi (Manganas;* ☎ 2284 031 246) serves robust traditional fare. *Margarita* (☎ 2284 031 058), nearby, is also worth seeking out.

Faros (☎ 2284 071 452) Dishes €1.50-11.75, fish by the kilo. This small taverna is the place to go for fish in Faros.

On the Rocks (☎ 2284 031 817, Faros) Dishes €3-5.50. Near Fasolou, this little cafe, serving crepes and pizzas, has a playful nautical theme.

Serifos Σέριφος

postcode 840 05 • pop 1020
Serifos is a barren, rocky island with a few pockets of greenery that are the result of tomato and vine cultivation. Livadi, the port, is on the south-east coast; the beautiful whitewashed capital, Hora, clings onto a hillside 2km inland.

Getting To/From Serifos
Ferry & Catamaran There are daily ferries from Serifos to Piraeus (4½ hours, €11.90), Sifnos (one hour, €4.40), Milos (two hours, €5.30) and Kimolos (2½ hours, €5.90).

Four times weekly the Piraeus ferry stops at Kythnos (1½ hours, €5.60), and twice weekly boats go to Paros (two hours, €6.10), Syros (three to five hours, €5.90) and Folegandros (five hours, €5.30).

There are weekly boats to Santorini (seven hours, €10.50), Ios (six hours, €8.80) and Sikinos (five hours, €8.40).

One daily catamaran runs to Sifnos (20 minutes, €7.30), Milos (1¼ hours, €8.80) and Piraeus (2¼ hours, €23.20), and one weekly runs to Kythnos (45 minutes, €9).

Getting Around Serifos
There are frequent buses between Livadi and Hora (€0.80); a timetable is posted at the bus stop by the yacht marina. Motorcycles and cars can be hired from Krinas Travel (see the Livadi entry for contact details).

LIVADI Λιβάδι
This rather scrappy port is at the top end of an elongated bay. Continue around the bay

or the ordinary town beach or climb over the headland that rises from the ferry quay or the pleasant, tamarisk-fringed beach at ivadakia. **Karavi Beach**, a walk farther outh over the next headland, is the unofficial nudist beach. There is an Alpha Bank, with ATM, on the waterfront.

There is a useful tourist information office (☎ 2281 051 466) on the waterfront, which has a domatia list (in Greek). It's open 10am to 2pm and 6pm to 10pm daily.

Krinas Travel (☎ 2281 051 488, fax 2281 051 073, e sertrau@otenet.gr), upstairs next to Captain Hook Bar, 50m from the quay, offers a wide range of services, including car hire. The port police (☎ 2281 051 470) are up steps from the quay.

Places to Stay & Eat

Coralli Camping (☎ 2281 051 500, fax 2281 051 073, e coralli@mail.otenet.gr) Adult/tent €4.40/2, double bungalows with mountain/sea view €52/64. This excellent site, shaded by tall eucalypts, is a step away from sandy Livadakia Beach. The bungalows have phone, TV, fan. There's also a restaurant and minimarket, and a minibus meets all ferries. Part of the camping ground *Heaven Pool Bar*, fuelled by cocktail shakes, bare flesh and dance music, has a bit of a scene going on.

Anna Domatia (☎ 2281 051 263) Doubles €29. Anna's, about 500m along the waterfront next to Hotel Asteria, has airy rooms.

Eliza (☎/fax 2281 051 763) Doubles from €49, family rooms €75.40. Eliza's has a lovely garden. It's 100m from the beach on the turn-off road to the Hora.

Anastasia Rooms (☎ 2281 051 247, mobile ☎ 69 7225 1878) Doubles/Apartments €43.50/52. Next door to Meli on the waterfront, Anastasia has nice rooms.

Hotel Areti (☎ 2281 051 479, fax 2281 051 547) Singles/doubles €34.90/43.50. This light and bright hotel, on the hill above the ferry quay, has lovely rooms.

Rooms to Let Marianna (☎ 2281 051 338, fax 2281 052 057) Doubles/apartments €43.50/52.50. This is a nice, secluded, shady place which is set back a little from the waterfront.

Meli (☎ 2281 051 749) is a breezy little cafe with great sandwiches and crepes but mercilessly slow service – perhaps ask for a takeaway...

Perseus (☎ 2281 051 273) Dishes €2.35-13, seafood by the kilo. Farther along the waterfront, Perseus serves the best Greek standards.

Serifos Yacht Club (☎ 2281 051 888) Crowds spill out of this small bar onto the waterfront late in the evening. It's all very sedate during the daylight hours though, when it reverts to a bright little cafe.

Captain Hook Bar, above Krinas Travel, is another lively spot.

There are a couple of reasonable *tavernas* on the beach at Livadakia.

AROUND SERIFOS

The dazzling white **Hora**, clinging to a crag above Livadi, is one of the most striking Cycladic capitals. It can be reached either by bus or by walking up the steps from Livadi. The atmospheric town square is filled with tables from the eateries on its edge, watched over by the imposing neoclassical town hall. From here, more steps lead to a ruined 15th-century **Venetian Kastro** above the village. A peripheral path, hugging the cliff's edge, skirts the **Hora**.

The post office is by the first bus stop. A small **archaeological museum** (☎ 2281 031 022; admission free; 8.30am-3pm Tues-Sun), also off the central square, has pottery and sculpture uncovered from the fortress.

There are several small art workshops, including **Nikos Kourouniotis** (☎ 2281 033 668), a talented, but refreshingly humble, jeweller and illustrator; you'll find him on the main pedestrian thoroughfare.

A short walk downhill from the Hora leads to the tiny, pebbled beach of **Seralia**, which has several excellent fish tavernas. About an hour's walk north of Livadi (or a shorter drive) along a track (negotiable by motorbike) is **Psili Ammos Beach**. A path from Hora heads north to the pretty village of **Kendarhos** (also called Kallitsos), from where you can continue to the 17th-century fortified **Moni Taxiarhon**, which has impressive 18th-century frescoes. The walk from the town to the monastery takes about two hours, but you will need to take food and water as there are no facilities in Kendarhos.

Places to Stay & Eat

The Hora appears to remain relatively alive in the winter months and many places remain open.

Aegean Eye (☎ *2281 032 020/033 109)* Double studios from €59, family rooms €72.50. On the edge of the cliff, Aegean Eye is a good down-to-earth option. All rooms have a kitchen (and a heater making it perfect for a winter break).

In the main square, the bar-cafe *Stou Stratou (mobile* ☎ *69-7233 7786)* has a hint of Paris about it, while *Zorba's*, the taverna opposite the town hall, is worth investigating. Nearer the bus stop, *Leonidas* is recommended.

Kafe Bar Sunrise is a homey little alfresco bar perched on a mountain edge (accessible from the peripheral path), and somewhat surprisingly has a kids' playground – ideal for parents who want to imbibe in peace.

Remezzo (☎ *2281 031 930)*, on the main pedestrian thoroughfare, is a chilled alfresco cafe. Snacks are available early in the day, and ambient music sets the scene in the evening.

Kythnos Κύθνος

postcode 840 06 • pop 1632
Kythnos, the next island north of Serifos, is virtually barren. It is popular mainly with Athenian holiday-makers, as evidenced by the number of yachts moored at the marina, and there is little to enthuse about unless you're looking for a cure for rheumatism at the thermal baths.

The main settlements are the port of Merihas and the capital, Hora, also known as Kythnos. Merihas has an OTE, and there is an agency of the National Bank of Greece at Cava Kythnos travel agency and minimarket. Antonios Larentzakis Travel Agency (☎ 2281 032 104, 2281 032 291) sells ferry tickets, can arrange accommodation and

KYTHNOS

To Syros & Andros
Cape Kefalos
AEGEAN SEA
297m
Loutra
To Kea & Lavrio
KYTHNOS
Fikiado Beach
Apokrousi Beach
308m
Episkopi Beach
Hora (Kythnos)
To Piraeus
Merihas
Dryopida
Cape Tzoulis
Flambouria Beach
302m
To Santorini & Folegandros
To Serifos, Sifnos, Milos & Kimolos
Kanala
Dimitrios Beach
Cape Berou

Daily Ferries
Low Frequency Ferries
Hydrofoil/Catamaran
Excursion Boat

rents cars and motorbikes. It's up the short flight of stairs near Ostria Taverna. Psaras Travel (☎ 2281 032 242, fax 2281 032 025), on the waterfront, also sells ferry tickets. Hora has the island's post office and police (☎ 2281 031 201). The port police (☎ 2281 032 290) are on the waterfront in Merihas.

Getting To/From Kythnos

Ferry There are at least three boats to Piraeus daily (2½ hours, €9.60). Most services coming from Piraeus continue to Serifos (1½ hours, €5.60), Sifnos (2½ hours, €5.90), Kimolos (three hours, €7.40) and Milos (3½ hours, €8.20).

There are three weekly ferries to Lavrio (3½ hours, €7), and Kea (1¼ hours, €4.65), and two to Folegandros (six hours, €9), Sikinos (seven hours, €9.30), Santorini (eight hours, €10.30) and Syros (two hours, €5.90).

A ferry runs once weekly to Andros (5 hours, €11.70).

Fast Boat & Catamaran There are four services weekly to Piraeus (1½ hours, €18.20), and Sifnos (1¼ hours, €9.90) and regular services to Milos. One weekly service goes to Serifos (45 minutes, €9).

Getting Around Kythnos

There are regular buses from Merihas to Dryopida (€0.90), continuing to Kanala (€1.50) or Hora (€0.90). Less regular services run to Loutra (€1.50). The buses supposedly meet the ferries, but usually they leave from the turn-off to Hora in Merihas.

Taxis are a better bet, except at siesta time. There are only three taxis on the island; call ☎ 69 4474 3791, ☎ 69 4427 6656 or ☎ 69 4427 7609.

MERIHAS Μέριχας

Merihas does not have a lot going for it other than a small, dirty-brown beach. But it's a reasonable base and has most of the island's accommodation. There are better beaches within walking distance north of the quay (turn left facing inland).

Places to Stay & Eat

Domatia owners usually meet the boats, but if no-one is waiting, wander around the waterfront and backstreets and you'll see plenty of signs advertising rooms; alternatively head for Larentzakis Travel.

Kythnos Hotel (☎ 2281 032 092) Doubles/triples €36.30/42. If you want to stay in this, the town's one hotel, you must book ahead. It's up the first set of steps on the way into town from the harbour and has decent rooms.

Ostria (☎ 2281 032 263) Dishes €2.10-14.70, seafood by the kilo. On the waterfront near the ferry quay, Ostria has reasonable Greek fare. Try the black-eyed bean salad (€3). *Restaurant Kissos*, farther along the waterfront, also serves good standards.

Taverna to Kandouni (☎ 2281 032 220) Dishes €2.10-11.75. Near the port police on the waterfront, Kandouni specialises in grilled meats; it also has *rooms* to let.

AROUND KYTHNOS

The capital, **Hora** (also known as Kythnos), lacks the charm of other Cycladic capitals.

The main reason for visiting is the walk south to **Dryopida**, a picturesque town of red-tiled roofs and winding streets that was the island's capital in the Middle Ages. It takes about 1½ hours to cover the 6km. From Dryopida, you can either walk the 6km back to Merihas or catch a bus or taxi.

Loutra offers the only accommodation outside Merihas. The **thermal baths** at Loutra in the north-east are reputedly the most potent in the Cyclades. The best **beaches** are on the south-east coast, near the village of Kanala.

Places to Stay

There are several *domatia* at Loutra, while *Hotel Porto Klaras* (☎/fax 2281 031 276) is reputed to be the best on the island, with doubles/self-contained studios for €43.50/52.50.

Kea Κέα or Τζία

postcode 840 02 • pop 2400
Kea, to the north of Kythnos, is the closest of the Cyclades to the mainland. The island is a popular summer weekend escape for Athenians, but remains relatively untouched by tourism. While it appears largely barren from a distance, there is ample water and the bare hills hide fertile valleys filled with orchards, olive groves, and almond and oak trees (acorns, a raw material used by the tanneries, made the inhabitants rich in the 18th century). The main settlements are the port of Korissia, and the capital, Ioulida, 5km inland.

Getting To/From Kea

Services connect Kea with Lavrio (1¼ hours, €5.30) on the mainland at least twice daily and also with Kythnos (1¼ hours, €4.65) three times weekly. In addition, a direct service runs twice weekly to Kythnos and Syros (four hours, €8.20). One weekly service runs to Kea (€13.20).

Getting Around Kea

In July and August there are, in theory, regular buses from Korissia to Vourkari,

KEA

To Lavrio
To Syros
AEGEAN SEA
Agia Irini
Otzias
Moni Panagias Kastriani
Vourkari
Korissia
To Kythnos
Gialiskari Beach
Flea
Ioulida
Pera Meria
Cape Spathi
570m
Astra
Ellinika
Kea Camping
KEA
Pisses Beach
Koundouros
450m
Havouna
Karthea
Cape Tamelos

0   2   4km
0   1   2mi

Daily Ferries	– – – – –
Low Frequency Ferries	- - - - -
Hydrofoil/Catamaran	— · — · —
Excursion Boat	· · · · · · · ·

Otzias, Ioulida and Pisses. In practice, how-ever, the bus driver operates at his own whim; if there isn't a bus waiting for the boat, you're better off catching one of the taxis (☎ 2288 021 021 or 2288 021 228) that hang about near the port. There are two expensive motorcycle-rental outlets and a ridiculously expensive car-rental monopoly that is best avoided.

KORISSIA Κορησσία
The port of Korissia is an uninspiring place in spite of its setting on a large bay with a long, sandy beach.

The tourist police (☎ 2288 021 100) can be found one block back from the waterfront between June and September. The well-meaning but clueless tourist information office (☎ 2288 021 500), opposite the ferry quay, has lists of domatia in Greek. Stefanos Lepouras, next door at Stegali Bookshop (☎ 2288 021 435, fax 2288 021 012) is, in fact, the unofficial tourist information officer

and is an excellent source of information (in-cluding bus timetables), so make sure you repay the favour and buy all your postcards and books from him! He also changes money.

Art Café (☎ 2288 021 181), on the wa-terfront, has Internet access (€2.10 per 20 minutes, €4.65 one hour). There is an ATM near the supermarket to the right of Hotel Karthea, and the Piraeus Bank (with ATM) is to the left of Hotel Karthea. There is a small ferry ticket office next to the car-rental agency on the waterfront.

Places to Stay & Eat
Domatia owners don't meet ferries, so if you're arriving late, make sure you have something booked.

Hotel Karthea (☎ 2288 021 204, fax 2288 021 417) Singles/doubles €38/52.50. This glum C-class hotel with ordinary rooms and lots of stairs is the tall, concrete box at the corner of the bay.

There are better places along the road that runs behind the beach, including a cou-ple of *domatia*.

Hotel Tzia (☎ 2288 021 305, fax 2288 021 140) Doubles with breakfast €49. Tzia has lovely rooms that open right onto the beach.

Hotel Korissia (☎ 2288 021 484) Singles/doubles €38/46.60, double/triple studios €59/67.90. Korissia has large, modern rooms. Turn right off the beach road at the canal; the hotel is on the right after about 150m.

Lagoudera, near the tourist office has good home-cooked local specialities, and *Taverna Akri* (☎ 2288 021 196), near the Hotel Karthea, is popular with locals; how-ever, the menu is only in Greek.

Head to Vourkari's hip cafes for any hope of cosmopolitan nightlife.

IOULIDA Ιουλίδα
Ioulida is a delightful higgledy-piggledy hillside town, full of alleyways and steps that beg to be explored. The architecture here is quite different from other Cycladic capitals – the houses have red-tiled roofs.

The bus turnaround is on a square just at the edge of town. An archway leads to Ioulida proper, and Ilia Malavazou, the main thoroughfare, leads uphill to the

CYCLADES

right. The post office is also along here on the right. The pathway continues uphill and crosses a small square, just beyond which, on the right, is an agency of the National Bank of Greece, signposted above a minimarket.

Things to See

The **archaeological museum** (☎ 2288 022 079; admission free; open 8.30am-3pm Tues-Sun), on the main thoroughfare, houses local finds, mostly from Agia Irini. It was closed for renovations at the time of writing.

The celebrated **Kea Lion**, chiselled from a huge chunk of slate in the 6th century BC, lies on the hillside an easy, pleasant 10-minute walk north-east of town. The path to the lion leads off to the left (the main path goes sharp right). Keep walking past the cemetery and you'll find the gate that leads downhill to the watchful lion, which is surrounded by whitewashed rocks.

Places to Stay & Eat

There are a sprinkling of *domatia* in Ioulida, and several decent tavernas.

Estiatorio I Piatsa (☎ 2288 022 195) Dishes €1.70-5.90. There are a couple of decent tavernas, including this one, just inside the archway, which serve generous plates of fresh fish.

Kalofagadon Dishes €1.70-8.20. Carnivores should not dilly-dally: go directly to Kalofagadon, on the main square, and order the lamb chops.

AROUND KEA

The beach road from Korissia leads past the lovely eucalyptus grove sheltering **Gialiskari Beach** to the ambient, tiny port of **Vourkari**, lined with yachts and cafes, 2.5km away. **Voukariani Art Gallery** (☎ 2288 021 458), nestled in among all the smart cafes and restaurants, has changing exhibitions of world-class art works over the summer – it's well worth a visit.

Just north of Vourkari you will find the ancient site of **Agia Irini** (which is named after a nearby church). This is the site where a Minoan palace has since been excavated.

The road continues for another 3km to a sandy beach at **Otzias**. A dirt road continues beyond here for another 5km to the 18th-century **Moni Panagias Kastriani** (☎ 2288 024 348), with a commanding position and terrific views; accommodation is a possibility here.

The island's best beach, 8km south-west of Ioulida, has the unfortunate name of **Pisses**. It is long and sandy and backed by a verdant valley of orchards and olive groves. **Flea**, also with an interesting name, occupies a lush valley and makes a nice walking destination from either Korissia or Ioulida.

Places to Stay & Eat

Kea Camping (☎ 2288 031 302, fax 2288 031 303, Pisses Beach) Adult/tent €4.40/ 4.40, bungalows €43.50. Pines and eucalypts provide shade at this camping ground. It has a shop, bar and restaurant nearby. Self-contained bungalows are also available nearby.

Fanni & John's (☎ 2288 021 316) Doubles €34.90. At Otzias, this friendly pension is set in a lush garden a short walk from the beach.

Gialiskari (☎ 2288 021 197) Doubles €46.60. Overlooking the water just before Vourkari, this pretty pension has comfortable rooms.

Tastra is a dreamy little beach bar-cafe at Gialiskari Beach. All the eateries in Voukari are worthy establishments, but a new taverna, *Ennea Kores*, right around the end of the bay, is the one that is consistently recommended by the resident Athenian jet set for its service and food.

CYCLADES

Crete Κρήτη

Crete is Greece's largest and most southerly island, and arguably the most beautiful. A spectacular mountain chain runs from east to west across the island, split into three ranges: the Mt Dikti Range in the east, the Mt Ida (or Mt Psiloritis) Range in the centre and the Lefka Ori (White Mountains) in the west. The mountains are dotted with agricultural plains and plateaus, and sliced by numerous dramatic gorges. Long, sandy beaches speckle the coastline, and the east coast boasts Europe's only palm-tree forest.

Administratively, the island is divided into four prefectures: Lasithi, Iraklio, Rethymno and Hania. Apart from Lasithi, with its capital of Agios Nikolaos, the prefectures are named after their major cities. The island's capital is Iraklio which is Greece's fifth-largest city. Nearly all Crete's major population centres are on the north coast. Most of the south coast is too precipitous to support large settlements.

Scenery and beaches aside, the island is also the birthplace of Europe's first advanced civilisation, the Minoan. If you intend to spend much time at the many Minoan sites, *Palaces of Minoan Crete* by Gerald Cadogan is an excellent guide.

Crete's size and its distance from the rest of Greece allowed an independent culture to evolve. Vibrant Cretan weavings are sold in many of the island's towns and villages. The traditional Cretan songs differ from those heard elsewhere in Greece. Called *mantinades*, these songs are highly emotive, expressing the age-old concerns of love, death and the yearning for freedom. You will still come across men wearing the traditional dress of breeches tucked into knee-high leather boots, and black-fringed kerchiefs tied tightly around their heads.

The attractions of Crete have not gone unnoticed by tour operators, and the island has the dubious honour of playing host to almost a quarter of Greece's tourists. The result is that much of the north coast is packed solid with hastily constructed hotels

Highlights

- Iraklio's Archaeological Museum and the Historical Museum of Crete
- The ancient Minoan site of Knossos
- The stunning expanse of the Lasithi Plateau
- Walking the gorge between Zakros and Kato Zakros, site of ancient Zakros
- Hania's beautiful old Venetian quarter
- Trekking the spectacular Samaria Gorge
- The lovely sand beaches and coves at Elafonisi
- Myrtos and Plakias – two south-coast villages that still welcome independent travellers

for package tourists, particularly between Iraklio and Agios Nikolaos and west of Hania. The tour operators have also taken over several of the southern coastal villages that were once backpacker favourites. The wild and rugged west coast, however, remains relatively untouched.

The best times to visit are from April to June and from mid-September to the end of October. Outside the major population centres, most places close down in winter.

For details on Crete see the Web sites: W www.interkriti.org, W www.infocrete .com and W www.explorecrete.com.

SUGGESTED ITINERARIES

One week

Spend two days in Iraklio; visit the Archaeological Museum, Historical Museum of Crete and Minoan site of Knossos. Have two days in Rethymno to visit the fortress and museums and explore the old quarter. If you have time take a day trip to the mountain town of Spili, or the resort of Plakias, if you prefer a beach. Spend three days in Hania to visit the museums, explore the old quarter and hike the Samaria Gorge. Recuperate the following day on the beach at Falasarna. Round off your trip with an evening of music and drinking at Café Kriti in Hania.

Two weeks

As above for the first two days. Overnight at one of the Lassithi Plateau villages and explore the Dikteon Cave and the plateau. Spend two nights in Sitia; visit the archaeological museum, walk the gorge to Kato Zakros, visit Ancient Zakros and have a swim. If you have time, visit Ancient Lato. Have two days in Rethymno to visit the fortress and museums and explore the old quarter. Overnight in Agia Galini to visit Phaestos and Agia Triada. Spend two nights in the mountain town of Spili, or the beach resort of Plakias, and visit Moni Preveli. Spend two nights in Hania to explore the old town and visit the museums. Head down to Paleohora for two nights and spend a day hiking the Samaria Gorge. If you have time, unwind on Elafonisi Beach the following day.

History

Although Crete has been inhabited since Neolithic times (7000–3000 BC), as far as most people are concerned its history begins with the Minoan civilisation. The glories of Crete's Minoan past remained hidden until British archaeologist Sir Arthur Evans made his dramatic discoveries at Knossos in the early 1900s. The term 'Minoan' was coined by Evans and derived from the King Minos of Greek mythology. Nobody knows what the Minoans called themselves.

Among the ruins unearthed by Evans were the famous Knossos frescoes. Artistically, the frescoes are superlative; the figures that grace them have a naturalism lacking in contemporary Cycladic figurines, ancient Egyptian artwork (which they resemble in certain respects), and the Archaic sculpture that came later. Compared with candle-smoke-blackened Byzantine frescoes, the Minoan frescoes, with their fresh, bright colours, look as if they were painted yesterday (see the boxed text 'The Mysterious Minoans').

But no matter how much speculation the frescoes inspire about the Minoans, all we really know is that early in the 3rd millennium BC an advanced people migrated to Crete and brought with them the art of metallurgy. Many elements of Neolithic culture lived on in the Early Minoan period (3000–2100 BC), but the Middle Minoan period (2100–1500 BC) saw the emergence of a society with unprecedented artistic, engineering and cultural achievements. It was during this time that the famous palace complexes were built at Knossos, Phaestos, Malia and Zakros.

Also during this time, the Minoans began producing their exquisite Kamares pottery (see Iraklio's Archaeological Museum section later in this chapter) and silverware, and became a maritime power trading with Egypt and Asia Minor.

Around 1700 BC all four palace complexes were destroyed by an earthquake. Undeterred, the Minoans built bigger and better palaces on the sites of the originals, as well as new settlements in other parts of the island.

Around 1500 BC, when the Minoan civilisation was at its peak, the palaces were destroyed again, signalling the start of the Late Minoan period (1500–1100 BC). This destruction was probably caused by Mycenaean invasions, although the massive volcanic eruption on the island of Santorini (Thira) may also have had something to do with it. The Knossos palace was the only one to be salvaged. It was finally destroyed by fire around 1400 BC.

The Minoan civilisation was a hard act to follow. The war-orientated Dorians, who arrived in 1100 BC, were pedestrian by comparison. The 5th century BC found Crete, like the rest of Greece, divided into

CRETE

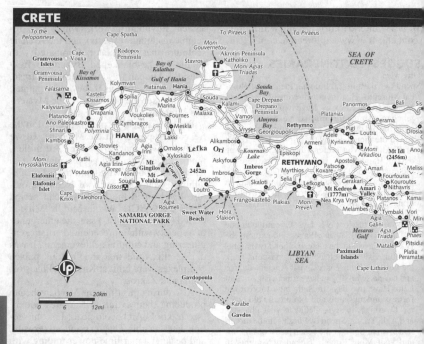

CRETE

city-states. The glorious classical age of mainland Greece had little impact on Crete, and the Persians bypassed the island. It was also ignored by Alexander the Great, so was never part of the Macedonian Empire.

By 67 BC, Crete had fallen to the Romans. The town of Gortyna in the south became the capital of Cyrenaica, a province that included large chunks of North Africa. Crete, along with the rest of Greece, became part of the Byzantine Empire in AD 395. In 1210 the island was occupied by the Venetians, whose legacy is one of mighty fortresses, ornate public buildings and monuments, and the handsome dwellings of nobles and merchants.

Despite the massive Venetian fortifications, which sprang up all over the island, by 1669 the whole of the Cretan mainland was under Turkish rule. The first uprising against the Turks was led by Ioannis Daskalogiannis in 1770. This set the precedent for many more insurrections, and in 1898 the Great

Powers intervened and made the island a British protectorate. It was not until the signing of the Treaty of Bucharest in 1913 that Crete officially became part of Greece, although the island's parliament had declared a de facto union in 1905.

The island saw heavy fighting during WWII. Germany wanted the island as an air base in the Mediterranean, and on 20 May 1941 German parachutists landed on Crete. It was the start of 10 days of fierce fighting that became known as the Battle of Crete. For two days the battle hung in the balance until Germany won a bridgehead for its air force at Maleme, near Hania. The Allied forces of Britain, Australia, New Zealand and Greece then fought a valiant rearguard action which enabled the British Navy to evacuate 18,000 of the 32,000 Allied troops trapped on the island. The German occupation of Crete lasted until the end of WWII.

During the war a large active resistance movement drew heavy reprisals from the

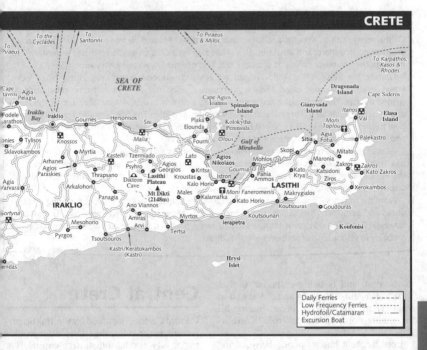

CRETE

To the Cyclades
To Santorini
To Piraeus
To Piraeus & Milos
To Karpathos, Kasos & Rhodes

SEA OF CRETE

Cape Stavros
Agia Pelagia
Iraklio
Iraklio Bay
Fodele
Arathos
Gournes
Hersonisos
Sisi
Cape Agios Ioannis
Spinalonga Island
Plaka
Elounda
Kolokytha Peninsula
Dragonada Island
Cape Sideros
Gianysada Island
Itanos
Moni Toplou
Vaï
Elasa Island

Tylisos
Sklavokambos
Knossos
Myrtia
Kastelli
Tzermiado
Psyhro
Agios Georgios
Lasithi Plateau
Dikteon Cave
Kritsa
Fourni
Malia
Lato
Agios Nikolaos
Olous
Gulf of Mirabello
Skopi
Agia Fotia
Sitia
Palekastro
Mitato
Maronia
Zakros
Kato Zakros
Zakros

Arhanes
Agios Paraskies
Thrapsano
Arkalohori
Panagia
Males
Kalamafka
Moni Faneromenis
Kato Horio
Kato Krya
Katsidoni
Ziros
Xerokambos

Agia Varvara
Ano Viannos
Myrtos
Ierapetra
Koutsounari
Makrygialos
Koutsouras
Goudouras

Gortyna
Mesohorio
Pyrgos
Tsoutsouros
Amiras
Arvi
Tertsa
Kastri/Keratokambos (Kastri)

Koufonisi

Hrysi Islet

IRAKLIO
LASITHI

Istron
Pahia Ammos
Gournia
Mohlos

Kroustas
Kalo Horio
Mt Dikti (2148m)

Daily Ferries	– – – – –
Low Frequency Ferries	·········
Hydrofoil/Catamaran	— · —
Excursion Boat	··········

Germans. Many mountain villages were temporarily bombed 'off the map' and their occupants were shot. Among the bravest members of this resistance movement were the 'runners' who relayed messages on foot over the mountains. One of these runners, George Psyhoundakis, wrote a book based on his experiences entitled *The Cretan Runner*.

Getting To/From Crete

The following section provides a brief overview of air and boat options to and from Crete. For more comprehensive information, see the relevant sections under specific town entries.

Air Crete has two international airports. The principal one is at Iraklio and there is a smaller one at Hania. In addition there is a domestic airport at Sitia. All three airports have flights to Athens. Iraklio and Hania have flights to Thessaloniki; Iraklio also has flights to Rhodes and Santorini.

Ferry Crete has ports at Iraklio, Hania, Rethymno, Agios Nikolaos, Sitia and Kastelli-Kissamos. The following are high-season schedules; services are reduced by about half during low season.

Direct daily ferries travel to Piraeus from Iraklio, Hania and Rethymno. There are three ferries weekly from Sitia via Agios Nikolaos to Piraeus, stopping at Milos. Three ferries weekly go from Iraklio to Thessaloniki via Santorini stopping twice a week at Paros and Tinos and once a week at Naxos, Skiathos, Syros and Volos. There are also three boats weekly to Rhodes from Agios Nikolaos via Sitia stopping at Kasos, Karpathos and Halki. Five ferries weekly sail from Kastelli-Kissamos to Antikythira, Kythira and Gythio with further stops at Kalamata and Piraeus.

Getting Around Crete

A fast national highway skirts the north coast from Hania in the west to Agios Nikolaos

CRETE

The Mysterious Minoans

Of the many finds at Knossos and other sites, it is the celebrated frescoes that have captured the imagination of experts and amateurs alike, shedding light on a civilisation hitherto a mystery. The message they communicate is of a society that was powerful, wealthy, joyful and optimistic.

Gracing the frescoes are white-skinned women with elaborately coiffured glossy black locks. Proud, graceful and uninhibited, these women were dressed in stylish gowns that revealed perfectly shaped breasts. The bronze-skinned men were tall, with tiny waists, narrow hips, broad shoulders and muscular thighs and biceps; the children were slim and lithe. The Minoans also seemed to know how to enjoy themselves. They played board games, boxed and wrestled, played leap-frog over bulls and over one another, and performed bold acrobatic feats.

As well as being literate, they were religious, as frescoes and models of people partaking in rituals testify. The Minoans' beliefs, like many other aspects of their society, remain an enigma, but there is sufficient evidence to confirm that they worshipped a nature goddess, often depicted with serpents and lions. Male deities were distinctly secondary.

From the frescoes it appears that women enjoyed a respected position in society, leading religious rituals and participating in games, sports and hunting. Minoan society may have had its dark side, however. There is evidence of human sacrifice being practised on at least one occasion, although probably in response to an extreme external threat.

---

in the east, and is being extended farther west to Kastelli-Kissamos and to the east to Sitia. There are frequent buses linking all the major northern towns from Kastelli-Kissamos to Sitia.

Less frequent buses operate between the north-coast towns and resorts and places of interest on the south coast, via the mountain villages of the interior. These routes are Hania to Paleohora, Omalos (for the Samaria Gorge) and Hora Sfakion; Rethymno to Plakias, Agia Galini, Phaestos and Matala; Iraklio to Agia Galini, Phaestos, Matala and the Lasithi Plateau; Agios Nikolaos to Ierapetra; and Sitia to Ierapetra, Vaï, Palekastro and Kato Zakros.

There is nothing comparable to the national highway on the south coast and parts of this area have no roads at all. There is no road between Paleohora and Hora Sfakion, the most precipitous part of the south coast; a boat (daily from June through August) connects the two resorts via Sougia and Agia Roumeli.

As well as the bus schedules given in this chapter, clapped-out 'village buses' travel to just about every village which has a road to it. These usually leave in the early morning and return in the afternoon.

Central Crete

Central Crete is occupied by the Iraklio prefecture, named after the island's burgeoning major city and administrative capital. The area's major attractions are the Minoan sites of Knossos, Malia and Phaestos. The north coast east of Iraklio has been heavily exploited by the package tourism industry, particularly around Hersonisos.

IRAKLIO Ηράκλειο
postcode 710 01 • pop 115,124
The Cretan capital of Iraklio is a bustling modern city and the fifth largest in Greece. It has none of the charm of Hania or Rethymno, but it is a dynamic city boasting the highest average per capita income in Greece. That wealth stems largely from Iraklio's position as the island's trading capital, but also from the year-round flow of visitors who flock to nearby Knossos.

History
The Arabs who ruled Crete from AD 824 to 961 were the first people to govern from the site of modern Iraklio. It was known then as El Khandak, after the moat that

IRAKLIO

PLACES TO STAY
2 Hotel Kronos
8 Hotel Lena
9 Iraklio Youth Hostel
11 Hotel Kastro
12 Hotel Mirabello
16 Vergina Rooms
17 Hotel Rea
20 Rent Rooms Hellas
34 Hotel Irini
36 Hotel Lato
38 Hotel Ilaira
43 Atlantis Hotel
48 Astoria Hotel

PLACES TO EAT
3 Ippokambos Ouzeri
4 O Vrakas
7 Katsina Ouzeri
13 Baxes
14 I Avli tou Defkaliona
49 Loukoulos
50 Giovanni Taverna
52 Loukoumades Cafe
54 Restaurant Ionia
55 Giakoumis Taverna

THINGS TO SEE
1 Venetian Fortress (Rocca al Mare)
15 Historical Museum of Crete
25 Morosini Fountain
26 Basilica of San Marco
28 Venetian Loggia
45 Battle of Crete Museum
46 Archaeological Museum
57 Church of Agia Ekaterini
57 Agios Minos Cathedral
63 Bembo Fountain
64 Kazantzakis' Tomb

OTHER
5 Sportc@fe
6 Prince Travel
10 OTE
18 Jasmin
19 Guernica
21 Road Editions
22 Laundry Washsalon
23 Planet International Bookshop
24 Loggeta Cars & Bikes
27 Buses to Knossos
29 Take Five
30 Alpha Bank
31 National Bank of Greece
32 Porto Club Travel Services
33 Adamis Travel Bureau
35 Summerland Travel
37 Creta Travel
39 Buses to Hania & Rethymno
40 Buses to Knossos & Airport
41 Bus Station A
42 Istos Cyber Cafe
44 Inter Laundry
47 EOT
51 Ideon Antron
53 Tourist Police
58 Post Office
59 Olympic Airways
60 EOS
61 Buses to Airport
62 Aegean Airlines

surrounded the town, and was reputedly the slave-trade capital of the eastern Mediterranean.

El Khandak became Khandakos after Byzantine troops finally dislodged the Arabs, and then Candia under the Venetians who ruled the island for more than 400 years. While the Turks quickly overran the Venetian defences at Hania and Rethymno, Candia's fortifications proved as effective as they looked – an unusual combination. They withstood a siege of 21 years before the garrison finally surrendered in 1669.

Hania became the capital of independent Crete at the end of Turkish rule in 1898, and Candia was renamed Iraklio. Because of its central location, Iraklio became a commercial centre, and resumed its position as the island's administrative centre in 1971.

The city suffered badly in WWII, when most of the old Venetian and Turkish town was destroyed by bombing.

Orientation

Iraklio's two main squares are Plateia Venizelou and Plateia Eleftherias. Plateia Venizelou, instantly recognisable by its famous

CRETE

Morosini Fountain (better known as the Lion Fountain), is the heart of Iraklio and the best place from which to familiarise yourself with the layout of the city. The city's major intersection is a few steps south of the square. From here, 25 Avgoustou runs north-east to the harbour; Dikeosynis runs south-east to Plateia Eleftherias; Kalokerinou runs west to the Hania Gate; 1866 (the market street) runs south; and 1821 runs to the south-west. To reach Plateia Venizelou from the New Harbour, turn right, walk along the waterfront and turn left onto 25 Avgoustou.

Iraklio has three intercity bus stations. Station A, on the waterfront between the port and 25 Avgoustou, serves eastern Crete. A special bus station for Hania and Rethymno only is opposite Station A. Station B, just beyond the Hania Gate, serves Phaestos, Agia Galini and Matala. To reach the city centre from Station B walk through the Hania Gate and along Kalokerinou. For details on bus schedules, see the Iraklio Getting There & Away section.

Information

Tourist Offices EOT (☎ 281 022 8225, fax 281 022 6020) is just north of Plateia Eleftherias at Xanthoudidou 1. The staff at the information desk hand out maps and photocopied lists of ferry and bus schedules. Opening times are 8am to 2pm Monday to Friday. In high season it also opens on Saturday and Sunday.

The tourist police (☎ 281 028 3190) are found on Dikeosynis 10, are open 7am to 11pm.

Money Most of the city's banks are on 25 Avgoustou, including the National Bank of Greece at No 35. It has a 24-hour automatic exchange machine, as does the Alpha Bank at No 94. There is a handy Ergo Bank ATM at bus station A.

American Express is represented by Adamis Travel Bureau, (☎ 281 034 6202), 25 Avgoustou 23, open 8am to 2pm Monday to Saturday. Thomas Cook (☎ 281 024 1108) is represented by Summerland Travel, Epimenidou 30.

Post & Communications The central post office is on Plateia Daskalogianni. Opening hours are 7.30am to 8pm Monday to Friday, and 7.30am to 2pm Saturday. From June through August there is a mobile post office at El Greco Park, just north of Plateia Venizelou, open 8am to 6pm Monday to Friday, and 8am to 1.30pm Saturday. The OTE, on Theotokopoulou just north of El Greco Park, opens 7.30am to 11pm daily.

Sportc@fe (☎ 281 028 8217), on the corner of 25 Avgoustou and Zotou, has fast modern machines and serves up coffee, beers and soft drinks while you surf. Istos Cyber Cafe (☎ 281 022 2120), Malikouti 2, charges €3.80 an hour to use its computers and also scans, prints, and faxes documents. There are a half-dozen computers with fast connections. It's open 9am to 1am daily.

Bookshops The huge Planet International Bookshop (☎ 281 028 1558) on the corner of Hortatson and Kydonias stocks most of the books recommended in this guide and has a large selection of Lonely Planet titles. Road Editions (☎/fax 281 034 4610, e road@her.forthnet.gr) at Handakos 29 has the best selection of maps in Iraklio as well as a good range of Lonely Planet titles.

Laundry There are two self-service laundrettes: Laundry Washsalon at Handakos 18, and Inter Laundry at Mirabelou 25 near the Archaeological Museum. Both charge €5.90 for a wash and dry.

Luggage Storage The left-luggage office at Bus Station A charges €1 per day and is open 6.30am to 8pm daily. Other options are Prince Travel (☎ 281 028 2706), at 25 Avgoustou 30, which also charges €1.50, Washsalon (see Laundry) which charges €1.50 and the youth hostel at Vyronos 5 which charges €1.50.

Emergency The modern University Hospital (☎ 281 039 2111) at Voutes, 5km south of Iraklio, is the city's best-equipped medical facility. The Apollonia Hospital (☎ 281 022 9713), inside the old walls on Mousourou, is more convenient.

Archaeological Museum

Second in size and importance only to the National Archaeological Museum in Athens, this outstanding museum (☎ 281 022 6092, Xanthoudidou; admission €4.40; open 8am-7pm Tues-Sun, 12.30pm-7pm Mon) is just north of Plateia Eleftherias. If you are seriously interested in the Minoans you will want more than one visit, but even a fairly superficial perusal of the contents requires half a day. The museum closes at 5pm from late October to early April.

The exhibits, arranged in chronological order, include pottery, jewellery, figurines and sarcophagi as well as some famous frescoes, mostly from Knossos and Agia Triada. All testify to the remarkable imagination and advanced skills of the Minoans. Unfortunately, the exhibits are not very well explained. If they were, there would be no need to part with €6.50 for a copy of the glossy illustrated museum guide.

Room 1 is devoted to the Neolithic and Early Minoan periods. Room 2 has a collection from the Middle Minoan period. Among the most fascinating exhibits here are the tiny glazed reliefs of Minoan houses from Knossos.

Room 3 covers the same period with finds from Phaestos, including the famous **Phaestos disc**. The symbols inscribed on the disc have not been deciphered. Here also are the famous **Kamares pottery vases**, named after the sacred cave of Kamares where the pottery was first discovered. The four large vases in case 43 were part of a royal banquet set. They are of exceptional quality and are some of the finest examples of Kamares pottery.

Exhibits in Room 4 are also from the Middle Minoan period. Most striking is the 20cm black stone **Bull's Head**, which was a libation vessel. The bull has a fine head of curls, from which sprout horns of gold. The eyes of painted crystal are extremely lifelike. Also in this room are relics from a shrine at Knossos, including two fine figurines of **snake goddesses**. Snakes symbolised immortality for the Minoans.

Pottery, bronze figurines and seals are some of the exhibits displayed in Room 5.

These include vases imported from Egypt and some Linear A and B tablets (see the boxed text 'Linear B Script'). The inscriptions on the tablets displayed here have been translated as household or business accounts from the palace at Knossos.

Room 6 is devoted to finds from Minoan cemeteries. Especially intriguing are two small clay models of grouped figures which were found in a *tholos* (Mycenaean tomb shaped like a beehive). One depicts four male dancers in a circle, their arms around each other's shoulders, possibly participating in a funeral ritual. The other model depicts two groups of three figures in a room flanked by two columns. Each group features two large seated figures being offered libations by a smaller figure. It is not known whether the large figures represent gods or departed mortals. On a more grisly level, there is a display of the bones of a horse sacrificed as part of Minoan worship.

Finds in Room 7 include the beautiful **bee pendant** found at Malia. It's a remarkably fine piece of gold jewellery depicting two bees dropping honey into a comb. Also in this room are the three celebrated vases from Agia Triada. The **Harvester Vase**, of which only the top part remains, depicts a light-hearted scene of young farm workers returning from olive picking. The **Boxer Vase** depicts Minoans indulging in two of their favourite pastimes – wrestling and bull grappling. The **Chieftain Cup** depicts a more cryptic scene: a chief holding a staff and three men carrying animal skins.

Room 8 holds finds from the palace at Zakros. Don't miss the gorgeous little crystal vase which was found in over 300 pieces and was painstakingly reconstructed by museum staff.

Room 10 covers the postpalatial period (1350–1100 BC) when the Minoan civilisation was in decline and being overtaken by the warrior-like Mycenaeans. Nevertheless, there are still some fine exhibits, including a child (headless) on a swing.

Room 13 is devoted to Minoan sarcophagi. However, the most famous and spectacular of these, the **sarcophagus from Agia Triada**, is upstairs in Room 14 (the

CRETE

Linear B Script

The methodical decipherment of the Linear B script by English architect and part-time linguist Michael Ventris was the first tangible evidence that the Greek language had a recorded history longer than any scholar had previously believed. The decipherment demonstrated that the language disguised by these mysterious scribblings was an archaic form of Greek 500 years older than the Ionic Greek used by Homer.

Linear B was written on clay tablets that lay undisturbed for centuries until they were unearthed at Knossos in Crete. Further clay tablets were unearthed later on the mainland at Mycenae, Tiryns and Pylos on the Peloponnese and at Thebes in Boeotia.

The clay tablets, found to be mainly inventories and records of commercial transactions, consist of about 90 different signs and date from the 14th to the 13th centuries BC. Little of the social and political life of these times can be deduced from the tablets, though there is enough to give a glimpse of a fairly complex and well-organised commercial structure.

For linguists, the script did not provide a detailed image of the actual language spoken, since the symbols were used primarily as syllabic clusters designed to give an approximation of the pronunciation of the underlying language. Typically, the syllabic cluster 'A-re-ka-sa-da-ra' is the woman's name Alexandra, but the exact pronunciation remains unknown.

Importantly, what is clear is that the language is undeniably Greek, thus giving the modern-day Greek language the second-longest recorded written history, after Chinese. The language of an earlier script, Linear A, remains to this day undeciphered. It is believed to be of either Anatolian or Semitic origin, though even this remains pure conjecture.

Hall of Frescoes). This stone coffin, painted with floral and abstract designs and ritual scenes, is regarded as one of the supreme examples of Minoan art.

The most famous of the Minoan frescoes are also displayed in Room 14. Frescoes from Knossos include the **Procession Fresco**, the **Griffin Fresco** (from the Throne Room), the **Dolphin Fresco** (from the Queen's Room) and the amazing **Bull-Leaping Fresco**, which depicts a seemingly double-jointed acrobat somersaulting on the back of a charging bull. Other frescoes here include the two lovely **Frescoes of the Lilies** from Amisos and fragments of frescoes from Agia Triada. More frescoes can be seen in Rooms 15 and 16. In Room 16 there is a large wooden model of Knossos.

Historical Museum of Crete

A fascinating range of bits and pieces from Crete's more recent past is housed in this museum (*☎ 281 028 3219, Lysimahou Kalokerinou 7; admission €3; open 9am-5pm Mon-Fri, 9am-2pm Sat summer; 9am-3pm Mon-Sat winter*), just back from the waterfront. The ground floor covers the period from Byzantine to Turkish rule, with plans, charts, photographs, ceramics and maps. On the 1st floor is the only **El Greco painting** on display in Crete. Other rooms contain fragments of 13th- and 14th-century frescoes, coins, jewellery, liturgical ornaments and vestments, and medieval pottery.

The 2nd floor has a reconstruction of the **library of author Nikos Kazantzakis**, with displays of his letters, manuscripts and books. Another room is devoted to Emmanouil Tsouderos, who was born in Rethymno and who was prime minister in 1941. There are some dramatic photographs of a ruined Iraklio in the **Battle of Crete** section. On the 3rd floor there is an outstanding **folklore collection**.

Other Attractions

Iraklio burst its **city walls** long ago but these massive fortifications, with seven bastions and four gates, are still very conspicuous, dwarfing the concrete structures of the 20th century. Venetians built the defences between 1462 and 1562. At the end of the Old

Harbour's jetty is another Venetian fortress, the 16th-century **Rocca al Mare** (☎ *281 024 6211, Iraklio Harbour; admission €1.50; open 8am-6pm Mon-Sat, 10am-3pm Sun).*

Several other notable vestiges from Venetian times survive in the city. Most famous is the **Morosini Fountain** on Plateia Venizelou. The fountain, built in 1628, was commissioned by Francesco Morosini, the governor of Crete. Opposite is the three-aisled 13th-century **Basilica of San Marco**. It has been reconstructed many times and is now an exhibition gallery. A little north of here is the attractively reconstructed 17th-century **Venetian loggia**. It was a Venetian version of a gentleman's club where the male aristocracy came to drink and gossip.

The delightful **Bembo Fountain**, at the southern end of 1866, is shown on local maps as the Turkish Fountain, but it was actually built by the Venetians in the 16th century. It was constructed from a hotchpotch of building materials including an ancient statue. The ornate edifice next to the fountain was added by the Turks, and now functions as a snack bar.

The former Church of Agia Ekaterini, next to Agios Minos Cathedral, is now a **museum** (☎ *281 028 8825, Monis Odigitrias; admission €1.50; open 9am-1.30pm Mon-Sat, 5pm-8pm Tues, Thur & Fri).* It houses an impressive collection of icons, most notably those painted by Mihail Damaskinos, the mentor of El Greco.

The **Battle of Crete Museum** *(Cnr Doukos Beaufort & Hatzidaki; admission free; open 9am-1pm daily)* chronicles this historic battle through photographs, letters, uniforms and weapons.

You can pay homage to Crete's most acclaimed contemporary writer, Nikos Kazantzakis (1883–1957), by visiting his **tomb** at the Martinenga Bastion (the best-preserved bastion) in the southern part of town. The epitaph on his grave, 'I hope for nothing, I fear nothing, I am free', is taken from one of his works.

Trekking
The Iraklio branch of the **EOS** (☎ *281 022 7609, Dikeosynis 53)* operates the Prinos

Refuge on Mt Ida, a 1½-hour walk from the village of Melisses, 25km south-west of Iraklio.

Organised Tours
Iraklio's travel agents run coach tours the length and breadth of Crete. ***Creta Travel*** *(☎ 281 022 7002, Epimenidou 20–22)* has a good range.

Places to Stay – Budget
The nearest ***camping grounds*** are 26km away at Hersonisos.

Iraklio Youth Hostel *(☎ 281 028 6281, fax 281 022 2947, Vyronos 5)* Dorm beds/doubles/triples €7.40/17.60/25. This GYHO establishment is a clean, well-run place, though a little on the quiet side. The dorms are single-sex and the rooms are basic. Luggage storage is available for €1.50 per piece and breakfast and dinner are served, if required.

Rent Rooms Hellas *(☎ 281 028 8851, fax 281 028 4442, Handakos 24)* Dorm beds €6.80, doubles/triples/quads €22/26.50/31.70. Many travellers enjoy the lively atmosphere at this de facto youth hostel which has a roof garden and a bar. Luggage storage is free.

There are few ***domatia*** in Iraklio and not enough cheap hotels to cope with the number of budget travellers who arrive in high season.

Vergina Rooms *(☎ 281 024 2739, Hortatson 32)* Doubles/triples €20.50/26.50. The pleasant Vergina Rooms is a characterful century-old house with a small courtyard and spacious, high-ceilinged rooms. Bathrooms are on the terrace and hot water is available upon request.

Hotel Rea *(☎ 281 022 3638, fax 281 024 2189, Kalimeraki-Handakos)* Singles/doubles €19/23.50, doubles/triples with bathroom €26.50/35.30. This handy place is clean, quiet and friendly.

Hotel Mirabello *(☎ 281 028 5052, fax 281 022 5852, @ mirabhot@otenet.gr, Theotokopoulou 20)* Singles/doubles €22/29.50, with bathroom €29.50/35.30. One of the nicest low-priced places in Iraklio would have to be the spiffy Mirabello on a

CRETE

Nikos Kazantzakis – Crete's prodigal son

Crete's most famous contemporary literary son is Nikos Kazantzakis. Born in 1883 in Iraklio, the then Turkish-dominated capital city of Crete, Kazantzakis spent his early childhood in the ferment of revolution and change that was creeping upon his homeland. In 1897 the revolution against Turkish rule that finally broke out forced him to leave Crete for studies in Naxos, Athens and later Paris. It wasn't until he was 31, in 1914, that he finally turned his hand to writing by translating philosophical books into Greek. For a number of years he travelled throughout Europe – Switzerland, Germany, Austria, Russia and Britain – thus laying the groundwork for a series of travelogues in his later literary career.

Nikos Kazantzakis was a complex writer and his early work was heavily influenced by the prevailing philosophical ideas of the time. The nihilistic philosophies of Nietzsche influenced his writings through which he is tormented by a tangible metaphysical and existentialist anguish. His relationship with religion was always troubling – his official stance being that of a non-believer, yet he seemed to always toy with the idea that perhaps God did exist. His self-professed greatest work is his *Odyssey*, a modern-day epic loosely based on the trials and travels of the ancient hero Odysseas (Ulysses). A weighty and complex opus of 33,333 seventeen syllable iambic verses, *Odyssey* never fully vindicated Kazantzakis' aspirations to be held in the same league as the Ancient's Greeks' Homer, the Romans' Virgil or the Renaissance Italians' Tasso.

Ironically it was much later in his career where Kazantzakis belatedly turned to novel writing that his star finally shone. It was through works like *Christ Recrucified* (1948), *Kapetan Mihalis* (1950) and *The Life and Manners of Alexis Zorbas* (1946) that he became internationally known. This last work gave rise the image of the ultimate, modern Greek male 'Zorba the Greek', immortalised in the Anthony Quinn and Melina Mercouri movie of the same name, and countless restaurants throughout Crete and Greece in general.

Kazantzakis died in Freiburg, Germany on 26 October 1957 while on yet one more of his many travels. Despite resistance from the orthodox church, he was given a religious funeral and buried in the southernmost bastion of the old walls of Iraklio. Among the writer's more optimistic quotes is: 'Happy is the man who before dying has the good fortune to travel the Aegean Seas. Nowhere else can one pass so easily from reality to the dream'. (Nikos Kazantzakis 1883–1957).

MARTIN HARRIS

---

quiet street in the centre of town. The rooms are immaculate.

Hotel Lena (☎ *281 022 3280, fax 281 024 2826, Lahana 10*) Singles/doubles €23.50/32.50, doubles with bathroom €38.20. Hotel Lena has comfortable, airy rooms with phones and double-glazed windows; some have air-con, others have fans.

Places to Stay – Mid-Range

Hotel Kastro (☎ *281 0284 185, fax 281 022 3622,* **W** *www.kastro-hotel.gr, Theotokopoulou 22*) Singles/doubles with breakfast €26.40/35.20. This is one of the cheapest B-class hotels. The rooms are large, contain telephones and have air-con.

Hotel Kronos (☎ *281 028 2240, fax 281 028 5853,* **e** *kronosht@otenet.gr, Sofokli Venizelou 2*) Singles/doubles €32.30/41. This place, which has large rooms in excellent condition, is the best-value C-class hotel. Try to get a room overlooking the sea.

Hotel Ilaira (☎ *281 022 7103, fax 281 024 2367, Ariadnis 1*) Singles/doubles €41/52.80. These pleasant stucco and wood rooms have telephones and showers; some have TVs and others have small balconies with sea views.

Hotel Irini (☎ 281 022 6561, fax 281 022 6407, Idomeneos 4) Singles/doubles €47/ 61.60. This is a modern establishment with 59 large, airy rooms with TV (local stations only), radio, telephone and air-con.

Places to Stay – Top End

Hotel Lato (☎ 281 022 8103, fax 281 024 0350, e info@lato.gr, Epimenidou 15) Singles/doubles with buffet breakfast €67/ 84. The Lato has rooms with spectacular sea views.

Atlantis Hotel (☎ 281 022 9103, fax 281 022 6265, e atlantis@atl.grecotel.gr, Ygias 2) Singles/doubles with buffet breakfast €70.50/100. This A-class hotel offers comfortable rooms with air-conditioning. Facilities include a health studio, sauna and indoor swimming pool.

Astoria Hotel (☎ 281 034 3080, fax 281 022 9078, e astoria@her.forthnet.gr, Plateia Eleftherias 11) Singles/doubles with buffet breakfast €83.70/106. This A-class hotel is the best place in town. Facilities include a glorious outdoor swimming pool.

Places to Eat – Budget

Iraklio has some excellent restaurants, and there's something to suit all tastes and budgets.

Giakoumis Taverna (Theodosaki 5-8) Mayirefta €2.30-4.40. Open noon-3pm & 7pm-10pm Mon-Sat. Theodosaki is lined with tavernas catering to the market on 1866 and this is one of the best. There's a full menu of Cretan specialities and turnover is heavy which means that the dishes are freshly cooked.

Restaurant Ionia (☎ 281 028 3213, Evans 3) Mayirefta €2.60-4.40. Open 7pm-midnight Mon-Sat. This is the place for good Cretan home cooking. Choose your meal from the pots and pans of pre-prepared food (mayirefta) on display.

O Vrakas (mobile ☎ 69-7789 3973, Plateia Anglon) Mains €2.90-3.50. Vrakas is a small street-side ouzeri that grills fresh fish al fresco in front of the diners. It's cheap and unassuming and the menu is limited,

but still very popular with locals. Grilled octopus (€3.22) with ouzo is a good choice.

Ippokambos Ouzeri (☎ 281 028 0240, Mitsotaki 2) Mains €3.50-5.30. This place is as good as taverna-style eating gets. The interior is attractively decorated with cooking pots but most people prefer to squeeze onto one of the street-side tables.

Katsina Ouzeri (☎ 281 022 1027, Marineli 12) Mezedes €1.50-4.40. Open 7pm-1am Tues-Sun. This is an old neighbourhood favourite. Most people come for the lamb and pork roasted in a brick oven or the excellent stewed goat.

Baxes (☎ 281 027 7057, Gianni Hronaki 14) Mains €3.22-5. Open 11am-2am daily. Now run by country folk, this simple restaurant offers Cretan special-occasion cooking. Lamb and goat are stewed for hours or roasted in a brick oven.

I Avli tou Defkaliona (☎ 281 024 4215, Kalokerinou 8) Mains €3.80-6.20. Open 8pm-4am Mon-Sat. In this charming taverna you'll soon forget you're in Crete's largest and least picturesque city. It offers a wide range of reasonably priced, imaginative mezedes and main dishes. It really gets rolling around 11pm when the tourists leave and the Cretans arrive.

Loukoumades Cafe (☎ 281 034 6005, Dikeosynis 8) Open 5am-midnight daily. If you haven't yet tried loukoumades (fritters with syrup; €1.50), then this is a good place to sample this gooey confection.

Whether you're self-catering or not, you'll enjoy a stroll up *1866* (the market street). This narrow street is always packed, and stalls spill over with produce of every description.

Places to Eat – Top End

Giovanni Taverna (☎ 281 034 6338, Koraï 12) Open noon-2.30pm & 7.30pm-midnight Mon-Sat. This is a splendid place with two floors of large, airy rooms and, in summer, outdoor eating on a quiet pedestrian street. The food is a winning Mediterranean combination of Greek and Italian specialities. The seafood platter for two costs €32.30.

Loukoulos (☎ 281 022 4435, Koraï 5) Grills €13-16. Open noon-3pm & 7pm-

CRETE

midnight Mon-Sat. Loukoulos offers luscious Mediterranean specialities. You can either choose the elegant interior or dine on the outdoor terrace under a lemon tree. All the vegetables are organically grown and vegetarians are well catered for.

Entertainment

Guernica (☎ *281 028 2988, Apokoronou Kritis 2)* Open 10am-midnight daily. Guernica boasts traditional decor and contemporary rock which mix well to create one of Iraklio's hippest bar-cafes.

Take Five (☎ *281 022 6564, Akroleondos 7)* Open 10am-midnight daily. This is an old favourite on the edge of El Greco Park that doesn't get going until after sundown when the outside tables fill up with a diverse crowd of regulars. It's a gay-friendly place, and the music and ambience are low-key.

Jasmin (☎ *281 028 8880, Handakos 45)* Open noon-midnight daily. This is a friendly bar-cafe with a back terrace that specialises in herbal tea but also serves alcoholic beverages. The nightly DJs play rock and world music as well as techno.

Ideon Antron (☎ *281 024 2041, Perdikari 1)* Open 10am-1am daily. On trendy Koraï with its rows of post-modern kafeneia, this is a throwback to the past. The stone interior with its shiny wood bar creates a relaxed, inviting place.

Getting There & Away

Air – Domestic Olympic Airways has at least six flights daily to Athens (€70.45) from Iraklio's Nikos Kazantzakis airport. It also has flights to Thessaloniki (€97, three weekly), Rhodes (€79.50, two weekly) and Santorini (€56, two weekly). The Olympic Airways office (☎ 281 022 9191) is at Plateia Eleftherias 42. The airport number is ☎ 281 024 5644.

Aegean Airlines has flights to Athens (€79.50, three daily) and Thessaloniki (€98.60, two daily). The Aegean Airlines office (☎ 281 034 4324, fax 281 034 4330) is at Leoforos Dimokratias 11. Its office is at the airport (☎ 281 033 0475).

Axon Airlines has flights to Athens (€70, two daily). The Axon Airlines office (☎ 281 033 1310) is located on Ethnikis Andistasis 134.

Air – International Olympic Airways flies to Larnaka, in Cyprus, from Iraklio (€148, two weekly).

Cronus Airlines offers direct connections to Paris and, in association with its partner Aegean Airlines, one-stop connections to Cologne/Bonn, Munich, Rome and Stuttgart.

Iraklio has lots of charter flights from all over Europe. Prince Travel (☎ 281 028 2706), 25 Avgoustou 30, advertises cheap last-minute tickets on these flights. Sample fares include London for €88 and Munich for €125.

Bus There are buses every half-hour (hourly in winter) to Rethymno (1½ hours, €5.60) and Hania (three hours, €10.90) from the Rethymno/Hania bus station opposite Bus Station A. Following is a list of other destinations from Bus Station A (☎ 281 024 5020, fax 281 034 6284, ✉ ktelirla@otenet.gr):

destination	duration	fare	frequency
Agia Pelagia	45 min	€2.20	5 daily
Agios Nikolaos	1½ hr	€4.50	half-hourly
Arhanes	30 min	€1.20	15 daily
Hersonisos/Malia	1 hr	€2	half-hourly
Ierapetra	2½ hr	€6.80	7 daily
Lasithi Plateau	2 hr	€4.50	2 daily
Milatos	1½ hr	€3.50	1 daily
Sitia	3½ hr	€8.80	5 daily

Buses leave Bus Station B for:

destination	duration	fare	frequency
Agia Galini	2½ hr	€5	7 daily
Anogia	1 hr	€2.30	6 daily
Matala	2 hr	€5	9 daily
Phaestos	2 hr	€4.10	8 daily

Taxi There are long-distance taxis (☎ 281 021 0102 or 281 021 0168) from Plateia Eleftherias, opposite the Astoria Hotel and Bus Station B, to all parts of Crete. Sample fares include Agios Nikolaos (€33.80), Rethymno (€42.50) and Hania (€69). A taxi to the airport costs around €5.90.

Ferry Minoan Lines and ANEK Lines operate ferries every evening each way between Iraklio and Piraeus (10 hours). They depart from both Piraeus and Iraklio between 7.45pm and 8pm. Fares are €21.70 deck class and €41.70 for cabins. The Minoan Lines' Highspeed boats, the F/B *Festos Palace* and F/B *Knossos Palace*, are much more modern and more comfortable than their ANEK rivals.

In summer and on weekends only, Minoan Lines runs six-hour day services on *Festos Palace* and *Knossos Palace*, departing Iraklio and Piraeus at 12.30pm and arriving at 6.30pm. This is by far the most convenient way to get to and from Crete.

Minoan also have three ferries weekly to Thessaloniki (23 hours, €38) via Santorini (3¾ hours, €12.05) and Mykonos (nine hours, €18.80). These services also stop at Paros (7½ hours, €16.15) and Tinos (10¼ hours, €20) twice weekly, and at Naxos (seven hours, €16.15), Syros (10 hours, €17.60) and Skiathos (17¾ hours, €30.80) once a week.

Iraklio's port police can be contacted on ☎ 281 024 4912.

Getting Around

To/From the Airport Bus No 1 goes to and from the airport every 15 minutes between 6am and 1am (€0.60). It leaves the city from near the Astoria Hotel on Plateia Eleftherias.

Bus Bus No 2 goes to Knossos every 10 minutes from Bus Station A (20 minutes, €0.80). It also stops on 25 Avgoustou and 1821.

Car, Motorcycle & Bicycle Most of the car- and motorcycle-rental outlets are on 25 Avgoustou. You'll get the best deal from local companies like Sun Rise (☎ 281 022 1609) at 25 Avgoustou 46, Loggeta Cars & Bikes (☎ 281 028 9462) at Plateia Kallergon 6, next to El Greco Park, or Ritz Rent-A-Car at Hotel Rea (see Places to Stay), which offers discounts for hotel guests. There are also many car rental outlets at the airport.

Mountain bicycles can be hired from Porto Club Travel Services (☎ 281 028 5264), 25 Avgoustou 20.

KNOSSOS Κνωσσός

Knossos *(k-nos-os)*, 5km from Iraklio, was the capital of Minoan Crete. Nowadays the site *(☎ 281 023 1940; admission €4.40; open 8am-7pm daily Apr-Oct, 8am-5pm daily winter)* is the island's major tourist attraction.

The ruins of Knossos were uncovered in 1900 by the British archaeologist Sir Arthur Evans. Heinrich Schliemann, who had earlier uncovered the ancient cities of Troy and Mycenae, had had his eye on the spot (a low, flat-topped mound), believing an ancient city was buried there, but was unable to strike a deal with the local landowner.

Evans was so enthralled by his discovery that he spent 35 years and £250,000 of his own money excavating and reconstructing sections of the palace. Some archaeologists have disparaged Evans' reconstruction, believing he sacrificed accuracy to his overly vivid imagination. However, most non-specialists agree that Sir Arthur did a good job and that Knossos is a knockout. Without these reconstructions it would be impossible to visualise what a Minoan palace looked like.

You will need to spend about four hours at Knossos to explore it thoroughly. There is absolutely no signage, so unless you have a travel guidebook, or hire a guide, you will have no idea what you are looking at. The cafe at the site is expensive – you'd do better to bring a picnic along.

History

The first palace at Knossos was built around 1900 BC. In 1700 BC it was destroyed by an earthquake and rebuilt to a grander and more sophisticated design. It is this palace that Evans reconstructed. It was partially destroyed again sometime between 1500 and 1450 BC. It was inhabited for another 50 years before it was devastated once and for all by fire.

The city of Knossos consisted of an immense palace, residences of officials and

CRETE

PALACE OF KNOSSOS

1 Lustral Basin
2 Bull Fresco
3 Giant Pithoi
4 Throne Room
5 Western Court
6 Corridor of the Procession Fresco
7 Grand Staircase
8 Hall of the Double Axes
9 Queen's Megaron
10 Water Closet
11 Priest King Fresco
12 South House
13 South-East House

CRETE

priests, the homes of ordinary people, and burial grounds. The palace comprised royal domestic quarters, public reception rooms, shrines, workshops, treasuries and store-rooms, all built around a central court. Like all Minoan palaces, it also doubled as a city hall, accommodating all the bureaucracy necessary for the smooth running of a complex society.

Until 1997 it was possible to enter the royal apartments, but the area was cordoned off before it disappeared altogether under the continual pounding of tourists' feet. Extensive repairs are under way but it is unlikely to open to the public again.

Exploring the Site

Numerous rooms, corridors, dogleg passages, nooks and crannies, and staircases prohibit a detailed walk-through description of the palace. However, Knossos is not a site where you'll be perplexed by heaps of rubble, trying to fathom whether you're looking at the throne room or a workshop. Thanks to Evans' reconstruction, the most significant parts of the complex are instantly recognisable (if not instantly found). On your wanders you will come across many of Evans' reconstructed columns, most painted deep brown-red with gold-trimmed black capitals. Like all Minoan columns, they taper at the bottom.

It is not only the vibrant frescoes and mighty columns which impress at Knossos; keep your eyes open for the little details which are evidence of a highly sophisticated society. Things to look out for include the drainage system, the placement of light wells, and the relationship of rooms to passages, porches, light wells and verandas, which kept rooms cool in summer and warm in winter.

The usual entrance to the palace complex is across the Western Court and along the **Corridor of the Procession Fresco**. The fresco depicted a long line of people carrying gifts to present to the king; only fragments remain. A copy of one of these fragments, called the **Priest King Fresco**, can be seen to the south of the Central Court.

If you leave the Corridor of the Procession Fresco and walk straight ahead to enter the site from the northern end, you will come to the **theatral area**, a series of steps, the function of which remains unknown. The area could have been a theatre where spectators watched acrobatic and dance performances, or the place where people gathered to welcome important visitors arriving by the Royal Road.

The **Royal Road** leads off to the west. The road, Europe's first (Knossos has lots of firsts), was flanked by workshops and the houses of ordinary people. The **lustral basin** is also in this area. Evans speculated that this was where the Minoans performed a ritual cleansing with water before religious ceremonies.

Entering the **Central Court** from the north, you pass the relief **Bull Fresco** which depicts a charging bull. Relief frescoes were made by moulding wet plaster, and then painting it while still wet.

Also worth seeking out in the northern section of the palace are the **giant pithoi**. Pithoi were ceramic jars used for storing olive oil, wine and grain. Evans found over 100 of these huge jars at Knossos, some 2m high. The ropes used to move them inspired the raised patterns decorating the jars.

Once you have reached the Central Court, which in Minoan times was surrounded by the high walls of the palace, you can begin exploring the most important rooms of the complex.

From the northern end of the west side of the Central Court, steps lead down to the **throne room**. This room is fenced off but you can still get a pretty good view of it. The centrepiece, the simple, beautifully proportioned throne, is flanked by the **Griffin Fresco**. (Griffins were mythical beasts regarded as sacred by the ancient Minoans.) The room is thought to have been a shrine, and the throne the seat of a high priestess, rather than a king. The Minoans did not worship their deities in great temples

but in small shrines, and each palace had several.

On the 1st floor of the west side of the palace is the section Evans called the **Piano Nobile**, for he believed the reception and state rooms were here. A room at the northern end of this floor displays copies of some of the frescoes found at Knossos.

Returning to the Central Court, the impressive **grand staircase** leads from the middle of the eastern side of the palace to the royal apartments, which Evans called the Domestic Quarter. This section of the site is now cordoned off. Within the royal apartments is the **Hall of the Double Axes**. This was the king's *megaron*, a spacious double room in which the ruler both slept and carried out certain court duties. The room had a light well at one end and a balcony at the other to ensure air circulation.

The room takes its name from the double axe marks on its light well. These marks appear in many places at Knossos. The double axe was a sacred symbol to the Minoans. *Labrys* was Minoan for 'double axe' and the origin of our word 'labyrinth'.

A passage leads from the Hall of the Double Axes to the **queen's megaron**. Above the door is a copy of the **Dolphin Fresco**, one of the most exquisite Minoan artworks, and a blue floral design decorates the portal. Next to this room is the queen's bathroom, complete with terracotta bathtub and **water closet**, touted as the first ever to work on the flush principle; water was poured down by hand.

Getting There & Away

Regular buses operate from Iraklio. See Iraklio's Getting Around section for details.

GORTYNA Γόρτυνα

Conveniently, Crete's three other major archaeological sites lie close to each other forming a rough triangle some 50km south of Iraklio. They are best all visited together.

Lying 46km south-west of Iraklio, and 15km from Phaestos, on the plain of Mesara, is the archaeological site of Gortyna (**gor-tih-nah**; ☎ 2892 031 144; admission €2.30; open 8am-7pm daily), also called Gortys. It's a vast and wonderfully intriguing site

CRETE

with bits and pieces from various ages strewn all over the place. The site was a settlement from Minoan to Christian times. In Roman times, Gortyna was the capital of the province of Cyrenaica.

The most significant find at the site was the massive stone tablets inscribed with the **Laws of Gortyna**, dating from the 5th century BC. The laws deal with just about every imaginable offence. The tablets are on display at the site.

The 6th-century **basilica** is dedicated to Agios Titos, a protege of St Paul and the first bishop of Crete.

Other ruins at Gortyna include the 2nd-century AD **praetorium**, which was the residence of the governor of the province, a **nymphaeum**, and the **Temple of Pythian Apollo**. The ruins are on both sides of the main Iraklio-Phaestos road.

PHAESTOS Φαιστός

The Minoan site of Phaestos (*fes-***tos***; ☎ 2982 042 315; admission €3.50; open 8am-7pm daily, 8am-5pm daily Nov-Apr*), 63km from Iraklio, was the second most important palace city of Minoan Crete. Of all the Minoan sites, Phaestos has the most awe-inspiring location, with all-embracing views of the Mesara Plain and Mt Ida. The layout of the palace is identical to Knossos, with rooms arranged around a central court.

In contrast to Knossos, Phaestos has yielded very few frescoes. It seems the palace walls were mostly covered with a layer of white gypsum. Evans didn't get his hands on the ruins of Phaestos, so there has been no reconstruction. Like the other palatial period complexes, there was an old palace here which was destroyed at the end of the Middle Minoan period. Unlike the other sites, parts of this old palace have been excavated and its ruins are partially super-imposed upon the new palace.

The entrance to the new palace is by the 15m-wide **Grand Staircase**. The stairs lead to the west side of the **Central Court**. The best-preserved parts of the palace complex are the reception rooms and private apartments to the north of the Central Court; excavations continue here. This section was entered by

an imposing portal with half columns at either side, the lower parts of which are still *in situ*. Unlike the Minoan freestanding columns, these do not taper at the base. The celebrated Phaestos disc was found in a building to the north of the palace. The disc is in Iraklio's Archaeological Museum.

Getting There & Away

There are buses to Phaestos from Iraklio's Bus Station B (1½ hours, €4.10, eight daily). There are also buses from Agia Galini (40 minutes, €1.50, six daily) and Matala (30 minutes, €1.20, five daily). Services are halved from December through February.

AGIA TRIADA Αγία Τριάδα

Agia Triada (*ah-***yee***-ah trih-***ah***-dha; ☎ 2892 091 564; admission €2.90; open 8.30am-3pm daily*) is a small Minoan site 3km west of Phaestos. Its principal building was smaller than the other royal palaces but built to a similar design. This, and the opulence of the objects found at the site, indicate that it was a royal residence, possibly a summer palace of Phaestos' rulers. To the north of the palace is a small town where remains of a *stoa* (long colonnaded building) have been unearthed.

Finds from the palace, now in Iraklio's Archaeological Museum, include a sarcophagus, two superlative frescoes and three vases: the Harvester Vase, Boxer Vase and Chieftain Cup.

The road to Agia Triada takes off to the right about 500m from Phaestos on the road to Matala. There is no public transport to the site.

MATALA Μάταλα
postcode 702 00 ● pop 300

Matala (**mah**-tah-lah), on the coast 11km south-west of Phaestos, was once one of Crete's best-known hippie hang-outs. These days, Matala is a decidedly tacky tourist resort packed out in summer and bleak and deserted in winter. The sandy beach below the caves is, however, one of Crete's best, and the resort is a convenient base from which to visit Phaestos and Agia Triada.

JULIET COOMBE

he Erechtheion (named after the Athenian hero Erichthonius) stands above the city of Athens.

JOHN ELK III

emains of the theatre at Delphi's 4th-century Sanctuary of Apollo set above a rich, green valley.

Withstanding the test of time – Doric columns and entablature of the Tholos at Delphi

Apollo watches over a contemplative Plato.

The graceful Caryatids look out over Athens.

The impressive palace of Knossos, Crete

It was the old Roman **caves** at the northern end of the beach that made Matala famous in the 1960s. There are dozens of them dotted over the cliff-face. They were originally tombs, cut out of the sandstone rock in the 1st century AD. In the 1960s, they were discovered by hippies, who turned the caves into a modern troglodyte city – moving ever higher up the cliff to avoid sporadic attempts by the local police to evict them.

Orientation & Information

Matala's layout is easy to fathom. The bus stop is on the central square, one block back from the waterfront. There is a mobile post office near the beach, on the right of the main road as you come into Matala. There is no bank or ATM; you can change money at Monza Travel (☎ 2892 045 757). The OTE is beyond here in the beach car park. Check your email at the Coffee Shop (☎ 2892 045 460), or at Zafiria Internet (☎ 2892 045 498); both charge around €4.40 per hour.

Places to Stay

Matala Community Camping (☎/fax 2892 045 340) Adult/tent €3.50/2.60. This is a reasonable site just back from the beach.

Komos Beach camp site (☎ 2892 042 332, Komos Pitsidion) Adult/tent €3.50/2.50. This site is at Komos Beach, about 4km before Matala on the road from Phaestos.

There are several pleasant options in Matala proper. Walk back along the main road from the bus station and turn right at Hotel Zafiria. This street is lined with budget accommodation.

Fantastic Rooms to Rent (☎ 2892 045 362, fax 2892 045 292) Doubles/triples €17.60/23.50. One of the cheapest accommodation options in Matala is this place, on the road leading inland. The comfortable rooms have a bathroom.

Pension Antonios (☎ 2892 045 123, fax 2892 045 690) Singles/doubles €11.70/17.60, double/triple apartments €23.50/26.40. Opposite Fantastic, this pension has attractively furnished rooms and apartments.

Hotel Zafiria (☎ 2892 045 366, fax 2892 045 725) Singles/doubles with breakfast €29.30/38.10. The sprawling Hotel Zafiria takes up a good portion of Matala's main road into town. At the hotel there is a spacious lobby-bar and rooms have balconies, sea views, and telephones.

Places to Eat

Eating in Matala is not an experience in haute cuisine, but you won't starve.

Taverna Manolis (☎ 2892 045 122) Grills €5.30-10.30. Split over two sides of the main street, this largish restaurant serves up standard fare at much the same prices as elsewhere.

Lions (☎ 2892 045 108) Daily specials €5.30-8.80. Overlooking the beach, Lions has been a popular place for quite a while. Its food is better than average.

Restaurant Zafiria (☎ 2892 045 455) Mains €5.30-8.80. A little more expensive than other places, this eatery has reasonably good food, though its location overlooking the car park is not the best.

Getting There & Away

There are buses between Iraklio and Matala (two hours, €5, nine daily), and between Matala and Phaestos (30 minutes, €1.20, five daily).

MALIA Μάλια

The Minoan site of Malia (☎ 2897 031 597; admission €2.30; open 8.30am-3pm daily), 3km east of the resort of Malia, is the only cultural diversion on the stretch of coast east of Iraklio, which otherwise has surrendered lock, stock and barrel to the package-tourist industry. Malia is smaller than Knossos and Phaestos, but like them consisted of a palace complex and a town. Unlike Knossos and Phaestos, the palace was built on a flat, fertile plain, not on a hill.

Entrance to the ruins is from the **West Court**. At the extreme southern end of this court there are eight circular pits which archaeologists think were used to store grain. To the east of the pits is the main entrance to the palace which leads to the southern end of the **Central Court**. At the south-west corner of this court you will find the **Kernos Stone**, a disc with 34 holes around its edge.

CRETE

Archaeologists still don't know what it was used for.

The **central staircase** is at the north end of the west side of the palace. The **loggia**, just north of the staircase, is where religious ceremonies took place.

Any bus going to or from Iraklio along the north coast can drop you at the site.

Eastern Crete

The eastern quarter of the island is occupied by the prefecture of Lasithi, named after the quaint plateau tucked high in the Mt Dikti Ranges rather than its uninspiring administrative capital of Agios Nikolaos, which is becoming something of a monument to package tourism. The main attractions, apart from the Lasithi Plateau, are the palm forest and beach at Vaï and the remote Minoan palace site of Zakros.

LASITHI PLATEAU
Οροπέδιο Λασιθίου
postcode 720 52
The first view of the mountain-fringed Lasithi Plateau, laid out like an immense patchwork quilt, is quite stunning. The plateau, 900m above sea level, is a vast expanse of pear and apple orchards, almond trees and fields of crops, dotted by some 7000 windmills. These are not conventional stone windmills, but slender metal constructions with white canvas sails. They were built in the 17th century to irrigate the rich farmland but few of the original windmills are now in service. Most have been replaced by less-attractive mechanical pumps. There are 20 villages dotted around the periphery of the plateau, the largest of which is **Tzermiado**, with 1300 inhabitants, a bank, post office and OTE. The other two major villages are **Psyhro** and **Agios Georgios**.

The plateau's rich soil has been cultivated since Minoan times. The inaccessibility of the region made it a hotbed of insurrection during Venetian and Turkish rule. Following an uprising in the 13th century, the Venetians drove out the inhabitants of

Lasithi and destroyed their orchards. The plateau lay abandoned for 200 years.

Most people come to Lasithi on coach trips, but it deserves an overnight stay. Once the package tourists have departed clutching their plastic windmill souvenirs, the villages return to pastoral serenity.

Dikteon Cave Δίκταιον Αντρον
Lasithi's major sight is Dikteon Cave (☎ 2844 031 316, Psyhro; admission €2.40; open 8am-4pm daily), just outside the village of **Psyhro**. Here, according to mythology, Rhea hid the newborn Zeus from Cronos, his offspring-gobbling father. The cave, which has both stalactites and stalagmites, was excavated in 1900 by British archaeologist David Hogarth. He found numerous votive offerings, indicating the cave was a place of cult worship. These finds are housed in the Archaeological Museum in Iraklio.

It is a steep 15-minute walk up to the cave entrance along a fairly rough track, but you can opt to take a rather expensive donkey ride (€8.80) instead. There is a less obvious paved trail to the cave that starts from the left side of the carpark. It is not as well-shaded as the rougher track. Walk between the two restaurants and you will see people coming down from the paved track.

Places to Stay
Zeus Hotel (☎ 2844 031 284, Psyhro) Singles/doubles with bathroom €20.50/26.50. This is a modern D-class hotel on the west side of the village of Psyhro near the start of the Dikteon Cave road.

Hotel Dias (☎ 2844 031 207, Agios Georgios) Singles/doubles €12/14.50. On the main street in the village of Agios Georgios, Hotel Dias has pleasant rooms above the restaurant of the same name.

Rent Rooms Maria (☎ 2844 031 209, Agios Georgios) Singles/doubles €18/20.50. On the north side of Agios Georgios, Maria has spacious stucco rooms decorated with weavings. The plant-filled enclosed garden is a pleasant place to relax.

Hotel Kourites (☎ 2844 022 194, Tzermiado) Singles/doubles with breakfast €29.50/35.50. On the left as you enter Tzermiado from the east side you'll see this hotel. There is free use of the hotel's bicycles.

Places to Eat

Stavros (☎ 2844 031 453, Psyhro) Mains €3-4.50. Stavros has a neat folksy interior and serves a good range of traditional Cretan dishes. Try goat in lemon and rice sauce (€4.40).

Platanos (☎ 2844 031 668, Psyhro) Ladera €2.70-3.80. Set under a large plane tree opposite Stavros is this alternative eatery. There's a good range of vegetable-based dishes, some of which are also cooked with snails (€3).

Taverna Rea (☎ 2844 031 209, Agios Georgios) Grills €4.50. Opposite the school on Agios Georgios' main street, Taverna Rea rustles up locally produced grilled meats and other staple Cretan fare.

Restaurant Kourites (☎ 2844 022 054, Tzermiado) Grills €4-5. Part of the hotel of the same name in Tzermiado, but 50m farther along the street, is this large restaurant that often has tour groups stopping by for lunch. Food is filling and wholesome.

Taverna Kri-Kri (☎ 2844 022 170, Tzermiado) Mayirefta €3.50-4. This little eatery on Tzermiado's main street serves simple, unfussy meals.

Getting There & Away

Public transport to the Dikteon Cave is problematic if you don't have your own wheels. From Agios Nikolaos there's an afternoon bus to Lasithi on Monday, Wednesday and Friday (2½ hrs, €5.60) and a morning bus from Lasithi to Agios Nikolaos also on Monday, Wednesday and Friday. From Iraklio there are two buses on weekdays to Lasithi (two hours, €4.50), and three on weekdays returning to Iraklio.

All buses go through Tzermiado and Agios Georgios before terminating at Psyhro at the foot of the road leading to Dikteon Cave.

AGIOS NIKOLAOS

Άγιος Νικόλαος
postcode 721 00 • pop 8093
Agios Nikolaos (**ah**-yee-os nih-**ko**-laos) is an undeniably pretty former fishing village.

Today it is one of Crete's more attractive resort destinations. Boasting a fetching combination of port, lake, narrow streets and aquamarine seas, 'Agios' attracts a lot of people. By the early 1960s, it had become a chic hideaway for the likes of Jules Dassin and Walt Disney. By the end of the decade, package tourists were arriving in force. While there is superficially little to attract the independent traveller, there is reasonable accommodation, prices are not too horrendous and there is quite a bit of activity to keep all tastes catered for. A 40% drop in tourism in the summer of 2001 left the village reeling. The years to come may see Agios Nikolaos return to less frenetic levels of tourism and it may yet become a decent place once more.

Orientation

The town centre is Plateia Venizelou, 150m up Sofias Venizelou from the bus station (☎ 2841 022 234). The most interesting part of town is the picturesque Voulismeni Lake, which is ringed with tavernas. The lake is 200m from Plateia Venizelou. Walk northeast along Koundourou and turn left at the bottom and you will come to a bridge that separates the lake from the harbour. The tourist office is at the far side of the bridge.

Once over the bridge, if you turn right and follow the road as it veers left, you will come to the northern stretch of waterfront which is the road to Elounda. A number of large and expensive hotels are along here.

Alternatively, if you turn right at the bottom of Koundourou you will come to a stretch of waterfront with steps leading up to the right. These lead to the streets that have the highest concentration of small hotels and pensions.

Information

The municipal tourist office (☎ 2841 022 357, fax 2841 082 354, e detadan@agn .forthnet.gr), by the bridge, is open 8am to 9.30pm daily from the start of April to mid-November. The tourist police (☎ 2841 026 900), Kondogianni 34, open between 7.30am and 2.30pm daily.

The National Bank of Greece on Nikolaou Plastira has a 24-hour automatic exchange

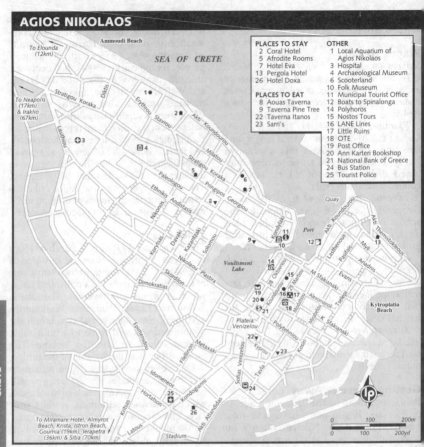

AGIOS NIKOLAOS

To Elounda (12km)

Ammoudi Beach

SEA OF CRETE

To Neapolis (17km) & Iraklio (67km)

Stratigou Koraka
Erythrou Stavrou
Diktis
Akti Koundourou
Milatou
Stratigou Koraka
Paleologou
Pringipos Georgiou
Ethnikis Andistasis
Nikiforos
Korytsas
Davaki
Kazantzaki
Solomou
Nikolaou
Plastira
Skordilon
Dimokratias
Epimenidou
Filellinon
Metaxaki
Idomeneos
Kritsas
Hortatson
Kondogianni
Latous
Akti Atlantidos
Stadium

Voulismeni Lake

Quay
Port
Akti Koundourou
Akti Themistokleous
Lastheous
Pasifais
Myli
Ariadnis
Evans
M Sfakanaki
Alexomanoli Teloga
Koraï
K Sfakanaki
Polythelniou
Kyprou
Koseti
Tavla
Sofias Venizelou
28 Oktovriou
25 Martiou
Kondylaki

Plateia Venizelou

Kytroplatia Beach

To Miramare Hotel, Almyros Beach, Krista, Istron Beach, Gournia (19km), Ierapetra (36km) & Sitia (70km)

0   100   200m
0   100   200yd

PLACES TO STAY
2 Coral Hotel
5 Afrodite Rooms
7 Hotel Eva
13 Pergola Hotel
26 Hotel Doxa

PLACES TO EAT
8 Aouas Taverna
9 Taverna Pine Tree
22 Taverna Itanos
23 Sarri's

OTHER
1 Local Aquarium of Agios Nikolaos
3 Hospital
4 Archaeological Museum
6 Scooterland
10 Folk Museum
11 Municipal Tourist Office
12 Boats to Spinalonga
14 Polyhoros
15 Nostos Tours
16 LANE Lines
17 Little Ruins
18 OTE
19 Post Office
20 Ann Karteri Bookshop
21 National Bank of Greece
24 Bus Station
25 Tourist Police

CRETE

machine. The tourist office also changes money. The post office, 28 Oktovriou 9, is open 7.30am to 2pm Monday to Friday. The OTE is on the corner of 25 Martiou and K Sfakianaki. It is open 7am to 11pm daily.

Internet access is available at the pleasant Polyhoros (☎ 2841 024 876), 28 Oktovriou 13, open 9am to 2am daily. The well-stocked Anna Karteri Bookshop (☎ 2841 022 272) at Koundourou 5 next to the bank has maps, books in English and other languages and some Lonely Planet titles.

The general hospital (☎ 2841 025 221) is at Knossou 3.

Things to See

The **folk museum** (☎ 2841 025 093, Paleologou 4; admission €0.90; open 10am-3pm Sun-Fri), next to the tourist office, has a well-displayed collection of traditional handcrafts and costumes.

The **archaeological museum** (☎ 2841 022 943, Paleologou 74; admission €1.50; open 8.30am-3pm Tues-Sun), housed in a modern building, has a large, well-displayed collection from eastern Crete.

The **Local Aquarium of Agios Nikolaos** (☎ 2841 028 030, Akti Koundourou 30; admission €3.80; open 10am-9pm daily) has interesting displays of fish and information about diving (including PADI courses) and snorkelling throughout Crete.

Voulismeni Lake (Λίμνη Βουλισμένη) is the subject of many stories about its depth and origins. The locals have given it various names, including Xepatomeni (Bottomless), Voulismeni (Sunken) and Vromolimni (Dirty). The lake isn't bottomless – it is 64m deep. The 'dirty' tag came about because the lake used to be stagnant and gave off quite a pong in summer. This was rectified in 1867 when a canal was built linking it to the sea.

Beaches
The popularity of Agios Nikolaos has nothing to do with its beaches. The town beach, south of the bus station, and Kytroplatia Beach, have more people than pebbles. Ammoudi Beach, on the road to Elounda, is equally uninspiring.

The sandy beach at Almyros about 1km south of town is the best of the lot and tends to be less crowded than the others. There's little shade but you can rent umbrellas for €2 a day.

Organised Tours
Travel agencies in Agios Nikolaos offer coach outings to all Crete's top attractions.

Nostos Tours (☎ 2841 022 819, fax 2841 025 336, e nostos@agn.forthnet.gr, Koundourou 30) Nostos has boat trips to Spinalonga (€8.80) as well as guided tours of Phaestos and Matala (€30.80), the Samaria Gorge (€36.70) and the Lasithi Plateau (€23.50).

Places to Stay – Budget
The nearest *camping ground* to Agios Nikolaos is near the Minoan site of Gournia (see Gournia later in this chapter).

Afrodite Rooms (☎ 2841 028 058, Korytsas 27) Singles/doubles with shared facilities €16.20/20.50. There's a tiny communal kitchen here.

Pergola Hotel (☎ 2841 028 152, fax 2841 025 568, Sarolidi 20) Singles/doubles with bathroom €17.60/23.50. Rooms here are comfortable and have fridges. There is

a pleasant outdoor veranda under a pergola to relax on.

Hotel Eva (☎ 2841 022 587, Stratigou Koraka 20) Singles/doubles €23.50/26.50. A neat little place close to the centre of action, this has smallish but quite reasonable rooms.

Hotel Doxa (☎ 2841 024 214, fax 2841 024 614, Idomeneos 7) Singles/doubles €23.50/29.50 The plant-filled lobby sets a homely tone for this hotel that also boasts an attractive terrace for breakfast or drinks. Rooms are small but inviting and are equipped with telephones and balconies.

Places to Stay – Mid-Range
Coral Hotel (☎ 2841 028 363, fax 2841 028 754, Akti Koundourou 68) Singles/doubles with buffet breakfast €47/58.70. This opulent B-class hotel on the northern waterfront is about as upmarket as places get in town. There's also a swimming pool.

Miramare Hotel (☎ 2841 023 875, fax 2841 024 164) Singles/doubles with buffet breakfast €65/82. About 1km south of the town centre, Miramare Hotel has been attractively landscaped into a hillside. The skilfully decorated rooms are outfitted with air-con on demand, satellite TV, fridges, telephones and balconies. There's a swimming pool, tennis courts and fitness centre. Try to get a room near the top of the hill for the stunning views of the sea.

Places to Eat
Agios Nikolaos' waterfront tavernas are expensive – head inland for better value.

Sarri's (☎ 2841 028 059, Kyprou 15) Breakfast €3. Open 8am-midnight daily. This is the best breakfast spot in town and it stays open until the wee hours serving up mouth-watering food to locals.

Taverna Itanos (☎ 2841 025 340, Kyprou 1) Ladera €2.50-4. This is a vast place with beamed ceilings and stucco walls. It has a few tables on the sidewalk as well as comfortable banquettes. The food is traditional Cretan.

Taverna Pine Tree (☎ 2841 023 890 Paleologou 18) Mezedes €2.80-4.90. Dining alongside scenic Voulismeni Lake is one of

CRETE

the great pleasures of Agios Nikolaos and this is a good choice.

Aouas Taverna (☎ 2841 023 231, Paleologou 44) Mezedes €1.80-8. This is the kind of family-run place where your waiter may be a 10-year-old and the cook is her aunt. The interior is plain but the enclosed garden is refreshing and the mezedes are wonderful.

Getting There & Away
Bus Buses leave the Agios Nikolaos bus station for Elounda (€0.90, 20 daily), Kritsa (€0.90, 12 daily), Ierapetra (€2.40, eight daily), Iraklio (€4.60, half-hourly), Istron (€0.90, 11 daily), Lasithi Plateau (€5.60, one daily) and Sitia (€4.90, six daily).

Ferry LANE Lines (☎ 2841 026 465, fax 023 090), at K Sfakianaki 5, has ferries three times a week to Piraeus (12 hours, €23.20), Karpathos (seven hours, €13) and Rhodes (10½ hours, €19). Tickets can be bought from LANE Lines or from other travel agents advertising ferry ticket sales.

Getting Around
You will find many car and motorcycle-hire outlets on the northern waterfront. Scooterland (☎ 2841 026 340), Koundourou 10, has a huge range of scooters and motorcycles. Prices begin at €11.80 a day for a scooter and go up to €44 a day for a Kawasaki EN.

ELOUNDA Ελούντα
postcode 720 53 • pop 1600
There are magnificent mountain and sea views along the 11km road from Agios Nikolaos to Elounda. Although formerly a quiet fishing village, Elounda is now bristling with tourists and is only marginally calmer than Agios Nikolaos. But the harbour is attractive, and there's a sheltered lagoon-like stretch of water formed by the Kolokytha Peninsula.

Orientation & Information
Elounda's post office is opposite the bus stop. From the bus stop walk straight ahead to the clock tower and church which are on the central square. There is a small OTE office next to the church. Elounda doesn't have tourist police, but there is a helpful tourist office (☎ 2841 042 464) opposite the church. Staff will help you find accommodation and change money.

Places to Stay & Eat
There's some good accommodation around, but nothing particularly cheap.

Corali Studios (☎/fax 2841 041 712) Double studios €35.30. On the north side of Elounda, about 800m from the clocktower, are these handy self-catering studios, set in lush lawns with a shaded patio.

Hotel Aristea (☎ 2841 041 300, fax 2841 041 302) Singles/doubles €29.50/44. This hotel is in the town centre and most rooms have a sea view.

Nikos (☎ 2841 041 439) Grills €3.80-6.20. This is a decent choice for fish, which has outdoor tables under a canopy. Service can be erratic but food is reasonably cheap.

The Ferryman Taverna (☎ 2841 041 230) Greek specialities €7.40-9. The Ferryman is *the* place to eat in Elounda. It is expensive, but worth it. Dining is waterside and service is top class.

Getting There & Away
There are 20 buses daily from Agios Nikolaos to Elounda (20 minutes, €0.90).

KOLOKYTHA PENINSULA
Χερσόνησος Κολοκύθα
Just before Elounda (coming from Agios Nikolaos), a sign points right to **ancient Olous**, once the port of Lato. The city stood on and around the narrow isthmus (now a causeway) which joined the southern end of the Kolokytha Peninsula to the mainland. Most of the ruins lie beneath the water, and if you go snorkelling near the causeway you will see outlines of buildings and the tops of columns. The water around here appears to be paradise for sea urchins. The peninsula is a pleasant place to stroll and there is an early Christian mosaic near the causeway.

There is an excellent sandy beach 1km along a dirt road (just driveable) on the east side of the peninsula. The beach is sheltered, the water pristine and few visitors use it.

SPINALONGA ISLAND
Νήσος Σπιναλόγκα

Spinalonga Island lies just north of the Kolokytha Peninsula. The island's massive **fortress** *(admission €1.50; open 8am-7pm daily)* was built by the Venetians in 1579 to protect Elounda Bay and the Gulf of Mirabello. It withstood Turkish sieges for longer than any other Cretan stronghold, finally surrendering in 1715, some 30 years after the rest of Crete. The Turks used the island as a base for smuggling. Following the reunion of Crete with Greece, Spinalonga Island became a leper colony. The last leper died there in 1953 and the island has been uninhabited ever since. It is still known among locals as 'the island of the living dead'.

The island is a fascinating place to explore. It has an aura that is both macabre and poignant. The **cemetery**, with its open graves, is an especially strange place. Dead lepers came in three classes: those who saved up money from their government pension for a place in a concrete box; those whose funeral was paid for by relations and who therefore got a proper grave; and the destitute, whose remains were thrown into a charnel house.

Getting There & Away
There are regular excursion boats to Spinalonga Island from Agios Nikolaos and a boat every half-hour from the port in Elounda (€5.90). Alternatively, you can negotiate with the fishermen in Elounda and Plaka (a fishing village 5km farther north) to take you across. The boats from Agios Nikolaos pass Bird Island and Kri-Kri Island, one of the last habitats of the *kri-kri*, Crete's wild goat. Both these islands are uninhabited and designated wildlife sanctuaries.

KRITSA Κριτσά
The village of Kritsa (krit-**sah**), perched 600m up the mountainside 11km from Agios Nikolaos, is on every package itinerary. Tourists come in busloads to the village

every day in summer. The villagers exploit these invasions to the full, and craft shops of every description line the main streets.

The tiny triple-aisled **Church of Panagia Kera** (☎ 2841 051 525; admission €2.30; open 8.30am-3pm Mon-Fri, 8.30am-2pm Sat) is on the right 1km before Kritsa on the Agios Nikolaos road. The frescoes that cover its interior walls are considered the most outstanding examples of Byzantine art on Crete. Unfortunately the church is usually packed with tourists.

Rooms Argyro (☎ 2841 051 174) Singles/doubles €17.60/29.50. There's very little accommodation in Kritsa, but this is the best place to stay. Each room is immaculate and there is a little shaded restaurant downstairs for breakfast and light meals. The rooms are on the left as you enter the village.

O Kastellos (☎ 2841 051 254) Mains €5.60-7.40. Grab a pizza or a hearty meal to eat under a plane tree here in the centre of town. Oven-cooked veal and pasta in a pot (€5.30) is recommended.

There are 12 buses daily from Agios Nikolaos to Kritsa (15 minutes, €0.70).

ANCIENT LATO Λατώ
The ancient city of Lato *(lah-*to; admission €1.50; open 8.30am-3pm Tues-Sun), 4km north of Kritsa, is one of Crete's few non-Minoan ancient sites. Lato was founded in the 7th century BC by the Dorians and at its height was one of the most powerful cities on Crete. It sprawls over the slopes of two acropolises in a lonely mountain setting, commanding stunning views down to the Gulf of Mirabello.

The city's name derived from the goddess Leto whose union with Zeus produced Artemis and Apollo, both of whom were worshipped here. Lato is far less visited than Crete's Minoan sites.

In the centre of the site is a deep well, which is cordoned off. As you face the Gulf of Mirabello, to the left of the well are some steps which are the remains of a **theatre**.

Above the theatre was the **prytaneion**, where the city's governing body met. The circle of stones behind the well was a

CRETE

threshing floor. The columns next to it are the remains of a stoa which stood in the *agora* (commercial area). There are remains of a pebble mosaic nearby. A path to the right leads up to the **Temple of Apollo**.

There are no buses to Lato. The road to the site is signposted to the right on the approach to Kritsa. If you don't have your own transport, it's a pleasant walk through olive groves along this road.

GOURNIA Γουρνιά

The important Minoan site of Gournia (*goor*-**nyah**; ☎ *2841 024 943; admission €1.50; open 8.30am-3pm Tues-Sun*) lies just off the coast road, 19km south-east of Agios Nikolaos. The ruins, which date from 1550 to 1450 BC, consist of a town overlooked by a small palace. The palace was far less ostentatious than the ones at Knossos and Phaestos because it was the residence of an overlord rather than a king. The town is a network of streets and stairways flanked by houses with walls up to 2m in height. Trade, domestic and agricultural implements found on the site indicate Gournia was a thriving little community.

Gournia is on the Sitia and Ierapetra bus routes from Agios Nikolaos and buses can drop you at the site.

Near the Minoan site is *Gournia Moon Camping* (☎/*fax 2842 093 243, Gournia*), the closest camping ground to Agios Nikolaos. It charges €3.50/2.60 per adult/tent. There's a swimming pool, restaurant, snack bar and minimarket. Buses to Sitia can drop you off outside.

MOHLOS Μόχλος
postcode 72 057 • pop 80

Mohlos (**moh**-los) is a pretty fishing village bedecked in hibiscus, bougainvillea and bitter laurel and reached by a 6km winding road from the main Sitia–Agios Nikolaos highway. It was once joined in antiquity to the homonymous island that now sits 200m offshore and was at one time a thriving Minoan community dating back to the Early Minoan period (3000–2000 BC).

Mohlos sees mainly French and German independent travellers seeking peace and quiet from the noise and hype farther west. There is a small pebble-and-grey-sand beach from which swimming is reasonable. Mohlos is an ideal travellers' rest stop with a high chill-out factor.

Orientation & Information

Mohlos is all contained within two or three blocks, all walkable within 10 minutes. There is no bank, or post office in Mohlos and very few tourist facilities at all, other than a couple of gift shops. There are two minimarkets.

Places to Stay & Eat

There is quite a bit of accommodation for independent travellers.

Hotel Sofia (☎/*fax 2843 094 554)* Doubles/triples €29.50/32.30. These comfortable rooms are above the Sofia restaurant. The owner also has fully equipped two- to three-person studios 200m east of the harbour.

Spyros Rooms (☎/*fax 2843 094 204)* Doubles €29.50. These very pleasant and modern rooms all have a fridge and air-conditioning and are a little way outside the village.

The restaurants abutting the harbour are all good. To start with, kick off with these two.

To Bogazi (☎ *2843 094 200)* Mezedes €1.50-4.50. With a sea view on two sides, To Bogazi is nearest the island and serves up over 30 inventive mezedes, many of which are vegetarian. The cuttlefish and pan-tossed greens is a suggested mains course (€5.30).

Sofia (☎ *2843 094 554)* Mayirefta €2.50-3.50. Mama's home cooking is the key ingredient on the menu at Sofia. Try artichokes with peas (€2.70), or cauliflower in wine sauce (€2.50). Vegetarians will love them.

Getting There & Away

There is no public transport travelling directly to Mohlos. Buses between Sitia and Agios Nikolaos will drop you off at the Mohlos turn-off. From there you'll need to hitch or walk the 6km to Mohlos village.

SITIA Σητεία
postcode 723 00 • pop 8000

Sitia (sih-**tee**-ah) is a good deal quieter than Agios Nikolaos. It is a pleasant traveller-friendly town and makes a good jumping-off point for the Dodecanese islands. A sandy beach skirts a wide bay to the east of town. The main part of the town is terraced up a hillside, overlooking the port. The buildings are a pleasing mixture of new and fading Venetian architecture.

Orientation & Information

The bus station is at the eastern end of Karamanli, which runs behind the bay. The town's main square, Plateia El Venizelou – recognisable by its palm trees and statue of a dying soldier – is at the western end of Karamanli.

There's no tourist office but Tzortzakis Travel (☎ 2843 025 080), Kornarou 150, is a good source of information. There are lots of ATMs and places to change money. The National Bank of Greece on the main square has a 24-hour exchange machine.

The harbour near the square is for small boats. Ferries use the large quay farther out, about 500m from Plateia Agnostou.

The post office is on Dimokritou. To get there from the main square, follow El Venizelou inland and take the first left. The OTE is on Kapetan Sifi, which runs uphill directly off Plateia El Venizelou.

Things to See & Do

Sitia's **archaeological museum** (☎ 2843 023 917, Pisokefalou; admission €1.50; open 8.30am-3pm Tues-Sun) houses a well-displayed collection of local finds spanning from Neolithic to Roman times, with emphasis on the Minoan. The museum is on the left side of the road to Ierapetra.

Sitia produces superior sultanas, and a **sultana festival** is held in the town in the last week of August, during which wine flows freely and there are performances of Cretan dances.

Places to Stay

Sitia Youth Hostel (☎ 2843 028 062, Therisou 4) Dorm beds/doubles €5/11.80.

Sitia's youth hostel is on the road to Iraklio. It's a well-run place with hot showers and a communal kitchen and dining room.

Hotel Arhontiko (☎ 2843 028 172, Kondylaki 16) Singles/doubles with shared facilities €17.70/20.50. This D-class hotel two streets uphill from the port is beautifully maintained and spotless. The owner enjoys sharing a bottle of raki with guests on the communal terrace.

Rooms to Let Apostolis (☎ 2843 028 172, Kazantzaki 27) Doubles with fridge €23.50. This upmarket domatio is co-owned with Hotel Arhontiko. Kazantzaki runs uphill from the waterfront, one street north of the OTE.

Kazarma Rooms to Rent (☎ 2843 023 211, Ionias 10) Doubles with bathroom €26.50. This is an attractive place to stay, and is signposted from Patriarhou Metaxaki. There is a communal lounge and a well-equipped kitchen.

El Greco Hotel (☎ 2843 023 133, fax 2843 026 391, Arkadiou 13) Singles/doubles with bathroom €28/38. The well-signposted El Greco has more character than the town's other C-class places. Rooms are comfortable.

Itanos Hotel (☎ 2843 022 900, fax 2843 022 915, ℮ itanoshotel@yahoo.com, Karamanli 4) Singles/doubles €28/47. The B-class Itanos has a conspicuous location on the waterfront and a popular terrace restaurant. The comfortable rooms are outfitted with air-con, satellite TV, balconies and sound-proofing.

Places to Eat

There is a string of tavernas along the quay side on El Venizelou that offer an array of mezedes and fish dishes at comparable prices.

Mihos Taverna (Kornarou 117) Grills €4-5.50. This taverna on the waterfront has excellent charcoal-grilled souvlaki. This is one of the few decent waterfront eateries.

Kali Kardia Taverna (☎ 2843 022 249, Foundalidou 22) Mains €4-5.50. Open 10am-midnight daily. This place is excellent value and popular with locals. Walk up Kazantzaki from the waterfront, take the second right and the taverna is on the right.

CRETE

Cafe Nato (mobile ☎ 69-7282 8503, Mastropavlou 43) Mezedes €1.50-2.50. Open noon-midnight daily. Cafe Nato, up from Hotel Nora, is a laid-back little taverna with outdoor tables that serves a variety of grilled meat, artisanal cheeses and good raki.

Symposio (☎ 2843 025 856, Karamanli 12) Mains €5.30-6.80. Symposio utilises all-Cretan natural products such as organic olive oil from the Toplou monastery. The food is top class. Rabbit in rosemary and wine sauce (€5.30) is recommended.

The Balcony (☎ 2843 025 084, Foundalidou 18) Mains €8.50-10.50. Open noon-3pm & 6.30pm-midnight. Providing the finest dining in Sitia, this has an extraordinarily creative menu that combines Greek, Italian and Mexican food.

Getting There & Away
Air The Olympic Airways office (☎ 2843 022 270) is at 4 Septemvriou 3. Sitia's tiny airport has flights to Athens twice a week for €75.40.

Bus There are six buses a day to Ierapetra (1½ hours, €3.80), five buses a day to Iraklio (3½ hours, €8.80) via Agios Nikolaos (1½ hours, €4.90), five to Vaï (one hour, €1.90), and two to Kato Zakros via Palekastro and Zakros (one hour, €3.40). The buses to Vaï and Kato Zakros run only between May and October; during the rest of the year, the Vaï service terminates at Palekastro and the Kato Zakros service at Zakros.

Ferry The F/B *Vitsentzos Kornaros* and F/B *Ierapetra* of LANE Lines link Sitia with Piraeus (14½ hours, €24), Kasos (four hours, €8.50), Karpathos (six hours, €11) and Rhodes (10 hours, €20) three times weekly. Departure times change annually, so check locally for latest information. Buy tickets at Tzortzakis Travel Agency (☎ 2843 022 631, 2843 28 900), Kornarou 150.

Getting Around
The airport (signposted) is 1km out of town. There is no airport bus; a taxi costs about €3.80.

AROUND SITIA
Moni Toplou Μονή Τοπλού
The imposing Moni Toplou (☎ 2843 061 226, Lasithi; admission €2.40; open 9am-1pm & 2pm-6pm daily), 18km east of Sitia on the back road to Vaï, looks more like a fortress than a monastery. It was often treated as such, being ravaged by both the Knights of St John and the Turks. It holds an 18th-century icon by Ioannis Kornaros, one of Crete's most celebrated icon painters.

From the Sitia-Paleokastro road it is a 3km walk. Buses can drop you off at the junction.

Vaï Βάι
The beach at Vaï, on Crete's east coast 24km from Sitia, is famous for its palm forest.

There are many stories about the origin of these palms, including the theory that they sprouted from date pits spread by Roman legionaries relaxing on their way back from conquering Egypt. While these palms are closely related to the date, they are a separate species unique to Crete.

You'll need to arrive early to appreciate the setting, because the place gets packed in July and August. It's possible to escape the worst of the ballyhoo – jet skis and all – by clambering over a rocky outcrop (to the right, facing the sea) to a small secluded beach. Alternatively, you can go over the hill in the other direction to a quiet beach frequented by nudists.

There are two *tavernas* at Vaï but no accommodation. If you're after more secluded beaches, head north for another 3km to the ancient Minoan site of **Itanos**. Below the site are several good swimming spots.

There are buses to Vaï from Sitia (one hour, €1.80, five daily).

ZAKROS & KATO ZAKROS
Ζάκρος & Κάτω Ζάκρος
postcode 72 300 • pop 765
The village of Zakros (**zah**-kros), 37km south-east of Sitia, is the nearest permanent settlement to the Minoan site of Zakros, a further 7km away (see Ancient Zakros following).

Kato Zakros, next to the site, is a beautiful little seaside settlement that springs to life between March and October. If the weather is dry, there is a lovely two-hour walk from Zakros to Kato Zakros through a gorge known as the Valley of the Dead because of the cave tombs dotted along the cliffs. The gorge emerges close to the Minoan site.

Places to Stay
It's much better to stay at Kato Zakros, where there are four places to choose from, than at Zakros.

Poseidon Rooms (☎ 2843 026 893, fax 2843 026 894, e akrogiali@sit.forthnet.gr) Doubles with/without bathroom €26.50/17.60. At the southern end of the waterfront, these rooms are small but very neat and clean and make for a good budget choice.

Athena Rooms (☎ 2843 026 893, fax 2843 026 894, e akrogiali@sit.forthnet.gr) Doubles with bathroom €26.50. A good-quality choice, these rooms are very pleasant with heavy stone walls and views of the beach from the balcony.

George's Villas (☎/fax 2843 026 833) Singles/doubles with bathroom €26.50/32.30. George's has spotless, beautifully furnished rooms with terraces. The villas are in a verdant, pine-fringed setting 800m along the old road to Zakros.

Rooms Coral (☎/fax 2843 027 064, e katozakrosgr@yahoo.com) Doubles €35.50. The excellent, smallish, spotlessly clean rooms here are equipped with Internet connectivity and all enjoy superb sea views from the communal balcony. There's a kitchen and fridge for guests' use.

Places to Eat
There are three decent restaurants in Kato Zakros, all next to each other.

Taverna Akrogiali (☎ 2843 026 893) Mains €4.40-7.40. There's soothing, seaside dining here with excellent service from owner Nikos Perakis. The speciality is grilled swordfish steak (€7.40).

Georgios Taverna Anesis (☎ 2843 026 890) Ladera €1.50-3.30. The owner specialises in home-cooked food and ladera dishes. Dining is under trees overlooking the beach.

Restaurant Nikos Platanakis (☎ 2843 026 887) Ladera €3-3.80. A wide range of Greek staples is available at this waterside spot as well as rarities such as rabbit, pheasant and partridge.

Getting There & Away
There are buses to Zakros via Palekastro from Sitia (one hour, €3, two daily). They leave Sitia at 11am and 2.30pm and return at 12.30pm and 4pm. From June through August, the buses continue to Kato Zakros.

ANCIENT ZAKROS
The smallest of Crete's four palatial complexes, ancient Zakros (☎ 2843 026 987, Kato Zakros; admission €1.50; open 8am-7pm daily) was a major port in Minoan times, maintaining trade links with Egypt, Syria, Anatolia and Cyprus. The palace comprised royal apartments, storerooms and workshops flanking a central courtyard.

The town occupied a low plain close to the shore. Water levels have risen over the years so that some parts of the palace complex are submerged. The ruins are not well preserved, but a visit to the site is worthwhile for its wild and remote setting.

XEROKAMBOS Ξερόκαμπος
postcode 720 59 • pop 25
Xerokambos (kseh-**roh**-kam-bos) is a quiet, unassuming agricultural village on the far south-eastern flank of Crete. Its isolation has so far meant that tourism is pretty much low-key and most certainly of the unpackaged kind. It attraction lies in its isolation, a couple of splendid beaches, a few scattered tavernas and a scattering of studio accommodation that is ideal for people with peace and quiet in mind.

Ambelos Beach Studios (☎/fax 2842 026 759) Double/triple studios €29.50/32.50. These smallish, but cosy studios have kitchenettes and fridges. There is a BBQ and outdoor wood oven for guests, and a tree-shaded courtyard.

Akrogiali Taverna (☎ 2842 026 777) Mains €3. The only beachside taverna in

CRETE

Xerokambos, Akrogiali is 50m from Ambelos Beach. The food ranges from grills to fish, to home-cooked mayirefta. Look for it near Ambelos Beach Studios.

There are no buses to Xerokambos. To get there from Zakros take the Kato Zakros road, and on the outskirts of Zakros turn left at the signpost for Livyko View Restaurant. This 8km dirt road to Xerokambos is driveable in a conventional vehicle. Otherwise there is a good paved road from Ziros.

IERAPETRA Ιεράπετρα
postcode 722 00 • pop 9541

Ierapetra (yeh-**rah**-pet-rah) is Crete's most southerly major town. It was a major port of call for the Romans in their conquest of Egypt. After the tourist hype of Agios Nikolaos, the unpretentiousness of Ierapetra is refreshing, and the main business continues to be agriculture, not tourism.

Orientation & Information

The bus station (☎ 2842 028 237) is on the eastern side of town on Lasthenous, one street back from the beachfront. From the ticket office, turn right and after about 50m you'll come to a six-road intersection. There are signposts to the beach via Patriarhou Metaxaki, and to the city centre via the pedestrian mall section of Lasthenous.

The mall emerges after about 150m on to the central square of Plateia Eleftherias. To the north of the square is the National Bank of Greece and on the south side is Eurobank. Both banks have ATMs.

If you continue straight ahead from Plateia Eleftherias you will come to Plateia Georgiou Kounoupaki, where you'll find the post office at Vitsenzou Kornarou 7.

There is no tourist office, but South Crete Tours (☎ 2842 022 892), opposite the bus station, might have maps of Ierapetra. To reach it, turn right from Plateia Georgiou Kounoupaki.

You can check your email at the Polycafe Orpheas (☎ 2842 080 462), Koundouriotou 25, or The Net Internet Cafe (☎ 2842 025 900, e the_net_ier@yahoo.com), Koundourou 16.

Things to See

The one-room **archaeological museum** (☎ 2842 028 721, Adrianou 2; admission €1.50; open 8.30am-3pm Tues-Sun) is perfect for those with a short concentration span. Pride of place is given to an exquisite statue of Demeter.

If you walk south along the waterfront from the central square you will come to the **Venetian Fortress** (Kato Meran; admission free; open 8.30am-3pm Tues-Sun), built in the early years of Venetian rule and strengthened by Francesco Morosini in 1626. It's in a pretty fragile state.

Inland from the fortress is the labyrinthine **old quarter**, a delightful place to lose yourself for a while. Look out for the Turkish mosque and Turkish fountain.

Beaches

Ierapetra has two beaches. The main town beach is near the harbour and the other beach stretches east from the bottom of Patriarhou Metaxaki. Both have coarse, grey sand.

The beaches to the east of Ierapetra tend to get crowded. For greater tranquillity, head for **Gaïdouronisi**, known also as **Hrysi**, where there are good, uncrowded sandy beaches, three tavernas and a stand of cedars of Lebanon, the only one in Europe. From June through August excursion boats (€16) leave for the islet every morning and return in the afternoon.

Places to Stay

Koutsounari Camping (☎ 2842 061 213, fax 2842 061 186, Koutsounari) Adult/tent €3.50/2.60. The nearest camping ground to Ierapetra is 7km east of Ierapetra at Koutsounari. It has a restaurant, snack bar and minimarket. Ierapetra-Sitia buses pass the site.

Hotel Coral (☎ 2842 022 846, Katzonovatsi 12) Singles/doubles €15/18, with bathroom €17.60/23.50. Rooms here are well kept and apartments are comfortable. The hotel is two blocks inland in the old town.

Katerina Rooms (☎ 2842 028 345, fax 2842 028 591, Markopoulou 95) Doubles with bathroom €32.50. On the seafront, Katerina has pleasant rooms. To reach the hotel from the bus station, follow Patriarhou Metaxaki to the waterfront.

Cretan Villa Hotel (☎/fax 2842 028 522, e cretan-villa@cretan-villa.com, W www cretan-villa.com, Lakerda 16) Singles/doubles €26.50/35.50. This is a well-maintained 18th-century house with traditionally furnished rooms and a peaceful courtyard. It is a five-minute walk from the bus station.

Astron Hotel (☎ 2842 025 114, fax 2842 025 91, Kothri 56) Singles/doubles with breakfast €41/73.50. The best hotel in town is the B-class Astron at the beach end of Patriarhou Metaxaki. The rooms here are comfortably furnished with satellite TV, telephone and air-conditioning.

Places to Eat

Most of the souvlaki outlets are on Kyrva and there is a swathe of restaurant along the promenade.

Taverna Babis (☎ 2842 024 048, Stratigou Samouil 68) Mains €3.50-5.50. Babis is one of the better tavernas along the waterfront. It has an enormous range of mezes dishes. Ask for *kakavia* (fish soup), or *steka* – a cream cheese made from curds.

Mezedokamomata (☎ 2842 028 286, Stratigou Samouil 74) Mezedes €1.70-3.80. Similar to Babis and only 50m farther along the street is this imaginative restaurant serving up a range of mezedes. If you like offal, ask for *splinandero*, or *omaties* rice and offal sausages.

Getting There & Away

In summer, there are six buses a day to Iraklio (2½ hours, €6.75) via Agios Nikolaos (one hour, €2.40), Gournia and Istron; eight to Makrygialos (30 minutes, €1.90); six to Sitia (1½ hours, €4.10) via Koutsounari (for camp sites); six to Myrtos (30 minutes, €1.20); and two a week to Ano Viannos (one hour, €2.50).

MYRTOS Μύρτος

postcode 722 00 • pop 433

Myrtos (**myr**-tos), on the coast 17km west of Ierapetra, is a sparkling village full of whitewashed houses with flower-filled balconies. It is a magnet for independent travellers, many of whom come only for a day or so, yet often stay on for a week or two. The village has a cosy, lived-in ambience where everyone seems to know each other.

You'll soon find your way around Myrtos which is built on a grid system. To get to the waterfront from the bus stop, facing south, take the road to the right passing Mertiza Studios on the right.

There is no post office, bank or OTE, but Aris Travel Agency (☎ 2842 051 017) on the main street has currency exchange. Internet access is available upstairs at Edem Cafe (☎ 2842 051 551), two blocks back from the waterfront.

Places to Stay

Hotel Myrtos (☎ 2842 051 227, fax 2842 051 215, W www.myrtoshotel.com) Singles/doubles with bathroom €17.50/23.50. This superior C-class place has large, well-kept rooms.

Cretan Rooms (☎ 2842 051 427) Doubles €26.50. These excellent traditional-styled rooms with balconies, fridges and shared kitchens are popular with independent travellers. They are prominently signposted from the village centre.

Nikos House (☎ 2842 051 116) 2-person /4-person apartments €35/40. Two blocks back from the waterfront, beneath the leaves of a large mulberry tree, are these large and comfortable apartments.

Big Blue (☎ 2842 051 094, fax 2842 051 121, e big-blue@ier.forthnet.gr) Singles/doubles with bathroom €23.50, 2-room apartments with 2 bathrooms & kitchenette €59. This nifty property is high up on the western edge of town.

Places to Eat

Myrtos Taverna (☎ 2842 051 227) Mains €3-6. Myrtos is popular with both locals and tourists both for its wide range of mezedes as well as for its vegetarian dishes. Rabbit in red wine sauce (€4.70) is recommended by the owner.

Taverna Akti (☎ 2842 051 584) Grills €4.40-6. Pleasant seafood dining and good

CRETE

food are Akti's attraction. Look for the 'daily specials' board to see what's on. Order octopus in red wine sauce (€6.50) if you see it.

Getting There & Away
There are six buses a day from Ierapetra to Myrtos (30 minutes, €1.20). The twice-weekly Ano Viannos–Ierapetra bus also passes through Myrtos.

MYRTOS TO ANO VIANNOS
Ano Viannos, 16km west of Myrtos, is a delightful village built on the southern flanks of Mt Dikti. The flower-decked **folklore museum** (☎ 2895 022 778, Ano Viannos; admission €1.50; open 10am-2pm daily) presents colourful costumes and traditional implements such as an olive press and key-making tools.

The village's 14th-century **Church of Agia Pelagia** (Ano Viannos; admission free; open 9am-8pm summer) is a tiny structure. The interior walls, covered with luscious frescoes by Nikoforos Fokas, are in need of restoration but can still be appreciated.

From Ano Viannos it's 13km south to the unspoilt and now contiguous villages of **Kastri** and **Keratokambos**, where there's a pleasant tree-lined beach.

The turn-off for **Arvi** (population 298) is 3km east of Ano Viannos. Arvi is bigger than Keratokambos, but only gets crowded during July and August. Hemmed in by cliffs, Arvi is a sun trap where bananas grow in abundance. The main street skirts a long sand-and-pebble beach. It's about a 15-minute walk inland to Moni Agiou Andoniou.

Places to Stay
Taverna & Rooms Lefkes (☎ 2895 022 719, Ano Viannos) Singles/doubles with bathroom €11.80/14.70. Ano Viannos' one domatia, this is 50m downhill from the large church. The rooms are over the taverna which has good Cretan specialities and a pleasant shady terrace.

Filoxenia Appartments (☎ 2895 051 371, Kastri) Double studios €35.30. The pickings in Kastri and Keratokambos are

much better than Ano Viannos. These two- to three-person studios, wrapped in a flower shaded garden, are beautiful. Equipped with kitchenette and fridge, they make an ideal mid-range accommodation option.

Komis Studios (☎ 2895 051 390, fax 2895 051 593, e pervass@otenet.gr, Keratokambos) Rooms €73.50. These stunningly decorated three-level apartments on the sea are built from stone, wood and stucco and outfitted with air-conditioning among other amenities. They are worth every cent.

Pension Gorgona (☎ 2895 071 353, Arvi) Doubles with bathroom €28. One of a few places to stay in Arvi, this pension on the main street has pleasant rooms.

Hotel Ariadne (☎ 2895 071 300, Arvi) Singles/doubles with bathroom €14.70/22. Farther west from Pension Gorgona, Hotel Ariadne has well-kept rooms.

Apartments Kyma (☎ 2895 071 344, Arvi) Apartments €23.50. At the eastern end of Arvi village you'll find these luxurious apartments.

Places to Eat
Morning Star Taverna (☎ 2895 051 209, Kastri) Mains €4.10-4.70. Grills and fish feature at this place in Kastri, with a mixed fish grill (€3.80) being a good bet. Tasty artichoke stew (€3) is a good choice for vegetarians.

Taverna Nikitas (☎ 2895 051 477, Keratokambos) Grills €4-5. By the sea in the centre of Keratokambos, this place offers delicious grills. Roast lamb and pork (€5) is recommended.

Restaurant Ariadne (☎ 2895 071 353, Arvi) Mains €3-4.50. Part of the hotel of the same name in Arvi, the restaurant here serves reasonable food with a mixture of grills and fish on offer.

Taverna Diktina (☎ 2895 071 249, Arvi) Mains around €4.50. This place features vegetarian food such as beans or stuffed tomatoes, both €3.

Getting There & Away
Public transport is poor. From Ano Viannos there are two buses weekly to Iraklio (2½

CRETE

hours, €6.20) and Ierapetra (one hour, €2.80) via Myrtos. There is no bus service to Keratokambos or Arvi, but in term time it may be possible to use the school buses from Ano Viannos.

You can easily drive the 8km coastal dirt road between Kastri-Keratokambos and Arvi.

Western Crete

The western part of Crete comprises the prefectures of Hania and Rethymno, which take their names from the old Venetian cities which are their capitals. The two towns rank as two of the region's main attractions, although the most famous is the spectacular Samaria Gorge. The south-coast towns of Paleohora and Plakias are popular resorts.

RETHYMNO Ρέθυμνο
postcode 741 00 • pop 23,355
Rethymno (**reh**-thim-no) is Crete's third-largest town. The main attraction is the old Venetian-Ottoman quarter that occupies the headland beneath the massive Venetian *fortezza* (fortress). The place is a maze of narrow streets, graceful wood-balconied houses and ornate Venetian monuments; several minarets add a touch of the Orient. The architectural similarities invite comparison with Hania, but Rethymno has a character of its own. An added attraction is a beach right in town.

The approaches to the town couldn't be less inviting. The modern town has sprawled out along the coast, dotted with big package hotels attracted by a reasonable beach.

History
The site of modern Rethymno has been occupied since Late Minoan times – the evidence can be found in the city's archaeological museum. In the 3rd and 4th centuries BC, the town was known as Rithymna, an autonomous state of sufficient stature to issue its own coinage. A scarcity of references to the city in Roman and Byzantine periods suggest it was of minor importance at that time.

The town prospered once more under the Venetians, who ruled from 1210 until 1645, when the Turks took over. Turkish forces held the town until 1897, when it was taken by Russia as part of the occupation of Crete by the Great Powers.

Rethymno became an artistic and intellectual centre after the arrival of a large number of refugees from Constantinople in 1923. The city has a campus of the University of Crete, bringing a student population that keeps the town alive outside the tourist season.

Orientation
Rethymno is a fairly compact city with most of the major sights and places to stay and eat within a small central area. It is hard to get lost in the city though the maze of narrow and often winding streets may make you think the opposite.

Ethnikis Andistasis which leads into the Old Town via the Puerto Guora is the main drag in central Rethymno, while Eleftheriou Venizelou running south of the town beach is the main beachside drag.

To the east of Eleftheriou Venizelou stretches a long sandy beach and an uninterrupted stretch of hotels, cafes, bars and restaurants. The most atmospheric places to stay and eat are all close to the centre.

Boats arrive conveniently within a couple of hundred metres of the old port, while buses arrive on the western side of the city. You can walk from both the port and bus station to the centre within minutes. If you are driving or biking into town from the expressway, there are three possible entry points.

Information
Tourist Offices Rethymno's municipal tourist office (☎ 2831 029 148) is on the beach side of El Venizelou, opposite the junction with Kalergi. It's open 8.30am to 2.30pm Monday to Friday. The tourist police (☎ 2831 028 156) occupy the same building and are open from 7am to 10pm every day.

CRETE

RETHYMNO

PLACES TO STAY
1. Rooms Lefteris
6. Hotel Fortezza
20. Olga's Pension
23. Garden House
26. Rooms for Rent Anda
29. Park Hotel
31. Rethymno Youth Hostel
34. Rent Rooms Sea Front

PLACES TO EAT
5. Taverna Pontios
8. Knosos

14. Taverna Kyria Maria
19. Stella's Kitchen
21. Taverna Old Town
22. Gounakis Taverna & Bar

THINGS TO SEE
2. Archaeological Museum
3. Entrance to Fortress
13. Loggia
16. Rimondi Fountain
24. Historical & Folk Art Museum
25. Nerantzes Mosque

30. Porto Guora
36. Kara Musa Pasa Mosque

OTHER
4. Notes
7. ANEK
9. Fortezza Disco
10. Rock Club Cafe
11. International Press Bookshop
12. Paradise Dive Centre
15. Galero
17. Motor Stavros
18. Ilias Spondidakis Bookshop

27. Katerina Karaoglani
28. I Melissa
32. Laundry Mat
33. The Happy Walker
35. Municipal Tourist Office; Tourist Police
37. National Mortgage Bank
38. Town Hall
39. OTE
40. Alpha Bank
41. National Bank of Greece
42. EOS
43. Post Office
44. Olympic Airways
45. Hospital
46. Bus Station

Money Banks are concentrated around the junction of Dimokratias and Pavlou Kountouriotou. The National Bank of Greece is on Dimokratias, on the far side of the square opposite the town hall. The Alpha Bank, at Pavlou Koundouriotou 29, and the National Mortgage Bank, next to the town hall, have 24-hour automatic exchange machines and ATMs.

Post & Communications The OTE is at Koundouriotou 28, and the post office is a block south at Moatsou 21. In summer there is a mobile post office about 200m south-east of the tourist office on El Venizelou. You can check your email at Galero (☎ 2831 054 345) on Plateia Rimini. It is open from very early to very late and charges €3.50 per hour.

Bookshops The International Press Bookshop (☎ 2831 024 111), Petihaki 15, stocks English novels, travel guides and history books. The Ilias Spondidakis bookshop (☎ 2831 054 307), Souliou 43, stocks novels in English, books about Greece, tapes of Greek music and has a small second-hand section.

Laundry The Laundry Mat self-service laundry (☎ 2831 056 196) at Tombazi 45, next door to the youth hostel, charges €7.50 for a wash and dry.

Things to See

Rethymno's 16th-century **fortress** (☎ 2831 028 101, Paleokastro Hill; admission €2.40; open 8am-8pm daily) is the site of the city's ancient acropolis. Within its massive walls once stood a great number of buildings, of which only a church and a mosque survive intact. The ramparts offer good views, while the site has lots of ruins to explore.

The **archaeological museum** (☎ 2831 029 975, Fortezza; admission €1.50; open 8.30am-3pm daily) is opposite the entrance to the fortress. The finds displayed here include an important coin collection. Rethymno has an excellent **Historical & Folk Art Museum** (☎ 2831 023 398, Vernardou 28–30; admission €3; open 9.30am-2.30pm Mon-Sat) which gives an excellent overview of the region's rural lifestyle with a collection of old clothes, baskets, weavings and farm tools.

Pride of place among the many vestiges of Venetian rule in the old quarter goes to the **Rimondi Fountain** with its spouting lion heads, and the 16th-century **loggia**.

At the southern end of Ethnikis Andistasis is the well-preserved **Porto Guora**, a remnant of the Venetian defensive wall. Turkish legacies in the old quarter include the **Kara Musa Pasa Mosque** near Plateia Iroön and the **Neradjes Mosque**, which was converted from a Franciscan church.

Activities

The **Happy Walker** (☎/fax 2831 052 920, ⓔ info@happywalker.nl, Ⓦ www.happywalker.nl, Tombazi 56) runs a varied program of mountain walks in the region. Most walks start in the early morning and finish with lunch and cost from about €20 onwards.

There is an **EOS** (☎ 2831 057 766, Dimokratias 12) in Rethymno.

The **Paradise Dive Centre** (☎ 2831 026 317, fax 2831 020 464, ⓔ pdcr@otenet.gr, El Venizelou 76) has activities and a PADI course for all grades of divers.

Special Events

Rethymno's main cultural event is the annual Renaissance Festival that runs during July and August. It features dance, drama and films as well as art exhibitions.

Some years there's a Wine Festival in mid-July held in the municipal park. Ask the tourist office for details.

Places to Stay – Budget

Elizabeth Camping (☎ 2831 028 694, fax 2831 050 401, Mysiria) Adult/tent €5/3.50. The nearest camping ground is near Mysiria Beach 3km east of Rethymno. The site has a taverna, snack bar and minimarket. There is a communal fridge, iced water 24 hours a day and free beach umbrellas and loungers. An Iraklio-bound bus can drop you at the site.

Rethymno Youth Hostel (☎ 2831 022 848, ⓔ manolis@yhrethymno.com, Ⓦ www.yhrethymno.com, Tombazi 41) Beds €5.30. The hostel is friendly and well run with free hot showers. Breakfast is available and there's a bar in the evening. There is no curfew and the place is open all year.

Rent Rooms Sea Front (☎ 2831 051 981, fax 2831 051 062, ⓔ elotia@ret.forthnet.gr, El Venizelou 45) Singles/doubles with bathroom €20.50/26.50. This is a delightful pension which has only six very clean studio/apartments. The front rooms can be noisy at night, but you are close to the beach.

Olga's Pension (☎ 2831 028 665, Souliou 57) Singles/studios €20.50/29.50. The friendly Olga's is tucked away on the touristy but colourful Souliou. A network of terraces, all bursting with greenery, connects a wide range of rooms, some with bath and sea views and others without.

Rooms Lefteris (☎ 2831 023 803, Kefalogianni 25–26) Singles/doubles with bathroom €23.50/29.50. All rooms are pleasant but the front rooms have stunning sea views although they can be noisy at night.

Rooms for Rent Anda (☎ 2831 023 479, Nikiforou Foka 33) Singles/doubles €27/33.

CRETE

This is a great choice if you have kids because it's just a short walk from Rethymno's municipal park. The prettily furnished rooms have private bathrooms but no other amenities, although the owner will gladly help you with anything you need.

Garden House (*☎ 2831 028 586, Nikiforou Foka 82*) Doubles/triples with bathroom €32.50/47. On a quiet street in Rethymno's Old Town, this is an impeccably maintained 600-year-old Venetian house retaining many of its original features including impressive doors and a gorgeous grape-arboured garden. The rooms are simple, comfortable and tasteful.

Places to Stay – Mid-Range
Park Hotel (*☎ 2831 029 958, Igoumenou Gavriil 9*) Singles/doubles with breakfast €32.50/41. The only missing ingredient here is an elevator to take you to rooms that are spread over two floors. The rooms are comfortable with air-con, TV, telephone, sound-proofing and balconies offering a view of the municipal park.

Hotel Fortezza (*☎ 2831 055 551, fax 2831 054 073, e mliodak@ret.forthnet.gr, Melissinou 16*) Singles/doubles with buffet breakfast €55.80/€70.50. Housed in a refurbished old building in the heart of the old town, these tastefully furnished rooms have TVs, telephones and air-con on demand.

Places to Eat
The waterfront along El Venizelou is lined with amazingly similar tourist restaurants staffed by fast-talking waiters desperately cajoling passers-by into eating at their establishments. The situation is much the same around the Venetian Harbour, except the setting is better and the prices higher.

To find cheaper food and a more authentic atmosphere, wander inland down the little side streets.

Stella's Kitchen (*☎ 2831 028 665, Souliou 55*) Breakfast €4.50-5.90. Open 8am-midnight daily. This tiny, homely spot on one of Rethymno's oldest streets serves up tasty snacks and a few meals. It's a good bet for breakfast as well.

Taverna Kyria Maria (*☎ 2831 029 078, Moshovitou 20*) Cretan dishes €2.40-6.50. Open 8am-1am daily. Wander down the little side streets to Kyria Maria, behind the Rimondi Fountain. This cosy, traditional taverna has outdoor seating under a leafy trellis with twittering birds.

Taverna Old Town (*☎ 2831 026 436, Vernardou 31*) 2-person set menus €12.30-15.30. Open noon-3pm & 7pm-midnight daily. The traditional Cretan food is well prepared and there are good-value set-price menus with wine.

Taverna Pontios (*☎ 2831 057 624, Melissinou 34*) Mains €2.70-4.50. Open noon-2.30pm & 6pm-midnight daily. This place proves once again that some of the best Cretan food comes from unassuming places. A convivial group of locals come here for the delicious cheese-stuffed calamari, among other dishes.

Gounakis Taverna (*☎ 2831 028 816, Koroneou 6*) Mains €3.50-5.60. This place is worth visiting for its food as much as for its music (see Entertainment).

Knosos (*☎ 2831 025 582, Limani*) 2-person fish platter €35.30. Of all the harbourside restaurants, only at the diminutive Knosos can you guarantee fish freshness and honest service at a reasonable price. The most popular fish dish is *tsipoura* (bream, €29.50 per kilogram).

Entertainment
Gounakis Bar (*☎ 2831 028 816, Koroneou 6*) Open 8pm-1am. If you love drinking cheap wine and listening to live Cretan folk music, this is the place to go. There's music and impromptu dancing most nights.

Rock Club Cafe (*☎ 2831 031 047, Petihaki 8*) Open 9pm-dawn. RCC is having its moment in the sun as Rethymno's trendiest hang-out. The crowd of young professionals that fills the club nightly may move on soon but right now this is where the action is.

Fortezza Disco (*Nearhou 20*) Open 11pm-dawn. This is the town's showpiece disco. It's big and flashy with three bars, a laser show and a well-groomed international crowd that starts drifting in around midnight.

Notes (☎ 2831 029 785, Himaras 27) Open 0am-midnight. Notes, a quiet bar-cafe, was pened by a musician who has an excellent election of Greek music. It's a good place to scape the crowds along El Venizelou.

Shopping

Katerina Karaoglani (☎ 2831 024 301, Katehaki 4) Open 10am-11pm Mon-Sat. Friendly Katerina Karaoglani makes her pottery in the store. You'll find the standard blue-glazed Cretan ceramics of a better quality than the tourist shops deliver.

I Melissa (☎ 2831 029 601, Ethnikis Antistasis 23) Open 9am-8pm Mon-Sat. In addition to hand-made icons, Melissa sells candles, incense, oil lamps and other odorous objects.

Getting There & Away

Bus There are numerous services to both Hania (one hour, €5.30) and Iraklio (1½ hours, €5.60). There's a bus in each direction every half-hour in summer, every hour in winter. In summer there are also four buses a day to Plakias (one hour, €3.10), four to Agia Galini (1½ hours, €4.25), three to Moni Arkadiou (30 minutes, €1.80), one to Omalos (two hours, €8.50) and two to Preveli (€2.80). The morning bus to Plakias continues to Hora Sfakion (two hours, €4.70). Services to these destinations are greatly reduced in winter.

Ferry ANEK (☎ 2831 029 221, fax 2831 055 519, W www.anek.gr, Arkadiou 250) operates a daily ferry between Rethymno and Piraeus (10 hours, €22) leaving Rethymno and Piraeus at 7.30pm. Tickets are available from the company's office.

Getting Around

Most of the car-rental firms are near Plateia Iroön. Motor Stavros (☎ 2831 022 858), Paleologou 14, has a wide range of motorcycles and also rents bicycles.

AROUND RETHYMNO

Moni Arkadiou Μονή Αρκαδίου
Surrounded by attractive hill country, this 16th-century monastery *(Arkadi; monastery*

admission free, small museum €2; open 8am-1pm & 3.30pm-8pm daily)* is 23km south-east of Rethymno. The most impressive of the buildings is the Venetian baroque church. Its striking facade, which used to feature on the old 100 dr note, has eight slender Corinthian columns and an ornate triple-belled tower.

In November 1866 the Turks sent massive forces to quell insurrections which were gathering momentum throughout the island. Hundreds of men, women and children who had fled their villages used the monastery as a safe haven. When 2000 Turkish soldiers attacked the building, rather than surrender, the Cretans set light to a store of gunpowder. The explosion killed everyone, Turks included, except one small girl, who lived to a ripe old age in a village nearby. Busts of the woman, and the abbot who lit the gun powder, stand outside the monastery.

There are buses from Rethymno to the monastery (30 minutes, €1.80) at 6am, 10.30am and 2.30pm, returning at 7am, noon and 4pm.

Amari Valley Κοιλάδα Αμαρίου
If you have your own transport you can explore the enchanting Amari Valley, southeast of Rethymno, between Mts Ida and Kedros. The region harbours around 40 well-watered, unspoilt villages set amid olive groves and almond and cherry trees.

The valley begins at the picturesque village of **Apostoli**, 25km south-east of Rethymno. The turn-off for Apostoli is on the coast 3km east of Rethymno. The road forks at Apostoli and then joins up again 38km to the south, making it possible to do a circular drive around the valley. Alternatively, you can continue south to Agia Galini.

There is an EOS refuge on **Mt Ida**, a 10km walk from the small village of **Kouroutes**, 5km south of Fourfouras. For information contact the Rethymno EOS (see Activities in the Rethymno section).

RETHYMNO TO SPILI

Heading south from Rethymno, there is a turn-off to the right to the Late-Minoan cemetery of **Armeni** 2km before the modern village of Armeni. The main road south continues through woodland, which gradually gives way to a bare and dramatic landscape. After 18km there is a turn-off to the right for **Selia** and **Frangokastello** and, a little beyond, another turn-off for Plakias (this turn-off is referred to on timetables as the Koxare junction or Bale). The main road continues for 9km to Spili.

SPILI Σπήλι
postcode 740 53 • pop 710
Spili is a gorgeous mountain town with cobbled streets, rustic houses and plane trees. Its centrepiece is a unique Venetian fountain which spurts water from 19 lion heads. Tourist buses hurtle through but Spili deserves an overnight stay.

The post office and bank are on the main street. The huge building at the northern end of town is an ecclesiastic conference centre. The OTE is up a side street, north of the central square. The bus stop is just south of the square. Spili is on the Rethymno–Agia Galini bus route.

Places to Stay & Eat
Green Hotel (☎ *2832 022 225*) Doubles with bathroom €19. Across from the police station on the main street, this is a homely place practically buried under plants and vines that also fill the interior. Rooms are attractive.

Heracles Rooms (☎ *2832 022 111, fax 2832 022 411*) Singles/doubles with bathroom €23.50/29.50. Signposted from the main road are these excellent rooms which are sparkling and beautifully furnished.

Costas Inn (☎ *2832 022 040, fax 2832 022 043*) Doubles/triples with bathroom €35.30/44. Farther along from Heracles, on the left, Costas Inn has well-kept, ornate rooms with satellite TV, radio and the use of a washing machine.

Taverna Costas (☎ *2832 022 040*) Cretan dishes €2.50-4.50. Under the inn of the same name, this popular eatery is a very good choice. Food products including wine are organic. Try the traditional sweets for dessert.

Taverna Stratidakis (☎ *2832 022 006*) Mayirefta €2.5-4.70. Opposite Costas Inn this place serves excellent traditional Greek dishes. The specials of the day are in pots at the back of the room.

AROUND SPILI
Most people come to the alluring little village of **Patsos** to visit the nearby **Church of Agios Antonios** in a cave above a picturesque gorge. You can drive here from Rethymno, or you can walk from Spili along a scenic 10km dirt track.

To reach the track, walk along 28 Oktovriou, passing the lion fountain on your right. Turn right onto Thermopylon and ascend to the Spili-Gerakari road. Turn right here and eventually you will come to a sign for Gerakari. Take the dirt track to the left, and at the fork bear right. At the crossroads turn right, and continue on the main track for about one hour to a T-junction on the outskirts of Patsos. Turn left to get to the cave.

Heading west of Spili then south towards the coast at Plakias you will pass through the dramatic **Kourtaliotis Gorge** through which the river Megalopotamos rumbles on its way to the sea at **Preveli Beach**. About 8km before Plakias there is a turn-off to the left for Preveli Beach and **Moni Preveli** (see the Around Plakias section later in this chapter).

PLAKIAS Πλακιάς
postcode 740 60 • pop 139
The south-coast town of Plakias was once a tranquil fishing village before it became a retreat for adventurous backpackers. Plakias offers a good range of independent accommodation, some pretty decent eating options, a brace of good regional walks, a large sandy beach and enough nightlife to keep the nightbirds singing until dawn. All in all, Plakias is one of the better choices for independent travellers looking for a hang-out in Crete.

Orientation & Information
It's easy to find your way around Plakias. One street skirts the beach and another runs

arallel to it one block back. The bus stop
s at the middle of the waterfront. The 30-
inute path to Myrthios begins just before
e youth hostel.

Plakias doesn't have a bank, but Monza
ravel Agency (☎ 2832 031 882, fax 2832
31 883), near the bus stop, offers currency
xchange. From June to August a mobile
ost office is on the waterfront. Check your
mail at the one PC in the Ostraco Bar
☎ 2832 031 710) for €4.50 per hour.

Places to Stay

Camping Apollonia (☎ 2832 031 318)
Adult/tent €3.80/2.20. On the right of the
ain approach road to Plakias, this place
as a restaurant, minimarket, bar and swim-
ing pool. While the site is at least shaded,
all looks rather scruffy and run-down.

Youth Hostel Plakias (☎ 2832 032 118,
info@yhplakias.com, www.yhplakias
om) Dorm beds €6. Open 1 Apr-end Oct.
or independent travellers this is *the* place
stay in Plakias. Manager Chris from the
K has created a very packie-friendly place
ith spotless dorms, green lawns, volley-
all court, and Internet access. Partying is
uch in evidence here, helped along by
hris' eclectic music collection. Follow the
gns from the waterfront. The hostel is
cked away in the olive trees behind the
wn, a 10-minute walk from the bus stop.
There is a wide range of independent do-
atia on offer. Most are signposted on a
ommunal wooden sign board next to
Monza Travel. Try these for starters.

Pension Kyriakos (☎ 2832 031 307, fax
832 031 631) Doubles €20.50. 'If you
on't like raki, stay away from here', says
wner Kyriakos. His small, clean rooms
ave only coffee-making facilities, but that
made up for by ample raki, supplied by
e gregarious owner.

Ippokambos (☎ 2832 031 525) Studios
€23.50. The large, clean rooms here have
ower-bedecked balconies, a fridge but no
ooking facilities other than to make coffee
r tea.

Morfeas Rent Rooms (☎/fax 2832 031
83) Singles/doubles with bathroom €20.50/
9.50. Close to the bus stop and above a
supermarket, Morfeas has light, airy and attractively furnished rooms with fridge,
phone and air-con.

Pension Thetis (☎ 2832 031 430, fax
2832 031 987) Double studios €29.50.
Thetis is a very pleasant, family-oriented
set of studios. Rooms have fridge and cooking facilities Relax in the cool and shady
garden.

Castello (☎/fax 2832 031 112) Double
studios €35.30. It is the relaxed owner
Christos and his cool and shady garden that
makes this place a happy haven. All rooms
are cool, clean and fridge-equipped and
have cooking facilities.

Places to Eat

Nikos Souvlaki (☎ 2832 031 921) All-in
grill €4.70. Popular with packies and just
inland from Monza Travel Agency, this is a
good souvlaki place, where a monster
mixed grill of gyros, souvlaki, sausage,
hamburger and chips won't break the bank.

Taverna Sofia (☎ 2832 031 333) Cretan
specials €3-5.90. In business since 1969,
Sofia's is a solid choice. Check the meals
on display from the trays in the window.
The jovial gastronome owner recommends
lamb in yogurt (€5.90).

Siroko (☎ 2832 032 055) Mains €3.50-
7. On the far west side of the village, Siroko
is a family-run place popular with travellers. Try the lamb in egg and lemon sauce
(€5.60) or a mixed seafood grill (€7). Vegetarians are also catered for.

Getting There & Away

Plakias has good bus connections in summer, but virtually none in winter. A
timetable is displayed at the bus stop. Summer services include four buses a day to
Rethymno (one hour, €3.10) and one to
Hora Sfakion. In winter there are three
buses a day to Rethymno, two at weekends.
It's possible to get to Agia Galini from
Plakias by catching a Rethymno bus to the
Koxare junction (referred to as Bale on
timetables) and waiting for a bus to Agia
Galini. This works best with the 11.30pm
bus from Plakias, linking with the 12.45pm
service from Rethymno to Agia Galini.

CRETE

Getting Around

Cars Allianthos (☎ 2832 031 851) is a reliable car-rental outlet. Odyssia (☎ 2832 031 596), on the waterfront, has a large range of motorcycles and mountain bikes available for hire.

AROUND PLAKIAS
Myrthios Μύρθιος

This pleasant village is perched on a hillside overlooking Plakias and the surrounding coast. Apart from taking in the views, the main activity is walking, which you'll be doing a lot of unless you have your own transport.

Niki's Studios & Rooms (☎ 2832 031 593) Singles/doubles with bathroom €13.20/19, 2-person studios €26.50. There are a few domatia in the village, including this comfortable place just below Restaurant Panorama.

Restaurant Panorama (☎ 2832 032 077) Mains €4-5. This place lives up to its name; it has great views. It also does good food, including vegetarian dishes and delicious desserts.

Moni Preveli Μονή Πρέβελη

Standing in splendid isolation high above the Libyan Sea, 14km east of Plakias, is the well-maintained Moni Preveli (☎ 2832 031 246, Preveli; admission €2; open 8am-7pm daily mid-Mar–May, 8am-1.30pm & 3.30pm-7.30pm daily June-Oct). Like most of Crete's monasteries, it played a significant role in the islanders' rebellion against Turkish rule. It became a centre of resistance during 1866, causing the Turks to set fire to it and destroy surrounding crops. After the Battle of Crete in 1941, many Allied soldiers were sheltered here by Abbot Agathangelos before their evacuation to Egypt. In retaliation the Germans plundered the monastery. The monastery's **museum** contains a candelabra presented by grateful British soldiers after the war.

From the road to the monastery, a road leads downhill to a large car park from where a steep foot track leads down to Preveli Beach.

From June through August there are two buses daily from Rethymno to Moni Preveli.

Beaches

Preveli Beach – known officially as Paralia Finikodasous (Palm Beach) – at the mouth of the Kourtaliotis Gorge, is one of Crete's most photographed and popular beaches. The river Megalopotamos meets the back end of the beach before it conveniently loops around its assorted bathers and empties into the Libyan Sea. The beach is fringed with oleander bushes and palm trees and used to be popular with freelance campers before camping was officially outlawed.

A steep path leads down to it from a large car park below Moni Preveli, or you can bike to within several hundred metres of the beach by following a signposted 5km rough dirt road from a stone bridge to the left just off the Moni Preveli main road. You can also get to Preveli Beach from Plakias by boat from June through August for €8.80 return, or by taxi boat from Agia Galini for €17.50 return.

Between Plakias and Preveli Beach there are several secluded **coves** popular with freelance campers and nudists. Some are within walking distance of Plakias, via **Damnoni Beach**. To reach them ascend the path behind Plakias Bay Hotel. Just before the track starts to descend turn right into an olive grove. At the first T-junction turn left and at the second turn right. Where six tracks meet, take the one signposted to the beach. Walk to the end of Damnoni Beach and take the track to the right, which passes above the coves. Damnoni Beach itself is pleasant out of high season, despite being dominated by the giant Hapimag tourist complex.

AGIA GALINI Αγία Γαλήνη
postcode 740 56 • pop 1009

Agia Galini (ah-**yee**-ah ga-**lee**-nee) is another picturesque erstwhile fishing village which really has gone down the tubes due to an overdose of tourism. Hemmed in against the sea by large sandstone cliffs and phalanxes of hotels and domatia, Agia Galini is rather claustrophobic – an ambience which is not ameliorated by an ugly, cement-block-littered harbour. Still, it does boast 340 days of sunshine a year, and some places remain open out of season. It's a convenient base from which to visit Phaestos and Agia Triada, and although the town beach is mediocre, there are boats to better beaches.

Orientation & Information
The bus station is at the top of Eleftheriou Venizelou, which is a continuation of the approach road. The central square, overlooking the harbour, is downhill from the bus station. You'll walk past the post office on the way and the OTE is on the square. There is no bank but there are lots of travel agencies with currency exchange. Check your email at Cosmos Internet (☎ 2832 091 262, e damvax@yahoo .com). It's open from 9am until late and charges €3.50 per hour.

Places to Stay
Agia Galini Camping (☎ 2832 091 386) Adult/tent €3.80/2.30. This camping ground is next to the beach, 2.5km east of the town. It is signposted from the Iraklio– Agia Galini road. The site is well shaded and has a restaurant, snack bar and minimarket.

Candia Rooms (☎ 2832 091 203) Singles/ doubles with bathroom €14.70/17.60. This place has very basic rooms. To get there take the first left opposite the post office.

Areti (☎ 2832 091 240) Singles/doubles with bathroom & balcony €17.60/29.50. This place with pleasant rooms is on the road to town.

Hotel Selena (☎ 2832 091 273) Singles/ doubles with bathroom €29.50/35.30. Open all year. The rooms here are D class. To reach the hotel, walk downhill from the bus station, turn left after the post office, take the second turning right and turn left at the steps.

Stohos Rooms (☎ 2832 091 433) 2-person/ 3-person studios €36/39. This is the only accommodation on the beach.

Places to Eat
Restaurant Megalonisos Mains €2.40-3.80. Open 9am-midnight daily. Near the bus stop, this is one of the town's cheapest restaurants, if not the friendliest.

Medousa Taverna (☎ 2832 091 487) Grills €4.50-5.50. Open noon-2am daily Apr-Oct. In the town centre, this taverna is owned by a German/Greek couple and presents a menu of specialities from both countries.

Onar (☎ 2832 091 288) Mezedes €1.70-5.30. Open 8am-1am daily Mar-Nov. Onar (meaning 'dream' in Homeric Greek) overlooks the harbour and is a good place to come for breakfast, mezedes, or cocktails.

Madame Hortense (☎ 2832 091 215) Mains €6.20-11.80. Open 11am-midnight daily. The most elaborate restaurant-bar in town is on the top floor of the three-level Zorbas complex on the harbour. Cuisine is Greek Mediterranean, with a touch of the East. Try chicken in curry sauce (€6.50).

Getting There & Away
Bus The story is the same as at the other beach resorts: heaps of buses in summer, skeletal services in winter. In peak season there are seven buses a day to Iraklio (2½ hours, €4.90), four to Rethymno (1½ hours, €4.25), six to Matala (45 minutes, €2) and six to Phaestos (40 minutes, €1.40). You can get to Plakias by taking a Rethymno-bound bus and changing at Koxare (Bale).

Taxi Boat In summer there are daily taxi boats from the harbour to the beaches of Agios Giorgios, Agios Pavlos and Preveli (Palm Beach). These beaches, which are west of Agia Galini, are difficult to get to by land. Both are less crowded than, and far superior to, the Agia Galini beach. Departures are between 9.30am and 10.30am.

AROUND AGIA GALINI
The outstanding **Museum of Cretan Ethnology** (☎ 2892 091 112, Vori; admission €3; open 9am-3pm Mon-Fri Nov-Mar, 10am-6pm Apr-Oct) is in the pleasant, unspoilt village of Vori, 14km from Agia

CRETE

HANIA

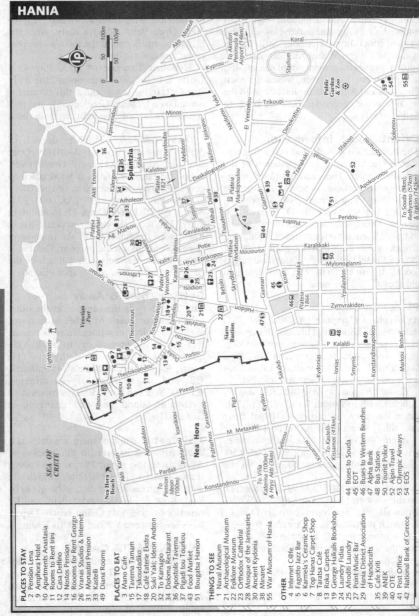

PLACES TO STAY
2 Pension Lena
9 Amphora Hotel
10 Apartments Anastasia
11 Rooms to Rent Irini
12 Casa Delfino
14 Nostos Pension
16 Roooms for Rent George
26 Vranas Studios & Internet
31 Monastiri Pension
33 Kastelli
49 Diana Rooms

PLACES TO EAT
3 Mano Cafe
15 Taverna Tamam
17 Tsikoudadiko
18 Café Eaterie Ekstra
20 Suki Yaki; Ideon Andron
32 To Karnagio
34 Doloma Restaurant
36 Apostolis Taverna
37 Pigadi tou Tourkou
43 Food Market
51 Bougatsa Hanion

THINGS TO SEE
1 Naval Museum
21 Archaeological Museum
22 Folklore Museum
23 Orthodox Cathedral
28 Mosque of the Janissaries
30 Ancient Kydonia
38 Minaret
55 War Museum of Hania

OTHER
4 Internet C@fe
5 Fagotto Jazz Bar
6 Karmela's Ceramic Shop
7 Top Hanas Carpet Shop
8 Taratsa Café
13 Roka Carpets
19 George Halkalis Bookshop
24 Laundry Fidias
25 Afroditi Laundry
27 Point Music Bar
29 Hania District Association
   of Handicrafts
35 Cafe Kriti
39 ANEK
40 OTE
41 Post Office
42 National Bank of Greece
44 Buses to Souda
45 EOT
46 Buses to Western Beaches
47 Alpha Bank
48 Bus Station
50 Tourist Police
52 Alpin Travel
53 Olympic Airways
54 EOS

Galini, just north of the main Agia Galini–Iraklio road.

HANIA Χανιά
ostcode 731 00 • pop 65,000

Hania (hahn-**yah**) is Crete's second city and former capital. The beautiful, crumbling Venetian quarter of Hania that surrounds the Old Harbour is one of Crete's best attractions. A lot of money has been spent on restoring the old buildings. Some of them have been converted into very fine accommodation while others now house chic restaurants, bars and shops.

The Hania district gets a lot of package tourists, but most of them stick to the beach developments that stretch out endlessly to the west. Even in a town this size many hotels and restaurants are closed from November to April.

Hania is a main transit point for trekkers going to the Samaria Gorge.

History
Hania is the site of the Minoan settlement of Kydonia, which was centred on the hill to the east of the harbour. Little excavation work has been done, but the finding of clay tablets with Linear B script has led archaeologists to believe that Kydonia was both a palace site and an important town.

Kydonia met the same fiery fate as most other Minoan settlements in 1450 BC, but soon re-emerged as a force. It was a flourishing city-state during Hellenistic times and continued to prosper under Roman and Byzantine rule.

The city became Venetian at the beginning of the 13th century, and the name was changed to La Canea. The Venetians spent a lot of time constructing massive fortifications to protect the city from marauding pirates and invading Turks. This did not prove very effective against the latter, who took Hania in 1645 after a two-month siege.

The Great Powers made Hania the island capital in 1898 and it remained so until 1971, when the administration was transferred to Iraklio.

Hania was heavily bombed during WWII, but enough of the old town survives

for it to be regarded as Crete's most beautiful city.

Orientation
The town's bus station is on Kydonias, two blocks south-west of Plateia 1866, one of the city's main squares. From Plateia 1866 to the Old Harbour is a short walk north down Halidon.

The main hotel area is to the left as you face the harbour, where Akti Koundourioti leads around to the old fortress on the headland. The headland separates the Venetian port from the crowded town beach in the quarter called Nea Hora.

Zambeliou, which dissects Halidon just before the harbour, was once the town's main thoroughfare. It's a narrow, winding street, lined with craft shops, hotels and tavernas.

Information
Tourist Offices Hania's EOT (☎ 2821 092 943, fax 2821 092 624) is at Kriari 40, close to Plateia 1866. It is well organised and considerably more helpful than most. Opening hours are 7.30am to 2.30pm weekdays. The tourist police (☎ 2821 073 333) are at Kudonias 29 and are open the same hours.

Money The National Bank of Greece on the corner of Tzanakaki and Giannari and the Alpha Bank at the junction of Halidon and Sakalidi have 24-hour automatic exchange machines. There are numerous places to change money outside banking hours. Most are willing to negotiate the amount of commission, so check around.

Post & Communications The central post office is at Tzanakaki 3, open 7.30am to 8pm Monday to Friday, and 7.30am to 2pm Saturday. The OTE is next door at Tzanakaki 5, open 7.30am to 10pm daily. Internet access is available at Vranas Studios (☎ 2821 058 618), on Agion Deka, open 9am to 2am, or at Internet C@fe (☎ 2821 073 300) on Theotokopoulou 53; open 8am-3am; €3.50 per hour.

Bookshops The George Haïkalis Bookshop (☎ 2821 042 197), situated on Plateia

CRETE

Venizelou, sells English-language newspapers, books and maps.

Laundry Both Laundry Fidias at Sarpaki 6 and the Afroditi Laundry at Agion Deka 18 charge €5.90 for a wash and dry.

Left Luggage Luggage can be stored at the bus station for €1.50 per day.

Museums

Housed in the 16th-century Venetian Church of San Francisco is the **archaeological museum** (☎ 2821 090 334, Halidon 21; admission €1.50; open 8am-4.30pm Tues-Sun). The Turkish fountain in the grounds is a relic from the building's days as a mosque.

The museum houses a well-displayed collection of finds from western Crete dating from the Neolithic to the Roman era. Exhibits include statues, pottery, coins, jewellery, three splendid floor mosaics and some impressive painted sarcophagi from the Late-Minoan cemetery of Armeni.

The **naval museum** (☎ 2821 091 875; Akti Koundourioti; admission €1.80; open 10am-4pm daily) has an interesting collection of model ships, naval instruments, paintings and photographs. It is housed in the fortress on the headland overlooking the Venetian port.

Hania has an interesting **folklore museum** (☎ 2821 090 816, Halidon 46B; admission €1.50; open 9am-3pm & 6pm-9pm Mon-Fri). There is also the new **War Museum of Hania** (Tzanakaki; admission free; open 9am-1pm Tues-Sat).

Other Attractions

The area to the east of the Old Harbour, between Akti Tombazi and Karaoli Dimitriou, is the site of **ancient Kydonia**.

The search for Minoan remains began in the early 1960s and excavation work continues sporadically. The site can be seen at the junction of Kanevaro and Kandanoleu, and many of the finds are on display in the archaeological museum.

Kydonia has been remodelled by a succession of occupiers. After ejecting the Arabs, the Byzantines set about building their *kastelli* (castle) on the same site, on top of the old walls in some places and using the same materials. It was here, too, that the Venetians first settled. Modern Kanevaro was the Corso of their city. It was this part of town that bore the brunt of the bombing in WWII.

The massive **fortifications** built by the Venetians to protect their city remain impressive today. The best-preserved section is the western wall, running from the fortezza to the **Siavo Bastion**. It was part of a defensive system begun in 1538 by engineer Michele Sanmichele, who also designed Iraklio's defences.

The **lighthouse** at the entrance to the harbour is the most visible of the Venetian monuments. It looks in need of tender loving care these days, but the 30-minute walk around the sea wall to get there is worth it.

You can escape the crowds of the Venetian quarter by taking a stroll around the **Splantzia quarter** – a delightful tangle of narrow streets and little plateies.

Whether you are self-catering or not you should at least feast your eyes on Hania's magnificent covered **food market**. It makes all other food markets look like stalls at a church bazaar. Unfortunately, the central bastion of the city wall had to be demolished to make way for this fine cruciform creation, built in 1911.

Activities

Alpin Travel (☎ 2821 053 309, Boniali 11–19; open 9am-2pm Mon-Fri & sometimes after 7pm) offers many trekking programs. The owner, George Andonakakis, helps run the **EOS** (☎ 2821 044 647, Tzanakaki 90) and is the guy to talk to about serious climbing in the Lefka Ori. George can provide information on Greece's mountain refuges, the E4 trail, and climbing and trekking in Crete in general.

Trekking Plan (☎ 2821 060 861), in Agia Marina, on the main road next to Santa Marina Hotel, offers treks (around €23.50) to the Agia Irini Gorge and climbs of Mt Gingilos, among other destinations. It also offers a full program of mountain-bike ours (from €26.50) at varying levels of difficulty.

Children's Activities

If your five-year-old has lost interest in Venetian architecture before the end of the first street, head for the **public garden** between Tzanakaki and Dimokratias. There's plenty to occupy children here, including a playground, a small zoo with a resident krikri (the Cretan wild goat) and a children's resource centre that has a small selection of books in English.

Organised Tours

Tony Fennymore (☎ 2821 087 139, mobile 69-7253 7055, e FennysCrete@hotmail com, w www.fennyscrete.ws) 2hr walks €10.30. This historian is a wealth of information about Hania's history and culture. From April to July and September to October his two-hour walking tours begin at the 'Hand' monument on Plateia Talo at the bottom of Theotokopoulou. He also runs various guided minibus tours around the region. His witty and indispensable walking guide *Fenny's Hania* (€7.40) is available at Roka Carpets (see Shopping).

Places to Stay – Budget

Hania Camping (☎ 2821 031 138, fax 2821 033 371, Hrysi Akti) Adult/tent €4.40/3.20. This facility, 3km west of town on the beach, is the nearest camping ground to Hania. It is shaded and has a restaurant, bar and minimarket. Take a Kalamaki Beach bus (every 20 minutes) from the south-east corner of Plateia 1866 and ask to be let off there.

The most interesting accommodation in town is around the Venetian port, but bear in mind it's a noisy area with numerous music bars. If you get a room in the back you'll have a better shot at a good night's sleep but you may swelter in the summer heat without the harbour breeze.

Rooms for Rent George (☎ 2821 088 715, Zambeliou 30) Singles/doubles €14.70/20.50. If it's character you're after, you can't do better than this 600-year-old house dotted with antique furniture.

Diana Rooms (☎ 2821 097 888, P Kalaïdi 33) Singles/doubles with bathroom €14.70/20.50. If you want to hop straight out of bed and onto an early morning bus bound for the Samaria Gorge, the best rooms around the bus station are here. They are light, airy and clean.

Monastiri Pension (☎ 2821 054 776, Ag Markou 18) Doubles €32.50. This pension has a great setting right next to the ruins of the Moni Santa Maria de Miracolioco in the heart of the old kastelli. Rooms are fair value; they're simple with shared bathrooms but some have a sea view. There's a convenient communal kitchen for preparing meals.

Pension Lena (☎ 2821 086 860, e lenachania@hotmail.com, Ritsou 3) Singles/doubles €26.50/32.50. This friendly pension is in an old Turkish building. There is a common kitchen for guests and owner Lena from Hamburg makes guests feel very welcome.

Rooms to Rent Irini (☎ 2821 093 909, Theotokopoulou 9) Doubles with bathroom €35.30. Irini has clean, simply furnished rooms.

Apartments Anastasia (☎ 2821 088 001, fax 2821 046 582, Theotokopoulou 21) Studios €38.20. These are stylish, well-equipped studios.

Kastelli (☎ 2821 057 057, fax 2821 045 314, Kanevaro 39) Singles/doubles €26.50/29.50, apartments €47-58.70 depending on size. At the quieter, eastern end of the harbour, Kastelli has renovated apartments with high ceilings, white walls and pine floors. There's no TV or telephone, but some rooms have attractive views.

Places to Stay – Mid-Range

Most places in this category are renovated Venetian houses, and there are some very stylish ones about.

Nostos Pension (☎ 2821 094 740, fax 2821 094 743, Zambeliou 42–46) Singles/doubles with bathroom €41/64.50. Mixing Venetian style and modern fixtures, this is a 600-year-old building which has been modelled into classy split-level rooms/units, all with kitchens. Try to get a room in front for the harbour view.

CRETE

Vranas Studios *(☎/fax 2821 058 618, Agion Deka 10)* Studios €44 in Aug. This place (at which prices are discounted by at least 40% outside August) is on a lively pedestrian street and has spacious, immaculately maintained studios which come with kitchenettes. All the rooms have polished wooden floors, balconies, TV and telephones and they can provide air-conditioning for a supplement.

Places to Stay – Top End
Amphora Hotel *(☎ 2821 093 224, fax 2821 093 226, e reception@amphora.gr, w www .amphora.gr, Parodos Theotoko-poulou 20)* Singles/doubles with buffet breakfast €60/85. This is Hania's most historically evocative hotel. It is located in an immaculately restored Venetian mansion with rooms around a courtyard. There's no elevator and no air-con but the rooms are elegantly decorated and some have views of the harbour. Front rooms can be noisy in the summer.

Casa Delfino *(☎ 2821 093 098, fax 2821 096 500, e casadel@cha.forthnet.gr, Theofanous 7)* Doubles/apartments with buffet breakfast €117/205. This modernised 17th-century mansion features a splendid courtyard of traditionally patterned cobblestones and 19 individually decorated suites. All have air-con, satellite TV, telephones, hair dryers, minibars and safes.

Places to Eat – Budget
The two restaurants in the *food market* are good places to seek out traditional cuisine. Their prices are almost identical. You can get a solid chunk of swordfish with chips for €4.50. More adventurous eaters can tuck into a bowl of garlic-laden snail and potato casserole for €3.80.

Doloma Restaurant *(☎ 2821 051 196, Kalergon 8)* Mayirefta €3-4.70. Open 7.30pm-1am Mon-Sat. You'll find very similar fare to the market restaurants here. This place is a great favourite with students from the nearby university.

Bougatsa Hanion *(☎ 2821 043 978, Apokoronou 37)* For a treat try the excellent *bougatsa tyri* (filo pastry filled with local myzithra cheese; €1.80) which come sprinkled with a little sugar.

Mano Cafe *(☎ 2821 072 265, Theo tokopoulou 62)* Continental breakfast €3.70. Open 8am-midnight daily. This is a tiny place and has very little seating, but of fers good-value breakfasts and snacks.

Places to Eat – Mid-Range
The port is the place to go for seafood. The prices are not cheap especially considering most of the seafood is frozen, but the setting is great. There are some chic places in the streets behind the port.

Apostolis Taverna *(☎ 2821 045 470, Enosis 6)* 2-person seafood platter €23.40. Open noon-midnight daily. This taverna is a favourite with locals.

Taverna Tamam *(☎ 2821 058 639, Zam beliou 49)* Vegetarian specials €3-5.50. Open 1pm-12.30am daily. An old Turkish *hammam* (bathhouse) here has been converted into this taverna, where you'll find tasty soups and a good range of well-prepared main dishes.

Cafe Eaterie Ekstra *(☎ 2821 075 725, Zambeliou 8)* Vegetarian dishes €3.50-4.20. This place offers a choice of Greek and international dishes. There are se menus and many vegetarian dishes.

Tsikoudadiko *(☎ 2821 072 873, Zambe liou 31)* Cretan specials €4-7.50. Tsik oudadiko offers a good mixed plate of mezedes in a splendid old plant-filled courtyard.

Pigadi tou Tourkou *(☎ 2821 054 547, Sarpaki 1–3)* Mains €5.80-8. Open 7pm-midnight Wed-Mon. This is in the heart of the old Turkish residential district of Splantzia and has a wide range of Middle Eastern dishes, as well as occasional live music.

Suki Yaki *(☎ 2821 074 264, Halidon 28)* 2-person set menu €25-35. Open noon-midnight daily. Entered through an archway, this is a Chinese restaurant run by a Thai family. The result is a large Chinese menu supported by a small selection of Tha favourites.

To Karnagio *(☎ 2821 053 336, Plateia Katehaki 8)* Cretan specialities €3.50-7.60

Open noon-1am. This is the best place in Hania for outstanding Cretan specialities, including the zucchini-cheese pies known as *bourekia*.

Entertainment

Café Kriti (☎ 2821 058 661, Kalergon 22) Open 6pm-1am. This is a rough-and-ready joint but it's the best place in Hania to hear live Cretan music. Music starts after 8.30pm.

Ideon Andron (☎ 2821 095 598, Halidon 26) Open noon-midnight. In the middle of busy, touristy Halidon, this place offers a sophisticated atmosphere with discreet music and garden seating. It serves good mezedes.

Fagotto Jazz Bar (☎ 2821 071 887, Angelou 16) Open 7pm-2am. Black-and-white photographs of jazz greats line the walls here. It's housed in a restored Venetian building and offers the smooth sounds of jazz and light rock.

Point Music Bar (☎ 2821 057 556, Sourmeli 2) Open 9.30pm-2am. This is a good rock bar for those allergic to techno. When the interior gets steamy you can cool off on the 1st-floor balcony overlooking the harbour.

Taratsa Café (☎ 2821 074 960, Koundourioti 54) Open 8am-1am. On the waterfront, this place plays rock music at a volume that renders conversation possible only for lip readers but you can escape to the outdoor terrace.

Shopping

Good-quality hand-made leather goods are available from shoemakers on Skrydlof, off Halidon, where shoes cost from €30. The old town has many craft shops.

Roka Carpets (☎ 2821 074 736, Zambeliou 61) You can watch Mihalis Manousakis weave his wondrous rugs on a 400-year-old loom using methods that have remained essentially unchanged since Minoan times. This is one of the few places in Greece where you can buy the genuine item. Prices begin at €23.50 for a small rug.

Top Hanas Carpet Shop (☎ 2821 058 571, Angelou 3) This place specialises in old Cretan *kilims* (flat-woven rugs) that were traditional dowry gifts; prices start at €88.

Karmela's Ceramic Shop (☎ 2821 040 487, Angelou 7) Karmelà's produces ceramics using ancient techniques and also displays unusual jewellery handcrafted by young Greek artisans.

Hania District Association of Handicrafts (☎ 2821 056 386, Akti Tombazi 15) The embroidery, weaving and ceramics are well executed but the sculptures of Greek mythological figures are unusually fine.

Getting There & Away

Air Olympic Airways has at least four flights a day to Athens which range in price from €53-76.60. There are also two flights a week to Thessaloniki (€103.30). The Olympic Airways office (☎ 2821 057 701) is at Tzanakaki 88.

Aegean Airlines has up to six daily flights to Athens (€55) and two to Thessaloniki (€90). Their office (☎ 2821 063 366, fax 2821 063 669) is at the airport. The airport is on the Akrotiri Peninsula, 14km from Hania.

Axon Airlines has flights to Athens (€70, two daily). The Axon Airlines office (☎ 2821 020 928) is at Hania airport.

Bus Buses depart from Hania's bus station for the following destinations:

destination	duration	fare	frequency
Elafonisi	2 hr	€7.40	1 daily
Falasarna	1½ hr	€4.90	2 daily
Hora Sfakion	2 hr	€4.90	3 daily
Iraklio	2½ hr	€10	half-hourly
Kastelli-Kissamos	1 hour	€3.10	14 daily
Kolymbari	45 min	€2	half-hourly
Lakki	1 hr	€2	4 daily
Moni Agias Triadas	30 mins	€1.30	3 daily
Omalos	1 hr	€4.50 (for Samaria Gorge)	4 daily
Paleohora	2 hr	€4.90	4 daily
Rethymno	1 hr	€5.30	half-hourly
Sougia	2 hr	€4.50	1 daily
Stavros	30 min	€1.20	6 daily

Ferry Ferries for Hania dock at Souda, about 7km east of town. There is at least one ferry

CRETE

The Good Oil

The olive has been part of life in the eastern Mediterranean since the beginnings of civilisation. Olive cultivation can be traced back about 6000 years. It was the farmers of the Levant (modern Syria and Lebanon) who first spotted the potential of the wild European olive *(Olea europaea)* – a sparse, thorny tree that was common in the region. These farmers began the process of selection that led to the more compact, thornless, oil-rich varieties that now dominate the Mediterranean.

Whereas most Westerners think of olive oil as being just a cooking oil, to the people of the ancient Mediterranean civilisations it was very much more. As well as being an important foodstuff, it was burned in lamps to provide light, it could be used as a lubricant and it was blended with essences to produce fragrant oils.

The Minoans were among the first to grow wealthy on the olive, and western Crete remains an important olive-growing area, specialising in high-quality salad oils. The region's showpiece Kolymvari Cooperative markets its extra-virgin oil in both the USA (Athena brand) and Britain (Kydonia brand).

Locals will tell you that the finest oil is produced from trees grown on the rocky soils of the Akrotiri Peninsula, west of Hania. The oil that is prized above all others, however, is *agourelaio*, meaning unripe, which is pressed from green olives.

Few trees outlive the olive. Some of the fantastically gnarled and twisted olive trees that dot the countryside of western Crete are more than 1000 years old. The tree known as *dekaoktoura*, in the mountain village of Anisaraki – near Kandanos on the road from Hania to Paleohora – is claimed to be more than 1500 years old.

Many of these older trees are being cut down to make way for improved varieties. The wood is burnt in potters' kilns and provides woodturners with the raw material to produce the ultimate salad bowl for connoisseurs. The dense yellow-brown timber has a beautiful swirling grain.

a day for the 10-hour trip to/from Piraeus. ANEK has a boat nightly at 8.30pm for €20.50. The ANEK office (☎ 2821 027 500) is opposite the food market. Souda's port police can be contacted on ☎ 2821 089 240.

Getting Around

There is no airport bus. A taxi to the airport costs about €11.80.

Local buses (blue) for the port of Souda leave from outside the food market. Buses for the western beaches leave from Plateia 1866.

Car rental outlets include Avis (☎ 2821 050 510), Tzanakaki 58; Budget (☎ 2821 092 778), Karaïskaki 39; and Europrent (☎ 2821 040 810, 2821 27 810), Halidon 87. Most motorcycle-rental outlets are on Halidon.

AKROTIRI PENINSULA
Χερσόνησος Ακρωτήρι

The Akrotiri (ahk-ro-**tee**-rih) Peninsula, to the east of Hania, has a few places of fairly minor interest, as well as being the site of

Hania's airport, port and a military base There is an immaculate **military cemetery** at Souda, where about 1500 British, Australian and New Zealand soldiers who lost their lives in the Battle of Crete are buried. The buses to Souda port from outside the Hania food market can drop you at the cemetery.

If you haven't yet had your fill of Cretan monasteries, there are three on the Akrotiri Peninsula. The impressive 17th-century **Moni Agias Triadas** *(Akrotiri; admission €1.20; open 6am-2pm & 5pm-7pm daily)* was founded by the Venetian monks Jeremiah and Laurentio Giancarolo. The brothers were converts to the Orthodox faith.

The 16th-century **Moni Gouvernetou** *(Our Lady of the Angels; Akrotiri; open 8am-12.30pm & 4.30pm-7.30pm daily)* is 4km north of Moni Agias Triada. The church inside the monastery has an ornate sculptured Venetian facade. Both Moni Agias Triadas and Moni Gouvernetou are still in use.

From Moni Gouvernetou, it's a 15-minute walk on the path leading down to the coast to the ruins of **Moni Ioannou Erimiti**, known also as **Moni Katholikou**. The monastery is dedicated to St John the Hermit who lived in the cave behind the ruins. It takes another 30 minutes to reach the sea.

There are three buses daily (except Sunday) to Moni Agias Triadas from Hania's bus station (€1.30).

HANIA TO XYLOSKALO

The road from Hania to the beginning of the Samaria Gorge is one of the most spectacular routes on Crete. It heads through orange groves to the village of **Fournes** where a left fork leads to **Meskla**. The main road continues to the village of **Lakki**, 24km from Hania. This unspoilt village in the Lefka Ori Mountains affords stunning views wherever you look. The village was a centre of resistance during the uprising against the Turks, and during WWII.

From Lakki, the road continues to **Omalos** and **Xyloskalo**, start of the Samaria Gorge.

Places to Stay & Eat

Hotel Gigilos (☎ 2825 067 181, Omalos) singles/doubles €11.80/17.60. This is the friendliest hotel in Omalos. Rooms are rather barely furnished but are quite large and very clean.

Hotel Exari (☎ 2825 067 180, fax 2825 067 124, Omalos) Rooms €20.50. Exari was renovated in 2000 and has pleasant, well-furnished rooms as well as an attached restaurant. The owners give lifts to walkers to the start of the Samaria Gorge.

Kallergi Hut (☎ 2825 033 199, Omalos) Bunk beds €4.50. The EOS (Greek Mountaineering Club) maintains this hut located in the hills between Omalos and the Samaria Gorge. It has 45 beds, electricity (no hot water) and makes a good base for exploring Mt Gingilos and surrounding peaks.

SAMARIA GORGE
Φαράγγι της Σαμαριάς

It's a wonder the stones and rocks underfoot haven't worn away completely, given the number of people who tramp through the Samaria (sah-mah-rih-**ah**) Gorge (☎ 2825 067 179; admission €3.50; open 6am-3pm daily 1 May–mid-Oct). Despite the crowds, a trek through this stupendous gorge is still an experience to remember.

At 18km, the gorge is supposedly the longest in Europe. It begins just below the Omalos Plateau, carved out by the river that flows between Mt Psiristra (1766m) and Mt Volakias (2115m). Its width varies from 150m to 3m and its vertical walls reach 500m at their highest points. The gorge has an incredible number of wildflowers, which are at their best in April and May.

It is also home to a large number of endangered species. They include the Cretan wild goat, the kri-kri, which survives in the wild only here and on the islet of Kri-Kri, off the coast of Agios Nikolaos. The gorge was made a national park in 1962 to save the kri-kri from extinction. You are unlikely to see too many of these shy animals, which show a marked aversion to trekkers.

An early start helps to avoid the worst of the crowds, but during July and August even the early bus from Hania to the top of the gorge can be packed.

The trek from Xyloskalo, the name of the steep wooden staircase that gives access to the gorge, to Agia Roumeli takes around six hours. Early in the season it's sometimes necessary to wade through the stream. Later, as the flow drops, it's possible to use rocks as stepping stones.

The gorge is wide and open for the first 6km, until you reach the abandoned village of Samaria. The inhabitants were relocated when the gorge became a national park. Just south of the village is a small church dedicated to Saint Maria of Egypt, after whom the gorge is named.

The gorge then narrows and becomes more dramatic until, at the 12km mark, the walls are only 3.5m apart – the famous **Iron Gates**.

The gorge ends just north of the almost abandoned village of Old Agia Roumeli. From here the path continues to the small, messy and crowded resort of Agia Roumeli,

CRETE

with a much-appreciated pebble beach and sparkling sea.

Spending the night in the gorge is not permitted.

What to Bring

Rugged footwear is essential for walking on the uneven ground covered by sharp stones. Don't attempt the walk in unsuitable footwear – you will regret it. You'll also need a hat and sunscreen. There's no need to take water. While it's inadvisable to drink water from the main stream, there are plenty of springs along the way spurting delicious cool water straight from the rock. There is nowhere to buy food, so bring something to snack on.

Getting There & Away

There are excursions to the Samaria Gorge from every sizable town and resort on Crete. Most travel agents have two excursions: 'Samaria Gorge Long Way' and 'Samaria Gorge Easy Way'. The first comprises the regular trek from the Omalos Plateau to Agia Roumeli; the second starts at Agia Roumeli and takes you as far as the Iron Gates.

Obviously it's cheaper to trek the Samaria Gorge under your own steam. Hania is the most convenient base. There are buses to Xyloskalo (Omalos; one hour, €4.50) at 6.15am, 7.30am, 8.30am and 1.45pm. There's also a direct bus to Xyloskalo from Paleohora (1½ hours, €4.55) at 6am.

AGIA ROUMELI TO HORA SFAKION

Agia Roumeli (Αγία Ρούμελη) has little going for it, but if you have just trekked through the Samaria Gorge and are too exhausted to face a further journey, there is a hotel here – see Places to Stay & Eat.

The small but rapidly expanding fishing village of Loutro (Λουτρό) lies between Agia Roumeli and Hora Sfakion. Loutro doesn't have a beach but there are rocks from which you can swim.

An extremely steep path leads up from Loutro to the village of Anopolis. Alterna-

tively, you can save yourself the walk by taking the Hania-Skaloti bus – see Getting There & Away.

From Loutro it's a moderate 2½ hour walk along a coastal path to Hora Sfakion. On the way you will pass the celebrated Sweet Water Beach, named after freshwater springs which seep from the rocks. Free lance campers spend months at a time here. Even if you don't feel inclined to join them you won't be able to resist a swim in the translucent sea.

Places to Stay & Eat

Hotel Agia Roumeli (☎ 2825 091 232, fax 2825 091 232, Agia Roumeli) Singles/doubles with bathroom €20.50/26.40 This D-class property is the only hotel in Agia Roumeli.

Porto Loutro (☎ 2825 091 433, Loutro) Doubles with bathroom €26.40. This place is in, as the name suggests, Porto Loutro.

There are also a number of domatia and tavernas in Agia Roumeli, Loutro and Anopolis, where you'll pay around €23.50 for a double.

Getting There & Away

There are three boats daily from Agia Roumeli to Hora Sfakion (1¼ hours, €4.50) via Loutro (45 minutes, €2.70). They connect with the bus back to Hania, leaving you in Hora Sfakion just long enough to spend a few euros. There's also a boat from Agia Roumeli to Paleohora (€6.50) at 4.45pm calling at Sougia (€3.20).

The Hania-Skaloti bus runs via Anopolis. It leaves Hania at 2pm and returns the following morning, calling in at Anopolis at 7am.

HORA SFAKION Χώρα Σφακίων
postcode 730 01 • pop 340

Hora Sfakion (ho-rah sfah-kee-on) is a small coastal port where hordes of walkers from the Samaria Gorge spill off the boat and onto the bus. As such, in high season it can seem like Piccadilly Circus at rush hour. Most people pause only long enough to catch the next bus out.

Hora Sfakion played a prominent role during WWII when thousands of Allied

NEIL SETCHFIELD

spectacular view of the Acropolis, a silent monument to times gone by

RICK GERHARTER

A closer look through columns at the Parthenon of Athens

JOHN ELK III

The Acropolis in all its night-time splendour viewed from Filopappos Hill

The sea is an intrinsic part of Greek life – Mykonos island, Cyclades.

Outdoor street cafe in Nafplio

Colourful facade of Symi's Maritime Museum

roops were evacuated by sea from the town
fter the Battle of Crete.

Orientation & Information

The ferry quay is at the eastern side of the
harbour. Buses leave from the square on
the eastern side. The post office and OTE
are on the square, and the police station
overlooks it. There is no tourist office or
ourist police.

Places to Stay & Eat

Accommodation in the village is of a rea-
onable quality and value. Some of the bet-
er accommodation is on the waterfront.

Rooms Stavris (☎ *2825 091 220, fax
2825 091 152,* e *info@sfakia-crete.com)*
Singles/doubles €17.60/19. Up the steps at
he western end of the port, Hotel Stavros
has clean rooms with bathrooms.

Hotel Samaria (☎ *2825 091 261, fax
2825 091 161)* Singles/doubles with bathroom €14.70/20.50. This decent hotel is on
he waterfront.

Livikon (☎ *2825 091 211, fax 2825 091
922)* Singles/doubles in high season
€35.30/38.20. Livikon has large, brightly
decorated rooms with stone floors and sea
views.

The adjoining Samaria and Livikon ho-
els have a *taverna* (☎ *2825 091 320)* down-
tairs that has a good selection of mayirefta
and vegetarian dishes. Main dishes cost
€2.70-4.20.

Getting There & Away

Bus There are three buses a day from Hora
Sfakion to Hania (two hours, €4.50). In
ummer only there are two daily buses to
Plakias (1¼ hours, €3.50) via Frangokastello, leaving at 10.30am and 5.30pm,
and two to Rethymno (two hours, €5.30), at
10.30am and 7.30pm.

Boat From June through August there are
daily boats from Hora Sfakion to Paleohora
three hours, €8) via Loutro, Agia Roumeli
and Sougia. The boat leaves at 10.30am and
2.30pm. There are also three or four boats
a day to Agia Roumeli (one hour, €4.50) via
Loutro (15 minutes, €1.50). From 1 June

there are boats to Gavdos Island (€8) on
Thursday, Friday, Saturday and Sunday
leaving at 10.30am and returning at 2.45pm.

AROUND HORA SFAKION

The road from Vryses to Hora Sfakion cuts
through the heart of the Sfakia region in the
eastern Lefka Ori. The inhabitants of this
region have long had a reputation for fear-
lessness and independence – characteristics
they retain to this day. Cretans are regarded
by other Greeks as being immensely proud
and there is none more so than the Sfakiot.

One of Crete's most celebrated heroes,
Ioannis Daskalogiannis, was from Sfakia.
In 1770, Daskalogiannis led the first Cretan
insurrection against Ottoman rule. When
help promised by Russia failed to materi-
alise, he gave himself up to the Turks to
save his followers. As punishment the
Turks skinned him alive in Iraklio. Wit-
nesses related that Daskalogiannis suffered
this excruciating death in dignified silence.

The Turks never succeeded in control-
ling the Sfakiots, and this rugged mountainous region was the scene of fierce
fighting. The story of their resistance lives
on in the form of folk tales and *rizitika*
(local folk songs).

The village of **Imbros**, 23km from Vryses, is at the head of the beautiful 10km Imbros Gorge, which is far less visited than the
Samaria Gorge. To get there, take any bus
bound for Hora Sfakion from the north
coast and get off at Imbros. Walk out of the
village towards Hora Sfakion and a path to
the left leads down to the gorge. The gorge
path ends at the village of **Komitades**, from
where it is an easy walk by road to Hora
Sfakion. You can of course do the trek in reverse, beginning at Komitades. The Happy
Walker organises treks through this gorge
(see Activities in the Rethymno section).

Frangokastello Φραγκοκάστελλο

Frangokastello is a magnificent fortress on
the coast 15km east of Hora Sfakion. It was
built by the Venetians in 1371 as a defence
against pirates and rebel Sfakiots, who re-
sented the Venetian occupation as much as
they did the Turkish.

CRETE

Restless Spirits

The Frangokastello bloodshed of 17 May 1828 gave rise to the legend of the *Drosoulites*. The name comes from the Greek word *drosia* meaning 'moisture', which could refer to the dawn moisture that is around when the ghosts are said to appear, or the watery content of the spirits themselves. On the anniversary of the decisive battle (or in late May around dawn) it's said that a procession of ghostly figures – the ghosts of Hadzi Mihalis Dalanis and his followers – materialises around the fort and marches to the sea. The phenomenon has been verified by a number of independent observers. Although locals believe the figures are the ghosts of the slaughtered rebels, others theorise that it may be an optical illusion created by certain atmospheric conditions and that the figures may be a reflection of camels or soldiers in the Libyan Desert. When questioned about the ghostly phenomenon, locals are understandably a little reticent, but remain convinced that something does in fact happen. Most claim that the older residents of Frangokastello have seen the apparitions. Whether you will depends on your luck – or belief in ghosts.

It was here in 1770 that Ioannis Daskalogiannis surrendered to the Turks. On 17 May 1828 many Cretan rebels, led by Hadzi Mihalis Dalanis, were killed here by the Turks. Legend has it that at dawn each anniversary their ghosts can be seen marching along the beach (see the boxed text 'Restless Spirits').

The castle overlooks a gently sloping, sandy beach. Domatia and tavernas are springing up rapidly here, but it's still relatively unspoilt.

Buses between Hora Sfakion and Plakias go via Frangokastello.

SOUGIA Σούγια
postcode 730 01 • pop 50

It's surprising that Sougia (**soo**-yiah) hasn't yet been commandeered by the package-tour crowd. With a wide curve of sand-and-pebble beach and a shady, tree-lined coastal road Sougia's tranquillity has been preserved only because it lies at the foot of a narrow, twisting road that would deter most tour buses.

If you arrive by boat, walk about 150m along the coast to the town centre. If you arrive by bus, the bus will drop you on the coastal road in front of Santa Irene Hotel. The only other road intersects the coastal road by Santa Irene Hotel and runs north to the Agia Irini Gorge and Hania.

Sougia doesn't have a post office, OTE or bank, but you can change money at several places, including Polifimos Travel (☎ 2823 051 022) and Roxana's Office (☎ 2823 051 362). Both are just off the coastal road or the road to Hania. Check your email at Internet Lotos (☎ 2823 051 191) for €3 per hour at one of its six computers.

Places to Stay
There's no camping ground, but the eastern end of the long, pebbled beach is popular with freelance campers.

Pension Galini (☎/fax 2823 051 488) Singles/doubles with bathroom €20.50/23.50, single/double studios €26.50/32.50. Next door to Aretousa, this pension has beautiful rooms.

Rooms Maria (☎ 2823 051 337) Doubles/triples with bathroom €29.50/35.30. This place is a block farther east on the coast from Santa Irene and has clean, white rooms.

Rooms Ririka (☎ 2823 051 167) Doubles €29.50. Next door to Rooms Maria is the equally attractive Rooms Ririka, also with rooms overlooking the sea.

Aretousa Rooms to Rent (☎ 2823 051 178, fax 2823 051 178) Singles/doubles €23.50/29.50. Inland, on the road to Hania, Aretousa has lovely rooms with wood panelled ceilings and balconies.

Santa Irene Hotel (☎ 2823 051 342, fax 2823 051 182, @ nanadakis@cha.forthnet.gr) Single/double studios €23.50/35.30. The smartest accommodation is here. Air conditioning costs €5.90 extra.

Places to Eat
Restaurants line the waterfront and there are more on the main street.

Kyma (☎ *2823 051 670*) Fish dishes €17.60-23.50. Just on the seafront as you enter town, Kyma has a good selection of ready-made food as well as fresh fish dishes.

Taverna Rembetiko (☎ *2823 051 510*) Ladera €2.70-3.50. Located on the road to Hania, this taverna has an extensive menu including various Cretan specialities such as boureki and stuffed zucchini flowers.

Getting There & Away

There's a daily bus travelling from Hania to Sougia (2½ hours, €4.70) at 1.30pm. Buses going from Sougia to Hania leave at 7am. Sougia is on the Paleohora–Hora Sfakion boat route. Boats leave at 10.15am for Agia Roumeli (one hour, €3), Loutro (1½ hours, €5.50) and Hora Sfakion (two hours, €5.90). For Paleohora (one hour, €3.80) to the west there is a departure at 5.30pm.

PALEOHORA Παλαιοχώρα
postcode 730 01 • pop 1826

Paleohora was discovered by hippies back in the 60s and from then on its days as a tranquil fishing village were numbered. However, the resort operators have not gone way over the top – yet. The place retains a laid-back feel. It is also the only beach resort on Crete that does not close down in winter.

The little town is set on a narrow peninsula with a long, curving sandy beach exposed to the wind on one side and a sheltered pebbly beach on the other. On summer evenings the main street is closed to traffic and the tavernas move onto the road.

It's worth clambering up the ruins of the 13th-century **Venetian castle** for the splendid view of the sea and mountains. The most picturesque part of Paleohora is the narrow streets huddled around the castle.

From Paleohora, a six-hour walk along a scenic coastal path leads to Sougia, passing the ancient site of Lissos.

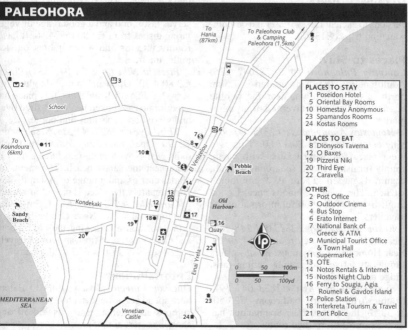

PALEOHORA

To Hania (87km)

To Paleohora Club & Camping Paleohora (1.5km)

To Koundoura (6km)

School

Pebble Beach

Old Harbour

Quay

Kondekaki

El Venizelou

Einai Yrela

Sandy Beach

MEDITERRANEAN SEA

Venetian Castle

0   50   100m
0   50   100yd

PLACES TO STAY
1 Poseidon Hotel
5 Oriental Bay Rooms
10 Homestay Anonymous
23 Spamandos Rooms
24 Kostas Rooms

PLACES TO EAT
8 Dionysos Taverna
12 O Baxes
19 Pizzeria Niki
20 Third Eye
22 Caravella

OTHER
2 Post Office
3 Outdoor Cinema
4 Bus Stop
6 Erato Internet
7 National Bank of Greece & ATM
9 Municipal Tourist Office & Town Hall
11 Supermarket
13 OTE
14 Notos Rentals & Internet
15 Nostos Night Club
16 Ferry to Sougia, Agia Roumeli & Gavdos Island
17 Police Station
18 Interkreta Tourism & Travel
21 Port Police

CRETE

Orientation & Information

Paleohora's main street, El Venizelou, runs north to south, with several streets leading off east to the pebble beach. Boats leave from the old harbour at the southern end of this beach. At the southern end of El Venizelou, a west turn onto Kondekaki leads to the tamarisk-shaded sandy beach.

The municipal tourist office (☎ 2823 041 507) is next to the town hall on El Venizelou. It is open 10am to 1pm and 6pm to 9pm Wednesday to Monday between May and October.

The post office is on the road that skirts the sandy beach. On El Venizelou are the National Bank of Greece, with ATM, and the OTE (on the west side, just north of Kondekaki). Internet access is provided at Notos Internet (☎ 2823 042 110, e notos@grecian.net) and at Erato Internet (☎ 2823 083 010, e erato@chania-cci.gr). Both charge €4.50 per hour.

Organised Tours

Various travel agents around town offer excursions to ancient Lissos (€22) and dolphin-watching trips (€13.20).

Places to Stay

Camping Paleohora (☎ 2823 041 225) Adult/tent €3.20/2. This ground is 1.5km north-east of the town, near the pebble beach. The site has a taverna but no mini-market.

Homestay Anonymous (☎ 2823 041 509) Singles/doubles €11.80/17.60. This is a great place for backpackers, with clean, simply furnished rooms set around a small, beautiful garden. There is a communal kitchen. The owner, Manolis speaks good English and is full of useful information for travellers.

Kostas Rooms (☎/fax 2823 041 248) Singles/doubles with bathroom €14.70/19. Near Homestay Anonymous, Kostas offers simple attractive rooms with ceiling fans, fridge and sea views.

Spamandos Rooms (☎ 2823 041 197) Doubles/triples with bathroom €23.50/26.50. In the old quarter, Spamandos has spotless, nicely furnished rooms.

Poseidon Hotel (☎ 2823 041 374/115 fax 2823 041 115) Singles/double studio €20.50/26.50. The studios here come equipped with fridges, air-con and kitchenettes and all have a little balcony.

Oriental Bay Rooms (☎ 2823 041 076 Singles/doubles with bathroom & ceiling fans €26.50/29.50. This place occupies the large modern building at the northern end of the pebble beach. The owner, Thalia, keep the rooms immaculate. There's also a shaded terrace-restaurant overlooking the sea that serves decent meals.

Places to Eat

The eating choices are reasonably good.

O Baxes Grills €3.80-5.60. Open noon midnight daily. In the street behind the OTE this is a fine little taverna which does a good job on old favourites like fried aubergine (€2.40), or *dakos* (€2.40).

Dionysos Taverna (☎ 2823 041 243 Cretan dishes €3-5.30. Open 7pm-1am daily Mar-Oct. The very popular Dionyso is a bit more expensive than Baxes but also serves tasty food and a good range of vegetarian dishes from €1.80 to €4.50. It has a roomy interior and a few tables outside under the trees.

Pizzeria Niki (☎ 2823 041 534) Pizza €3.80-4.70. Open 6.30pm-midnight daily Apr-Oct. Just off Kondekaki, this place has superior pizzas cooked in a wood-fired oven and served on a spacious outdoor terrace.

Third Eye (☎ 2823 041 234) Meals under €5.90. Open 8am-3pm & 6pm-midnight daily Mar-Nov. Vegetarians have a treat in store near the sandy beach. The menu includes curries and a range of Asian dishes Unfortunately the place is closed in winter.

Caravella (☎ 2823 041 131) Open 11am midnight daily Apr-Nov. Caravella has a prime position overlooking the old harbour and offers an array of fresh and competitively priced seafood. Fish is €22 a kilogram.

Entertainment

Outdoor Cinema Most visitors to Paleohora spend at least one evening at this well signposted cinema. Entry is €4.50 and showings start at 9.45pm.

Paleohora Club (☎ 2823 042 230) This is another option for a night out. It is next to Camping Paleohora 1.5km north-east of the village. It kicks in after 11pm.

Nostos Night Club (☎ 2823 042 145) Open 6pm-2am. If you've seen the movie and don't fancy the trek to the disco, try this place right in town, between El Venizelou and the Old Harbour.

Getting There & Away

Bus In summer there are three buses a day to Hania (two hours, €4.70); in winter there are two. In summer, this service goes via Omalos at 6.30 am (1½ hours, €4.30) to cash in on the Samaria Gorge trade. For information call the bus station on ☎ 2823 041 914.

Boat In summer there are daily ferries from Paleohora to Hora Sfakion (three hours, €8) via Sougia (one hour, €3.80), Agia Roumeli (two hours, €6.50) and Loutro (2½ hours, €7.90). The ferry leaves Paleohora at 9.30am, and returns from Hora Sfakion at 12.30pm. There's also a boat three/two times a week in summer/winter to Gavdos (four hours, €9.40) that leaves Paleohora at 8.30am. Tickets for all of these boats can be bought at Interkreta Tourism & Travel (☎ 2823 041 393, fax 2823 041 050), Kondekaki 4.

Getting Around

Car, Motorcycle & Bicycle All three can be hired from Notos Rentals (☎ 2823 042 110, e notos@grecian.net) on El Venizelou. Cars rent for around €23.50, a motorbike for €14.70 and bicycle for €3.

Excursion Boat The M/B *Elafonisos* gets cranked into action in mid-April ferrying people to the west-coast beach of Elafonisi (one hour, €3.80). The service builds up from three times a week to daily in June through September. It departs at 10am and returns at 4pm.

AROUND PALEOHORA

Gavdos Island Νήσος Γαύδος
Gavdos Island (population 50), in the Libyan Sea 65km from Paleohora, is the most southerly place in Europe. It is an excellent choice for those craving isolation and peace. The island has three small villages and pleasant beaches. There is a post office, OTE, police officer and doctor. There are no hotels but several of the locals let rooms, and there are tavernas. Fishermen from Gavdos Island take tourists to the remote, uninhabited island of Gavdopoula. The best source of information about the island is Interkreta Tourism & Travel in Paleohora.

Getting There & Away A small post boat operates between Paleohora and Gavdos on Monday and Thursday all year, weather permitting. It leaves Paleohora at 8.30am and takes about four hours (€9.40). In summer there's also a Tuesday boat. The boats turn around from Gavdos almost immediately.

There are also four boats a week from Hora Sfakion to Gavdos (€8) and a weekly boat from Sougia (€7).

Elafonisi Ελαφονήσι
As one of the loveliest sand beaches in Crete it's easy to understand why people enthuse so much about Elafonisi, at the southern extremity of Crete's west coast. The beach is long and wide and is separated from Elafonisi Islet by about 50m of knee-deep water on its northern side. The islet is marked by low dunes and a string of semi-secluded coves that attract a sprinkling of naturists.

Places to Stay *Rooms Elafonissos* (☎ 2825 061 548) Double/triple studios €23.50/29.50. This place has a taverna overlooking the sea from its commanding position on a bluff.

Rooms Elafonissi (☎ 2825 061 274, fax 2825 097 907) Singles/doubles with bathroom €20.50/26.50. These rooms have fridges, an outdoor patio and attached restaurant.

Innahorion (☎ 2825 061 111) Singles/doubles with bathroom €23.50/29.50. This is perhaps the least attractive of the three options. The 15 rooms each have a fridge

CRETE

and kitchenette, but are set back a fair way from the beach. Innahorion also has a restaurant.

Getting There & Away There is one boat daily from Paleohora to Elafonisi (one hour, €3.80) from June through August, as well as daily buses from Hania (2½ hours, €7.40) and Kastelli-Kissamos (1½ hours, €3). The buses leave Hania at 7.30am and Kastelli-Kissamos at 8.30am, and both depart from Elafonisi at 4pm.

KASTELLI-KISSAMOS
Καστέλλι-Κίσσαμος
postcode 734 00 • pop 2936

If you find yourself in the north-coast town of Kastelli-Kissamos, you've probably arrived by ferry from the Peloponnese or Kythira. The most remarkable part of Kastelli-Kissamos is its unremarkableness. It's simply a quiet town that neither expects nor attracts much tourism.

In antiquity, its name was Kissamos; it was the main town of the province of the same name. When the Venetians came along and built a castle here, the place became known as Kastelli. The name persisted until 1966 when authorities decided that too many people were confusing this Kastelli with Crete's other Kastelli, 40km south-east of Iraklio. The official name reverted to Kissamos, and that's what appears on bus and shipping schedules. Local people still prefer Kastelli, and many books and maps agree with them. An alternative that is emerging is to combine the two into Kastelli-Kissamos, which leaves no room for misunderstanding.

Orientation & Information
The port is 3km west of town. From June through August a bus meets the boats; otherwise a taxi costs around €3. The bus station is just below the square, Plateia Kissamou, and the main street, Skalidi, runs east from Plateia Kissamou.

Kastelli-Kissamos has no tourist office. The post office is on the main road. Signs from the bus station direct you through an alley on the right of Skalidi which takes you to the post office. Turn right at the post office and you'll come to the National Bank of Greece on the central square. Turn left at the post office and the OTE office is opposite you about 50m along the main road. There is also a string of pensions and tavernas along the sea below the bus station.

Places to Stay
There are three camping grounds to choose from.

Camping Kissamos (☎ 2822 023 444, fax 2822 023 464) Adult/tent €4.10/2.40. Close to the city centre, this place is convenient for the huge supermarket next door and for the bus station, but not much else. It's got great views of the olive-processing plant next door. Signs direct you there from the city centre.

Camping Mithymna (☎ 2822 031 444, fax 2822 031 000, Paralia Drapania) Adult/tent €4.50/2.40. This is a much better choice than Camping Kissamos. It's 6km east of town, on an excellent shady site near the best stretch of beach. Facilities include a restaurant, bar and shop. Getting there involves a bus trip to the village of Drapanias – from where it's a pleasant 15-minute walk through olive groves to the site.

Camping Nopigia (☎ 2822 031 111, fax 2822 031 700, ℮ info@campingnopigia.gr, Nopigia) Adult/tent €3.90/2.50. This is a good site, 2km west of Camping Mithymna. While the beach is no good for swimming, the swimming pool here makes up for that.

Koutsounakis Rooms (☎ 2822 023 753) Singles/doubles with bathroom €13/19. One of the best deals in town, this is adjacent to the bus station. The rooms are spotless.

Hotel Kissamos (☎ 2822 022 086) Singles/doubles with bathroom & breakfast €19/25. This C-class hotel, west of the bus station on the north side of the main road, is in an uninspiring location but has good-value rooms.

Argo Rooms for Rent (☎/fax 2822 023 563, Plateia Teloniou) Singles/doubles with bathroom €20.50/29.50. The C-class Argo has spacious rooms. From the central square, walk down to the seafront, turn left, and you will come to the rooms on the left.

Thalassa ☎ *2822 031 231,* e *skoulakis@ otenet.gr,* w *www.thalassa-apts.gr, Paralia Drapania)* Double studios €35.30. If you have your own transport, this is an ideal spot to retreat to. All studios (sleeping two to five persons) are immaculate and are 50m from the beach. Thalassa is 6km east of Kissamos near Camping Mythimna.

Places to Eat

Restaurant Makedonas (☎ *2822 022 844)* Ladera €2-2.70. For local colour go to this no-frills place just west of Plateia Kissamou, where you can dine on oil-based, home-cooked food. The beef patties in tomato sauce (*bifteki stifado*; €3.50) is recommended by the owner.

Papadakis Taverna (☎ *2822 022 340, Paralia Kissamou)* Open 11am-midnight daily. Opposite Argo Rooms for Rent, this taverna has a good setting overlooking the beach and serves well-prepared fish dishes such as oven-baked fish (€5), or fish soup (€5). Fish is €29.50 per kilogram.

Getting There & Away

Bus There are 14 buses a day to Hania (one hour, €3), where you can change for Rethymno and Iraklio; and two buses a day for Falasarna (€1.90) at 10am and 5.30pm.

Ferry ANEN Ferries operates the F/B *Myrtidiotissa* on a route that takes in Antikythira (two hours, €6.50), Kythira (four hours, €12.90), Gythio (seven hours, €15.60), Kalamata (10 hours, €17.60) and Piraeus (19 hours, €17.60). It leaves Kastelli-Kissamos five times a week between 8am and 11am. You can buy tickets from Horeftakis Tours (☎ 2822 023 250) and the ANEN Office (☎ 2822 022 009 or 2822 024 030), both of which are on the right side of Skalidi, east of Plateia Kissamou.

Getting Around

Cars can be hired from Hermes (☎ 2822 022 980) on Skalidi, and motorcycles from Motor Fun (☎ 2822 023 400) on Plateia Kissamos.

AROUND KASTELLI-KISSAMOS
Falasarna Φαλάσαρνα

Falasarna, 16km west of Kastelli-Kissamos, was a Cretan city-state in the 4th century BC. There's not much to see, and most people are here for the superb beach, which is long, sandy and interspersed with boulders. There are several *domatia* at the beach.

From June through August there are three buses daily from Kastelli-Kissamos to Falasarna (€1.90) as well as buses from Hania (€4.90).

Gramvousa Peninsula
Χερσόνησος Γραμβούσα

North of Falasarna is the wild and remote Gramvousa Peninsula. There is a wide track, which eventually degenerates into a path, along the east-coast side to the sandy beach of **Tigani**, on the west side of the peninsula's narrow tip. The beach is overlooked by the two islets of Agria (wild) and Imeri (tame) Gramvousa. To reach the track, take a west-bound bus from Kastelli-Kissamos and ask to be let off at the turnoff for the village of **Kalyviani** (5km from Kastelli-Kissamos). Walk the 2km to Kalyviani, then take the path that begins at the far end of the main street. The shadeless walk takes around three hours – wear a hat and take plenty of water.

You don't have to inflict this punishment upon yourself to see the beautiful peninsula. From June through August there are daily cruises around the peninsula in the *Gramvousa Express* (€14.70). The boat leaves Kastelli-Kissamos at 9am and returns at 6pm.

Ennia Horia Εννιά Χωριά

Ennia Horia (Nine Villages) is the name given to the highly scenic mountainous region south of Kastelli-Kissamos, renowned for its chestnut trees. If you have your own transport you can drive through the region en route to Moni Hrysoskalitissas and Elafonisi or, with a little backtracking, to Paleohora. Alternatively, you can take a circular route, returning via the chestnut road. The village of **Elos** stages a chestnut festival on the third Sunday of October when sweets made

CRETE

from chestnuts are eaten. The road to the region heads inland 5km east of Kastelli-Kissamos.

Polyrrinia Πολυρρηνία

The ruins of the ancient city of Polyrrinia (po-lih-reh-**nee**-ah) lie 7km south of Kastelli-Kissamos, above the village of Ano Paleokastro (which is sometimes called Polyrrinia). It's a steep climb to reach the ruins but the views are stunning.

The city was founded by the Dorians and was continuously inhabited until Venetian times. There are remains of city walls, and an aqueduct built by Hadrian. It's a scenic walk from Kastelli-Kissamos to Polyrrinia, otherwise there is a very infrequent bus service – ask at the Kastelli-Kissamos bus station.

To reach the Polyrrinia road, walk east along Kastelli-Kissamos' main road, and turn right after the OTE.

Ano Paleokastro has only one taverna, *Taverna Odysseos*, which has mains at €3.50 to €5. Unfortunately there's no accommodation.

Dodecanese Δωδεκάνησα

Strung along the coast of western Turkey like jewels upon an aquamarine sea, the Dodecanese archipelago is closer to Asia Minor than mainland Greece. Because of their strategic and vulnerable position, they have encountered a greater catalogue of invasions and occupations than the rest of Greece.

The name Dodecanese ('dodecka' means 12 in Greek) derives from the time of the Ottoman Empire when 12 of the 18 islands were granted special privileges for having willingly submitted to the new Ottoman overlords, a rule which began in earnest in 1478. Intriguingly, the original Dodecanese did not include the largest and richest islands of Rhodes and Kos, as they had unwillingly been subjugated to the Ottomans; they consisted only of Patmos, Lipsi, Leros, Kalymnos, Astypalea, Nisyros, Symi, Halki, Karpathos, Kasos and Kastellorizo.

The islands' vicissitudinous history has endowed them with a wealth of diverse archaeological remains, but these are not the islands' only attractions. The highly developed resorts of Rhodes and Kos have beaches and bars galore, while Lipsi and Tilos have appealing beaches, but without the crowds. The far-flung islands of Agathonisi, Arki, Kasos and Kastellorizo await Greek-island aficionados in pursuit of traditional island life, while everyone gapes at the extraordinary landscape that geological turbulence has created on Nisyros.

SUGGESTED ITINERARIES
One week
Spend two days on Rhodes, and explore the capital's medieval city. Visit either Lindos or the ancient city of Kamiros, or both if you hire a car and cross Rhodes' unspoilt mountainous interior. Spend the next two days chilling out on the beaches of tranquil Tilos or walking around the island. You may fit in a couple of days on Nisyros, with its extraordinary volcanic landscape, the picturesque villages of Emboreios and Nikea and an impressive ruined kastro on its ancient acropolis. Otherwise, make for Kos, birthplace of Hippocrates, to see its extensive ruins and enjoy its wild nightlife.

Highlights

- Sense Patmos, the stunning island of St John with an inimitable spirit of place. Here, it is said, God delivered the Book of Revelations

- Lie back and relax in Lipsi, an island where time stands still and which most people pass by. The annual feast of Panagia tou Harou draws pilgrims from all over the Dodecanese

- See the Asklipion in Kos, religious sanctuary to Asklepios, the god of healing, and home to a healing centre and a school of medicine where trainees followed the teachings of Hippocrates

- Walk around the Old Town of Rhodes, the splendid fortress city built by the Knights of St John and the largest inhabited medieval town in Europe

- Smell the sulphur from the rim of the volcano on the extraordinary island of Nisyros

- Head for Kastellorizo – a tiny rock in the sun, Greece's furthest outpost and location for the cult film *Mediterraneo*

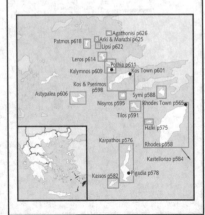

Agathonisi p626
Arki & Marathi p625
Lipsi p622
Patmos p618
Leros p614
Pothia p611
Kalymnos p609
Kos Town p601
Kos & Pserimos p598
Astypalea p606
Symi p588
Nisyros p595
Rhodes Town p565
Tilos p591
Halki p575
Karpathos p576
Rhodes p558
Kastellorizo p584
Kassos p582
Pigadia p578

DODECANESE

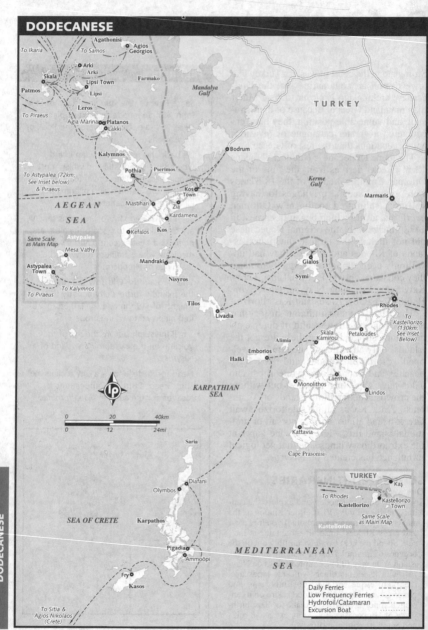

DODECANESE

To Ikaria
Agathonisi
To Samos
Agios Georgios
Arki
Arki
Skala
Lipsi Town
Patmos
Lipsi
To Piraeus
Leros
Farmako
Mandalya Gulf
TURKEY
Agia Marina
Platanos
Lakki
Bodrum
Kalymnos
Pserimos
Kerme Gulf
To Astypalea (72km; See Inset below) & Piraeus
Pothia
Marmaris
AEGEAN SEA
Kos Town
Mastihari
Kardamena
Zia
Same Scale as Main Map
Astypalea
Kefalos
Kos
Mesa Vathy
Astypalea Town
Mandraki
Gialos
To Piraeus
To Kalymnos
Nisyros
Symi
Tilos
Livadia
Rhodes
To Kastellorizo (130km; See Inset Below)
Alimia
Skala Kamirou
Petaloudes
Emborios
Halki
Rhodes
KARPATHIAN SEA
Monolithos
Laerma
Lindos
Kattavia
Cape Prasonisi
TURKEY
Kaş
Saria
To Rhodes
Kastellorizo Town
Diafani
Kastellorizo
Olymbos
Same Scale as Main Map
SEA OF CRETE
Karpathos
Kastellorizo
Pigadia
MEDITERRANEAN SEA
Ammoöpi
Fry
Kasos
To Sitia & Agios Nikolaos (Crete)

Daily Ferries	--------
Low Frequency Ferries	--------
Hydrofoil/Catamaran	——
Excursion Boat	....

0   20   40km
0   12   24mi

DODECANESE

Two weeks
Follow the one week itinerary, but spend three days on Rhodes to see more of the interior. Spend the night on Nisyros and enjoy a drink and dinner on Mandraki's delightful central square – the town undergoes a metamorphosis when the day-trippers leave. To recuperate from the liveliness of Kos, spend three days relaxing on Lipsi's un-crowded beaches, do more walking and take a day trip to remote and traditional Arki. Or, if even Lipsi sounds too touristy for you, go to quieter Agathonisi. Finally, en route to Piraeus, spend a day on Patmos to explore its monasteries.

History
The Dodecanese islands have been inhabited since pre-Minoan times; by the archaic period Rhodes and Kos had emerged as the dominant islands of the group. Distance from Athens gave the Dodecanese considerable autonomy and they were, for the most part, free to prosper unencumbered by subjugation to imperial Athens. Following Alexander the Great's death, Ptolemy I of Egypt ruled the Dodecanese.

The Dodecanese islanders were the first Greeks to become Christians. This was through the tireless efforts of St Paul, who made two journeys to the archipelago, and through St John, who was banished to Patmos, where he had his revelation.

The early Byzantine era saw the islands prosper, but by the 7th century AD they were plundered by a string of invaders. By the early 14th century it was the turn of the crusaders – the Knights of St John of Jerusalem, or Knights Hospitallers. The knights eventually became rulers of almost all the Dodecanese, building mighty fortifications, but not mighty enough to keep out the Turks in 1522.

The Turks were ousted by the Italians in 1912 during a tussle over possession of Libya. The Greeks, inspired by Mussolini's vision of a vast Mediterranean empire, made Italian the official language and prohibited the practice of Orthodoxy. The Italians constructed grandiose public buildings in the Fascist style, which was the antithesis of archetypal Greek architecture. More beneficially, they excavated and restored many archaeological monuments.

After the Italian surrender of 1943, the islands became battleground for British and German forces, with much suffering inflicted upon the population. The Dodecanese were formally returned to Greece in 1947.

Getting To/From The Dodecanese
Air Astypalea, Karpathos, Kasos, Kos, Leros and Rhodes have flights going to Athens. In addition, Rhodes has flights to Iraklio on Crete, Thessaloniki, and in summer to Mykonos and Santorini (Thira) in the Cyclades.

Ferry – Domestic Ferry schedules to the Dodecanese are fairly complex, but they do follow a predictable and rarely varying pattern. Departure times in both directions tend to be geared to an early morning arrival at both Piraeus and Rhodes. This means that island-hopping southwards can often involve some anti-social hours.

The following table gives an overall view of ferry connections to the Dodecanese from the mainland and Crete in high season. The services from Alexandroupolis are subject to seasonal demand so check before committing yourself to the trip.

Connecting from the Dodecanese to the Cyclades can sometimes be difficult. It is possible to reach Astypalea from the Dodecanese and connect with ferries serving the Cyclades from there, but this is more by luck than by design.

Hydrofoil – Domestic Kyriacoulis Hydrofoils operates daily services from the North-East Aegean island of Samos to the northern Dodecanese, and occasional services from Ikaria.

Ferry & Hydrofoil – International There are ferries and hydrofoils to the Turkish ports of Marmaris and Bodrum from Rhodes and Kos respectively, and day trips to Turkey from Kastellorizo and Symi. Boats en route from Piraeus to Cyprus and Israel call at Rhodes.

DODECANESE

Ferry Connections to the Dodecanese

origin	destination	duration	price	frequency
Alexandroupolis	Kos	26 hours	€33.50	1 weekly
Alexandroupolis	Rhodes	30 hours	€35.50 dr	1 weekly
Piraeus	Astypalea	12 hours	€21.40	3 weekly
Piraeus	Halki	22 hours	€29.50	2 weekly
Piraeus	Kalymnos	10–13 hours	€21.80	1 daily
Piraeus	Karpathos	18½ hours	€24.40	4 weekly
Piraeus	Kasos	17 hours	€24	4 weekly
Piraeus	Kos	12–15 hours	€23.20	2 daily
Piraeus	Leros	11 hours	€19.70	1 daily
Piraeus	Lipsi	16 hours	€28	1 weekly
Piraeus	Nisyros	13–15 hours	€23.20	2 weekly
Piraeus	Patmos	9½ hours	€21	1 daily
Piraeus	Rhodes	15–18 hours	€26.70	2 daily
Piraeus	Symi	15–17 hours	€21.20	2 weekly
Piraeus	Tilos	15 hours	€21.80	2 weekly
Sitia	Halki	5½ hours	€11.90	2 weekly
Sitia	Karpathos	4 hours	€10.60	4 weekly
Sitia	Kasos	2½ hours	€7.70	4 weekly
Sitia	Rhodes	11 hours	€19	3 weekly
Thessaloniki	Kos	18 hours	€39	1 weekly
Thessaloniki	Rhodes	21 hours	€45	1 weekly

Rhodes Ρόδος

Rhodes (ro-dos in Greek), the largest island in the Dodecanese, with a population of over 98,000, is the number one package tour destination of the group. With 300 days of sunshine a year, and an east coast of virtually uninterrupted sandy beaches, it fulfils the two prerequisites of the sun-starved British, Scandinavians and Germans who flock there.

But beaches and sunshine are not its only attributes. Rhodes is a beautiful island with unspoilt villages nestling in the foothills of its mountains. The landscape varies from arid and rocky around the coast to lush and forested in the interior.

The World Heritage-listed Old Town of Rhodes stands as the largest inhabited medieval town in Europe, and its mighty fortifications are the finest surviving example of defensive architecture of the time.

History & Mythology

As is the case elsewhere in Greece, the early history of Rhodes is interwoven with mythology. The sun god Helios chose Rhodes as his bride and bestowed upon her light, warmth and vegetation. Their son, Cercafos, had three sons, Camiros, Ialysos and Lindos, who each founded the cities that were named after them.

The Minoans and Mycenaeans had outposts on the islands, but it was not until the Dorians arrived in 1100 BC that Rhodes began to exert power and influence. The Dorians settled in the cities of Kamiros, Ialysos and Lindos and made each an autonomous state. They utilised trade routes to the east which had been established during Minoan and Mycenaean times, and the island flourished as an important centre of commerce.

Rhodes continued to prosper until Roman times. It was allied to Athens in the Battle of Marathon (490 BC), in which the Persians

The Colossus of Rhodes

Whether the famous Colossus of Rhodes ever actually existed can never be proven, since there are no remains and no tangible evidence other than the reports of ancient travellers. The statue was apparently commissioned by Demetrius Poliorketes in 305 BC after he finally capitulated to Rhodian defiance following his long and ultimately failed siege of Rhodes in that same year.

The bronze statue was built over 12 years (294–282 BC) and when completed stood 32m high. What is not clear is where this gargantuan statue stood. Popular medieval belief has it astride the harbour at Mandraki (as depicted on today's T-shirts and tourist trinkets), but it is highly unlikely that this is the case and it's also technically unfeasible.

An earthquake in either AD 225 or 226 toppled the statue, most likely on land, where the remains lay undisturbed for 880 years. In AD 654 invading Saracens had the remains broken up and sold for scrap to a Jewish merchant in Edessa (in modern-day Turkey). The story goes that after being shipped to Syria, it took almost 1000 camels to convey it to its final destination.

were defeated, but had shifted to the Persian side by the time of the Battle of Salamis (480 BC). After the unexpected Athenian victory at Salamis, Rhodes hastily became an ally of Athens again, joining the Delian League in 478 BC. After the disastrous Sicilian Expedition (416–412 BC), Rhodes revolted against Athens and formed an alliance with Sparta, which it aided in the Peloponnesian Wars.

In 408 BC, the cities of Kamiros, Ialysos and Lindos, consolidated their powers for mutual protection and expansion by co-founding the city of Rhodes. The architect Hippodamos, who came to be regarded as the father of town planning, planned the city. The result was one of the most harmonious cities of antiquity, with wide, straight streets connecting its four distinct parts: the acropolis, agora, harbour and residential quarter.

Rhodes became Athens' ally again, and together they defeated Sparta at the Battle of Knidos, in 394 BC. Rhodes then joined forces with Persia in a battle against Alexander the Great, but when Alexander proved invincible, hastily allied itself with him. In the skirmishes following Alexander's death, Rhodes sided with Ptolemy I.

In 305 BC, Antigonus, one of Ptolemy's rivals, sent his son, the formidable Demetrius Poliorketes (the Besieger of Cities), to conquer the city. Rhodes managed to repel Demetrius after a long siege. To celebrate this victory, the 32m-high bronze statue of Helios Apollo (Colossus of Rhodes), one of the Seven Wonders of the Ancient World, was built (see the boxed text).

After the defeat of Demetrius, Rhodes knew no bounds. It built the biggest navy in the Aegean and its port became a principal Mediterranean trading centre. The arts also flourished, and the Rhodian school of sculpture supplanted that of Athens as the foremost in Greece. Its most esteemed sculptor was Pythocretes, whose works included the *Victory of Samothrace*, and the relief of the *trireme* (warship) at Lindos.

When Greece became the battleground upon which Roman generals fought for leadership of the empire, Rhodes allied itself with Julius Caesar. After Caesar's assassination in 44 BC, Cassius besieged Rhodes, destroying its ships and stripping the city of its artworks, which were then taken to Rome. This marked the beginning of Rhodes' decline. In AD 70, Rhodes became part of the Roman Empire.

In AD 155, Rhodes Town was badly damaged by an earthquake, and in 269 the Goths invaded, rendering further damage. When the Roman Empire split, Rhodes became part of the Byzantine province of the Dodecanese. Raid upon raid followed: the Persians in 620, the Saracens in 653, then the Turks.

Phone numbers listed incorporate changes due in Oct 2002; see p83

DODECANESE

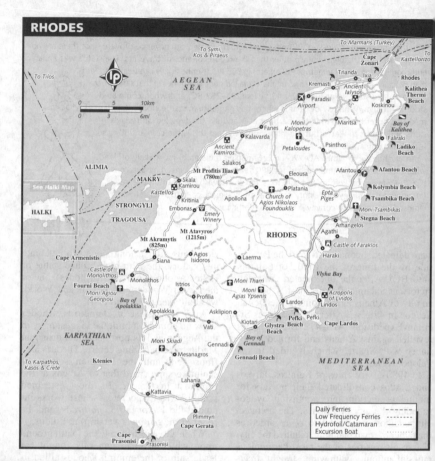

RHODES

When the crusaders seized Constantinople, Rhodes was given independence. Later the Genoese gained control. The Knights of St John arrived in Rhodes in 1309 and ruled for 213 years until they were ousted by the Ottomans. Rhodes suffered several earthquakes during the 19th century, but greater damage was rendered to the city in 1856 by an explosion of gunpowder which had been stored and forgotten – almost 1000 people were killed and many buildings were wrecked. In 1947, after 35 years of Italian occupation, Rhodes became part of Greece along with the other Dodecanese islands.

Getting To/From Rhodes

All the addresses listed in this section are in Rhodes Town.

Air Olympic Airways has at least five flights daily travelling to Athens (€84), two daily to Karpathos (€44.30), one daily to Kastellorizo (€35.80), six weekly to Santorini (€76.90), four weekly to Iraklio (€79.50), three weekly to Kasos (€44.30) and two weekly to Thessaloniki (€105.40) and Mykonos (€78). The Olympic Airways office (☎ 2241 024 571) is located at Ierou Lohou 9.

Aegean Airlines and Axon Airlines offer cheaper options. Aegean Airlines has flights to Athens (€75, four daily), Thessaloniki (€107.50, one daily) and Iraklio (€75, one daily). Through its partner Cronus Airlines, Aegean Airlines offers one stop connections to a number of European destinations. Aegean Airlines (☎ 2241 024 166, fax 2241 024 431) is at Ethelondon Dodekanision 20 while Cronus (☎ 2241 025 444, fax 2241 028 468, e info@cronus.gr) is at 25 Martiou 5.

Axon Airlines has flights to Athens (€73.40, two daily). The Axon Airlines office (☎ 2241 032 224) is at Ethelondon Dodekanision 20.

Castellania Travel Service (☎ 2241 075 860, fax 2241 075 861, e castell@otenet.gr), on Plateia Ippokratous, specialises in youth and student fares, and is one of the best places for low-cost air tickets.

Ferry – Domestic Rhodes is the main port of the Dodecanese and offers a complex array of departures.

The following table lists scheduled domestic ferries from Rhodes to other islands in the Dodecanese in high season.

The EOT and the municipal tourist office located in Rhodes Town can provide you with schedules.

destination	duration	price	frequency
Astypalea	10 hours	€15	2 weekly
Halki	1½ hours	€5.90	9 weekly
Kalymnos	5½ hours	€13.20	1 daily
Karpathos	3½ hours	€13.50	3 weekly
Kasos	5 hours	€16	2 weekly
Kastellorizo	3½ hours	€12	2 weekly
Kos	3½ hours	€10.30	1 daily
Leros	7½ hours	€14	1 daily
Lipsi	9½ hours	€15.30	1 weekly
Nisyros	3¾ hours	€8.80	3 weekly
Patmos	8½ hours	€17	1 daily
Piraeus	15–18 hours	€26.70	2 daily
Symi	2 hours	€5.40	1 daily
Tilos	2½ hours	€8.50	4 weekly

The weekly ferry from Rhodes to Alexandroupolis also stops at Samos (nine hours, €21) in the North-East Aegean.

Ferry – International Poseidon Lines and Salamis Lines both stop at Rhodes en route from Piraeus to Cyprus (Lemesos/Limassol) and Israel (Haifa). From Rhodes to Cyprus takes 15 hours (€70.50), with a further 11 hours to Haifa (€117.40). There is an additional €17.60 port tax on top of these fares. The boats leave Rhodes on Tuesday and Friday. You can buy tickets from Kydon Tours (☎ 2241 023 000, fax 2241 032 741) at Ethelondon Dodekanision 14, in the New Town, or Kouros Travel (☎ 2241 024 377, 2241 022 400), Karpathou 34.

There are no scheduled car ferry services between Marmaris in Turkey and Rhodes. Travellers with a vehicle may have to wait up to four days for an unscheduled crossing to be arranged. A ferry will be dispatched from Marmaris to pick up passengers with a vehicle only if there is also a vehicle to be transported from Marmaris. The crossing takes 2½ hours.

Fares for crossings to Marmaris were as follows at the time of research: passenger €47, motorbike €88, car €176. Greek port taxes are an extra €8.80. Turkish port taxes are US$10 per person and US$3 per vehicle.

If you do plan to cross to Turkey, be prepared to wait. Contact Triton Holidays (☎ 2241 021 690, fax 2241 031 625, e info@tritondmc.gr), Plastira 9, Mandraki, upon arrival to arrange a crossing.

Immigration and customs are on the quay.

Hydrofoil – Domestic Kyriacoulis Hydrofoils (☎ 2241 024 000, fax 2241 020 272), on the quay at Plateia Neoriou 6, operates the following services from Rhodes in high season:

destination	duration	price	frequency
Astypalea	5½ hours	€30.50	1 weekly
Kalymnos	3½ hours	€26	1 weekly
Os	2 hours	€20.60	2 daily
Leros	3½ hours	€28	3 weekly
Nysiros	2¼ hours	€17.20	1 weekly
Patmos	3½ hours	€32.20	3 weekly
Symi	1 hour	€9.80	2 weekly
Tilos	1¼ hours	€17.10	2 weekly

DODECANESE

Tickets are available from Triton Holidays (see Ferry – International). There is an additional daily hydrofoil, the *Aegli*, run and owned by the island Symi, with a daily service (€9.40/18.50 one way/return) to and from Gialos on Symi.

Hydrofoil – International There are two or three daily hydrofoils to Marmaris (one hour, weather permitting) April to October. Fares are currently cheaper than ferries at €32.30/ 39.70 one way/return (plus US$10 Turkish port tax, payable in Turkey). You buy tickets from Triton Holidays, but you must submit your passport a day before your journey. This is currently the only scheduled transport option to and from Turkey.

Catamaran The *Dodekanisos Express* starts its daily run up the Dodecanese at around 8.30am each day stopping at Kos, Kalymnos and Leros daily with stops at other times in Symi, Halki, Tilos, Nisyros, Lipsi and Patmos. Kastellorizo was on the schedule when we were there; check to see if it is included when you travel.

Tickets may be bought at Skevos Travel (☎ 2241 022 461, fax 2241 022 354, ℯ skeyos@rho.forthnet.gr) at Amerikis 11, or from the offices of Dodekanisos Naftiliaki (☎ 2241 070 590, fax 2241 070 591, ℯ info@12ne.gr) at Afstralias 3.

The Tilos-owned *Sea Star* departs Rhodes each morning at 9am for Tilos (55 minutes, €16.20) and Nisyros (€16.50). See Triton Holidays for tickets.

Caique See the Getting There & Away section for Halki for information about caiques between Rhodes and Halki.

Excursion Boat There are excursion boats to Symi (€12 return) every day in summer, leaving Mandraki Harbour at 9am and returning at 6pm. You can buy tickets at most travel agencies, but it is better to buy them at the harbour, where you can check out the boats and haggle. Look for shade and the size and condition of the boat, as these vary greatly. You can buy an open return if you want to stay on Symi.

Getting Around Rhodes

To/From the Airport The airport is 16km south-west of Rhodes Town, near Paradisi. There are 21 buses daily between the airport and Rhodes Town's west side bus station (for routes down the west side of Rhodes; €1.50). The first leaves Rhodes Town at 5am and the last at 11pm; from the airport, the first leaves at 5.55am and the last at 11.45pm.

Bus Rhodes Town has two bus stations. From the east side bus station on Plateia Rimini there are 18 buses daily to Faliraki (€1.50), 14 to Lindos (€3.10), three to Kolymbia (€1.50), nine to Gennadi (€3.70) via Lardos, and four to Psinthos (€1.60).

From the west side station next to the New Market there are buses every half hour to Kalithea Thermi (€1.50), 10 to Koskinou (€1.50), five to Salakos (€2.70), two to ancient Kamiros (€3.40), one to Monolithos (€4.40) via Skala Kamirou, and Embonas (€3.90). The EOT and municipal tourist office give out schedules.

Car & Motorcycle There are numerous car and motorcycle rental outlets in Rhodes Town's New Town. Shop around and bargain because the competition is fierce.

Taxi Rhodes Town's main taxi rank is east of Plateia Rimini. There are two zones on the island for taxi meters: zone one is Rhodes Town and zone two (slightly higher) is everywhere else. Rates are a little higher between midnight and 6am. Sample fares are: airport €10.30, Filerimos €8, Petaloudes €14.70, ancient Kamiros €20.60, Lindos €25 and Monolithos €32.30. Taxi company contact phone numbers include ☎ 2241 064 712, ☎ 2241 064 734 and ☎ 2241 064 778.

Disabled travellers may call Savvas Kafkakis who runs a special taxi on mobile ☎ 697 413 1882.

Bicycle The Bicycle Centre (☎ 2241 028 315), Griva 39, Rhodes Town, has three-speed bikes for €2.70 and mountain bikes for €3.80.

Excursion Boat There are excursion boats to Lindos (€15 return) every day in summer, leaving Mandraki Harbour at 9am and returning at 6pm.

RHODES TOWN
postcode 851 00 • pop 42,400

The heart of Rhodes Town is the Old Town, enclosed within massive walls. Avoid the worst of the tourist hordes by beginning your exploration early in the morning. But at any time, away from the main thoroughfares and squares, you will find deserted labyrinthine alleyways. Much of the New Town to the

north is dominated by package tourism, but it does have a few places of interest to visitors.

Orientation

The Old Town is nominally divided into three sectors: the Kollakio or Knights' Quarter, the Hora and the Jewish quarter. The Kollakio comprises the northern sector and is roughly bordered by Agisandrou and Theofiliskou which run east to west. The Kollakio contains most of the medieval historical sights of the Old Town. The Hora, often known as the Turkish Quarter, is primarily the commercial sector and contains most of the shops and

RHODES OLD TOWN

PLACES TO STAY			
26 Maria's Rooms			
27 Mike and Mama's Pension			
30 Pension Olympos			
31 Marco Polo Mansion			
38 Hotel Cava d'Oro			
39 Hotel Spot			
41 Hotel Via Via			
48 Mango Rooms & Cafe Bar			
51 Pension Minos			
52 Apollo Tourist House			
53 Pension Andreas			
54 Pink Elephant			

PLACES TO EAT			
22 Myrovolos			
28 Diafani Garden Restaurant			

32 Cleo's Italian Restaurant			
37 Mystagogia			
43 Taverna Kostas			
45 Araliki			
46 Nisyros			
50 L'Auberge Bistrot			

THINGS TO SEE
1 Temple of Aphrodite
3 Palace of the Grand Masters
4 Entrance to Moat #2
6 Inn of Spain
7 Inn of Provence
8 Chapelle Française
9 Inn of France
10 Museum of Decorative Arts
11 Inn of Auvergne

12 Old Knights' Hospital
13 Inn of the Order of the Tongue of Italy
14 Palace of Villiers de l'Ile Adam
21 Archaeological Museum
23 Clock Tower
24 Mosque of Süleyman
25 Turkish Library
29 Mustafa Pasha Baths (Hammam)
33 Agios Spyridon Church (Kavakli Mosque)
35 Castellania Fountain
40 Kahal Shalom Synagogue
42 Ibrahim Pasha Mosque
49 Recep Pasha Mosque
55 Entrance to Moat

OTHER
2 Commercial Bank of Greece
5 Old Town Post Office Branch
15 National Bank of Greece
16 Departure Point for F/B Nisos Kalymnos & Dodekanisos Express Catamaran
17 Departure Point for Boats to Turkey
18 Customs Office
19 Commercial Bank ATM
20 Port Police
34 Castellenia Travel Service
36 Resalto Club
44 Kafe Besara
47 Folk Dance Theatre

DODECANESE

Phone numbers listed incorporate changes due in Oct 2002; see p83

restaurants. Sokratous and its northerly extension Orfeos are the Hora's main thoroughfares. The sector is bordered to the east by Perikleous, beyond which is the quieter, mainly residential Jewish Quarter. The Old Town is accessed by nine main gates *(pyles)* and two rampart-access portals. The whole town is a mesh of Byzantine, Turkish and Latin architecture with quiet, twisting alleyways punctuated by lively squares. While you will inevitably get lost at some point, it will never be for long.

The commercial centre of the New Town lies north of the Old Town and is easily explored on foot. Most commercial activity is centred on two blocks surrounding Plateia Kyprou. The hotel district is centred on a large sector bordered by 28 Oktovriou and G Papanikolaou. The main square of the New Town is Plateia Rimini, just north of the Old Town. The tourist offices, bus stations and main taxi rank are on or near this square.

The commercial harbour, for international ferries and large inter-island ferries, is east of the Old Town. Excursion boats, small ferries, hydrofoils and private yachts use Mandraki Harbour, farther north.

Information
Tourist Offices The EOT (☎ 2241 023 255, fax 2241 026 955, e eot-rodos@otenet.gr), on the corner of Makariou and Papagou, supplies brochures and maps of the city, and will helps find accommodation. It's open 7.30am to 3pm Monday to Friday. In summer the same service is provided by Rhodes' municipal tourist office (☎ 2241 035 945), Plateia Rimini. Opening times are 8am to 8pm Monday to Saturday and 8am to noon on Sunday; it's closed in winter.

From either of these you can pick up the *Rodos News*, a free English-language newspaper.

The tourist police (☎ 2241 027 423) are next door to the EOT and open 24 hours daily. The port police may be contacted on ☎ 2241 022 220.

Money The main National Bank of Greece and the Alpha Credit Bank are on Plateia Kyprou. In the Old Town there is a National Bank of Greece on Plateia Mousiou, and a Commercial Bank of Greece nearby. All have ATMs. Opening times are 8am to 2pm Monday to Thursday, 8am to 1.30pm Friday.

American Express (☎ 2241 021 010) is represented by Rhodos Tours, Ammohostou 18.

Post & Communications The main post office is on Mandraki Harbour. Opening times are 7.30am to 8pm Monday to Friday. The Old Town post office branch is open seven days. The OTE at Amerikis 91 is open 7am to 11pm daily.

For Internet access try Rock Style Internet Cafe (☎ 2241 027 502, e info@rockstyle .gr), Dimokratias 7, just south of the Old Town, or Mango Cafe Bar (☎ 2241 024 877, e karelas@hotmail.com), Plateia Dorieos 3, in the Old Town.

Bookshops Second Story Books (mobile ☎ 697 759 4320), Amarantou 24, in the New Town has a broad selection of second-hand foreign-language books.

Laundry Wash your clothes at Lavomatique, 28 Oktovriou 32, or Express Servis, Dilberaki 97 (off Orfanidou). Both charge around €3 a load. Express Laundry, Kosta Palama 5, does service washes for €3.50.

Luggage Storage You can store luggage at Planet Holidays (☎ 2241 035 722), Gallias 6, for €2.60 for two hours and €3.50 for up to two days. You can negotiate a price for a longer period.

Emergency Rhodes' general hospital (☎ 2241 080 000) is at Papalouka, just north-west of the Old Town. For emergency first aid and the ambulance service, call ☎ 2241 025 555 or ☎ 2241 022 222.

Old Town
In medieval times, the Knights of St John lived in the Knights' Quarter and other inhabitants lived in the Hora. The 12m-thick city walls are closed to the public, but you can do **guided walks** (☎ *2241 023 359; €3.50, 2.45pm Tues & Sat)*, starting at the courtyard of the Palace of the Grand Masters.

Knights' Quarter An appropriate place to begin an exploration of the Old Town is the imposing cobblestone **Avenue of the Knights** (Ippoton), where the knights lived. The knights were divided into seven tongues' or languages, according to their place of origin – England, France, Germany, Italy, Aragon, Auvergne and Provence – each responsible for protecting a section of the bastion. The Grand Master, who was in charge, lived in the palace, and each tongue was under the auspices of a bailiff. The knights were divided into soldiers, chaplains and ministers to the sick.

To this day the street exudes a noble and forbidding aura, despite modern offices now occupying most of the inns. Its lofty buildings stretch in a 600m-long unbroken wall of honey-coloured stone blocks, and its flat facade is punctuated by huge doorways and arched windows. The inns reflect the Gothic styles of architecture of the knights' countries of origin. They form a harmonious whole in their bastion-like structure, but on closer inspection each possesses its own graceful and individual embellishments.

First on the right, if you begin at the eastern end of the Avenue of the Knights, is the **Inn of the Order of the Tongue of Italy** (1519); next to it is the **Palace of Villiers de l'Île Adam**. After Sultan Süleyman had taken the city, it was Villiers de l'Île who had the humiliating task of arranging the knights' departure from the island. Next along is the **Inn of France**, the most ornate and distinctive of all the inns. On the opposite side of the street is a wrought-iron gate in front of a Turkish garden.

Back on the right side is the **Chapelle Française** (Chapel of the Tongue of France), embellished with a statue of the Virgin and Child. Next door is the residence of the Chaplain of the Tongue of France. Across the alleyway is the **Inn of Provence**, with four coats of arms forming the shape of a cross, and opposite is the **Inn of Spain**.

On the right is the magnificent 14th-century **Palace of the Grand Masters** (☎ 2241 023 359, Ippoton; admission €3.50; open 8.30am-3pm Tues-Sunday). It was destroyed

in the gunpowder explosion of 1856 and the Italians rebuilt it in a grandiose manner, with a lavish interior, intending it as a holiday home for Mussolini and King Emmanuel III. It is now a museum, containing sculpture, mosaics taken from Kos by the Italians, and antique furniture.

In the 15th-century knights' hospital is the **archaeological museum** (☎ 2241 027 657, Plateia Mousiou; admission €2.40; open 8.30am-3pm Tues-Sat; 8.30am-3pm Sun). Its most famous exhibit is the exquisite Parian marble statuette, the Aphrodite of Rhodes, a 1st-century BC adaptation of a Hellenistic statue. Less charming to most people is the 4th-century BC Afroditi Thalassia in the next room. However, writer Lawrence Durrell was so enamoured of this statue that he named his book Reflections on a Marine Venus after it. Also in this room is the 2nd-century BC marble Head of Helios, found near the Palace of the Grand Masters where a Temple of Helios once stood.

MARTIN HARRIS

DODECANESE

Aphrodite of Rhodes, found in Rhodes Old Town's archaeological museum

The **Museum of the Decorative Arts** (☎ *2241 072 674, Plateia Argyrokastrou; admission €1.50; open 8.30am-3pm Tues-Sun*), farther north, houses a collection of artefacts from around the Dodecanese.

On Plateia Symis, there are the remains of a 3rd-century BC **Temple of Aphrodite**, one of the few ancient ruins in the Old Town.

Hora The Hora has many Ottoman legacies. During Turkish times, churches were converted to mosques, and many more were built from scratch. Most are now dilapidated. The most important one is the newly renovated, pink-domed **Mosque of Süleyman**, at the top of Sokratous. It was built in 1522 to commemorate the Ottoman victory against the knights, then rebuilt in 1808.

Opposite is the 18th-century **Turkish library** *(Plateia Arionos; admission free; open 9.30am-4pm Mon-Sat)*. It was founded in 1794 by Turkish Rhodian Ahmed Hasuf and houses a small collection of Persian and Arabic manuscripts and a collection of Korans written by hand on parchment.

The Jewish Quarter The Jewish Quarter of the Old Town is an almost forgotten sector of Rhodes Town, where life continues at an unhurried pace and where local residents live almost oblivious to the hubbub of the Hora, no more than a few blocks away. This area of quiet streets and sometimes dilapidated houses was once home to a thriving Jewish community. Descendants of Sephardic Jews from Spain, the Jewish community here spoke Ladino (a dialect based on Spanish) and numbered over 2000 souls at the height of its prosperity.

The **Kahal Shalom synagogue** on Dosiadou has a commemorative plaque to the many members of Hora's large Jewish population who were sent to Auschwitz during the Nazi occupation. Jews still worship here and it is usually open in the morning. Close by is Plateia Martyron Evreon (Square of the Jewish Martyrs).

New Town

The **Acropolis of Rhodes**, south-west of the Old Town on Monte Smith, was the site of the ancient Hellenistic city of Rhodes. The hill is named after the English admiral Sir Sydney Smith, who watched for Napoleon's fleet from here in 1802. It has superb views.

The site's restored 2nd-century **stadium** once staged competitions in preparation for the Olympic Games. The adjacent **theatre** is a reconstruction of one used for lectures by the Rhodes School of Rhetoric. Steps above here lead to the **Temple of Pythian Apollo**, with four re-erected columns. The unenclosed site can be reached on city bus No 5.

North of Mandraki, at the eastern end of G Papanikolaou, is the graceful **Mosque of Murad Reis**. In its grounds are a Turkish cemetery and the Villa Cleobolus, where Lawrence Durrell lived in the 1940s, writing *Reflections on a Marine Venus*.

The town **beach** begins north of Mandraki and continues around the island's northernmost point and down the west side of the New Town. The best spot is on the northernmost point, where it's not quite as crowded.

Activities

Scuba Diving Three diving schools operate out of Mandraki: **Waterhoppers Diving Centre** (☎/*fax 2241 038 146, mobile* ☎ *69 3296 3173,* e *water-hoppers@rodos.com, Perikleous 29*), **Diving Centres** (☎ *2241 061 115, fax 2241 066 584, Lissavonas 33*) and **Scuba Diving Trident School** (☎/*fax 2241 029 160, S. Zervou 2*). All offer a range of courses including a 'One Day Try Dive' for €40 to €50. You can get information from their boats at Mandraki. Kalithea Thermi is the only site around Rhodes where diving is permitted.

Greek Dancing Lessons The **Nelly Dimoglou Dance Company** (☎ *2241 020 157, Folk Dance Theatre, Andronikou; admission €10.30 per person, group €7.40 per person; performances 9.30pm Mon, Wed, Fri*), gives lessons and stages performances.

Organised Tours

Triton Holidays (☎ *2241 021 690, fax 2241 031 625,* e *info@tritondmc.gr, Plastira 9, Mandraki*) This place offers a wide range of

RHODES TOWN

OTHER
1 Aquarium
3 National Bank
5 Mosque of Murad Reis
6 Skevos Travel
10 Second Story Books
12 The Bicycle Centre
16 Express Servis
19 Lavomatique
21 Olympic Airways
22 OTE
23 Cronus Airlines
24 Manuel Music Center
25 Port Police
26 Post Office
27 The Stag & Doe
28 Departure Points for Hydrofoils, Diving & Excursion Boats
29 Kydon Tours
30 Aegean Airlines; Axon Airlines
31 Rhodos Tours
32 Hospital
33 EOT
34 Tourist Police
35 National Bank of Greece
36 Alpha Credit Bank
37 Triton Holidays
38 Planet Holidays
39 Bus Station (West Side)
40 Kouros Travel
41 Express Laundry
42 Bus Station (East Side)
44 Municipal Tourist Office
45 Taxi Rank
46 Kyriacoulis Hydrofoils
47 Rock Style Internet Cafe

PLACES TO STAY
2 Grand Hotel Rhodes
8 New Village Inn
18 Hotel Anastasia

PLACES TO EAT
4 Restaurant Ellinikon
7 Chalki
9 Princess
11 Kringlan Swedish Bakery
17 Thomas & Charlotte's Taverna
20 7,5 Thavma
43 Nirefs, Demetriades & Cofea Pâtisseries
48 To Steki tou Tsima

ENTERTAINMENT
13 Colorado Entertainment Centre
14 Down Under Bar
15 Red Lion

tours, and provides specialist advice on any of the islands and Turkey.

Places to Stay – Budget

The Old Town has a reasonable selection of budget accommodation.

Mike and Mama's Pension (☎ 2241 025 359, *Menekleous 28*) Singles/doubles €20.50/ 23.50. This pension is a reasonably comfortable option.

Pension Andreas (☎ 2241 034 156, fax 2241 074 285, ⓔ *andreasch@otenet.gr*, Ⓦ *www.hotelandreas.com, Omirou 28D*) Singles/doubles with bathroom €32.50. This exceptionally friendly pension has clean, pleasant rooms and a terrace bar with terrific views and does great breakfasts. There is a private garden, library and Internet centre for guests across the street.

Apollo Tourist House (☎ 2241 032 003, ⓔ *hotelapollo@email.com*, Ⓦ *www.apollo -touristhouse.com, Omirou 28C*) Singles/ doubles €20/41. This is a small cosy pension, with shared bathrooms and kitchen, a small courtyard and friendly Spanish-Chilean owner. Renovations are planned for 2002.

Pension Minos (☎ 2241 031 813, *Omirou 5*) Singles/doubles €26.50/32.30. This pension has spotless, spacious rooms and a roof garden with views of the Old Town.

Maria's Rooms (☎ 2241 022 169, *Menekleous 147*) Doubles without/with bathroom €29.50/35.20. This establishment, just off Sokratous, has pleasant, clean-smelling rooms.

Hotel Spot (☎/fax 2241 034 737, ⓔ *spothot@otenet.gr, Perikleous 21*) Singles/ doubles with bathroom €32.30/ 35.20. The Spot has exceptionally clean, pleasant rooms. There is also a small book exchange, left luggage facilities and Internet access for guests.

Pink Elephant (☎/fax 2241 022 469, *Irodotou 42*) Doubles without/with bathroom €26.50/29.50, triples with bathroom €35.20. Despite the name, this hotel's attractive decor is blue and white.

Pension Olympos (☎/fax 2241 033 567, *Agiou Fanouriou*) Singles/doubles €29.30/

41. This pension has pleasant rooms with bathroom and television, and an attractive little courtyard.

Most of the New Town's hotels are modern and characterless, but there are some exceptions.

New Village Inn (☎/fax 2241 034 937, ⓔ *newvillageinn@rho.forthnet.gr, Konstantopedos 10*) Singles/doubles €23.50/ 35.20. This New Town inn has tastefully furnished rooms with refrigerator and fan, and a traditional stone-walled courtyard, festooned with plants.

Places to Stay – Mid-Range

Mango Rooms (☎/fax 2241 024 877, ⓔ *karelas@hotmail.com, Plateia Dorieos 3*) Doubles/triples €44/45. This place has clean, nicely furnished rooms with bathroom, TV, ceiling fan, safety box and refrigerator.

Hotel Via Via (☎/fax 2241 077 027, ⓔ *viavia@rho.forthnet.gr, Lisipou 2*) Doubles/triples with bathroom €47/58.70. Just off Pythagora, this pristine hotel has tastefully furnished rooms and is open in winter.

Hotel Cava D'Oro (☎ 2241 036 980, *Kistiniou 15*) Doubles triples €40/61. Michael Palin stayed in one of the very tasteful old stone rooms during the series *Pole to Pole*. Rooms have air-con, TV and telephone.

Hotel Anastasia (☎ 2241 028 007, fax 021 815, ⓔ *finikas2@otenet.gr, 28 Oktovriou 46*). Doubles/triples €42.50/52.80. This New Town hotel, in a former Italian mansion, is set back from the road, and is reasonably quiet. The high-ceilinged rooms, with tiled floors, are spotless, and the rates include breakfast.

Places to Stay – Top End

Rhodes is full of top-end resort-style accommodation. Try these two for starters.

Marco Polo Mansion (☎/fax 2241 025 562, ⓔ *marcopolo@rho.forthnet.gr, Agiou Fanouriou 40-42*). Doubles €80-130; min 1 week. Featured in glossy European magazines is this old-fashioned Anatolian inn decorated in rich Ottoman-era colours. This cool and shady lodging, right in the heart of the Old Town, is run by the ebullient Effie Dede

Grand Hotel Rhodes (☎ *2241 0026 284, fax 2241 035 589, Akti Miaouli)* Singles/doubles €80/120. Next to the beach is the pretty but pricey Grand Hotel with bars, restaurant and swimming pools. It is open all year and has rooms with either a pleasant garden or sea view; the price includes breakfast.

Places to Eat – Budget

Old Town Avoid the touts and tack along Sokratous and around Plateia Ippokratous. Hit the back streets to find less touristy places to eat.

Taverna Kostas (☎ *2241 026 217, Pythagora 62)* Mains €5-7. Popular Kostas' is good value and has stood the test of time with its repeat clientele and good grills and fish dishes.

Diafani Garden Restaurant (☎ *2241 026 053, Plateia Arionos)* Mayirefta €4-5. Back in the Old Town, this restaurant on a quiet square serves home-style, reasonably priced dishes. Try the excellent mousakas (€5) or stifado (€7.40).

Araliki (☎ *2241 073 708, Aristofanous 45)* Mezedes €2.50-3.50. This atmospheric kafeneio serves creative mezedes including several vegetarian versions.

Myrovolos (☎ *2241 038 693, Lahitos 13)* Mains €4.50-6. Minuscule Myrovolos is a welcome antidote to Rhodes' tacky tourist restaurants. Excellent, imaginative food is served up and there is live music from 6pm to 8pm. Sample the seafood with ouzo special (€11.80).

New Town The New Town has some surprisingly good places to eat, as long as you are prepared to look.

Kringlan Swedish Bakery (☎ *2241 039 090, I Dragoumi 14)* Breakfast €5.50. This bakery in the New Town serves sandwiches and pastries that are out of this world; great for breakfast.

Chalki (☎ *2241 033 198, Kathopouli 30)* Mezedes €2.50-5. Chalki is a down-to-earth and thoroughly idiosyncratic eatery. Choose from an enticing display of mezedes, and down them with excellent draught wine.

7,5 Thavma (☎ *2241 039 805, Dilberaki 15)* Mains €5.50-7.50. 7,5 Thavma is a Swedish-influenced diner with Greek and Swedish dishes alternating on an inventive fusion menu. Recommended dishes are tiger prawns (€7.60) and salmon (€7).

Thomas & Charlotte's Taverna (☎ *2241 073 557, Georgiou Leondos 8)* Mains €5-6.50. This taverna serves a wide selection of standard Greek dishes. Try the tasty *kleftiko* (€6.50), a slow-cooked mixture of meat and vegetables served wrapped in greaseproof paper.

Places to Eat – Mid-Range & Top End

Old Town *Nisyros* (☎ *2241 031 741, Agiou Fanouriou 45-47)* Mains €7.30-13. A beautiful and tastefully decorated restaurant with impeccable service and a wide range of Greek dishes. Dining is in a leafy, secluded courtyard.

Cleo's Italian Restaurant (☎ *2241 028 415, Agiou Fanouriou 17)* Pasta dishes €5.40-10. This is a sophisticated place with a cool, elegant interior and a quiet courtyard.

Mystagogia (☎ *2241 032 981, Themistokleous 5)* Mezedes €2-7. Opened in late 1999, Mystagogia draws its charm as much from the open fireplace for winter meals as from its carefully cooked dishes. *Bekri mezes* or 'drunkard's mezes' (spicy pork or beef cubes in tomato sauce; €11.50) is recommended for the curious and hungry.

L'Auberge Bistrot (☎ *2241 034 292, Praxitelous 21)* Mains €6.50-8. If you crave something other than Greek food, this bistro serves terrific French dishes. Enjoy a fine Côte du Rhône Rouge (€11.80) to wash it all down.

New Town *Restaurant Ellinikon* (☎ *2241 028 111, G Papanikolaou 6)* Mains €5-6.50. This restaurant excels in traditional Greek fare. The stifado is highly recommended, but leave room for the luscious iced caramel, which often features as dessert of the day.

Princess (☎ *2241 020 068, Mandilara 26)* Mains €6-8. This is a classy place offering Mediterranean dishes from Greece, Spain, Italy and the Middle East. Great for that special, romantic night out; the chef's recommendation: gorgonzola chicken (€9.40).

To Steki tou Tsima (☎ *2241 074 390, Peloponisou 22)* Seafood mezedes €4.50-5.50. To Steki is an unpretentious and totally untouristy fish restaurant on the south side of New Town. Sample from an imaginative and occasionally unusual array of fish (such as *yermanos*, €7.50) and shellfish-based mezedes (try *fouskes*, €3.50).

Cafes

Feverish touting reaches its acme at the patisseries for people-watching, with names like *Nirefs*, *Demetriades* and *Cofea* bordering the New Market. Nevertheless, they're convivial meeting places. Coffee and cake costs around €5.50.

There's a lively cafe strip on S. Venizelou.

Entertainment

Old Town *Son et Lumière* (☎ *2241 021 922, entrance Plateia Rimini)* Admission €3.50. This sound-and-light show, staged in the grounds of the Palace of the Grand Masters, depicts the Turkish siege of Rhodes and is superior to most such efforts. A noticeboard outside gives the times for performances.

Kafe Besara (☎ *2241 030 363, Sofokleous 11-12)* This Aussie-owned place is one of the Old Town's liveliest bars, and a great place to hang about.

Mango Cafe Bar (☎ *2241 024 877, Dorieos 3)* This bar claims to have the cheapest drinks in the Old Town as well as Internet access and is the preferred haunt of local expats, scuba divers and diehard travellers.

Resalto Club (☎ *2241 020 520, Plateia Damagitou)* Admission free, beer €6, cocktails €9. Open 11pm until late. This Greek music centre features live music on weekends. The repertoire ranges from *entehno* (artistic compositional) to *laïko* (popular) to *rembetiko* (blues).

New Town There is a plethora of discos and bars in New Town – over 600 at last count and rising. The two main areas are called Top Street and the Street of Bars. Top Street is Alexandrou Diakou and the Street of Bars is Orfanidou, where a

cacophony of Western music blares from every establishment.

Down Under Bar (☎ *2241 032 982, Orfanidou 37)* Shots €3. For a wild night of dancing on the bar, make for this place.

Red Lion (*Orfanidou 9)* Pints €2.30. For something more subdued, this bar has the relaxed atmosphere of a British pub. Ron and Vasilis will gladly answer questions about Rhodes for the price of a drink.

Colorado Entertainment Centre (☎ *2241 075 120, Akti Miaouli & Orfanidou 57)* This is a popular place. The Colorado consists of three venues in one – the Dancing Club, the Heaven Night Club and a live band venue. There is more than enough fun for a week in this enormous palace of hype.

Shopping

Good buys in Rhodes' Old Town are gold and silver jewellery, leather goods and ceramics (although leather goods are cheaper in Turkey). Look around and be discriminating – it's quite acceptable to haggle.

Manuel Music Center (☎ *2241 028 266, 25 Martiou 10-13)* For good-quality Greek music, ie, not 'Zorba the Greek does Syrtaki' tourist music, all the latest and more Greek CDs are on sale here.

Getting Around Rhodes Town

Local buses leave from Mandraki. Bus No 2 goes to Analipsi, No 3 to Rodini, No 4 to Agios Dimitrios and No 5 to Monte Smith. You can buy tickets at the kiosk on Mandraki.

EASTERN RHODES

Rhodes' best beaches are on the east coast. There are frequent buses to Lindos, but some beaches are a bit of a trek from the road. It's possible to find uncrowded stretches of coast even in high season.

Kalithea Thermi, 10km from Rhodes Town, is a derelict Italian-built spa. Within the complex are crumbling colonnades, domed ceilings and mosaic floors. Buses from Rhodes Town stop opposite the turnoff to the spa. The beach is used by Rhodes diving schools (see Activities in the Rhodes Town section). To the right there's a small sandy beach (with a snack bar); take the track which veers right from the turn-off to the spa. Kalithea is currently being restored.

Faliraki Beach, 5km farther south, is the island's premier resort and comes complete with high-rise hotels, fast-food joints and bars. Although the main stretch of beach is crowded, the bay at the extreme southern end is uncrowded and popular with nude bathers. The bus stop is close to the beach.

Ladiko Beach is next along. Touted locally as 'Anthony Quinn Beach', this is in fact two back-to-back coves with a pebbly beach on the north side and volcanic rock platforms on the south. The swimming is good and development is relatively low-key.

At Kolymbia, further down the coast, a right turn leads in over 4km of pine-fringed road to the **Epta Piges** (Seven Springs), a beautiful spot where a lake fed by springs can be reached either along a path or through a tunnel. There are no buses around here, so take a Lindos bus and get off at the turn-off.

Back on the coast, **Kolymbia** and **Tsambika** are good but crowded beaches. A steep road (signposted) leads in 1.5km to reach **Moni Tsambikas**, from where there are terrific views. The monastery is a place of pilgrimage for childless women. On 18 September, the monastery's festival day, women climb up to it on their knees and then pray to conceive.

Arhangelos, 4km farther on and inland, is a large agricultural village with a tradition of carpet weaving and handmade goatskin boots production. Just before Arhangelos here is a turn-off to **Stegna Beach**, and just after to the lovely sandy cove of **Agathi**; both are reasonably quiet. The **Castle of Faraklos** above Agathi was a prison for recalcitrant knights and the island's last stronghold to fall to the Turks. The fishing port of **Haraki**, just south of the castle, has a pebbled beach. There are more beaches between here and Vlyha Bay, 2km from Lindos.

Places to Stay & Eat Accommodation at Faliraki Beach is monopolised by package tour companies, so you are advised to move on, or camp if you have the gear.

Faliraki Camping (☎ *2241 085 358, Faliraki*) Adult/tent €3.50/2.70. This once pleasant ground with restaurant, bar and minimarket is now marred by ugly construction work for new studios.

Dining in Faliraki is basically hit-and-miss. If you are serious about eating here, you might as well have a curry or a pizza.

Faliraki Raj (☎ *2241 086 986, Lindou*) Curry €6-7. Opposite the church, Faliraki Raj won't be same as home, but will make a spicy change from mousakas.

La Strada Ristorante (☎ *2241 085 878, Lindou*) Pizzas €4-5. Apart from crispy, wood-oven pizzas, La Strada offers up over 100 variations of pasta, fish and meat.

Lindos Λίνδος
postcode 851 07 • pop 724

Lindos village, 47km from Rhodes, lies below the Acropolis and is a showpiece of dazzling-white 17th-century houses, many with courtyards with black-and-white *hohlakia* (pebble mosaic) floors. Once the dwellings of wealthy admirals, many have been bought and restored by foreign celebrities. The main thoroughfares are lined with tourist shops and cafes, so you need to explore the labyrinthine alleyways to fully appreciate the place.

Lindos is the most famous of the Dodecanese's ancient cities, receiving 500,000 visitors a year. It was an important Doric settlement because of its excellent vantage point and good harbour. It was first established around 2000 BC and is overlaid with a conglomeration of Byzantine, Frankish and Turkish remains.

After the founding of the city of Rhodes, Lindos declined in commercial importance, but remained an important place of worship. The ubiquitous St Paul landed here en route to Rome. The Byzantine fortress was strengthened by the knights, and also used by the Turks.

The 15th-century **Church of Agia Panagia** on Acropolis is festooned with 18th-century frescoes.

Orientation & Information The town is pedestrianised. All vehicular traffic terminates on the central square of Plateia

DODECANESE

Eleftherias, from where the main drag, Acropolis, begins. The donkey terminus is a little way along here.

The municipal tourist information office (☎ 2244 031 900) is on Plateia Eleftherias, open 7.30am to 9pm daily. Pallas Travel (☎ 2244 031 494, fax 2244 031 595) and Lindos Sun Tours (☎ 2244 031 333), both on Acropolis, have room-letting services. The latter also rents cars and motorcycles.

The Commercial Bank of Greece, with ATM, is by the donkey terminus. The National Bank of Greece is on the street opposite the Church of Agia Panagia. Turn right at the donkey terminus for the post office. There is no OTE, but there are cardphones on Plateia Eleftherias and the Acropolis. Lindos' two Internet cafes are near the post office.

The privately owned Lindos Lending Library, on Acropolis, is well stocked with English books. It also has a laundrette (€7.30 per load).

The Acropolis of Lindos The Acropolis (☎ 2244 031 258; admission €3.50; open 8am-6.30pm Tues-Sun, 12.30pm-6.30pm Mon) is spectacularly perched atop a 116m-high rock. It's about a 10-minute climb to the well-signposted entrance gate. Once inside, a flight of steps leads to a large square. On the left (facing the next flight of steps) is a trireme (warship) hewn out of the rock by the sculptor Pythocretes. A statue of Hagesandros, priest of Poseidon, originally stood on the deck of the ship. At the top of the steps ahead, you enter the Acropolis by a vaulted corridor. At the other end, turn sharp left through an enclosed room to reach a row of storerooms on the right. The stairway on the right leads to the remains of a 20-columned **Hellenistic stoa** (200 BC). The Byzantine **Church of Agios Ioannis** is to the right of this stairway. The wide stairway behind the stoa leads to a 5th-century BC propylaeum, beyond which is the 4th-century **Temple to Athena**, the site's most important ancient ruin. Athena was worshipped on Lindos as early as the 10th century BC, so this temple has replaced earlier ones on the site. From its far side there are splendid views of Lindos village and its beach.

Donkey rides to the Acropolis cost €3.50 one way.

Places to Stay & Eat Accommodation is expensive and reservations are essential in summer. The following two places are near each other on the north side of the village.

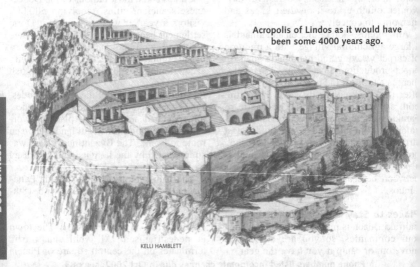

Acropolis of Lindos as it would have been some 4000 years ago.

KELLI HAMBLETT

Follow the donkeys heading to the Acropolis for about 150m to find them.

Lindos Pension (☎ 2244 031 369) Doubles €35.20. This is the cheapest option. Rooms are small and plain, but clean and pleasant.

Pension Electra (☎ 2244 031 266, Lindos) Doubles with bathroom €50. Electra has a roof terrace with superb views and a beautiful shady garden. Rooms have air-con.

Kalypso (☎ 2244 031 669) Mains €5.50-7. Set in one of Lindos' historic buildings, Kalypso is open for lunch and dinner. Try either sausages in mustard, chicken in coconut sauce or rabbit stew in red wine.

WESTERN RHODES

Western Rhodes is more green and forested than the east coast, but it's more exposed to winds so the sea tends to be rough, and the beaches are mostly of pebbles or stones. Nevertheless, tourist development is rampant, and consists of the suburb resorts of Ixia, Trianda and Kremasti. Paradisi, despite being next to the airport, has retained some of the feel of a traditional village.

Ialysos Ιαλυσός

Like Lindos, Ialysos, 10km from Rhodes, is a hotchpotch of Doric, Byzantine and medieval remains. The Doric city was built on Filerimos Hill, which was an excellent vantage point, attracting successive invaders. The only ancient remains are the foundations of a 3rd-century BC temple and a restored 4th-century BC fountain. Also at the site are the restored **Monastery of Our Lady** and the **Chapel of Agios Georgios**.

The ruined **fortress** *(admission €2.40; open 8am-5pm Tues-Sun)* was used by Süleyman the Magnificent during his siege of Rhodes Town. No buses go to ancient Ialysos. The airport bus stops at Trianda, on the coast. Ialysos is 5km inland from here.

Ancient Kamiros

Αρχαία Κάμειρος

The extensive **ruins** *(admission €2.40; open 8am-5pm Tues-Sun)* of the Doric city of Kamiros stand on a hillside above the west coast, 34km from Rhodes Town. The ancient city, known for its figs, oil and wine, reached the height of its powers in the 6th century BC. By the 4th century BC, it had been superseded by Rhodes. Most of the city was destroyed by earthquakes in 226 and 142 BC, but the layout is easily discernible.

From the entrance, walk straight ahead and down the steps. The semicircular rostrum on the right is where officials made speeches to the public. Opposite are the remains of a **Doric temple** with one standing column. The area next to it, with a row of intact columns, was probably where the public watched priests performing rites in the temple. Ascend the wide stairway to the ancient city's main street. Opposite the top of the stairs is one of the best preserved of the **Hellenistic houses** that lined the street. Walk along the street, ascend three flights of steps, and continue ahead to the ruins of the 3rd-century **great stoa**, which had a 206m portico supported by two rows of Doric columns. It was built on top of a huge 6th-century cistern which supplied the houses with rainwater through an advanced drainage system. Behind the stoa, at the city's highest point, stood the **Temple to Athena**, with terrific views inland.

Buses from Rhodes Town to Kamiros stop on the coast road, 1km from the site.

Kamiros to Monolithos

Skala Kamirou, 13.5km south of Ancient Kamiros, is a fairly unremarkable place sporting a few market gardens, a scattering of tavernas and a petrol station. More importantly, it serves as the access port for travellers heading to and from the island of Halki (see the Halki section later). The road south from here to Monolithos has some of the island's most impressive scenery. From Skala Kamirou the road winds uphill with great views across to Halki. This is just a taste of what's to come at the ruined 16th-century **Castle of Kastellos**, reached along a rough road from the main road, 2km beyond Skala Kamirou. There is a left fork to Embonas (see The Interior, later in this section) 8km farther along. The main road continues for another 9km to **Siana**, a picturesque village below Mt Akramytis (825m), famed for its honey and *souma*, a local firewater.

DODECANESE

The village of Monolithos, 5km beyond Siana, has the spectacularly sited **Castle of Monolithos** perched on a sheer 240m high rock and reached along a dirt track. Continuing along this track, at the fork bear right for **Moni Georgiou** and left for the very pleasant shingled **Fourni Beach**.

Places to Stay & Eat There is little accommodation along this stretch of coast.

Hotel Thomas (☎ 2246 061 291, *Monolithos*) Doubles €29.50. You could try this hotel in Monolithos village.

Althemeni Restaurant (☎ 2246 031 303, *Skala Kamirou*) Fish €40 per kg. This place is right on the harbourfront and offers a wide range of fish, as well as grills and mayirefta.

SOUTHERN RHODES
South of Lindos, Rhodes becomes progressively less developed. Although **Pefki**, 2km south of Lindos, does get package tourists, it's still possible to get out of earshot of other tourists, away from the main beach.

Lardos is a pleasant village 6km west of Lindos and 2km inland from Lardos Beach. From the far side of Lardos a right turn leads in 4km to **Moni Agias Ypsenis** (Monastery of Our Lady) through hilly, green countryside.

Heading south from Lardos, don't miss the almost hidden **Glystra Beach**, 4km south along the coast road. This diminutive bay is one of the best swimming spots along the whole eastern coastline.

The well-watered village of **Laerma** is 12km north-west of Lardos. From here it's another 5km to the beautifully sited 9th-century **Moni Tharri**, which was the island's first monastery and has been re-established as a monastic community. It contains some fine 13th-century frescoes.

Asklipion, 8km north of Gennadi, is an unspoilt village with the ruins of yet another castle and the 11th-century **Church of Kimisis Theotokou**, which has fine Byzantine wall paintings.

Gennadi Γεννάδι
postcode 851 09 • pop 542
Gennadi, (ye-**nah**-dhi) 13km south of Lardos is an attractive, largely untouched

agricultural village masquerading as a holiday centre. For independent travellers it i probably the best base for a protracted stay in the south. The village itself, a patchwork of narrow streets and whitewashed houses is set several hundred metres back from the beach.

Places to Stay & Eat *Effie's Dream Apartments* (☎ 2244 043 410, fax 2244 04. 437, ⓔ dreams@srh.forthnet.gr, ⓦ www .rodosnet.gr) Doubles/triples €35.50/44 This place, right by an enormous 800-year old mulberry tree, has modern, spotlessly clean studios with lovely rural and sea vis tas from the communal balcony. The friendly Greek-Australian owners will mee you if you call ahead. Internet access is also available.

Effie's Dream Cafe Bar (☎ 2244 04. 410) Snacks €2.50-4. Below the apart ments of the same name, Effie's serve drinks and tasty snacks such as village sausage with onions and peppers (€2.40).

I Kouzina tis Mamas (☎ 2244 043 547 Pasta dishes €3.50. You will find this pizza and pasta restaurant along the main street dishing up a wide range of Greek grills a well.

Gennadi to Prasonisi
From Gennadi an almost uninterrupted beach of pebbles, shingle and sand dune extends down to **Plimmyri**, 11km south. It's easy to find deserted stretches.

From Plimmyri the main road continues to **Kattavia**, Rhodes' most southerly village The 11km dirt road north to Messanagros winds through terrific scenery. From Kat tavia a 10km road leads south to the remote **Prasonisi**, the island's southernmost point once joined to Rhodes by a narrow sandy isthmus now split by encroaching seas. It' a popular spot for windsurfing.

Places to Stay & Eat *Studios Platanos* (☎ 2244 046 027, *Lahania*) Studio €26.50-30. Owned by the proprietors o Taverna Platanos, each air-conditioned stu dio has a kitchenette and fridge. Lahania i signposted 2km off the main highway.

Taverna Platanos (☎ *2244 046 027, Plateia Iroön Polytehniou, Lahania*) Mains €3-5. Platanos makes for a popular Sunday outing, dining on the tiny village square amid running water. The food served is wholesome and filling village fare; try chickpeas (€2.60) or locally produced pork chops (€5).

The Faros Taverna (☎ *2244 091 030, Prasonisi*) Doubles €30; meals €7-8. One of two tavernas on the beach, Faros has comfortable rooms that attract windsurfers. The attached restaurant serves up tasty, filling fare.

South of Monolithos

Rhodes' south-west coast doesn't see as many visitors as other parts of the island. It is lonely and exposed and has only recently acquired a sealed road, completing the network around this southern quadrant of the island. Forest fires in recent years have devastated many of the west-facing hillsides and there is a general end-of-the-world feeling about the whole region.

The beaches south of Monolithos are prone to strong winds. From the important crossroads village of **Apolakkia**, 10km south of Monolithos, a road crosses the island to Gennadi, passing through the unspoilt villages of **Arnitha** and **Vati** with an optional detour to **Istrios** and **Profilia**. A turn-off to the left 7km south of Apolakkia leads to the 18th-century **Moni Skiadi**. It's a serene place with terrific views down to the coast, and there is free basic accommodation for visitors.

THE INTERIOR

The east-west roads that cross the island have great scenery and very little traffic. If you have transport they're well worth exploring. It's also good cycling territory if you have a suitably geared bicycle.

Petaloudes Πεταλούδες

Petaloudes (*Valley of the Butterflies; admission €2.20; open 8.30am-sunset 1 May-30 Sept*), one of the more popular 'sights' on the package tour itinerary, is reached along a 6km turn-off from the west coast road, 2.5km south of Paradisi.

The so-called 'butterflies' (*Callimorpha quadripunctarea*) are in fact strikingly coloured moths that are lured to this gorge of rustic footbridges, streams and pools by the scent of the resin exuded by the styrax trees. Regardless of what you may see other tourists doing, do not make any noises to disturb the butterflies; their numbers are declining rapidly, largely due to noise disturbance. Better still, don't visit and leave them alone. If you must, there are buses to Petaloudes from Rhodes Town.

Around Petaloudes

From Petaloudes a winding cross-island road leads to the 18th-century **Moni Kalopetras** built by Alexander Ypsilandis, the grandfather of the Greek freedom fighter. This same road leads across the central mountain spine of roads through a rather dry landscape full of olive trees to the pretty village of **Psinthos** which makes for a very pleasant lunch break.

From Psinthos you can choose to loop back to Rhodes Town (22km) via a fast but undistinguished direct route passing through **Kalythies**, or head further south and pick up the very pretty cross island route from **Kolymbia** to **Salakos**.

Places to Stay & Eat *Artemidis Restaurant & Rooms* (☎ *2241 051 735, Psinthos*) Doubles €30. This restaurant serves tasty traditional Greek fare and has a swimming pool. The rooms are above the restaurant.

Pigi Fasouli Estiatorio (☎ *2241 050 071, Psinthos*). Mains €4.50-6. Dine on succulent steaks or mezedes under cool plane trees next to running water. Look for signs from the main square in Psinthos to find it.

Salakos & Mt Profitis Ilias
Σάλακος & Ορος Προφήτης Ηλίας
This route to Mt Profitis Ilias (pro-**fee**-tis ee-**lee**-as) and Salakos (**sah**-la-kos) across the north central highlands of Rhodes is perhaps the most scenic of all the day-trip drives or rides. It can be tackled from either the west or the east coast of Rhodes, though the most attractive way is from east to west.

Start at the signposted turn-off near **Kolymbia**. Shortly beyond you may wish to stop briefly to visit **Epta Piges** (Seven Springs), a cool, shady valley with running water and, you guessed it, seven springs. This is a popular tourist attraction in its own right. Heading up and inland you will next come to the villages of **Arhipoli** and **Eleousa**, once used by the Italians as hill stations. The road now climbs through a landscape that becomes more and more forested. Two kilometres from Eleousa you will pass the small Byzantine church of **Agios Nikolaos Foundouklis** with its faded frescoes. This is a good picnic spot – there are tables, chairs and spring water.

It is a further 6km along a winding, pine-shrouded road to the summit of **Mt Profitis Ilias** (780m). The surrounding forest is lush and cool and a pleasant relief for cyclists.

It is downhill from here and a further 12km of winding and cruising will bring you to the village of **Salakos**. If you are on foot you can walk down on an established track that begins near the easy-to-find **Moni Profiti Ilia**. It will take you about 45 minutes to walk down to Salakos. The village is a cheery place, with a small square and fountain and several cafes for coffee or cold beers.

From Salakos it is only 9.5km downhill to the west coast village of **Kalavarda**.

Wine Country

From Salakos you may detour to **Embonas** on the slopes of Mt Attavyros (1215m), the island's highest mountain. Embonas is the wine capital of Rhodes and produces some of the island's best tipples. The red Cava Emery, or Zacosta and white Villare from Emery wines in Embonas in Rhodes are good choices. You can taste and buy them in the **Emery Winery** (☎ 2246 029 111, Embonas; free wine tasting to 3pm Mon-Fri).

Embonas village is no great shakes, despite being touted by EOT as a 'traditional village'. You may wish to detour around Mt Attavyros to **Agios Isidoros**, 14km south of Embona, a prettier and still unspoilt wine-producing village that you can visit en route to Siana.

Halki Χάλκη

postcode 851 10 • pop 280

Halki is a small rocky island just 16km of the west coast of Rhodes. Like many small islands in the Dodecanese it has suffered the depredations of a failed economy (sponge diving), a chronic lack of water and subsequent population depletion due to migration. Many Halkiots now live in Tarpon Springs, Florida, where they have established a buoyant sponge-fishing community. Still, Halki has undergone a rejuvenation in recent years thanks to rather select visitors who come to Halki with discreet villa and studio rental.

Getting To/From Halki

Ferry L.A.N.E. Lines of Crete includes Halki on its long, twice weekly 'milk run' from Rhodes to Piraeus via Crete and Milos.

Such destinations include Rhodes (two hours, €6), Karpathos-Pigadia (three hours €6.30), Crete-Sitia (7½ hours, €11.90) and Piraeus (22 hours, €29.50).

Hydrofoil One hydrofoil a week connects Halki with Rhodes (1¼ hours, €11.50), Tilos (3¼ hours, €18) and Kalymnos (4½ hours €24.50). Check for current departure days.

Catamaran The *Dodekanisos Express* catamaran calls in twice a week at Halki on its run up the Dodecanese to Patmos. From Halki the departure north is at around 9.55am and back to Rhodes at around 7.40pm.

Caique Halki is linked to Skala Kamirou on Rhodes. Departures (1½ hours, €5.50) from Halki are at 6am (Monday to Saturday) and 9am (Sunday). From Skala Kamirou departures are 2.30pm (Monday to Saturday) and 4pm (Sunday).

To get to Skala Kamirou from Rhodes Town, take the 1.30pm Monolithos bus from the west side bus station (€3.50). There are no connecting buses on Sunday morning.

Getting Around Halki

There are no buses or taxis on the island, or rental cars or motorbikes, but there are

HALKI

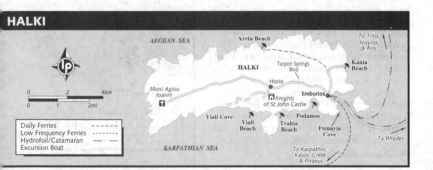

vater taxis to the main beaches and the is-
and of Alimnia. Better bring a stout pair of
valking shoes.

EMBORIOS Εμπορειός
The attractive port town of Emborios resembles Gialos on Symi, but on a smaller
scale. The port is draped around a horseshoe bay and former sea captains' mansions – some renovated, others still in a
state of disrepair – rise up around the bay
in a colourful architectural display. Cars
are all but banned from the harbour, so the
Emborios waterside enjoys a tranquil,
motor-free setting.

Orientation & Information
The quay is in the middle of the harbour.
There is one road out of Emborios, grandly
named Tarpon Springs Boulevard for the
ex-Halkiots in Florida, who financed most
of its construction. It passes Podamos, the
island's only sandy beach, and goes as far
as Moni Agiou Ioanni.

There is no official tourist office on
Halki. The two travel agents on the harbour
may help out with queries. There is no bank
or ATM on Halki – the nearest is on Rhodes.
The travel agents will exchange money.

Things to See
The impressive stone **clock tower** at the
southern side of the harbour is a gift from
the Halkiots of Florida. While the clock
tower may look good, don't rely on it for
the time. Each of the four faces is stuck on
a different hour of the day.

The **Church of Agios Nikolaos** has the
tallest belfry in the Dodecanese and boasts
a particularly well-made and impressive
hohlaki courtyard on the east side.

Places to Stay & Eat
Accommodation is in short supply. Book
beforehand wherever possible.

Captain's House (☎ 2246 045 201) Doubles with bathroom €29.50. This beautiful
19th-century mansion with period furniture
and a tranquil, tree-shaded garden is the most
pleasant place to stay. It is owned by a retired
Greek sea captain and his British wife.

Argyrenia Rooms (☎ 2246 045 205)
Doubles €20.50. Rooms are small but clean
and this place is open all year. It is at the
junction with the road to Kania beach.

Mavri Thalassa (☎ 2246 045 021) Mains
€4-5. This restaurant at the end of the harbour is well regarded by locals and does
good fish dishes. The shrimp with rice (€5)
is recommended.

Taverna Maria (☎ 2246 045 089)
Mayirefta €3. This is a friendly family
restaurant with good mayirefta dishes. The
owners' special is lamb fricassee (€5.30).

AROUND HALKI
Podamos beach is the closest and the best
beach. It is a 15-minute walk from Emborios in the direction of Horio. There is one
cantina and one restaurant.

Horio, a 30-minute walk along Tarpon
Springs Boulevard from Emborios, was the
'pirate-proof' inland town. Once a thriving
community of 3000 people, it's now derelict

DODECANESE

and uninhabited. A path leads from Horio's churchyard to a Knights of St John castle.

Moni Agiou Ioanni is a two-hour, 8km, unshaded walk along a concrete road from Horio. The church and courtyard, protected by the shade of an enormous cypress tree, is a quiet, tranquil place, but it comes alive each year from 28–29 August during the feast of the church's patron, St John. During this time there is music and dancing and free food and wine. Beds are available all year for a small donation to the church.

Karpathos
Κάρπαθος

postcode 857 00 • pop 5323

If ever there was a Greek island that combined the right proportions of size, attractiveness, remoteness, water activities and general good feel, that island might just be the elongated island of Karpathos (**kar**-pahthos), midway between Crete and Rhodes. Karpathos has rugged mountains, numerous beaches – among the best in the Aegean – and unspoilt villages. So far, it has not succumbed to the worst excesses of mass tourism.

The island is traversed by a north-south mountain range. For hundreds of years the north and south parts of the island were isolated from one another and so they developed independently. It is even thought that the northerners and southerners have different ethnic origins. The northern village of Olymbos is of endless fascination to ethnologists for the age-old customs of its inhabitants.

Karpathos has a relatively uneventful history. Unlike almost all other Dodecanese islands, it was never under the auspices of the Knights of St John. It is a wealthy island, receiving more money from emigrants living abroad (mostly in the USA) than any other Greek island.

Getting To/From Karpathos

Air There are four flights weekly to and from Athens (€88.40), up to two daily to

Rhodes (€44.30) and three weekly to Kasos (€23.50). The Olympic Airways office (☎ 2245 022 150) is on the central square in Pigadia. The airport is 18km south-west of Pigadia.

Ferry Karpathos shares the same essentially limited ferry services as its neighbours Halki and Kasos. Windy weather can sometimes delay arrivals and departures.

L.A.N.E. Lines of Crete provides three services weekly to Rhodes (four hours, €13.50) via Halki (three hours, €8.20) as well as to Piraeus (18½ hours, €24.40) via Milos (13 hours, €22). Kasos (1½ hours, €5.60) is served by three weekly services.

Note that these ferries also serve the ports of Sitia (4¼ hours, €10.60) and Agios Nikolaos (seven hours, €12.90) in Crete.

Getting Around Karpathos

To/From the Airport There is no airport bus. Travellers must take a taxi (€8.80) or seek independent transport.

Bus Pigadia is the transport hub of the island; a schedule is posted at the bus terminal. Buses serve most of the settlements in southern Karpathos. The fare is between €1 and €1.30. There is no bus between Pigadia and Olymbos or Diafani, but a bus meets the excursion boats from Pigadia at Diafani and transports people up to Olymbos.

Car, Motorcycle & Bicycle Gatoulis Car Hire (☎ 2245 022 747, fax 2245 022 814), on the east side of Pigadia on the road to Aperi, rents cars, motorcycles and bicycles. Possi Travel (☎ 2245 022 235) also arranges car and motorcycle hire.

The 19.5km stretch of road from Spoa to Olymbos is unsurfaced, but you can drive it, with care. Do not tackle this road by motorcycle or scooter. If you rent a vehicle, make it a small jeep and fill up your tank before you leave.

Taxi Pigadia's taxi rank (☎ 2245 022 705) is on Dimokratias, near the bus station. A price list is displayed. Sample taxi fares from Pigadia are as follows: Ammoöpi (€4.40),

Arkasa (€8.80), Pyles (€8.80), Kyra Panagia (€14.70) and Diafani (€61.60).

Excursion Boat In summer there are daily excursion boats from Pigadia to Diafani for €14.70 return. There are also frequent boats to the beaches of Kyra Panagia and Apella for €9. Tickets can be bought at the quay.

From Diafani, excursion boats go to nearby beaches and occasionally to the uninhabited islet of Saria where there are some Byzantine remains.

PIGADIA Πηγάδια
pop 1692
Pigadia (pi-**gha**-dhi-ya) is the island's capital and main port. It's a modern town, pleasant enough, but without any eminent buildings or sites. The town is built on the edge of Vrondi Bay, a 4km-long sandy beach where you can rent water sports equipment. On the beach are the remains of the early Christian basilica of Agia Fotini.

Orientation & Information
From the quay, turn right and take the left fork onto Apodimon Karpathion, Pigadia's main thoroughfare, which leads to the central square of Plateia 5 Oktovriou.

Pigadia doesn't have an EOT but there is a local tourist information office (☎ 2245 023 835, fax 2245 023 836) in a kiosk in the middle of the harbourfront. The police (☎ 2245 022 224) are near the hospital. Nearby are the post office and OTE. Possi Travel (☎ 2245 022 148, fax 2245 022 252) is the main travel agency for ferry and air tickets.

The National Bank of Greece, which has an ATM, is situated on Apodimon Karpathion. The bus station is one block up from the waterfront on Dimokratias. There's a laundrette, Laundro Express, on Mitropolitou Apostolou.

Caffe Galileo Internet 2000 (☎ 2245 023 606, ⓔ caffegal@otenet.gr), on Apodimon Karpathion, has Internet access.

Places to Stay
There's plenty of accommodation and owners usually meet the boats.

DODECANESE

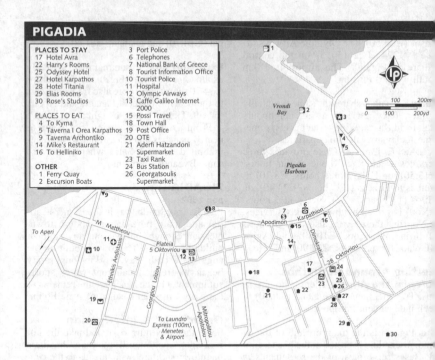

PIGADIA

PLACES TO STAY
17 Hotel Avra
22 Harry's Rooms
25 Odyssey Hotel
27 Hotel Karpathos
28 Hotel Titania
29 Elias Rooms
30 Rose's Studios

PLACES TO EAT
4 To Kyma
5 Taverna I Orea Karpathos
9 Taverna Archontiko
14 Mike's Restaurant
16 To Helliniko

OTHER
1 Ferry Quay
2 Excursion Boats

3 Port Police
6 Telephones
7 National Bank of Greece
8 Tourist Information Office
10 Tourist Police
11 Hospital
12 Olympic Airways
13 Caffe Galileo Internet 2000
15 Possi Travel
18 Town Hall
19 Post Office
20 OTE
21 Aderfi Hatzandoni Supermarket
23 Taxi Rank
24 Bus Station
26 Georgatsoulis Supermarket

Harry's Rooms (☎ 2245 022 188, Kyprou 2) Singles/doubles €17.60/20.50. These rooms, just off 28 Oktovriou, are spotless.

Elias Rooms (☎ 2245 022 446, e elias rooms@hotmail.com) Singles/doubles with bathroom €20.50/23.50. These cosy rooms are in a quiet part of town with great views. The owner is friendly and helpful.

Rose's Studios (☎/fax 2245 022 284) Double studios €23.50 with kitchen. Fairly high up behind Pigadia are these well-kept studios with bathroom and kitchen.

Hotel Karpathos (☎ 2245 022 347) Singles/ doubles with bathroom €23.50/25. This C-class hotel has light, airy rooms.

Hotel Avra (☎ 2245 022 388, 2245 023 486, 28 Oktovriou 50) Doubles €29.50. This E-class hotel has small but comfortable rooms with ceiling fan, fridge and a small common kitchen.

Hotel Titania (☎ 2245 022 144, fax 2245 023 307) Singles/doubles €38/45. This C-class hotel, opposite the Karpathos, has spacious, pleasant rooms and is open all year.

Odyssey Hotel (☎ 2245 023 240, fax 2245 023 762) Double/triple studios €35.20/41. Each studio has a kitchenette, phone, music, TV, fridge, room safe and balcony, and fans are available on demand.

Places to Eat

Mike's Restaurant (☎ 2245 022 727, Apodimon Karpathion) Grills €4.20-10.80. One of the longer-standing and more popular eateries, Mike's serves up consistently good, solid fare at reasonable prices.

Taverna I Orea Karpathos (☎ 2245 022 501, Limani) Mains €3.50-5. Near the quay, I Orea Karpathos serves a wide range of traditional Karpathian dishes and reputedly the best *makarounes* (€4.40) in Pigadia.

To Helliniko (☎ 2245 023 932, Apodimon Karpathion) Daily specials €3.80-8.80. Boasting a pleasant outdoor terrace and a tasteful interior, the Helliniko's

Karpathian goat stifado (€5) is particularly commendable.

To Kyma (☎ *2245 022 496, Limani*) Fish €28/kg. To Kyma is known for its top-class fish dishes and offers fine harbourside dining.

Taverna Archontiko (☎ *2245 022 531*) Mains €5-9.50. Open evenings only. Rooftop dining is at its best at this popular restaurant. Try the green pepper chicken (€6.50).

Karpathos has several *supermarkets* (try Georgatsoulis or Aderfi Hatzandoni) and *bakeries*.

SOUTHERN KARPATHOS
Ammoöpi Αμμοοπή

If you are seeking sun and sand and some of the best and clearest water in the whole of the Aegean head for Ammoöpi (Amm-oh-oh-pee), 8km south of Pigadia. This is *the* place on the island to enjoy eating, sleeping, drinking, swimming and snorkelling to the max. There are four buses daily from Pigadia. Ammoöpi is a scattered beach resort without any centre or easily identifiable landmarks, so ask the bus or taxi driver to drop you off at whichever establishment you decide to check.

Places to Stay & Eat Ammoöpi Beach Rooms (☎ *2245 081 123, Mikri Ammoöpi*) Doubles €12. With spotless, simply furnished rooms, this is the cheapest place to stay. The rooms are at the northern end of Ammoöpi.

Hotel Sophia (☎/*fax 2245 081 078*) Doubles/triples €36/44. This hotel is farther back along the main road, behind the Blue Sea Hotel.

Blue Sea Hotel (☎ *2245 081 036, fax 2245 081 095,* e *huguette@hellasnet.gr*) Doubles €44. Each of the 27 comfortable double rooms has a fridge and ceiling fan and the owners host a 'Karpathos Night' playing Karpathos music) every Wednesday evening.

Vardes (☎ *2245 081 111, fax 2245 081 112*) Double studios €44. For seekers of total quiet relaxation consider Vardes – a small block of very tasteful, spacious and airy studios set back against the hillside. All have phone and kitchenette.

Taverna Ilios (☎ *2245 081 148*) Mains €4.70-6. Offering Greek and international cuisine, Ilios serves up large portions and is just back from the beach. The chef recommends the Ilios fillet (€9.50) for hungry diners.

Ammoopi Taverna (☎ *2245 081 138*) At the far northern end of Ammoöpi and right on the beach is this mid-range eatery. Food is good but service is brusque. There is a Greek music night once a week.

Menetes Μενετές

Menetes (Me-ne-**tes**) is perched on top of a sheer cliff which is 8km above Pigadia. It's a picturesque, unspoilt village with pastel-coloured neoclassical houses lining its main street. Behind the main street are narrow, stepped alleyways that wind between more modest whitewashed dwellings. The village has a little **museum** on the right as you come from Pigadia. The owner of Taverna Manolis will open it up for you.

Places to Stay & Eat *Mike Rigas domatia* (☎ *2245 081 269*) Doubles/triples with bathroom €16.20/20.50. These domatia are in a traditional Karpathian house on the north side of Menetes down a side road. The garden brims with trees and flowers.

Taverna Manolis (☎ *2245 081 103*) Mains €4.50-7. This taverna dishes up generous helpings of grilled meat.

Fiesta Dionysos (☎ *2245 081 269*) Mains €4-6. This place specialises in local dishes, including omelette made with artichokes and Karpathian sausages.

Arkasa & Finiki Αρκάσα & Φοινίκι

Arkasa (ar-**ka**-sa), 9km farther on, straddles a ravine. It is changing from a traditional village to holiday resort. Turn right at the T-junction to reach the authentic village square.

A turn-off left, just before the ravine, leads after 500m to the remains of the 5th-century Basilica of Agia Sophia. Two chapels stand amid mosaic fragments and columns. Agios Nikolaos beach is just south across the headland from here.

DODECANESE

The serene fishing village of Finiki (fi-ni-ki) lies 2km north of Arkasa. There is no decent swimming here as in Arkasa, but it is a pretty diversion while on your way north. The little sculpture at the harbour commemorates the heroism of seven local fishers during WWII – locals will tell you the story.

Places to Stay & Eat *Glaros Studios* (☎ 2245 061 015, 2245 061 016, *Agios Nikolaos*) Double studios €44-50. Done out in Karpathiot style and right on Agios Nikolaos beach, these studios have raised sofa-style beds and large terraces with sun beds, and enjoy a cool sea breeze.

Eleni Studios (☎/fax 2245 061 248, *Arkasa*) Double apartments €44. These fully-equipped apartments are on the left along the road to Finiki. The tidy complex boasts a swimming pool.

Pine Tree Studios (*mobile* ☎ 69 7736 9948, *Adia*) Doubles €35. Above the restaurant of the same name, these comfortable fridge- and kitchenette-equipped studios make for a quiet rural retreat.

Dimitrios Fisherman's Taverna (☎ 2245 061 294, *Finiki*) Fish platter for 2 €14.70. Locals come from all over the island to eat the fresh fish at this cosy taverna just off Finiki harbour.

Pine Tree Restaurant (*mobile* ☎ 69 7736 9948, *Adia*) Ladera €3-4.50. About 9km north of Finiki you will find this peaceful oasis under pine trees overlooking the sea. Try the homemade bread, makarounes and stifado.

Lefkos Λεύκος

Lefkos (**lef**-kos), 13km north of Finiki, and 2km from the coast road, is a burgeoning resort centred around a little fishing quay. It is a beach-lover's paradise with five superb sandy beaches. In summer Lefkos gets crowded, but at other times it still has a rugged, off-the-beaten-track feel about it.

Local boat owners sometimes take visitors to the islet of Sokastro where there is a ruined castle. Another diversion from the beaches is the ancient catacombs, reached by walking inland and looking for the brown and yellow signpost to the catacombs.

Places to Stay & Eat Accommodation tends to be block-booked by tour companies in Lefkos. Call either of the following before turning up.

Sunset Studios (☎ 2245 071 171, *fax 2245 071 407*) Double studios €38. Sunset Studios are high up, overlooking Golden Beach. Rooms all have sea views and are immaculate.

Golden Sands Studios (☎ 2245 071 175, *fax 2245 071 219*) Double studios €35. These conveniently located, breezy studios abutting Golden Beach, have well-equipped kitchens.

Small Paradise Taverna (☎ 2245 071 184) Ladera €2.40-3. This taverna serves tasty local dishes and fresh seafood on a vine-shaded terrace.

Tou Kalymniou to Steki (☎ 2245 071 449, *Lefkos*) Mains €4.40-6. Also known as 'O Kalymnios' and located right by the little fishing harbour, this restaurant dishes up fish (€26.50 per kg) as well as many traditional Greek dishes. Try the crayfish salad (€3.30).

Getting There & Around There are two buses weekly to Lefkos and a taxi costs €20.50. Hitching is dicey as there is not much traffic.

Lefkos Rent A Car (☎/fax 2245 071 057) is a reliable outlet with competitive prices. The owner will deliver vehicles free of charge to anywhere in southern Karpathos.

CENTRAL KARPATHOS

Aperi, Volada, Othos and Pyles, the well watered mountain villages to the north of Pigadia, are largely unaffected by tourism. None has any accommodation, but all have tavernas and kafeneia. **Aperi** was the island's capital from 1700 until 1892. Its ostentatious houses were built by wealthy emigrants returning from the USA. Like Aperi, **Volada** has an air of prosperity.

Othos (altitude 510m) is the island's highest village. It has a small ethnographic museum. From Othos the road winds downhill to **Pyles**, a gorgeous village of twisting streets, pastel houses and citrus groves. It clings to the slopes of Mt Kali Limni (1215m), the Dodecanese's second-highest peak.

The fine beaches of **Ahata**, **Kyra Panagia** and **Apella** can be reached along mostly dirt roads off the east coast road, but are most easily reached by excursion boat from Piadia. Kyra Panagia and Apella both offer accommodation and tavernas. These are the best places on Karpathos for snorkelling and skin diving.

Mesohori, 4km beyond the turn-off for Lefkos, is a pretty village of whitewashed houses and stepped streets. **Spoa** village is 6km farther on at the beginning of the 9.5km dirt road to Olymbos. It overlooks the east coast and has a track down to **Agios Nikolaos Beach**.

NORTHERN KARPATHOS
Diafani & Olymbos
Διαφάνι & Ολυμπος

Diafani is Karpathos' small northern port, where scheduled ferries stop six times weekly. There's no post office or bank, but Orfanos Travel Holidays (☎ 2245 051 410), as currency exchange. There's no OTE but there are cardphones.

Clinging to the ridge of barren Mt Profitis Ilias, 4km above Diafani, Olymbos is a living museum (population 330). Women wear bright, embroidered skirts, waistcoats and headscarves, and goatskin boots. The interiors of the houses are decorated with embroidered cloth and their facades feature brightly painted, ornate plaster reliefs. The inhabitants speak in a vernacular which contains some Doric words, and some of the houses have wooden locks of a kind described by Homer. Olymbos is a matrilineal society – a family's property passes down from the mother to the first-born daughter. The women still grind corn in windmills and bake bread in outdoor communal ovens.

Olymbos, alas, is no longer a pristine backwater caught in a time warp. Tourism has taken hold in a big way and is the village's main money spinner. The 'traditional' village is finding it ever harder to remain traditional and is in danger of becoming a kind of kitsch eco-Disney for day-trippers from Pigadia. Olymbos is still fascinating, but sadly rather overrated for what it ultimately has to offer.

Places to Stay & Eat – *Olymbos* Pension **Olymbos** (☎ 2245 051 252) Singles/doubles €14.70/17.60. These clean, simply furnished rooms are just off the main street.

Mike's Rooms (☎ 2245 051 304) Doubles €20.50. These rooms are just beyond the bus turnaround.

Hotel Aphrodite (☎ 2245 051 307) Doubles with bathroom €30. This hotel, near the central square, has immaculate rooms.

Makarounes are served at all the restaurants in Olymbos.

Olymbos Taverna (☎ 2245 051 252) Mains €2.90-4. You'll eat solidly here; go for the makarounes (€2.90). The service, however, can be very slow.

Mike's Taverna (☎ 2245 051 304) Mains €2-4.50. This place, directly below Mike's Rooms, is also a good option, but can get busy with the day trippers.

Samiotiko '1769' (☎ 2245 051 272) Makarounes €3.50. For a good view and top-rate loukoumades and makarounes seek out this little cafe-restaurant on the main street.

Diafani *Vananda Camping* (☎ 2245 051 288) Adult/tent €3.20/2.30. If you walk 30 minutes (2km) north you will reach this well-watered camping ground and hippy-style kafeneio, 50m from pebbly Vananda Beach.

Nikos Hotel (☎ 2245 051 289) Singles/doubles €20.50/25. This hotel, with comfortable rooms and breakfast included, is on the left as you enter Diafani.

Hrysi Akti (☎ 2245 051 315, fax 2245 051 215) Doubles with bathroom €29.50. This hotel is opposite the caique quay in Diafani. The first floor rooms are better and have TV and fridge.

Balaskas Hotel (☎/fax 2245 051 320, ✉ balaskashotel@yahoo.com) Doubles €29.50. This modern property, 100m inland from the harbour, has good rooms and breakfast is included.

Chrysi Akti Taverna (☎ 2245 051 215) Mains €3.80-5.30. This taverna is popular and the service is friendly.

Mayflower (☎ 2245 051 302) Mains €5.90. Next door to Hrysi Akti, Mayflower is about your only other convenient harbourside choice.

DODECANESE

Kasos Κάσος

postcode 858 00 • pop 1088

Kasos, 11km south of Karpathos, is really
the end of the line. It's the last Dodecanese
island before Crete and looking south, it is
the last Greek island before Egypt. It is neither particularly easy to get to, nor to get
away from if the weather in these parts is
inclement. Kasos is a rocky little island
with prickly pear trees, sparse olive and fig
trees, drystone walls, sheep and goats.

History

Despite being diminutive and remote,
Kasos has an eventful history. During Turkish rule it flourished, and by 1820 it had
11,000 inhabitants and a large mercantile
fleet. Mohammad Ali, the Turkish governor
of Egypt, regarded this fleet as an impedi-
ment to his plan to establish a base on Crete
from which to attack the Peloponnese and

quell the uprising. So, on 7 June 1824, Ali
men landed on Kasos and killed arour
7000 inhabitants. This massacre is com
memorated annually on the anniversary o
the slaughter and Kasiots return fro
around the world to participate.

During the late 19th century, many Ka
iots emigrated to Egypt and around 5000 o
them helped build the Suez Canal. Last cen
tury many emigrated to the USA.

Getting To/From Kasos

Air There are five flights weekly to Rhode
(€44.30), and two to Karpathos (€23.50
The Olympic Airways office (☎ 041 555)
on Kritis.

Ferry L.A.N.E. Lines of Crete include
Kasos on its long run to/from Rhodes an
Piraeus via Karpathos, Crete and Milo
Sample fares are: Piraeus €24 (17 hours
Rhodes €16.20 (6½ hours) and Sitia €7.7
(2½ hours).

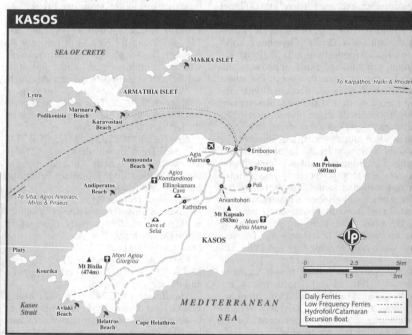

KASOS

SEA OF CRETE

MAKRA ISLET

Lytra

ARMATHIA ISLET

To Karpathos, Halki & Rhodes

Marmara
Beach
Podikonisia
Karavostasi
Beach

Fry
Emborios

Agia
Marina
Ammounda
Beach

Panagia

Mt Prionas
(601m)

Agios
Konstandinos
Ellinokamara
Cave

Poli

Andiperatos
Beach

To Sitia, Agios Nikolaos,
Milos & Piraeus

Arvanitohori

Kathistres

Mt Kapsalo
(583m)

Moni
Agiou Mama

Cave of
Selaï

KASOS

Platy

Moni Agiou
Giorgiou

Kourika

Mt Bixila
(474m)

Kasos
Strait

Avlaki
Beach

Helatros
Beach

Cape Helatros

*MEDITERRANEAN
SEA*

| | | 2.5 | 5km |
| 0 | 1.5 | | 3mi |

Daily Ferries	- - - - - -
Low Frequency Ferries	— - — -
Hydrofoil/Catamaran	— · · —
Excursion Boat	· · · · · · ·

DODECANESE

xcursion Boat In summer the *Athina*
xcursion boat (☎ 2245 041 047) travels
om Fry to the uninhabited Armathia Islet
€5.90 return) where there are sandy
eaches.

ietting Around Kasos
here is no bus on Kasos. The airport is
nly 800m along the coast road from Fry.
   There are just two taxis (☎ 2245 041 158,
245 041 278) on Kasos. Motorbikes can be
:nted from Frangiskos Moto Rentals
☎ 2245 041 746) for €10.30 per day.

'RY Φρυ
ry **(free)** is the island's capital and port. It
an be thoroughly explored in under an hour.
's a pleasant, ramshackle kind of place with
ttle tourism. Its narrow whitewashed streets
re usually busy with locals in animated dis-
ussion. The town's focal point is the pic-
uresque old fishing harbour of Bouka. The
uburb of Emborios is 1km east of Fry.

)rientation & Information
'urn left at the quay to reach Bouka. Veer
:ft, and then right, and continue along the
vaterfront to the central square of Plateia
roön Kasou. Turn right here to reach Kri-
is, Fry's main street. To reach Emborios,
ontinue along the waterfront passing the
urn-off (signposted 'Ai Mammas') for
³anagia, Poli and Moni Agiou Mamma.
   Kasos does not have an EOT or tourist
•olice, but Emmanuel Manousos, at Kasos
Maritime and Travel Agency (☎ 2245 041
$95, @ kassos@kassos-island.gr), Plateia
roön Kasou, is helpful.
   The National Bank of Greece is repre-
ented by the supermarket on Kritis. There is
ι Commercial Bank ATM on the south side
•f Fry. Kasos Maritime and Travel Agency
vill exchange money. The post office is near
he ATM. The OTE is behind Plateia
)imokratias. Check your email at Kasosnet
☎ 2245 041 705, @ kasos@kasosnet.gr)
tear Bouka for €4.40 per hour.
   The port police (☎ 2245 041 288) are be-
ιind the Church of Agios Spyridon. The
•olice (☎ 2245 041 222) are just beyond the
•ost office.

Places to Stay
All of the island's accommodation is in Fry,
except for one place in Emborios.
   Ilias Koutlakis Rooms (☎ 2245 041 284,
2245 041 230, Hohlakoulia) Doubles with
bathroom €29.50. These tidy, seafront
rooms are on the left 300m along the road
to Emborios.
   Anesis Hotel (☎ 2245 041 234, Kritis 20)
Singles/doubles with bathroom €20.50/25.
This hotel is above a supermarket. Ask in
the supermarket for the owner.
   Anagennisis Hotel (☎ 2245 041 495, fax
041 036, @ kassos@kassos-island.gr, Plateia
Iroön Kasou) Singles/doubles €22/28, with
bathroom €28/36.70. This hotel has clean and
comfortable rooms.
   Blue Sky (☎ 2245 041 047) 2/3 person
studios €54.30/64.60. Some 400m metres
inland these comfortable studios are another
good choice for two or three persons.
   Borianoula (☎ 2245 041 495, fax 2245
041 036, @ kassos@kassos-island.gr,
Emborios) 2/3 person studios €54.30/64.60.
See Kasos Maritime and Travel Agency for
the keys for these three reasonable-sized
apartments.

Places to Eat
There are several restaurants and snack bars
available in Fry.
   O Mylos (☎ 2245 041 825, Plateia Iroön
Kasou) Mains €3.50-4. Open year-round.
This good restaurant offers tasty casserole
dishes and grilled meat and fish.
   Restaurant Mihail Karagiannis (☎ 2245
041 390) Mains €4-5. Open year-round.
This dependable eating place opposite
Kasos Maritime and Travel Agency is
rough and ready but without a sign. Expect
no frills grills and solid staple fare.
   Astravi (☎ 2245 041 880, Bouka) Pizzas
€5. Open evenings only. Above the Zan-
tana Cafe is this pizzeria and snack bar with
great harbour views.
   I Orea Bouka (☎ 2245 041 460, Bouka)
Mains €4.50-5.50. This neat taverna has
perhaps the most interesting food. I Orea
Bouka, overlooking Bouka harbour, serves
Greek fish and meat dishes and, occasionally, Egyptian specialities.

DODECANESE

Entertainment

Cafe Zantana *(☎ 2245 041 880, Bouka)*
Open 9am-late. Kasiots congregate at this
trendy cafe which overlooks Bouka harbour. Mihalis, the owner, makes excellent
cappuccino and cocktails.

Perigiali Bar *(☎ 2245 041 767, Bouka)*
This diminutive bar between Bouka and
Plateia Iroön Kasou is Kasos' night club.
The music played is predominantly Greek.

AROUND KASOS

Kasos' best beach is the isolated, pebbled
cove of **Helatros**, near Moni Agiou Georgiou.
The beach has no facilities and little shade.
You can get there along an 11km paved road
and then a dirt road which bears left (downhill) from the road to the monastery, or along
a slightly longer unpaved road from the
monastery. **Avlaki** is another decent beach
reached along a path from the monastery.

The mediocre **Ammounda beach**, beyond
the airport near the blue-domed church of
Agios Konstandinos, is the nearest to Fry.
There are slightly better beaches farther
along this stretch of coast, one of them the
fine-pebble **Andiperatos beach** at the end of
the road system. Neither has shade.

Agia Marina, 1km south-west of Fry, is a
pretty village with a gleaming white-and-
blue church. On 17 July the Festival of Agia
Marina is celebrated here. From Agia Marina the road continues to verdant **Arvanitohori**, with fig and pomegranate trees.

Poli, 3km south-east of Fry, is the former
capital, built on the ancient acropolis. **Panagia**, between Fry and Poli, has fewer than 50
inhabitants. Its once-grand sea captains' and
ship owners' mansions are now derelict.

Monasteries

The island has two monasteries: **Moni
Agiou Mamma** and **Moni Agiou Georgiou**.
The uninhabited Moni Agiou Mamma on
the south coast is a 1½ hour walk from Fry.
Take the Poli road and turn left just before
the village (signposted 'Ai Mammas'). The
road winds uphill through a dramatic,
eroded landscape of rock-strewn mountains,
crumbling terraces and soaring cliffs. Eventually you will come to a sharp turn right

(signposted again). From here the track descends to the blue-and-white monastery.

An 11km asphalt road leads from Fry to
Moni Agiou Georgiou. There are no monks
but there is a resident caretaker for most of
the year. Free accommodation *may* be
available for visitors, but don't bank on it.

Kastellorizo (Megisti)
Καστελλόριζο (Μεγίστη)

postcode 851 11 • pop 275

It takes a certain amount of decisiveness
and a sense of adventure to come to tiny
rocky Kastellorizo (kah-stel-**o**-rih-zo), a
mere speck on the map 118km east of
Rhodes, its nearest Greek neighbour, yet
only 2.5km from the southern coast of
Turkey and its nearest neighbouring town
Kaş. Kastellorizo is so-named for the 'red
castle' that once dominated the main port
but is also known as 'Megisti' (the largest)

KASTELLORIZO (MEGISTI)

1 Moni Agiou Stefanou
2 Paleokastro
3 Moni Agias Triadas
4 Knights of St John Castle
5 Moni Agiou Georgiou
6 Blue Cave

To Ro, Agios Georgios & Rhodes

Kastellorizo Town

To Kaş (Turkey)

To Strongyli

Mandraki

▲ Vikla (273m)

Horafia

KASTELLORIZO (MEGISTI)

0   500   1000m
0   500   1000yd

MEDITERRANEAN SEA

Daily Ferries
Low Frequency Ferries
Hydrofoil/Catamaran
Excursion Boat

DODECANESE

or it is the largest of a group of 14 islets that surround this isolated Hellenic outpost. Tourism is low-key, yet there are more Australian-Greek Kastellorizians here in summer than there are locals. There are no stunning beaches, but there are rocky inlets from where you can swim and snorkel.

The island featured in the Oscar-winning Italian film *Mediterraneo* (1991) which was based on a book by an Italian army sergeant.

History

Kastellorizo has suffered a tragic history. Once a thriving trade port serving Dorians, Romans, Crusaders, Egyptians, Turks and Venetians, Kastellorizo came under Ottoman control in 1552. The island was allowed to preserve its language, religion and traditions, and its cargo fleet became the largest in the Dodecanese, allowing the islanders to achieve a high degree of culture and education.

Kastellorizo lost all strategic and economic importance after the 1923 Greece-Turkey population exchange. In 1928 it was ceded to the Italians, who severely oppressed the islanders. Many islanders chose to emigrate Australia, where today a disproportionate number still live.

During WWII, Kastellorizo suffered bombardment, and English commanders ordered the few remaining inhabitants to abandon the island. Most fled to Cyprus, Palestine and Egypt. When they returned they found their houses in ruins and re-migrated. Subsequently, the island has never fully recovered from its population loss. In recent years, returnees have been slowly restoring buildings and the island now enjoys a tenuous, but pleasant resurgence of resettlement.

Getting To/From Kastellorizo

Air In July and August there are daily flights to and from Rhodes (€35.80), dropping to three weekly at other times. You can buy tickets from Dizi Tours & Travel (☎ 2246 049 241, fax 2246 049 240, e dizivas@otenet.gr) in Kastellorizo Town. A ramshackle bus ferries passengers between the airport and the port (€1.50).

Ferry & Catamaran Kastellorizo is the least well-connected island in the whole of the Dodecanese archipelago. Ferry links are subject to seasonal changes and the only direct domestic destination is Rhodes (four hours, €10.90). Check locally with Dizi Travel or Papoutsis Travel (☎ 2246 070 830, fax 2246 049 286, e paptrv@rho.forthnet .gr) for the latest details.

At the time of research the *Dodekanisos Express* catamaran was running to Kastellorizo twice a week. Contact Dodekanisos Naftiliaki (☎ 2241 070 590, e info@12ne .gr) in Rhodes for the current schedules.

Excursion Boat to Turkey Islanders go on frequent shopping trips to Kaş in Turkey and day trips (€14.70) are also offered to tourists. Look for the signs along the waterfront.

Note that one-way travellers may theoretically enter and exit Greece legally via this route. Report to the police if arriving from Kaş.

Getting Around Kastellorizo

Excursion boats go to the islets of **Ro**, **Agios Georgios** and **Strongyli** and the spectacular **Blue Cave** (Parasta), named for its brilliant blue water, due to refracted sunlight. All of these trips cost around €14.70 and leave at around 8.30am daily.

KASTELLORIZO TOWN

Along with Mandraki, its satellite neighbourhood over the hill and to the west, Kastellorizo Town is the only settlement on the island. Built around a U-shaped bay, its waterfront is skirted with imposing, spruced-up, three-storey mansions with wooden balconies and red-tiled roofs. It is undoubtedly pretty nowadays, but the alluring facade of today's waterfront contrasts starkly with backstreets of abandoned houses overgrown with ivy, crumbling stairways and stony pathways winding between them.

Orientation & Information

The quay is at the eastern side of the bay. The central square, Plateia Ethelondon Kastellorizou, abuts the waterfront almost

DODECANESE

Mediterraneo – the Movie

If you have not seen the movie before you come to Kastellorizo, do so when you go home. You will enjoy it immensely. If you cannot recognise a lot of the places depicted in the film, don't be surprised. Many of the scenes depicting a 1940s Kastellorizo were shot away from today's busy waterfront and centred instead on Mandraki Bay and the square abutting the church of Agiou Konstantinou & Elenis and the nearby school in the area known as Horafia. The famous soccer scene was shot at a then unpaved airport, while other scenes were shot at locations along the coastline.

The legacy of the movie still lingers, and many Italians now come in search of the locations, or simply to satisfy their curiosity about an island that had so obviously enchanted the protagonists of this 1991 classic. One of the main characters of the movie, the unassuming Antonio (Claudio Bigagli), who marries the prostitute Vasilissa (Vanna Barba), was spotted arriving, pack on back, at Kastellorizo airport one summer recently. Some old habits die hard.

halfway round the bay, next to the yachting jetty. The suburbs of Horafia and Mandraki are reached by ascending the wide steps at the east side of the bay.

On the bay's western side are the post office and police station (☎ 2246 049 333). There's no OTE but there are cardphones. The National Bank of Greece (with ATM) is near the waterfront. The port police (☎ 2246 049 333) are at the eastern tip of the bay.

Things to See

The **Knights of St John Castle** stands above the quay. A metal staircase leads to the top from where there are splendid views of Turkey. Within the castle, a well-displayed collection is held at the **museum** (☎ 2246 049 283; admission free; open 7am-2.30pm Tues-Sun). Beyond the museum, steps lead down to a coastal pathway, from where more steps go up the cliff to a **Lycian tomb** with a Doric facade. There are several along the Anatolian coast in Turkey, but this is the only known one in Greece.

Moni Agiou Georgiou is the largest of the monasteries that dot the island. Within its church is the subterranean Chapel of Agios Haralambos reached by steep stone steps. Here Greek children were given religious instruction during Turkish times. The church kept locked; ask around the waterfront for the whereabouts of the caretaker. To reach the monastery ascend the conspicuous zigzag white stone steps behind the town and at the top take the path straight ahead.

Moni Agiou Stefanou, on the north coast, is the setting for one of the island's most important celebrations, Agios Stefanos Day on 1 August. The path to the little white monastery begins behind the post office. From the monastery, a path leads to a bay where you can swim.

Paleokastro was the island's ancient capital. Within its Hellenistic walls are an ancient tower, a water cistern and three churches. Concrete steps, just beyond a soldier's sentry box on the airport road, are the beginning of the steep path to Paleokastro.

Places to Stay – Budget

Accommodation is generally of a high standard. Most domatia do not display signs but it's not hard to find the owners – that is, if they don't find you first when you disembark.

Villa Kaserma (☎ 2246 049 370, fax 2246 049 365) Doubles/triples with bathroom €28/34. This red-and-white building standing above the western waterfront has very pleasant rooms.

Pension Palameria (☎ 2246 049 282, fax 2246 049 071) Doubles with bathroom €29.50. This converted building on the small square at the north-west corner of the waterfront has spotless rooms with kitchen dining area. Inquire about them at To Mikro Parisi restaurant.

I Anaviosi (☎ 2246 049 302) Singles/doubles €17.60/23.50, doubles with bathroom €29.50. These rooms are above the Sydney Restaurant.

Panorama Studios (☎/fax 2246 049 098, mobile ☎ 697 247 7186, Mandraki) Doubles

DODECANESE

ith bathroom €35.50. These are roomy, idge-equipped studios. Some have balonies and views across to Kaş in Turkey.

Places to Stay – Mid-Range
Carnagio Apartments (☎/fax 2246 049 66) 2-3/5 person apartments €53/73.50. These traditionally furnished apartments 'e housed in a beautifully restored red-and-chre mansion near the top of the harbour's est side.

Kastellorizo Hotel Appartments (☎ 2246 49 044, fax 2246 049 279, e kastel@otenet gr, W www.kastellorizohotel.gr) Singles/oubles €44. These are beautiful, fully quipped rooms.

Pension Mediterraneo (☎ 2246 049 368) ingles/doubles €59. Farther along the ame side of the bay are these equally well-ppointed rooms.

Places to Eat
Most restaurants are clustered along the usy waterfront.

Restaurant Orea Megisti (☎ 2246 049 82, Plateia Ethelondon Kastellorizou) This restaurant serves a range of well pre-ared casserole dishes (goat casserole €5.80) and also spit-roast goat and lamb, oth of which are accompanied with rice ooked with herbs.

To Mikro Parisi (☎ 2246 049 282) Mains €4.50-5. To Mikro Parisi has been going trong for over 30 years. It serves generous elpings of grilled fish and meat. Fish soup €6) is the speciality, but the stifado €4.40) is also good.

Sydney Restaurant (☎ 2246 049 302) Mayirefta €3.50-4. This restaurant, a little arther around from To Mikro Parisi, serves p mayirefta and fish dishes and is also ighly recommended.

Tis Ypomonis (☎ 2246 049 224) This corner restaurant does a nightly roaring trade in ouvlaki (€4.70), sausage and steaks.

Akrothalassa (☎ 2246 049 052) Grills €4.10. Dine under the vines at this relaxed averna on the south side of the harbour, where good grills and fish are served up.

Restaurant Platania (☎ 2246 049 206, Plateia Mihail & Patricias Kaïli) Breakfast

€6. This is an out-of-the-way, unpretentious place that appeared in the film *Mediterraneo*. Come here for good breakfasts and their *revithokeftedes* (chickpea rissoles, €2.60).

There are several easy-going cafeterias on the waterfront. *Kaz Bar* is a good place to kick off, since you can check your email first. Next, *Meltemi* (☎ 2246 049 214) has tempting waterside chairs and cold beers. You can hardly miss *Mythos Bar*, the brightly painted watering hole on the east side of the harbour.

Symi Σύμη

postcode 856 00 • pop 2300
Symi is a rocky, dry island 24km north of Rhodes. It lies within the geographical embrace of Turkey, 10km from the Turkish peninsula of Datça. The island has scenic rocky interior, with pine and cypress woods. It has a deeply indented coast with precipitous cliffs and numerous small bays with pebbled beaches, and is enormously popular with day trippers from Rhodes. Symi has good accommodation and eating choices and enjoys excellent transport links to the outside world. However, the island suffers from a severe water shortage and the day-tripper crowds can get a bit overwhelming at times.

History
Symi has a long tradition of both sponge-diving and shipbuilding. During Ottoman times it was granted the right to fish for sponges in Turkish waters. In return, Symi supplied the sultan with first-class boat builders and top-quality sponges.

These factors, and a lucrative shipbuilding industry, brought prosperity to the island. Gracious mansions were built and culture and education flourished. By the beginning of the 20th century the population was 22,500 and the island was launching some 500 ships a year. But the Italian occupation, the introduction of the steamship and Kalymnos' rise as the Aegean's principal sponge producer put an end to Symi's prosperity.

The treaty surrendering the Dodecanese islands to the Allies was signed on Symi on 8 May 1945.

DODECANESE

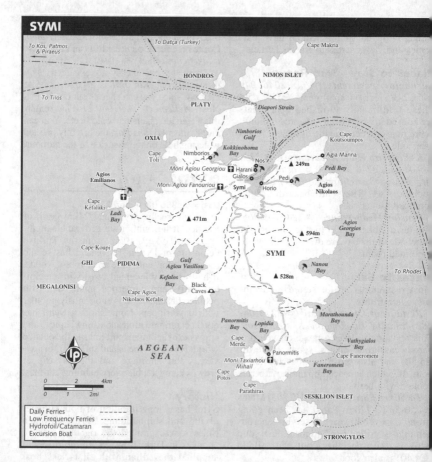

Getting To/From Symi

Ferry, Catamaran & Hydrofoil Symi has up to four mainline ferries a week heading north to other Dodecanese islands and Piraeus. Additional links are provided by the F/B *Nisos Kalymnos*, or F/B *Hioni*. Services to Rhodes are much more frequent.

The *Dodekanisos Express* catamaran services the island at least twice a week.

Symi is connected by hydrofoil to Kos (one hour, €15.40), Kalymnos (1½ hours, €21.30), Astypalea (four hours, €26.70) and Rhodes (50 minutes, €9.80). Services tend to be weekend-oriented. The Symi-owned *Aigli* hydrofoil leaves Symi for Rhodes at 7.15am and returns to Symi at 5pm or 6pm.

Excursion Boat There are daily excursion boats running between Symi and Rhodes' Mandraki Harbour. The Symi-based *Symi I* and *Symi II* are the cheapest. They are owned cooperatively by the people of Symi and operate as excursion boats as well as regular passenger boats. Tickets cost €10.30 return and can be bought on board.

Symi Tours has excursion trips to Datça in Turkey. The cost is a rather steep €59 return (including Turkish port taxes).

Getting Around Symi

Bus & Taxi A minibus makes frequent runs between Gialos and Pedi Beach (via Horio). Check the current schedule with Symi Tours. The flat fare is €0.65. The bus stop and taxi rank are on the east side of the harbour. Sample taxi tariffs are Horio €2.40, Pedi €2.70 and Nimborios €4.20.

Excursion Boat Several excursion boats do trips to Moni Taxiarhou Mihail and Sesklia islet where there's a shady beach. Check the boards for the best value tickets. Symi Tours also has trips to the monastery (€30).

Excursion boats also go to some of the island's more remote beaches.

Taxi boats These small boats do trips to many of the island's beaches. The cost on average is about €8.

GIALOS Γιαλός

Gialos, Symi's port town, is a Greek treasure. Neoclassical mansions in a harmonious medley of colours are heaped up the steep hills flanking its U-shaped harbour. Behind their strikingly beautiful facades, however, many of the buildings are derelict. The town is divided into two parts: Gialos, the harbour, and Horio, above, crowned by the kastro (castle).

Gialos' beach is the crowded, minuscule Nos Beach. Turn left at the Italian-era clock tower at the north-eastern end of the harbour.

Orientation & Information

Arriving ferries, hydrofoils and the catamaran dock just to the left of the quay's clock tower. Excursion boats dock a little further along. The centre of activity in Gialos is focused upon the promenade at the centre of the harbour. Kali Strata, a broad stairway, leads from here to hilltop Horio.

There is no EOT in Symi Town, but the staff at Symi Tours (☎ 2246 071 307, fax 2246 072 292) is helpful. There is a Symi Visitor Office sharing space with the ANES ticket office on the north side of the harbour.

The post office, police (☎ 2246 071 111) and port police (☎ 2246 071 205) are by the ferry quay. The OTE is signposted from the eastern side of the central square. The National Bank of Greece is at the top of the harbour. The Ionian Bank on the waterfront has an ATM.

There are two Internet cafes: the Roloï Bar and The Club Upstairs.

Things to See & Do

Horio consists of narrow, labyrinthine streets crossed by crumbling archways. As you approach the kastro, the once-grand 19th-century neoclassical mansions give way to modest stone dwellings of the 18th century.

On the way to the castle, archaeological and folklore exhibits are held in the **Museum of Symi** (admission €1.45; open 10am-2pm Tues-Sun).

The castle incorporates blocks from the ancient acropolis, and the **Church of Megali Panagia** is within its walls. Behind the central square is the **Symi Maritime Museum** (admission €1.45; open 12.30-2.30pm Tues-Sun).

Symi Tours has multilingual guides who lead **guided walks** around the island. The publication *Walking on Symi* by Francis Noble (€5.90) is on sale at Kalodoukas Holidays at the beginning of Kali Strata.

Places to Stay

There is very little budget accommodation. The cheapest doubles cost around €35. Some accommodation owners meet the boats.

Hotel Kokona (☎ 2246 071 549, fax 2246 072 620) Singles/doubles with bathroom €35/41. This hotel has comfortable rooms. It's on the street to the left of the large church.

Pension Catherinettes (☎/fax 2246 072 698, e marina-epe@rho.forthnet.gr) Doubles with/without sea view €44/28. Some of this pension's rooms have magnificent painted ceilings.

Hotel Fiona (☎ 2246 072 755, fax 2246 072 088) Doubles/triples with bathroom €44/53. This hotel in Horio has lovely rooms with wood-panelled ceilings and great views. To reach it turn left immediately after To Klima Restaurant.

DODECANESE

Hotel Nireus (☎ *2246 072 400, fax 2246 072 404,* e *nireus@altavista.com, Akti Georgiou Genista)* Singles/doubles €47/59. This hotel has elegant, traditional rooms and suites.

Opera House Hotel (☎ *2246 072 034, fax 2246 072 035)* Double/triple studios €65/80. These spacious studios in a peaceful garden are well signposted from the harbour.

Hotel Aliki (☎/fax *2246 071 665, Akti Georgiou Gennimata)* Singles/doubles €82/105. This pricey, A-class, traditional-style hotel is farther along from Hotel Nireus.

Places to Eat

Gialos Many of Gialos' restaurants are mediocre, catering for day-trippers. The following are exceptions.

Vigla Restaurant (☎ *2246 072 056)* Fish €9-11. This restaurant is at the top of the harbour and features fresh fish.

O Meraklis Taverna (☎ *2246 071 003)* Grills €4.70. This taverna is quietly popular and does good grills and mayirefta.

Taverna Neraïda (☎ *2246 071 841)* Mains €4-5. This excellent, low-priced option is beyond Hotel Glafkos. Fish souvlaki (€7.40) makes an interesting change.

O Ilios (☎ *2246 072 172)* Snacks €2-3. This English-run vegetarian restaurant is at the top of the harbour. It serves snacks and homemade cakes during the day and three-course meals in the evening. Service can be very slow at busy times.

Restaurant Les Catherinettes (☎ *2246 072 698)* Mixed mezedes €7.40. This restaurant, below the pension of the same name, offers an extensive range of well-prepared dishes.

Estiatorio Mythos (☎ *2246 071 488)* Mezedes €3-4.50. This is an unpretentious little place with top-class food. At lunchtime Mythos serves mainly pasta dishes, while mezedes feature in the evening.

Horio There are a couple of good restaurants at the top of the long staircase from Gialos.

To Klima (☎ *2246 072 693, Kali Strata)* Mains €6-7. To Klima serves well prepared Greek dishes and offers an enticing vegetarian menu.

Restaurant Syllogos (☎ *2246 072 148, Kali Strata)* Mains €5-7. This restaurant offers imaginative fare such as chicken with prunes and pork with leek (€5.90).

Entertainment

There are several lively bars in the streets behind the south side of the harbour.

White House Cafe (☎ *2246 071 372)* Drop by here in the evenings and enjoy occasional live music.

Jean & Tonic (☎ *2246 071 819)* Open 8pm-6am. Haul yourself up Kali Strata, work up a thirst and enjoy this expat-owned watering hole.

AROUND SYMI

Pedi is a little fishing village and burgeoning holiday resort in a fertile valley 2km downhill from Horio. It has some sandy stretches on its narrow beach. There are domatia, hotels and tavernas.

Nos Beach is the closest beach to Gialos. It's a five-minute walk north of the campanile. There is a taverna, bar and sun beds.

Nimborios is a long, pebbled beach 2km west of Gialos. It has some natural shade as well as sun beds and umbrellas. Water quality can be dicey and the one taverna here serves good but expensive food delivered with a rather sulky attitude. You can walk there from Gialos along a scenic path. Take the road by the east side of the central square, and continue straight ahead; the way is fairly obvious. Just bear left after the church and follow the stone trail.

Taxi boats go to **Agios Georgios Bay** and the more developed **Nanou Beach**, which has sun beds, umbrellas and a taverna, and **Agia Marina**, which also has a taverna. These are all shingle beaches. Symi's only sandy beach is the tamarisk-shaded **Agios Nikolaos**.

The remote **Marathounda** and **Agios Emilianos** beaches are reached by excursion boat.

Moni Taxiarhou Mihail

Μονή Ταξιάρχου Μιχαήλ

Symi's principal sight is the large Moni Taxiarhou Mihail (Monastery of Michael of

Panormitis) in Panormitis Bay, and it's the stopping-off point for many of the day trippers from Rhodes. A monastery was first built here in the 5th or 6th century, but the present building dates from the 18th century. The katholikon contains an intricately carved wooden iconostasis, frescoes, and an icon of St Michael which supposedly appeared miraculously where the monastery now stands. St Michael is the patron saint of Symi, and protector of sailors.

The monastery complex comprises a museum, restaurant and basic guest rooms, where beds cost around €12; reservations are necessary in July and August.

Tilos Τήλος

postcode 850 02 • pop 280

Tilos is one of the few islands left in the Dodecanese that still retains something of its traditional character and where tourism has not widely impacted on the slow and carefree lifestyle of the islanders. Tilos lies 65km west of Rhodes, has good, uncrowded beaches, two abandoned, evocative villages, a well-kept monastery at the end of a spectacularly scenic road, and keeps its authentic Greek-island image intact. It's a terrific island for walkers, with vistas of high cliffs, rocky inlets and sea, valleys of cypress, walnut and almond trees, and bucolic meadows.

Tilos' agricultural potential is not utilised, since, rather than work the land for a pittance, young Tiliots prefer to leave for the mainland or emigrate to Australia or the USA.

There are two settlements: the port of Livadia, and Megalo Horio, 8km north.

History

Mastodon bones – midget elephants that became extinct around 4600 BC – were found in a cave on the island in 1974. The cave, **Harkadio**, is signposted from the Livadia-Megalo

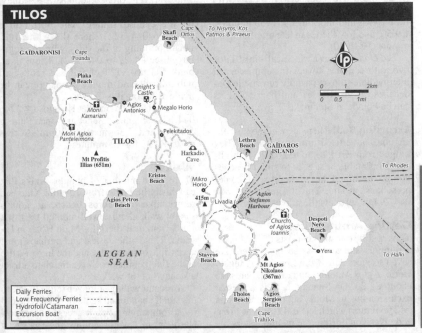

TILOS

GAÏDARONISI
Cape Pounda
Skafi Beach
Cape Orfos
To Nisyros, Kos Patmos & Piraeus
Plaka Beach
Knight's Castle
Moni Kamariani
Agios Antonios
Megalo Horio
Moni Agiou Panteleimona
TILOS
Pelekitados
Mt Profitis Illias (651m)
Lethra Beach
GAÏDAROS ISLAND
Harkadio Cave
To Rhodes
Eristos Beach
Mikro Horio
Agios Petros Beach
415m
Livadia
Agios Stefanos Harbour
AEGEAN SEA
Stavros Beach
Church of Agios Ioannis
Despoti Nero Beach
Yera
To Halki
Mt Agios Nikolaos (367m)
Tholos Beach
Agios Sergios Beach
Cape Trahilos

Daily Ferries
Low Frequency Ferries
Hydrofoil/Catamaran
Excursion Boat

DODECANESE

Horio road, but is kept locked. Erinna, one of the least-known of ancient Greece's female poets, lived on Tilos in the 4th century BC.

Elephants and poetry aside, Tilos' history shares the same catalogue of invasions and occupations as the rest of the archipelago.

Getting To/From Tilos

Ferry Tilos is served by G&A Ferries, D.A.N.E. Sea Lines, the Kalymnos-based F/B *Nisos Kalymnos* and Chios-based F/B *Hioni* with up to four services a week in high season. Tickets can be bought at Stefanakis Travel Agency (☎ 2246 044 360) in Livadia.

Hydrofoil Tilos sees only one or two hydrofoils a week. Check locally for departure/arrival days. Destinations include Rhodes (one hour, €17.10), Nisyros (40 minutes, €9.50) and Kos (1½ hours, €12.15), with connections further afield.

Catamaran The Tilos-owned *Sea Star* (☎ 2246 077 048) connects Tilos daily with Nisyros and Rhodes. *Sea Star* departs Tilos for Nisyros mid-morning daily (35 minutes, €9.50) and for Rhodes in late afternoon (55 minutes, €16.20).

The *Dodekanisos Express* calls in at Tilos two to three times a week in summer as an intermediate stop on its daily run up the Dodecanese from Rhodes and back. Tickets can be bought at Stefanakis Travel Agency.

Excursion Boat There are a number of excursions advertised around Livadia. They range from €14.70 to €20.60. A high-speed inflatable boat goes to small beaches around the island, but it's a pricey €22 per person; ask at Tilos Travel Agency (☎ 2246 044 294, [e] office@tilostravel.co.uk).

Getting Around Tilos

Tilos' public transport consists of two buses: a minibus and a full-sized bus. There are seven services daily from Livadia to Megalo Horio, Agios Antonios and Eristos. Fares are about €1.20. On Sunday there is a special excursion bus to Moni Agiou Panteleimona (€2.95 return) which leaves Livadia at 11am and gives you one hour at the monastery.

Tilos has two taxis: Taxi Mike (mobile ☎ 69 4520 0436) and Nikos Logotheti (mobile ☎ 69 4498 1727). Both are available at any time.

LIVADIA Λιβάδεια

Livadia is the main town and port, though not the capital: that honour belongs to Megalo Horio. It's a sleepy, pleasant enough place, though it can be a bit more hot and humid than other parts of the island. In Livadia you will find most services and shops and the bulk of the island's accommodation.

Orientation & Information

From the quay, turn left, ascend the steps beside Stefanakis Travel, and continue ahead to the central square. If you continue straight ahead, the road curves and turns right, passing the Church of Agios Nikolaos, to skirt the beach.

Tilos has no EOT but the staff at both Stefanakis Travel (☎ 2246 044 310) and Tilos Travel Agency, opposite the quay, are helpful. The post office and OTE are on the central square. The port police (☎ 2246 044 322) share the white Italianate building at the quay with the regular police (☎ 2246 044 222). There is no bank and no ATM on Tilos. Credit card withdrawals and money exchange can be made at Stefanakis Travel.

You can check email at Kosmos (☎ 2246 044 074, [e] pnut@otenet.gr), open 9am to 1.30pm and 7.30pm to 11.30pm. Access costs €2.95 for 30 minutes.

Walks

There are a number of popular walks that can easily be made from Livadia. One is a return hike to **Stavros beach**, an hour's steady walk along a well-marked trail that starts from near the Tilos Mare Hotel in Livadia. This is the easiest and perhaps most accessible of the walks, and the lure of a dip at the fine-pebble beach is enough to attract a steady line of walkers.

A second walk is a longer return track to the small abandoned settlement of **Yera** and its accompanying beach access at **Despoti Nero**. From Livadia follow the road past

Agios Stefanos on the east side of the bay and keep walking. Allow half a day for this hike.

Another walk, mostly bypassing the main road system, leads from Livadia to the abandoned ghost-village of **Mikro Horio**. This will take about 45 minutes.

Places to Stay

The information kiosk at the harbour opens whenever a ferry arrives and has photos and prices of Tilos' accommodation.

Casa Italiana Rooms (☎ *2246 044 253*) Doubles with bathroom €24. These well-kept rooms with refrigerator overlook the quay.

Paraskevi Rooms (☎ *2246 044 280*) Doubles with bathroom €29.50. The best of the three domatia on the Livadia waterfront, this place has clean, nicely furnished rooms with well-equipped kitchens.

Stefanakis Studios (☎ *2246 044 310,* e *stefanakis@rho.forthnet.gr*) Doubles €32.50. These studios above Stefanakis Travel are just as commendable as Paraskevi.

Hotel Eleni (☎ *2246 044 062, fax 2246 044 063,* e *elenihtl@otenet.gr*) Singles/doubles with bathroom €35.20/41. This hotel, 400m along the beach road, has beautiful, tastefully furnished double rooms with refrigerator, telephone; breakfast is included in the room rate.

Marina Beach Rooms (☎ *2246 044 066, fax 2246 044 169,* e *marinaroom@otenet.gr*) Doubles €41. These immaculate and compact rooms with sea-view balconies are on the bay's eastern side, 1km from the quay.

Faros Rooms (☎ *2246 044 068, fax 2246 044 029,* e *dimkouk@otenet.gr*) Doubles/triples €41/48.50. A little farther along from Marina Beach, rooms here are spotless and tastefully furnished.

Places to Eat

Sofia's Taverna (☎ *2246 044 340*) Mayirefta €3. This taverna, 100m along the beach road, serves delicious, home-cooked food.

Taverna Blue Sky (☎ *2246 044 259*) Mezedes €1.80-3.20. Blue Sky, on the harbour, is good for grilled fish and vegetarian mezedes.

Taverna Michalis (☎ *2246 044 359*) Grills €5.30. Head to this popular tourist taverna, beyond the central square, for tasty grilled meat.

Restaurant Irina (☎ *2246 044 206*) Mayirefta €4-5. With its relaxing waterside location, Irina does great home-made food, including excellent mousakas and aubergine slippers (*papoutsakia*).

Joanna's Cafe Bar (☎ *2246 044 145*) Pizza €4.50-6. This cafe bar is a popular breakfast and brunch hang-out, serving excellent coffee, yogurt and muesli, pizza and delicious home-made cakes.

Entertainment

There are one or two bars on Livadia's waterfront, but serious ravers head for the spooky abandoned village of Mikro Horio 3km from Livadia.

Mikro Horio Music Bar (☎ *2246 044 081, Mikro Horio*) Take the minibus provided and enjoy this place where the music belts out until 4am in summer.

MEGALO HORIO Μεγάλο Χωριό

Megalo Horio, the island's capital, is a serene whitewashed village. Its alleyways are fun to explore and the village makes a great alternative base if you are looking for a taste of rural life in Tilos. There are domatia, a couple of restaurants and two lively, atmospheric bars to keep visitors bedded, fed and suitably watered. From here you can visit the **Knight's Castle**, a taxing 40-minute walk along a track starting at the north end of the village.

The little **museum** on the main street houses finds from the Harkadio Cave. It's locked, but if you ask at the town hall on the first floor someone will show you around.

Places to Stay & Eat

Miliou Rooms & Apartments (☎ *2246 044 204*) Doubles €19. This reasonable place is on the main street.

Elefantakia Studios (☎ *2246 044 242*) Doubles €29. These kitchenette- and fridge-equipped studios are next to Miliou Rooms & Apartments.

To Kastro (☎ *2246 044 232*) Grills €4.50. This is the best place to eat. It is on the

DODECANESE

village's south side, overlooking the Eristos plain below. Great barbecue-grilled meats and home cooking are the highlights here.

Entertainment

Megalo Horio has two atmospheric bars. *Ilakati*, on the steep road signposted Kastro, plays rock and blues, and *Anemona* (☎ 2246 044 090), at the top of the steps that start by the To Kastro restaurant, plays mainly Greek music.

AROUND MEGALO HORIO

Just before Megalo Horio, a turn-off to the left leads after 2.5km to the pleasant, tamarisk-shaded **Eristos Beach**, a mixture of gritty sand and shingle. A signposted turn-off to the right from this road leads to the quiet settlement of **Agios Antonios**. **Plaka Beach**, 3km farther west, is dotted with trees and affords some free camping.

The 18th-century **Moni Agiou Panteleimona** is 5km beyond here along a scenic road. It is uninhabited but well maintained, with fine 18th-century frescoes. The island's minibus driver takes groups of visitors here on Sunday. A three-day festival takes place at the monastery, beginning on 25 July.

Places to Stay & Eat

The Megalo Horio municipality is finally getting around to formalising a *camping ground* on Eristos Beach, but no details were available at time of research. Expect to pay around €5 for one person and a tent.

Tropicana Taverna & Rooms (☎ 2246 044 020, Eristos) Doubles/triples €17.50/22. Tropicana is on the Eristos road and its restaurant serves up good mayirefta dishes (€2.60-3.20).

Eristos Beach Hotel (☎/fax 2246 044 024, Eristos) Doubles €32. This hotel, right on the beach, has excellent, airy studios for up to four persons with fridge and kitchenette.

Nisyros Νίσυρος

☎ 2242 • postcode 853 03 • pop 1000

Nisyros (**nee**-sih-ros) is one of those quirky Greek islands that is not on the usual island-hopping circuit. It has no stunning sandy beaches and supports a rather low-key tourist infrastructure that favours individuals, yachties and lost souls.

Nisyros is an almost round, rocky island and has something that no other Greek island has – its own volcano. The landscape is at the same time rocky, lush and green, yet it has no natural water.

The lunar landscape of the interior is off set by craggy peaks and rolling hillsides leading down to brown pebbly beaches that see relatively few visitors. The island's settlements are the capital of Mandraki, the fishing village of Pali and the crater-top villages of Emborios and Nikea.

Getting To/From Nisyros

Nisyros is linked to the Dodecanese by almost daily ferries. There is an additional service four times a week sailing to Kardamena on Kos with the caique *Chrysoula* (two hours, €3).

The island is serviced by two hydrofoils a week heading both north and south and catamarans three to five times a week.

In summer there are daily excursion boats from Kardamena, Kefalos and Kos Town on Kos (€13-18).

Getting Around Nisyros

Bus There are two companies running up to 10 excursion buses every day to the volcano (€6 return) with 40 minutes waiting time between 9.30am and 3pm. There are in addition three daily buses to Nikea (€1.60) via Pali. The bus stop is at the quay.

Motorcycle There are three motorcycle-rental outlets on Mandraki's main street.

Taxi There are two taxis on Nisyros: Babis Taxi (☎ 2242 031 460) and Irene's Taxi (☎ 2242 031 474). Sample fares are: the volcano €17.60 return, Nikea €10.30 and Pali €4.70.

Excursion Boat From June to September there are excursion boats (€8 return) to the pumice-stone islet of Giali where there is a good sandy beach.

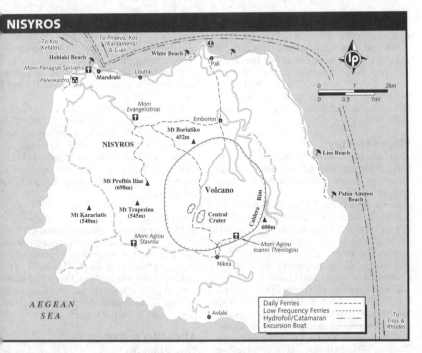

NISYROS

Map showing Nisyros island with Mandraki, Paleokastro, Moni Panagias Spilianis, Hohlaki Beach, White Beach, Loutra, Pali, Emborios, Moni Evangelistrias, Mt Boriatiko 452m, Mt Profitis Ilias (698m), Volcano, Central Crater, Caldera Rim, 600m, Mt Karariatis (540m), Mt Trapezina (545m), Moni Agiou Stavrou, Moni Agiou Ioanni Theologou, Nikea, Lies Beach, Pahia Ammos Beach, Avlaki, AEGEAN SEA.

Legend: Daily Ferries, Low Frequency Ferries, Hydrofoil/Catamaran, Excursion Boat

MANDRAKI Μανδράκι

Mandraki is the attractive port and capital of Nisyros. Its two-storey houses have brightly painted wooden balconies. Some are whitewashed but many are painted in bright colours, predominantly ochre and turquoise. The web of streets huddled below the monastery and the central square are especially charming.

Orientation & Information

To reach Mandraki's centre, walk straight ahead from the quay. At the fork bear right; the left fork leads to Hotel Porfyris. Beyond here a large square adjoins the main street, which proceeds to Plateia Aristotelous Foriadou, then continues diagonally opposite, passing the town hall. Turn left at the T-junction for the central square of Plateia Ilikiomeni.

Tourist information is willingly dispensed by Nisyrian Travel (☎ 2242 031 204) at the quay, open 10am to 1pm and 6pm to 8pm daily. The staff here, and at Enetikon Travel on the main street, is helpful.

The post office, port police (☎ 2242 031 222) and the regular police (☎ 2242 031 201) share premises opposite the quay. The Co-operative Bank of the Dodecanese offers currency exchange and credit card withdrawals, but has no ATM. Travel agents will usually exchange money with no hassles.

Things to See

Mandraki's greatest tourist attraction is the clifftop 14th-century **Moni Panagias Spilianis** *(Virgin of the Cave; ☎ 2242 031 125; admission free; open 10.30am-3pm)*, crammed with ecclesiastical paraphernalia. Turn right at the end of the main street to reach the steps up to the monastery.

The impressive Mycenaean-era acropolis, **Paleokastro** (Old Kastro), above Mandraki, has well-preserved Cyclopean walls built of massive blocks of volcanic rock. Follow the route signposted 'kastro', near the monastery

DODECANESE

steps. This eventually becomes a path. At the road turn right and the kastro is on the left.

Hohlaki is a black-stone beach and can usually be relied upon for swimming unless the wind is up and then the water can get rough. To get there, walk to the end of the waterfront, go up the steps and turn right onto a stone-laid path. It's a five-minute walk away.

Places to Stay

Mandraki has a fair amount of accommodation, but owners do not usually meet incoming ferries. There is no camping ground here.

Hotel Romantzo (☎/fax 2242 031 340) Singles/doubles with bathroom €23.50/30. If you turn left from the quay, you will come to this hotel with clean, well-kept rooms. The rooms are above a snack bar and there is a large communal terrace with a refrigerator, tables and chairs.

Three Brothers Hotel (☎ 2242 031 344, fax 2242 031 640) Singles/doubles with bathroom €20.50/30. This hotel, opposite Hotel Romantzo, is another pleasant option.

Iliovasilema Rooms (☎ 2242 031 159) Doubles €24. This place is in an excellent location, but right in the middle of the tourist traffic on the waterfront.

Haritos Hotel (☎ 2242 031 322, fax 2242 031 122) Doubles/triples €44/53. Open year-round. These are well-appointed rooms all with fridge, TV and telephone. Look for them on the Pali road.

Hotel Porfyris (☎/fax 2242 031 376) Singles/doubles €30/53. This C-class hotel, Mandraki's best, has a swimming pool.

Places to Eat

On Nisyros, be sure to try the non-alcoholic local beverage called *soumada*, made from almond extract. Another speciality of the island is *pitties* (chickpea and onion patties).

Taverna Nisyros (☎ 2242 031 460) Grills €4-5. This taverna, just off the main street, is a cheap and cheerful little place and is open all day. Good charcoal grills and souvlakia.

Tony's Tavern (☎ 2242 031 460) Breakfast €3.50. Tony's, on the waterfront, does great breakfasts and superb meat dishes, and has a wide range of vegetarian choices. Try the excellent gyros – the best on the island according to Tony.

Kleanthes Taverna (☎ 2242 031 484) Mezedes €3. This taverna beyond Tony's has good mezedes.

Restaurant Irini (☎ 2242 031 365, Plateia Ilikiomeni) Mayirefta €2.60. This restaurant on the central square is recommended for its low-priced home cooking.

Taverna Panorama (☎ 2242 031 185) Grills €3.80. Near Hotel Porfyris, this is another commendable option. Try suckling pig or goat.

Shopping

Artin Caracasian Studio (mobile ☎ 69 4566 8413) This art photographer is now based in Nisyros. See and buy his excellent photographs of Nisyros (€2.90-7.30). You can also hear and buy the *Visions of Nisyros* CD (€14.60) – a dreamy musical work by two German musicians and on sale in Artin's studio on the waterfront.

AROUND NISYROS
The Volcano

Nisyros is on a volcanic line which passes through the islands of Aegina, Paros, Milos, Santorini, Nisyros, Giali and Kos. The island originally culminated in a mountain of 850m, but the centre collapsed 30,000– 40,000 years ago after three violent eruptions. Their legacy is the white and orange pumice stones that can still be seen on the northern, eastern and southern flanks of the island, and the large lava flow that covers the whole southwest of the island around Nikea village. The first eruption partially blew off the top of the ancestral cone, but the majority of the sinking of the central part of the island came about as a result of the removal of magma from within the reservoir underground.

Another violent eruption occurred in 1422 on the western side of the caldera depression (called Lakki), but this, like all others since, emitted steam, gases and mud, but no lava. The islanders call the volcano Polyvotis, because during the Great War between the gods and the Titans, the Titan

Polyvotis annoyed Poseidon so much that Poseidon tore off a chunk of Kos and threw it at Polyvotis. This rock pinned Polyvotis under it and the rock became the island of Nisyros. The hapless Polyvotis from that day has been groaning and sighing while trying to escape – hence the volcano's name.

There are five craters in the **caldera** (admission €1). A path descends into the largest one, Stefanos, where you can examine the multicoloured fumaroles, listen to their hissing and smell their sulphurous vapours. The surface is soft and hot, making sturdy footwear essential.

The easiest way to visit the volcano is by tourist bus, but you will share your experience with the hoards of mid-morning daytrippers. Better still, walk in from Nikea, or even Mandraki, or take a cab before 10.30am.

Emborios & Nikea
Εμπορειός & Νίκαια
Emborios and Nikea perch on the volcano's rim. From each, there are stunning views down into the caldera. Only a handful of inhabitants linger on in Emborios. You may encounter a few elderly women sitting on their doorsteps crocheting, and their husbands at the kafeneio. But generally, the winding, stepped streets are empty, the silence broken only by the occasional braying of a donkey or the grunting of pigs.

In contrast to Emborios, picturesque Nikea, with 50 inhabitants, buzzes with life. It has dazzling white houses with vibrant gardens and a central square with a lovely pebble mosaic. The bus terminates on Plateia Nikolaou Hartofyli. Nikea's main street links the two squares.

The steep path down to the volcano begins from Plateia Nikolaou Hartofili. It takes about 40 minutes to walk it one way. Near the beginning you can detour to the signposted **Moni Agiou Ioanni Theologou**.

Places to Stay & Eat Emborios has no accommodation for tourists and no tavernas, but there is at least one place to eat.

To Balkoni (☎ 2242 031 607) Meals €5-6. Enjoy the view of the crater over lunch.

Community Hostel (☎ 2242 031 401, Plateia Nikolaou Hartofili) Doubles €19. This simple community-run hostel is Nikea's only accommodation.

Pali Πάλοι
Pali is a small yachtie port with some simple accommodation and plenty of places to eat. The island's best beaches are here and at **Lies**, 5.5km farther on. **Pahia Ammos** beach is a further 15 minutes' walk from Lies along a coastal track.

Places to Stay & Eat *Hotel Ellinis* (☎ 2242 031 453) Doubles €30. Rooms here are small and fairly basic but are OK for a night or two's stay.

Afroditi Restaurant (☎ 2242 031 242) Grills €5-6. This is the best of the bunch of Pali's five eateries. Dining is waterside, though motorbikes and cars weave between tables. The owners of the restaurant rent a *house* in Pali for €44, which accommodates up to five people.

Kos Κως

postcode 853 00 (Psalidi 852 00)
• pop 30,000

Kos is the third-largest island of the Dodecanese and one of its most fertile and well watered. It lies only 5km from the Turkish peninsula of Bodrum. It is second only to Rhodes in its wealth of archaeological remains and its tourist development, with most of its beautiful beaches wall-to-wall with sun beds and parasols. It's a long, narrow island with a mountainous spine.

Pserimos is a small island between Kos and Kalymnos. It has a good sandy beach, but unfortunately becomes overrun with daytrippers from both of its larger neighbours.

History
Kos' fertile land attracted settlers from the earliest times. So many people lived here by Mycenaean times that it sent 30 ships to the Trojan War. During the 7th and 6th centuries BC, Kos flourished as an ally of the powerful Rhodian cities of Ialysos, Kamiros

DODECANESE

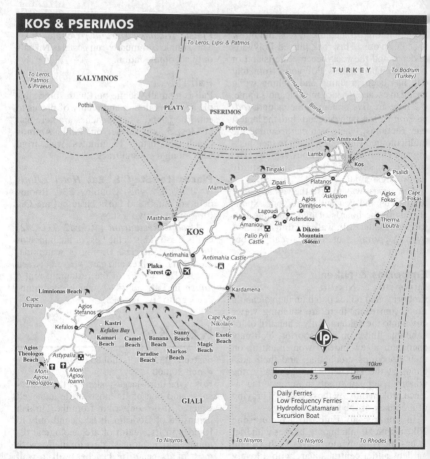

KOS & PSERIMOS

and Lindos. In 477 BC, after suffering an earthquake and subjugation to the Persians, it joined the Delian League and flourished. Hippocrates (460–377 BC), the father of medicine, was born and lived on the island. After Hippocrates' death, the Sanctuary of Asclepius and a medical school were built, which perpetuated his teachings and made Kos famous throughout the Greek world.

Ptolemy II of Egypt was born on Kos, thus securing it the protection of Egypt, under which it became a prosperous trading centre. In 130 BC, Kos came under Roman domination, and in the 1st century AD it

was administered by Rhodes, with which it came to share the same vicissitudes, right up to the tourist deluge of the present day.

Getting To/From Kos

Air There are three flights daily to Athens (€76.60). The Olympic Airways office (☎ 2242 028 330) is at Vasileos Pavlou 22, in Kos Town. The airport (☎ 2242 051 229) is 27.5km from Kos Town near the village of Andimahia.

Ferry – Domestic Kos is well connected with all the islands in the Dodecanese and

Hippocrates – the First GP

Hippocrates is often called the father of medicine yet little is known for certain about his life. He is believed to have lived between 460 and 377 BC, but 'facts' about his birth and medical practices owe more to mythology and legends than to hardcore evidence. The earliest known biography of him is *Life of Hippocrates*, by Soranus, a Roman physician. This work was published about AD 100, more than 400 years after Hippocrates' death.

Hippocrates' fame probably resulted from about 80 anonymously written medical works that became part of the collection of the Library of Alexandria after about 200 BC. Those writings became linked with Hippocrates and are known by scholars as the *Hippocratic corpus*. However, it cannot be proved that Hippocrates actually wrote any of these works.

Hippocrates' medicine challenged the methods of many physicians who used magic and witchcraft to treat disease. It taught that diseases had natural causes and could therefore be studied and possibly cured according to the workings of nature. Under Hippocratic medicine, a well-trained physician could cure illness with knowledge gained from medical writings or from experience. Modern medicine is based on this assumption.

MARTIN HARRIS

Piraeus. In summer there is a weekly ferry service to Samos and Thessaloniki. Services are offered by three major companies: D.A.N.E. Sealines (☎ 2242 027 311), G&A Ferries (☎ 2242 028 545), the F/B *Nisos Kalymnos* and sometimes the F/B *Hioni*. Sample fares are: Rhodes (3½ hours) €10.30, Piraeus (12 to 15 hours) €23.20, Patmos (4 hours) €8.50.

Ferry – International There are daily ferries in summer travelling from Kos Town to Bodrum (otherwise known as ancient Halicarnassus) in Turkey (one hour, €30 to €38 return, including Turkish port tax). Boats leave at 8.30am and return at 4pm. Many travel agents around Kos Town sell tickets; Exas Travel (☎ 2242 028 545) is a good bet.

Hydrofoil & Catamaran Kos is served by Kyriacoulis Hydrofoils and the *Dodekanisos Express* catamaran. In high season there are daily shuttles, morning and evening, to and from Rhodes (two hours, €20.60), with good connections to all the major islands in the group, as well as Samos (four hours, 24.50), Ikaria (three3½ hours, €19.50), Ikaria (2¾ hours, €23) and Fourni (3-½three hours, €22) in the North-Eastern

Aegean. From Samos you can easily connect with the Cyclades.

Information and tickets are readily available from the many travel agents.

Excursion Boat From Kos Town there are many boat excursions, around the island and to other islands. Examples of return fares are: Kalymnos €9; Pserimos, Kalymnos and Platy €18; and Nisyros and Giali €19. There is also a daily excursion boat from Kardamena to Nisyros (€12 return) and from Mastihari to Pserimos and Kalymnos.

Getting Around Kos

To/From the Airport An Olympic Airways bus (€3) leaves the airline's office two hours before each flight. The airport is 26km south-west of Kos Town, near the village of Antimahia, and is poorly served by public transport, though buses to and from Kardamena and Kefalos stop at the roundabout nearby.

Many travellers choose to share a taxi into town (€13 to €14).

Bus The bus station (☎ 2242 022 292, fax 2242 020 263) is at Kleopatras 7, just west of the Olympic Airways office. There are

DODECANESE

10 buses daily to Tingaki (€1.20), three to Zia (€1.20), five to Pyli (€1.20), five to Mastihari (€1.70), six to Kardamena (€1.90) and six to Kefalos (€2.50) via Paradise, Agios Stefanos and Kamari beaches. There are frequent local buses to the Asklipion, Lambi and Agios Fokas from the bus stop on Akti Koundourioti in Kos Town.

Car, Motorcycle & Bicycle There are numerous car, motorcycle and moped rental outlets.

You'll be tripping over bikes to rent. Prices range from €3.50 for an old boneshaker to €10 for a top-notch mountain bike.

Tourist Train You can take a guided tour of Kos in the city's (vehicular) Tourist Train (20 minutes, €1.50), which runs 10am to 2pm and 6pm to 10pm starting from the Municipality Building. Or take a train to the Asklipion and back (€2.05 return), departing on the hour 9am to 6pm Tuesday to Sunday.

Excursion Boat These boats line the southern side of Akti Koundourioti in Kos Town and make trips around the island.

KOS TOWN

Kos Town, on the north-east coast, is the island's capital and main port. The Old Town was destroyed by an earthquake in 1933. The New Town, although modern, is picturesque and lush, with an abundance of palms, pines, oleander and hibiscus. The Castle of the Knights dominates the port, and Hellenistic and Roman ruins are strewn everywhere. It's a pleasant enough place and can easily be covered on foot in half a day.

Orientation

The ferry quay is north of the castle. Excursion boats dock on Akti Koundourioti to the south-west of the castle. The central square of Plateia Eleftherias is south of Akti Koundourioti along Vasileos Pavlou. Kos' so-called Old Town is on Ifestou; its souvenir shops, jewellers and boutiques denude it of any old-world charm, though.

South-east of the castle, the waterfront is called Akti Miaouli. It continues as Vasileos Georgiou and then G Papandreou which leads to the beaches of Psalidi, Agios Fokas and Therma Loutra.

Information

Kos Town's municipal tourist office (☎ 2242 024 460, fax 2242 021 111 e dotkos@hol.gr) is at Vasileos Georgiou 1. The staff is efficient and helpful, and the office is open 8am to 8pm Monday to Friday and 8am to 3pm Saturday May to October.

The tourist police (☎ 2242 022 444) and regular police (☎ 2242 022 222) share the yellow Municipality Building opposite the quay. The port police (☎ 2242 028 507) are at the corner of Akti Koundourioti and Megalou Alexandrou.

The post office is on Vasileos Pavlou and the OTE is at Vyronos 6. Kos Town has two good Internet cafes: Cafe Del Mare (☎ 2242 024 244, e sotiris@cybercafe.gr) at Megalou Alexandrou 4 and Multi Tech Internet Services (☎ 2242 023 584, e info @multitech.gr) at El Venizelou 55.

Both the National Bank of Greece on Antinavarhou Ioannidi and the Alpha Bank on El Venizelou have ATMs. The Alpha Bank on Akti Koundourioti has a 24-hour automatic exchange machine.

The hospital (☎ 2242 022 300) is at Ippokratous 32. The Happy Wash laundrette is at Mitropolis 20 and the Laundromat Center is at Alikarnassou 124.

Archaeological Museum

There are many statues from various periods and a fine 3rd-century AD mosaic in the vestibule of the archaeological museum (☎ 2242 028 326, Plateia Eleftherias; admission €2.40; open 8am-2.30pm Tues-Sun). The most renowned statue is that of Hippocrates.

Archaeological Sites

The **ancient agora** (admission free) is an open site south of the castle. A massive 3rd-century BC stoa, with some reconstructed columns, stands on its western side. On the north side are the ruins of a **Shrine of**

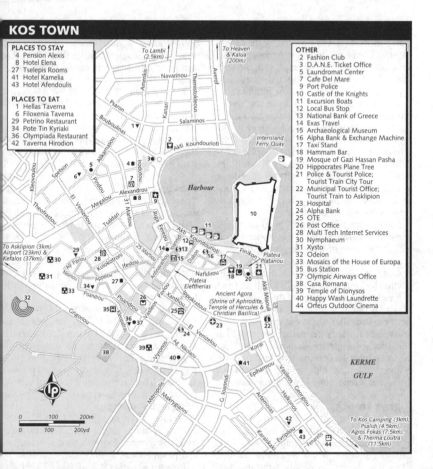

KOS TOWN

PLACES TO STAY
4 Pension Alexis
8 Hotel Elena
27 Tselepis Rooms
41 Hotel Kamelia
43 Hotel Afendoulis

PLACES TO EAT
1 Hellas Taverna
6 Filoxenia Taverna
29 Petrino Restaurant
34 Pote Tin Kyriaki
36 Olympiada Restaurant
42 Taverna Hirodion

OTHER
2 Fashion Club
3 D.A.N.E. Ticket Office
5 Laundromat Center
7 Cafe Del Mare
9 Port Police
10 Castle of the Knights
11 Excursion Boats
12 Local Bus Stop
13 National Bank of Greece
14 Exas Travel
15 Archaeological Museum
16 Alpha Bank & Exchange Machine
17 Taxi Stand
18 Hammam Bar
19 Mosque of Gazi Hassan Pasha
20 Hippocrates Plane Tree
21 Police & Tourist Police;
     Tourist Train City Tour
22 Municipal Tourist Office;
     Tourist Train to Asklipion
23 Hospital
24 Alpha Bank
25 OTE
26 Post Office
28 Multi Tech Internet Services
30 Nymphaeum
31 Xysto
32 Odeion
33 Mosaics of the House of Europa
35 Bus Station
37 Olympic Airways Office
38 Casa Romana
39 Temple of Dionysos
40 Happy Wash Laundrette
44 Orfeus Outdoor Cinema

Aphrodite, **Temple of Hercules** and a 5th-century **Christian basilica**.

North of the agora is the lovely cobblestone Plateia Platanou where you can pay your respects to the **Hippocrates Plane Tree**, under which Hippocrates is said to have taught his pupils. Plane trees don't usually live for more than 200 years – so much for the power of the Hippocratic oath – though in all fairness it is certainly one of Europe's oldest. This once-magnificent tree is held up with scaffolding, and looks to be in its death throes. Beneath it is an old sarcophagus converted by the Turks into a fountain.

Opposite the tree is the well-preserved 18th-century **Mosque of Gazi Hassan Pasha**, its ground floor loggia now converted into souvenir shops.

From Plateia Platanou a bridge leads across Finikon (called the Avenue of Palms) to the **Castle of the Knights** (☎ 2242 027 927, Leoforos Finikon; admission €2.40; open 8am-2.30pm Tues-Sun). Along with the castles of Rhodes Town and Bodrum, this impregnable fortress was the knights' most stalwart defence against the encroaching Ottomans. The castle, which had massive outer walls and an inner keep, was built

DODECANESE

in the 14th century. Damaged by an earthquake in 1495, it was restored by the Grand Masters d'Aubuisson and d'Amboise (each a master of a 'tongue' of knights) in the 16th century. The keep was originally separated from the town by a moat (now Finikon).

The other ruins are mostly in the southern part of the town. Walk along Vasileos Pavlou to Grigoriou and cross over to the restored **Casa Romana** (☎ 2242 023 234, Grigoriou 5; admission €1.40; open 8am-2.30pm Tues-Sun), an opulent 3rd-century Roman villa which was built on the site of a larger 1st-century Hellenistic house. Opposite here are the scant ruins of the 3rd-century **Temple of Dionysos**.

Facing Grigoriou, turn right to reach the **western excavation** site. Two wooden shelters at the back of the site protect the 3rd-century mosaics of the **House of Europa**. The best-preserved mosaic depicts Europa's abduction by Zeus in the guise of a bull. In front of here an exposed section of the Decumanus Maximus (the Roman city's main thoroughfare) runs parallel to the modern road, then turns right towards the **nymphaeum**, which consisted of once-lavish latrines, and the **xysto**, a large Hellenistic gymnasium, with restored columns. On the opposite side of Grigoriou is the restored 3rd-century **odeion**.

Places to Stay

Kos Camping (☎ 2242 023 910, Psalidi) Adult/tent €4.40/2.30. This facility, 3km along the eastern waterfront, is Kos' one camping ground. It's a well-kept, shaded site with a taverna, snack bar, minimarket, kitchen and laundry.

Pension Alexis (☎ 2242 028 798, fax 2242 025 797, Irodotou 9) Singles/doubles €17.60/25. This convivial pension with clean rooms is highly recommended. The friendly, English-speaking Alexis promises never to turn anyone away, and he's a mine of information.

Hotel Afendoulis (☎ 2242 025 321, fax 2242 025 797, Evripilou 1) Singles/doubles with bathroom €29.50/35.50. On the other side of town, and also owned by Alexis, is this tastefully furnished hotel. Laundry for guests costs €5.80 a load.

Hotel Kamelia (☎ 2242 028 983, fax 027 391, e kamelia_hotel@hotmail.com) Open year-round. Singles/doubles €16.50/41. On a quiet tree-lined street, this is a pleasant C-class hotel.

Hotel Elena (☎ 2242 022 740, Megalou Alexandrou 7) Doubles/triples with bathroom €23.50/31. This D-class hotel is a commendable budget option. Another recommended place is *Tselepis Rooms* (☎ 2242 028 896, Metsovou 8), where singles/doubles with bathroom cost €30.80/36.50.

Places to Eat

The restaurants lining the central waterfront are generally expensive and poor value; avoid them and head for the back streets.

Taverna Hirodion (☎ 2242 026 634, Artemisias 27) Mains €5-6. This taverna serves good and inexpensive food, though it's a little out of the way. The pork fillet in brandy sauce (€10.30) is considered the house speciality.

Olympiada Restaurant (☎ 2242 023 031, Kleopatras 2) Pasta €3.50. This unpretentious place behind the Olympic Airways office serves reasonably priced, tasty food.

Filoxenia Taverna (☎ 2242 024 967, Cnr Pindou & Alikarnassou) Mixed platters €7-8.50. This taverna has a good reputation for traditional home-cooked food. Try the filling gyros platter.

Hellas Taverna (☎ 2242 022 609, Psaron 7) Mains €4.50-6. This restaurant is highly recommended with good *bekri mezes* and pastitsio among the dishes on offer.

Pote tin Kyriaki (☎ 2242 027 872, Pisandrou 9) Pittes €3.50. Open evenings only, closed Sunday. This is another fine choice, with a good line in home-made pittes.

Petrino Restaurant (☎ 2242 027 251, Plateia Ioannou Theologou) Mains €8-9. Open evenings only. This is a stylish place in a stone mansion, with outdoor eating in a romantic garden setting. Try chicken stuffed with spinach, cheese and mint sauce.

Entertainment

Kos Town has two streets of bars, Diakon and Nafklirou, that positively pulsate in high season. Most bars belt out techno, but

Hammam Bar (*Akti Koundourioti 1*) plays Greek music.

Kos Town has five discos among which are the following.

Fashion Club (☎ *2242 022 592, Kanari 2*) This indoor venue has three air-con bars.

Heaven (☎ *2242 023 874, Akti Zouroudi 5*) This outdoor venue plays mostly house and has a swimming pool.

Kalua (☎ *2242 024 938, Akti Zouroudi 3*) Next door to Heaven, the music here is more mixed and includes R&B. It's an outdoor venue and also has a swimming pool.

There is also an outdoor cinema, *Orfeus* (☎ *2242 025 036, Fenaretis 3*), open summer only; entry costs €5.90.

AROUND KOS TOWN

Asklipion Ασκληπιείον

The island's most important ancient site is the Asklipion (☎ *2242 028 763, Platani; admission €2.40; open 8.30am-6pm Tues-Sun*), built on a pine-covered hill 4km south-west of Kos Town. From the top there is a wonderful view of Kos Town and Turkey. The Asklipion consisted of a religious sanctuary to Asclepius, the god of healing, a healing centre, and a school of medicine, where the training followed the teachings of Hippocrates.

Hippocrates was the first doctor to have a rational approach to diagnosing and treating illnesses. Until AD 554 people came from far and wide to be treated here, as well as for medical training.

The ruins occupy three levels. The **propylaea**, Roman-era public **baths** and remains of guest rooms are on the first level. On the next level is a 4th-century BC **altar of Kyparissios Apollo**. West of this is the **first Temple of Asclepius**, built in the 4th century BC. To the east is the 1st-century BC **Temple to Apollo**; seven of its graceful columns have been re-erected. On the third level are the remains of the once-magnificent 2nd-century BC **Temple of Asclepius**.

Frequent buses go to the site, but it is pleasant to cycle or walk there.

AROUND KOS

Kos' main road runs south-west from Kos Town with turn-offs for the mountain villages and the resorts of Tingaki and Marmari. Between the main road and the coast, a quiet road, ideal for cycling, winds through flat agricultural land as far as Marmari.

The nearest decent beach to Kos Town is the crowded **Lambi Beach**, 4km to the north. Farther round the coast, **Tingaki**, 9km from Kos Town, has an excellent, long, pale sand beach. **Marmari Beach**, 4km west of Tingaki, is slightly less crowded. Windsurfing is popular at all three beaches.

Vasileos Georgiou (later G Papandreou) in Kos Town leads to the three crowded beaches of **Psalidi**, 3km from Kos Town; **Agios Fokas**, 7km away; and **Therma Loutra**, 11km away. The latter has hot mineral springs which warm the sea.

Antimahia (near the airport) is a major island crossroads. A worthwhile detour is to the **Castle of Antimahia** on a turn-off to the left, 1km before Antimahia. There's a ruined settlement within its well-preserved walls.

The Asklipion as it may have looked 2000 years ago

KELLI HAMBLETT

DODECANESE

Kardamena, 27km from Kos Town and 5km south-east of Antimahia, is an over-developed, tacky resort best avoided, unless you want to take an excursion boat to Nisyros (see the Getting To/From Kos section).

Mastihari Μαστιχάρι

Mastihari, (mas-ti-**ha**-ri) north of Andimahia and 30km from Kos Town, is an important village in its own right. It's a resort destination, but also an arrival/departure point for ferries to Pothia on Kalymnos. It is better equipped to cater for independent travellers, with a good selection of domatia. Mastihari is just that little bit more 'Greek' than its resort neighbours further east, Marmari and Tingaki. From here there are excursion boats to Kalymnos and the island of **Pserimos**.

Places to Stay & Eat There's loads of accommodation in Mastihari.

Rooms to Rent Anna (☎ 2242 059 041) Doubles €20.50. Walk 200m inland along the main road to these rooms, on the left.

To Kyma (☎ 2242 059 045) Singles/doubles €17.60/23.50. This is a pleasant, small, family-run hotel with smallish but presentable rooms which enjoy a good sea breeze. There is a clean and homely communal kitchen for guests' use.

Rooms Panorama (☎/fax 2242 059 145) Double studios €29.50. Most of these tidy studios with kitchenette overlook the west beach.

Kali Kardia Restaurant (☎ 2242 059 289) Fish dishes €6.50-7.50. Right on the central square, this busy eatery is commendable and the fish is particularly good.

Mountain Villages

Several attractive villages are scattered on the northern slopes of the green and wooded, alpine-like Dikeos mountain range. At **Zipari**, 10km from the capital, a road to the south-east leads to **Asfendiou**. From Asfendiou, a turn-off to the left leads to the pristine hamlets of **Agios Georgios** and **Agios Dimitrios**. The road straight ahead leads to the village of **Zia**, which is touristy but worth a visit for the surrounding countryside and some great sunsets.

Lagoudi is a small, unspoilt village to the west of Zia. From here you can continue to **Amaniou** (just before modern Pyli) where there is a left turn to the ruins of the medieval village of **Pyli**, overlooked by a ruined castle.

Places to Eat *Palia Pygi* (☎ 2242 041 510, Pyli) Grills €5. Just off the central square at modern Pyli, this little taverna overlooking a lion-headed fountain serves tasty grills and mayirefta.

Taverna Olympia (☎ 2242 069 121, Zia) Mains €4.50-5. Open year-round. This establishment cashes in not on its view (which is nonexistent), but its solid, reliable local cuisine and repeat clientele.

Taverna Panorama (☎ 2242 069 367, Bagiati-Asfendiou) Open evenings only. Mezedes €3-3.50. With nary a tourist in sight, good mezedes and excellent service, Panorama enjoys a great night-time view. It's 3km from Zipari on the Asfendiou road.

Kamari & Kefalos
Καμάρι & Κέφαλος

From Antimahia the main road continues south-west to the huge Kefalos Bay, fringed by a 5km stretch of sandy beaches which are divided into roughly six 'name' beaches, each signposted from the main road. The most popular is **Paradise Beach**, while the most undeveloped is **Exotic Beach**. **Banana Beach** (also known as **Langada Beach**) is a good compromise.

Agios Stefanos Beach at the far western end is taken up by a vast Club Med complex. The beach, reached along a short turn-off from the main road, is still worth a visit to see the island of Agios Stefanos (named after its church), which is within swimming distance, and the ruins of two 5th-century basilicas to the left of the beach as you face the sea. The beach continues to Kamari.

Kefalos, 43km south-west of Kos Town, is the sprawling village perched high above Kamari beach. It's a pleasant place with few concessions to tourism. The central square, where the bus terminates, is at the top of the 2km road from the coast. There is a post office and bank with an ATM here.

The southern peninsula has the island's most wild and rugged scenery. **Agios Theologos beach** is on the east coast, 7km from Kefalos at the end of a good sealed road. Body surfing is popular here and boards can be rented. Sunsets are stunning.

Limnionas, 10km north of Kefalos, is a little fishing harbour. Its two small sandy beaches rarely get crowded.

Places to Stay & Eat Much of the accommodation in Kefalos Bay is monopolised by tour groups. Try these two independent operators for starters. Both are on the Kamari seafront about 200m on the right from Sebastian Tours.

Anthoula Studios (☎ 2242 071 904, mobile ☎ 694 633 5950, Kamari) Double apartments €41. This is spotless ground floor accommodation with kitchen, fridge and balcony with lounger. Bookings are essential.

Rooms to Let Katerina (☎ 2242 071 397, Kamari) Double studios €38.50. These are nearby and also a good choice, although they are a bit smaller.

Kamari is full of picture menu restaurants catering to package-tourist diners from the UK. Be adventurous; seek further afield.

Psarotaverna (mobile ☎ 69 4456 0770, Limnionas) Catering mainly to a Greek clientele, Miltos delivers the freshest fish – guaranteed (sea bream costs €7.50 to €8.50).

Restaurant Agios Theologos (mobile ☎ 69 7450 3556, Agios Theologos) This restaurant abutting Agios Theologos beach serves good fish dishes (white snapper is €9 to €10), home-made goat cheese and scrumptious home-baked bread. It's the best place on Kos to watch the sunset over dinner.

Astypalea
Αστυπάλαια

postcode 859 00 • pop 1000

Astypalea (ah-stih-**pah**-lia), the most westerly island of the archipelago, is an island in search of a sense of belonging. Geographically and architecturally it is more akin to the Cyclades islands, but administratively it is a Dodecanese island. Sited more or less equidistant between its nearest Cycladic neighbour, Amorgos, to the west and its fellow Dodecanese island, Kos, to the east, Astypalea effectively has a foot in both camps.

With a wonderfully picturesque hilltop hora and bare, gently contoured hills, high mountains, green valleys and sheltered coves, it's surprising Astypalea does not get more foreign tourists. It is, however, very popular with Athenians.

Getting To/From Astypalea

Air There are five flights weekly from Astypalea to Athens (€66). Astypalea Tours (☎ 2243 061 571), in Astypalea Town, is the agent for Olympic Airways.

Ferry Lying between the Cyclades and the Dodecanese, Astypalea is the most easterly destination of some Cyclades services, and the most westerly of the Dodecanese services. Departure times are more favourable when heading west and north.

The F/B *Nisos Kalymnos* or F/B *Hioni* do round trips to Astypalea from Kalymnos twice a week. Other services are provided by D.A.N.E. Sealines and G&A Ferries. Tickets are available from the Paradisos Ferries Agency (☎ 2243 061 224, fax 2243 061 450).

Hydrofoil Between June and September there is one hydrofoil a week plying a round trip from Rhodes (5½ hours, €30.50) to Astypalea via Symi, Kos and Kalymnos.

Getting Around Astypalea

Bus From Skala a bus travels fairly frequently to Hora and Livadia (€0.60), and from Hora and Skala to Maltezana (€0.90) via Marmari.

Excursion Boat In summer there are daily excursion boats to the island's less accessible beaches and to Agia Kyriaki Islet (€6). Tickets can be bought from the stalls by the boats.

DODECANESE

Phone numbers listed incorporate changes due in Oct 2002; see p83

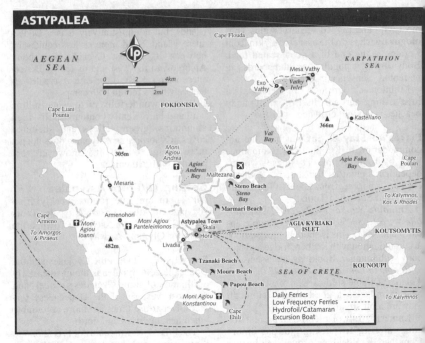

ASTYPALEA

ASTYPALEA TOWN

Astypalea Town, the capital, consists of the port of Skala and hilltop district of Hora, crowned by a fortress. Skala can be a noisy, busy place despite its small size, and few linger here to relax. Most visitors head uphill to Hora to so-called Windmill Square, where the windmills lining the square are perhaps Hora's most enduring feature. Hora has streets of dazzling-white cubic houses with brightly painted balconies, doors and banisters. The castle peering above this jumble of houses and balconies completes the picture.

Orientation & Information

From Skala's quay, turn right to reach the waterfront. The steep road to Hora begins beyond the white Italianate building. In Skala the waterfront road skirts the beach and then veers right to continue along the coast to Marmari and beyond.

A municipal tourist office adjoins the quayside cafe. The helpful owner of Astypalea Tours (☎ 2243 061 571, fax 2243 061 328) below Vivamare Apartments, is the agen for Olympic Airways and ferry lines.

The post office is at the top of the Skala Hora road. The OTE is close to Skala's waterfront. The Commercial Bank, with a ATM, is on the waterfront.

The police (☎ 2243 061 207) and port po lice (☎ 2243 061 208) are in the Italianat building.

Castle

During the time of the Knights of St John Astypalea was occupied by the Venetia Quirini family, who built the imposing cas tle. In the Middle Ages the population live within its walls, but gradually the settle ment outgrew them. The last inhabitants le in 1948 and the stone houses are now i ruins. Above the tunnel-like entrance is th Church of Our Lady of the Castle an within the walls is the Church of Agio Giorgios.

Archaeological Museum

Skala sports a small but well-presented archaeological museum (☎ 2243 061 206; admission €1.50; open 8am-2.30pm Tuesun). The whole island of Astypalea is in fact a rich trove of archaeological treasure and many of the finds are on display here. The collection runs from the prehistoric-Mycenaean period through to the Middle Ages. Look out for a fine selection of grave offerings from two Mycenaean chamber tombs excavated at Armenohori and the little bronze Roman statue of Aphrodite found at Trito Marmari. The museum is a little way up the Skala-Hora road on the right.

Places to Stay

Hotel and domatia owners usually meet incoming boats. Campers have one option.

Camping Astypalea (☎ 2243 061 338, Marmari) Adult/tent €3.50/2. This shaded ground is 3km east of Skala right next to the narrow sand-and-pebble beach.

Hotel Australia (☎ 2243 061 275, Pera Gialos) Doubles/triples €35/38. This hotel, back from the waterfront, has well-kept rooms with fridge and phone and a friendly Greek-Australian owner.

Karlos Rooms (☎ 2243 061 330, fax 2243 061 477, Pera Gialos) Doubles €35. These comfortable waterside rooms overlook Pera Gialos beach.

Akti Rooms (☎ 2243 061 114, Pera Gialos) Doubles/triples €38/44. These fridge-and phone-equipped rooms are beyond Karlos Rooms. There are good sea views from the balconies.

Hotel Paradisos (☎ 2243 061 224, fax 2243 061 450, Skala) Singles/doubles with bathroom €29.50/40. This ageing but well-maintained hotel has comfortable rooms.

Aphrodite Studios (☎ 2243 061 478, fax 2243 061 087, Skala) Double/triple studios €38/44. These beautiful, well-equipped studios are between Skala and Hora. Take the Hora road, turn left after the shoe shop and it's on the left.

Places to Eat

There' a decent selection of good restaurants both in Skala and up in Hora.

Karavos (☎ 2243 061 072, Pera Gialos) Vegetarian dishes €3-4. Excellent home-cooked food is served up at this homey and diminutive eatery right on the Pera Gialos waterfront. Try stuffed zucchini flowers, or *poungia* (cheese foldovers).

Restaurant Australia (☎ 2243 061 067, Skala) This old-style restaurant, below Hotel Australia, serves delicious fish; the speciality is lobster and macaroni (€8.80).

Restaurant Astropalia (☎ 2243 061 387, Skala) Grills €6. Enjoy wonderful views down to Skala from the terrace at this place.

Ouzeri Meltemi (☎ 2243 061 479, Hora) Mezedes €3.20. Opposite the windmills in Hora, this is a great place to hang out to watch the sunset.

Egeon Mezedopolio (☎ 2243 061 730, Hora) Snacks €3.50. Just a couple of doors along from Meltemi, this mezes cafe serves up excellent snacks and mezedes.

LIVADIA Λιβάδια

The little resort of Livadia lies in the heart of a fertile valley 2km from Hora. Its beach is the best on the island, but also the most crowded.

Quieter beaches can be found farther south at **Tzanaki**, the island's unofficial nudist beach, and at **Agios Konstantinos** below the monastery of the same name. You can drive to Agios Konstantinos beach along a reasonably-surfaced dirt road, or walk the 3km in about 40 minutes.

Places to Stay & Eat

There are a few comfortable places to stay in Livadi and a sprinkling of restaurants.

Gerani Rooms (☎ 2243 061 484) Doubles/triples with bathroom €29.50/32. This place is a pleasant budget option; the rooms come with refrigerator.

Kaloudis Domatia (☎ 2243 061 318) Doubles €32.50. These domatia with a communal kitchen are another good option.

Jim Venetos Studios & Apartments (☎ 2243 061 490, fax 2243 061 423) Double studios €38, 4-person apartments €59. A sign at the western end of the waterfront points to this place, which has attractive studios and apartments.

DODECANESE

Trapezakia Exo (☎ 2243 061 083) Mains €3.50-4.50. A neat little snack bar-cum-restaurant, Trapezakia Exo is right on the beach at the western end of the waterfront. Snack on sandwiches or enjoy the cuttlefish speciality (€3.50).

OTHER BEACHES

Marmari, 2km north-east of Skala, has three bays with pebble-and-sand beaches. **Steno Beach**, 2km further along, is one of the better but least frequented beaches on the island. It's sandy, has shade and is well-protected. **Maltezana** (also known as **Analipsi**) is 7km beyond Marmari in a fertile valley on the isthmus. A former Maltese pirates' lair, it's a scattered, pleasantly laid-back settlement, but its two beaches are somewhat grubby. There are some remains of Roman baths with mosaics on the settlement's outskirts.

The road from Maltezana is reasonable as far as **Vaï**, and is gradually improving beyond. **Mesa Vathy** is a fishing hamlet with a beach at the end of a narrow inlet. It takes about 1½ hours to walk here from Vaï. From Mesa Vathy a dirt road leads to **Exo Vathy**, another hamlet with a beach.

Places to Stay & Eat

There are quite a few accommodation options in Maltezana, but many only operate during the summer.

Maltezana Rooms (☎ 2243 061 446, *Maltezana*) Doubles €25. These fairly standard rooms are 50m east of the quay, just back from the beach.

Villa Varvara (☎ 2243 061 443, *Maltezana*) Double/triple studios €44/50. Varvara has fourteen blue-and-white painted studios over-look a vegetable garden 100m from the beach. All have TVs and fridges.

Ovelix Taverna (☎ 2243 061 260, *Maltezana*) Fish dishes €7-8. This recommended taverna 100m inland from the quay does good fish meals.

Almyra Restaurant (☎ 2243 061 451, *Maltezana*) Fish dishes €7.50-8.50. Next to the quay, this is another recommended spot for seafood. Both this and Ovelix operate 1 June to 30 September.

Kalymnos Κάλυμνος

postcode 852 00 • pop 18,200

Kalymnos (**kah-lim-nos**), only 2.5km south of Leros, is a mountainous, arid island, speckled with fertile valleys. Kalymnos is renowned as the 'sponge-fishing island', but with the demise of this industry it is now exploiting its tourist potential. It faces a tough job. While there is plenty on offer to entice travellers – good food, accommodation and rugged scenery – the pull of neighbouring Kos on the package tourism industry is just too strong and the majority of people flying into the region stay on Kos. The modest numbers that do make it across to Kalymnos via the local ferry find an island that is still in touch with its traditions and where the euro goes just that little bit further.

Getting To/From Kalymnos

Air Most people wishing to fly to Kalymnos fly to Kos and transfer to the Mastihari-Pothia local ferry.

Olympic Airways is represented by Kapellas Travel (☎ 2243 029 265) in Pothia

Ferry Kalymnos is on the main north-south route for ferries to and from Rhodes and Piraeus and is reasonably well serviced with one or more daily departures. Services are provided by D.A.N.E. Lines, G&A Ferries, Miniotis Lines and the local F/B *Nisos Kalymnos*. Sample destinations are: Piraeus (10 to 13 hours) €21.80, Rhodes (five hours) €13.20, Astypalea (three hours) €7.40, Kos (1½ hours) €4.40 and, Patmos (2½ hours) €7.70 and Samos (four hours) €10.

The car and passenger ferries F/B *Olympios Apollon* and F/B *Atromitos* leave between three and six times daily between 7am and 8pm from Pothia to Mastihari or Kos (50 minutes, €2.80).

Hydrofoil & Catamaran Kalymnos is currently served by Kyriacoulis Hydrofoils linking Kalymnos with most islands in the north and south Dodecanese group. Sample destinations are: Rhodes (3½ hours, €26), Patmos (1½ hours, €15), Astypalea (two

KALYMNOS

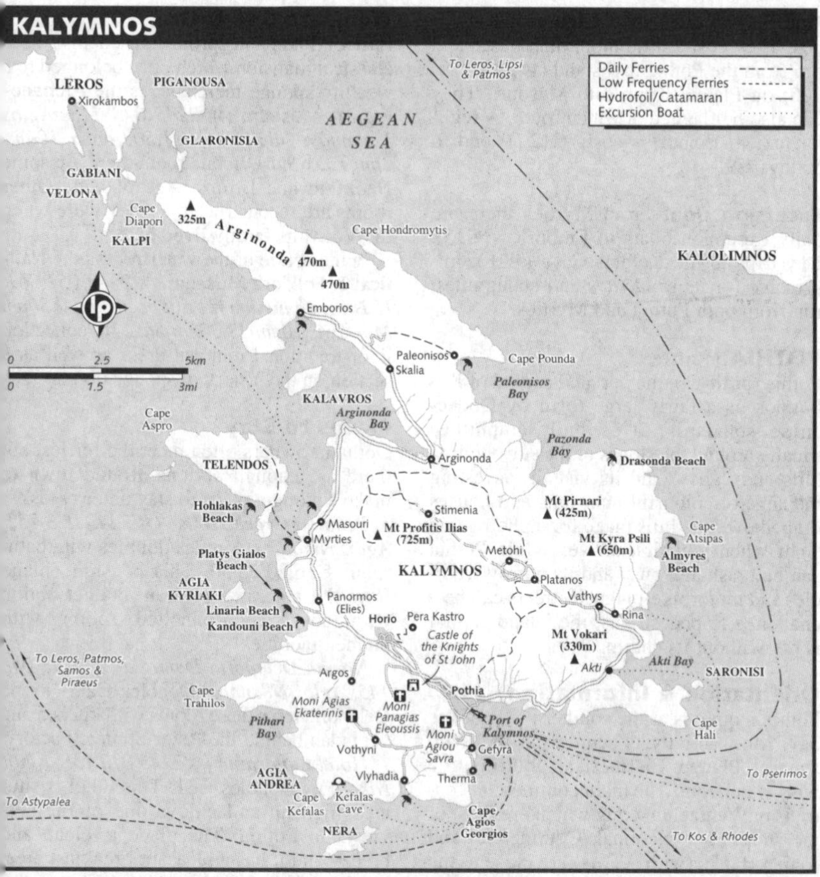
Daily Ferries
Low Frequency Ferries
Hydrofoil/Catamaran
Excursion Boat
To Leros, Lipsi & Patmos
LEROS
Xirokambos
PIGANOUSA
AEGEAN SEA
GLARONISIA
GABIANI
VELONA
Cape Diapori
325m
Arginonda
KALPI
Cape Hondromytis
470m
470m
KALOLIMNOS
Emborios
0 2.5 5km
0 1.5 3mi
Paleonisos
Skalia
Cape Pounda
Paleonisos Bay
KALAVROS
Arginonda Bay
Cape Aspro
Pazonda Bay
Arginonda
Drasonda Beach
TELENDOS
Hohlakas Beach
Masouri
Myrties
Stimenia
Mt Profitis Ilias (725m)
Mt Pirnari (425m)
Mt Kyra Psili (650m)
Cape Atsipas
Almyres Beach
Metohi
Platys Gialos Beach
KALYMNOS
Platanos
AGIA KYRIAKI
Panormos (Elies)
Vathys
Rina
Linaria Beach
Kandouni Beach
Horio
Pera Kastro
Castle of the Knights of St John
Mt Vokari (330m)
Akti
Akti Bay
To Leros, Patmos, Samos & Piraeus
Argos
SARONISI
Cape Trahilos
Pothia
Moni Agias Ekaterinis
Moni Panagias Eleoussis
Port of Kalymnos
Pithari Bay
Moni Agiou Savra
Cape Hali
Vothyni
Gefyra
AGIA ANDREA
Vlyhadia
Therma
To Pserimos
To Astypalea
Cape Kefalas
Kefalas Cave
NERA
Cape Agios Georgios
To Kos & Rhodes

ours, €14.80) and Samos (3½ hours, €19.50). Tickets can be bought from Mikes Magos Travel Agency (☎ 2243 028 777, fax 2243 022 608).

The *Dodekanisos Express* catamaran calls in once daily during Ssummer on its run up and down the Dodecanese chain. Fares are similar to those of the hydrofoil.

Excursion Boat In summer there are three excursion boats daily from Pothia to Mastichari on Kos, and one to Pserimos (€6). Other excursions run by the caique *Irini* include Nera, Vlyhadia, Platys Island, Akti and Vathys and Kefala cave. There are also daily excursions from Myrties to Xirokambos on Leros (€4.40 one way).

Getting Around Kalymnos

Bus In summer there is a bus on the hour from Pothia to Masouri (€0.80) via Myrties, to Emborios (€0.90) three times weekly and to Vathys (€0.90) four times daily. Buy tickets from Themis Minimarket in Pothia as they are not available on the bus.

Motorcycle There are several motorcycle rental outlets along Pothia's waterfront.

Taxi Shared taxis are a feature of Kalymnos. They cost a little more than buses and run from the Pothia taxi stand (☎ 2243 050 300) on Plateia Kyprou to Masouri. They can also be flagged down en route. A regular taxi to Emborios costs €12.50 and to Vathys €9.

Excursion Boat From Myrties there are daily excursion boats to Emborios (€15). Day trips to the Kefalas Cave (€18), impressive for its stalactites and stalagmites, run from both Pothia and Myrties.

POTHIA Πόθια

Pothia (**poth**-ya), the port and capital of Kalymnos, is a fairly large town by Dodecanese standards. It is built amphitheatrically around the slopes of the surrounding hills and valley, and its visually arresting melange of colourful mansions and houses draped over the hills make for a photogenic sight when you first arrive. While Pothia can be brash and busy and its narrow vehicle- and motorbike-plagued streets can be a challenge to pedestrians, the island capital is not without its charm.

Orientation & Information

Pothia's quay is at the southern side of the bay. Most activity is centred on the main square, Plateia Eleftherias, abutting the busy waterfront. The main commercial centre is on Venizelou along which are most of the shops. The National, Commercial and Ionian Banks (with ATMs) are close to the waterfront.

In the middle of the central promenade is a seasonal tourist information kiosk (☎ 2243 050 879), open 7.30am to 10pm in summer. There are two Internet cafes in Pothia: Neon Internet Cafe 3 (☎ 2243 028 343, Agios Nikolaos) and Neon Internet Cafe 1 (☎ 2243 048 318, Hristos). Rates are €1.50 for 30 minutes and they are open 8.30am to midnight. The post office is a 10 minute walk north-west of Plateia Eleftherias.

The police (☎ 2243 029 301) are on Patriarhou Maximimou before the post office while the port police (☎ 2243 029 304) are at the start of the quay.

Things to See & Do

East of Plateia Kyprou, housed in a neoclassical mansion which once belonged to a wealthy sponge merchant, is the **Archaeological Museum** (☎ 2243 023 113, Agios Mammas; admission €1.50; open 10am-2pm Tues-Sun). In one room there are some Neolithic and Bronze Age objects. Other rooms are reconstructed as they were when the Vouvalis family lived here.

In the centre of the waterfront is the **Nautical & Folklore Museum** (☎ 2243 051 361, Hristos; admission €1.50; open 8am-1.30pm Mon-Fri, 10am-12.30pm Sat). Its collection is of traditional regional dress as well as a section on the history of sponge diving.

Places to Stay

Domatia owners often meet the ferries, but there are enough options around town to make finding a place to stay an easy task.

Pension Greek House (☎ 2243 023 752, Agios Nikolaos) Singles/doubles with bathroom €16.20/23.50. This pension, inland from the port, is a pleasant budget option with cosy wood-panelled rooms with kitchen facilities.

Norma Delaporta Domatia (☎ 2243 048 145, Agios Nikolaos) Doubles €20. Norma Delaporta rents these rooms with kitchen and verandah behind the Astor Sponge Factory.

Hotel Panorama (☎ 2243 022 138, Agios Nikolaos) Doubles €31. This hotel is situated high up and enjoys one of the best views in Pothia. The place is clean and breezy and it has a pleasant breakfast area; breakfast is included in the room rates.

Archontiko Hotel (☎/fax 2243 024 149, Agios Nikolaos) Singles/doubles €28/38. Open year-round. At the south of the quay is a cool and pleasant hotel in a renovated century-old mansion. Rooms all have fridges, TV and phone and breakfast is included.

Places to Eat

Xefteris Taverna (☎ 2243 028 642, Hristos) Stifado €4.40. Open lunch & dinner daily. This century-old and pretty basic taverna serves delicious, inexpensive food. The meal-sized dolmades and the stifado are recommended.

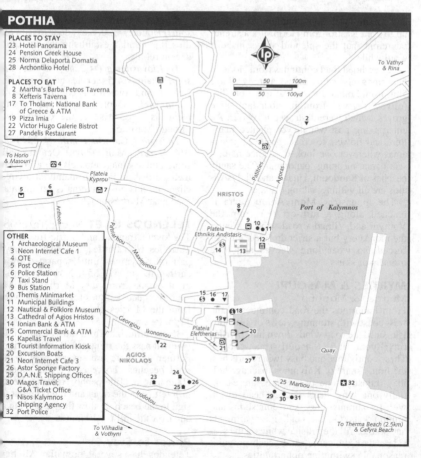

POTHIA

PLACES TO STAY
23 Hotel Panorama
24 Pension Greek House
25 Norma Delaporta Domatia
28 Archontiko Hotel

PLACES TO EAT
2 Martha's Barba Petros Taverna
8 Xefteris Taverna
17 To Tholami; National Bank
   of Greece & ATM
19 Pizza Imia
22 Victor Hugo Galerie Bistrot
27 Pandelis Restaurant

OTHER
1 Archaeological Museum
3 Neon Internet Cafe 1
4 OTE
5 Post Office
6 Police Station
7 Taxi Stand
9 Bus Station
10 Themis Minimarket
11 Municipal Buildings
12 Nautical & Folklore Museum
13 Cathedral of Agios Hristos
14 Ionian Bank & ATM
15 Commercial Bank & ATM
16 Kapellas Travel
18 Tourist Information Kiosk
20 Excursion Boats
21 Neon Internet Cafe 3
26 Astor Sponge Factory
29 D.A.N.E. Shipping Offices
30 Magos Travel;
   G&A Ticket Office
31 Nisos Kalymnos
   Shipping Agency
32 Port Police

Pizza Imia (☎ 2243 050 809, *Hristos*) Pizza for 2 €6.50. Devour scrumptious wood-oven pizza in all permutations and flavours at this place.

To Tholami (☎ 2243 051 900, *Hristos*) This well-established eatery is popular with locals. Suggested dishes are octopus balls (*ohtapodokeftedes*) and grilled tuna steaks (€5.90).

Martha's Barba Petros Taverna (☎ 2243 029 678, *Hristos*) Of the fish tavernas on the eastern waterfront, this is the best; the crab salad (€4.50) is a delicious and filling starter.

Pandelis Restaurant (☎ 2243 051 508, *Agios Nikolaos*) Open all day year-round. Meat dishes €4.50. The specialities at this homely eatery are goat in red wine sauce and the home-made dolmades.

AROUND POTHIA

The ruined **Castle of the Knights of St John** (or Kastro Hrysoherias) looms to the left of the Pothia-Horio road. There is a small **church** inside the battlements.

Pera Kastro was a pirate-proof village inhabited until the 18th century. Within the crumbling walls are the ruins of stone houses

DODECANESE

Phone numbers listed incorporate changes due in Oct 2002; see p83

and six tiny, well-kept churches. Steps lead up to Pera Kastro from Horio. It's a strenuous climb but the splendid views make it worthwhile.

A tree-lined road continues from Horio to **Panormos** (also called Elies), a pretty village 5km from Pothia. Its pre-war name of Elies (olives) derived from its abundant olive groves, which were destroyed in WWII. An enterprising post-war mayor planted many trees and flowers to create beautiful panoramas wherever one looked – hence its present name, meaning 'panorama'. The sandy beaches of **Kandouni**, **Linaria** and **Platys Gialos** are all within walking distance.

The monastery **Moni Agiou Savra** is reached along a turn-off left from the Vothyni and Vlihadia road. You can enter the monastery but a strict dress code is enforced, so wear long sleeves and long trousers or skirts.

MYRTIES & MASOURI
Μυρτιές & Μασούρι

From Panormos the road continues to the west coast with stunning views of Telendos Islet until the road winds down into **Myrties** (myr-**tyez**) and **Masouri** (mah-**soo**-ri). These contiguous and busy twin resorts host the lion's share of Kalymnos' package holiday industry. The two centres are essentially one long street packed head to tail with restaurants, bars, souvenir shops and minimarkets. On the land side apartments and studios fill the hillside while on the seaside a dark, volcanic sand beach provides reasonable swimming opportunities.

Come here if you like an active holiday. There are exchange bureaus, car and motorbike rental outlets and even an Internet cafe. From Myrties there's a daily caique to Xirokambos on Leros (€4.40 one way).

Places to Stay & Eat

Most accommodation in Masouri and Myrties is block-booked by tour groups. There are a couple of places that deal with walk-ins.

Rita Studios (☎ 2243 024 021, *Masouri*) Doubles €30. Rita's has largish, airy rooms with kitchenette and big balconies for outdoor dining.

Studios Sevasti (☎ 2243 047 854, *Masouri*) Doubles €30. Next door to Rita Studios this similar establishment has quiet, decent rooms.

To Iliovasilema (☎ 2243 047 683, *Masouri*) Mains €4-5. Service here is truly excellent and the food equally so. The kontosouvli (Cypriot-style, spit roasted meat) is tops. It's on the central road through Masouri.

Taverna I Galazia Limni (☎ 2243 047 016, *Myrties*) Mains €4.50. Octopus ball, squid and saganaki mussels are all recommended dishes. Pitched mainly at a Greek clientele, this cosy taverna is off the main road near Myrties beach.

TELENDOS ISLET Νήσος Τέλενδος

The lovely, tranquil and traffic-free islet of Telendos, with a little quayside hamlet, was part of Kalymnos until separated by an earthquake in AD 554. Nowadays it's a great escape from busy Myrties and Masouri. Frequent caiques for Telendos depart from the Myrties quay between 8am and 11pm (€2 return).

If you turn right from the Telendos quay you will pass the ruins of a Roman basilica. Farther on, there are several pebble-and-sand beaches. To reach the far superior 100m long and fine-pebbly **Hohlakas Beach** turn left from the quay and then right at the sign to the beach. Follow the paved path up and over the hill for 10 minutes.

Places to Stay

Telendos has several domatia. All have pleasant, clean rooms with bathroom. Opposite the quay is **Pension & Restaurant Uncle George** (☎ 2243 047 502, 2243 2855, e unclegeorgeingreece@hotmail.com) with studios for €24. **Nicky Rooms** (☎ 2243 047 584), with pleasant doubles for €19.50 is to the right of the quay. Adjoining the cafe of the same name is **On the Rocks Cafe Rooms** (☎ 2243 048 260, *fax 2243 048 260*, e otr@telendos.com), with two- or three-person apartments for €32.50.

Hotel Porto Potha (☎ 2243 047 321, *fax 2243 048 108*, e portopotha@kal.forthnet.gr) Doubles/triples €28/37. The

otel, beyond On the Rocks Cafe, has well-
kept rooms and a swimming pool.

Places to Eat

On the Rocks Cafe (*☎ 2243 048 260*) Souvlaki €5. The Greek-Australian owner serves
well-prepared meat and fish dishes as well as
vegetarian mousakas and souvlaki. It becomes a lively music bar at night and on Friday and Monday evenings it's 'Greek Night'.

Barba Stathis (*☎ 2243 047 953*) Mains
€5-6. Barba Stathis does a great spin on octopus in red sauce (*ohtapodi stifado*), as
well as octopus balls. Look for it in a little
lane behind the waterfront.

EMBORIOS Εμπορειός

The scenic west-coast road continues 11.5km
farther to Emborios, where there's a pleasant, shaded sand-and-pebble beach. One of
the nicest places to stay is **Harry's Apartments** (*☎ 2243 040 062*), where double/
triple apartments cost €26.50/32.50.

Paradise Restaurant (*☎ 2243 040 062*)
Harry's Apartments also runs the adjoining
restaurant. There's a good line in vegetarian
dishes (€6) such as chickpea croquettes (*rev-
hokeftedes*) and pies (*pittes*) with fillings
such as aubergine, vegetables and onion.

VATHYS & RINA Βαψύς & Ρίνα

Vathys, 13km north-east of Pothia, is one of
the most beautiful and peaceful parts of the
island. Vathys means 'deep' in Greek and
refers to the slender fjord that cuts through
high cliffs into a fertile valley, where narrow roads wind between citrus orchards.
There is no beach at Vathys' harbour, Rina,
but you can swim off the jetty at the south
side of the harbour. Water taxis (*☎ 2243
031 316*) take tourists to quiet coves nearby.

Places to Stay & Eat

Vathys has two places to stay, both at Rina.
Hotel Galini (*☎ 2243 031 241, fax 2243
031 100*) Doubles with bathroom €24. This
C-class hotel has well-kept rooms with balcony and breakfast included.

Pension Manolis (*☎ 2243 031 300,
Rina*) Singles/doubles with bathroom €19/
2. This pension, above the right side of the

harbour, has beautiful rooms. There is a
communal kitchen and terraces surrounded
by an attractive garden.

Restaurant Galini (*☎ 2243 031 241,
Rina*) Mains €4-5. Part of Hotel Galini, this
is a friendly place to eat. Roast local pork
(€4.40) and grilled octopus (€4) are two
recommended dishes.

Taverna tou Limaniou (*☎ 2243 031 206*)
Mains €4.50-5.50. In a stone-clad building
is this cosy family taverna. Ask for the pork
and chicken special (€5.80), or the garlic
prawn saganaki (€7.40).

Leros Λέρος

postcode 854 00 • pop 8059

Travellers looking for an island that is un-
mistakably Greek and still relatively untouched by mass commercial tourism will
find it on Leros, a destination surprisingly
little known by foreign travellers, though
well known for years by the discerning
Greek public. Leros is a medium-sized island in the northern Dodecanese offering an
attractive mix of sun, sea, rest and recreation, a stunning medieval castle and some
excellent dining opportunities.

The island offers gentle, hilly countryside dotted with small holdings and huge,
impressive, almost landlocked bays, which
look more like lakes than open sea. The immense natural harbour at Lakki was the
principal naval base of the Italians in the
eastern Mediterranean, and is now a curious
living architectural museum of Italian fascist Art Deco buildings.

Getting To/From Leros

Air There is a flight daily to Athens (€69).
The Olympic Airways office (*☎ 2247 022
844*) is in Platanos, before the turn-off for
Pandeli. The airport (*☎ 2247 022 777*) is in at
Partheni in the north. There is no airport bus.

Ferry Leros is on the main north-south
route for ferries between Rhodes and Piraeus. There are daily departures from
Lakki to Piraeus (11 hours, €19.70), Kos
(3¼ hours, €6.20) and Rhodes (7¼ hours,

DODECANESE

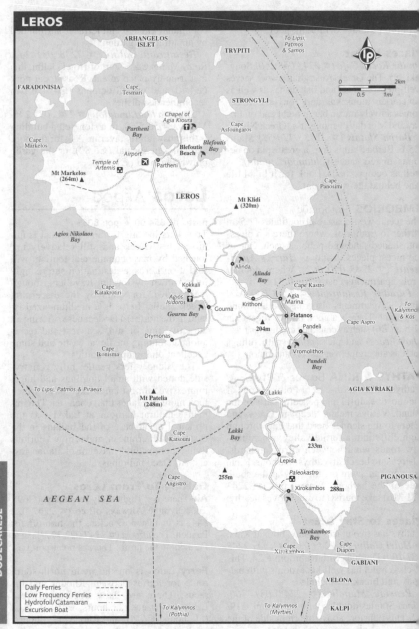

LEROS

ARHANGELOS
ISLET

TRYPITI

To Lipsi,
Patmos
& Samos

FARADONISIA

Cape
Tesmari

STRONGYLI

Chapel of
Agia Kioura

Cape
Asfoungaros

Partheni
Bay

Cape
Markelos

Blefoutis
Beach

Blefoutis
Bay

Airport

Temple of
Artemis

Partheni

Mt Markelos
(264m) ▲

LEROS

Mt Klidi
(320m) ▲

Cape
Panosimi

Agios Nikolaos
Bay

Cape
Katakrotiri

Alinda

Alinda
Bay

Cape Kastro

Kokkali

Agios
Isidoros

Krithoni

Agia
Marina

To
Kalymno
& Kos

Gourna Bay

Gourna

Platanos

Cape Aspro

Drymonas

204m ▲

Pandeli

Cape
Ikonisma

Vromolithos

Pandeli
Bay

To Lipsi, Patmos & Piraeus

AGIA KYRIAKI

Mt Patelia
(248m) ▲

Lakki

Lakki
Bay

233m ▲

Cape
Katsouni

Lepida

PIGANOUSA

Cape
Angistro

255m ▲

Paleokastro

Xirokambos

288m ▲

AEGEAN SEA

Xirokambos
Bay

Cape
Xirokambos

Cape
Diapori

GABIANI

VELONA

KALPI

Daily Ferries
Low Frequency Ferries
Hydrofoil/Catamaran
Excursion Boat

To Kalymnos
(Pothia)

To Kalymnos
(Myrties)

DODECANESE

14), as well as two weekly to Samos (3½ ours, €5.50).

ydrofoil & Catamaran In summer there e hydrofoils and a catamaran every day to atmos (45 minutes, €9.50), Lipsi (20 min-es, €7.20), Samos (two hours, €15), Kos ne hour, €12.30) and Rhodes (3¼ hours, 28). Hydrofoils and the catamaran leave om Agia Marina.

xcursion Boat The caique leaves Xiro-ambos 7.30am daily for Myrties on Kalym-s (€4.70 one way). In summer Lipsi-based iques make daily trips between Agia Mar-a and Lipsi. The trip costs €14.70 return.

etting Around Leros
he hub for Leros' buses is Platanos. There e four buses daily to Partheni via Alinda d six buses to Xirokambos via Lakki €0.60 flat fare).

There is no shortage of car, motorcycle d bicycle rental outlets around the island.

AKKI Λακκί
rriving at Lakki (lah-**kee**) by boat is like epping into an abandoned Fellini film set. he grandiose buildings and wide tree-lined ulevards dotted around the Dodecanese e best (or worst) shown here, for Lakki as built as a Fascist showpiece during the alian occupation. Few people linger in akki, though it has decent accommodation d restaurants and there are some secluded wimming opportunities on the road past e port. Check your email at Barrage In-rnet Café (☎ 2247 024 813) in Lakki, pen 8am to 1am, with rates of €3 per hour.

IROKAMBOS Ξηρόκαμπος
irokambos Bay, on the south of the island, a low-key resort with a gravel-and-sand each and some good spots for snorkelling. ust before the camping ground, on the op-osite side, a signposted path leads up to the ined fortress of **Paleokastro**.

Diving courses are offered by the **Panos iving Club** (☎ 2247 023 372, mobile 694 763 3146; 10-day course around 366 all-inclusive).

Places to Stay & Eat
Camping Leros (☎ 2247 023 372) Adult/tent €4.50/2.30. The island's only camping ground, this is on the right coming from Lakki. It's pleasant and shaded though the ground is a little hard. There is a small restaurant and bar.

Villa Alexandros (☎ 2247 022 202) Doubles €44. About 100m from the beach, this is a better but more expensive choice.

To Kyma (☎ 2247 025 248) Mayirefta €3.50-4. Straddling the road at the eastern side of the bay and under the shade of tamarisk trees is this relaxing restaurant. Try fried calamari, or a dish from the daily mayirefta selection.

PLATANOS & AGIA MARINA
ΠλάτανοVϖ & Αγία Μαρίνα
Platanos (**plah**-ta-nos), the capital of Leros, is 3km north of Lakki. It's a picturesque place spilling over a narrow hill pouring down to the port of Agia Marina to the north, and Pandeli to the south, both within walk-ing distance. The port of **Agia Marina** (ay-i-a ma-**ri**-na) has a more authentic ambience than Alinda resort to the north. Platanos is the main shopping area for the island, and while it doesn't offer much in the way of eat-ing or accommodation options, it's a very pleasant place to spend a leisurely hour or so browsing. It is also the starting point for path up to the **Castle of Pandeli** *(admission €0.88 castle, €1.50 castle & museum; open 8am-1pm & 5pm-8.30pm daily)*.

Orientation & Information
The focal point of Platanos is the lively cen-tral square, Plateia N Roussou. Harami links this square with Agia Marina.

There is a tourist information kiosk at the quay. Laskarina Tours (☎ 2247 024 550, fax 2247 024 551), at the Eleftheria Hotel, and Kastis Travel & Tourist Agency (☎ 2247 022 140), near the quay in Agia Marina, are very helpful. Laskarina Tours organises trips around the island (€11 to €18).

The post office and OTE share premises on the right side of Harami. You can access the Internet at Enallaktiko Cafe (☎ 2247 025 746) in Agia Marina.

The National Bank of Greece is on the central square. There is a Commercial Bank ATM in Agia Marina. The police station (☎ 2247 022 222) is in Agia Marina. The bus station and taxi rank are both on the Lakki-Platanos road, just before the central square.

Places to Stay & Eat
Eleftheria Hotel (☎ 2247 023 550) Doubles with bathroom €32.50. This C-class hotel, near the taxi rank, has pleasant, well-kept rooms.

You are probably better off heading down to Agia Marina to eat, as the only real option in Platanos is the *cafe* on the central square.

Ouzeri-Taverna Neromylos (☎ 2247 024 894, Agia Marina) Mains €4-5.50. There are several tavernas at Agia Marina, the most atmospheric of which is this one next to a former watermill. Night-time dining is best when lights illuminate the watermill.

Entertainment
Agia Marina is the heart of the island's nightlife, with several late-night music bars.

Enallaktiko Cafe (*Agia Marina*) Beer €1.50. This popular hang-out has pool, video games and Internet access.

PANDELI
Walking south from Platanos, you'll arrive at **Pandeli**, a little fishing village-cum-resort with a sand-and-shingle beach. Just outside of Platanos, beyond the turn-off for Pandeli, a road winds steeply down to **Vromolithos** where there's a good shingle beach.

Places to Stay
At *Pension Roza* (☎ 2247 022 798) on the waterfront doubles/triples cost €17.50/23.50.

Rooms to Rent Kavos (☎ 2247 023 247) has reasonable doubles for €32.50, a bit farther along from Pension Roza.

Pension Happiness (☎ 2247 023 498) Singles/doubles with bathroom €29.50/32.50. Pension Happiness, on the left down from Platanos, has modern, sunny rooms.

Pension Rodon (☎ 2247 022 075) Doubles €26.50-32.50. Open year-round. This place is up near the main road halfway between Pandeli and Vromolithos, next to Dimitris Taverna. It is an excellent and popular choice.

Places to Eat
Dimitris Taverna (☎ 2247 025 626) Mezedes €3-4.50. This is one of Leros' best tavernas. Its delicious mezedes include cheese courgettes, stuffed calamari, and onion and cheese pies; main courses include chicken in retsina and pork in red sauce. It's high up near the main road.

Psaropoula (☎ 2247 025 200) Mains €. Right on the beach, Psaropoula has a wide ranging menu featuring fish; prawn souvlaki with bacon is a good choice.

Entertainment
Savana Bar Open mid-afternoon-late. In Pandeli, head for this bar, run by two English guys. It has a great music policy: you can choose what you want.

KRITHONI & ALINDA
Κριθώνι & Αλιντα
Krithoni and Alinda are contiguous resorts on the wide Alinda Bay, 3km north-west of Agia Marina. On Krithoni's waterfront there is a poignant, well-kept **war cemetery**. After the Italian surrender in WWII, Leros saw fierce fighting between German and British forces. The cemetery contains the graves of 179 British, two Canadian and two South African soldiers.

Alinda, the island's biggest resort, has a long, tree-shaded sand-and-gravel beach. If you walk beyond the development you'll find some quiet coves.

Places to Stay & Eat
Hotel Gianna (☎/fax 2247 024 135, Alinda) Singles/doubles €26.50/38. Just beyond the war cemetery, a road veers left to this place which has nicely furnished rooms.

Studios & Apartments Diamantis (☎ 2247 022 378, Alinda) Doubles/triples €35.50/44. This sparkling, pine-furnished place is behind the cemetery.

Tassos Studios I (☎ 2247 022 769, fax 023 769, Krithoni) 2-4 person studios €47. Beautiful fully-equipped mini-apartments lose to Krithoni beach, with the same own-rs as Tassos II in Agia Marina.

Finikas Taverna (☎ *2247 022 695, linda*) Mezedes €2.50-4.20. This water-ont taverna in Alinda offers up 15 types of alad and 16 different mezedes and has an qually extensive menu of well-prepared reek specialities.

GOURNA Γούρνα

he wide bay of Gourna, on the west coast, as a similar beach to Alinda but is less de-eloped. At the northern side, the chapel of gios Isidoros is on a tranquil islet reached y a causeway.

NORTHERN LEROS

artheni is a scattered settlement north of the irport. Despite having a large army camp, 's an attractive area of hills, olive groves, elds of beehives and two large bays.

Artemis, the goddess of the hunt, was vorshipped on Leros in ancient times. Just outh of the airport there's a signposted turn o the left that leads to the **Temple of Artemis**. A dirt track turns right 300m along . Where the track peters out, clamber up to he left. You will see the little derelict Chapel of Agia Irini. There's little in the vay of ancient ruins but it's a strangely vocative, slightly eerie place.

Farther along the main road there is a urn-off to the right to **Blefoutis Bay**, which as a shaded sand-and-pebble beach and a ood taverna. Beyond this turn-off, the main road skirts **Partheni Bay** and its poor each. But if you continue straight ahead, urn right at the T-junction, go through a ate to pass the **Chapel of Agia Kioura**, then hrough another gate and bear right, you'll ome to a lovely secluded pebbled cove.

Patmos Πάτμος

ostcode 855 00 • pop 2663

Patmos could well be *the* ideal Greek island destination. It has a beguiling mix of qual-ties that make it a seductively pleasant oliday destination. It appeals in equal doses o the culturally inclined, the religiously

motivated, gastronomes and sun-worshippers, shoppers, yachties, bookaholics and trav-ellers simply seeking to unwind. Patmos is a place of pilgrimage for both Orthodox and Western Christians, for it was here that St John wrote his divinely inspired revelation (the Apocalypse). Patmos is instantly palat-able and entices the visitor to linger and to almost certainly return another time.

History

In AD 95, St John the Divine was banished to Patmos from Ephesus by the pagan Roman Emperor Domitian. While residing in a cave on the island, St John wrote the *Book of Revelations*. In 1088 the Blessed Christodoulos, an abbot who came from Asia Minor to Patmos, obtained permission from the Byzantine Emperor Alexis I Komninos to build a monastery to com-memorate St John. Pirate raids necessitated powerful fortifications, so the monastery looks like a mighty castle.

Under the Duke of Naxos, Patmos be-came a semi-autonomous monastic state, and achieved such wealth and influence that it was able to resist Turkish oppression. In the early 18th century, a school of theology and philosophy was founded by Makarios and it flourished until the 19th century.

Gradually the island's wealth polarised into secular and monastic entities. The sec-ular wealth was acquired through ship-building, an industry that diminished with the arrival of the steam ship.

Getting To/From Patmos

Ferry Patmos is on the main north-south route for ferries to and from Rhodes and Pi-raeus and is reasonably well serviced with at least one and sometimes more daily depar-tures from Skala. Services are provided by D.A.N.E. Lines and G&A Ferries, while the F/B *Nisos Kalymnos* or F/B *Hioni* provide additional links to Agathonisi and Samos.

Hydrofoil & Catamaran There are daily hydrofoils to Rhodes (five hours, €32.20), via Kalymnos (1½ hours, €15) and Kos (2¼ hours, €16.75), and to Fourni (40 min-utes, €10.50), Ikaria (1¼ hours, €10.90)

DODECANESE

PATMOS

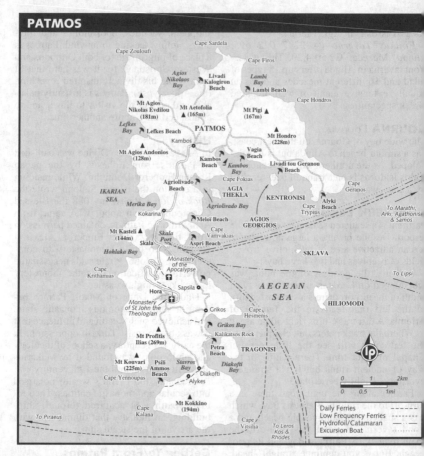

and Samos (one hour, €10.801). Twice a week, a hydrofoil runs to and from Agathonisi (40 minutes, €10).

The *Dodekanisos Express* catamaran calls in at Patmos six times a week during summer. Tickets can be bought at the Dodekanisos Shipping Agency (☎ 2247 029 303, ⓔ liapi@klm.forthnet.gr) in Skala. Prices are similar to hydrofoil ticket prices.

Excursion Boat The local *Patmos Express* leaves Patmos daily for Lipsi at 10am (€6 return) and returns from Lipsi at 4pm.

The Patmos-based *Delfini* (☎ 2247 03 995) goes to Marathi every day in high season – Monday and Thursday at other time Twice a week it also calls in at Arki. Fro Marathi a local caique will take you acros to Arki.

Getting Around Patmos

Bus From Skala there are 11 buses daily July and August to Hora (€0.65), eight Grikos (€0.70) and four to Kambo (€0.70). The frequency drops off during th rest of the year. There is no bus service Lambi.

Motorcycle There are lots of motorcycle and car rental outlets in Skala. Competition is fierce, so shop around. Australis Motor Rentals (☎ 2247 032 284) rents scooters for between €8.80 and €18 per day.

Taxi Taxis congregate at Skala's taxi rank. Sample fares are: Meloï Beach €2.40, Lambi €4.40, Grikos €3.50 and Hora €3.

Excursion Boat Boats go to all the island's beaches from Skala, leaving about 11am and returning about 4pm.

SKALA Σκάλα

Patmos' port town is Skala (**ska**-la), a bright and glitzy town draped around a curving bay and only visible from arriving ships once the protective headland has been rounded. It's a busy port and large cruise ships are often anchored offshore and smaller ones at Skala's harbour. Once the cruise ships and daily ferries depart, Skala reverts to being a fairly normal, livable port town. It has a wide range of good accommodation and restaurants, and all the island's major facilities are here.

Orientation & Information

Facing inland from the quay, turn right to reach the main stretch of waterfront where excursion boats and yachts dock. The right side of the large, white Italianate building opposite the quay overlooks the central square. For the road to Hora, turn left from the quay and right at Taverna Grigoris.

The generally useless municipal tourist office (☎ 2247 031 666), open summer only, shares the Italianate building with the post office and police station. Astoria Travel (☎ 2247 031 205, fax 2247 031 975), on the waterfront near the quay, and Travel Point (☎ 2247 032 801, fax 2247 032 802, info@travelpoint.gr), just inland from the central square, are helpful. The latter has a room-finding service.

The National Bank of Greece on the central square has an ATM. Inland from the central square is another smaller square; the OTE is on the left side of the road heading inland from here. The hospital (☎ 2247 031 211) is 2km along the road to Hora.

Patmos' port police (☎ 2247 031 231) are behind the large quay's passenger-transit building. The bus terminal and taxi rank (☎ 2247 031 225) are at the large quay.

Places to Stay – Budget

Domatia owners meet the boat. If you are not scooped up by one, there are a couple of budget places along the Hora road.

Pension Sofia (☎ 2247 031 876) Doubles/triples with bathroom €23.50/26.50. Head up along the Hora road and look for this comfortable pension 250m on the left. The rooms have balconies.

Pension Maria Pascalidis (☎ 2247 032 152), farther up the Hora road, is similar to Sofia and has singles/doubles for €14.50/23.50.

Hotel Rex (☎ 2247 031 242) Singles/doubles with bathroom €20.50/26.50. This fairly basic D-class hotel is on a narrow street opposite the cafeteria/passenger-transit building.

About 500m north of the main harbour is Netia, a quieter district with a number of accommodation options.

Pension Avgerinos (☎/fax 2247 032 118, Netia) Doubles with bathroom €44. Pension Avgerinos is run by a welcoming Greek-Australian couple. The rooms' views are very good.

Villa Knossos (☎ 2247 032 189, fax 2247 032 284, Netia) Doubles/triples with bathroom €41/44. This villa, set in a lovely garden, has immaculate rooms with balcony.

Australis Apartments (☎ 2247 032 562, fax 2247 032 284, Netia) Doubles €47. Nearby and easy to find is Australia Apartments where rooms have TV and fully equipped kitchenette.

Australis Hotel (☎ 2247 032 189, 2247 032 284, Netia) Singles/doubles €38/44. Set amidst a leafy garden, the Australis also has larger rooms for up to six persons.

Places to Stay – Mid-Range

On the south side of the harbour are other pricier options.

Hotel Delfini (☎ 2247 032 060, fax 2247 032 061) Singles/doubles €35.50/54.30. This C-class hotel has well-kept rooms. The

DODECANESE

front rooms have individual balconies with blue-and-white tables and cane chairs overlooking the street.

Hotel Blue Bay (☎ *2247 031 165, fax 2247 032 303,* e *bluebayhotel@yahoo .com,* W *www.bluebay.50g.com)* Singles/doubles €44/59. This Australian-Greek owned waterfront hotel has very clean, pleasantly furnished rooms.

Hotel Byzance (☎ *2247 031 052 fax 2247 031 663)* Singles/doubles €53/62. Rooms here have air-conditioning, TV, fridge, phone and music.

Captain's House (☎ *2247 031 793, fax 2247 034 077)* Singles/doubles €53/73. Each comfortable room has air-con, TV, fridge and phone. Breakfast is included in the room rate.

Places to Eat

Hiliomodi Ouzeri (☎ *2247 034 080)* Mezes platter €6. Head to this ouzeri for excellent seafood. The tasty appetisers plate is excellent value.

Grigoris Taverna (☎ *2247 031 515)* Mains €.3.80. Grigoris is very popular and his dolmades are recommended.

Loukas Restaurant (☎ *2247 031 832)* Grills €4.50. Succulent grill dishes are served in a leafy, shaded garden, in the back streets 150m inland from the harbour.

Pandelis Taverna (☎ *2247 031 230)* Ladera €2.35-2.90. A busy little taverna that caters to cruise groups and travellers alike. The service is efficient and the street dining is atmospheric.

Giagia (☎ *2247 033 226)* Mains €8-10. For a spicy change try this classy Indonesian restaurant, serving excellent *nasi goreng* and other dishes such as vegetarian fried bean curd in chilli sauce. It has a good selection of wines; the organic Mantinea Spyropoulou white (€13.20) is recommended.

Entertainment

Skala's music nightlife revolves around a scattering of bars and the odd club or two. *Consolato Music Club* (☎ *2247 031 194)* is a popular bar that is open year-round.

Aman (☎ *2247 032 323)* Nearby is another popular spot. This is more a place to sit outside on its tree-shaded patio and relax to music while nursing a cold beer or cocktail.

MONASTERIES & HORA

The immense **Monastery of St John the Theologian**, with its buttressed grey walls, crowns the island of Patmos. A 4km asphalt road leads in from Skala, but many people prefer to walk up the Byzantine path. To do this, walk up the Skala-Hora road and take the steps to the right 100m beyond the far side of the football field. The path begins opposite the top of these steps.

A little way along, a dirt path to the left leads through pine trees to the **Monastery of the Apocalypse** (☎ *2247 031 234; admission free, treasury €2.90; open 8am-1pm Mon-Sat, 8am-noon Sun, 4pm-6pm Tues, Thur & Sun),* built around the cave where St John received his divine revelation. In the cave you can see the rock that the saint used as a pillow, and the triple fissure in the roof, from which the voice of God issued, and which supposedly symbolises the Holy Trinity.

To rejoin the Byzantine path, walk across the monastery's car park and bear left onto the (uphill) asphalt road. After 60m, turn sharp left onto an asphalt road, and almost immediately the path veers off to the right. Soon you will reach the main road again. Cross straight over and continue ahead to reach Hora and the Monastery of St John the Theologian.

The finest frescoes of this monastery are those in the outer narthex. The priceless contents in the monastery's **treasury** include icons, ecclesiastical ornaments, embroideries and pendants made of precious stones.

Huddled around the monastery are the immaculate whitewashed houses of **Hora**. The houses are a legacy of the island's great wealth of the 17th and 18th centuries. Some of them have been bought and renovated by wealthy Greeks and foreigners.

Places to Stay & Eat

There are no hotel or domatia signs in Hora. There is accommodation but it is expensive and the best places are pre-booked months in advance. Try Travel Point in Skala, who have at least 10 traditional houses for rent

Vangelis Taverna (☎ 2247 031 967) Mains €4.50. This taverna on the central quare is deservedly popular. Good bets are ekri mezes (pork cubes in a spicy sauce vith vegetables) and the similar spetsofaï.

To Balkoni (☎ 2247 032 115) Mains €5-.50. The best dining views from Hora are fforded by 'The Balcony' which affords tunning views at night down to Skala. The ood is excellent; beef and liver with onions s one of the specials.

NORTH OF SKALA

The pleasant, tree-shaded **Meloï Beach** is ust 2km north-east of Skala, along a turn-ff from the main road.

Two kilometres farther along the main oad there's a turn-off right to the relatively quiet **Agriolivado Beach**. The main road ontinues to the inland village of **Kambos** nd then descends to the shingle beach from vhere you can walk to the secluded pebbled Vagia Beach. The main road ends at **Lambi**, km from Skala, where there is a beautiful each of multicoloured pebbles.

Places to Stay & Eat

Stefanos Camping (☎ 2247 031 821, Meloï) Adult/tent €3.80/2. This good camping ground, with bamboo-shaded sites, a mini-narket, cafe bar and motorcycle rental fa-ilities, is at Meloï. The rainbow-coloured ninibus meets most boats.

Rooms to Rent (☎ 2247 031 213, Meloï) Doubles €22. These basic domatia are 50m ack from the beach. The family also owns some newer rooms nearby, where doubles vith bathroom are €24.

Ta Kavourakia (☎ 2247 031 745, Kam-os) Meals €8-9. Ta Kavourakia is popular vith Italians and serves up good fish dishes.

George's Place (☎ 2247 031 881, Kam-os) Snacks €3-5. George's is on the beach and serves light snacks and drinks. You can play backgammon to laid-back music.

Psistaria Leonidas (☎ 2247 031 490, Lambi) Mayirefta €2.50-3.50. Leonidas on Lambi beach rustles up a wide range of homemade mayirefta dishes, various fish of the day plates and highly recommended saganaki (€3.80).

SOUTH OF SKALA

Sapsila is a quiet little corner 3km south of Skala, ideal for book lovers who want space and quiet and an underused beach to read on. **Grikos**, 1km further along over the hill, is a relaxed low-key resort with a narrow sandy beach. Farther south, the long, sandy, tree-shaded **Psili Ammos** can be reached by excursion boat or walking track.

Places to Stay & Eat

Matheos Studios (☎ 2247 032 119, Sapsila) Double/triple studios €29/41. This relaxed getaway is a neat place to stay for a week or so. The seven self-contained studios are set in a quiet, leafy garden 200m from Sapsila beach.

Stamatis Rooms (☎ 2247 031 302, Grikos) Doubles with bathroom €35. The rooms at this, the cheapest place to stay in Grikos, are comfortable enough.

Flisvos Restaurant (☎ 2247 031 764, Grikos) Full meals €8-9. Flisvos is a well-shaded, modern taverna. Accompany your meal with their fruity, slightly spritzig draft wine. There is also a seasonal *taverna* on Psili Ammos.

Lipsi Λειψοί

postcode 850 01 • pop 606

Lipsi (lip-**see**), 12km east of Patmos and 11km north of Leros, is the kind of place that few people know about, and once they have discovered it feel disinclined to share their discovery with others. It's a friendly, cheery place with just about the right balance of remoteness and 'civilisation'. There is comfortable accommodation, a pleasing choice of quality restaurants and a good selection of underpopulated beaches. Apart from two or three days a year when pilgrims and revellers descend upon Lipsi for its major festival, you can have most of it to yourself.

Getting To/From Lipsi

Ferry Lipsi is not well served by ferries. The F/B *Nisos Kalymnos* or F/B *Hioni* make up for the deficit somewhat with at least four

DODECANESE

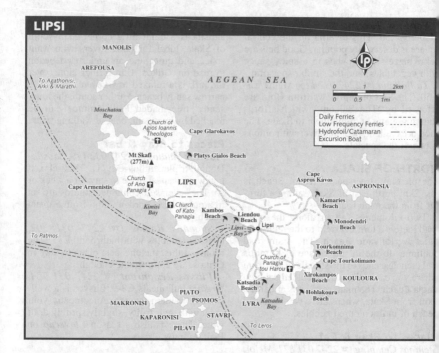

LIPSI

MANOLIS

AREFOUSA

To Agathonisi,
Arki & Marathi

AEGEAN SEA

Moschatou
Bay

Church of
Agios Ioannis
Theologos

Cape Glarokavos

Mt Skafi
(277m)▲

Platys Gialos Beach

Cape
Aspros Kavos

Church of
Ano
Panagia

LIPSI

ASPRONISIA

Cape Armenistis

Kimisi
Bay

Church
of Kato
Panagia

Kambos
Beach

Liendou
Beach

Lipsi

Kamaries
Beach

To Patmos

Lipsi
Bay

Monodendri
Beach

Tourkomnima
Beach

Church of
Panagia
tou Harou

Cape Tourkolimano

Xirokampos
Beach

KOULOURA

Katsadia
Beach

Hohlakoura
Beach

PIATO

MAKRONISI

PSOMOS

LYRA *Katsadia*
Bay

KAPARONISI

STAVRI

PILAVI

To Leros

Daily Ferries	– – – – –
Low Frequency Ferries	- - - - - - -
Hydrofoil/Catamaran	— · — ·
Excursion Boat	· · · · · · ·

0   1   2km
0   0.5   1mi

visits a week providing links both north and south. Hellas Ferries occasionally call in.

Hydrofoil & Catamaran In summer, hydrofoils call at Lipsi at least twice daily on their routes north and south between Samos, in the North-Eastern Aegean, and Rhodes. The *Dodekanisos Express* catamaran calls in three times a week. Sample fares are Rhodes (4½ hours) €29.70 and Patmos (20 minutes) €7.

Excursion Boat The *Captain Makis* and *Anna Express* do daily trips in summer to Agia Marina on Leros and to Skala on Patmos (both €14.70 return). *Black Beauty* and *Margarita* do 'Five Island' trips for around the same price. All four excursion boats can be found at the small quay and all depart at around 10am each day.

Getting Around Lipsi
Lipsi has three minibuses going to Platys Gialos (€0.90), Katsadia and Hohlakoura (both €0.80). Two taxis also operate on the island. There are several motorcycle rental outlets.

LIPSI TOWN
Orientation & Information
All boats dock at Lipsi Town, where there are two quays. The ferries, hydrofoils and catamaran all dock at the larger, outer jetty, while excursion boats dock at a smaller jetty nearer the centre of Lipsi town.

From the large quay, facing inland, turn right. Continue along the waterfront to the large Plateia Nikiforios, which is just beyond Hotel Calypso. Ascend the wide steps at the far side of Plateia Nikiforios and bear right to reach the central square. The left fork leads to a second, smaller square.

The municipal tourist office (☎ 2247 041 288) is on the central square, but you may find Laid Back Holidays (☎ 2247 041 141, fax 2247 041 343) or Lipsos Travel (☎/fax 2247 041 215) more helpful. The post office and OTE are on the central square, and there is a freestanding Commercial Bank ATM near the wide steps. Paradisis Travel changes money and cashes Eurocheques. The police (☎ 2247 041 222) are in the large white building opposite Paradisis Travel. The port police (☎ 2247 041 133) are in the long white building to the right of the wide steps.

Things to See & Do

Lipsi's **museum** *(Plateia, admission free; open 11am-1pm)* is on the central square. Its small display of exhibits include pebbles and plastic bottles of holy water from around the world.

The town beach of **Liendou** is a short walk from the waterfront. More strenuous entertainment can be enjoyed by walking to each of the island's beaches (see Beaches later).

Places to Stay

Studios Kalymnos (☎ 2247 041 141, fax 2247 041 343, e lbh@otenet.gr) Doubles €32. One of the more appealing and certainly the most friendly place to stay is at these neat and airy studios, a 10-minute walk from the quay. Studios Kalymnos are set in a cool garden with a barbecue for guests, with soothing chill-out music played during the day. Owner Nick can usually be found at the Laid Back Holidays booth on the ferry quay.

O Glaros (☎ 2247 041 360) Doubles €23.50. Set back on the hill about 100m from Plateia Nikiforios is this choice. There are a few smallish but airy and comfortable rooms with a wide communal balcony and a well-equipped communal kitchen.

Flisvos Pension (☎ 2247 041 261) Doubles/triples €29.50/35.20. This simple pension is just beyond the police station.

Hotel Calypso (☎/fax 2247 041 420) Doubles/ triples with bathroom €29.50/35.20. Opposite the excursion boat quay you'll find this D-class hotel with comfortable rooms.

Rooms Galini (☎ 2247 041 212, 2247 041 012) Doubles with bathroom €35.20. High up overlooking the harbour, Galini has pleasant, light rooms with refrigerator, cooking ring and balcony.

Rizos Studios (☎/fax 2247 041 215) Doubles/triples €44/50. These exceptionally well-equipped and well-located studios

are brand new. Each unit is equipped with every kitchen utensil imaginable and enjoys a view over Liendou Bay. Contact Lipsos Travel for location details.

Places to Eat & Drink

There's a string of restaurants and cafes on the waterfront between the two quays as well as one or two places up near the main square.

Yiannis Restaurant (☎ 2247 045 395) Grills €4.70. This place near the main ferry quay is popular and highly recommended.

Psarotaverna Theologos (☎ 2247 041 248) Fish €20.50/kg. Further along the quay, Theologos only opens when the owner has fish to cook and that is not every day. However, the fish is guaranteed to be very fresh.

The Rock (☎ 2247 041 180) Mezedes €1-2. This coffee bar and ouzeri offers some unusual mezedes such as sea urchins with ouzo (€1.50). The tasty grilled octopus is a standard mezes.

Kalipso Restaurant (☎ 2247 041 060) Grills €4-5. Adjoining the hotel of the same name, Kalipso serves very tasty, low-priced food.

Cafe du Moulin (☎ 2247 041 416) Snacks €3-4. Up on the main square is this French- and Greek-speaking establishment. It's good for light lunches – omelettes, mousakas and the like.

Meltemi Night Club Night owls head here for music and drinks. Greek music usually kicks in later on and it stays open until late – or early, depending on how you view your day.

AROUND THE ISLAND
Beaches

Lipsi has quite a few beaches and all are within walking distance. Some are shaded, some are not. Some are sandy, others gravelly. At least one is for nudism. Getting there makes for pleasant walks passing through countryside dotted with smallholdings, olive groves and cypresses, but buses also go to most of them.

Liendou Beach is the most accessible and naturally most popular beach. The water is very shallow and calm; this is the best beach for children.

DODECANESE

The Miracle of Lipsi

Every year a small miracle happens on the small island of Lipsi. An icon of the Virgin Mary in the blue-domed church of Agios Ioannis in Lipsi Town has small sprig of dried lilies encased within the glass protecting the icon. Every year on August 24 the dried lily sprig comes to life and a cluster of white buds appears thereon and blossoms. Amid much pomp and ceremony, the icon is taken in procession from the church of Agios Ioannis to the small chapel of the Panagia tou Harou – the curiously-named Virgin of Charon, so-named because this is the only icon in the Orthodox world that shows the Virgin holding a dead Jesus. Here a ceremony, attended by nearly all the islanders and hundreds of visiting pilgrims, takes place. The religious ceremony is followed by a night-long feast (*paneyiri*).

The story goes that a young woman once prayed for assistance for her son from the Virgin. Her prayer was duly answered and, in gratitude, she left a small bouquet of lilies near the icon of the Virgin. The lilies withered in due course, but on 24 August, the day of the Virgin's Assumption into Heaven, the lilies sprang to life once more and have done so ever since. This once sceptical writer took part in the procession and did indeed espy the revitalised lily buds popping up under the protective glass. Sleight-of-hand, or a true miracle? Decide for yourselves next 24 August.

Next along is sandy **Kambos Beach** a 1km, 15-minute walk along the same road that leads to Platys Gialos. Take the dirt road off to the left. There is some shade available.

Beyond Kambos Beach the road takes you, after about 40 minutes, to **Platys Gialos**, a lovely but narrow sandy beach with a decent taverna. The water is turquoise-coloured, shallow and ideal for children. The minibus runs here.

South 2km from Lipsi town is the sand-and-pebble **Katsadia Beach**, shaded with tamarisk trees and easily reached on foot, or by the hourly minibus. There are a couple of restaurants here and the water is clean and protected.

The pebble **Hohlakoura Beach**, to the east of Katsadia, is near the **Church of Panagia tou Harou** but offers neither shade nor facilities. Farther north, **Monodendri** is the island's unofficial nudist beach. It stands on a rocky peninsula, and there are no facilities. It is a 3km, 50-minute walk to get there, though it is reachable by motor bike.

Places to Eat

Gambieris Taverna (☎ 2247 041 087, *Katsadia*) Ladera €2.50-3.50. This small, rustic taverna, above the beach at Katsadia, is owned by an elderly couple who serve simple meat and fish dishes.

Dilaila Cafe Restaurant (☎ 2247 041 041, *Katsadia*) Mains €3-5. Nearer the beach, this modern spot is owned by English-speaking Christodoulos. Recommended dishes include vegetarian mousakas (€4.40) and chickpea patties (€3).

Kostas Restaurant (mobile ☎ 69 4496 3303, *Platys Gialos*). Grills €4-5; fish €5-7. Open 8am-6pm Jul-Aug, later on Wed & Sat. Owner Kostas Makris dishes up excellent fish and grill dishes as well as suckling pig (€6) in his restaurant overlooking the beach at Platys Gialos.

Arki & Marathi

Getting To/From Arki & Marathi

The F/B *Nisos Kalymnos* or *F/B Hioni* call in once a week, but this depends on the weather. In summer the Lipsi-based excursion boats visit Arki and Marathi, and the Patmos-based caique *Delfini* (☎ 2247 031 995) does frequent trips (€11.80 return).

ARKI Αρκοί
postcode 850 01 • pop 50

Tiny Arki, 5km north of Lipsi, is hilly, with shrubs but few trees. Its only settlement, the little west coast port, is also called Arki. Islanders make a meagre living from fishing.

There is no post office, OTE or police on the island, but there is a cardphone. Away from its little settlement, the island seems almost mystical in its peace and stillness.

ARKI & MARATHI

AEGEAN SEA

ARKI

🏛 Church of Metamorfosis

Arki

MARATHI

Tiganakia Bay

Church of Agios Nikolaos

Marathi Beach

To Lipsi

To Patmos

Daily Ferries	------
Low Frequency Ferries	--------
Hydrofoil/Catamaran	— · —
Excursion Boat	··········

Things to See & Do
The **Church of Metamorfosis** stands on a hill behind the settlement. From its terrace are superb views of Arki and its surrounding islets. The cement road between Taverna Trypas and Taverna Nikolaos leads to the path up to the church. The church is locked but ask a local if it's possible to look inside.

Several secluded sandy coves can be reached along a path skirting the right side of the bay. To reach the path, walk around the last house at the far right of the bay, go through a little wooden gate in the stone wall, near the sea, and continue ahead.

Tiganakia Bay on the south-east coast has a good sandy beach. To walk there from Arki village, take the cement road which skirts the north side of the bay. The bay is reached by a network of goat tracks and lies at the far side of the headland. You will recognise it by the incredibly bright turquoise water and the offshore islets.

Places to Stay & Eat
Arki has three tavernas, two of which have double rooms.

O Trypas Taverna & Rooms (☎ 2247 032 507) Doubles with bathroom €23.50;

meals €5-6. This restaurant and hostelry is to the right of the quay, as you face inland. Suggested dishes are black-eyed beans (*fasolia mavromatika*) and *pastos tou Trypa*, a kind of salted fish dish.

Taverna Nikolaos Rooms (☎ 2247 032 477), open all year, has doubles for €24 and meals for around €6; try the potatoes *au gratin*. *Taverna Manolas*, opposite the quay with meals from €5 to €6, is also highly commendable.

MARATHI Μαράθι
Marathi is the largest of Arki's satellite islets. Before WWII it had a dozen or so inhabitants, but now has only one family. The old settlement, with an immaculate little church, stands on a hill above the harbour. The island has a superb sandy beach.

Places to Stay & Eat
Marathi has two tavernas, both of which rent rooms and are owned by the island's only permanent inhabitants, who speak English.

Taverna Mihalis (☎ 2247 031 580) Doubles €23.50; meals €4-6. This taverna, the friendlier and cheaper of the two places to eat and sleep at, has comfortable doubles.

Taverna Pandelis (☎ 2247 032 609) has comfortable doubles for €30 and meals for €4 to €6.

Agathonisi
Αγαθονήσι

postcode 850 01 • pop 112
Agathonisi is a sun-bleached, often ignored speck of rock an hour's sail south of Samos. The island attracts yachties, serious island hoppers and the curious as well as latter-day Robinson Crusoes all seeking what Agathonisi has to offer – plain peace and quiet. Bring a stack of novels to this island and relax. There are only three settlements of any stature in the island: the port of Agios Georgios, the uphill and inland village of Megalo Horio and the smaller settlement of Mikro Horio all of which are less than 1km apart.

DODECANESE

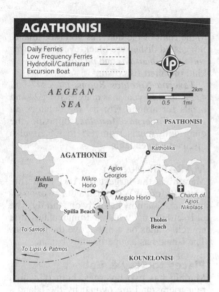

AGATHONISI

Daily Ferries — — — — —
Low Frequency Ferries - - - - - - -
Hydrofoil/Catamaran — · · — · ·
Excursion Boat · · · · · · · · · · ·

AEGEAN
SEA

0   1   2km
0   0.5   1mi

PSATHONISI

AGATHONISI

Katholika

Agios
Georgios

Hohlia   Mikro
Bay   Horio
              Megalo Horio   Church of
                                 Agios
Spilia Beach   Nikolaos

To Samos   Tholos
                          Beach
To Lipsi & Patmos

KOUNELONISI

Getting To/From Agathonisi

Agathonisi is linked to Samos and Patmos about four times a week by the F/B *Nisos Kalymnos* and the F/B *Hioni*. A hydrofoil also links the island with Samos and destinations further south Monday to Saturday.

Getting Around Agathonisi

There is no public transport, but it takes less than 15 minutes to walk from Mikro Horio to Megalo Horio or to Agios Giorgios.

AGIOS GIORGIOS Άγιος Γεώργιος

The village of Agios Giorgios (**agh**-ios ye-**or**-yi-os) is a delightful little place with just enough waterfront activity to stop you sinking into a state of inertia. It has a pebbled beach and **Spilia Beach**, also pebbled, is close by, reached along the track around the far side of the bay.

Orientation & Information

Boats dock at Agios Giorgios from where cement roads ascend right (facing inland) to Megalo Horio and left to Mikro Horio. There is no tourist information, post office, bank or OTE, but there are cardphones.

The one police officer, who is also the port police and customs officer, has an office in the white building at the beginning of the Megalo Horio road.

Places to Stay & Eat

Domatia Giannis (☎ 2247 029 062) Doubles/triples €24/26. The newest establishment on the scene comprises comfortable rooms, each of which takes between two and three persons, with four at a pinch. Inquire at the Glaros Restaurant.

Pension Maria Kamitsi (☎/fax 2247 029 003) Doubles with bathroom €22. This pleasant and friendly establishment is easy to find.

Theologias Rooms (☎ 2247 029 005) Doubles with bathroom €22. This place is next door to Pension Maria Kamitsi.

Glaros Restaurant (☎ 2247 029 062) Grills €4.50-5. This is perhaps the best place to eat. Try *markakia* – feta cheese fingers in vine leaves with a special sauce. Owners Voula and Yiannis speak English.

George's Taverna (☎ 2247 029 007) Fish €7-8. This excellent taverna is the closest to the quay. George and his German wife speak English.

AROUND AGATHONISI

Megalo Horio is Agathonisi's biggest village. It doesn't have accommodation for tourists. **Tholos Beach** and **Katholika**, an abandoned fishing hamlet, are reached by the cement road from Megalo Horio. At the T-junction turn left to reach Tholos Beach near a fish farm. You can visit the **Church of Agios Nikolaos**; ask a local if it's possible to look inside. **Katholika** is reached by turning left at the T-junction. There's not much to see but the walk is worth it for the views.

Places to Eat

Restaurant I Irini (☎ 2247 029 054, *Megalo Horio*) Meals €5-6. This restaurant on the central square has good solid meals.

Kafeneio/Pantopoleio Ta 13 Adelfic (*Megalo Horio*) Meals €4.50-6. Also on the central square, this kafeneio is a good budget place to eat.

North-Eastern Aegean Islands
Τα Νησιά του Βορειοανατολικού Αιγαίου

The North-Eastern Aegean Islands are grouped together more for convenience than for any historical, geographical or administrative reason. Apart from Thasos and Samothraki, they are, like the Dodecanese, much closer to Turkey than to the Greek mainland, but, unlike the Dodecanese, they are not close to one another. This means island-hopping is not the easy matter it is within the Dodecanese and Cyclades, although, with the exception of Thasos and Samothraki, it is possible.

These islands are less visited than either the Dodecanese or the Cyclades. Scenically, they also differ from these groups. Mountainous, green and mantled with forests, they are ideal for hiking but most are also blessed with long stretches of delightful beaches.

Although historically diverse, a list of the islands' inhabitants from classical times reads like a who's who of the ancient world. Some of the North-Eastern Aegean Islands also boast important ancient sites. All of them became part of the Ottoman Empire and were then reunited with Greece after the Balkan Wars in 1912.

There are seven major islands in the group: Chios, Ikaria, Lesvos (Mytilini), Limnos, Samos, Samothraki and Thasos. Fourni situated near Ikaria, Psara and Inousses near Chios, and Agios Efstratios near Limnos are small, little-visited islands in the group.

Accommodation throughout the island chain tends to be a little more expensive than on some of the more touristed islands, but bear in mind that the high-season (July to August) prices quoted in this chapter are 30% to 50% cheaper out of season.

SUGGESTED ITINERARIES

One week
With only seven days, you will be a bit pushed, so plan your ferry trips carefully, or just spend the whole week on one island. Fly out to Lesvos (Mytilini) or take a fast boat. Make sure you visit Mithymna (Molyvos) and the capital, Mytilini. If you're interested in hiking, head for

Highlights

- Lush, subtropical Samos – a paradise for lovers of nature

- The olive trails in Lesvos' Plomari region – great for long, magical walks

- The mystical Sanctuary of the Great Gods on remote Samothraki

- Thasos' dense forests, traditional villages and multitude of superb beaches

- Ikaria's Caribbean-like beaches and quirky, laid-back inland villages

- Village festivals on Lesvos and Ikaria

- Medieval Mesta, the most atmospheric of Chios' mastic villages

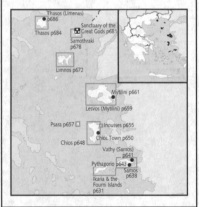

Thasos (Limenas) p686
Thasos p684
Sanctuary of the Great Gods p681
Samothraki p678
Limnos p672
Mytilini p661
Lesvos (Mytilini) p659
Psara p657
Inousses p655
Chios Town p650
Chios p648
Vathy (Samos) p641
Pythagorio p643
Samos p638
Ikaria & the Fourni Islands p631

hills near Plomari, where there are nice trails through olive groves. Those interested in beaches, should spend a couple of days at Skala Eresou. You could easily spend a week on Lesvos, but if you fancy a change take a ferry to Chios and spend a night in one of the atmospheric and intriguing Mastihohoria (mastic villages). Fly or sail back to the mainland.

If you're interested in spending the whole week on one island, Thasos makes a good alternative to Lesvos. To get there, fly to Kavala and take the ferry from Keramoti.

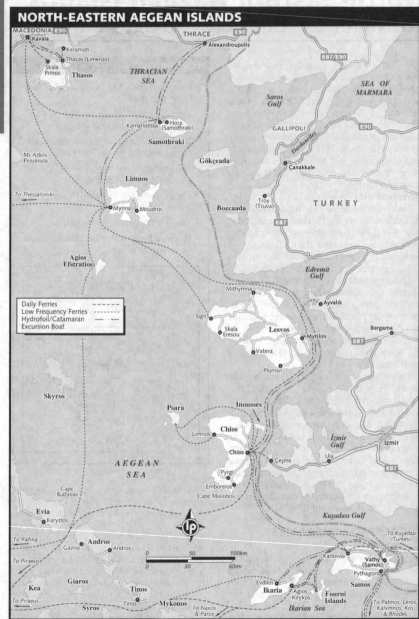

NORTH-EASTERN AEGEAN ISLANDS

MACEDONIA E90
Kavala
Keramoti
Thasos (Limenas)
Skala Prinos
Thasos

THRACE E90
Alexandroupolis

E87/E90

THRACIAN SEA

SEA OF MARMARA

Saros Gulf

Kamariotissa
Hora (Samothraki)
Samothraki

GALLIPOLI E90
Dardanelles
Çanakkale

Gökçeada

Limnos
Myrina Moudros

Bozcaada

Troy (Truva)
E87

TURKEY

To Thessaloniki

Mt Athos Peninsula

Agios Efstratios

Edremit Gulf

Mithymna
Ayvalık

Daily Ferries
Low Frequency Ferries
Hydrofoil/Catamaran
Excursion Boat

Sigri
Skala Eresou
Lesvos
Mytilini
E87
Bergama

Vatera
Plomari

Skyros

Psara
Inousses

Limnos
Chios

İzmir Gulf

AEGEAN SEA

Chios
Pyrgi
Emboreios
Cape Mastihos

Çeşme
Ula
İzmir
E87

Cape Kafireas

Kuşadası Gulf

Evia
Karystos

To Kuşadası (Turkey)

To Rafina

Andros
Gavrio Andros

Karlovasi
Vathy (Samos)
Pythagorio

To Piraeus

Kea
Giaros

Tinos
Tinos

Evdilos
Ikaria
Agios Kirykos
Fourni Islands
Samos

To Piraeus
Syros
Mykonos
To Naxos & Paros
Ikarian Sea
To Patmos, Leros, Kalymnos, Kos & Rhodes

0   50   100km
0   30   60mi

Ferry Connections to the North-Eastern Aegean Islands

origin	destination	duration	price	frequency
Alexandroupolis	Agios Efstratios	7 hours	€13.50	1 weekly
Alexandroupolis	Chios	16 hours	€26	2 weekly
Alexandroupolis	Limnos	5 hours	€12	2 weekly
Alexandroupolis	Samos	20 hours	€25	1 weekly
Alexandroupolis	Samothraki	2 hours	€7	1 daily
Kavala	Agios Efstratios	6 hours	€6.50	1 weekly
Kavala	Chios	16 hours	€24	1 weekly
Kavala	Lesvos (Mytilini)	10 hours	€20	2 weekly
Kavala	Limnos	5 hours	€11.50	4 weekly
Kavala	Samothraki	4 hours	€9	2 weekly
Kavala	Thasos (Skala Prinos)	1½ hours	€3	hourly
Kavala	Thasos (Limenas)	1¾ hours	€3	1 daily
Keramoti	Thasos (Limenas)	35 mins	€1.5	hourly
Piraeus	Chios	8 hours	€17	1 daily
Piraeus	Ikaria	9 hours	€17	1 daily
Piraeus	Lesvos (Mytilini)	12 hours	€22.50	1 daily
Piraeus	Limnos	13 hours	€21	4 weekly
Piraeus	Samos	13 hours	€20.50	2 daily
Rafina	Agios Efstratios	8½ hours	€15	2 weekly
Rafina	Limnos	10 hours	€17	4 weekly
Thessaloniki	Chios	18 hours	€32	2 weekly
Thessaloniki	Lesvos	13 hours	€25	2 weekly
Thessaloniki	Limnos	7 hours	€16.50	2 weekly

Two weeks
Fly or take a ferry to Lesvos and follow the one-week itinerary to Chios. Continue on to Samos, which has interesting ruins, lovely scenery, and a reasonably busy nightlife, then on to Ikaria, if you want a laid-back and idiosyncratic few days. Spend a night or two on Fourni en route to Ikaria if quiet beaches are more your thing. Take the overnight boat back to Piraeus or fly to Athens from Samos or Ikaria to finish your trip.

Getting To/From the North-Eastern Aegean Islands

Air Samos, Chios, Lesvos, Limnos and Ikaria have air links with Athens. In addition, Samos, Chios, Lesvos and Limnos have flights to Thessaloniki. Lesvos is connected to both Limnos and Chios by local flights.

Ferry – Domestic The above table gives an overview of the scheduled domestic ferries to this island group travelling from mainland ports during the high season. Further details and information on inter-island links can be found under individual island entries.

Ferry – International In summer there are daily ferries from Samos to Kuşadası (for Ephesus) and from Chios to Çeşme. Ferries from Lesvos to Ayvalık run four times weekly.

Hydrofoil In summer there are regular hydrofoil links running between Kavala and Thasos and there are also some hydrofoils travelling between Alexandroupolis and Samothraki. Hydrofoils also operate out of Samos where they head west towards Ikaria, south towards the Dodecanese as well as north towards Chios and Lesvos.

Phone numbers listed incorporate changes due in Oct 2002; see p83

Ikaria & the Fourni Islands

pop 9000

Ikaria (Ικαρία; ih-kah-**ree**-ah) is a rocky and mountainous island which is fertile, with an abundance of cypress trees, pine forests, olive and fruit trees – Ikarian apricots are especially luscious. At present the island's tourism is low-key, but Ikaria is slowly being 'discovered' by Germans and Austrians seeking a quiet alternative. Ikaria's beaches at Livadia and Mesahti, near Armenistis on the north coast, have to be rated as among the best in Greece.

Ailing Greeks have visited Ikaria since ancient times because of its therapeutic radioactive springs which they believe to be the most efficacious in Europe. One spring is so highly radioactive that it was deemed unsafe and forced to close.

The name Ikaria originates from the mythical Icarus. Another myth ascribes the island as the birthplace of Dionysos, the Greek god of wine, fruitfulness and vegetation.

Ikaria has two ports, Agios Kirykos on the south coast, and Evdilos on the north coast. The island's best beaches are on the north coast, west of Evdilos.

Ikaria is a bit of an oddity as a tourist destination. Long neglected by mainland Greece and used as a dumping ground for left-wing political dissidents by various right-wing governments, Ikaria and Ikarians have a rather devil-may-care approach to things, including tourism. The islanders, while welcoming tourists, are taking a slow approach to cultivating the tourist dollar. The result is that Ikaria is an island that may take a bit of getting used to at first, but will surely remain long in your memory.

Getting To/From Ikaria

Air In summer there are six flights weekly to Athens (€66), usually departing in the early afternoon. The Olympic Airways office (☎ 2275 022 214) is in Agios Kirykos, though tickets can also be bought from Blue Nice Agency (☎ 2275 031 990, fax 2775

031 752) in Evdilos. There is no bus to the airport and a taxi will cost around €10.

Ferry Nearly all ferries that call at Ikaria's ports of Evdilos and Agios Kirykos are on the Piraeus-Samos route. Generally there are departures daily from Agios Kirykos and three to four weekly from Evdilos. There are five ferries a week to Mykonos (2½ hours, €9.60) and Samos (five hours, €15.40); four to Tinos (3½ hours) and Syros (2½ hours), and three to Paros (four hours, €10) and Naxos (3½ hours, €9). Buy tickets at Roustas Travel (☎ 2275 022 441, fax 2275 031 428) and the GA Ferries agency (☎ 2275 022 426) in Agios Kirykos or from Roustas Travel and Blue Nice Agency in Evdilos.

Chios-based Miniotis Lines also runs a couple of small boats twice weekly to Chios (8½ hours, €15) from Agios Kirykos via Fourni and Samos.

Hydrofoil Agios Kirykos handles the majority of Ikaria's hydrofoil services. In summer there are five connections weekly to the Fourni Islands (20 minutes, €6), four to Pythagorio on Samos (1¼ hours, €13.50), three to Patmos (1¼ hours, €11) and Kos (2¾ hours, €23), and weekly services to Chios, Kalymnos and Leros.

Hydrofoils to/from Evdilos are not as frequent, but they do exist. Check with Dolihi Tours (☎ 2275 023 230, fax 2275 022 346) for the latest information.

Caique A caique leaves Agios Kirykos at 1pm on Monday, Wednesday and Friday for Fourni, the largest island in the miniature Fourni archipelago. The caique calls at the main settlement and usually at Hrysomilia or Thymena, where there are domatia and tavernas. Tickets cost €3 one way. Day excursion boats to Fourni from Agios Kirykos cost around €9, a bit more from Evdilos on the north coast.

Getting Around Ikaria

Bus Ikaria's bus services are almost as mythical as Icarus, but they do occasionally exist. In summer a bus is supposed leave Evdilos for Agios Kirykos at 8am daily and return to

IKARIA & THE FOURNI ISLANDS

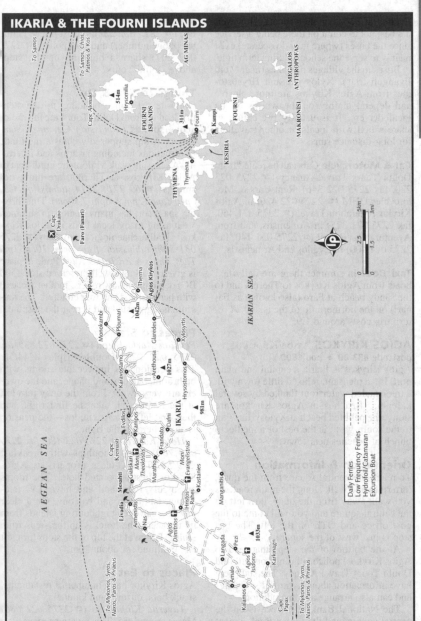

Daily Ferries	
Low Frequency Ferries	
Hydrofoil/Catamaran	
Excursion Boat	

Evdilos at noon, or thereabouts. However, it's best not to count on there being a service since the buses (where they do operate) exist mainly to serve the schools during term time.

Buses to the villages of Rahes (near Moni Evangelistrias), Xylosyrtis and Hrysostomos from Agios Kirykos are more elusive and depend mainly on the whims of the local drivers. It is usually preferable to share a taxi with locals or other travellers for long-distance runs.

Car & Motorcycle Cars can be rented from Dolihi Tours Travel Agency (☎ 2275 023 230, fax 2275 022 346), Rent Cars & Motorcycles DHM (☎ 2275 022 426) in Agios Kirykos, Marabou Travel (☎ 2275 071 460, fax 2275 071 325) in Armenistis, and from Aventura Car Rental (☎ 2275 031 140, fax 2275 071 400) in Evdilos and Armenistis.

Taxi Boat In summer there are daily taxi boats from Agios Kirykos to Therma and to the sandy beach at Faro (also known as Fanari) on the northern tip of the island. A return trip costs around €9.

AGIOS KIRYKOS Αγιος Κήρυκος
postcode 833 00 • pop 1800

Agios Kirykos is Ikaria's capital and main port. It's a pleasant, relaxed little town with a tree-shaded waterfront flanked by several kafeneia. Beaches in Agios Kirykos are stony; the pebbled beach at Xylosyrtis, 7km to the south-west, is the best of a mediocre bunch of beaches near town.

Orientation & Information

To reach the central square from the quay, turn right and walk along the main road. As you walk away from the quay, turn left on the central square and you will come to the post office and OTE on the left. The bus stop is just west of the square.

At the bottom of the steps that lead to Agios Kirykos' police building you will find Dolihi Tours Travel Agency. The staff here have information about hydrofoil schedules and can also arrange accommodation.

The National Bank of Greece is on the central square, and the Ionian Bank is next

to Dolihi Tours; both have ATMs. The police (☎ 2275 022 222), tourist police (same telephone number) and port police (☎ 2275 022 207) share a building up the steps above Dolihi Tours.

Things to See & Do

Opposite the police building, up the steps that lead up from Dolihi Tours, are the **radioactive springs** (Admission €2; open 8am-11am). A dip supposedly cures a multitude of afflictions including arthritis and infertility. A pleasant walk a kilometre north-east of Agios Kirykos, at Therma, are more **hot springs** (☎ 69 7714 7014, admission €3; open 8am-12pm & 6pm-7.30pm). This thriving spa resort has many visitors in summer.

Housing many local finds is Agios Kirykos' small **archaeological museum** (☎ 2275 031 300; admission free; open 10am-1pm Tues, Thurs & Fri July & Aug). Pride of place is given to a large, well-preserved stele (500 BC) depicting in low relief a mother (seated) with her husband and four children. The museum is signposted and is near the hospital.

Places to Stay

Pension Maria-Elena (☎ 2275 022 835, fax 2275 022 223) Doubles/triples €44/53. This pension has impeccable rooms with bathroom, balcony and phone, and the owners are very sweet. From the quay turn left at the main road, take the first right, and then first left into Artemidos – the pension is along here on the right.

Hotel Kastro (☎ 2275 023 480, fax 2275 023 700) Singles/doubles with breakfast €49/58. This C-class property is Agios Kirykos' best-appointed hotel. The rooms are nicely furnished and have TV, telephone, bathroom and balcony. On a clear day you can see neighbouring islands from its terraces. The hotel is up the steps from Dolihi Tours; at the top of the steps turn left and continue for about 20m.

Places to Eat

Agios Kirykos has a number of restaurants, snack bars, ouzeria and kafeneia.

Taverna Klimataria (☎ 2275 022 686) Mains around €5. This taverna serves good grilled meats in a neat little courtyard hidden away in the backstreets and is open all year.

Restaurant Dedalos (☎ 2275 022 473) Mains around €4.50. On the main square, this restaurant offers delicious fresh fish including a good fish soup. Its draught wine is highly recommended.

Filoti Pizzeria Restaurant (☎ 2275 023 088) Small/large pizza €4.50/10.50. This is one of the town's best regarded restaurants. Apart from the smokily delectable wood-fired pizza, there are good pasta, souvlaki and chicken dishes. The restaurant is at the top of the cobbled street that leads from the butcher's shop.

To Tzaki (☎ 2275 022 113) Mains around €4. If you feel like a brisk walk and fancy a change of scenery, try this nifty little taverna in the village of Glaredes, about 4km west of Agios Kirykos.

Entertainment
At the top of the steps leading south from the central square, is *Ftero*, looking out over the port towards Fourni – it's a very pleasant spot for a tipple.

AGIOS KIRYKOS TO THE NORTH COAST
The island's main north-south asphalt road begins west of Agios Kirykos and links the capital with the north coast. As the road climbs up to the island's mountainous spine there are dramatic mountain, coastal and sea vistas. The road winds through several villages, some with traditional stone houses topped with rough-hewn slate roofs. It then descends to the island's second port of Evdilos, 41km by road from Agios Kirykos.

This journey is worth taking for the views, but if you are based in Agios Kirykos and want to travel by bus you will more than likely have to stay overnight in Evdilos or Armenistis. A taxi down to Agios Kirykos will cost around €24. Hitching is usually OK, but there's not much traffic.

EVDILOS Εύδηλος
postcode 833 00 • pop 440
Evdilos, the island's second port, is a small fishing village. Like Agios Kirykos it's a

pleasant and relaxing place, though its charms only reveal themselves in the evening, when the waterfront gets quite lively. To see some lovely old houses and a cute little church, walk up Kalliopis Katsouli, the cobbled street leading uphill from the waterfront square.

You may prefer to head further west to the island's best beaches. There is, nonetheless, a reasonable beach to the east of Evdilos. Walk 100m up the hill from the square and take the path down past the last house on the left. If you are heading to Ikaria by boat and intend to base yourself on the north coast, take a boat direct to Evdilos rather than Agios Kirykos.

Information
There is an ATM (the only one on this side of the island) at the western end of the waterfront, where you'll also find the ticket agencies for NEL (☎ 2275 031 572) and Hellas Ferries (☎ 2275 031 990). Aventura (☎ 2275 031 140), in a side street leading from the centre of the waterfront, rents cars and bikes, sells tickets and gives general information.

Courses
Hellenic Cultural Centre (☎ 2275 031 982, 2275 031 978, **W** www.hcc.gr/courses/english/index.htm) May-Oct. This centre offers courses in Greek language, culture, literature, dancing and cooking. All levels of language proficiency are catered for; many professional translators undertake the three-month intensive course.

Places to Stay
Spyros Rossos Domatia (☎ 2275 031 518) Doubles with bathroom €29.50. Facing the sea from the middle of the waterfront is this plush-looking building on the far right with black wrought-iron balconies and orange life buoys.

Korali Rooms (☎ 2275 031 924) Doubles with bathroom €35. These clean and simple rooms (some with balcony overlooking the waterfront) are above the restaurant of the same name, at the western end of the harbour. Look for the blue and white facade.

Ikarian Panigyria

Throughout the summer there are *panigyria*, night-long festivals held on saints' days. The festas offer the islanders a chance to get to know one another and also serve as important fundraisers for the local community – which is why the food and wine can be a little more expensive than you might expect. Make sure you get in the spirit of things though – don't just order a salad!

Festivals held in villages in the western end of the island take place on the following dates:

14 May – Agios Isidoros
40 days after Orthodox Easter – Armenistis
29 June – Pezi
6 August – Hristos Rahes
15 August – Langada

Evdilos has two good-quality hotels.

Hotel Atheras (☎ *2275 031 434, fax 2275 031 926*) Singles/doubles €47/53. This B-class hotel is a breezy, friendly place with modern rooms with balconies. There's also a small pool and bar. It's in the backstreets, about 200m from the port. The hotel has cheaper studios and rooms in nearby Kerame.

Hotel Evdoxia (☎ *2275 031 502, fax 2275 031 571*) Doubles €60. Open year-round. At the top of the hill is this small B-class hotel, worth considering if you don't mind the petty house rules and the climb home from the centre of town. There is a minimarket with basic provisions, a laundry service, money exchange and restaurant (see Places to Eat).

For a quiet stay upon arrival in Evdilos you might consider making the 3km (40-minute) walk to Kampos (see West of Evdilos), where there are *domatia*, a couple of excellent beaches and restaurants. Take a taxi if you have a lot of luggage.

Places to Eat

To Keïmali (☎ *2275 031 923, Plateia Evdilou*) Mains around €4.50. Open from 7pm. In summer, there are a number of eateries to choose from, including this nice little place on the waterfront square. Try the grilled meat dishes or the souvlaki in pita €1.

Cuckoo's Nest (☎ *2275 031 540, Plateia Evdilou*) Mezedes around €2, mains from €4. Open from 7pm. This ouzeri, also on the harbour, serves tasty mezedes and mains and has a comprehensive selection of bottled Ikarian wine. All the meat is local.

Hotel Evdoxia Restaurant (☎ *2275 031 502*) Mains €3.50-6. With home-cooked food and a view, this is a good meeting place for travellers. You can even order your favourite dish if you are staying at the hotel.

WEST OF EVDILOS
Kampos Κάμπος
postcode 833 01 • pop 127

Kampos, 3km west of Evdilos, is an unspoilt little village with few concessions to tourism. Although it takes some believing, sleepy little Kampos was the island's ancient capital of Oinoe (etymologically derived from the Greek word for wine). The name comes from the myth that the Ikarians were the first people to make wine. In ancient times Ikarian wine was considered the best in Greece, but a phylloxera outbreak in the mid-1960s put paid to many of the vines. Production is now low-key and mainly for local consumption. Ancient coins found in the vicinity of Kampos have a picture of Dionysos, the wine god, on them. Kampos' sandy beach is excellent and easily accessible.

Information The irrepressible Vasilis Dionysos, who speaks English, is a fount of information on Ikarian history and walking in the mountains. You will often find him in his gloomy but well-stocked village store – on the right as you come from Evdilos. The village's post box is outside this shop and inside there is a metered telephone. There is also a cardphone nearby.

Things to See & Do As you enter Kampos from Evdilos, the ruins of a **Byzantine palace** can be seen up on the right. In the centre of the village there is a small **museum** (☎ *2275 031 300; admission free; open 8am-2pm*). It houses Neolithic tools,

CLINT CURÉ

Dionysos – God Of Wine

geometric vases, fragments of classical sculpture, figurines and a fine 'horse head' knife sheath carved from ivory.

Next to the museum is the 12th-century **Agia Irini**, the island's oldest church. It is built on the site of a 4th-century basilica, and columns standing in the grounds are from this original church. Agia Irini's frescoes are currently covered with whitewash because of insufficient funds to pay for its removal. Vasilis Dionysos has the keys to the museum and church.

The village is also a good base for mountain walking. A one-day circular walk along dirt roads can be made, taking in the village of **Dafni**, the remains of the 10th-century Byzantine **Castle of Koskinas** and the villages of **Frandato** and **Maratho**. The trek up to the little Byzantine **Chapel of Theoskepasti**, jammed in beneath an overhanging lump of granite, is worth the effort. Inside you will be shown the skulls of a couple of macabre internees. To get to the chapel and the neighbouring **Moni Theoktistis**, where there are beautiful 300-year-old frescoes, look for the signs at the village of Pigi on the road to Frandato. A lovely woman named Evangelia runs a kafeneio at the monastery.

Places to Stay & Eat *Vasilis & Yiannis Dionysos Domatia (☎ 2275 031 300, ☎/fax 2275 031 688)* Doubles with bathroom

€26.50. These two brothers create a wonderful family atmosphere for their guests, and the rooms are very pleasant. The optional enormous breakfasts are something to be experienced and are accompanied by good Greek music. From Evdilos, take the dirt road to the right from near the cardphone and follow it round to the blue and white building on your left. Alternatively, make your presence known at the village store. Call in advance and Vasilis will organise a taxi from the port.

Vasilis cooks delicious fish for his guests and his original pita recipe is exquisite.

Klimataria (☎ 2275 030 470) Mains around €4. This moderately priced taverna is in the village.

Pashalia (☎ 2275 031 346) Mains around €4.50. This taverna is nearby and is probably the better of the two.

Armenistis Αρμενιστής
postcode 833 01 • pop 70

Armenistis, 15km west of Evdilos, is the island's largest resort. It has two beautiful long beaches of pale golden sand, separated by a narrow headland. Places to stay are springing up quickly here, but it's still visited predominantly by independent travellers. Marabou Travel (☎ 2275 071 460, fax 2275 071 325), on the road which skirts the sea, organises walking tours and jeep safaris on the island. Aventura (☎ 2275 071 117), by the zaharoplasteio before the bridge, rents cars and sells tickets. Just east of Armenistis a road leads inland to **Moni Evangelistrias** and the thriving community of **Rahes**, which offers excellent opportunities for hiking (see the boxed text 'Strange Rahes').

From Armenistis a road continues 3.5km west to the small and secluded pebbled beach of **Nas** at the mouth of a stream. This is Ikaria's unofficial nudist beach. Behind the beach are some scant remains of a **temple of Artemis**. Nas has in recent times begun to witness a mini-boom and there are now quite a few domatia and tavernas.

Places to Stay – Budget *Rooms Ikaros (☎ 2275 071 238)* Most doubles €15, single/double rooftop 'penthouse' €18/23.50 (less

Strange Rahes

The hillside town of Hristos Rahes, and its neighbouring villages (which are collectively known as Rahes), is famous for the strange hours it keeps. No-one is quite sure why, but the villages in these parts like to stay up late – shops are open 9pm till 3am!

Another oddity of this region is the design of the older houses. Many of them were built out of the local stone and have a sloping, one-sided roof. There are no windows or chimneys, just a low door that's obscured by a high wall in front. This unique design served to camouflage the villages in the days when the threat of pirate raids was very real.

If you have the time and energy, it's best to explore the region on foot. The local community has published a walking map with excellent notes called *The Round of Rahes on Foot*; it's available at most tourist shops and supermarkets.

for longer stays). This is one of Armenistis' cheapest places to stay. It has a cool shady garden nestled in among the village's oldest houses. The elderly owner, Dimitris Hroussis, speaks a little English and is friendly. The place is signposted as you enter the village.

Kirki (☎ 2275 071 254, fax 2275 071 083) Double rooms/studios with bathroom €29/41. These rooms are on the right as you approach town. Each room has a private terrace overlooking the sea.

Pashalia Restaurant Domatia (☎/fax 2275 071 226) Doubles with bathroom €35. These domatia, above the restaurant of the same name, have a superb location at the eastern end of Armenistis beach, right on the water. Rooms are clean and nicely furnished, some have kitchens and most have sea-view balconies.

Rooms Fotinos (☎ 2275 071 235) Doubles with/without bathroom €29/18. At the approach to the village, before the road forks, you will see these rooms on the left. They are light, airy and nicely furnished.

Pension Thea (☎ 2275 071 491) Doubles €29. This new pension is at Nas, but the

rooms are quite exposed to the sun. Still, they have a fridge and sea view.

Places to Stay – Mid-Range *Hotel Daidalos* (☎ 2275 071 390, fax 2275 071 393) Singles/doubles with breakfast €53/67.50. This C-class property, around to the west of the village, is one of Armenistis' best hotels. It has a cool and inviting interior and nicely furnished rooms. The hotel has a sea-water swimming pool.

Villa Dimitri (☎/fax 2275 071 310, **W** www.villa-dimitri.de) 2-person studios & apartments with private patios €38-61. The most exquisite accommodation on the island is this Cycladic-inspired pension belonging to Dimitris Ioannidopoulos. The individual studios and apartments, 800m west of Armenistis, spill down a cliff that overlooks the sea amid a riotous profusion of flowers and plants. Bookings are essential and should be for a minimum of one week.

Places to Eat Wherever you eat, see if you can try some of the locally made light but potent wine.

Pashalia Taverna (☎ 2275 071 302) Mains around €5. The first place along the harbour road, this taverna offers prompt service and a variety of excellent ready-made dishes. Try the filling pasta and veal in a clay pot or the *katsikaki* (kid goat).

Delfini (☎ 2275 071 254) Mains around €5. Directly opposite and below the Pashalia Taverna is this folksy restaurant offering great grilled souvlaki (and good fish) to complement the view over the water. The meat here is local.

Kafestiatorio O Ilios (☎ 2275 071 045). Mains around €4.50. This simple place at the end of the harbour road has some of the best seafood – the owner is a fisherman.

To Mouragio Mains around €5. This harbourside option is known for its large souvlakia.

To Symposio (☎ 2275 071 222) Mains around €7. This place on the Armenistis harbourside offers unusual though overly complicated fare, some of it with a German twist.

Astra (☎ 2275 071 255) Mains around €5. Nas now has six tavernas, of which this one is probably the best. Some dishes are wood-oven cooked. Try the potato salad – almost a meal in itself – or ask to sample the oven-cooked kid and wash it down with the mean draught red wine.

FOURNI ISLANDS Οι Φούρνοι
postcode 834 00 • pop 1030
The Fourni Islands are a miniature archipelago lying between Ikaria and Samos. Two of the islands are inhabited: Fourni and Thymena. The capital of the group is **Fourni** (also called Kampos), which is the port of Fourni Island. Fourni has one other village, tiny Hrysomilia, 10km north of the port; the island's only road connects the two. The islands are mountainous and a good number of beaches are dotted around the coast.

The telephone number of Fourni's port police is ☎ 2275 051 207. Fourni has local police (☎ 2275 051 222) and a doctor (☎ 2275 051 202).

Fourni is the only island with accommodation for tourists and is ideal for those seeking a quiet retreat. Other than the settlement of Fourni itself and a beach south over the headland at **Kampi**, the island offers little else besides eating, sleeping and swimming. Most of the islanders make a living from fishing, sending their catch to the Athens fish market.

Places to Stay & Eat
Manolis & Patra Markaki Rooms (☎ 2275 051 268, ☎/fax 2275 051 355) Doubles €23.50, 4-person apartments €41. These gorgeous rooms and apartments are decorated with heirlooms, pretty curtains and old furniture. The rooms are opposite the ferry pier, above the Markakis Cafe-Bar. Ask also about the rooms and apartments they have elsewhere on the island.

Maria & Kostas Markakis Pension (☎ 2275 051 148) Doubles €33. This tidy pension is at the south end of the waterfront.

Taverna Nikos (☎ 2275 051 253) Mains around €4.50. This taverna on the waterfront will keep you amply supplied with fresh fish and other grilled dishes.

Miltos (☎ 2275 051 407) Mains around €4.50. Also on the waterfront, Miltos serves similar fare to Taverna Nikos.

Getting To/From Fourni
Ferry Fourni lies on the ferry route between Piraeus and Samos. As well as daily boats to Ikaria (40 minutes, €3), there are five ferries weekly to Samos (two hours, €6), and three weekly to Piraeus via Paros (3¼ hours, €9) and Naxos (four hours, €8). These ferries stop at Mykonos (4½ hours, €9) and Syros (5½ hours, €13) once a week. Tickets are available from an office on the corner of the waterfront and the main shopping street.

Hydrofoil Hydrofoils call at Fourni on the route from Ikaria to Samos and the Dodecanese. See the Getting To/From Ikaria section for details of services.

Getting Around Fourni
There are three boats a week from Fourni to Hrysomilia and Thymena.

Samos Σάμος

pop 32,000
Samos is the closest of all the Greek islands to Turkey, from which it is separated by the 3km-wide Mykale Straits. The island is the most visited of the North-Eastern Aegean group. Charter flights of tourists descend on the island from many northern European countries. Samos is a popular transit point for travellers heading from the Cyclades to Turkey and vice versa. Most barely pause in Samos, which is a pity because the island has a lot to offer.

Despite the package tourists, Samos is still a destination worth visiting. Forays into its hinterland are rewarded with unspoilt villages and mountain vistas. In summer the humid air is permeated with heavy floral scents, especially jasmine. This, and the prolific greenery of the landscape, lends Samos an exotic and tropical air. Orchids are grown here for export and an excellent table wine is made from the local muscat grapes.

Samos has three ports: Vathy (Samos) and Karlovasi on the north coast, and Pythagorio on the south coast.

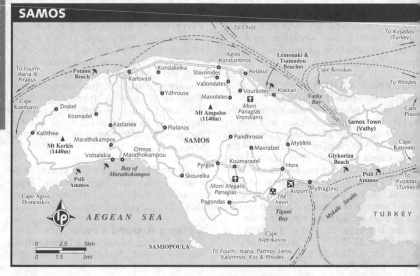

SAMOS

History

The first inhabitants of Samos, the Pelasgian tribes, worshipped Hera, whose birthplace was Samos. Pythagoras was born on Samos in the 6th century BC. Unfortunately, his life coincided with that of the tyrant Polycrates, who in 550 BC deposed the Samian oligarchy. As the two did not see eye to eye, Pythagoras spent much of his time in exile in Italy. Despite this, Samos became a mighty naval power under Polycrates, and the arts and sciences also flourished. 'Big is beautiful' seems to have been Polycrates' maxim – almost every construction and artwork he commissioned appears to have been ancient Greece's biggest. The historian Herodotus wrote glowingly of the tyrant's achievements, stating that the Samians had accomplished the three greatest projects in Greece at that time: the Sanctuary of Hera (one of the Seven Wonders of the Ancient World), the Evpalinos Tunnel and a huge jetty.

After the decisive Battle of Plataea (479 BC), in which Athens had been aided by the Samians, Samos allied itself to Athens and returned to democracy. In the Battle of Mykale, which took place on the same day as the Battle of Plataea, the Greek navy

(with many Samian sailors) defeated the Persian fleet. However, during the Peloponnesian Wars, Samos was taken by Sparta.

Under Roman rule Samos enjoyed many privileges, but after successive occupations by the Venetians and Genoese it was conquered by the Turks in 1453. Samos played a major role in the uprising against the Turks in the early 19th century, much to the detriment of its neighbour, Chios (see the Chios section later in this chapter).

Trekking

Samos is a popular place for rambling, or more demanding mountain treks. Its natural fecundity and appealing combination of mountains and sea make it a popular destination for walkers from all over Europe. Should you be planning a hike on Samos, Brian and Eileen Anderson's *Landscapes of Samos*, a pocket guide to walks on the island, contains descriptions of over 20 walks.

Getting To/From Samos

Air There are at least four flights daily from Samos to Athens (€63) and three flights weekly to Thessaloniki (€88). The Olympic Airways office (☎ 2273 027 237) is on

e corner of Kanari and Smyrnis in Vathy
Samos). There is also an Olympic Airways
ffice (☎ 2273 061 213) on Lykourgou Lo-
otheti in Pythagorio. The airport is 4km
est of Pythagorio.

erry – Domestic Samos is the transport
ub of the North-Eastern Aegean, with feres to the Dodecanese and Cyclades as well
s to the other North-Eastern Aegean Is-
nds. Schedules are subject to seasonal
nanges, so consult any of the ticket offices
or the latest versions. ITSA Travel (☎ 2273
23 605, fax 2273 027 955, e itsa@gemini
iavlos.gr) is the closest agency to the ferry
rminal in Vathy (Samos). Your luggage
an also be stored for free whether you buy
ticket or not. Ferries depart from both
athy (Samos) and Pythagorio.

To Piraeus there are at least two ferries
aily (13 hours, €20.50). Two to three ferries
aily go to Ikaria (2½ hours, €6) and four
oats a week to Fourni (two hours, €6); three
eekly to Chios (four hours, €9); one weekly
Lesvos (seven hours, €12.50), Limnos (11
ours, €20), Alexandroupolis (20 hours,
25) and sometimes Kavala (20 hours, €25).
hree to four ferries per week to Naxos (6
ours, €15.50) and Paros (6½ hours, €13.50),
ith connections to Mykonos, Ios, Santorini
nd Syros. There are about three ferries a
eek to Patmos (2½ hours, €6.50), two to
eros (3½ hours, €5.50) and Kalymnos (four
ours, €10), and one to Kos (5½ hours,
11.50) and Rhodes (nine hours, €21).

erry – International In summer two feres go daily from Vathy (Samos) to
uşadası (for Ephesus) in Turkey. From
ythagorio there is one boat a week. From
ovember to March there are one to two
erries weekly. Tickets cost around €41
olus €21 port taxes). Daily excursions are
lso available from 1 April to 31 October
nd for an additional €25 you can visit
phesus. Tickets are available from many
utlets but the main agent is ITSA Travel.
Bear in mind that the ticket office will re-
uire your passport in advance for port for-
alities. Turkish visas, where required, are
sued upon arrival in Turkey for US$45.

Check with the Turkish diplomatic mission
in your home country for the requirements
since these change frequently.

Hydrofoil In summer hydrofoils link Pythagorio twice daily with Patmos (one hour,
€11), Leros (two hours, €15), Kos (3½
hours, €19.50) and Kalymnos (2½ hours,
€19.50). Also from Pythagorio there are dolphins four times per week to Fourni (50 mins,
€11.50) and Ikaria (1½ hours, €13.50), daily
to Lipsi (1½ hours, €11.50) and twice a week
to Agathonisi (35 minutes, €9).

There are also two services weekly from
Vathy (Samos) to Fourni (1¾ hours, €11.50)
and Ikaria (2¼ hours, €13.50). Also from
Vathy (Samos) there are three dolphins a
week to Chios (1½ hours, €18), two a week
to Lesvos (4 hours, €25), at least three times
a week to Patmos (€17), Kos (€24.50),
Leros (€21) and Kalymnos (€23.50). Schedules are subject to frequent changes, so contact the tourist office in Pythagorio or the
port police (☎ 2273 061 225) for up-to-date
information. Tickets are available from By
Ship Travel in Pythagorio (☎ 2273 062 285,
fax 2273 061 914) and Vathy (☎ 2273 022
116) or ITSA Travel in Vathy.

Excursion Boat In summer there are excursion boats four times weekly between
Pythagorio and Patmos (€29.50 return)
leaving at 8am. For an additional €18.50
you can visit the monastery. Daily excursion boats also go to the little island of
Samiopoula for €18/9 with/without lunch.
There is also a boat tour of Samos once or
twice a week, leaving from Pythagorio; it
costs €32.50 and does not include lunch.

Getting Around Samos
To/From the Airport There are no
Olympic Airways buses to the airport. A
taxi from Vathy (Samos) should cost about
€9. Alternatively, you can take a local bus
to Pythagorio and a taxi to the airport from
there for about €3.50.

Bus Samos has an adequate bus service that
continues till about 8pm in summer. On
weekdays, there are 14 buses daily from

Vathy (Samos) bus station (☎ 2273 027 262) to both Kokkari (20 minutes, €1.50) and Pythagorio (25 minutes, €1), seven to Agios Konstantinos (40 minutes, €1.50) and Karlovasi (via the north coast, one hour, €2.50), five to the Ireon (25 minutes, €2), five to Mytilinii (20 minutes, €1), and two to Ormos and Votsalakia (two hours, €4.50).

In addition to frequent buses to/from Vathy (Samos) there are five buses from Pythagorio to the Ireon and four to Mytilinii. Pay for your tickets on the bus. Services are greatly reduced on weekends, with virtually no buses running on Sundays.

Car & Motorcycle Samos has many car-rental outlets, including Hertz (☎ 2273 061 730), Lykourgou Logotheti 77, and Europcar (☎ 2273 061 522), Lykourgou Logotheti 65, both in Pythagorio.

There are also many motorcycle-rental outlets on Lykourgou Logotheti. Many of the larger hotels can arrange motorcycle or car rental for you.

Taxi From the taxi rank (☎ 2273 028 404) on Plateia Pythagorou in Vathy (Samos), approximate tariffs are as follows: Kokkari €9, Pythagorio €8, Psili Ammos €7.50, Avlakia €8.50, the airport €9, and the Ireon €9.

VATHY (SAMOS) Βαθύ (Σάμος)
postcode 831 00 • pop 5790
The island's capital is the large and bustling Vathy, also called Samos, on the north-east coast. The waterfront is crowded with tourists who rarely venture to the older and extremely attractive upper town of Ano Vathy where 19th-century, red-tiled houses perch on a hillside. The lower and newer town is strung out along Vathy Bay and it is quite a walk from one end to the other.

Orientation
From the ferry terminal (facing inland) turn right to reach the central square of Plateia Pythagorou on the waterfront. It's recognisable by its four palm trees and statue of a lion. A little farther along and a block inland are the shady municipal gardens. The waterfront road is called Themistokleous Sofouli.

Information
The municipal tourist office (☎ 2273 028 530) is just north of Plateia Pythagorou in a little side street, but it only operates during the summer season. The staff will assist in finding accommodation.

The tourist police (☎ 2273 027 980) and the regular police are at Themistokleous Sofouli 129 on the south side of the waterfront

The National Bank of Greece is on the waterfront just south of Plateia Pythagorou and the Commercial Bank is on the east side of the square. Both sport ATMs.

The post office is on Smyrnis, four blocks from the waterfront. The OTE is on Plateia Iroön, behind the municipal gardens.

The Diavlos NetCafe (☎ 2273 022 469) is at Themistoklous Sofouli 160, near the police station. Access is fast and costs €3 per hour. It's open 8am to 11.30pm, year-round.

The island's bus station (KTEL) is on Ioannou Lekati. The taxi rank (☎ 2273 028 404) is on Plateia Pythagorou. Samos' hospital (☎ 2273 027 407) is on the waterfront north of the ferry quay.

The port police (☎ 2273 027 318) are just north of the quay, one block back from the waterfront.

Things to See
Apart from the charming old quarter of Ano Vathy, which is a peaceful place to stroll and the municipal gardens, which are a pleasant place to sit, the main attraction of Vathy (Samos) is the **archaeological museum** (☎ 2273 027 469, adult/student €2.50/1.50; open 8.30am-3pm Tues-Sun).

Many of the fine exhibits in this well laid out museum are a legacy of Polycrates' time. They include a gargantuan (4.5m) kouro statue found in the Ireon (Sanctuary of Hera). In true Polycrates fashion, it was the largest standing kouros ever produced. The collection includes many statues, mostly from the Ireon, bronze sculptures, stelae and pottery.

Places to Stay – Budget
Vathy does not have a camping ground. Be wary of touts who may approach you as you disembark and tell you that places listed in this guide are closed – it's usually not true.

VATHY (SAMOS)

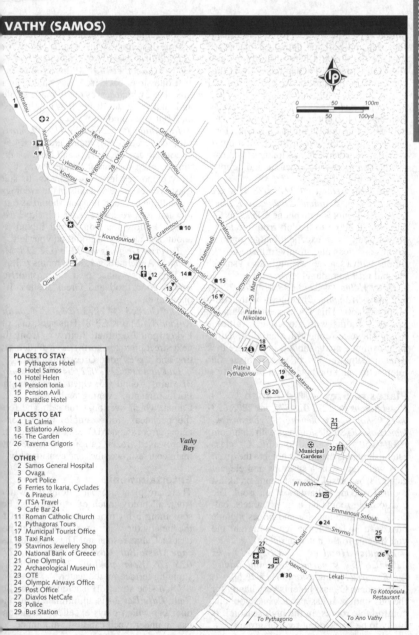

PLACES TO STAY
1 Pythagoras Hotel
8 Hotel Samos
10 Hotel Helen
14 Pension Ionia
15 Pension Avli
30 Paradise Hotel

PLACES TO EAT
4 La Calma
13 Estiatorio Alekos
16 The Garden
26 Taverna Grigoris

OTHER
2 Samos General Hospital
3 Ovaga
5 Port Police
6 Ferries to Ikaria, Cyclades
   & Piraeus
7 ITSA Travel
9 Cafe Bar 24
11 Roman Catholic Church
12 Pythagoras Tours
17 Municipal Tourist Office
18 Taxi Rank
19 Stavrinos Jewellery Shop
20 National Bank of Greece
21 Cine Olympia
22 Archaeological Museum
23 OTE
24 Olympic Airways Office
25 Post Office
27 Diavlos NetCafe
28 Police
29 Bus Station

Pension Ionia (☎ 2273 028 782, *Manoli Kalomiri 5*) Singles/doubles €15/18. The cheapest and perhaps homeliest places to stay are the domatia here – the rooms are clean and pretty. To get there from the quay, turn right onto the waterfront, left at Stamatiadi, then left into Manoli Kalomiri.

Pension Avli (☎ 2273 022 939, *Areos 2*) Doubles with bathroom €23.50. Close to Pension Ionia, this traditional place is a former Roman Catholic convent, built around a lovely courtyard. It has loads of atmosphere. The rooms are spacious and simply but tastefully furnished.

Pythagoras Hotel (☎ 2273 028 422, *fax 2273 028 893*, ℮ *smicha@otenet.gr, Kallistratou 12*) Doubles with phone €28. This C-class hotel, 800m to the left from the ferry arrival point, is an excellent budget option. Rooms are clean and simply furnished. Ask for one with a sea view. There's also a snack bar and nice communal terrace.

Hotel Helen (☎ 2273 028 215, *fax 2273 022 866, Grammou 2*) Doubles with bathroom €29.50. This C-class establishment has cosy rooms with attractive furniture. Rooms have air-con, fridge and TV. Turn right from the quay, and left just before the Roman Catholic church, veer right at the intersection and the hotel is on the right.

Places to Stay – Mid-Range

Hotel Samos (☎ 2273 028 377, *fax 2273 023 771*, ℮ *hotsamos@otenet.gr, 11 Themistokleous Sofouli*) Singles/doubles with bathroom €32/40.50. This grand-looking, C- class establishment is the nearest hotel to the quay. It is well kept with a spacious and elegant cafeteria, bar, snack bar, restaurant, breakfast room, TV room, billiard room and pool. The comfortable rooms have fitted carpets, balcony, telephone and TV and prices include breakfast. On leaving the quay turn right and you'll come to the hotel on the left.

Paradise Hotel (☎ 2273 023 911, *fax 2273 028 754*, ℮ *paradise@gemini.diavlos .gr, Kanari 21*) Singles/doubles €26.50/ 41. This modern C-class hotel is very handy for the bus station. It has a snack bar, pool and comfortable rooms. In the high season it is likely to be booked out by tour groups.

Places to Eat

When dining out on Samos don't forget to sample the Samian wine, extolled by Byron.

Estiatorio Alekos (☎ 2273 092 629, *Lykourgou Logotheti 49*) Mains around €5. Just one street back from the waterfront in this place, which serves ready-made staple and made-to-order dishes. It's nothing special, but you could do worse.

Kotopoula (☎ 2273 028 415, *Vlamaris*) Mezedes around €3, mains around €4.50. Greeks escape the tourists and head for this vine-cloaked restaurant, hidden away by a leafy plane tree in the backstreets. Its spit roasted chicken (served only in the evenings) is the thing to order, but you should also try the delicious *revithokeftedes* (chickpea rissoles). Follow Ioannou Lekati inland for about 800m until you find it on your left.

Taverna Grigoris (☎ 2273 022 718, *Mihalis 5*) Appetisers €1.50-3, mains €3.50-6. This folksy place near the post office serves good food and Greek dishes. It's open all day.

The Garden (☎ 2273 024 033, *Manoli Kalomiris*) Mains €3-8. This spot, just of Lykourgou Logotheti (entry is from the next street up to the north) has a garden setting and serves good Greek standards.

La Calma (☎ 2273 022 654, *Kefalopoulo 7*) Mains around €5. Open 7pm-midnight. For a romantic evening ambience, try La Calma, which overlooks the sea. The food (pepper steak, for example) makes for a change from standard Greek fare, though the microwaved frozen carrots that come with main courses lower the tone considerably.

Entertainment

There are plenty of bars along the waterfront, all pretty much of a muchness. For something a bit more interesting, head to the bars by the water on Kefalopoulou, just past La Calma restaurant. These include *Escape Music Bar*, *Cosy* and *Ovaga* (☎ 227 025 476, *Kefalopoulou 13*), which has a stunning terrace by the water.

On a side street off Themistokleous Sofouli, *Cafe Bar 24* is an intimate little outdoor bar which plays excellent music and has an underhyped candle-lit ambience.

Cine Olympia (☎ 2273 025 011, *Gymasiarhou Kateraini 27*) Admission €6. Sessions at 9.30pm. This cinema shows recent Hollywood releases, in English with Greek subtitles.

Shopping

Vathy has some interesting little shops tucked in behind the waterfront Plateia Pythagora. If you're interested in jewellery and old things, stop by *Stavrinos jewellery shop* (☎ 2273 027 273, *Cnr Kontaxi & Cyrillou*). The shop has been around since 1870 and so has some of the stock. Mihali Stavrinos is quite a character and will help you choose something special.

PYTHAGORIO Πυθαγόρειο
postcode 831 03 • pop 1400

Pythagorio, on the south east coast of the island, is 14km from Vathy (Samos). Today, it's a busy yet pretty tourist resort with streets lined with red hibiscus and pink oleander. It has a somewhat upmarket feel and is a convenient base from which to visit the ancient sites of Samos.

Pythagorio stands on the site of the now World Heritage listed ancient city of Samos. Although the settlement dates from the Neolithic era, most of the remains are from Polycrates' time (around 550 BC). The mighty jetty of Samos projected almost 450m into the sea, protecting the city and its powerful fleet from the vagaries of the Aegean. Remains of this jetty lie below and beyond the smaller modern jetty, which is on the opposite side of the harbour to the quay. The town beach begins just beyond the jetty. All boats coming from Patmos, and other points south of Samos, dock at Pythagorio.

Orientation

From the ferry quay, turn right and follow the waterfront to the main thoroughfare of Lykourgou Logotheti, a turn-off to the left. Here there are supermarkets, greengrocers,

PYTHAGORIO

To Evpalinos Tunnel & Moni Panagias Spilianis

To Evpalinos Tunnel

To Vathy (Samos) & Psili Ammos Beach

To Airport & Ireon

Polykratous
Aristarhou
Odyssea Onloga
Polykratous
A. Fanouriou
Damos
Esopou
Egeou
Erpalinou
Egeou Pelagos
Melissou
Iras
Lykourgou Logotheti
Despoti Kyrillou
Sotiros
Pythagora
Roikou
Plateia Irinis
Nikolaou
Kapetan
S. Georgiadi
Metamorfosis
Despoti Kyrillou
Konstantinou Kanari
G. Vatikioti
D. Rafalla
A. Lykourgou
Pythagora
Kontaxi
Themistokli Sofouli
Plateia Tarsana

Harbour

AEGEAN SEA

PLACES TO STAY
18 Polixeni Hotel
19 Hotel Elpis
20 Pension Arokaria
22 Hotel Evripoli
23 Hotel Damo

PLACES TO EAT
12 Symposium
13 Taverna ta Platania
16 Poseidonas
17 Restaurant Remataki

0   40   80m
0   40   80yd

OTHER
1 Olympic Airways
2 Police
3 Post Office
4 Bus Stop
5 National Bank of Greece
6 Parking
7 Temple of Aphrodite
8 Commercial Bank ATM
9 By Ship Travel
10 Tourist Office
11 Taxi Rank
14 Pythagorio Museum
15 Port Police
21 Castle of Lykourgos Logothetis
24 OTE
25 Ferries to Patmos, Lipsi, Agathonisi, Leros, Kalymnos, Kos, Fourni & Ikaria

Quay

bakers, travel agents and numerous car, motorcycle and bicycle rental outlets. The central square of Plateia Irinis is farther along the waterfront.

Information

The tourist office (☎ 2273 062 274, fax 2273 061 022) is on the south side of Lykourgou Logetheti. The English-speaking staff is particularly friendly and helpful and give out a town map, bus timetable and information about ferry schedules. It's also a currency exchange, and is open 8am to 10pm daily.

The tourist police (☎ 2273 061 100) are also on Lykourgou Logetheti, to the left of the tourist office.

The post office and the National Bank of Greece are both on Lykourgou Logotheti. The OTE is on the waterfront near the quay.

The bus station (actually a bus stop) is on the south side of Lykourgou Logotheti. There is a taxi rank (☎ 2273 061 450) on the corner of the waterfront and Lykourgou Logotheti.

Things to See

Walking north-east on Polykratous from the town centre, a path left passes traces of an ancient theatre. The **Evpalinos Tunnel** can also be reached along this path: take the left fork after the theatre. The right fork leads up to **Moni Panagias Spilianis** (Monastery of the Virgin of the Grotto). The city walls extend from here to the Evpalinos Tunnel.

Back in town, the remains of the **Castle of Lykourgos Logothetis** are at the southern end of Metamorfosis. The castle was built in 1824 and became a stronghold of Greek resistance during the War of Independence.

In the town hall at the back of Plateia Irinis, is the **Pythagorio Museum** (☎ 2273 061 400, Plateia Irinis; admission free; open 8.45am-2pm Tues-Sat). It has some finds from the Ireon.

Between Lokourgou and the car park are the **ruins of Aphrodite.**

Evpalinos Tunnel The 1034m-long Evpalinos Tunnel (☎ 2273 061 400; adult/ student/senior €1.50/1/1, EU students free; open 8.45am-2.45pm Tues-Sun) completed

in 524 BC, is named after its architect. I penetrated through a mountainside to chan nel gushing mountain water to the city. Th tunnel is, in effect, two tunnels: a servic tunnel and a lower water tunnel seen at var ious points along the narrow walkway. Th diggers began at each end and met in th middle, an achievement of precision engin eering that is still considered remarkable.

In the Middle Ages the inhabitants o Pythagorio used the tunnel as a hide-ou during pirate raids. The tunnel is fun to ex plore, though access to it is via a very con stricted stairway. If you are tall, portly, o suffer from claustrophobia, give it a miss!

The tunnel is most easily reached from th western end of Lykourgou Logotheti, from where it is signposted. If you arrive by road a sign points you to the tunnel's southern mouth as you enter Pythagorio from Samos

Places to Stay

Many of Pythagorio's places to stay ar block-booked by tour companies.

Hotel Elpis (☎ 2273 061 144, Metamor fosis Sotiros) Singles/doubles with fridg €21/23.50. This is a neat and clean D-clas hotel.

Pension Arokaria (☎ 2273 061 287 Metamorfosis Sotiros) Doubles €35.50 This is a pleasant and quiet place for inde pendent travellers. It has a cool and leafy garden, and a lovely owner.

Hotel Evripili (☎ 2273 061 096, fax 227. 061 897) Single/doubles €35.50/44. This i a friendly place occupying a stone building not far from the waterfront. The rooms are cosy and nicely furnished.

Polixeni Hotel (☎ 2273 061 590, fax 2273 061 359) Doubles with balcony and air-con around €59. This homely place or the waterfront has nicely furnished, clean and comfortable rooms.

Hotel Damo (☎ 2273 061 303, fax 2273 061 745) 2-3 person studios €60. This C class place is near the OTE and has agree able self-contained studios.

Places to Eat

The waterfront is packed with restaurants all offering much the same fare.

Restaurant Remataki (☎ 2273 061 104) Mezedes €2-6, mains €4-7. This restaurant is at the beginning of the town beach. It has an imaginative menu of carefully prepared, delicious food – it's a miracle that a place this good has survived in a tourist enclave. Try a meal of various mezedes for a change: revithokeftedes, *piperies Florinis* (Florina peppers) and *gigantes* (lima beans) make a good combination. The artichoke soup and *dolmadakia* are also excellent.

Poseidonas (☎ 2273 062 530) Mains €5-12. Next door to Remataki, this popular restaurant serves some interesting dishes, including Chinese-inspired seafood.

Taverna ta Platania (☎ 2273 061 817, *Plateia Irinis*) Mains €4-6. This taverna is a block inland from Restaurant Remataki, opposite the museum, and away from the more expensive waterfront eateries.

Symposium (☎ 2273 061 938) Mains €5-11. This upmarket restaurant is known for its steaks and Greek classics.

AROUND PYTHAGORIO
Ireon Ηραίον
The Sacred Way, once flanked by thousands of statues, led from the city to the Ireon (☎ 2273 095 277; *adult/student €2.50/1.50, free for EU students; open 8.30am-3pm Tues-Sun*). The Ireon was a sanctuary to Hera, built at the legendary place of her birth, on swampy land where the River Imbrasos enters the sea.

There had been a temple on the site since Mycenaean times, but the one built in the time of Polycrates was the most extraordinary: it was four times the size of the Parthenon. As a result of plunderings and earthquakes only one column remains standing, although the extent of the temple can be gleaned from the foundations. Other remains on the site include a stoa, more temples and a 5th-century basilica.

The Ireon is now listed as a World Heritage Site. It is on the coast 8km west of Pythagorio.

Mytilinii Μυτιληνιοί
The fascinating **palaeontology museum** (☎ 2273 052 055; *admission €1.50, free Sun;*

open 9am-2pm, 5pm-7pm Mon-Sat, 10.30am-2.30pm Sun), on the main thoroughfare of the inland village of Mytilinii, between Pythagorio and Vathy (Samos), houses skeletons of prehistoric animals. Included in the collection are remains of animals that were the antecedents of the giraffe and elephant. From the museum it's a nice walk to Agia Triada monastery, where there's an ossuary.

Beaches
Sandy **Psili Ammos** (not to be confused with a beach of the same name near Votsalakia) is the finest beach near Pythagorio. This gently sloping beach is ideal for families and is popular, so be there early to grab your spot. The beach can be reached by car or scooter from the Vathy-Pythagorio road (signposted), or by excursion boat (€9) from Pythagorio, leaving each morning at 9am and returning at 4pm. There are also buses from Vathy (Samos). **Glykoriza Beach,** nearer Pythagorio, is dominated by a few hotels nearby, but is a clean, public beach of pebbles and sand and is a good alternative to the sometimes very busy Psili Ammos.

Places to Stay & Eat
The following places are all at PsiliAmmos.

Elena Apartments (☎ 2273 023 645, fax 2273 028 959) Double apartments €41. This place, right on the beach, has rather cramped self-contained double apartments.

Apartments Psili Ammos (☎ 2273 025 140, mobile ☎ 69 7482 9025, fax 2273 025 140) 2-person studios €41. Near Elena Apartments is this place, which has self-contained rooms.

Restaurant Psili Ammos (☎ 2273 028 301) Prices €3-5.50. This taverna is favourably located overlooking the beach; the food is good.

Sunrise Mains around €4. This is a more intimate eatery, also with a good beach outlook.

SOUTH-WEST SAMOS
The south-west coast of Samos remained unspoilt for longer than the north coast, but in recent years a series of resorts has sprung up alongside the best beaches. The area east

of Marathkampos was ravaged by fires in 2000, and it will be some years before the forests recover.

Ormos, 50km from Vathy, has a pebble beach. From here a road leads 6km to the inland village of **Marathokampos**, which is worth a visit for the stunning view down to the immense Bay of Marathokampos. **Votsalakia**, 4km west of Ormos and known officially as Kampos, and the much nicer **Psili Ammos** (not to be confused with the Psili Ammos near Pythagorio), 2km beyond, have long, sandy beaches. There are many domatia and tavernas on this stretch of coast though it has a rather scrappy feel to it and lacks the intimacy of smaller coastal resorts.

With your own transport you may like to continue from Psili Ammos along a stunning route that skirts mighty Mt Kerkis, high above the totally undeveloped and isolated west coast. The road passes through the village of **Kallithea**, and continues to **Drakeï**, where it terminates.

WEST OF VATHY (SAMOS)

The road which skirts the north coast passes many beaches and resorts. The fishing village of **Kokkari**, 10km from Vathy (Samos), is also a holiday resort with a pebble beach. The place is very popular with tourists, but it is exposed to the frequent summer winds and for that reason is a favourite of windsurfers. Rooms, studios and tavernas abound, all offering much the same quality.

Beaches extend from here to **Avlakia**, with **Lemonaki** and **Tsamadou** beaches being the most accessible for walkers staying in Kokkari. Clothing is optional at these two secluded beaches. Continuing west, beyond Avlakia, the road is flanked by trees, a foretaste of the scenery encountered on the roads leading inland from the coast. A turnoff south along this stretch leads to the delightful mountain village of **Vourliotes**, from where you can walk another 3km to **Moni Panagias Vrondianis**. Built in the 1550s, it is the island's oldest extant monastery; a sign in the village points the way.

Continuing along the coast, a 5km road winds its way up the lower slopes of Mt Ampelos through thick, well-watered

woodlands of pine and deciduous trees, the gorgeous village of **Manolates**. The are is rich in bird life, with a proliferation nightingales, warblers and thrushes. The are no buses to Manolates, so you'll have find your own way (Agios Konstantinos the nearest bus stop). The Samians say th if you have not visited either Vourliotes Manolates, then you have not seen Samos

Back on the coast, the road continues t the pretty flower-filled village of **Agic Konstantinos**. Beyond here it winds throug rugged coastal scenery to the town c **Karlovasi**, Samos' third port. The town cor sists of three contiguous settlements: Pale (old), Meson (middle) and Neo (new). once boasted a thriving tanning industry, bu now it's a lacklustre town with little of ir terest for visitors. The nearest beach is th sand and pebble **Potami**, 2km west of tow

Places to Stay

Despite the onset of package tourism Kokkari still has many accommodation op tions for independent travellers.

In the high season the EOT (☎ 2273 09 217) operates in the village and will assis in finding accommodation. The bus stop on the main road at a large stone church and the EOT is a little way down the stree opposite the church.

Pension Eleni *(☎ 2273 092 317, fax 227. 092 620)* Doubles €29.50. This pension ha immaculate, tastefully furnished rooms witl bathroom. From the large stone church i Kokkari, continue along the main road; at the T-junction veer left and, 50m along on th left, next to the Dionyssos Garden restaurant there's a sign pointing to the pension. There are many more domatia, apartments an small hotels along this stretch of road, which is just one block back from the waterfront.

Kalypso Rooms to Rent *(☎ 2273 094 124* Doubles €23.50. Farther west along the coas road, close to a beach, are these rooms named after their friendly and kind owner They are well kept and surrounded by a gor geous garden. Doubles have bathrooms anc use of a communal kitchen. Coming from Kokkari, turn right opposite the turn-off fo Manolates (signposted) and after 50m you will come to a sign pointing to the rooms. The bus stop is just before the Manolates turn-off.

Studios Sandy (☎ 2273 094 415) Double & triple studios €29.50. Next door to Kalypso, these pleasant and cosy studios are a good option.

Studio Angella (☎ 2273 094 478, Athens 2105 059 708, mobile ☎ 69 7297 5722) Doubles €26.50. In Manolates try this studio.

Traditional Greek House (☎ 2273 094 331) Doubles €20.50. Phone to inquire about rooms in this nice little unnamed house in Manolates.

If you get stuck in Karlovasi there are several budget *hotels* and *domatia*, some signposted from the central square where the bus terminates.

Places to Eat

There are many reasonably priced restaurants to be found in Kokkari, all offering 'English menus' and the usual range of bland tourist fare.

Paradisos Restaurant (☎ 2273 094 208) Mains around €6, with wine or beer around €10.50. This restaurant, at the turn-off to Manolates, serves delectable dishes.

Loukas Taverna (☎ 2273 094 541) Mains €3-4. In Manolates, head for this taverna for the best and cheapest food around as well as great views. Try the stuffed courgette flowers and the special home-made *moshato* wines. Follow the prominent signs to the back end of the village.

Chios Χίος

pop 54,000

Chios (**hee**-os) does not feature prominently on the travel circuit. Situated rather awkwardly on the ferry routes and without a tangible international profile, the island attracts curious travellers and expat Greeks rather than hordes of package tourists, though those that do come find the island subtly rewarding in its own distinct way. Like its neighbours Samos and Lesvos, Chios is a large island covering 859 sq km. It is separated from the Turkish Karaburun Peninsula by the 8km-wide Chios Straits.

A large number of highly successful ship owners come from Chios and its dependencies, Inousses and Psara. This, and its mastic production, have meant that Chios has not needed to develop a large tourist industry. In recent years, however, package tourism has begun to make inroads, though it's limited to a fairly small coastal stretch south of Chios. The mastic villages of the south and its role as a stepping stone to Turkey is what primarily brings travellers to Chios.

History

In ancient times, Chios, like Samos, excelled in the arts, which reached their peak in the 7th century BC when the Chios school of sculpture produced some of Greece's most eminent sculptors of the time. The technique of soldering iron was invented in this school. During the Persian Wars, Chios was allied to Athens, but after the Battle of Plataea it became independent, and prospered because it didn't have to pay the annual tribute to Athens.

In Roman times Chios was invaded by Constantine, who helped himself to its fine sculptures. After the fall of Byzantium, the island fell prey to attacks by pirates, Venetians, Catalans and Turks. It revived somewhat under the Genoese, who took control in the 14th century. However, it was recaptured by the Turks in 1566 and became part of the Ottoman Empire.

In the 19th century, Chios suffered two devastations. In 1822 the Samians cajoled the people of Chios into assisting them in an uprising against Ottoman rule. The Turks retaliated by sacking Chios, killing 25,000 of its inhabitants and taking almost twice that number into slavery. The massacre was the subject of Victor Hugo's poem *L'Enfant de Chios* and Eugène Delacroix's painting *Le Massacre de Chios* (in the Louvre). In 1881 the island suffered a violent earthquake which killed almost 6000 people and destroyed many of the buildings in the capital.

Getting To/From Chios

Air Chios has on average five flights daily to Athens (€59), three weekly to Thessaloniki (€76.30) and one weekly to Lesvos

CHIOS

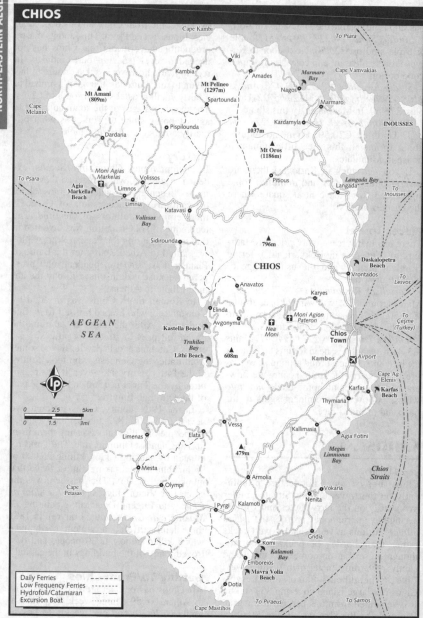

Cape Kambi

To Psara

Viki

Cape Vamvakias

Kambia

Mt Pelineo
(1297m)

Amades

Marmaro
Bay

Nagos

Mt Amani
(809m)

Spartounda

Marmaro

Cape
Melanio

INOUSSES

1037m

Pispilounda

Kardamyla

Dardaria

Mt Oros
(1186m)

Moni Agias
Markelas

Pitious

Langada Bay

To Psara

Agia
Markella
Beach

Limnos

Volissos

Langada

To
Inousses

Limnia

Katavasi

Volissos
Bay

Sidirounda

796m

CHIOS

Daskalopetra
Beach

Vrontados

Anavatos

To
Lesvos

AEGEAN
SEA

Karyes

Elinda

Moni Agion
Pateron

To
Çeşme
(Turkey)

Avgonyma

Kastella Beach

Nea
Moni

Chios
Town

Trahilos
Bay

608m

Airport

Lithi Beach

Kambos

Cape Ag
Elenis

Karfas

Karfas
Beach

0   2.5   5km
0   1.5   3mi

Thymiana

Vessa

Kallimasia

Agia Fotini

Limenas

Elata

Megas
Limnionas
Bay

Chios
Straits

Mesta

479m

Armolia

Cape
Petasas

Olympi

Vokaria

Pyrgi

Kalamoti

Nenita

Gridia

Komi

Kalamoti
Bay

Emboreios

Mavra Volia
Beach

Dotia

Cape Mastihos

To Piraeus

To Samos

Daily Ferries	– – – –
Low Frequency Ferries	— — —
Hydrofoil/Catamaran	— · — ·
Excursion Boat	· · · · · ·

(€41.50). The Olympic Airways office (☎ 2271 020 359) is on Leoforos Aigaiou in Chios. The airport is 4km from Chios. There is no Olympic Airways bus, but a taxi to/from the airport should cost about €4.

Ferry – Domestic In summer at least one ferry goes daily to Piraeus (eight hours, €17) and Lesvos (three hours, €10.50). There's one per week to Kavala (16 hours, €24) and two to Thessaloniki (18 hours, €32), via Limnos (11 hours, €16), and Alexandroupolis (16 hours, €26), via Limnos and Samothraki (14 hours, €23). There are three boats weekly to Samos (four hours, €9) and one per week to Kos (nine hours, €15.30) and Rhodes (15 hours, €21.50). Tickets for these routes can be bought from the NEL office (☎ 2271 023 971, fax 2271 041 319) at Leoforos Aigaiou 16 in Chios.

Miniotis Lines (☎ 2271 024 670, fax 2271 025 371, ⓔ miniotis@compulink.gr, ⓦ www.miniotis.gr) at Neorion 23 in Chios is smaller, and runs small boats to Karlovasi (four hours, €8), Vathy (4½ hours, €9.50) and Pythagorio (five hours, €9.50) on Samos twice a week. Three times a week these boats continue on to Fourni (7½ hours, €15) and Ikaria (8½ hours, €18). It also has three boats weekly to Psara (3½ hours, €8). Miniotis boats occasionally dock at the eastern end of the harbour, at the corner of Aigaiou and Kokali.

The *Oinoussai II*, another small local boat, runs to and from Oinousses (1¼ hours, €3, purchase tickets on board) every day except Thursday and Sunday. It leaves Chios at 2pm and Inousses at 9am, so you must stay overnight. There are also daily water taxis between Langada and Inousses (€30, shared between the passengers).

Ferry – International Boats to Turkey run all year from Chios. During April and October there are usually three ferries weekly to Çeşme, leaving Chios at 8.30am and returning at 6.30pm. During May there is an additional sailing and from July to September there are daily sailings. The fare is €38.50/50 one-way/return (not including the €9 port tax). Further information and

tickets can be obtained from Miniotis Lines. There are special daily excursion rates that often work out cheaper. Check with local agencies offering such trips.

Travellers requiring visas for Turkey can obtain them upon arrival in Çeşme for around US$45.

Hydrofoil In summer there are about three hydrofoils a week to Samos (3½ hours, €23) and Lesvos (1½ hours, €20).

Getting Around Chios
Bus From the long-distance bus station in Chios there are, in summer, eight buses daily to Pyrgi (€2), five to Mesta (€2.50) and six to Kardamyla (€2) via Langada. There are four buses a week to Volissos (€2.50). Only one or two buses weekly do the journey to Anavatos (€1.50) via Nea Moni and Avgonyma. There are fairly regular buses to the main beaches of Emborios, Komi, Nagos and Lithi. Buses to Karfas Beach are serviced by the blue (city) bus company. Schedules are posted at both bus stations.

Car & Motorcycle The numerous car-rental outlets in the town of Chios include Aegean Travel (☎ 2271 041 277, ⓔ aegeantr@otenet.gr, Aigaiou 114), at the northern end of the waterfront. In summer it's a good idea to book in advance for weekends.

Taxi Call ☎ 2271 041 111 for a taxi.

CHIOS TOWN
postcode 821 00 • pop 22,900
The town of Chios, on the east coast, is the island's port and capital. It's a large settlement, home to almost half of the island's inhabitants. Its waterfront, flanked by concrete buildings and trendy bars, is noisy in the extreme, with an inordinate number of cars and motorcycles careering up and down. The atmospheric old quarter, with many Turkish houses built around a Genoese castle, and the lively market area, are both worth a stroll. Chios doesn't have a beach; the nearest is the sandy beach at Karfas, 6km south.

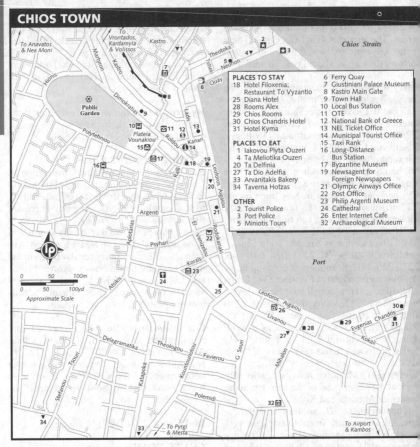

CHIOS TOWN

PLACES TO STAY	6	Ferry Quay
18	Hotel Filoxenia;	7	Giustiniani Palace Museum
	Restaurant To Vyzantio	8	Kastro Main Gate
25	Diana Hotel	9	Town Hall
28	Rooms Alex	10	Local Bus Station
29	Chios Rooms	11	OTE
30	Chios Chandris Hotel	12	National Bank of Greece
31	Hotel Kyma	13	NEL Ticket Office
		14	Municipal Tourist Office
PLACES TO EAT	15	Taxi Rank
1	Iakovou Plyta Ouzeri	16	Long-Distance
4	Ta Meliotika Ouzeri		Bus Station
20	Ta Delfinia	17	Byzantine Museum
27	Ta Dio Adelfia	19	Newsagent for
33	Arvanitakis Bakery		Foreign Newspapers
34	Taverna Hotzas	21	Olympic Airways Office
		22	Post Office
OTHER	23	Philip Argenti Museum
2	Tourist Police	24	Cathedral
3	Port Police	26	Enter Internet Cafe
5	Miniotis Tours	32	Archaeological Museum

Orientation

Most ferries dock at the northern end of the waterfront at the western end of Neorion. Bear in mind that some ferries from Piraeus arrive at the very inconvenient time of 4am – worth remembering if you are planning to find a room. The old Turkish quarter (called Kastro) is to the north of the ferry quay. To reach the town centre from here, follow the waterfront round to the left and walk along Leoforos Aigaiou. Turn right onto Kanari to reach the central square of Plateia Vounakiou. To the north-west of the square are the public gardens, and to the south-east

is the market area. The main shopping street are south of the square. As you face inland the bus station for local buses (blue; ☎ 227 022 079) is on the right side of the publi gardens, and the station for long-distanc buses (green; ☎ 2271 027 507) is on the lef

Information

The municipal tourist office (☎ 2271 04 389, fax 2271 044 343, e infochio@oten .gr) is at Kanari 18. The extremely helpfu and friendly staff can provide informatio on accommodation, car rental, bus and boa schedules, and more. The book *Hikin outes on Chios* is available here for €4.50. he office is open 7am to 10pm daily.

The post office and OTE are both one lock back from the waterfront while most anks are between Kanari and Plateia 'ounakiou. There is an ATM halfway long Aplotarias.

The Enter Internet Cafe (☎ 2271 041 058) at Aigaiou 48 (upstairs), on the southern aterfront, and charges €4 an hour.

The tourist police (☎ 2271 044 427) and e port police (☎ 2271 044 432) are at the astern end of Neorion.

Museums

he most interesting museum is the **Philip rgenti Museum** (☎ *2271 023 463, Koraïs; dmission €1.50; museum & library open am-2pm Mon-Thur, 5pm-7.30pm Fri, am-12.30pm Sat)*. Situated in the same uilding as the **Koraïs Library**, one of the ountry's largest libraries. The museum, hich is near the cathedral, contains em- roideries, traditional costumes and por- aits of the wealthy Argenti family.

The town's other museums are not so ompelling. The **archaeological museum** ☎ *2271 044 239, Mihalon 10; admission €1.50; open 8am-7pm Tues-Sun)* contains culptures, pottery and coins. It sometimes as interesting temporary exhibits. The **yzantine Museum** (☎ *2271 026 866, lateia Vounakiou; admission free; open 0am-1pm Tues-Sun)* is housed in a former nosque, the Medjitie Djami.

Just inside the Kastro's main gate, is the ny **Giustiniani Palace Museum** (☎ *2271 22 819; €1.50 Mon-Sat, admission €1 Sun; pen 8am-7pm Mon-Sat, 8am-3pm Sun)*. It olds a few restored wall paintings of rophets, and other Byzantine bits and pieces.

Places to Stay – Budget

With over 30 *domatia* to choose from, bud- et accommodation is fairly plentiful in 'hios. Call into the municipal tourist office or a full listing. Be aware, though, that ac- ommodation in central Chios can be very oisy – choose carefully.

Chios Rooms (☎ *2271 020 198, mobile 69 7283 3841, Aigaiou 110)* Singles/

doubles/triples €18/24/35.50, some with private bathroom. This beautifully decked- out neoclassical place is a real find. It's clean, comfortable and full of interesting artworks and old pieces of furniture. It's upstairs, above Aegean Travel, at the east end of the waterfront.

Rooms Alex (☎ *2271 026 054, Livanou 29)* Doubles with bathroom €29.50. This is another domatia option. Alex has six dou- bles and there is a relaxing roof garden fes- tooned with flags. Alex will pick you up at your boat if you call him. He will also help with car or bike rentals and give general in- formation on Chios.

Places to Stay – Mid-Range & Top End

Diana Hotel (☎ *2271 044 180, fax 2271 026 748, El Venizelou 92)* Singles/doubles with breakfast €43/53. This D-class place is a good hotel aimed primarily at the Greek business market.

Hotel Filoxenia (☎ *2271 026 559, fax 2271 028 447, Voupalou 8)* Doubles with bathroom, fridge, air-con & balcony €59. This is signposted from the waterfront and is above Restaurant To Vyzantio. The foyer has a lovely faded decadence about it, but the rooms are lacking such charm and are somewhat overpriced.

Hotel Kyma (☎ *2271 044 500, fax 2271 044 600,* e *kyma@chi.forthnet.gr, Evge- nias Chandris 1)* Singles/doubles with TV, air-con & phone €44/64.56. The C-class Kyma occupies a century-old mansion and has lots of character. Try to get one of the rooms overlooking the sea. The breakfast is magnificent (and included in the room rate). The helpful owners can organise driving itineraries that include accommodation in Mesta and Volissos.

Chios Chandris Hotel (☎ *2271 025 768, Evgenias Chandris 2,* e *chios@chandris .gr,* w *www.chandris.gr)* Singles/doubles with breakfast €79.50/106, 3-person stu- dios & 2-person suites €176. This classy international-style hotel is the best on the is- land. All rooms have a balcony with sea view. There's a pool, restaurant and bar, full room service and many other facilities.

Places to Eat

Arvanitakis Bakery (Cnr Katapoka & Kountouriotou) The bread baked here is some of the best you'll find in Greece. Try the whole wheat.

Restaurant To Vyzantio (☎ 2271 041 035, Cnr Ralli & Roïdou) Mains around €3.50. This bright, cheerful and unpretentious place serves good traditional Greek fare at low prices.

Iakovou Plyta Ouzeri (☎ 2271 023 858, Agiou Georgiou Frouriou 20) Mezedes from around €3. Tucked away in the old town is this ouzeri specialising in tasty fish mezedes.

Ta Meliotiko Ouzeri (☎ 2271 040 407) Salads and vegetable dishes around €2.50, seafood around €6. This basic place on the waterfront near the police station dishes out huge helpings of delicious Greek salads, seafood and vegetable appetisers. Be hungry.

Ta Delfinia (☎ 2271 022 607, Aigaiou 36) Mains from around €3.50. This waterfront taverna is a bit touristy (with photo menus), but the food and service are good and it's the best place to watch street life.

Ta Dio Adelfia (☎ 2271 021 313, Livanou 38) Mains around €4.50. This taverna with a pleasant walled garden is opposite Rooms Alex.

Taverna Hotzas (☎ 2271 042 787, Kondyli 3) Most dishes around €3.50. Open evenings Mon-Sat year round. This taverna at the southern end of town is an institution, with lots of ugly cats and a lovely garden littered with lemon trees. Try the fava, the *mastelo* (grilled cheese) and the grilled fish. To get there, walk up Aplotarias and turn right at the fork along Stefanou Tsouri; follow it until you come across the restaurant.

CENTRAL CHIOS

North of the town of Chios is an elongated beachside suburb leading to **Vrontados** where you can sit on the supposed stone chair of Homer, the Daskalopetra, though it is quietly accepted that it's unlikely to have been used by Homer himself. It's a serene spot though, and it would not be hard to imagine Homer and his acolytes reciting epic verses to their admiring followers.

Immediately south of Chios is a warren of walled mansions, some restored, other crumbling, called the **Kampos**. This was the preferred place of abode of wealthy Genoese and Greek merchant families from the 14th century onwards. It's easy to get los here so keep your wits about you. It's bes to tour the area by bicycle, moped or car since it is fairly extensive. Chios' mair beach resort, **Karfas**, is here too, 7km south of Chios. The beach is sandy though comparatively small with some moderate development and some A-class hotels; if you like your beaches quiet, look elsewhere.

In the centre of the island is the 11th century **Nea Moni** (*admission free; oper 8am-1pm, 4pm-8pm*). This large monastery now World Heritage-listed, stands in a beautiful mountain setting, 14km from Chios Like many monasteries in Greece it wa built to house an icon of the Virgin Mary who appeared before the eyes of three shepherds. In its heyday the monastery was one of the richest in Greece with the most preeminent artists of Byzantium commissioned to create the mosaics in its katholikon.

During the 1822 atrocities the buildings were set on fire and all the resident monks were massacred. There is a macabre display of their skulls in the ossuary at the monastery's little chapel. In the earthquake of 1881 the katholikon's dome caved in, causing damage to the mosaics. Nonetheless, the mosaics, esteemed for the striking contrast of their vivid colours and the fluidity and juxtapositions of the figures, still rank among the most outstanding examples of Byzantine art in Greece. A few nuns live at the monastery. The bus service to the monastery is poor, but travel agents in Chios have excursions here and to the village of Anavatos

Ten kilometres from Nea Moni, at the end of a road that leads to nowhere, stands the forlorn ghost village of **Anavatos**. Its abandoned grey-stone houses stand as lonely sentinels to one of Chios' great tragedies. Nearly all the inhabitants of the village perished in 1822 and today only a small number of elderly people live there, mostly in houses at the base of the village. Anavatos is a striking village, built on a precipitous cliff which th illagers chose to hurl themselves over, ather than be taken captive by the Turks. arrow, stepped pathways wind between the ouses to the summit of the village.

The beaches on the mid-west coast are ot spectacular, but they are quiet and gen-rally undeveloped. **Lithi Beach**, the south-rnmost, is popular with weekenders and an get busy.

OUTHERN CHIOS

outhern Chios is dominated by medieval illages that look as though they were trans-lanted from the Levant rather than built by ienoese colonisers in the 14th century. The olling, scrubby hills are covered in low mas-c trees that for many years were the main ource of income for these scattered settle-nents (see the boxed text 'Gum Mastic').

There are some 20 *Mastihohoria* (mastic illages); the two best preserved are Pyrgi nd Mesta. As mastic was a lucrative com-nodity in the Middle Ages, many an invader ast an acquisitive eye upon the villages, ne-essitating sturdy fortifications. The arch-vays spanning the streets were to prevent the ouses from collapsing during earthquakes. secause of the sultan's fondness for mastic hewing gum, the inhabitants of the Masti-ohoria were spared in the 1822 massacre.

Pyrgi Πυργί
op 1300

'he largest of the Mastihohoria, and one of ne most extraordinary villages in the whole f Greece, is the fortified village of Pyrgi, 4km south-west of Chios. The vaulted treets of the fortified village are narrow nd labyrinthine, but what makes Pyrgi nique are the building facades, decorated vith intricate grey and white designs. Some f the patterns are geometric and others are ased on flowers, leaves and animals. The echnique used, called *xysta*, is achieved by oating the walls with a mixture of cement nd black volcanic sand, painting over this vith white lime, and then scraping off parts f the lime with the bent prong of a fork, to eveal the matt grey beneath.

From the main road, a fork heading to he right (coming from Chios) leads to the

Gum Mastic

Gum mastic comes from the lentisk bush, and conditions in southern Chios are ideal for its growth. Many ancient Greeks, including Hip-pocrates, proclaimed the pharmaceutical benefits of mastic. Ailments it was claimed to cure included stomach upsets, chronic coughs and diseases of the liver, intestines and blad-der. It was also used as an antidote for snake bites. During Turkish rule Chios received pref-erential treatment from the sultans who, along with the ladies of the harem, were hooked on chewing gum made from mastic.

Until recently, mastic was widely used in the pharmaceutical industry, as well as in the manufacture of chewing gum and certain al-coholic drinks, particularly arak, a Middle East-ern liqueur. In most cases mastic has now been replaced by *raki*, a Greek firewater. But mas-tic production may yet have a future. Some adherents of alternative medicine claim that it stimulates the immune system and reduces blood pressure and cholesterol levels. Chew-ing gum made from mastic can be bought on Chios, under the brand name Elma.

heart of the village and the central square. The little 12th-century **Church of Agios Apostolos**, just off the square, is profusely decorated with well-preserved 17th-century frescoes. Ask at the taverna or kafeneio for the church's caretaker, who will open it up for you. The facade of the larger church, on the opposite side of the square, has the most impressive xysta of all the buildings here.

Places to Stay & Eat *Giannaki Rooms* (☎ 2271 025 888, mobile ☎ 69 4595 9889, fax 2271 022 846) Doubles €44. This old house has been fully renovated and offers rooms with TV and air-con. Book ahead.

Taverna Kanios (☎ 2271 072 150) Most dishes around €2.50. This little taverna on the central square (on the right as you face the large church) is the main eating option.

There's an upstairs *pizzeria* on the square but it's not always open.

Emboreios Εμπορειός

Six kilometres to the south of Pyrgi, Emboreios was the port of Pyrgi in the days when mastic production was big business. These days Emboreios is a quiet place, perfect for people who like to relax. As you come from Chios, a signpost points left to Emboreios, just before you arrive at Pyrgi.

Mavra Volia Beach is at the end of the road and has unusual black volcanic pebbles as its main attraction. There is another more secluded beach, just over the headland along a paved track.

Places to Stay & Eat *Studio Apartments Vasiliki* (☎ 2271 071 422) Doubles €35.50. These studios in Emboreios are often full, but the same people also have rooms in Mavra Volia.

Neptune (☎ 2271 070 020) Seafood around €4.50. This taverna has the most prominent position in Emboreios.

Porto Emborios (☎ 2271 070 025) Mains around €4.50, appetisers €3. On the main square this shady place is very pleasant, with an old stone facade decorated with hanging strings of chillies and garlic and fishing nets. It has good home-cooked food, including roast lamb.

Mesta Μεστά

Continuing on the main road from Pyrgi, after 5km you will reach the mastic village of **Olympi**. It's less immediately attractive than its two neighbours but still worth a brief stop.

Mesta, 5km on, has a very different atmosphere from that created by the striking visuals of Pyrgi and should be on any visitor's itinerary. Nested among low hills, the village is exquisite and completely enclosed within massive fortified walls. Entrance to the maze of streets is via one of four gates. This method of limiting entry to the settlement and its disorienting maze of streets and tunnels is a prime example of 14th-century defence architecture, as protection against pirates and marauders. The labyrinthine cobbled streets of bare stone houses and arches have a melancholy aura, though it's a cheerful place, with women chatting on their front steps as

they shell almonds and fresh *revithia* (chickpeas) or tie bundles of sweet-smelling herbs.

The village has two churches of the Taxiarhes (archangels). The older one dates from Byzantine times and has a magnificent 17th-century iconostasis. The second one, built in the 19th century, has very fine frescoes.

Orientation Buses stop on Plateia Nikolaou Poumpaki, on the main road outside Mesta. To reach the central square of Plateia Taxiarhon, with your back to the bus shelter, turn right, and then immediately left, and you will see a sign pointing to the centre of the village.

Places to Stay & Eat *Despina Floris Rooms* (☎ 2271 076 050, fax 2271 076 529) Double studios around €32.50. This clearing house for renovated rooms is perhaps the best place to start if you're looking for somewhere to stay. Despina, who also runs Mesaonas restaurant on the square, speaks good English.

Anna Floradis Rooms (☎ 2271 028 891, 2271 076 455/176) Doubles €38. These five, very comfortable rooms are next to the church.

Karambelas Apartments (☎ 2271 022 068, 10 Ilia Mandalaka) Doubles €59. These exquisite, spotless studios in a renovated medieval house belong to the family that run the O Morias Sta Mesta taverna. Rooms contain beautiful handmade textiles and stone wall niches. You can negotiate a much better rate outside high season. Ask at the taverna if no-one answers the phone.

O Morias Sta Mesta (☎ 2271 076 400, Plateia Taxiarhon) Mains around €4.50. Dionyssis Karambelas, the affable owner of this restaurant – one of the two on Plateia Taxiarhon in romantic courtyard settings – is originally from the Peloponnese (hence the name of the restaurant: Morias is the old name for the Peloponnese). Dionyssis will provide you with superb country cooking. Ask to try the *hortokeftedes* (vegetable patties) and an unusual wild green, *kritamos* (rock samphire), that grows by the sea. The bread is homemade and the unusually sweet olives taste like mastic. You may be given a glass of *souma*, an ouzo made from figs, or a mastic firewater.

Mesaonas (☎ 2271 076 050, Plateia Tax-*arhon*) Mains around €4.50. This restaurant on the square is also very good. It specialises in traditional recipes made with local ingredients. The wine, oil, cheese and, of course, the souma, are all from Mesta.

NORTHERN CHIOS

Northern Chios is characterised by its craggy peaks (Mt Pelineo, Mt Oros and Mt Amani), deserted villages and scrawny hillsides once blanketed in rich pine forests. The area is mainly for the adventurous and those not fazed by tortuous roads.

Volissos is the main focus for the villages of the north-western quarter. Reputedly Homer's place of birth, it is today a quiet settlement, capped with an impressive Genoese fort. Volissos' port is **Limnia**, a workaday fishing harbour. It's not especially appealing, but has a welcoming *taverna*. You can continue to **Limnos**, a kilometre away, where caiques sometimes leave for Psara. The road onwards round the north end is very winding and passes some isolated villages.

On the eastern side a picturesque road leads out of Vrontados through a landscape that is somewhat more visitor-friendly than the western side. **Langada** is the first village, wedged at the end of a bay looking out towards Inousses. Next are **Kardamyla** and **Marmaro**, the two main settlements. If you fancy a dip, head a few kilometres farther to the lush little fishing hamlet of **Nagos**. It has a nice beach with coloured pebbles.

Beyond Nagos, the road winds upwards, skirting the craggy Mt Pelineo. The scenery is green enough, but settlements are fewer and more remote. **Amades** and **Viki** are two villages you will traverse before hitting the last village, **Kambia**, perched high up on a ridge overlooking bare hillsides and the sea far below. From here a mostly sealed road leads you round Mt Pelineo, past a futuristic phalanx of 10 huge wind-driven generators on the opposite side of the valley, and back to the trans-island route near Volissos.

Places to Stay

Hotel Kardamyla (☎ 2272 023 353, fax 2271 044 600) Doubles €65. If you choose to stay up in Marmaro, try this comfortable hotel run by the same management as Hotel Kyma in Chios.

Volissos Restored Houses (☎ 2274 021 413/421, fax 2274 021 521) Studios from €44. These beautifully renovated village houses, some with patios, look out over the gently sloping landscape towards the sea. It's a nice spot if you're looking for peace and quiet.

Inousses Οινούσσες

Off the north-eastern coast of Chios lie nine tiny islets, collectively called Inousses. Only one of these, also called Inousses, is inhabited. Those who live here permanently make their living from fishing and sheep farming. The island has three fish farms and exports small amounts of fish to Italy and France. Inousses is hilly and covered in scrub and has good beaches.

However, these facts apart, this is no ordinary Greek island. Inousses may be small, but it is the ancestral home of around 30% of Greece's ship owners. Most of these wealthy maritime barons conduct their business from Athens, London and New York, but in summer return with their families to Inousses, where they own luxurious mansions.

There is a rumour that these ship owners offer financial incentives to discourage people from opening tavernas or domatia on

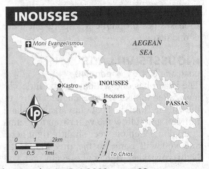

INOUSSES

Moni Evangelismou · AEGEAN SEA · Kastro · INOUSSES · Inousses · PASSAS · 0 1 2km · 0 0.5 1mi · To Chios

the island, because they don't want to attract foreign tourists. It may not be possible to vouch for the truth of this but certainly tourism is not encouraged on the island: no domatia owners come to meet the boat, there are no domatia signs and wandering around the streets fails to bring offers of accommodation. The place has a curiously barren and sterile air since there are few tourist facilities and even fewer visitors. Several islanders have stated that Inousses has a few domatia, but they are vague as to their whereabouts.

On a more positive note – and if these quirks have not discouraged you from going to Inousses – the island's town has some nice neoclassical mansions and abandoned houses; good beaches (**Kastro Beach** is the usual swimming stop for day-trippers); and no tourists. In the town of Inousses there is a large naval boarding school. If you visit during term time you may well encounter the pupils parading around town to bellowed marching orders.

Getting To/From Inousses

The island is served only by the local ferry boat *Oinoussai II*, which plies everyday (except Thursday and Sunday) between the island and the town of Chios. It leaves Chios at 2pm and Inousses at 9am, so is of no use for day trips. Purchase tickets on board for €3 (one way). The trip takes about one hour. There are also daily water taxis (☎ 69 4416 8104) to/from Langada. The one-way fare is €30, which is split between the passengers. In summer there are sometimes excursion boats from Chios to the island.

Getting Around Inousses

Inousses has no public transport, but there is one taxi.

INOUSSES VILLAGE

postcode 821 01 • pop 640

The island has one settlement, the little village called Inousses. To reach the 'centre' of the village from the boat quay, facing inland turn left and follow the waterfront to Plateia Antoniou P Lemou; veer slightly right here, and you will come to the tiny Plateia tis Naftisynis; veer right once again and you

will see ahead Restaurant & Kafeneio Pateroniso, near the highly decorated cream and brick-red building. Facing this establishment turn right and ascend the steps. There's not a lot to see in the centre, apart from the church but it is near the island's only hotel.

If you turn left at Restaurant Pateroniso and then take the first right into Konstantinou Antonopoulou you will come to the National Bank of Greece which, one can surmise, is kept very busy. Next door to the bank is a combined post office and OTE.

The police (☎ 2271 055 222) are at the top of the steps that lead to the town centre

Maritime Museum

This museum (☎ 2271 055 182; admission €1.50; open 10am-1.30pm) is between the Restaurant Pateroniso and the National Bank of Greece. It opened in 1990 and the benefactors were wealthy ship owners from the island. Many island families donated nautical memorabilia, which includes *objets d'art*, photographs, models of early ships, cannons and nautical instruments.

Places to Stay & Eat

There is no camping ground on the island and camping freelance would definitely be frowned upon.

Hotel Thalassoporos (☎ 2271 055 475 Singles/doubles with bathroom €23.50 35.50. Inousses' one hotel is this bland C class property at the top of the steps that lead to the village centre. It's unlikely ever to be full, but just in case, phone ahead in July and August.

Restaurant Pateroniso (☎ 2271 055 586 Mains around €4.50. This is Inousses' only restaurant outside the summer months. The food is reasonably priced and well prepared, but you will not be made to feel welcome – if it's busy with locals, you'll be ignored altogether.

The little fish taverna *Zepagas* – open only in summer – is at the far western end of the harbour.

There are a couple of bars. *Remezzo* is a small bar on the waterfront, while *Trigono* is up in the village and mainly patronised by the few local young people left on the island

The town has four *grocery stores*. One of the two on the waterfront thankfully serves as a bit of a snack bar (though your options are limited to cheese pies, canned dolmades and whatever else you can glean from its shelves) and has tables out the front. The other two are in the centre of the village, on the road that leads up to the prominent Agios Nikolaos church.

ISLAND WALK

Although most of this three-hour circular walk is along a narrow cement road, you are unlikely to meet much traffic. Take plenty of water and a snack with you as there are no refreshments available along the way. Also take your swimming gear as you will pass many of the island's beaches and coves.

Just beyond the maritime museum you will see a signpost to **Moni Evangelismou**. This will take you along the cement road that skirts the west coast. Along the way you will pass several inviting beaches and coves. Only **Apiganos Beach** is signposted, but there are others which are easily accessible from the road. After about one hour the road loops inland, and a little farther along is the entrance to the palatial Moni Evangelismou, surrounded by extensive grounds.

Within the convent is the mummified body of Irini Pateras, daughter of the late Panagos Pateras, a multimillionaire ship owner. Irini became a nun in her late teens and died in the early 1960s when she was 20. Her distraught mother decided built the convent in memory of her daughter. In the Greek Orthodox religion, three years after burial the body is exhumed and the bones cleaned and reburied in a casket. When Irini's body was exhumed it was found to have mummified rather than decomposed; this phenomenon is regarded in Greece as evidence of sainthood. Irini's mother is now abbess of the convent, which houses around 20 nuns. Only women may visit the convent and of course they must be appropriately (modestly) dressed.

Continuing along the cement road, beyond the entrance to the convent, you will come to two stone pillars on the left. The wide path between the pillars leads in 10 minutes to an enormous white cross which is a **memorial** to St Irini. This is the highest point of the island and commands stunning views over to northern Chios and the Karaburun Peninsula in Turkey. About 20 minutes farther along, the cement road gives way to a dirt track. Continue straight ahead to reach the town of Inousses.

Psara Ψαρά

postcode 821 04 • pop 500

Psara (psah-**rah**) lies off the north-west coast of Chios. The island is 9km long and 5km wide and is rocky with little vegetation. During Ottoman times Greeks settled on the remote island to escape Turkish oppression. By the 19th century, many of these inhabitants, like those of Chios and Inousses, had become successful ship owners. When the rallying cry for self-determination reverberated through the country, the Psariots zealously took up arms and contributed a large number of ships to the Greek cause. In retaliation the Turks stormed the island and killed all but 3000 of the 20,000 inhabitants. The island never regained its former glory and today all of the inhabitants live in the island's one settlement, also called Psara.

Like Inousses, Psara sees few tourists.

Places to Stay

EOT Guesthouse (☎ *2274 061 293*) Single/double rooms €53/59, single/double studios €41/47. The old parliament building has been converted into an EOT guesthouse. Breakfast is included in the price of

PSARA

0   2   4km
0   1   2mi

ANTIPSARA

Moni Kimisis
Theotokou

546m
PSARA

Kaminaki

Psara

Cape Agios
Georgios

To Chios

NORTH-EASTERN AEGEAN

all rooms. Information may be obtained by either telephoning the guesthouse or ringing ☎ 2251 027 908 in Lesvos.

There are also *domatia* in Psara and a small number of *tavernas*.

Getting To/From Psara
Ferries leave Chios for Psara (3½ hours, €8) at 7am three times weekly, returning at noon. Call Miniotis Lines (☎ 2271 024 670) in Chios or check with a local agent for current departure days since these change from year to year. Local caiques also run from Limnos (three hours, €4.50) on the west coast of Chios about once a week, but departure times are unpredictable and often depend on the prevailing weather conditions.

Lesvos (Mytilini)
Λέσβος (Μυτιλήνη)

pop 88,800
Lesvos is the third-largest island in Greece, after Crete and Evia. It's north of Chios and south-east of Limnos. Most Greeks call the island Mytilini, also the name of the capital. The island is mountainous with two bottleneck gulfs penetrating its south coast. The south and east of the island are fertile, with numerous olive groves. In contrast to the south and east, the west has rocky and barren mountains, creating a dramatic moonscape.

Lesvos produces the best olive oil in Greece and has many olive oil refineries. Many abandoned olive oil and soap factories are now being renovated and revived as cultural centres. Aside from olive oil, Lesvos is famous for its ouzo, its sardines from the Gulf of Kalloni (eaten raw, like sashimi marinated in salt, and very good with ouzo) and its *ladotyri*, a sheep's milk cheese that is kept in oil for one to two years. If you go in search of ladotyri, make sure you ask for the real thing – the commercial stuff is coated with paraffin.

Lesvos is becoming a popular package-holiday destination, but is large enough to absorb tourists without seeming to be overrun. Still, it's best to visit outside the peak tourist months of July and August. Early spring and late autumn are ideal for trekking. There's a lot to see here; you could easily spend two weeks taking in the sights and still feel you've run out of time to see everything.

History
In the 6th century BC, Lesvos was unified under the rule of the tyrant Pittakos, one of ancient Greece's Seven Sages. Pittakos succeeded in resolving the long-standing animosity between the island's two cities of Mytilini and Mithymna. This new-found peace generated an atmosphere conducive to creativity, and Lesvos became a centre of artistic and philosophical achievement.

Terpander, the musical composer, and Arion, the poet, were both born on Lesvos in the 7th century BC. Arion's works influenced the tragedians of the 5th century BC such as Sophocles and Euripides. In the 4th century BC, Aristotle and Epicurus taught at an exceptional school of philosophy which flourished on Lesvos.

Sappho, one of the greatest poets of ancient Greece, was born on Lesvos around 630 BC. Unfortunately little of her poetry is extant, but what remains reveals a genius for combining passion with simplicity and detachment, in verses ofx beauty and power.

On a more prosaic level, Lesvos suffered at the hands of invaders and occupiers to the same extent as all other Greek islands. In 527 BC the Persians conquered the island, but in 479 BC it was captured by Athens and became a member of the Delian League. In the following centuries the island suffered numerous invasions, and in 88 BC it was conquered by Julius Caesar. Byzantines, Venetians, Genoese and Turks followed.

However, through all these vicissitudes the arts retained a high degree of importance. The primitive painter Theophilos (1866–1934) and the Nobel Prize-winning poet Odysseus Elytis (1911–96) were born on Lesvos. The island is to this day a spawning ground for innovative ideas in the arts and politics, and is the headquarters of the University of the Aegean. The Lesvos campus of the university is the home of the environmental studies and social anthropology departments.

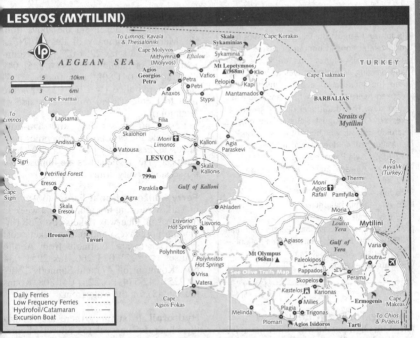

LESVOS (MYTILINI)

AEGEAN SEA

TURKEY

To Limnos, Kavala & Thessaloniki

Cape Korakas

Skala Sykaminias

Cape Molyvos

Mithymna (Molyvos)   Eftalou   Sykaminia   Mt Lepetymnos ▲(968m)   Klio

Cape Tsakmaki

Agios Georgios Petra   Petra   Vafios   Pelopi   Kapi

0   5   10km
0   3   6mi

Cape Fournia

Anaxos   Petri   Stypsi   Mantamados

BARBALIAS

Lapsarna

Straits of Mytilini

To Limnos

Filia

Andissa   Skalohori

Moni Limonos   Kalloni   Agia Paraskevi

Vatousa

LESVOS

Sigri

Petrified Forest

Eresos   ▲ 799m   Skala Kallonis

To Ayvalik (Turkey)

Thermi

Cape Sigri

Skala Eresou   Parakila   Agra

Gulf of Kalloni

Moni Agios Rafail   Pamfylla

Moria

Hrousas   Tavari

Ahladeri

Loutra Yera   Mytilini

Lisvorio Hot Springs   Lisvorio

Agiasos   Gulf of Yera   Varia

Polyhnitos

Polyhnitos Hot Springs   Mt Olympus (968m) ▲   Paleokipos   Loutra

Vrisa

See Olive Trails Map   Pappados   Perama

Vatera   Kastelos   Karionas

Cape Agios Fokas   Skopelos   Ermogenis   Cape Makeas

Melinda   Milies

Plagia   Trigonas   To Chios & Piraeus

Plomari   Agios Isidoros   Tarti

Daily Ferries — — —
Low Frequency Ferries - - - - - -
Hydrofoil/Catamaran — · —
Excursion Boat ....

Trekking

Lesvos has some nice trekking trails in the north and south. Some of these were marked with colour-coded signs, but these days only a few signs are left; nonetheless, the trails are easy to follow. These walks can be taken in sections, or over a few days, stopping off along the way where appropriate. They are a mixture of dirt vehicle tracks and pedestrian trails. The main trails are **Vatera to Yera**, **Petra to Lapsarna**, **Kapi to Sykaminia** and **Sigri to Eresos**. There are many other walking trails on the island, including those in the olive-growing region around Plomari (see the boxed text 'Olive Trails' in this chapter). Of these, the **Skopelos-Karionas-Kastelos-Trigonas/Plagia** day trek is the most popular.

Bird-Watching

Bird-watching – or 'birding', as experts call it – is big business in Lesvos. The island is the transit point and home to over 279 species of birds ranging from raptors to waders. As a result, Lesvos is attracting an ever-increasing number of visitors – human and feathered – particularly in spring. There are four main observation areas centred on Eresos, Petra, Skala Kallonis and Agiasos. The major aim of birders seems to be spotting the elusive Cinereous bunting and Kruper's nuthatch.

A folksy and detailed handbook to the hobby is Richard Brooks' *Birding in Lesbos*, which is available on Lesvos.

Special Events

Throughout summer, villages hold festivals on the name day of their church. These two-day festas with very ancient origins usually involve the racing of beautifully decorated horses and the sacrifice of a bull. For a list of dates and villages, see the boxed text 'Festival Time'.

If you're visiting the island in February, don't miss carnival in the town of Agiasos – among other things, the locals perform hilariously vulgar comedies.

Festival Time

In July and August the villages of Lesvos hold wild celebrations in honour of patron saints. There's usually a lot of food, drink, live music and dancing all night, as well as horse races and the sacrifice of a bull, which is then cooked overnight with wheat and eaten the next day. This traditional dish is known as *keskek*. On 6 August Skala Kalloni holds a sardine festival, which is not to be missed.

Major festival dates are as follows:

1 July – Agia Paraskevi
20 July – Agiasos, Eresos, Plomari, Vrisa
22 July – Skopelos
24 July – Eresos
25 July – Skala Kalloni
26 July – Paleokipos, Plomari
27 July – Eresos, Gavathas, Perama, Plomari
  6 August – Eresos, Andissa, Skala Kalloni
15 August – Agiasos, Kerami
30 August – Vafios

Getting To/From Lesvos

Air With Olympic Airways there are at least four flights daily from Lesvos to Athens (€71.60) and around one daily to Thessaloniki (€76.30), as well as one flight weekly to Chios (€41.50) and four flights a week to Limnos (€48.50). Aegean (☎ 2251 061 120, fax 2251 061 801) flies between Lesvos and Athens three times a day and Thessaloniki once a day. Note that Lesvos is always referred to as Mytilini on air schedules. The Olympic Airways office (☎ 2251 028 659) in Mytilini is at Kavetsou 44 (Kavetsou is a southerly continuation of Ermou). The airport is 8km south of Mytilini. A taxi to/from the airport will cost about €6.

Ferry – Domestic In summer there is at least one ferry daily to Piraeus (12 hours, €22.50) via Chios (3 hours, €10.50) and two weekly highspeed services (6 hours, €40). There are two ferries weekly to Kavala (10 hours, €20) via Limnos (6 hours, €15.50), two weekly to Thessaloniki (13 hours, €25) via Limnos and one to Alexandroupolis (11½ hours, €16.50). Ferry ticket

offices line the eastern side of Kountourioti, in Mytilini. Get tickets for the above from the Maritime Company of Lesvos (NEL; ☎ 2251 028 480, fax 2251 028 601), Kountourioti 67, or Samiotis Tours (☎ 2251 042 574, fax 2251 041 808), Kountourioti 43.

The port police (☎ 2251 028 827) are next to Picolo Travel on the east side of Kountourioti.

Lesvos now has a very strict anti-drug policy, and the port police sometimes conduct searches of ferry passengers who look 'suspect'. Heavy penalties are imposed for possession of any drugs.

Ferry – International Ferries to Ayvalık in Turkey run roughly four times a week in high season. One-way tickets cost €38 (including port taxes) and return tickets cost €47. Tickets are available from Aeolic Cruises (☎ 2251 023 266, fax 2251 034 694, Kountourioti 47) and Samiotis Tours (☎ 2251 042 574, fax 2251 041 808, Kountourioti 43), on the waterfront.

Hydrofoil In summer there are around three hydrofoils a week to Chios (1½ hours, €20) and Samos (five hours, €25). Call Kyriacoulis (☎ 2251 020 716), Kountourioti 73, for the latest schedule.

Getting Around Lesvos

Bus Lesvos' transport hub is the capital, Mytilini. In summer, from the long-distance bus station (☎ 2251 028 873) there are three buses daily to Skala Eresou (2½ hours, €6.50) via Eresos, five buses daily to Mithymna (1¾ hours, €4.50) via Petra, and two buses to Sigri (2½ hours, €6.50). There are no direct buses between Eresos, Sigri and Mithymna. If you wish to travel from one of these villages to another, change buses in the town of Kalloni, which is 48km from Eresos and 22km from Mithymna. There are five buses daily to the south-coast resort of Plomari (1¼ hours, €3). A timetable is posted in the window at the bus station.

Car & Motorcycle The many car-hire outlets in Mytilini include Hertz (☎ 2251 042 576, mobile ☎ 69 3605 7676), which is based at Samiotis Tours (☎ 2251 042 574, fax 2251 041 808), Kountourioti 43, on the waterfront, and Troho Kinisi (☎ 2251 046 511, mobile ☎ 69 3223 7900), which operates from the Erato Hotel just south of the Olympic Airways office.

Many motorcycle-rental firms are located along the same stretch of waterfront. You will, however, be better off hiring a motorcycle or scooter in Mithymna or Skala Eresou, since Lesvos is a large island and an underpowered two-wheeler is not really a practical mode of transport for getting around.

Ferry In summer there are hourly ferries (5 minutes, €1) between Perama and Koundouroudia, near Loutra. Buses to Mytilini meet all ferries.

MYTILINI TOWN Μυτιλήνη
postcode 811 00 ● pop 23,970

Mytilini, the capital and port of Lesvos, is a large workaday town. If you are enthralled by pretty towns like Mykonos you won't necessarily find the same ambience in Mytilini. However, this town has its own attractions, including a lively harbour and nightlife, once-grand 19th-century mansions

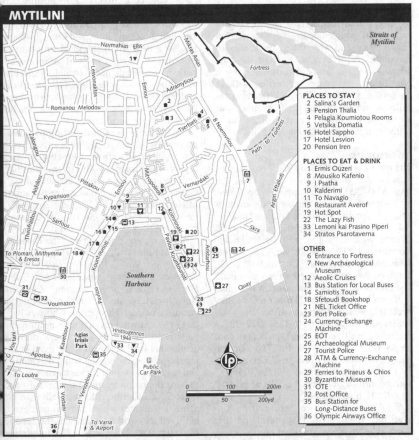

MYTILINI

Straits of Mytilini

PLACES TO STAY
2 Salina's Garden
3 Pension Thalia
4 Pelagia Koumiotou Rooms
5 Vetsika Domatia
16 Hotel Sappho
17 Hotel Lesvion
20 Pension Iren

PLACES TO EAT & DRINK
1 Ermis Ouzeri
8 Mousiko Kafenio
9 I Psatha
10 Kalderimi
11 To Navagio
15 Restaurant Averof
19 Hot Spot
22 The Lazy Fish
33 Lemoni kai Prasino Piperi
34 Stratos Psarotaverna

OTHER
6 Entrance to Fortress
7 New Archaeological Museum
12 Aeolic Cruises
13 Bus Station for Local Buses
14 Samiotis Tours
18 Sfetoudi Bookshop
21 NEL Ticket Office
23 Port Police
24 Currency-Exchange Machine
25 EOT
26 Archaeological Museum
27 Tourist Police
28 ATM & Currency-Exchange Machine
29 Ferries to Piraeus & Chios
30 Byzantine Museum
31 OTE
32 Post Office
35 Bus Station for Long-Distance Buses
36 Olympic Airways Office

Phone numbers listed incorporate changes due in Oct 2002; see p83

(which are gradually being renovated), and jumbled streets. You will love Mytilini if you enjoy seeking out traditional kafeneia and little backstreet ouzeria, or if you take pleasure in wandering through unfamiliar towns. With a large university campus and a year-round population, Mytilini – unlike most island towns – is also lively in winter.

The northern end of Ermou, the town's main commercial thoroughfare, is a wonderful ramshackle street full of character. It has old-fashioned zaharoplasteia, grocers, fruit and vegetable stores, bakers, and antique, embroidery, ceramic and jewellery shops.

Orientation

Mytilini is built around two harbours (north and south) which occupy both sides of a promontory and are linked by the main thoroughfare of Ermou. East of the harbours is a large fortress surrounded by a pine forest. All passenger ferries dock at the southern harbour. The waterfront here is called Kountourioti and the ferry quay is at its southern end. The northern harbour's waterfront is called Navmahias Ellis.

Information

The tourist police (☎ 2251 022 776) have an office at the entrance to the quay. The EOT (☎ 2251 042 511), 6 Aristarhou, is open 8am to 2.30pm Sunday to Friday and can help with information about the entire island.

Banks, including the National Bank of Greece with an ATM, can be found on Kountourioti. There is also an ATM and an exchange machine at the Commercial Bank booth on this street, near the ferry terminal. The post office is on Vournazon, west of the southern harbour. The OTE is on the same street just west of the post office.

Sfetoudi Bookshop (☎ 2251 022 287), Ermou 51, sells good maps, postcards and books on Lesvos. Look for *The Sacred Water: the Mineral Springs of Lesvos* and *39 Coffee Houses and a Barber's Shop*, both beautifully produced books of photos by Jelly Hadjidimitriou.

You can find more information on Mytilini, and Lesvos in general, on the Internet at ⓦ www.greeknet.com.

Things to See & Do

Mytilini's imposing **castle** *(adult/student €1.50/1; open 8.30am-3pm)* was built in early Byzantine times, renovated in the 14th century by Fragistco Gatelouzo, and subsequently enlarged by the Turks. The surrounding pine forest is a pleasant place for a picnic.

One block north of the quay and housed in a neoclassical mansion is the **archaeological museum** *(☎ 2251 022 087; admission €1.50 both museums; open 8.30am-3pm Tues-Sun)*. It has a large array of impressive finds from Neolithic to Roman times. It's a fascinating collection, with interesting ceramic figurines, including some somersaulting women, and gold jewellery. There are excellent notes in Greek and English. There is also a **new archaeological museum** *(8 Noemvriou; open 8am-7pm)*, 400m away, with impressive displays, including spectacular mosaics – whole housefuls – laid out under glass so that you can walk over them. Admission is included in the ticket for the other archaeological museum.

The dome of the **Church of Agios Therapon** can be spotted from almost anywhere on the southern waterfront. The church has a highly ornate interior with a huge chandelier, an intricately carved iconostasis and priest's throne, and a frescoed dome. The **Byzantine Museum** *(☎ 2251 028 916; admission €1; open 10am-1pm Mon-Sat)* in the church's courtyard houses some fine icons.

Whatever you do, don't miss the **Theophilos Museum** *(☎ 2251 041 644; admission €1.50; open 9am-2.30pm & 6pm-8pm Tues-Sun May-Sept, 9am-1pm & 4pm-6pm Tues-Sun Oct & Apr, 9am-2pm Tues-Sun Nov-Mar)*. It houses the works of the prolific primitive painter Theophilos, who was born on Lesvos. Several prestigious museums and galleries around the country now proudly display his works. However, he lived in abject poverty, painting the walls of kafeneia and tavernas in return for sustenance.

Next door, commemorating the artist and critic Stratis Eleftheriadis (he Gallicised his name to Teriade) who was born on Lesvos but lived and worked in Paris, is the **Teriade Museum** *(☎ 2251 023 372; admission*

€1.50; open 9am-8pm Tues-Sun). It was largely due to Teriade's efforts that Theophilos' work gained international renown. On display are reproductions of Teriade's own illustrations and his collection of works by 20th-century artists, including such greats as Picasso, Chagall and Matisse.

These museums are 4km from Mytilini in the village of **Varia**, where Theophilos was born. Take a local bus from the bus station at the northernmost section of Kountourioti.

Loutra Yera (Admission €1.50; open 7am-8pm daily), 5km west of Mytilini on the Gulf of Yera, is worth a visit if you're interested in hot springs. The cool white marble interior is steamy and dreamy.

Places to Stay – Budget

Most of these domatia are in little side streets off Ermou, near the northern harbour.

Pension Iren (☎ 2251 022 787, Komninaki 41) Doubles/triples with breakfast €25/30. This place has the nearest domatia to the quay. It has clean and simply furnished rooms. Komninaki is one block behind the eastern section of Kountourioti.

Salina's Garden (☎ 2251 042 073, Fokeas 7 & Kinikiou 1) Singles/doubles €21/22. These cosy and clean rooms are in a delightful garden, and guests can use the lovely kitchen to prepare their own meals. The rooms are signposted from the corner of Ermou and Adramytiou.

Pension Thalia (☎ 2251 024 640, Kinikiou 1) Doubles/triples with bathroom €23.50/26.50. Coming from Ermou, if you turn right opposite Salina's rooms you will reach these clean, bright rooms in a large family house.

Vetsika Domatia (☎ 2251 024 968, Tsertseti 1) Singles/doubles €18/23.50. These rooms in an old neoclassical house near the castle are nothing fancy but they are clean and quiet.

Pelagia Koumiotou Rooms (☎ 2251 020 643, Tsertseti 6) Doubles/triples €21/26.50. These rooms near the castle are quite nice and the owner is very friendly. Walk along Mikras Asias and turn left into Tsertseti; the rooms are on the right.

Places to Stay – Mid-Range

There are several hotels on the southern waterfront.

Hotel Lesvion (☎ 2251 022 037, fax 2251 042 493, Kountourioti 27a) Singles/doubles with TV & phone €29.50/51.50. This hotel is on the west side of the harbour. The rooms are a bit scruffy but they're passable. Better rates can usually be negotiated.

Hotel Sappho (☎ 2251 022 888, fax 2251 024 522, Kountourioti 31) Singles/doubles €32.50/53. This place is just two doors away from Hotel Lesvion.

Places to Eat

You will eat well on Lesvos whether you enjoy fish dishes, traditional Greek food, international cuisine or vegetarian meals. You might wish to avoid the restaurants on the western section of the southern waterfront where the waiters tout for customers. These restaurants are atypical of Mytilini as they pander to tourists and serve bland, overpriced food.

Restaurant Averof (☎ 2251 022 180, Ermou 52 & Prokymaia) Mains around €3.50. This place, in the middle of the southern waterfront, is a no-nonsense traditional restaurant serving hearty Greek staples like patsas (tripe soup). Despite its earthy cuisine it has a classy romantic ambience and excellent service.

Kalderimi (☎ 2251 046 577, Thasou 3) Appetisers €1.50-3, mains around €6. Closer to the main harbour, locals congregate at this little ouzeri with tables that spill out into the street. The food is very good – in contrast to the service, which is indifferent.

Ermis Ouzeri (☎ 2251 026 232, Kornarou 2) Mezedes-style meal with beer around €9. This small, mildly ramshackle, but delightfully atmospheric ouzeri has yet to be discovered by the mass tourist crowd. It is at the north end of Ermou on the corner with Kornarou. Its interior is decorated with scattered antiques, old watercolour paintings and old black and white photos of previous clients.

I Psatha (☎ 2251 045 922, on Hrysostomou) Open evenings only. Mains €4.50. If you want some good-value meat dishes such as souvlaki, check out this place off Ermou. There is an old jukebox that actually works.

Stratos Psarotaverna (☎ *2251 021 739, Hristougennon 1944*) Mains around €7.50. Head to this place at the bottom end of the main harbour for top-quality fish dishes. Tables from all the surrounding restaurants take over the road in summer.

Lemoni kai Prasino Piperi (☎ *2251 024 014, Cnr Koundouroti & Hristougennon*) Mains €6-12. If you're looking for a change, check out this classy Italian-Mediterranean place overlooking the harbour. It's upstairs, above a souvlaki joint.

Aspros Gatos (☎ *2251 061 670*) Mains €5.50-13.50. In Neapolis Mytilinis, towards the airport, is this great steak house with a Greek-Mediterranean menu. Most of the recipes are traditional Greek, but some Asian ingredients are also used. It's in a big garden and there's a kids' playground on site.

Entertainment
Mousiko Kafenio (*Cnr Mitropoleos & Vernardaki*) Open 7.30am-2am. This is a hip place – arty without being pretentious. Drinks are mid-price range rather than cheap, but worth it for the terrific atmosphere.

The Lazy Fish (☎ *2251 044 831, Imvrou 5*) Open Sept-July. For good beer and a nibble try this establishment, which is especially cosy and popular in the winter. It's set back from the southern end of Komninaki and is a bit difficult to find – look for a stone building with black wrought-iron wall lamps at the entrance.

Hot Spot On the east side of the harbour, this joint is known for its good music, and you can borrow board games here. It's a nice place to be at sunset.

To Navagio (☎ *2251 021 310, Arhipelagos 23*) This upmarket yet casual place in the centre of the waterfront serves a good variety of alcoholic beverages as well as fresh juices, hearty breakfasts and great coffee.

Getting To/From Mytilini
Mytilini has two bus stations: the one for long-distance buses is just beyond the south-western end of Kountourioti; the bus station for buses to local villages is on the northernmost section of Kountourioti. For motorists, there is a large free parking area just south of the main harbour.

NORTHERN LESVOS
Northern Lesvos is dominated economically and physically by the exquisitely preserved traditional town of Mithymna, a town of historical, and modern, importance in Lesvos' commercial life. The neighbouring beach resort of Petra, 6km south, receives low-key package tourism, and the villages surrounding Mt Lepetymnos are authentic, picturesque and worth a day or two of exploration. Sykaminia, Mantamados and Agia Paraskevi in particular, are very pretty. Moni Taxiarhon, near Mantamados, is also worth a visit. Skala Sykaminias is a nice beach.

Mithymna Μήθυμνα
postcode 811 08 • pop 1333
Although this town has officially reverted to its ancient name of Mithymna (Methymna), most locals still refer to it as **Molyvos**. It is 62km from Mytilini and is the principal town of northern Lesvos. The one-time rival to Mytilini, picturesque Mithymna is nowadays the antithesis of the island capital. Its impeccable stone houses with brightly coloured shutters reach down to the harbour from a castle-crowned hill. Its two main thoroughfares of Kastrou and 17 Noemvriou are winding, cobbled and shaded by vines. In contrast to Mytilini, Mithymna's pretty streets are lined with souvenir shops.

Orientation & Information From the bus stop, walk straight ahead towards the town. Where the road forks, take the right fork into 17 Noemvriou. At the top of the hill, the road forks again; the right fork is Kastrou and the post office is along here on the left. The left fork is a continuation of 17 Noemvriou.

There is a small municipal tourist office (☎ 2253 071 347), on the left, between the bus stop and the fork in the road. The National Bank of Greece is on the left, next to the tourist office and has an ATM. There is also a Commercial Bank booth with an ATM directly opposite.

A Balm for the Soul

Lesvos has many mineral springs, most dating back to ancient times. The baths are usually housed in old whitewashed buildings that look like sunken church domes. Small holes in the roof let in rays of sunlight, creating a magical dappled effect on the water. The pools are usually made of marble.

In times past, before houses had their own bathrooms, these communal baths were the place people came to bathe and talk.

With the exception of the ramshackle abandoned hot springs at Thermi (which are worth a visit, if you like faded grandeur), it's possible to take a dip at all of the baths. There are springs at Loutra Yera (near Mytilini) and Eftalou (near Mithymna) and two in the vicinity of Polyhnitos. The properties of the waters are outlined in the following text.

Loutra Yera

These springs are west of Mytilini, on the Gulf of Yera. It's thought that there was once a temple to Hera at this site, where ancient beauty pageants took place. The springs contain radium and are 39.7°C. They are recommended for infertility, rheumatism, arthritis, diabetes, bronchitis, gall stones, dropsy and more.

Polyhnitos

South-east of Polyhnitos, these springs are in a pretty, renovated Byzantine building. These are some of the hottest springs in all of Continental Europe, with a temperature of 87.6°C, and are recommended for rheumatism, arthritis, skin diseases and gynaecological problems.

Lisvorio

About 5km north of the Polyhnitos springs, these are just outside the little village of Lisvorio. There are two quaint little baths here, situated on either side of a stream, with pretty vegetation all around. At the time of writing these buildings were in disrepair, but it is thought they will be renovated soon. One of the baths is in reasonable condition and it's possible to have a soak. The temperature and the properties of the waters are similar to those at Polyhnitos.

Eftalou

These baths on the beach not far from Mithymna are idyllic. The bathhouse is an old whitewashed vault with a pebbled floor. The water is perfectly clear and is 46.5°C. These springs are recommended for rheumatism, arthritis, neuralgia, hypertension, gall stones and gynaecological and skin problems.

hings to See & Do One of the most easant things to do in Mithymna is to stroll ong its gorgeous streets. If you have the energy, the ruined 14th-century **Genoese cas-** e (☎ 2253 071 803; admission €1.50; open ues-Sun 8am-7pm) is worth clambering up for fine views of the coastline and over the a to Turkey. From this castle in the 15th ntury, Onetta d'Oria, wife of the Genoese vernor, repulsed an onslaught by the Turks putting on her husband's armour and ading the people of Mithymna into battle. summer the castle is the venue for a drama stival; ask for details at the tourist office.

The beach at Mithymna is pebbled and crowded, but in summer **excursion boats** leave at 10.30am daily for the superior beaches of Eftalou, Skala Sykaminias and Petra. Trips cost around €16 and up, depending on the itinerary; sunset cruises and boat 'safaris' are also available. Contact Faonas Travel (☎ 2253 071 630, e tekes@otenet.gr), down at the port, for more information.

Eftalou's **hot spring** (☎ 2253 071 245; admission €2.50; open 8am-1pm & 3pm-8pm) is an entrancing place right on the beach – don't miss it.

Phone numbers listed incorporate changes due in Oct 2002; see p83

Places to Stay – Budget *Camping Mithymna* (☎ 2253 071 169) Adult/tent €3/2. Open early June. This excellent and refreshingly shady camping ground is 1.5km from town and signposted from near the tourist office. Although it opens in early June, you can usually camp if you arrive a bit earlier than that.

There are over 50 official domatia in Mithymna; most consist of only one or two rooms. All display domatia signs and most are of a high standard. The municipal tourist office will help you if you can't be bothered looking; otherwise, the best street to start at is 17 Noemvriou.

Nassos Guest House (☎ 2253 071 022, *Arionos*) Rooms about €23.50. Among the first signposted rooms you will come to are those in this old Turkish house run by the lovely Betty Katsaris. Arionos leads off 17 Noemvriou to the right. The rooms are simply furnished and most have a panoramic view. Stop by Betty's restaurant (see Places to Eat) if there's no-one at the rooms.

Myrsina Baliaka Domatia (☎ 2253 071 414, *Myrasillou*) Doubles around €26.50. A beautifully restored stone building houses these domatia. From the bus stop walk towards the town and take the second right by the cardphone. The domatia are 50m on your right. Look out for the prominent green shutters.

Molyvos Hotel I (☎ 2253 071 556, fax 2253 071 640) Doubles with bath & phone €32.50. This pleasant hotel has spacious clean rooms and friendly staff. There's a lovely terrace overlooking the water, and they serve a good breakfast. It's down there near the beach.

Places to Stay – Mid-Range *Amfitriti Hotel* (☎ 2253 071 741, fax 2253 071 744) Singles/doubles with breakfast €38.50/62. This very lux-looking place is down near the water and the old olive press, not far from the town beach and its cluster of bars. There's a lovely swimming pool and the hotel itself is quite classy.

Hotel Olive Press (☎ 2253 071 205, fax 2253 071 647) Singles/doubles with bath, phone, fridge & air-con €54.50/79.50. This

converted olive-oil factory on the beach i often full, but call ahead and you might b in luck.

Hotel Sea Horse (☎ 2253 071 630, fa 2253 071 374, [e] *tekes@otenet.gr*) Double €73.50. Down at the fishing harbour, th hotel has bright breezy rooms with balcon and all mod-cons.

Hotel Eftalou (☎ 2253 071 584, fax 225 071 669, [e] *parmakel@otenet.gr*) Double €59. This pleasant C-class hotel with con fortable rooms is among the cluster small, low-key resort hotels on the road o to Eftalou. There's a swimming pool and restaurant.

Hotel Delfinia (☎ 2253 071 315, fax 225 071 524, [e] *delfinia@otenet.gr*) Single doubles with sea view & breakfast €55.5 73.50. This older but superior hotel cate mainly to packages, but is very accomme dating to independent travellers. It's a kil metre out of Mithymna on the road to Petr

Places to Eat The streets 17 Noemvrio and Kastrou have a wide range of restau ants serving typical Greek fare.

Betty's (☎ 2253 071 421, 17 Noemvrio Mains around €5. If you're looking for lovely atmosphere try this place which o cupies an old bordello. Good grills a home-cooked meals such as pastitsio a mousakas are the specialities. The elega rooms upstairs provide a view of the wat from on high. To get there, take the downh fork after passing uphill through the tunne

O Gatos (☎ 2253 071 661, 17 Noe vriou) Mains around €5. With a sleepi cat on its doorstep, this little place has classy feel and a great view from its gia balcony. Heading uphill, it's on the left you come out of the tunnel.

Captain's Table (☎ 2253 071 241) A petisers €2-6, mains €5-10. For more o fishing-village ambience, head down to far end of the little harbour where there i clutch of restaurants, the best of which this Australian-Greek place. The mezed are exquisite: try *adjuka* – a Ukrainia inspired spicy aubergine dish – or the uniq spinach salad. There is live bouzouki mu once a week.

Taverna tou Ilia (☎ 2253 071 536) Mains around €4.50. For a change of scenery and a meal with a view, head up to this taverna at Vafios, 8km inland from Mithymna. The food is top-notch. *Pikilia* (a plate of mixed appetisers) costs around €4 per person, while lamb dishes are around €5. All of the meat is local and the food is very traditional.

Petra Πέτρα
postcode 811 09 • pop 1150

Petra, 5km south of Mithymna, is a popular coastal resort with a long sandy beach shaded by tamarisk trees. Despite tourist development it remains an attractive village retaining some traditional houses. Petra means 'rock', and looming over the village is an enormous, almost perpendicular rock which looks as if it's been lifted from Meteora in Thessaly. The rock is crowned by the 18th-century **Panagia Glykophilousa** (Church of the Sweet Kissing Virgin). You can reach it by climbing the 114 rock-hewn steps – worth it for the view. Petra, like many settlements on Lesvos, is a 'preserved' village. It has not and will not make any concessions to the concrete monstrosities that characterise tourist development elsewhere in Greece. The nearby village of Petri, to the east, has some nice old kafeneia and provides an excellent vantage point from which you can survey Petra and its surrounding landscape.

Petra has a post office, OTE, bank, medical facilities and bus connections. There's also an interesting refurbished Turkish mansion known as **Vareltzidaina's House** (*admission free; open 8am-7pm Tues-Sun*) between the rock and the waterfront, it can be difficult to find, but the locals can point you in the right direction.

Places to Stay *Women's Agricultural Tourism Collective* (☎ 2253 041 238, fax 2253 041 309) Singles/doubles around €15/21. There are about 120 private rooms available in Petra, but your best bet for accommodation is to head straight for this women's collective, Greece's first. The women can arrange for you to stay with a family in the village. The office is on the central square, upstairs in the restaurant

above Cantina; enter from the street behind the waterfront.

Studio Niki (☎ 2253 041 601) Doubles with kitchenette around €29.50. Of the cluster of small pensions at the western end of Petra's waterfront, this place with tidy rooms is a good bet. Book well in advance for peak season.

Places to Eat *Syneterismos* (☎ 2253 041 238, fax 2253 041 309) Mains €4. This very popular and friendly place, belonging to the Women's Agricultural Tourism Collective, has mouth-watering mousakas and Greek salad. It's upstairs on the waterfront square, above Cantina; enter from the street running one block behind the waterfront.

To Tyhero Petalo (☎ 2253 041 755) Mains around €5. This taverna, towards the eastern end of the waterfront, has attractive decor and sells ready-made food.

O Rigas (☎ 2253 041 405) Mains around €4.50. Open 7pm. For something very authentic, head up to the old village to this wisteria-swathed taverna, which is the oldest in Petra. It has a very laid-back feel and the music is excellent. To get there walk uphill around the rock and keep going straight ahead for about 500m.

WESTERN LESVOS

Western Lesvos is different from the rest of the island and this becomes apparent almost immediately as you wind westward out of Kalloni. The landscape becomes drier and barer and there are fewer settlements, though they look very tidy and their red-tiled roofs add vital colour to an otherwise mottled green-brown landscape. The far western end is almost devoid of trees other than the petrified kind. Here you will find Lesvos' 'petrified forest' on a windswept and barren hillside. One resort, a remote fishing village, and the birthplace of Sappho are what attract people to western Lesvos.

Eresos & Skala Eresou
Ερεσός & Σκάλα Ερεσού
postcode 881 05 • pop 1560

Eresos, 90km from Mytilini, is a traditional inland village. It is reached via the road

Sappho

Sappho is renowned chiefly for her poems that speak out in favour of lesbian relationships, though her range of lyric poetry extends beyond works of an erotic nature. She was born around 630 BC in the town of Eresos on the western side of Lesvos. Little is known about her private life other than that she was married, had a daughter and was exiled to Sicily in about 600 BC. Only fragments remain of her nine books of poems, the most famous of which are the marriage songs. Among her works were hymns, mythological poems and personal love songs. Most of these seem to have been addressed to a close inner-circle of female companions. Sappho uses sensuous images of nature to create her own special brand of erotic lyric poetry. It is a simple yet melodious style, later copied by the Roman poet Catullus.

Lesvos, and Eresos in particular, is today visited by many lesbians paying homage to Sappho.

MARTIN HARRIS

junction just after the hillside village of Andissa. The road leading down to Eresos, through what looks like a moonscape, belies what is ahead. Beyond the village of Eresos a riotously fertile agricultural plain leads to Eresos' beach annexe, Skala Eresou, which is 4km beyond on the west coast. It is a popular resort linked to Eresos by an attractive, very straight tree-lined road. A new sealed road links Eresos with Kalloni via Parakila and Agra.

Skala Eresou is built over ancient Eresos, where Sappho (c630–568 BC) was born. Although it gets crowded in summer it has a good, laid-back atmosphere. It is also a popular destination for lesbians who come on a kind of pilgrimage in honour of the poet. If you're a beach-lover you should certainly visit – there is almost 2km of coarse silvery-brown sand.

Orientation & Information From the bus turnaround at Skala Eresou, walk towards the sea to reach the central square of Plateia Anthis & Evristhenous abutting the waterfront. The beach stretches to the left and right of this square. Turn right at the square onto Gyrinnis and just under 50m along you will come to a sign pointing left to the post office; the OTE is next door.

Krinellos Travel (☎ 2253 053 246, 2253 053 982, e krinellos@otenet.gr), close to the main square, is helpful. They arrange accommodation, car, motorcycle and bicycle hire and treks on foot or on horses and donkeys. Neither Skala Eresou nor Eresos has a bank.

Things to See Eresos' archaeological museum (admission free; open 8.30am-3pm Tues-Sun) houses archaic, classical Greek and Roman finds including statues, coins and grave stelae. The museum, in the centre of Skala Eresou, stands near the remains of the early Christian Basilica of Agios Andreas.

The **Petrified Forest** (☎ 2253 054 434, admission €1.50, open 8am-4pm daily), as the EOT hyperbolically refers to this scattering of ancient tree stumps, is near the village of Sigri, on the west coast north of Skala Eresou. Experts reckon the petrified wood is at least 500,000, but possibly 20 million, years old. If you're intrigued, the forest is easiest reached as an excursion from Skala Eresou; inquire at travel agencies. If you're making your own way, the turn-off to the forest is signposted 7km before the village of Sigri.

Sigri itself is a beautiful, peaceful fishing port with a delicious edge-of-the-world feeling. In Sigri, the **Natural History Museum of the Lesvos Petrified Forest** (☎ 2253 054 434, admission €1.50, open 8am-9pm daily) is a very swish place with background information on the forest, and, of course, a few tree stumps.

Places to Stay There are a few domatia in Eresos but most people head for Skala Eresou, where there are a number of domatia, pensions and hotels.

Pete Metaxas Studios (☎ 2253 053 506) Singles/doubles €21/23.50. These small studios are at the north-west end of the waterfront, one block back from the beach.

Sappho Hotel (☎ 2253 053 233, fax 2253 053 174) Singles/doubles with breakfast & sea view €26.50/48.50; doubles without view €41. This C-class property is a small women-only hotel on the waterfront. It can be noisy here, though.

Hotel Galini (☎ 2253 053 137/174, fax 2253 053 155) Doubles with bathroom €48. This C-class property has small but airy rooms with private balcony. It is clearly signposted.

Places to Eat The shady promenade offers many eating options, most with beach and sea views across to Chios and Psara.

Gorgona (☎ 2253 053 320) Appetisers €2-4, mains €4.50-6. Gorgona, with its stone-clad facade, is as good a place to start as any. It's at the south-eastern end of the promenade.

Soulatso (☎ 2253 052 078) Appetisers & salads around €2, mains around €4.50. Fresh fish (from €4.50) and a nice array of appetisers (including a decent ladotyri) are served at this place in the middle of the waterfront.

Margaritatari (☎ 2253 053 042) For a good breakfast or afternoon tea, head to this waterfront cafe to sample scrumptious Austrian pastries, including apple strudel (€5.50).

Popular watering holes include *Tenth Muse*, on the square, which is a favourite lesbian bar; *Parasol*, on the waterfront, with funky tropical feel and exotic cocktails; and *Notorious*, at the far south-eastern end of the promenade, in an isolated, romantic spot overlooking the water.

SOUTHERN LESVOS

Southern Lesvos is dominated by Mt Olympus (968m). Pine forests and olive groves decorate its flanks.

Fascinating Fossil Find

Lesvos is hardly the kind of place that you would associate with great excitement in the musty and dusty world of palaeontology. Nonetheless, the island has been thrust onto centre stage recently with the extraordinary discovery of fossils of animals, fish and plants at Vatera, a sleepy beach resort located on the south coast of Lesvos, hitherto more associated with sun and sand than fossilised fish.

Among the fossils found in the Vatera region are elephants, mastodons, giraffes, bones of rhinoceros and hippopotamus, deer, tortoises, snails, fish, and pieces of a gigantic prehistoric horse. Dated up to 5.5 million years old, the fossils are being temporarily displayed at the Museum of Natural History in the neighbouring village of Vrisa, just 2km from the excavation sites.

The large village of **Agiasos** on the northern flank of Mt Olympus features prominently in local tourist publications and is a popular day-trip destination. Agiasos is picturesque but not tacky, with artisan workshops making everything from handcrafted furniture to pottery. Its winding, cobbled streets lead you to the church of the Panagia Vrefokratousa with its Byzantine Museum and Popular Museum in the courtyard.

Plomari on the south coast is a pleasant, crumbling resort town. A large, traditional village, it also has a laid-back beach settlement. Most people stay at **Agios Isidoros**, 3km to the east where there is a narrow, overcrowded beach. **Tarti**, east of Agios Isidoros, is a much nicer beach. On the other side of Plomari, **Melinda** is a very pretty, serene fishing village with a beach. There are three tavernas in Melinda, all offering rooms and cheap hearty food.

About one hour's walk from Melinda, west along the coast, the **Panagia Krifti** is a little church built in a cave near a hot spring.

Low-key, though slightly desolate, family resort of **Vatera** is over to the east and reached via the inland town of **Polyhnitos**.

Olive Trails

In the vicinity of Plomari, the old paths that link the hill villages are being restored and it's now possible to spend anywhere from an afternoon to a few days exploring this pretty region on foot. Local clubs have been clearing the paths since 1997 and a government program has been sponsoring their efforts since 2000. The preservation of the paths is an ongoing project, and volunteers are welcome.

All walks traverse olive groves with old *setia* (dry-walled terraces) and *damia* (small one-storey stone houses). You'll also pass through lush dells filled with old oaks, wild pears and pistachios, plane trees, pink hollyhocks and other wildflowers, and herbs, as well as higher, drier forests of pine and juniper. There are startling views down to the sea. Along the way there are many springs, rivers and streams as well as old mills and olive presses. In general, it's best to walk these paths in spring or autumn. The trails are clearly signposted, and there are maps in villages and at the airport.

The major routes are as follows:

Melinda-Paleohori
Distance: 1.2km. Duration: 30 minutes. This trail starts at the fishing village of Melinda and follows the Selandas river for 200m. It ascends to the living village of Paleohori, passing a spring with potable water along the way. The trail ends at one of the village's two olive presses, where there is now a museum.

Paleohori-Rahidi
Distance: 1km. Duration: 30 minutes. The path here is 2m to 4m wide and paved with white stone. It ascends to Rahidi, which used to be the summer residence of the villagers from Paleohori. There are two springs along the way, and vineyards. There are about 40 nice old houses in Rahidi and a kafeneio that opens in summer. Rahidi, which now has a population of about five, first received electricity in 2001. There are stunning views from here. If you like, you can continue to Agios Ioannis along the same path.

Melinda-Kournela
Distance: 1.8km. Duration: 40 minutes. An old stone path climbs from the beach at Melinda to Kournela, a village of about 50 houses, with a current population of three to four people. There are big shady plane trees, a triple-spouted fountain where people used to wash clothes, and an old steam-driven olive mill. There are good views across to Paleiohori and Rahidi.

Kournela-Milos
Distance: 800m. Duration: 20 minutes. This trail descends to Milos, where there's an old flour mill. The village is at a crossroads, with paths leading to Paleohori, Melinda, Kournela and Megalohori.

Melinda-Milos
Distance: 2km. Duration: 1 hour. This level trail follows the Selandas River and passes a few houses, some ruined olive mills, one spring and two bridges. There is some unusual vegetation, including orange and mandarin trees. It's a shady trail, good for summer.

Milos-Amaxo
Distance: 1.75km. Duration: 1 hour. This very level trail follows the Melinda River, through vineyards and plane, poplar and pine forests. There are springs and fountains with good drinking water

In Polyhnitos there are **hot springs** (see Activities) and a **folk museum** (☎ 2253 041 007; open 10am-1pm Tues-Sun). There is a small **museum of natural history** (*admission €1; open 9am-3pm*) at Vrisa, between Polyhnitos and Vatera.

Activities

There are many opportunities for **walkin** on old olive trails in the hills above Ploma (see the boxed text 'Olive Trails'). You ca go **horse-riding** (€15/hr) on the trails; co tact Kostas Moukas (mobile ☎ 69 3244 751

Olive Trails

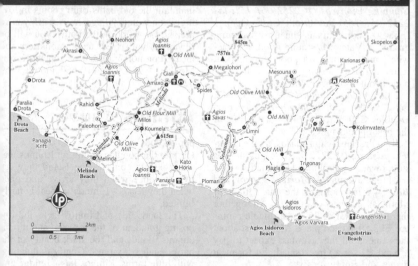

along the way. Nice wooden bridges made of chestnut cross the river. It's possible to start this walk from Amaxo, after driving from Plomari. If you're a good rider, you can mountain bike all the way from Amaxo down to Melinda.

Amaxo-Giali-Spides
Distance: 1.5km. Duration: 45 minutes. This trail follows a dirt road for about 500m to Giali, then ascends to Spides on a path. Halfway between Amaxo and Giali there's a little church with a picnic table that makes a nice spot for lunch.

Skopelos-Karionas-Kastelos-Trigonas/Plagia
Distance: 8km. Duration: 3 hours. This route follows a dirt road from Skopelos to Karionas, but there are cobbled paths the rest of the way. At the ruined castle known as Kastelos, there's now a small church. It's possible to take a detour to the village of Milies, where there is a fountain and some nice old houses. A path from Milies continues to Kolimvatera.

Plomari-Mesouna
Distance: 6km. Duration: 3 hours. The trail follows the Sedoundas River past many old houses. There's an olive processing plant in the village of Limni and about 4km upriver there's an old watermill that used to crush olives.

or details. Good-quality **mountain bikes** an be rented from Kostas for €23.50 a day.

A visit to the Polyhnitos **hot springs** ☎ 2252 041 449, fax 2252 042 678; open 7am-10am & 4pm-6pm daily), where there's a renovated bathhouse that dates from the

Byzantine period, is worthwhile. There are also hot springs at Lisvorio, clearly signposted from the village. The facilities near the spring are currently undergoing repair, but the old caretaker will let you have a soak if he's there.

Phone numbers listed incorporate changes due in Oct 2002; see p83

Places to Stay & Eat

Camping Dionysos (☎ *2252 061 151, fax 2252 061 155*) Adult/tent €6/6. Open 1 June-30 Sept. This is the only camping ground at Vatera. It's quite good, if somewhat small, and has a pool, minimarket, restaurant and cooking facilities. It is set back about 100m from the beach.

Hotel Vatera Beach (☎ *2252 061 212, fax 2252 061 164,* ⓔ *hovatera@otenet.gr*) Doubles €59. This C-class hotel is one of the best options in Vatera.

If you're hungry in Agiasos, try the nameless *psistaria* (☎ *2252 022 236*), by the bus stop, owned by Prokopis Douladellis.

Three tavernas – *Maries*, *Psaros* and *Bill's* – offer rooms in the cute village of Melinda, just west of Plomari. All together there are a total of 35 beds; double rooms are €23.50 at each place. Meals cost about the same at all the tavernas; expect to pay around €1 for a Greek salad, €4 for meat dishes and €6-12 for fish.

In Milies, near Plomari, the people who maintain the old paths offer rooms in lovingly renovated village houses. If you're prepared to work on the paths, you will be rewarded with free accommodation and meals. For more information contact Kostas Moukas (☎ 2252 032 719/660, mobile ☎ 69 3244 7517).

Limnos Λήμνος

pop 16,000

Despite the popular saying on Limnos that when people come to the island they cry twice – once when they arrive and once when they leave – Limnos' appeal is fairly limited.

The landscape of Limnos lacks the imposing grandeur of the forested and mountainous islands and the stark beauty of the barren and rocky ones. Gently undulating with little farms, Limnos has a unique and

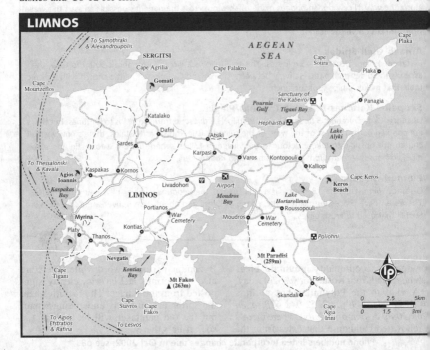

LIMNOS

Old Venetian Quarter, Hania

Peeling blue, Kasos island

Arched doorway of the Ahmed Hasuf Turkish Library, Rhodes

Santorini island sporting bright colours

Kastellorizo island

A long way down! Fira, the town on the lip of the caldera – Santorini (Thira) island, Cyclades

A typical stairway on the crater side of Fira

The sun sets over a church dome – Santorini.

understated appeal. In spring vibrant wild flowers dot the landscape, and in autumn purple crocuses sprout forth in profusion. Large numbers of flamingoes grace the lakes of eastern Limnos and the coastline boasts some fine beaches. The island is sufficiently off the beaten track to have escaped the adverse effects of mass tourism.

History

Limnos' position near the Straits of the Dardanelles, midway between the Mt Athos Peninsula and Turkey, has given it a traumatic history. To this day it maintains a large garrison, and jets from the huge air base loudly punctuate the daily routine.

Limnos had advanced Neolithic and Bronze Age civilisations, and during these times had contact with peoples in western Anatolia, including the Trojans. In classical times the twin sea gods, the Kabeiroi, were worshipped at a sanctuary on the island, but later the Sanctuary of the Great Gods on Samothraki became the centre of this cult.

During the Peloponnesian Wars, Limnos sided with Athens and suffered many Persian attacks. After the split of the Roman Empire in AD 395 it became an important outpost of Byzantium. In 1462 it came under the domination of the Genoese who ruled Lesvos. The Turks succeeded in conquering the island in 1478 and Limnos remained under Turkish rule until 1912. Moudros Bay was the Allies' base for the disastrous Gallipoli campaign in WWI.

Getting To/From Limnos

Air In summer there are two to three flights daily to Limnos from Athens (€55.50), six weekly from Thessaloniki (€56) and four flights weekly to Lesvos (€48.50). The Olympic Airways office (☎ 2254 022 214) is on Nikolaou Garoufallidou, opposite Hotel Paris, in Myrina.

The airport is 22km east of Myrina. An Olympic Airways bus from Myrina to the airport (€3) connects with all flights. Alternatively, a taxi will cost you about €12.

Ferry In summer four ferries weekly go from Limnos to Kavala (4-5 hours, €9.70)

and to Rafina (10 hours, €17) via Agios Efstratios (1½ hours, €5). In high season there is usually one boat per week to Sigri in Lesvos (six hours, €13.50). There are also three boats weekly to Chios (11 hours, €16) and Piraeus (13 hours, €21) via Lesvos, and one or two to Piraeus directly. There are two boats weekly to Thessaloniki (seven hours, €16.50) and one to two to Alexandroupolis (five hours, €12) via Samothraki (three hours, €7.50).

In addition, *Aiolis*, a small local ferry, does the run to Agios Efstratios (2½ hours, €5) three times weekly. Tickets can be bought at Myrina Tourist & Travel Agency (☎ 2254 022 460, fax 2254 023 560, e root@mirina.lim.forthnet.gr) on the harbourfront in Myrina.

Hydrofoil In July and August there are around two hydrofoils weekly to and from Alexandroupolis (three hours, €23.50) via Samothraki (1½ hours, €15). The hydrofoil schedule is notoriously unreliable, so check with Myrina Tourist & Travel Agency (☎ 2254 022 460, fax 2254 023 560, e root@mirina.lim.forthnet.gr) for the latest version.

Excursion Boat Every Sunday in July and August *Aiolis* does a roundtrip to the small island of Agios Efstratios (see Agios Efstratios, later in the chapter). The boat usually leaves at about 8am and returns from Agios Efstratios at 5pm.

Getting Around Limnos

Bus Bus services on Limnos are poor. In summer there are two buses daily from Myrina to most of the villages. Check the schedule (scribbled on a blackboard in Greek) at the bus station (☎ 2254 022 464) on Plateia Eleftheriou Venizelou.

Car & Motorcycle In Myrina, cars and jeeps can be rented from Myrina Rent a Car (☎ 2254 024 476, fax 2254 022 484) on Kyda near the waterfront. Prices range from €30 to €45 for a small car or jeep, depending on the season. There are several motorcycle-hire outlets on Kyda.

MYRINA Μύρινα
postcode 814 00 • pop 4340

Myrina is the capital and port of Limnos. Surrounded by massive hunks of volcanic rock, it is not immediately perceived as a picturesque town, but it is animated, full of character and unfettered by establishments pandering to tourism.

The main thoroughfare of Kyda is a charming paved street with clothing stores, traditional shops selling nuts and honey, old-fashioned kafeneia and barber shops – the latter are testimony to the island's military presence. Down the side streets you'll see (interspersed with modern buildings) little whitewashed stone dwellings, decaying neoclassical mansions and 19th-century wattle-and-daub houses with overhanging wooden balconies. A Genoese castle looms dramatically over the town.

Orientation & Information
From the end of the quay turn right onto Plateia Ilia Iliou. Continue along the waterfront passing the Hotel Lemnos and the town hall. A little farther along you will see the Hotel Aktaion, set back from the waterfront. Turn left here, then immediately veer half-left onto Kyda. Proceeding up here you will reach the central square where the National Bank of Greece and the OTE are located. The taxi rank (☎ 2254 023 033) is also on this square. Continue up Kyda and take the next turn right onto Nikolaou Garoufallidou. The post office is here on the right. Back on Kyda, continue for another 100m and you will come to Plateia Eleftheriou Venizelou where you will see the bus station.

There is a small tourist information kiosk on the quay. A laundrette (☎ 2254 024 392) is on Nikolaou Garoufallidou, opposite the Olympic Airways office. The police station (☎ 2254 022 201) is at the far end of Nikolaou Garoufallidou – on the right coming from Kyda. The port police (☎ 2254 022 225) are on the waterfront near the quay.

Things to See & Do
As with any Greek island castle, the one towering over Myrina is worth climbing up to. From its vantage point there are

magnificent views over the sea to Mt Athos. As you walk from the harbour, take the first side street to the left by an old Turkish fountain. An inconspicuous sign here points you to the castle.

Myrina has two decent sandy beaches right in town. The first, known as Romeïkos Gialos, stretches north from the castle and can be reached by walking along Kyda from the harbour, and taking any of the streets off to the left. The next one, separated by a small headland, is known as Riha Nera (shallow water), so named because of its gently shelving beach which is ideal for children.

In Myrina, and housed in a neoclassical mansion, is the archaeological museum (admission €1.50; open 8am-2.30pm Mon-Sat, 9am-2.30pm Sun & public holidays). Worth a visit, it contains finds from all the three sites on Limnos. The museum overlooks the beach, next to the Hotel Castor.

Organised Tours
Theodoros Petridis Travel Agency (☎ 2254 022 039, fax 2254 022 129) Tours €35.50 June-Sept. This travel agency organises round-the-island boat trips. They include stops for swimming and lunch.

Places to Stay – Budget
There is an information board with a map of the island and the names and telephone numbers of all domatia and hotels in Limnos on the harbourfront square. Budget accommodation is thin on the ground in Myrina.

Apollo Pavillion (☎/fax 2254 023 712, e apollo47@otenet.gr) Dorm beds €9 per person, double studios with/without air-con €50/44. This neoclassical place, with friendly English-speaking owners, has spacious and clean rooms with a variety of accommodation options. Book ahead in summer. Walk along Nikolaou Garoufallidou from Kyda and you will see the sign 150m along on the right.

Hotel Lemnos (☎ 2254 022 153, fax 2254 023 329) Doubles €50. This place on the harbourfront is about the cheapest hotel accommodation you will find. Most rooms have TV, phone, bath and balcony.

Places to Stay – Mid-Range & Top End

Blue Waters Hotel (☎ 2254 024 403, fax 2254 025 004, ⓔ bwkon@otenet.gr) Doubles €68. This clean and comfortable place on the beachfront at Romeïkos Gialos, north of the Kastro, has spacious rooms with aircon, phone, TV and fridge. It's the most centrally located of the mid-range options.

Hotel Filoktitis (☎/fax 2254 023 344, Ethnikis Antistaseos 14) Singles/doubles with balcony, TV & fridge €44/50. Above the restaurant of the same name, this pleasant hotel inland from Riha Nera has very friendly owners. The rooms are nice and big. To get there follow Maroulas (the continuation of Kyma) and take Ethnikis Antistaseos at the fork in the road, or head inland for a few blocks from the beach.

Arion Beach Apartments (☎ 2254 022 144, fax 2254 022 147) Doubles/triples €47/57.50. Thirty metres from the Riha Nera beach is this lovely homely place with friendly English-speaking owners. The rooms are huge with fridge, air-con and stove and have big balconies. To get there, take Seferi, the first street on your right as you walk over the hill to Riha Nera from Romeïkos Gialos. Look for the Arion's sign just a few doors up.

Diamantidis Hotel (☎ 2254 022 397, fax 2254 023 187) Singles/doubles with breakfast €59/94. This A-class property is one of the island's best hotels. Rooms are spacious and airy. The hotel is located inland from Myrina town on the main road.

Places to Eat

Restaurants are of a high standard on Limnos. Several fish restaurants line the waterfront.

Taverna Glaropoula (☎ 2254 024 069) Meal of small fish, salad & wine €12. Locals give top marks to this cosy little taverna with a nice harbourside location.

O Platanos Taverna (☎ 2254 022 070) Main course, salad & local wine around €10.50. Halfway along Kyda is this small, unassuming but very pleasant taverna, on the left as you walk from the waterfront. It is on a small square under a couple of huge plane trees and makes an attractive alternative to the waterfront establishments.

Filoktitis (☎ 2254 023 344, Ethnikis Antistaseos 14) Mains around €4. Open lunch & dinner. This exceedingly popular and jolly restaurant is 200m inland from Riha Nera beach. The food is excellent and less expensive than the harbourside joints. It offers a range of ready-made dishes, including a good pastitsio. To find it follow Maroulas (the continuation of Kyma) and take Ethnikis Antistaseos at the fork in the road, or head inland for a few blocks from the beach.

WESTERN LIMNOS

North of Myrina, turn left just past the little village of **Kaspakas** and a narrow road will lead you down to the beach at **Agios Ioannis**. The beach is pleasant enough, but Agios Ioannis consists of a few desultory fishing shacks, scattered beach houses and a couple of tavernas, one of which has its tables set out in the embrace of a large volcanic rock.

Inland from Kaspakas, the barren hilly landscape dotted with sheep and rocks (particularly on the road to Katalako via Sardes and Dafni) reminds you more of the English Peak District than an Aegean island. The villages themselves have little to cause you to pause and you will certainly be an object of curiosity if you do. There is a remote and completely undeveloped beach at Gomati on the north coast and it can be reached by a good dirt road from Katalako.

Heading 3km south from Myrina you will reach **Platy**. It's a fairly scrappy little resort, but the beach is okay.

Back on the beach road, if you continue past the Lemnos Village Resort Hotel, you will come to a sheltered sandy cove with an islet in the bay. The beach here is usually less crowded than Platy. **Thanos Beach** is the next bay around from Platy; it is also less crowded, and long and sandy. To get there, continue on the main road from Platy to the cute little village of Thanos, where a sign points to the beach. **Nevgatis**, the next bay along, is deserted but a trifle windy. Continuing along the coast road you'll come to the almost picturesque village of **Kontias**, marked by a row of old windmills.

CENTRAL LIMNOS

Central Limnos is flat and agricultural with wheat fields, small vineyards, and cattle and sheep farms. The island's huge air-force base is ominously surrounded by endless barbed-wire fences. The muddy and bleak Moudros Bay cuts deep into the interior, with **Moudros**, the second-largest town, positioned on the eastern side of the bay. Moudros does not offer much for the tourist other than a couple of small hotels with tavernas on the waterfront. The harbour has none of Myrina's picturesque qualities.

One kilometre out of Moudros on the road to Roussopouli, you will come across the **East Moudros Military Cemetery**, where Commonwealth soldiers from the Gallipoli campaign are buried. Limnos, with its large protected anchorage, was occupied by a force of Royal Marines on 23 February 1915 and was the principal base for this ill-fated campaign. A metal plaque, inside the gates, gives a short history of the Gallipoli campaign. A second Commonwealth cemetery, **Portianos War Cemetery**, is at Portianos, about 6km south of Livadohori on the trans-island highway. The cemetery is not as obvious as the Australian-style blue and white street sign with the name Anzac St. Follow Anzac St to the church and you will find the cemetery off a little lane behind the church.

EASTERN LIMNOS

Eastern Limnos has three archaeological sites *(admission free; all open 8am-7pm)*. The Italian School of Archaeologists has uncovered four ancient settlements at **Poliohni**, on the island's east coast. The most interesting was a sophisticated pre-Mycenaean city, which predated Troy VI (1800–1275 BC). The site is well laid-out and there are good descriptions in Greek, Italian and English. However, there is nothing too exciting to be seen; the site is probably of greater interest to archaeological buffs than casual visitors.

The second site is that of the **Sanctuary of the Kabeiroi** (Ta Kaviria) in north-eastern Limnos on the shores of remote Tigani Bay. This was originally a site for the worship of Kabeiroi gods predating those of Samothraki

(see Sanctuary of the Great Gods, under Samothraki, later in this chapter). There is little of the Sanctuary of Samothraki's splendour, but the layout of the site is obvious and excavations are still being carried out.

The major site, which has 11 columns, is that of a Hellenistic sanctuary. The older site is farther back and is still being excavated. Of additional interest is the cave of Philoctetes, the hero of the Trojan War, who was abandoned here while a gangrenous leg (a result of snakebite) healed. The sea cave can be reached by a path that leads down from the site. The cave can actually be entered by a hidden, narrow entrance (unmarked) to the left of the main entrance.

You can reach the sanctuary easily, if you have your own transport, via a fast road that was built for the expensive (and now white elephant) tourist enclave, Kaviria Palace. The turn-off is 5km to the left, after the village of **Kontopouli**. From Kontopouli you can make a detour to the third site, along a rough dirt track to **Hephaistia** (Ta Ifestia), once the most important city on the island. Hephaestus was the god of fire and metallurgy and, according to mythology, was thrown here from Mt Olympus by Zeus. The site is widely scattered over a scrub-covered, but otherwise desolate, small peninsula. There is not much to see of the ancient city other than low walls and a partially excavated theatre. Excavations are still under way.

The road to the northern tip of the island is worth exploring. There are some typical Limnian villages in the area and the often deserted beach at **Keros** is popular with windsurfers. Flocks of flamingoes can sometimes be seen on shallow **Lake Alyki**. From the cape at the north eastern tip of Limnos you can see the islands of Samothraki and Imvros (Gökçeada) in Turkey.

Agios Efstratios
Αγιος Ευστράτιος

postcode 815 00 • pop 290
The little-known island of Agios Efstratios, called locally Aï-Stratis, merits the title of

erhaps the most isolated island in the
Aegean. Stuck more or less plumb centre in
he North Aegean some distance from its
earest neighbour Limnos, it has few cars
nd fewer roads, but a steady trickle of cur-
ous foreign island-hoppers seeking to find
ome peace and quiet.

Large numbers of political exiles were
ent here for enforced peace and quiet be-
ore and after WWII. Among the exiled
uests were such luminaries as composer
Mikis Theodorakis and poets Kostas Var-
alis and Giannis Ritsos.

The little village of Aï-Stratis was once
icturesque, but in the early hours of the
morning of 21 February 1968 a violent
arthquake, with its epicentre in the seas
etween Limnos and Aï-Stratis, virtually
destroyed the vibrant village in one fell
woop. Many people emigrated as a result
nd there are now large numbers of is-
anders living in Australia and elsewhere.

Ham-fisted intervention by the then rul-
ng junta saw the demolition of most of the
emaining traditional homes and in their
lace, cheaply built concrete boxes were
rected to house the islanders. Needless to
ay, the islanders are still pretty miffed over
0 years after the event, and the remaining
illside ruins stand silent sentinel over a
ather lacklustre village today.

Still, if you yearn for serenity and traffic-
ree bliss, and enjoy walking, Aï-Stratis is a
reat place to visit. It has some fine beaches
- though most are only accessible by caique
- ample accommodation, simple island
ood and a surprisingly busy nightlife.

There is a post office, one cardphone and
ne metered phone for the public.

Getting To/From Agios Efstratios

Agios Efstratios is on the Kavala-Rafina
erry route, which includes Limnos. There
re two services weekly to Rafina (8½
ours, €15), six to Limnos (1½ hours, €5)
nd one per week to Alexandroupolis (6¾
ours, €13.50).

In addition, the small local ferry *Aiolis*
utters to and from Limnos three times a
veek on Monday, Wednesday and Friday.
On the off-days, during summer, *Aiolis*

does a more or less daily excursion run
from Limnos. But the harbour is exposed to
the west winds, causing ferry services to
often be cancelled or delayed.

Beaches

Apart from the reasonable village beach of
dark volcanic sand, the nearest beach worth
making the effort to visit is **Alonitsi** on the
north-east side of the island. It is a long, totally undeveloped, pristine strand and it can
be all yours if you are prepared to walk the
90 minutes to reach it. To get there take the
little track from the north-east side of the village, starting by a small bridge, and follow it
up towards the power pylons. Halfway along
the track splits; take the right track for
Alonitsi, or the left track for the **military
lookout** for great views. **Lidario**, a beach on
the west side can be reached – with difficulty
– on foot, but is better approached by sea, if
you can get someone to take you there.

Places to Stay & Eat

Accommodation options in Agios Efstratios are now pretty good. There is no hotel
on the island but there are currently about
100 beds available and you will always find
somewhere to stay unless you turn up at the
height of the summer season without a
reservation.

Xenonas Aï-Strati (☎ 2254 093 329)
Doubles €35.50. This spotless and airy
place is run by Julia and Odysseas Galan-
akis. The rooms are in one of the few buildings that survived the earthquake on the
north-eastern side of the village.

Malama Panera Domatia (☎ 2254 093
209) Doubles €35.50. These domatia, on
the south side of the village, are as equally
well appointed as Xenonas Aï-Strati.

There are also other unofficial *domatia*
available. Ask at the little convenience
store, if you get stuck. You can fax the community fax machine (fax 2254 093 210) if
you want to make a booking.

Places to eat are fairly inexpensive,
though fish still tends to be a bit on the
steep side.

Thanasis Taverna (☎ 2254 093 269)
Mains around €4.50. This fairly obvious

community-run taverna stands overlooking the harbour.

Tasos Ouzeri Mains around €4.50. Open only in summer. This place is diagonally opposite Thanasis Taverna and offers similar fare.

Samothraki
Σαμοθράκη

pop 2800

The egg-shaped island of Samothraki is 32km south-west of Alexandroupolis. Scenically it is one of the most awe-inspiring of all Greek islands. It is a small island, but a great deal of diverse landscape is packed into its 176 sq km. Its natural attributes are dramatic, big and untamed, culminating in the mighty peak of Mt Fengari (1611m), the highest mountain in the Aegean. Homer related that Poseidon watched the Trojan War from Mt Fengari's summit.

The jagged, boulder-strewn Mt Fengari looms over valleys of massive gnarled oak and plane trees, thick forests of olive and pine, dense shrubbery and damp, dark

glades where waterfalls plunge into dee icy pools. On the gentler, western slopes the island there are corn fields studded wi poppies and other wild flowers in sprin Samothraki is also rich in fauna. Its spring are the habitat of a large number of frog toads and turtles; in its meadows you wi see swarms of butterflies and may con across the occasional lumbering tortoise. C the mountain slopes there are an inordina number of bell-clanking goats. The island beaches, with one exception, are pebbly.

Samothraki's ancient site, the Sanctu ary of the Great Gods, at Paleopolis, is or of Greece's most evocative ancient site Historians are unable to ascertain the na ture of the rites performed here, and i aura of potent mysticism prevails over th whole island.

The island's culinary speciality is *ka sikaki* (kid goat), prepared in a multitude ways; restaurants usually serve it roasted.

History

Samothraki was first settled around 100 BC by Thracians who worshipped the Grea Gods, a cult of Anatolian origin. In 700 B the island was colonised by people from

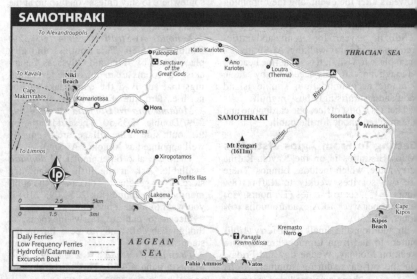

SAMOTHRAKI

To Alexandroupolis

Paleopolis
Kato Kariotes
THRACIAN SEA

Sanctuary of the Great Gods
Ano Kariotes
Loutra (Therma)

To Kavala
Niki Beach

Cape Makrivrahos
Kamariotissa

Hora
SAMOTHRAKI
Isomata

Mnimoria

Alonia
Fonias River

To Limnos
Mt Fengari (1611m)

Xiropotamos

Profitis Ilias

0   2.5   5km
0   1.5   3mi

Lakoma

Cape Kipos

Kremasto Nero
Kipos Beach

Daily Ferries
Low Frequency Ferries
Hydrofoil/Catamaran
Excursion Boat

AEGEAN SEA

Panagia Kremniotissa

Pahia Ammos
Vatos

esvos, who absorbed the Thracian cult
ato the worship of the Olympian gods.

This marriage of two cults was highly
uccessful and by the 5th century BC
amothraki had become one of Greece's
najor religious centres, attracting prospec-
ve initiates from far and wide to its Sanc-
uary of the Great Gods. Among the
uminaries initiated into the cult were King
.ysander of Sparta, Philip II of Macedon
nd Cornelius Piso, Julius Caesar's father-
n-law. One famous visitor who did not
ome to be initiated was St Paul, who
.ropped in en route to Philippi.

The cult survived until paganism was out-
awed in the 4th century AD. After this the
sland became insignificant. Falling to the
urks in 1457, it was united with Greece,
long with the other North-Eastern Aegean
slands, in 1912. During WWII Samothraki
vas occupied by the Bulgarians.

Getting To/From Samothraki

Ferry In summer, Samothraki has daily
erry connections with Alexandroupolis
two hours, €7.50), at least two per week to
Kavala (four hours, €9.70), and one per
veek to Limnos (three hours, €8). There
ire also a couple of boats a week to Sigri
Lesvos) in peak season. Outside high sea-
on, boats to/from Kavala are nonexistent.
Schedules are listed on the window of a
.iosk (☎ 2551 041 505) opposite the pier.
'erry tickets can be bought at Niki Tours
☎ 2551 041 465, fax 2551 041 304), in
Kamariotissa, and from the kiosk.

Hydrofoil In summer there are two to
.hree hydrofoils daily between Samothraki
ind Alexandroupolis (one hour, €14.70).
For departure details contact Niki Tours
.r the ticket kiosk (☎ 2551 041 505) in
Kamariotissa.

Getting Around Samothraki

Bus In summer there are at least four buses
daily from Kamariotissa to Hora (€0.75)
.nd Loutra (Therma), via Paleopolis. Some
.f the Loutra buses continue to the nearby
:amping grounds. There are four buses
daily to Profitis Ilias (via Lakoma).

Car & Motorcycle Cars and small jeeps
can be rented from Niki Tours (☎ 2551 041
465, fax 2551 041 304) and Kyrkos Rent a
Car (☎ 2551 041 620, mobile ☎ 69 7283
9231). A small car is about €45. Motorcycles
can be rented from Rent A Motor Bike
(☎ 2551 041 057), opposite the ferry quay.

Taxi For a taxi, call ☎ 2551 041 733, 2551
041 341 or 2551 041 077.

Excursion Boat Depending on demand,
caiques do trips from the Kamariotissa jetty
to Pahia Ammos and Kipos beaches, and
the *Samothraki* excursion boat does trips
around the island.

KAMARIOTISSA Καμαριώτισσα
postcode 680 02 • pop 826

Kamariotissa, on the north-west coast, is
Samothraki's port. Hora (also called Samothraki), the island's capital, is 5km inland
from here. Kamariotissa is the transport hub
of the island, so you may wish to use it as a
base. It's a cheerful flower-filled place with
vaguely lively nightlife.

Orientation & Information

The bus station is on the waterfront just east
of the quay (turn left when you disembark).
There is no EOT or tourist police, and the
regular police are in Hora. Opposite the bus
station you will find Niki Tours, which is
marginally helpful. There are two ATMs on
the waterfront, but no post office or OTE –
those are in Hora. Cafe Parapente, just back
from the waterfront on the left side of the
road leading up to Hora, offers Internet access for €3 an hour. The port police (☎ 2551
041 305) are east along the waterfront.

General information about the island,
including boat schedules, can be found at
W www.samothraki.com.

Places to Stay

Domatia owners often meet ferries in Kamariotissa, and *domatia* are easy to find in
the compact port.

Hotel Kyma (☎ 2551 041 263) Singles
with shared bath €30, doubles/triples with
bathroom, fridge & air-con €40/48. This

little hotel, along the tree-lined waterfront road, has comfortable, homely rooms and friendly owners.

Niki Beach Hotel (☎ *2551 041 545, fax 2551 041 461*) Singles/doubles with bathroom & TV €40/47. This spacious C-class hotel, just past the Hotel Kyma, has a lovely garden and is fronted by poplar trees.

Aeolos Hotel (☎ *2551 041 595, fax 2551 041 810*) Singles/doubles with breakfast €50/60. Behind the Niki Beach, this B-class property has a swimming pool and a commanding position on a hill overlooking the sea. The rooms, which come with bathroom, fridge, TV, telephone and air-con, are comfortable enough but nothing special.

Places to Eat

Despite an abundance of cafe-bars, breakfast joints and ouzeria, Kamariotissa's eating establishments are all pretty run of the mill.

If you are just looking for a quick bite, try one of the *gyros stands* on the waterfront. A souvlaki or gyros costs about €4.50.

Klimitaria Restaurant (☎ *2551 041 535*) Mains from €4.50. At the eastern end of the waterfront road, this pleasant restaurant serves an unusual speciality called *gianiotiko*, an oven-baked dish of diced pork, potatoes, egg and other goodies (€5.50). It also serves a good pastitsio (€4.50).

I Synantisi (☎ *2551 041 308*) Fish from €5. For simple fresh fish, try this ouzeria on the waterfront between the ferry dock and the bus stop. The food is straightforward but excellent.

Psistaria Pizzeria Skorpios (☎ *2551 041 920*) Pizzas €6-9, grilled meat dishes from €4.50. A few doors up from Klimitaria, Skorpios serves decent home-made pizzas (take-away available) and grilled meat in no-frills surroundings.

HORA Χώρα

Hora, concealed in a fold of the mountains above Kamariotissa, occupies a striking site. The crumbling red-tiled houses – some of grey stone, others whitewashed – are stacked up two steep rocky mountainsides cloaked with pine trees. The twisting cobbled streets resound with cockerels crowing,

dogs barking and donkeys braying, rather than the ubiquitous roar of motorcycles. The village is totally authentic with no concessions to tourism. The ruined castle at the top of the main thoroughfare offers sweeping vistas down to Kamariotissa. It is an open site with free entrance.

Orientation & Information

To get to Hora's narrow winding main street, follow the signs for the kastro from the central square where the bus turns around. Here on the main street, which is nameless (as are all of Hora's streets; houses are distinguished by numbers), are the OTE the Agricultural Bank and the post office.

The police (☎ 2551 041 203) station is in the ruined castle at the top of Hora's main street. Further up on the main street, on the right, a fountain gushes refreshing mountain water.

Places to Stay & Eat

There are no hotels in Hora. There are two reasonably priced *pensions* just off the central square, but the best places to stay in Hora are *domatia* in private houses. Almost all of these are unofficial and do not display signs. If you ask in one of the kafeneia you will be put in touch with a room owner.

Taverna-Ouzeri I Plateia Mains from €3. This taverna on the central square offers grilled meat and a couple of vegetarian options. The tomato-and-feta saganaki is not bad.

SANCTUARY OF THE GREAT GODS

Το Ιερό των Μεγάλων Θεών

Next to the little village of Paleopolis, 6km north-east of Kamariotissa, is the Sanctuary of the Great Gods *(admission free; open 8.30am-8.30pm Tues-Sun)*. The extensive site, lying in a valley of luxuriant vegetation between Mt Fengari and the sea, is one of the most magical in the whole of Greece. The Great Gods were of greater antiquity than the Olympian gods worshipped in the official religion of ancient Greece. The principal deity, the Great Mother (Alceros Cybele), was worshipped as a fertility goddess

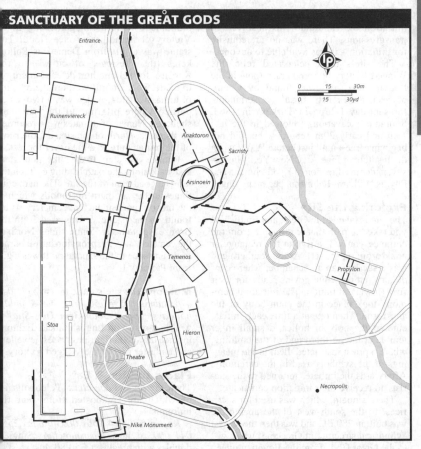

SANCTUARY OF THE GREAT GODS

Entrance

Ruinenviereck

Anaktoron

Sacristy

Arsinoein

Temenos

Propylon

Stoa

Hieron

Theatre

Necropolis

Nike Monument

0   15   30m
0   15   30yd

When the original Thracian religion became integrated with the state religion, the Great Mother was merged with the Olympian female deities Demeter, Aphrodite and Hecate. The last of these was a mysterious goddess, associated with darkness, the underworld and witchcraft. Other deities worshipped here were the Great Mother's consort, the virile young Kadmilos (god of the phallus), who was later integrated with the Olympian god Hermes; as well as the demonic Kabeiroi twins, Dardanos and Aeton, who were integrated with Castor and Pollux (the Dioscuri), the twin sons of Zeus and Leda. These twins were invoked by mariners to protect them against the perils of the sea. The formidable deities of Samothraki were venerated for their immense power. In comparison, the Olympian gods were a frivolous and fickle lot.

Initiates were sworn on punishment of death not to reveal what went on at the sanctuary; so there is only very flimsy knowledge of what these initiations involved. All that the archaeological evidence reveals is that there were two initiations, a lower and a higher. In the first initiation, gods were invoked to bring about a spiritual rebirth within the candidate. In the second initiation the candidate was absolved of transgressions. There was no prerequisite for initiation – it was available to anyone.

The site's most celebrated relic, the Winged Victory of Samothrace (now in the Louvre in Paris), was found by Champoiseau, the French consul, at Adrianople (present-day Edirne in Turkey) in 1863. Sporadic excavations followed in the late 19th and early 20th centuries, but did not begin in earnest until just before WWII when the Institute of Fine Arts, New York University, under the direction of Karl Lehmann and Phyllis Williams Lehmann, began digging.

Exploring the Site

The site is labelled in Greek and English. If you take the path that leads south from the entrance you will arrive at the rectangular **anaktoron**, on the left. At the southern end was a **sacristy**, an antechamber where candidates put on white gowns ready for their first (lower) initiation. The initiation ceremony took place in the main body of the anaktoron. Then one at a time each initiate entered the holy of holies, a small inner temple at the northern end of the building, where a priest instructed them in the meanings of the symbols used in the ceremony. Afterwards the initiates returned to the sacristy to receive their initiation certificate.

The **arsinoein**, which was used for sacrifices, to the south-west of the anaktoron, was built in 289 BC and was then the largest cylindrical structure in Greece. It was a gift to the Great Gods from the Egyptian queen Arsinou. To the south-east of here you will see the **sacred rock**, the site's earliest altar, which was used by the Thracians.

The initiations were followed by a celebratory feast which probably took place in the **temenos**, to the south of the arsinoein. This building was a gift from Philip II. The next building is the prominent Doric **hieron**, which is the most photographed ruin on the site; five of its columns have been reassembled. It was in this temple that candidates received the second initiation.

On the west side of the main path (opposite the hieron) are a few remnants of a

theatre. Nearby, a path ascends to the **Nike monument** where the magnificent Winged Victory of Samothrace once stood. The statue was a gift from Demetrius Poliorketes (the 'besieger of cities') to the Kabeiroi for helping him defeat Ptolemy in battle. To the north-west are the remains of a massive **stoa**, which was a two-aisled portico where pilgrims to the sanctuary sheltered. Names of initiates were recorded on its walls. North of the stoa are the ruins of the **ruinenviereck**, a medieval fortress.

Retrace your steps to the Nike monument and walk along the path leading east; on the left is a good plan of the site. The path continues to the southern **necropolis** which is the most important ancient cemetery so far found on the island. It was used from the Bronze Age to early Roman times. North of the cemetery was the **propylon**, an elaborate Ionic entrance to the sanctuary; it was a gift from Ptolemy II.

Museum The site's museum (☎ 2551 041 474; admission €1.50, free Sun & public holidays; open 8.30am-3pm Tues-Sun) is well laid out, with English labels. Exhibits include terracotta figurines, vases, jewellery and a plaster cast of the Winged Victory.

Places to Stay & Eat

There are several *domatia* at Paleopolis, all of which are signposted from near the museum.

Kastro Hotel (☎ 2551 089 400, fax 2551 041 000, **W** www.kastrohotel.gr) Singles/doubles with breakfast €50/80. Just west of Paleopolis, above the coast road, this C class property offers simple but comfortable rooms with a sea view. The hotel has a swimming pool.

I Asprovalta (☎ 2551 098 250) Fish from around €5. Overlooking the sea, this serene little taverna in Kato Kariotes, just past Paleopolis, serves delicious fresh seafood.

AROUND SAMOTHRAKI
Loutra (Therma) Λουτρά (Θερμά)
Loutra, also called Therma, is 14km east of Kamariotissa and a short walk inland from the coast. It's in an attractive setting with

rofusion of plane and horse-chestnut trees, ense greenery and gurgling creeks. While ot an authentic village, it is the nearest amothraki comes to having a holiday resort. Many of its buildings are purpose-built omatia, and most visitors to the island em to stay here. If you visit before midlay, be prepared to find most places closed.

The village takes both its names from its therapeutic, sulphurous, mineral springs. Whether or not you are arthritic you may njoy a **thermal bath** (*☎ 2551 098 229; admission €1.50; open 6am-11am & 5pm-pm*). The baths are in the large white uilding by the bus stop.

Places to Stay Samothraki's two official amping grounds are both near Loutra, on ae beach, and both are signposted 'Multiary Campings'. Rest assured, the authories mean municipal, not military, camping rounds.

Multilary Camping (Camping Plateia; 2551 041 784, 2551 098 291) Adult/tent 3/3. Open June-Aug. This site is to the left f the main road, 2km beyond the turn-off or Loutra, coming from Kamariotissa. It is nady, with toilets and cold showers but no ther amenities.

Multilary Camping (☎ 2551 041 491, 551 098 244) Adult/tent €3/3. Open Juneug. This second site is 2km farther along ae road. It has a minimarket, restaurant and ot showers, but is a rather dry camping round.

Domatia owners meet the buses at outra.

Mariva Bungalows (☎ 2551 098 230, fax 551 098 374) Doubles with bathroom & reakfast €48. These spacious C-class bunalows, set on a hillside in a secluded part f the island, near a waterfall, are perhaps ae loveliest place to stay on Samothraki. o reach the hotel take the first turn left long the road which leads from the coast p to Loutra. Follow the signs to the hotel, vhich is 600m along this road.

Kaviros Hotel (☎ 2551 098 277, fax 2551 98 278) Singles/doubles €38/41. This B-lass hotel is bang in the middle of Loutra, ast beyond the central square. It looks like a concrete bunker but is a pleasant family-run place surrounded by greenery.

Places to Eat In Loutra there are a number of restaurants and tavernas scattered throughout the upper and lower village.

Paradisos Restaurant (☎ 2551 095 267) Mains from €4. In the upper village try this restaurant, which plies its trade under a huge plane tree and its welcome shade. Take the road to the right from the bus stop to find it.

Fengari Restaurant (☎ 2551 098 321) Mains from €4. This restaurant, signposted from near the bus stop, cooks its food in traditional Samothraki ovens. It is hidden away on a backstreet – follow the signs from Kaviros Hotel.

Kafeneio Ta Therma (☎ 2551 098 325), next to the bus stop and baths, serves excellent coffee, drinks and mezedes, as well as superb homemade sweets. Try the figs in syrup.

Fonias River

Visitors to the north coast should not miss the walk along the Fonias River to the **Vathres** rock pools. The walk starts at the bridge over the river 4.7km east of Loutra – the track being over-optimistically signposted as a vehicular road. After an easy 40-minute walk along a fairly well-marked track you will come to a large rock pool fed by a dramatic 12m-high waterfall. The water is pretty cold but very welcome on a hot day. Locals call the river the 'Murderer' – winter rains can transform the waters into a raging torrent.

Beaches

The gods did not over-endow Samothraki with good beaches. However, its one sandy beach, **Pahia Ammos**, on the south coast, is superb. You can reach this 800m stretch of sand along an 8km winding road from Lakoma. In summer there are caiques from Kamariotissa to the beach. Around the headland is the equally superb **Vatos Beach**, used mainly by nudists.

Opposite Pahia Ammos, on a good day, you can see the mass of the former Greek island of Imvros (Gökçeada), ceded to the Turks under the Treaty of Lausanne in 1923.

Samothraki's other decent beach is the pebbled **Kipos Beach** on the south-east coast. It can be reached via the road skirting the north coast. However, there are no facilities here other than a shower and a freshwater fountain, and there is no shade. It pales in comparison to Pahia Ammos. Kipos Beach can also be reached by caique from Kamariotissa.

Places to Stay & Eat *Yiannis Kapelas Rooms* (☎ 2551 095 119, 2551 095 139) Doubles with breakfast €35. These domatia at Pahia Ammos are on the beach, above the *Taverna Pahia Ammos*, which serves fresh fish and other dishes on it's beautiful terrace. Book ahead if you want to stay here.

Other Villages

The small villages of **Profitis Ilias**, **Lakoma** and **Xiropotamos** in the south-west, and **Alonia** near Hora, are serene unspoilt villages all worth a visit. The hillside Profitis Ilias, with many trees and springs, is particularly delightful and has several tavernas, of which *Vrahos* (☎ 2551 095 264) is famous for its delicious roast kid. Asphalt roads lead to all of these villages.

Thasos Θάσος

pop 13,530

Thasos lies 10km south-east of Kavala. It is almost circular in shape and although its scenery is not quite as awesome as Samothraki's it has some pleasing mountain vistas. The EOT brochures tout it as the 'emerald isle', and despite bad fires in recent years it is indeed a marvel of lushness and greenery. Villages are shaded by huge oaks and plane trees watered by streams and springs. The main attractions of Thasos, aside from its villages and forests, are its many excellent white-sand beaches and the archaeological remains in and around the capital, Thasos (Limenas). A good asphalt road goes around the island, so all the beaches are easily accessible.

Although Thasos can get quite crowded with tourists, including many on package tours, there are enough rooms for everyone even in the high season and Thasos has no less than five camping grounds dotted around its coast. A notice opposite the bus station in Limenas lists the town's hotels and also, very helpfully, indicates which hotels remain open in the winter.

It's worth seeking out the local olive oil, salted olives, figs and green walnuts in syrup, and honey.

History

Thasos has been continuously inhabited since the Stone Age. Its ancient city was founded in 700 BC by Parians, led there by a message from the Delphic oracle. The oracle told them to 'find a city in the Isle of Mists'. From Thasos, the Parians established settlements in Macedonia and Thrace where they mined for gold at Mt Pangaion.

Gold was also mined on Thasos, and the islanders were able to develop a lucrative export trade based on ore, marble, timber and wine, as well as gold. As a result Thasos built a powerful navy, and culture flourished. Famous ancient Thassiots included he painters Polygnotos, Aglafon Aristofon nd the sculptors Polyclitos and Sosicles. The merchants of Thasos traded with Asia Minor, Egypt and Italy.

After the Battle of Plataea, Thasos beame an ally of Athens, but war broke out etween the two cities when Athens atempted to curtail Thasos' trade with Egypt nd Asia Minor. The islanders were deeated and forced into joining the Delian League; the heavy tax imposed crippled its conomy. Thasos' decline continued through Macedonian and Roman times. Heavy taxes were imposed by the Turks, and many inabitants left the island; during the 18th entury the population dropped from 8000 o 2500.

Thasos was revived in the 19th century when Mohammed Ali Pasha of Egypt beame governor of Kavala and Thasos. Ali alwed the islanders to govern themselves and xempted them from paying taxes. The reival was, however, short-lived. The Egyptan governors who superseded Ali Pasha plundered the island's natural resources and mposed heavy taxes. In 1912, along with the other islands of the group, Thasos was united with Greece. Thasos was occupied by Bulgarians and Germans in WWII.

In recent years Thasos has once again truck 'gold'. This time it's 'black gold', in he form of oil which has been found in the ea around the island. Oil derricks can now be spotted at sea at various locations around Thasos. It's also a major provider of very white marble – the quarries are fast creating uge holes in the island's mountainsides.

Getting To/From Thasos

Ferry There are ferries every two hours between Kavala, on the mainland, and Skala Prinos (1¼ hours, €2.65). There is one ferry daily between Limenas and Kavala, departng at 6am and returning at 2pm. Ferries dir-ct to Limenas leave every hour or so in ummer from Keramoti (40 minutes, €1.20), 6km south-east of Kavala. If you are comng from Kavala airport, catch a taxi (15 min-tes, €9) to the ferry at Keramoti instead of Kavala – it's much closer, the ferries go di-ect to Thasos (Limenas), and the ferry ride

itself is much quicker. Ferry schedules are posted at the ticket sales booths (☎ 2593 022 318) and port police (☎ 2593 022 106) in Limenas and Skala Prinos.

Hydrofoil There are six hydrofoils every day between Limenas and Kavala (45 minutes, €6).

Getting Around Thasos

Bus Thasos (Limenas) is the transport hub of the island. There are at least seven buses daily to Limenaria (via the west coast villages, €3) and many to Skala Potamia at the south end of Hrysi Ammoudia (Golden Beach) via Panagia and Potamia. There are five buses a day to Theologos and three to Alyki (€2.50). Three buses daily journey in a clockwise direction all the way around the island (3½ hours, €7) and another three go anticlockwise. Timetables are available from the bus station (☎ 2593 022 162).

Car & Motorcycle Cars can be hired from Avis Rent a Car (☎ 2593 022 535, fax 2593 023 124) on the central square in Limenas or in Skala Prinos (☎ 2593 072 075) and Potamia (☎ 2593 061 735). There are many other agencies, so you may want to shop around. In Limenas you can hire motorcycles and mopeds from Billy's Bikes (☎ 2593 022 490), opposite the foreign-language newspaper agency, and 2 Wheels (☎ 2593 023 267), on the road from Prinos.

The coast road is about 100km all in all, but due to winding mountain roads a full circuit with stops takes about a day.

Bicycle Bicycles can be hired from Babis Bikes (☎ 2593 022 129), on a side street between 18 Oktovriou and the central square in Limenas.

Excursion Boat The *Eros 2* excursion boat (☎ 2593 022 704) makes trips around the island three to four times a week, with stops for swimming and a barbecue. The boat leaves from the old harbour at 9.45am (but you should be there at 9.30am) and returns at 5.30pm. The price is €23.50, including barbecue. There are also a couple of water taxis running regularly to Hrysi Ammoudia (Golden Beach) and Makryammos beaches.

THASOS (LIMENAS)
Θάσος (Λιμένας)
postcode 640 04 • pop 2610

Thasos, on the north-east coast, is the main port and capital of the island. Confusingly, it is also called Limenas and Limin. The island's other port is Skala Prinos, on the west coast. Thasos is built on top of the ancient city, so ruins are scattered all over the place. It is also the island's transport hub, with a reasonable bus service to the coastal resorts and villages.

Orientation & Information

The quay for ferries and hydrofoils is at the centre of the waterfront. The port police (☎ 2593 022 106) and ferry ticket booths (☎ 2593 022 318) are here, opposite the Hotel Timoleon. The central square is straight ahead from the waterfront. The town's main

thoroughfare is 18 Oktovriou, which is parallel to the waterfront, before the central square. Turn left into 18 Oktovriou from the quay to reach the OTE on the right. Take the next turn right into Theogenous and the second turn right for the post office, which is on the left. Millennium Internet Cafe (☎ 2593 058 089), on the waterfront, is open 8am-1am and has Web access for €3 an hour.

Laundry Express (☎ 2593 022 235), just off the central square, provides laundry and dry-cleaning services.

The helpful tourist police (☎ 2593 023 111) are on the waterfront near the bus station. They will assist in finding accommodation if necessary.

The National Bank of Greece is on the waterfront opposite the quay and has an exchange machine and ATM. The newsagent on Theogenous sells English-language newspapers.

The bus station is on the waterfront; to reach it turn left from the quay. To reach the

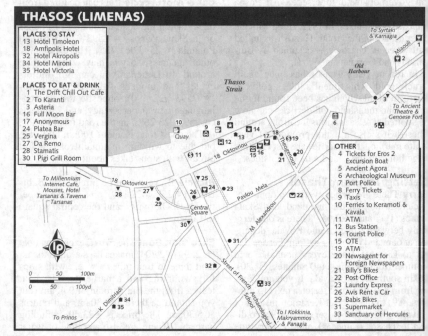

THASOS (LIMENAS)

PLACES TO STAY
13 Hotel Timoleon
18 Amfipolis Hotel
32 Hotel Akropolis
34 Hotel Mironi
35 Hotel Victoria

PLACES TO EAT & DRINK
1 The Drift Chill Out Cafe
2 To Karanti
3 Asteria
16 Full Moon Bar
17 Anonymous
24 Platea Bar
25 Vergina
27 Da Remo
28 Stamatis
30 I Pigi Grill Room

OTHER
4 Tickets for Eros 2 Excursion Boat
5 Ancient Agora
6 Archaeological Museum
7 Port Police
8 Ferry Tickets
9 Taxis
10 Ferries to Keramoti & Kavala
11 ATM
12 Bus Station
14 Tourist Police
15 OTE
19 ATM
20 Newsagent for Foreign Newspapers
21 Billy's Bikes
22 Post Office
23 Laundry Express
26 Avis Rent a Car
29 Babis Bikes
31 Supermarket
33 Sanctuary of Hercules

town's picturesque small harbour, turn left from the quay and walk along the waterfront. There are town beaches both east and west of the waterfront.

Things to See

Thasos' **archaeological museum** (☎ 2593 022 180), next to the ancient agora at the small harbour, has been closed for years but is expected to reopen in 2002. The most striking exhibit is a very elongated 6th-century-BC **kouros** statue that stands in the foyer. It was found on the acropolis of the ancient city of Thasos. Other exhibits include pottery and terracotta figurines and a large well-preserved head of a rather effeminate Dionysos. The ancient city of Thasos was excavated by the French School of Archaeology, so the museum's labelling is in French and Greek.

The **ancient agora** *(admission free)* next to the museum was the bustling marketplace of ancient and Roman Thasos – the centre of its civic, social and business life. It's a pleasant, verdant site with the foundations of stoas, shops and dwellings.

The **ancient theatre**, nearby, has also been closed for almost a decade but is expected to reopen early 2002. When the theatre reopens, performances of ancient dramas and comedies will be staged annually. The theatre is signposted from the small harbour.

From the theatre a path leads up to the **acropolis** of ancient Thasos where there are substantial remains of a medieval fortress built on the foundations of the ancient walls that encompassed the entire city. From the topmost point of the acropolis there are magnificent views. From the far side of the acropolis, steps carved into the rock lead down to the foundations of the ancient wall. From here it's a short walk to the Limenas-Panagia road at the southern edge of town.

Special Events

In July and August, pending the reopening of the ancient theatre, performances of ancient plays are held as part of the Kavala Festival of Drama. Information and tickets can be obtained from the EOT in Kavala or the tourist police on Thasos.

Courses

Holiday workshops in a variety of disciplines are held each summer at Markyammos, a couple of kilometres from Thasos (Limenas). Courses include traditional Greek dance, Greek cooking, ceramics, painting, Pilates body control, hatha yoga, aromatherapy, reflexology, shiatsu massage, and trekking and climbing. Prices vary; seven yoga classes costs around €73.50, while a 6-hour trek on Mt Ipsario is €37 including lunch. Call ☎ 2593 022 101 for more information.

Places to Stay – Budget

Limenas has many reasonably priced *domatia*. If you are not offered anything when you arrive, look for signs around the small harbour and the road to Prinos.

Hotel Victoria (☎ 2593 022 556, fax 2593 022 132) Doubles €38.50. This comfortable place is next door to Hotel Mironi and is run by the same owner.

Hotel Tarsanas (☎ 2593 023 933) Doubles €41. This little hotel is a kilometre west of town on a quiet beach. Rooms have bathroom and kitchen. It has a very good restaurant and bar.

Hotel Mironi (☎ 2593 023 256, fax 2593 022 132) Singles/doubles with bathroom, air-con & fridge €29.50/47. This is a modern and spacious hotel with lots of cool marble. From the ferry quay walk to 18 Oktovriou and turn right and then left on the road signposted to Prinos. The hotel is along here on the left.

Hotel Akropolis (☎/fax 2593 022 488, [e] fivos3@otenet.gr) Singles/doubles with bathroom, TV, fridge & air-con €41/53. This well-maintained, century-old mansion on the Street of the French Archaeological School one block south of the central square, has a lovely garden out front and a foyer filled with wondrous family heirlooms. The rooms are somewhat pokey and cramped but comfortable enough.

Places to Stay – Mid-Range & Top End

Hotel Timoleon (☎ 2593 022 177, fax 2593 023 277) Singles/doubles with breakfast €44/53. This B-class property has clean spacious rooms with balcony, air-con, TV and phone. It is on the waterfront, just beyond the bus station, and provides a free minibus to/from Nysteri Beach.

Amfipolis Hotel (☎ 2593 023 101, fax 2593 022 110, cnr 18 Oktovriou & Theogenous) Singles/doubles/suites with buffet breakfast €45.50/73.50/103. This A-class hotel occupies a grand old tobacco factory. Rooms are elegantly furnished and have interesting wood-panelled ceilings. The hotel has two bars, a restaurant and a pool.

Makryammos Bungalows (☎ 2593 022 101, fax 2593 022 761, e makryamo@mail .otenet.gr) Singles/doubles with breakfast €75/91. This attractive, slightly hippie-ish resort was the first on the island and is situated on an idyllic beach a couple of kilometres south-east of Thasos (Limenas). There are around 200 bungalows hidden in the forest behind the beach, all very private and furnished in an elegant traditional style with marble floors. Incorporated into the complex is a restaurant, taverna, tennis court, swimming pools, water-sports equipment, etc. Excellent child-minding facilities are provided free of charge. The hotel also serves as the venue for 'alternative holiday workshops' (see Courses) that have a new-age bent.

Places to Eat

Limenas has a great selection of restaurants serving well-prepared food.

I Kokkinia (☎ 2593 023 729) Appetisers €2.50, mains €4-6. This little taverna is on the Street of the French Archaeology School, on the outskirts of Limenas, on the way to Panagia and Makryammos. Fish is the speciality (the owner's father is a fisherman), but chargrilled meat and other traditional dishes are also offered.

I Pigi Grill Room (☎ 2593 022 941) Mains €3-5. This restaurant, on the central square, is an inviting, unpretentious place next to a spring. The food is good and the service friendly and attentive. Try *stifado* (stew in tomato sauce) or mussel saganaki.

Vergina (☎ 2593 023 807) Mains around €4.50. On one of the streets leading from the main square to 18 Oktovriou, this place

with tables outside has good grills, including souvlaki.

Mouses (☎ 2593 023 697) Mains €3-8 Named in honour of the seven muses (nemices), this beachside place west of the por specialises in fish but also serves other thing. Try the *taramokeftedes* (fish roe rissoles There's live music several nights a week.

Asteria (☎ 2593 022 403) Mains €4 7.50. On the old harbour, this restaurar serves classic Greek cuisine such a mousakas, pastitsio, *kleftiko* (lamb stuffe with feta and tomato, and baked in a whit sauce) and *fasolakia*.

Syrtaki (☎ 2593 023 353) Mains aroun €5. Just beyond the old harbour, along th beach, this place serves good traditiona Greek fare. Try the lamb kleftiko or th *stamnato* (pork and vegetables in a cla pot).

Da Remo (☎ 2593 022 890, 18 Ok tovriou) Pizzas €4-12. This pizza place is cut above usual Greek pizzerias; home de livery is an option.

*Taverna Tarsanas (☎ 2593 023 933 Mezedes €2.50, mains €3-20. This lovel place, a kilometre west of Thasos on the sit of a former boatbuilders, serves the mos exquisite seafood on the island. There ar lots of interesting seafood mezedes that yo won't find anywhere else. Fresh lobste (€44/kg) – difficult to find on Thasos – always available. Traditional meat dishe are also served.

Stamatis (☎ 2593 022 131, 18 Ok tovriou) This zaharoplasteio has been goin since 1958. It's the best place for coffe and sweets.

Entertainment

Platea Bar (☎ 2593 022 144) This earthy quirky little bar with shaman-style hand crafted decor is a local favourite. It's know for its reliably good music and casual, wel coming atmosphere. Look for it on the cen tral square.

To Karanti (☎ 2593 024 014) This out door ouzeri next to the fishing boats on th old harbour, has one of the most beautifu settings in Thasos. Its relaxed atmosphere i enhanced by excellent Greek music. Asid from a full bar, breakfast and mezedes are available.

The Drift Chill Out Cafe With a nice laid-back outdoor setting by the water north-east of the old harbour, this bar is a refreshing option.

Beyond the old harbour, *Karnagia* is a lovely place to have a drink at sunset. Sited where wooden boats are still built, it has a dramatic locale at the end of the promontory.

Anonymous (☎ 2593 022 847, 18 Oktovriou) this bar serves English-style snacks and Guinness in a can, as well as many other beers.

Full Moon (☎ 2593 023 230) Next door to Anonymous Cafe, this watering hole has an Australian owner and is also very popular.

EAST COAST

The hillside villages of **Panagia** and **Potamia** are a bit touristy but very picturesque. Both are 4km west of Golden Beach. The Greek-American artist Polygnotos Vagis was born in Potamia in 1894 and some of his work can be seen in the **Polygnotos Vagis Museum** (☎ 2593 061 400; open 9.30am-12.30pm & 6pm-9pm Tues-Sat, 10am-1pm Sun & holidays) in the village next to the main church. (The municipal museum in Kavala also has a collection of Vagis' work.)

The long and sandy **Hrysi Ammoudia** (Golden Beach) is one of the island's best beaches, though it can get a trifle crowded. Roads from both Panagia and Potamia lead down to it, and the bus from Limenas calls at both villages before continuing to the southern end of the beach, which is known as Skala Potamia.

The next beach south is at the village of **Kinira**, and just south of here is the very pleasant **Paradise Beach**. The little islet just off the coast here is also called Kinira. **Alyki**, on the south-east coast, is a magical, spectacular place consisting of two quiet beaches back to back on a headland and some quaint old houses. The southernmost beach is the better of the two. There is a small archaeological site near the beach and an ancient, submerged marble quarry. Here marble was cut and loaded on ships from the 6th century BC to the 6th century AD.

The road linking the east side with the west side runs high across the cliffs, providing some great views of the bays at the bottom of the island. Along here you will come to **Moni Arhangelou**, an old monastery built on top of cliffs directly opposite Mt Athos on the mainland. It's possible to visit, and the nuns sell some handpainted icons, crosses and other paraphernalia.

Places to Stay & Eat

Golden Beach Camping (☎ 2593 061 472, fax 2593 061 473) Adult/tent €4/2.50. This place, smack in the middle of Hrysi Ammoudia, is the only camping ground on this side of the island; it's only a stone's throw from the inviting water. Facilities are good and include a minimarket.

Hotel Emerald (☎ 2593 061 979, fax 2593 061 451) Self-contained double/quad studios with kitchen €59/73.50. This hotel up the hill at the northern end of Hrysi Ammoudia has a pool and other facilities and very nice rooms; it's often prebooked by package tours.

Apartments Kavouri (☎ 2593 062 031). 2-3 person apartments €47. These spacious studios have balconies and fully equipped kitchens. They are at the far southern end of Skala Potamia, near the bus turnaround.

Hotel Elvetia (☎ 2593 061 231, fax 2593 061 451) Doubles with fridge €35. This hotel in Panagia has pleasant doubles. With your back to the fountain in the central square of Panagia (where the bus stops), turn left and take the first main road to the left; the hotel is on the left.

Hotel Hrysafis (☎/fax 2593 061 451) Doubles with bathroom €35.50. This vine-covered hotel is just beyond Hotel Elvetia, on the right, and has the same owners as the Elvetia.

Thassos Inn (☎ 2593 061 612, fax 2593 061 027) Doubles with TV, bathroom, phone, heating & balcony €47. Open summer & winter. This lovely hotel in Panagia is up the hill, in the cool of the forest. Built in traditional style, it has views over the slate rooftops of the village. From the bus stop, follow the small street leading from the fountain. Turn right at the sign to the hotel about 20m up the street, just past the honey shop, and follow the babbling brook.

There are *domatia* at both Kinira and Alyki.

Drosia/Platanos (☎ *2593 062 172, 2593 061 340*) Salads €2-4, mains €4-5. This popular taverna is on Panagia's central square.

Phedra Mains €4-10. In the middle of Hrysi Ammoudia (Golden Beach), this was one of the first restaurants on Thasos and is deservedly popular.

Avalon (☎ *2593 062 060*) Mains €4-10. In an imposing old monastery at the southern end of Hrysi Ammoudia in Skala Potamia, this establishment serves traditional fare as well as pizza and fish.

Taverna Captain (☎ *2593 061 160*). Fish €5.50-9. In Skala Potamia, this somewhat touristy place offers up decent fish.

Psarotaverna O Glaros Fish meals €5-10. This is perhaps the best of the tavernas at Alyki, and it offers a nice view over the bay.

I Oraia Alyki (☎ *2593 053 074*) Mains €4-6. On the beach at Alyki is this simple taverna with good fish, and sometimes, homemade cheese.

WEST COAST

The west coast consists of a series of beaches and seaside villages, most with Skala (literally 'step' or 'ladder', but also meaning a little pier) before their names. Roads lead from each of these to inland villages with the same name (minus the 'skala'). Travelling from north to south the first beach is Glifoneri, closely followed by Pahia Ammos (Pahis Beach). The first village of any size is Skala Rahoni. This is Thasos' latest development, having recently been discovered by the package-tour companies. It has an excellent camping ground and the inland village of Rahoni remains unspoilt. A wide range of water-sports equipment can be hired from Skala Rachoni Watersports (☎ 2593 081 056).

Skala Prinos, the next coastal village, and Thasos' second port, is nothing special. There is an ATM here. Vasiliou, about 1km south of the port, is a very nice beach backed by trees. The hillside villages of Mikros Prinos and Megalos Prinos, collectively known as Kasaviti, are gorgeous and lush with excellent tavernas (see Places to Eat).

Skala Sotira and Skala Kallirahis are pleasant and both have small beaches. Kallirahi, 2km inland from Skala Kallirahis, is a peaceful village with steep narrow streets and old stone houses. It has a large population of skinny, anxious-looking cats and word has it that the locals are scared of dogs. Judging by the graffiti and posters, there are also a lot of communists (though not as many as in Skala Potamia).

Skala Maries is a delightful fishing village and one of the least touristy places around the coast. It was from here, early in the 20th century, that the German Speidel Metal Company exported iron ore from Thasos to Europe. There are beaches at both sides of the village, and between here and Limenaria there are stretches of uncrowded beach. Maries, Skala Marie's inland sister village, is very pretty and has a lovely square.

Limenaria is Thasos' second-largest town. It's a crowded though pleasant resort with a narrow sandy beach. The town was built in 1903 by the Speidel Metal Company. There are slightly less crowded beaches around the coast at Pefkari and Potos.

From Potos a scenic 10km road leads inland to Theologos, which was the capital of the island in medieval and Turkish times. This one of the island's most beautiful villages and the only mountain settlement served by public transport. The village houses are of whitewashed stone with slate roofs. It's a serene place, still unblemished by mass tourism.

Places to Stay

Camping Perseus (☎/fax *2593 081 242*) Adult/tent €3/2. This facility, at Skala Rahoni, is a pleasant, grassy camping ground among olive trees. The cook at the site's taverna will prepare any Greek dish you wish if you place your order a day in advance.

Camping Prinos (☎ *2593 071 171*) Adult/tent around €3.50/2.50. This EOT-owned site, at Skala Prinos, is well maintained with lots of greenery and shade and s about a kilometre or so south of the ferry quay, in Vasiliou.

Camping Daedalos (☎/fax 2593 058 251) Adult/tent around €3.50/2. This camping ground is just north of Skala Sotira right on the beach. It has a minimarket, restaurant and bar. Sailing, windsurfing and water-skiing lessons are also on offer.

Camping Pefkari (☎ 2593 051 190) Adult/tent around €3/3. This nifty camping ground is at Pefkari Beach, south of Limenaria. It requires a minimum three-night stay. Look carefully for the sign; it is not so obvious.

All of the seaside villages have **hotels** and **domatia** and the inland villages have rooms in private houses. For information about these inquire at kafeneia or look for signs.

Alexandra Beach Hotel (☎ 2593 052 391, fax 2593 051 185, e alexandra@ tha.forthnet.gr) Singles/doubles with all mod-cons €84/116.50. Rates considerably less outside high season. This resort-like complex is near Potos and is one of the island's best hotels. Aside from the very nice beach there's a restaurant, pool, bar, tennis court and more. Breakfast and dinner are included in the room rate.

Places to Eat

Psisteria Glifoneri Mains around €4. At Glifoneri Beach, on the way from Thasos (Limenas) to Skala Rahoni, this place is on a small beach with a freshwater spring. Try the excellent homemade mussel saganaki with feta.

Pefkospilia (☎ 2593 081 051) Appetisers €1.50-3, mains €3.50-18. This cute traditional family-run taverna by the water at Pahis, just off the road between Thasos (Limenas) and Skala Rahoni, is in a beautiful spot under a large pine tree. It serves delectable local specialities, including the sought-after fish known as *mourmoures*

(€23.50/kg), *kravourosalata* (crab salad, €3) and *htapodokeftedes* (octopus rissoles, €2.50).

Taverna Drosia (☎ 2593 081 270) Most mains €3-5. This taverna in a grove of plane and oak trees on the outskirts of Rahoni features live bouzouki on Friday, Saturday and Sunday evenings. Chargrilled meat is the speciality of the house, though they also have fresh seafood and precooked dishes.

Taverna O Andreas (☎ 2593 071 760) Mains from €3. This homespun taverna on Kasaviti's serene central square shaded by ancient plane trees, serves excellent soup, vegetable dishes, meat and oven-cooked foods. The whole family participates in cooking, and, judging by the food, they're passionate about it. Chirping birds, and cute cats chasing each other around the plane tree will entertain you as you quietly savour your meal.

Vasilis (☎ 2593 072 016). Mains around €4. This beautiful, traditional wooden place on the road into Kasaviti has very good local food but is worth visiting for its stunning old-world architecture alone.

Taverna Orizontes (☎ 2593 031 389) Mains around €4. This taverna, the first on the left as you enter Theologos, features *rembetika* nights.

Augustus Mains €4-7.50. Specialising in grilled meat, including goat and lamb, this bouzouki joint is also in Theologos. The bouzouki action takes place on Friday, Saturday and Sunday nights. Strangely passive ducks swim around in a floodlit pond – just one of the kitschy highlights that await you.

Ciao Tropical Beach Bar (☎ 2593 081 136) Open day & night. More Hawaiian than Hawaii, this beach bar in Pahis is quite a work of art. The owner has meticulously created everything by hand, from the umbrellas to the wood-carved lamps and furniture. You have to see it to believe it.

Evia & the Sporades
Εύβοια & Οι Σποράδες

Evia, Greece's second-largest island, is so close to the mainland historically, physically and topographically that one tends not to regard it as an island at all. Athenians regard Evia as a convenient destination for a weekend break, so consequently it gets packed. Except for the resort of Eretria, however, it is not frequently visited by foreign tourists.

The Sporades lie to the north and east of Evia and to the east and south-east of the Pelion Peninsula, to which they were joined in prehistoric times. With their dense vegetation and mountainous terrain, they seem like a continuation of this peninsula. There are 11 islands in the archipelago, four of which are inhabited: Skiathos, Skopelos, Alonnisos and Skyros. The first two have a highly developed tourist industry, whereas Alonnisos and Skyros, although by no means remote, are far less visited and retain more local character.

SUGGESTED ITINERARIES
One week
Starting in Athens, take the bus to Kymi in Evia and then the ferry to Linaria in Skyros. Give delectable Skyros at least two days of your time. Take a hydrofoil to Alonnisos and work your way towards Volos on the mainland, visiting the islands of Skopelos and Skiathos en route.

Two weeks
Try this adventurous route if you have time. From Athens head to Rafina in Attica and take the ferry to Karystos in Evia. Work your way up to Kymi in Evia, perhaps taking in Eretria on Evia's west side and some walking up Mt Dirfys from the inland village of Steni. From Kymi in Evia follow the one-week itinerary, allowing two to three days on each island of the Sporades. Finally exit from Skiathos to Thessaloniki (ferry or hydrofoil) and return to Athens by train.

Getting To/From Evia & the Sporades
Air Skiathos airport receives charter flights from northern Europe and there are also

Highlights

- The changing tides of the Evripous Channel that so puzzled Aristotle
- Skiathos' golden beaches – among the best in Greece
- Getting delightfully lost in the labyrinthine streets of picturesque Skopelos Town
- Quirky Skyros and pretty Skyrian houses – Greece's hidden island treasure
- Relaxing on Alonnisos, one of the Aegean's greenest and most underrated islands

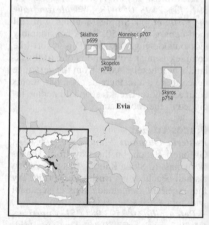

domestic flights to Athens. Skyros airport has domestic flights to Athens and occasional charter flights from the Netherlands.

Bus From Athens' Terminal B bus station there are buses every half-hour to Halkida from 5.45am to 9.45pm (one hour, €4.30), two daily to Paralia Kymis (3¼ hours, €9.70) and three daily to Loutra Edipsou (3½ hours, €8.50). From the Mavromateon terminal in Athens, there are buses every 45 minutes to Rafina (for Karystos and Marmari; one hour, €1.30).

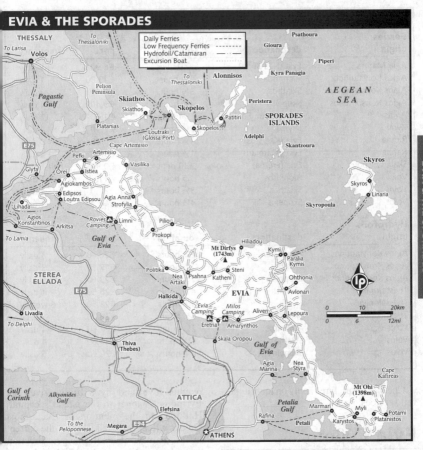

EVIA & THE SPORADES

Daily Ferries	------
Low Frequency Ferries	--------
Hydrofoil/Catamaran	-·-·-
Excursion Boat	········

Train There are hourly trains from Athens' Larisis station to Halkida (1½ hours, €3.55).

Ferry There is no ferry from Thessaloniki to the Sporades, but from 29 June to 16 September there is a daily catamaran to Alonnisos (3¾ hours, €21), Skopelos (three hours, €26), Skiathos (four hours, €32.30) and Agios Konstantinos (6½ hours, €44).

The table following gives an overall view of the available ferries to this island group from mainland ports in high season. Further details and inter-island links can be found under each island entry.

Hydrofoil Hydrofoil links by and large follow similar routes as the ferries, except for the Evia (Kymi) to Skyros (Linaria) link. The table following gives an overall view of the hydrofoil connections in high season. Further details and inter-island links can be found under each island entry. The summer hydrofoil timetable is usually available in late April from Minoan Flying Dolphin (☎ 21 0428 0001, fax 21 0428 3526), Akti Themistokleous 8, Piraeus GR-185 36. The Athens office (☎ 21 0324 4600) is at Filellinon 3. The timetable is also available from local hydrofoil booking offices.

Phone numbers listed incorporate changes due in Oct 2002; see p83

Ferry & Hydrofoil Connections to Evia & the Sporades

Ferries

origin	destination	duration	price	frequency
Agia Marina	Evia (Nea Styra)	40 mins	€1.90	5 daily
Agios Konstantinos	Alonnisos	5½ hours	€13.30	1 daily
Agios Konstantinos	Skiathos	3½ hours	€9.40	2 daily
Agios Konstantinos	Skopelos	4½ hours	€9.40	4 daily
Arkitsa	Evia (Loutra Edipsou)	1 hour	€1.60	12 daily
Kymi	Skyros	2¼ hours	€7.10	2 daily
Rafina	Evia (Karystos)	1¾ hours	€5.60	2 daily
Rafina	Evia (Marmari)	1¼ hours	€3.80	4 daily
Skala Oropou	Evia (Eretria)	30 mins	€0.90	half-hourly
Volos	Alonnisos	5 hours	€11.50	3 daily
Volos	Skiathos	3½ hours	€8	4 daily
Volos	Skopelos	4½ hours	€10	4 daily

Hydrofoils

origin	destination	duration	price	frequency
Agios Konstantinos	Alonnisos	2½ hours	€26.40	3 daily
Agios Konstantinos	Skiathos	1½ hours	€17.10	3 daily
Agios Konstantinos	Skopelos	2¼ hours	€23.60	3 daily
Thessaloniki	Alonnisos	4½ hours	€25.50	1 daily
Thessaloniki	Skiathos	3½ hours	€23.50	6 weekly
Thessaloniki	Skopelos	4¾ hours	€26.40	1 daily
Volos	Alonnisos	2½ hours	€22.60	4 daily
Volos	Skiathos	1¼ hours	€16.80	4 daily
Volos	Skopelos	2¼ hours	€20.60	5 daily

Cheaper return fares apply on most hydrofoil services.

Evia Εύβοια

The island of Evia (**eh**-vih-ah) will probably never be a prime destination for foreign tourists, but if you're based in Athens with a few days to spare, and (preferably) your own transport, a foray into Evia is well worthwhile for its scenic mountain roads, pristine inland villages, and a look at some resorts which cater for Greeks (including one for ailing Greeks), rather than for foreign tourists.

A mountainous spine runs north-south; the east coast consists of precipitous cliffs, whereas the gentler west coast has a string of beaches and resorts. The island is reached overland by a bridge over the Evripous Channel to the island's capital, Halkida. At the mention of Evia, most Greeks will eagerly tell you that the current in this narrow channel changes direction around seven times daily, which it does, if you are prepared to hang around to watch it. The next bit of the story, that Aristotle became so perplexed at not finding an explanation for this mystifying occurrence that he threw himself into the channel and drowned, can almost certainly be taken with a grain of salt.

Getting Around Evia

Halkida is the transport hub of Evia. There are buses to Kymi Town (2½ hours, €5.30, nine daily) via Eretria, two of which continue to Paralia Kymis to link up with the ferry arrivals/departures. There are also buses to Steni (one hour, €1.90, six daily), Limni (2½ hours, €4.70, four daily), Loutra Edipsou (3½ hours, €6.70, two daily) and Karystos (3½ hours, €6.70, three daily) via Eretria. Timetables are outside the ticket office.

HALKIDA Χαλκίδα
postcode 341 00 • pop 45,000
Halkida was an important city-state in ancient times, with several colonies dotted around the Mediterranean. The name derives from the bronze manufactured here in antiquity (*halkos* means 'bronze' in Greek). Today it's a lively industrial and agricultural town, but with nothing of sufficient note to warrant an overnight stay.

However, if you have an hour or two to spare between buses then have a look at the **archaeological museum** (*☎ 2221 025 131, Leoforos Venizelou 13; admission €1.50; open 8.30am-3pm Tues-Sun)*; it's worth a mosey around. It houses finds from Evia's three ancient cities of Halkida, Eretria and Karystos, including a chunk from the pediment of the Temple of Dafniforos Apollo at Eretria.

The Halkida train station is on the mainland side of the bridge. To reach central Halkida, turn right outside the train station, walk over the bridge, turn left and you will find Leoforos Venizelou, Halkida's main drag, off to the right.

The phone number of the Halkida tourist police is ☎ 2221 087 000.

Diving
Sport Apollon Scuba Diving Centre (*☎ 2221 086 369)* in Halkida offers a range of diving activities for all grades. The dives take place off the Alikes coast, north of Evia.

CENTRAL EVIA
Steni Στενή
postcode 340 03 • pop 1300
From Halkida, it's 31km to the lovely mountain village of Steni, with gurgling springs and plane trees.

Steni is the starting point for the climb up **Mt Dirfys** (1743m), Evia's highest mountain. The EOS-owned *Dirfys Refuge* (*☎ 2228 051 285)*, at 1120m, can be

reached along a 9km dirt road, or after a three-hour walk along a forest footpath. From the refuge it's two hours to the summit. You should not attempt this walk unless you are an experienced trekker and take a reliable trekking guidebook with you. For further information contact the EOS (*☎ 2228 025 230)*, Angeli Gyviou 22, Halkida.

A road continues from Steni to **Hiliadou**, on the north coast, where there is a fine pebble-and-sand beach.

Places to Stay & Eat *Hotel Dirfys* (*☎ 2228 051 217)* Singles/doubles €23.50/ 35.30. This is the best value of Steni's two hotels, and is located 50m uphill from the bus terminal. It has comfortable, carpeted rooms with great views from the balconies.

Mouria Ouzeri (*☎ 2228 051 234)* Mains €2.90-5.90. This ouzeri on the central square serves generous portions of tender chargrilled chicken (€4.10) and lamb chops (€5.90) and very palatable local bulk wine.

Ouzeri Vrachos (*☎ 2228 051 546)* Mains €2.90-5.90. A huge helping of fried gavros and Greek salad is €5.90 at this little eatery on the central square.

Taverna Platanos (*☎ 2228 051 225)* Mains €3.50-7.30 It's worth the short walk from Steni, 500m along the Steni-Hiliadou road, to this taverna in a verdant setting by a brook. Char-grilled lamb, chicken or goat is €5.30.

Kymi Κύμη
postcode 340 03 • pop 3850
The town of Kymi is built on a cliff 250m above the sea. The port of Kymi (called Paralia Kymis), 4km downhill, is the only natural harbour on the precipitous east coast, and the departure point for ferries to Skyros.

Kymi is quite attractive in a rather ramshackle way. If you like untouristy, lively workaday towns, you may enjoy an overnight stay. However, Paralia Kymis, squeezed between cliff and sea, is a drab place and there's little reason to linger.

The **folklore museum** (*☎ 2222 022 011; admission free; open 5pm-7.30pm Wed & Sat, 10am-1pm Sun)*, on the road to Paralia

Kymis, has an impressive collection of local costumes and memorabilia, including a display commemorating Kymi-born Dr George Papanikolaou, inventor of the Pap smear test.

Places to Stay & Eat *Hotel Beis* (☎ 2222 022 604, fax 2222 029 113, ✉ hotelbeis@ yahoo.gr) Singles/doubles €26.40/38.20. This hotel on the waterfront has comfortable, well-maintained rooms and is the better of Paralia Kymis' two hotels.

Chalkidou Domatia (☎ 2222 023 896, Athinon 14) Singles/doubles €23.50/29.40. These well-kept domatia, 100m south of the central square, have great views down to Paralia Kymis from the balconies.

To Kouzouli Mezedopeio (☎ 2222 023 786, Galani 34) Mains €2.90-5.90. This little blue-and-white eatery 100m north of the central square has tasty offerings such as saganaki, stuffed green peppers and meatballs.

In Paralia Kymis a string of *restaurants* lines the waterfront.

NORTHERN EVIA

From Halkida a road heads north to **Psahna**, the gateway to the highly scenic mountainous interior of northern Evia. The road climbs through pine forests to the beautiful agricultural village of **Prokopi**, 52km from Halkida. The inhabitants are descendants of refugees who, in 1923, came from Prokopion (present-day Ürgüp) in Turkey, bringing with them the relics of St John the Russian. On 27 May (St John's festival), hordes of pilgrims come to worship his relics in the Church of Agios Ioannis Rosses.

At Strofylia, 14km beyond Prokopi, a road heads south-west to **Limni**, a pretty (but crowded) fishing village with whitewashed houses and a beach. With your own transport or a penchant for walking, you can visit the 16th-century **Convent of Galataki**, 8km south-east of Limni. Its *katholikon* (main church) has fine frescoes. Limni has several *hotels* and *domatia*. There's one camping ground, *Rovies Camping* (☎ 2227 071 120), on the coast, 13km north-west of Limni.

The road continues to the sedate spa resort of **Loutra Edipsou** (119km from Halkida) whose therapeutic sulphur waters have been celebrated since antiquity. Many luminaries, including Aristotle, Plutarch, Strabo and Plinius, sang the praises of these waters. The waters are reputed to cure many ills, mostly of a rheumatic, arthritic or gynaecological nature. Today the town has Greece's most up-to-date hydrotherapy-physiotherapy centre. If you're interested, contact any EOT or the EOT Hydrotherapy-Physiotherapy Centre (☎ 2226 023 501), Loutra Edipsou. Even if you don't rank among the infirm you may enjoy a visit to this resort with its attractive setting, a beach, many domatia and hotels.

SOUTHERN EVIA
Eretria Ερέτρια
postcode 340 08 • pop 5000
As you head east from Halkida, Eretria is the first major place of interest. Ancient Eretria was a major maritime power and also had an eminent school of philosophy. The city was destroyed in AD 87 during the Mithridatic War, fought between Mithridates (king of Pontos) and the Roman commander Sulla. The modern town was founded in the 1820s by islanders from Psara fleeing the Turkish. Once Evia's major archaeological site, it has metamorphosed into a tacky package-tourist resort.

Things to See From the top of the **ancient acropolis**, at the northern end of town, there are splendid views over to the mainland. West of the acropolis are the remains of a palace, temple, and a theatre with a subterranean passage once used by actors. Close by, the **Museum of Eretria** (☎ 2211 062 206; admission €1.50; open 8am-3pm Tues-Sun) contains well-displayed finds from ancient Eretria. In the centre of town are the remains of the **Temple of Dafniforos Apollo** and a mosaic from an ancient bath.

Places to Stay Eretria has loads of *hotels* and *domatia*. The two camping grounds nearby are used more by visitors with motor campers than with tents.

Eva Camping (☎ 2211 068 081, fax 2211 068 083) Adult/tent €3.50/4.40. This is a well-organised site at Malakonda, 5km west of Eretria, with a restaurant, bar and clean facilities.

Milos Camping (☎ 2211 060 460, fax 2211 060 360) Adult/tent €2.90/4.40 This camping ground on the coast 1km west of Eretria has good shade and all the amenities expected of a well-run site.

Karystos Κάρυστος
postcode 340 01 • pop 4500

Continuing east from Eretria, the road branches at Lepoura: the left fork leads to Kymi, the right to Karystos (kah-ris-tos). Set on the wide Karystian Bay, below Mt Ohi (1398m), Karystos is the most attractive of southern Evia's resorts and is flanked by two long sandy beaches. The town was designed on a grid system by the Bavarian architect Bierbach, who was commissioned by King Otho. If you turn right from the quay you will come to the central square of Plateia Amalias which abuts the waterfront. Further along the waterfront is the remains of a 14th-century Venetian castle, the **Bourtzi**, which has marble from a temple dedicated to Apollo incorporated into its walls.

Organised Tours *South Evia Tours Travel Agency (☎ 2224 025 700, fax 2224 029 011, e root@set.hlk.forthnet.gr, w www.setours tripod.com, Plateia Amalias 7)* With helpful English speaking staff, this company offers a range of services including car hire, accommodation and excursions. The latter include walks in the foothills of Mt Ohi and a cruise around the Petali Islands.

Places to Stay & Eat Karystos has three easy-to-find hotels on the waterfront.

Hotel Als (☎ 2224 022 202, Opposite ferry quay) Singles/doubles €23.50/38. Although somewhat lacklustre, the rooms are comfortable and clean here.

Hotel Galaxy (☎ 2224 022 600, fax 2224 022 463, Cnr Kriezotou & Odysseos) Singles/doubles with breakfast €29.40/44.80. This hotel has air-con rooms with TV, music channels and balconies.

Hotel Karystion (☎ 2224 022 391, fax 2224 022 727, Kriezotou 2) Singles/doubles/triples

with breakfast €41/52.80/ 64.50. The modern, carpeted rooms at this hotel 100m east of the Bourtzi have air-con, satellite TV, and balconies with sea views.

Cavo d'Oro (☎ 2224 022 326) Mains €2.90-5.90. Join the locals in this cheery little alleyway restaurant one block west of the main square, where tasty oil-based dishes *(ladera)* cost from €2.90 and meat dishes are €4.40.

Marinos Restaurant (☎ 2224 024 126, Opposite ferry quay) Mains €2.90-7.60. The pick of the bunch from the restaurants lining the waterfront, the Marinos has ladera and fresh fish. Whitebait is €3.80 a portion and most other fish is €38 a kilogram.

Around Karystos

The ruins of **Castello Rossa** (Red Castle), a 13th-century Frankish fortress, are a short walk from **Myli**, a delightful, well-watered village 4km inland from Karystos. The aqueduct behind the castle once carried water from the mountain springs and a tunnel led from this castle to the Bourtzi in Karystos. A little beyond Myli there is an **ancient quarry** scattered with fragments of the once-prized Karystian marble.

With your own transport you can explore the sleepy villages nestling in the southern foothills of Mt Ohi. From the charming village of **Platanistos** a 5km dirt road (driveable) leads to the coastal village of **Potami** with its sand-and-pebble beach.

Skiathos Σκιάθος

postcode 370 02 • pop 4100

The good news is that much of the pine-covered coast of Skiathos is blessed with exquisite beaches of golden sand. The bad news is that in July and August the island is overrun with package tourists and is expensive. Despite the large presence of sun-starved northern Europeans, and the ensuing tourist excess, Skiathos is still a pretty island and not surprisingly one of Greece's premier resorts.

The island has only one settlement, the port and capital of Skiathos Town, on the south-east coast. The rest of the south coast is one long chain of holiday villas and hotels. The north coast is precipitous and less accessible. Most people come to the island for the beaches and nightlife, but the truly curious will discover some picturesque walks, hidden valleys and even quiet beaches.

Getting To/From Skiathos

Air As well as the numerous charter flights from northern Europe to Skiathos, during summer there are up to five flights daily to Athens (€56.95). The Olympic Airways office (☎ 2427 022 200) is in Skiathos Town on the right side of Papadiamanti, the main thoroughfare, as you walk inland.

Ferry In summer, there are ferries from Skiathos to Volos (3½ hours, €8, three to four daily), Agios Konstantinos (3½ hours, €9.40, two daily) and Alonnisos (two hours, €5.30, four to six daily) via Glossa (Skopelos) and Skopelos Town (1½ hours, €4.10).

From mid June to late September, Minoan Lines has a weekly service north to Thessaloniki (5¾ hours, €13.30), and south to Tinos (7½ hours, €17.60), Mykonos (8½ hours, €18.80), Paros (10 hours, €20), Santorini (13½ hours, €25) and Iraklio (17¾ hours, €30.80).

Tickets can be bought from Alkyon Tourist Office (☎ 2427 022 029) at the bottom of Papadiamanti in Skiathos Town. The port police can be contacted on ☎ 2427 022 017.

Hydrofoil In summer, there is a bewildering array of hydrofoils from Skiathos and around the Sporades in general. Among the main services, there are hydrofoils from Skiathos to Volos (1¼ hours, €16.80, three or four daily), and Alonnisos (one hour, €11.20, eight to 10 daily) via Glossa (Skopelos) and Skopelos Town (35 minutes, €8.50). There are also hydrofoils to Agios Konstantinos (1½ hours, €17.10, two or three daily) and Thessaloniki (4½ hours, €26, one daily). There are also services to the Pelion Peninsula and various ports in northern Evia. Hydrofoil tickets may be purchased from Alkyon Tourist Office.

Getting Around Skiathos

Bus Crowded buses leave Skiathos Town for Koukounaries Beach (30 minutes, €0.90) every half-hour between 7.30am and 10.30pm. The buses stop at all the access points to the beaches along the south coast.

Car & Motorcycle Car-hire outlets in Skiathos Town including Alamo (☎ 2427 023 025) and Euronet (☎ 2427 024 410), as well as heaps of motorcycle-hire outlets, are along the town's waterfront.

Excursion Boat Excursion boats travel to most of the south-coast beaches from the old harbour. Trips around the island cost about €13.20 and include a visit to Kastro, Lalaria Beach and the three caves of Halkini Spilia, Skotini Spilia and Galazia Spilia, which are only accessible by boat.

SKIATHOS TOWN

Skiathos Town, with its red-roofed, whitewashed houses, is built on two low hills. It is picturesque enough, although it doesn't have the picture-postcard attractiveness of Skopelos or Skyros Towns. The islet of Bourtzi (reached by a causeway) between the two harbours is covered with pine forest. The town is a major tourist centre, with hotels, souvenir shops, travel agents and bars dominating the waterfront and main thoroughfares.

Orientation

The quay is in the middle of the waterfront, just north of Bourtzi Islet. To the right (as you face inland) is the straight, new harbour; to the left, and with more character, is the curving old harbour used by local fishing and excursion boats. The main thoroughfare of Papadiamanti strikes inland from opposite the quay. The central square of Plateia Trion Ierarhon is just back from the middle of the old harbour and has a large church in the middle.

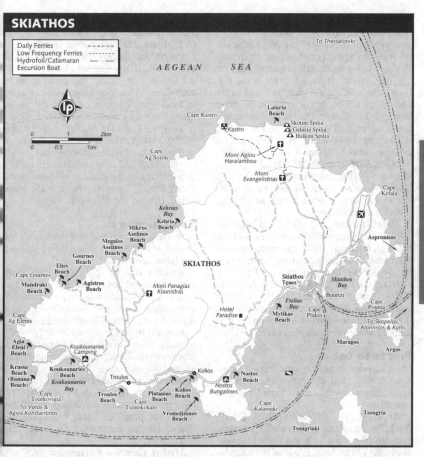

SKIATHOS

Daily Ferries	-------
Low Frequency Ferries	--------
Hydrofoil/Catamaran	—··—
Excursion Boat	··········

AEGEAN   SEA

To Thessaloniki

To Volos &
Agios Konstantinos

To Skopelos,
Alonnisos & Kymi

EVIA & THE SPORADES

Information

The tourist police office (☎ 2427 023 172), opposite the regular police about halfway along Papadiamanti, next to the high school, operates 8am to 9pm daily during the summer season.

The post office, OTE and National Bank of Greece are all located on Papadiamanti. The bus terminus is at the northern end of the new harbour. There are several ATMs and a couple of automatic exchange machines around town. The Skiathos Internet Centre (☎ 2427 022 021) is at Miaouli 12.

Museum

Skiathos was the birthplace of the Greek short-story writer and poet Alexandros Papadiamantis, as well as the novelist Alexandros Moraïtidis. Papadiamantis' house is now a museum (☎ 2427 023 843, Plateia Papadiamantis; admission €0.90; open 9am-1pm & 5pm-8pm Tues-Sun). It holds a small collection documenting his life.

Organised Tours

Various local operators run excursion-boat trips around the island. See Getting Around Skiathos.

Phone numbers listed incorporate changes due in Oct 2002; see p83

Places to Stay

Most accommodation is booked solid by package-tour operators from July to the end of August, when prices are often double those of low season. Prices quoted here are for high season. There is a kiosk on the harbourfront with information on room availability. If you're brave enough to arrive during the summer rush, then just about any travel agent will endeavour to fix you up with accommodation. Worth trying is Alkyon Tourist Office (☎ 2427 022 029).

Hotel Karafelas (☎ *2427 021 235, Papadiamanti 59*) Singles/doubles €29.40/52.80. The pleasant rooms at this hotel have verandas overlooking a small garden and there's a communal kitchen.

Hotel Marlton (☎ *2427 022 552, Evagelistrias 10*) Singles/doubles/triples €41/50/60. This hotel has well-kept modern rooms with air-con and refrigerators. Some rooms have balconies overlooking a garden.

Hotel Akti (☎ *2427 022 024, fax 2427 022 430*) Singles/doubles €41/53, 4-person apartments €88. For a central location with a waterfront views, try this hotel on the new harbour waterfront with pleasant airy rooms.

Places to Eat

Most eateries in Skiathos are geared to the tourist trade and are expensive. Finding some decent cuisine can be a matter of trial and error.

Avra (☎ *2427 021 008*) Mains €4.10-5.60. The Avra, one of the swathe of restaurants just down from Plateia Trion Ierarhon, above the old harbour, is one of the bargains of Skiathos. It serves huge helpings of succulent chicken (€4.40), pork (€5) and lamb (€5.60) with french fries and salad.

O Kavouras (☎ *2427 021 094, Opposite hydrofoil terminal*) Mains €4.70-6. The food here is consistently tasty and reasonably priced. Popular starters are baked potato with butter (€0.60) and crab salad (€3.30); mains include octopus casserole (€5.20) and chicken with okra (€4.70).

Taverna Ouzeri Kabourelia (☎ *2427 021 112*) Mains €4.70-7.40. If you're partial to hummus you'll enjoy this delicious version (pea puree on the menu) costing €2.65 at the Kabourelia, on the old harbour waterfront. The beef stifado (€5.60) and lamb giouvets (€5.60) are also highly commendable.

Psaradika Ouzeri (☎ *2427 023 412*) Mains €4.10-10. Not surprisingly, as it's next to the fish market, this place at the far end of the old harbour waterfront specialises in fresh fish. If you're on a limited budget then plump for gavros at €4.10 a portion.

Taverna Folia (☎ *2427 023 196*) Mains €2.90-5.90. Tables at this taverna are set out in a peaceful tree-shaded alley. Well prepared hot and cold mezedes are offered and grilled fish, meat and ready-made food. From Plateia Trion Ierarhon, walk along Athan Diakou and follow the signs.

Entertainment

Scan Papadiamanti and Polytehniou (better known as Bar Street) to see which disco or bar takes your fancy.

Banana Bar (☎ *2427 021 232, Polytehniou*) In high season this wild bar seethes with UK and Scandinavian tourists indulging in marathon boozing sessions. Give it a miss if you don't like punishingly loud music.

Borzoï (☎ *mobile 69-4496 4351, Polytehniou*) The Borzoï has an atmospheric stone-walled interior and a pretty garden set around an old olive press. Greek, Latin American, jazz, blues and rock is played.

Kentavros Bar (☎ *2427 022 980, Off Plateia Papadiamantis*) The long-established Kentavros promises rock, soul, jazz and blues, and gets the thumbs up from locals and expats.

Mythos Paradiso Cinema (☎ *2427 023 975*) Entry €5.90. You can catch an English-language movie at this outdoor cinema signposted from the ring road.

Shopping

Loupos & his Dolphins (☎ *2427 023 777, Plateia Padiamantis*) This high-class place sells original icons and very fine ceramics and jewellery.

AROUND SKIATHOS
Beaches

With some 65 beaches to choose from, beach-hopping on Skiathos can become a full-time occupation. Many are only accessible by caique and the ones that are more easily accessible tend to get crowded.

Buses ply the south coast stopping at the beach access points. The ones nearest town are extremely crowded; the first one worth getting off the bus for is the pine-fringed, long and sandy **Vromolimnos Beach**, which has been awarded an EU blue flag for cleanliness. Farther along, **Platanias** and **Troulos Beaches** are also good but both, alas, are very popular. The bus continues to **Koukounaries Beach**, backed by pine trees and a lagoon and touted as the best beach in Greece. Nowadays it's best viewed at a distance, from where the 1200m long sweep of pale gold sand does indeed look beautiful.

Krassa Beach, at the other side of a narrow headland, is more commonly known as **Banana Beach**, because of its curving shape and soft yellow sand. It is nominally a nudist beach, though the skinny-dippers tend to abscond to **Little Banana Beach** around the corner if things get too crowded.

Agia Eleni Beach, a short walk west of Koukounaries, is reputedly the best beach for windsurfing. All the south-coast beaches have water-skiing and windsurfing outlets, and motorboats are available for hire at Koukounaries Beach.

The north coast's beaches are less crowded but are exposed to the strong summer *meltemi* winds. From Troulos a road heads north to sandy **Megalos Aselinos Beach**. Turn left onto a dirt road to reach this beach. A right fork leads to **Mikros Aselinos Beach** and farther on to **Kehria Beach**, also reachable by a dirt road from nearer Skiathos Town.

Lalaria, on the northern coast, is a striking beach of pale grey, egg-shaped pebbles, much featured in tourist brochures. It is most easily reached by excursion boat from Skiathos Town.

Diving

Dolphin Diving (☎ 2427 021 599, 2427 022 025) Located on Nostos Beach, this is the only diving school in the Sporades. Both the Beginners and Advanced Dives cost €35.30. The Discovery Dive, which explores locations 30m deep, is €44.80.

Kastro Κάστρο
Kastro, perched dramatically on a rocky headland above the north coast, was the fortified pirate-proof capital of the island from 1540 to 1829. It consisted of some 300 houses and 20 churches and the only access was by a drawbridge. Except for two churches, it is now in ruins. Access is by steps, and the views from it are tremendous. Excursion boats come to the beach below Kastro, from where it's an easy clamber up to the ruins.

Moni Evangelistrias
Μονή Ευαγγελίστριας
The 18th-century Moni Evangelistrias is the most appealing of the island's monasteries. It is in a delightful setting, poised above a gorge, 450m above sea level, and surrounded by pine and cypress trees. The monastery, like many in Greece, was a refuge for freedom fighters during the War of Independence, and the islanders claim the first Greek flag was raised here in 1807.

The monastery is an hour's walk from town or you can drive here. It's signposted off the Skiathos Town ring road, close to the turn-off to the airport.

Places to Stay & Eat
Koukounaries Camping (☎/fax 2427 049 250) Adult/tent €5.85/2.95. This excellent site at the eastern end of Koukounaries Beach is the only officially recognised camping ground in the Sporades. It has clean toilets and showers, a minimarket and taverna.

Nostos Bungalows (☎ 2427 022 420, fax 2427 022 525) 2/4-person bungalows €97/181. These gorgeous, stylishly furnished bungalows overlooking Nostos Beach, 5km from Skiathos Town, are in a well-designed complex, with bars, a restaurant, pool and tennis court.

Hotel Paradise (☎ 2427 021 939, fax 2427 023 346) Doubles €100. This smallish hotel is in a tranquil setting surrounded by a pine forest high above the coast, 4km west of Skiathos Town. It has tastefully furnished air-con rooms and a restaurant and bar. If you're driving, look for the hotel sign along the coast road. Otherwise book ahead to arrange a lift from town in the hotel's bus.

Skopelos Σκόπελος

postcode 370 03 • pop 5000

Skopelos is less commercialised than Skiathos, but until recently seemed to be following hot on its trail. However, in recent years locals seem to have become determined to keep the island's traditions and character intact and not succumb to the worst accesses of mass tourism. Skopelos is a beautiful island. It is heavily pine-forested and has vineyards, olive groves and fruit orchards. It is noted for its plums and almonds, which are used in many local dishes.

Like Skiathos, the north-west coast is exposed, with high cliffs. The sheltered southeast coast harbours many beaches but, unlike Skiathos, most are pebbled. There are two large settlements: the capital and main port of Skopelos Town on the east coast; and the lovely, unspoilt hill village of Glossa, the island's second port, 3km north of Loutraki on the west coast.

Skopelos has yielded an exciting archaeological find. In ancient times the island was an important Minoan outpost ruled by Staphylos, who, according to mythology, was the son of Ariadne and Dionysos. *Staphylos* means grape in Greek and the Minoan ruler is said to have introduced wine making to the island. In the 1930s a tomb containing gold treasures, and believed to be that of Staphylos, was unearthed at Staphylos, now a resort.

Getting To/From Skopelos

Ferry In summer there are three ferries daily to Alonnisos from Glossa (1¼ hours, €3.20) and Skopelos Town (30 minutes, €3.20). There are also ferries to Volos (4½ hours, €10, four daily), to Agios Konstantinos (4½ hours, €9.40, two daily) and to Skiathos (1½ hours, €4.40, four or five daily). The times given are from Skopelos Town; from Glossa it's one hour less. Boats from Glossa actually depart from Loutraki, on the coast. Tickets are available from

Lemonis Agents (☎ 2424 023 055, fax 242 023 095) on the waterfront near the old qua in Skopelos Town. The telephone number Skopelos' port police is ☎ 2424 022 180.

Hydrofoil Like Skiathos, Skopelos linked to a number of destinations by h drofoil. The main services during summ include: to Alonnisos (20 minutes, €6.5 eight or nine daily), to Skiathos (one hou €8.50, 10 to 12 daily), to Volos (2¼ hour €20.60, five daily), to Agios Konstantino (2¼ hours, €23.60, three daily) and to The saloniki (4½ hours, €26.40, five or six week). In addition, there are also services the Pelion Peninsula and to various ports i Evia. Purchase tickets from Kosifis Trave (☎ 2424 022 767, fax 2424 023 608) o posite the new quay in Skopelos Town.

Getting Around Skopelos

Bus There are buses from Skopelos Tow all the way to Glossa/Loutraki (one hou €2.35, eight daily), a further three that g only as far as Milia (35 minutes, €1.80) an another two that go only as far as Agnonta (15 minutes, €0.80).

Car & Motorcycle There are a fair num ber of car- and motorcycle-rental outlets i Skopelos Town, mostly at the eastern en of the waterfront. Among them is Mote Tours (☎ 2424 022 986, fax 2424 022 602 next to Hotel Eleni.

SKOPELOS TOWN

Skopelos Town is one of the most captiva ing towns in the Sporades. It skirts a sem circular bay and clambers in tiers up hillside, culminating in a ruined fortres Dozens of churches are interspersed amon tall, dazzlingly white houses with bright shuttered windows and flower-adorned ba conies. Traditionally, roofs in Skopelo Town were tiled with beautiful rough-hew bluestone, but these are gradually being re placed with mass-produced red tiles.

Orientation

Skopelos Town's waterfront is flanked b two quays. The old quay is at the wester

SKOPELOS

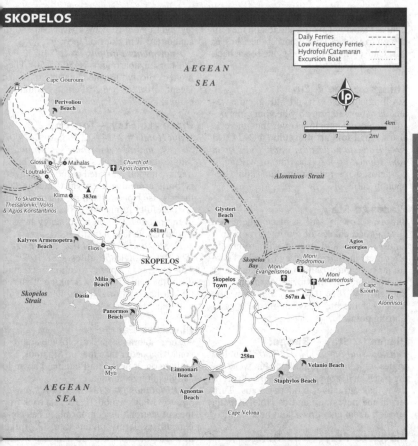

Map legend:
Daily Ferries — — — — — —
Low Frequency Ferries — — — — — — —
Hydrofoil/Catamaran — ·· — ·· —
Excursion Boat ············

AEGEAN SEA

Cape Gourouni

Perivoliou Beach

Glossa
Mahalas
Loutraki
Church of Agios Ioannis

To Skiathos, Thessaloniki, Volos & Agios Konstantinos

Klima
383m

Alonnisos Strait

Glysteri Beach

Kalyves Armenopetra Beach

Elios
681m

Agios Georgios

SKOPELOS

Skopelos Bay
Moni Evangelismou
Moni Prodromou
Moni Metamorfosis

Milia Beach

Skopelos Town

Cape Kiourto

To Alonnisos

Skopelos Strait

Dasia

Panormos Beach

567m

Cape Myti

258m

Velanio Beach

Limnonari Beach

Agnontas Beach

Staphylos Beach

AEGEAN SEA

Cape Velona

EVIA & THE SPORADES

...nd of the harbour and the new quay is at ...e eastern end. All ferries and hydrofoils ...ow use the new quay. From the ferry, turn ...ght to reach the bustling waterfront lined ...ith cafes, souvenir shops and travel agen...ies. The bus station is to the left of the ...uay.

...nformation

...here is no tourist office on Skopelos. How-...ver, the staff at the privately owned Thalpos ...eisure & Services (☎ 2424 022 947, fax ...424 023 057, e thalpos@otenet.gr, w www ...olidayislands.com), on the waterfront, are helpful offering a wide range of services, including booking accommodation and tours around the island.

There is no tourist police. The regular police station (☎ 2424 022 235) is above the National Bank. The post office lurks in an obscure alleyway: walk up the road opposite the bus station, take the first left, the first right and the first left and it's on the right. A sign in the middle of the waterfront points inland to the OTE.

The National Bank of Greece is on the waterfront near the old quay; it has an ATM. To reach Skopelos' self-service laundrette go up the street opposite the bus station, turn right at Platanos Taverna and it's on the left.

You can check your email at the Click & Surf Café (☎ 2424 023 093), one block back from the waterfront.

Things to See & Do

Strolling around town and sitting at the waterside cafes will probably be your chief occupations in Skopelos Town, but there is also a small **folk art museum** (☎ 2424 023 494, Hatzistamati; admission free; open 7am-10pm daily). At the time of writing, it was closed for renovation but should reopen in 2002.

Places to Stay

Skopelos Town is still a place where you have a good chance of renting a room in a family house, and people with rooms to offer meet the ferries and hydrofoils. There are no camping grounds on the island.

The Rooms & Apartments Association of Skopelos (☎ 2424 024 567), on the waterfront near the old quay, might be a good starting point.

Places to Stay – Budget

Pension Soula (☎ 2424 022 930) Doubles/triples with bath €38.20/50. This welcoming place, in a large garden in a quiet part of town, has attractive, modern rooms. Turn left at the new quay and at Hotel Amalia turn left again and after 200m bear right.

Places to Stay – Mid-Range

Kyr Sotos (☎ 2424 022 549, fax 2424 023 668) Doubles/triples €52.80/63.40. The delightful and popular rooms at this characterful pension in the middle of the waterfront have wooden floors and ceilings. There's a little courtyard and well-equipped communal kitchen. In low season, doubles cost only €19.10.

Perivoli Studios (☎ 2424 022 640, fax 2424 023 668, ⓔ perivoli@otenet.gr) Doubles/triples €52.80/58.70. These charming studios occupy a single-storey traditional building. Each is simply but stylishly furnished with a well-equipped kitchen and a terrace overlooking an orchard. At the new quay turn left

and walk 300m to the T-junction. Take a dog leg right onto a road by a river bed and th studios are 40m along on the right.

Apartments Philipos (☎ 2424 022 930 2/4-person apartments €56/67.50. Thes modern, nicely furnished apartments are ac jacent to the co-owned Pension Soula (se earlier).

Places to Stay – Top End

Ionia Hotel (☎ 2424 022 568, fax 2424 02 301, ⓔ ionia@vol.forthnet.gr, Manolak Singles/doubles/triples €47/76/90. This a tractive hostelry, located in the back street is built around a courtyard and garden there's also a pool. The light and airy room are tastefully furnished. It's a steep hike u to the hotel, so if you have heavy luggag it's advisable take a taxi.

Hotel Adonis (☎ 2424 022 231, fax 242 023 239) Singles/doubles €58.70/79.20 This hotel is in a prime location in the mid dle of the waterfront, overlooking all the ac tion. It has comfortable and homely room with balconies.

Places to Eat

At the restaurants on Skopelos the quality i somewhat better than that on Skiathos. Sev eral are on or near Tria Platania, known lo cally as Souvlaki Square.

O Platanos (☎ 2424 023 067, Souvlak Square) Mains €5.60-10.30. Just back from the bus station this popular place has table beneath a large plane tree. A mixe mezedes for two is €21.15 and mixed souv laki special is €10.30.

Ilias Restaurant (☎ 2424 023 971, Souv laki Square) Mains €5.90-14.70. The Ilia offers a wide variety of mezedes; grills, how ever, are its speciality. If you're feeling glu tonous then plump for the 'variety of me plate' – a huge wooden platter piled high wit sausages, beefburgers, pork and chicke kebab, french fries and salad garnish.

Taverna Finikas (☎ 2424 023 247 Mains €2.90-5.90. This charming restaur ant, signposted from the OTE, is set roun an enormous palm tree. The imaginativ cuisine includes stuffed pork with prune and apples (€5.60), beef in wine sauce wit

oni Agias Triados perched high on a pinnacle

Moni Hozoviotissis, built into a cliff – Amorgos

ete's local villages dot the hilly landscape.

The lush green of Cretan farmland

Picturesque local lodging – Keratokambos

GEORGE TSAFOS

IZZET KERIBAR

GEORGE TSAFOS

Traditional windmills, whose styles vary throughout the different regions, are still an important part of rural life in Greece.

pices (€5.90) and vegetable au gratin €4.40).

Taverna Alexander (☎ *2424 022 324*) Mains €5.90-8.80 This taverna, signposted from the OTE, serves excellent local specialities such as Skopelos cheese pie, *tyropitta* and pork with prunes (€7.30). You dine in a cosy walled garden which also sports a deep well that is floodlit at night.

Ouzeri Anatoli Mains €2.90-7.30. Open summer only. For mezedes and live music, head to this ouzeri, high up above the town in the Kastro. Here from 11pm onwards, you will hear rembetika music sung by Skopelos' own exponent of the Greek blues, Georgos Xindaris. The easiest though most strenuous way there is to follow the path up past the church at the northern end of the quay.

Perivoli Taverna (☎ *2424 023 758, North of Souvlaki Square*) Mains €5.90-11.20. At this sophisticated taverna you dine under a vine arbor in a pretty garden. The Greek and international menu includes chicken with almonds in white sauce, sole with spinach in wine sauce and Malaysian chicken with soya sauce (all €7.35). The menu also includes vegetarian dishes and there's a good selection of Greek wines.

Alpha-Pi supermarket (*Doulidi*) This is a well-stocked supermarket, just inland from the bus station.

Entertainment
Dionos Blue Bar (☎ *2424 023 731, Near OTE*) This cool little bar offers jazz, blues, soul and ethnic music. It serves 17 beers, 25 malt whiskies and a wide range of cocktails.

Platanos Jazz Bar (☎ *2424 023 661, Opposite old quay*) You can hear jazz, blues and Latin American music at this long-established atmospheric place. It's open all day and serves breakfast on its shady terrace – an ideal place to recover from a hangover.

For more lively entertainment there is a strip of clubs along Doulidi, just off Souvlaki Square. Each attracts its own age group; poke your nose in to see if you fit in.

Panselinos (☎ *2424 024 488, Doulidi*) If you would like to hear some live rembetika then this is the place to head for.

Dancing Club Kounos (☎ *2424 023 623, Doulidi*) The DJ spins house, acid, and hard rock at this hot spot. Some Greek music is also played.

GLOSSA Γλώσσα
Glossa, Skopelos' other major settlement, is another whitewashed delight and is also considerably quieter than the capital. It has managed to retain the feel of a pristine Greek village.

The bus stops in front of a large church at a T-junction. As you face the church, the left road winds down to Loutraki and the right to the main thoroughfare of Agiou Riginou. Along here you'll find a bank and a few small stores.

Skopelos' beaches are just as accessible by bus from Glossa as they are from Skopelos Town; Milia, the island's best beach, is actually closer to Glossa. There are also places to stay and tavernas at Loutraki, but there's not a lot to do other than hang around, eat, sleep and drink since the narrow pebble beach is not so inviting.

Places to Stay & Eat
Hotel Atlantes (☎ *2424 033 223, Opposite bus stop*) Singles/doubles €29.40/50. This pleasant hotel was closed for renovation at the time of writing, but is scheduled to reopen in 2002.

Rooms Kerasia (☎ *2424 033 373*) Doubles €41. This modern place, in a tranquil setting, has clean, well-maintained rooms with balconies. Just before you enter Glossa from Skopelos Town turn left down a narrow road to reach the rooms.

Glossa also has a few other rooms in private houses – inquire at *kafeneia*.

Agnanti Taverna & Bar (☎ *2424 033 076, Agiou Riginou*) Mains €4.50-8.20. It's worth a trip to Glossa just to eat at this taverna, where local produce is used to create imaginative and delectable food. Herb fritters (€3.50) are just one of the many delicious starters. The mains also offer plenty of choice with such offerings as goat with artichokes (€7.90) and chicken with okra (€5.30). There are superb views over to Evia from the taverna's roof terrace.

EVIA & THE SPORADES

EVIA & THE SPORADES

AROUND SKOPELOS
Monasteries
Skopelos has many monasteries, several of which can be visited on a scenic, although quite strenuous, one-day trek from Skopelos Town. Facing inland from the waterfront, turn left and follow the road which skirts the bay and then climbs inland (signposted 'Hotel Aegeon'). Continue beyond the hotel and you will come to a fork. Take the left fork for the 18th-century **Moni Evangelismou** (now a convent). From here there are breathtaking views of Skopelos Town, 4km away. The monastery's prize piece is a beautiful and ornately carved and gilded iconostasis in which there is an 11th-century icon of the Virgin Mary.

The right fork leads to the uninhabited 16th-century **Moni Metamorfosis**, the island's oldest monastery. From here the track continues to the 18th-century **Moni Prodromou** (now a nunnery), 8km from Skopelos Town.

Walking Tours
There is a useful English-language walking guide to Skopelos called *Skopelos Trails* by Heather Parsons (☎ 2424 024 022, 🌐 www .skopelos.net/walks). It costs €11.15 and is available in waterfront stores.

Heather also leads guided walks. Her evening walk to Panormos Beach (€10) is very popular as you finish off the four-hour hike with a swim and a meal.

Beaches
Skopelos' beaches are mostly pebbled, and almost all are on the sheltered south-west and west coasts. All the buses stop at the beginning of paths which lead down to them. The first beach along is the crowded sand-and-pebble **Staphylos Beach** (site of Staphylos' tomb), 4km south-east from Skopelos Town. From the eastern end of the beach a path leads over a small headland to the quieter **Velanio Beach**, the island's official nudist beach. **Agnontas**, 3km west of Staphylos, has a small pebble beach and from here caiques sail to the superior and sandy **Limnonari Beach**, in a sheltered bay flanked by rocky outcrops.

From Agnontas the road cuts inland through pine forests before re-emerging at the sheltered and steeply shelving **Panormos Beach**. This is the only beach which has organised water sports. The next beach along, **Milia**, is considered the island's best – a long swathe of tiny pebbles.

Places to Stay & Eat
There are hotels and domatia at Staphylos, Limnonari, Panormos and Milia.

Limnonari Rooms (☎ 2424 023 046, 📧 lemonisk@otenet.gr, Behind Limnonari Beach) Doubles €55.70. This domatia, in a peaceful setting, has airy, nicely furnished rooms. There is a well-equipped communal kitchen and a large terrace.

Taverna Pefkos (☎ 2424 022 080, Overlooking Staphylos Beach) Mains €2.90-7.30. This welcoming taverna serves tasty traditional Greek dishes and pastas. There are romantic views from its terrace when there is a full moon.

Taverna Pavlos (☎ 2424 022 409) Mains €2.90-5.90. Reputedly the best of the three waterside tavernas at Agnontas, the Pavlos specialises in fish. Sardines are €14.70 and red mullet is €38.10 a kilogram.

Alonnisos
Αλόννησος

postcode 370 05 • pop 3000

Alonnisos is still a serene island despite having been ferreted out by 'high-quality' package-tour companies. Package tourism would no doubt have taken off in a bigger way had the airport (erroneously and optimistically shown on island maps) materialised. This project was begun in the mid-1980s, but the rocks of Alonnisos proved unyielding and the politics Byzantine, making the construction of a runway impossible.

Alonnisos once had a flourishing wine industry, but in 1950 the vines were struck with the disease phylloxera and, robbed of their livelihood, many islanders moved away. Fate struck another cruel blow in 1965 when a violent earthquake destroyed

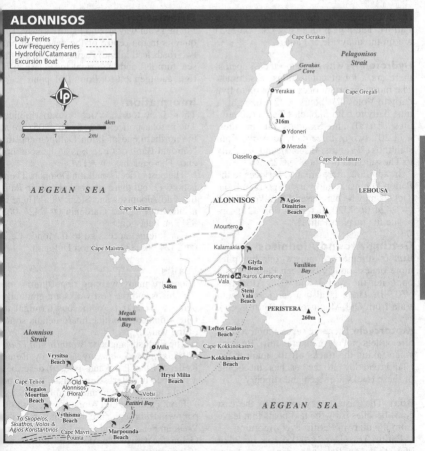

ALONNISOS

Legend:
Daily Ferries — — — —
Low Frequency Ferries — — — — —
Hydrofoil/Catamaran — · — · —
Excursion Boat · · · · · · · ·

Pelagonisos Strait

Cape Gerakas

Gerakas Cove

Yerakas

Cape Gregali

▲ 316m

Ydoneri

Merada

Diasello

Cape Paliofanaro

AEGEAN SEA

ALONNISOS

LEHOUSA

Cape Kalami

Mourtero

▲ Agios Dimitrios Beach

▲ 180m

Kalamakia

Cape Maistra

Glyfa Beach

Steni Vala ▲ *Ikaros Camping*

Vasilikos Bay

Steni Vala Beach

▲ 348m

PERISTERA ▲ 260m

Megali Ammos Bay

▲ Leftos Gialos Beach

Alonnisos Strait

Cape Kokkinokastro

Milia

▲ Kokkinokastro Beach

Vrysitsa Beach

Hrysi Milia Beach

Cape Telion
Megalos Mourtias Beach

Old Alonnisos (Hora)

Votsi

Patitiri *Patitiri Bay*

AEGEAN SEA

Vythisma Beach

To Skopelos, Skiathos, Volos & Agios Konstantinos

Cape Mavri Pounta

Marpounda Beach

EVIA & THE SPORADES

---

the hill-top capital of Alonnisos Town (now called Old Alonnisos, Hora or Palio Horio). The inhabitants abandoned their hill-top homes and were subsequently rehoused in hastily assembled concrete dwellings at Patitiri. In recent years many of the derelict houses in the capital have been bought for a song from the government and renovated by British and German settlers. There is now a flourishing expat artist community, several of whom reside here year-round.

Alonnisos is a green island with pine and oak trees, mastic and arbutus bushes, and fruit trees. The west coast is mostly precipitous cliffs but the east coast is speckled with pebbled beaches. The water around Alonnisos has been declared a marine park, and is the cleanest in the Aegean. Every house has a cesspit, so no sewage enters the sea.

Getting To/From Alonnisos

Ferry There are ferries from Alonnisos to Volos (five hours, €11.50, two or three daily), four to five daily to both Skopelos Town (30 minutes, €3.20) and Skiathos (two hours, €5.60), and one daily to Agios Konstantinos (5½ hours, €13.30). Tickets can be purchased from Alonnisos Travel

(☎ 2424 065 198, fax 2424 065 511) in Patitiri. The port police (☎ 2424 065 595) are on the quayside at Patitiri.

Hydrofoil As with Skiathos and Skopelos, there are a lot of connections in summer. The more important ones include up to five daily to Volos (2½ hours, €22.60), eight or nine daily to both Skopelos Town (20 minutes, €6.50) and Skiathos (40 minutes, €11.20), two or three daily to Agios Konstantinos (2½ hours, €26.40), and one daily to Thessaloniki (4½ hours, €25.50).

In addition, there are also services to the Pelion Peninsula and various ports in Evia. Tickets may be purchased from Ikos Travel (☎ 2424 065 320, fax 2424 065 321), opposite the quay in Patitiri.

Getting Around Alonnisos

Bus In summer, Alonnisos' one bus plies more or less hourly between Patitiri (from opposite the quay) and Old Alonnisos (€0.90). There is also a service to Steni Vala from Old Alonnisos via Patitiri (€1).

Motorcycle There are several motorcycle-hire outlets on Pelagson, in Patitiri. Be wary when taking the tracks off the main trans-island road down to the beaches since some of these tracks are steep and slippery.

Boat The easiest way to get to the east coast beaches is by the taxi boats that leave from the quay in Patitiri every morning.

Patitiri Travel (☎ 2424 065 154, fax 2424 066 277), on Pelagson, rents out four-person 15-horsepower motor boats. The cost is €52.85/132/293.50 for one day/three days/one week in August. Prices are lower at other times.

PATITIRI Πατητήρι

Patitiri sits between two sandstone cliffs at the southern end of the east coast. Not surprisingly, considering its origins, it's not a traditionally picturesque place, but it nevertheless makes a convenient base and has a relaxed atmosphere. Patitiri means 'wine press' and is where, in fact, grapes were processed prior to the demise of the wine industry.

Orientation

Finding your way around Patitiri is easy. The quay is in the centre of the waterfront and two roads lead inland. Facing away from the sea, turn left and then right for Pelasgon or right and then left for Ikion Dolopon.

Information

There is no tourist office or tourist police. The regular police (☎ 2424 065 205) are at the northern end of Ikion Dolopon and the National Bank of Greece is at the southern end. The bank has an ATM.

The post office is on Ikion Dolopon. There is no OTE but there are card phones in Patitiri, Old Alonnisos and Steni Vala. There is a laundrette called Gardenia (☎ 2424 065 831) on Pelasgon.

For Internet access go to Il Monde Café (☎ 2424 065 834) on Ikion Dolopon.

Walks

There are many walking opportunities on Alonnisos and the best walks are gradually being waymarked. At the bus terminal in Old Alonnisos a notice board details some of the walks.

The English-language *Alonnisos on Foot: A Walking & Swimming Guide* by Bente Keller & Elias Tsoukanas (€8.20) describes a number of interesting walks. It can be bought at Ikos Travel and local bookshops.

From Patitiri to Old Alonnisos a delightful path winds through shrubbery and orchards. Walk up Pelasgon and, 80m beyond Pension Galini, the path to Old Alonnisos starts. After 10 minutes turn right at a water tap, which may not be functioning. After about 15 minutes the path is intersected by a dirt road. Continue straight ahead on the path and after about 25 minutes you will come to the main road. Walk straight along this road and you will see Old Alonnisos ahead.

If you are coming from Old Alonnisos walk down the main road to Patitiri for about 350m and look for the sign on the right.

Organised Tours

Ikos Travel (☎ 2424 065 320, fax 2424 065 321) This company offers several excursions; talk to the genial and knowledgeable manager, Pakis Athanasiou, about these. They include one to Kyra Panagia, Psathoura and Peristera islets (€41.0) which includes a good picnic lunch on a beach, and a round-the-island excursion (€35.20). It also organises guided walks which usually include a picnic lunch and a swim. Stout walking shoes, trousers and a long-sleeved shirt are recommended. Ikos Travel will provide you with a locally produced, but very detailed, walking map.

Places to Stay

Accommodation standards are good on Alonnisos and, except for the first two weeks of August, you shouldn't have any difficulty finding a room.

The Rooms to Let service (☎ 2424 065 577), opposite the quay, will help you find a room on any part of the island.

Places to Stay – Budget

Pension Panorama (☎ 2424 065 240, fax 2424 065 598) 3-person studios/family apartments €41/70.40. The highly commendable Panorama has well-equipped studios and apartments in a sparkling white, blue-shuttered building high above the harbour. The owner, Eleni Athanasiou, often meets the incoming boats. Take the first left off Ikion Dolopon and follow the path upwards until you see the rooms on your right.

Ilias Rent Rooms (☎ 2424 065 451, fax 2424 065 972, Pelasgon 27) Doubles/2-person/3-person studios €29.40/41/44.80. The pleasant rooms and studios here are very clean. The rooms have a communal kitchen with kettle and sink, and the studios have a well-equipped kitchen area.

Pension Galini (☎ 2424 065 573, fax 2424 065 094, Pelasgon) Singles/doubles/5-person/6-person apartments €35.30/41/52.80/64.50. This pension, on the left 400m up Pelasgon, has beautifully furnished blue, white and yellow rooms and a fine flower-festooned terrace.

Places to Stay – Mid-Range

Liadromia Hotel (☎ 2424 065 521, fax 2424 065 096, e liadromia@alonnisos.com) Doubles €50, triple studios €70.40. This

impeccably maintained hotel was the first to open in Patitiri. The attractive rooms are full of character with stucco walls, hand-embroidered curtains, stone floors and traditional carved-wood furniture. Walk inland up Ikion Dolopon and take the first turn right up the steps, follow the path around and the hotel is on the left.

Hotel Haravgi (☎ 2424 065 090, fax 2424 065 189) Singles/doubles/triples with breakfast €41/52.80/64.50, double/triple studios €52.80/64.50. This hotel has modern rooms and there is a peaceful communal terrace overlooking the sea. To reach the hotel, turn left at the port and beyond the waterfront tavernas take the steps up to the right. At the top turn right to reach the hotel.

Places to Eat

Greek-island-hopping gourmets should definitely include Alonnisos on their 'must visit' lists as it has some top-notch eateries. Weight-watchers should, however, scrutinise menus carefully as many dishes contain liberal amounts of cream.

To Kamaki Ouzeri (☎ 2424 065 245, Ikion Dolopon) Mains €4.40-5.90. Mezedes are the speciality of this little ouzeri although the mains are also commendable. Among the delicious offerings are chickpea puree (€2.90) and cuttlefish in green sauce (€4.40).

Karavi Ouzeri (☎ 2424 066 100, Opposite National Bank) Mains €4.40-7.30. This superlative ouzeri has a delectable choice of mezedes and mains. There is cheese pie (€0.90), mussel pilaf (€5.90), chicken filled with bacon, chilli peppers, cream and cheese (€5.90) and many other delectable dishes to choose from.

The waterfront restaurants are all much of a muchness – take your pick and hope for the best.

Entertainment

Symvolo Bar (☎ 2424 066 156) You can enjoy jazz, blues, funk and rock at the Symvolo, two doors down from the National Bank. The atmospheric interior is a medley of traditional north African and Greek furniture and decorations. Cocktails include the lethal Rusty Nail (whisky and Drambuie) and the gentler Alexander (cognac, milk and cinnamon).

Bar Dennis (☎ 2424 065 569) This long-established bar on the southern waterfront is open all day and plays jazz, blues and Greek music. As well as alcoholic beverages and coffees it serves luscious ice cream.

Enigma Disco (☎ 2424 065 333, Pelasgon) Enigma rocks to teenybopper tunes when the tourist season kicks in.

OLD ALONNISOS

Old Alonnisos (Hora or Palio Horio) with its winding stepped alleys is a tranquil, picturesque place with lovely views. From the main road just outside the village a path leads down to pebbled Megalos Mourtias Beach and other paths lead south to Vythisma and Marpounda Beaches.

Places to Stay

There are no hotels in Old Alonnisos, but there is a growing number of domatia.

Fadasia House (☎ 2424 065 186, Plateia Hristou) Singles/doubles/2-person studios €23.50/35.30/44.80. This good-value place, near the central square, has attractive modern rooms and most have wood-raftered ceilings. The studios have a sink, refrigerator and hot plates. There is also a little snack bar and garden.

Rooms & Studios Hiliadromia (☎/fax 2424 065 814, Plateia Hristou) Doubles/2-person studios €35.30/44.80. The attractive rooms at the Hiliadromia have white stucco walls and stone floors. The studios have well-equipped kitchens and some have good sea views.

Konstantina Studios (☎ 2424 065 900, fax 2424 066 165, postal address: Alonnisos, North Sporades, Greece 370 05) This accommodation is the most luxurious in Old Alonnisos. It comprises spacious, traditionally furnished 2-/3-person studios with well-equipped kitchens and marble bathrooms; all with balconies with sea views. There is a garden with a barbecue for guests' use. Prices depend on the time of year and length of stay. For more information contact the proprietor, Konstantina Vlakou.

Places to Eat

Taverna Aloni (☎ 2424 065 550, Near bus terminal) Mains €4.10-5.30. At the Aloni you can tuck into good traditional taverna food while enjoying the superb sea views from its terrace.

Nappo (☎ 2424 065 579) Mains €5-6.20. The Italian owner, Paolo, serves up top-rate pizzas at this restaurant, signposted from the main street.

Astrofengia (☎ 2424 065 182) Mains €5.30-11.70. This sophisticated restaurant signposted from the bus terminal, offers exquisite mezedes such as hummus (€0.60) and rosti made with baked potato, bacon and cream (€3.50). The equally stimulating mains include vegetarian cannelloni (€5.90), beef and beer casserole (€7.30) and ostrich stroganoff (€11.70). Tempting desserts are on offer too (all €2.34).

Paraport Taverna (☎ 2424 065 608, main street) Mains €5-8.80. This taverna features some unusual and delicious items on its menu. Paraport pie (made from bacon, cheese and peppers) is €4.40 and seafood risotto is €4.70.

AROUND ALONNISOS

Most of Alonnisos' beaches are on the east coast which also means they avoid the strong summer meltemi winds and the flotsam that gets dumped on the west coast beaches. Apart from the road from Patitiri to Old Alonnisos, the only road is one which goes north to the tip of the island. It is driveable and sealed all the way though the last settlement, Yerakas (19km), is a bit of a let-down when you get there. Dirt tracks lead off to the beaches. Another sealed road leads to the yacht port of Steni Vala and a little farther as far as Kalamakia.

The first beach is the gently shelving **Hrysi Milia Beach**, which is the best beach for children. The next one up is **Kokkinokastro**, a beach of red pebbles. This is the site of the ancient city of Ikos (once the capital); there are remains of city walls and a necropolis under the sea.

Steni Vala is a small fishing village with a permanent population of 30 and good beach nearby. There are three tavernas and

Alonnisos Marine Park

The National Marine Park of Alonnisos – Northern Sporades is an ambitious but belatedly conceived project begun in May 1992. Its prime aim was the protection of the endangered Mediterranean monk seal, but also the preservation of other rare plant and animal species threatened with extinction.

The park is divided into two zones. Zone B, west of Alonnisos, is the less accessible of the two areas and comprises the islets of Kyra Panagia, Gioura, Psathoura, Skantzoura and Piperi. Restrictions on activities apply on all islands and in the case of Piperi, visitors are banned, since the island is home to around 33 species of bird, including 350 to 400 pairs of Eleanora's falcon. Other threatened sea birds found on Piperi include the shag and Audouin's gull. Visitors may approach other islands with private vessels or on day trips organised from Alonnisos.

Zone A comprises Alonnisos Island itself and the island of Peristera off Alonnisos' east coast. Most nautical visitors base themselves here at the yacht port of Steni Vala, though in theory the little harbour of Yerakas in the north of the island could serve as a base, though there are no facilities whatsoever. Restrictions on activities here are less stringent.

For the casual visitor the Alonnisos Marine Park is somewhat inaccessible since tours to the various islands are fairly limited and run during summer only. Bear in mind also that the park exists for the protection of marine animals and not for the entertainment of human visitors, so do not be surprised if you see very few animals at all. In a country not noted in its recent history for long-sightedness in the protection of its fauna, the Alonnisos Marine Park is a welcome and long-overdue innovation.

EVIA & THE SPORADES

30-odd rooms in *domatia*, as well as *Ikaros Camping* (☎ 2424 065 258). This is a small camping ground, but it is right on the beach and has reasonable shade from olive trees. Try *Taverna Steni Vala* (☎ 2424 065 590) for both food and lodgings. Mind you don't trip over the posing yachties; they're thick on the ground.

Kalamakia, 3km farther north, has a good beach, rooms and tavernas. **Agios Dimitrios Beach**, farther up still, is an unofficial nudist beach. There are no organised water sports on Alonnisos.

ISLETS AROUND ALONNISOS

Alonnisos is surrounded by eight uninhabited islets, all of which have rich flora and fauna. The largest remaining population of the monk seal *(Monachus monachus)*, a Mediterranean sea mammal faced with extinction, lives in the waters around the Sporades. These factors were the incentive behind the formation of the **marine park** in 1983, which encompasses the sea and islets around Alonnisos. Its research station is on Alonnisos, near Gerakas Cove. See the boxed text 'Alonnisos Marine Park'.

Piperi, to the north-east of Alonnisos, is a refuge for the monk seal and it is forbidden to set foot there without a licence to carry out research.

Also north-east of Alonnisos, **Gioura** has many rare plants and a rare species of wild goat. **Kyra Panagia** has good beaches and two abandoned monasteries. **Psathoura** has the submerged remains of an ancient city and the brightest lighthouse in the Aegean.

Peristera, just off Alonnisos' east coast, has several sandy beaches and the remains of a castle. **Lehousa** sits immediately northwest of here.

Skantzoura, to the south-east of Alonnisos, is the habitat of falcons and the rare Aegean seagull. The eighth islet is tiny **Adelphi**, between Peristera and Skantzoura.

Skyros Σκύρος

postcode 340 07 • pop 2800

Skyros is some distance from the rest of the group and differs topographically. Almost bisected, its northern half has rolling, cultivated hills and pine forests, but the largely

Skyros Carnival

In this pre-Lenten festival, which takes place on the last two Sundays before *Kathara Deftera* (Clean Monday – the first Monday in Lent), young men don goat masks, hairy jackets and dozens of copper goat bells. They then proceed to clank and dance around town, each with a partner (another man), dressed up as a Skyrian bride but also wearing a goat mask. Women and children also wear fancy dress. During these revelries there is singing and dancing, performances of plays, recitations of satirical poems and drinking and feasting. These riotous goings-on are overtly pagan, with elements of Dionysian festivals, goat worship (in ancient times Skyros was renowned for its excellent goat meat and milk), and the cult of Achilles, the principal deity worshipped here. The transvestism evident in the carnival may derive from the fact that Achilles hid on Skyros dressed as a girl to escape the oracle's prophecy that he would die in battle at Troy.

uninhabited south is barren and rocky. It is less visited by tourists than other islands of the Sporades, and with the demise in 2000 of the hydrofoil link with the other Sporades and Volos this trend will probably continue. A number of expats, particularly English and Dutch, have made Skyros their home.

There are only two settlements of any worth on the island: the small port of Linaria, and Skyros Town, the capital, 10km away on the east coast. Skyros is visited by poseurs rather than package tourists – and as many of these are wealthy young Athenians as foreigners. Skyros also has quite a different atmosphere from other islands in this region, reminding you more of the Cyclades than the Sporades, especially the stark, cubist architecture of Skyros Town.

Some visitors come to Skyros to attend courses at the Skyros Centre, a centre for holistic health and fitness. See the Skyros Town section for details. Solo women travellers are increasingly drawn to Skyros because of its reputation as a safe, hassle-free island.

Skyros' factual history was mundane in comparison to its mythological origins until Byzantine times, when rogues and criminals from the mainland were exiled on Skyros. Rather than driving away invading pirates, these opportunistic exiles entered into a mutually lucrative collaboration with them.

The exiles became the elite of Skyrian society, furnishing and decorating their houses with elaborately hand-carved furniture, plates and copper ornaments from Europe, the Middle East and East Asia. Some of these items were brought by seafarers and some were looted by pirates from merchant ships.

Those people on the island before the mainland exiles arrived soon began to emulate the elite in their choice of decor, so local artisans cashed in by making copies of the furniture and plates, a tradition which continues to this day. Almost every Skyrian house is festooned with plates, copperware and hand-carved furniture.

Other traditions also endure. Many elderly Skyrian males still dress in the traditional baggy pantaloons and *trohadia* (multi-thonged footwear unique to the island). The Skyros Lenten Carnival is Greece's weirdest and most wonderful festival, and is the subject of Joy Koulentianou's book *The Goat Dance of Skyros*. See the 'Skyros Carnival' boxed text.

Another special feature of Skyros which shouldn't go unmentioned, although it will probably go unseen, is the wild Skyrian pony, a breed unique to Skyros. The ponies used to roam freely but are now almost extinct. The only ones you are likely to see are tame ones kept as domestic pets.

Finally, Skyros was the last port of call for the English poet Rupert Brooke (1887–1915), who died of septicaemia at the age of 28 on a ship off the coast of Skyros in 1915, en route to Gallipoli.

Getting To/From Skyros

Air In summer there are only two flights weekly (Wednesday and Sunday) between Athens and Skyros (50 minutes, €47). It is rumoured that a private air service will eventually supplement Olympic's severely reduced schedule. For tickets see Skyros Travel Agency, in Skyros Town.

Ferry There are ferry services at least twice daily in summer, provided by F/B *Lyko-midis*, between the port of Kymi (Evia) and Skyros (two hours, €7.10). You can buy ferry tickets from Lykomidis Ticket Office (☎ 2222 091 789, fax 2222 091 791), on Agoras in Skyros Town. There is also a ferry ticket office at Linaria.

Skyros Travel Agency also sells tickets for the Kymi-Athens bus (3¼ hours, €8.60) which meets the ferry on arrival at Kymi.

Getting Around Skyros

In addition to the options listed here, it is also possible to join a boat trip to sites around the island. See Organised Tours under the Skyros Town entry.

Bus In high season there are five buses daily from Skyros Town to Linaria (€0.70) and Molos (via Magazia). Buses for both Skyros Town and Molos meet the boats at Linaria. However, outside of high season there are only two buses to Linaria (to coincide with the ferry arrivals) and none to Molos. Bus services to Kalamitsa, Pefkos and Atsitsa are organised on an ad hoc basis during summer. Contact Skyros Travel for full details.

Car & Motorcycle Cars and 4WD vehicles can be rented from Skyros Travel Agency. A car goes for between €38.20 and €41 and a 4WD from €44.80 to €55.80. Motorcycles can be rented from Motorbikes (☎ 2222 092 022). To find it, walk north and take the first turn right past Skyros Travel.

SKYROS TOWN

Skyros' capital is a striking, dazzlingly white town of flat-roofed Cycladic-style houses draped over a high rocky bluff, topped by a 13th-century fortress and the monastery of Agios Georgios. It is a gem of a place and a wander around its labyrinthine, whitewashed streets will probably produce an invitation to admire a traditional Skyrian house by its proud and hospitable owner.

Orientation

The bus terminal is at the southern end of town on the main thoroughfare of Agoras, an animated street lined with tavernas, snack bars and grocery shops, and flanked by narrow winding alleyways. To reach the central square of Plateia Iroön walk straight ahead up the hill.

Beyond Plateia Iroön, Agoras forks, with the right fork leading up to the fortress and Moni Agiou Georgiou (with fine frescoes), from where there are breathtaking views. The left fork leads to Plateia Rupert Brooke, dominated by a disconcerting bronze statue of a nude Rupert Brooke. The frankness of the statue caused an outcry among the islanders when it was first installed in the 1930s. From this square a cobbled, stepped path leads in 15 minutes to Magazia Beach.

Information

Skyros does not have an EOT or tourist police, but you can find most information from Skyros Travel Agency (☎ 2222 091 600, fax 2222 092 123, e skyrostravel@hol.gr) on Agoras, including room bookings. To get to the regular police (☎ 2222 091 274) take the first right after Skyros Travel Agency, and turn right at the T-junction.

The National Bank of Greece is on Agoras next to the central square. It sports an ATM. Foreign-language newspapers and magazines can be bought at an agency opposite the bank.

The post office is on the west side of the central square. The OTE is opposite the police station. Internet access is available from 9am to 11pm at Mepoh Café Bar on Agoras.

Things to See & Do

Skyros Town has two museums. The **archaeological museum** (☎ *2222 091 327, Near Plateia Rupert Brooke; admission €1.50; open 8.30am-3pm Tues-Sun*) features an impressive collection of artefacts from Mycenaean to Roman times, as well as a traditional Skyrian house interior, transported in its entirety from the home of the benefactor.

The **Faltaïts Museum** (☎ *2222 091 232, Near Plateia Rupert Brooke; admission €1.50; open 10am-1pm & 5.30pm-8pm daily*)

SKYROS

Cape Aloni

Palamari Beach

Cape Vathy

Frokala

Katounes

Kyra Panagia

Atsitsa

Cape Pouria

Molos
Magazia
Skyros Town

Moni Agiou Dimitriou

SKYROS

Moni Agiou Georgiou

AEGEAN SEA

Cape Oros

Agios Fokas

Alyko Bay

KOULOURI

Aspous

Mealos Bay

Katholiko Bay

Pefkos

Cape Souliotis

Pefkos Bay

Aherounes

Loutro

Aherounes Bay

Linaria

Kalamitsa

RINIA

VALAXA

Kalamitsa Bay

Mt Dafni (734m)

Mt Kohilas (792m)

Mt Vouva (727m)

Caves

Cape Latomio

Cape Exo Myti

Rupert Brooke's Grave

Tris Boukes Bay

Tris Boukes

Cape Castelli

To Kymi (Evia)

PLATIA

Renes Bay

Cape Marmaro

SARAKINO

Daily Ferries
Low Frequency Ferries
Hydrofoil/Catamaran
Excursion Boat

0   2   4km
0   1   2mi

is a private museum housing the outstanding collection of a Skyrian ethnologist, Manos Faltaïts. The collection includes costumes, furniture, books, ceramics and photographs.

The English co-owner of Mepoh Café Bar (see Information), Janet Smith, is a Reiki Master and, at the time of writing, planned to open a **Reiki Centre** (☎ 2222 029 039, e janetinskyros@hotmail.com) opposite the cafe.

The versatile Niko Sikkes (☎ 2222 092 707 or 2222 092 158) leads **walking tours** around Skyros. He also gives **talks** on the traditions and culture of Skyros (in Dutch and English) at the Faltaïts Museum. For more information phone him or call at his shop, the Argos.

Courses

Skyros Centre (☎ 020-7267 4424, fax 728-3063, e skyros@easynet.co.uk, 92 Prince of Wales Rd, London NW5 3NE, UK) This centre runs courses on a whole range of subjects from yoga and dancing, to massage and windsurfing. The emphasis is on developing a holistic approach to life. There is a branch in Skyros Town, but the main 'outdoor' complex is at Atsitsa Beach, on the west oast. For detailed information on its fortightly programs contact the Skyros Centre.

Kristina's Cooking School Course \$600 (€319.90) In the off season, Australian and long-term Skyros resident Kristina Brooks-Tsalapatani of Kristina's at Pegasus (see Places to Eat) runs this cooking school. Her Greek cookery course runs over five mornings, teaching a maximum of eight nascent gastronomes all about cooking Greek-style. Bookings are essential.

Organised Tours

Skyros Travel Agency (☎ 2222 091 600, fax 2222 092 123) This agency runs a boat excursion (€16.15) to Sarakino Islet and the Pendekali and Gerania sea caves.

Places to Stay

Accommodation in Skyros Town is usually in the form of rooms, often decorated with traditional plates, in family houses. Since these can be hard to find yourself, you will often be met at the bus stop with offers of domatia from the women who run them. It's not a bad idea to take up one of these offers, at least for starters. Prices should be in the €22.40 to €34 range for a double, though as elsewhere there are seasonal fluctuations.

Failing that, head for Skyros Travel Agency (see Information) for references to suitable rooms.

Hotel Elena (☎ 2222 091 738, 091 070) singles/doubles €11.70/23.50, singles/doubles/triples with bath €15/30/35.20. This aged hotel has clean rooms and most have a refrigerator and a balcony. From the bus terminal walk north and take the first right.

Pension Nikolas (☎ 2222 091 778, fax 2222 093 400) Rooms €44.80-58.70. This pension has attractive, well-maintained rooms and is a good option for visitors wanting a quiet place to stay. From the bus terminal walk back towards Linaria for 50m and where the main road veers left, continue straight ahead and uphill following the signs.

Hotel Nefeli & Skyriana Spitia Studios (☎ 2222 091 964, fax 2222 092 061) Singles/doubles/3-person studios €50/62/79. The Nefeli has lovely rooms with old photographs depicting traditional Skyrian life. It sports a large swimming pool. The hotel is on the left just before you enter Skyros Town. The adjoining studios are well equipped and furnished in traditional Skyrian style.

Places to Eat

In recent times good restaurants in Skyros have proliferated like mushrooms in a dark cellar.

O Pappous kai Ego (☎ 2222 093 200, Agoras) Mains €4.70-7.30. This popular place with a stylish interior serves unusual mezedes such as mushrooms with cream (€3.20) and squid with aniseed; tasty mains include chicken in wine (€4.70) and pork in soya sauce (€7.30).

Margetis (☎ 2222 091 311, Agoras) Mains €8.80-17.60. This is the place to go for fresh fish. Other restaurants sell fish but Margetis specialises in it. Red mullet and sea bream are €30.10 a kilogram.

Kristina's at Pegasus (☎ 2222 091 897) Mains €4.70-6.50. Open Mon-Sat. This longestablished place, signposted from the central square, was something of a gastronomic trail blazer on Skyros. Kristina conjures up delectable Greek and international dishes using local produce. The *kaseri* and *sac* cheeses (local specialities), chicken fricassee and cheesecake are highly recommended. Mains include a vegetarian mixed plate (€4.70). Dining is on a relaxing little terrace.

Liakos Café & Restaurant (☎ 2222 093 509) Mains €5.60-8.20. During the day you can have a drink or meal in the Liakos' serene interior where botanical prints grace the walls. In the evening most people prefer to sit out on the roof terrace. The imaginative menu includes fava (€2.60), aubergines stuffed with feta (€2.90), rice with mussels and tomato sauce (€5.90) and chicken with yoghurt (€5.40). Turn right after Skyros Travel Agency.

Anemos Cafe & Ouzeri (☎ 2222 092 822, Near Plateia Rupert Brooke) Mains €4.10-7.30. At Anemos you can enjoy a relaxing drink, snack or main meal on a romantic terrace overlooking Magazia. Among the interesting mezedes offered are cuttlefish with spinach (€4.70) and the intriguing-sounding vegetarian aphrodisiac (€3.80). There's an equally creative range of main dishes and desserts, and the wines include regional favourites from all over Greece.

Entertainment

Nightlife centres around the bars on Athinos, all of which are tastefully decorated. One gets the impression neither the locals or expats would tolerate tackiness. There's always some place open all year due to the large transient population of young soldiers.

Kata Lathos (☎ 2222 091 671, Opposite central square) Popular with a young crowd, this bar which has a roof garden plays rock, jazz and blues.

Apokalypsis (mobile 69-7238 7599, Next to post office) This place gets top marks for its stylish interior. The evening kicks in with soul, followed by hits from the 60s and 70s, and finishes off in the wee hours with Greek music.

Iröon (☎ 2222 093 122, Opposite central square) This bar is another favourite with the young crowd; it belts out rock, soul and funk.

Kalypso (☎ 2222 092 160) The farther north you go along Agoras the more mellow the sounds. At the classy little Kalypso, where Agoras forks, mostly jazz and blues is played.

Neoptolemos (☎ 2222 092 484, Next to Kalypso) Like its neighbour, this pleasant bar is one of the quieter ones. As well as breakfasts, coffees and juices, it offers 70 different cocktails.

Mepoh Café Bar (☎ 2222 091 016, Agoras) When the computers shut down at the Mepoh everyone gets down to the serious business of drinking and listening to an eclectic range of music.

Stone (☎ 2222 092 355) Skyros has three discos. Stone, just south of Skyros Town, was the 'in' disco at the time of writing.

Kavos Bar (☎ 2222 093 213) Kavos, at Linaria, is a popular spot for drinks and evening gossip. Try to be here when the Lykomidis ferry comes in and witness the impressive sound when Richard Strauss' *Also Sprach Zarathustra* is blasted out over the bay from huge speakers. Better still, listen out for it while on the ferry – the sound is better.

MAGAZIA & MOLOS
Μαγαζιά & Μώλος

The resort of Magazia is at the southern end of a splendid, long sandy beach, a short distance north of Skyros Town; quieter Molos is at the northern end of the beach. Although the two are contiguous, Magazia is a compact and attractive place of winding alleys, whereas, with the exception of its windmill and the adjacent rock-hewn Church of Agios Nikolaos, Molos is a characterless, spread-out development.

Places to Stay – Budget & Mid-Range

Skyros Camping (☎ 2222 092 458, Adult/tent €4.40/4.40. In Magazia, opposite the steps up to Skyros Town, is this camping ground, Skyros' only one. It's unofficial and rather run-down, with thirsty-looking olive trees offering shade.

Ferogia Domatia (☎ 2222 091 828, Magazia) Singles/doubles/triples/4-person apartment €23.50/35.30/41/58.70. These spotless rooms, on the beach, have pleasant modern furniture, refrigerators and balconies. The apartment is beautifully furnished and contains lovely antique Skyrian ceramics displayed on carved-wood shelves

To Perigiali (☎ 2222 091 889, fax 2222 092 770, e perigiali@skyrosnet.gr) Singles/doubles/2/4-person studios €44.80/50/52.80/64.50. These well-equipped and attractive studios near the southern end of Magazia Beach are surrounded by a beautiful garden

Diadameia Domatia (☎ 2222 092 008, fax 2222 092 009, Near Skyros Camping) Doubles/triples €55.70/64.70. These spacious and beautifully furnished rooms above the family ceramics shop in Magazia have air-con and a refrigerator.

Hotel Paradise (☎ 2222 091 220/560, fax 2222 091 443, next to bus terminal) Doubles/triples €58.70/73.50. This pleasant Molos hotel has rooms with cream marble floors and white walls. Each room has air-con, refrigerator and TV.

Places to Stay – Top End

Skyros Palace (☎ 2222 091 994, fax 2222 092 070) Doubles/triples €60/74.80. This i the island's most luxurious hotel. It's a complex of tasteful apartments, north of Molos. Each apartment has air-con, verandas and music channels. The complex has a cafe, bar, restaurant, TV lounge and swimming pool, and is 50m from a good beach. Mosquitoes can be a problem: ask for a mosquito zapper.

Places to Eat

Stefanos (☎ 2222 091 272) Mains €3.50-7.30. This restaurant has a great location overlooking Magazia Beach, at the southern end. A range of ready-made food and grilled meat and fish is offered.

Tou Thoma to Magazi (☎ 2222 091 903) At this taverna on the beach at Molos the freshness of the fish is guaranteed as it's caught by the owner's father, a local fisherman. A portion of lobster and spaghetti is €14.70 and red mullet is €20.50 a kilogram.

Anemomilos Ouzeri & Bar (☎ 2222 093 873) Mains €3.80-7.30. In a splendid setting at Molos' 19th-century windmill near the little rock-hewn Church of Agios Nikalaos, the Anemomilos serves well-prepared food during the day, and in the evening metamorphoses into a lively bar. Mezedes include fava (€2.60), squid (€2.60) and calamari (€3.50); chicken souvlaki (€5.30) and shrimps in tomato sauce (€7.30) feature in the mains.

Shopping

Diadameia Ceramic Shop (☎ 2222 92 008) A good selection of Skyrian ceramics is on sale at this shop in Magazi below the domatia of the same name.

Skyros Shop It's hard to imagine any non-Skyrian wanting to wear the multi-thonged *trohadia*, except maybe a foot fetishist who is into bondage. They can be bought at this shop on the street leading to Plateia Rupert Brooke.

Argo Shop (☎ 2222 92 158, Opposite Skyros Shop) This shop, owned by expat Dutchman, Niko Sikkes, sells high-quality copies of ceramics from the Faltaïts Museum.

Woodcarvings are a classy buy, though they can be expensive. There are several *workshops* scattered round town.

AROUND SKYROS
Beaches

At **Atsitsa**, on the west coast, there's a tranquil pebble beach shaded by pines. The beach attracts freelance campers, and there's the main outdoor centre of the Skyros Centre and a *taverna* with domatia here. Just to the north is the even less crowded beach of **Kyra Panagia** (also with freelance campers).

At **Pefkos**, 10km south-east of Atsitsa, there is another good but small beach and a taverna. If you don't have transport take a Skyros Town-Linaria bus and ask to be let off at the turn-off. It's a 3km walk from there to the beach. Farther east, the pebble-and-sand beach at **Kalamitsa** is reasonable but not really worth the extra effort to get there and there is not much shade. There are no organised water sports on Skyros.

Palamari, near the airport, is a long stretch of sandy beach which does not get crowded.

Rupert Brooke's Grave

Rupert Brooke's well-tended grave is in a quiet olive grove just inland from Tris Boukes Bay in the south of the island. The actual grave is poorly marked with a rough wooden sign in Greek on the roadside, but you can hardly miss it. The gravestone is inscribed with some verses of Brooke's among which is the following apt epitaph:

If I should die think only this of me:
That there's some corner of a foreign field
That is forever England.

No buses go to this corner of the island. However, you can take an excursion boat to Sarakino Islet, or drive or walk along a good, graded scenic road from Kalamitsa, built for the Greek navy, which now has a naval station on Tris Boukes Bay.

If you walk it will take about 1½ hours; take food and water. If you have come this far with the aim of getting to the sea, you will have to turn back since the area farther down the hill is restricted by the Greek navy and the road onwards is closed.

Phone numbers listed incorporate changes due in Oct 2002; see p83

The Ionian group, known in Greek as the Heptanisa or 'the Seven Islands', consists of seven main islands anchored in the Ionian Sea: Corfu, Paxi, Kefallonia, Zakynthos, Ithaki, Lefkada and Kythira (the last is more accessible from the Peloponnese). The islands differ from other island groups – they're more reminiscent of Corfu's neighbour Italy, not least in light, and their colours are mellow and green compared with the stark, dazzling brightness of the Aegean.

These islands receive a lot of rain (Corfu has the nation's highest rainfall) and, consequently, the vegetation, with the exception of the more exposed Kythira, is more luxuriant. Overall, vegetation combines elements of the tropical with forests that could be northern European: Exotic orchids as well as wildflowers emerge below spring snowlines, and eucalypts and acacias share soil with plane, oak and maple trees. The islands do not experience the *meltemi*, and as a result they can be extremely hot in summer.

The culture and cuisine of each Ionian island is unique and differs from the Aegean islands and Crete. Influences from Mediterranean Europe and Britain have also been stronger, yet have developed with special individuality on each island.

For information on this region on the Internet, see **W** www.ionianislands.gr.

SUGGESTED ITINERARIES

One week

Northern Ionians Spend two days in Corfu Town; explore the narrow streets of the old town and visit the museums. Visit Durrell territory in the pretty north-east coast. Spend one night in Paleokastritsa or Lakones; see the sights of the area, and have a meal at one of the restaurants on the Lakones-Makrades road. Spend a day at a west-coast resort and catch a sunset at Pelekas, or head to the unspoilt Diapondia Islands. Spend one or two nights on Paxi, and be sure to visit Antipaxi.

Southern Ionians Spend a couple of days on Lefkada, explore the capital and relax on a west-coast beach, plus visit Meganisi on a day trip or overnight there. Spend two days on Ithaki, visiting

Highlights

- Wandering the narrow streets of Corfu's old town and admiring the fine Venetian buildings
- Walking the ancient olive groves of Paxi and swimming in the crystal-clear water of Antipaxi
- Travelling the dramatic west coast of Lefkada, with its incredible beaches and exquisite blue water
- Exploring the traditional, unspoilt villages and fine pebble beaches of Meganisi
- Unwinding on the beautiful white-sand beach of Myrtos in Kefallonia with a bottle of the island's unique Robola white wine
- Relaxing in the picturesque fishing villages of Frikes and Kioni on Ithaki, Odysseus' homeland
- Visiting the tranquil inland villages of Kythira, and swimming at the island's lovely undeveloped beaches

Vathy and the villages of Anogi, Frikes and Kioni. Have two days in Fiskardo on Kefallonia (in the high season stay elsewhere and visit on a day trip), to see Assos village and Myrtos Beach.

Spend one day in Sami to visit the nearby caves and Antisamos Beach, or a day in Argostoli.

Two weeks
Combine the above itineraries, but allow an extra day for travel between the two island groups.

History & Mythology

The origin of the name Ionian is obscure but is thought to derive from the goddess Io. Yet another of Zeus' paramours, Io, while fleeing the wrath of a jealous Hera (in the shape of a heifer), happened to pass through the waters now known as the Ionian Sea.

If we are to believe Homer, the islands were important during Mycenaean times; however, no magnificent palaces or even modest villages from that period have been revealed, although Mycenaean tombs have been unearthed. Ancient history lies buried beneath tonnes of earthquake rubble – seismic activity has been constant on all Ionian islands, including Kythira.

According to Homer, Odysseus' kingdom consisted not only of Ithaca (Ithaki) but also encompassed Kefallonia, Zakynthos and Lefkada. Ithaca has long been controversial. Classicists and archaeologists in the 19th century concluded that Homer's Ithaca was modern Ithaki, his Sami was Sami on Kefallonia, and his Zakynthos was today's Zakynthos, which sounded credible. But in the early 20th century German archaeologist Wilhelm Dorpfeld put a spanner in the works by claiming that Lefkada was ancient Ithaca, modern Ithaki was ancient Sami and Kefallonia was ancient Doulichion. His theories have now fallen from favour with everyone except the people of Lefkada.

By the 8th century BC, the Ionian islands were in the clutches of the mighty city-state of Corinth, which regarded them as stepping stones on the route to Sicily and Italy. A century later, Corfu staged a successful revolt against Corinth, which was allied to Sparta, and became an ally of Sparta's archenemy, Athens. This alliance provoked Sparta into challenging Athens, thus precipitating the Peloponnesian Wars (431–404 BC). The wars left Corfu depleted, as they did all participants, and Corfu became little more than

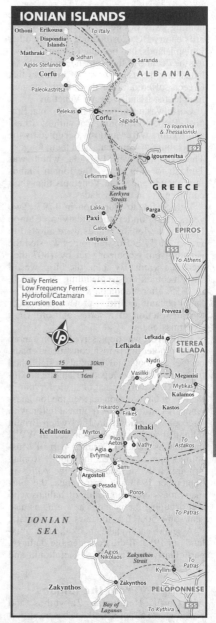

IONIAN ISLANDS

a staging post for whoever happened to be holding sway in Greece. By the end of the 3rd century BC, Corfu, along with the other Ionian islands, had become Roman. Following the decline of the Roman Empire, the islands saw the usual waves of invaders that Greece suffered. After the fall of Constantinople, the islands became Venetian.

Corfu was never part of the Ottoman Empire. Paxi, Kefallonia, Zakynthos, Ithaki and Kythira were variously occupied by the Turks, but the Venetians held them longest. The exception was Lefkada, which was Turkish for 200 years. The Ionian islands fared better under the Venetians than their counterparts in the Cyclades.

Venice fell to Napoleon in 1797. Two years later, under the Treaty of Campo Formio, the Ionian islands were allotted to France. In 1799 Russian forces wrested the islands from Napoleon, but by 1807 they were his again. By then, the all-powerful British couldn't resist meddling. As a result, in 1815, after Napoleon's downfall, the islands became a British protectorate under the jurisdiction of a series of Lord High Commissioners.

British rule was oppressive but, on a more positive note, the British constructed roads, bridges, schools and hospitals, established trade links and developed agriculture and industry. However, the nationalistic fervour in the rest of Greece soon reached the Ionian islands. A call for *enosis* (political union with Greece) was realised in 1864 when Britain relinquished the islands to Greece. In WWII the Italians invaded Corfu as part of Mussolini's plan to resurrect the mighty Roman Empire. Italy surrendered to the Allies in September 1943 and, in revenge, the Germans massacred thousands of Italians who had occupied the island. The Germans also sent some 5000 Corfiot Jews to Auschwitz.

A severe earthquake shook the Ionian islands in 1953. It did considerable damage, particularly on Zakynthos, Kefallonia and Ithaki.

Getting To/From the Ionians

Air Corfu, Kefallonia, Zakynthos and Kythira have airports; Lefkada has no airport but Aktion airport, near Preveza on the mainland, is a 30-minute bus journey away. All these airports have frequent flights to/from Athens. See W www.olympic-airways.gr for information.

Many charter flights come from northern Europe and the UK to Corfu, and Kefallonia, Zakynthos and Aktion also receive such tourist flights.

Bus Buses run between Corfu and both Athens and Thessaloniki, and between Athens and Paxi, Kefallonia and Zakynthos. Lefkada is joined to the mainland by a causeway and can be reached by bus from Athens as well as Patras. Buses from Athens to Corfu, Lefkada, Kefallonia and Zakynthos depart from the intercity bus terminal at Kifissou 100, 7km north-west of Omonia.

See W www.ktel.org for limited schedule details.

Ferry – Domestic The Peloponnese has several departure ports for the Ionian islands: Patras for ferries to Kefallonia, Ithaki, Paxi and Corfu; Kyllini for ferries to Kefallonia and Zakynthos; and Piraeus, Kalamata, Neapoli and Gythio for Kythira, which is also connected with Crete (Kastelli-Kissamos) by ferry. Epiros has one port, Igoumenitsa, for Corfu and Paxi; and Sterea Ellada has one, Astakos, for Ithaki and Kefallonia (although this service is limited to the high season). There are numerous Internet sites offering information on ferry timetables; among the best is W www.ferries.gr.

The following table gives an overall view of the available scheduled domestic ferries to this island group from mainland ports in high season. Further details and inter-island links can be found under each island entry.

Ferry – International From Corfu, ferries depart for Brindisi, Bari, Ancona, Trieste and Venice in Italy. At least three times weekly in summer, a ferry goes from Kefallonia to Brindisi via Igoumenitsa and Corfu. In July and August this ferry also calls at Zakynthos and Paxi.

From Corfu it's also possible to catch a ferry to Albania.

Ferry Connections to the Ionian Islands

origin	destination	duration	price	frequency
Astakos	Piso Aetos (Ithaki)	2¾ hours	€5	1 daily
Gythio	Diakofti (Kythira)	2½ hours	€7.05	3 weekly
Igoumenitsa	Corfu Town	1¾ hours	€4.10	up to 14 daily
Igoumenitsa	Lefkimmi (Corfu)	1 hour	€2.50	6 daily
Igoumenitsa	Gaïos (Paxi)	1¾ hours	€5	1 daily
Kyllini	Zakynthos Town	1¼ hours	€4.40	up to 7 daily
Kyllini	Argostoli (Kefallonia)	2¾ hours	€8.80	2 daily
Kyllini	Poros (Kefallonia)	1½ hours	€6.20	2 daily
Neapoli	Agia Pelagia (Kythira)	1 hour	€5.90	2-3 daily
Patras	Corfu Town	7 hours	€17.90	
Patras	Sami (Kefallonia)	2½ hours	€10	2 daily
Patras	Vathy (Ithaki)	3½ hours	€10.90	2 daily
Piraeus	Diakofti	6½ hours	€16.50	2 weekly
Sagiada	Corfu Town	45 mins	€3.80	1 weekly

Hydrofoil There are a few useful hydrofoil services between the mainland and the Ionians. Between May and September there is a triangular service linking Igoumenitsa, Corfu and Paxi. From June to August a fast service links Kythira with Piraeus (usually via a few ports in the eastern Peloponnese).

Corfu & the Diapondia Islands

postcode 491 00 • pop 111,040

Corfu is the second-largest and greenest Ionian island, and also the best known. In Greek, the island's name is Kerkyra (Κέρκυρα; **ker**-kih-rah). It was Homer's 'beautiful and rich land', and Odysseus' last stop on his journey home to Ithaca. Shakespeare reputedly used it as a background for *The Tempest*. In the 20th century, the Durrell brothers, among others, extolled its virtues.

With its beguiling landscape of vibrant wildflowers and slender cypress trees rising out of shimmering olive groves, Corfu is considered by many as Greece's most beautiful island. With the highest rainfall, it's also the nation's major vegetable garden and produces scores of herbs, and the mountain air is heavily scented.

There's a lot of information about Corfu on the Internet, but surprisingly we've yet to find the definitive site offering all the information you'll need, as exists for the other Ionian islands.

Getting To/From Corfu

Air Corfu has at least three Olympic Airways flights to/from Athens daily (€84), and three flights a week to/from Thessaloniki (€73.40). The Olympic Airways office (☎ 2661 038 694) is at Polyla 11, Corfu Town.

Aegean Air (☎ 2661 027 100) has two or three flights daily between Athens and Corfu for a similar price. Aegean Air's office is at the airport.

Bus KTEL buses run two or three times daily between Corfu Town and Athens (11 hours, €26.70) – some services go via Lefkimmi in the island's south. There is also a service once or twice daily to/from Thessaloniki (nine hours, €25.70); for both destinations budget an additional €3 for the ferry between Corfu and the mainland. Tickets must be bought in advance; Corfu's KTEL long-distance bus station and ticket office is on Avramiou, inland from the new port.

Phone numbers listed incorporate changes due in Oct 2002; see p83

IONIAN ISLANDS

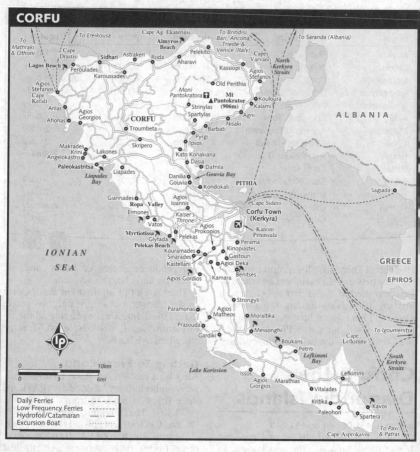

CORFU

Ferry – Domestic Hourly ferries run between Corfu and Igoumenitsa (1¾ hours, €4.10). Every Friday a ferry goes to Sagiada on the mainland (45 minutes, €3.80). Car ferries go to Paxi (3½ hours, €8.80) four times weekly, via Igoumenitsa (but the hydrofoil is more frequent, faster and not much more expensive). You can travel to Patras on one of the frequent international ferries that call at Corfu in summer. Corfu's port police can be contacted on ☎ 2661 032 655.

There are also half a dozen ferries daily between Lefkimmi in the island's south and Igoumenitsa (one hour, €2.50). Lefkimmi's port police are on ☎ 2662 023 277.

Ferry – International Corfu is on the Patras-Igoumenitsa ferry route to Italy (Brindisi, Bari, Ancona, Trieste, Venice), though some ferries originate in Igoumenitsa. Ferries go a few times daily to Brindisi (seven hours, €42 to €48 depending on the company), and in summer usually once daily to Bari (10 hours, €45), Ancona (14 hours, €64.60), Trieste (21 hours, €70.50) and Venice (30 hours, €64.60). See also the Igoumenitsa Getting There &

Away section in the Northern Greece chapter and the Patras Getting There & Away section in the Peloponnese chapter.

Italian Ferries and Ventouris Ferries operate high-speed catamaran services between Corfu and Brindisi. There are daily services from May to mid-September. The journey takes 3¼ hours and fares are €56 in low season, €65 in high season (passengers aged under 26 are eligible for a 20% discount).

Shipping agencies selling tickets are found mostly on Xenofondos Stratigou. Alsi Travel & Shipping (☎ 2661 080 030, fax 2661 044 148), directly across from Corfu's new port at Ethnikis Antistaseos 1, can help with information on most shipping lines – the assortment of companies, routes and prices can get confusing!

Much less popular than the Italy-bound ferries is the twice-daily ferry between Corfu and Saranda in Albania (one hour, €11.80). Most travellers to Albania need a visa, so it's best to investigate this before you leave home. Alternatively, Petrakis Lines (☎ 2661 031 649), Eleftherious Venizelou, offers regular day trips to the historical areas around Agiou Saranda for around €52.80. No visa is required for this trip.

Hydrofoil Petrakis Lines operates passenger-only hydrofoils between Corfu, Igoumenitsa and Paxi from May until September. There are at least two services daily between Corfu and Paxi (one hour direct or 1¾ hours via Igoumenitsa, €11.20). There's one hydrofoil daily except Monday from Corfu to Igoumenitsa, and four weekly from Igoumenitsa to Corfu.

Getting Around Corfu

To/From the Airport There is no bus service between Corfu Town and the airport. Bus Nos 6 and 10 from Plateia San Rocco in Corfu Town stop on the main road 500m from the airport (en route to Benitses and Ahillion).

Bus Destinations of KTEL buses (green-and-cream) from Corfu Town's long-distance bus station (☎ 2661 030 627), on Avramiou, are as follows:

destination	duration	frequency	via
Agios Gordios	40 mins	5 daily	Sinarades
Agios Stefanos	1½ hours	3 daily	Sidhari
Aharavi	1¼ hours	4 daily	Roda
Glyfada	45 mins	6 daily	Vatos
Kavos	1½ hours	10 daily	Lefkimmi
Loutses	1¼ hours	2 daily	Kassiopi
Messonghi	45 mins	3 daily	Benitses
Paleokastritsa	45 mins	7 daily	Gouvia
Pyrgi	30 mins	7 daily	Ipsos

Fares range from €1 to €2.80. Sunday and holiday services are reduced considerably, and some routes don't run at all.

The numbers and destinations of local buses (dark blue) from the bus station (☎ 2661 031 595) at Plateia San Rocco, Corfu Town, are:

destination (bus no)	duration	frequency	via
Agios Ioannis (11)	30 min	7 daily	Pelekas
Ahillion (10)	20 min	6 daily	Gastouri
Aqualand (8)	20 min	12 daily	
Kanoni (2)	20 min	half-hourly	
Kastellani (5)	25 min	13 daily	Kourmades
Kontokali (7)	30 min	half-hourly	Gouvia & Dasia
Perama (6)	30 min	13 daily	Benitses
Potamos (4)	45 min	11 daily	Evroupoli & Tembloni

Tickets are either €0.50 or €0.70 depending on the length of journey. They can be bought on board or from the booth on Plateia San Rocco.

Car & Motorcycle Car and motorbike rental places are plentiful in Corfu Town and in most of the resort towns on the island. There are numerous agencies opposite the old and new ports in Corfu Town, plus most travel agencies will be able to organise a vehicle for you. It's worth shopping around to get a good deal.

Car-hire companies in Corfu Town include Sunrise (☎ 2661 026 511), Ethnikis Antistasis 16, and Sixt (☎ 2661 044 017),

IONIAN ISLANDS

Eleftheriou Venizelou 22. Budget (☎ 2661 028 590) and Europcar (☎ 2661 046 931) share an office at Eleftheriou Venizelou 32.

Easy Rider (☎ 2661 043 026), Eleftheriou Venizelou 50 (at the new port), rents scooters and motorbikes.

CORFU TOWN
pop 36,000

The island's capital is Corfu Town (Kerkyra), built on a promontory. It's a gracious medley of many occupying influences, which never included the Turks. The Spianada (Esplanade) is green, gardened and boasts Greece's only cricket ground, a legacy of the British. The Liston, a row of arcaded buildings flanking the north-western side of the Spianada, was built during the French occupation and modelled on Paris' Rue de Rivoli. The buildings function as up-market cafes, lamplit by night. Georgian mansions and Byzantine churches complete the picture. The Venetian influence prevails, particularly in the old town, wedged between two fortresses. Narrow alleyways of 18th-century shuttered tenements in muted ochres and pinks are more reminiscent of Venice or Naples than Greece.

Orientation

The town is separated into northern and southern sections. The old town is in the northern section between the Spianada and the New Fortress to the west. The Old Fortress is east of here and projects out to sea, cut off from the town by a moat. The southern section is the new town.

The old port is north of the old town, and the new port is west. Between them is the hulking New Fortress. The long-distance bus station is off Avramiou, inland from the new port. The local bus station is on Plateia San Rocco. Local buses serve the town and nearby villages.

Information

Tourist Offices Corfu's EOT office (☎ 2661 037 520, fax 2661 030 298) is well hidden on the 1st floor of a building on the corner of Rizospaston Voulefton and Polyla; it's open 8am to 2pm weekdays.

The tourist police (☎ 2661 030 265) are on the 3rd floor of Samartzi 4, just off Plateia San Rocco.

Money Banks can be found around Plateia San Rocco and by both ports. The National Bank of Greece is where Voulgareos becomes Theotoki. Alpha Bank has a large branch on Kapodistria behind the Liston. There is a handy bureau de change booth on the southern corner of the cricket ground.

Post & Communications The post office is on Leoforos Alexandras, and the OTE phone office is nearby at Mantzarou 9.

There are now a handful of Internet cafes in Corfu: Netoikos at Kaloxairetou 14, between Agios Spyridon church and the Liston; On Line Internet Cafe at Kapodistria 28, opposite the Spianada; Hobby.Net at Solomou 32, by the steps leading to the New Fortress; and Cyber Café Corfu, about 200m west of the new port at Gardikioti 3 (turn left at the Yamaha store). The going rate is €4.40 to €5.90 per hour.

Medical Services The Corfu General Hospital (☎ 2661 088 200, 2661 045 811) is on I Andreadi. Readers have recommended Dr Yannopapas (☎ 2661 049 350), a British-trained doctor with rooms at Mantzarou 1, by the OTE.

Things to See & Do

The star exhibit of the **Archaeological Museum** (☎ *2661 030 680, Vraïla 5; admission €2.40; open 8.30am-3pm Tues-Sun*) is the *Gorgon Medusa* sculpture, one of the best-preserved pieces of Archaic sculpture found in Greece. It was part of the west pediment of the 6th-century-BC Temple of Artemis at Corcyra (the ancient capital), a Doric temple that stood on the Kanoni Peninsula south of the town. The petrifying Medusa is depicted in the instant before she was beheaded by Perseus. This precipitated the birth of her sons, Chrysaor and Pegasus (the winged horse), who emerged from her headless body. Note the disturbing snakes that emerge from Medusa's hair.

CORFU TOWN

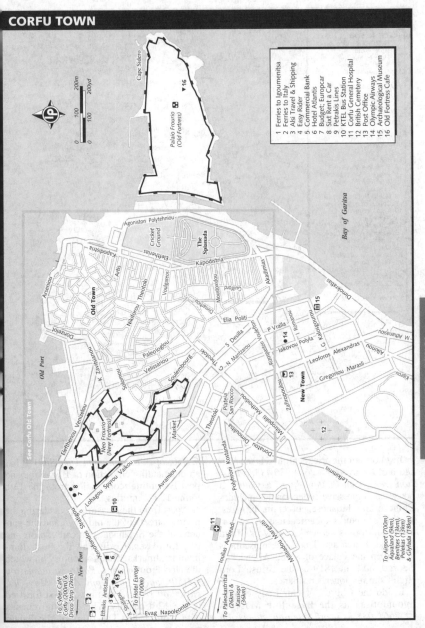

See Corfu Old Town

Old Town

Old Port

New Port

New Town

The Spianada

Cricket Ground

Cape Sidero

Palaio Frourio
(Old Fortress)

Neo Frourio
(New Fortress)

Market

Bay of Garitsa

1 Ferries to Igoumenitsa
2 Ferries to Italy
3 Alsi Travel & Shipping
4 Easy Rider
5 Commercial Bank
6 Hotel Atlantis
7 Budget; Europcar
8 Sixt Rent a Car
9 Petrakis Lines
10 KTEL Bus Station
11 Corfu General Hospital
12 British Cemetery
13 Post Office
14 Olympic Airways
15 Archaeological Museum
16 Old Fortress Cafe

Agoniston Polytehniou
Eleftheras
Kapodistria
Kapodistria
Artis
Arseniou
Nikiforou Theotoki
Voulgareos
Guilford
Moustoxidou
Dimarhi
Akadimias
Donzelot
Paleologou
Velissariou
Solomou
K. Zavitsianou
Solomou
Eleftheriou Venizelou
Sollembourg
G. N. Maltzarou
I Theotoki
Elia Politi
S. Desilla
P Vraila
Romanou
Iakovou Polyla
Theotoki
Plateia
San Rocco
Mitropolii Methodiou
Rigosospaston Voulefton
Zafiropoulou
G. Kalogeorgou
Leoforos Alexandras
Gregoriou Marasli
Dimoulitsa
Donaton
Polyhroni Kostanda
Avramiou
Lohagou Spyrou Vaikou
Ksenofondos
Ioulias Andreadi
Miltiadou Margariti
Ethnikis Antistasis
Evag. Napoleontos
M Athanasiou
Alkinou
Kipriou
Lefkimmis
Dimokratis

To Cyber Café
Corfu (200m) &
Disco Strip (2km)

To Hotel Europi
(100m)

To Paleokastritsa
(26km) &
Kassiopi
(36km)

To Airport (700m)
Aqualand (9km),
Benitses (13km),
Pelekas (13km)
& Glyfada (18km)

200m
200yd

IONIAN ISLANDS

CORFU OLD TOWN

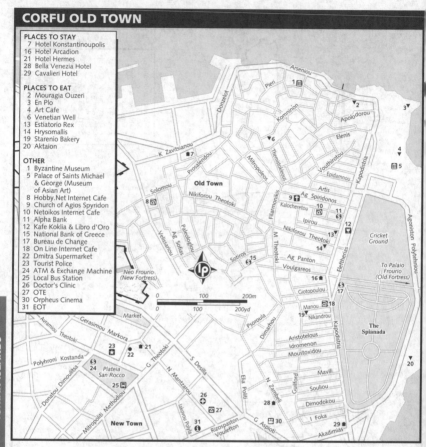

PLACES TO STAY
7 Hotel Konstantinoupolis
16 Hotel Arcadion
21 Hotel Hermes
28 Bella Venezia Hotel
29 Cavalieri Hotel

PLACES TO EAT
2 Mouragia Ouzeri
3 En Plo
4 Art Cafe
6 Venetian Well
13 Estiatorio Rex
14 Hrysomallis
19 Starenio Bakery
20 Aktaion

OTHER
1 Byzantine Museum
5 Palace of Saints Michael & George (Museum of Asian Art)
8 Hobby.Net Internet Cafe
9 Church of Agios Spyridon
10 Netoikos Internet Cafe
11 Alpha Bank
12 Kafe Koklia & Libro d'Oro
15 National Bank of Greece
17 Bureau de Change
18 On Line Internet Cafe
22 Dmitra Supermarket
23 Tourist Police
24 ATM & Exchange Machine
25 Local Bus Station
26 Doctor's Clinic
27 OTE
30 Orpheus Cinema
31 EOT

Just north of the cricket ground is the **Museum of Asian Art** (☎ 2661 030 433; admission free; open 8.30am-3pm Tues-Sun). It houses an impressive collection that includes Chinese and Japanese porcelain, bronzes, screens, sculptures, theatrical masks, armour, books and prints, as well as artworks from Thailand, Korea and Tibet. The museum is housed in the Palace of Saints Michael & George, built in 1819 as the British Lord High Commissioner's residence.

Inside the Church of Our Lady of Antivouniotissa, is the **Byzantine Museum** (☎ 2661 038 313, off Arseniou; admission €1.50; open 8.30am-3pm Tues-Sun). It has an outstanding collection of Byzantine and post-Byzantine icons dating from the 13th to the 17th centuries.

Apart from the pleasure of wandering the narrow streets of the old town and the gardens of the Spianada, you can explore the two fortresses, Corfu Town's most dominant landmarks. The promontory on which the **Neo Frourio** (New Fortress; admission €1.50; open 9am-9pm daily May-Oct, closed off season) stands was first fortified in the 12th century. The existing remains date from 1588. The ruins of the **Palaio**

Is it Cricket?

Newcomers to Corfu's Liston promenade cafe scene may be puzzled by the sight of men dressed in white surrounding another man dressed in white attempting to hit a hard leather ball out of the rather scruffy park with a long willow bat. This is cricket – Greek-style. Travellers from the former British Empire will recognise and delight at this eccentric and quintessentially British game replete with its sixes, fours, LBWs and owzats!

The game was imported to Corfu by the British during their 49-year hegemony of the island from 1815 to 1864. It has remained firmly entrenched in Corfu ever since. The few teams around the island gather to battle it out on sunny Sundays. While the pitch has seen better days and the distance from the batting crease to the tables of the Liston cafes can seem alarmingly close, the game is played with unusual verve and enthusiasm. This is also the only place in Greece where cricket is played.

The basic aim, for those unfamiliar with the game, is to score 'runs' by hitting the ball as far as possible and then running to and fro between the wooden wickets before the ball is returned by the fielders. Batters are considered 'out' when the ball hits their wickets, when a fielder catches the ball before it bounces, when the ball hits the leg when it could have hit the wicket, or when the fielder hits the wickets before the batter has returned to the crease after running.

It's a complex game and spectators enjoy its subtleties as well as its seemingly slow pace as much as the players do. Good cricket-watching is almost always accompanied by copious amounts of beer, the occasional shouts of encouragement from the sidelines and the odd comment on the weather. It wouldn't be cricket any other way – even in Greece.

Frourio (*Old Fortress;* ☎ *2661 048 310; admission €2.40; open 8.30am-7pm Tues-Sun*) date from the mid-12th century.

In Corfu, many males are christened Spyros after the island's miracle-working patron St Spyridon. His mummified body lies in a silver, glass-fronted coffin in the 16th-century **Church of Agios Spyridon** on Agiou Spyridonos. It is paraded on Palm Sunday, Easter Sunday, 11 August and the first Sunday in November.

For something completely different and to contrast the old with the new, visit the heavily promoted **Aqualand** (☎ *2661 052 963,* W *www.aqualand.com.gr; adult/child under 12 €16.20/10.30, discounted entry after 3pm; open 10am-6pm daily May-Oct, 10am-7pm July-Aug*). This garish waterpark is 9km from town in Agios Ioannis and is chock-full of countless waterslides, pools and other family-oriented attractions (all included in the entry price).

Places to Stay – Budget
There are no EOT-approved *domatia* but locals who unofficially let rooms often meet the boats.

Hotel Europi (☎ *2661 039 304*) Singles/doubles €17.60/29.40, with bath €23.50/35.20. Small and basic, the Europi has little to recommend it other than being cheap and near the new port (convenient for those arriving or departing by ferry). A sign points to the hotel at the western end of Xenofondos Stratigou.

Hotel Hermes (☎ *2661 039 268, fax 2661 031 747, G Markora 14*) Singles/doubles €26.40/30.80, with bath €30.80/38.15. The Hermes is in an atmospheric if noisy location, directly opposite one end of the bustling daily fruit and vegetable market. It has basic, timeworn rooms and is popular with backpackers.

Places to Stay – Mid-Range & Top End
Hotel Atlantis (☎ *2661 035 560, fax 2661 046 480,* ℮ *atlanker@mail.otenet.gr, Xenofondos Stratigou 48*) Singles/doubles €61.60/76.30. Directly opposite the new port, Atlantis is handy if you are arriving late or leaving early. It has pleasant air-conditioned rooms, but the location can be noisy.

Phone numbers listed incorporate changes due in Oct 2002; see p83

Hotel Konstantinopoulis (☎ *2661 048 716, fax 2661 048 718, Zavitsianou 11)* Singles/doubles €52.80/70.50. Renovation has reincarnated this shabby backpacker's favourite into a fine Art Nouveau hostelry. Although there's no air-conditioning, its position makes it one of Corfu's best deals. Note that the hotel does not accept credit cards.

Bella Venezia Hotel (☎ *2661 046 500, fax 2661 020 708,* e *belvenht@hol.gr, Zambeli 4)* Singles/doubles €61.60/73.40. In a quietish location in the southern part of town is this well-maintained, neoclassical-style hotel. Wake up to breakfast in the lovely large garden.

Hotel Arcadion (☎ *2661 037 670, fax 2661 045 087,* e *arcadion@otenet.gr, Kapodistria 44)* Singles/doubles €61.60/79.20. This smartly refurbished central hotel is right by the Liston and offers pleasant, comfortable rooms. Entrance is not via the new ground-floor McDonald's, but on the side street to the right.

Cavalieri Hotel (☎ *2661 039 041, fax 2661 039 283, Kapodistria 4)* Singles/doubles €73.40/102.70. Occupying a 300-year-old building just south of the Spianada, the Cavalieri has an interior of classical elegance. Be sure to check out the magical view from the rooftop bar.

Places to Eat

As it was not conquered by the Turks, Corfu maintains a distinctive cuisine influenced by other parts of Europe.

Starenio Bakery (☎ *2661 047 370, Guildford 59)* Pies €1.80. This lovely little food store offers a great assortment of home-made vegetable pies (the usual – cheese and spinach – plus more unusual fare like zucchini, leek or eggplant, and a very tasty wild herb). It also sells a tempting array of cakes and pastries and divinely gooey baklava.

Hrysomallis (☎ *2661 030 342, Nikiforou Theotoki 6)* Mains average €5. Just behind the expensive Liston cafe strip is one of Corfu's oldest restaurants, a no-frills place where you can dine on staples such as *mousakas* (layers of eggplant and zucchini, minced meat and potatoes topped with cheese sauce and baked), *yemista* (stuffe tomatoes or green peppers), *pastitsi* (baked cheese-topped macaroni) and loca dishes like *sofrito* (lamb or veal with garlic vinegar and parsley) and *pastitsada* (bee with macaroni, cloves, garlic, tomatoes an cheese). Prices are extremely reasonable and the quality high, which must be why th locals flock here.

Indulge in a little people-watching on the Liston. You will pay around €4.10 t €4.70 for coffee and croissant at any of the cafes, and can sit either under the loggia o across the road in the open-air terraces tha border the cricket ground. The place come alive with locals in the late evening.

Venetian Well (☎ *2661 044 761, Platei Kremasti)* Mains €13.50-19. Just inlan from the old port is this delightful, well-hidden eatery (turn left past the cathedra and look for the signs). The romantic set ting includes plenty of outdoor tables in the square, which features (funnily enough) a decorative Venetian well. Meals are no cheap, but the food is excellent and include creative dishes such as duck served wit cumquats and lamb with sun-dried tomatoe and goat's milk cheese.

Mouragia Ouzeri (*Arseniou 15)* Appetisers around €2.05. Despite not being absolute waterfront like its neighbouring eateries, Mouragia is the pick of the trio o restaurants here due to its great range o *mezedes*.

Estiatorio Rex (☎ *2661 039 649, Kapodistria 66)* Mains €11. This well-established restaurant has operated behind the Liston since 1932. It's now a popula upmarket eatery offering well-prepared dishes, including quality seafood and traditional Greek favourites.

Cafes There are a number of cafes in Corfu Town that are not really 'places to eat' so much as places to linger over a *nes frappé* (and a light snack perhaps) and rest weary sightseeing bones. Their real attraction is usually a lovely setting and invariably a stupendous view. Among the best of these cafes are the peaceful and shady *Art Cafe*, in gardens behind the Palace of Saints

Michael and George; the *Old Fortress Cafe*, inside the (surprise!) Old Fortress complex; *En Plo*, meaning 'by the sea' and is, literally, inches from the water at the corner of Arseniou and Kapodistria (you need to go down a sloping road to the Faliraki area – this is a popular spot for sunbathing and swimming); and *Aktaion*, on the waterfront opposite the Spianada.

Self-Catering Head to the colourful stalls of the bustling *produce market*, open from morning to early afternoon daily except Sunday, for fresh fruit, vegetables and fish. It's north of Plateia San Rocco, by the southern wall of the New Fortress. *Dimitra supermarket*, next to Hotel Hermes on G Markora, will supply you with the groceries you can't pick up at the nearby produce market.

Entertainment
Having fun in Corfu is comprised mainly of strolling around, sitting at the cafes on the Liston or being cool at the multitude of little cafes and bars that dot the old and new town. Popular Liston bars include *Kafe Koklia* and *Libro d'Oro*.

Corfu's disco strip is 2km north-west of the new port. Here, high-tech palaces cater mainly to locals and to holidaying Greeks and Italians in high season. The holidaying northern Europeans tend to stay and party in their resort areas – the most popular are Dasia, Ipsos, Kassiopi, Sidhari and Agios Gordios (ie, the Pink Palace). Don't expect an evening at any of the 'disco strip' clubs to be a cheap night out. Drinks cost around €4.40 each and you usually pay a sizable cover charge to get in. The big and flashy *Hippodrome* and *Apokalipsis!* are very popular with holidaying Italians. If you ask the locals, *Coca* is the place to go to late, with good DJs and mostly foreign music. *Sodoma*, next to Coca, also has its fans and offers a mixture of overseas and Greek music.

If it's visual entertainment you want, Corfu Town has the *Orpheus* cinema (☎ 2661 039 768, Aspioti), which shows English-language films with Greek subtitles for about €5.30.

NORTH OF CORFU TOWN
Most of the coast of northern Corfu is package-tourist saturated, and thoroughly de-Greeked, though once you venture beyond the main package resorts ending at Pyrgi you enter some of Corfu's most privileged scenery. Writers Lawrence and Gerald Durrell spent much of their creative years along this coastline which, in parts, is little more than a short boat hop to the Albanian coastline opposite.

Dasia and **Ipsos** are brash tourist strips full of bars, restaurants and cafes. The beach is narrow and a busy road separates the sea from the fun and entertainment. More or less extending out of Ipsos is **Pyrgi**, 16km north of Corfu Town, where a road continues east around the base of **Mt Pantokrator** (906m), the island's highest peak. From Pyrgi, another road snakes north and inland over the western flank of the mountain to the north coast. A detour can be made to the picturesque village of **Strinylas** from where a road leads through stark terrain to the summit, Moni Pantokratora and stupendous views.

Heading west around the winding coastal road you will first hit **Nisaki**, little more than a small cove with a pebble beach, a couple of tavernas and some domatia. The tiny cove of **Agni** offers three excellent tavernas (and nothing else). The next village of interest is **Kalami**, where the White House was the home of the Durrell brothers. The building is perched right on the water's edge and must have been idyllic during the writers' sojourn here.

Just round the next headland is the pretty little harbour of **Kouloura**, home to a pleasant restaurant. From both Kalami and Kouloura the houses and buildings of Butrint in neighbouring Albania can be seen quite clearly.

Kassiopi is the next major port of call. It is a sizable resort village around a circular harbour. There is a reasonable beach just west of Kassiopi round the headland. The coast road continues past the lovely long (and surprisingly undeveloped) beach of **Almyros** to the resort of **Roda**, a rather uninspiring place after the arresting scenery of

IONIAN ISLANDS

IONIAN ISLANDS

The Brothers Durrell

The name Durrell is synonymous with Corfu, though it is perhaps surprising that of the two brothers – Lawrence (1912–90) and Gerald (1925–95) – it is the naturalist Gerald rather than the poet and novelist Lawrence who has so inextricably linked the name of this famous duo with the island of Corfu and the little village of Kalami on Corfu's north-eastern coast.

Gerald Durrell was born in India and gained considerable repute among conservationists for his role in breeding endangered animal species for eventual release in the wild. He was also a prolific author, producing more than 35 informative yet amusing books about animals. Durrell's love of animals started when living in Corfu in the 1930s. His best-known books were *The Overloaded Ark* (1953), *Three Singles to Adventure* (1953), *My Family and other Animals* (1956), *A Zoo in My Luggage* (1960) and *Birds, Beasts and Relatives* (1969).

MARTIN HARRIS

Brother Lawrence, also born in India, was the dedicated writer in the family. He was at once a novelist, poet, writer of topographical books, verse plays and farcical short stories. He is best known for the Alexandria Quartet, a series of four interconnected novels. His Greek trilogy included *Prospero's Cell* (1945), in which he describes his life in Corfu during 1937 and 1938, *Reflections on a Marine Venus* (1953), for which he spent two years in Rhodes in 1945–46 as press officer for the Allied government, and *Bitter Lemons of Cyprus* (1957), where he spent 1952 to 1956 as a teacher and government official – latterly during the Cypriot insurgency.

Both brothers were well known around Corfu and some of the older restaurant owners near Corfu Town's Liston still remember their illustrious literary patrons. Their former house overlooking the sea at the village of Kalami is now a fish restaurant.

the north-eastern coast and the beach scene is not all that brilliant. **Sidhari**, also a rather tacky tourist resort, is not much better.

Pleasant **Agios Stefanos**, farther around the coast (and not to be confused with the small village of Agios Stefanos on the north-eastern coast), has a long sandy beach extending under the lee of high sand cliffs. Regular boats to the Diapondia islands (see the Diapondia Islands section) leave from the little harbour 1.5km from the village centre.

Places to Stay & Eat

There are a number of good camping grounds along the north-eastern coast.

Dionysus Camping Village (☎/fax 2661 091 760, e laskari7@otenet.gr). Adult/tent €4.10/2.40, bungalows €7.40 per person. Large, shady Dionysus is well signposted on the right between Dafnila and Dasia. It

boasts good facilities, including a pool shop and restaurant. Bungalows are little more than simple huts with two or four bed and no facilities.

Karda Beach Camping (☎/fax 2661 09 595, e campco@otenet.gr) Adult/ten €4.70/3.50, bungalows €32.30 plus €4.7 per person. Continuing along the road from Dasia to Ipsos is this quite luxurious camping ground, close to the beach and with ex cellent facilities including a pool an restaurant. Bungalows are a good option they're small but fully equipped and hav their own bathroom.

Manessis Apartments (☎ 2661 081 47 e diana@otenet.gr) Apartments €73.4 sleeping up to 4. By Aleka's lace shop at th end of Kassiopi's harbour are these appea ing two-bedroom apartments, with bou gainvillea cascading down the balconie The owner, an Irish woman with grea information about the area, only rents to independent travellers.

San Stefanos Golden Beach Hotel (☎ 2663 051 053) Double rooms €32.30, double studios €41.10, 4-person apartments €73.40. This pleasant hotel, with comfortable rooms and a small apartment complex nearby, is on the way to the port and has a great view over the bay.

White House (☎ 2661 091 251) Mains €5-10.60. If you're a Durrell fan, you can have a nostalgic meal at Kalami's White House and ponder the view as you search for your own literary inspiration. The restaurant slightly trades off its name and position, but a decent fish meal is reasonable value at around €9.40.

SOUTH OF CORFU TOWN

The Kanoni Peninsula, 4km from Corfu Town, was the site of the ancient capital but little has been excavated. **Mon Repos Villa**, at its north-eastern tip, was Prince Philip's birthplace. The beautiful wooded grounds (*admission free; open 8am-7pm daily*) can be explored, and the residence has finally been restored to its former glory and is open to the public as a museum. Opposite the entrance are two excavation sites; one is the ruins of the 5th-century **Basilica of Agia Kerkyra**, built on the site of a 5th-century-BC temple.

The coast road continues south with a turn-off to **Ahillion Palace** (☎ 2661 056 245; *admission €3; open 9am-6pm daily*), near the village of Gastouri and well signposted. In the 1890s it was the summer palace of Austria's Empress Elizabeth (King Otho of Greece was her uncle), and she dedicated the villa to Achilles. The beautifully landscaped garden is guarded by kitsch statues of the empress' other mythological heroes.

The resort of **Benitses** used to be the playground of holiday hooligans, but in recent times has made strenuous efforts to get its act together. Still, the excesses of too much package tourism in the past have taken the sheen off the little fishing village, but the narrow winding streets of the old village still maintain an air of authenticity.

Heading farther south you will next hit **Moraïtika** and **Messonghi**, two resorts that have merged into one. They're similar to Benitses but quieter. The beach scene, while not ideal, is certainly better than its neighbour farther north. The winding coastal road between Messonghi and **Boukaris** is decidedly more appealing and is dotted with a few tavernas and small pebbly beaches.

Places to Stay & Eat

There is accommodation aplenty around Benitses and farther south along the coast, but as there's not much here to hold the independent traveller for long, you're better off staying elsewhere.

Tripa (☎ 2661 056 333) Set banquet €29.40. This friendly, well-known taverna is touristy and a bit over the top, but it's very popular. It's been around a long time and the food is surprisingly good – and plentiful (come hungry!). It's in the little inland village of Kinopiastes (8km from Corfu Town), and has hosted its fair share of illustrious patrons. The sumptuous set banquet has a wide range of original Corfiot dishes, and the price includes drinks (beer, wine and soft drink) and a floor show of Greek dancing.

THE WEST COAST

Corfu's best beaches are on the west coast. **Paleokastritsa**, 26km from Corfu, is the coast's largest resort. Built around sandy and pebbled coves with a green mountain backdrop, it's incredibly beautiful. Once paradisal, it's been the victim of development. While the water here looks enticing, it is generally considerably colder than at other parts of the island – but then this area is Corfu's prime diving location and snorkelling is also a popular activity. **Corkyra Dive Club** (☎/fax 2663 041 206, @ cfudiveclub@ker.forthnet.gr, ⓦ www.corfuxenos.gr/sports/cdiveclub.htm) is based in Paleokastritsa and offers dives and diving courses for beginners and experienced divers. Dives, with equipment supplied, start from €41.10.

Moni Theotokou (*admission free, donation expected; open 7am-1pm & 3pm-8pm daily*) perches on the rocky promontory at Paleokastritsa. The monastery was founded

IONIAN ISLANDS

in the 13th century but the present building dates from the 18th century. A small adjacent museum contains icons.

From Paleokastritsa a path ascends to the unspoilt village of **Lakones**, 5km inland. Walk back along the approach road and you'll see a signposted footpath on the left. There are superb views along the 6km road west to **Makrades** and **Krini**. The restaurants along the way extol the views from their terraces.

Farther south, the beach at **Ermones** is near **Corfu Golf Club** (☎/fax 2661 094 220, e cfugolf@hol.gr, w www.corfugolfclub .com), among the largest in Europe. Hill-top **Pelekas**, 4km away, is renowned for its spectacular sunsets. It can be as busy as the coast, but with young independent travellers rather than package tourists (see the excellent Web site at w www.pelekas .com). Pelekas is close to three lovely sandy beaches, **Glyfada**, **Pelekas** and **Myrtiotissa**, the last an unofficial nudist beach. Don't miss the superb panoramic views over Corfu from **Kaiser's Throne**, a lookout high up above Pelekas village.

Agios Gordios, home to the infamous Pink Palace, is a popular backpacker hangout 8km south of Glyfada. It's a laid-back kind of place and will appeal to travellers interested primarily in the booze-and-beach scene.

Places to Stay & Eat

Paleokastritsa Camping (☎ 2663 041 204, fax 2663 041 104) Adult/tent €3.80/3.30. You'll find this camping ground right of the main approach road to town. It's a shady and well-organised place, with a restaurant on site and lots of conveniences very close by (ie, minimarket, swimming pool), but is a fair way back from the beaches.

Paleokastritsa also has many hotels, studios and domatia. A good starting point is the family-run *Astakos Taverna* (☎ 2663 041 068, e alex_ziniatis@hotmail.com), in the centre of town between the main beach and the most northerly beach. The owners offer rooms for €17.60 to €26.40 – they have rooms above the taverna and also in the quieter side street.

Golden Fox (☎ 2663 049 101/2, fax 049 319, e goldfox@otenet.gr, w www.gol enfox.gr) High up overlooking Paleokas tritsa and just beyond the village of Lakones is this scenic spot with magnificent views over the coast. The Golden Fox has terraces on three levels and includes a restaurant, a snack bar and a pool bar. The swimming pool here (open to the public and free of charge) must have the best view in the whole of Greece. This complex also has a few well-maintained studios to rent (from €44 to €64.60 depending on season).

Pension Tellis & Brigitte (☎ 2661 094 326, e martini@pelekas.com) Rooms €17.60-23.50. A good-value option in Pelekas and close to the central square is the bougainvillea-smothered Tellis & Brigitte. The rooms are simple and the service friendly. Prices vary depending on season and length of stay.

Levant Hotel (☎ 2661 094 230, fax 266 094 115, e levant@otenet.gr, w www.levan -hotel.com) Doubles €93.90. Open year round. This stylish, neoclassical building once a private house, is one of the most el egant hotels on the island. It's near Kaiser' Throne lookout and has charming, helpful staff, magnificent rooms and a restauran terrace with awesome views.

Pink Palace (☎ 2661 053 103/4, fa 2661 053 025, e pink-palace@ker.forthne .gr, w www.thepinkpalace.com) A/B-clas rooms €26.40/22 per person with breakfas & dinner. Open year-round. You'll eithe love or hate this huge, garish complex. It' definitely not everyone's cup of tea, but it' pretty much considered a 'must do' on the Europe backpacker circuit, and it's de signed for under-25s who want fun and sun without the hassles of having to look for it. There are two categories of accommodatio and, somewhat surprisingly, the new A class rooms are extremely pleasant; B clas is hostel-style rooms that can sleep up to four. The drawcard is the debauchery for which this place is (in)famous. There's a nightly disco until late, a 24-hour bar theme parties and lots of watersports op portunities. A big pink bus will pick you up from the port.

Sunrock (☎ *2661 094 637, fax 2661 094 056,* e *sunrock@nettaxi.com,* w *www geocities.com/sunrock_corfu*) 4-person rooms €16.20 per person, with bathroom €19.10 per person. Open year-round. Prices include breakfast and dinner. Behind Pelekas Beach is family-run Sunrock (formerly known as Vrachos), which is becoming another backpacker favourite. The market is quite clearly hostel-going young backpackers, and meals (home-cooked) are included in the price. You can be picked up from the port. The bar and taverna are open to the public.

Jimmy's Restaurant & Rooms (☎ *2661 094 284,* e *jimmyspelekas@hotmail.com*) Doubles €23.50-29.40, triples €38.20-44. At the intersection of the roads to Pelekas Beach, Kaiser's Throne and Corfu Town is Jimmy's, a popular hang-out with friendly multilingual staff. Its specialities are Corfiot dishes such as sofrito, pastitsada and *ourdeto* (fish with paprika and cayenne), and it has excellent choices for vegetarians, including vegetarian mousakas. Jimmy's also has pleasant rooms for rent above the restaurant.

Mirtiotisa (☎ *2661 094 113,* e *sks_mirtia@ hotmail.com*) Five minutes uphill from Myrtiotissa beach is this busy restaurant, in an idyllic setting and serving the usual taverna fare. It also has simple, agreeable rooms (singles/doubles €17.60/29.40 year-round) and the garden doubles as an unofficial beach car park.

THE DIAPONDIA ISLANDS
Τα Διαπόντια Νησιά
Scattered like forgotten stepping stones to Puglia in Italy lie a cluster of little-known and even less-visited satellite islands belonging administratively to Corfu. Of the five islands only three are inhabited, though many of their original residents have long since departed for the lure of New York City and only return in the summer months to renew their ties.

Ereikousa (Ερείκουσα; population 702) is the closest Diapondia island to Corfu and therefore perhaps the most visited. Wild and wooded **Mathraki** (Μαθράκι;

population 297) is the least developed of the trio but offers solitude and some fine walking. **Othoni** (Οθονοί; population 648) is largest of the group and also the farthest out; it's popular with Italian yachties.

Often isolated by tricky seas, the islands are worth the extra effort to visit them and serious island collectors should place them high on their agenda. Development is proceeding slowly and cautiously and all offer one or two places to stay and eat. Most people visit on day trips from Sidhari or Agios Stefanos, though regular ferries do link the islands with both Agios Stefanos, on the north-western tip of Corfu, and Corfu Town.

If you're keen on visiting the Diapondia islands, your best bet is to contact San Stefano Travel (☎/fax 2663 051 910, e steftrav@ otenet.gr) located in Agios Stefanos. Friendly Noula and her super-helpful staff will give you the lowdown on all the ferry options from Agios Stefanos and know of the various accommodation possibilities on each island.

Getting To/From the Diapondia
The most reliable link is the thrice-weekly service from Corfu Town with the *Alexandros II*, which leaves at around 6.30am Tuesday, Thursday and Saturday for the long haul round Corfu to bring supplies and the odd vehicle. It leaves from opposite the BP petrol station between the new and old ports, and a one-way journey will cost €5 to €5.60.

From Agios Stefanos a small passenger boat, the *Nearchos* (information on ☎ 69 4499 9771), services Mathraki and Othoni twice a week (€3 to €3.50 one way, Monday and Wednesday, weather permitting), and a different boat (information on ☎ 2633 071 586) services Erikousa and Othoni, also twice weekly (Tuesday and Thursday; similar prices). Schedules vary without warning so check beforehand.

The easiest solution may be to jump on a day excursion out of Sidhari or Agios Stefanos. Excursions are advertised widely around hotels and travel agencies in the area.

IONIAN ISLANDS

Paxi & Antipaxi

PAXI Παξοί
postcode 490 82 • pop 2440

Paxi (pahx-ee), 10km long and 4km wide, is the smallest main Ionian island. It has a captivating landscape of dense, centuries-old olive groves, snaking drystone walls, derelict farmhouses and abandoned stone olive presses. The olive trees have amazingly twisted, gnarled and hollowed trunks, which gives them the look of sinister, ancient monsters.

Paxi has escaped the mass tourism of Corfu and caters for small, discriminating tour companies. People come here because they have fallen in love with Paxi's inimitable cosy feel, or have heard about its friendly islanders and its captivating scenery.

There are only three coastal settlements – Gaïos, Longos and Lakka – and a few inland villages. The whole island is walkable, though good roads do cover its length. Paxi is an absolute must for any serious island-hopper and is worth the extra effort needed to get here.

For information on the Internet, see Ⓦ www.paxos-greece.com.

PAXI & ANTIPAXI

PAXI
To Corfu & Brindisi
To Igoumenitsa
South Kerkyra Straits
To Parga
Lakka
Kastanitha Cave
Longos
Fontana
Magazia
Panagia Islet
Ortholithos Stack
Bogdanatika
Gaïos
Agios Nikolaos Islet
Agrilas Bay
Agrilas
Vellianitatika
Ozias
MONGONISI
Tryptos

ANTIPAXI
Vrika Beach
Voutoumi Beach
Vigla
Agrapidia
IONIAN SEA

0   2   4km
0   1   2mi

Daily Ferries
Low Frequency Ferries
Hydrofoil/Catamaran
Excursion Boat

Getting To/From Paxi

Bus There is a direct bus service to Athen (7½ hours, €27.20 plus €10.30 hydrofoi ticket between Paxi and Igoumenitsa) twic weekly. Tickets are available from Boua Travel (☎ 2662 032 401) on the Gaïo waterfront. Buses from Athens to Paxi de part from Hotel Vienni (☎ 21 052 9143/4/5), Pireos 20 in Athens (near Platei Omonias) twice weekly.

Ferry – Domestic A daily car ferry, th *Theologos*, sails between Paxi and Igou menitsa on the mainland, and twice a wee it sails on to Corfu (otherwise you need t change ferries in Igoumenitsa). The Paxi Igoumenitsa trip takes 1¾ hours and cost €5; Paxi-Corfu (via Igoumenitsa) takes 3¼ hours and costs €5.60. A second car ferry the *Agia Theodora*, also runs the Paxi Igoumenitsa route twice weekly. Ferrie dock at Gaïos' new port 1km east of th central square, though excursion boats doc by the central square and along the quay to wards the new port.

Tickets for Corfu and Igoumenitsa can b obtained from most of the travel agencies o the island. Staff at Paxos Magic Holiday are very helpful, and its Web site (Ⓦ ww .paxosmagic.com) has up-to-date links wit the ferry timetables.

Paxi's port police can be contacted o ☎ 2662 031 222.

Ferry – International Italian Ferries an Ventouris Ferries both operate high-spee catamaran services between Brindisi an Paxi (4¾ hours, €82.20). Both run thre times weekly from 27 July to 2 Septembe Tickets and information can be obtaine from Paxos Magic Holidays in Gaïos.

Hydrofoil Petrakis Lines operates popula passenger-only hydrofoils between Corf Igoumenitsa and Paxi from May until Sep tember. There are at least two services dail between Corfu and Paxi – these often sto in Igoumenitsa en route. Prices from Pa are €10.30 to Igoumenitsa (one hour) an €11.20 to Corfu (one hour direct or 1 hours via Igoumenitsa).

For detailed information in Paxi contact
Bouas Travel (☎ 2662 032 401), or Petrakis
Lines (☎ 2661 031 649) in Corfu.

Getting Around Paxi

The island's bus links Gaïos and Lakka via
Longos up to five times daily (€1.20). A
taxi from Gaïos to Lakka or Longos costs
around €8.80; the taxi rank in Gaïos is on
the waterfront by the main square.

Alfa Hire (☎ 2662 032 505, fax 2662 032
188) in Gaïos rents cars, and Rent a Scooter
Vassilis (☎ 2662 032 598) opposite the bus
top in Gaïos has the biggest range of scooters and mopeds on the island.

Gaïos Γάιος

Gaïos, on a wide, east-coast bay, is the island's capital. It's a delightfully attractive
place with crumbling, 19th-century red-
tiled pink, cream and whitewashed buildings. The fortified Agios Nikolaos Islet
almost fills its harbour. Panagia Islet,
named after its monastery, lies at the northern entrance to the bay.

Orientation & Information The main
square abuts the central waterfront. The main
street of Panagioti Kanga runs inland from
here to another square where you'll find the
bus stop. The post office is just beyond here
and the OTE is next door. (The only Internet
cafe on the island at the time of research was
Akis Bar in the town of Lakka.)

There is no tourist office, but staff at
Paxos Magic Holidays (☎ 2662 032 269,
fax 2662 032 122, e info@paxosmagic
com, W www.paxosmagic.com), on Panagioti Kanga, are very helpful.

Things to See & Do The excellent Cultural Museum of Paxi (☎ 2662 032 556; admission €1.50; open 11am-1.30pm &
8.30pm-11pm daily), in an old school on the
waterfront, has a well-displayed eclectic
collection. Don't miss the mind-boggling
stirrups hanging from a four-poster bed – a
19th-century sex aid.

The best way to get to know Paxi is to walk
the island along its many pathways lined with
drystone walls through the countless olive

groves that blanket the island. Pick up a
copy of the excellent *Bleasdale Walking
Map of Paxos* (€8.80), available at most of
the travel agencies around town, which
comes with an explanatory booklet.

Places to Stay Accommodation tends to
mostly consist of prebooked studios and
apartments, though you can usually find
somewhere private to stay. All the island's
agencies can help, and all produce glossy
brochures detailing the villas and apartments on their books.

San Giorgio Rooms to Rent (☎ 2662 032
223) Double rooms €44, double studios
€52.80. This is the first accommodation option you'll encounter if you're walking from
the new port. The large pension, with well-
kept, airy rooms, is signposted above the
waterfront, 200m north of the central square.

Up the hill opposite the bus stop are a
few reasonably priced domatia, including
Magda's Domatia (☎ 2662 032 573), with
cheap, basic rooms, and, next door, *Spiro's
Domatia* (☎ 2662 031 172), with rooms in
better nick than his neighbour's.

Thekli Zenebisis (☎/fax 2662 032 313) 2-
person studios €64.60. Possibly the best-
value studios in Gaïos are run by the
delightful Thekli. Her immaculate and well-
equipped rooms all have balconies and good
views. They're tricky to find (up two sets of
steps behind the museum) – call ahead and
Thekli will meet you at the port. Prices drop
to as low as €29.40 in low season.

Paxos Beach Hotel (☎ 2662 032 211,
fax 2662 032 695, e zerbas1@otenet.gr,
W www.paxosbeachhotel.gr) Doubles/
triples with half-board €102.70/133.50.
This bungalow complex, 1.5km south of
Gaïos and overlooking the sea, has tastefully furnished rooms in a pretty setting.
The complex has a tennis court, beach, bar
and restaurant.

Places to Eat Gaïos has a glut of generally
good eating places.

Restaurant Mambo (☎ 2662 032 670)
Mains €5-11.75. Countless locals and return visitors alike agree that this waterfront
restaurant is the best place for an evening

meal, and the always-full tables attest to its popularity. There's the added attraction of perhaps the best baked feta in all of Greece.

Taverna Dodos (☎ *2662 032 265)* Mains to €8.80. In a pretty, colourful garden in the southern part of town (back from the waterfront – follow the signs) is this relaxed family taverna. All the taverna favourites are featured on the menu, and there are good choices for vegetarians.

Authentiko (☎ *2662 032 647)* Mains €4.40-8.80. Great eating can be had at friendly Authentiko, with a vine-covered canopy area close to the bus stop. This place does home-cooked dishes, and the specials change regularly. Enticing offerings include char-grill tuna steak, oven-baked lamb with yogurt and stewed duck in red-pepper sauce.

George's Corner Mains to €7, sandwiches & pittas €0.90-5.30. Cheap and cheerful, plus popular and quick, George's is on the main square and offers great pittas and burgers and an array of other snacks.

Self-catering supplies can be picked up at the *Paxos Market & Delicatessen* (☎ *2662 031 160)* on the central square. There's a good *bakery* next door to *Cafe Kalimera Espresso Bar* (the latter serves up excellent coffee), just west of the central square.

Around Paxi

Paxi's gentle east coast has small pebble beaches, while the west coast has awesome vistas of precipitous cliffs, punctuated by several grottoes only accessible by boat. You can walk to **Trypitos**, a high cliff from where there are stunning views of Antipaxi. From Gaïos, walk south-west along the Makratika road and turn right uphill at Villa Billy's, marked with a small sign on the wall. Stay on the main track and just before it ends turn left onto a narrow path which leads to Trypitos.

The small fishing village-cum-resort of **Longos** is 5km north of Gaïos, and has a few beaches nearby. It's much smaller than Gaïos and has a more intimate feel. The village consists of little more than a cramped square and a winding waterfront. It's a great base if you want a quieter stay.

The pretty harbour of **Lakka** lies at the end of a deep, narrow bay on the north coast

and is a popular yachtie call. There are a couple of decent beaches around either side of the bay's headland (including Harami Beach, with water sports on offer), and there are some great walks from here.

Places to Stay & Eat *Babis Dendias* (☎/fax *2662 031 597)* 4-person studios €102.70, one-week stay preferred. Most of the accommodation in Longos is monopolised by tour companies, and your best independent bet is Babis Dendias – inquire at his *pantopoleio* (general store), 20m beyond the bus stop. Babis has fully equipped accommodation for up to four people – he has properties both in town and just outside, plus knows of locals with rooms to rent. Prices fall to a bargain €52.80 in low season.

Routsis Holidays (☎ *2662 031 807*, fax *2662 031 161,* e *routsis-holidays@ke .forthnet.gr,* w *www.forthnet.gr/routsisho idays/)* This waterfront agency in Lakka is the agent for many rooms and villas in and around town. Properties on the books include two hotels – the *Lefkothea* has good value rooms with shared bathroom and communal kitchen and feels a little like hostel. The *Ilios* is similar but all rooms have private bathrooms.

There are good eating options in Longos and Lakka, mostly scattered around their waterfronts.

Vassilis (☎ *2662 031 587)* Mains €5.30-12. Smart, waterfront Vassilis in Longos has been widely praised, and indeed it's tough to get an outside table without pre booking. The food is very good – bordering on 'gourmet Greek' – but portions are disappointingly small.

I Gonia (☎ *2662 031 060)* Mains average €7.40. Longos locals insist that 'the Corner' is the most authentic place on the waterfront, offering tasty, good-value grilled meats as well as standard taverna fare.

Taxidi (☎ *2662 031 325)* Right at the end of the Longos harbour, in a whitewashed building with two seafront terraces, is this inviting cocktail bar run by friendly Spiro Even if you don't fancy one of his intoxicating fresh melon and vodka mega cocktails, it's worth calling in for some local advice. He usually knows of several individuals who have private rooms to rent.

La Rosa di Paxos (☎ 2662 031 471) Mains to €13.20. On the eastern side of the Lakka waterfront is this upmarket place, one of the prettiest restaurants in the Ionians. Tables spill over two terraces and are surrounded by flowering plants. The international menu gives a nod to Greek cuisine but there's also a heavy Italian influence (including tiramisu for dessert), plus lots of grilled vegetables in local olive oil and fresh fish displayed in a fridge on the waterside.

Klimataria (☎ 2662 030 075) Mains to €10.30. Under a vineyard-covered canopy on the main square of Lakka is this English-run place, offering a few well-done Greek dishes but also some real variety, including chicken balti, lemon stir-fry chicken and a vegie bake. There's a good selection of home-made cakes, plus you can pre-order sandwiches for a picnic.

In the evening, there are a number of central waterside bars good for a drink or three. *Akis* (☎ 2662 031 665) has the distinction of being the only place on Paxi where you can access the Internet.

ANTIPAXI Αντίπαξοι

Diminutive Antipaxi, 2km south of Paxi, is covered with grape vines from which excellent wine is produced. Caiques and tourist boats run daily out of Gaïos and usually pull in at a couple of beaches offering good swimming in exquisitely clear water. Vrika Beach at the north-eastern tip is sandy and gently sloping. Two restaurants, *Spiro's Taverna* and *Vrika Taverna*, serve the often-busy tourist trade, plus provide beach umbrellas for hire. Spiros (☎ 2662 031 172 during the day in season; ☎ 2662 032 417 at night and in winter) from Spiro's Taverna offers accommodation on the island for those who like isolation. Fully equipped houses go for €88 for two people, €146.80 for four people.

A path links Vrika Beach with Voutoumi Beach, farther south around a couple of headlands. Voutoumi Beach is very pretty, but is made up of large pebbles, a *taverna* high up on the bluff serves hungry bathers,

and a new beachside restaurant was under construction at the time of research.

If you don't fancy just beach bumming, take a walk up to the scattered settlement of **Vigla**, stopping to admire the many little vineyards along the way and dotted throughout the village.

Getting To/From Antipaxi

The cheapest way to get to Antipaxi is via the boat run by Antipaxos Lines (known as 'Nicos Boat') from Gaïos that leaves at 10am and returns from Vrika Beach at 5pm. The cost is €3.50 return.

In high season there are half a dozen high-speed express boats that leave the Gaïos waterfront between 10am and 1pm. The return boats leave Vrika Beach at 2.30pm and 5pm (and will pick up from Voutoumi Beach if requested). Tickets cost €4.40 return and can be bought from the kiosk on the quay. Most round-the-island excursions stop in at Antipaxos.

Lefkada & Meganisi

LEFKADA Λευκάδα
postcode 311 00 • pop 22,500

Lefkada is the fourth-largest island in the Ionians. Joined to the mainland by a narrow isthmus until the occupying Corinthians dug a canal in the 8th century BC, its 25m strait is spanned from the mainland by a causeway.

Lefkada has 10 satellite islets: Meganisi, Kalamos, Kastos, Madouri, Skorpidi, Skorpios, Sparti, Thilia, Petalou and Kythros.

Lefkada is mountainous with several peaks over 1000m. It is also fertile, well watered by underground streams, with cotton fields, acres of dense olive groves, vineyards, fir and pine forests.

Once a very poor island, Lefkada's beauty is also in its people who display intense pride in their island. Many of the older women wear traditional costume. A festival of 'speech and art' takes place every summer and includes a well-established international folklore festival in late August.

For information on the Internet, see W www.lefkas.net.

IONIAN ISLANDS

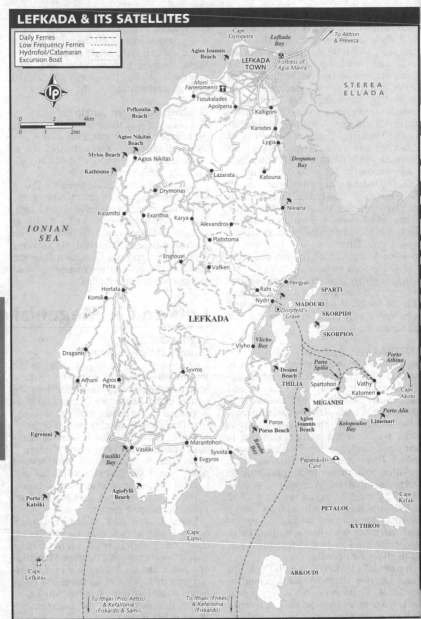

LEFKADA & ITS SATELLITES

Daily Ferries	-------
Low Frequency Ferries	-------
Hydrofoil/Catamaran	-------
Excursion Boat	....

Getting To/From Lefkada

Air Lefkada has no airport but Aktion airport, near Preveza on the mainland, is a 30-minute bus journey away. It has daily flights in summer between Athens and Preveza (€52.25). Lefkada's Olympic Airways office (☎ 2645 022 881) is at Dorpfeld 1; Preveza's (☎ 2682 028 343) is at Irinis 37.

Bus From Lefkada Town's KTEL bus station (☎ 2645 022 364) there are buses to Athens (5½ to six hours, €20.55, four or five daily), Patras (three hours, €9.10, two weekly), Thessaloniki (eight hours, €25, at least two weekly) and Aktion airport (20 to 30 minutes, €1.50, four or five daily).

Ferry The F/B *Agia Marina* runs between Vasiliki and Fiskardo (one hour, €3.30) on Kefallonia, Piso Aetos (two hours, €4.30) on Ithaki and then to Sami back on Kefallonia (2½ hours, €5.90). In summer it runs once or twice daily. Also in high season a ferry leaves daily from Nydri for Frikes on Ithaki and then Fiskardo.

You can contact Lefkada Town's port police on ☎ 2645 022 322, Vasiliki's on ☎ 2645 031 323.

Getting Around Lefkada

From Lefkada Town, frequent buses go to Nydri and Vlyho (up to 18 daily in high season), Poros (two daily) and Vasiliki (five daily). There are regular buses to Karya (seven daily), Agios Nikitas (up to six daily), Kalamitsi (two daily) and Athani (two daily). Other villages are served by one or two buses daily. Sunday services are reduced.

Cars can be hired in Lefkada Town from Europcar (☎ 2645 023 581), Panagou 6, by the harbour, and Budget (☎ 2645 024 643), its neighbour. Rent a motorbike from Motorcycle Rental Santas (☎ 2645 025 250), next to the new Ionian Star Hotel, near the docks. Many of the large car-rental companies are also represented in Nydri.

Lefkada Town

pop 6800

Lefkada Town, the island's capital and primarily a yachting port, is built on a promontory at the south-eastern corner of a salty lagoon, which is used as a fish hatchery.

The town was devastated by earthquakes in 1867 and 1948. After 1948, many houses were rebuilt in a unique style, with upper floors of painted sheet metal or corrugated iron that is strangely attractive, constructed in the hope they would withstand future earthquakes. The belfries of churches are made of metal girders – another earthquake precaution. Damage from the 1953 earthquake was minimal.

Orientation The bus station is on the eastern waterfront. The town's animated main thoroughfare, Dorpfeld, starts just south of the causeway at Hotel Nirikos. This street is named after 19th-century archaeologist Wilhelm Dorpfeld, who is held in high esteem for postulating that Lefkada, not Ithaki, was the home of Odysseus. Dorpfeld leads to Plateia Agiou Spyridonos, the main square. After the square the thoroughfare's name changes to Ioannou Mela. It is lined with interesting shops and several *kafeneia*.

Information There is no tourist office on Lefkada. The tourist police (☎ 2645 026 450) are in the same building as the regular police on Dimitriou Golemi, but they are not particularly helpful.

The National Bank of Greece and the Ionian Bank (both with ATMs) and the post office are on the eastern side of Ioannou Mela. The OTE is on Plateia Zambelou. You can get onto the Net at the large Internet Cafe (☎ 2645 021 507) on Koutroubi, just off 8th Merarchias (next to the Commercial Bank of Greece). It's a few minutes' walk south-west of the bus station.

Things to See Housed in a new building at the corner of Sikelianou and Svoronou (part of the cultural centre) is the **Archaeological Museum** *(☎ 2645 021 635; admission free; open 8.30am-3pm Tues-Sun)*. It has a small, well displayed and labelled collection of artefacts found on the island. One of the earliest objects, dating from the late 6th century BC, is a delicate terracotta figurine of nymphs dancing around a flute

IONIAN ISLANDS

player. Other figurines date from the Archaic and Hellenistic periods.

Works by icon painters from the Ionian school are displayed in a **collection of post-Byzantine icons** (☎ 2645 078 062; admission free; open 8.30am-1.30pm Tues-Sat, 5pm-7.30pm Tues & Thurs). It's housed in a late-19th-century building off Ioannou Mela (if it appears to be closed, ask at the Public Library of Lefkada upstairs).

The 14th-century Venetian **Fortress of Agia Mavra** is on the mainland. It was first established by the crusaders but the remains mainly date from the Venetian and Turkish occupations of the island. **Moni Faneromenis**, 3km west of town, was founded in 1634, destroyed by fire in 1886 and rebuilt. It's now inhabited by a few monks and nuns, and the monastery's church can be visited. The views of the lagoon and town are worth the ascent.

West of the lagoon, past windmills, is **Agios Ioannis Beach**, a great place to view the sunset. The nearest beaches to town are at the northern side of the lagoon, about a 2km walk away.

Places to Stay
Kariotes Beach Camping (☎ 2645 071 103) Adult/tent €5/4.40. This is the nearest camping ground to Lefkada Town – it's 5km south of the capital on the east coast. It's a pleasant if overgrown ground offering plenty of shade plus a pool to cool off in.

Hotel Byzantio (☎/fax 2645 022 629, ☎ 2645 021 315, Dorpfeld 4) Doubles €35.20. This slightly scruffy, hostel-style place has good-value rooms in a very central location.

Hotel Santa Maura (☎ 2645 021 308, fax 2645 026 253) Singles/doubles €41.10/49.90. The nicest place to stay in Lefkada Town is this bright and breezy place off Dorpfeld, halfway between the main square and the waterfront. The immaculate rooms are large and airy, and each has a balcony, TV, fridge and air-con.

Hotel Lefkas (☎ 2645 023 916, fax 2645 024 579, Panagou 2) Singles/doubles €55.80/88. The Lefkas, with its palatial lobby, faces the port. Rooms are not nearly as grand as the hotel's exterior and lobby would have you expect, but they certainly offer all you'll need for a comfortable stay.

Places to Eat
Karaboulias Restauran (☎ 2645 021 367) Mains to €10.30. Karaboulias fish taverna, on the eastern waterfront, offers traditional fare with flair. As well as its pavement tables, it has seating across the road on the quayfront, but sadly the view is of construction of the new marina, due for completion in 2004.

Regantos Taverna (☎ 2645 022 855 Vergioti 17) Mains to €8.80. Tucked away west of the main thoroughfare is this atmospheric little place, painted an eye-catching and appealing combination of blue and yellow. The menu features all the grilled and baked Greek standards, plus well-prepared seafood dishes.

Lighthouse Taverna (☎ 2645 025 117 Filarmonikis 14) Mains to €8.80. We must admit to some cynicism when we saw all the guidebook recommendations photocopied and pasted in this taverna's window but we came to the conclusion that all were genuine. Sotiris and his family have a good time running this friendly eatery and they offer tasty, good-value Greek favourites in their delightful, vine-covered garden.

The western side of the waterfront is lined with hip bars and cafes frequented by fashionable Lefkadians. *Il Posto*, at the end of Dorpfeld, is a cool place to hang out. *Cafe Casbah* on Plateia Agiou Spyridono offers excellent people-watching and is a great venue for chilling out.

Around Lefkada
Nydri A sleepy fishing village not so long ago, Nydri, 16km south of Lefkada Town fell hook, line and sinker to the lure of the tourist trade. Now it's a busy, commercialised but fun town from where you can cruise around the islets of **Madouri**, **Sparti**, **Skorpidi** and **Skorpios**, plus visit **Meganisi** Shop around for the full range of excursions – a day trip taking in Meganisi and Skorpios costs from €8.80 to €14.70 (the higher price will usually include an extra such as a beach barbecue lunch).

The privately owned Madouri islet, where the Greek poet Aristotelis Valaoritis (1824–79) spent his last 10 years, is off limits. It's not officially possible to land on Skorpios, where Aristotle, sister Artemis and children Alexander and Christina Onassis are buried in a cemetery visible from the sea, but you can swim off a sandy beach on the northern side of the island.

If you would rather explore the islets independently, boats can be hired from Trident Travel Agency (☎ 2645 092 978, fax 2645 092 037, ⓔ trident@otenet.gr) on the main street.

The quiet village of **Vlyho** is 3km south of Nydri. Beyond here, a road leads to a peninsula where Wilhelm Dorpfeld is buried. Just west of the Nydri-Vlyho road are the Bronze Age ruins that he excavated, leading him to believe Lefkada was Homer's Ithaca.

Places to Stay & Eat There are a large number of rooms and studios in Nydri though a fair few get block-booked by tour companies. Try Samba Tours (☎ 2645 092 658, fax 2645 092 659) for assistance with accommodation and most other tourist services.

Dessimi Beach Camping (☎ 2645 095 225, fax 2645 095 190) Adult/tent €5/3.80. This basic but pleasant camping ground is south of Nydri, signposted after the village of Vlyho. It's right on the beach, but the waterfront sites are tough to come by. There's boat rental directly in front.

Gorgona Hotel (☎/fax 2645 092 268) Double rooms €29.40, double studios €58.70. In a side street off the main road opposite the Avis car-rental office, you'll find this friendly, family-run place. Set in a shady, flower-filled garden that's home to a few ducks, the Gorgon offers simple, spotlessly clean rooms and studios.

Ta Kalamia (☎ 2645 092 983) Mains €5.30-11.80. One of the most interesting eateries in town is this stylish place, on the main drag and with a large garden area out back. The English version of the menu is a delightful read – fancy some 'mashroom's ala Hellinic', 'baby goad', 'scared rabbit in beer' or 'saute shrimps with in poef garlic'? No matter – the food is excellent.

Poros Beach This little village overlooks Rouda Bay and makes a great alternative base to the often-raucous Nydri, although your own transport is an asset. The beach is good and there are boats for hire.

Poros Beach Camping & Bungalows (☎ 2645 095 452, fax 2645 095 152) Adult/tent €5.90/5.30, doubles €41.10, 2-bedroom bungalows (sleeping 4) €82.20. This large, popular complex on the way into the village has something for everyone, and facilities are excellent – there's a restaurant, mini-market, bar and swimming pool.

Rouda Bay Hotel (☎ 2645 095 600, fax 2645 095 631, ⓔ roudabay@corfu-island.com) Double studios €58.70. This 'hotel' is a very attractive complex of studios and maisonettes set around a courtyard smack in the middle of the beachfront. The spacious rooms are beautifully furnished and are a cut above those you normally encounter.

Vasiliki Purported to be *the* best windsurfing location in Europe, Vasiliki is a pretty fishing village with a below-average beach (but that's OK as most visitors are here to engage in more active pursuits than sunbathing and paddling). It attracts a sizable, largely youthful, crowd each season and you can hop over to Kefallonia and Ithaki from here if you are heading south.

If they're not already booked solid, you can rent windsurfing equipment from **Club Vass** (*Greece* ☎ 2645 031 588, *UK* ☎ 01920-484121, Ⓦ www.clubvass.com) on the beach, and possibly get some lessons too. Priority is, understandably, given to people who have come on one of their all-inclusive package holidays from the UK, but it's worth asking if you're keen to give it a go.

Next door to Club Vass, **Wildwind** (*Greece* ☎/fax 2645 031 610, *UK* ☎ 01920-484516, Ⓦ www.wildwind.co.uk) rents out catamarans and offers instruction on a similar basis (ie, if equipment is not being used by their guests).

Caiques take visitors from Vasiliki to swim at the best beaches on the west coast, and a boat will also take you to the unspoilt **Agiofylli Beach**, to the town's south.

IONIAN ISLANDS

Places to Stay & Eat The best bet for accommodation is to drop in to Samba Tours
(☎ 2645 031 520, fax 2645 031 522) on the
main road into town.

Camping Vassiliki Beach (☎ *2645 031
308, fax 2645 031 458*) Adult/tent €5.60/
5.30. This happening camping ground is a
very popular place for windsurfers – that
much is clear by the amount of equipment
scattered around. This well-shaded place is
well run and has good facilities.

Pension Holidays (☎/fax 2645 031 426)
Doubles €44. Friendly Spiros offers simply
furnished rooms with air-con, TV, fridge
and balcony at reasonable prices. Head
down the main street to the waterfront, turn
left and you'll come across the pension.

Alexander Restaurant (☎ *2645 031 858*)
Mains to €9.70. Busy Alexander, on the
waterfront, offers an excellent range of well-
prepared Italian and Greek dishes, and judging by the crowds the punters are happy.

West Coast Beach lovers should skip
Lefkada's east coast and head straight for
the west. The sea here is possibly the best
in the Ionian – an incredible pale turquoise
blue that is almost iridescent – and most
beaches feature pale golden or white sand.
The best beaches include **Porto Katsiki**,
Egremni and **Kathisma**. All are signposted
off the road leading to the island's south-
western promontory (a sanctuary of Apollo
once stood at **Cape Lefkatas**).

The town of **Agios Nikitas** is hardly
Lefkada's best-kept secret, but it is the island's most picturesque and tasteful resort.
There's not much of a beach to speak of here,
so most people head to beautiful **Mylos
Beach** just around the headland, which is inaccessible by road – you have to take a taxi
boat from the tiny Agios Nikitas beach.

Olive Tree Hotel (☎ *2645 097 453, fax
2645 097 153,* ℮ *olivetreehotel@hotmail
.com*) Doubles/triples €52.80/58.70. Set,
as its name suggests, among olive trees
(signposted down a small path off the main
road just north of Agios Nikitas), this
friendly place has simple but pleasant
rooms, all with balcony and with some
kitchen facilities.

MEGANISI Μεγανήσι
postcode 310 83 • pop 1250
Meganisi has the largest population of Lefkada's three inhabited satellite islets and is
the easiest to visit, but like many small Greek
islands it has suffered population depletion.
It's easily visited on a day trip, independently or on one of the excursion boats from
Nydri that visit a few of the satellite islands.

Meganisi's a tranquil islet with a lovely,
verdant landscape and deep bays of
turquoise water, fringed by pebbled beaches.
It's visited primarily by yachties and is untouched by package-tour operators. It has
three settlements: the capital of Spartohori
(above the small port of Spilia), the port of
Vathy and the village of Katomeri.

Getting To/From Meganisi
The *Meganisi* ferry boat runs about six
times daily between Nydri (the southern
end of the quay) and Meganisi (35 to 45
minutes, €1.40). It usually calls in first at
Porto Spilia and then into Vathy before
heading back to Nydri.

Whether you're visiting for a day on the
ferry or plan to stay longer, you may want to
bring over a car or moped from Nydri, as there
is nowhere to rent transport on the island.

Spartohori & Porto Spilia
Quiet Spartohori, with narrow, winding
lanes and pretty, flower-bedecked houses,
perches on a plateau above Porto Spilia,
where the ferry docks. No-one lives at
Spilia, but there are several popular tavernas. A road ascends steeply to Spartohori or
you can walk the 1km there up steps. To
reach Spartohori's main street and central
square turn right at Tropicana Pizzeria. Alternatively, take the road out of Porto Spilia
and instead of veering right to Spartohori,
veer left to reach a pleasant pebble beach.

One of the island's best beaches is **Agios
Ioannis**, a long stretch of small pebbles 3km
south-west of Spartohori.

Places to Stay & Eat There's no official
camping ground, but wild camping is tolerated at Porto Spilia, in the area behind the
restaurant Locanta Salitzo (☎ 2645 051

546). Inquire here before setting up, and expect to pay about €4.40 per person.

Tropicana Pizzeria (☎ *2645 051 846*) Pizzas to €5.60. Friendly Giorgios is the man to see if you want good home-made pizzas, or if you're after a place to stay in Spartohori. Giorgios can contact a room-owner for you, who will meet you at the pizzeria and guide you to your lodgings. *Nikos* (☎ *2645 051 050*), *Yiannis* (☎ *2645 051 695*) and *Giorgios* (☎ *2645 051 409*) all have rooms in the €23.50 to €29.40 range, and it's wise to book ahead for July and August.

Taverna Porto Spilia, down in the ferry-docking area below Spartohori, is a sprawling, bustling waterside eatery offering all the local favourites. *Taverna Lakis*, on Spartohori's square, offers tasty Greek fare and features Greek evenings, which tourists from Nydri often attend (brought over by excursion boat). When things really get going, Mamma Lakis, who is no spring chicken, has been known to dance with a table on her head.

Vathy & Katomeri

Vathy is the island's second port. The post office is on the waterfront near the quay. Farther round there's a children's playground in an area resembling a town square. Beyond here, the road climbs to Katomeri, 700m away. From Katomeri you can visit a number of good beaches, including Fanari and Limonari.

Hotel Meganisi (☎ *2645 051 240, fax 2645 051 639*) Doubles €64.60. The island's only hotel is the cosy Meganisi, well signposted in Katomeri. It offers spotless, modern rooms with air-con, a lovely swimming pool and outdoor area, plus a restaurant serving tasty traditional dishes.

To find private accommodation in Vathy and surrounds, the best contact is helpful, English-speaking Kiki at *Cafe Risko* (☎ *2645 051 134*, e *vathi_blues@hotmail.com*), on the square in Vathy. Kiki can help find you one of the 20-odd rooms in town priced (very roughly) from €23.50 in low season, €44 in high. Risko is an excellent place to stop by anyway – it offers pizza, pasta and gelati in a pleasant garden, there's a computer set up for Internet access, plus you can change money or browse the book exchange.

Another good dining option is *Taverna Porto Vathy*, a charming fish taverna right next to the ferry quay.

Kefallonia & Ithaki

KEFALLONIA Κεφαλλονιά
pop 39,579

Kefallonia, the largest of the Ionian islands, has rugged, towering mountains. The highest, Mt Enos (1627m), is the Mediterranean's only mountain with a unique fir forest species, *Abies Cephalonica*. While not as tropical as Corfu, Kefallonia has many species of heavily scented herbs and wildflowers.

Kefallonia's capital is Argostoli but the main port is Sami, on the south-eastern coast. As the island is so big and mountainous, travelling between towns is time consuming.

A good Web site to gather information on the island is W www.kefaloniathewaytogo .com.

Getting To/From Kefallonia

Air There is at least one flight daily between Kefallonia and Athens (€65.50). The Olympic Airways office (☎ 2671 028 808) in Argostoli is at Rokou Vergoti 1.

Bus There are a few options for the bus journey to Athens from Kefallonia. There is a daily bus plying the Argostoli-Poros-Kyllini-Patras-Athens route (€24.50 to Athens), a bus taking the Argostoli-Kyllini-Athens route (€25) and another on the Argostoli-Sami-Patras-Athens route (€23.90). Prices include ferry tickets, and all journeys take around eight hours. For information contact the KTEL bus station (☎ 2671 022 276) on the southern waterfront in Argostoli.

Ferry – Domestic Kefallonia has six ports: Sami (port police ☎ 2674 022 031), Argostoli (☎ 2671 022 224), Poros (☎ 2674 072 460), Lixouri (☎ 2671 094 100), Pesada and Fiskardo (☎ 2674 041 400).

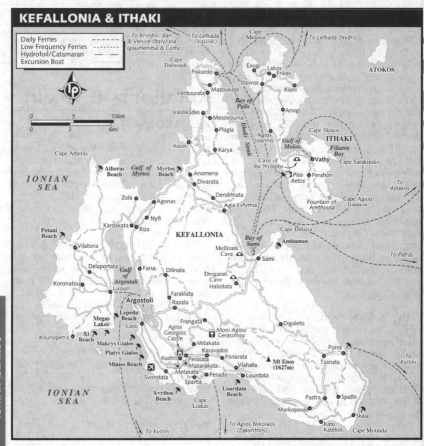

KEFALLONIA & ITHAKI

Daily Ferries
Low Frequency Ferries
Hydrofoil/Catamaran
Excursion Boat

To Brindisi, Bari
& Venice (Italy) via
Igoumenitsa & Corfu

To Lefkada
(Vasiliki)

Cape
Melissa

To Lefkada (Nydri)

Cape
Dafnoudi

Exogi   Lakos
Fiskardo   Frikes

ATOKOS

Ventourata   Mazoukata   Stavros   Kioni

Vasilikades   Mesovounia

Bay of
Polis

Anogi

Plagia

Agios
Ioannis

Cape Skinos

ITHAKI

Assos   Karya

Ithaki Strait

Gulf of
Molos

Filiatro
Bay

Vathy   Cape Sarakiniko

IONIAN
SEA

Cape Atheras

Atheras
Beach

Gulf of
Myrtos

Myrtos
Beach

Anomeria

Cave of
the Nymphs

Piso
Aetos   Perahori

To
Astakos

Divarata

Zola   Agonas

Dendrinata

Fountain of
Arethousa

Cape Agiou
Ioannou

Kardakata   Nyfi   Riza

Agia Evfymia

Petani
Beach

Vilatoria

KEFALLONIA

Bay of
Sami

Cape Bihalia

Delaportata   Gulf
of
Argostoli

Farsa

Mellisani
Cave

Antisamos

To Patras

Koronatou   Lixouri

Dilinata

Sami

Argostoli

Faraklata

Drogarati
Cave
Haliotata

Megas
Lakos

Lepeda
Beach

Razata

Frangata

Digaleto

Kounopetra   Xi
Beach

Lassi

Agios
Georgios
Castle

Moni Agiou
Gerasimou

Poros

Makrys Gialos

Mitakata

Karavados

Tzanata

To
Kyllini

Platys Gialos

Kastro

Peratata

Poriarata

Minies Beach

Mazarakata

Vlahata

Mt Enos
(1627m)

Svorotata

Metaxata   Pesada

Lourdata

Spartia

Lourdata
Beach

Pastra   Spathi

IONIAN
SEA

Avythos
Beach

Cape
Liakas

Markopoulo

Skala

To Agios Nikolaos
(Zakynthos)

Kato
Katelios   Cape Mounda

To Kyllini

0   5   10km
0   3   6mi

At least two ferries daily connect Sami with Patras (2½ hours, €10) and Vathy on Ithaki (one hour, €3.80). From Poros (1¼ hours, €6.15) and Argostoli (2¼ hours, €8.80), at least two ferries ply daily to Kyllini in the Peloponnese.

In summer, boats leave Sami to go Piso Aetos in Ithaki (40 minutes, €1.80), then Fiskardo (1½ hours, €3.30). From Fiskardo they continue to Vasiliki in Lefkada (three hours, €5.90) and return to Kefallonia later in the day. Daily ferries also run in high season on a route between Fiskardo, Frikes (Ithaki) and Nydri (Lefkada).

From Pesada in the south there are two high-season services daily (1¼ hours, €3.80) travelling to Agios Nikolaos on Zakynthos (travel agents in Kefallonia sell tickets to 'Skinari', but the port town is actually called Agios Nikolaos). There is inexplicably no bus to the remote port of Pesada, and virtually no buses from Agios Nikolaos to anywhere in Zakynthos, making crossing without your own transport quite difficult – not to mention costly if you rely on taxis. Both these ports are quite a distance from the major towns in the respective islands.

The Cult of Captain Corelli

Kefallonia receives its fair share of package tourists but not on the same scale as Corfu and Zakynthos, although that may soon change due to some heavy Hollywood exposure.

The island has received unprecedented publicity in recent years thanks to Louis de Bernières' novel *Captain Corelli's Mandolin* (released in the USA as *Corelli's Mandolin*). It was on a package holiday to Kefallonia that the author, a former soldier, received his inspiration for the story. Instead of relaxing on the beach he spent his holiday learning about the island's history, and the resulting book tells the emotional story of a young Italian army officer sent to Kefallonia during WWII and his relationships with the locals, his fellow soldiers and German commanders. Most beach bums will have a dog-eared copy of the novel, and copies are available in almost every minimarket and bookstore on the island.

Publicity for the island reached fever pitch in the summer of 2001 with the release of the movie based on the book, starring Nicholas Cage as Corelli and co-starring Penelope Cruz and John Hurt (plus hundreds of Kefallonian extras, as photos in shops, hotels and restaurants all over the island will attest). The movie was filmed entirely on location in Kefallonia in 2000, largely in and around the town of Sami. You'll be disappointed if you see the film then visit Sami hoping to marvel at its pretty Venetian architecture. Sami was largely reduced to rubble in the 1953 earthquake that devastated most of the island, and the town you see in the movie was all a cleverly constructed set.

Ferry – International In high season there is a regular ferry plying the route between Patras, Sami, Igoumenitsa and Brindisi in Italy. To get to other ports in Italy, you need to take the ferry first from Sami to Patras.

Tickets can be obtained from Vassilatos Shipping (☎ 2671 022 618, fax 2671 024 992) on Metaxa 54, opposite the port authority in Argostoli. In Sami, inquire at Blue Sea Travel (☎ 2674 023 007, e bluemare@ otenet.gr).

Getting Around Kefallonia
To/From the Airport The airport is 9km south of Argostoli. There is no airport bus. A taxi costs €7.40.

Ferry Car ferries run hourly between Lixouri and Argostoli. The journey takes 30 minutes, and tickets (€0.90 per person) are sold on board.

In summer, you can catch a morning ferry from Sami to Fiskardo (via Piso Aetos on Ithaki), or sometimes an afternoon ferry, which runs direct.

Bus From Argostoli's bus station there are seven buses daily to the Lassi Peninsula (€0.90), four buses to Sami (€2), two to Poros (€3), two to Skala (€2.70) and two

to Fiskardo (€3.30). There is a daily east-coast service linking Katelios with Skala, Poros, Sami, Agia Efimia and Fiskardo. No buses operate on Sunday.

Car & Motorcycle In Argostoli, cars can be hired from Reliable Rent a Car (☎ 2671 023 613), next to the Olympic Airways office at R Vergoti 3, and motorcycles from Sunbird Motor Rent (☎ 2671 023 723), on the waterfront. The Avis representative is CBR Travel (☎ 2671 022 770) at the southern end of the central square.

Argostoli Αργοστόλι
postcode 281 00 • pop 7300
Argostoli, unlike Zakynthos Town, was not restored to its former Venetian splendour after the 1953 earthquake. It's a modern, lively port set on a peninsula. Its harbour is divided from Koutavos lagoon by a British-built causeway connecting it with the rest of Kefallonia.

Orientation & Information The modern and (for once) user-friendly KTEL bus station is on the southern waterfront near the causeway; the main ferry quay is at the waterfront's northern end. The EOT (☎ 2671 022 248), on the northern waterfront beside

IONIAN ISLANDS

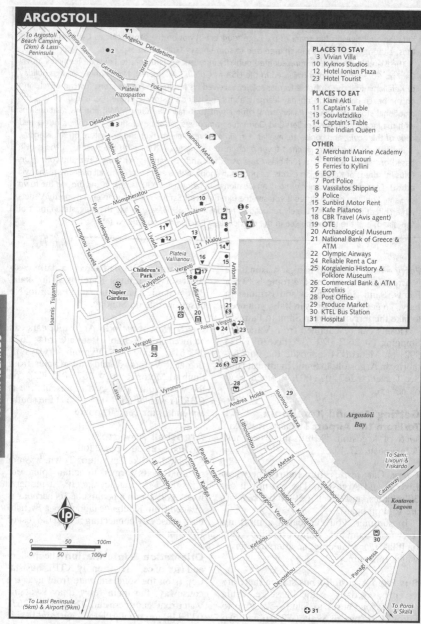

ARGOSTOLI

PLACES TO STAY
3 Vivian Villa
10 Kyknos Studios
12 Hotel Ionian Plaza
23 Hotel Tourist

PLACES TO EAT
1 Kiani Akti
11 Captain's Table
13 Souvlatzidiko
14 Captain's Table
16 The Indian Queen

OTHER
2 Merchant Marine Academy
4 Ferries to Lixouri
5 Ferries to Kyllini
6 EOT
7 Port Police
8 Vassilatos Shipping
9 Police
15 Sunbird Motor Rent
17 Kafe Platanos
18 CBR Travel (Avis agent)
19 OTE
20 Archaeological Museum
21 National Bank of Greece & ATM
22 Olympic Airways
24 Reliable Rent a Car
25 Korgialenio History & Folklore Museum
26 Commercial Bank & ATM
27 Excelixis
28 Post Office
29 Produce Market
30 KTEL Bus Station
31 Hospital

To Argostoli Beach Camping (2km) & Lassi Peninsula

Plateia Rizospaston

Plateia Vallianou

Children's Park

Napier Gardens

Argostoli Bay

To Sami, Lixouri & Fiskardo

Causeway

Koutavos Lagoon

To Lassi Peninsula (5km) & Airport (9km)

To Poros & Skala

0   50   100m
0   50   100yd

IONIAN ISLANDS

the port police, is open 8am to 2.30pm weekdays (in July and August it also opens 5pm to 9.30pm weekdays, and in August it often opens on weekends).

The centre of Argostoli's activity is Plateia Vallianou, the huge palm-treed central square up from the waterfront off 21 Maïou, and its surrounding streets. Other hubs are the waterfront (Antoni Tristi, which becomes Ioannou Metaxa to the south), and pedestrianised Lithostrotou, two blocks inland, lined with smart shops and cafes.

There are banks with ATMs along the northern waterfront and on Lithostrotou. The post office is on Lithostrotou and the OTE is on G Vergoti. Excelixis (☎ 2671 025 530), signposted off Lithostrotou (behind the Greek Orthodox Church), offers Internet access.

Things to See Argostoli's **archaeological museum** (☎ 2671 028 300, R Vergoti; admission €1.50; open 8.30am-3pm Tues-Sun) has a well-displayed collection of island relics including Mycenaean finds from tombs.

The **Korgialenio History and Folklore Museum** (☎ 2671 028 835, R Vergoti; admission €3; open 9am-2pm Mon-Sat) has a busy but good collection of traditional costumes, furniture and tools, items which belonged to British occupiers, and photographs of pre- and post-earthquake Argostoli.

KTEL organises day tours of the island (taking in Drogarati Cave, Melissani Lake and Fiskardo) for €17.60, and day trips to Ithaki for €29.40. Inquire at the bus station.

The town's closest sandy beaches are **Makrys Gialos** and **Platys Gialos**, 5km south in the package-resort area of the Lassi Peninsula. Regular buses serve the area.

Places to Stay The EOT should be able to give you a list of locals offering inexpensive domatia.

Argostoli Beach Camping (☎ 2671 023 487, fax 2671 024 525) Adult/tent €4.70/ 4.40. This OK camping ground – one of only two on the island – is on the coast, 2km north of town. It has decent enough facilities but is not a patch on the camping ground at Sami.

Vivian Villa (☎ 2671 023 396, fax 2671 028 670, e villaviv@otenet.gr, Deladetsima 9) Doubles €49.90, double studios €58.70 (for triples add 20%); 4-person apartments €88. Easily the nicest place in town is this small complex, run by super-friendly, English-speaking Vivian and Nick. They offer spacious, spotless accommodation and if they're full, they'll always attempt to find you somewhere else to stay.

Kyknos Studios (☎ 2671 023 398, fax 2671 025 943, M Geroulanou 4) Double studios €35.20. Another good option is these pleasant, simple studios set behind a garden not far from the square.

There's a string of hotels along the waterfront, and a number around the bustling main square.

Hotel Tourist (☎/fax 2671 022 510, Antoni Tristi 109) Singles/doubles €35.20/52.80. The refurbished Tourist, on the waterfront, offers pleasant rooms and good facilities.

Hotel Ionian Plaza (☎ 2671 025 581, fax 2671 025 585, Plateia Vallianou) Singles/ doubles €40.50/62.50. Argostoli's smartest hotel is the marble-decorated Ionian Plaza, right on the main square. The lobby and public areas are impressively stylish; the rooms – all with balconies overlooking the square – are very pleasant.

Places to Eat Among the pricey cafes on the main square is the very popular *Souvlatzidiko*, next to Hotel Aeon, offering tasty gyros for about €1.50.

Captain's Table (☎ 2671 023 896, Rizospaston 3) Mains €4.40-14.50. Just off the central square (behind Hotel Ionian Plaza), upmarket Captain's is one of Argostoli's top restaurants and the place to go for a splurge. Despite the fact that the place prides itself on its fish and seafood, choosing either can inflate the bill considerably. You'll do well with any of the meat dishes, and there are gourmet offerings such as duck in orange sauce and even ostrich fillet. There's a sister restaurant, also called the *Captain's Table* (☎ 2671 027 170), on the corner of the waterfront and 21 Maïou. This place also has high-quality food but a more casual feel, and more casual prices.

IONIAN ISLANDS

The Indian Queen (☎ *2671 022 632, Lavraga 2*) Mains €5.20-10.30. Give your tastebuds a rest from fish, feta and mousakas and head to this place just off the main square (opposite Hotel Mirabel). A good selection of curries and tandoori and balti dishes is on offer, and vegetarians should fare well.

Kiani Akti (☎ *2671 026 680*) Mains €5-13.20. The fish and the mezes here are excellent, but it's the setting that's the main attraction. Located on a jetty opposite the Merchant Marine Academy at the northern end of the waterfront, you can dine while the water laps under your feet.

Pick up self-catering supplies from the huge waterfront ***produce market***. Opposite are good bakeries and grocery stores.

No surprises that the main hub for nightlife are the cafe-bars on the main square, with tables spilling out onto the road and music pumping out of the speakers until late. ***Kafe Platanos*** (☎ *2671 028 282, Plateia Vallianou*) is the classiest of the bunch, with chandeliers inside and tables and wicker chairs scattered around a lovely large plane tree outside.

Sami Σάμη
postcode 280 82 • pop 1000

Sami, 25km north-east of Argostoli and the main port of Kefallonia, was also devastated by the 1953 earthquake. It now has undistinguished buildings, but its setting is pretty, nestled in a bay and flanked by steep hills. It's worth an overnight stay to visit the nearby caves and beach. A post office, OTE and bank are in town. Buses for Argostoli usually meet ferries.

Places to Stay & Eat ***Karavomylos Beach Camping*** (☎ *2674 022 480, fax 2674 022 932,* ℮ *valettas@hol.gr*) Adult/tent €4.70/4.40. This well-kept beachfront ground is 800m west of Sami – turn right from the quay and follow the coast. It's a large, shady place and offers all manner of facilities: minimarket, laundry, restaurant, playground and Internet access.

Hotel Melissani (☎*/fax 2674 022 464*) Singles/doubles €38.20/49.90. This pleasant

older-style hotel is signposted from the eastern end of the waterfront. Rooms are comfortable and offer comforts such as TV and fridge.

Delfinia (☎ *2674 022 008*) Mains €3.80-10.30. All the places to eat in Sami are clustered along the harbour, and the tavernas are much of a muchness. One of the better places – and popular with the locals – is Delfinia, which does fish and meat on the grill, has a wider than normal choice of vegetarian Greek dishes and often features a musician serenading diners (not with a mandolin – at least not yet).

Riviera (☎ *2674 023 233*) Mains €3-6.50. Riviera is a pleasant waterfront place where you can while away some time over good coffee, breakfast or a light meal (omelette, pizza, pasta, etc). Simple, inexpensive domatia are offered above the cafe.

Around Sami

Be sure to visit gorgeous **Antisamos Beach**, 4km north-east of Sami. The long, stony beach is in a lovely green setting backed by verdant hills. The drive here is also a highlight, offering dramatic views.

Mellisani Cave (*admission €4.70, including boat trip*) is a subterranean seawater lake. When the sun is overhead its rays shine through an opening in the cave ceiling, lighting the water's many shades of blue. The cave is 2.5km from Sami, well signposted beyond the seaside village of Karavomylos. The large **Drogarati Cave** (*admission €3*) has impressive stalactites. It's signposted from the Argostoli road, 4km from Sami. Both caves are open all day.

The fishing village of **Agia Evfymia** with its pebbled beach is 10km north of Sami. It is another popular yachting stop, and there are a few hotels and some studios and domatia here.

Fiskardo Φισκάρδο
postcode 280 84 • pop 300

Fiskardo, 50km north of Argostoli, was the only village not devastated by the 1953 earthquake. Framed by cypress-mantled hills, and with fine Venetian buildings, it's a delightful place, even if it is a little dolled up for the tourists. It's especially popular with yachties.

The bus will drop you off on the road that bypasses Fiskardo. Walk across the car park, descend the steps to the left of the church and continue ahead to Fiskardo's central square and waterfront.

You can get to Fiskardo by ferry from Lefkada and Ithaki or by bus from Argostoli.

Places to Stay & Eat It will be tough to find accommodation in high season if you haven't prebooked. At other times it's OK, but prices are high.

Regina's Rooms (☎ 2674 041 125) Doubles with/without bath €44/35.20. Behind the town, by the car park area, is this reasonably priced place run by friendly Regina. Rooms are simple and among the cheapest in town, and there's a good-value cafe here too.

Stella Apartments (☎ 2674 041 211, fax 2674 041 262, e stella@kef.forthnet.gr) Double studios €67.50. This yellow-and-green complex around from the harbour offers comfortable studios in a very pleasant setting. Across the road from the apartments is a set of steps leading down to a cove for swimming.

Nicholas Taverna (☎/fax 2674 041 307) Mains €4.70-11.20. To the right as you disembark the ferry is this excellent taverna with a great view over Fiskardo, run by exuberant Nicholas and sons. Food is very good, and the studio accommodation offered here is first class (studios priced from €93.90).

The Captain's Cabin (☎ 2674 041 007) Mains to €8.80. You can't miss Captain's on the seafront, a popular watering hole for visiting yachties. Food on offer here is from a limited version of the standard Greek/international menu.

Lagoudera (☎ 2674 041 275) Gyros €1.50, mains €3.30-8.20. In a pretty setting just back from the harbourfront is Lagoudera, known for its grilled meat and serving up tasty gyros, souvlaki, steaks and lamb chops.

Around Fiskardo

Assos is a gem of whitewashed and pastel houses, straddling the isthmus of a peninsula on which stands a Venetian fortress.

Assos was damaged in the 1953 earthquake but sensitively restored with the help of a donation from the city of Paris. There's some accommodation on the road into town. Try *Linardos Studios* (☎/fax 2674 051 563), with immaculate double studios for €55.80.

There's an outstanding white sandy beach at **Myrtos**, 3km south of Assos. If you explore by boat, you'll find nearby hidden coves between tall limestone cliffs.

Southern Kefallonia

Kastro, above the village of **Peratata**, 9km south-east of Argostoli, was the island's capital in the Middle Ages. Ruined houses stand beneath the 13th-century castle of **Agios Georgios**, which affords magnificent views.

The villages of **Vlahata** on the principal Argostoli-Poros road and Lourdata (or Lourdas) down the hillside on the coast have merged into one. **Lourdata Beach** is long and sandy. **Kato Katelios** is a charming little place, not quite a thriving resort but no longer the small farming and fishing community that it once was.

Poros is overdeveloped and has a rather scruffy, pebbled beach. **Skala**, on the southern tip, is a preferable resort with a long, fine, sand beach backed by a pine wood, but at the time of research it was extremely tough to find accommodation in Skala that was not block-booked by tour operators. Poros has better accommodation options for the independent traveller.

Odyssia (☎ 2671 081 615, fax 2671 081 614) 4-person apartments €73.40. In Kato Katelios, just back from the waterfront, these apartments are incredibly spacious and fully equipped for a pleasant longer stay.

If you wish to stay in Skala, contact Vangelis at Skalina Tours (☎ 2671 083 275, fax 2671 083 475) for assistance with independent accommodation.

Makis Studios & Apartments (☎/fax 2674 072 501) Double studios €52.80, 4-person apartments €73.40. These immaculate studios in Poros are run by friendly, helpful folk.

IONIAN ISLANDS

ITHAKI Ιθάκη
postcode 283 00 • pop 3100

Ithaki (ancient Ithaca) was Odysseus' long-lost home, the island where the stoical Penelope sat patiently, weaving a shroud. She told her suitors, who believed Odysseus was dead, that she would choose one of them once she had completed the shroud. Cunningly, she unravelled it every night in order to keep her suitors at bay, as she awaited Odysseus' return.

Ithaki is separated from Kefallonia by a strait only 2km to 4km wide. The unspoilt island has a harsh, precipitous east coast and a soft, green west coast. The interior is mountainous and rocky with pockets of pine forest, stands of cypresses, olive groves and vineyards. Because of its general lack of good beaches, Ithaki doesn't attract large crowds, but it's a great place to spend a relaxing, quiet holiday.

A decent Web site to find more information is **W** www.ithaki.org.

Getting To/From Ithaki

There are two ferries daily connecting Vathy with Patras (3¾ hours, €10.90) via Sami (one hour, €3.80) on Kefallonia. There's also a ferry doing a circular route between Piso Aetos on the west coast and Vasiliki on Lefkada via Fiskardo and on to Sami on Kefallonia. (Piso Aetos has no settlement and consists of a dock, a small ticket booth and a canteen. Taxis usually meet boats.)

In high season, a daily ferry sails between Frikes (northern Ithaki), Fiskardo and Nydri on Lefkada, and a daily ferry also runs between Piso Aetos and Astakos on the mainland (2¾ hours, €5). Ithaki's port police can be contacted on ☎ 2674 032 909.

Getting Around Ithaki

The island's one bus runs twice daily to Kioni (via Stavros and Frikes) from Vathy (€1.50). It's primarily a bus for getting children to school so its limited schedule is not well suited to travellers on day trips. Taxis are quite expensive (eg, €17.60 for the Vathy-Frikes trip). In Vathy, Spiros & Nikos Rent a Bike (☎ 2674 033 243) is behind the nautical & folklore museum, and AGS Rent a Car (☎ 2674 032 702, fax 2674 033 551) is on the waterfront beside the town hall.

Vathy Βαθύ
pop 1800

Vathy (also known as Ithaki Town) is small with a few twisting streets, a central square, nice cafes and restaurants, and a few tourist shops, grocers and the like. Old mansions rise up from the seafront.

Orientation & Information The ferry quay is on the western side of the bay. To reach the central square of Plateia Efstathiou Drakouli, turn left and follow the waterfront. The main thoroughfare, Kallinikou, is parallel to, and one block inland from, the waterfront.

Ithaki has no tourist office, but there are agencies on the main square that can help with information. The tourist police (☎ 2674 032 205) are on Evmeou, which runs south from the middle of the waterfront.

The National Bank of Greece (with ATM) is just south-west of the central square. The post office is on the central square and the OTE is farther east along the waterfront. Ogygia Net-Café, a few metres inland from the harbour (turn up the alley by Café Lo Spuntino, signposted 'Flowers'), offers Internet access for €3 per hour.

Things to See & Do Behind Hotel Mentor, is a small **archaeological museum** *(☎ 2674 032 200; admission free; open 8.30am-3pm Tues-Sun)*. The charming **nautical & folklore museum** *(admission €0.70; open 9.30am-3.30pm Mon-Fri)* is housed in an old generating station just back from the waterfront (signposted) and displays clothing (including traditional dress), household items and furniture as well as shipping paraphernalia.

Boat excursions leave from Vathy harbour in the summer months and include a round-Ithaki trip and a day trip to Lefkada. There is also a taxi boat to lovely **Gidaki Beach**, north-east of Vathy.

Places to Stay *Vasiliki Vlassopoulou Domatia (☎ 2674 032 119)* Doubles €23.50. Turn left from the quay and right at the town hall, take the steps ahead, and you will see the sign for these pleasant, older-style domatia, set around a pretty garden terrace. The owners speak very little English.

Dimitrios Maroudas Rooms & Apartments (*☎/fax 2674 032 751*) Double rooms with shared bath €23.50, 2-/4-person apartments with kitchen & bathroom €52.80. Just off the eastern waterfront, this place is signposted 180m beyond the OTE (two blocks behind Century Music Club). It's a family-run place providing clean, simple rooms and apartments.

Captain Yiannis Hotel (*☎ 2674 033 311, fax 2674 032 849*) Double rooms €58.70, studios & apartments from €73.40. This hotel complex is on the opposite side of the harbour to the ferry dock and is not well signposted. It's about 1km from town and you'll know you've reached it by the smart swimming pool and bar area (there's also a tennis court). There's a feeling of space, as the clean, comfortable rooms and apartments are well spread out over the property.

Perantzada 1811 (*☎ 2674 023 914, fax 2674 033 493, @ arthotel@otenet.gr*) Double rooms with/without sea view €200/170.20. With rooms straight out of a magazine, this gorgeous boutique hotel oozes style (and prices to match). Funky furniture, interesting artwork, colourful rooms, gourmet breakfast and lovely outdoor areas (including bean-bags to relax in) combine to make this hotel quite unique in all the Ionians. The pretty, pale-blue building is one block back from the waterfront on the eastern side of town.

Places to Eat Try the sweet, gooey *rovani*, the local speciality made with rice, honey and cloves, at one of the *zaharoplasteia* on or near the main square.

Sirens Yacht Club Restaurant & Bar (*☎ 2674 033 001*) Mains €4.10-8.50. This classy place is tucked away well back from the waterfront, not far from the bank. It's run by locals who have returned to Ithaki after migrating to New York and their imaginative menu offers lots of great small dishes you can really make a meal from. Try the mini cheese pies and the baked feta with tomato and peppers.

Kantouni (*☎ 2674 032 918*) Mains to €10.30. Make your selection from a kitchen full of freshly prepared home-style fare at this restaurant on the waterfront. There's a great selection of pies with fillings such as spinach, cheese, onion, leek and chicken, and tasty oven-baked casserole dishes like lamb with potatoes and beef in red sauce.

Gregory's Taverna (*☎ 2674 032 573*) Mains €4.40-9.10. On the eastern side of the harbour, a 15-minute walk from town, is this friendly place serving up a great selection of starters, plus well-prepared meats (lamb chops, fillet steak) and seafood (this is a great place to splurge on lobster).

Drakouli Café (*☎ 2674 033 435*) Young locals meet at this stylish cafe in a waterfront mansion, which was the home of George Drakoulis, a wealthy Ithakan shipowner. It's a good spot for a drink but the snack menu is limited. Other popular cafebars line the eastern harbourfront, and this is where the nightlife is centred.

Around Ithaki

Ithaki has a few sites associated with Homer's *Odyssey*. Though none is impressive, you may enjoy (or endure) the scenic walks to them. The most renowned is the **Fountain of Arethousa**, where Odysseus' swineherd, Eumaeus, brought his pigs to drink and where Odysseus, on his return to Ithaca, went to meet him disguised as a beggar after receiving directions from the goddess Athena. Lesser mortals have to deal with inadequate signposting. The walk takes 1½ to two hours. Take plenty of water as the spring shrinks in summer.

A shorter trek is to the **Cave of the Nymphs**, where Odysseus concealed the splendid gifts of gold, copper and fine fabrics that the Phaeacians had given him. The cave is signposted from the town. Below the cave is the **Bay of Dexa** (where there is decent swimming and usually some watersports), thought to be ancient Phorkys where the Phaeacians disembarked and laid the sleeping Odysseus on the sand.

The location of Odysseus' palace has been much disputed and archaeologists have been unable to find conclusive evidence.

IONIAN ISLANDS

Odysseus & Ithaki

Ithaki (Ithaca) has long been the symbolic image for the end of a long journey. For mythical hero Odysseus (Ulysses), Ithaki was the home he left to fight in the Trojan Wars. According to the often wild tales recounted in Homer's *Iliad,* though more specifically in the *Odyssey,* it took the wily hero Odysseus 10 long years to return home to Ithaki from Troy on the Asia Minor coast.

Tossed by tempestuous seas, attacked by sea monsters, delayed by a cunning siren yet helped on his way by friendly Phaeacians, Odysseus finally made landfall on Ithaki. Here, disguised as a beggar, he teamed up with his son Telemachus and his old swineherd Eumaeus, and slayed a castleful of conniving suitors who had been eating him out of home and fortune while trying unsuccessfully to woo the ever-patient and faithful Penelope, Odysseus' long-suffering wife who had waited 20 years for him to return.

Despite Ithaki owing its fame to such illustrious classical connections, no mention of the island appears in writings of the Middle Ages. As late as AD 1504 Ithaki was almost uninhabited following repeated depredations by pirates. The Venetians were obliged to induce settlers from neighbouring islands to repopulate Ithaki. Yet the island is described in considerable detail in the *Odyssey,* which matches in many respects the physical nature of the island today. 'The Fountain of Arethousa' has been identified with a spring rising at the foot of a sea cliff in the south of the island and the 'Cave of the Nymphs' with a fairly nondescript cave up from the Bay of Phorkys. However, many Homerists have been hard-pressed to ascribe other locales described in the *Odyssey* – particularly Odysseus' castle – to actual places on the islands since scant archaeological remains assist the researcher. Other Homerists conclude that Ithaki may well have been Lefkada, a theory espoused by German archaeologist Willem Dorpfeld, though this idea seems to have fallen on rocky ground in more recent times.

Odysseus as a mythical man is everyone's hero, a pre-classical Robin Hood or John Wayne, both villain and king bundled into one well-marketed package. Classical Greek writers presented him sometimes as an unscrupulous politician, and sometimes as a wise and honourable statesman. Philosophers usually admired his intelligence and wisdom. To listeners of yore he was the hero underdog that everyone wanted to see win. Whether he actually existed or not is almost irrelevant since the universal human qualities that he embodied are those that most of us, whether we want to or not, admire and aspire to.

Schliemann erroneously believed it was near Vathy, whereas present-day archaeologists speculate it was on a hill near Stavros.

Anogi Fourteen kilometres north of Vathy is Anogi, the old capital. The restored 12th-century church of **Agia Panagia** has beautiful Byzantine frescoes. Ask in the kafeneio on the square for Gerasimos who has the key.

Frikes There's really not much to this charming fishing village in among windswept cliffs – a few waterfront restaurants and stores and that's it. Kiki Travel Agency (☎/fax 2674 031 387, e kikitrav@otenet.gr), owned by helpful Angeliki Digaletou, has a range of services including accommodation help, moped hire and sailing trips.

Kiki Domatia (☎/fax 2674 031 387, e kikitrav@otenet.gr) Doubles €41.10. These spotless domatia are in a lovely blue-and-yellow harbourfront building and the simple rooms include basics such as kettle, toaster and fridge.

Aristotelis Apartments (☎ 2674 031 079, fax 031 179, e arisvill@otenet.gr) Double studios €47, 4-person maisonette €58.70. This smart new development of eight apartments is near Hotel Nostos as you come into Frikes and offers excellent value. Rooms are well sized and attractively furnished; all have fully equipped kitchens, plus there's a nice outdoor barbecue area.

Restaurant Ulysses (☎ 2674 031 733) Mains to €7.40, fish and lobster priced by the kilogram. This casual waterfront restaurant offers fresh fish and lobster (which you choose from a large tank), plus good grilled meats and favourite pasta dishes.

Kioni Four kilometres south-east of Frikes, Kioni is perhaps one of Ithaki's better-kept secrets. It is a small village draped around a verdant hillside spilling down to a picturesque little harbour where yachties congregate. There are tavernas and a couple of bars, though it's not the best place to swim. Instead, seek out the little bays between Kioni and Frikes.

Maroudas Apartments (☎ 2674 031 691, fax 2674 031 753) Double studios €41.10. This place, opposite the doctor's surgery on the narrow road into town, is probably Kioni's cheapest accommodation. It has well-maintained, well-equipped studios. Inquire in person at the nearby souvenir store across from the small supermarket.

Captain's Apartments (☎ 2674 031 481, fax 2674 031 090) Double studios/4-person apartments €47/64.60. Signposted as you enter Kioni are these tastefully furnished and spacious apartments run by the very friendly Dellaporta family. Each of the units has a phone, TV and outdoor verandah area.

Kalipso (☎ 2674 031 066) Mains to €10.30. Sit right by the colourful small boats lining this tiny harbour and enjoy Kalipso's house speciality, its famous onion pie. There's also a good selection of seafood and traditional dishes on offer at this popular yachtie restaurant.

Zakynthos
Ζάκυνθος

postcode 291 00 • pop 32,560

Zakynthos (**zahk**-in-thos) has inspired many superlatives. The Venetians called it Fior' di Levante (flower of the orient). The poet Dionysios Solomos wrote that 'Zakynthos could make one forget the Elysian Fields'. Indeed, it is an island of exceptional natural beauty and outstanding beaches.

Unfortunately, Zakynthos' coastline has been the victim of the most unacceptable manifestations of package tourism. The lack of general budget accommodation and a rapacious attitude to tourism on the part of islanders make Zakynthos the least attractive of the Ionian islands as a destination for independent travellers. Even worse, tourism is endangering the loggerhead turtle, *Caretta caretta* (see the boxed text later in this section), and the Mediterranean monk seal, *Monachus monachus*.

There is more information available on the Internet, see Ⓦ www.zakynthos-net.gr or Ⓦ www.zanteweb.gr.

Getting To/From Zakynthos

Air There is at least one daily flight between Zakynthos and Athens (€63.40). The Olympic Airways office (☎ 2695 028 611) in Zakynthos Town is at Alexandrou Roma 16.

Bus There are five buses daily from Zakynthos Town to Patras (3½ hours, €9.10). The same buses continue on to Athens (seven hours, €20.85). There is also a twice-weekly service to Thessaloniki (€34.50). Ticket prices include the ferry fare between Zakynthos and Kyllini.

Ferry Depending on the season, between three and seven ferries daily operate from Zakynthos Town to Kyllini in the Peloponnese (1½ hours, €4.40). Tickets can be obtained from the Zakynthos Shipping Cooperative (☎ 2695 041 500, fax 2695 048 301) at Lombardou 40 in Zakynthos Town.

From the northern port of Agios Nikolaos a car ferry shuttles across to Pesada on Kefallonia from May to October (1¼ hours, €3.80). There is inexplicably no bus from Pesada to anywhere else on Kefallonia, and virtually no buses from Agios Nikolaos to anywhere in Zakynthos, making crossing without your own transport quite difficult – not to mention costly if you rely on taxis. Both these ports are quite a distance from the major towns on the respective islands (although Agios Nikolaos has a few tavernas and rooms for rent). Check with the port police (☎ 2695 042 417) for the times of the ferry; there are usually two services daily, in the morning and evening.

IONIAN ISLANDS

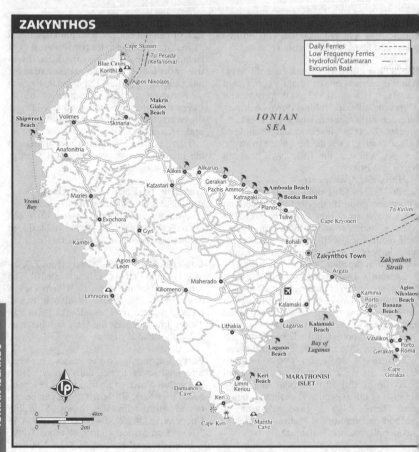

ZAKYNTHOS

Daily Ferries	– – – – –
Low Frequency Ferries	– – – – – –
Hydrofoil/Catamaran	— · · —
Excursion Boat	– · – · –

Getting Around Zakynthos

To/From the Airport There is no shuttle service between Zakynthos Town and the airport, 6km to the south-west. A taxi costs between €4.40 and €5.90.

Bus Frequent buses go from Zakynthos Town's modern bus station (☎ 2695 022 255) on Filita, one block back from the waterfront, to Alikes (€1), Tsilivi (€0.80), Argasi (€0.80) and Laganas (€0.80). Bus services to other villages are poor (one or two daily). Check the current schedule at the bus station.

Car & Motorcycle Avis (☎ 2695 027 512 fax 2695 026 330) has an office just b Plateia Agiou Markou. Ionian Renta (☎ 2695 048 946) rents cars and bikes. I office in Zakynthos Town is on Makri, an it has branches in a number of resort town on the island.

ZAKYNTHOS TOWN

pop 10,250

Zakynthos Town is the capital and port o the island. The town was devastated by th 1953 earthquake but was reconstructed wit its former layout preserved in wide arcade

treets, imposing squares and gracious neo-
lassical public buildings. It is hardly cosy,
iven its strung-out feel, but it is a reason-
ble place for an overnight stop and in com-
arison to many of the overtouristed parts
f the island there is at least a semblance of
ireekness left in the town.

Orientation & Information
he central Plateia Solomou is on the
vaterfront of Lombardou, opposite the
erry quay. Another large square, Plateia
giou Markou, is behind it. The bus station
s on Filita, one block back from the water-
ront and south of the quay. The main thor-
ughfare is Alexandrou Roma, parallel to
ie waterfront and several blocks inland.

Zakynthos Town has no tourist office.
he tourist police (☎ 2695 027 367) are at
ombardou 62.

The National Bank of Greece is just west
f Plateia Solomou, and directly next door is
Commercial Bank. Both have ATMs. The
ost office is at Tertseti 27, one block west
f Alexandrou Roma. The OTE is just off
'lateia Solomou. Top's (☎ 2695 026 650) at
ilita 34, near the bus station, has Internet
ccess. Zakynthos' hospital (☎ 2695 042
14) is west of town.

Things to See
he **Byzantine museum** (☎ 2695 042 714,
'lateia Solomou; admission €2.40; open
am-2.30pm Tues-Sun) houses an impres-
ve collection of ecclesiastical art which
'as rescued from churches razed in the
arthquake.

The **Museum of Solomos** (☎ 2695 028
82, Plateia Agiou Markou; admission
2.40; open 9am-2pm daily) is dedicated to
)ionysios Solomos (1798–1857), who was
orn on Zakynthos and is regarded as the
ather of modern Greek poetry. His work
'ymn to Liberty became the stirring Greek
ational anthem. The museum houses mem-
rabilia associated with his life, but the
ocus is really for Greek visitors.

Places to Stay
here are plenty of mid-range hotels in Za-
ynthos Town, but the problem is quality

rather than quantity. The hotels are all generally dated, and rooms are usually small
and quite dreary.

Zante Camping (☎ 2695 061 710, fax
2695 063 030) Adult/tent €4.40/3.50. This
site at Tragaki in the Tsilivi area, is the
nearest camping ground to Zakynthos Town
(about 5km away). It's a pleasant shaded
ground with a minimarket and its own path
down to the beach.

Saint Loukas Rooms for Rent (☎ 2695
026 809, Plateia Agiou Louka 2) Double
studios €41.10. Just back from the waterfront, behind the Europcar car-rental office,
is a building of well-kept rooms and studios
run by friendly owners who lived in Canada
for 12 years. The front rooms have balconies overlooking the harbour but you may
suffer with traffic noise.

Phoenix (☎ 2695 023 514, fax 2695 045
083, Plateia Solomou) Singles/doubles
€35.20/47. This unremarkable hotel, conveniently located on the main square and close
to the ferry quay, has clean, standard rooms.

Hotel Alba (☎ 2695 026 641, fax 2695
026 642, L Ziva 38) Singles/doubles €44.90/
57.20. Just off Plateia Agiou Markou is this
pleasant, good-value hotel with small but
adequate rooms.

Hotel Palatino (☎/fax 2695 045 400,
e palatzak@otenet.gr, Kolkotroni 10) Doubles €73.40. This newly refurbished hotel,
five minutes' walk north of the main square,
offers the most spacious and modern rooms
in town. It's popular with businesspeople
mid-week so it's worth booking ahead.

Places to Eat
Cafes featuring mandolato, a local nougat
sweet, are found along Alexandrou Roma,
as are good souvlaki and gyros places.
Street vendors on Plateia Solomou sell
cheap, barbecued corn on the cob. There's
a **fresh-produce market** on Filioti, and a
well-stocked **supermarket** on the corner of
Filioti and the waterfront.

Arekia (☎ 2695 026 346) There is no
menu at this popular, non-touristy place, a
10-minute walk north of the main square
along the waterfront. The owner tells you
what's been made that day and you choose,

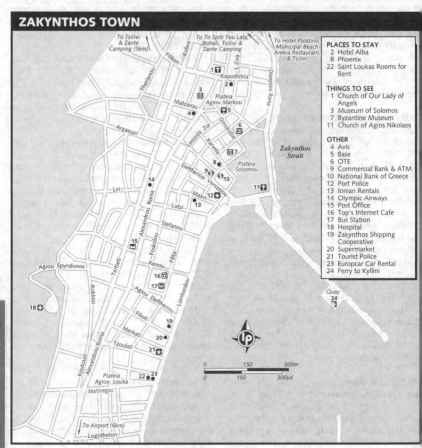

ZAKYNTHOS TOWN

To Tsilivi & Zante Camping (5km)

To To Spiti Tou Lata, Bohali, Tsilivi & Zante Camping

To Hotel Palatino, Municipal Beach Arekia Restaurant, & Tsilivi

Zakynthos Strait

Quay

To Airport (6km)

PLACES TO STAY
2 Hotel Alba
8 Phoenix
22 Saint Loukas Rooms for Rent

THINGS TO SEE
1 Church of Our Lady of Angels
3 Museum of Solomos
7 Byzantine Museum
11 Church of Agios Nikolaos

OTHER
4 Avis
5 Base
6 OTE
9 Commercial Bank & ATM
10 National Bank of Greece
12 Port Police
13 Ionian Rentals
14 Olympic Airways
15 Post Office
16 Top's Internet Cafe
17 Bus Station
18 Hospital
19 Zakynthos Shipping Cooperative
20 Supermarket
21 Tourist Police
23 Europcar Car Rental
24 Ferry to Kyllini

IONIAN ISLANDS

---

and although the food is good hearty Greek fare and very reasonably priced, it's not really what you come for. There is live music – kantades and the *arekia* of the restaurant's name – most nights from about 10pm. You'll probably have as much fun as the singers, even if you don't understand a word of the songs.

To Spiti tou Lata (*House of Latas;* ☎ 2695 041 585) Mains to €11.20. The setting here is wonderful, with tables spread out under a bougainvillea-covered pergola and fabulous views over Zakynthos Town to Mt Skopos. Head out of town, up to Bochali

near the Venetian *kastro* (walled town). Take Dionysiou Roma north, turn left at Plaza Hotel following signs to Bochali and then first left after the Maritime Museum. The menu includes a good selection of mezedes and Greek cooked dishes but the to-order grilled meats and fish are the speciality. There's also traditional music.

Base (☎ 2695 042 409, *Plateia Agiou Markou*) This hip bar is a good place for a daytime coffee or evening drink. It's particularly popular with young Zantiots as a night-time hangout, and there is often a DJ playing music.

At Loggerheads

The loggerhead turtle *(Caretta caretta)* is one of Europe's most beautiful yet most endangered marine species. In Greece the loggerhead turtle nests on two of the Ionian islands, on the Peloponnese coast and in Crete. It prefers large tracts of clean, flat and uninhabited sand. So too do basking tourists from northern Europe and it is this fateful convergence of interests that has led to the turtle being placed under the threat of extinction.

The female turtle lays about 120 eggs the size of ping-pong balls in the sand in preferred sites. After laying her eggs she returns to the sea and the eggs must lie undisturbed for up to 60 days before the hatchlings emerge. For at least 150 million years the turtle has survived geological and climatic changes but the changes to its environment caused by modern mass tourism has rung alarm bells within the conservation world.

Zakynthos hosts the largest congregation of nests. There is an average of 1300 nests per year along the 5km stretch of the Bay of Laganas on the island's south coast alone. In recent years this popular resort has come under repeated fire with conservation lobbies clashing with local authorities and businesses involved in the lucrative tourist trade. Operators who make handsome profits from renting out beach umbrellas and sunbeds have attracted particular criticism. Umbrella poles indiscriminately destroy eggs and nests and the very existence of humans anywhere near the nesting sites is totally counterproductive to the turtles' survival.

In 1999 the Greek government declared the Bay of Laganas area a National Marine Park (W www.nmp-zak.org) and strict regulations are now in force regarding boating, mooring, fishing and watersports in designated maritime zones. At the resort of Laganas itself much of the damage has already been done, but other beaches in the area, such as Gerakas, are now completely off-limits between dusk and dawn during the breeding season (nesting occurs from late May to late August, hatching from late July to late October). There are other regulations in effect (ie, cars, bikes and horses are not allowed on nesting beaches, umbrellas are only allowed in designated areas, lights cannot be shone directly onto nesting beaches), but unfortunately these laws are not particularly well enforced.

The Zakynthos branch of Archelon (W www.archelon.gr), the Sea Turtle Protection Society of Greece, has an excellent public information centre at Gerakas and regularly hosts informative slide shows at hotels in the area. The organisation accepts volunteers (minimum one-month commitment) for all its monitoring and research programs.

IONIAN ISLANDS

ROUND ZAKYNTHOS

oggerhead turtles come ashore to lay their ggs on the golden-sand beaches of the uge Bay of Laganas, on Zakynthos' south ⸱ast. Laganas is a highly developed, tacky ⸱sort and is a truly dreadful place to spend ⸱holiday unless you like lager and loud dis- ⸱s and would rather be in the UK than ⸱reece. Avoid it like the plague, or at least ⸱op by to see how Mammon and mass ⸱urism have met in the most abominable ⸱t of circumstances.

Kalamaki is not much quieter than La- ⸱nas and it's tough to find accommodation ⸱at hasn't been block-booked by tour op- ⸱ators. Beachside **Keri** (follow the sign off ⸱e main road indicating Limni Keriou) is a

better choice, although its narrow, stony beach is not much to write home about.

The Vasilikos Peninsula, south-east of Zakynthos Town beyond the busy resort of Argasi, offers a number of small, beachfront settlements off the main road, and there are tavernas and accommodation options at all these places. The first decent place to stop is **Kaminia**, followed by the sandy cove of **Porto Zoro**. Virtually at the tip of the east coast, **Banana Beach** is a more pleasant place to hang out with a long (albeit narrow) strip of golden sand. There are plenty of watersports, umbrellas and sun lounges. **Agios Nikolaos** at the very end of the peninsula also has great (turtle-free) watersports facilities.

Shipwreck Beach

The famous Shipwreck Beach (Navagio), whose photos grace virtually every tourist brochure about Zakynthos, is at the north-western tip of the island. It truly is a splendid beach with crystalline, aquamarine waters, but when some seven large excursion boats on round-the-island cruises pull up here at around midday every day and offload their passengers by the hundreds, the place really loses its appeal. Don't go on one of these cruises unless you fancy nine hours on a crowded boat offering overpriced snack food and generally travelling too far from the coastline to allow you to see much of interest.

You're better off taking a small boat trip to Shipwreck Beach or the Blue Caves (in the island's north-east), and these are best done from the lighthouse at Cape Skinari at the far northern tip of the island (3km after Agios Nikolaos). From here, the Potamitis brothers (☎ 2695 031 132) take small boats (many with glass bottoms) at frequent intervals to either venue for €5.90 (they will also act as a taxi boat to Shipwreck Beach, taking you there and picking you up a pre-arranged time). You can also visit Shipwreck Beach on a small excursion boat from the little harbour of Vromi Bay on the west coast, which in turn is reached from Anafonitria. Avoid the crowds by visiting in the morning or from mid-afternoon, and take food, drink and a beach umbrella as there are no facilities. And be sure to visit the precariously perched lookout platform over Shipwreck Beach, on the west coast, signposted between Anafonitria and Volimes. Be warned that this is not a place for those afraid of heights, but the view is definitely worth it.

Beyond ghastly Mavratzis (dominated by the mock fortress of the Zante Palace Hotel) is the more pleasant beach of **Porto Roma**, although this narrow strip of sand can get crowded. On the other side of the peninsula, facing Laganas Bay, is Zakynthos' best beach, the long and sandy **Gerakas**. This is one of the main turtle-nesting beaches (see boxed text 'At Loggerheads') and access to the beach is strictly forbidden between dusk and dawn during the breeding season.

You can semi-escape from the tourist hype by visiting the accessible west-coast coves such as lovely **Limnionas** or **Kambi** (the latter has great tavernas for sunset-watching). Get even more off the beaten path by touring the inland farming villages, and make an effort to visit tiny **Gyri** in the centre of the island, where there is a cosy taverna with live arekia music on weekends.

Places to Stay & Eat

Tartaruga Camping (☎ 2695 051 967, fax 2695 053 023) Adult/tent €4.40/3. If you're travelling on the road from Laganas to Keri, you'll pass the well-signposted turn-off to this lovely camping ground, with a wonderful setting amid terraced olive groves and vineyards and a trail down to the beach. There are also some rooms for rent here but these usually need to be booked advance.

Seaside Apartments to Let (☎ 2695 04 297) Double studios €44, 4-bed apartment €73.40. These delightful rooms are above the beachfront Keri Tourist Center (a glorified minimarket and gift shop). Their bright, modern decor is fabulously enhanced by artwork done by the friendly owner.

Sea View Village (☎ 2695 035 178, fax 2695 035 152, e seaview@zakynthos-net.gr) Doubles/triples/quads €73.40/88/ 102.70 Easily one of the nicest new complexes we've seen is this smart, 26-room resort just south of the turn-off to Kaminia Beach, well positioned for exploration of the area's beaches. Modern, spacious studios and apartments are a cut above many others on offer and the central pool and bar area is lovely.

Gerakas Taverna & Bar (☎ 2695 03 248) Mains €4.40-9.40. This pleasant family-run place is on the road heading to the Gerakas beach. It offers an extensive menu featuring many Greek favourites, grilled meats, oven-baked dishes, lots of fish etc. There's also a cocktail bar, plus sales of ocal organic produce (oil, honey, olives, vine and cheese), and the owners have a few easonably priced studios to rent.

Kythira & Antikythira

KYTHIRA Κύθηρα
ostcode 80 100 • pop 3100

he island of Kythira (kee-thih-rah) is to many Greeks the Holy Grail of island-hopping. The *Road to Kythira*, a well-known 1973 ong by Dimitris Mitropanos, epitomises what for most people is the end of a line that s never reached. Indeed, given its location, ou have to make a special effort get here.

Some 30km long and 18km wide, Kythira dangles off the Laconian Peninsula f the Peloponnese between the often turulent Ionian and Aegean Seas. It is a curiusly barren island in parts, with misty noors, hidden valleys and winding lanes. More than 40 villages are scattered evenly cross the island, and ghosts are said to oam the inland villages. Kythira was part f the British Ionian protectorate for many ears, evidenced by the sprinkling of arched tone bridges around the island.

Kythira is the least 'Ionian' of the Ionian sland group. Physically separated from its earest neighbour Zakynthos by a long tretch of sea, it is administered from Piaeus and mostly resembles the Cyclades in ppearance and architecture.

Mythology suggests that Aphrodite was orn in Kythira. She is supposed to have sen from the foam where Zeus had thrown 'ronos' sex organ after castrating him. The oddess of love then re-emerged near Pafos a Cyprus, so both islands haggle over her irthplace.

The EOT has begun encouraging tourists o visit Kythira but it's still unspoilt. Its atactions are its relatively undeveloped eaches, its enduring feel as a special island nd the fact that it is 'the end of the line'.

Kythira's main port is Agia Pelagia, lough hydrofoils depart from and arrive at le custom-built port of Diakofti (as do

ferries when the weather is bad). Public transport on Kythira ranges from abysmal to nonexistent, so bringing your own wheels or renting them locally is advisable.

For information on the Internet, see the Web sites W www.kythira.com and W www .kytheranet.com.

Getting To/From Kythira
Air There are daily flights between Kythira and Athens (€52.80). The airport is 10km east of Potamos, and the Olympic Airways office (☎ 2736 033 362) is on the central square in Potamos. Book also at Kythira Travel (☎ 2736 031 390) in Hora.

Ferry ANEN Lines operates the *Myrtidiotissa* on a weekly schedule between Piraeus, Kythira, Antikythira, Kastelli-Kissamos (Crete), Kalamata and Gythio (both in the Peloponnese). Twice a week the ferry runs directly between Piraeus and Kythira (6½ hours, €16.50). The ferry arrives at and departs from Diakofti.

From mid-June to mid-September there are three weekly connections between Kythira and Gythio (2½ hours, €7.10). Four times a week the ferry runs between Kythira and Kastelli-Kisamos (four hours, €12.90). Information and tickets are available from Porfyra Travel (☎/fax 2736 031 888, e porfyra@otenet.gr) in Livadi.

The *Nisos Kythira* shuttles two or three times daily between Agia Pelagia and Neapoli (one hour, €4.40). Tickets are sold at the quay before departure, or by Sirenes Travel Club (☎ 2736 034 371) in Potamos. In case of bad weather, the boat arrives at and departs from Diakofti, not Agia Pelagia.

The port police (☎ 2736 033 280) are at Agia Pelagia on the waterfront. Diakofti's port police are on ☎ 2736 034 222.

Hydrofoil From June to mid-September, there are daily hydrofoils from Diakofti to Zea in Piraeus (€30.80). It takes 3½ hours direct (three times a week), or five hours via Neapoli, Monemvassia, Kiparissi and Leonidio, in the eastern Peloponnese (four times a week). Tickets are available at Kythira Travel (☎ 2736 031 490) on the main square in Hora.

IONIAN ISLANDS

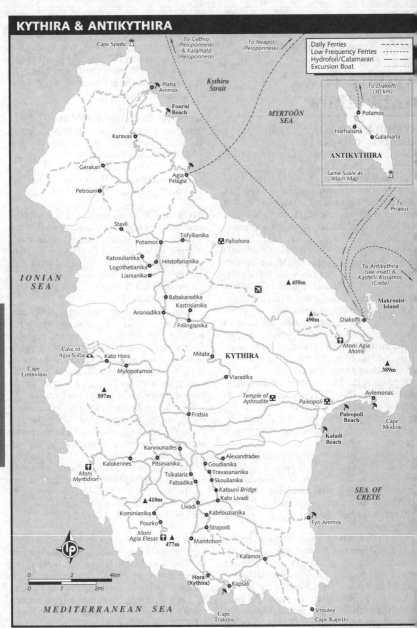

KYTHIRA & ANTIKYTHIRA

Daily Ferries ----
Low Frequency Ferries -----
Hydrofoil/Catamaran ----
Excursion Boat ....

Cape Spathi

To Gythio
(Peloponnese)
& Kalamata
(Peloponnese)

To Neapoli
(Peloponnese)

Kythira Strait

Platia Ammos

Fourni Beach

MYRTOÖN SEA

To Diakofti
(30 km)

Potamos

Harhaliana
Galaniana

ANTIKYTHIRA

Same Scale as
Main Map

Karavas

Gerakari

Agia Pelagia

Petrouni

To Piraeus

Stavli

Trifyllianika

Paliohora

Potamos

Katsoulianika
Logothetianika
Lianianika

Hristoforianika

To Antikythira
(see inset) &
Kastelli-Kissamos
(Crete)

IONIAN SEA

Babakaradika
Kastrisianika

Aroniadika

Frilingianika

▲458m

Makronisi
Island

Cape
Limnionas

Cave of
Agia Sofia

Kato Hora

Mylopotamos

Mitata

KYTHIRA

490m

Diakofti

Moni Agia Monis

▲389m

Viaradika

Temple of
Aphrodite

Paleopoli

Avlemonas

Fratsia

Paleopoli
Beach

Cape
Modoni

Kaladi
Beach

Karvounades

Alexandrades

Kalokerines

Pitsinianika

Goudianika
Travasarianika

Tsikalaria
Fatsadika

Skoulianika

Katouni Bridge

Kato Livadi

▲410m

Livadi

Katelouzianika

*SEA OF
CRETE*

Kominianika

Pourko

*Moni
Agia Elesas*

▲477m

Strapodi

Manitohori

Fyri Ammos

Kalamos

IONIAN ISLANDS

0   2   4km
0   1   2mi

Hora
(Kythira)

Kapsali

MEDITERRANEAN SEA

Cape
Trahilos

Vroulea
Cape Kapello

Getting Around Kythira

There is no regular public transport on the island. Not surprisingly, there are many axis, but the best way to see the island and explore the small villages and difficult-to-access beaches is with your own transport. Helpful Panayotis at Moto Rent (☎ 2736 31 600, fax 2736 031 789) on Kapsali's waterfront rents cars and mopeds.

Hora Χώρα
pop 550

Hora (or Kythira), the pretty capital, with white, blue-shuttered houses, perches on a long, slender ridge 2km uphill from Kapsali. The central square, planted with hibiscus, bougainvillea and palms, is Plateia Dimitriou Staï. The main street runs south of it.

The post office is on the square, as are the National Bank of Greece and Agricultural Bank, both with ATMs. Just south of the square is Anonymo (also called Cafe No-Name), a cafe-bar offering Internet access (€5.90 per hour). The police station (☎ 2736 31 206) is near the kastro.

Hora has no tourist office but English-speaking Panayotis offers information to tourists at his Moto Rent office (☎ 2736 31 600) on Kapsali's waterfront.

Things to See
Hora's Venetian **kastro**, built in the 13th century, is at the southern end of town. If you walk to its southern extremity, passing the Church of Panagia, you will come to a sheer cliff – from here there's a stunning view of Kapsali and on a good day of Antikythira.

North of the central square, near the turn-off to Kapsali, is the **archaeological museum** (☎ 2736 031 789; admission free; open 8.45am-3pm Tues-Sat, 9.30am-2.30pm Sun). It features gravestones of British soldiers and their infants who died on the island in the 19th century. A large marble lion from around 550 BC is also exhibited.

Call in to **Stavros** (☎ 2736 031 857), a store north of the square (opposite the turn-off to Kapsali) and pick up some of the local produce, including some of Greece's best honey.

Places to Stay *Castello Rooms* (☎ 2736 031 069, fax 2736 031 869, ⓔ jfatseas@ otenet.gr) Doubles €35.20, studios sleeping up to three €44. There's a sign at the southern end of the main street to these spacious rooms and studios.

Papadonicos Rooms (☎ 2736 031 126) Double studios €35.20, 4-person apartments €52.80. These pleasant studios are a bit farther south from Castello Rooms, in an old converted house with a pleasant terrace garden area. This is one of few places in this part of the island open year-round.

Hotel Margarita (☎ 2736 031 711, fax 2736 031 325, ⓔ fatseasp@otenet.gr) Singles/doubles €70.50/82.20 high season. This charming hotel, off the main street between the central square and kastro, offers very pleasant rooms (all with TV and telephone) in a renovated 19th-century mansion featuring a lovely old staircase. Breakfast is served on a pretty whitewashed terrace.

Places to Eat There are not a lot of restaurant choices in Hora, but there's a decent selection of cafes offering snacks, largely clustered around the central square and with a few along the main street.

Fournos (☎ 2736 034 289) Snacks €2.10-11.80. Run by Lili, a Greek-Australian, this place offers a good selection of snacks a cut above the usual fare – eg, tasty antipasto plates, homemade quiche and pies and a very decent burger. There are tables and chairs on the square, although the cafe itself is tucked away slightly off a side street.

Zorba's (☎ 2736 031 655) There's no menu as such here at this *psistaria* south of the square, and vegetarians will struggle. Customers choose from a display of freshly prepared meat and the owners grill it for you, and will whip up a salad to accompany it. Prices vary according to what's on offer, but costs are very reasonable.

Kapsali Καψάλι
postcode 801 00 • pop 70

Kapsali is a picturesque village down a winding road from Hora. It looks particularly captivating from Hora's castle, with its twin sandy bays and curving waterfront.

Restaurants and cafes line the beach, and safe sheltered swimming is Kapsali's trademark. Not surprisingly, this is a very popular place so accommodation can be scarce unless you book well ahead. It can also get pretty crowded in high season, so if you like your beach in solitude look elsewhere.

Offshore you can see the stark rock island known as the **Avgo** (Egg) rearing above the water. It is here that Kytherians claim Aphrodite sprang from the sea.

As well as cars and mopeds, bicycles, canoes and pedal boats can be hired from Panayotis at Moto Rent (☎ 2736 031 600), on the waterfront. He also offers waterskiing opportunities.

Places to Stay & Eat *Camping Kapsali* (☎ 2736 031 580) Adult/tent €3.30/3. Open June-mid Sept. This small pine-shaded ground (well signposted off the road from Hora) is 400m from Kapsali's quay, behind the village. It's a quiet spot with minimal facilities and is better suited to small tents rather than large campervan setups.

Vassilis Studios (☎ 2736 031 125, fax 2736 031 553) Double studios €73.40. On the road between Hora and Kapsali is this attractive green-and-white complex of studios, not far from the beach. Olga, the friendly owner, offers spacious studios with lovely wooden floors and good bay views.

Raikos Hotel (☎ 2736 031 629, fax 2736 031 801, e raikoshotel@techlink.gr) Doubles/triples €85.10/102.70. Signposted off the Hora-Kapsali road is this very smart, friendly hotel, offering spacious, pleasantly decorated rooms with terraces overlooking Kapsali and Hora's kastro. There's a lovely pool and bar area too.

Hydragogio (☎ 2736 031 065) Mains to €12.30, lobster and fish priced by the kilogram. This lively eatery at the far end by the rocks specialises in fresh fish and mezedes. It's a good place to splurge on lobster, if your budget stretches that far. The wine list is comprehensive and excellent.

There are numerous restaurants and cafes lining Kapsali's waterfront, plus a good assortment of bars – this is probably the liveliest town on the island as far as nightlife goes. *Shaker* and *Barbarossa* are popular.

Potamos Ποταμός
pop 680
Potamos, 10km from Agia Pelagia, is the island's commercial hub. On Sunday morning it attracts almost every islander to market. The National Bank of Greece (with ATM) is on the central square. The post office is just north of the central square.

Hotel Porfyra (☎ 2736 033 329, 2736 033 924) Double/triple studios €47/52.80, 4-person apartments €61.60. At Potamos one hotel, spotless self-contained units surround a pleasant internal courtyard. The sign is in Greek only – look for it almost opposite the post office north of the main square.

Taverna Panaretos (☎ 2736 034 290) Mains to €8.80. This bustling taverna on the central square serves well-prepared international and Greek dishes, including tempting seafood risotto and pasta.

Ta Katsigouro (☎ 2736 033 880) Snacks to €4.40. This place is also known as the Greek-Aussie snack bar and has a logo incorporating a kangaroo's body and a goat's head. It's just south of the square and serves up great souvlaki, gyros and burgers.

Mylopotamos Μυλοπόταμος
pop 90
Mylopotamos is an alluring, verdant village. Its central square is flanked by a much-photographed church and kafeneio *O Platanos*, which offers simple, excellent fare in a gorgeous setting. It's worth a stroll to the **Neraïda** (water nymph) waterfall with luxuriant greenery and mature, shady trees. As you reach the church, take the right fork and follow the signs to an unpaved road leading down to the falls.

To reach the abandoned **kastro** of Mylopotamos, take the left fork after the kafeneio and follow the sign for Kato Hora (lower village). The road leads to the centre of Kato Hora, from where a portal leads into the spooky kastro, with derelict houses and well-preserved little churches (usually locked).

Farther along the same road is the **Cave of Agia Sofia**, reached by a precipitous, unpaved 2km road. Irregular opening times are usually pinned on the side of the church in Mylopotamos.

Agia Pelagia Αγία Πελαγία
pop 280
Kythira's northern port of Agia Pelagia is a simple, friendly waterfront village ideal for relaxing and swimming. Mixed sand-and-pebble beaches are either side of the quay.

Places to Stay & Eat Prebooking in high season is almost essential in Agia Pelagia.

Georgos Kambouris Domatia (☎ 2736 033 480) Doubles €49.90. This is one of the friendliest and most pleasant places to stay. Georgos' wife, Maria, maintains spotless, airy rooms. The building is just in front of Hotel Romantica.

Hotel Kytheria (☎ 2736 033 321, fax 2736 033 825) Doubles €64.60. This welcoming hotel, on the beach and owned by helpful Angelo from Australia, has very comfortable, tidy rooms.

Venardos Hotel (☎ 2736 034 205, fax 2736 033 850, ℮ venardos@otenet.gr) Singles/doubles/triples €64.60/76.30/88. Open year-round. This large hotel has sizable, airy rooms and a lovely terrace area. Australians get a special welcome.

Faros Taverna (☎ 2736 033 343) Mains to €7.40. This blue-and-white taverna close to the quay serves good, economical Greek staples.

Moustakias (☎ 2736 033 519) Mains to €8.80. This ouzeri, next to the minimarket, offers food ranging from mezedes to grilled meats to seafood, including all the traditional Greek favourites.

Sempreviva Patisserie (☎ 2736 033 390) Cakes & pastries to €3. For breakfast, Sempreviva serves wickedly delicious Greek cakes and freshly brewed coffee.

Around Kythira
If you have transport, a tour round the island is rewarding. The monasteries of **Agia Moni** and **Agia Elesa** are mountain refuges with superb views. **Moni Myrtidion** is a beautiful monastery surrounded by trees. From Hora, drive north-east to the picturesque village of **Avlemonas** via **Paleopoli** with its wide, pebbled beach. Here, archaeologists spent years searching for evidence of a temple at Aphrodite's birthplace. Be sure to also visit the spectacularly situated ruins of the Byzantine capital of **Paleohora**, in the island's north-east.

Just north of the village of Kato Livadi make a detour to see the remarkable, and seemingly out-of-place, British-made **Katouni Bridge**, a legacy of Kythira's time as part of the British protectorate in the 19th century. In the far north of the island the village of **Karavas** is verdant and very attractive and close to both Agia Pelagia and the reasonable beach at **Platia Ammos**. Beachcombers should seek out **Kaladi Beach**, near Paleopoli. Another good beach is **Fyri Ammos**, closer to Hora.

Places to Eat *Filio* (☎ 2736 031 549) Mains to €8.80. It's well worth going out of your way to visit this great restaurant in Kalamos, one of the nicest on the island. In a lovely garden setting you'll be offered countless traditional Kytherian dishes by friendly, helpful staff.

Estiatorion Pierros (☎ 2736 031 014). While heading out across the island, stop in at great little roadside establishment in Livadi, where you'll find no-nonsense traditional Greek staples. There's no menu – visit the kitchen to see what's been freshly cooked.

Sotiris (☎ 2736 033 722) Seasonal fish and lobster priced by the kilogram. This popular fish taverna in pretty Avlemonas offers well-prepared fresh catch and is known for its lobster and excellent fish soup.

ANTIKYTHIRA Αντικύθηρα
pop 70
The tiny island of Antikythira, 38km south-east of Kythira, is the most remote island in the Ionian group. It has only one settlement, **Potamos**, one doctor, one police officer, one teacher (with a only handful of pupils), one telephone and a monastery. It doesn't have a post office or

Phone numbers listed incorporate changes due in Oct 2002; see p83

IONIAN ISLANDS

bank. The only accommodation for tourists is 10 basic rooms in two purpose-built blocks, open in summer only. Potamos has a kafeneio and taverna.

Getting To/From Antikythira Surprisingly, there's only bare-bones ferry connections between Kythira and Antikythira, even in high season. ANEN Lines' *Mirtidiotissa* calls in twice weekly – on Saturday in the wee small hours on the way from Kythira to Crete, and Sunday going the opposite way, so technically a brief stay is possible, if you don't mind arriving on the island at 2.45am! Outside of high season schedules are even less conducive to a visit. The journey from Kythira to Antikythira costs €6.20 and takes two hours. This is not an island for tourists on a tight schedule and will probably only appeal to those who really like their isolation. For information and tickets, contact Porfyra Travel (☎/fax 2736 031 888, ⓔ porfyra@otenet.gr) in Livadi on Kythira.

Language

The Greek language is probably the oldest European language, with an oral tradition of 4000 years and a written tradition of approximately 3000 years. Its evolution over the four millennia was characterised by its strength during the golden age of Athens and the Democracy (mid-5th century BC); its use as a lingua franca throughout the Middle Eastern world, spread by Alexander the Great and his successors as far as India during the Hellenistic period (330 BC to AD 100); its adaptation as the language of the new religion, Christianity; its use as the official language of the Eastern Roman Empire; and its eventual proclamation as the language of the Byzantine Empire (380–1453).

Greek maintained its status and prestige during the rise of the European Renaissance and was employed as the linguistic perspective for all contemporary sciences and terminologies during the period of Enlightenment. Today, Greek constitutes a large part of the vocabulary of any Indo-European language, and much of the lexicon of any scientific repertoire.

The modern Greek language is a southern Greek dialect which is now used by most Greek speakers both in Greece and abroad. It is the result of an intralinguistic influence and synthesis of the ancient vocabulary combined with words from Greek regional dialects, namely Cretan, Cypriot and Macedonian.

Greek is spoken throughout Greece by a population of around 10 million, and by some five million Greeks who live abroad.

Pronunciation

All Greek words of two or more syllables have an acute accent which indicates where the stress falls. For instance, άγαλμα (statue) is pronounced *aghalma*, and αγάπη (love) is pronounced *aghapi*. In the following transliterations, bold lettering indicates where stress falls. Note also that **dh** is pronounced as 'th' in 'then'; **gh** is a softer, slightly guttural version of 'g'.

Greetings & Civilities

Hello.
*ya*sas   Γειά σας.
*ya*su (informal)   Γειά σου.
Goodbye.
an*dio*   Αντίο.
Good morning.
kali*mera*   Καλημέρα.
Good afternoon.
*here*te   Χαίρετε.
Good evening.
kalis*pera*   Καλησπέρα.
Good night.
kali*nihta*   Καληνύχτα.
Please.
paraka*lo*   Παρακαλώ.
Thank you.
efharis*to*   Ευχαριστώ.
Yes.
ne   Ναι.
No.
ohi   Όχι.
Sorry. (excuse me, forgive me)
sigh*nomi*   Συγγνώμη.
How are you?
ti *kane*te?   Τι κάνετε;
ti *kanis?*   Τι κάνεις;
(informal)
I'm well, thanks.
kala efharis*to*   Καλά ευχαριστώ.

Essentials

Do you speak English?
mi*late* anglika?   Μιλάτε Αγγλικά;
I understand.
katala*veno*   Καταλαβαίνω.
I don't understand.
dhen katala*veno*   Δεν καταλαβαίνω.
Where is ...?
pou *ine* ...?   Πού είναι ...;
How much?
poso kani?   Πόσο κάνει;
When?
pote?   Πότε;

LANGUAGE

The Greek Alphabet & Pronunciation

Greek	Pronunciation Guide		Example		
Α α	a	as in 'father'	αγάπη	*aghapi*	love
Β β	v	as in 'vine'	βήμα	*vima*	step
Γ γ	gh	like a rough 'g'	γάτα	*ghata*	cat
	y	as in 'yes'	για	*ya*	for
Δ δ	dh	as in 'there'	δέμα	*dhema*	parcel
Ε ε	e	as in 'egg'	ένας	*enas*	one (m)
Ζ ζ	z	as in 'zoo'	ζώο	*zoo*	animal
Η η	i	as in 'feet'	ήταν	*itan*	was
Θ θ	th	as in 'throw'	θέμα	*thema*	theme
Ι ι	i	as in 'feet'	ίδιος	*idhyos*	same
Κ κ	k	as in 'kite'	καλά	*kala*	well
Λ λ	l	as in 'leg'	λάθος	*lathos*	mistake
Μ μ	m	as in 'man'	μαμά	*mama*	mother
Ν ν	n	as in 'net'	νερό	*nero*	water
Ξ ξ	x	as in 'ox'	ξύδι	*ksidhi*	vinegar
Ο ο	o	as in 'hot'	όλα	*ola*	all
Π π	p	as in 'pup'	πάω	*pao*	I go
Ρ ρ	r	as in 'road'	ρέμα	*rema*	stream
		a slightly trilled r	ρόδα	*rodha*	tyre
Σ σ, ς	s	as in 'sand'	σημάδι	*simadhi*	mark
Τ τ	t	as in 'tap'	τόπι	*topi*	ball
Υ υ	i	as in 'feet'	ύστερα	*istera*	after
Φ φ	f	as in 'find'	φύλλο	*filo*	leaf
Χ χ	h	as the ch in Scottish *loch*, or like a rough h	χάνω	*hano*	I lose
			χέρι	*heri*	hand
Ψ ψ	ps	as in 'lapse'	ψωμί	*psomi*	bread
Ω ω	o	as in 'hot'	ώρα	*ora*	time

Combinations of Letters

The combinations of letters shown here are pronounced as follows:

Greek	Pronunciation Guide		Example		
ει	i	as in 'feet'	είδα	*idha*	I saw
οι	i	as in 'feet'	οικόπεδο	*ikopedho*	land
αι	e	as in 'bet'	αίμα	*ema*	blood
ου	u	as in 'mood'	πού	*pou*	who/what
μπ	b	as in 'beer'	μπάλα	*bala*	ball
	mb	as in 'amber'	κάμπος	*kambos*	forest
ντ	d	as in 'dot'	ντουλάπα	*doulapa*	wardrobe
	nd	as in 'bend'	πέντε	*pende*	five
γκ	g	as in 'God'	γκάζι	*gazi*	gas
γγ	ng	as in 'angle'	αγγελία	*angelia*	classified
γξ	ks	as in 'minks'	σφιγξ	*sfinks*	sphynx
τζ	dz	as in 'hands'	τζάκι	*dzaki*	fireplace

The pairs of vowels shown above are pronounced separately if the first has an acute accent, or the second a dieresis, as in the examples below:

γαϊδουράκι	*gaidhouraki*	little donkey
Κάιρο	*kairo*	Cairo

Some Greek consonant sounds have no English equivalent. The υ of the groups αυ, ευ and ηυ is generally pronounced 'v'. The Greek question mark is represented with the English equivalent of a semicolon ';'.

Small Talk

What's your name?
pos sas lene?   Πώς σας λένε;
My name is ...
me lene ...   Με λένε ...
Where are you from?
apo pou iste?   Από πού είστε;

I'm from ...
ime apo ...   Είμαι από ...
America
tin ameriki   την Αμερική
Australia
tin afstralia   την Αυστραλία
England
tin anglia   την Αγγλία
Ireland
tin irlandhia   την Ιρλανδία
New Zealand
ti nea zilandhia   τη Νέα Ζηλανδία
Scotland
ti skotia   τη Σκωτία

How old are you?
poson hronon iste?   Πόσων χρονών είστε;
I'm ... years old.
ime ... hronon   Είμαι ... χρονών.

Getting Around

What time does he ... leave/arrive?
ti ora fevyi/ ftani to ...?   Τι ώρα φεύγει/ φτάνει το ...;

plane   *aeroplano*   αεροπλάνο
boat   *karavi*   καράβι
bus (city)   *astiko*   αστικό
bus (intercity)   *leoforio*   λεωφορείο
train   *treno*   τραίνο

I'd like ...
tha ithela ...   Θα ήθελα ...
a return ticket
isitirio me epistrofi   εισιτήριο με επιστροφή
two tickets
dhio isitiria   δυο εισιτήρια
a student's fare
fititiko isitirio   φοιτητικό εισιτήριο

Signs

ΕΙΣΟΔΟΣ	**Entry**
ΕΞΟΔΟΣ	**Exit**
ΩΘΗΣΑΤΕ	**Push**
ΣΥΡΑΤΕ	**Pull**
ΓΥΝΑΙΚΩΝ	**Women (toilets)**
ΑΝΔΡΩΝ	**Men (toilets)**
ΝΟΣΟΚΟΜΕΙΟ	**Hospital**
ΑΣΤΥΝΟΜΙΑ	**Police**
ΑΠΑΓΟΡΕΥΕΤΑΙ	**Prohibited**
ΕΙΣΙΤΗΡΙΑ	**Tickets**

first class
proti thesi   πρώτη θέση
economy
touristiki thesi   τουριστική θέση

train station
sidhirodhro- mikos stathmos   σιδηροδρομικός σταθμός
timetable
dhromologio   δρομολόγιο
taxi
taxi   ταξί

Where can I hire a car?
pou boro na nikyaso ena aftokinito?
Πού μπορώ να νοικιάσω ένα αυτοκίνητο;

Directions

How do I get to ...?
pos tha pao sto/ sti ...?   Πώς θα πάω στο/ στη ...;
Where is ...?
pou ine ...?   Πού είναι...;
Is it near?
ine konda?   Είναι κοντά;
Is it far?
ine makria?   Είναι μακριά;

straight ahead   *efthia*   ευθεία
left   *aristera*   αριστερά
right   *dexia*   δεξιά
behind   *piso*   πίσω
far   *makria*   μακριά
near   *konda*   κοντά
opposite   *apenandi*   απέναντι

Can you show me on the map?
borite na mou to dhixete sto harti?
Μπορείτε να μου το δείξετε
στο χάρτη;

Around Town

I'm looking for (the) ...
psahno ya ...
Ψάχνω για ...

bank	*trapeza*	τράπεζα
beach	*paralia*	παραλία
castle	*kastro*	κάστρο
church	*ekklisia*	εκκλησία
... embassy	*tin ... presvia*	την ... προσβεία
market	*aghora*	αγορά
museum	*musio*	μουσείο
police	*astynomia*	αστυνομία
post office	*tahydhromio*	ταχυδρομείο
ruins	*arhea*	αρχαία

I want to exchange some money.
thelo na exaryiroso lefta
Θέλω να εξαργυρώσω λεφτά.

Accommodation

Where is ...?
pou ine ...? Πού είναι ...;
I'd like ...
thelo ena ... Θέλω ένα ...

a cheap hotel
ftino xenodohio φτηνό ξενοδοχείο
a clean room
katharo dho-matio καθαρό δωμάτιο
a good hotel
kalo xenodohio καλό ξενοδοχείο
a camp site
kamping κάμπινγκ

single	*mono*	μονό
double	*dhiplo*	διπλό
room	*dhomatio*	δωμάτιο
with bathroom	*me banio*	με μπάνιο
key	*klidhi*	κλειδί

How much is it ...?
poso kani ...? Πόσο κάνει ...;
per night
ti vradhya τη βραδυά

Emergencies

Help!
voithya! Βοήθεια!
Police!
astynomia! Αστυνομία!
There's been an accident.
eyine atihima Εγινε ατύχημα.
Call a doctor!
fonaxte ena yatro! Φωνάξτε ένα ιατρό!
Call an ambulance!
tilefoniste ya asthenoforo! Τηλεφωνήστε για ασθενοφόρο!
I'm ill.
ime arostos (m) Είμαι άρρωστος
ime arosti (f) Είμαι άρρωστη
I'm lost.
eho hathi Εχω χαθεί
Thief!
klefti! Κλέφτη!
Go away!
fiye! Φύγε!
I've been raped.
me viase kapyos Με βίασε κάποιος.
I've been robbed.
meklepse kapyos Μ'έκλεψε κάποιος.
Where are the toilets?
pou ine i toualetez? Πού είναι οι τουαλέτες;

for ... nights
ya ... vradhyez για ... βραδυές
Is breakfast included?
symberilamvani ke pro-ino? Συμπεριλαμβάνει και πρωϊνό;
May I see it?
boro na to dho? Μπορώ να το δω;
Where is the bathroom?
pou ine tobanio? Πού είναι το μπάνιο;
It's expensive.
ine akrivo Είναι ακριβό.
I'm leaving today.
fevgho simera Φεύγω σήμερα.

Food

breakfast	pro-ino	πρωϊνό
lunch	mesimvrino	μεσημβρινό
dinner	vradhyno	βραδυνό
beef	vodhino	βοδινό
bread	psomi	ψωμί
beer	byra	μπύρα
cheese	tyri	τυρί
chicken	kotopoulo	κοτόπουλο
Greek coffee	ellinikos kafes	ελληνικός καφές
iced coffee	frappe	φραππέ
lamb	arni	αρνί
milk	ghala	γάλα
mineral	metalliko	μεταλλικό
water	nero	νερό
tea	tsai	τσάι
wine	krasi	κρασί

I'm a vegetarian.
ime hortofaghos Είμαι χορτοφάγος.

Shopping

How much is it?
poso kani?
Πόσο κάνει;
I'm just looking.
aplos kitazo
Απλώς κοιτάζω.
I'd like to buy ...
thelo n'aghoraso ...
Θέλω ν΄αγοράσω ...
Do you accept credit cards?
pernete pistotikez kartez?
Παίρνετε πιστωτικές κάρτες;
Could you lower the price?
borite na mou kanete mya kaliteri timi?
Μπορείτε να μου κάνετε μια καλύτερη τιμή;

Time & Dates

What time is it?
ti ora ine? Τι ώρα είναι;

It's ...	ine ...	είναι ...
1 o'clock	mia i ora	μία η ώρα
2 o'clock	dhio i ora	δύο η ώρα
7.30	efta ke misi	εφτά και μισή
am	to pro-i	το πρωί
pm	to apoyevma	το απόγευμα
today	simera	σήμερα

tonight	apopse	απόψε
now	tora	τώρα
yesterday	hthes	χθες
tomorrow	avrio	αύριο

Sunday	kyriaki	Κυριακή
Monday	dheftera	Δευτέρα
Tuesday	triti	Τρίτη
Wednesday	tetarti	Τετάρτη
Thursday	pempti	Πέμπτη
Friday	paraskevi	Παρασκευή
Saturday	savato	Σάββατο

January	ianouarios	Ιανουάριος
February	fevrouarios	Φεβρουάριος
March	martios	Μάρτιος
April	aprilios	Απρίλιος
May	maïos	Μάιος
June	iounios	Ιούνιος
July	ioulios	Ιούλιος
August	avghoustos	Αύγουστος
September	septemvrios	Σεπτέμβριος
October	oktovrios	Οκτώβριος
November	noemvrios	Νοέμβριος
December	dhekemvrios	Δεκέμβριος

Health

I need a doctor.
hriazome yatro Χρειάζομαι ιατρό.
Can you take me
to hospital?
borite na me pate Μπορείτε να με πάτε
sto nosokomio? στο νοσοκομείο;
I want something for ...
thelo kati ya ... Θέλω κάτι για ...
diarrhoea
dhiaria διάρροια
insect bites
tsimbimata apo τσιμπήματα από
endoma έντομα
travel sickness
naftia taxidhiou ναυτία ταξιδιού

aspirin		
aspirini		ασπιρίνη
condoms		
profylaktika		προφυλακτικά
(kapotez)		(καπότες)
contact lenses		
faki epafis		φακοί επαφής
medical insurance		
yatriki asfalya		ιατρική ασφάλεια

Numbers

0	*mi**dhen***	μηδέν		20	*i**kosi***	είκοσι
1	*e**nas***	ένας (m)		30	*tri**anda***	τριάντα
	mia	μία (f)		40	*sa**ran**da*	σαράντα
	*e**na***	ένα (n)		50	*pe**ninda***	πενήντα
2	*dhio*	δύο		60	*e**xinda***	εξήντα
3	*tris*	τρεις (m & f)		70	*evdho**minda***	εβδομήντα
	tria	τρία (n)		80	*ogh**dhon**da*	ογδόντα
4	*te**seris***	τέσσερεις (m & f)		90	*ene**ninda***	ενενήντα
	*te**sera***	τέσσερα (n)		100	*e**kato***	εκατό
5	*pen**de***	πέντε		1000	*hilii*	χίλιοι (m)
6	*exi*	έξη			*hiliez*	χίλιες (f)
7	*ep**ta***	επτά			*hilia*	χίλια (n)
8	*oh**to***	οχτώ				
9	*e**nea***	εννέα				
10	*dhe**ka***	δέκα				

one million

*e**na** ekato**my**rio*   ένα εκατομμύριο

Glossary

Achaean civilisation – see *Mycenaean civilisation*

acropolis – citadel; highest point of an ancient city

AEK – Athens football club

agia (f), agios (m) – saint

agora – commercial area of an ancient city; shopping precinct in modern Greece

amphora – large two-handled vase in which wine or oil was kept

ANEK – Anonymi Naftiliaki Eteria Kritis; main shipping line to Crete

Archaic period (800–480 BC) – also known as the Middle Age; period in which the city-states emerged from the 'dark age' and traded their way to wealth and power; the city-states were unified by a Greek alphabet and common cultural pursuits, engendering a sense of national identity

architrave – part of the *entablature* which rests on the columns of a temple

arhontika – 17th- and 18th-century AD mansions which belonged to arhons, the leading citizens of a town

Arvanites – Albanian-speakers of northwestern Greece

Asia Minor – the Aegean littoral of Turkey centred around İzmir but also including İstanbul; formerly populated by Greeks

askitiria – mini-chapels; places of solitary worship

baglamas – miniature *bouzouki* with a tinny sound

basilica – early Christian church

bouleuterion – council house

bouzouki – stringed lute-like instrument associated with *rembetika* music

bouzoukia – 'bouzoukis'; used to mean any nightclub where the *bouzouki* is played and low-grade blues songs are sung; see *skyladika*

buttress – support built against the outside of a wall

Byzantine Empire – characterised by the merging of Hellenistic culture and Christianity and named after Byzantium, the city on the Bosphorus which became the capital of the Roman Empire in AD 324; when the Roman Empire was formally divided in AD 395, Rome went into decline and the eastern capital, renamed Constantinople after Emperor Constantine I, flourished; the Byzantine Empire dissolved after the fall of Constantinople to the Turks in 1453

caique – small, sturdy fishing boat often used to carry passengers

capital – top of a column

cella – room in a temple where the cult statue stood

choregos – wealthy citizen who financed choral and dramatic performances

city-states – states comprising a sovereign city and its dependencies; the city-states of Athens and Sparta were famous rivals

classical Greece – period in which the city-states reached the height of their wealth and power after the defeat of the Persians in the 5th century BC; ended with the decline of the city-states as a result of the Peloponnesian Wars, and the expansionist aspirations of Philip II, King of Macedon (ruled 359–336 BC), and his son, Alexander the Great (ruled 336–323 BC)

Corinthian – order of Greek architecture recognisable by columns with bell-shaped capitals with sculpted elaborate ornaments based on acanthus leaves

cornice – the upper part of the *entablature*, extending beyond the *frieze*

crypt – lowest part of a church, often a burial chamber

Cycladic civilisation (3000–1100 BC) – civilisation which emerged following the settlement of Phoenician colonists on the Cycladic islands

cyclopes – mythical one-eyed giants

dark age (1200–800 BC) – period in which Greece was under Dorian rule

delfini – dolphin; a common name for a hydrofoil

diglossy – the existence of two forms of one language within a country; has existed in Greece for most of its modern history

dimarhio – town hall

Dimotiki – Demotic Greek language; the official spoken language of Greece

domatio (s), domatia (pl) – room; a cheap accommodation option available in most tourist areas

Dorians – Hellenic warriors who invaded Greece around 1200 BC, demolishing the city-states and destroying the Mycenaean civilisation; heralded Greece's 'dark age', when the artistic and cultural advancements of the Mycenaeans and Minoans were abandoned; the Dorians later developed into land-holding aristocrats which encouraged the resurgence of independent city-states led by wealthy aristocrats

Doric – order of Greek architecture characterised by a column which has no base, a fluted shaft and a relatively plain capital, when compared with the flourishes evident on Ionic and Corinthian capitals

ELPA – Elliniki Leshi Periigiseon & Aftokinitou; Greek motoring and touring club

ELTA – Ellinika Tahydromia; Greek post office

entablature – part of a temple between the tops of the columns and the roof

EOS – Ellinikos Orivatikos Syllogos; Greek alpine club

EOT – Ellinikos Organismos Tourismou; national tourism organisation which has offices in most major towns

Epitaphios – picture on cloth of Christ on his bier

estiatorio – restaurant serving ready-made food as well as a la carte dishes

ET – Elliniki Tileorasi; state television company

evzones – famous border guards from the northern Greek village of Evzoni; they also guard the Parliament building

Filiki Eteria – friendly society; a group of Greeks in exile; formed during Ottoman rule to organise an uprising against the Turks

flokati – shaggy woollen rug produced in central and northern Greece

fluted – (of a column) having vertical indentations on the shaft

frappé – iced coffee

frieze – part of the *entablature* which is above the *architrave*

galaktopoleio (s), galaktopoleia (pl) – a shop which sells dairy products

Geometric period (1200–800 BC) – period characterised by pottery decorated with geometric designs; sometimes referred to as Greece's 'dark age'

GESEE – Greek trade union association

giouvetsi – casserole of meat and pasta

Hellas, Ellas or Ellada – the Greek name for Greece

Hellenistic period – prosperous, influential period of Greek civilisation ushered in by Alexander the Great's empire-building and lasting until the Roman sacking of Corinth in 146 BC

Helots – original inhabitants of Lakonia whom the Spartans used as slaves

hora – main town (usually on an island)

iconostasis – altar screen embellished with icons

Ionic – order of Greek architecture characterised by a column with truncated flutes and capitals with ornaments resembling scrolls

kafeneio (s), kafeneia (pl) – traditionally a male-only coffee house where cards and backgammon are played

kafeteria – upmarket *kafeneio*, mainly for younger people

kalderimi – cobbled footpath

kasseri – mild, slightly rubbery sheep's milk cheese

kastro – walled-in town

Katharevousa – purist Greek language very rarely used these days

katholikon – principal church of a monastic complex

kefi – an undefinable feeling of good spirit without which no Greek can have a good time

KE – Kommounistiko Komma Elladas; Greek communist party

oine – Greek language used in pre-Byzantine times; the language of the church liturgy

ore – female statue of the Archaic period; see *kouros*

ouros – male statue of the Archaic period, characterised by a stiff body posture and enigmatic smile

TEL – Kino Tamio Ispraxeon Leoforion; national bus cooperative; runs all long-distance bus services

ypriako – the 'Cyprus issue'; politically sensitive and never forgotten by Greeks and Greek Cypriots

dera – oil-based dishes

bation – in ancient Greece, wine or food which was offered to the gods

inear A – Minoan script; so far undeciphered

inear B – Mycenaean script; has been deciphered

ra – small violin-like instrument, played on the knee; common in Cretan and Pontian music

akarounes – pasta dish stirfried in butter and onions and sprinkled with cheese

alakas – literally 'wanker'; used as a familiar term of address, or as an insult, depending on context

angas – 'wide boy' or 'dude'; originally a person of the underworld, now any street-wise person

ayirefta – pre-cooked food usually served in cheaper restaurants

ayiria – cook houses

egaron – central room of a Mycenaean palace

eltemi – north-easterly wind which blows throughout much of Greece during the summer

etope – sculpted section of a Doric *ieze*

eze (s), mezedes (pl) – appetiser

iddle Age – see *Archaic period*

inoan civilisation (3000–1100 BC) – Bronze Age culture of Crete named after the mythical king Minos and characterised

by pottery and metalwork of great beauty and artisanship

moni – monastery or convent

Mycenaean civilisation (1900–1100 BC) – first great civilisation of the Greek mainland, characterised by powerful independent city-states ruled by kings; also known as the Achaean civilisation

myzithra – soft sheep's-milk cheese

narthex – porch of a church

nave – aisle of a church

Nea Dimokratia – New Democracy; conservative political party

necropolis – literally 'city of the dead'; ancient cemetery

nefos – cloud; usually used to refer to pollution in Athens

NEL – Naftiliaki Eteria Lesvou; Lesvos shipping company

neo kyma – 'new wave'; left-wing music of the boites and clubs of 1960s Athens

nomarhia – prefecture building

nomos – prefectures into which the regions and island groups of Greece are divided

nymphaeum – in ancient Greece, building containing a fountain and often dedicated to nymphs

OA – Olympiaki Aeroporia or Olympic Airways; Greece's national airline and major domestic air carrier

odeion – ancient Greek indoor theatre

odos – street

ohi – 'no'; what the Greeks said to Mussolini's ultimatum when he said surrender or be invaded; the Italians were subsequently repelled and the event is celebrated on 28 October

omphalos – sacred stone at Delphi which the ancient Greeks believed marked the centre of the world

OSE – Organismos Sidirodromon Ellados; Greek railways organisation

OTE – Organismos Tilepikinonion Ellados; Greece's major telecommunications carrier

oud – a bulbous, stringed instrument with a sharply raked-back head

ouzeri (s), ouzeria (pl) – place which serves *ouzo* and light snacks

ouzo – a distilled spirit made from grapes and flavoured with aniseed

Panagia – Mother of God; name frequently used for churches
panigyria – night-long festivals held on saints' days
Pantokrator – painting or mosaic of Christ in the centre of the dome of a Byzantine church
pantopoleio – general store
PAO – Panathinaïkos football club
PAOK – main Thessaloniki football club
paralia – waterfront
PASOK – Panellinio Sosialistiko Komma; Greek socialist party
pediment – triangular section (often filled with sculpture) above columns, found at the front and back of a classical Greek temple
periptero (s), periptera (pl) – street kiosk
peristyle – columns surrounding a building (usually a temple) or courtyard
pinakotheke – picture gallery
pithos (s), pithoi (pl) – large Minoan storage jar
pittes – pies; usually filled with cheese, vegetables or meat
plateia – square
Politiki Anixi – Political Spring; centrist political party
Pomaks – minority, non-Turkic Muslim people from northern Greece
Pontians – Greeks whose ancestral home was on the Black Sea coast of Turkey
PRO-PO – Prognostiko Podosferou; Greek football pools
propylon (s), propylaia (pl) – elaborately built main entrance to an ancient city or sanctuary; a propylon had one gateway and a propylaia more than one
psarotaverna – taverna specialising in seafood
psistaria – restaurant serving grilled food

rembetika – blues songs commonly associated with the underworld of the 1920s
retsina – resinated white wine
rhyton – another name for a libation vessel
rizitika – traditional, patriotic songs of Crete

sacristy – room attached to a church wher sacred vessels etc are kept
sandouri – hammered dulcimer from As Minor
Sarakatsani – Greek-speaking nomad shepherd community from northern Gree
SEO – Syllogos Ellinon Orivaton; Gree mountaineers' association
skites (s), skiti (pl) – hermit's dwelling
Skopia – what the Greeks call the Form Yugoslav Republic of Macedonia (FYRON
skyladika – literally 'dog songs'; popula but not lyrically challenging, blues son often sung in *bouzoukia* nightclubs
spilia – cave
stele (s), stelae (pl) – grave stone whic stands upright
stoa – long colonnaded building, usually an *agora*; used as a meeting place and she ter in ancient Greece

taverna – traditional restaurant whic serves food and wine
temblon – votive screen
tholos – Mycenaean tomb shaped like beehive
toumberleki – small lap drum played wi the fingers
triglyph – sections of a Doric *frieze* b tween the *metopes*
trireme – ancient Greek galley with thr rows of oars on each side
tsikoudia – Cretan version of *tsipouro*
Tsingani – Gypsies or Roma
tsipouro – distilled spirit made from grap

vaulted – having an arched roof, normal of brick or stone
velentza – *flokati* rug
Vlach – traditional, semi-nomadic she herds from northern Greece who speak Latin-based dialect
volta – promenade; evening stroll
volute – spiral decoration on Ionic capita

xythomyzithra – soft sheep's-milk chee

zaharoplasteio (s), zaharoplasteia (p – patisserie; shop which sells cakes, choc lates, sweets and, sometimes, alcohol drinks

Thanks

Many thanks to the travellers who used the last edition and wrote to us with helpful hints, useful advice and interesting anecdotes:

Ruth Alexander, Peter H Allan, John Allen, Jane Alston, Ronny & Pia Anderson, Per Axel Andrin, Costa Androulakis, Maria Apostolides, Matthew Bronson, Kenneth Austin, Aspy & Homai Ayrton, Theo Baak, Michael Bacash, Joan & Al Bailey, Amanda Baker, Niki Bales, George Bangian, Jenny Barnes, Amy Bartlett, Joanna Beals, John Bedford, Jochen Beier, C B Belcher, Jeff Bell, Gordon Betteray, Lars Bjork, F Blackwood, Ursula Blum, J Boisbonnard, Sarah Boniface, Joanna & Don Box, Romi Branger, Abra Brayman, John & Louise Brekelmans, M Brennan, Katie Buchanan, Tracy Budge, Jan Bullerdieck, Matt Burch, Ann Burnett, Chris Cale, Pete & Kris Callaway, Roderick Campbell, John Cappelletti, Scott Casban, John Chapman, Jin Chin, Eugene Chow, Sandy Clendenen, Diana Clough, Colin Coates, Bevan Cobb, John Cole, Russ Conley, Nick Constantinou, Helen Conway, Susan Cook Summer, Ruth Cookson, Esteban Corrales, Diane Cotter, Michael Counsell, Anthony Crawford, Andrew Crompton, Stephen Cross, Madi Dale, Eddy De Boer, Victoriano de Sasi, Michael R Decker, Marius den Hartog, Chanon deValois, Kostis Diamantopoulos, Tina Doukas, Helen Durham, John Dynan, Esther Ebbing, Scott Eden, Helene Eichholz, Robin Eley Jones, Paul England, Alex Estrada, Nick Evangelios, Trasy Fahle, Gillian Farley, Guy Farline, Linda Casoranti, Debroah Filcoff, Toby & Lisa Fisher, Emily Ford, Gemma French, Lucie Frenette, Adam Galbraith, Gaelen Gates, James Gill, Paul W Gioffi, Wolfgang Glebe, Maria Godwin, Athina Gorezis, Helen Goss, Harry Gousopoulos, Paul Graalman, Thomas Graf, Patrick Grange, Jonathan Granger, Nancy Grant, Richard Green, Sue Green, Frank Greenhill, Arne Gudde, Karen Marie Gujord, Ty Gwyn, Samantha Gynn, Siamak x Pat Habibiyan, Pamela Hagedorn, Louise Hait, Susie Hansen, Steve Harper, Bruce Harpham, Thomas Haunstein, Allan Healy, Esther Hecht, Masami Heiser, Brendan Hickey, Luke Hildmard, Katia Hiliopoulos, John & Rosemary Hillard, Marianne Hirthe, David Hitch, Gerald Holt, Clarie Hood, Reynold Humphries, Pirmin Hunn, Joanne Hutchinson, Christian Ilcus, Millie Ireland, Bernard Jacks, Jay Jaggard, Romanna Jakymec, Jocelyn James, Jennifer Jansma, T Jellings, Maureen Jensonm, Robert Jeremy Cavin, Penny Jones, Eivind Jorgensen, Ira Kalb, Michael Karakatsanis, Marilyn Karasopoulos, Patrick Kinsella, Petra Kubalcik, Wan Kwong Young, Stephen Lamb, Baylor Lancaster, Birgith Lange Nielsen, Radka Langhammerova, Espen Lauritzen, Michael Lautman, Denise Lee, John Lennan, Birgitte Lerno, Racheal Levine, George Liangas, Vasilis Ligonis, Jeroen Lintjens, Robert Lipske, Miroslav Lovcinsky, Benedict Lowe, Christina Lowe, Carl Mackander, Alec MacKaye, Philip Makedon, Jim Manion, Jo Mann, Deborah Marchant, Lia Marcote, Remco Measmeijer, Peter Mazis, Andy McCosh, Carrie McCrum, Brenda McDowell, John & Audrey McLennan, Marianthe McLiesh, Jeff & Kristen Meltesen, Mark Melville, R S Merrillees, Patrice Meunier, Stuart Michael, Markella Mikkelsen, Cynthia Miller, Marilyn Milota, Laura Milsom, Nicki Miquel, Arkajyoti Misra, Kimberly Moore, Simon Munt, Mat Murray, Prue Murray, Trish Murray, Irene Ngu, Vicky Nicholas, Birgith Lange Nielsen, Judith Nielsen, Mette Nygerd, Ahmet Okal, Jacquie Olsen, Lisa Olszewski, Michele Orme, Len Outram, Jacki Owen, A Panagiotopoulos, Joanne Parker, Thea Parkin, Leigh Pate, Ian Paton, Sonia Pereira, Michel-Antoine Perrault, Frank Phelan, Ntinos Pissimissis, Sean Plamondon, Beth Powell, Marcelo Horacio Pozzo, Jo Price, Michael Richards, Anthony Riems, E Rood, Brenda Roscoe, Steven Rosner, Matthew Rothschild, John Rowe, Keith W Rowland, Emma Ryan, Krysztof Rybak, John Sadler, Gerard Sayers, Inge Schimmel, Amy Schuler, Storrm Rodwell, Ian & Jan Scott, Phil Scott, Philippa H Scriven, Adrian Serafin, Tracey Seslen, U Shalit, Nidhi Sharma, Mark & Stephanie Shattuck, Andrew & Ingrid Shepherd, Norman Shepherd, Bill Sheridan, Matthew Shirrell, Vern & Cindy Simpson, Mme Sita Pottacheruva, Simon Skerritt, Maureen Slattery-Nassoufi, Kara Slaughter, Richard Smith, Richard E Smith, John Spilos, Robyn St Clare, Karen A Stafford, Ruth Stanley, John Steedman,

Stuart Suckling, Bruce Sudds, Timothy Sullivan, Eldon H Sund, Matthias Sunkler, Hiroyuki Tanaka, Martin Tatuch, Linus Tay, Jan Tepper, Mie Bogo Thaysen, Cinkler Tibor, Alan Timmins, Jacob Tjoernholm, O G Trawt, Dimitra Triadafilu, Metaxia Tsoukatos, Andrew Turner, Anna Vardakastanis, Nikos Ververidis, Fabrizio Vianello, Stefan Vogel, Alice Voigt, George S Vrontos, Pauline Waddell, Paul Waldman, Alan Walker, James Walker, Karen Walsh, Jeremy Watts, Joan Weaver, Mike Webber, Ray West, Craig Weston, Tony Weston, Oyvind Westvik, Paul White, Karl Whittenbarge, Ben & Dale Williams, Lauren Williams, Ellie Windmill, Joanne Woo, Brodie Woodland, Peta Woodland, Jennifer Woznesensky, Claire Wright, Li Zavazal, Erhard Zedelmayer, Laura Zurowski.

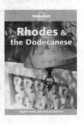

LONELY PLANET

ON THE ROAD

Travel Guides explore cities, regions and countries, and supply information on transport, restaurants and accommodation, covering all budgets. They come with reliable, easy-to-use maps, practical advice, cultural and historical facts and a rundown on attractions both on and off the beaten track. There are over 200 titles in this classic series, covering nearly every country in the world.

 Lonely Planet Upgrades extend the shelf life of existing travel guides by detailing any changes that may affect travel in a region since a book has been published. Upgrades can be downloaded for free from **www.lonelyplanet.com/upgrades**

For travellers with more time than money, **Shoestring** guides offer dependable, first-hand information with hundreds of detailed maps, plus insider tips for stretching money as far as possible. Covering entire continents in most cases, the six-volume shoestring guides are known around the world as 'backpackers bibles'.

For the discerning short-term visitor, **Condensed** guides highlight the best a destination has to offer in a full-colour, pocket-sized format designed for quick access. They include everything from top sights and walking tours to opinionated reviews of where to eat, stay, shop and have fun.

CitySync lets travellers use their Palm™ or Visor™ hand-held computers to guide them through a city with handy tips on transport, history, cultural life, major sights, and shopping and entertainment options. It can also quickly search and sort hundreds of reviews of hotels, restaurants and attractions, and pinpoint their location on scrollable street maps. CitySync can be downloaded from **www.citysync.com**

MAPS & ATLASES

Lonely Planet's **City Maps** feature downtown and metropolitan maps, as well as transit routes and walking tours. The maps come complete with an index of streets, a listing of sights and a plastic coat for extra durability.

Road Atlases are an essential navigation tool for serious travellers. Cross-referenced with the guidebooks, they also feature distance and climate charts and a complete site index.

LONELY PLANET

ESSENTIALS

Read This First books help new travellers to hit the road with confidence. These invaluable predeparture guides give step-by-step advice on preparing for a trip, budgeting, arranging a visa, planning an itinerary and staying safe while still getting off the beaten track.

Healthy Travel pocket guides offer a regional rundown on disease hot spots and practical advice on predeparture health measures, staying well on the road and what to do in emergencies. The guides come with a user-friendly design and helpful diagrams and tables.

Lonely Planet's **Phrasebooks** cover the essential words and phrases travellers need when they're strangers in a strange land. They come in a pocket-sized format with colour tabs for quick reference, extensive vocabulary lists, easy-to-follow pronunciation keys and two-way dictionaries.

Miffed by blurry photos of the Taj Mahal? Tired of the classic 'top of the head cut off' shot? **Travel Photography: A Guide to Taking Better Pictures** will help you turn ordinary holiday snaps into striking images and give you the know-how to capture every scene, from frenetic festivals to peaceful beach sunrises.

Lonely Planet's **Travel Journal** is a lightweight but sturdy travel diary for jotting down all those on-the-road observations and significant travel moments. It comes with a handy time-zone wheel, a world map and useful travel information.

Lonely Planet's eKno is an all-in-one communication service developed especially for travellers. It offers low-cost international calls and free email and voicemail so that you can keep in touch while on the road. Check it out on **www.ekno.lonelyplanet.com**

FOOD & RESTAURANT GUIDES

Lonely Planet's **Out to Eat** guides recommend the brightest and best places to eat and drink in top international cities. These gourmet companions are arranged by neighbourhood, packed with dependable maps, garnished with scene-setting photos and served with quirky features.

For people who live to eat, drink and travel, **World Food** guides explore the culinary culture of each country. Entertaining and adventurous, each guide is packed with detail on staples and specialities, regional cuisine and local markets, as well as sumptuous recipes, comprehensive culinary dictionaries and lavish photos good enough to eat.

LONELY PLANET

OUTDOOR GUIDES

For those who believe the best way to see the world is on foot, Lonely Planet's **Walking Guides** detail everything from family strolls to difficult treks, with 'when to go and how to do it' advice supplemented by reliable maps and essential travel information.

Cycling Guides map a destination's best bike tours, long and short, in day-by-day detail. They contain all the information a cyclist needs, including advice on bike maintenance, places to eat and stay, innovative maps with detailed cues to the rides, and elevation charts.

The **Watching Wildlife** series is perfect for travellers who want authoritative information but don't want to tote a heavy field guide. Packed with advice on where, when and how to view a region's wildlife, each title features photos of over 300 species and contains engaging comments on the local flora and fauna.

With underwater colour photos throughout, **Pisces Books** explore the world's best diving and snorkelling areas. Each book contains listings of diving services and dive resorts, detailed information on depth, visibility and difficulty of dives, and a roundup of the marine life you're likely to see through your mask.

OFF THE ROAD

Journeys, the travel literature series written by renowned travel authors, capture the spirit of a place or illuminate a culture with a journalist's attention to detail and a novelist's flair for words. These are tales to soak up while you're actually on the road or dip into as an at-home armchair indulgence.

The range of lavishly illustrated **Pictorial** books is just the ticket for both travellers and dreamers. Off-beat tales and vivid photographs bring the adventure of travel to your doorstep long before the journey begins and long after it is over.

Lonely Planet **Videos** encourage the same independent, tough-minded approach as the guidebooks. Currently airing throughout the world, this award-winning series features innovative footage and an original soundtrack.

Yes, we know, work is tough, so do a little bit of deskside dreaming with the spiral-bound Lonely Planet **Diary** or a Lonely Planet **Wall Calendar**, filled with great photos from around the world.

TRAVELLERS NETWORK

Lonely Planet Online. Lonely Planet's award-winning Web site has insider information on hundreds of destinations, from Amsterdam to Zimbabwe, complete with interactive maps and relevant links. The site also offers the latest travel news, recent reports from travellers on the road, guidebook upgrades, a travel links site, an online book-buying option and a lively travellers bulletin board. It can be viewed at **www.lonelyplanet.com** or AOL keyword: lp.

Planet Talk is a quarterly print newsletter, full of gossip, advice, anecdotes and author articles. It provides an antidote to the being-at-home blues and lets you plan and dream for the next trip. Contact the nearest Lonely Planet office for your free copy.

Comet, the free Lonely Planet newsletter, comes via email once a month. It's loaded with travel news, advice, dispatches from authors, travel competitions and letters from readers. To subscribe, click on the Comet subscription link on the front page of the Web site.

Lonely Planet Guides by Region

Lonely Planet is known worldwide for publishing practical, reliable and no-nonsense travel information in our guides and on our Web site. The Lonely Planet list covers just about every accessible part of the world. Currently there are 16 series: Travel guides, Shoestring guides, Condensed guides, Phrasebooks, Read This First, Healthy Travel, Walking guides, Cycling guides, Watching Wildlife guides, Pisces Diving & Snorkeling guides, City Maps, Road Atlases, Out to Eat, World Food, Journeys travel literature and Pictorials.

AFRICA Africa on a shoestring • Botswana • Cairo • Cairo City Map • Cape Town • Cape Town City Map • East Africa • Egypt • Egyptian Arabic phrasebook • Ethiopia, Eritrea & Djibouti • Ethiopian Amharic phrasebook • The Gambia & Senegal • Healthy Travel Africa • Kenya • Malawi • Morocco • Moroccan Arabic phrasebook • Mozambique • Namibia • Read This First: Africa • South Africa, Lesotho & Swaziland • Southern Africa • Southern Africa Road Atlas • Swahili phrasebook • Tanzania, Zanzibar & Pemba • Trekking in East Africa • Tunisia • Watching Wildlife East Africa • Watching Wildlife Southern Africa • West Africa • World Food Morocco • Zambia • Zimbabwe, Botswana & Namibia
Travel Literature: Mali Blues: Traveling to an African Beat • The Rainbird: A Central African Journey • Songs to an African Sunset: A Zimbabwean Story

AUSTRALIA & THE PACIFIC Aboriginal Australia & the Torres Strait Islands •Auckland • Australia • Australian phrasebook • Australia Road Atlas • Cycling Australia • Cycling New Zealand • Fiji • Fijian phrasebook • Healthy Travel Australia, NZ & the Pacific • Islands of Australia's Great Barrier Reef • Melbourne • Melbourne City Map • Micronesia • New Caledonia • New South Wales • New Zealand • Northern Territory • Outback Australia • Out to Eat – Melbourne • Out to Eat – Sydney • Papua New Guinea • Pidgin phrasebook • Queensland • Rarotonga & the Cook Islands • Samoa • Solomon Islands • South Australia • South Pacific • South Pacific phrasebook • Sydney • Sydney City Map • Sydney Condensed • Tahiti & French Polynesia • Tasmania • Tonga • Tramping in New Zealand • Vanuatu • Victoria • Walking in Australia • Watching Wildlife Australia • Western Australia
Travel Literature: Islands in the Clouds: Travels in the Highlands of New Guinea • Kiwi Tracks: A New Zealand Journey • Sean & David's Long Drive

CENTRAL AMERICA & THE CARIBBEAN Bahamas, Turks & Caicos • Baja California • Belize, Guatemala & Yucatán • Bermuda • Central America on a shoestring • Costa Rica • Costa Rica Spanish phrasebook • Cuba • Cycling Cuba • Dominican Republic & Haiti • Eastern Caribbean • Guatemala • Havana • Healthy Travel Central & South America • Jamaica • Mexico • Mexico City • Panama • Puerto Rico • Read This First: Central & South America • Virgin Islands • World Food Caribbean • World Food Mexico • Yucatán
Travel Literature: Green Dreams: Travels in Central America

EUROPE Amsterdam • Amsterdam City Map • Amsterdam Condensed • Andalucía • Athens • Austria • Baltic States phrasebook • Barcelona • Barcelona City Map • Belgium & Luxembourg • Berlin • Berlin City Map • Britain • British phrasebook • Brussels, Bruges & Antwerp • Brussels City Map • Budapest • Budapest City Map • Canary Islands • Catalunya & the Costa Brava • Central Europe • Central Europe phrasebook • Copenhagen • Corfu & the Ionians • Corsica • Crete • Crete Condensed • Croatia • Cycling Britain • Cycling France • Cyprus • Czech & Slovak Republics • Czech phrasebook • Denmark • Dublin • Dublin City Map • Dublin Condensed • Eastern Europe • Eastern Europe phrasebook • Edinburgh • Edinburgh City Map • England • Estonia, Latvia & Lithuania • Europe on a shoestring • Europe phrasebook • Finland • Florence • Florence City Map • France • Frankfurt City Map • Frankfurt Condensed • French phrasebook • Georgia, Armenia & Azerbaijan • Germany • German phrasebook • Greece • Greek Islands • Greek phrasebook • Hungary • Iceland, Greenland & the Faroe Islands • Ireland • Italian phrasebook • Italy • Kraków • Lisbon • The Loire • London • London City Map • London Condensed • Madrid • Madrid City Map • Malta • Mediterranean Europe • Milan, Turin & Genoa • Moscow • Munich • Netherlands • Normandy • Norway • Out to Eat – London • Out to Eat – Paris • Paris • Paris City Map • Paris Condensed • Poland • Polish phrasebook • Portugal • Portuguese phrasebook • Prague • Prague City Map • Provence & the Côte d'Azur • Read This First: Europe • Rhodes & the Dodecanese • Romania & Moldova • Rome • Rome City Map • Rome Condensed • Russia, Ukraine & Belarus • Russian phrasebook • Scandinavian & Baltic Europe • Scandinavian phrasebook • Scotland • Sicily • Slovenia • South-West France • Spain • Spanish phrasebook • Stockholm • St Petersburg • St Petersburg City Map • Sweden • Switzerland • Tuscany • Ukrainian phrasebook • Venice • Vienna • Wales • Walking in Britain • Walking in France • Walking in Ireland • Walking in Italy • Walking in Scotland • Walking in Spain • Walking in Switzerland • Western Europe • World Food France • World Food Greece • World Food Ireland • World Food Italy • World Food Spain **Travel Literature:** After Yugoslavia • Love and War in the Apennines • The Olive Grove: Travels in Greece • On the Shores of the Mediterranean • Round Ireland in Low Gear • A Small Place in Italy

Lonely Planet Mail Order

Lonely Planet products are distributed worldwide. They are also available by mail order from Lonely Planet, so if you have difficulty finding a title please write to us. North and South American residents should write to 150 Linden St, Oakland, CA 94607, USA; European and African residents should write to 10a Spring Place, London NW5 3BH, UK; and residents of other countries to Locked Bag 1, Footscray, Victoria 3011, Australia.

INDIAN SUBCONTINENT & THE INDIAN OCEAN Bangladesh • Bengali phrasebook • Bhutan • Delhi • Goa • Healthy Travel Asia & India • Hindi & Urdu phrasebook • India • India & Bangladesh City Map • Indian Himalaya • Karakoram Highway • Kathmandu City Map • Kerala • Madagascar • Maldives • Mauritius, Réunion & Seychelles • Mumbai (Bombay) • Nepal • Nepali phrasebook • North India • Pakistan • Rajasthan • Read This First: Asia & India • South India • Sri Lanka • Sri Lanka phrasebook • Tibet • Tibetan phrasebook • Trekking in the Indian Himalaya • Trekking in the Karakoram & Hindukush • Trekking in the Nepal Himalaya • World Food India **Travel Literature:** The Age of Kali: Indian Travels and Encounters • Hello Goodnight: A Life of Goa • In Rajasthan • Maverick in Madagascar • A Season in Heaven: True Tales from the Road to Kathmandu • Shopping for Buddhas • A Short Walk in the Hindu Kush • Slowly Down the Ganges

MIDDLE EAST & CENTRAL ASIA Bahrain, Kuwait & Qatar • Central Asia • Central Asia phrasebook • Dubai • Farsi (Persian) phrasebook • Hebrew phrasebook • Iran • Israel & the Palestinian Territories • Istanbul • Istanbul City Map • Istanbul to Cairo • Istanbul to Kathmandu • Jerusalem • Jerusalem City Map • Jordan • Lebanon • Middle East • Oman & the United Arab Emirates • Syria • Turkey • Turkish phrasebook • World Food Turkey • Yemen **Travel Literature:** Black on Black: Iran Revisited • Breaking Ranks: Turbulent Travels in the Promised Land • The Gates of Damascus • Kingdom of the Film Stars: Journey into Jordan

NORTH AMERICA Alaska • Boston • Boston City Map • Boston Condensed • British Columbia • California & Nevada • California Condensed • Canada • Chicago • Chicago City Map • Chicago Condensed • Florida • Georgia & the Carolinas • Great Lakes • Hawaii • Hiking in Alaska • Hiking in the USA • Honolulu & Oahu City Map • Las Vegas • Los Angeles • Los Angeles City Map • Louisiana & the Deep South • Miami • Miami City Map • Montreal • New England • New Orleans • New Orleans City Map • New York City • New York City City Map • New York City Condensed • New York, New Jersey & Pennsylvania • Oahu • Out to Eat – San Francisco • Pacific Northwest • Rocky Mountains • San Diego & Tijuana • San Francisco • San Francisco City Map • Seattle • Seattle City Map • Southwest • Texas • Toronto • USA • USA phrasebook • Vancouver • Vancouver City Map • Virginia & the Capital Region • Washington, DC • Washington, DC City Map • World Food New Orleans **Travel Literature**: Caught Inside: A Surfer's Year on the California Coast • Drive Thru America

NORTH-EAST ASIA Beijing • Beijing City Map • Cantonese phrasebook • China • Hiking in Japan • Hong Kong & Macau • Hong Kong City Map • Hong Kong Condensed • Japan • Japanese phrasebook • Korea • Korean phrasebook • Kyoto • Mandarin phrasebook • Mongolia • Mongolian phrasebook • Seoul • Shanghai • South-West China • Taiwan • Tokyo • Tokyo Condensed • World Food Hong Kong • World Food Japan **Travel Literature:** In Xanadu: A Quest • Lost Japan

SOUTH AMERICA Argentina, Uruguay & Paraguay • Bolivia • Brazil • Brazilian phrasebook • Buenos Aires • Buenos Aires City Map • Chile & Easter Island • Colombia • Ecuador & the Galapagos Islands • Healthy Travel Central & South America • Latin American Spanish phrasebook • Peru • Quechua phrasebook • Read This First: Central & South America • Rio de Janeiro • Rio de Janeiro City Map • Santiago de Chile • South America on a shoestring • Trekking in the Patagonian Andes • Venezuela **Travel Literature**: Full Circle: A South American Journey

SOUTH-EAST ASIA Bali & Lombok • Bangkok • Bangkok City Map • Burmese phrasebook • Cambodia • Cycling Vietnam, Laos & Cambodia • East Timor phrasebook • Hanoi • Healthy Travel Asia & India • Hill Tribes phrasebook • Ho Chi Minh City (Saigon) • Indonesia • Indonesian phrasebook • Indonesia's Eastern Islands • Java • Lao phrasebook • Laos • Malay phrasebook • Malaysia, Singapore & Brunei • Myanmar (Burma) • Philippines • Pilipino (Tagalog) phrasebook • Read This First: Asia & India • Singapore • Singapore City Map • South-East Asia on a shoestring • South-East Asia phrasebook • Thailand • Thailand's Islands & Beaches • Thailand, Vietnam, Laos & Cambodia Road Atlas • Thai phrasebook • Vietnam • Vietnamese phrasebook • World Food Indonesia • World Food Thailand • World Food Vietnam

ALSO AVAILABLE: Antarctica • The Arctic • The Blue Man: Tales of Travel, Love and Coffee • Brief Encounters: Stories of Love, Sex & Travel • Buddhist Stupas in Asia: The Shape of Perfection • Chasing Rickshaws • The Last Grain Race • Lonely Planet ... On the Edge: Adventurous Escapades from Around the World • Lonely Planet Unpacked • Lonely Planet Unpacked Again • Not the Only Planet: Science Fiction Travel Stories • Ports of Call: A Journey by Sea • Sacred India • Travel Photography: A Guide to Taking Better Pictures • Travel with Children • Tuvalu: Portrait of an Island Nation

Index

Abbreviations

Ath – Athens
Cen – Central Greece
Cre – Crete
Cyc – Cyclades
Dod – Dodecanese

Evi – Evia
Ion – Ionian Islands
NEA – North-Eastern Aegean
  Islands
NG – Northern Greece

Pel – Peloponnese
SG – Saronic Gulf Islands
Spo – Sporades

Text

A

accommodation 103-5
Achaïa (Pel) 212-20
Acrocorinth 224
Acropolis (Ath) 150-6, **151**
activities 101-2, see also
  individual activities
Adamas (Cyc) 484-6
Aegiali (Cyc) 460-1
Aegina (SG) 392-6, **393**
Aegina Town (SG) 393-5
Agathonisi (Dod) 625-6, **626**
Agia Galini (Cre) 534-5
Agia Kyriaki (Cen) 304-13
Agia Marina (Dod) 615-16
Agia Pelagia (Ion) 763
Agia Roumeli (Cre) 544
Agia Triada (Cre) 512
Agios Efstratios (NEA) 676-8
Agios Germanos (NG) 360-1
Agios Giorgios (Dod) 626
Agios Kirykos (Ika) 632-3
Agios Konstantinos (Cen) 292
Agios Nikolaos (Cre) 515-18
Agios Nikolaos (Ion) 757
Ahillion Palace (Ion) 731
air travel
  glossary 114
  to/from Greece 113-20
  within Greece 125-7
Akrotiri Peninsula (Cre) 542-3
Alexander the Great 25
Alexandroupolis (NG) 383-6,
  384
Ali Pasha 321
Alinda (Dod) 616-17
Alonnisos (Spo) 706-11, **707**
Alonnisos Marine Park (Spo)
  711

Bold indicates maps.

Amari Valley (Cre) 531-2
Amfilohia (Cen) 286
Ammoöpi (Dod) 579
Amorgos (Cyc) 458-61, **459**
Anafi (Cyc) 477-8, **477**
Anavatos (NEA) 652-3
Anavryti (Pel) 246-7
Ancient Akrotiri (Cyc) 473-7
ancient sites
  Acropolis (Ath) 150-6, **151**
  Acropolis of Lindos (Dod)
    570
  Acropolis of Rhodes (Dod)
    564
  Agia Triada (Cre) 512
  Akrotiri (Cyc) 473-7
  Ancient Agora (Ath) 157-8,
    157
  Asklipion (Dod) 603-4
  Basilica of Agia Kerkyra
    (Ion) 731
  Byzantine Palace (NEA) 634
  Corinth (Pel) 223-4
  Delos (Cyc) 434-6, **435**
  Delphi (Cen) 277-80, **277**
  Dion (NG) 354
  Dodoni (Cyc) 321-2
  Elefsina/Eleusis (Ath) 207-8
  Epidaurus (Pel) 234-6
  Erechtheion (Ath) 155
  Exobourgo (Cyc) 420
  Gournia (Cre) 520
  Kamiros (Dod) 571
  Kassopi (NG) 336
  Keramikos (Ath) 158-9
  Knossos (Cre) 509-11, **510**
  Kydonia (Cre) 538
  Lato (Cre) 519-20
  Marathon Tomb (Ath) 206
  Mavromati/ancient Messini
    (Pel) 262-3
  Mycenae 227-9, **228**
  Mystras (Pel) 244-6
  Nekromanteio of Afyra (NG)
    331-2

Nikopolis (NG) 336
Olympia (Pel) 269-71, **270**
Olynthos 365
Paleohora (SG) 395
Parthenon (Ath) 153
Pella (NG) 349-50
Phaestos (Cre) 512
Philippi (NG) 378-81
Pirgos Himarrou (Cyc) 452
Poliohni (NEA) 676
Roman Athens 159-61
Sanctuary of Apollo (Cen)
  279, **277**
Sanctuary of Poseidon &
  Amphitrite (Cyc) 420
Sanctuary of the Great Gods
  (NEA) 680-2, **681**
Sanctuary of the Kabeiroi
  (NEA) 676
Sparta (Pel) 241
Temple of Aphaia (SG) 395
Temple of Aphrodite (Dod)
  564
Temple of Apollo (SG) 394
Temple of Athena Nike
  (Ath) 152-3
Temple of Dafniforos (Evi)
  696
Temple of Dionysos (Dod)
  602
Temple of Hephaestus (Ath)
  158
Temple of Olympian Zeus
  (Ath) 160
Temple of Poseidon (Ath)
  203
Temple of Poseidon (SG)
  398
Temple of Pythian Apollo
  (Dod) 564
Temple of Vasses (Pel) 272
Temple to Athena (Dod) 570
Theatre of Dionysos (Ath)
  156

ancient sites *(cont)*
  Thira (Cyc) 473
  Troizen (SG) 398-9
  Zakros (Cre) 523
  Zalongo (NG) 336
Andirio (Cen) 284
Andritsena (Pel) 272-3
Andros (Cyc) 413-16, **414**
Andros Hora (Cyc) 415-16
animals, see fauna
Ano Mera (Cyc) 433-4
Ano Meria (Cyc) 482-3
Ano Viannos (Cre) 526-7
Antikythira (Ion) 763-4, **760**
Antiparos (Cyc) 443-6, **437**
Antipaxi (Ion) 737-54, **734**
Apiranthos (Cyc) 452
Apollonas (Cyc) 453
Apollonia (Cyc) 489
Arahova (Cen) 281-2
Arcadia (Pel) 236-41
Archaeological Museums
  Athens 195
  Central Greece 276, 296-7,
  Crete 503-504, 529, 538
  Cyclades 415, 418, 439,
    447, 470, 495
  Dodecanese 563, 600, 607,
  Evia 695
  Ionian Islands 724, 739,
    747, 750, 761
  National Archaeological
    Museum (Ath) 161-5,
    162
  North-Eastern Aegean
    Islands 632, 640, 662,
    668, 687
  Northern Greece 318, 342,
    355, 358, 376, 382
  Peloponnese 214-15, 226,
    231, 236, 260
  Sporades 713
archaeological sites, see
  ancient sites
Argolis (Pel) 225-36
Argos (Pel) 225-7
Argostoli (Ion) 745-8, **746**
Aristi (NG) 322
Aristotle 45
Arkasa (Dod) 579-80
Arki (Dod) 624-5, **625**
Armenistis (NEA) 635-7
Arta (NG) 336-7
arts 46-65
  architecture 51-5
  cinema 65
  dance 46, (Dod) 564, (Ath)
    183-4
  decorative arts 63
  drama 65
  embroidery 63
  jewellery 63
  literature 48-65
  metalwork 63
  mosaics 63
  music 46-8, (Ath) 183
  painting 59-63
  pottery 58-9
  sculpture 55-8
  weaving 63
Asklipion (Dod) 603-4
Assos (Ion) 749
Astakos (Cen) 287
Astypalea (Dod) 605-8, **606**
Astypalea Town (Dod) 606-7
Athens 138-208, **between
    pp144 & 145, 160**
  Acropolis 150-6, **151**
  activities 169
  Ancient Agora 157-8, **157**
  Byzantine Athens 161
  children's activities 170
  courses 169-70
  entertainment 181-5
  getting around 189-204
  getting there & away 187-9
  Hellenic festival 170-1
  hills 167-8
  history 139-41
  information 143-6
  National Archaeological
    Museum 161-5, **162**
  Neoclassical Athens 161
  organised tours 170
  orientation 141-3
  parks & gardens 168-9
  places to eat 175-81
  places to stay 171-5
  Roman Athens 159-61
  shopping 186
  spectator sports 185-6
  walking tour 146-50
Athos Peninsular (secular
  Athos; NG) 368-9, **368**
Attica (Ath) 201-8, **202**
automobile association 98

B

bargaining, see money
Batsi (Cyc) 413-15
birds, see fauna
bird watching
  (NEA) 659, (NG) 360, 387,
    (Spo) 711

boat travel
  to/from Greece 122-4
  within Greece 132-6, **133**
books 85-8
bookshops 88
Bouboulina, Lascarina 405
bus travel
  local transport 136
  to/from Greece 120
  within Greece 127-8
business hours 98-9
Byron, Lord 29, 285

C

Cape Sounion (Ath) 203-4
car travel
  rental 130-7
  road distances **133**
  road rules 130
  to/from Greece 120
  within Greece 129-31
castles
  Agios Georgios (Ion) 749
  Astypalea Castle (Dod) 606
  Castello Rossa (Evi) 697
  Castle of Antimahia (Dod)
    603
  Castle of Faraklos (Dod) 569
  Castle of Kastellos (Dod)
    571
  Castle of Koskinas (NEA)
    635
  Castle of Lykourgos
    Logothetis (NEA) 644
  Castle of Pandeli (Dod) 615
  Castle of the Knights (Dod)
    601
  Genoese Castle (NEA) 665
  Knight's Castle (Dod) 593
  Knights of St John Castle
    (Dod) 586
  Mytilini Castle (NEA) 662
  Neo Kastro (Pel) 266
  Nestor's Palace (Pel) 267
  Paleokastro (Pel) 267
caves
  Cave of Antiparos (Cyc) 444
  Cave of the Lakes (Pel) 220
  Cave of the Nymphs (Ion)
    751
  Dikteon Cave (Cre) 514
  Diros Caves (Pel) 254
  Drogarati Cave (Ion) 748
  Mellisani Cave (Ion) 748
  Nestor's Cave (Pel) 267
  Perama Cave (NG) 320
  Petralona Cave (NG) 365-6

cemeteries
Athens' First Cemetery
168-9
Military Cemetery (Cre) 542
War Cemetery (Dod) 616
Central Greece 274-313
children, travel with 97
Chios (NEA) 647-55, **648**
Chios Town (NEA) 649-52, **650**
churches
Agia Irini (NEA) 635
Agia Marina (Dod) 584
Agios Nikolaos Foundouklis
(Dod) 574
Church of Agia Panagia
(Dod) 569
Church of Agios Apostolos
(NEA) 653
Church of Agios Ioannis
(Dod) 570
Church of Agios Nikolaos
(Dod) 592
Church of Agios Spyridon
(Ion) 727
Church of Agios Therapon
(NEA) 662
Church of the Holy Apostles
(Ath) 157
Church of Megali Panagia
(Dod) 589
Church of Metamorfosis
(Dod) 625
Church of Panagia
Evangelistria (Cyc) 418
Church of Panagia Kera
(Cre) 519
Church of Panagia
Paraportiani (Cyc) 430
Church of the Holy Apostles
(Ath) 158
Panagia Ekatontapyliani
(Cyc) 439
Classical Age 22-4
climate 37-9
conduct, see society & conduct
conservation, see environment
consulates, see embassies &
consulates
Corfu (Ion) 721-33, **722**
Corfu Town (Ion) 724-9, **723**
Corinth (Pel) 220-3, **221**
Corinth Canal (Pel) 224
Corinthia (Pel) 220
costs, see money

Bold indicates maps.

courses 102
credit cards, see money
Crete 496-552, **498-9**
cultural events, see special
events & festivals
customs 79
Cyclades 408-95, **409**
cycling 131

D
Dadia Forest Reserve (NG)
387-9
Dafni (Ath) 207-8
dance, see arts
Delos (Cyc) 433-6
Delphi (Cen) 277-80, **277**
Delphic oracle (Cen) 278
Diafani (Dod) 581-2
Diakofto (Pel) 217
Diakofto-Kalavryta railway
(Pel) 218
Diapondia Islands (Ion) 733
Didymotiho (NG) 388-9
Dimitsana (Pel) 239
Dion (NG) 354
disabled travellers 97
Distomo (Cen) 283
diving 101
(Ath) 202-3, (Cre) 529,
(Cyc) 430, 441, 444,
476, 485, (Dod) 564,
(Evi) 695, (Ion) 731,
(Spo) 701
documents 76
Dodecanese 553-626, **554**
Dodoni (NG) 321-2
Donousa (Cyc) 457-8
drinks 109-11
driving licence 76
drugs 98
Durrell, Lawrence & Gerald
730

E
ecology 39
economy 42-3
Edessa (NG) 356-8
education 43-5
Elafonisi (Cre) 549-50
electricity 90
Elefsina/Eleusis (Ath) 207-8
Elia (Pel) 267-73
Elounda (Cre) 518
email access, see Internet
embassies & consulates 77-9
foreign embassies in Greece
77-9
Greek embassies abroad 77

Embonas 574
Emboreios (NEA) 654-5
Emborios (Dod) 575, 597, 613
Ennia Horia (Cre) 551-2
entertainment 111-12
environment 39
Epidaurus (Pel) 234
Epiros (NG) 314-37, **315**
Erechtheion (Ath) 155
Ereikousa (Ion) 733
Eresos (NEA) 667-70
Eretria (Evi) 696-7
Ermoupolis (Cyc) 422-5
Evdilos (NEA) 633-4
Evia 692-7, **693**
evil eye 419
Evros Delta (NG) 387

F
Falasarna (Cre) 551
fauna 40-1
birds 40
endangered species 41-2
Hellenic Wildlife Rehabilitation Centre (SG) 395-6
loggerhead turtle 757
olives 542
sea turtle rescue centre
(Ath) 202
treatment of animals 70-2
fax services 84
ferry travel, see boat travel
films 88
Finiki (Dod) 579-80
Finikounda (Pel) 264
Fira (Cyc) 468-73, **470**
Fiskardo (Ion) 748-9
flokati rugs 307
flora 39-40
citron 451
olives 39, 139, 262
wild flowers 40
Florina (NG) 358-9
Folegandros (Cyc) 479-83, **480**
Folegandros Hora (Cyc) 481-2
Fonias River (NEA) 683
food 105-9
Greek specialities 106-8
self catering 109
vegetarian 108
fortresses
Akronafplia fortress (Pel) 231
Bourtzi fortress (Pel) 231
Fortress of Agia Mavra (Ion)
740
Frangokastello (Cre) 545-6

fortresses *(cont)*
  Methoni fortress (Pel) 265
  Neo Frourio (Ion) 726
  Palmidi fortress (Pel) 231
  Rethymno (Cre) 527-31
Fountain of Arethousa (Ion)
  751
Fourni Islands (NEA) 637, **631**
Fourni Town (NEA) 637

G

Gaïos (Ion) 735-6
Galaxidi (Cen) 283-4
Galissas (Cyc) 425-6
galleries, *see* museums
gardens & parks
  Areos Park (Ath) 168
  National Gardens (Ath) 168
  Zappeio Gardens (Ath) 168
Gavdos Island (Cre) 549
Gavrio (Cyc) 413
gay travellers 96-7
Gefyra (Pel) 247-9
Gennadi (Dod) 572
geography 37
Gerolimenas (Pel) 255
Gialos (Dod) 589-90
Glossa (Spo) 705
Glyfada (Ath) 201-4
golf (Ath) 169
Gortyna (Cre) 511-12
Gourna (Dod) 617
Gournia (Cre) 520
government 42
Gramvousa Peninsula (Cre)
  551
gum mastic 653
Gythio (Pel) 250-3

H

Halki (Dod) 574-6, **575**
Halkida (Evi) 695
Halkidiki (NG) 364-74
Hania (Cre) 537-42, **536**, 543
health 90-6
  diseases 93
  environmental hazards 92-3
  hospital treatment 96-7
  predeparture planning 90-1
hiking, *see* trekking
Hippocrates 599, 601
history 19-37
  Alexander the Great 25
  Archaic Age 21-2
  Balkan Wars 30
  Bronze Age 19-20

Byzantine Empire 26
Christianity 26
Civil War 32-3
Classical Age 22-4
Crusades 27
Cycladic civilisation 19-20
Cyprus issue 33-4
foreign policy 36-9
Geometric Age 20-1
Great Idea 30
Macedonian expansion 24-5
martial law 34
Minoan civilisation 19-20
Mycenaean civilisation 20
Ottoman Empire 27-8
Peloponnesian Wars 23
Persian Wars 22
recent developments 35-6
Republic (1924–35) 31-2
Roman rule 26
Socialism 35
Stone Age 19
War of Independence 28-9
WWI 31
WWII 32
hitching 131-2
holidays, *see* public holidays
Hora Sfakion (Cre) 544-5
Horto (Cen) 304
hot springs, see spas
Hydra (SG) 399-403, **400**
Hydra Town (SG) 400-2, **401**
hydrofoil travel, *see* boat travel

I

Ialysos (Dod) 571
Ierapetra (Cre) 524-5
Igoumentisa 328-30, **328**
Ikaria (NEA) 630-7, **631**
Inousses (NEA) 655-7, **655**
Inousses Town (NEA) 656-7
insurance, travel 76, 116
Internet
  access to 84
  resources 84-5
Ioannina (NG) 316-20, **317**
Ionian Islands 718-64, **719**
Ios (Cyc) 461-6, **462**
Ios Hora (Cyc) 462-5
Ioulida (Cyc) 494-5
Iraklia (Cyc) 454-5
Iraklio (Cre) 500-9, **501**
Ireon (NEA) 645
Isthmia (Pel) 224-5
Ithaki (Ion) 750-4, **744**
Iti National Park (Cen) 291

Itilo (Pel) 256-7
itineraries 73
  Athens 139
  Central Greece 274
  Crete 497-500
  Cyclades 408-9
  Dodecanese 553-61
  Evia & the Sporades 692
  Ionian Islands 718-19
  North-Eastern Aegean
    Islands 627-9
  Northern Greece 314
  Peloponnese 209
  Saronic Gulf Islands 391

K

Kalamaki (Ion) 757
Kalamata (Pel) 259-62, **260**
Kalambaka (Cen) 311-12, **309**
Kalavryta (Pel) 218-20
Kalymnos (Dod) 608-13, **609**
Kamares (Cyc) 488-9
Kamari (Cyc) 475-6
Kamari (Dod) 604-5
Kamariotissa (NEA) 679-80
Kamariotissa Hora (NEA) 680
Kaminia (Ion) 757
Kampos (NEA) 634-5
Kapsali (Ion) 761-2
Karavostasis (Cyc) 480-1
Kardamyla (NEA) 655
Kardamyli (Pel) 258-9
Karfas (NEA) 652
Karitena (Pel) 238
Karpathos (Dod) 576-81, **576**
Karpenisi (Cen) 287
Karterados (Cyc) 475
Karyes (NG) 372, **372**
Karystos (Evi) 697
Kasos (Dod) 582-4, **582**
Kaspakas (NEA) 675
Kassandra Peninsula (NG) 366
Kassiopi (Ion) 729
Kastelli-Kissamos (Cre) 550-1
Kastellorizo/Megisti (Dod)
  584-7, **584**
Kastellorizo Town (Dod) 585-9
Kastoria (NG) 362-4, **363**
Kastraki (Cen) 312-13, **309**
Katapola (Cyc) 458-60
Katapola Hora (Cyc) 460
Kato Zakros (Cre) 522-3
Katomeri (Ion) 743
Kavala (NG) 374-8, **375**
Kazantzakis, Nikos 506
Kea (Cyc) 493-5, **494**
Kefallonia (Ion) 743-54, **744**

Kefalos (Dod) 604-5
Kimolos (Cyc) 487-8, **484**
Kioni (Ion) 753
Kolokytha Peninsula (Cre) 518-19
Komotini (NG) 382-3
Konitsa (NG) 325-6
Korissia (Cyc) 494
Koroni (Pel) 263-4
Koryshades (Cen) 288
Kos (Dod) 597-605, **598**
Kos Town (Dod) 600-3, **601**
Kotronas (Pel) 256
Koufonisia (Cyc) 456-7
Koumbara (Cyc) 464
Krithoni (Dod) 616-17
Kritsa (Cre) 519
Kyllini (Pel) 273
Kymi (Evi) 695-6
Kynouria (Pel) 240-1
Kythira (Ion) 759-64, **760**
Kythira Hora (Ion) 761
Kythnos (Cyc) 492-3, **492**

L

Lagio (Pel) 255-6
lakes
    Drakolimni (NG) 324
    Lake Kremasta (CG) 289
    Lake Marathon (Ath) 206
    Lake Pamvotis (NG) 316
    Prespa Lakes (NG) 359-62, **360**
Lakki (Dod) 615
Lakonian Mani (Pel) 253-7
Lamia (Cen) 289-91, **290**
Langada (NEA) 655
Langada Pass (Pel) 247
Langadas (NG) 349-50
language 71, 765-70
language courses, see language
Larisa (Cen) 292-6, **294**
Lasithi Plateau (Cre) 514-15
Lato (Cre) 519-20
laundry 90
Lavrio 204-6
Lefkada (Ion) 737-54, **738**
Lefkada Town (Ion) 739-40
Lefkes (Cyc) 443
Lefkos (Dod) 580-1
legal matters 98
Leonidio (Pel) 240

Leros (Dod) 613-17, **614**
lesbian travellers 96-7
Lesvos/Mytilini (NEA) 658-72, **659**
Limenaria (NEA) 690
Limeni (Pel) 256
Limnia (NEA) 655
Limnos (NEA) 655
Limnos (NEA) 672-6, **672**
Lindos (Dod) 569-71
Lipsi (Dod) 621-4, **622**
Lipsi Town (Dod) 622-3
literature, see arts
Litohoro (NG) 350-4
Little Cyclades 453-8, **454**
Livadi (Cyc) 490-1
Livadia (Cen) 276-7
Livadia (Dod) 592-3
Livadia (Dod) 607-8
local transport 136
Loutra/Therma (NEA) 682-3
Loutraki (Pel) 225
Lykavittos Hill (Ath) 167

M

Macedonia (NG) 337-9, **338**
Magazia (Spo) 716-17
magazines 88
Makrynitsa (Cen) 301
Malia (Cre) 513-14
Mandraki (Dod) 595-6
Mani, the (Pel) 252-9
maps 73-4
Marathi (Dod) 625, **625**
Marathi Maraqi (Cyc) 443
Marathon (Ath) 206
Marathonisi Islet (Pel) 250
markets (Ath) 186
Marmaro (NEA) 655
Masouri (Dod) 612
Mastihari (Dod) 604
Matala (Cre) 512-13
Mathraki (Ion) 733
Mavromati (Pel) 262-3
medical treatment, see health
Megalo Horio (Cen) 288
Megalo Horio (Dod) 593-4
Megalo Papingo 322
Megalopoli (Pel) 237-8
Meganisi (Ion) 742-54, **730**
Melanes (Cyc) 452
Menetes (Dod) 579
Merihas (Cyc) 493
Mesogeia 204-6
Messaria (Cyc) 475
Messinia (Pel) 259-67
Messinian Mani (Pel) 257-9
Messolongi (Cen) 285-6
Mesta (NEA) 654-5

Meteora (Cen) 308-11, **309**
Methoni (Pel) 264-5
metro travel 136
Metsovo (NG) 326-8
Mikro Horio (Cen) 288
Mikro Papingo (NG) 322
Milies (Cen) 303
Milina (Cen) 304
Milopotas (Cyc) 462-5
Milos (Cyc) 483-7, **484**
Minoan civilisation 19-20, 500
Mithymna (NEA) 664-7
Mohlos (Cre) 520-2
Molos (Spo) 716-17
monasteries
    Agia Elesa (Ion) 763
    Agia Moni (Ion) 763
    Agios Ioannis (Cyc) 424
    Koutloumousiou (NG) 372
    Monastery of the Apocalypse (Dod) 620
    Monastery of Our Lady (Dod) 571
    Monastery of Perivleptos (Pel) 246
    Monastery of the Virgin of Proussiotissa (Cen) 288
    Moni Agias Lavras (Pel) 220
    Moni Agias Paraskevis (NG) 323
    Moni Agias Triadas (SG) 403
    Moni Agias Triados (Cen) 310
    Moni Agias Varvaras Rousanou (Cen) 310
    Moni Agias Ypsenis (Dod) 572
    Moni Agios Nikolaos (SG) 403
    Moni Agiou Georgiou (Dod) 584, 586
    Moni Agiou Mamma (Dod) 584
    Moni Agiou Nikolaou (NG) 327
    Moni Agiou Nikolaou Anapafsa (Cen) 308
    Moni Agiou Panteleimona (Dod) 594
    Moni Agiou Stefanou (Cen) 310
    Moni Agiou Stefanou (Dod) 586
    Moni Angiou Antoniou (Cyc) 443
    Moni Arhangelou (NEA) 689
    Moni Arkadiou (Cre) 531
    Moni Dafniou (Ath) 207
    Moni Efpraxias (SG) 402
    Moni Evangelismou (NEA) 657

monasteries (cont)
Moni Evangelismou (Spo) 706
Moni Evangelistrias (Spo) 701
Moni Faneromenis (Ion) 740
Moni Hozoviotissis (Cyc) 460
Moni Kalamiotissas (Cyc) 477
Moni Kaissarianis (Ath) 201-4
Moni Kalopetras (Dod) 573
Moni Mavriotissas (NG) 364
Moni Mega Spileou (Pel) 217-18
Moni Megalou Meteorou (Cen) 310
Moni Metamorfosis (Spo) 706
Moni Myrtidion (Ion) 763
Moni Osiou Louka (Cen) 282-3
Moni Panagias Spilianis (Dod) 595
Moni Panagias Spilianis (NEA) 644
Moni Panagias Vrondianis (NEA) 646
Moni Pandeleïmonos (NG) 320
Moni Preveli (Cre) 534
Moni Prodomou (Spo) 706
Moni Profiti Ilia (Cyc) 473
Moni Profiti Ilias (SG) 402
Moni Taxiarhou Mihail (Dod) 590-1
Moni Tharri (Dod) 572
Moni Theoktistis (NEA) 635
Moni Theotokou (Ion) 731-732
Moni Toplou (Cre) 522
Moni Tsambikas (Dod) 569
Moni Varlaam (Cen) 310
Moni Zoödohou Pigis (Cyc) 416
Moni Zoödohou Pigis (Cyc) 478
Moni Zoödohou Pigis (SG) 398
Moni Zourvas (SG) 403
Nea Moni (NEA) 652
Stomio Monastery 325
Monemvasia (Pel) 247-9
money 79-82
ATMs 80-112
bargaining 82
costs 81-2
credit cards 80-112
currency 79
exchange rates 80

exchanging money 80-1
tipping 82
Monodendri (NG) 322
mosques
Aslan Pasha (NG) 318
Koursouri Tzami (Cen) 306
Mosque of Gazi Hassan Pasha (Dod) 601
Mosque of Murad Reis (Dod) 564
Mosque of Süleyman (Dod) 564
motorcycle travel
rental 131-7
to/from Greece 120-2
within Greece 129-31
Moudros (NEA) 676
mountaineering club 97-8
Moutsouna (Cyc) 452-3
Mt Athos (NG) 369-74
permits 342
Mt Dirfys (Evi) 695
Mt Gamila (NG) 324
Mt Olympus (NG) 350-4, 351
Mt Pantokrator (Ion) 729
Mt Parnassos (Cen) 280-2
Mt Parnitha 208
Mt Profitis Ilias (Dod) 573-4
museums
Acropolis Museum (Ath) 155-6
Aegean Maritime Museum (Cyc) 430
agricultural museum (Cyc) 430
Archaeological Museum see under Archaeological Museums
Archaeology Museum (Cyc) 486
art gallery of Larisa (Cen) 295
Atatürk's House (NG) 342
Averof Gallery (NG) 327
Battle of Crete Museum (Cre) 505
Benaki Museum (Ath) 165
Byzantine Museum (Ath) 166
Byzantine Museum (Cyc) 441
Byzantine Museum (Ion) 726
Byzantine Museum (Ion) 755
Byzantine Museum (NEA) 651
Byzantine Museum (NEA) 662
Byzantine Museum (NG) 318

Byzantine Museum (NG) 363
Byzantine Museum (SG) 401
Centre of Folk Arts & Traditions (Ath) 167
City of Athens Museum (Ath) 167
Cultural Museum of Paxi (Ion) 735
Della Rocca-Barozzi Venetian Museum (Cyc) 447
Ecclesiastical Art Museum of Alexandroupolis (NG) 385
ethnographical & historical museum (Cen) 295
Falaïts Museum (Spo) 713-14
folk art museum (Spo) 704
folk museum (Pel) 221-2
folklore collection of Naoussa (Cyc) 441
folklore museum (Cen) 288
folklore museum (Cre) 538
folklore museum (Cyc) 430, 471
folklore museum (Evi) 695
Folkloric & Historical Museum (NG) 385
Folkloric Museum (NG) 318, 337
Giustiniani Palace Museum (NEA) 651
Goulandris Museum of Cycladic & Ancient Greek Art (Ath) 165-6
Greek History Museum (NG) 318
Hellenic Maritime Museum (Ath) 195
Historical & Folk Art Museum (Cre) 529
Historical Archives Museum of Hydra (SG) 401
Historical Museum of Crete (Cre) 504
Historical Museum of the Olympic Games (Pel) 269
Jewish Museum (Ath) 167
John Coumantarios Art Gallery (Pel) 243
Kastorian Museum of Folklore (NG) 364
Kitsos Makris Folk Art Centre (Cen) 297
Korgialenio History & Folklore Museum (Ion) 747
Lena's House (Cyc) 430
maritime museum (Cyc) 474

museums (cont)
Maritime Museum (NEA) 656
Megaron Gyzi Museum (Cyc) 470
Milies folk museum (Cen) 303
Military Museum (Pel) 231
Milos Folk & Arts Museum (Cyc) 486
Mining Museum (Cyc) 485
Monemvasia Archaeological Museum (Pel) 248
Municipal Museum (NG) 376
Museum of Asian Art (Ion) 726
Museum of Byzantine Culture (NG) 343
Museum of Cretan Ethnology (Cre) 535
Museum of Decorative Arts (Dod) 564
Museum of Eretria (Evi) 696
Museum of Greek Folk Art (Ath) 166
Museum of Greek Popular Instruments (Ath) 167
Museum of History & Art of Thessaloniki (NG) 342
Museum of Macedonian Struggle (NG) 342
Museum of Modern Art (Cyc) 415
Museum of Modern Art (NG) 358
Museum of Popular Aegean Civilisation (Cyc) 443
Museum of Prehistoric Thera (Cyc) 470
Museum of Solomos (Ion) 755
Museum of the History of Greek Costume (Ath) 167
Museum of the Komboloi (Pel) 232
Museum of Traditional Greek Ceramics (Ath) 150
National Art Gallery (Ath) 166
National Historical Museum (Ath) 166-7
Natural History Museum of the Lesvos Petrified Forest (NEA) 668
Nautical & Folklore Museum (Dod) 610

Nautical & Folklore Museum (Ion) 750
Nautical Museum (Cyc) 415
naval museum (Cre) 538
Numismatic Museum (Ath) 166
Oberlaender Museum (Ath) 159
Open Air Water Power Museum (Pel) 239
Paul & Alexandra Kanellopoulos Museum (Ath) 149
Peloponnese Folklore Foundation Museum (Pel) 231
Philip Argenti Museum (NEA) 651
Polygnotos Vagis Museum (NEA) 689
Popular Art Museum (NG) 318
Pythagorio Museum (NEA) 644
Skiathos Museum (Spo) 699
Symi Maritime Museum (Dod) 589
Teriade Museum (NEA) 662-3
Theatre Museum (Ath) 167
Theophilos Museum (NEA) 662
Vrellis Wax Museum (NG) 318
War Museum (Ath) 167
War Museum of Hania (Cre) 538
music, see arts
Mycenae (Pel) 227-9
Mykonos (Cyc) 426-33, **427**
Mykonos Hora (Cyc) 428-32, **429**
Mylopotamos (Ion) 762-3
Myrina (NEA) 674-5
Myrthios (Cre) 534
Myrties (Dod) 612
Myrtos (Cre) 525-6
Mystras (Pel) 244-6, **245**
mythology 66, 752
Mytikas (Cen) 287
Mytilini (NEA) 661-4
Mytilinii (NEA) 645

N
Nafpaktos (Cen) 284
Nafplio (Pel) 229-34
Naoussa (Cyc) 441-2
national parks 42
Alkazar park (Cen) 295

Iti National Park (Cen) 291-2
Mt Parnitha National Park (Ath) 208
Vikos-Aoös National Park (NG) 322
Naxos (Cyc) 445-53, **446**
Naxos Hora (Cyc) 446-50, **448**
Nea Itilo (Pel) 256-7
Neapoli (Pel) 249-50
Nekromanteio of Afyra (NG) 331
Nemea (Pel) 225
newspapers 88
Nikea (Dod) 597
Nikopolis (NG) 336
Nisyros (Dod) 594-7, **595**
Nisyros volcano (Dod) 596-7
North-Eastern Aegean Islands 627-91, **628**
Northern Greece 314-90
Nydri (Ion) 740-64

O
Oia (Cyc) 473-5
Old Alonnisos (Spo) 710
olive trails (NEA) 670-1, **671**
Olymbos (Dod) 581-2
Olympia (Pel) 268-72
Olympic Games 184-5
organised tours
to/from Greece 124
within Greece 136
Ormos (Cyc) 462-5
Othoni (Ion) 733
Ouranoupolis (NG) 369
ouzeria 105-6, 299

P
Paleohora (Cre) 547-9, **510**
Paleokastro (Pel) 267
Pali (Dod) 597
Palio Trikeri (Cen) 305-13
Panagia (NEA) 689
Pandeli (Dod) 616
Parga (NG) 331-4, **332**
Parikia (Cyc) 437-41, **438**
Paros (Cyc) 436-43, **437**
Parthenon (Ath) 153-4
Patitiri (Spo) 708-10
Patmos (Dod) 617-21, **618**
Patras (Pel) 213-17, **214**
Paxi (Ion) 734-54, **734**
Pelion Peninsula (Cen) 299-305, **300**
Pella (NG) 349

Bold indicates maps.

Peloponnese 209-73, **210-11**
people 43
Peratata (Ion) 749
Petaloudes (Cyc) 443
Petaloudes (Dod) 573
Petra (NEA) 667
Phaestos (Cre) 512
Philippi (NG) 378-81
philosophy 44
photography 89
Pigadia (Dod) 577-9, **578**
Piraeus (Ath) 194-204, **196**
Plaka (Cyc) 486
Plakias (Cre) 532-4
planning 73-4
Platanias (Cen) 305
Platanos (Dod) 615-16
Plato 44
politics 42
Polygyros (NG) 365-90
Polyrrinia (Cre) 552
population 43
Poros (SG) 396-9, **397**
Poros Town (SG) 397-8
Porto Kagio (Pel) 255
Porto Spilia (Ion) 742-3
postal services 82
Potamia (NEA) 689
Potamos (Ion) 762
Pothia (Dod) 610-11, **611**
Prespa Lakes (NG) 359-62
Preveza (NG) 334-5
Proussos (Cen) 288
Psara (NEA) 657-8
Psarades (NG) 361-2
Pserimos (Dod) 597, **598**
public holidays 99
Pyli (Cen) 307
Pylos (Pel) 265-7
Pyrgi (NEA) 653
Pyrgos (Pel) 268
Pyrgos Dirou (Pel) 254-5
Pythagorio (NEA) 643-5, **643**

R
radio 89
Rafina (Ath) 205-6
Ramnous (Ath) 206-7
religion 70-2
rembetika music (Ath) 183,
  see also arts
responsible tourism 74-5
Rethymno (Cre) 527-31, **528**
retsina 110
Rhodes (Dod) 556-74, **558**
Rhodes Town (Dod) 561-8,
  561, 565

Rina (Dod) 613-15
Rupert Brooke's Grave (Spo)
  717

S
safety 98, 148
Sagiada (NG) 330-1
Salakos (Dod) 573-4
Samaria Gorge (Cre) 543-4
Sami (Ion) 748
Samos (NEA) 637-47, **638**
Samothraki (NEA) 678-84, **678**
Santorini/Thira (Cyc) 466-77,
  467
Sappho 668
Saronic Gulf Islands 391-407,
  392
science 45-6
scuba diving, see diving
sculpture, see arts
senior travellers 97
Serifos (Cyc) 490-2, **490**
Shinias (Ath) 207
Shinousa (Cyc) 455-6
Shipwreck Beach (Ion) 758
shopping 112
Sifnos (Cyc) 487-90, **488**
Sikinos (Cyc) 478-9, **479**
Sithonian Peninsula (NG)
  366-8
Sitia (Cre) 521-2
Skala (Dod) 619-20
Skala Eresou (NEA) 667-70
Skiathos (Spo) 697-702, **699**
Skiathos Town (Spo) 698-700
skiing 102, (Ath) 169, (NG)
  327, (Pel) 220
Skopelos (Spo) 702-6, **703**
Skopelos Town (Spo) 702-5
Skoutari (Pel) 256
Skyros (Spo) 711-17
Skyros Town (Spo) 713-16
snorkelling 101, see also diving
society & conduct 65-70
Socrates 44
Soufli (NG) 387
Sougia (Cre) 546-7
Sparta (Pel) 241-4, **242**
Spartohori (Ion) 742-3
spas
  Kalithea Therma (Dod) 568
  Lisvorio (NEA) 665
  Livadia (NEA) 665
  Louta Edipsou (Evi) 696
  Loutra Yera (NEA) 663, 665
  Polyhnitos (NEA) 665

special events & festivals
  99-101
  festival of Agios Georgios
    (Cen) 281
  Hellenic festival (Ath) 170-1
  Milos festival (Cyc) 485
  Olynthos Olive Festival (NG)
    365
  Patras Carnival (Pel) 215
  Skyros Carnival (Spo) 712
spectator sports 112
Spetses (SG) 403-7, **404**
Spetses Town (SG) 404-6
Spetsopoula (SG) 407
Spili (Cre) 532
Spinalonga Island (Cre) 519
Sporades 698-717, **693**
Stemnitsa (Pel) 238-9
Steni (Evi) 695
Sterea Ellada 274-92, **275**
Stoupa (Pel) 257-8
Symi (Dod) 587-91, **588**
Syros (Cyc) 420-6, **421**
Syvota (NG) 331

T
taxes & refunds 81
taxi travel 136
Telendos Islet (Dod) 612-13
telephone services 82-4
  mobile phones 84
television 89
Temple of Vasses 272
tennis (Ath) 169
Thasos (NEA) 684-91, **684**
Thasos/Limenas (NEA) 686-9,
  686
Theologos (NEA) 690
Thessaloniki (NG) 337-48, **340**
  entertainment 346
  getting around 348-9
  getting there & away 347-8
  history 339
  organised tours 344
  places to eat 345-6
  places to stay 344-5
  shopping 346-7
  special events 344
  things to see & do 342-3
Thessaly (Cen) 292-313, **293**
Thirasia (Cyc) 477-80
Thiva/Thebes (Cen) 276
Tholos (Pel) 268
Thrace (NG) 379-90, **380**
Tilos (Dod) 591-4, **591**
Tinos (Cyc) 416-20, **417**

Tinos Hora (Cyc) 418-19
Tiryns (Pel) 234
toilets 90
tourist offices 75-6
tourist police 75-6
traditions 68-9
Tragaea (Cyc) 450-2
train travel
    to/from Greece 120
    within Greece 128-9
trekking 101, (Cre) 505, 529,
    543-4, 538, (NEA) 659,
    670, (NG) 318, 352-3, (Pel)
    239, 258-73
Trikala (Cen) 305-7
Trikeri (Cen) 304
Tripolis (Pel) 236-7
Trypiti (Cyc) 486
Tsangarada (Cen) 302
Tsepelovo (NG) 322

V
Vaï (Cre) 522-3
Vasiliki (Ion) 741-64
Vathy (Dod) 613-15
Vathy (Ion) 743

Vathy (Ion) 750-1
Vathy/Samos (NEA) 640-5,
    641
vegetarian food 108
Vergina (NG) 356
Veria (NG) 354-6
video systems 89
Vikos (NG) 322
Vikos Gorge (NG) 322-4
Vikos-Aoös National Park (NG)
    322
visas 76
Vlahata (Ion) 749
Volos (Cen) 296-9, 297
Vonitsa (Cen) 286-7
Vravrona/Brauron (Ath) 205-6
Vrontados (NEA) 652
Vyzitsa (Cen) 303-4

W
walking 132, (Dod) 592,
    see also trekking
water skiing 101
windsurfing 101, (Cyc) 430,
    (Ion) 741

wineries
    Emery Winery (Dod) 574
    Santorini (Cyc) 473
    Kamari (Cyc) 476
women travellers 96
    health 96
work 102-3
    permits 102

X
Xanthi (NG) 381-2
Xerokambos (Cre) 523-4
Xirokambos (Dod) 615
Xyloskalo (Cre) 543

Z
Zagoria Villages (NG) 322-5,
    323
Zagorohoria (NG) 322-5
Zahlorou (Pel) 217-18
Zakros (Cre) 522-3
Zakynthos (Ion) 753-9, 754
Zakynthos Town (Ion) 754-6, 756

Boxed Text

Ali Pasha 321
Alonnisos Marine Park 711
Ancient Greek Mythology 66-8
At Loggerheads 757
Athena & the Olive Tree 139
Balm for the Soul, A 665
Beware the Evil Eye 419
Combes Beware! 466
Brothers Durrell, The 730
Colossus of Rhodes, The 557
Corfu Bus Timetables 723
Cult of Captain Corelli, The
    745
Dangers & Annoyances 148-9
Delphic Oracle, The 278
Diakofto–Kalavryta Railway
    218
Evil Olive, The 39
Fancy a Flokati? 307
Fascinating Fossil Find 669
Ferries from Piraeus 198-9
Ferry Connections to the
    Cyclades 412
Ferry Connections to the
    Ionian Islands 721
Festival Time 660

Getting it Straight – Things You
    Should Know Before You Go
    410
Glory Days of the Citron 451
Good Oil, The 542
Gum Mastic 653
Hippocrates – the First GP 599
Hydrofoils from Piraeus 200
Ikarian Panigyria 634
Is it Cricket? 727
Kalamata Olives 262
Lascarina Bouboulina 405
Linear B Script 504
Mediterraneo – the Movie 586
Mt Olympus Trails 352-3
Miracle of Lipsi, The 624
Mysterious Minoans 500, The
    Name days 70
Nikos Kazantzakis – Crete's
    prodigal son 506
Odysseus & Ithaki 752
Olive Trails 670
Olympian Creation Myth 69
Olympic Airways Services
    Within Greece 126-7
Ouzeri, The 299

Paradise Club Scene, The 433
Restless Spirits 546
Rocky Road to 2004, The
    184-5
Santorini Wines 475
Santorini's Unsettling Past 469
Sappho 668
Shipwreck Beach 758
Skyros Carnival 712
Spartan Existence, A 243
Strange Rahes 636
Story of Silk, The 388
Survival Guide to Mt Athos, A
    371
Three Pillars of Western
    Philosophy 44-5
Transliteration & Variant
    Spellings: An Explanation 71
Urban Guerilla Terror 34
Useful Phone Numbers 84
Warning: Phone Number
    Changes 83
Who are the Pontians? 349
Wildflowers 40
Wily Pelops, The 212
Wine+Pine=Retsina 110

MAP LEGEND

CITY ROUTES

Freeway	Freeway		Unsealed Road
Highway	Primary Road		One Way Street
Road	Secondary Road		Pedestrian Street
Street	Street		Stepped Street
Lane	Lane		Tunnel
	On/Off Ramp		Footbridge

REGIONAL ROUTES

Tollway, Freeway
Primary Road
Secondary Road
Minor Road

BOUNDARIES

International
State
Disputed
Fortified Wall

AREA FEATURES

Building
Park, Gardens
Market
Beach
Cemetery
Plaza

TRANSPORT ROUTES & STATIONS

Train — Walking Trail
Underground Train — Walking Tour
Metro — Path
Cable Car, Funicular — Pier or Jetty

WATER TRANSPORT

Daily Ferry
Low Frequency Ferry
Hydrofoil
Excursion Boat

HYDROGRAPHY

River, Creek — Dry Lake, Salt Lake
Canal — Spring, Rapids
Lake — Waterfalls

POPULATION SYMBOLS

✪ **CAPITAL**	National Capital	● **CITY**	City	● Village	Village
◉ **CAPITAL**	Regional Capital	● **Town**	Town		Urban Area

MAP SYMBOLS

■ Place to Stay	▼ Place to Eat	● Point of Interest

✕	Airport	✝	Church, Cathedral	🏛	Monument	🚕 Taxi Rank
✪	Archaeological Site	🎬	Cinema	▲	Mountain	☎ Telephone
§	Bank	◥	Dive Site	🏛 🎭	Museum, Theatre	■ Tomb
🍷 ♫	Bar, Music Venue	📷	Embassy, Consulate	℗ ⊙	Parking, Petrol	ℹ Tourist Information
⊟ ◙	Bus Stop, Terminal	✚	Hospital, Clinic	⊞	Police Station	⊟ Transport (General)
🏰	Castle, Fortress	ⓐ	Internet Cafe	✉	Post Office	☼ Winery
⌂	Cave	☼ ※	Lighthouse, Lookout	⊗	Shopping Centre	✗ Windmill

Note: not all symbols displayed above appear in this book

LONELY PLANET OFFICES

Australia
Locked Bag 1, Footscray, Victoria 3011
☎ 03 8379 8000 fax 03 8379 8111
email: talk2us@lonelyplanet.com.au

USA
150 Linden St, Oakland, CA 94607
☎ 510 893 8555 TOLL FREE: 800 275 8555
fax 510 893 8572
email: info@lonelyplanet.com

UK
10a Spring Place, London NW5 3BH
☎ 020 7428 4800 fax 020 7428 4828
email: go@lonelyplanet.co.uk

France
1 rue du Dahomey, 75011 Paris
☎ 01 55 25 33 00 fax 01 55 25 33 01
email: bip@lonelyplanet.fr
www.lonelyplanet.fr

World Wide Web: www.lonelyplanet.com or AOL keyword: lp
Lonely Planet Images: lpi@lonelyplanet.com.au